D1104469

❖ SEARCHING THE SCRIPTURES

Volume Two:
A Feminist Commentary

In Celebration
of the Centennial Anniversary
of The Woman's Bible

Now, to my mind, the Revising Committee of "The Woman's Bible," in denying divine inspiration for such demoralizing ideas shows a more worshipful reverence for the great Spirit of All Good than does the Church. We have made a fetich (*sic*) of the Bible long enough. The time has come to read it as we do all other books, acccepting the good and rejecting the evil it teaches.

Elizabeth Cady Stanton
Preface to vol. 2 of The Women's Bible

Searching
the Scriptures

Volume Two:
A Feminist Commentary

Edited by
ELISABETH SCHÜSSLER FIORENZA
with the assistance of Ann Brock
and Shelly Matthews

CROSSROAD ◆ NEW YORK

1994

The Crossroad Publishing Company
370 Lexington Avenue, New York, NY 10017

Printed in the United States of America

Library of Congress Cataloguing-in-Publication Data
(Rev. for vol. 2)

Searching the Scriptures.

    Vol. 2 has author statement: edited by Elisabeth Schüssler Fiorenza with the assistance of Ann Brock and Shelly Matthews.
    Includes bibliographical references and index.
    Contents: v. 1. A feminist introduction–
v. 2. A feminist commentary.
    1. Bible. N.T.–Feminist criticism. 2. Bible. N.T.–
Criticism, interpretation, etc. 3. Women in
Christianity–History–Early church, ca. 30–600.
I. Schüssler Fiorenza, Elisabeth, 1938–
II. Matthews, Shelly. III. Brock, Ann.
BS2379.S43   1993   220.6'082   93-31336

ISBN 0-8245-1381-9 (v. 1)
ISBN 0-8245-1424-6 (v. 2)

Contents

Part III: Biographical Discourses: Envoys of Sophia

Preface

As I POINTED OUT in the introduction to the first volume, *Searching the Scriptures* is the fruit of several years of panel discussions on the topic "Rethinking the *Woman's Bible*," which were sponsored by the Women in the Biblical World Section of the Society of Biblical Literature at its annual meetings. Discussions of this project were initiated by Professor Esther Fuchs, who approached me to collaborate on a revision of *The Woman's Bible* in light of the approaching centennial of its first publication. Rather than start with such a revision immediately, I suggested that we initiate a series of panel discussions on Rethinking the *Woman's Bible* for exploring the theoretical boundaries and implications of the *Woman's Bible*. Westminster/John Knox Press took up Professor Fuchs's idea directly and published in 1992 *The Women's Bible Commentary,* which was edited by Carol Newsom and Sharon Ringe.

Inspired by the numerous insights and queries raised at the panels on Rethinking the *Woman's Bible,* the present project adopted a different theoretical conceptualization. I am very grateful to all the participants in these discussions as well as to the members of the advisory board for their ideas, suggestions, and assistance. Without the support of my feminist colleagues in biblical and religious studies, I could not have undertaken or completed this project. My profound appreciation and gratitude go particularly to all the authors who have contributed their scholarly expertise, feminist insights, and painstaking research to this second volume of Searching the Scriptures. Their variegated theoretical voices, interreligious approaches, and international perspectives document that feminist biblical scholarship has come of age.

Rev. Ann Brock has joined Rev. Shelly Matthews and myself in the preparation of this volume for publication. I am very indebted to both young scholars for their assistance in commenting on contributions, contacting straggling authors, and in proofing the manuscript of Searching the Scriptures during the preparation of this volume. This feminist project has greatly benefited from their meticulous editorial work, critical feedback, and patient enthusiasm. I was fortunate to have been able to engage such able coworkers. To them, as well as to my research assistant Solveig Nielsen-Goodin, I am especially grateful. Finally, I want to thank Harvard Divinity School, and especially Dean Ronald F. Thiemann, for the support of this work.

We were able to complete this feminist commentary project because of the tremendous support not only of women scholars but also of two publishing houses. Without the enthusiastic encouragement and the financial commitment first of Werner Linz and Frank Oveis, now of Continuum Publishing Company, and later of Gwendolin Herder and Michael Leach of the Crossroad Publishing Company, *Searching the Scriptures* would never have seen the day of publication. By relinquishing all editorial control and "the power of naming," both publishing companies have taken considerable promotional and financial risks.

Special thanks are due to Maurya Horgan of The HK Scriptorium, who very expertly has navigated this volume through the hazards and perils of the copyediting and publication process. Her enthusiasm and great care in preparing this volume were invaluable. Thanks are also due to Stefan Killen for designing the cover of this volume.

As always, I am indebted to Francis and Chris Schüssler Fiorenza for their indefatigable support. It is my hope that this interreligious commentary work will enrich the critical historical and cultural religious imagination of women in all walks of life.

Elisabeth Schüssler Fiorenza

❖ SEARCHING THE SCRIPTURES

Volume Two:
A Feminist Commentary

Transgressing
Canonical Boundaries

ELISABETH SCHÜSSLER FIORENZA ◆

Searching the Scriptures is dedicated to two of our nineteenth-century fore-mothers: Anna Julia Cooper and Elizabeth Cady Stanton. Focusing on these two feminist foremothers not only marks a historical milestone in feminist religious thought but also honors the nineteenth-century dual roots of American feminist religious vision and struggle. Whereas the first volume, *A Feminist Introduction,* honored the inclusive vision of the African American womanist thinker Anna Julia Cooper,[1] this second volume celebrates the centennial publication of the *Woman's Bible,* edited by the suffragist Elizabeth Cady Stanton.

By conceptualizing and publishing the *Woman's Bible,* Cady Stanton sought to interrupt the conservative trend in the suffrage movement. This trend was fueled, she believed, by the influx of evangelical women after the National Woman's Christian Temperance Union (WCTU) adopted a suffrage platform, swelling the ranks of local and national suffrage associations. With the project of the *Woman's Bible,* Cady Stanton tried to force the National American Woman's Suffrage Association (NAWSA) to engage in a public discussion of the conservative social trend of narrowly focusing on the ballot, rather than on the full emancipation from "woman's sphere."[2] Over and against those who saw the project as a waste of time, Cady Stanton insisted on its political necessity. She argued that it is important for women to interpret the Bible, because scripture and its authority have been and continue to be used against women struggling for emancipation. Moreover, women as well as men have internalized scripture's misogynist teachings as the Word of God. Hence, she and her collaborators utilized historical-critical scholarship to argue that the Bible is the word of *men* who have projected their own selfish interests into it. Texts that speak negatively about women are either mistranslated and misinterpreted relics of past time or are not true at all because they contradict the principles of reason and science. Since men have also been the Bible's authoritative interpreters throughout the centuries, she argued, women must now claim their right to biblical interpretation.[3]

Cady Stanton's efforts, however, backfired. She had great difficulty persuading well-known suffragists to sponsor or write for this project of biblical revision, because they believed it would engender an antisuffrage backlash in the churches. Rather than disturb this conservative trend, the project of the *Woman's Bible* consolidated the alliance between nonreligious political pragmatists and evangelical conservatives. In 1896, NAWSA publicly distanced itself from the project. More importantly, Cady Stanton's call for a feminist political engagement with biblical religion was widely disregarded not only in the nineteenth century but also by the second wave of the women's movement in this century. Whereas white feminists in the academy and the women's movements have always seen education as a site of political struggle for change, they have tended to abandon rather than re-vision biblical religions.

As at the end of the last century, so also today, the historical-religious legacy of Elizabeth Cady Stanton is much debated, but for quite different reasons. Like other suffragists and social reformers, she was limited by her social status and class position. Not only did she express anti-immigrant sentiments by arguing that women's suffrage would increase Anglo-Saxon voters, but she also appealed to ethnic and racial prejudices when she exhorted, "American women of wealth and refinement, if you do not wish the lower orders of Chinese, Africans, Germans, and Irish, with their low ideas of womanhood to make laws for you . . . demand that woman, too, shall be represented in the government."[4] Unlike Clara Colby, for instance, Cady Stanton did not concern herself with labor problems and the different struggles of African American and Native American women. The *Woman's Bible* uncritically repeats many of the anti-Jewish stereotypes prevalent in Christian popular and scholarly discourses. Although Elizabeth Cady Stanton and the suffragist movement must be taken to task for their shortcomings and prejudices, nevertheless their contributions to the feminist movement and feminist thought must be critically honored. What Adrienne Rich concludes in her poem "Heroines" also holds true for the intention of this feminist commentary project:

> You draw your long skirts
>
>   deviant
>
>   across the nineteenth century
>
>   registering injustice
>
>   failing to make it whole
>
> How can I fail to love
>
>   your clarity and fury
>
> How can I give you
>
>   all your due
>
>   take courage from your courage

> honor your exact
> > > legacy as it is
> > recognizing
> > > as well
> > > > that it is not enough[5]

By celebrating both the work of Elizabeth Cady Stanton and that of Anna Julia Cooper, *Searching the Scriptures* seeks to underscore the partialness of white women's historical vision, even though this vision often claims to represent feminist history and vision in its entirety. It does so by inviting feminist scholars in religion from around the world to bring their expertise and perspectives to this celebration of our foresisters. *Searching the Scriptures* thereby seeks to internationalize the ongoing common feminist struggles and ecumenical-interreligious conversations regarding the cultural heritage of ancient Christian and Jewish writings.

Despite the polyphony of voices from very different social, geographical, and religious locations gathered again in this volume, it is important to reiterate what I pointed out in the first volume. The academy in general and biblical studies in particular have not been hospitable to women of all colors. Whereas Euro-American feminists have struggled for admission to biblical studies and theology in the 1960s and 1970s, only in the 1970s and 1980s have women of other ethnic or racial backgrounds entered the academy in greater numbers. Only a very few have made it through Euro-American credentializing processes and professional ranks, and these few are often overburdened by a host of demands on them. Hence, this commentary project still remains limited by its sociohistorical institutional location.

Elizabeth Cady Stanton had to twist the arms of well-known suffragists to list them on the editorial committee. Only seven of them actually contributed commentaries. Hence, she began and primarily wrote the *Woman's Bible* herself. Since Cady Stanton and her collaborators wrote without the aid of scholars who knew Hebrew and Greek, they focused on social-political commentary rather than on philological and historical discussions. *Searching the Scriptures,* in contrast, had no such problems. Most of the well-known feminist scholars in biblical studies eagerly accepted the invitation to contribute to this commentary. Those who declined did so not because they objected to the project but because of time constraints and other work commitments.

In contrast to Elizabeth Cady Stanton's *Woman's Bible,* which was extremely controverted from its very inception, the first published volume of *Searching the Scriptures* has found an enthusiastic reception both within and outside of the academy. As with the first volume, contributors to this second volume had complete freedom regarding the conceptualization, method, and feminist perspective of their commentary. For practical reasons of publication, their only limitation was with respect to length. Hence, this volume not only brings together very different feminist voices, theoretical perspectives, and interpretive methods; it also set out to include and give voice to feminist approaches that are exclusive of each other. Nonetheless, readers who are not as familiar with the intricacies of feminist theoretical discussion or the multiplicity of exegetical methods need not worry that they will be lost in a maze of contradictions. Every commentator was asked to spell out her own exegetical method and feminist hermeneutical perspective and to take into account the function of the ancient text in the multiplicative oppressions of most women.

The overall method and conceptualization of this volume of *Feminist Commentary* differ in crucial ways from the method and conceptualization of the *Woman's Bible*. When Elizabeth Cady Stanton, her daughter Harriot Stanton Blatch, and the British suffragist Frances Lord began their interpretive work in 1886, they literally cut out the passages about women which they wanted to exegete. They pasted them on blank pages, collected them in a book, and added their own commentaries to each page. Such a reductive critical method was first employed by Marcion (ca. 130), who accepted only a freely edited collection of ten Pauline letters and the Gospel of Luke in his canon.[6] He also rejected the Israelite scriptures because he sought to purify early Christian scriptures from all judaizing tendencies. Such a reductive method was also utilized by Luther and other Reformers who judged scriptural texts according to their "canon within the canon."[7] Therefore, this method has strongly determined Protestant theological traditions of interpretation. Consequently, the *Woman's Bible* is firmly rooted in the Protestant Christian tradition. It is a compilation of critical reflections on key scriptural passages and principles, but not a biblical commentary in the strict sense.

Even more so than the *Woman's Bible,* the present feminist commentary utilizes biblical-historical and literary scholarship for a feminist reading of the scriptures but differs in significant ways from the *Woman's Bible.* Whereas the authors of the *Woman's Bible* used a reductive approach, singling out passages *about women,* this commentary for the most part has adopted a *transgressive method of proliferation.* Rather than focusing only on the women's passages, it generally seeks to analyze writings in their entirety. This method is used in order to assess how much the texts religiously advocate and foster all women's and marginalized men's subordination and exploitation and how much they transgress the kyriarchal boundaries of their time. Its contributors "search the scriptures" in a double sense.[8] They scrutinize and interrogate the scriptures to uncover their "crimes" of silencing and marginalization. Moreover, most of them also seek to bring to the fore and make audible again the subjugated voices and suppressed traditions that have left traces in ancient writings. To that end they not only employ a multiplicity of theoretical perspectives and interpretive frameworks but also interpret a variety of early

Christian and Jewish writings. They go beyond the canon to explore extra-canonical writings which are often only known by and accessible to scholars. By making such extracanonical writings available to a wider audience, this commentary seeks to expand our historical-critical imagination and religious-communal vision.

The transgressive method and approach of the present commentary presuppose inherited Christian socioreligious boundaries insofar as this work includes all of the writings of the Christian Testament; however, the texts are not read simply from a Christian feminist perspective. This commentary is unique in that several of the contributors to it treat the canonical Christian text from within a Jewish or post-Christian frame of reference. Because of limitations of space and resources, it includes neither the books of the Hebrew Bible nor the canon of the rabbis.[9] Rather, it focuses on the reigning canon of Christian Scriptures, the so-called New Testament, but it is not limited to these works.

In short, this commentary seeks to transgress canonical boundaries in order both to undo the exclusionary kyriarchal tendencies of the ruling canon and to renew the debate on the limits, functions, and extent of the canon. Feminist discussions have tended to reduce this debate to the question of the authority of the canon.[10] Revitalizing this debate is necessary because the historical silencing and textual marginalization of women are the by-products of the so-called patristic kyriarchal selection and exclusionary canonization process.[11]

By proliferating and destabilizing the dominant canon of the Christian churches, this work seeks to undo such exclusionary tendencies. It does so by bringing to public awareness that the present canon of Christian Scriptures is a collection of diverse writings that were gathered into an authoritative edition. The motivation for the authoritative collection was not only religious but also political. Struggles between orthodoxy and heresy, as well as the political goal of establishing the unified church as the consolidating power of the Roman Empire, drove the exclusionary selection and canonization process.

Orthodoxy and heresy are not independent facts but interrelated constructions that were defined by those Christians who sought to articulate their self-identity as "orthodox" by creating a pejorative image of their opponents as "heretics."[12] This exclusionary construction of the tandem notion orthodoxy—heresy was developed in the second and third centuries. It asserts the temporal priority of orthodoxy and the sinful character of heresy.[13] According to Origen, all heretics were first orthodox but then strayed from the true faith. Heresy, then, is not only a freely chosen defection but also a mutilation and corruption of the original "canon" or "rule of faith." In a similar fashion the rabbis insisted that their interpretation of Judaism was always orthodox.[14] This dualistic conceptualization of the history of faith in a Christian context was supported by the idea of apostolic succession, which was also developed after the first century. This construct holds that Jesus founded the church and gave his revelation to the apostles, who in turn proclaimed and preserved his teaching. The "orthodox" church is said to be the only legitimate one because it alone continues this line of "apostolic" succession.

This understanding of orthodoxy and heresy was shared by all groups and factions in early Christianity; hence, they all attempted to prove that their teaching and community were in continuity with Jesus and the first disciples. In order to prove that they were the "orthodox" preservers of the "canon" of faith, Montanists, so-called gnostic Christian groups of various theological persuasions, and the so-called patristic churches all claimed prophetic revelation and apostolic succession. In this struggle for legitimacy and ecclesial hegemony, the "orthodox" canonization of prophetic and apostolic writings played a decisive role.[15] The consequence was the exclusion, co-optation or destruction of all writings championed by those who were not aligned with the orthodox—the so-called heretics. This drive for the "orthodox" self-identity of the "patristic" churches was motivated by political factors and had as an attendant outcome the identification of women's ecclesial leadership with heresy.

Moreover, the drive for the unitary, exclusive self-identity of the church was a political struggle to ensure the unity of the empire. It engendered the desire for an established canon of Christian Scriptures, a collection of writings accepted by the dominant "orthodox patristic" churches. The scholarly conjecture that a particular intervention of the emperor accelerated the process of canonization underscores the political interests at work in this process of canonization. In 331 Bishop Eusebius of Caesarea received a letter from the emperor Constantine requesting the production of fifty Bibles, to be used in the churches of Constantinople. Eusebius was asked to use expensive parchment for these copies of the "divine scriptures," to be paid for by the emperor, and to ship the completed copies in two imperial carriages. Eusebius, the principal architect of the political theology of the newly christianized state, "knew that Constantine was concerned about the unity of the church and the unity of the state . . . and that these new Bibles prepared for the capital city would play an important role in the unity of the Church."[16] Therefore, it was not just theological arguments but also the needs of the imperial state and church that settled the list of writings included in the Christian Testament. This process of selection and canonization excluded or destroyed all those writings attributed to the so-called heretical "others."

Recent research on the function of early Christian letters illuminates the roots of this political process of canonization in two ways.[17] First, scholars describe three types of letters in antiquity: the *private* letter between individuals; the *public* letter or published letter or published correspondence of educated writers and philosophers; and the *official* letter, which served the interests of imperial administration and colonial communication. Both the

Pauline letters and subsequent early Christian letters were addressed to the Christian *ekklēsia,* the voting assembly of free citizens. Thus, like the "official" letters of the imperial administration the Christian letters were political communications. Just as the colonial imperial correspondence between emperor, local governors, and imperial administration was the most important instrument for controlling and governing the affairs of the vast Roman imperium, so the Pauline and other early Christian letters functioned to foster the maintenance and unification of the multicultural Christian *ekklēsiai.* Second, scholars argue that the subsequent collection of the Pauline correspondence and its modification through the addition of letters written in Paul's name after his death served as a model for the process of canon building. This collection sought not only to foster the authority of the local church officers and the organizational unity of the church but also to inculcate the kyriarchal pattern of submission that was the backbone of the imperial order. It is no accident that the so-called Household Codes that advocate this kyriarchal political ethos of subordination for the Christian household and the whole community are found only in the post-Pauline literature and the writings of the "apostolic fathers." They not only advocate the adaptation of the Christian *ekklēsia* to the imperial order of the classical city-state but also argue for the subordination and exclusion of women from ecclesial leadership.

Virginia Burrus has maintained that "patristic" heresiologists created "the figure of the heretical female as a negative expression of their own orthodox male self-identity."[18] Yet I would add that such a portrayal and utilization of the figure of the "heretical woman" are not just an individualist symbolic gender projection. Rather, this image has its roots in the bitter struggle over the character of the *ekklēsia.* The "radical democratic" understanding of *ekklēsia* entitled all those gifted with the charisms of the Spirit to ecclesial leadership. Not only propertied freeborn men but also slave women and men and freeborn women were full "citizens" of the *ekklēsia* and were therefore called to public responsibility and leadership. The understanding of church that won out advocated accommodation to the kyriarchal order of the Roman state. Consequently, the orthodox "fathers" argued not only against women's ecclesial leadership but also against their public speaking and writing of books. The acid polemics of these male leaders, however, not only document an insecure "orthodox" male identity but also indicate how much the question of women's ecclesial office was still alive in the "patristic" malestream church.[19]

In this debate the appeal to the scriptures plays a significant role. Egalitarian Christian groups, for example, trace their apostolic authority through the scriptures back to Mary of Magdala, emphasizing that women as well as men have received revelations from the resurrected One. In turn, "patristic" writers pit the authority of Peter over against that of Mary of Magdala also with reference to the scriptures. Christians who acknowledge the leadership of women search their Bible, the Hebrew Scriptures, and early Christian writings for precedents and passages mentioning women. "Patristic" theologians, on the contrary, seek to explain away or to play down the importance of positive scriptural statements about women.

Origen, for instance, concedes that women had been prophets in the beginnings of the church, but he argues that they did not speak in public. John Chrysostom acknowledges that women missionaries preached the gospel, but he insists that they did so only because the "angelic conditions" of the very beginning allowed for it. Whereas Montanists legitimized the prophetic authority of women with reference to the biblical women prophets, the emerging malestream church orders utilized the same reference to support the subordinate institution of deaconesses. Against women who called on the example of the apostle Thecla for legitimizing their preaching and baptizing activities, Tertullian maintained that the *Acts of Paul and Thecla* were a fraud. While it is generally difficult to establish an explicit link between the "patristic" polemics against women's leadership and the process of canonization, Tertullian's claim indicates how the process of canonization was affected by the bitter polemics of the struggle concerning the leadership of women in early Christianity.

Hence, it is plausible that the canon reflects an androcentric selection process and that it has functioned to inculcate a kyriarchal imperial church order. The frequent association of women with heresy is not just a symbolic projection but is rooted in a particular historical situation. In this situation, boundary delimitations and the unity of the churches have become the most pressing issues, especially after Constantine's conversion to Christianity. This concern with boundaries, self-identity, and unity of church and empire was probably generated by the desire to control the large influx of new, barely converted members into the imperial church. Yet the effects on the radical democratic understanding of *ekklēsia* and the ecclesial rights and citizenship of all women and marginalized men were devastating. Recognizing these harmful effects of the early Christian struggles over canonization as a means to the kyriarchal co-optation of the *ekklēsia,* feminist biblical scholarship cannot remain within the limits drawn by the established canon. Rather it must transgress them for the sake of a different theological self-understanding and historical imagination.

Yet it cannot be overemphasized that this transgressive approach of proliferation and analysis, which has been adopted by this commentary, does *not* seek to establish a new *feminist* canon.[20] Its aim is not constructive but deconstructive insofar as it seeks to unsettle and destabilize the fixation of feminist debates on the canon and its claims to authority. By destabilizing canonical authority, this commentary seeks to deconstruct oppressive cultural and religious identity formations engendered by the ruling Christian canon. Its goal is not a rehabilitation of the canon but an increase in historical-religious knowledge and imagination. Such a proliferating transgression of canon and critical rejection of its exclusive formation apply to all four meanings of canon.[21]

First, the Greek word *ho kanōn,* from which all metaphorical senses are derived, means literally "straight rod" or "ruler." Canon, in this first sense, provides a criterion, norm, and standard that can be used to determine the truth of opinions or the rectitude of actions. Paul uses this expression in Gal 6:16 in its customary meaning as standard or norm. Later Christian writers employ it in the sense of the "rule of faith," "rule of tradition," "canon of truth," or the "norm of sound preaching." Malestream as well as feminist debates on whether such a standard or norm of truth is to be found in scripture or on how to define "the canon within the canon" utilize this sense of the term. *Searching the Scriptures* in no way seeks to reconstruct such a historical "canon of truth"; rather, its overall conceptualization subscribes to a feminist liberation theological hermeneutics which insists that the "criterion" for evaluating biblical texts must be articulated today in and through women's struggles for liberation.

The *second* meaning of *kanōn* in antiquity was a model or type to be respected and imitated. Hence, classical texts speak of the exemplary person as a standard and measure of the good or of the truth. In this sense Jesus Christ has become the *kanōn* for Christians. The ancients also used this term for characterizing written works that, on the basis of style and language, they considered to be classics[22] and as such deserving of respect and imitation. Certain classical works of art or epochal historical periods were considered as *kanōn,* as public standard and norm. The heated academic discussions on the "legacy" of the Western canon in the humanities and its relation to a multicultural education employ the term in this sense. The "canon" is here understood as the premier story of Western civilization, an instrument of cultural power and influence.[23] Again *Searching the Scriptures* does not intend to create a feminist "classic" in this sense, since it does not claim that those books which were added to the established canon are *feminist* writings.

The *third* meaning of *kanōn* connotes a public list, index, table, or catalogue. In this sense, *kanōn* can refer to a "table of contents," an official list of persons, or a collection of writings. It was not until the second half of the fourth century C.E. that *kanōn, kanonikos,* and *kanonizein* were applied to the scriptures. In 367 Athanasius distinguished between canonical *biblia kanonizomena* and noncanonical books (*ta akanonista*), and the clearest instance of the use of *kanōn* for the whole collection is found only around 380 C.E. The expression "canon of the New Testament" (*kanōn tēs kainēs diathēkēs*) is not found until around 400 C.E.

No single canon has in fact ever been accepted by all Christian churches. The lists of canonical writings accepted by the ancient churches vary greatly. For instance, the canonicity of the book of Revelation, the *Shepherd of*

Hermas, or the *Acts of Thecla* was debated for a long time. The Muratorian Canon lists such additional books as the Wisdom of Solomon and the *Revelation of Peter* among the accepted writings. In 397, the Synod of Carthage gave the following rationale for establishing a canonical list of writings: "for these are the things that we have received from our fathers to be read in church."[24] If official proclamation and public [re]reading of the accepted books in church constitute their canonicity, then some readers might be tempted to assume that *Searching the Scriptures* seeks to initiate such a process of canonization. It is conceivable that in a process of public acknowledgment and [re]reading, local communities of the *ekklēsia of women* could decide on a new feminist canon of scriptures. To initiate such a canonization process of kyriocentric writings, however, is decidedly not the goal of this feminist commentary project.

The *fourth* and last meaning of *kanōn* has been suggested by Patricia Cox Miller in a discussion of Valentinian hermeneutics.[25] Over against Irenaeus's definition of canon as "rule of faith" and authoritative standard, she argues for a meaning of canon that has often been occluded. This sense of canon understands it as something used to keep a thing straight, such as the reeds of a wind organ or a weaver's rod:

> A canon, in this sense, gives shape, frame and support for weavings and musical fantasias. Here, canon is not identical with its content, since many tapestries can be woven upon the same loom. Rather canon is a figure for the shaping element within any message; it is rather the *activity* of weaving (or writing), not the cloth or the exegesis itself. Thus canon is not a content or a collection of texts so much as a texture of relationships undergirded by the desire in language signified by both its disseminative and its polyvalent dynamics. "The written canon is undermined by its own writing," and the search goes on.[26]

Hence, Cox Miller argues that the disagreements between the Valentinians and Irenaeus over scripture were engendered by conflicting understandings of *canon* and not so much by a reaction against Marcion's canon proposal. Whereas Irenaeus's understanding of canon was that of an original revelation rooted in the past, the Valentinians held that canon is not a fixed entity or given authority but rather the loom upon which sacred writings are created.

Such a notion of canon comes close to that of *Searching the Scriptures* yet still differs from it. The method of canonical transgression and proliferation adopted by this volume shares in both the historical rootedness of canon and the postmodern hermeneutics of canon as the unceasing activity of interpretation. But this volume seeks not only to read the contents of the ruling canon against itself but also to question the very form of the "loom" and its historical function of setting exclusive religious boundaries. It does so because it realizes the continuing impact of the historical canon and its authority on the lives of women in Christian churches and cultures; it does so also because it seeks to challenge the exclusive political functions of historical canon formation. Hence, it does not want to engage in feminist religious identity formation but rather seeks for a different historical-religious imagination.

The Jewish feminist Asphodel Long has likened the Bible to a

> magnificent garden of brilliant plants, some flowering, some fruiting, some in seed, or in bud, shaded by trees of age old, luxurious growth. Yet in the very soil which gives it life the poison has been inserted . . . . This poison is that of misogyny, the hatred of women, half of the human race. . . .[27]

I would like to take the image of the garden in a different direction. Rather than likening the canon to a loom, I would compare it with a wall that not only protects the garden with its flowers and fruits but also separates it from the rest of the fields and meadows. More important, it excludes people who do not own the garden and those who are not invited into it. Patriarchal walls and enclosures have always served not only to protect women but also to control and limit them. One of the earliest feminist midrashim, which has been recorded by Judith Plaskow, tells the story of Eve and Lilith, the first wife of Adam, who are separated by a high wall.[28] Only when Eve overcomes her fear of the demonized Lilith and climbs over the wall of the garden in order to get to know and to join Lilith as her sister, can she become liberated and experience new worlds of possibilities. In a similar way, I argue here that feminist interpretation must transgress the boundaries and walls erected by the canon of the "fathers" in order to discover the historical-religious world of our "heretical" sisters that borders on the garden but is separated by the canonical wall of exclusion.

Hence, the image of the enclosed garden brings into focus the need for a deconstructive, transgressive method of interpretation; however, it is not able to articulate a positive image for the function of scripture in feminist struggles to transform religion and society. Such an image, I suggest, is found in the scriptures. It is the open, cosmic house of divine Wisdom. Her dwelling of cosmic dimensions has no walls; she permeates the whole world. Her inviting table, with the bread of sustenance and the wine of celebration, is set between seven cosmic pillars that allow the spirit of fresh air to blow where it will. This image does not allow for an understanding of canonical authority as exclusive and commanding. Rather, it grasps the original Latin meaning of *augere/auctoritas* as nurturing creativity, flowering growth, and enhancing enrichment. Biblical authority should foster such creativity, strength, and freedom.

The three sections of this commentary work extend the call of divine Wisdom. They invite readers to read these ancient works in light of Sophia's manifold revelations; they trace some of the submerged struggles and subjugated knowledges of inclusive Wisdom communities which still come to the fore in the diverse correspondence preserved in the canon; and finally they tell the life stories and recount the sayings of the prophets of Sophia who are her embodied presence. Like the envoys of divine Sophia/Wisdom, the contributors to this feminist commentary invite readers: "Come eat of Her bread and drink of Her wine" (Prov 9:1–6). By transgressing canonical boundaries and engaging in the adventurous process of reading against the kyriarchal grain, our interpretive journey can become the home/habitat[29] of divine Wisdom and her sister-outsiders.[30]

NOTES

1. See Karen Baker Fletcher, "Anna Julia Cooper and Sojourner Truth," in *Searching the Scriptures: A Feminist Introduction,* ed. Elisabeth Schüssler Fiorenza (New York: Crossroad, 1993), 41–52.

2. For this interpretation, see Kathi L. Kern, "Rereading Eve: Elizabeth Cady Stanton and The Woman's Bible, 1885–1896," *Women's Studies* 19 (1991): 371–83.

3. See also Suzan E. Hill, "The Woman's Bible: Reformulating Tradition," *Radical Religion* 3/2 (1977): 23–30; James Smylie, "The Woman's Bible and the Spiritual Crisis," *Soundings* 59/3 (1976): 305–28; Anne McGrew Bennett, *From Woman-Pain to Woman-Vision,* ed. Mary Hunt (Minneapolis: Fortress, 1989), 71–77; and Carolyn de Swarte Gifford, "Elizabeth Cady Stanton and the Woman's Bible," in *Searching the Scriptures: A Feminist Introduction,* 52–64.

4. As quoted by Barbara Hilkert Andolsen, *"Daughters of Jefferson, Daughters of Bootblacks," Racism and American Feminism* (Macon: Mercer University Press, 1986), 31.

5. Adrienne Rich, *A Wild Patience Has Taken Me This Far: Poems 1978–1981* (New York: Norton, 1981), 35–36.

6. See Lee Martin McDonald, *The Formation of the Christian Biblical Canon* (Nashville: Abingdon, 1992), 88. He suggests that the canon of Marcion was in keeping with an earlier tradition but that Marcion structured his canon according to "the sayings of Jesus and the writings of the apostles rather than as law, gospel, apostles."

7. For discussion, see James Barr, *Holy Scripture: Canon, Authority, Criticism* (Philadelphia: Westminster, 1983); Harry Y. Gamble, *The New Testament Canon: Its Making and Meaning* (Philadelphia: Fortress, 1985).

8. See my introduction "Transforming the Legacy of *The Woman's Bible,*" in *Searching the Scriptures: A Feminist Introduction,* 1–26.

9. Jacob Neusner insists that Bible and Torah do not refer to the same category or classification (*Jews and Christians: The Myth of a Common Tradition* [Philadelphia: Trinity Press International, 1991], 146–47). Torah never received closure, since in Judaism revelation does not end; rather, God speaks all the time through the sages. Whereas the Christian biblical canon emerged from the process of establishing church order and doctrine, Torah derives from the process of working out three different systems—the Pentateuch, the Mishnah, and the Bavli (Talmud).

10. See the excellent discussion of Ellen K. Wondra, "By Whose Authority? The Status of Scripture in Contemporary Feminist Theologies," *Anglican Theological Review* 75/1 (1993): 83–101.

11. David M. Bossman argues that a social group depends on a canon that defines its social symbol system ("Canon and Culture: A Call for Biblical Theology in Context," *Biblical Theology Bulletin* 23 [1993]: 4–13). The Christian canon represents the collective experience of the early church whose boundaries it defines. Hence, it is clear that canon is a normative social symbol system of the "patristic" church; it does not represent the collective experience of early Christian women.

12. Allain Le Boulluec, *La notion d'hérésie dans la littérature grecque, IIe–IIIe siècles* (Paris: Études Augustiniennes, 1985).

13. On this topic, see the classic work of Walter Bauer, *Orthodoxy and Heresy in Earliest Christianity* (Philadelphia: Fortress, 1971).

14. See, e.g., Alan F. Segal, *Two Powers in Heaven: Early Rabbinic Reports About Christianity and Gnosticism* (Leiden: Brill, 1977), 5 n. 3. He also points to an interesting possible philological connection between heretic and sex/gender. He argues for the interpretation of the Hebrew *min*, meaning "heretic/sectarian," as derived from the Hebrew *MYN* meaning "kind/species" or "sex/gender." The word is also associated with the Hebrew word *NH*, meaning to "commit adultery." Heresy and sexual unfaithfulness/idolatry are thus linked and gendered in the tradition the rabbis and the "fathers" inherited.

15. See, e.g., Jaroslav Pelikan, *The Emergence of the Catholic Tradition* (Chicago: University of Chicago Press, 1971).

16. Roy W. Hoover, "How the Books of the New Testament Were Chosen," *Bible Review* 9 (1993): 44–47.

17. Helmut Koester, "Writings and the Spirit: Authority and Politics in Ancient Christianity," *Harvard Theological Review* 84 (1991): 353–72, who traces this political process. It seems more likely, however, that early Christian letters as well as their collection and canonization as authoritative literature have been engendered by interests of administration and control rather than by a progressive democratization of the church.

18. Virginia Burrus, "The Heretical Woman as a Symbol in Alexander, Athanasius, Epiphanius, and Jerome," *Harvard Theological Review* 84 (1991): 49.

19. For elaboration and documentation, see my book *In Memory of Her: A Feminist Theological Reconstruction of Christian Origins* (New York: Crossroad, 1983).

20. For such an attempt, see Rosemary Radford Ruether, *Womanguides: Readings Toward a Feminist Theology* (Boston: Beacon, 1985).

21. For a history of the meanings of canon and different Christian canon formations, see Hans von Campenhausen, *The Formation of the Christian Bible* (Philadelphia: Fortress, 1972); and Bruce Metzger, *The Canon of the New Testament* (Oxford: Oxford University Press, 1987), 289–315.

22. For such a notion of canon as a "poetic classic" and a "classic model" of early Christianity, see Sally McFague, *Metaphorical Theology: Models of God in Religious Language* (Philadelphia: Fortress, 1982), 54–66.

23. See Cornel West, "Minority Discourse and the Pitfalls of Canon Formation," *The Yale Journal of Criticism* 1/1 (1987): 193–201 for the problems connected with attempts to establish a "new canon."

24. C. J. Hefele, *A History of the Councils of the Church, From the Original Documents* (Edinburgh, 1876), 2:252–53.

25. Patricia Cox Miller, "'Words With an Alien Voice': Gnostics, Scripture, and Canon," *Journal of the American Academy of Religion* 57 (1989): 459–84.

26. Ibid., 479.

27. Asphodel P. Long, *In A Chariot Drawn By Lions: The Search for the Female in Deity* (London: The Woman's Press, 1992), 195.

28. See her contribution in Rosemary Radford Ruether, ed., *Religion and Sexism: Images of Women in the Jewish and Christian Traditions* (New York: Simon & Schuster, 1974).

29. For this expression, see Nelle Morton, *The Journey is Home* (Boston: Beacon, 1985).

30. I owe this expression to Audre Lorde. For the hermeneutical position of feminists as insiders/outsiders or resident aliens, see my book *But She Said: Feminist Practices of Biblical Interpretation* (Boston: Beacon, 1992).

PART ONE

Revelatory Discourses: Manifestations of Sophia

The Book of Sophia
Thunder, Perfect Mind
Trimorphic Protennoia
The Book of Norea
The Odes of Solomon
The Sibylline Oracles
The Revelation to John
Montanist Oracles
The Daughters of Job

The Book of Sophia

Silvia Schroer ◆

INTRODUCTION

A Feminist Approach to the Figure and the Book of Wisdom

The book of Wisdom, written in Greek, is probably the latest Jewish writing accepted as part of the Greek canon of the Jewish Scriptures. In Protestant churches it is reckoned among the Apocrypha and, as a consequence, is often missing from Protestant editions of the Bible. In line with tradition, this writing is most often entitled "Wisdom of Solomon," an attribution that may be explained by the fact that in the central section of the book the already legendary King Solomon speaks. In the traditions of Israel he was considered the foremost patron of wisdom and wisdom literature.[1]

The book of Wisdom is interesting for a feminist reading of the Bible because here, as in other postexilic writings, the text speaks of personified Wisdom (Hebrew ḥokmâ; Greek sophia), a female figure who is immediately associated with Israel's God and who advances a divine claim. In their search for new images of God, Christian women have discovered in "Lady" Wisdom a point of departure for a feminist spirituality and theology. Feminist exegesis has paid close attention to the meaning of the image of God as Wisdom in the writings of the Hebrew Scriptures, but also to the great influence exercised by Sophia and the theology of wisdom on early Christian circles—their image of God and their interpretation of the person and destiny of Jesus of Nazareth. A few of the essential results of previous research may be presented here in the briefest form.

Personified Wisdom appears for the first time in biblical writings from the period after the Babylonian exile: within the book of Proverbs (chaps. 1–9) and in Job 28. In the second century B.C.E., Jesus Sirach shaped important chapters of his book around Wisdom (Sirach 1; 6; 14–15; 24; 51), and the book of Wisdom itself was probably composed in the last decades of the first century B.C.E. In all these writings, the relationship of (Lady) Wisdom to the God of Israel is difficult to determine in any systematic way.

Traditional exegesis has not succeeded in reaching a consensus about the meaning of Sophia in these writings or in the religious symbol system of post-exilic Israel, because the figure of Wisdom is difficult to reconcile with the patriarchal concepts of a monotheistic religion. Although studies in the history of religions have repeatedly emphasized the influence of Egyptian and Hellenistic goddesses on the figure of Sophia, as soon as the discussion turned to her importance within Israel and her theological meaning very little attention was paid to her femaleness.

Claudia Camp, with her book *Wisdom and the Feminine in the Book of Proverbs* (1985), a groundbreaking work both in its methodology and in its content, has furnished us with a basis for further feminist research on Wisdom. She demonstrates a connection, within the book of Proverbs, between womanly wisdom and Lady Wisdom, between the wise women in Israelite history and literature and the roles of Wisdom in Proverbs 1–9. At the same time, the personification of wisdom within the framework of Proverbs combines the pluriform teaching and sentences on wisdom within this book into a *single* doctrine embodying Israel's wisdom traditions and the life-sustaining wisdom of women. Thus, it offers a new religious identity in an era when the sacred institutions of the monarchy had vanished. But in doing so it not only assumes the role of mediator between the distant God of Israel and the people, as the situation is often interpreted. In addition, personified Wisdom is an attempt on the part of wisdom circles in the postexilic period to speak of the God of Israel through the image of a woman, and so to relate the image of God to new experiences and to the daily life of Israel in the period of rebuilding after the exile.

Claudia Camp's work shows how important it is for a feminist exegesis of the wisdom writings, methodologically speaking, to move from texts to contexts. Personified Wisdom must be examined concerning its functions and must be interpreted in feminist terms in the immediate context of each of the wisdom writings. The results will be different in each case, since Sophia assumes different functions and roles in the various writings. Moving from text to context also means methodologically to understand shifting images of God in their interaction with the social, political, cultural, and religious changes of a particular epoch.

The following exposition is situated within the framework of Elisabeth Schüssler Fiorenza's feminist-critical hermeneutics.[2] We will use historical inquiry to clarify the meaning of Sophia in the book of Wisdom and in the theological history of Israel. This theological history must be reconstructed in feminist theological terms as a part of the history of Jewish women at the end of the first century B.C.E. This critical work of remembering encounters through the hermeneutics of suspicion a biblical text that it is marked by androcentric translation, composition, selection, and projection. In addition, a feminist dialogue with a God-image, in particular, must presume a priori that Sophia's femaleness does not in itself constitute a viable theological criterion. Only when we know what meaning the figure and the book of Wisdom had for Jewish women of that time, and whether they promoted women's oppression or liberation from patriarchal power in society and in the religious community will we find a standpoint from which to judge whether this writing is adequate to the demands of today's more far-reaching liberation of women.

THE CHARACTER, STRUCTURE, AND CONTENT OF THE BOOK OF WISDOM

The book of Wisdom seems at first abstract, even cerebral. Lines of thought from the wisdom tradition and from philosophy are interwoven but offer contemporary women readers no concrete points for orientation within this complex of reflections. People are addressed (e.g., in 1:1), but we have no clear idea who it is who calls out for justice and who is being summoned. There are no names of persons, nations, or places—not even when a knowledge of Israel's history makes the identification seem obvious. The book of Wisdom seeks anonymity by clothing biblical traditions in disguises of Greek and Hellenistic language and forms. The avoidance of concrete figures and identifications at the same time lends the work an appearance of universal validity, something that is characteristic of wisdom literature; it thus seems to claim that these teachings have timeless importance and apply to all human beings.

This writing is fond of poetic language rich in imagery and likes to use rare Greek words, rhetorical stylistic figures, and redundant formulas. Scholars assign it to the genre of *protreptikos*, an encouraging and admonitory promotional writing on behalf of an art or science. Structurally speaking, we can distinguish three principal sections.

Part I (chaps. 1–5) begins with an admonition in wisdom style to love justice and seek God (1:1–15) and to give no place to death in one's life. In 1:16–2:24 there follows a counterexample: the first foolish speech of the godless, who have dedicated themselves to death. Their attitude is disclosed in a "thought quotation" as a deep-seated skepticism in the face of the ephemeral nature of life (cf. Qoheleth's position). Since the godless acknowledge no meaning in the laws governing the world, they have no goal but luxury, enjoyment, and uninhibited pleasure. Their resignation and cynicism make them reckless profiteers and practitioners of violence for whom the righteous, with their "pious" attitudes, are only objects of ridicule. In 3:1–10, however, it is emphatically said in opposition to this philosophy of life that the souls of the righteous are in God's hand and that they receive a manifold reward from God, while the godless are punished. In this section, against the older biblical tradition, there is expectation of another or eternal life for righteous people, in combination with a judgment at the end of time. In 3:11–4:6 the implications of such expectations are clear. Barren women and men are promised fruitfulness "at the visitation of souls," while a bitter end is prophesied for the numerous tribes of the children of adulterers and adulteresses. According to 4:7–20, again contrary to Israelite tradition, an early death can even be the sign of the election of a righteous person, while the godless will finally be thrown down like idols from their pedestals. Wis 5:1–14 impressively describes the scenario of the reversal of fortunes on Day X with a further penitent speech depicting the thoughts of the godless who now see the error of their ways. Wis 5:15–23 emphasizes that eternal life with God is promised to the righteous and, in fact, that God, together with the whole universe, will fight against people without understanding who know no law and whose actions reveal their wickedness, until, in a general desolation of the earth, even the thrones of the rulers will be overturned.

Part II (chaps. 6–10) is a so-called encomium, a speech in praise of Wisdom. First, a judgment speech threatens the kings and judges with a harsh divine reckoning (6:1–11) because they have not paid heed to law and justice. At the same time, the wisdom teacher who is speaking invites the tyrants to learn wisdom and thus to avoid judgment. In 6:12–21 there follows a first song of praise in honor of Wisdom, who is so easy to find. The search for Wisdom begins with a striving for instruction, which brings one near to God and is for rulers the only genuine guarantee of a long-lasting reign. In 6:22–7:21 follows a self-recommendation on the part of the wisdom teacher. In 6:22–25 he announces that he will "publish" everything concerning the origin and source of Wisdom, since a multitude of wise people will mean salvation for the world. Although no name is given, it will become clear in what follows that the speaker represents the prototype of the wise king of Israel, namely, Solomon. In 7:1–14, he emphasizes his human origins. He has acquired Wisdom through prayer. According to 7:15–21, God is the personal source and guide behind Wisdom and gives unerring knowledge of the sciences. Wisdom, the teacher of the wise, is the "fashioner" of all things. The whole encomium centers on the song in praise of the nature of Wisdom and the evidence of her power, in 7:22–8:1. Here Wisdom is described, by means of a great many attributes, as an emanation (outflow, effervescence) of God. In 8:2–21 follows a love song of the wise person (Solomon) to the mystic (initiate) of divine knowledge. She teaches the four (Greek) cardinal virtues of self-control and prudence, justice and courage. The wise one cannot attain to the longed-for marital communion with Wisdom by unassisted personal effort and accomplishment. Therefore in his great prayer (9:1–18) he begs God to send down the companion of God's throne (*paredros*). The concluding verse, "they [human beings] were saved by Wisdom" is simultaneously the introduction to chapter 10 and Part III (chaps. 11–19).

In 10:1–11:1 follows a hymnic retrospect of the saving activity of Wisdom in "human history." Without any names being mentioned, that activity is illustrated by examples from the biblical narratives of Adam, Cain and Abel, Noah, Abraham, Joseph, and finally the departure of Israel from Egypt. The motif of salvation and preservation of the just runs like a refrain through the text.

In Part III (chaps. 11:2–19:22) there is a hymnic reminiscence of the exodus. The principal theme, that God's punishments of enemies correspond to God's favors to the just (11:5) is illustrated in 11:6–14 through the example of the Nile turned to blood and the life-giving water from the rock. According to a second major theme, there is also a correspondence between sin and punishment (11:16). Four sets of comparisons (plague of frogs and gift of quail; plague of locusts, stinging flies, poisonous snakes, and the brass serpent; hail, storms, and bread from heaven; darkness and light, the column of fire) illustrate this principle in 16:1–18:4. Previously, an excursus (11:15–12:27) discusses God's kindness and love for creation, God's justice and care for humanity. A further excursus (13:1–15:19) is devoted to a detailed description of various forms of false notions of God and the worship of idols. In 18:5–19:9, again, two comparisons are put forward (death of the firstborn and death in the wilderness, on the one hand, and the protection of the just on the other). The third part concludes with a kind of epilogue containing retrospective views and new comparisons in which the Egyptians' hatred of foreigners is described as the reason for a divine judgment on them. As God stood by Israel in those days by reversing the laws of creation for the benefit of God's people, so God stands by Israel at all times and in all places. With this confident assertion, the book ends.

PLACE AND TIME OF COMPOSITION,
AUTHORSHIP, AND PURPOSE

We do not know who wrote the book of Wisdom. It could be the work of a single male author (such as Jesus Sirach) or female author. Many exegetes, however, find that the three nonhomogeneous principal sections lack unity. They therefore see this writing as more probably the product of a school, put together over time in a collective process. There is an increasing consensus about the place of origin and the date of the book of Wisdom.[3] According to this consensus, the book was written by Greek-speaking and Greek-educated authors at Alexandria in Egypt, where many wealthy Jews lived. According to C. Larcher, the three principal parts could have been composed in succession during the last three decades B.C.E.[4] Larcher's detailed justification for this late dating in fact explains many of the puzzling allusions in the text and helps us to make some progress toward decoding the *Sitz im Leben* of the book in spite of its generalizing character as a piece of wisdom literature. Hypothetically, the historical background, the purpose of the work, and the situation of its intended audience can be sketched as follows:

Part I is addressed to diaspora Jews in Egypt, around 31 B.C.E. The congregation is in turmoil because, under the strong influence of Hellenism, many have fallen away from Jewish belief (3:10–12), no longer practice it, or are even persecuting their fellow believers. The renegades are profiting and prospering, while those faithful to Jewish belief have apparently fallen into difficulties. Although no pogroms or persecutions are attested for this period, the destabilized political situation after the victory of Octavian over his rival, Marc Antony, in the naval battle at Actium (31 B.C.E.) could explain how and why the situation of the Jewish communities in Egypt had gotten worse. But it is also possible that the first major section was written with an eye to the events of the first year of Herod's reign in Palestine. With Roman support, Herod had conquered Antigonus, the last Hasmonean king, and after the conquest of Jetusalem in 37 B.C.E. he beheaded Antigonus at Antioch. Ruthlessly, Herod had many of his opponents executed and ordered the high priest, Aristobulus III, to be drowned at Jericho. For the Jewish population, Herod, as a half-Jew, a Roman vassal, and the representative of the Hellenistic style of life, was a hated tyrant. In addition to domestic political turmoil, there was a severe earthquake in 31 B.C.E. that cost many people their lives (see the possible reference in Wis 5:17–23).

After the suicides of Antony and Cleopatra VII (Philopator) in 30 B.C.E., Egypt became a Roman province under the control of the emperor. In light of these important events in secular history and the increasing pressure on the Jewish population in Palestine and in the Egyptian diaspora, the book of Wisdom sought with the utmost seriousness to stabilize Jewish identity by aiming its barbs outward against apostates and at the same time turning its attention inward to securing those who had remained true to Judaism in their faith.

Part II may have been written in the years after Octavian, now Caesar Augustus, seized power over Egypt in 30 B.C.E. (see 6:1–3). The Roman rulers exercised their judicial power through their representatives to the ends of the earth (6:1b); the Pax Romana was also being felt in Egypt. The author or authors, at the beginning of this new era, raised the voice of reason, issued reminders about the humanity and mortality of kings (against the Ptolemaic image of the ruler and the novel institution of the imperial cult), and presented, in the image of Wisdom and of the ideal wise king (Solomon), the indispensable preconditions for an enduring rulership, which simultaneously satisfied the highest demands of intelligence and ethics.

Part III presumes an increasing degree of anti-Semitism on the part of the Egyptian populace (see 19:13, the accusation of hatred of foreigners). The background may be the disadvantages accruing to Jewish men and women from the introduction, under Augustus, of a poll tax on all those who did not enjoy full citizenship. Opportunities for advancement in the city and imperial government were open only to Egyptians, provided they could demonstrate that they had had a Greek education in a gymnasium. The reference to the increasing growth of the Roman imperial cult (14:16b–22), longing for the Palestinian homeland (12:3, 7), and thoughts of national liberation (18:9) make it probable that this section was written sometime around the middle of Augustus's reign—that is, shortly before the beginning of the Common Era. The Jewish community, remembering the exodus from Egypt and the gift of the promised land, confirms its hope that God will again intervene within history on behalf of the just among God's people.

THE MANIFESTATIONS AND ATTRIBUTES OF SOPHIA IN WISDOM 6–10

In the first chapters of the book there is only marginal reference to Wisdom. It is primarily the middle section (chaps. 6–10) that is devoted to the personified Sophia.[5] In the introduction to his speech to the kings and tyrants of the earth (6:1–2, 9) the teacher of wisdom (Solomon) proclaims that he will teach Wisdom (6:9, 11, 25). When, in what follows, the text speaks of Sophia as a female figure, the nonpersonified meaning of wisdom (i.e., study, knowledge, experience, cleverness) is always implied, even when it recedes into the background.

In the descriptive song in 6:12–16, Sophia is first described, in line with sayings in Proverbs 1 and 8 as well as Sirach 4; 6; 15; 51, as a woman whom the students of wisdom seek and love. The wisdom teacher who speaks in 6:22–25 emphasizes expressly that Wisdom has nothing to do with "mysteries" (secrets). He will openly proclaim her existence and her origin; he will bring knowledge of her before the public and will not (selfishly) keep it to himself.

Even the legendary sage and king, Solomon, received Wisdom like every other mortal, through prayer and appeal to God (7:7). It was more valuable to him than kingly power, wealth, health, well-being, or light. According to 7:15–21, wisdom and knowledge come from God. Insight into all the scientific disciplines of Hellenism (philosophy, cosmology, chronology, astronomy, zoology, demonology, psychology, biology) is ultimately the gift of God, but it is Wisdom who, as architect or builder (Greek *technitis*) of all things, undertakes the teaching or instruction of the wise. The nature of Sophia is described hymnically in 7:22–8:1 in twenty-one epithets. The triple perfect number (3 x 7) of the attributes simultaneously signals the impossibility of adequately describing her essence. Sophia is lauded, in a manner similar to the praise of the Egyptian or Greek divinities, as a being of many names and many forms. To speak of her in a perfect way is as difficult as it was for Cleanthes (262–232

B.C.E.), a student of the Stoic founder Zeno, to speak of "the good," so that he selected some thirty attributes for his hymn in praise of the good:

> You ask me about the nature of the good? Then listen: It is full of order, just, godfearing, pious, full of self-control, valuable, lovely and dutiful. . . .[6]

Many of the things that are said about Sophia in 7:22ff. contain references drawn from the corpus of Stoic philosophy and its descriptions of the divine. While the first eleven attributes describe the nature of Wisdom "in itself" (v. 22), the remainder give more attention to her relationship to the world and to human beings.

Chapter 8, with its biography of the "ideal" sage, takes up the idea already expressed in 7:28, that God cannot love any human being who does not live with wisdom (i.e., sleep with her, have intercourse with her). The love relationship between the student of wisdom (Solomon) and Sophia is described in strongly erotic language: Solomon falls in love with Wisdom, is enamored of her beauty (8:1–3), decides to wed her (8:9) and sleep with her (8:16), and tries to take her for himself (8:18). The erotic language of these images is nothing new: even in Proverbs, but especially in the work of Jesus Sirach (e.g., 51:13–17) the longing of the student of wisdom for Sophia is depicted as an erotic and sexual desire. In Qumran literature (11QPs^a 21.11–17) SHE (Wisdom) is unmistakably praised as a desired lover. But what is new in contrast to the older texts is that Sophia is called the beloved and the companion (8:3) of God. The erotic-feminine aspects do not become independent, however; they always remain embedded in larger contexts. Sophia's marital communion with God explains pictorially why she is *the* mystic of divine knowledge pure and simple. Again, it is Sophia's omniscience, not her beauty, that is the motive for the sage to marry her. Only Wisdom, that is, because of her knowledge of the divine and of all things, can be a perfect counselor to a wise king (cf. Prov. 8:12–16). Only the well-qualified advice of Wisdom guarantees the young king renown, the ability to judge rightly, an immortal name, governance over nations, and success in war. The chapter closes with the acknowledgment that Sophia is a gift of God (8:21).

The middle section of the book reaches its climax in the prayer of the wise king in chapter 9 (cf. Solomon's great prayer in 1 Kings 8). The sage asks God for the *paredros* (the one-who-sits-beside) of the divine throne (9:4). Both the concept of the *paredros* and the image of the enthroned couple are, in the history of religions, very closely connected with the divine couples in polytheistic religions (Greece, ancient Orient). The authors of the book of Wisdom, however, as the marital metaphors have already shown, have no hesitation about employing daring images when it is a question of describing divine reality in its various aspects. A fundamental attitude of skepticism and the consideration derived from it, that Wisdom's teaching is indispensable for the salvation of human beings, conclude the prayer. Almost imperceptibly, a transition has taken place in the progressive unfolding of the text: the wise king who speaks describes himself as a weak human being and refers at nearly every point to the "human condition" in general and the importance of Sophia for (all) human beings. Thus, the programmatically formulated humanity of the ideal ruler and sage in 7:1 also has a "democratizing effect." What is said in the middle section of the book about Solomon and Sophia is fundamentally true of all human beings; it thus possesses general validity even beyond the bounds of Judaism.

This general validity is preserved also in chapter 10. While it is true that exclusively biblical stories and persons are cited there as historical examples of the salvation of human beings by Wisdom, the names of those persons are omitted in order to avoid a narrowing of that salvation to the biblical and Jewish tradition. Through this universalistic reading of the biblical writings, sympathizers attracted to Judaism are offered a means of access to these texts.[7] The often-repeated motif of saving, guarding, and preserving determines the flow of the text. Sophia saves Adam, Cain, the earth, and Noah, Abraham, Lot, Jacob, and Joseph (10:1–14); it is she also who rescues "a holy people and blameless race" (Israel) from the nation of oppressors (Egypt) (10:15–21). Thus God's saving deeds in and for Israel are retold, with the name of Sophia taking the place of the traditional name of God. Wisdom is the God of Israel in the image of a woman.

But the femaleness of this divine figure is by no means only eroticism; it is also and primarily bound up with knowledge, rule, teaching, counsel, the most exalted origins, the power to form and create, trustworthiness, salvation, guidance, and virtue, especially justice. Most of these characteristics are not ordinarily associated with the roles assigned to women in a patriarchal society.[8] This makes it all the more important to ask whether we can find clues to the reason why, toward the end of the first century B.C.E., Sophia was able to become a persuasive religious symbol even within these female roles. Is there a connection between this female image of God and the image of women at the same period? What influences impelled Jewish women and men in Egypt to develop such an image of God? What ends are served by the female personification of "Wisdom" in this text?

FROM TEXT TO CONTEXT

At an initial level, the book of Wisdom contains little direct information about women. In the fiction employed, a male sage directs his teaching to male kings. Women are mentioned explicitly only in 3:12 (the foolish wives/women of the godless), in 3:13 (barren women), and in 9:7 (the daughters as well as the sons of Israel). It is noteworthy that according to 3:13ff. the

childlessness of a woman (and of a man), contrary to the older Israelite tradition, is no longer regarded as the greatest misfortune that can befall a person.[9]
The barren woman, so long as she is "undefiled" and "has not entered into a
sinful union" (had pre- or extramarital sexual relations) is promised fruit at the
"visitation of souls," that is, at the day of divine judgment or at the end of the
ages. It is true that similar ideas are suggested as early as Isaiah 54; 56:3–5, and
in Sir 16:1–4, but this is the first place where a fundamental preference is
expressed for virtuous, voluntary sexual abstinence over a less virtuous manner
of life accompanied by the bearing of many children. Concretely, this means
that women who could not (or did not wish to) bear children and who voluntarily lived as virgins, single women, or widows were accorded the same status
in the religious congregation as married mothers.[10] We encounter this unusual
image of the childless and "virginal" woman in a similar fashion in a short writing by Philo of Alexandria, *De vita contemplativa*. This little book reveals a
number of connections to the book of Wisdom that are highly suggestive for
feminist research.

THE THERAPEUTRIDES: JEWISH WOMEN IN
CONTEMPLATIVE COMMUNITIES

Philo of Alexandria (25 B.C.E.–ca. 40 C.E.) wrote short works on a variety of
Jewish groups of his own time. In *De vita contemplativa* he reports on the
community of the Therapeutae and Therapeutrides, who, in rural isolation in
the vicinity of Alexandria, far removed from the cares of the city, devoted
themselves entirely to prayer, the study of the scriptures, and an ascetic style of
life, their material demands being as modest as possible.[11] We must, of course,
take into account that the image Philo sketches of these groups is shaped by
his personal opinion and subjective depiction. But since we have no other
sources on the Therapeutae and Therapeutrides, we must search with the
utmost thoroughness for historical information in *De vita contemplativa*,
which remains an important document for the history of Jewish women.

The Therapeutae or Therapeutrides, whose name so puzzles Philo that he
apparently can make only stabs at interpretation (*Vit. cont.* 2), are "dropouts."
Out of a longing for eternal blessedness, they leave earthly life behind them;
that is, they bestow their property on their relatives and abandon family, associates, friends, and their homeland and flee into the countryside (*Vit. cont.* 13,
18). There, sheltered in small settlements, they lead a strongly regimented
common life. During the week, the members spend most of their time in individual cells, engaging in philosophical and theological studies and composing
hymns. On the sabbath, then, they all assemble to hear a lecture:

> This common sanctuary in which they meet every seventh day is a double enclosure, one portion set apart for the use of the men, the other for the women. For women too regularly make part of the audience with the same ardour and the same sense of their calling. The wall between the two chambers rises up from the ground to three or four cubits. . . . [T]he modesty becoming to the female sex is preserved, while the women sitting within ear-shot can easily follow what is said since there is nothing to obstruct the voice of the speaker. (*Vit. cont.* 32)

Thus, men and women, even though they seem to live and study separately during the week, form a single community in which women have fundamentally the same status as men. Women are also fully integrated in the principal festival of the Therapeutae and Therapeutrides, a simple but festive meal followed by a liturgy. In this connection, Philo adds that the female members are mainly "aged virgins" who voluntarily live in a state of sexual abstinence (*Vit. cont.* 68).

Ross S. Kraemer supposes that the "aged virgins" may not have been only unmarried, childless women or real virgins but also older women who had already passed through menopause. Interestingly, Philo gives as a reason for these women's choice of sexual abstinence that they desire to live with Sophia and are striving for an immortal posterity. In fact, Philo may have written this unusual notion of women who seek to live with (wifely) Lady Wisdom under the impression that these women, through their style of life, their age, and their spiritual efforts, had already divested themselves of femaleness and, as he elsewhere describes the spiritual goal, had become "male."[12] We do not know whether Philo's depiction also corresponds to the Therapeutrides' self-conception. In any case, personified Wisdom had a central importance in the spiritual life of the community.

The teaching of Sophia is a kind of heavenly food to the ascetic Therapeutae and Therapeutrides, from which they seek to live in the most literal sense of the word (*Vit. cont.* 35). Still, jubilant singing and festivals are also part of this life with Wisdom. In the community's evening celebration after the *agapē* meal, a choir of women and men makes present in song the rescue of Israel at the exodus from Egypt. The presentation closes with a common choral song, in which the men are led by the prophet Moses and the women by the prophetess Miriam (*Vit. cont.* 83–84). Thus, in shaping their liturgical practices the Therapeutae and Therapeutrides had a regard for traditions of particular importance to women and included them alongside the dominant patriarchal traditions.

We can conclude from *De vita contemplativa* that in Greco-Roman Egypt there were monastic Jewish groups to which certain women were admitted. These communities may have recruited primarily well-to-do, educated members who in several respects made a break with the norms of their Jewish and

Greco-Roman-Egyptian milieu. They withdrew from their family ties in order to live together in a new, spiritual family (much like the Jesus movement). They considered childlessness an admirable form of life. They despised material wealth and well-being as well as all the excesses of social life. They refused to be served by slaves, since they regarded slavery as contrary to nature and a consequence of greed and violence (*Vit. cont.* 70). The women living in the community seem to have enjoyed, for the most part, the same rights as men. At any rate they are depicted by Philo, in this writing, as religious subjects of full maturity who not only brought to the community the consciousness of their history as women (Miriam[13]) but perceived themselves also as life companions of divine wisdom.

Research on the book of Wisdom has repeatedly postulated connections with the Therapeutrides. In fact, there are points of contact in the structure and content of both writings that cannot be peripheral or accidental. Philo contrasts the Therapeutae and Therapeutrides with other (pagan) groups who worship the elements, the stars, demigods, statues, or animals (*Vit. cont.* 3–9). This distinction has repeated parallels, especially in the third section of the book of Wisdom (chaps. 12–15), which attacks various forms of false knowledge and worship of God as well as idol worship. Personified Sophia plays a central role in the spirituality both of the Therapeutae and Therapeutrides and of the authors of the book of Wisdom. In addition, both of them combine recollection of the exodus (Wis 10:15–21; chaps. 11 and 19) with songs of praise. In each case, this exodus is led by female figures, namely, the prophetess Miriam or Sophia. Both in the circles of the Therapeutae and Therapeutrides and in those of sapiential thought it appears that the consciousness of a special kind of friendship with God was cultivated (Wis 7:27; *Vit. cont.* 90); it could be achieved through the study of wisdom and would lead to blessedness. Also common to both writings is an internal posture of distance toward current attitudes to life in their cultural environment (cf., e.g., Wisdom 3–4) and a strong orientation toward a divine or heavenly world and order of things that could be experienced in the past and present and was accepted as a certainty for the future. For the Therapeutae and Therapeutrides, however, this worldview effected a very drastic turning away from the world that cannot be demonstrated in the book of Wisdom. Nevertheless, the connections between the two writings are so marked that we must suppose that they originated in a similar milieu and that there was a spiritual kinship between the two groups. Comparable examples of connections between radical "dropout" groups and a broader circle of sympathizers who did not share their extreme style of life but did participate in their ideas include Qumran and the Essenes and also the itinerant charismatics of the Jesus movement and their resident associates. Thus, we may suppose that the book of Wisdom originated in circles in which Jewish women from Egypt/Alexandria had a place, perhaps an unusual one, and in which women's religious traditions as well as a female image of God as Sophia were cultivated. In the Palestinian region as well there is a famous example from the first century B.C.E. of a female figure who led a new exodus of Israel. The eponymous heroine of the Judith novel, who possibly was meant to invite Jewish women and men from the diaspora to return to Jerusalem, corresponds in many ways to the image of women and of Wisdom described above. She came from wealthy circumstances and remained voluntarily a widow and childless after the loss of her husband. She is to be remembered as a model of piety and virtue by all Israelites after her death. But especially she undertakes an extraordinarily courageous action in a dramatic situation in order to rescue her people from the oppression of a tyrant. Judith (like Sophia) is the savior of Israel who (like Moses) accomplishes the will of God with a strong hand and leads the exodus.[14]

THE POWER OF THE GODDESS: ISIS AND SOPHIA

Even in the frame of the book of Proverbs, in Job 28, and in the book of Jesus Sirach, the figure of personified Wisdom is strongly inspired by the images and mythology of the ancient oriental and Egyptian goddess cults. Maat, Hathor, the tree goddesses of Egypt, and even the Syrian goddess lent to Sophia her image and her power of fascination. The observation that Sophia in the book of Wisdom is shaped by the figure of Isis and the theology of Isis in late Ptolemaic or early Roman Egypt was expressed, in partial studies, as early as the first half of the twentieth century. Major publications by J. M. Reese, B. L. Mack, and J. S. Kloppenborg contributed to a more precise development of the connections between Isis and Sophia.[15]

In mythology, the Egyptian goddess Isis is the sister-spouse of Osiris and the mother of Horus, whom she, as a goddess expert in magic, shields from danger. In late Egypt, this goddess attained a preeminent place. Her cult spread throughout the realm of the Ptolemies, in the Aegean region, and in the western Mediterranean. By way of Greece it reached Italy near the end of the second century B.C.E, where temples, mysteries, processions, and books were devoted to the goddess.[16] The popularity and increasing spread of the Isis cult were attributable to the unlimited variety of the goddess. Through an equation of Isis with other divinities, the "many-formed one" in the Egyptian divine realm had developed more and more into a universal goddess. As described in the mythology, her functions of creating and protecting life as wife and mother made her ruler over the mystery of life. In the fates of Osiris and Horus, human beings recognized their own story, and Isis assumed an important mediating role between the living and the dead. To her was attributed rule over cosmic and earthly powers and over destiny. In particular, her role as ruler of destiny, which enabled her to break through the fatalistic order of the world because, unlike the Greek divinities, she was not subject to Heimarmene, the Greek goddess of unavoidable fate, made Isis a most attractive figure in Hellenism also. Isis was worshiped across almost all groups of the population (with the exception of the military), by men and women; nevertheless, her cult exercised a special attraction for women and probably had a positive influence on women's position in society. It is said of Isis in the aretalogies:[17]

> Thou didst make the power of women equal to that of men.

Or:
> It is I whom the women call Goddess . . .
> I have brought woman and man together . . .
> I invented marriage contracts.

Kloppenborg distinguishes three types of Isis worship in the first century B.C.E.: the Isis worshiped by the simple people, the Isis of the Ptolemaic and Roman royal theology, and the Isis of the Greeks as we find her in the aretalogies or the writings of someone like Plutarch (*De Iside et Osiride*) or Diodorus Siculus. While the first type had scarcely any influence on Alexandrian Judaism, the authors of the book of Wisdom deliberately entered into dialogue with the royal theology, and even more so with the strongly missionary Isis worship of the Greeks.

The relationship between Solomon and Wisdom, extensively described in the middle section of the book, acquires a special mythological dimension against the background of the royal Isis theology. As King Solomon attains immortality through Wisdom, so Osiris and Horus achieve immortality through Isis. As Sophia is at the same time "goddess" and (desired) spouse of the king, so Isis is goddess and royal spouse, counselor and guarantor of the ruling house.[18] Through Wisdom, the divine agent, Solomon obtains his kingdom, rule, wisdom, and power. In one of the Isis hymns of Isidore, from a Ptolemaic temple near Fayum (85 B.C.E.), it is said of Isis:

> All those who live most happily, the outstanding men,
> scepter-bearing kings and all who rule,
> reign, if they cling to thee, unto old age, . . .
> But that ruler whom the Queen loves best
> reigns over both Asia and Europe,
> he obtains peace . . .[19]

According to the statement of a great many aretalogies, Isis puts an end to injustice, tyranny, and wars.[20] The Ptolemaic queens identified with Isis. We know that Cleopatra VII dressed as Isis and had herself called Nea Isis.

Isis is honored in many dedicatory inscriptions as the (universal) savior. She (like Maat before her) is responsible for law and custom, gives laws, and takes care that they are obeyed, so that all human beings may live in peace as equals. The saving power of Sophia is described in like terms, especially in Wisdom 10 but also in many other passages. She knows how to steer a ship (10:4 and 14:1–6); she comes to prisoners in their dungeons (10:14); she brings riches to the just (3:3–6), and so on.[21]

In summary, we may say that the statements about Sophia in the book of Wisdom are imbued to the highest degree with features from Isis mythology; in fact, they apparently quote and allude to the language of the Isis mission quite deliberately when sketching the portrait of Sophia. Sophia is the Jewish response to the challenge of Isis and mystery cult piety in Egypt before the end of the era. What is noteworthy in this response is that it consists not of negative rejection but of constructive integration.[22] The book of Wisdom is addressed to Jews, and perhaps also to Jewish sympathizers, who came into immediate contact with Isis religion in Alexandria and for whom the Isis cult quite possibly furnished a very real religious alternative. Rather than demonizing Isis religion, the book of Wisdom attempts to develop an equal and equally attractive figure out of Jewish tradition and set her over against Isis. The social position of Jews in Alexandria is also reflected in this attempt. In relation to the Egyptian population, the Jews had enjoyed a thoroughly privileged position, but at the beginning of Roman rule in Egypt that position was threatened (see "Introduction," above). In spite of their disadvantages in relation to the Hellenistic population, and despite their critical attitude toward a society in which "might was the law of right" (2:11), where a few "strong," at the expense of the "weak" (cf. 2:1–11), gave themselves up to hedonism, and where a great gulf existed between poor and rich, Judaism aspired to Greek culture, education and religious observance.[23] Behind the constructive Jewish reaction to Isis theology, a fragment of women's history also emerges. Both the Egyptian and the Greek women in Egypt possessed a notable degree of legal and economic freedom. The Hellenistic queens such as Olympias, Arisinoë II, and Cleopatra VII, as powerful politicians, influenced the image of women in the Hellenistic epoch, even though improved opportunities for education, birth control, or political activity were accorded to only a minority of women. In the philosophical schools, however, there was discussion of the traditional roles of women. Poets and painters concerned themselves with women's feelings of sexual pleasure.[24] The Hellenistic emancipation of the individual had the additional consequence that the practice of religion was partly transferred to the charge of private cultic associations and became a matter of individual choice.

These changes did not wash over the Jewish groups living in Alexandria without leaving a trace. Jewish women (at least the upper class) may have formulated to an increasing degree their own self-concept, as well as their demand to take an active part in the shaping of religious life and to formulate "modern" approaches to faith that were capable of offering contemporary and attractive images of God. While the positive indications of such developments are sparse, many early Jewish writings confirm, by their androcentric and negative reaction, how strongly Jewish men were upset and made insecure by women. With an enormous vehemence, they attempted to eroticize the biblical stories about women and to demonize the female figures in order to counter the strength, knowledge, and demands of Jewish women by means of androcentric projections of the image of women.[25]

FEMINIST THEOLOGICAL EVALUATION

THE FUNCTION OF THE PERSONIFICATION OF SOPHIA

The stylistic device of personification functions primarily to unite diverse features and to identify something abstract ("wisdom") with something concrete and familiar ("woman"). Thus personified *ḥokmâ* in Proverbs 1–9 combines the various wisdom teachings in Proverbs 10–31 and Israel's wisdom traditions into a *single* teaching. It unites the wisdom of women and the image of God.[26]

Sophia, as a religious symbol in the book of Wisdom, inherits the features of the older personification of Wisdom but introduces new accents as well. As a personification, she serves less to combine the various teachings in the Jewish tradition than to unite the whole Jewish wisdom tradition with that of Greece and Hellenism. Thus, she mediates between the strongly ethical dimensions of biblical wisdom teaching with their interest in a just order of things and the intellectual concept of wisdom of Greek antiquity, which, in turn, concerned itself with the philosophical and ethical search for the highest good and the greatest happiness. What the Hellenists call *philosophia,* the striving for wisdom, exists also in the Jewish tradition: that is the message of this writing. The effort to achieve knowledge and education is seen as a weighty common interest of both cultural groups and a basis for intercultural dialogue. The religious and national identity of educated Jewish circles in Alexandria revealed itself, even in times of crisis, as strong enough to react to the challenges of the Hellenistic world by maintaining a dialogue.[27] Nationalism and the independence of Israel are combined in Sophia with universalism and a considered and deliberate theological inculturation. This dialogue is not uncritical. Wisdom, as Alexandrian Jews understood it, is not a private matter and is not reserved to a few initiates in the mysteries.[28] She is open to communication and yet is more than acquired knowledge of things. Wisdom, as Jews understood her, is the sole guarantee of the continuance even of a Hellenistic or Roman empire, since education is indispensable for just rule. Against the background of the expanding Pax Romana (cf. the reference in 14:22), Sophia is a symbol critical of the governing power, directed against arbitrariness and tyranny.

She appears in the image of a wise, omniscient, just, and saving woman whose autonomy is transparent both to the God of Israel and to the goddess Isis. Isis herself, though originally an Egyptian goddess, had entered the Hellenistic-Roman world as a religious symbol with an unusual capacity to create unity. By incorporating the mythology and theology of Isis in the figure of Sophia, Egyptian Judaism sought to lend power to its own integrating forces through the use of a female symbol of the divine.

The importance of personified Sophia as a creator of unity is also manifest in the theological structure of the book of Wisdom. The first section begins with the programmatic appeal: "love righteousness, you rulers of the earth." What constitutes righteousness according to God's will is made evident in chapters 1–5, primarily through the contrast of the righteous and the godless. The purpose of the first section of the book is to demonstrate that the righteous, contrary to appearances, are on the better and more productive way—in fact, that God's rules of governance will ultimately triumph. The real world with its unjust order of things and its striving for riches is contrasted with a just world, a contrast-world, whose symbolism already strongly resembles the Christian Testament ideas about a "reign of God" (cf. 10:10, 14). This contrast-world really exists; it is possible to live according to its laws; its rules are valid. But it is also utopian to the degree that it will only be fully revealed and accomplished in a "then." "Then" the godless will come to a realization of the truth; the "righteous man" will be rehabilitated; God "with all creation will fight against the frenzied foes" (5:20) and establish justice. The second section of the book shows that these ideas are not purely apocalyptic. Wisdom, who is here presented, is not withdrawn and unattainable; she is accessible. She is the teacher of righteousness. Righteousness and wisdom are like the outer and inner sides of a life pleasing to God. Without wisdom, there can be no just "reign of God." In the first and second sections of the book, to begin with, the striving for this "reign of God" is initiated by individual human beings. But when, in the third section, Wisdom as a divine agent of salvation and leader of the exodus is called to mind, she unites herself expressly with the collective history of the whole people of Israel. At the same time she transforms the old Jewish traditions, which are newly selected and narrated in "sophialogical" terms. Thus, the striving toward a just world is assigned to individuals but is also eased by a collective, salvation-historical assurance.

SOPHIA: SYMBOL OF UNITY IN DIVERSITY
AND TEACHER OF RIGHTEOUSNESS

Sophia in the book of Wisdom is the symbol of an interreligious and intercultural dialogue in a multicultural society of the first century B.C.E. She attempts a positive interaction with the existing religious and cultural pluralism by reinterpreting her own tradition, readily opening herself to foreign influences and taking inspiration from them. The "contextual theology" of the work is not averse to speaking about the God of Israel in new language and in images similar to those of the goddess. This process of reformulation, however, does not lead to a surrender of accepted tradition, to a leveling of the independence of Jewish thought and belief, or to esoteric indifference. The common history affords identity ("at all times and in all places"; cf. 19:22). The irreplaceable measure that endures through all changes is the justice of God. Not without reason does the book of Wisdom engage itself intensively with the widest variety of forms of false knowledge of God, with idolatry and the blasphemous worship of rulers (chaps. 11–19). Despite all openness, there is no surrender of the right to criticize humanly unworthy tendencies in other religions and the idolatry of the imperial cult. There is also resistance to the increasing hatred of foreigners, that is, anti-Judaism, in Egypt (cf. 19:14–16).

Sophia shows the way to a just Jewish life amid a pluralistic world. Certainly, the optimistic attitude toward the power for change afforded by knowledge, education, and consciousness may be traced to the fact that, in the book of Wisdom, educated and probably well-situated Jews are speaking their minds. Nevertheless, this option is worthy of consideration even and especially for our own time. In an attempt to work toward a just world order at the end of the twentieth century, one that could offer resistance to the "new" world orders of existing systems of power, the experience and knowledge of women—womanly wisdom—will stand in the forefront. Wisdom, the collected experience and education of women, can save women; she could even lead a worldwide exodus from patriarchal oppression. As an integrative religious symbol, Sophia is well suited to create community between religions; as a cosmopolitan symbol she can contribute to the struggle against nationalism through a national identity that is open to the whole world.[29]

Sophia, as an authentic biblical image of God, offers remarkable possibilities for breaking up the petrifactions and ontologizations of androcentric God language, and for doing so on the basis of a Jewish tradition. Her attributes are the attributes of God; when she speaks, God speaks; what she proclaims and does is God's will. She is the "wholly other," yet she makes herself known. The authors of the work dared to think of Sophia within the horizons of the imagery of the goddess Isis, who promises salvation because she stands above the powers of destiny.

The message of Wisdom is as current today as it was then: it is a program against fatalism and necrophilia, a challenge to love all living things as God loves and an expression of confidence that God, together with the whole universe, intervenes against the powers of death.

Love righteousness! ... (1:1)
Do not invite death by the error of your life,

or bring on destruction by the works of your hands!
because God did not make death,
and does not delight in the death of the living.
For God created all things so that they might exist.... (1:12–14a)

Translated by Linda M. Maloney

NOTES

1. In the original German edition of this essay, citations are from Dieter Georgi's translation (1980). English citations are adapted from the NRSV.

2. Elisabeth Schüssler Fiorenza, *In Memory of Her: A Feminist Theological Reconstruction of Christian Origins* (New York: Crossroad, 1983); eadem, *Bread Not Stone: The Challenge of Feminist Biblical Interpretation* (Boston: Beacon, 1984).

3. For the date and place of origin, see John S. Kloppenborg, "Isis and Sophia in the Book of Wisdom," *Harvard Theological Review* 75 (1982): 57–84; Helmut Engel, "Was Weisheit ist und wie sie entstand, will ich verkünden," in *Lehrerin der Gerechtigkeit,* ed. G. Hentschel and E. Zenger (Erfurter Theologische Schriften 19; Leipzig: St. Benno, 1991), 67–102.

4. C. Larcher, *Le Livre de la Sagesse ou la Sagesse de Salomon* (Etudes bibliques n.s. 1; 3 vols.; Paris: Gabalda, 1983, 1984, 1985).

5. On the structure and content of the encomium, see esp. Engel, "Was Weisheit ist."

6. *Stoicorum Veterum Fragmenta,* ed. I. ab Arnim (Leipzig, 1905), 237 frag. 557.

7. I am grateful to Dr. Daniel Kosch of Zürich for calling my attention to the important fact that the book of Wisdom, with this kind of universalistic reading of scripture, represents an independent alternative both to an allegorical exegesis influenced by Hellenism that denies the literal meaning of the scriptures and also to the combination of allegorical and literal interpretation later represented by Philo.

8. See D. Georgi, "Frau Weisheit oder Das Recht auf Freiheit als schöpferische Kraft," in *Verdrängte Vergangenheit, die uns bedrängt: Feministische Theologie in der Verantwortung für die Geschichte,* ed. Leonore Siegele-Wenschkewitz (Munich: Kaiser, 1988), 252–53.

9. In fact, it appears that in the Hellenistic and Roman period it was not so common for Jewish women to have a great many children as has often been supposed. Ancient documents, including those from Egypt, for example, show that a substantial percentage of women had only one (surviving) child. See G. Mayer, *Die jüdische Frau in der hellenistisch-römische Antike* (Stuttgart: Kohlhammer, 1987), 71–76.

10. We cannot exclude the possibility that 4:1–2, otherwise so difficult to understand, also refers to such women. (In that case, the subject would be "she," the childless woman, rather than "she," virtue.) They are promised immortality, that is, a continuing memory and recognition before God and human beings. They function as models for imitation (4:2) in life and after their death, and "throughout all time" they will be given the highest honor for their "undefiled" victory.

11. We do not know when this work was written, and it is uncertain whether Philo is referring to older documents or to contemporary data. A comparison with the book of Wisdom, however, is reliable, since the difference in time cannot be more than fifty years at the most. Quotations from Philo are from the Loeb edition: *Philo,* with an English translation by F. H. Colson (Loeb Classical Library ; 10 vols.; London: Heinemann; Cambridge, MA: Harvard University Press, 1941), vol. 9.

12. Ross S. Kraemer, "Monastic Jewish Women in Greco-Roman Egypt: Philo Judaeus on the Therapeutrides," *Signs: Journal of Women in Culture and Society* 14 (1989): esp. 352ff.

13. Miriam or Marion was, in Hellenistic-Roman times, by far the most common name for Jewish women, in Egypt as well (see Mayer, *Die jüdische Frau,* 33–42).

14. An indication of the virulence of Wisdom as a female image of God in the time before and after the end of the era is found in Philo's work *De fuga et inventione* 51ff. (on Gen 25:20). In a very daring exegesis, Philo arrives at the idea that the daughter of God, Wisdom, should be called Father because, while her name is female, her nature is male, as is the case with all the virtues. Philo sees great importance in the fact that Wisdom is to be distinguished from the creator of the universe "as a male being" and must be given the second place, which is appropriate for all things female. He does this in order, finally, to deny her femaleness altogether. Such complicated twistings are to be seen as an indication of the fact that Philo knew of Jewish groups for whom Sophia's femaleness was very important and who understood Wisdom precisely *not* as a hypostasis subordinated to the male God or as a secondary principle. See also Georgi, "Frau Weisheit," 249–51.

15. James M. Reese, *Hellenistic Influence on the Book of Wisdom and Its Consequences* (Analecta Biblica 41; Rome: Pontifical Biblical Institute, 1970); Burton L. Mack, *Logos und Sophia: Untersuchungen zur Weisheitstheologie im hellenistischen Judentum* (Göttingen: Vandenhoeck & Ruprecht, 1973); Kloppenborg, "Isis and Sophia."

16. Despite repeated measures taken by the Roman emperor against the Isis religion, the cult could not be confined. The principal temple of Isis in Philea was not closed until the year 537 C.E. by the emperor Justinian.

17. The first quotation comes from an Egyptian papyrus from Oxyrhynchus (2nd century C.E.) (cited according to B. P. Grenfell and A. S. Hunt, *The Oxyrhynchus Papyri,* Part XI [London, 1915], no. 1380, col. x, lines 214–15). The other quotations come from the well-known Isis aretalogy from Cyme on the coast of Asia Minor (cited from Jan Bergmann, *Ich bin Isis: Studien zum memphitischen Hintergrund der griechischen Isisaretalogien* [Uppsala: Universitetet, 1968], 301–3, lines 10, 17, 30) (first–second century C.E.).

18. One epithet of Ptolemaic rulers and Roman emperors was "beloved of Isis."

19. Greek text from the *Supplementum Epigraphicum Graecum* VIII, No. 550, lines 7–19.

20. Thus, in the Isis aretalogy from Cyme (see n. 17 above), line 25 (cf. also line 34 and Oxyrhynchus papyrus no. 1380, line 240): "I have overthrown the rule of tyrants."

21. It is true that all these statements relate to older biblical traditions, but the image of personified Wisdom as savior is clearly new, since in the faith of Israel saving activity is otherwise the preserve of God (Deut 26:5–9; Josh 24:2–13; Psalms 78; 105; 106; 136; Sirach 44–50, etc.).

22. Certain special emphases are inserted. Thus, the maternal features of Isis are not included in the image of Sophia (differing from Jesus Sirach). This may again be regarded as an indication of the self-understanding of women in the corresponding groups (see what was said of the Therapeutrides above).

23. The book of Wisdom responds in concentrated form, with a new interpretation of Jewish tradition, to the most important achievements and new ventures of Hellenism—the founding of a public school system, the enormous value of education and training, the new forms of poetic creativity, the importance of the erotic, the growing respect for the scholarly disciplines cultivated in centers like Alexandria, and philosophical concern for questions of the proper manner of life. The emphasis on the equality of all human beings at birth (7:1–5) could indicate that the authors of the book, like the Isis cult or the Therapeutae and Therapeutrides, fundamentally rejected the institution of slavery.

24. On the history of women in Hellenism, see S. B. Pomeroy, *Goddesses, Whores, Wives and Slaves: Women in Classical Antiquity* (New York: Schoken, 1984).

25. The "counter-test" of androcentric polemic against strong women cannot be pursued here. There is an outstanding collection of material and interpretation in the monograph by

Max Küchler, *Schweigen, Schmuck und Schleier: Drei neutestamentliche Vorschriften zur Verdrängung der Frauen auf dem Hintergrund einer frauenfeindlichen Exegese des Alten Testaments im antiken Judentum* (Fribourg: Universitätsverlag; Göttingen: Vandenhoeck & Ruprecht, 1986).

26. On personification, see esp. Claudia V. Camp, *Wisdom and the Feminine in the Book of Proverbs* (Sheffield: Almond, 1985), 209–25; and S. Schroer, "Die göttliche Weisheit and der nachexilische Monotheismus," in *Der eine Gott und die Göttin: Gottesvorstellungen des biblischen Israel im Horizont feministischer Theologie,* ed. Marie-Thérès Wacker and Erich Zenger (Quaestiones Disputatae 135; Freiburg: Herder, 1991), esp. 163–69.

27. This reaction had a certain tradition in Egyptian diaspora Judaism. The community at Elephantine had already gone its own way in its worship of YHWH, also under the influence of openness to religious impulses from its environment (e.g., in the question of a *paredros* of YHWH). It is true, however, that in the third section, probably against a background of political threat, the book reveals a marked degree of self-righteousness and, combined with it, enmity and hatred directed at the Egyptian population.

28. The fact that there were sharply controversial Jewish views on this question is indicated by the LXX translation of Job 28 and Proverbs 8, which determinedly retract the openness of the older biblical figure of Wisdom and make Sophia accessible to only a chosen few. On this, see the important new contribution by Max Küchler, "Gott und seine Weisheit in der Septuaginta (Ijob 28; Spr 8)," in *Monotheismus und Christologie,* ed. H.-J. Klauck (Quaestiones Disputatae 138; Freiburg im Breisgau: Herder, 1992), 117–42.

29. Early Christian groups may well have been influenced, at least indirectly, by Alexandrian Jewish wisdom theology; however, they shift the integrative function of Sophia more strongly into the realm of inner-Jewish religious practice, so that Wisdom is experienced as the hostess and shelterer of the marginalized.

RECOMMENDED READINGS

Camp, Claudia V. *Wisdom and the Feminine in the Book of Proverbs.* Sheffield: Almond, 1985. A methodologically important feminist work on the function and backgrounds of personified Ḥokmâ in the book of Proverbs.

Engel, Helmut. "Was Weisheit ist und wie sie entstand, will ich verkünden." In *Lehrerin der Gerechtigkeit,* edited by Georg Hentschel and Erich Zenger, 67–102. Erfurter Theologische Schriften 19. Leipzig: St. Benno, 1991. A very rich collection of materials on the encomium in Wisdom 6–9, continuing the work of Kloppenborg and adding a useful collection of the most important Isis aretalogies in German translation.

Georgi, Dieter. "Frau Weisheit oder Das Recht auf Freiheit als schöpferische Kraft." In *Verdrängte Vergangenheit, die uns bedrängt: Feministische Theologie in der Verantwortung für die Geschichte,* edited by Leonore Siegele-Wenschkewitz, 243–76. Munich: Kaiser, 1988. A creative attempt at a feminist theological reading by a male author who is able to draw connections on the basis of his own abundant knowledge.

———. *Weisheit Salomos.* Jüdische Schriften aus hellenistisch-römischer Zeit III/4. Gütersloh: Mohn, 1980. German translation of the Greek text with a brief commentary in the footnotes. The translation is distinguished by its precision and is, in my opinion, not androcentric, since the translator/author includes feminist initiatives in his own work (see also the preceding title).

Kloppenborg, John S. "Isis and Sophia in the Book of Wisdom." *Harvard Theological Review* 75 (1982): 57–84. An exegetical and theological extension of other, primarily religious-historically oriented work comparing Isis and Sophia. A closely written but lucid contribution that has justly attracted a good deal of attention.

Kraemer, Ross S. "Monastic Jewish Women in Greco-Roman Egypt: Philo Judaeus on the Therapeutrides." *Signs: Journal of Women in Culture and Society* 14 (1989): 342–70. A feminist essay on Philo's writing on the Therapeutrides.

Larcher, Chrysostome. *Le Livre de la Sagesse ou la Sagesse de Salomon.* Etudes bibliques n. s. 1. 3 vols. Paris: Gabalda, 1983, 1984, 1985. The most recent commentary on Wisdom in French. Very detailed and well grounded, but little interested in the personification of Sophia or in comparisons with the cult of Isis.

Mack, Burton L. *Logos und Sophia: Untersuchungen zur Weisheitstheologie im hellenistischen Judentum.* Göttingen: Vandenhoeck & Ruprecht, 1973. A monograph with a fullness of material, especially on the theology of the Isis-king.

Mayer, Günter. *Die jüdische Frau in der hellenistisch-römischen Antike.* Stuttgart: Kohlhammer, 1987. A monograph with some useful social-historical material and statistics on the period, but strongly androcentric.

Pomeroy, Sarah B. *Goddesses, Whores, Wives and Slaves: Women in Classical Antiquity.* New York: Schocken, 1984. An easy-to-read history of women in classical antiquity written by a classical scholar who works with a feminist perspective. It sheds light on the broader background as well as on the cult of Isis and the world of Hellenistic women, but without a detailed citation of literature and sources.

Reese, James M. *Hellenistic Influence on the Book of Wisdom and its Consequences.* Analecta Biblica 41. Rome: Pontifical Biblical Institute, 1970. A monograph in exegesis and history of religions, with a great deal of comparative material on Isis and Sophia.

Schroer, Silvia. "Die göttliche Weisheit und der nachexilische Monotheismus." In *Der eine Gott und die Göttin: Gottesvorstellungen des biblischen Israel im Horizont feministischer Theologie,* edited by Marie Thérès Wacker and Erich Zenger. Quaestiones Disputatae 135. Freiburg: Herder, 1991. This essay builds on Claudia Camp's research and contains a great many citations of feminist writings on Sophia.

Winston, David. *The Wisdom of Solomon.* Anchor Bible. Garden City, NY: Doubleday, 1979. A commentary in English.

Thunder, Perfect Mind

ANNE McGUIRE ◆

I am the harlot and the holy one.
I am the wife and the virgin.
I am the m[oth]er and the daughter.
I am the members of my mother. . . .
Hear me, you listeners, and be taught my utterances, you who know me!
I am the hearing that is acceptable in every matter,
I am the utterance that cannot be restrained. . . .
For I am the one who alone exists,
And I have no one who will judge me.
Thunder, Perfect Mind (13,18–22; 20,26–31; 21,18–20)[1]

INTRODUCTION

THUNDER, PERFECT MIND, which survives only in the Coptic version found at
Nag Hammadi, presents the revelation discourse of a mysterious female divinity. Throughout the text, the voice of this divinity alternates between "I AM"
proclamations and second-person address. While this alternating structure
works to differentiate and connect the "I" who speaks and the "you" she
addresses, the text's rhetorical features, especially its imagery of paradox, gender, and language, set in motion a reconstruction of the speaker's identity and
her relation to those who hear her, especially women.

The author, date, and place of composition are unknown, but *Thunder* was
probably composed in Greek well before 350 C.E., the approximate date of the
Coptic manuscript. There is no scholarly consensus on the social and historical setting of *Thunder*, but its sophisticated reworking of images and ideas
from a variety of sources,[2] including Jewish and Christian wisdom, Isis worship, Middle Platonism, Stoicism, and Gnostic traditions,[3] helps to mark
Thunder as the product of a syncretistic and revisionary religious imagination.

In presenting this commentary, I write as a feminist scholar of early Christian literature who seeks to cross boundaries that devalue, silence, or exclude voices from outside the canon, as I seek to bring to those voices a wider readership as well as a critical feminist perspective.[4] The task of this commentary is to offer a reading that highlights the literary form and religious perspectives of *Thunder* and exposes its dual relation to patriarchal cultural patterns. My analysis thus seeks both to subject the text to feminist suspicion and critique and to uncover in it potential resources for contemporary feminist reflection and spiritual transformation.[5] Such resources, I would argue, are located particularly in the ways *Thunder* affirms multiplicity and particularity, as it re-images the divine and her relation to humankind, to language, and to culture.[6]

In addition to searching for revisionary voices within the text, I also bring critical perspectives from outside the text, especially from feminist theoretical perspectives on gender. The first and most important of these is the view that gender is both a category of classification and a representation of male and female difference, produced and transmitted through such means as social practices, literary works, and religious traditions.[7] Second is the view that religious texts and traditions often play a powerful role in "producing and perpetuating gender asymmetries,"[8] particularly by locating patriarchal constructions of male and female difference in the "natural" or "sacred" order of things. Viewed critically as the result of social and cultural production, rather than of biological sexual difference, or "nature,"[9] conceptions of gender emerge as culturally variable and changeable representations of difference, rather than as universal, permanent, or fixed structures of the "natural order."

Third is the perspective that the construction of gender is itself the result of a complex metaphorical process in which categories from a "source domain," such as the biological, social, or economic realm, are transferred onto the "target" domain of gender.[10] Gender can also serve as a powerful source domain for a variety of other cultural domains, especially those involving other categories of difference, such as kinship, ethnicity, race, class, religious affiliation, space and time, or of being itself, as in the distinction of divine and human.[11] It follows from this that both cultural construction of gender and gendered imagery belong to "a web of metaphors that have to do with many things other than gender per se."[12] Finally, my approach is indebted to the perspective that the meanings of texts are not stable and fixed but arise out of the interaction of readers and the possibilities offered by the text. Invariably, the social and theoretical positions, sensitivities, and interests of readers shape the range and force of their interpretations.[13]

While these perspectives suggest that gender-related symbols may, in some cases, have little or nothing to do with the social domain of male and female roles,[14] even the most figurative uses of gendered imagery may have something, or quite a lot, to do with the social construction and reconstruction of gender. Just as gendered metaphors transfer associations from the source domain of gender to a target domain, such as theological reflection on the divine, the juxtaposition of domains brings new associations back to the source domain, thereby effecting a mutual or two-way transfer of associations. Interpretive caution in charting such movement is essential, since the metaphorical process is complex and the social implications of mythic imagery remain particularly unclear.[15] What is clear, however, is that gender imagery can play a crucial role in the figurative "argument of images" by which human beings reorganize their social and cultural worlds and shape new individual and group identities.[16]

As a commentator, I am particularly concerned to bring to *Thunder* a sensitivity to its complex interweaving of themes and its multiple metaphors for the divine.[17] The commentary is organized around three of these interwoven themes. First is the text's use of paradox and gender imagery to represent the revealer and her relationships. Second is its elaboration of a theory of language,[18] manifested particularly in statements about the linguistic and intellective faculties of the revealer.[19] Third is its focus on the speaker's relationships, disclosing the centrality of relationality itself to the identity of the revealer and her "members." All of these contribute significantly to, as they generate questions about, the complex identity of the speaker, particularly the way unity and multiplicity, immanence and transcendence, universality and particularity are conjoined within her identity.[20] In this commentary, I hope to suggest ways in which the symbolic world inscribed in the text might be interpreted, criticized, and/or appropriated by ancient and contemporary readers.

COMMENTARY

Thunder, Perfect Mind opens with the announcement of the speaker's origin and quickly shifts to exhortation, as the revealer admonishes her audience to use their faculties of sight, hearing, and speech to enter into relation with her.

It is from the Power that I was sent,
And it is to those who reflect upon me that I have come,
And I was found among those who seek after me.
Look at me, you who reflect upon me;
And you hearers, hear me!
You who are waiting for me, take me to yourselves.
And do not drive me from your sight.
And do not make your sound hate me, nor your hearing.
Do not be ignorant of me at any place or any time.
Be on guard! Do not be ignorant of me. (13,2–15)

While several of these exhortations suggest an opposition between two distinct responses to the speaker, the final warning distinguishes more specifically between the ways of ignorance and knowledge (*gnōsis*). If this distinction points to a rigid boundary between "non-gnostic" and "gnostic" social groups, *Thunder* would appear to privilege the gnostic "self" or "group," and to exclude the non-gnostic "other." But if the distinction refers instead to epistemological perspectives, the warning may work not to exclude socially the ignorant or "non-gnostics," but rather to invite all who "hear" to turn and enter into a receptive and "knowing" relation with the one who calls herself both "gnosis and ignorance."[21] While this reading allows the possibility of crossing the boundary from ignorance to gnosis, it indicates, at the same time, the liminality of the speaker as one who exists "betwixt and between" such antithetical categories as gnosis and ignorance, shame and boldness, alien and citizen.[22]

GENDER AND PARADOX IN THE IDENTITY
OF THE REVEALER AND HER MEMBERS

This initial series of admonitions leads directly to a series of self-predications, or "I AM" statements, which recall the imagery of a wide range of divine figures, including Isis, Wisdom/Sophia, Jesus (Gospel of John), and Barbelo/Protennoia (several Nag Hammadi sources). The interweaving of paradox with the imagery of gender and kinship, however, resonates beyond such allusions and discloses the complex identity and relations of the speaker. While the first of these echoes biblical statements of divine transcendence, the rest associate the speaker with the antithetical roles of women in patriarchal culture, within the family, and in sexual reproduction.

> For I am the first and the last.
> I am the honored and the scorned,
> I am the harlot and the holy one.
> I am the wife and the virgin.
> I am the m[oth]er and the daughter.
> I am the members of my mother.
> I am the barren one and the one with many children.
> I am she whose marriage is manifold,
>   and I have not taken a husband.
> I am the midwife and she who does not give birth.
> I am the comforting of my labor pains.
> I am the bride and the bridegroom. (13,15–29)

The antithetically paired terms of these self-predications mirror the bipolar construction of the female gender in the patriarchal culture of antiquity. At the same time, however, the paradoxical conjunction of terms in divine self-predication breaks down some of the restrictive functions of these polarities. In some cases, the text does so by including polarity, particularity, and multiplicity within the divine; in others, it displaces the duality of apparent opposites with paradoxes that cross and nullify the boundaries between them.

In proclaiming herself to be "the harlot and the holy one," the speaker associates herself metaphorically with a pair of female roles that frequently serve to divide and reduce women to the polar opposites of harlot (*pornē*) and holy one (*semnē*). The juxtaposition of this polarity to that of honored and scorned appears even more to reinforce the oppressive polarization of scorned harlots and honored holy ones.[23] Yet, by including both sides of these two polarities within the divine, *Thunder* not only pushes both beyond their literal sense and valuation but links the speaker directly to the conflicting, though sometimes overlapping, roles of women. In this way, the text opens new possibilities for the critique and reinterpretation of such polarities, the identities they shape, and the values they ascribe to the female gender in its divine and human manifestations.

The following lines move from sharply antithetical polarities to the relational language of gender, kinship, and childbirth. The conjunction of "wife and virgin" identifies the speaker as one who both shares in and transcends the usually conflicting roles of unmarried virgins and married wives. As mother and daughter, she identifies herself with the most fundamental kinship roles by which women are related to others, and to one another. The claim to be "the members of my mother" extends these characteristics further, as it echoes the metaphor of the body and its "members" (1 Cor 12:12–26) and asserts the multiplicity of the speaker's identity in relation to her own mother. In this case, however, the image is a figure not for the coexistence of multiplicity and unity within Christ and the church but for the relation of immanence and transcendence, particularity and universality, within the divine and her "members." Even more important, it points to the speaker's identity with the role of "daughter," with the dispersed spiritual "members" of her mother, and with the "mother" from whom they come and in whom they reside.

The relation of the speaker to the roles of women becomes even clearer with a series of metaphors that connect the divine to female roles in sexual relations and reproduction. The paradoxical pairing of such identities as "the barren one and the one with many children," however, undermines the polarity that defines and values women by their reproductive capacity or incapacity, their fertility or infertility, and revalues both by placing them together within the divine. The speaker's association with reproduction becomes even more complex, as the "mother" with many children identifies herself as "the midwife and she who does not give birth." The following claim, in turn, refers paradoxically to the comforting of the labor pains of this one "who does not give birth." Even more important, it places both the experience of pain ("my labor pains") and the power to comfort these specifically female pains within the identity of the divine. Echoing simultaneously the curse on Eve (Gen 3:16) and the association of Isis with pregnancy, childbirth, and the comforting of pain, these statements illustrate the speaker's relation to the divine powers of healing and to the experience of women in the pains of childbirth and infertility alike.[24]

While these statements identify the speaker almost exclusively with female roles, the final line in the quotation above introduces a series of statements that include several male figures. Some of these exist in paradoxical relation to the speaker, while others reside within her ambiguously gendered identity.

> I am the bride and the bridegroom.
> And it is my husband who brought me forth.
> I am the mother of my father and the sister of my husband.
> And he is my offspring.
> I am the servant of him who prepared me.
> I am the lord of my offspring.
> But he is the one who br[ought me forth]
>   before time on a day of birth.
> And he is my offspring in time and my power is from him.
> I am the staff of his power in his youth
> And he is the rod of my old age.
> And whatever he wills happens to me. (13,27–14,9)

In most of these lines, the revealer distinguishes herself from the male character(s) she names. The first statement, however, suggests that "she" encompasses both female and male characteristics within her identity. With its allusion to the bridegroom–bride metaphor for the relation of God and Israel, or Christ and the church, this self-predication associates the speaker simultaneously with the traditionally "male" role of divine bridegroom (God or Christ) and the traditionally "female" role of the human bride (Israel or the church). The speaker thus claims an identity that is both male and female, singular and plural, and, perhaps, both divine and human.

From this assertion of female–male union, the text moves to a series of paradoxical statements about the speaker's relation to various male figures: the "husband" who "brought" her "forth," the "father" to whom she is "mother," the "husband" to whom she is "sister," and the "offspring." These roles and relations may belong to different figures, or they may refer to the same figure at different "moments,"[25] or in distinct manifestations. What is more important, in acknowledging one or several male figures who brought her forth, sent her, and gave her power, the text appears to reinscribe conventional or patriarchal patterns of gender relations, with the image of a superior male power empowering a subordinate female figure to realize his will, articulate his thought, and utter his name in the world.[26] She may be "the staff of his power," but ultimately the power appears to be his.

Over against this image, however, stand several statements that reverse the relation of female and male to support the image of a reciprocal sharing and exchange of roles. In this way, the paradoxical mixing of gender and kinship relations undermines a rigid stratification of male dominance and female subordination and sets in its place a more dynamic structure of reciprocity and exchange. The multiplicity and paradox of these images function neither to establish a single gendered identity for the speaker, nor to assert uniformity in "her" relations, but to suggest that the various self-descriptions of the divine point to, but cannot exhaust, the mysterious identity of the divine or her "members."[27] The speaking voice of *Thunder* may thus be described as a single yet multifaceted character who exists in the union and dynamic interrelationship of various female and male roles.

Language and Multiplicity in the Identity of the Divine

Concluding the text's initial series of self-predications is the first of three passages that highlight the linguistic character of the speaker and reveal the complex relation between the unity and multiplicity of the divine and her linguistic utterances.[28]

I am the silence that is incomprehensible,
And the conception whose remembrance is manifold.
I am the voice whose sound is manifold,
And the utterance whose appearance is manifold.
I am the utterance of my name. (14,9–15)

These statements present a model for understanding the paradoxical and antithetical metaphors of the text, locating their significance within the incomprehensible silence and linguistic manifestations of the divine. Just as earlier statements illustrate the conjunction of unity and multiplicity in the divine, these relate the unity of divine conception, voice, and utterance to the multiplicity of remembrance, sound, and appearance. Finally, in defining herself as "the utterance of my name," the "voice" of the text links her identity directly to philosophical and religious reflection on the divine "name" and to the central activity of the text, the self-revelatory utterance of that name.

The Relationality of the Revealer

Together, the themes of gender, paradox, and language disclose the multiple relations of the speaker and point to the centrality of relationality itself to her identity and that of her "members." Even more important, several lines of the text employ antithetical images of relation which link the identity of the speaker to the varied, and sometimes opposed, responses of the audience. In second-person statements, in particular, the speaker challenges her audience to recognize the antithetical character of their responses and to relate these to her identity and their own:

> I am the disgraced and the exalted one.
> Give heed to my poverty and my wealth.
> Do not be haughty to me when I am discarded
>   upon the earth,
> And you will find me among [those] that are to come.
> And do not look upon me on the garbage heap and go
>   and leave me discarded.
> And you will find me in the kingdoms.
> And do not look upon me when I am discarded among
>   those who are disgraced and in the least places,
> And then laugh at me.
> And do not cast me down among those who are slain
>   in violence. (14,33–15,14)

In these and other lines, the voice of *Thunder* speaks poignantly as the subject and object of conflicting responses. She is the object not only of honor, exaltation, and love, but of derision, disgrace, and hatred. And insofar as these opposed responses, and the pain that accompanies them, constitute her very identity, she is the subject who experiences, and exists within, the poles of negative and positive response. On the negative side of derision and disgrace, she has solidarity with the vulnerable, the oppressed, and the outcast. On the positive side, she is also "the exalted one," who speaks in the future tense of being found "among those that are to come" and "in the kingdoms" (15,4–9). In the present voice of the text, however, her existence is characterized by the dualities of poverty and wealth, weakness and power, fear and pride, silence and speech (14,34–15,35). She who speaks is "disgraced and exalted," as she is "hated everywhere and . . . . loved everywhere" (16,9–11). She urges her audience to recognize the dualities in which she exists, to acknowledge their complicity, and to change their vision, attitudes, and relation to her.[29]

In most passages, the polarities of human response appear to transcend ethnic and cultural boundaries (she is hated and loved "everywhere"). Other passages, however, highlight the differing but sometimes overlapping, representations of the divine among distinct social and ethnic groups. The speaker claims to be "the wisdom of Greeks (*hellēn*)" and "the gnosis of non-Greeks (*barbaros*)" yet also "the judgment of Greeks and non-Greeks" alike (16,4–6). Among non-Greeks, she is a "non-Greek" (16,2–3), and yet she has no image or appearance (16,8–9). In Egypt, however, she is "the one whose appearance is manifold" (16,6–7). Together, these statements suggest that various social and ethnic groups play a central role in defining the speaker, even as the fullness of her identity transcends singular or local representations. Her identity, the text suggests, arises from the juxtaposition and interaction of distinct, and often opposed, categories of difference, including those of ethnicity (Greek and non-Greek), epistemology (gnosis and ignorance), representation (iconic and aniconic), gender (female and male), and being itself (divine and human).

As the speaker acknowledges the role of conflicting responses in her identity, she admonishes her hearers to enter into relation with her and her "members," even out of unpleasant situations and pain.

Take me [. . .] [underst]anding out of pain,
and receive me to yourselves out of understanding
    [and] pain.
Receive me to yourselves out of disgraceful places and contrition.
And seize me from those which are good even though
    in disgrace.
Out of shame, receive me to yourselves in shamelessness.
And out of shamelessness and shame, upbraid my
    members among yourselves.
And come forward to me, you who know me and who know
    my members. (17,19–22)

While these lines reinforce the importance of the relation between speaker and hearers, they also extend the domain of significant relations to those of the audience with others ("the great ones," "the small first creatures"), as the speaker urges them neither to separate her from that which appears to be small, nor to cast out or turn anyone away (17,36–18,6).

In one of *Thunder*'s most striking passages, the speaker identifies herself with the intellective faculties of mind, repose, and gnosis, and declares her relation to multiple categories of being, including angels, gods, the spirits of all human beings, and women.

But I am the [perfect] mind and the repose of the [. . .]
I am the gnosis of my seeking, and the finding of those
    who seek after me.
And the command of those who ask of me.
And the power of the powers by my gnosis,
Of the angels who have been sent by my word,
And the gods among the gods by my command.
And it is with me that the spirits of all humans exist,
And it is within me that women exist.

I am she who is honored and praised and who is despised scornfully.
I am peace and because of me war has come to be.
And I am an alien and a citizen.
I am substance and she who has no substance. (18,9–28)

In parallel statements, this passage invites all its hearers, both male and female, to perceive their "spirits" as dwelling *with* the divine, but it leads women to understand themselves as dwelling *within* her.[30] At the same time, the conjunction of polarities, especially that of "alien and citizen," places the speaker both within and outside the boundaries of divine and human "society." Simultaneously insider and outsider, the speaking voice of *Thunder* is both a liminal figure and a figure of liminality itself, existing at the threshold of, or betwixt and between, the known and unknown, the visible and invisible, the immanent and transcendent, the accepted and rejected.

In these, as in other images, the speaker exists in the violation and crossing of boundaries, as further antitheses emphasize the paradoxical duality of her activities:

[I am] restraint and unrestraint.
I am the union and the dissolution.
I am the abiding and I am the loosing.
I am descent and they come up to me.
I am the judgment and the acquittal. (19,9–15)

In attaching no specific objects to these abstract terms, *Thunder* leaves open the ways in which the speaker manifests herself as "the union and the dissolution." This ambiguity invites the interpretive claim that the speaker works both to unite and to dissolve all things, including even the duality of divine speaker and human audience, the "I" and "you" of the text.

The dissolution of this duality is supported further not only by the figurative devices of the text but by statements that place the linguistic faculties of speaking, hearing, and writing within the divine and her hearers:

Hear me, you listeners, and be taught my utterances,
    you who know me!
I am the hearing that is acceptable in every matter;
I am the utterance that cannot be restrained.
I am the name of the sound and the sound of the name.
I am the sign of writing and the manifestation of difference.
                                      (20,26–35)

As hearing, these lines suggest, the divine is available to all (19,20–22; 20,28–29), but as silence or singular utterance, she cannot be grasped (14,9–10; 19,22–23; 20,30–31), or reduced to a singular word, conception, or interpretation (14,10–14; 19,22–25). She is, rather, to be imaged as a "mute who does not speak," yet whose multitude of words are manifold" (19,23–25) in number and in polysemic significance. Together, these and other lines which link the speaker to the linguistic and intellective faculties, point suggestively toward the identity of the speaker with the text and its "hearing." In this way, the text implies, the divine is present and active not only in the self-revelatory utterances of the text, but in the audience's hearing of them as well.

With the speaker's claim to be "the name of the sound and the sound of the name," the text focuses attention on the reflexive identity of the speaker as divine name and as the thundering sound which utters that name. By juxtaposing this self-description with the claim to be "the sign of writing and the manifestation of difference," the text extends the media of divine manifestation beyond the activities of reflecting, speaking, hearing, and naming to the activities of reading, writing, and differentiating. In identifying the divine as the "sign (*sēmeion*) of writing," the text reflects back upon itself, identifying the divine with the hidden significance of writing generally and, more particularly, with the hidden significance of this text. Finally, as "the manifestation of difference," the text suggests that the speaker's significance is manifested in the differentiation of features, the distinction of categories, the processes of separation and dissolution, and the multiplicity of expression and interpretation.

If the "members" listen and respond as she commands, the divine voice asserts, they will discover in the text and in themselves both the one who "cries out" and the one who "listens."

> Give heed, then, listeners, and you also, angels,
> And those who have been sent,
> And you spirits who have arisen from the dead,
> For I am the one who alone exists,
> And I have no one who will judge me. (21,13–20)

With the claim to be "the one who alone exists," *Thunder* introduces a perspective on the identity of the speaker and her relations with "others" that appears strikingly new yet serves both to solve and to dis-solve the mystery of the speaker's identity. The "one" who speaks in *Thunder, Perfect Mind* is the unity that encompasses all duality and multiplicity, including those of her utterances and her "members." She is the union and the dissolution; indeed, she is "the one who alone exists," whom knowing readers will discover within themselves as they discover themselves within the divine.

This redemptive moment comes, the text suggests, when those who have embraced the "many pleasant aspects" of sin, unrestrained acts, and passions "become sober and go up to the place of rest." There, the speaker claims, "they will find me" and "live" and "not die again" (21,20–32). Within the symbolic world of the text, this redemptive "place" or state may be available already to those who understand the mysterious utterances of the text. For in understanding the text, they operate with the divine faculties of hearing, seeing, and knowing, which are grounded in the divine and manifested in themselves. At the crucial moment, such knowing or "gnostic" readers understand the speaker's claim to be "the union and the dissolution," as they realize the conjunction and dissolution of the central duality of the text: the distinction between the divine "I" who speaks and the human "you" she calls to listen. When such members of the audience hear the divine voice, they become sober, discover the divine faculties within, and transport themselves "upward" to the "place of rest" as restored "members" of the divine. The symbolic world and rhetorical features of the text thus work together to break down and dissolve the boundaries separating the "I" and "you" of the text, as the divine voice shares her faculties and empowers her "members" to speak her/their name and discover her/themselves.

Within a religious setting, recitation of *Thunder, Perfect Mind* may have had the effect not only of invoking divine presence but also of awakening a new understanding of the self and of the divine. As recitation allows both reciters and hearers to become speakers and hearers of the divine, so it invites them to enter into relation with the divine. In this way, they come to know the divine as the union and dissolution of multiplicity and duality, as these are manifested in the organizing categories of her utterances, and of their own culture, identity, and experience. Without denying or negating the particularity and multiplicity of those categories, *Thunder* leads its readers to discover in the text and in themselves "the name of the voice and the voice of the name," she who is "honored and scorned," "she who cries out" and "the one who listens." The gendered metaphors of the text invite female readers, in particular, to recognize the polarities of female identity both in patriarchal culture and within the divine. In realizing their shared identity with the divine, female and male readers alike might come to a new understanding of the categories of difference that shape their understanding of themselves and the world, including those of strong-weak, inside-outside, Greek-non-Greek, transcendent-immanent, divine-human. In perceiving the conjunction and dissolution of such categories within the divine, they not only reconceive the divine but reconstitute their member-ship within her complex and multifaceted identity.

Thunder, Perfect Mind uses the imagery of gender, paradox, language, and relation to communicate a distinctive conception of the divine and her "members." Through its complex literary form and rhetorical devices, *Thunder* effects a new understanding of the identity of the divine with her human hearers, as it places the "divine" powers of language and interpretation within them. With these powers, they in turn are able to speak and hear the divine utterances with gnosis, as they come to understand themselves in the divine "place of rest," joined to "the one who alone exists," the divine female voice of revelation and redemption in *Thunder, Perfect Mind*.[31]

NOTES

1. All translations are my own. The standard edition of the Coptic text with English translation is George W. MacRae, "The Thunder: Perfect Mind: VI,2: 13,1-21,32," in *Nag Hammadi Codices V,2–5 and VI with Papyrus Berolinensis 8502,1 and 4,* ed. D. M. Parrott (Leiden: E. J. Brill, 1979), 231–55. MacRae's translation also appears in *The Nag Hammadi Library in English*, 3rd ed., ed. James M. Robinson (San Francisco: Harper & Row, 1988), 295–303. Other valuable translations include Bentley Layton, "The Thunder-Perfect Intellect (Th)," in *The Gnostic Scriptures* (New York: Doubleday, 1987), 77–85, and the forthcoming edition and translation by Paul-Hubert Poirier for the Bibliothèque Copte de Nag Hammadi series (BCNH). I am very grateful to Prof. Poirier for sharing this and other work with me before publication.

2. Paul-Hubert Poirier argues for a sapiential Jewish milieu, universalist and missionary, perhaps from late second century Alexandria ("Interprétation et situation du traité Le Tonnerre, intellect parfait [NH VI,2]," presented to the Colloquium on the Texts of Nag Hammadi and The Problem of Their Classification [Université Laval, Québec, Sept. 15–19, 1993]). Bentley Layton argues that *Thunder*'s multiple resonances with such Nag Hammadi texts as the *Apocryphon of John, Trimorphic Protennoia,* and the *Hypostasis of the Archons* place it in close relation to the Sethian or "Gnostic" tradition ("The Riddle of the Thunder [NHC VI,2]: The Function of Paradox in a Gnostic Text from Nag Hammadi,"in *Nag Hammadi, Gnosticism, and Early Christianity*, ed. C. W. Hedrick and R. Hodgson, Jr. [Peabody, MA: Hendrickson, 1986], 37–54).

3. At the 1993 annual meeting of the Society of Biblical Literature (Washington, D.C.), Michael A. Williams and Karen King presented compelling critiques of the category "Gnosticism." In response to Williams's affirmative answer to his title, "Should We Replace Gnosticism as a Category?" I argued for a critical redefinition of the term as a polythetic category of classification. In this essay, I use the terms "gnostic" and "non-gnostic" not to designate members of a specific religious phenomenon ("Gnosticism") but to designate a way of being religious which was associated in ancient religious texts like *Thunder* with a particular conception of *gnōsis*.

4. I am currently working toward completion of a book on gender imagery in selected Nag Hammadi texts, including *Thunder*. The inclusion of such texts as *Thunder* in the present volume illustrates well the editor's decision to create "a forum and space where different voices and discourses can be heard" (Elisabeth Schüssler Fiorenza, "Rethinking *The Woman's Bible*," in *Searching the Scriptures: A Feminist Introduction* [New York: Crossroad, 1993], ix).

5. The text's dual relation to patriarchal patterns—that is, its reinforcement and subversion of patterns of domination, marginalization, or exclusion—can usefully be related to the "doubled vision" of feminist hermeneutics outlined by Elisabeth Schüssler Fiorenza ("Transforming the Legacy," in *Searching the Scriptures*, 1:11).

6. *Thunder* has recently appeared as a resource in the work of two major African American women artists. Toni Morrison (*Jazz* [New York: Knopf, 1992]) and filmmaker Julie Dash (*Daughters of the Dust* [1991]) both use quotations from *Thunder* at the beginning of their works. The epigraph to *Jazz* is a quotation from *Thunder* 20,31–35 ("I am the name of the sound and the sound of the name. I am the sign of the letter and the designation of the divi-

sion"). Dash's film opens with an off-camera female voice reciting *Thunder* 13,15–14,15 ("I am the first and the last, I am the honored and the scorned one, I am the whore and the holy one . . ."). Danna Nolan Fewell and David Gunn use the same passage as an epigraph, attributing the lines to Dash (*Gender, Power, and Promise: The Subject of the Bible's First Story* [Nashville: Abingdon, 1993], 6).

7. Teresa de Lauretis, "The Technology of Gender," in *Technologies of Gender: Essays on Theory, Film, and Fiction* (Bloomington: Indiana University Press, 1987), 1–3.

8. Peggy Day, "Introduction," in *Gender and Difference in Ancient Israel*, ed. Peggy Day (Minneapolis: Augsburg-Fortress, 1989), 4.

9. Elizabeth Castelli and James McBride, "Beyond the Language and Memory of the Fathers: Feminist Perspectives in Religious Studies," in *Transcending Boundaries: Multi-Disciplinary Approaches to the Study of Gender*, ed. Pamela R. Frese and John M. Coggeshall (New York: Bergin & Garvey, 1991), 113–50.

10. Deborah Durham and James Fernandez, "Tropical Dominions: The Figurative Struggle over Domains of Belonging and Apartness in Africa," in *Beyond Metaphor: The Theory of Tropes in Anthropology*, ed. James Fernandez (Stanford: Stanford University Press, 1991), 191: "Metaphor juxtaposes two apparently distinct domains to effect a transfer of meaning from one to the other."

11. Judith Shapiro compares the metaphorical system of gender to that of totemism: "The biological opposition between female and male [gender], like the array of animal species [totemism] provides a powerful natural model for representing differences between social groups and oppositions between culturally significant categories. . . . At the same time, gender differences themselves are defined through categories of the economy, the polity– of the wider social universe in which they are located" ("Gender Totemism," in *Dialectics and Gender: Anthropological Approaches,* ed. Richard R. Randolph, D. M. Schneider, and M. N. Diaz [Boulder, CO, and London: Westview Press, 1988], 2–3).

12. Shapiro, "Gender Totemism," 3, citing Marilyn Strathern on the variety of purposes for which gender symbols can be used. A similar point is made by Caroline Bynum, "Introduction: The Complexity of Symbols," in *Gender and Religion: On the Complexity of Symbols*, ed. C. Bynum, S. Harrell, and P. Richman (Boston: Beacon, 1986), 2: "Gender-related symbols are sometime 'about' values other than gender."

13. Mieke Bal, "Introduction," in *Anti-Covenant: Counter-Reading Women's Lives in the Hebrew Bible* (Sheffield: Almond Press, 1989), 15: "Meaning is a readerly product, yet based on an elaboration of the possibilities offered by the text. . . . the text is, in a way, itself a reading, for which it is called to account."

14. This insight from Bynum is central to the important contribution of Michael A. Williams, "Variety in Gnostic Perspectives on Gender," in *Images of the Feminine in Gnosticism*, ed. Karen L. King (Philadelphia: Fortress, 1988), 2–22. I agree with Williams that gendered imagery is often used to reflect on non-gendered categories, but I am more interested in the mutual transfer of associations between gendered and non-gendered categories.

15. This is especially true for the study of Nag Hammadi texts, given the very limited evidence for their social worlds. See the remarks of Karen King, "Editor's Foreword," in *Images of the Feminine*, xiii–xiv; and Mary Rose D'Angelo, "Response to 'Pursuing the Spiritual Eve' by Elaine Pagels," in *Images of the Feminine*, 207–8.

16. James Fernandez, *Persuasions and Performances: The Play of Tropes in Culture* (Bloomington: Indiana University Press, 1986), viii.

17. Claudia Camp writes about the imaginative power of metaphor, especially the female metaphor of Woman Wisdom in Proverbs, in ways that correlate interestingly with *Thunder*. Such correlations are not surprising, in view of the close relation of *Thunder* to Wisdom tradi-

tions ("Feminist Theological Hermeneutics: Canon and Christian Identity," in *Searching the Scriptures*, 1:165–66).

18. Patricia Cox Miller relates *Thunder* to ancient theories of language, with special attention to conceptions of the relation between language and divinity ("In Praise of Nonsense," in *Classical Mediterranean Spirituality*, ed. A. H. Armstrong [New York: Crossroad, 1986], 481–505).

19. Edward M. Bruner and Phyllis Gorfain, "Dialogic Narration and the Paradoxes of Masada," in *Text, Play, and Story: The Construction and Reconstruction of Self and Society*, ed. E. M. Bruner (Prospect Heights: Waveland Press, 1984), 64: "Precisely because in paradox one meaning is not dominant, interpretation not singular, and truth not apparent, paradox operates as a figure of thought which foregrounds the multiplicity of meaning, interpretation, and truth."

20. Jorunn J. Buckley, "Two Female Gnostic Revealers," *History of Religions* 19 (1979–80): 259–69.

21. *Thunder* 14,26–27; see also 16,3–5; 18,11–12; 18,28–34.

22. *Thunder* 14,26–32; 18,25–26. The category of liminality is most fully developed in Victor Turner, *The Ritual Process: Structure and Anti-Structure* (Ithaca, NY: Cornell University Press, 1977). For a useful adaptation of the concept to Proverbs, see Claudia Camp, "Wise and Strange: An Interpretation of the Female Imagery in Proverbs in Light of Trickster Mythology," in *Reasoning with the Foxes* (*Semeia* 42; Atlanta: Scholars Press, 1988), esp. 30–31. On the relevance of liminality to *Thunder*, I am indebted to my students Melissa Demian, "The Liminal Mirror: Paradox and Identity in *Thunder: Perfect Mind*"; and Alisa Conner, "The Latticed Window: Liminality in *Thunder: Perfect Mind* and Proverbs 1-9."

23. On the cultural paradigm of honor and shame, see Karen Jo Torjesen, "Reconstruction of Women's Early Christian History," in *Searching the Scriptures*, 1:290–91.

24. R. E. Witt discusses the role of Isis as "goddess of the family in Egypt and later in the Graeco-Roman world" (*Isis in the Graeco-Roman World* [Ithaca, NY: Cornell University Press, 1971], 18–19). Diodorus Siculus (*Geography* 1.25) reports that Egyptians say Isis was "the discoverer of many health-giving drugs" and "versed in the science of healing." In the Kyme Aretalogy, Isis claims: "I appointed to women to bring their infants to birth in the tenth month."

25. I owe this insight to Mark Auslander, colleague in anthropology, who observed that *Thunder*'s complex and paradoxical manipulations of cultural categories work to subvert conventional categories of space, time, the body, and kinship, and to produce new forms of relationality and temporality.

26. On the sapiential and philosophical sources of this imagery, see Poirier, "Interprétation et situation," 23–33.

27. On the relation between poetic language and the mystery of divine identity, see Cox Miller, "In Praise of Nonsense," 481–82.

28. *Thunder* 14,9–15; 19,20–35; 20,26–21,13. In the first, the speaker claims to be "the utterance of my name" (14,14–15); in the second, "the gnosis of my name" (19,32–33); and in the third, "the name of the sound and the sound of the name" (20,31–33).

29. On the duality of the speaker, see Buckley, "Two Female Gnostic Revealers," 259-269.

30. MacRae's translation, paralleled by those of Layton and Poirier, reads: "And of spirits of every **man** who exists with me, and of women who dwell within me." My translation attends to the generic sense of the Coptic noun *rōme* (human being) and to the possibility that the verb (*ey-shoop*, to exist or dwell) is a verbal form (the second tense) that emphasizes the prepositional phrase.

31. I owe much to students and colleagues with whom I have discussed *Thunder*, especially Jennifer Almquist, Mark Auslander, Alisa Conner, Melissa Demian, Kim Everett, Kate Felmet, Jessica Jernigan, Karen King, Julie Netherland, Catherine Partridge, Elizabeth Penland, and Rob Shea.

RECOMMENDED READINGS

Buckley, Jorunn J. "Thunder, Perfect Mind, The (NHC VI,2)." In *The Anchor Bible Dictionary,* edited by David N. Freedman, 6:545–46. New York: Doubleday, 1992.

———. "Two Female Gnostic Revealers." *History of Religions* 19 (1979–80): 259–69.

King, Karen L., ed. *Images of the Feminine in Gnosticism*. Philadelphia: Fortress, 1988.

Layton, Bentley. "The Riddle of the Thunder (NHC VI,2): The Function of Paradox in a Gnostic Text from Nag Hammadi." In *Nag Hammadi, Gnosticism, and Early Christianity*, edited by C. W. Hedrick and R. Hodgson, Jr., 37–54. Peabody, MA: Hendrickson, 1986.

———. "The Thunder–Perfect Intellect (Th)." In *The Gnostic Scriptures*, edited by B. Layton, 77–85. New York: Doubleday, 1987.

MacRae, George W. "Discourses of the Gnostic Revealer." In *Proceedings of the International Colloquium on Gnosticism, Stockholm, August 20-25, 1973*, edited by G. Widengren, 111–22. Stockholm: Almqvist & Wiksell, 1977.

———. "The Thunder: Perfect Mind: VI,2: 13,1–21,32." In *Nag Hammadi Codices V,2–5 and VI with Papyrus Berolinensis 8502,1 and 4* (The Coptic Gnostic Library edited with English Translation, Introduction and Notes published under the auspices of the Institute for Antiquity and Christianity; Nag Hammadi Studies 11), edited by D. M. Parrott, 231–55. Leiden: E. J. Brill, 1979.

MacRae, George W. [intro. and trans.] and Douglas M. Parrott. "The Thunder, Perfect Mind (VI,2)." In *The Nag Hammadi Library in English,* 3rd ed., translated by members of the Coptic Gnostic Library Project of the Institute for Antiquity and Christianity, James M. Robinson, Director; managing ed., Marvin W. Meyer, 295–303. San Francisco: Harper & Row; Leiden: E. J. Brill, 1988.

Miller, Patricia Cox. "In Praise of Nonsense." In *Ancient Mediterranean Spirituality*, edited by A. H. Armstrong, 481–505. New York: Crossroad, 1986.

Poirier, Paul-Hubert. "Structure et intention du traité intitulé 'Le tonnerre, intellect parfait.'" In *Actes du IVe congrès copte, Louvain-la-neuve, 5-10 septembre 1988, II. De la linguistique au gnosticisme,* edited by M. Rassart-Debergh and J. Ries, 372–80. Louvain-la-Neuve: Publications de l'Institut orientale de Louvain 41, 1992.

Tardieu, Michel. "Le titre de CG VI,2 (Addenda)." *Muséon* 88 (1975): 365–69.

———. "Le titre du deuxième Écrit du Codex VI." *Muséon* 87 (1974): 523–30.

Trimorphic Protennoia

INGVILD SÆLID GILHUS ◆

THE GNOSTIC WISDOM MONOLOGUE *Trimorphic Protennoia* is a rich and complex text, covering roughly fifteen and one-half pages of Coptic text. Most of the text is written in the first person and ascribed to a female spiritual redeemer—Trimorphic Protennoia, First Thought in Three Forms, who is the female aspect of God. The text describes her three descents into the world and how she brings—first as Voice (Father), then as Speech (Mother), and finally as Word (Son—Christ)—the message of salvation to those living in the world. The traditional Gnostic myth of the fall is implied and referred to but not systematically exposed.

TRIMORPHIC PROTENNOIA AND THE PROLOGUE OF THE GOSPEL OF JOHN

The main issue in research so far has been the text's relationship to Christianity and especially to the prologue in the Gospel of John.[1] The two texts probably have a common background in Jewish wisdom speculations, which were developed in different directions: In the prologue the Word is *the* incarnation of God, while in *Tri. Prot.* the Word is only one of three manifestations of God and is dependent on the other two. And whereas the Christians made the Word into flesh, the Gnostics gave it a spiritual descent from the female Thought of God and at the same time denied a true connection between Word and flesh. Jesus is referred to in *Tri. Prot.*, but its christological interpretation is docetic and separates the Jesus of the Gospels and of the church completely from the spiritual Christ.

Thus far there has been no specific feminist research on the text; however, two editions with translations and commentaries (both made by women) have laid a useful foundation.[2] The fact that the protagonist of the text is a female aspect of God makes it interesting for feminist research, which long has discussed the impact of goddesses and feminine imagery of the godhead. More particularly the text is of interest for feminist research in Christian Testament studies because of its connection with the prologue of John: *Tri. Prot.* challenges the theology of the prologue by suggesting that the male Word was derived from Speech and Voice and was originally dependent on a spiritual mother. By removing this maternal symbol, Christianity lost one of its possibilities of developing a female image of God.

GOD THE MOTHER AND
A HERMENEUTICS OF SUSPICION

In contrast to Christianity, Gnosticism developed a concept of God the Mother. But a consecrated female figure is not necessarily a female-type character, nor is it necessarily friendly to women. It might as well be a male-type character built on a male construct of reality. Whether Protennoia is the one or the other is an underlying question in the present investigation.

Of special interest in the analysis will be the relationship between mythological structure and meanings, the connection between sensorial and ideological values, and how a special vision of the world is reflected throughout. The theoretical framework for the analysis draws on postmodernism and feminist theory in general and especially on Julia Kristeva's analysis of the sacred mother (Mary) and its implications for a general understanding of motherhood and femininity.[3] Through her deconstruction of the image of Mary, Kristeva has analyzed the discourse of motherhood offered by the cult of the Virgin. Her point is that consecrated motherhood is "the *fantasy* that is nurtured by the adult, man or woman, of a lost territory; what is more, it involves less an idealized archaic mother than the idealization of the *relationship* that binds us to her."[4] Kristeva says further: "Christianity is doubtless the most refined symbolic construct in which femininity, to the extent that it transpires through it— and it does so incessantly— is focused on *Maternality.*"[5] *Tri. Prot.* offers an alternative discourse on maternity and an alternative maternal symbolic construct. What sort of gender ethics did that symbolic construct of motherhood provide for women and men?

It is most unlikely that the text was ever meant to answer questions about gender; however, it reveals unintentional meanings about gender and values connected with gender: for instance, its use of gendered imagery to describe the connection between spirit and matter; its use of kin roles to describe the mythological figures; its implicit use of male gender in the Jewish-Christian-Gnostic myth of the human made in the image of God; its consistent use of an androcentric inclusive language with male generic terms to describe those to be saved.

THE TEXT AND ITS CONTEXT

Tri. Prot. reflects a background in Jewish sapiental traditions. It presupposes a developed form of Sethian Gnosticism that has undergone a secondary christianization.[6] The text teaches a spiritual Christ-myth fit into a Gnostic revelation structure, but it denies the human Jesus salvific power. This suggests an origin in a group that has rejected the developing Christology of the church and made its own polemical reinterpretation of it. The setting of the group is unknown, but the text's stress on baptism suggests a gnosticized baptist sect. It is not possible to give a precise description of the sociopolitical and ecclesial location of the writing. The impression left is that of people in bitter opposition to this world and to the church. The text is especially eloquent and detailed when it comes to the destruction of the world-maker and his rulers and reflects a certain malice on this point. Its lingering on the final destruction of the powers of this world combined with its glorification of the believers as kings in the world to come suggests a minority group, probably thrust away by the church and therefore strongly on the defensive.

PROTENNOIA AND HER DESCENTS

In general the text is spiritual and cryptic; it is therefore demanding on the reader. The mythology of the text is complicated: Protennoia is present in virtually all beings that exist, Gnostics as well as archons. She is a pantheistic figure, existing both above and below, and she has three forms. The descriptions of the eternal Protennoia are woven into the descriptions of her three specific descents. The narrative moves continually back and forth between them. The text was probably meant for those who were initiated in knowledge and presupposes detailed information from other Gnostic sources. In its present form it is difficult to understand and requires a systematic sorting out.

PROTENNOIA

Protennoia is the First Thought dwelling in the Thought of the Father. Her qualities are light, life, and movement. She existed before the All and is the one through which the All took shape. The perfect Son, the Christ, was begotten through her. In her universal aspect she is thus the female part of a triad consisting of the unbegotten Father, the only-begotten Son, and herself—the Mother. She is androgynous, mother and father, copulating with herself and with those that love her. In addition, she is the Womb and gives shape to the All. She both casts Speech into the ears of those who know her and speaks within every creature. The relationships between her three descents are described both in linguistic and patriarchal terms: Father Voice is perceptible through Mother Speech, who has within her the Son, the Word.

THE FIRST DESCENT

The Voice was revealed after the demiurge, Ialdabaoth, had come forth and produced his aeons. It inspired Ialdabaoth to produce a man in its likeness and proclaimed that this man meant destruction for Ialdabaoth. The Voice reached down and stayed with the lost portions of light hidden in the man, empowering it and giving it form. Through a passage seething with metaphors of war, the Voice relates how it would break and destroy the demons of the underworld, their walls of darkness, their forces, and their defenses. While the evil forces were destroyed, the spiritual part of the souls was prepared: The Voice had secretly spoken its mysteries through the language of the Archons and Authorities and borne fruit in the lost portions of light. It is called Father and has three masculinities (37:26). Protennoia as Voice is called "He who is syzygetic" (42:5), while Protennoia as "the unchanging Speech" is called "She who is syzygetic" (42:7–8).

THE SECOND DESCENT

The Speech came in the likeness of a female. Her mission was to instruct about the coming end of the present aeon and the beginning of the aeon to come. The approaching destruction of this aeon frightened the authorities: their thrones were disturbed, the earth shaking and the firmament trembling. The rulers of the planets and the authorities were bewildered and confused. Neither did they understand what was happening—for they did not know the Speech and the Voice that they heard—nor did their maker, Ialdabaoth. And they wept and mourned:

> For as for our tree from which we grew, a fruit of ignorance is what it has; and also its leaves, it is death that dwells in them, and darkness dwells under the shadow of its boughs. And it was in deceit and lust that we harvested it, this (tree) through which ignorant Chaos became for us a dwelling place. For behold, even he, the Archigenetor of our birth, about whom we boast, even he did not know this Speech. (44:20–29)[7]

THE THIRD DESCENT

The Word became perceptible through the Speech of the Mother. In its transcendental aspect the Word was the begotten Son, anointed by the Mother and perfect. He was both hidden within everyone because of his being an aspect of Protennoia and had in his descendant state taken on a special form. The mission of the Word was to save the portion of Sophia lost in the world. This salvation took place through a baptism of water that stripped the one baptized of Chaos and put upon him shining light. The one baptized was delivered to different groups of mythological beings; he was given a robe, baptized and immersed in the Water of Life, enthroned, glorified, snatched away, and brought to the lightplace of the Fatherhood, where he would finally receive "the five Seals from [the Light] of the Mother, Protennoia" (48:31–32). He would then become a Light in Light stripped from all ignorance. In his self-revelation the Word proclaimed that he was revealed in "their tents as Word" (47:15) and further that "I revealed myself in the likeness of their shape. And I wore everyone's garment and I hid myself within them" (47:15–18). This passage refers to a specific Gnostic interpretation of the incarnation of Christ. The Word even said that he clothed himself as the Son of the Archigenetor and appeared as "their Christ" (49:8). And he said: "As for me, I put on Jesus. I bore him from the cursed wood, and established him in the dwelling places of his Father" (50:12–15).

THE FEMALE PRINCIPLE

The three descents of Protennoia are described chronologically and happened at different stages in human history. They refer to mythological events and figures and are elaborations upon them. These elaborations were made in interaction with the mythology of the universal Protennoia and were systematized into a threefold scheme of Voice-Speech-Word. A comparison with other Sethian texts, especially the *Apocryphon of John* with the Pronoia hymn in the long versions, suggests that the three descents refer to (1) the revelation of a spiritual male image that inspired the demiurge to make man in its likeness; (2) the spiritual Eve, who hid herself in Adam and subsequently acted as a spiritual stimulant to him and to the lost portions of light; (3) Christ, whose main act of salvation was to reveal a baptism or an unction.

In *Tri. Prot.* the personalities of the mythological figures are weakened, and their universal mission and actions are emphasized. This is in accordance with a general tendency in *Tri. Prot.* to give importance to the action at the cost of the actors. In several of the Sethian texts the spiritual Eve acts as a veritable mother goddess. But in *Tri. Prot.* the mythology of Eve has receded into the background; she has been reduced from being a person to becoming a principle. The highly developed mythology of Eve was one of the strongest elements in the construction of a goddess in Sethian Gnosticism. The hymnic passages to her in the *Hypostasis of the Archons* (89:11–17) and the *Origin of the World* (113:32–114:15) reflect a rich measure of personal piety. The absence of the mythological person of Eve in *Tri. Prot.* points to a weakening of female mythology and of personal commitment to a goddess.

The unbegotten Father is the great transcendent signifier. All successful creative activity has its ultimate source in him. His elevated state prevents a direct contact with creation; therefore he made Protennoia and acted through her. Protennoia has no independent existence. Thus, the female principle is secondary and derived from the male principle. Independent female creative activity is unsuccessful. That must be understood with reference to Aristotelian embryology, where the male provides form at the conception of the child while the female provides matter. An utter female conception would therefore be formless. Sophia conceived Ialdabaoth alone, which resulted in his becoming a hybrid with animal features. In *Tri. Prot.* the myth of the fallen Sophia is partly overworked.[8] Sophia is referred to as "the innocent one" (39:29), but also as "her from whom he (Ialdabaoth) had come forth originally" (39:31–32). The motif of Sophia's fall has obviously moved into the background in this text and no blame falls on her. The burden of being a scoundrel is placed on Ialdabaoth alone.

Some observations about the female principle can be made with a basis in the text's mythological triads, which are (1) the transcendent triad of the unbegotten Father, Protennoia, and the begotten Son; (2) the incomplete triad of Sophia and Ialdabaoth; (3) the descendant triad of Voice, Speech, and Word. The second and third triads relate to the first: the transcendent Son is the origin of the second triad, while the third triad consists of Protennoia's three forms. All triads have only *one* female element and show quantitatively less value to the female principle than to the male. The triads are built up as patriarchal nuclear families. The second one is defective and therefore unsuccessful. Even if Protennoia is conceived of both as the unbegotten father's spouse and as his daughter, there exists no mother–daughter relationship in either of the triads.

Generally the female elements in the triads mediate between the two male elements, and they also mediate between above and below. Sophia mediates between the Son (who created her) and Ialdabaoth, between the aeons above and below. Protennoia mediates between the unbegotten Father and the begotten Son, between the aeons above and the portions of light below, between the transcendent triad and the descendant triad. The descendant triad consists of the three forms of Protennoia; but, more important, the descendant triad is a direct reflection of the transcendent triad. The divine triad of Sethian literature (Father, Mother, and Son) is in this text repeated in a descendant state. The most important being in the descendant triad is the Son. He is the last of the redeemers and the one who completes the process of salvation by transmitting the baptism with the five seals. He is the only one who is present in the world through incarnation. Even if the descendant Son became perceptible through the Speech of the Mother, the connection between the transcendent Son and the descendant Son is closer, as explicated by the descendant Son: "it is a male offspring [that supports me] as my foundation" (46:9–10). The transcendent Mother plays the main role in the text, but her descendant Son threatens her position, because it is he who completes the process of salvation. Accordingly, Protennoia's most important function lies in manifesting her Son both in his transcendent and descendant aspect.

The text is thus a Gnostic variant of that mother–son relationship in which the Western world has been living for two thousand years.

GOD THE ANDROGYNE MOTHER

In her universal aspect Protennoia is designated Mother, but she has also the epithet "male Virgin" (46:21). Her masculinity and her femininity are distinguished and projected in the Voice and the Speech respectively. The Voice and the Speech are syzygetic and dependent on each other. Protennoia could be characterized as a female androgyne with distinct sex characteristics. Ialdabaoth, in contrast, is different. He is also androgynous, but his sex distinctions are blurred, probably a consequence of his being formless.

Protennoia's power of reproduction is dual, owing to her double sex. In her universal aspect she combines the procreative functions of the male and the female. She is both the Womb from which everything goes forth and the one who gives shape to the All. To give shape is usually a male function and probably connected with Protennoia's male aspect. The Voice, called Father, reflects the male aspect and carries on its shape-giving activity: The Voice is hidden in "his own," "empowering [them and] giving them shape" (40:32–33), usually a male prerogative. Man was produced in the likeness of the Voice, and is for that reason presumably male. Those belonging to the Father are referred to as "the Sons of the Light" (37:19–20; 41:1; 49:25). To save his own and to destroy the evil forces the Father acts as a warrior.

Accordingly, Protennoia as Voice is consistently male and has no part in Protennoia's female aspect. Her female aspect is limited to only one of the three descents, the Speech. The Speech comes to "the Sons of the Thought" (44:30) to teach them; she has put breath into "her own" and cast the eternally holy Spirit into them. The other part of the mission of the Speech applies to the archons. To them her voice appeared unstructured as Thunder. The descent of the Speech brought severe disturbance to the archontic mechanisms of chronological time and of the spheres. Most interesting, the approaching destruction is described as a birth: "just as in the pangs of the parturient it (the time) had drawn near, so also had the destruction approached" (43:6–8). The conception of this world as an evil womb shines through. A biological perspective is also present in the metaphor of the evil tree of the archons with its fruit of ignorance, its leaves of death, and its boughs of darkness, all harvested in deceit and lust.

It is rather peculiar that the mythology of the female descent of Protennoia has so few positive female features. They are restricted to her function as instructor and life-giver. But these functions are not elaborated mythologically and are only pale reminiscences of the similar functions of the powerful Eve in other Sethian texts. At the same time, the image of birth is used in a destructive way.

Like Father Voice, the Son (the Word) is utterly male. The Son fools the archons with his different disguises and in the bargain shows the impermanence of all fleshly "robes." The theme of the robes is carried on at the baptism of those to be saved, to whom he will give a permanent robe of light. The Son is a model for those to be saved because he was anointed and made perfect from the beginning. They are his seed, and he is in reality the father of everyone. Seen in relation to Aristotelian embryology, the theme of the "fleshly robes" reveals that the female contribution at the birth of the child in reality is archontic and evil. In contrast, the male seed as the element which gives shape, contains the divine spirit. The Father–Son relation thus guaranteed spiritual succession. It got its final apotheosis in the baptism through which the Sons become kings.

Where does all this leave Protennoia? Protennoia is a remote mother, even if she is universally present, and she suffers from a lack of personality. At best she is a pale reflection of the all-goddess of late antiquity. She may have constituted the female context of a Logos Christology, but this spiritual maternity turned out to be a dead end and was left behind before Christianity introduced the apotheosed maternity of Mary.[9] The concept of the spiritual mother was apparently built on reason more than on emotion. Still, an emotional substratum clings to this figure, growing out of her peculiar relationship with those that are called her own: They were not fully formed and were therefore still part of her, different from her, and at the same time identical with her. Only through knowledge of her secrets, the *nomina sacra* of the five seals, would they be fully formed and placed in "the incomprehensible Silence" (50:20). A deep psychological truth is hidden: the result of knowing the innermost secrets of the Mother is inevitable—to obtain the ultimate state of lack of difference, that is, to return to her womb.

In line with their longing for this state of being, Protennoia's adherents' fascination with her lay not in her maternal personality but rather in her being the maternal source of being—the womb without a face—and in her being the quality of *life* in everything. Protennoia also includes within herself the tightest parenthood structure possible: the patriarchal nuclear family—Father, Mother, and Son—constituting an absolute totality but with interchanging roles. One more tribute to the return to oneness without difference.

WOMEN

The text is full of metaphors describing the original nondifferentiated state of being as invisible, incomprehensible, ineffable, immeasurable, silent, hidden. From them are developed a descending series of interrelated metaphors to describe the contact between spirit and matter and the process of salvation. These metaphors are primarily related to sight and hearing. The superior metaphoric system is auditive and applied to Protennoia and her descents: Silence-Thought-Voice-Speech-Word. The visual system with plays on Light and Image is appended to the auditive. But their sensorial qualities are not restricted to the auditive and the visual. Through the text's use of gendered imagery the process of attaining knowledge has been eroticized. The ear has been developed into an erotic organ through which a spiritual fertilization takes place, a point made by Kristeva in relation to Mary.[10]

The universe of the text is dualistic, with a sharp division between the spiritual world and the world of the archons. This dualism is not established by means of polarized sexual values. On the contrary, throughout the text male and female values are described as relational in terms of kin roles with complementary functions in the process of salvation.

How does this text relate to women? On the one hand, it does not give any indication that women were excluded from the process of salvation. For instance, man was probably made in a male image, but his sex does not seem significant; and the text shows no special interest in Sophia's fall as a female fault. On the other hand, it does not reflect any explicit interest in women either, and uses a male generic language. Most significantly, the model of salvation is wholly male: the Son is the one created perfect, and the ones to be saved shall become "Sons of Light" or "Sons of the Thought." Protennoia, the Mother, is unique, the only one of her sex. In contrast to her son, she is not a model for anyone.

Conception and birth are used as powerful symbols, but they have no positive meaning as physiological and biological events. Sexuality has moved from the sexual organs and is subsumed into the process of obtaining knowledge through the ears and the eyes. Femininity is absorbed in maternity and reduced through a profound spiritualization. *Tri. Prot.*'s discourse on maternity takes place within a traditional patriarchal structure. The construct of the mother is the result of systematic philosophical thought combined with longing for the maternal origin—marred by a strong effort to make her male. It bears witness to an idealization of the mother—child relationship, which went in the paradoxical direction of masculinization and repression of the female element.

If we presume that this text was available to women and that its ascetic implications were realized, one could claim that it had a liberating function for women because it gave them a possibility for salvation in line with men and freed them from their biology and their burdens of motherhood. But one could also say the opposite, that it denied their existence as women, deprived them of their biology, devaluated the meaning of birth, and thus reduced them to second-rate men.

Generally speaking, the deconstruction of this female image of God will be one more obstacle to the popular understanding of Gnosticism as a religion that was "better" for women than the Christianity of the victorious church. It is easy to deconstruct *Trimorphic Protennoia,* but it is difficult to make a reconstruction of it that is friendly to women.

NOTES

1. See Gesine Robinson, "The Trimorphic Protennoia and the Prologue of the Fourth Gospel," in *Gnosticism and the Early Christian World: In Honor of James M. Robinson,* ed. J. E. Goehring, C. W. Hedrick, J. T. Sanders, with H. D. Betz (Sonoma, CA: Polebridge, 1990), 37–50.

2. Yvonne Janssens, "Le Codex XIII de Nag Hammadi," *Le Muséon* 87/3–4 (1974): 341–413; Gesine Schenke, *Die Dreigestaltige Protennoia (Nag Hammadi Codex XIII)* (Berlin: Akademie-Verlag, 1984).

3. Julia Kristeva, "Stabat Mater," in *The Kristeva Reader,* ed. Toril Moi (Oxford: Basil Blackwell, 1986), 160–86.

4. Ibid., 161.

5. Ibid.

6. Sethian is a current designation of one of the main branches of Gnosticism; the other main branch is Valentinianism.

7. The citations are made from the translation of John D. Turner in *The Nag Hammadi Library in English* (Leiden: Brill, 1988).

8. The passage is obscure, and it may seem as though it was the male light Eleleth who called Ialdabaoth into existence. But because of 39:31–32, where Sophia is called "her from whom he (Ialdabaoth) had come forth originally," it is more likely that Eleleth's call took place after Ialdabaoth's birth by Sophia.

9. See Marina Warner, *Alone of All Her Sex: The Myth and the Cult of the Virgin Mary* (London: Weidefeld, 1976).

10. Kristeva, "Stabat Mater," 172–73.

RECOMMENDED READINGS

Janssens, Yvonne. "Le Codex XIII de Nag Hammadi." *Le Muséon* 87/3–4 (1974): 341–413.

———. "The Trimorphic Protennoia and the Fourth Gospel." In *The New Testament and Gnosis: Essays in honour of Robert McL. Wilson,* edited by A. H. B. Logan and A. J. M. Wedderburn, 229–44. Edinburgh: T. & T. Clark, 1983.

Kristeva, Julia. "Stabat Mater." In *The Kristeva Reader,* edited by Toril Moi, 160–86. Oxford: Basil Blackwell, 1986.

Robinson, Gesine. "The Trimorphic Protennoia and the Prologue of the Fourth Gospel." In *Gnosticism and the Early Christian World: In Honor of James M. Robinson,* edited by J. E. Goehring, C. W. Hedrick, J. T. Sanders, with H. D. Betz, 37–50. Sonoma, CA: Polebridge, 1990.

Schenke, Gesine. *Die Dreigestaltige Protennoia (Nag Hammadi Codex XIII).* Berlin: Akademie-Verlag, 1984.

Warner, Marina. *Alone of All Her Sex: The Myth and the Cult of the Virgin Mary.* London: Weidefeld, 1976.

The Book of Norea, Daughter of Eve

KAREN L. KING ◆

FEMINIST HERMENEUTICS

THE BOOK OF NOREA (entitled *Hypostasis of the Archons*) illustrates the critical appropriation of tradition through *retelling* the stories of Eve and Norea. It applies a kind of "hermeneutics of suspicion" in that it does not approach scripture as fixed or universally authoritative.[1] Instead, the text demonstrates a freedom to reimagine the contours and contexts of religious belief and experience in the face of suffering and injustice. By its own model, the text invites the reader to do the same, to rechart the system of power relations and to identity formations residing in the narrative.

Retelling provides a fruitful hermeneutic for theological exploration and appropriation without requiring a decision *either* to reject the canonical text *or* to authorize one particular interpretation of it. Retelling thereby raises the possibility that a text can be appropriated critically without denying the variety of human experiences and situations. The story of Eve and Norea in the *Hypostasis of the Archons* shows that already in antiquity the Genesis narrative could be read as a story about powerful female spirituality, not as proof of women's natural inferiority.

Retelling also addresses a painful issue in feminist hermeneutics: given the value of religious tradition on the one hand, and given the use of religion for violence and oppression on the other, how is it possible to appropriate this heritage for a common, inclusive, and mature spirituality without unknowingly reaffirming traditions used to support violence and oppression? The story of Eve's rape gives us a disturbing but compelling reminder that no text, even one as seemingly positive in its attitudes toward women as the *Hypostasis of the Archons,* is "pure" or "safe." A hermeneutics of suspicion must be applied to interpretations and retellings, both ancient and modern, as much as to their base narratives.

This commentary aims at a participatory hermeneutic, that is, one that extends an invitation to readers to engage actively in the process of interpretation, an interpretation that is not presented as definitive but whose meaning is open. My intention here is to open a dialogue with readers by offering my interpretation as one view. Moreover, to illustrate the process of modern retelling as participatory hermeneutics, an example is given of a retelling of the rape of Eve at the conclusion of the commentary.

REDISCOVERY

In 1945, a clay jar was discovered in the desert of middle Egypt near the town of Nag Hammadi. In it were papyrus codices dating to the fourth century C.E. Among the most startling of the discoveries was a short text in which Norea, the daughter of Eve, appears as the savior of humankind. She is portrayed as the pure and undefiled mother of humanity and the source of true teaching about the nature of the arrogant world rulers.

The title of the text, which is inscribed at the end of the manuscript, is the *Hypostasis of the Archons,*[2] sometimes translated as the "*Nature* (or *Reality*) *of the Rulers.*" This title points to one of the main aims of the text: to give the reader true information about the history and character of the arrogant and wicked forces that rule the world. Some modern scholars have also referred to the text as "the book of Norea," since her voice fuses with that of the narrator toward the end of the text (from 93.13 to the end). This fusion has the effect of turning the account into a direct narrative from Norea to the reader.

SUMMARY OF STRUCTURE AND PLOT

Following the prologue, the narrative can be divided into two main sections. In the first section (86.25–91.11), we are given an account of the origins and character of the world creator and his cronies, the rulers (also referred to as authorities, archons, and forces). Their arrogance and impotence are illustrated by their unsuccessful attempts to dominate the Female Spiritual Principle.

The modern reader will immediately recognize elements from Genesis throughout this section but will also no doubt be shocked by the startling ways that this familiar story is told. Here the world creator of Genesis appears not as the true, good God, but as an arrogant, ignorant, and somewhat powerless being, androgynous and shaped like a lion (see 87.27–28; 94.16–19; 95.1–4). Above him exists the true, transcendent Father of Light, who is neither the world creator nor its ruler, although he determines everything that takes place in the lower world in order to bring about the salvation of the children of light.[3] The text thus posits two deities: a lower world creator and the heavenly Father of Light above.

The story begins with the lower creator's arrogant claim to be the only God. As a rebuke to him, the image of divine Incorruptibility (a female figure) appears out of the Light realm above and is reflected on the waters. Immediately the rulers are enamored and want to possess her. They attempt a variety of strategies, including the creation of humanity and the rape of Eve. Their efforts, however, are unsuccessful because of their inferiority and because the goddess Sophia is keeping watch. She sends down the Female Spiritual Principle, who first appears in Eve and instructs Adam, and then, taking the form of a serpent, encourages Adam and Eve to eat from the tree of the knowledge of good and evil.

In short, the meaning of the Genesis creation story is turned upside down: the creation of humanity is portrayed as a wicked attempt to dominate the Spirit; eating of the tree is good; and Eve and the snake are savior figures!

The second section (91.11–97.21) continues the narrative with the story of the children of Eve, focusing especially on her daughter Norea. The rulers again make a series of attempts to dominate her but fail utterly. Norea overcomes them with her fiery breath and spiritual power, exposing their ignorance and impotence.

The text concludes with a dialogue between Norea and the angel Eleleth, who comes to aid her against the rulers. He answers her questions about the origin of the rulers and the salvation of her children, concluding with a prophecy about the coming of the True Man at the end of time.

COMMENTARY

THE NATURE OF THE RULERS (86.25–87.11)

The theological universe of the Hebrew Bible is here decentered for the first time. We are told that above Samael (who is identified with the creator God of Genesis) there is a higher, incorruptible realm. Not knowing this, he claims to be the only God.[4] A voice from that realm exposes his ignorance and calls him "God of the blind."[5]

The creator God (also called Samael, Saklas, or Yaldabaoth) is not physically sightless, but spiritually ignorant and impiously arrogant.[6] The paragraph is structured to contrast the sinful and limited perspective of Samael with that of the higher spiritual plane of the Entirety and Incorruptibility.[7]

Rather than repent, the creator God persists in his blasphemy. The account of the resulting creation is very compressed and nearly unintelligible, but it gives us three important bits of information. First, the parentage of Samael is chaos and darkness, a heritage that suggests his true character. Second, we learn that Samael is not successful at creating, in contrast to the Genesis account. What he thinks is his "power" is really just empty words, blasphemy. It is not he who orders chaos but a female figure new to the story—Pistis Sophia (Faith Wisdom). It is she who establishes the offspring of Samael in their appropriate places.[8] (We will hear more of Sophia later.) Third, the author remarks that the model Pistis Sophia uses to order the visible world is the invisible world of Incorruptibility above. Here the text draws its conceptuality from Plato's account of the creation of the world in the *Timaeus,* where the cosmos is formed by a demiurge after the model of the eternal Ideas.

THE RULERS' ATTEMPTS TO DOMINATE THE FEMALE SPIRITUAL PRINCIPLE (87.11–91.11)

Episode 1: The Creation of Adam to Ensnare Incorruptibility

When Incorruptibility rebuked the arrogance of the chief ruler, her image appeared on the waters and the rulers were enamored of it. They desired to possess and control it. They then devise the creation of Adam as a plot to trap the image of Incorruptibility within a material body, but all they have to work with is earth, so they shape the man after their own bodily likeness according to the divine image that had appeared in the waters.[9] But their plan fails, as it was destined to. Although they are able to give the earthman a soul (since they can give him what they possess), like them he is weak and is even unable to rise. The text portrays them as impotent fools and ridicules their ineffectual attempts to enliven Adam by blowing on him "like storm winds" (88.6–7). They are ignorant of the true identity of the image they desire, and for this the text ridicules them, adding a certain comic humor to the narrative.

The Spirit is now sent to enliven Adam and dwell with him. She comes down from the "Adamantine land," a place whose name indicates its unyielding, metaliclike strength.[10] She comes to him first as a voice, the power of effective language. It is she who gives Adam his name. Now with her assistance, Adam is able to name all the animals brought to him by the Rulers, demonstrating his powers of discernment. Meanwhile the Rulers unwittingly become complicit in the plan of Incorruptibility by placing Adam in the garden within reach of the tree of the knowledge of good and evil. Even though they tell him not to eat of it and threaten him with death if he does, we know what will happen: Adam will eat and gain higher discernment. The veil of his ignorance will be partially lifted, so that his understanding will no longer be that of a purely material nature.

Episode 2: The Surgical Violation of Adam and the Rape of Eve

The rulers now attempt to extract the Spirit from Adam by surgical removal. After anesthetizing him with some of their own ignorance (sleep is used here as a metaphor for reduced consciousness), they open his side and replace it with flesh. The Living Woman (Spirit) is removed from him, leaving Adam only matter and soul.

The Living Woman awakens Adam from the sleep of ignorance. He immediately recognizes her true identity as his life-giver: "It is you who have given me life; you will be called 'Mother of the living.' For it is she who is my mother. It is she who is the physician,[11] and the woman, and she who has given birth" (89.13–17).[12]

In contrast to Adam's acknowledgment of the Woman's spiritual nature, the rulers react with immediate violence. Their lust is aroused and they pursue the Spiritual Woman in order to rape her. The narrative moves rapidly: they see her; they become agitated and aroused; they agree together to the rape and begin the pursuit. But contrary to antiquity's usual literary portrayal of the victim's reaction as fear and powerlessness, the Spiritual Woman laughs at them and—just as she falls into their clutches—she transfers her self from the material body of Eve to a tree.[13] But the rulers are oblivious to the movements of the Spirit; they seize the abandoned body of the carnal woman and rape her.[14]

The scene is one both of victory and horror. The laughter of the Female Spiritual Principle exposes the authorities as fools; the Spirit has again evaded their attempts at domination and destruction—and they haven't even noticed! Again the text ridicules their powerlessness. Her laughter exposes the nature of absolute power for what it is—wicked, blind, and ignorant. The *Hypostasis of the Archons* explicitly and decisively condemns rape, making it clear that rape is less an act of sexual passion than an attempt to dominate and degrade.

But the comedy is also painfully poignant and shockingly violent. Like so much comedy, it trades its humor against the humiliation of nonpersons. And the victory of the Spiritual Woman is traded against the division of her self, against the denial of her material body, the carnal Eve.

The psychic dissociation depicted here is a common, although painful survival response by victims of rape and incest. While psychic dissociation can be effective at maintaining some personal integrity in the face of attempts to destroy one's self, ultimately it is an extremely painful solution to violence, insofar as it abandons the body as one's self.

In the *Hypostasis of the Archons,* there is no attempt to purify the "defiled" carnal woman; rather, her utter loss of spiritual elevation is emphasized. The text says that the rulers defiled the stamp of her voice. The association of voice and speech with the spiritual emissary of Incorruptibility, combined with the association of the mouth and the vagina as orifices of penetration, makes it clear that, for this text, sexual impurity has defiled Eve's capacity for spiritual elevation. She is even disavowed later in the text by her own daughter, Norea, who denies that Eve is her true mother and accepts only the Spiritual Woman as her legitimate parent. The text has turned its back on the victimized woman—and both the Spiritual Woman and Norea have traded their purity and spiritual power against this discourse.[15]

Episode 3: The Forbidden Tree

After leaving Eve, the Spiritual Woman enters the snake and instructs the carnal woman through it. The dialogue follows Gen 3:1–5 with only some modification, adding that the motivation for the prohibition against eating of the tree was the rulers' jealousy. The account here also deletes the woman's reflective deliberation (Gen 3:6a), possibly to emphasize her lowered state. She eats and gives some to her husband. They immediately recognize that they lack Spirit. Here the snake works for the salvation of Adam and Eve, and Eve participates in Adam's enlightenment by giving him fruit to eat.

Episode 4: The Curses

The chief ruler now appears on the scene. He has to ask where Adam is because he lacks the capacity to discern the latest turn of events. Adam provides the necessary clues and the ruler realizes that they have eaten from the tree.

As a last resort, the rulers attempt to keep humankind in ignorance by throwing them out of the garden into a life of toil. Unlike the Genesis account, which portrays work as punishment, the *Hypostasis of the Archons* emphasizes that the constant need to meet the needs of the body serves as a ploy to keep people from devoting themselves to higher spiritual matters.

THE CHILDREN OF EVE (91.11–92.4)

The text now turns to the propagation of humanity. Eve's first child is Cain, the product of her rape by the authorities. She produces a second child by Adam: Abel. Cain, being of a material nature, cultivates the land. Abel, possessing the soul nature of his parents, herds living animals (sheep). God recognizes the superiority of Abel's nature; in jealousy (typical of his carnal fathers), Cain kills Abel and is cursed.

After this, Adam produces another son with Eve: Seth. He is of a soul-nature, replacing Abel.

No father is named for the last child. We are simply told that Eve bore a daughter named Norea, whom she says will be "an assistance for many generations of humankind." The editor adds, pointing ahead in the story: "She is the virgin whom the forces did not defile." With Norea's birth, humankind begins to multiply and improve.

Norea

Before continuing with the commentary, a few words about Norea are necessary. Norea appears in the *Hypostasis of the Archons* as the daughter of Eve and the mother of spiritual humanity. She is the "virgin whom the forces did not defile" (92.2–3). She brings knowledge and truth to people suffering under the false enslavement of the world rulers.

But to readers acquainted only with the canonical Bible, her existence may come as something of a surprise. Norea is not a biblical figure. She seems to have developed from Jewish speculation about Naamah (Gen 4:22).[16] Birger Pearson summarizes this development:

> Norea appears in a wide range of gnostic literature (including Manichaean and Mandaean) under the following names: Norea, Noraia, Orea, Oraia, Horaia, Nora, Noria, Nuraita, and Nhuraita. She is represented in the sources as the daughter of Adam and Eve, as the wife-sister of Seth, or even the wife of Noah or Shem. She is typically portrayed as the intended victim of rape by the creator-archons. Comparative analysis of the gnostic sources, together with certain Jewish haggadoth concerning the biblical Naamah (cf. Gen. 4:22), reveals that the gnostic figure of Norea has been developed out of the Jewish material featuring Naamah. . . . In certain Jewish traditions Naamah is presented as a Cainite woman with a reputation for lewdness. Her role as a seductress of the "sons of God" (Gen. 6:2) has, in fact, been transposed in the gnostic literature, in a typically gnostic hermeneutical inversion, as a successful evasion of rape by the wicked archons. In the gnostic sources Norea is featured as a "saved savior," whose own salvation is a paradigm for that of her spiritual race, that is, gnostic humankind.[17]

The *Hypostasis of the Archons* indicates a knowledge of many of these traditions, but deploys them for its own ends. Norea appears as the sister of Seth but fully displaces him as the primal parent and savior of spiritual humanity.[18] She is also associated with Noah, but the text reverses the spiritual valence of earlier portrayals, which had her working with the devil to thwart God's plan for the construction of the ark. Similarly, in retelling the story of Gen 6:1–4,

Norea appears in neither of her traditional roles as a seductress or as a victim of rape. Rather, she exposes the rulers' ignorance and evil, successfully escaping them without harm.[19] By consuming the ark and denouncing the rulers, she is a model for rebellion against illegitimate forces of domination.

NOREA AGAINST THE RULERS (92.4–32)

Episode 1: The Flood

Having failed to capture the Spiritual Principle and seeing that humanity is improving, the rulers attempt to destroy humanity and all other living things through a flood. The ruler of the forces attempts to save Noah, his children, the beasts, and the birds by warning him to build an ark and hide in it. Orea (an alternate spelling of Norea) tries to board the ark, but Noah refuses. In an astonishing display of tremendous power, her fiery breath consumes the ark, and Noah is forced to build a second time. Here the episode ends.

Several aspects of this story require further explication. Why does the ruler of the forces attempt to save Noah? Why does Noah attempt to keep Norea from boarding the ark? Why does the story end so abruptly?

Later in the narrative (95.13–25), we learn that one of the authorities, Sabaoth, had repented upon learning about the power of Pistis Sophia. She then placed him in charge of the seventh heaven. He was named "God of the forces" (95.22–25). Some scholars have plausibly argued that it is Sabaoth, not his father, Samael, who sought to aid Noah and the others.[20] In this text, Sabaoth takes on many of the positive qualities of the Hebrew God, while his negative qualities (such as jealousy) are attributed to Samael.

Comparison with other writings from antiquity is useful here. Epiphanius, a fourth-century heresiologist, says that a group of heretics called Gnostics possessed books of Noria, the wife of Noah. These Gnostics, he says:

> suggest the reason why Noria was not allowed to join Noah in the ark, though she would often have liked to. The archon who made the world, they say, wanted to destroy her in the flood with all the rest. But they say that she laid siege to the ark and burned it, a first and a second time, and a third. And this is why Noah's own ark took many years to build—it was burned often by Noria. For Noah was obedient to the archon, they say, but Noria revealed the powers on high. . . . (*Panarion* 26.1, 7–9)[21]

Perhaps a similar story lies behind our narrative. Sabaoth may have favored Noah and attempted to save the best of humanity from destruction. Noah might also be protecting his own favored status by denying Norea entrance. We can only speculate, for the author does not bother to give a full and lucid account. The text shows less interest in the particulars of the story than in repeating its main theme: the rulers attempt to destroy and dominate humankind because of their jealousy and ignorance, but they are ineffectual in the face of the superior power of the Spirit represented by Norea.[22]

Episode 2: The Attempted Rape of Norea

The rulers now attempt rape. They first try to persuade her by resorting to a lie: "Your mother Eve came to us," they claim. But the readers know that in fact she fled from them. Norea too is not fooled. She exposes the rulers' true nature and disempowers them by naming them as the accursed rulers of darkness and unrighteousness.[23] She affirms her spiritual home in the world above, even as she rejects the carnal woman they raped as her mother.

Norea's uncompliant response angers the rulers and they become even more arrogant. Their leader prepares to force her "to render them service as did also your mother Eve" (92.30–31). But Norea calls out for help to the holy and true God. Her call is answered in the appearance of the great angel Eleleth, whose arrival prompts the rulers to withdraw quietly.

THE DIALOGUE OF NOREA AND ELELETH (92.34–97.21)

Norea's cry for help is a practical complement to her bold speech. The great angel Eleleth comes down from the heavens in response to her call, and the stage is set for the final episode of the text: the dialogue between Norea and Eleleth.[24] There are five exchanges between the two: the initial cry for help and then four questions from Norea, each followed by a response from Eleleth.

The First Question (93.6–32)

Norea begins by asking the angel who he is. He replies that his name is Eleleth;[25] he is one of the four light-givers;[26] he is sagacity and understanding. He has come from the presence of the holy spirit to save Norea from the dominion[27] of the lawless ones by teaching her about her "root."[28]

In the middle of his response, the narrator breaks in with an awe-filled description of Eleleth's power and appearance. He clearly is a counterimage to the rulers. Where they are ignorant, he is sagacity and understanding; where they are impotent, his power is beyond telling; where they are bestial and androgynous, he is handsome and male; where they are rulers of darkness, he is brilliant light.

At 93.18–19, the narrator speaks for the first time in the first person, the narrator's voice melding with the voice of Norea for the remainder of the tractate.

This shift has the effect of turning the dialogue into an eyewitness report by Norea.[29]

Eleleth tells Norea that because she comes from the heavenly abode (of "Incorruptibility"), the authorities have no real power over her.[30] Her "root" is the truth, against which no power can prevail.

The Second Question (93.32–96.17)

Norea now asks to be taught about the rulers. The response is a complete cosmogony, beginning with a very brief description of the divine realm of Incorruptibility. The description repeats some elements already related at the beginning of the text, but now in more detail.

The story of creation begins with Pistis Sophia's desire to create. Although her child is a celestial being, it is deficient because she created alone without a male consort.[31] It is cast forth from Incorruptibility "like an aborted fetus," a simile that draws heavily for its signification upon the ancient practice of exposing malformed infants.[32] The deficient character of the being is furthered by its contact with matter. The result is a being who is bestial[33] in form, ignorant, arrogant, androgynous, blind, and jealous. This is the creator God.

Samael boasts that he is the only God. To confute him, Sophia introduces light into matter by stretching forth her finger. This act results in the introduction of divine light into the world below.[34]

Samael proceeds to create a vast realm for himself, including the seven (planetary) rulers. He boasts to them that he is the god of everything that exists.

Again a rebuttal comes from the higher realm, this time from Zoe, the daughter of Pistis Sophia. In a mockery of Yaldabaoth's impotent attempts to breathe life into Adam, Zoe's potent, fiery breath becomes an angel who binds Yaldabaoth and casts him into the underworld.

Strangely enough, when Sabaoth, one of Yaldabaoth's children, sees the power of the angel, he repents, condemning his parents and turning his allegiance to Sophia and Zoe. His behavior models the pattern of "repentance" for the children of light, who are called upon to reject both female materiality[35] and the world ruler, and turn to the Female Spiritual Principle. Most important, his repentance indicates the possibility that the offspring of the world ruler are not predestined for damnation but are condemned for their actions and intentions.[36] His portrayal undermines any interpretation of the text as racially or biologically determinist.[37]

Sabaoth is established by Sophia as the God of justice and sovereignty. Yaldabaoth is envious of Sabaoth's power, and from his envy springs death.

THE THIRD QUESTION

Norea next asks Eleleth about her relation to the rulers. Eleleth assures her that her nature is not material, but that she and her offspring derive from the light, that is, the spirit of truth, the seed that Sophia ejected into matter when she stretched forth her finger (94.29–30). Therefore they are not subject to the dominion of death (96.25–27), because they come from the primeval Father above. The knowledge of the spirit of truth will become known after three generations (Eve, Norea, her children), at which time the error of the authorities will cease to have power to bind the children of the light.

THE FOURTH QUESTION

Although Eleleth has said that after three generations the truth will be made known, Norea impatiently pleas, "How much longer?" Eleleth assures her that the moment will come when the True Man will reveal the Spirit of truth. Eleleth's final response culminates in a poetic declaration about the final salvation of Norea's children and the destruction of the lower world, ending with praise to the father and the son.

Although no explicitly Christian terminology is used, the description of the True Man strongly suggests a Johannine-like Christ figure. He is sent from the Father, and will come in a "modeled form" (a physical body); he will be a teacher, trampling death underfoot and leading the souls to ascend back to the light; his coming will signal the destruction of the authorities and initiate his own rule over the Entirety above. The True Man is an eschatological savior who will effect the last stage of the Father's plan to save Norea's children.

GENDER, MYTH, AND POWER POLITICS

The concluding speech of Eleleth clearly shows that there is no intention in the text to initiate a social program for the overthrow of patriarchy; the ideal of the text is a return to the legitimate rule of the father and the son. Yet while gendered language is not primarily aimed at criticism of gendered social roles, it does point to the social world, not to change or redeem it but to expose it.[38]

The primary object of criticism is not the oppression of women by men but absolute power, which degrades and oppresses men and women alike. Illegitimate power is shown to be wicked, arrogant, and ignorant, and it is contrasted with the Spirit of truth, whose power is goodness, light, and knowledge.

Moreover, the use of rape as a primary metaphor to condemn the rulers has the effect of undermining the patriarchal politics that trade on women's bodies against violence and domination. The patriarchal schema is further undermined by the illuminating presence of the female redeemers. Eve brings knowledge to Adam; Zoe instructs Sabaoth about the higher realm; Norea brings spiritual knowledge to humanity. Ultimately these female redeemers undermine the power politics of patriarchy, based on force and illegitimate attempts to dominate. The authoritarianism of the father-creator is ridiculed and displaced, and even revenge against him is limited. Anne McGuire concludes:

> The mythic narrative of the *Hypostasis of the Archons* invites the reader to dwell in the imaginative world depicted in the text, to see things as the revelation of Eleleth and Norea's confrontation with the powers reveals them, and to discern their respective modes of exercising power. Under this reading, the *Hypostasis of the Archons* invites its readers to dwell in a world marked by struggle between spiritual and archontic powers, but it also empowers its readers to recognize the powers at work in their world, and to participate in the exercise of Norea's virginal power against the powers of the Rulers. In this way, the *Hypostasis of the Archons* challenges its readers to identify with the "children of Norea," to inherit the promise, to resist and rename those powers that would claim falsely to rule in their world, as Norea renames and subverts the false powers of her world.[39]

Several figures model this process of spiritual advancement:[40] Adam's awakening by the Spiritual Woman; Adam and Eve's eating of the tree and realizing their lack of the spiritual element; Norea's defiance of the world rulers and receipt of higher spiritual instruction from Eleleth; Sabaoth's repentance and instruction by Zoe. Ultimately the most important model is Norea, since she will be the savior of all humankind; but each model contributes to the readers' growing comprehension of the nature of spiritual advancement. Some impetus is needed to awaken one out of the sleep of ignorance. One must realize one's own lack of spirit and the need for it; some must recognize, too, their complicity with the wicked rulers and repent. Rejection of the lies of this world and rebellion against the forces that seek to enslave one in humiliation and darkness are necessary before, finally, the higher teaching can be received and comprehended. Then no power on earth or in the starry spheres above the earth can keep the spirit from its true home.

The *Hypostasis of the Archons* seems to know that the soul, which exists in the degradation of entrapment in the material world and yet which is at the same time a most pure spark of true divinity and light, shares a metaphorical correspondence with the ambiguous nature of woman as she was culturally constructed in antiquity: she is at once associated more closely than man with sexuality and materiality, is considered to be in need of instruction, and is subordinate to male authority, but she is also the powerful, life-giving mother and the ideal of virginal purity. This ambiguity made the feminine an extremely attractive image for symbolizing the text's perception of the human condition:

caught between death and degradation, on the one hand, and a taste for eternity and illumination, on the other.

This ambiguity also makes the feminine useful in expressing mediation between the straining poles of material nature and transcendence. Only the female saviors are presented as both immanent in the world and capable of ascent from it. As such, feminine figures provide linkage between the worlds above and below.[41] The true man may ultimately be the savior, but he is distant and abstract; the female savior, Norea, is strong and present. She is the source of life and teaching.[42] Since she stands between the pleromatic home of the children of light and their temporary residence in the world below, the Female Spiritual Principle can help to transverse the distance between political exploitation and empowerment, between the experience of degradation and the knowledge of infinite self-worth, between despair and peace.

RETELLING

At a recent conference of the southwest Presbyterian Synod's Committee on Justice for Women, I asked participants to rewrite the stories of Eve and Norea, to interpret by thinking imaginatively and creatively with the narrative. One group took up the dissociative division of Eve during her rape by the Archons. The women felt an immediate and pressing need to get Eve out of the tree and back into her body. This is the solution they devised:

Re-Creation Story

Then Sophia called to the Future and said,
  Send me women skilled in mourning,
Send me Tamar, the raped princess,
  Send me Hagar, the abused slave,
Send me the Levite's murdered concubine.
  Send me a community for my daughter, Eve.
And from the forests of the future,
  women came.
Without a word, the women came
  Daughters of Silence
Daughters of Sophia.
  They took their places
around the broken body of their mother, Eve.

A voice was heard in the midst of them,
  wailing and weeping.

It was Rachel weeping for her children;
> It was Rachel weeping for her mother.
And the women tore their robes,
> and heaped ashes on their heads.
They swayed and chanted the story of rape,
> the story of betrayal,
And the story of mothers and daughters.

Then the women stood and danced,
> first slowly, then faster.
And the wails and the weeping
> became screams of fury, screams of rage.
They danced the warrior dance of Jael,
> who drove a peg through the head
of her enemy Sisera,
> while he was sleeping, powerless.
And they danced of nails and traps and burning beds.
> They danced of vengeance and hate.

Then from the rage came a bubble of joy.
> And they laughed with Eve
at the foolishness of her enemies.
> They shook and slapped each other's shoulders
when they thought of how she had escaped.
> Aged Sarah—she who giggled at angels
and old men,
> stole a glance around the circle and chuckled,
"The idiots plundered her body,
> and never noticed that the treasure was gone
—hidden in a tree, far above their addled heads!"
> The women rolled their eyes and laughed
until tears rolled down their faces,
> and their sides ached.

Then from the circle, came Shiphrah and Puah,
> skilled Hebrew midwives, saviors to Moses.
They carried oil from Egypt and healing herbs from the desert
> and they washed the blood and dirt from their mother Eve
and they put balm on her wounds.
> They stroked her skin and anointed it with sweet-
> > smelling perfumes and incense.

They oiled her hair and braided it in long dark coils.
     And taking soft silk and fine linen,
they draped her in vivid colors.
     Then the women joined hands
and sang a love song
     to the beauty and the life of their mother's body
and their own bodies.

When the song was over, the women sat and waited in silence for their
     mother's decision.
     And Eve spoke forth from the tree and said,
"You have honored my shame,
     and I will honor your honor.
I will be one with my body
     and one with my spirit.
And I will be WOMAN."
     And the feminine spiritual principle
went out of the tree
     and entered into the carnal woman
and she was Eve.

     And Sophia saw what she had created
and created again.
     She was pleased
and she said, "It is very good."

MANUSCRIPT, LANGUAGE, AUTHORSHIP, PROVENANCE, AND DATE

The only surviving copy of the *Hypostasis of the Archons* was discovered near Nag Hammadi in 1945 and is now stored in the Coptic Museum in Cairo. It occupies twelve pages of a fourth-century papyrus codex.[43] The manuscript is written in the Subachmimic (Lycopolitan) dialect of Coptic.[44] The text was originally written in Greek and later translated into Coptic.

The identity of the author is unknown. The text is not written by Norea; her first person narration is only a stylistic convention used to give the text the literary character and immediacy of an eyewitness account.

Scholars agree that editorial hands have been busily at work within the *Hypostasis* and that a wide variety of ancient traditions have found often startling places in its imaginative landscape. This fact complicates tracing the provenance of the text with any certainty. One or more literary sources may lie behind the text. Moreover, it contains quotations or allusions to materials known from Judaism, Christianity, and Sethian mythology.

Especially prominent are materials that echo Jewish sources.[45] Many elements from the interpretation of Genesis find their origins or closest parallels in Jewish circles. The figure of Norea, for example, developed from Jewish speculation about the biblical Naamah (Gen 4:22).[46] On the other hand, the treatment of Genesis and other Jewish traditions in the *Hypostasis of the Archons* is quite distinctive. The portrait of God as creator and ruler is split between Yaldabaoth and Sabaoth, while the God of mercy and truth is located beyond the realm of creation entirely. Moreover, the Hebrew Scriptures are treated with considerable ambivalence. On the one hand, they provide material central to the text's narrative of creation and history. On the other hand, the *Hypostasis of the Archons* retells the story in a highly creative and critical mode. God's claim to sovereignty in Isaiah is flatly denied and even ridiculed. Some have argued that this portrayal derives from critical circles within Judaism. Bernard Barc, for example, suggests that the figure of Noah is used to explain the origins of a falsified and partial Judaism. He argues that the redactor thinks he is purifying the Genesis text, removing the layers of subterfuge that have altered and falsified it, restoring it to its pristine truth.[47] Others argue that the portrayal of the world creator as an evil and ignorant sub-deity appears to promote an unequivocal Christian anti-Judaism. Yet orthodox Christianity accepted the Genesis portrait of God as creator, ruler, and judge without criticism. Defining the Jewish provenance of *Hypostasis of the Archons* remains an uncompleted task.

Christian elements also appear in the text.[48] Many modern readers will respond to echoes of Paul and the Gospel of John. Yet some scholars have denied that the text originally derived from a Christian milieu, suggesting that the most significant Christian elements were added secondarily by a later christianizing editor. This issue is still hotly debated.[49]

Historians have drawn attention also to the features that the *Hypostasis of the Archons* shares with Sethian mythology,[50] although in our text it is Norea, not Seth, who is the predominant figure. Elements include self-understanding as the children of Norea, Norea as the savior, the light-giver Eleleth, the appearance of the divine image as the result of the arrogance of Yaldabaoth, and the periodization of history (the age of Adam, the age of Norea, the age of Norea's offspring, and the present time). Moreover, the *Hypostasis of the Archons* is literarily related to another Sethian text found at Nag Hammadi, *On the Origin of the World* (NHC II,5). They are probably not directly dependent, but may have shared a mutual reliance on an earlier composition, now lost.

In light of the tentative state of analysis, any conclusion about the geographical provenance or date of the *Hypostasis of the Archons* would be highly speculative. The latest possible date for the composition is supplied by the dating of the fourth-century manuscript. Dates from the mid-second to the late third century have been suggested by scholars, depending on their understanding of the text's history of composition.

NOTES

1. This attitude is also found in the canonical Gospels, for example, in their interpretive reformulations of the parables. Comparing the different tellings of a single parable illustrates how each evangelist shaped his telling to fit his theological aims.

2. All citations of this text are taken from the translation of Bentley Layton in *Nag Hammadi Codex II,2-7* (Nag Hammadi Studies 20; Leiden: E. J. Brill, 1989), 1:235–59.

3. This point is repeated several times by the narrator (see 87.20–23; 88.10–11; 88.33–89:3; 96.12–14).

4. See Isa 45:5. The blasphemy of Samael combines the myth of the fall of the angels with prophetic condemnation of royal arrogance (see Bernard Barc, *L'Hypostase des Archontes: Traité gnostique sur l'origine de l'homme, du monde et des archontes* [Bibliothèque copte de Nag Hammadi, Section: "Textes" 5; Quebec: Presses de l'Université Laval; Louvain: Peeters, 1980], 34).

5. The reference may be to his followers as well as to his own character. The phrase might also be incorrect and should be simply "blind god" (see Bentley Layton, "The Hypostasis of the Archons or The Reality of the Rulers," *Harvard Theological Review* 69 (1976): 47.

6. For a discussion of the etymology of the name Samael, see Roger Aubrey Bullard, *The Hypostasis of the Archons: The Coptic Text with Translation and Commentary* (Berlin: de Gruyter, 1970), 52–54; Layton, "Hypostasis," 46–47. For the name Saklas, see Layton, "Hypostasis," 72–73. For the name Yaldabaoth, see Gershom Scholem, "Jaldabaoth Reconsidered," in *Mélanges d'Histoire des Religions offert à Henri-Charles Puech* (Paris: Presses universitaires de France, 1974), 405–21.

7. On the Entirety, see Layton, "Hypostasis," 46. Incorruptibility is portrayed both as a female divinity and as a place (see 87.12–14; 88.17–19; 93.29–30).

8. Her role here is positively evaluated, contrā Layton, "Hypostasis," 48.

9. Note the conflated interpretation of Gen 2:7 and 1:26–27. Note, too, how the *Hypostasis of the Archons* interprets the plural of Gen 1:26-27 to refer to the chief ruler and his cronies.

10. See Layton, "Hypostasis," 51–52.

11. "Physician" is sometimes mistranslated as "midwife." See Ingvild Gilhus's objections (*The Nature of the Archons: A Study in the Soteriology of a Gnostic Treatise from Nag Hammadi (CG II,4)* [Studies in Oriental Religions 12; Wiesbaden: Harrassowitz, 1985], 57–58).

12. Compare Gen 3:20. The speech also contains a complex wordplay based on the Aramaic name of Eve, which continues below where further wordplay in Aramaic associates the tree of life with the words for snake and instructor (89.31–33). See Layton, "Hypostasis," 55–56.

13. Mythological references to metamorphoses of women into trees to escape would-be rapists are well-documented in antiquity. See my comparison with Ovid's account of Daphne in "Ridicule and Rape, Rule and Rebellion: The Hypostasis of the Archons," in *Gnosticism and the Early Christian World*, ed. James E. Goehring, Charles W. Hedrick, Jack T. Sanders, with Hans Dieter Betz (Sonoma, CA: Polebridge Press, 1990), 12–15; Birger Pearson, "'She Became a Tree'"—A Note to CG II,4: 89,25–26" *Harvard Theological Review* 69 (1976): 413–15;

Stephen Gero, "The Seduction of Eve and the Trees of Paradise—A Note on a Gnostic Myth," *Harvard Theological Review* 71 (1978): 299–301.

14. Gilhus is mistaken in her belief that Eve seduces the authorities purposefully in order to capture their light (see *Nature of the Archons,* 53). The *Hypostasis of the Archons* never presents her as a seductress, nor does it give any indication that the authorities have any light to be captured.

15. For further consideration of this episode, see my "Ridicule and Rape."

16. See Birger Pearson, "The Figure of Norea in Gnostic Literature," in *Proceedings of the International Colloquium on Gnosticism, Stockholm, August 20–25, 1973,* ed. Geo Widengren (Filologisk-filosofiska serien 17; Stockholm: Almqvist & Wiksell; Leiden: E. J. Brill, 1977); idem, "Revisiting Norea," in *Images of the Feminine in Gnosticism,* ed. Karen L. King (Studies in Antiquity and Christianity 4; Philadelphia: Fortress, 1988). See also Layton, "Hypostasis," 366–71.

17. Pearson, "Revisiting Norea," 265–66.

18. Anne McGuire rightly points out that Norea is not merely the counterpart to Seth, "but a female figure of greater significance and power than her male counterpart Seth" ("Virginity and Subversion: Norea against the Powers in the *Hypostasis of the Archons,*" in *Images of the Feminine in Gnosticism,* ed. Karen L. King [Studies in Antiquity and Christianity 4; Philadelphia: Fortress, 1988], 247).

19. See Pheme Perkins, "The Rebellion Myth in Gnostic Apocalypses," in *Society of Biblical Literature 1978 Seminar Papers,* ed. Paul Achtemeier (Missoula, MT: Scholars Press, 1978), 1:15–30.

20. Layton ("Hypostasis," 62), Francis T. Fallon (*The Enthronement of Sabaoth: Jewish Elements in Gnostic Creation Myths* [Nag Hammadi Studies 10; Leiden: E. J. Brill, 1978], 76 n. 163), and Barc (*L'Hypostase,* 110–13) support the view that Sabaoth is meant here to be the "ruler of the forces"; Bullard (*Hypostasis of the Archons,* 94–95) and Gilhus (*Nature of the Archons,* 83–84) argue that he is to be identified with Yaldabaoth.

21. Trans. Frank Williams, *The Panarion of Epiphanius of Salamis. Book I (Sects 1-46)* (Nag Hammadi Studies 35. Leiden: E. J. Brill, 1987), 83.

22. See the further analysis of McGuire, "Virginity and Subversion," 250.

23. See the matchless analysis of this scene by McGuire in "Virginity and Subversion," 250–53.

24. The dialogue structure of a dialogue is a form common to revelation discourses. See Pheme Perkins, *The Gnostic Dialogue: The Early Church and the Crisis of Gnosticism* (New York: Paulist Press, 1980).

25. For possible etymologies of this name, see Barc, *L'Hypostase,* 113–14.

26. In Sethian mythology, there are four light-givers who are located in the realm of Autogenes and who will be the heavenly resting place for those who are saved (see Hans-Martin Schenke, "Das sethianische System nach Nag-Hammadi-Handschriften," in *Studia Coptica,* ed. Peter Nagel [Berlin: Akademie-Verlag, 1974], 166–67). Eleleth is the name of one of these four light-givers.

27. See Layton's comment, "Hypostasis," 65.

28. See my commentary on the *Gospel of Mary* (chapter 32 in this volume).

29. See the comments of Layton, "Hypostasis," 66–67.

30. The statement that "he appeared in the final ages" probably refers to the true man who will appear in the end-time (see 96.32–97:1).

31. See Richard Smith, "Sex Education in Gnostic Schools," in *Images of the Feminine in Gnosticism,* ed. Karen L. King (Studies in Antiquity and Christianity 4; Philadelphia: Fortress, 1988), esp. 349–51.

32. See Pheme Perkins, "Sophia as Goddess in the Nag Hammadi Codices," in *Images of the Feminine in Gnosticism*, ed. Karen L. King (Studies in Antiquity and Christianity 4; Philadelphia: Fortress, 1988), 111.

33. He is said to be leonine in form. Howard Jackson has shown that the lion as a symbol for the passions is a Platonic element found widely in early Christian and ascetic writings (*The Lion Becomes Man: The Gnostic Leontomorphic Creator and the Platonic Tradition* (SBLDS 81; Atlanta: Scholars Press, 1985).

34. Comparison with other stories of Sophia (*Apocryphon of John* II, 9.25–10.19; BG 36.16–38.15; *Letter of Peter to Philip* 153.8–136.15; *On the Origin of the World* 98.13–100.29; *Zostrianos* 9.16–11.9; *Gospel of Philip* 59.31–32; Irenaeus, *Adversus Haereses* 1.2.2–4; 30.2–4; and Hippolytus, *Refutatio* 6.30-31) shows that the portrait of Sophia in the *Hypostasis of the Archons* is extremely positive. Her desire to create with a spouse and her introduction of light into matter are never evaluated negatively. There is no condemnation of her actions and no scene of repentance. Her male sexual behavior is suggestively portrayed at 94.29–31, where the text says that she "stretched forth her finger and introduced light into matter." This ejaculation from her finger is called *sperma* (96.27). Nor is this *sperma* described as weak, female seed, but is the offspring from the imperishable light.

35. Note here again, as with the carnal Eve, how the female is rejected when associated primarily with materiality and sexual reproduction.

36. See Gilhus, *Nature of the Archons*, 77, 212–13, 291–22; Michael Williams, *The Immovable Race: A Gnostic Designation and the Theme of Stability in Late Antiquity* (Nag Hammadi Studies 29; Leiden: E. J. Brill, 1985), 158–85.

37. Most troubling is the way the text too easily lends itself to interpretation as an ancient paradigm of racial determinism. Although its system is not based on color, it can be interpreted as promoting discrimination among types of persons based on their racial progenitors: the children of Cain, the children of Abel, and the children of Seth. Yet closer study of the text undermines this interpretation, since salvation is open to all who reject the world rulers. See Gilhus, *Nature of the Archons*, 114–18.

38. For a fuller treatment of the gender symbolism of the *Hypostasis of the Archons*, see King, "Ridicule and Rape."

39. McGuire, "Virginity and Subversion," 257–58.

40. Gilhus also understands the text to give paradigms of different stages of knowledge (see *Nature of the Archons*, 112–13).

41. See Pheme Perkins, "Sophia and the Mother-Father: The Gnostic Goddess," in *The Book of the Goddess Past and Present*, ed. Carl Olson (New York: Crossroad, 1986), 107.

42. A point made by Gilhus, *Nature of the Archons*, 125.

43. For a more detailed description of the manuscript, see Layton, "Hypostasis," 351–62.

44. For a detailed analysis of language, see Layton, "Hypostasis," 374–83.

45. For a list of biblical parallels, see Layton, "Hypostasis," 36–43; Gilhus, *Nature of the Archons*, 14–17, 21–22. For additional parallels, see Bullard, *Hypostasis;* Ithamar Gruenwald, "Jewish Sources for the Gnostic Texts from Nag Hammadi?" in *Proceedings of the Sixth World Congress of Jewish Studies* 3, ed. Avigdor Shinan (Jerusalem: Hocohen Press, 1977), 45–56; G. Stroumsa, *Another Seed: Studies in Gnostic Mythology* (Nag Hammadi Studies 24; Leiden: E. J. Brill, 1984); Fallon, *Enthronement of Sabaoth*; Birger Pearson, "Jewish Sources in Gnostic Literature," in *The Literature of the Jewish People in the Period of the Second Temple and the Talmud,* ed. Michael Stone (Compendia rerum judaicarum ad novum testamentum; Philadelphia: Fortress, 1984), 2:443–81.

46. See Pearson, "Figure of Norea."

47. Barc, *L'Hypostase des Archontes*, 19–20, 26–27.

48. See the list of parallels to the Pauline corpus in E. Pagels, "Exegesis and Exposition of the Genesis Creation Accounts in Selected Texts from Nag Hammadi," in *Nag Hammadi, Gnosticism and Early Christianity,* ed. Charles W. Hedrick and Robert Hodgson, Jr. (Peabody, MA: Hendrickson, 1986), 279–85.

49. In favor of a Christian editor are, for example, Bullard (*Hypostasis,* 47–48) and Barc (*L'Hypostase des Archontes,* 5, 45–48); for the originally Christian character of the text argue Layton ("Hypostasis," 363–64) and E. Pagels ("Genesis Creation Accounts," 266–77).

50. See especially Schenke, "Das sethianische System nach Nag Hammadi Handscriften"; idem, "The Phenomenon and Significance of Gnostic Sethianism," in *The Rediscovery of Gnosticism: Proceedings of the International Conference on Gnosticism at Yale, New Haven, Connecticut, March 28-31, 1978,* ed. Bentley Layton (Leiden: E. J. Brill, 1981), 2:588–616.

RECOMMENDED READINGS

Barc, Bernard. *L'Hypostase des Archontes: Traité gnostique sur l'origine de l'homme, du monde et des archontes.* Bibliothèque copte de Nag Hammadi, Section: "Textes" 5. Quebec, Canada: Les Presses de l'Université Laval; Louvain: Peeters.

Gilhus, Ingvild Saelid. *The Nature of the Archons: A Study in the Soteriology of a Gnostic Treatise from Nag Hammadi (CG II,4).* Studies in Oriental Religions 12. Wiesbaden: Otto Harrassowitz, 1985.

King, Karen L. "Ridicule and Rape, Rule and Rebellion: The Hypostasis of the Archons." In *Gnosticism and the Early Christian World,* edited by James E. Goehring, Charles W. Hedrick, Jack T. Sanders, with Hans Dieter Betz, 3–24. Sonoma, CA: Polebridge Press, 1990.

Layton, Bentley. "The Hypostasis of the Archons or The Reality of the Rulers." *Harvard Theological Review* 67 (1974): 351–425; 69 (1976): 31–101.

McGuire, Anne. "Virginity and Subversion: Norea against the Powers in the *Hypostasis of the Archons.*" In *Images of the Feminine in Gnosticism,* edited by Karen L. King, 239–58. Studies in Antiquity and Christianity 4. Philadelphia: Fortress, 1988.

Pagels, Elaine. "Exegesis and Exposition of the Genesis Creation Accounts in Selected Texts from Nag Hammadi." In *Nag Hammadi, Gnosticism and Early Christianity,* edited by Charles W. Hedrick and Robert Hodgson, Jr., 257–85. Peabody, MA: Hendrickson, 1986.

———. "Pursuing the Spiritual Eve: Imagery and Hermeneutics in the *Hypostasis of the Archons* and the *Gospel of Philip.*" In *Images of the Feminine in Gnosticism,* edited by Karen L. King, 187–206. Studies in Antiquity and Christianity 4. Philadelphia: Fortress, 1988.

Pearson, Birger A. "The Figure of Norea in Gnostic Literature." In *Proceedings of the International Colloquium on Gnosticism, Stockholm, August 20-25, 1973,* edited by Geo Widengren, 143–52. Filologisk-filosofiska serien 17. Stockholm: Almqvist & Wiskell; Leiden: E. J. Brill, 1977. Reprinted in *Gnosticism, Judaism, and Egyptian Christianity.* Studies in Antiquity and Christianity 5. Philadelphia: Fortress, 1990.

———. "Revisiting Norea." In *Images of the Feminine in Gnosticism,* edited by Karen L. King, 265–75. Studies in Antiquity and Christianity 4. Philadelphia: Fortress, 1988.

Perkins, Pheme. "Sophia as Goddess in the Nag Hammadi Codices." In *Images of the Feminine in Gnosticism,* edited by Karen L. King. Studies in Antiquity and Christianity 4. Philadelphia: Fortress, 1988.

The Odes of Solomon

SUSAN ASHBROOK HARVEY ◆

INTRODUCTION

THE ODES OF SOLOMON is a collection of forty-two Christian hymns written probably in the second century and surviving to us in the Syriac language. Highly imagistic and rich in their poetic sensibility, these hymns have been used in modern feminist discussion because of their striking use of gendered imagery for the Trinity. In the *Odes of Solomon* the Holy Spirit is often presented as feminine in gender ("She") and in her actions (giving birth, nurturing), while Christ and God, here most often imaged as Savior, Creator, and Father, are also occasionally referred to with feminine imagery (breast-feeding, cradling; God as midwife). The use of gendered imagery is but one aspect of the "metaphorical theology" contained in these odes, which have thereby offered vivid testimony to the varied nature of early Christian God-language.

Feminists have long noted the impoverishment of Christian language about God, which has increased since the Industrial Revolution.[1] The fluid and multivalent imagery that pervaded biblical, early Christian, medieval, and Byzantine religious language—which drew from the world of nature as well as the realm of the human community—has shrunk in the industrial and modern era to draw almost solely on the monolithic, patriarchal language of God the Father. Feminist theologians have been concerned with the issue of how religious language, language used to talk about God, relates to the real situation of women. In simplistic terms, patriarchal language for God has been used to justify the exclusion of women from certain aspects of Christianity, particularly the clerical priesthood. In addition, it has been used to perpetuate oppressive understandings of human nature: for example, that women are not fully created in the image of God since the nature of divinity has so often, for Christians, been identified as masculine.

Ancient Christians no less than modern ones devoted much attention to the question of religious language. How can we use human, limited language to discuss that which is divine and unlimited? What relation does a word bear to its object? Can language capture anything of the divine, or is all language for God meaningless? Given that the divine is by nature incomprehensible to us, in what ways can language help us comprehend something of God? For the ancients, as often for us, the only valid use of language to discuss the divine was metaphorical: we must never mistake the word for the reality when speaking about God. But words may offer a glimpse of an aspect of the divine, if we can understand words as metaphorical, as not limited in their meaning to a literal sense. Sallie McFague has pointed out that the ancients were in fact far less literal in their understanding of religious language than moderns: a literalist reading of the Bible, or a literal interpretation of God-language (for example, that "God the Father" should mean that God is actually male) was impossible for the ancient mind-set, which saw the world as symbolic at every level of a greater and truer level of reality.[2] In a sense, modern Christians have been doubly hampered: first, by the reduction of their divine metaphors to monolithic dependence on those of fatherhood and sonship, and, second, by the instinct to read and interpret religious language, whether biblical or theological, as literal.

In discussing the *Odes of Solomon,* I will utilize historical-critical method to set the collection in the context of early Syriac literature and early Syrian Christian spirituality. I believe strongly that we cannot impose our contemporary categories of understanding onto ancient literature: for example, the concept of gender, and especially of gender in the divine realm, did not mean to the ancients what it does to us, even with the array of meanings we might give. Historical-critical method offers us insight into how the ancient Syrians used and understood their imagery. But as a feminist historian, I am concerned that we push further and ask what questions these ancient hymns can raise for us. How are we going to use language for the divine? How do the distinctions (or the polarities) between gender and person, body and soul, physical and spiritual affect our understanding of the human–divine relationship?

It is the task of the feminist historian to seek the voices that have been lost and to remind us that things have not always been "the way things are." For the Christian feminist, such as myself, this task carries the added responsibility to keep the tension always in sight between Christianity as liberating and Christianity as oppressive. Some issues are not new for Christianity. The matter of inclusive language is not a recent concern introduced to the religious sphere from the secular. Inclusive language and the challenges it offers the Christian have been a part of this religion from its origins. The *Odes of Solomon* remind us of that fact with particular power. My task in this essay is to recover the ancient voices of these odes to hear them within their historical context. Reclaiming a part of the Christian past more fully, the task remains to ask what tools they provide for fashioning a fuller Christian future.

THE ODES IN SCHOLARSHIP

The *Odes of Solomon* are among the most beautiful of early Syriac literature and also among the most puzzling.[3] Since the discovery of the *Odes* early
in this century, scholars have debated their date (first, second, third century?),
place of origin (Egypt? Syria? within the Syrian Orient, Edessa, or Antioch?),
original language (Greek? Syriac? Hebrew?) and religious orientation (Christian? Jewish? Gnostic?). While nothing is certain, most scholars would now
agree that the *Odes* date from the mid-second century, written somewhere in
Syria. Portions of the *Odes* survive to us in Coptic, Greek, and Latin; as a
whole, the collection survives only in Syriac. The linguistic evidence tells us
that the *Odes* somehow circulated across a broad geographical area, although
we have no idea how widely they were known or used.

The Syriac text itself shows interaction with the Greek language. No consensus has been reached as to whether Syriac or Greek was the original language of composition for these odes. The importance of this question is somewhat overstated, however. All Syriac literature that survives to us prior to the
mid-fourth century circulated and survives bilingually in both Syriac and
Greek. The Syrian Orient remained bilingual (and in places multilingual) until
well after the Arab conquest in the seventh century. During the early Christian
period the population of this region was diverse in culture and in language:
geographically, the Syrian Orient was the crossroad between the Orient and
the Mediterranean. A rich and fertile cultural matrix resulted. These *Odes* are
Syrian, whether or not they were first composed in Syriac. Most of the imagery
I will discuss would only be present in the Syriac version; this imagery is part of
the common Syriac religious language for the early Christian period.

The cultural matrix of the Syrian Orient also accounts for the confusion
scholars have displayed in identifying the religious orientation of the *Odes*.
The consensus now accepts the *Odes* as Christian, though debate continues as
to whether they might be Gnostic-Christian. The multicultural and highly
cosmopolitan nature of the Mediterranean world during the early Christian
period resulted in considerable interplay between religions; commonalities in
imagery and themes resulted. This situation accounts for how the *Odes* could
show similarities to the writings of different religious communities; their parallels to the Qumran hymns and to Johannine literature have also provoked
discussion. My own view is that the Gnostic threads in the *Odes of Solomon*
are inconsequential to the theological orientation of the collection and are
threads common to the general religious mind-set of the age rather than an
indication of a Gnostic author.

The *Odes of Solomon* date from the period of early Christianity displaying
the greatest diversity in beliefs and practices across the Christian communities.
Indeed, the *Odes* themselves represent that diversity not least in their use of

feminine imagery for the divine (though they are hardly unique in this for their time period). In other respects the *Odes* are consonant with that part of early Christianity that will eventually be called "orthodox." Most important, and most relevant to this essay, the *Odes* present a fully Trinitarian Godhead, with Father, Son, and Spirit each distinct yet fully integrated as the divine. Few Christian texts from this early date present such a balanced Trinity; in most second-century Christian writing, the Spirit is barely mentioned. Furthermore, the *Odes* celebrate the physical world and the physical human body as God's created order and as emphatically good. This celebration stands in sharp contrast to many religious writings of the period, particularly many Gnostic texts. The emphasis on Trinity and on the goodness of God's creation means that we cannot dismiss the *Odes of Solomon* as representing a marginal Christian community; to pick but one example, St. Ephrem, the great Syriac poet-theologian of the fourth century, an ardent defender of Nicene Christianity and one canonized in both the Catholic and Orthodox churches, shows deep affinities with the theology of the *Odes of Solomon*.

FEMININE IMAGERY FOR THE DIVINE

Feminists have long been interested in the use of feminine imagery for the divine in the *Odes of Solomon*. The majority of the *Odes* follow what might be considered more normative imagery for God as Father, his Messiah as Son, the Spirit as God's agent, and all three with imagery that is not gender-dependent. But in the course of the entire forty-two *Odes*, at one point or another, all three persons of the Trinity are presented in explicitly feminine terms. In 8:14, Christ (or God) speaks of his relation to humanity, "I fashioned their limbs/and my own breasts I prepared for them/that they might drink my holy milk and live by it."[4] In *Ode* 35, the odist speaks of the contemplation of God as the experience of a child nurtured by its mother:

> And I was carried like a child by its mother;
> And He gave me milk, the dew of the Lord.
> And I grew strong in His favour
> And rested in His perfection. (35:5–6)

In these examples we see the feminine images of breast-feeding and nurturing or child-rearing used in a manner properly considered as metaphor: "*this* is like *that*," and the likeness enables us to think differently about both parts of the metaphor. These two instances are also similar to the use of mother imagery for the divine both in biblical texts and in other early Christian literature. The case of the Holy Spirit, on the other hand, is different. For the Spirit, the presentation in the *Odes of Solomon* is sometimes metaphorical and sometimes a much more profound identification in a manner that exceeds the simple pattern of biologically defined gender roles. Before we can understand the Holy Spirit in the *Odes of Solomon,* however, we must understand the Spirit in the context of early Syriac spirituality more generally.

Prior to the year 400, in all Syriac literature that survives to us, the Holy Spirit is most often referred to as feminine. The basic reason was linguistic: in the Syriac language the word for spirit, *rûḥā,* is a feminine noun (related to *rûaḥ* in Hebrew). Thus, the Spirit is referred to as "She," and the attendant adjectives and verbs are also in the feminine since Semitic languages inflect verbs for gender. This grammatical usage did not require meanings that were gender-specific. When, for example, in *Odes of Solomon* 16:5 the odist says, "I will open my mouth,/and His Spirit will speak through me/the glory of the Lord and His beauty," the Spirit and its speaking are grammatically feminine in the Syriac, but the sense of the passage is not dependent on gender.

Nonetheless, the cue from grammar was not meaningless. Gender identification for the Spirit was furthered by the actions most commonly ascribed to the Spirit by Syriac writers. The verbs that were used with this feminine noun were often evocative of gendered activity. By far the most important was the verb *raḥḥef,* "to hover," used especially of a mother bird hovering over her nestlings. This, for the Syrians, was the archetypal action of the Spirit. Its use evoked a mother image, even when its sense did not necessarily require a gendered meaning. In the Syriac version of Gen 1:2, the Spirit hovers over the face of the waters at creation. When the fourth-century writer Aphrahat describes baptism, not only does the (feminine) Spirit hover over the waters of the font to consecrate them, but the font itself becomes the womb giving birth to Christians—an image that would become the most common one in Syriac literature about baptism.

> For by baptism we receive the Spirit of Christ, and at that moment when the priests invoke the Spirit, She opens the heavens and descends and hovers over the waters, and those who are baptized put Her on. For the Spirit is far from all who are from the body until they come to the birth from water, and then they receive the Holy Spirit.[5]

An exquisite passage from the *Odes of Solomon* captures this classical Syriac understanding of the Spirit as hovering bird:

> As the wings of doves over their nestlings
> And the mouths of the nestlings towards their mouths,
> So are the wings of the Spirit over my heart.
> My heart continually refreshes itself and leaps for joy,
> Like the babe who leaps for joy in his mother's womb. (28:1–2)

In this passage, the mother's nest is also her womb in which the believer is enfolded and nourished. The image evokes further, by the specific Syriac words used, the visitation of Mary and Elizabeth in Luke 1:41. Hence, just as John the Baptist leapt for joy in the womb of his mother when he encountered his Lord, so, too, does the believer (the odist) leap for joy when he encounters the Lord in the womb of the Spirit, an image that always carries the sense of baptism for the Syrians—the birth from the womb of the font and from the womb of the Spirit.

Hovering is the essential activity of the Spirit in Syrian tradition; it is the way that the Spirit is present within creation.[6] Other actions ascribed to the Spirit by Syriac writers also evoke the feminine: the Spirit gives birth, or comforts, or nurtures. In the *Odes of Solomon,* the Spirit appears as a dove fluttering over the head of Christ in a scene highly reminiscent of the baptism in the Jordan (24:1–4); in *Ode* 33 a figure named the Perfect Virgin exhorts and instructs in a manner recalling holy Wisdom in Proverbs 8–9, and this figure may well be an image for the Spirit. Still other actions ascribed to the Spirit carry no gendered sense at all: Syriac writers speak of the Spirit as coming, dwelling in, searching out, leading. In *Odes of Solomon* 3:10, the Spirit is grammatically feminine but the actions ascribed are not gendered: "This is the Spirit of the Lord, which is not false,/Who teaches people to know His ways."

As if to reinforce the elusive nature of the gendered sense, then, early Syriac writers sometimes use Spirit as a grammatically masculine noun. Even in the *Odes of Solomon,* where the Spirit is most often feminine, occasionally the words appear in the masculine when the sense does not require a feminine meaning:

> As the wind moves through the harp
> And the strings speak,
> So the Spirit of the Lord speaks through my limbs,
> And I speak through His love.
> . . . .
> Our spirits praise His Holy Spirit. (6:1–2, 7b)

Thus, feminine imagery was not the sole language for the Spirit in early Syriac writers, but it was an imagery taken for granted by our writers and assumed to be appropriate when speaking of the divine. It is clear that while grammatical considerations made this possible, the understanding was also based on how the Holy Spirit was actually experienced: Syriac Christians perceived the actions of the Spirit to be often those best expressed as feminine. But what did "feminine" mean for the early Syrian Christians? A closer look at two of the *Odes of Solomon* shows that gender was not reduced to obvious biological or socially constructed images when used with respect to the divine.

First, consider the description of the Spirit from *Ode* 36. It is far more complex than what we have seen so far.

> I rested on the Spirit of the Lord,
> And She lifted me up on high.
> And caused me to stand on my feet in the high place of the Lord,
> In the presence of His perfection and His glory,
> where I glorified [Him] with the composition of His hymns.
> She gave birth to me before the Lord's face,
> and although I was a man
> I was named a brilliant son of God. . . .
> For according to the greatness of the Most High, so did She make me;
> and according to His renewing He renewed me. (36:1–3, 5)[7]

In this ode the maternal image of Spirit as birth-giver, recalling for Syrians the role of the Spirit in baptism, is also the mighty image of Creator: "according to the greatness of the Most High, so did She make me." Nor is the Spirit merely described as the maternal aspect of God's activity. Here she is presented in a manner consonant with the later, orthodox understanding of the Trinity: She is both one with God, "the Spirit of the Lord," and distinct in her own activity. This activity is more than maternal. She is the place of rest for the believer, as well as the believer's way to God. She lifts him into the spiritual realm; she enables him to stand in God's presence. Neither the resting nor the standing is a static state for the believer. To rest in the Spirit is to be lifted by Her; to stand by Her power is to be born anew, a child of the divine. The Spirit is a mighty power of movement and that movement is the power of life itself. Even when portrayed as feminine, the Spirit is more than female. Her gender, in this ode, is crucial to understanding Her activity even as Her activity cannot be contained solely within gendered terms.

By far the most elusive and the most notorious of this collection is *Ode* 19. I translate it in full:

> A cup of milk was offered to me
> And I drank it with the sweetness of the Lord's kindness.
> The Son is the cup,
> And He who was milked is the Father.
> And She who milked Him is the Holy Spirit.
> Because His breasts were full,
> And it was not necessary for His milk to be poured out without cause.
> The Holy Spirit opened Her womb,
> And mixed the milk of the two breasts of the Father.
> And She gave the mixture to the world without their knowing,
> And those who received it are in the perfection of the right hand.

The womb of the Virgin caught it,
And she received conception and gave birth.
And the Virgin became a mother with many mercies.
And she labored and bore a son and there was no pain for her,
Because it was not without cause.
And she did not need a midwife
Because He (God) delivered her.
Like a man she gave birth by her will.
And she bore with manifestation
And she acquired with much power.
And she loved with redemption,
And she guarded with kindness
And she manifested with greatness.
Hallelujah.

In this ode, identity and gender, divine and human, are turned into inverted patterns. The ode begins with the image of grace, "the sweetness of the Lord's kindness," experienced as milk, the food of childhood. The image of the Son as cup evokes the Eucharist and possibly baptism, since second-century baptismal rites included the presentation to the newly baptized of a cup of milk and honey as well as the bread and wine.[8] We should expect the evocation of baptismal imagery for the Syrians to carry the sense of new birth, and, indeed, the milk in this cup is that of a nursing mother for her newborn. In this instance, however, the mother whose breasts are full is God the Father. Yet the maternal image for God cannot be contained in one person of the Trinity. The Spirit is God's womb in which life is conceived.[9] Not confined in Her activity, She is also the agent who milks Him, who takes His milk into Herself and gives it forth, life-giving food, to the creation.

Inversion follows inversion. The milk of God the Mother becomes the seed of God the Father received into the Virgin's womb, by which she conceives her son. The Virgin becomes a mother unlike any human mother. The language of this ode for the Virgin will sound familiar to all who know the exaltation of Mary in later Christian doctrine. But few texts this early, and no Western Christian writings for some centuries to come, refer to Mary in such glorified terms as are here used for the Virgin.[10] Here the Virgin is the "mother of many mercies," a title that will not be used for Mary by Latin Christians much before the tenth century.[11] Her birth is painless, one of the earliest meanings for Mary's "virgin birth"; being painless, it reverses the curse placed on Eve in Gen 3:16. Inversion follows again: God serves as her midwife, a role both female and human;[12] while she herself gives birth "like a man," "by her will"—the manner by which God refers to His creation of humanity elsewhere in the *Odes*

(8:18).[13] The final verses exalt the Virgin in terms that characterize God, Son, and Spirit throughout the *Odes.*

Who in this *Ode* is masculine and who is feminine? Who participates in human, and who participates in divine experience? None are who they appear to be. All are more than they appear to be: male is more than male—it is also female; female is more than female—it is also male; the divine exceeds any clear boundaries; even the human is more than human. The use of gender in *Ode* 19 jolts and disorients us with tremendous force. We are shown that gender is essential to understanding actions, and to some extent to understanding the nature of being, both for the divine and for the human person. Yet gendered action and gendered nature cannot adequately convey the fullness of the divine, nor even of the human. One gender does not and cannot suffice even as metaphor to express identity, especially in the divine persons.

Ode 19 returns us to our starting point: although feminine imagery for the divine most often and with the greatest complexity is used in the *Odes of Solomon* for the Holy Spirit, it is also used for Father and Son. In no case is it the only kind of imagery for the divine in the *Odes,* which contain masculine images as well as nongendered images for God, Son, and Spirit also. How, then, are we to understand this usage of gendered imagery?

In early Syriac tradition the Spirit is most often portrayed in the feminine gender, as we have seen, in part because of grammatical gender and in part because of the gendered nature of actions ascribed to the Spirit (hovering as a mother bird, comforting as a mother comforts, birthing, nurturing). We need to remember that religions in the ancient Mediterranean world understood divinity in explicitly gendered terms. There were gods and goddesses, although gender was not seen to function in the divine realm as it did in the realm of human society: sometimes gods could give birth; goddesses were often warriors. Along the Levant, it was common to find the worship of divine triads, gods and goddesses related as father, mother, and son. The Syrian goddess Atargatis was part of one such triad (as was the Egyptian Isis), and her worship was among the most powerful of the cults native to the Syrian Orient.[14] Some scholars would like to interpret the feminine Holy Spirit of early Syriac Christianity as related to, or parallel to, the Syrian goddess of the indigenous religious tradition. This is more accurately the case for the distinct female entities present in certain Gnostic texts (where the balancing of opposites, including gender, was important) or speculative cosmological systems. The concept that gender was somehow inherent in divinity was certainly inherited by the early Christians throughout the Mediterranean world. But it is important to notice that the understanding of the Holy Spirit as feminine and the use of feminine imagery for the divine more generally, as we have seen in the *Odes of Solomon,* represent a religious understanding at once less concrete and more nuanced than that evidenced by the male and female deities of paganism, or indeed of the Syrian goddess herself. Even the feminine Holy Spirit in early Syriac literature is never portrayed as a distinct female entity.

In the *Odes of Solomon* we are shown that gender is an appropriate image for understanding certain divine activities. The experience of the divine as the source of life or as life-giving led the odist to use feminine language of birthgiving and nursing to describe that aspect of divine activity, whether for God, for Christ, or for the Spirit. But gender is here also shown to be a part of the divine in terms that are less biologically oriented. The Spirit is referred to as "She" and as "He." As feminine, She teaches, gives life, gives speech and song to the odist; She is rest and protection, God's voice, and Perfect Wisdom; She is God's agent and Her own source of action. To refer to the gender of the Holy Spirit, no less than the gender of God or of the Son, is thus not an attempt to define divine identity. Gender is here shown to be an attribute of divine essence without being equivalent to it. Gender, but not a specific gender, is somehow an attribute of the divine, an identity that contains gender even as it transcends it.

The *Odes of Solomon* are poetry. Their writer uses language as a poet and not as a philosopher: his language is deliberately and intricately metaphorical in every line. Most early Syrian theology was in fact written in poetry and not in the form of philosophical discourse. There was a sense for Syriac writers that poetry was the most appropriate and effective way to write about God, since poetic language, because it was deliberately metaphorical, could reveal glimpses of the divine without in any way seeking to define or limit that which is beyond human comprehension. By nature, metaphor is revelatory rather than definitive. The language of the *Odes of Solomon* should be understood in this way: a use of imagery to reveal aspects of the divine, but not an attempt to speak literally about the divine. The discussion of religious language as metaphorical was carried out by the early Syriac poet-theologians, and the *Odes of Solomon* represent precisely this kind of theological writing.[15]

Yet there is more to the story. While early Christians of other languages occasionally used feminine imagery for the divine, no other language of the early Christian world allowed the specific feminine identification that Syriac afforded the Spirit. Early Christian theologians discussed the nature of gendered religious language with a stated degree of dispassion. Gregory of Nazianzus wrote that although we speak of God as Father, we know He is not male.[16] Jerome pointed out that the term for Spirit is feminine in Hebrew, masculine in Latin and neuter in Greek, instructing us that God is without gender.[17] But in Syriac the concept of a feminine Holy Spirit could be developed theologically because of the language itself, and it was. As we have seen in the *Odes of Solomon*, this development for the Spirit was far more complex than the simple use now and then of maternal imagery for the divine. At some point this became problematic for the larger church institution. Clearly, although theologians could claim that God was without gender, the feminine identification of the Spirit as more than simple metaphor was not acceptable to church leaders.

Around the year 400 a change appeared in Syriac writings. The Holy Spirit henceforth was referred to almost exclusively in masculine terms. After 400, the Spirit as "She" in Syriac literature is found only on rare occasions, in poetry where it might be required for metrical pattern, or in archaic prayers preserved in liturgical texts. When the word *rûḥā* was used to mean wind or spirit generally, it was construed in its feminine form; when used for the Holy Spirit, it was construed as masculine despite the grammatical strain this placed on the language. Other images took the place of the early feminine ones, in general keeping the sense of earlier images without involving gender: the Spirit overshadows, or indwells, or enfolds. These were no longer gendered images; a "masculine" Spirit did not emerge in Syriac theology or religious poetry as a "feminine" one had in the earlier period.

Other aspects of Syrian spirituality developed feminine imagery.[18] Devotion to the Virgin Mary flourished, as it had from the earliest period, along with the cults of female saints. The Syrian preference for following John 3:3–7 and portraying baptism as new birth led to rich imagery of the baptismal font as the womb and of baptism as Mother. Christ's life was imaged as a series of births: first from the womb of Mary, then from the womb of the Jordan at baptism, and finally from the womb of Sheol at the resurrection. In mystical writings, the ascetic's body became a womb in which to receive the Word. Yet no parallel to the Holy Spirit as feminine has ever reappeared in Syriac theology or spirituality. Indeed, all of the instances noted place the feminine imagery distinctly outside the Godhead.

We do not know why or how this change took place. No text survives that tells us. Instead, it simply happened. The fourth century was a period that saw the church as an institution seek to achieve a more concrete unity and conformity throughout the Roman Empire than had previously been the case. In the course of the fourth century, Christianity first became legalized as a religion; subsequently the first ecumenical councils were held at which, for example, the creed and scriptural canon were finally agreed upon; toward the end of the century Christianity was declared the state religion of the Roman Empire. These dramatic changes enabled the church to enact and enforce its desire for unity in ways previously not available. While complete conformity was never possible, the degree of difference allowed diminished substantially over what had been present in the earlier period. Christianity in the Syrian Orient, as elsewhere in the empire, was compelled to make certain changes. This is the only explanation we can find to account for the change in the gender of the Holy Spirit for Syriac Christianity. To the larger ecclesiastical structure of the Roman Empire, it would seem, some people perceived the idea of a feminine

Holy Spirit to be dangerous. For whatever reason, an image of great beauty and theological power was lost. In the *Odes of Solomon,* we can see how that image was used and what riches it revealed.

NOTES

1. E.g., E. McLaughlin, "'Christ My Mother': Feminine Naming and Metaphor in Medieval Spirituality," *Nashotah Review* 15 (1975): 228–48.

2. S. McFague, *Metaphorical Theology: Models of God in Religious Language* (Philadelphia: Fortress, 1982).

3. *The Odes of Solomon,* 2nd ed., ed. and trans. J. H. Charlesworth (Missoula, MT: Scholars Press, 1977). In this essay I follow Charlesworth's translations, because this edition is the most easily available to a general audience. I have occasionally altered the translations according to my own reading of the texts, and following the latest critical edition by M. Franzmann, *The Odes of Solomon: An Analysis of the Poetical Structure and Form* (Novum Testamentum et Orbis Antiquus 20; Freiburg: Universitätsverlag; Göttingen: Vandenhoeck & Ruprecht, 1991).

4. In Franzmann's edition of this ode (pp. 63–66), this verse appears as 8:16. As she rightly points out, the speaker is referred to only as "I." Charlesworth has kept the opinion of earlier scholars who identify this "I" as Christ. While Franzmann's discussion has made tremendous strides toward a more accurate and nuanced analysis of the speakers within the *Odes* as a whole, in the instance of *Ode* 8 I accept the identification of the speaker of this verse as Christ. I agree with Franzmann, however, that there is no reason to see this ode as representing the voice of more than one speaker. See Franzmann, *Odes,* 4, 295–301.

5. Aphrahat, *Demonstration* 6, sec. 14 (my trans.). Text edited by D. I. Parisot in *Patrologia Syriaca,* ed. R. Graffin (Paris, 1894) I, cols. 292.24–293.5, trans. J. Gwynn, in A Select Library of Nicene and Post-Nicene Fathers 13 (New York, 1898), 362–75.

6. See above all S. P. Brock, "The Holy Spirit as Feminine in Early Syriac Literature," in *After Eve: Women, Theology and the Christian Tradition,* ed. J. Soskice (London: Marshall Pickering, 1990), 73–88.

7. I accept the reading and analysis of G. R. Blaszcak, *A Formcritical Study of Selected Odes of Solomon* (Atlanta: Scholars Press, 1985), 9–25 for this ode.

8. See T. M. Finn, *Early Christian Baptism and the Catechumenate: West and East Syria* (Collegeville, MN: Michael Glazier, The Liturgical Press, 1992).

9. H. J. W. Drijvers has traced this image of God's womb back to the earliest Syriac version of John 1:18, which reads, "the only-begotten Son, which is from the womb of the Father," a wording kept in the Peshitta version ("The 19th Ode of Solomon," *Journal of Theological Studies* 31 [1980]: 337–55, at 342–43).

10. Notably the *Protevangelion of James,* which dates from the mid-second century and may well be Syrian in origin. The correlation is significant.

11. H. Graef, *Mary: A History of Doctrine and Devotion* (New York: Westminster, 1963), 1:34–35.

12. Undoubtedly the odist is recalling the Hebrew metaphor of God as midwife in Ps 22:9–10. The images of God as comforting mother (Isa 49:15; 66:13) and God in the throes of divine labor pangs (Isa 42:14b) may also lie in the background.

13. Franzmann's textual emendation results in a masculinized reading of this verse, and to some extent diminishes the strength of gender inversion throughout this ode. Thus, in her reading, the Father's milk is his sperm, and God impregnates the virgin "like a husband" (changing

the line divisions to place this phrase in apposition to God rather than the Virgin) (*Odes,* 146–52).

14. Our most important source is Lucian of Samosata, *The Syrian Goddess (De Dea Syria),* ed. and trans. H. W. Attridge and R. A. Oden (Missoula, MT: Scholars Press, 1976).

15. See my discussion in "Feminine Imagery for the Divine: The Holy Spirit, the Odes of Solomon, and Early Syriac Tradition," *St. Vladimir's Theological Quarterly* 37.2 (1993): 111–39.

16. Gregory of Nazianzus, *Fifth Theological Oration,* trans. E. R. Hardy and C. Richardson in *The Christology of the Later Fathers* (Library of Christian Classics 3; Philadelphia: Westminster, 1954), 198.

17. Jerome, *In Isa.* 11 (on 40:9–11), ed. M. Adriaen and F. Glorie, CCL 73:1 (1963), 459.

18. For citations and discussion of the following, see my "Feminine Imagery for the Divine."

RECOMMENDED READINGS

Brock, S. P. "The Holy Spirit as Feminine in Early Syriac Literature." In *After Eve: Women, Theology and the Christian Tradition,* edited by J. M. Soskice, 73–88. London: Marshall Pickering, 1990.

Charlesworth, J. H., ed. *The Odes of Solomon.* 2nd ed. Missoula, MT: Scholars Press, 1977. Provides a critical edition of the Syriac with English translation and some commentary. Does not entirely supersede the earlier editions by Harris-Mingana and Bernard, but is an easily available and helpful introduction.

Drijvers, H. J. W. "The 19th Ode of Solomon." *Journal of Theological Studies* 31 (1980): 337–55.

Franzmann, M. *The Odes of Solomon: An Analysis of the Poetical Structure and Form.* Novum Testamentum et Orbis Antiquus 20. Freiburg: Universitätsverlag; Göttingen: Vandenhoeck & Ruprecht, 1991. Critical edition with the most complete form-critical analysis to date. For the specialist; no serious work on the *Odes* can be done without it.

Harvey, S. A. "Feminine Imagery for the Divine: The Holy Spirit, the Odes of Solomon, and Early Syriac Tradition." *St. Vladimir's Theological Quarterly* 37.2 (1993): 111–39.

Lattke, M. *Die Oden Salomos in ihrer Bedeutung für Neues Testament und Gnosis.* Orbis Biblicus et Orientalis 25/1, 1a, 2, 3. Freiburg: Universitätsverlag; Göttingen: Vandenhoeck & Ruprecht, 1979–86. Critical edition (in German transliteration), German translation and commentary. The final volume (25/3) is an annotated bibliography of modern scholarship in English, French, and German, on the *Odes* from 1799–1984; this is an invaluable research tool.

McFague, S. *Metaphorical Theology: Models of God in Religious Language.* Philadelphia: Fortress, 1982.

McNeil, B. "The Odes of Solomon and the Scriptures." *Oriens Christianus* 67 (1983): 104–22.

Pierce, M. "Themes in the 'Odes of Solomon' and Other Early Christian Writings and their Baptismal Character." *Ephemerides Liturgicae* 98 (1984): 35–59.

Ruether, R. R. *Womanguides: Readings Toward a Feminist Theology.* Boston: Beacon, 1985.

The Sibylline Oracles

AMY-JILL LEVINE ◆

AS A JEWISH WOMAN working in a discipline and in a society conditioned by masculinist and Christian values and norms, I engage texts in pursuit of a feminist and Jewish agenda. I seek the recovery of both literary constructions and social roles of Jews and women in antiquity; such materials enrich my own history. Then, with a critical, ecumenical gesture, I turn this engagement back upon the institutions that would label it marginal and parochial: my work seeks to counter in particular those who would view Judaism as monolithic, as having ended at Golgotha, or as a singularly repressive foil to a more sexually egalitarian reading of Christian origins. To achieve these goals, my methodology combines a historical perspective informed by the analysis of cultural contact and by such categories as class and social status, gender, ethnic identity, and (religious) group affiliation with literary-critical observations sensitive to gaps in the text and the construction of the "other." The *Sibylline Oracles,* with their extracanonical status, various depictions of women, and uneasy combinations of Gentile, Jewish, and Christian motifs, well match my interests.

These twelve books of moral exhortations, political observations, and theological poetry ascribed to an antediluvian seer encompass material from the second century B.C.E. to the seventh century C.E. Written by Jews, the earlier oracles were edited by Christians, who in turn added new books of their own. Like Amos and Jeremiah, the Sibyl warns against immorality and predicts a series of disasters brought about by divine displeasure; like Zechariah and John the Baptist, she proclaims the eschatological punishment of the wicked. But while the *Sibylline Oracles* echo familiar Jewish and Christian concerns, their referents and their attributed authorship diverge significantly from canonical traditions. Not only are the Oracles replete with allusions to Greek and Roman history and myth; they are ascribed to a Gentile woman. Thus, they complicate our already problematic understanding of cross-cultural influence and gender roles in antiquity.

The Sibyl's value for reconstructing women's history is not unambiguous. On the one hand, she is not unique in antiquity: other women—Gentile, Jewish, and Christian—are said to possess prophetic gifts. Further, the proliferation of the Sibylline traditions among these various communities attests to a general recognition of women's visionary abilities. Yet this very proliferation, along with the attendant formalization of the oracular genre, prevents a confident claim for women's authorship. The form was utilized by authors—sex unknown—who hid behind the Sibyl's pseudepigraphic skirts.

GENTILE ANTECEDENTS

The Sibyl's earliest mentions by such figures as Heraclitus, Aristophanes, and Plato refer to a single individual. Hence, the Sibyl may have been a real woman with renowned prophetic abilities, whose personal name, Sybilla, was transformed into a professional title. Citing Varro, Lactantius states: "For in the Aeolic (or Doric) dialect, they used to call the gods by the word Sioi (Σιοί), not Theoi (Θεοί), and for 'counsel' they used the word bolla (βολλά), not Boule (βουλή), so that the Sibyl received her name as the Siobule (i.e., 'The counsel of god')." Pausanias proposes that Sibulla (Σίβυλλα) was a metathesis for Libussa (Λίβυσσα), "Libyan woman." Other suggestions include "the ancient one of G-d," "wise woman," "grandmother," and "god-appeasing."

Especially after Alexander the Great, the number of sibyls increased. The first to note the plurality was apparently the Sophist Sopater, himself the author of a work on prophetic women. Varro, cited by Lactantius, lists ten, including the Cumean, Libyan, Delphic, Erythrean, and Phrygian; later lists substitute the Hebrew, Chaldean, and Egyptian. The medieval church increased the number to twelve, corresponding to the twelve apostles.

The Sibyl's works were circulated in book form, as were the prophecies of Orpheus, Epimenides, Bacis, as well as Daniel, 4 Ezra, and John of Patmos. The most famous Gentile collection of oracles was the official one at Rome, sold, according to legend, by the Cumean Sibyl to Tarquinius Priscus. These Greek hexameters offered responses to particular circumstances with a combination of cryptic political observations and prescriptions for cultic activity. The most authoritative collection of prophecies in Rome, they were entrusted to special keepers and consulted only in times of national crisis and only with senatorial consent. Serving originally as resistance literature condemning oppressive regimes, the form was easily appropriated by those desiring political expression. Suetonius, for example, notes that when Augustus destroyed oracles that he found subversive, he also edited the Sibyllines.

On 16 July 83 B.C.E., the temple of Jupiter Optimus Maximus burned, and along with it the original deposit of Sibylline books. Yet their genre, and the mystique surrounding their author, survived. In 76 B.C.E. the Senate decreed that the collection be replaced; other books were generated in the Sibyl's name, and she herself was eventually accorded status befitting the use of her oracles: a coin from Erythrea refers to her as *Thea Sibylla,* or "the Goddess Sibyl." Her prophecy was said to continue after her death, and her appearance was preserved in the moon.

The pagan Sibyl had specific forms and functions. Originally a wandering prophet, like Jesus or Apollonias of Tyana, her independence distinguished her from her counterparts at Delphi. However, both the Cumean and Ery-threan Sibyls were associated with caves, which may indicate some connection to earth-goddess traditions. Also unlike her Delphic sisters, she spoke in gen-eral terms rather than issuing answers to specific questions or choices for specific questioners. The universal rather than local focus of her oracles, com-bined with their fatalistic nature, contributed to the genre's authority. Yet their frequent vagueness, which demanded interpretation, kept the works popular and useful. Thus, the Sibylline genre was at home in the apocalyptic imagina-tion of formative Judaism and early Christianity.

But the Sibyl herself was not at home in any domestic sense. Just as the Pythia dressed as an unmarried woman, so the Sibyl was independent of a hus-band. The association of repudiated sexuality and a woman's prophetic abili-ties permeates antiquity. On the Greek side, Cassandra is cursed with the gift of prophecy that no one would heed because of her refusal to submit to Apollo's sexual desires. The equation of women's sexual renunciation and prophetic abilities applies in Jewish circles to the daughters of Job (*Testament of Job* 46–53) and the Therapeutrides of Philo (*On the Contemplative Life* 1–11); Christian paradigms are represented by such figures as the widow Anna (Luke 2:36) and Philip's four virgin daughters (Acts 21:9, see also 1 Cor 11:15; Acts 2:17–21 following Joel 2:28–32). The Montanist prophets present even stronger parallels: not only did this Christian movement share a concern for celibacy; both the Montanists and the various Sibyls speak of a compulsion to prophesy. Some Jewish tradition was less concerned with questions of sexual-ity: included among the prophets are Rebecca (*Jubilees* 25:14, 21; *Targum Onkelos* Gen 27:13; *Targum Pseudo-Jonathan* Gen 27:5, 42; Josephus, *Antiquities* 1.19.1–5); Miriam (Pseudo-Philo, *Biblical Antiquities* 9:9ff.); and Deborah (Pseudo-Philo, *Biblical Antiquities* 30:2; 33:1). In the Babylonian Talmud, *b. Megilla* 14a lists Sarah, Miriam, Deborah, Hannah, Abigail, Hul-dah, and Esther as prophets. Yet we cannot determine if the communities that wrote these works had their own women prophets. Some may have viewed Ezra as signaling the end of the prophetic voice—of both women and men— in Israel.

A product of the past, the Sibyl was credited with great age (cf. Aeschylus, *Eum.* 38). Ovid (*Met.* 14.132) relates that she was granted by Apollo as many years as there were grains of sand on the seashore, then claims she is to live for a thousand years (14.136). Heraclitus (360–325 B.C.E.), who claims the Sibyl was even older than Orpheus, describes her as one "speaking with inspired (or frenzied) mouth, unsmiling, unperfumed, [who] penetrates through the centuries by the powers of the gods." Her age then allowed the Sibyl to "predict" much of which had already happened (*vaticinium ex eventu*).

THE JEWISH SIBYL

An adaptation of the classic literary form, the Jewish *Sibyllines* are apologetic literature: they testify to Hellenistic Jews the ancient truth of their own tradition and advise them on their relationship with their Gentile neighbors and Roman overlords. They may also have had the secondary function of introducing Judaism to Gentiles. Such appropriation is not unique to the *Sibyllines;* it appears in such diverse forms as the verse of Hecateaus of Abdera and the exhortations of Pseudo-Phocylides.

Connecting the Greek genre with biblical history, the Sibyl identifies herself as the daughter-in-law of Noah (*Sib. Or.* 1:289–90; 3:827); this connection is also depicted on third-century C.E. coins from Apamea-Kobotos. Alexander Polyhistor (first century B.C.E.) mentions a Sibyl named Saabe or Sambethe, whom he identifies as Chaldean or Hebrew. Pausanius mentions a later Sibyl who resided with the "Jews around Palestine" and adds that some suspected she was the daughter of Erymanthe and Berossus, the author of the Chaldean history (ca. 300–270 B.C.E.). He alludes as well to the appropriation of the genre by other groups, including but not limited to Alexandrian Jews. Josephus (*Antiquities* 1.4) ascribes *Sib. Or.* 3:97–104, generally believed to be from the Babylonian Sibyl, to a Hebrew prophetess. The Christian prologue to the full collection and other later sources based on Lactantius suggest that the Persian Sibyl was also the Chaldean or the Hebrew and that her name was Sambethe. The origins of this name are obscure. Derivations range from Sibtu, the prophetic queen of the Mari texts, to the queen of Sheba, to the goddess Sidurî-Sabitu, to the divine epithet Sabaoth ([Lord of] Hosts).

The bulk of the early Jewish *Sibyllines* (books 3, 5, 11–14, and parts of 1–2) likely achieved their present form in Alexandria. Book 4, also Jewish, was probably composed in the Jordan Valley or Syria. Books 3, 4, 5, and 11 predate the Bar Kochba revolt of 132–135 C.E.; the Jewish material in books 1 and 2 also likely bears a pre–second-century imprint. Books 12–14 are later, and book 8 preserves Jewish material that dates to the late second century C.E.

THE CHRISTIAN SIBYL

While the Jewish texts carefully construct a prophetess of Hebrew, or at least Babylonian, birth who repudiates her Erythrean and Cumean sisters and who speaks of her past iniquities, the Christian texts—books 1–2 in their present form and books 6–8– evince no additional interest in her background. She offers no personal testimony in book 6, and she speaks personally in book 7:195–210 to confess her pagan sins and to hope for Christian deliverance. But reconstruction of Christian attitudes toward the oracles is not restricted to the oracles themselves. The Christian prologue to the collection speaks of "the Chaldean, that is, the Persian, who is called Sambethe, who is of the family of Noah." Other sources erase any Jewish connection. The church fathers emphasize the Sibyl's Gentile origins and hence picture her as an independent witness to Christian truth. The *Shepherd of Hermas*'s second vision, which occurs on the road to Cumae, is of an aged woman carrying a book. He thinks—and so should the reader—that she is the Sibyl, but she corrects him: she is the church, and she is old because she is the earliest of G-d's creations. In this second-century text, the image of the human, inspired female is replaced by the institutional metaphor. In the *City of God,* for example, Augustine hails the acrostic of book 8 "as a genuine prophecy of Christ which had fallen from the lips of the Erythrean Sibyl." In turn, pagan sources such as Celsus mention the Christian heresy of the Sibyllistae and accuse Christians of interpolating into the *Oracles.* The Sibyl was popular among the patristic writers, who include some eight hundred lines of the *Oracles,* both Jewish and Christian, in twenty-two documents, as well as in the Middle Ages and the Renaissance. Her depiction as revealer to the Gentiles is enshrined on the Sistine Chapel opposite the Hebrew prophets.

BOOKS 1–2

Originally Jewish but showing signs of Christian redaction, the first two books are united in manuscript tradition. Like its pagan prototype, the first book schematizes history (cf. Hesiod's *Works and Days*) into four declining ages; a fifth inaugurates universal destruction, followed by a sixth—the first postdiluvian generation—the golden age. The second book details behaviors leading to salvation or destruction. Martyrdom and virginity are positively associated (2:45–55; cf. 4 Maccabees; Revelation). Explicitly Christian concern for virginity reappears in 2:311, where the Virgin Mary is accorded an intercessory role.

Accompanying the usual condemnations of idolatry, violence, and injustice is a particular interest in the treatment of widows and orphans (2:270–73) and parents (273–76). Among the sins, secret intercourse with a virgin and abortion are specifically noted (2:279–82). Book 2:56–148, an extract from Pseudo-Phocylides, introduces a major theme of the collection: the condemnation of homosexuality, and particularly of homosexual prostitution (2:73; cf. Leviticus 18; Romans 1; the earlier oracles of book 3, etc.). The various texts employ sexual offenses to explain the destruction of political enemies; for example, Rome will fall because of the immoral actions of its inhabitants. Ironically, although the collection begins in Eden (1:3–64), Eve is not seen as committing a sexual sin and her curses of childbirth and domination go unmentioned.

The notice that "Adam was persuaded by the woman's words" is also ironic, given that the genre itself insists the reader be persuaded by a woman's words. Book 1:5 speaks of divine compulsion (cf. 3:2–6, 295; 4:18; 5:53). Like Jeremiah, the Sibyl resists her role of prophesying destruction. Yet her situation is worse than that of her biblical counterparts. Book 2:4–5 notes that she lacks awareness of her prophecies. No independent representative of the divine, the Jewish/Christian Sibyl eventually becomes simply an exhausted, mantic mouthpiece. And book 2 (341–44) ends with her confession of her own sins: greed, self-absorption, lacking care for marriage and reason, shamelessness. She is hardly a figure to be emulated.

Interest in virginity, prophecy, and women's religious functions complement the note in 1:196–98 (cf. 1:262) suggesting a Phrygian connection to this material. Home also to the Montanists as well as to the cult of the Great Mother (Cybele), this area of Asia Minor was known for its women prophets as well as the sexual nature of its various religious offspring.

BOOKS 3–5

Similar in outlook and motifs, books 3, 4, and 5 share a periodization of history, a vision of the world destroyed by fire, and the legend of Nero's return. Book 3, the earliest of the three and the longest of the collection, may even contain passages from the Erythrean Sibyl. The composite text ranges from Ptolemaic times to the aftermath of Actium.

Book 3 emphasizes that the prophesied destruction of Rome will be caused not merely by idolatry and failure to support the Jerusalem Temple but also by sexual impropriety, notably, homosexuality and pederasty (3:185–86, 595–600, 601–7, 764–66). Ancillary to this concern for sexual morality, the book predicts the vengeance to be exacted on Rome by a *Despoina* (lady). This figure represents both Cleopatra and the goddess whom she claimed to incarnate, Isis. Clearly predating Actium, *Sib. Or.* 3:350–80 presents an ideal scenario, drawing from Isis aretalogies, in which the great queen would destroy an oppressive system and establish law and justice. Yet in a section postdating 30 B.C.E., the *Despoina* has become the "widow" who brings it desolation (75–92). More positive allusions to other Isis aretalogies appear, but these concern her sponsored "king from the sun" (3:652; cf. the Egyptian *Potter's Oracle*).

Feminine imagery continues to accompany the depictions of fallen Egypt and Rome. The latter is taunted in 3:357–58: "Virgin, often drunken with your weddings of many suitors, as a slave will you be wed, without decorum." Here and throughout the oracles, the political nature of the genre is expressed by means of the personal: sexual humiliation of the female-figured state (e.g., 3:454–56). And states fall because both men and women are sexually immoral. For example, *Sib. Or.* 3:43–45 notices widows engaging in secret affairs (cf. 1 Tim 5:13). Even the universal history is gender-coded. According to 3:120–55, battle lines among the gods were drawn according to the sexes: goddesses, including Rhea, Gaia, Aphrodite, and Demeter, ended the war between Chronos and Titan. When Rhea gave birth, the Titans killed her sons but allowed the daughters to live. This scenario creates an implicit parallel between the god whom Rhea hid and his Hebrew counterpart, Moses.

The Sibyl's own background is recounted in 3:827. Claiming to be the daughter-in-law of Noah, she counters rumors that she is the Erythrean Sibyl (3:808–9) and that she is a "crazy liar" (3:815–16) born to Circe and Gnostos (possibly from the LXX *gnōstēs,* "soothsayer"). Like the women in the Hebrew Scriptures whose ethnic origins are not explicitly noted (e.g., Tamar, Bathsheba), the Sibyl provided later commentators an opportunity to assign nationality (and hence ascribe loyalties). This same ethnic fluidity tends not to attach to male characters.

Book 4, a relatively short oracle, repeats the typical condemnations against idolatry (6–7), sexual offenses (32–34, including "the hateful and repulsive abuses of a male"; the Sibyl does not mention lesbianism), injustice and violence (161–77). Unique is its connections to later Ebionite and Elcasite baptist traditions. These data suggest, according to Collins, a provenance not of Alexandria but in Jewish baptist circles around the Jordan Valley. Like John the Baptist, book 4 treats baptism as a sign of repentance as well as a last hope to avert eschatological destruction.

Returning to the recitation of world history, book 5 opens with the end of the pharaohs and continues to Hadrian. Cleopatra, the "indomitable woman" of 5:18, receives brief notice. The remainder of the text, a long series of prophecies against various nations followed by the return of Nero, the coming of a savior, and the destruction of the world, repeats the dominant motifs of books 3 and 4. Rome is again denounced for crimes of immorality, adultery, incest, bestiality, and especially homosexuality and pederasty (5:166, 386–93, 430) and for its destruction of Jerusalem. While perhaps contemporary with book 4, this oracle includes a strong Temple focus the other lacks.

In a fascinating parallel, the Jewish Sibyl first describes herself as "thrice-wretched" (5:52) because she is compelled to prophesy disaster, she who is "the familiar friend of Isis" (5:53). The end of the oracle presents Isis as "thrice-wretched," a "speechless maenad" whose memory will not be preserved by the earth (5:4:84–86). The Sibyl is wretched because she must awaken the memories of others and because she must talk while Isis, her friend, is silent and forgotten. Being connected to the divine does not bode well for goddess or woman.

BOOKS 6–8

A short hymn to Christ comprises book 6. That a woman would be the ascribed author of such materials is not anomalous in either Jewish or Christian circles. While Josephus (*Antiquities*) robs Deborah and Hannah of their poetry, texts as wide-ranging as Pseudo-Philo (*Biblical Antiquities*), Judith, and the *Sayings of the Desert Mothers* attest to women's role in religious composition.

Book 7's oracles against the nations present incest (both mother/son and father/daughter) as the sign of anarchy. In the commentary on the baptism of the Christ, water sprinkled on fire, which releases a dove to heaven, is described as the "begetting of the Logos (Word) by the Father" (7:76–84). This passage immediately follows the list of the deity's noble "Mothers": Hope, Piety, and Holiness (7:72–73). Removed from female biology, the incarnation appears only in its abstract, Johannine version. Book 7 ends, as does book 2 (341–44) with the Sibyl's confession. To the earlier list of crimes, 7:150–63 adds fornication ("I have known innumerable beds, but no marriage concerned me") and faithlessness. The text ends with her plea that she be stoned.

Book 8's first half foresees the impending fall of Rome and hence the destruction of the world, ca. 195 C.E. Amid various political considerations, 8:217–50 presents an eschatological acrostic on *Iesous Chreistos Theou Huios soter stauros* (Jesus Christ, son of God, crucified savior), versions of which appear in Constantine's *Oratio ad Sanctos* and Augustine's *City of God*. Among the work's eschatological comments are a notice of socioeconomic egalitarianism (73–130) and the reign of an "abominable woman" in the tenth generation (194). This depiction may reflect Revelation 17–18 and 21 (the whore of Babylon; the connection would match the book's anti-Roman agenda). The principal female figure of book 8 is, conversely, the Virgin Mary.

BOOKS 11–14

The existence of two manuscript traditions creates an oddity in enumeration. Book 9 of one version contains parts of books 6, 7, 8, and book 10 is the same as book 4. Therefore, today the *Sibyllines* are numbered 1–8 and 11–14.

Book 11's review of history from Noah's flood to Cleopatra's death shares much with books 3 through 5. However, contrary to these texts' anti-Roman bias, this Alexandrian anti-Egyptian work refers to Cleopatra as the "female, destructive of mortals, betrayer of her own kingdom" (11:247). The motif of Cleopatra's/Egypt's widowhood (cf. 3:75–92) reappears in 11:279, but here her abusive marriage to Rome is described as an even worse fate (11:290).

Book 12, from the mid-third century, echoes the concerns about Cleopatra (12:22), but reserves its major condemnation for the personal crimes of the imperial households. One passage about Caligula, 12:63–66, may refer to the rape of a vestal virgin (an act attributed to Nero by Suetonius); another likely betrays knowledge of Commodus's incestuous relations with his sisters (12:217–20). Continuing the account of book 12, book 13 offers a brief political history of the empire from 240 to 260.

The last book in the collection is the least understood: the text is corrupt, the comments difficult to translate into historical references; the purpose unknown. Thus the Sibyl, who in earlier books fears being considered mad, here offers a good case for her detractors.

GENERAL OBSERVATIONS

As a woman apart from both synagogal and ecclesiastical identification, the Sibyl's representation contributes toward an understanding of gender constructs and cross-cultural borrowings in antiquity. While the genre may have been co-opted by men, its existence may attest to women's religious roles in the Greco-Roman world and within the two covenant communities. The antediluvian Sibyl does not directly translate into the social reality of those who produced and preserved her oracles. Yet, particularly when coupled with the evidence from other Jewish and Christian sources, she does indicate a possibility that women were and in some cases continued to be recognized as vehicles for divine speech and liturgical composition.

This recognition itself is problematic. The Sibyl can at best represent exceptional women. Like the daughters of Job and Philip, the Therapeutrides and the Montanists, she is unmarried and so free from domestic constraints. Yet in contrast to these women, her status is not celebrated even by the communities that record her oracles. Her self-confessed crimes, her prophetic distress, her ignorance, and even the perception of her insanity make her a figure of pity rather than of honor. For a woman to prophesy, according to these works, is a curse, not a blessing.

Her status also indicates an ambivalence toward sexuality. The destruction of kingdoms is both explained in part by sexual crimes (adultery, homosexuality) and cast in terms of sexual humiliation (the indecorous virgin, the widow, the whore). The Sibyl's own identity stands apart from these images: this literary persona recognizes neither the negative depictions of her own sex nor the existence of lesbianism.

Ethnic categories are also complicated by this depiction. A potential indicator of peaceful coexistence, Jewish appropriation of this Gentile genre showed the ease of movement between the two cultures. Yet, just as the Jewish Sibyl ultimately condemns the Gentiles (especially Rome) by means of the very literary form they valued as sacred, Christian texts co-opted the Jewish ones and then used them to condemn the Jews. The *Oracles* thus fulfill their predictions of distress for women and men, members of all religious groups.

RECOMMENDED READINGS

Collins, John J. "The Development of the Sibylline Tradition." In *Aufstieg und Niedergang der römischen Welt*," ii/20.1: 421–59. Berlin: de Gruyter.

———. "The Sibylline Oracles," translation and introduction. In *Old Testament Pseudepigrapha*, edited by James H. Charlesworth, 3:317–472. Garden City, NY: Doubleday, 1983.

———. *The Sibylline Oracles of Egyptian Judaism*. Missoula, MT: Scholars Press, 1972.

Geffcken, J. *Die Oracula Sibyllina*. Leipzig: Hinrichs, 1902.

Nikiprowetzky. V. "La Sibylle juive et le 'Troisième Livre' des 'Pseudo-Oracles Sibyllins' depuis Charles Alexandre." In *Aufstieg und Niedergang der römischen Welt, ii/20*: 460–542. Berlin: de Gruyter, 19??.

———. *La Troisième Sibylle*. Paris and The Hague: Mouton, 1970.

Parke, H. W. *Sibyls and Sibylline Prophecy in Classical Antiquity*. London and New York: Routledge, 1988.

Potter, D. S. *Prophecy and History in the Crisis of the Roman Empire: A Historical Commentary on the Thirteen Sibylline Oracles*. Oxford: Clarendon, 1990.

Schürer, E. *The History of the Jewish People in the Age of Jesus Christ*. 2d ed., edited by G. Vermes et al., 3:617–54. Edinburgh: T. and T. Clark, 1986.

Thompson, B. "The Patristic Use of the Sibylline Oracles." *Review of Religion* 16 (1952): 115–36.

The Revelation to John

Tina Pippin ◆

IN THE LATE TWENTIETH CENTURY, we are living on the edge of apocalypse. Natural disasters, wars, and new social and cultural movements are interpreted by some as signs and symbols of the end of time. Is the end of this millennium "closing time" (Norman O. Brown) or the beginning of what Rosemary Radford Ruether calls "the radical kingdom"? Is this time before the turn of the century the time when the prophetic scroll is rolled out as the script for the final battle (Revelation 20), as fundamentalist Christians propose? Or is this turn into a new century a postmodern turn—a turn into a mosaic of the wealth of global dreams and visions of the future?

Conflicting readings of these apocalyptic times produce a multiplicity of voices. These voices are not only conflicting but are competing for control and for acknowledgment as the authoritative voice. The biblical text of Revelation is the space of the interpretive battle. The dominant reading in popular Christian culture of Revelation has been a literal reading in which all the apocalyptic symbols are made static, and the text is ripped out of its first-century C.E. context. Many fundamentalists actually rewrite Revelation to fit their own conservative political agendas, which are based on cold war rhetoric of the Soviet Union as "other" or on any political threat perceived as "other." Although the second half of the twentieth century brought more biblical scholars of the academy to Revelation, most of these studies are caught in the slow trickle-down effect. For most mainline churches and biblical scholars, Revelation is still at best marginally canonical.

The end of a thousand years brings renewed fervor to studying Revelation, as the last decade of the second thousand years of Christianity shows. The Persian Gulf crisis in 1990 and 1991 received headlines such as "Armageddon Prophecy: Gulf Crisis May Herald War to End All Wars" and "Is the Gulf Conflict the Last Battle? Theological Forces Clash." Richard Lee, of Rehoboth Baptist Church in Atlanta, proclaimed Saddam Hussein the beast of Revelation, and a homemaker in Georgia was quoted on the war, "I believe the second coming of Christ is very close, so this is exciting to me personally, although of course I don't want anybody to die."[1]

At the end of the last century when the collaborators of *The Woman's Bible* were compiling their texts, they responded in their own (limited) way to the cries of oppression brought on by the Industrial Revolution and the Civil War and slavery and its aftermath. Women at the turn of this century are responding in similar ways, with, it is hoped, more knowledge of both the personal and systemic roots of oppression. The biblical books responded in their own ways to the oppression of their times, and apocalyptic literature responds to the present crisis by positing a near-future solution.

How are women to respond to Revelation? Matilda Joslyn Gage and Elizabeth Cady Stanton began the process a century ago in their writing on this "profoundly mystic book."[2] Stanton proclaims: "Why so many different revising committees of bishops and clergymen should have retained this book as holy and inspiring to the ordinary, is a mystery."[3] They searched for positive images of women to counter the negative interpretations of their time. They searched for new ways to encounter this canonical text and face the Apocalypse of John's vision. But these women faced the apocalypse of their own time with a creative political activism. The apocalypse of women underlies all their work; they dreamed of equal rights and total reform of the political and social system.

By the "apocalypse of women" I mean the misogyny and disenfranchisement that are at the roots of gender relations, accompanied by (hetero)sexism and racism, along with violence, poverty, disempowerment, and fear. This apocalypse of women is the destruction of women as women, through rape or pornography or stereotyping or any part of the mind–body dichotomy. How are women to respond to Revelation? By first of all listening to the voices of women past and present who speak out of their own apocalypses, their own crises and visions of the future. The text of Revelation, with its female archetypes of good and evil, virgin and whore, is an account of a political and religious and also gender crisis of the end of the first century C.E. Women readers are to bring a heightened hermeneutic of suspicion to the reading of this biblical text. In this chapter I examine what this hermeneutic might look like in the face of the ongoing apocalypse of women.

In imagining what the women of the 1895 commentary would write today, I find two correlations. First, their interest in astrology is our interest in the Goddess, ancient matrifocal societies, and the study of the rise of patriarchy. Second, their wish "to inspire our children with proper love and respect for the Mothers of the Race"[4] is shared by us, but the political focus is shifted from suffrage to survival in a nuclear age. A discussion of "women and war" brings the text of Revelation into a global context, since women bear the greatest losses from the modern ideology of war.

RE-VEILING/UN-VEILING: READING REVELATION

Matilda Joslyn Gage begins her reading of Revelation with this statement: "The Book of Revelation, properly Re-Veilings, cannot even be approximately explained without some knowledge of astrology. It is a purely esoteric work, largely referring to woman, her intuition, her spiritual powers, and all she represents."[5] This wordplay on the meaning of the Greek title "apocalypse," usually translated as an "uncovering," "revelation," "discovery," or "unveiling," is curious. Are the symbols and mysteries seen as re-veiling/revealing all at once; that is, covering at the moment they uncover meaning? Catherine Keller relates her definition of apocalypse as follows:

> "Apocalypse" . . . means "to remove the veil"—supposedly of the unknown virgin bride at the moment of consummation. Thus the warrior's initiation by destruction, "lifting the corner of the universe and looking at what is underneath," rips the veil off of a mystery that never was hidden. The veil was the separation imposed by the fathers and the father of the fathers. Another aesthetic, one not freed from human empathy to the horrors of transcendent destruction, invites us to its beauty.[6]

To unveil is to take the mystery away. In Keller's description the veil that twentieth-century societies have created is the patriarchal nuclear complex. To unveil is to face death and the machines of death. Keller relates: "*Facing . . .* turns out to be just what the warrior does not do, never did, and seeks with his apocalypse to avoid eternally."[7] To unveil is to see the whole. To unveil is to *face*.

Women have been socialized to fear such face-to-face encounters. Psychic numbing keeps the veil in place.[8] The desire for the end of the world is questioned only by a few, the politically powerless. Revelation unveils, unmasks the desire for death, and for utopia. It also reveils, remasks the ethics of violence and destruction. Gloria Anzaldua explores what an unveiling means in terms of "making face, making soul":

> Among Chicanas/*mexicanas, haciendo caras,* "making faces," means to put on a face, express feelings by distorting the face—frowning, grimacing, looking sad, glum or disapproving. For me, *haciendo caras* has the added connotation of making *gestos subversivos,* political subversive gestures, the piercing look that questions or challenges. . . .[9]

Making faces—at war, at patriarchy, at racism, at classism, at heterosexism, at destruction, at the desire for the violent consummation at the end of time, at the hope of freedom, at the hope of equality, at the dream of a better world—this facing is part of women's response to apocalypse. What the white women of the Revising Committee of *The Woman's Bible* were not completely aware of was their role in the system of oppression of women of color. A hundred years brings the call for the unveiling, which is the constant chipping away at the veil of privilege (white, male, and Western, in particular). Unveiling means change.

THE POETICS AND POLITICS OF DESTRUCTION

. . . to the hard of hearing you shout, and for the almost-blind you draw large and startling figures.

—Flannery O'Connor[10]

As part of our sacred canon, Revelation is about dealing with the end of the world. Revelation is, to draw from the words of Maurice Blanchot, "the writing of the disaster," and in this case, the ultimate disaster, the final holocaust. The writing of the disaster takes place in what Blanchot calls our bruised and wounded space.[11] This space is the reserve of the memory of the past—of wars and prisons and Hiroshima. Blanchot comments: "It is not you who will speak; let the disaster speak in you, even if it be by your forgetfulness or silence."[12] Revelation has a way of speaking even when silenced or placed on the margins of the canon and the lectionary. Regardless of critical stance, this telling of the disaster intrigues the reader. The eschatological disaster is always right at the tip of consciousness.

Recent readings in Revelation include studies in the historical and socio-political context, genre studies, literary analysis, and liberation readings. Both Adela Yarbro Collins and Elisabeth Schüssler Fiorenza focus on the social and literary context of Revelation. Since they are the two dominant women scholars of Revelation, I will focus on their readings as/of women, since they present the generally accepted views in the academy for reading Revelation.

A FEMINIST READING OF REVELATION:
ADELA YARBRO COLLINS

In *Crisis and Catharsis,* Yarbro Collins accepts the information given by Irenaeus that a prophet and seer John wrote Revelation at the end of Domitian's reign (95 or 96 C.E.). Persecution of Christians was not widespread at the end of the first century; rather, martyrdom was sporadic and localized, based on public indictment. Yarbro Collins calls the crisis in Revelation a "perceived crisis," based on broader factors of Roman imperialism: taxation and the imperial cult, in particular.[13] The telling of the disaster and subsequent "happy ending" for God's chosen is cathartic for the reader.[14] This tale of the destruction of the Roman Empire brings an emotional and psychological release of internalized frustration and disempowerment. For the reader/hearer, Revelation provides a prophetic hope for justice brought about by God's new order.

The outline of Revelation proposed by Yarbro Collins is as follows:

1. Prologue   1:1–8
     Preface   1:1–3
     Prescript and sayings   1:4–8
     The seven messages   1:9–3:22
     The seven seals   4:1–8:5
     The seven trumpets   8:2–11:19
2. Seven unnumbered visions   12:1–15:4
     The seven bowls   15:5–16:20
       Babylon appendix   17:1–19:10
     Seven unnumbered visions   19:11–21:8
       Jerusalem appendix   21:9–22:5
     Epilogue   22:6–21
       Sayings   22:6–20
       Benediction   22:21[15]

When Yarbro Collins reads for women in the text, she is also reading for history. The social context of women's lives in late first century Christianity can be discovered in Revelation. Yarbro Collins focuses on Rev 14:1–5, the description of the 144,000. The preparation of this all-male group of holy warriors includes sexual purity. Yarbro Collins compares this scene in Revelation with the fallen angels, who lie with women in the Book of the Watchers (*1 Enoch* 1–36): "Sexual intercourse with women is a narrative emblem for earthly existence."[16] Inherent in these purity laws is the exclusion of women and the conclusion that contact with women's bodies is dangerous. On the sexual purity of the 144,000 men "who have not defiled themselves with women" (Rev 14:4), Yarbro Collins comments: "Such a remark reveals a complex set of emotions, involving perhaps hatred and fear both of women and one's own body."[17] To go further with this line of reasoning, in Revelation the body of woman is marginalized (the Woman Clothed with the Sun and the Bride) or violently destroyed (Jezebel and the Whore). What is considered unclean and dangerous by the male hierarchy has to be placed outside the camp. Those on the inside—the inside of the Bride, the New Jerusalem—in this cultural system are all male. The scene of entry into the heavenly city becomes the ultimate sexual fulfillment—*jouissance*.

Using Yarbro Collins's historical reading as a base, I have devised a role play on Revelation to enable students to experience an imagined scene from the text. The role play is an example of feminist methodology in appropriating Revelation experientially. The text is the letter to the church in Pergamum

(Rev 2:12–17) in western Anatolia; the date is 95 C.E., before the death of Domitian. The setting is the local governor's court in the center of the city. The players are: (1) *The provincial governor.* He is concerned primarily for his career and prestige and wants to end conflicts quickly, so the report to Rome will make him look good. Usually played by the instructor. (2) *The Asiarchs.* These high priests of the Asian Koinon (assembly) presided over the imperial cult (worshiping Caesar Domitian as Lord God). The most prestigious position for a wealthy citizen was to serve as Asiarch. Tension built up when Christians began to refuse to offer incense to the Roman emperor as "their Lord and God." John in Revelation called for no compromise; the Asiarchs were loyal to the Roman Empire and its policies; they were wealthy and benefited from the oppressive economic system.[18] (3) *The Nicolaitans.* In Revelation it appears that this sect is promoting worshiping Caesar and eating meat sacrificed to idols. Whereas John holds a noncompromising position of choosing God or Caesar, the Nicolaitans promote participation in pagan rites and the imperial cult as a part of their Christian stance. (4) *The church members of Pergamum.* These Christians were under a lot of pressure to conform to the political and social environment of Roman-occupied Asia Minor. John's message was difficult, because it called on the Christians to risk their economic and social status. The Nicolaitans provided a middle way—a way to avoid oppression, persecution, and loss of social status. Antipas, a member of the church, had recently been murdered for his political stance against the Roman emperor. John was banished to the island of Patmos. The congregation was fearful of further suffering.

The groups gather before the provincial governor at a hearing to determine what the further course of action will be if members of the Pergamene church continue to refuse to offer incense to Caesar. All rise when the governor enters, saying with him, "Hail be to Caesar Domitian, our Lord and our God." If any refuse to give honor to Caesar, there is immediate trouble. In a brief preparation time before the role play the church members decide what stance they will take; sometimes the group is split on whether or not to agree with John's either-or ethic. There is usually an argument between some church members and the Nicolaitans about coopting into the Roman imperial system. The interaction is different each time I use the role play, but the governor and the Asiarchs usually decide to imprison or execute any dissenters if they do not comply with the local ordinance. The authorities remind the Christians of the fate of Antipas and of John. This role play stretches the so-called historical facts of Revelation, but it enables students to realize the choices some early Christians faced as the colonized, which I believe was a real rather than a "perceived" crisis. But I commit the referential fallacy in this role play for the sake of feminist pedagogy, and I do not posit any direct relation between the text and this imagined social setting.

A FEMINIST READING OF REVELATION:
ELISABETH SCHÜSSLER FIORENZA

Schüssler Fiorenza offers a feminist reading of Revelation. Her "feminist liberationist strategy of rhetorical reading" combines "literary-cultural but also historical-theological modes of analysis."[19] She is inclusive of issues of race, class, and gender in reading Revelation. Her concern is to relate the symbols to the political meanings in both the first-century context and today.

Schüssler Fiorenza approaches Revelation with suspicion in terms of finding any definite historical figures behind the symbols. She states, "I will therefore argue that Rev. must be understood as a poetic-rhetorical construction of an alternative symbolic universe that 'fits' its historical-rhetorical situation."[20] Schüssler Fiorenza is making the move toward more dialogue with literary and ideological studies, grounding her work in a political hermeneutic.

Schüssler Fiorenza outlines Revelation using structural analysis. The "surface structure" forms a chiasm as follows:

A	1:1–8
B	1:9–3:22
C	4:1–9:21; 11:15–19
D	10:1–15:4
C′	15:1, 5–19:10
B′	19:11–22:9
A′	22:10–21[21]

The examination of the units and patterns of the text reveals the epistolary form of Revelation and the central prophetic/parenetic/apocalyptic vision of the text: the little scroll of 10:1–15:4.[22] The effect of the composition of Revelation is cathartic and leads naturally to a more detailed literary analysis.

Schüssler Fiorenza is concerned with the total effect of Revelation. She notes:

Exegetes and theologians still have to discover what artists have long understood: the strength of the language and composition of Rev. lies not in its theological argumentation or historical information but in its evocative power inviting imaginative participation.[23]

This participation comes from an examination of the "rhetorical situation" of Revelation. Revelation has hermeneutical value in the contemporary situation "wherever a social-political-religious 'tension' generated by oppression and persecution persists or re-occurs."[24] The ethical choice in Revelation of either Christ or Caesar has been used by Daniel Berrigan, Ernesto Cardenal, and Alan Boesak to address the oppression of nuclear proliferation, the oppression of Nicaragua under Somoza's rule, and the apartheid system of South

Africa, respectively. Revelation is a cathartic text for Christians in oppressive systems.

I recently experimented with the radical ethic of "Christ against prevailing culture" in Revelation. The context is the protest of the presence of Oliver North as a speaker at the Pastors' Conference of the 1991 Southern Baptist Convention. Our small group of protestors standing with signs outside of the convention hall during North's speech received both positive and negative responses. One convention messenger who stopped to disagree with one of our signs, which read "Oliver North does not speak for me," began arguing for a theocracy. I decided to argue "apocalyptically" using the either-or ethic of Revelation as a base. Of course, my opponent immediately retreated to Jesus and Paul, neither one of whom argues a "Christ of culture" position, let alone a theocracy! The active resistance against Roman imperialism and the Roman state that Revelation presents in vivid form is impossible for the oppressor to affirm. The opponent from the religious right focused on the merger of church and state—the very "Christo-fascism" (Dorothee Sölle) which Revelation warns against.

Regarding this possibility of different responses to Revelation, Schüssler Fiorenza relates the characterization of women in the text. Rome and Israel are portrayed by female figures, and the believers are called from desiring the Whore to desiring the Bride. Schüssler Fiorenza argues:

> Rev. engages the imagination of the contemporary reader to perceive women in terms of good or evil, pure or impure, heavenly or destructive, helpless or powerful, bride or temptress, wife or whore. Rather than instill "hunger and thirst for justice," the symbolic action of Rev. therefore can perpetuate prejudice and injustice if it is not "translated" into a contemporary "rhetorical situation" to which it can be a "fitting" response.[25]

This response to the portrayal of women in Revelation is similar to that of Yarbro Collins. A hermeneutic of suspicion is utilized to unveil the dialectic of the female. Schüssler Fiorenza argues for a "feminist-liberationist strategy of rhetorical reading" in asserting "the interpreter's agency, subjecthood, contextuality, particularity, stance, and perspective when reading Revelation."[26] She wants to engage the text at the level of reconstruction rather than deconstruction.[27]

Feminist response to Revelation needs to include this initial active reading, but before women "translate," the original representation of women in Revelation needs to be examined. The making of archetypes of the female and the abuse of women's bodies in Revelation reveals a deep misogyny. Misogyny in the end of the twentieth century may be more technologically advanced, but the roots and results of woman-hatred are the same.

Schüssler Fiorenza's argument concerning the male identity of the 144,000 is helpful: "A literal ascetic interpretation is unlikely since such a misogynist stance is nowhere else found in the New Testament."[28] She chooses to focus on the overall liberating effect of the book rather than on gender, and this move rightly includes concerns of race, class, colonialism, and ethnicity.[29] Schüssler Fiorenza and Yarbro Collins both provide necessary positive readings of this canonical text.

Yet another feminist reading sees women as marginalized (the woman left in exile in Revelation 12) and/or used as sexual objects and abused (Jezebel, the Whore, and the Bride). This blatantly misogynist text has one advantage for contemporary readers; the reader is facing the sexism that developed into the exclusion of women from positions of equality and power in the early church.

The interest of the commentators of *The Woman's Bible* in 1895 was in the more positive, reconstructive reading of Revelation such as that now provided by Schüssler Fiorenza and Yarbro Collins. But further, the commentators of 1895 were interested in the study of astrology and the connection between ancient deities and the stars. I want to make a similar connection with a study of ancient goddesses and the interest of many contemporary feminists in neo-paganism.

REVELATION AND THE GODDESS

A woman in the shape of a monster
a monster in the shape of a woman
the skies are full of them
    —Adrienne Rich, "Planetarium"[30]

A thinking woman sleeps with monsters.
    —Adrienne Rich, "Snapshots of a Daughter-in-Law"[31]

Part of the patriarchal politics of Revelation is to focus on the so-called positive figures of women, the Woman Clothed with the Sun and the Bride. These are females who are controlled by the patriarchal politics and are made up and made passive. Along with the so-called evil women of Revelation (Jezebel and the Whore), all these females represent some form of the Goddess subdued and killed.[32] Catherine Keller defines the key issue here: "The defeat of female 'monsters' symbolizes the defeat of prepatriarchal modes of being, culturally, bodily and spiritually. . . . Do these women, these goddesses, these metaphors of female energy, become monstrous because they threaten the masculinist separatism, threaten to prevent its coming to be in the first place?"[33] Revelation is about many things, but the death of the Goddess looms large.

A student modeled these "good" and "evil" forms in a project on woman as virgin and whore in medieval art in a class of mine on early and medieval Christianity. Along with slides of representative art, this student dressed in the dichotomy: a sheet made into a toga tied over one shoulder with the other shoulder bare. Her face was divided by a line: one side was the virgin with the white face paint of a mime and hair pulled back (corresponding to the shoulder covered by the toga); the other side represented the whore with rouge and painted eyes and wild hair. What was striking about this portrayal was the split face, the binary opposition of good and evil all in one woman.

In artistic representations of the Whore in Revelation she is a beautiful presence. Especially striking is the smiling Whore of Lovis Corinth's 1916 lithograph "The Whore of Babylon." An angel trumpets while kings pull and eat hunks of flesh from the body of the Whore, who looks off to the side with an absent smile. This representation shows the subduing of the "erotic power" of women, along with the extreme fear of the power of women's bodies.[34]

Carol Christ and others point to the symbol of the Goddess as controlled and reimaged in terms of male power in both the virgin and whore archetypes. Christ states: "The simplest and most basic meaning of the symbol of the Goddess is the acknowledgment of the legitimacy of female power as a beneficent and independent power."[35] The representation of the evil state (political and psychological) as female in Revelation is no accident or anomaly. Revelation is "the writing of the disaster" of the history of women in male-dominated societies. The death of the Goddess signifies the death of women's power.

Yet there is some magic in the scene in Revelation 12 when the Woman Clothed with the Sun puts on the great eagle's wings and flies into the wilderness. The symbol of the goddess Isis is reflected in this winged Woman. The earth (Gaia) comes to the aid of the Woman: "it opened its mouth and swallowed the river that the dragon had poured from his mouth" (Rev 12:16). The winged Woman who flees from the dragon Satan is traditionally known as Israel, the church, or the virgin mother of the Messiah. Matilda Joslyn Gage states that the Woman Clothed with the Sun (feminine) with her feet on the moon (masculine) "portrays the ultimate triumph of spiritual things over material things—over the body, which man, or the male principle, corresponds to or represents."[36] The spiritual feminine is seen as subduing the material masculine. This view of the Woman is positive and helpful in revisioning the Goddess in this powerful scene.

In all of these metaphors of the religious body as female the Goddess is captured and subdued and molded (or in Revelation 12 is exiled) to fit male fantasies of the ideal female. The Bride is adorned, in contrast to the stripping and burning of the Whore. The marriage of the Bride counters the death/ funeral of the Whore. The ancient goddess in all her characteristic diversity of motherhood, erotic sexuality, virginity, and as warrior, justice giver, caretaker, creatrix of nature and arts, and destroyer is segmented into these binary oppositions of good and evil, whore and virgin-mother. The goddess is compartmentalized and stereotyped. Gloria Anzaldua relates this fragmentation:

> You say my name is ambivalence? Think of me as Shiva, a many-armed and legged body with one foot on brown soil, one on white, one in straight society, one in the gay world, the man's world, another in the working class, the socialist, and the occult worlds. A sort of spider woman hanging by one thin strand of web. Who, me confused? Ambivalent? Not so. Only your labels split me.[37]

Anzaldua calls for an end to the dominant ideology that determines the "ideal woman." She recalls that wild spirit of the Goddess, freeing woman to make her own definitions about her body, her self, and her salvation.

The judgment on women is vicious in Revelation. Women are left with no safe space. God's people are called out of the fallen city (the Whore) and into the new city, the New Jerusalem (the Bride). The love–hate relationship with the Whore is transferred to the Bride of Christ. The Bride is a beautiful virgin who marries the Lamb and becomes the heavenly city. The virginal 144,000 male followers of the Lamb, who represent the whole number of the pure and faithful, are allowed to enter the Bride. This scene is disturbing because the imagery is that of mass intercourse. After the holy war all the blessed (men) partake in a double ecstasy: killing the enemy woman and sharing in the victor's spoils of war. Women in this narrative are not safe. They are killed or "prepared as a bride adorned for her husband" (Rev 21:2). The female who is safe is in exile in the wilderness and is alone, her child taken from her. Women in Revelation are victims—victims of war and victims of patriarchy.[38] Revelation is not a safe space for women.

In effect, I am saying that Revelation is not liberating for women readers. This reading goes against the grain of traditional reconstructionist feminist hermeneutics. I find in Revelation only negative and male-dominated images of women. This biblical text of the end of time is so misogynist that I continue to be shocked by its blatant voice. The maternal and bridal images are often the points of redeeming this text for women, but both these images are patriarchal and heterosexist. In general, readings of Revelation ignore the gender roles and focus on the political implications. A political reading using liberation theology does reveal the call to endurance and hope in Revelation, and this reading is important. Having studied the evils of Roman imperial policy in the colonies, I find the violent destruction of Rome very cathartic. But when I looked into the face of Rome, I saw a woman.

A reading for political codes in the text is not enough. In her writing on Revelation, Mary Daly explains: "No one asks *who* are the agents of wickedness. It is enough to have a scapegoat, a victim for dismemberment."[39] The issue remains today as presented by Matilda Joslyn Gage a hundred years ago: "But our present quest is not what the mystic or the spiritual character of the Bible may be; we are investigating its influence upon woman under Judaism and Christianity and pronounce it evil."[40] I think Revelation calls for multiple responses—of catharsis, of hope, of fear, and of horror.

Revelation is an open text for finding some of the early roots of misogyny in the history of the Christian church. The function of this text in women's lives—both directly and indirectly—is especially vivid in the centuries of witch burning in Europe and North America. Those women with the ancient knowledge of midwifery, herbs, medicine, and the religions of old Europe were seen as a threat. Even more, the *Malleus Maleficarum* makes the claim that witches had intercourse with demons and that women are more susceptible to the charms of the devil.[41] Note that the Whore is seated on a scarlet beast with seven heads and ten horns (Rev 17:3), which finally all turn against the Whore: "they and the beast will hate the whore; they will make her desolate and naked; they will devour her flesh and burn her up with fire" (17:16). This image of fire became reality for women accused of witchcraft, a period of women's history Mary Daly refers to as "The Burning Times."[42] Daly continues:

> . . . the technological true believers of the Book of Revelation live their fatal faith, the faith of the Fathers. Knowing their own rightness/righteousness, they are participant observers in the stripping, eating, and burning of the "famous prostitute," the whore hated by god and by the kings (leaders) he has inspired. The harlot "deserves" to be hated and destroyed, of course, for she symbolizes the uncontrollable Babylon, the wicked city.[43]

As women readers of Revelation and of the history of patriarchal politics and misogyny in Christianity, have we not been too willing participants in this scapegoating of the Whore? Have we not accepted too readily the ideal image put before women by the patriarchy? Have we not sung too enthusiastically the taunt song at the funeral of the Whore and the triumphant hymn of the entry of the pure, male believers into the heavenly city?

DECOLONIZING APOCALYPTIC

As an elite female embedded in a system of white privilege, I am able to focus my attention on the sexism of Revelation. The ideology of gender in the text is a neglected area in studies on Revelation, so a focus on gender and misogyny is partially justified by the history of the neglect of these topics. But in this reading for gender I am promoting a Western, white feminist reading and hermeneutic. Gender oppression has to be linked with other forms of oppression that women experience. Since I am not from the Third World or living in poverty or in the midst of war, my voice is limited.[44] In my gender analysis of Revelation I cannot claim to speak for all (or any!) women readers of this text.

The majority of women suffer multiple oppression—sexism, racism, ableism, classism, ageism, heterosexism, colonialism—I am not listing these oppressions just to be "politically correct." Rather, I am called by women of color to face my own role in their multiple oppressions and our mutual enslavement. Gayatri Spivak's focus on the oppressed or nonelite "people" as "subaltern" (from Italian Marxist Antonio Gramsci) draws attention to the role of the intellectual/elite in cultural and political oppression.[45] The hegemonic relation is exposed. Spivak understands this relationship as follows: "The subaltern cannot speak. There is no virtue in global laundry lists with 'woman' as a pious item. Representation has not withered away. The female intellectual as intellectual has a circumscribed task which she must not disown with a flourish."[46] There is no universal experience of women reading Revelation. The voices that have been made Other or have been silenced—both in the fictional universe of the narrative and outside by the real readers of the text—have to be heard, have to be spoken to.

Revelation speaks to the subaltern of the Roman colony in western Anatolia who suffered the economic and political effects of the so-called "Pax Romana." When speaking of the Pax Romana, the powerful lines of George Orwell's *1984* come to mind: "War is peace/Freedom is Slavery/Ignorance is strength."[47] Roman occupation brought about a heightened sense of apocalyptic times for the conscienticized. Many chose not to face the multiple oppression brought about by Roman imperial policy: the economic hardships and extreme poverty in both urban and rural areas; the system of taxation and imposition by the local indigenous elite of the imperial cult; the presence of Roman military and Roman politicos. Revelation represents a minority view, or at least a view actively held by a minority of the colonized.

Thus, it is easy to see the immediate connections Third World Christians make with Revelation's response to oppression. Two comments by Alan Boesak serve as an example of the use of this text: "The Apocalypse is determined to keep the dream of God alive for God's people. It is a protest against and a call for resistance to evil. It depicts the dream of a new creation. . . ." Boesak continues:

> What we are learning is the truth that in order for a new South Africa to be born, we have to be willing to give up our lives. We are learning the meaning of the reply to the souls underneath the altar. And in the process we have exposed the

true nature of the South African state. Their only power is the power to destroy. They can never last.[48]

Revelation becomes a decolonizing text.[49]

It is difficult to read this ancient text for race and ethnicity, since the understandings of race were different in the Mediterranean basin under Roman rule, and inclusion in the "people of God" was based on covenant and not race. What is clear is that the 144,000 is an exclusive group. The outsiders of the Roman Empire, the colonized and Christian, become the insiders. As Yarbro Collins notes, "the ultimate insiders were the Roman citizens."[50] This reversal of power and status is connected with the defeat of the goddess Roma by God's army and the replacement of the throne of Rome with the throne of God and the Lamb (Rev 22:3).

The boundaries of the new covenant group are clear. Those people and groups not included but mentioned in the text are "the cowardly, the faithless, the polluted, the murderers, the fornicators, the sorcerers, the idolaters, and all liars" (Rev 21:8). Again: "Outside are the dogs and sorcerers and fornicators and murderers and idolaters, and everyone who loves and practices falsehood" (Rev 22:15). Inside the heavenly city are the faithful. As the unfaithful are known by the mark of the beast on their foreheads, the people of God have God's seal on their foreheads. The 144,000 come from every tribe of Israel (Rev 7:4–8). They represent the whole number of God's people, but they do not represent the Jews.

Along with the 144,000 is a countless group of redeemed: After this I looked, and there was a great multitude that no one could count, from every nation, from all tribes and all peoples and languages, standing before the throne and before the Lamb, robed in white, with palm branches in their hands (Rev 7:9). Are the redeemed then culturally diverse? I think the answer to this question is both yes and no. Yes, there are all nations and tribes and languages represented in the multitude. But no, only one religion is represented; there is no room for Jews or pagans or anyone who refuses to acknowledge the divinity of Jesus. Yarbro Collins notes: "In Revelation, idolatry is focused on a goddess, Roma."[51] It is, of course, impossible to separate the political from the religious; nonetheless, the idolatry of Roman colonialism is tied with worship of the Goddess. For all the people not in the covenant of God, the judgment is severe: "their place will be in the lake that burns with fire and sulfur, which is the second death" (Rev 21:8).

The boundary of the redeemed sets up a system of opposites expressed as insider and outsider, Christian and non-Christian, and fornicators and virgins. There is no room for dissent and no place for women's power and women's voices. The call to "patient endurance" (Rev 1:9) in the midst of suffering has always been bad news for women. Only certain ones of the marginalized will be included in the inside. The demand for purity in the heavenly city means that any "other" religion is dangerous.

The global dialogue and movement toward multiculturalism in the late twentieth century demand a breaking of these cultural boundaries. Difference is not affirmed in Revelation; everyone is called to be the same, regardless of their nation, tribe, or language. Revelation has an oppressive function in women's lives. This text encourages exclusivity and protectionism, rather than an openness to and sharing of different religious traditions. Revelation is decolonizing literature that turns around and recolonizes. A feminist reading of Revelation is necessarily deconstructive; Revelation is made up of conflicting readings that cannot be resolved.

WOMEN AND WAR

The apocalypse of women has always included the horrors of war. What does it mean for women to read the ultimate war narrative? Is this violent version of the end of time the story women want to tell—the story women want to be involved in?

Revelation describes the final eschatological battle in all its extreme violence and gory detail. There is a certain catharsis to this holy war. This war is "the war to end all wars." God's army conquers the evil powers. Both men and women are subject to death by this army. This holy war is by no means a "just war," mainly because civilian noncombatants are targeted. The believers who are called to "patient endurance" must resist nonviolently, but this resistance is active, not passive, since the result of being a witness (read "martyr") might be death. What are women's roles in this war? How are contemporary women readers to respond to God's war?

The violence and vengeance in Revelation come out of the persecution, both real and perceived, that was experienced by Christians in the Roman Empire at the end of the first century. The violence of the book is startling; violence is done to nature and people and supernatural beings. There are swords and slaughter and hunger and martyrs. The people of all classes who hide in the cave say to the mountain: "Fall on us and hide us from the face of the one seated on the throne and from the wrath of the Lamb; for the great day of their wrath has come, and who is able to stand?" (Rev 6:16–17). The wrath of God and the Lamb is so great that people cannot "face" them.

The war is bloody; there are casualties on both sides. Cannibalism is part of the warfare tactics—the kings and merchants eat the Whore and are in turn eaten by the birds of midheaven, who "gather for the great supper of God" (Rev 19:17). There is torture in the lake of fire and sulfur (Rev 20:10): "This is the second death, the lake of fire; and anyone whose name was not found written in the book of life was thrown into the lake of fire" (Rev 20:14–15). All the enemies and every impure thing (the old earth, especially the sea) is destroyed. "Then I saw a new heaven and a new earth; for the first heaven and the first earth had passed away, and the sea was no more" (Rev 21:1). The new Jerusalem comes down to replace the old city. There is no evil or pollution in the new world. The new world of God far surpasses the old Roman world.

The description of the final battle is fantastic. The symbolic universe of a supernatural battle involves the imagination of the reader. Yarbro Collins argues, "At least Revelation limits vengeance and envy to the imagination and clearly rules out violent deeds."[52] Revelation does call for a nonviolent ethical stance; God's army will do all the "dirty work." But the imagination is endless, and the connection between the desire of the reader and the desire in the text has endless possibilities.

When I describe the drama in Revelation as fantastic, I am referring to a mode (not genre) of literature, fantasy literature. The fantasy of the end-time has mimetic potential. Rosemary Jackson's definition of fantasy relates the political with the textual; fantasy is a politically subversive form of literature. Jackson states: "fantasies image the possibility of radical cultural transformation through attempting to dissolve or shatter the boundary lines between the imaginary and the symbolic."[53] Fantasy literature is not escapist; rather, fantasy exposes the reader to what is "real" through the symbols of the supernatural and the magical. The violence and vengeance that are part of this fantasy world in Revelation exposes the violence in the "real" world of the first century. But also exposed is the desire for the violent destruction of the enemy at the hands of God.

Is this desire for violence part of women's ways of knowing? Or is this desire the patriarchal image/imagining of the end? Do women desire a violent apocalypse? Literal interpretations of Revelation get caught up in the violent details. Jean Elshtain points to the effect of these fundamentalist readings: "Apocalyptic warnings may be balm to the spirit of many, rather than a way to strike terror and in so doing to promote action."[54] The bonds of such a passive response to Revelation have to be broken.

Alice Walker responds bluntly and honestly to "the hope for revenge" against the enemies: "*Let the earth marinate in poisons. Let the bombs cover the ground like rain. For nothing short of total destruction will ever teach them anything.*" Then Walker points to a different knowledge, a different response:

> So let me tell you: I intend to protect my home. Praying—not a curse—only the hope that my courage will not fail my love. But if by some miracle, and all our struggle, the earth is spared, only justice to every living thing (and everything is alive) will save humankind.

And we are not saved yet.
Only justice can stop a curse.[55]

The survivalist ethic of women of color turns curse into courage. Women set the terms of salvation, not the male God on his distant throne.

Walker speaks the account of her vision like Sojourner Truth, with a voice like "apocalyptic thunders."[56] Walker is able to face the nuclear apocalypse brought about by the white males in power. She shakes us out of our sleep. As Jonathan Schell warns, "We drowse our way toward the end of the world."[57] It takes voices of "apocalyptic thunders" to wake us.

Part of facing apocalypse is learning to "sustain the gaze."[58] This phrase from Joanna Macy means a breaking free of our denial of the nuclear apocalypse. As a concrete example of what women are doing to "sustain the gaze," Macy includes the women protesters of cruise missiles at Greenham Common. She calls their action "apocalyptic or 'uncovering' behavior."[59] In the late twentieth century, women are called to active resistance—to take part in facing the end. As Catherine Keller recognizes, "The nuclear complex must be faced and healed if it is not to bring on the end of time."[60] Helen Cauldicott, the women of Women's Action for Nuclear Disarmament, Physicians for Social Responsibility, the women speaking in the documentary "Women for America, For the World," and Sane/Freeze are all speaking of the doom to allow us to break out of our denial.

The holy war of Revelation is no longer an option. As Schell reveals, "The choices don't include war any longer. They consist now of peace, on the one hand, and annihilation, on the other."[61] Women's response to the coming apocalypse has to be a reinterpretation of what it means to choose Christ over Caesar. Choosing Christ no longer means desiring martyrdom. When two-thirds of the earth's population goes to bed hungry each night, martyrdom becomes another form of patriarchal abuse. Christ is more than a sacrificial lamb who resurrected into a mythic warrior hero. Women have to refuse the call to mimic such sacrifice. Women (and men!) must be involved in risk-taking for social change.[62]

War always involves a dialectic of yes and no, and women have said both yes and no to war. In an article entitled "Tales of War and Tears of Women," Nancy Huston argues that the telling or narrative of a war is necessary for its "reality." She shows how women play "supporting roles" in the war performance: as pretext, booty, recompense, casualties, miracle mothers and castrating bitches, and cooperative citizens, to name a few roles.[63] Of women who say no to war Huston elaborates on an example of women who laughed instead of wept at military power: "These women said no, they laughed in the face of the ineluctable, they refused to collaborate in the making of tragedy, they denounced it for what it is: a theatre of the absurd."[64] Is all war, even holy war, "theatre of the absurd"? I think women's response is to laugh and say yes.

Revelation ends after the war, after the destruction of the old earth. A utopia ("no place") is set up by God. "Death will be no more; mourning and crying and pain will be no more, for the first things have passed away" (Rev 21:4). God and the Lamb dwell inside the city with the chosen people. The new world is perfectly pure, and there is no more suffering. Is this male fantasy of a utopia of limited diversity and the war to make it happen what women want? For women who say no to supporting roles in this holy war, what is the alternative apocalyptic narrative?

REWRITING THE APOCALYPSE FOR WOMEN

The future for women is part of the subtext of Revelation. Women are to mimic the roles of the "good" archetypes of mother of the Messiah and Bride. The future for women is to become like the Bride, adorned for her husband and submissive to his wishes. Woman as city (Rome or the New Jerusalem) lays herself out as sacrifice. Like the goddess Tiamat, whose body is used to form the earth, the Bride becomes the heavenly city and God's church. But in contrast to the Tiamat story, there is no fight.

The Bride and the Woman Clothed with the Sun are kept safe from the war. There is even a wedding feast in the midst of the fighting (Rev 19:9). The Brussels Tapestry of the marriage of the Lamb (mid-sixteenth century) shows the festivities of the marriage supper, with a beautiful, smiling Bride with her arm around the Lamb. The guests around the table are worshiping the Lamb. But directly above the Bride's head lies the burning Whore, surrounded by flames with a look of horror on her face and a eucharistic-type cup in her hand. The juxtaposition of these two scenes is disturbing. Is the burning of the Whore the desire of women? Are we to identify with the smiling Bride as "ideal woman?"

I am not out to demythologize apocalyptic literature. I want to enter boldly into these mythical and fictional worlds—these fantastic landscapes—and see what there is to see. I want to encounter face to face the beasts and dragons and the Lamb and the heavenly angels. I want to encounter face to face the exiled and battered women. Here lies the call of Revelation for women readers: to face the divisions of women by the patriarchy and to face our own roles in the violence. This facing is no easy task; the images in Revelation are grotesque, and my reaction is to turn away from the violence—to seek some other text.

"Sustaining the gaze" at Revelation is important for women readers because the gaze is necessary for breaking through denial over the apocalypse of women. Gazing at the biblical apocalypse enables women to gaze at the contemporary apocalypse. The parousia, the coming of Christ, will not be brought about by the further sacrifice and martyrdom of women (or men). Revelation leaves women with no option for the future; the future is predetermined by God. But at the turn of the millennium women do have choices. Women in Revelation are silenced, but women readers today have voices to speak at, of, and about the biblical and contemporary apocalypses. We need to develop voices of "apocalyptic thunders."

The apocalyptic future, the utopia of Revelation is individualistic. There is competition for power and control—but most of all for place, a place, in the book of life and in the heavenly place. Charlotte Perkins Gilman imagined a different place in 1915 during World War I. She envisioned a women's utopia on this earth where there was no competition or war. One of the three men who discovered this utopian community comments:

> As I learned more and more to appreciate what these women had accomplished, the less proud I was of what we, with all our manhood, had done.
>
> You see, they had no wars. They had no kings, and no priests, and no aristocracies. They were sisters, and as they grew, they grew together—not by competition, but by united action.[65]

Gilman's vision is certainly idealistic, and she has been cited for her elitism and racism, which must be noted as we dream about the next millennium. But the dream of "united action," a global action, pushes women toward the future. Women will testify to a different apocalyptic vision, a different utopia.[66]

NOTES

1. The speaker is "Glynnis Mullis, age twenty-seven, homemaker and member of a charismatic church, St. Simons Island." From the *Atlanta Journal and Constitution*, 15 January 1991.

2. Elizabeth Cady Stanton, *The Woman's Bible* (Seattle: Coalition Task Force on Women and Religion, 1974), 176.

3. Ibid., 184.

4. Ibid.

5. Ibid., 176.

6. Catherine Keller, "Warriors, Women, and the Nuclear Complex: Toward a Postnuclear Postmodernity," in *Sacred Connections: Postmodern Spirituality, Political Economy, and Art*, ed. David Ray Griffin (Albany: State University of New York Press, 1990), 81.

7. Ibid., 67.

8. Psychic numbing is the first step in the grief process of denial. The term is also used by psychologists to refer to ignorance of the nuclear apocalypse—and the accompanying nonaction.

9. Gloria Anzaldua, "Haciendo caras, una entrada," in *Making Face, Making Soul/ Haciendo Caras: Creative and Critical Perspectives by Women of Color*, ed. Gloria Anzaldua (San Francisco: Aunt Lute Foundation, 1990), xv.

10. Flannery O'Connor, "The Fiction Writer and His Country," in *Mystery and Manners*, ed. Sally Fitzgerald and Robert Fitzgerald (New York: Farrar, Straus & Giroux, 1957), 34.

11. Maurice Blanchot, *The Writing of the Disaster*, trans. Ann Smock (Lincoln: University of Nebraska Press, 1986), 30, 55.

12. Ibid., 4.

13. Adela Yarbro Collins, *Crisis and Catharsis: The Power of the Apocalypse* (Philadelphia: Westminster, 1984), chapter 3 ("The Social Situation—Perceived Crisis").

14. "Catharsis" is a literary term originating in Aristotle's *Poetics*. Catharsis operates on the emotional and intellectual levels. According to Adnan K. Abdulla (*Catharsis in Literature* [Bloomington: Indiana University Press, 1985], 9), catharsis is defined as "an aesthetic response which begins with the audience's identification with the protagonist and leads to emotional arousal of two conflicting emotions (e.g., fear and pity). These emotions are resolved by their reconciliation, bringing to the audience a sense of elevated harmony, or peace, or repose, which can be thought of as understanding, whether moral, metaphysical, or psychological."

15. Ibid., 112.

16. Adela Yarbro Collins, "Women's History and the Book of Revelation," in *SBL 1987 Seminar Papers,* ed. Kent Harold Richards (Atlanta: Scholars Press, 1987), 89.

17. Yarbro Collins, *Crisis and Catharsis*, 159.

18. See Elisabeth Schüssler Fiorenza, *The Book of Revelation: Justice and Judgment* (Philadelphia: Fortress Press, 1985), 193–94.

19. Elisabeth Schüssler Fiorenza, *Revelation: Vision of a Just World* (Minneapolis: Fortress, 1991), 14–15.

20. Schüssler Fiorenza, *Book of Revelation*, 183.

21. Ibid., 175. See also Schüssler Fiorenza's earlier outline in *Invitation to the Book of Revelation* (New York: Image Books, 1981), 218–19, and an updated explanation in *Revelation: Vision of a Just World*.

22. Schüssler Fiorenza, *Book of Revelation*, 176–77.

23. Ibid., 22.

24. Ibid., 199.

25. Ibid.

26. Schüssler Fiorenza, *Revelation: Vision of a Just World*, 13.

27. *Deconstruction* is a literary theory usually associated with Jacques Derrida. Deconstruction relates to the difference between signifier and signified and the "warring forces of signification" (Barbara Johnson). Deconstruction reveals the power relations in the play between signifier and signified and shows the conflicting voices that speak in the text.

28. Schüssler Fiorenza, *Invitation to the Book of Revelation*, 139.

29. Ibid., 14.

30. Adrienne Rich, "Planetarium," in *The Fact of a Doorframe: Poems Selected and New 1950–1984* (New York: W. W. Norton, 1984), 114.

31. Adrienne Rich, "Snapshots of a Daughter-in-Law," in *The Fact of a Doorframe*, 36.

32. "Goddess or God/ess" is the elemental female power of divinity; the original mother/creatrix. Rosemary Radford Ruether defines God/ess as "a written symbol intended to combine both the masculine and feminine forms of the word for the divine while preserving the Judeo-Christian affirmation that divinity is one" (*Sexism and God-Talk: Toward A Feminist Theology* [Boston: Beacon, 1983], 46). "Whore" is generally a woman who has sexual intercourse for money—a prostitute. In many cultures economic deprivation is a cause of prostitution. In religious literature the Whore is an archetype of the evil female. The Whore is set up as evil so that violence against her is accepted and acceptable.

33. Keller, "Warriors, Women, and Nuclear Complex," 76.

34. The "erotic" or "erotic power" is defined by Audre Lorde as "the lifeforce of women; of that creative energy empowered, the knowledge and use of which we are now reclaiming in our language, our history, our dancing, our loving, our work, our lives" ("Uses of the Erotic: The Erotic as Power," in *Sister Outsider: Essays and Speeches* [Freedom, CA: The Crossing Press, 1984], 55).

35. Carol Christ, *Laughter of Aphrodite: Reflections on a Journey to the Goddess* (San Francisco: Harper & Row, 1987), 121.

36. *The Woman's Bible*, 183.

37. Gloria Anzaldua, "La Prieta," in *This Bridge Called My Back: Writings by Radical Women of Color*, ed. Cherrie Moraga and Gloria Anzaldua (New York: Kitchen Table: Women of Color Press, 1981), 205.

38. "Patriarchy" refers to the total system of oppression of women and men. For Rosemary Radford Ruether: "By patriarchy we mean not only the subordination of females to males, but the whole structure of Father-ruled society: aristocracy over serfs, masters over slaves, king over subjects, racial overlords over colonized peoples" (*Sexism and God-Talk,* 61).

39. Mary Daly, *Gyn/Ecology: The Metaethics of Radical Feminism* (Boston: Beacon, 1990), 105.

40. *The Woman's Bible*, 209.

41. Heinrich Kraemer, *Malleus Maleficarum* (London: Pushkin Press, 1951).

42. Daly, *Gyn/Ecology*, 216.

43. Ibid., 104–5.

44. On the use of the term "Third World," see Chandra Talpade Mohanty, Ann Russo, and Lourdes Torres, eds., *Third World Women and the Politics of Feminism* (Bloomington: Indiana University Press, 1991).

45. Gayatri Chakravorty Spivak, "Can the Subaltern Speak?" in *Marxism and the Interpretation of Culture*, ed. Cary Nelson and Lawrence Grossberg (Urbana: University of Illinois Press, 1988), 283.

46. Ibid., 308.

47. George Orwell, *Nineteen Eighty-Four* (New York: Harcourt, Brace & World, 1949), 5.

48. Allan A. Boesak, *Comfort and Protest: The Apocalypse from a South African Perspective* (Philadelphia: The Westminster Press, 1987), 35, 83–84.

49. "Decolonization" deals with reading from the "underside" of history—from the point of view of the colonized, the conquered. Decolonizing literature is that which represents a "reading from below" and exposes the dominant ideology of the imperial power.

50. Adela Yarbro Collins, "Insiders and Outsiders in the Book of Revelation and Its Social Context," in *"To See Ourselves as Others See Us": Christians, Jews, "Others" in Late Antiquity* (Chico, CA: Scholars Press, 1985), 188. Filmmaker and critic Trinh T. Minh-ha comments on the relationship of insider and outsider: ". . . where should the line between insider and outsider stop? How should it be defined? By skin color, by language, by geography, by nation or by political affinity? What about those, for example, with hyphenated identities and hybrid realities?" From "Not You/Like You: Post-Colonial Women and the Interlocking Questions of Identity and Difference," in *Making Face, Making Soul*, 374.

51. Yarbro Collins, "Insiders and Outsiders," 214.

52. Adela Yarbro Collins, "Persecution and Vengeance in the Book of Revelation," in *Apocalypticism in the Mediterranean World and the Near East*, ed. David Hellholm (Tübingen: J. C. B. Mohr, 1983), 747.

53. Rosemary Jackson, *Fantasy: The Literature of Subversion* (New York: Methuen, 1981), 178. "Fantasy" is a literary mode. Using Marxist ideology, Rosemary Jackson defines it as sub-

versive literature. Elements of the fantastic include the supernatural, fairy tales, the imaginary, the impossible, or the marvelous. Apocalyptic literature is an early form of fantasy literature.

54. Jean Bethke Elshtain, *Women and War* (New York: Basic Books, 1987), 247.

55. Alice Walker, "Only Justice Can Stop A Curse," in *Reweaving the Web of Life: Feminism and Nonviolence*, ed. Pam McAllister (Philadelphia: New Society Publishers, 1982), 264, 265.

56. Toinette M. Eugene, "Moral Values and Black Womanists," *Journal of Religious Thought* 41, 2 (1984–85): 28.

57. Jonathan Schell, *The Fate of the Earth* (New York: Avon Books, 1982), 239.

58. To gaze is to face, and facing means taking off the mask, breaking through psychic numbing, looking at the Other as Other. For a detailed literary reading, see Kaja Silverman, *The Acoustic Mirror: The Female Voice in Psychoanalysis and Cinema* (Bloomington: Indiana University Press, 1988).

59. Joanna Macy, "Learning to Sustain the Gaze," in *Facing Apocalypse*, ed. Valerie Andrews, Robert Bosnak, and Karen Walter Goodwin (Dallas: Spring Publications, 1987), 167.

60. Keller, "Warriors, Women, and the Nuclear Complex," 77.

61. Schell, *The Fate of the Earth*, 193.

62. On risk taking, see Sharon Welch, *A Feminist Ethic of Risk* (Minneapolis: Fortress, 1990).

63. Nancy Huston, "Tales of War and Tears of Women," *Women's Studies International Forum* 5, 3/4 (1982): 275.

64. Ibid., 282.

65. Charlotte Perkins Gilman, *Herland* (New York: Pantheon Books, 1979), 60.

66. The material in this chapter appears in different form in my *Death and Desire: The Rhetoric of Gender in the Apocalypse of John* (Louisville: Westminster/John Knox Press, 1992).

RECOMMENDED READINGS

Andrews, Valerie, Robert Bosnak, and Karen Walter Goodwin, eds. *Facing Apocalypse*. Dallas: Spring Publications, 1987.

Boesak, Allan A. *Comfort and Protest: The Apocalypse from a South African Perspective*. Philadelphia: Westminster, 1987.

Collins, Adela Yarbro. *Crisis and Catharsis: The Power of the Apocalypse*. Philadelphia: Westminster, 1984.

Collins, John J., ed. *Apocalypse: The Morphology of a Genre. Semeia 14*. Missoula, MT: Scholars Press, 1979.

Hellholm, David, ed. *Apocalypticism in the Mediterranean World and the Near East*. 2nd ed. Tübingen: Mohr-Siebeck, 1988.

Hemer, Colin J. *The Letters to the Seven Churches of Asia in Their Local Setting*. Journal for the Study of the New Testament Supplement 11. Sheffield: JSOT Press, 1986.

Pippin, Tina. *Death and Desire: The Rhetoric of Gender in the Apocalypse of John*. Louisville: Westminster, 1992.

Schüssler Fiorenza, Elisabeth. *The Book of Revelation: Justice and Judgment*. Philadelphia: Fortress, 1985.

——. *Invitation to the Book of Revelation*. Garden City, NY: Doubleday, 1981.

——. *Revelation: Vision of A Just World*. Proclamation Commentary. Minneapolis: Fortress, 1991.

Thompson, Leonard. *The Book of Revelation: Apocalypse and Empire*. New York: Oxford University Press, 1990.

Montanist Oracles

SUSANNA ELM ◆

MONTANISM IS ONE of the many hereticated movements within Christianity in which women as agents of prophetic visions held positions of vital importance and could thus exercise a high degree of leverage in the androcentric structure of early Christianity. Central to and thus formative within the movement from its outset, the fate of Montanist prophetesses and their oracles is intrinsically linked to that of Montanism as such. Montanism itself, clearly shaped by its underlying indigenous religious matrix characterized by centuries of worship to a powerful female deity, Cybele, and her companion, Attis, is paradigmatic for the processes operative in eliminating a more individualistic, locally diverse Christianity, soon denounced as "heretical," in favor of a hierarchically structured, centralized "orthodox" church. The role of women and that of prophecy, both capable of disrupting the gendered distribution of ecclesiastical power, are pivotal in this process.

Montanism exemplifies thus the strategies employed in the institutionalization of "charismatic movements." It furthermore demonstrates methodological approaches used to justify marginalization *ex post* and, conversely, highlights the difficulties involved in attempting to question the validity of that marginalization.

Marginalization or disempowerment is never simply a binary process but a highly complex and consistently evolving task employing a "multiplicity of force relations," intent on relegating entire groups to the shadows cast by the dominant institution.[1] To highlight these shadowy places becomes particularly difficult in antiquity, since virtually all our sources exist solely because they conformed to the dominant paradigm. Yet we cannot simply assume that the marginalized groups, of which women formed an essential component, simply thought, believed, and lived in a way directly opposite to the dominant ones; in the same way in which there is not simply one truth or one knowledge, there exist also a "plethora of ignorances."[2] The potential plurality of the shadowed places has to be borne in mind constantly. Women and "heretics" were not "mere victims of patriarchy . . . because no voice—past or present—is more than partially empowered or partially distinctive. . . . Women of every age speak in a variety of accents."[3] Here Montanist oracles acquire their true significance: however filtered, altered, and maligned, they are one of the rare instances in which ancient woman's voice has been preserved.

Montanism originated in the 150s and 160s C.E. in a specific region in Asia Minor, in Phrygia—more precisely in the town of Ardabau (Eusebius, *Church History* 4.27; Epiphanius, *Panarion* 48.1.2). Calling itself the "Prophecy," or "New Prophecy," but soon known as the "Phrygian" or "Cataphrygian heresy," the movement acquired the name Montanism only in the course of its heresiological "classification" in the fourth century, which favored identification of "sects" with their "founders."[4] Montanism spread quickly beyond Phrygia to Rome and then North Africa, where it counted Tertullian as well as the two important women martyrs Perpetua and Felicitas among its followers.

In the process, its message underwent constant, if at times subtle, change. Keeping with the heresiological tradition never to omit any heresy ever known, Western sources continue to mention Montanists well into the sixth, and Eastern well into the twelfth century C.E. While in the East forms of Montanism actually survived at least until the ninth century, despite occasionally massive repression, the same cannot be said for the West, where, by the beginning of the fourth century, Montanism had ceased to exist.[5]

Christian literature attests that the Montanist prophets and prophetesses produced numerous writings (e.g., Hippolytus, *Refutatio* 8.19.1). Most of these perished, with the exception of several treatises written during Tertullian's Montanist period. Our knowledge of Montanism is, therefore, based on those treatises, the descriptions given by its opponents, a number of inscriptions and archaeological findings, and nineteen oracles. These *Montanist Oracles* (*Or.*), fourteen of which are authentic and five of which are of questionable authenticity, have been preserved as part of the adversarial descriptions and date back to the first, original Phrygian phase of Montanism discussed in the following:[6]

> There is said to be a village called Ardabau in Phrygian Mysia. There, they say, first, . . . a recent convert to the faith named Montanus, . . . was carried away as by the Spirit, and suddenly experiencing some kind of possession and spurious ecstasy, he was inspired and began to speak and say strange things, prophesying. . . . [The devil] also raised up two other women and filled them with the spurious spirit, so that, . . . they spoke in a frenzied manner, unsuitably, and abnormally. (Anonymous in Eusebius, *Church History* 5.16–17)

> He is the one who taught the dissolution of marriages, who legislated fasts, who named Pepuza and Tymion Jerusalem (now these are two towns of Phrygia). (Apollonius in Eusebius, *Church History* 5.18)

. . . in Pepuza either Quintilla or Priscilla . . . had been asleep . . . and the Christ came to her and slept with her in the following manner, as that deluded woman described it: "Having assumed the form of a woman," she says," Christ came to me in a bright robe and put wisdom (*sophian*) into me, and revealed to me that this place is holy, and that it is here that Jerusalem will descend from heaven. (*Or.* 11 in Epiphanius, *Panarion* 49.1)

These quotes contain in a nutshell the aspects central to the movement: religious leadership of women and men through prophecy. The content of these prohecies, uttered in a state of rapture by "Montanus and his women," who were according to most sources called Maximilla and Priscilla (Prisca), was strongly eschatological and apocalyptic. "For the one they call Maximilla, the prophetess, declares: 'After me there will no longer be a prophet, but the fulfillment'" (*Or.* 6 in Epiphanius, *Panarion* 48.2.4).

This eschatology, however, was sufficiently flexible to secure the movement's survival after the end of its first phase, roughly coincidental with the death of the last of the three original founders, Maximilla, in ca. 179 C.E. (Gregory of Nazianzus, *Or.* 22.12; Eusebius, *Church History* 5.17.4).[7] Indeed, later catastrophes led to eschatological revivals, as, for example, in 235, when in the wake of earthquakes in Caesarea in Cappadocia a new prophetess appeared (Firmillian; see Cyprian, *Ep.* 75.10). Prophetic ecstasies, especially of women, remained prevalent throughout Montanism's documented history, as demonstrated by one Nanas, whose fourth-century epitaph evokes her "angel-visits and [the gifts] of tongues in great measure."[8]

One striking aspect of the original Montanist eschatology was its concreteness, its intrinsic link to a distinct "holy place." Pepuza and Tymion were the symbol of a fervent hope as the actual locus of the new Jerusalem, revealed by Christ as woman. Closely related to this concrete, enthusiastic eschatology is Montanism's ethical rigor. "Holiness," understood as chastity or pureness, was paramount: "Likewise the holy prophetess Prisca preaches that the holy minister should know how to administer holiness of life (*sanctimoniam*). 'For purification produces harmony,' she says, 'and they see visions, and when they turn their faces downward they also hear salutary voices, as clear as they are secret'" (*Or.* 10 in Tertullian, *Ex. chast.* 10.5). This emphasis on chastity and continence led to "new fasts, feasts, and the eating of dry food and cabbage . . . [as] taught by those females" (Hippolytus, *Refutatio* 8.19.1). Its intense asceticism did not, however, entail an absolute condemnation of the flesh. Thus, Prisca's saying "They are flesh, and they hate the flesh" implies criticism of contemporary Gnostic teachings, which explicitly condemn the body as evil on principle (*Or.* 9 in Tertullian, *De res. carn.* 11.2). Montanists preached the resurrection of the flesh and knew, in addition to baptism through their prophetesses, resurrection of the dead.[9]

Montanism, beyond question, emerged out of the teachings of Christianity. Yet its selection and appropriation of specific aspects of Christianity were deeply influenced by a preexisting cultural matrix, that of its native Phrygia. Thus, each of its defining characteristics finds its roots within the tradition of the Gospels as well as in its local religious inheritance.

Prophetic utterances were an integral part of both the Hebrew Bible and the Christian Testament (e.g., Acts 11:27; 13:1; 15:32; 1 Cor 12:1–13:3; 1 Thess 5:19). Notwithstanding potentially contentious oracles such as *Or.* 1: "I am the Lord God, the Almighty dwelling in humans (*en anthrōpō*)"; *Or.* 2: "Neither angel nor envoy, but I the Lord God the Father have come"; or *Or.* 7, attributed to Maximilla: "Hear not me, but hear Christ,"[10] which express the notion of the Lord "speaking through" his prophets, Montanism's doctrine, in particular its Christology, was in perfect accord with the teachings of the "Great Church."[11] Accusations to the contrary are a reflection of later sources.

Montanism was equally in accord with the gospel in its exaltation of women as prophetesses (Acts 2:17–18; Gal 3:28). Indeed, Montanist prophetesses claimed a line of ancestry that included not only Jewish figures such as Miriam, Deborah, and Hulda, but had far more recent precedent in Hannah and Mary, and in Asia Minor itself in the daughters of Philippus and in Ammia in Philadelphia (Acts 21:8–10; Eusebius, *Church History* 5.17.3).

The principal sources of Montanist eschatology were likewise scriptural. To mention but a few examples, Paul in Gal 4:26 speaks of the "heavenly Jerusalem" as "a free woman" (see also 1 Corinthians 15), and Revelation speaks directly of "that new Jerusalem which is coming down from heaven" (3:12). Indeed, the Johannine tradition, itself deeply rooted in Asia Minor, exercised a particular influence on Montanist teachings.[12] Montanus, in a questionable oracle, is said to have declared: "I am the Father, and I am the Son, and I am the Paraclete" (*Or.* 15 in *Dial. of a Mont.*)—in clear resonance of the opening passage of Revelation. A detailed comparison with the Gospel of John (esp. 14:16–26; 15:26; 16:7–15) reveals the extent to which "Montanus and his women" saw themselves as the vessel through which the Paraclete spoke to the disciples.

The notion that the prophet by necessity suffers for his or her message is likewise predominant in Revelation and finds its clear parallel in the heightened tendency for martyrdom among "Phrygians": "Wish not to choose to die in your beds, nor in miscarriages and mild fevers, but in martyrdoms, that he who has suffered for you may be glorified" (Montanus, *Or.* 14 in Tertullian, *De Fuga* 9.4; cf. *Martyrdom of Polycarp.* 4).[13]

The very nature of Montanism's Christianity also reveals its Phrygian roots. Recent archaeological findings have identified the "holy land of the Montanists" as the high valley between the ancient sites of Philadelphia, Eumeneia, Apamea, and Hierapolis.[14] This fairly circumscribed area was also the site of a major non-Christian sanctuary with its community of "sacred slaves"—that of Apollo Lairbenos and his mother Leto in Dionysopolis. This Apollo/Leto sanctuary flourished between the early second century and the third century C.E. and represents—in characteristic reversal of the male–female relation in favor of the male—a syncretistic reinterpretation of the central Phrygian cultic pair, Cybele and Attis. At the onset of his prophecies, Montanus was a recent convert to Christianity, and two fourth-century sources state that he had been a priest of Apollo. Indeed, Ardabau itself was located in the vicinity of Dionysopolis.

The preponderance of the matriarchal/female element in the Phrygian religious matrix is well known and finds its direct correlation in the Montanist hierarchy. Inscriptions near the Apollo/Leto sanctuary speak of virtually equal numbers of male and female priests. Montanism likewise knew not only prophetesses, who baptized and even celebrated the Eucharist, but female bishops and presbyters as well (Epiphanius, *Panarion* 49.2; can. 11 Laodicea).[15] The central Montanist ritual described by Epiphanius, that "in their assembly seven virgins dressed in white and carrying torches enter, coming, of course, to prophesy to the people," resembles mixed-gendered Phrygian cultic practice in its external arrangement as well as in content: Epiphanius's observation that "they pour forth tears as if they were sustaining the sorrow of repentance, . . . and lament the life of humans" (*Panarion* 49.2) echoes precisely the faithful's annual grieving over the fate of Apollo/Attis *and* that of humankind, now merged with the notion of Christ's passion and death (*De err. prof. rel.* 3.1).

Similar "pagan" echoes ring through Montanus's *Or.* 3: "Behold, a human (*ho anthrōpos*) is like a lyre, and I flit about like a plectron; a human sleeps, and I awaken him/her; behold, it is the Lord who excites the hearts of humans and gives humans a heart" (*Or.* 3 in Epiphanius, *Panarion* 48.4). The oracle does convey the fragmented nature of ecstatic experience, but beyond that it clearly alludes to Apollo, God of the lyre, Montanus's prior master: thus, the second Homeric hymn to Apollo describes the God's arrival in Pythos, his lyre emanating love-filled paeans elicited by the golden plectron (1.178f.; cf. *Odes of Solomon* 6.5.1).

Another oracle attributed to Maximilla, "The Lord has sent me as partisan (*hairestistēn*), revealer (*mnēnytēn*), and interpreter (*hermeneutēn*) of this suffering, covenant, and promise. I am compelled to come to understand the knowledge of God whether I want to or not," expresses a virtually physical sense of pressure forcing the prophetess to speak, as if a despotic God exercises his will through his priestly subject, much as Apollo ruled his "sacred slaves."[16]

The amalgamation of the Christian and the "Phrygian" heritage becomes especially acute in the choice of Pepuza and Tymion as the site of the new

Jerusalem. According to Rev 21:10, the holy Jerusalem will be seen from "a great high mountain." During the second century C.E., the story of Noah became localized in Phrygia and acquired a distinct eschatological element: based on Gen 6:3, Phrygia was considered the site of the holy mountain Ararat, where the 120 years of atonement would come to an end, and where a new generation would arise at the end of the days (*Sib. Or.* 1.196–97 and 261–62). Indeed, if Christ's death is assumed to have occurred in ca. 30 C.E., it is no wonder that the decades after 150 C.E. witnessed an intensified eschatological revival in Phrygia, precisely in the mountains "between" Pepuza and Tymion.[17]

Montanism's rapid spread from its heartland to Rome and from there throughout the Roman Empire, to North Africa in particular, was aided by the fact that, for all its local "color," Montanism touched upon issues then at the core of inner-Christian debates. What was the role of prophecies? What leadership roles should women occupy? What importance should be attributed to chastity? What was the nature of baptism? When should Easter be celebrated? How to account for the delay of eschatological expectations? How should local centers and their indigenous form of Christianity respond to broader, Greco-Roman tendencies in Christianity's development? The answers to these questions are complex and at the same time indicative of the intentions of those attempting to provide them, both in antiquity and within modern scholarship.

Protestant scholarship, here most prominently represented by A. von Harnack, has on the whole interpreted Montanism as representing a distant golden age of vibrant prophecy, forced into demise as the direct consequence of the development of canonical theology. This and similar interpretations convince by their internal logic but overlook the complexity of the sources, since "one continued to proclaim in theory the importance of prophecy,"[18] so that the reasons for its actual decline had to be sought elsewhere, for example, in the simultaneous shift within the ecclesiastical organization from communal authority to the monepiscopacy. In that context, an erratic, "frenzied," ecstatic style of leadership was no longer acceptable. Therefore, prophetic charisma was subsumed into the episcopal charisma and thus lost its individual standing. According to this view, Montanism represents a conservative movement, stymied by its adherence to an earlier model of institutional development.[19]

Feminist theories discussing the movement's demise derive from essentially the same premise: ecclesiastical hostility was a reaction to the preponderance of women in the movement. Women, like prophets, and especially prophetic women, could easily undermine the strengthening patriarchal hierarchy and thus had to be suppressed. The leadership of women in the movement is undeniable, as is its controversial nature. Yet this must not lead us to oversimplify its demise as a mere result of ecclesiastical misogyny. What marks the early Montanist movement is its egalitarianism: both women and men were engaged in its leadership; a nongendered hierarchical distribution based on the notion that the prophet and therefore her gender are incidental to the prophecy; the prophet is the mere mouthpiece of God's message.

Therefore, the rise and demise of the women within the movement must be seen as an intrinsic part of its fate as a whole: the strong imprint of the local, "pagan" religious matrix with its female priests favored charismatic, prophetic leadership, which in turn responded well to the loosely structured community of the adherents.[20] All these factors then combined to pressure Montanism with its men and women prophets and their subjective rendering of Christianity—"having assumed the form of a woman," she says,"Christ came to me"— into heresy.

NOTES

1. M. Foucault, *The History of Sexuality* (New York: Pantheon, 1978), 1:92–93; M. Douglas, *How Institutions Think* (Syracuse: Syracuse University Press, 1986), 69.

2. E. K. Sedgwick, *Epistemology of the Closet* (Berkeley: University of California Press, 1990), 8.

3. C. Walker Bynum, *Fragmentation and Redemption: Essays on Gender and the Human Body in Medieval Religion* (New York: Zone Books, 1991), 18–19.

4. H. Kraft, "Die altkirchliche Prophetie und die Entstehung des Montanismus," *Theologische Zeitschrift* 11 (1955): 249; K. Aland, "Bemerkungen zum Montanismus und zur frühchristlichen Eschatologie," in *Kirchengeschichtliche Entwürfe* (Gütersloh: Mohn, 1960), 149–61.

5. Aland, *Kirchengeschichtliche Entwürfe*, 164; A. Strobel, *Das heilige Land der Montanisten: Eine religionsgeographische Untersuchung* (Religionsgeschichtliche Versuche und Vorarbeiten 37; Berlin: de Gruyter, 1980), 10–29, 49–59.

6. Quoted according to R. E. Heine, *The Montanist Oracles and Testimonia* (Patristic Monograph Series 14; Macon, GA: Mercer University Press, 1989), 2–9; Aland, *Kirchengeschichtliche Entwürfe*, 143–48; Strobel, *Das heilige Land*, 65–221.

7. Aland, *Kirchengeschichtliche Entwürfe*, 118.

8. Strobel, *Das heilige Land*, 99.

9. Ibid., 244–47.

10. Heine, *Montanist*, 4–5.

11. Aland, *Kirchengeschichtliche Entwürfe*, 111–12.

12. Ibid., 127–32; Kraft, "Die altkirchliche Prophetie," 250–57.

13. Kraft, "Die altkirchliche Prophetie," 255–57.

14. Strobel, *Das heilige Land*, 60.

15. Ibid., 34–49, 230, 241, 267–77; R. Shepard Kraemer, *Her Share of the Blessings: Women's Religions among Pagans, Jews and Christians in the Graeco-Roman World* (New York: Oxford University Press, 1992), 157–90.

16. Strobel, *Das heilige Land*, 247–67, 277–84.

17. Kraft, "Die altkirchliche Prophetie," 249–50, 260; Strobel, *Das heilige Land*, 163–64, 288–91.

18. P. de Labriolle, *La crise Montaniste* (Paris: Leroux, 1913), 562.

19. L. Ash, "The Decline of Ecstatic Prophecy in the Early Church," *Theological Studies* 37 (1976): 227, 248–52; Kraft, "Die altkirchliche Prophetie," 266–71.
20. Kraemer, *Her Share of the Blessings,* 128–56, 174–208.

RECOMMENDED READINGS

Aland, K. "Bemerkungen zum Montanismus und zur frühchristlichen Eschatologie." In *Kirchengeschichtliche Entwürfe,* 105–48, 149–64. Gütersloh: Mohn, 1960.

Ash, L. "The Decline of Ecstatic Prophecy in the Early Church." *Theological Studies* 37 (1976): 227–52.

Bynum, C. Walker. *Fragmentation and Redemption: Essays on Gender and the Human Body in Medieval Religion.* New York: Zone Books, 1991.

Douglas, M. *How Institutions Think.* Syracuse: Syracuse University Press, 1986.

Foucault, M. *The History of Sexuality:* Volume 1, *An Introduction,* trans. R. Hurley. New York: Pantheon, 1978.

Heine, R. E. *The Montanist Oracles and Testimonia.* Patristic Monograph Series 14. Macon, GA: Mercer University Press, 1989.

Klawiter, F. C. "The Role of Martyrdom and Persecution in Developing the Priestly Authority of Women in Early Christianity: A Case Study of Montanism." *Church History* 49 (1980): 251–61.

Kraemer, R. Shepard. *Her Share of the Blessings: Women's Religions among Pagans, Jews and Christians in the Graeco-Roman World.* New York: Oxford University Press, 1992.

Kraft, H. "Die altkirchliche Prophetie und die Entstehung des Montanismus." *Theologische Zeitschrift* 11 (1955): 249–71.

Labriolle, P. de. *La crise Montaniste.* Paris: Leroux, 1913.

Sedgwick, E. K. *Epistemology of the Closet.* Berkeley: University of California Press, 1990.

Strobel, A. *Das heilige Land der Montanisten: Eine religionsgeographische Untersuchung.* Religionsgeschichtliche Versuche und Vorarbeiten 37. Berlin: de Gruyter, 1980.

The Daughters of Job

REBECCA LESSES ◆

INTRODUCTION

THE DAUGHTERS OF JOB is of particular interest to feminist scholars and researchers of Jewish women's history because of the clear ascription of mystical powers and insight to women. In this commentary I examine it as part of the process of reconstructing Jewish historical memory from a feminist perspective. Judith Plaskow defines one of the tasks of Jewish feminist historians as "surfacing forgotten processes and events, nameless persons and discarded sources."[1] The *Daughters of Job*, comprising chapters 46–53 of the *Testament of Job* (*T. Job*), is certainly a "discarded source" for Jewish history. It, like the other pseudepigrapha, was preserved by Christians, although written by Jews (see the section below on "Women's Leadership").[2] It belongs to the heritage of Greek-speaking Judaism, which was largely lost to later Jewish history with the ascendancy of the rabbinic tradition. Part of my purpose in writing this commentary is to show how "non-normative" Jewish sources can be used to reveal aspects of Jewish women's lives in antiquity that have otherwise been lost. This is a part of the larger Jewish feminist project articulated by Judith Plaskow of opening up the canon of Torah to encompass works not traditionally drawn upon for Jewish historical memory.[3]

As a Jewish feminist, I present this study within the context of a feminist commentary on early Christian works and related writings about women. My audience includes not only those concerned with the reconstruction of Jewish women's history but also those for whom the Christian Testament is a witness to their faith and to early Christian women's history. Given this dual audience, I am concerned that my commentary not contribute to anti-Jewish attitudes by supporting the idea that Jesus came to liberate women from the sexism of first-century Jewish society.[4] Inasmuch as the Christian movement began in the Jewish community of first-century Israel and then continued in Jewish communities in the Roman Empire, as well as expanding into non-Jewish communities, it is not correct to refer to first-century Judaism as the "background" for Christianity. Rather, first-century Christianity is one of several Jewish movements. Therefore, if Christian feminists discern "liberating" aspects of Jesus' message or of the early Christian message, this may be due to egalitarian tendencies within the various Jewish communities. This aspect cannot be used to separate "Jesus the feminist" from his "Jewish background" (a problematic proposal in any case, since Jesus was a Jew and Judaism was not part of his "background" but was an integral part of his life).

In this commentary I will explore two groups of questions. The first group is literary: What is the relation of the *Daughters of Job* to the rest of *T. Job?* Is it an integral part, or an independent work, and what are the implications in either case? What image of women and women's capacities does the *Daughters of Job* present, in possible contrast to the first part of *T. Job?* The second group of questions flows from these literary considerations: How does this work provide evidence for a type of Judaism in which it was thinkable that women could engage in mystical practices? How does it compare in this respect with other testamentary literature, particularly the *Testaments of the Twelve Patriarchs?* Does other literature with similar interests shed light on this question, such as the apocalyptic literature, *Joseph and Aseneth*, the Qumran literature, Philo's account of the Therapeutics, the Christian Testament, and, going farther afield, the Hekhalot literature?

CONTENTS OF THE TESTAMENT OF JOB

Chapters 1–45 of *T. Job* concentrate on the character of Job, in the form of an extensive development of chapters 1–2 of the Septuagint version of the book of Job. The last section leaves Job almost entirely behind and focuses on Hemera, Kasia, and Amaltheia's Horn (the three daughters born to Job and Dinah, his second wife)[5] and on the heavenly inheritance Job bequeaths to them. Chapters 1–45, spoken in the first person by Job, describe Job's contest with Satan (which Job, depicted as the king of Egypt, initiates because he destroys a temple dedicated to Satan), in which Job is ultimately victorious (chaps. 1–27) and Job's encounter with his friends (also depicted as kings, chaps. 28–45), in which he convinces the kings that he has been vindicated by God and that "[his] throne is in the upper world" (33:3).[6]

In chapter 46, Job's first-person testament turns to a third-person account of the daughters' inheritance. As Job is about to die, he distributes his estate to his sons. His daughters step forward and ask, "Our father, sir, are we not also your children? Why then did you not give us some of your goods?" (46:2). Job replies that they will receive an inheritance "better than that of your seven brothers" (46:4). Their inheritance consists of three shimmering cords, laid away in golden boxes, the same cords God gave Job to heal him from his afflictions (47:4–9). Job refers to them as a "protective amulet" (*phylaktērion*), a term replete with magical associations. When each woman puts them on in turn, she receives "another heart—no longer minded toward earthly things" (48:2) and is able to speak in one of the angelic languages in praise of God. Hemera speaks in the "angelic dialect" (48:3); Kasia speaks in the "dialect of the archons" and praises God for the "creation of the heights" (49:2); and Amaltheia's Horn speaks in the "dialect of those on high, . . . in the dialect of the cherubim" (50:2). Each woman's hymns are recorded: Kasia's in the "Hymns of Kasia" (49:3), Amaltheia's Horn's in the "Prayers of Amaltheia's Horn" (50:3), and in addition Nereus, Job's brother, writes down the hymns that each woman spoke (51:4). Not only do the cords enable them to participate in the heavenly liturgy in praise of God; they also bestow heavenly sight on the women. When Job is about to die, the three women are able to see "the gleaming chariots which had come for his soul" (52:6), which others cannot see. They see the one who sits in the great chariot descend and greet Job (52:8). He takes Job's soul, embraces it, mounts the chariot, and sets off for the east, while the three women sing hymns to God as Job's body is taken to the tomb (52:10–12).

STRUCTURE

The image of women in the two main sections of the book is strikingly different. In the first part, Job's first wife, Sitis, is well-meaning but lacks perception of the true state of affairs. The first part of *T. Job* praises women as wives and mothers but has a low opinion of their spiritual capabilities;[7] however, in chapters 46–53 Hemera, Kasia, and Amaltheia's Horn overshadow Job.[8] The three women do not remain in the status of the spiritually unperceptive; on the contrary, they gain access to heavenly realities that even the kings in the first part of *T. Job* are not able to see.

Because of the shifting image of women, and because Job's first-person testament ends abruptly at 45:3 and becomes a third-person account of the distribution of his estate, several scholars have questioned the unity of *T. Job*. M. R. James argues that chapters 46–53 are an addition made by the Christian paraphraser who translated *T. Job* from Hebrew to Greek and added the hymns; R. Spittler suggests a Montanist redaction; and P. W. van der Horst says that the differences in the book may be due to various aggadic traditions about Job and his family.[9] Against them, John J. Collins argues for the unity of the book. In chapters 1–45, Job's opposition first to Satan and then to the kings has been resolved, while his opposition to women has not been. These chapters serve to resolve the opposition between Job and the women in the rest of the book. The mystical and apocalyptic elements of chapters 46–53 are also congruent with chapters 1–45.[10] Susan Garrett also argues for the unity of the book: "In both parts of the document, women are those whose hearts are naturally preoccupied with 'earthly affairs.'" In her opinion, "Job's second set of daughters do not display such preoccupation with earthly affairs—but only because they have been given 'different' or 'changed' hearts." Only an external intervention (Job's gift) changes their nature.[11]

Whether or not chapters 46–53 come from a source or author different from the source or author of chapters 1–45, chapters 46–53 present a portrait of women significantly different from that of the first part of the book. For this reason alone, it is useful to examine these chapters separately to see what the author considered the possible capabilities of women. If the sections do come from different sources or authors, then it is obviously appropriate to consider them separately. If, however, chapters 46–53 are an integral part of *T. Job,* this raises the question of why the image of women changes so radically from the first part to the second part. Is the author of *T. Job* trying to make a particular point? Since there is no unequivocal evidence for the unity or disunity of *T. Job,* in the rest of this article I will focus on chapters 46–53, being conscious of the differing questions raised by the different hypotheses on the unity of the work.

CONTEXT OF THE DAUGHTERS OF JOB

Originally I wanted to consider the question of what group might have written *Daughters of Job* and whether the work could be considered evidence for Jewish women's involvement in mysticism. It is not, however, a treatise by or about a particular group (unlike Philo's account of the Therapeutics),[12] but a kind of midrash about Job's daughters, based on the biblical text. In addition, *T. Job* as a whole presents itself as Job's testament; as in the other pseudepigrapha, the author(s) hide(s) behind the name of a biblical character. Thus, it is very difficult to go beyond the text to find out who actually wrote it and whether it describes actual practices. Instead, by placing *Daughters of Job* in the context of the other testamentary literature, other literature that discusses contact with the heavenly realm, and the inscriptional evidence for Jewish women's leadership, I will consider what message and possibilities this work presents for women.

JOSEPH AND ASENETH

Joseph and Aseneth strikingly presents Aseneth as a woman whose contacts with the heavenly realm are even more extensive than those of the daughters of Job in *T. Job*. Aseneth is the virgin daughter of Pentephres, priest of Heliopolis, and fervent follower of the Egyptian gods. Her father proposes to give her in marriage to Joseph; she refuses initially because he is a follower of a false god. Eventually she is won over by the vision of Joseph's beauty and holiness. After her first meeting with him, she secludes herself in her tower (where she usually lives, shunning all contact with men) and repents of her idolatry in sackcloth and ashes for seven days. After her fervent prayers to God, a "man" descends to her from heaven (14:3). He is "chief of the house of the Lord and commander of the whole host of the Most High" (14:8). He feeds her from the honeycomb that the bees of paradise make, the food that the angels, the chosen of God, and the sons of the Most High eat (16:14–15). The man renames her "City of Refuge," because in her many nations will take refuge in God (15:7). Her contact with the "chief of the house of the Lord" brings her immortality (16:16). She has become equal to Joseph in holiness, and after the man from heaven leaves, she marries Joseph. Like the daughters of Job, Aseneth undergoes a transformation: in her case, from worshiper of the Egyptian gods to repentant proselyte. But her contact with heavenly realities does not preclude participation in earthly reality (her marriage to Joseph). The dualism between "heavenly" and "earthly" realities does not seem nearly so strong in *Joseph and Aseneth* as in *T. Job*.

TESTAMENTS OF THE TWELVE PATRIARCHS

Although *T. Job* as a whole is closest in genre to the other Jewish testaments,[13] its message about women is very different from theirs. The other testaments say that women are evil (*T. Reuben* 5:1); they warn men to be wary of women (*T. Reuben* 3:10; *T. Judah* 17:1); and they tell men to avoid promiscuity with women (*T. Reuben* 4:6; *T. Judah* 14:2). Women rule over both kings and poor men (*T. Judah* 15:5). In contrast to these depictions, even in the first part of *T. Job* the various women characters are, at the most, spiritually unperceptive, while Job's daughters are capable of communication with the divine realm—a capability that only men possess in the other testaments. For example, in *T. Levi* 2:5–12, Levi has a vision of heaven, and in 5:1 he sees God on the divine throne. These differences point to the presence of at least two strands of thought in early Judaism: one that thought only men capable of communication with heaven, and another in which both women and men could have connection with the divine realm.

WOMEN'S LEADERSHIP

Inscriptional evidence shows that women in several locations held positions of authority in the synagogue. Women held the titles of "head of the synagogue," "leader," "elder," "mother of the synagogue," and "priest."[14] There is some evidence to indicate that Asia Minor may have been a particularly hospitable location for Jewish women's religious leadership.[15] See, for example, the evidence of the Aphrodisias inscription (third century C.E.), where Iael is referred to as the *prostatēs* (president/patron) of the soup kitchen sponsored by the group of the scholars of the law.[16] The *Daughters of Job* should be placed within this context of Jewish women's religious leadership. The inscriptions provide evidence for women's involvement in institutional leadership, while the *Daughters of Job* shows a way of thinking that values women's prophetic or ecstatic activity and leadership.

Although the inscriptions do not refer to female prophetic or ecstatic activity, the Christian Testament does give evidence for women's ecstatic prophecy in early Christianity and uses language very reminiscent of the *Daughters of Job*. Chapters 11–14 of 1 Corinthians refer to the prophecy of both women and men,[17] and Paul discusses women's prophecy with the stipulation that women should cover their heads, "because of the angels" (1 Cor 11:10). 1 Cor 12:10 mentions prophecy, speaking in tongues, and the interpretation of tongues as several of the gifts of the spirit; 1 Cor 13:1 refers to the "tongues of angels;" and much of chapter 14 is taken up with Paul's rules for those who speak in tongues. The phrase "because of the angels" seems to refer to the belief that the angels were present in the congregation during worship,[18] when both women and men spoke in the "tongues of angels." Compare *Daughters of Job:* Hemera "spoke ecstatically in the angelic dialect, sending up a hymn to God in accord with the hymnic style of the angels" (*T. Job* 48:3). Despite these similarities, I do not suggest that *Daughters of Job* was produced by the group of ecstatic Christians in Corinth, because *Daughters of Job* is clearly a Jewish work.[19] There is no mention of Christ or use of explicitly Christian terminology. I bring this comparison from an early Christian group still close to Judaism because it exhibits the same willingness to contemplate women's ecstatic activity as *Daughters of Job* does.

The Therapeutics, an ascetic Egyptian Jewish group composed of women and men who withdrew from the world and engaged in contemplation, have often been cited as a possible origin for the *Testament of Job* because of the involvement of women (Therapeutrides) as well as men (Therapeutae) in the group.[20] In this community, according to Philo, women and men live alone in individual houses. During the six days of the week, each one prays and studies scriptures with allegorical interpretation and composes hymns and psalms to God. On every sabbath they gather together, men and women sitting apart in one room, and hear a discourse from the (male) senior among them. Once a year they come together for the great feast of Shavuot, or Pentecost. Philo refers to the women as "aged virgins" who have remained unmarried and without children because of their "ardent yearning for wisdom," whom they are "eager to have for their life mate." At this banquet the leader of the group discourses on the scriptures and sings a hymn to God, either one of his own composition or one written by the earlier poets. Then each member sings in turn, with other members joining in for the refrain. After the supper, they rise in two choirs, one of women and one of men, and "sing hymns to God," sometimes together and sometimes antiphonally, dancing as they sing. Then they join in one choir, like the choir of women and men led by Miriam and Moses who sang to God at the Red Sea, and sing together all night.[21]

The obvious points of comparison between *T. Job* and the Therapeutics are the composition of hymns and psalms to God and the ecstatic hymn-singing of the Therapeutrides and Therapeutae on the night of Shavuot. However, while the three women in *T. Job* learn the various languages of the angels and praise God in these languages, the hymn composition of the Therapeutics seems to be a more sober activity. Philo says, "They also compose hymns and psalms to God" in addition to contemplation.[22] He mentions nothing about the "hymnody of the angels" or the "language of the cherubim." As additional evidence against the hypothesis of Therapeutic origins, van der Horst points out that whereas among the Therapeutics only men lead the community and expound scripture in public, the *Daughters of Job* does not rule out women's participation in any activity. In *T. Job* only the three women see the chariots coming for Job's soul, and they lead the mourners in his burial procession (*T. Job* 52). *Testament of Job* as a whole does not promote asceticism, whereas the Therapeutics led a very ascetic life.[23] Although the question of Therapeutic origin of *T. Job* is open, Philo's account of the type of spirituality available to both women and men among them is evidence for a strand of Judaism in which both women and men are concerned with prayer, contemplation, and ecstatic song and dance. Philo may not refer to angelic speech as *T. Job* does, but both his account and *T. Job* provide evidence for female as well as male concern for spiritual realities.

APOCALYPTIC, HEKHALOT, AND QUMRAN LITERATURES

These three bodies of literature share with *Daughters of Job* a concern for the divine realm and human connection to it. Like Abraham in *Apocalypse of Abraham* 17, Isaiah in *Martyrdom of Isaiah* 8:17 and 9:33, and Zephaniah in *Apocalypse of Zephaniah* 8, Kasia, Hemera, and Amaltheia's Horn learn the heavenly liturgy and chant it with the angels. Then the women put on Job's cords themselves and partake in the liturgy while still on earth (although with their minds on heaven), whereas the apocalyptic figures are brought to heaven by an angel and there learn the angelic song. The voluntary quality of the women's experience is shared by the adepts described in the Hekhalot literature, who are not brought to heaven by angels but rather seek to ascend themselves.[24] These Jewish mystical texts from the fourth to eighth centuries C.E.

give instructions for heavenly ascents and adjurations of angels. As in *Daughters of Job,* there is emphasis on learning and recording the angelic hymns; many of the pages of these texts are taken up with the hymns the angels sing in their daily service of God. Sometimes learning the hymns is cited as one means of making the ascent to heaven;[25] however, the Hekhalot texts explicitly allow only men to take part in the ascents and adjurations.[26]

Participation in the heavenly liturgy while still on earth is important in several of the Qumran texts, and in fact seems to have been a central feature of worship at Qumran.[27] Although both *Daughters of Job* and the Qumran texts share a vivid sense of "being in heaven" while still on earth, the experience described in the Qumran texts was available only to men who wanted to live in the same cultic purity as the priests of the Jerusalem Temple. In contrast, in *T. Job* as a whole both men and women could be "minded towards heaven," and in *Daughters of Job* in particular, women were especially singled out for their connection with heaven and the angels.

CONCLUSIONS

The type of Judaism espoused in *Daughters of Job* is "heavenly-minded" and is concerned with participation in the angelic worship. It shares these characteristics with the apocalyptic literature, the Hekhalot texts, and the Qumran documents, but none of those texts specifies that a connection with heaven is available to women. The texts that seem closest are *Joseph and Aseneth,* 1 Corinthians, and Philo's description of the Therapeutics. Unlike 1 Corinthians and Philo's account, which either refer to an actual community or purport to, *Daughters of Job* does not pretend to describe a particular community. Because of the particular form (midrashic and pseudepigraphic) of *Daughters of Job,* it seems impossible to go behind the text and postulate a community that might have produced it. However, *Daughters of Job, Joseph and Aseneth,* and several other sources present the possibility (and in some places, the actuality) of women's ecstatic communion with the divine, in contrast to those that present this as available only to men. The author of *Daughters of Job,* like those responsible for the other documents discussed here, believes that the supremely holy heavenly world, containing the angels and the divine throne, is available to human beings, either through participating in the divine liturgy on earth (the Corinthians, the men of Qumran, *Daughters of Job*), the descent of angels to earth (*Joseph and Aseneth,* the Hekhalot literature) or by ascending to heaven (the apocalyptic literature, the Hekhalot literature). They differ on who is allowed to have this access. *Daughters of Job* (along with *Joseph and Aseneth,* 1 Corinthians, and *On the Contemplative Life*) provides evidence that some groups thought that this access was available to both women and men. While the testamentary literature describes women as evil temptresses, the opposite of the pure men (like Levi) who can ascend to heaven and see visions, *Daughters of Job* describes only women as seeing visions and participating in the angelic liturgy, and *T. Job* as a whole speaks of both female and male involvement in heavenly life (see *T. Job* 33).

The difference between *Daughters of Job, Joseph and Aseneth, On the Contemplative Life,* and those works that deny the possibility of women's access to divine realities may stem from their differing views of women's ability to attain to the purity necessary for human contact with the divine. The other testamentary literature denies that women can reach such purity. Both *Joseph and Aseneth* and *De Vita* state that such purity is possible for virgins, while *Daughters of Job* does not deal with the question explicitly. Such a view is not necessarily feminist in the modern sense of the word, but it leaves open the possibility of women's intimate contact with divine realities in a way closed off by the testamentary literature, the apocalyptic works, or the Hekhalot texts.[38] It is hoped that exploring one document that presents contact with heaven as a possibility for women will contribute to the discovery of other strands in early Judaism and will help to break down the monolithic picture of a patriarchal Judaism that results from reading androcentric texts such as the Mishna with an uncritical eye.[39]

NOTES

1. Judith Plaskow, *Standing Again at Sinai: Judaism from a Feminist Perspective* (New York: HarperCollins, 1990), 35.

2. Russell Spittler, ed. and trans., *Testament of Job,* in *The Old Testament Pseudepigrapha,* ed. J. H. Charlesworth (Garden City, NY: Doubleday, 1983), 1:830; and P. W. van der Horst, "Images of Women in the Testament of Job," in *Studies on the Testament of Job,* ed. Michael A. Knibb and P. W. van der Horst (Cambridge: Cambridge University Press, 1989), 109.

3. For a longer discussion of these issues, see Plaskow, *Standing Again at Sinai,* chapter 2.

4. See Adele Reinhartz, "From Narrative to History: The Resurrection of Mary and Martha," in *"Women Like This": New Perspectives on Jewish Women in the Greco-Roman World,* ed. Amy-Jill Levine (Atlanta: Scholars Press, 1991), 183.

5. In the biblical book of Job, Job's three daughters are named Jemimah (Dove), Keziah (Cinnamon), and Keren-happuch (Horn of Kohl, a type of eye shadow). See Marvin Pope, *The Book of Job* (Anchor Bible; Garden City, NY: Doubleday, 1973), 352-53 for more explanation of the Hebrew names. In the Septuagint, these names became Hemera ("Day" in Greek, a play on the first syllable of Jemimah, which means "day" in Hebrew), Kasia (the same word as the Hebrew, meaning the same thing), and Amaltheia's Horn. The last name is a play only on the first part of the Hebrew name. It refers to the "legendary horn of plenty (*cornucopia*) ascribed in Greek mythology to the broken horn of the she-goat who nursed Zeus" (Spittler, "Testament of Job," in *Old Testament Pseudepigrapha,* 1:838).

6. Unless otherwise noted, all translations of *T. Job* are from Spittler, "Testament of Job."

7. Van der Horst, "Images," 101.

8. John J. Collins, "Structure and Meaning in the Testament of Job," in *Society of Biblical Literature 1974 Seminar Papers,* ed. G. W. MacRae (Missoula, MT: Scholars Press, 1974), 44.

9. M. R. James, ed., *Apocrypha Anecdota,* 2nd Series (Cambridge: Cambridge University Press, 1897), xcvi; R. Spittler, "The Testament of Job: Introduction, Translation and Notes" (Ph.D. diss., HarvardUniversity, 1971), 58-59; van der Horst, "Images," 107.

10. Collins, "Structure and Meaning," 48.

11. Susan Garrett, "The 'Weaker Sex' in the *Testament of Job,"Journal of Biblical Literature* 112 (1993): 54.

12. Philo, *De Vita Contemplativa,* trans. F. H. Colson (Loeb Classical Library; Cambridge, MA: Harvard University Press; London: Heinemann, 1941).

13. Spittler, *"Testament of Job,"*in *Old Testament Pseudepigrapha,* 1:831-32.

14. Bernadette J. Brooten, *Women Leaders in the Ancient Synagogue: Inscriptional Evidence and Background Issues* (Brown Judaic Studies 36; Chico, CA: Scholars Press, 1982), 1-5.

15. Paul Trebilco, *Jewish Communities in Asia Minor* (Cambridge: Cambridge University Press, 1991), chapter 5.

16. Bernadette J. Brooten, "The Gender of Iael in the Jewish Inscription from Aphrodisias," in *Of Scribes and Scrolls,* ed. Harold Attridge, J. J. Collins, and T. H. Tobin (Lanham, MD: University Press of America, 1990), 165-66; and eadem, "Iael *Prostatēs* in the Jewish Donative Inscription from Aphrodisias," in *The Future of Early Christianity: Essays in Honor of Helmut Koester,* ed. B. A. Pearson (Minneapolis: Fortress, 1991), 153-56.

17. Elisabeth Schüssler Fiorenza, *In Memory of Her: A Feminist Theological Reconstruction of Christian Origins* (New York: Crossroad, 1983), 45.

18. J. A. Fitzmyer, "A Feature of Qumran Angelology and the Angels of 1 Cor. XI. 10," *New Testament Studies* 4 (1957-58): 55-57.

19. Van der Horst, "Images," 109. See, however, Spittler's arguments that *T. Job* was redacted by Montanists in the second century who added the section on the daughters of Job to justify the female prophets of the New Prophecy (*"Testament of Job,"* in *Old Testament Pseudepigrapha,* 1.834).

20. See Spittler's survey of theories on the provenance of the *Testament of Job* (*"Testament of Job,"* in *Old Testament Pseudepigrapha,* 1:833-34).

21. The descriptions in this paragraph are from Philo, *On the Contemplative Life* 29, 30–33, 68, 75, 80, 84, 87.

22. Ibid. 29.

23. Van der Horst, "Images," 115.

24. The term "Hekhalot" refers to the heavenly palaces to which the adepts journey.

25. *Synopse zur Hekhalot-Literatur,* ed. Peter Schäfer (Tübingen: Mohr-Siebeck, 1981), 81, 94, and 557. For further discussion, see Martha Himmelfarb, "Heavenly Ascent and the Relationship of the Apocalypses and the Hekhalot Literature," *Hebrew Union College Annual* 59 (1988): 73-100.

26. *Synopse,* 623,684.

27. Carol Newsom, *Songs of the Sabbath Sacrifice: A Critical Edition* (Atlanta: Scholars Press, 1985), 17.

28. Ross Kraemer, "Monastic Jewish Women in Greco-Roman Egypt: Philo Judaeus on the Therapeutrides," *Signs* 14 (1989): 342–70. See Garrett, "Weaker Sex," esp. p. 70, for a more negative view of *Testament of Job.*

29. See Schüssler Fiorenza, *"In Memory of Her,* 59.

BIBLIOGRAPHY

Brock, S.P. *Testamentum Iobi,* and J. C. Picard, *Apocalypsis Baruchi graece.* PVTG 2. Leiden: Brill, 1967.

Brooten, Bernadette J. *Women Leaders in the Ancient Synagogue: Inscriptional Evidence and Background Issues.* Brown Judaic Studies 36. Chico, CA: Scholars Press, 1982.

Garrett, Susan. "The 'Weaker Sex' in the Testament of Job." *Journal of Biblical Literature* 112 (1993): 55–70.

Himmelfarb, Martha. "Heavenly Ascent and the Relationship of the Apocalypses and the *Hekhalot* Literature." *Hebrew Union College Annual* 59 (1988): 73–100.

Knibb, Michael, and Pieter W. van der Horst, eds. *Studies on the Testament of Job.* Cambridge: Cambridge University Press, 1989.

Kraemer, Ross. "Monastic Jewish Women in Greco-Roman Egypt: Philo Judaeus on the Therapeutrides." *Signs* 14 (1989): 342–70.

Kraft, Robert, et al., eds. *The Testament of Job according to the SV Text: Greek Text and English Translation.* Missoula, MT: Scholars Press and Society of Biblical Literature, 1974.

Levine, Amy-Jill, ed. *"Women Like This": New Perspectives on Jewish Women in the Greco-Roman World.* Early Judaism and Its Literature 1. Atlanta: Scholars Press, 1991.

Plaskow, Judith. *Standing Again at Sinai: Judaism from a Feminist Perspective.* New York: HarperCollins, 1990.

Schäfer, Peter. "The Aim and Purpose of Early Jewish Mysticism." In Peter Schäfer, *Hekhalot-Studien,* 277–95. Tübingen: Mohr-Siebeck, 1988.

Spittler, Russell, ed. and trans. *"Testament of Job."* In *The Old Testament Pseudepigrapha,* edited by James H. Charlesworth, vol. 1. Garden City, NY: Doubleday, 1983.

Trebilco, Paul. *Jewish Communities in Asia Minor.* Cambridge: Cambridge University Press, 1991.

PART TWO

Epistolary Discourses: Submerged Traditions of Sophia

1 Corinthians
2 Corinthians
Galatians
Philippians
1 Thessalonians
2 Thessalonians
Romans
Philemon
Colossians
Ephesians
1 Peter
The Pastoral Epistles
James
Jude
2 Peter
The Johannine Epistles
Hebrews

1 Corinthians

Antoinette Wire ◆

INTRODUCTION

Corinth's Setting, History, and Social Structure

Situated on a rocky northwest promontory of the Peloponnesus, Corinth compensated for small agricultural output by trading in other people's produce, which moved on the isthmus to mainland Greece and on wooden tracks across it that carried sea cargo from the East to Rome. The ancient geographers Strabo and Pausanius offer delightful walking tours around the docks and the roads to Corinth and its forum, where crafts such as Paul's tents were made and sold, temples of Hera, Apollo, and Athena were visited, meat was sacrificed to sell, and springwater baths were taken.[1] Visible across the gulf to the north were Mount Parnassus and Delphi, where the Pythian priestess still sat on the tripod. A recent inscription there honored the victories of three sisters in the two hundred meter and war-chariot races of the Isthmian games near Corinth.

But Strabo's "thousand temple-slave prostitutes" at the temple of Aphrodite on Corinth's acropolis were in Paul's time a thing of the past. Old Corinth, an ancient independent city of Greece, had led the Achaean League against Rome's advance into Greece and, in 146 B.C.E., was burned to the ground, its men killed and women and children enslaved. Not until one hundred years later was it rebuilt by Julius Caesar as a Roman colony with strictly Roman citizenship and city government, settled by Roman freedmen and their households. The Roman historian Dio Cassius speaks of "such prosperity that they used to say if they had not been captured they could not have been saved."[2] But the Roman eye would not have the vision of the heirs of old Corinth, possibly including a colony of Jews attested in the nearby city of Sicyon in Corinth's absent century (1 Macc 15:23).[3] Imagine yourself as a child sleeping in a fine house, knowing that your stepfather killed the sister who used to sleep in your bed.

We meet the religious memory of Corinth's violation in Pausanius's tales about its sites. Glauce's well brings on the story of a mourning ritual of old Corinth in which all the children cut their hair and wailed in black to ward off revenge for the deaths of Medea's children. Medea, who had been abandoned by Jason for Glauce, sent Jason's sons to Corinth with a dress for Glauce that set her on fire. She jumped into a well to her death, and the boys were killed. Though the new settlers had discontinued this ritual, which mourned innocent death and harsh revenge, people could still visit in Poseidon's temple on the isthmus the crypt dedicated to the god Palemon. Drowned as a child with his mother Ino when she fled her husband into the sea, he was raised up and brought to his shrine on a dolphin by his mother, who had become the foam goddess Leucothea.[4] Reared on such stories by their mothers and nurses, Corinthian survivors could not have forgotten their own violation.[5] They would be ready to hear about the man crucified by a Roman governor, the man whom the women met on the road.

When Rome destroyed and rebuilt Corinth—and Carthage at the same time—it confirmed its political and economic control over the Mediterranean world. The first century B.C.E. was also the turning point in Rome's political life from an overgrown citizen-ruled city to an empire ruled by one man through his slaves, freedmen, and friends. Now everyone had to jockey for influence (even emperors could be assassinated), and influence came to be more and more identified with wealth. In Corinth the struggle for power was intensified by everyone bearing some stigma—the remnant Greek families for their disenfranchisement, most Roman citizens for their slave origins, rich merchants for their lack of education, powerful slave bureaucrats for their caste, women for family subordination, Jews for not honoring the gods. Yet many had some significant privilege, whether Roman citizenship or Greek pedigree or money or political influence or ethnic rights or at least membership in some new religious association.

The key social reality was insecurity, with a few experiencing significant changes in social status. Some who had been more secure in traditional times—such as Roman senators, Stoic popular philosophers, and Jewish communities with rights of self-rule—now had less confidence. Others once without any maneuvering room—freed people, entrepreneurs in crafts or trade, soldiers, and enterprising women—discovered space to move. Paul seems to have been among those tightening their belts after a youth that promised more, whereas many Corinthian Christians found themselves with options that they were not reared to expect. Though resources in the established group remained far greater, the two groups' perceptions of their lives were very different and the best attitudes on both sides could not prevent tensions, especially in small communities that cut across social boundaries as the churches did.

THE DEVELOPMENT OF THE CORINTHIAN CHURCH

When Paul first arrives in Corinth about 50 C.E., Christians may already be meeting in the home of two Jews named Prisca and Aquila, who were recently expelled from Rome after disruptions linked to Christians (Acts 18:1–11; Suetonius, *Claudius* 25.4). Paul's letters show the same couple hosting house-churches later in Ephesus and back in Rome (1 Cor 16:19; Rom 16:3–4). The report from Acts that Paul makes tents in their workshop while he preaches in the Corinthian synagogue suggests that he becomes part of a highly mobile group of female and male missioner-artisans.

In writing 1 Corinthians Paul gives prominence to certain early converts he baptized as households who have homes where the church can meet, and Luke suggests a synagogue ruler among them (1 Cor 1:14–16; 16:15–18; Acts 18:8). If Corinth's church were established among people such as Stephanus, they would not only have brought with them some of the traditional subordination of women, slaves, and children in their households, but also the expectation that the church would function like the synagogue with its own self-rule, welfare, and courts.

But after Paul leaves Corinth he writes them a warning letter (now lost, 5:9), implying that new people and issues have entered the church. Acts, written close to a half-century later, remembers this as the time that a gifted Jewish preacher of Christ named Apollos arrives in Ephesus from Alexandria and is instructed by Prisca and Aquila concerning baptism, after which they send him on to Corinth (Acts 18:24–19:7). If this reflects an early tradition, what Apollos teaches in Corinth may be a view of baptism already known or even recently developed in Corinth and transmitted to him by Prisca and Aquila. At any rate Apollos's preaching in Corinth strengthens a spiritual movement there and the church writes a letter to Paul (7:1). They do not ask him questions but make confident assertions about their Christian life, to which he responds with 1 Corinthians, conceding their claims on principle but calling for compromises in practice (6:12; 7:1; 8:1–7; 10:23; 16:12). At the same time he criticizes their conduct on the basis of oral reports, probably from his Corinthian converts, which project an alarm about recent disorders that he thinks can legitimate his calls for restriction.

Those who come in for the sharpest restrictions are the women prophets. Although not charged with any sexual offenses, they are expected to remarry or marry when men are not able to handle abstinence, in spite of the fact that marriage may disqualify a woman prophet (1 Corinthians 5–7). Paul concludes his warnings on idolatry with challenges to the church itself in matters of dress and meals. In both areas women are implicated, explicitly for not covering their heads while praying and prophesying, and implicitly for what Paul con-

siders disorderly in food service, a traditional female responsibility (chaps.
8–11). Paul's restrictions on prophecy and speaking in tongues at the end of
his discussion of spiritual gifts culminate in the demand that women not speak
in church (chaps. 12–14). Finally, the resurrection witness of women is omitted, both that of the earliest witnesses and, by Paul's sealing off the list with his
own experience, that of the women who prophesy in Corinth (chap. 15).
Though Paul does not choose to identify women who prophesy as the leaders
of the spiritual movement in Corinth, they are the group whose power he is
most persistently destabilizing, and this speaks for itself.

Women are among those in Greek society without education and political
power, but they were in this period beginning to take some semipublic space,
as in Corinth's church, in part because of its home location and in part because of widespread respect for women's prophetic powers. Although the situation in the church is doubtless very complex, a certain polarization of new
leaders and old leaders cannot be ignored. Note that Paul does not sustain his
opening neutral stance. After his final admonition he recommends to the
church the household of Stephanus, accepts them as Corinth's presence with
him, and—apparently entrusting his letter to them—calls on the church to recognize such people (16:15–17).

It is significant for understanding 1 Corinthians that 2 Corinthians shows
that the rift between Paul and the church deepened into a chasm (2 Corinthians 10–12). Yet he no longer singles out his early converts for praise, nor
does he single out women prophets for restriction. Unless we propose an
explosion of the church with an exodus to account for these changes, or full
compliance, which nothing in 2 Corinthians suggests, we must recognize that
his earlier letter and intervening contacts were not successful, either in restoring the first group or in subduing the second. What we see in 2 Corinthians is a
change in strategy. Paul determines to modify the spiritual movement in
Corinth's church not by taking sides but by making himself vulnerable in every
contrary way in order to demonstrate God's power and expose human foolishness. Yet he still does not question whether his particular social experience
in Christ can provide a universal model, and, unless we reorder 2 Corinthians
to make his correspondence with Corinth end in reconciliation, the alienation
remains. At the end of the century the letter *1 Clement,* written to Corinth to
protest the expelling of its church elders, not only demonstrates that Corinthian Christians remain independent but suggests by its choice of arguments
that women remain important leaders (*1 Clement* 1–2; 6; 12–13; 21; 54–56).

A METHOD IN HER MADNESS

I use the word "madness" to pick up on a likely critique of the interpretive
strategy behind my reading of 1 Corinthians. For a text that is of interest

almost exclusively to people who read it as scripture, it may seem suicidal to take an equal interest in major voices in the text other than the voice of the author, especially in a setting where they are in conflict. I do this not to spite the text or its authority in contemporary communities of faith but to recover it as a document with functioning authority. This requires that the issues engaged by the text be again seriously engaged by a full hearing of the contesting voices within their setting and that the authority of these voices be judged in the light of everything the text and our faith teach us to be true.

The problem with canonical texts is that believers tend to confuse the voice of the author with the voice of God. Where unable to accept the author's views, we put Paul or John through contortions to advocate what we believe. If letters arguing to convince people on the basis of many kinds of evidence are read on the assumption that the author's view is authoritative, the reader does not weigh the evidence and therefore cannot be persuaded, either by the author or by opposing voices. But if the text's authority is conceived more broadly as that of the full range of voices which speak through it and challenge the reader to take seriously the claims that are made, then there is the possibility of persuasion and of conviction that has authority. This also allows people who have been alienated from the texts by an idolatrous worship of the author to become reengaged in the contested issues and seek for truth.

It may also be seen as madness to think a reconstruction of these multiple voices possible. The letter from Corinth that Paul is answering is lost, as are any responding letters he received. Other relevant texts are few. An added factor making access difficult is that in imperial Greece probably less than 10 percent of the population read and fewer wrote. Not only were letters in first-century churches dictated and read aloud on arrival, functioning as speeches to hearers (Gal 6:11; 1 Thess 5:27; Col 4:16, 18; Rev 1:3), but the far greater part of communication was face to face or in oral messages. When only one side of a very partially written communication between the Corinthians and their itinerant leaders is accessible, can we possibly hear the interchange including the voices of the very largely nonliterate women?

Lacking record of either the voices that spoke before Paul's voice or the voices that spoke after his voice, we must find the voices speaking within his voice. Because everything Paul says is geared to persuade the Corinthians, the way that he seeks to persuade them in each successive part of his argument can tell us where he thinks they are and what response he anticipates from them. Therefore it is the study of Paul's rhetoric, his means of persuasion, that has the best chance of making possible a hearing of the voices from the Corinthian church, including the voices of women prophets.

The key elements in the study of rhetoric are the speaker, the intended hearers, and the message (also context and code can be treated as distinct factors). The speaker may start a text or a part of it by making him- or herself credible with what is called ethos argumentation, may continue in the body of the text to make the message clear with logos argumentation, and may close by appealing to the hearers in pathos argumentation. It can also be useful to distinguish the forensic rhetoric of the courtroom, which argues what was right or wrong conduct in a past event, from the celebrative (or epideictic) rhetoric of the cult or school, which argues what is worthy of praise and blame in a present attitude, and both of these from the deliberative rhetoric of the council chamber, which argues what will be good or bad conduct in the future. Yet the rhetoric of a letter can incorporate all of these functions without being reduced to any one. Therefore the goal of rhetorical analysis of a letter is not to determine whether speaker, message, or hearers are the prime focus, nor whether its rhetoric is dominated by forensic, celebrative, or deliberative argument, nor how to name and classify all the separate arguments used.

The aim of rhetoric is to read a whole text as persuasion and to understand how at each stage of that persuasion the speaker is drawing on what the hearers accept in an attempt to move them further toward the position or action the speaker is advocating. Of course the argumentative situation is always changing, as previous stages of the discussion influence how later stages will be received. Because arguments develop by a speaker's adapting to a specific audience in order to persuade them, the arguments can be used as a kind of mold to learn the way the intended hearers think and act. The precision of this mold depends not at all on the natural agreement of speaker and hearers but on the knowledge, skill, and motivation of the speaker to persuade, all of which we can gauge to be quite high for Paul in Corinth. Therefore the mold should be good. But it will have to be used with great care because it is the mold of a community and I ask some questions about specific groups in the community such as Paul's first converts and the women prophets. Each part of the mold will therefore have to provide evidence concerning the groups it reflects and what it can yield about them.

Readers cannot evade the task of evaluating what are and are not legitimate ways to argue. Although we should not disparage speakers in advance as manipulative, since it is the intended audience that determines what is persuasive, threats of force or self-fulfilling curses are not in most cases taken as legitimate argument. A key question is what constitutes fair opportunity for counterpersuasion, since speech is the vehicle of argument. This must be worked out on many levels, in the case of this text both to assure the right of people today to answer Paul in spite of certain interpretations of canonical authority and to recover the right that women in Corinth had, and doubtless used, to contest Paul's silencing of them.

As is by now evident, this contribution to feminist interpretation will be an attempt in historical reconstruction done by analysis of a writer's argumentative situation. In this task my own framework for understanding history is the women whose history it is. Christian women have long struggled with the history of the early church in Corinth and have special need to look at it more carefully. Other women and all readers are challenged to consider the uses of this history for themselves and to cultivate what they take as their history. The purpose of this rhetorically based historical reconstruction is both to expose the text where it is an instrument of oppression and to begin to recover the text as evidence of the social, theological, and liturgical leadership of certain early Christians, particularly of one group of early Christian women.

COMMENTARY

PAUL'S SELF-PRESENTATION (1:1–4:21)

Blessing and Thanksgiving (1:1–9)

Following Paul's usual style, the word of greeting one would expect in a Greek letter has become a Jewish blessing of peace from God—he adds grace, and from Christ—and the names of the sender and receiver, which come first, have been much elaborated (1:1–3). Paul identifies himself and the Corinthian church both as divinely called: he to be an apostle of Christ and they to be holy people consecrated to Christ. Neither stands alone because Sosthenes stands with him as sender of the letter—(Is Sosthenes taking dictation? He is not mentioned again.)—and with the Corinthians stand "all who call on the name of our Lord Jesus Christ in every place, theirs and ours." Whether the final words mean "their Lord and ours" or "their place and ours," the effect is to evoke a wide circle of people calling on one Lord, possibly to prepare for Paul's later appeals to other churches' conduct (4:17; 7:17; 11:16; 14:33). Paul's interest in the Corinthians' greater incorporation into this circle is confirmed in the last line of the section, "God is faithful, through whom you were called into the common life (solidarity) of his son . . ." (1:9).

The liturgical nature of Paul's opening lines, evident in his naming God six times and Christ nine times, centers on his praise to God for God's particular gift to the Corinthians. This gift is not faith (Rom 1:8; 1 Thess 1:3, 8) or endurance (1 Thess 1:2–3; 2 Cor 1:3–6) or solidarity (Phil 1:3–5) but speech and knowledge. Paul's thanksgiving has so many functions in his argument that only the reader can gauge which is dominant. It introduces the major issue he will address in this letter, their spiritual wisdom. It compliments them in order to make them more ready to hear his reproof, which begins immediately after. It also concedes the principle that their gifts of speech are from God and incontestable, which allows Paul to define their wealth as grounded in the witness of Christ among them, who alone can put them beyond accusation—"not to be called in"—in his day of judgment.

Yet when Paul stresses that the Corinthians are called into solidarity with everyone who calls on Christ and that they are strengthened in order finally to stand before Christ, we cannot jump to the conclusion that they are self-centered in relation to other believers and without humility before Christ. Paul's argument does suggest what becomes clearer as we read, that these people who "lack no spiritual gift" do not learn their practices from what is standard in other churches, nor are they intent on preparing for divine judgment. Apparently they experience directly and express confidently some present revealing of Christ. Paul presents himself here as one who recognizes their gifts from God but is stressing their dependence on God and solidarity with others.

Appeal for Agreement (1:10–17)

In many letters Paul does not begin his major appeal about local issues until after an extended proclamation (Rom 12:1; 2 Cor 10:1; Phil 4:1), but here he begins immediately with a triple call for agreement, an account of an oral report from Corinth, and an argument against divisions based on baptism. The call for agreement concerns their primary gift of speech and knowledge. It begins and ends positively—"speak the same," "be restored in the same mind and the same knowledge"—but between these it demands an end to "the schisms/splits/cleavings among you." Next Paul appeals to them concerning strife reported to him by Chloe's people, for the second time in two sentences calling them "brothers." The NRSV's "brothers and sisters" communicates the generic aspect of this kinship claim in Christ. Though both English words have the same spelling in Greek with different endings to indicate gender, Paul's use of the masculine plural for men and women together—the standard Greek syntax—reflects an androcentric culture in which women are subsumed into men's interactions without being recognized. So much "brothering" could make all Paul's hearers wary, particularly so the women, who may know from experience that even when he is talking about women, they have been known to vanish from his brotherly address (1 Thess 4:3–6; 1 Cor 14:24–29).

Chloe appears in Christian texts only here, where some of her followers have brought word to Paul. Their alarm about recent divisions suggests that she could be head of one of the first households and/or worship centers in the church whose members want Paul to help them recover an earlier order of life—an indication that the old guard is not all male-led. Paul's citing her name against his practice elsewhere (5:1; 11:18; 15:12) suggests that she has a reputation that can support his critique of the group's divisions, perhaps particularly among women.

The four slogans, "I belong to _____," should not be taken as a precise lineup in a four-sided battle in Corinth. The final "But I belong to Christ! Is Christ divided?" may well be Paul's own parody and retort and no part of their shouts. This is supported by the way Paul finally states his view of their right relations: "All things are yours, whether Paul or Apollos or Cephas . . . , and you are Christ's and Christ is God's" (3:21–23). Because Cephas appears only in these two references to the struggle, each time in third place, it is likely that he is being used as a standard apostolic figure (as in 9:5 and 15:5) to diffuse the polarity of a local conflict. The real "split" must be between followers of Paul and Apollos. This is confirmed in Paul's further description of the struggle (3:4), in his extended analogy of himself and Apollos as gardeners, builders and managers (3:5-4:5), and in his closing, "But I have applied these changing figures to myself and Apollos for your sake . . . (4:6)." The best evidence of a two-sided conflict is the focus of Paul's entire letter on criticizing one tendency in Corinth, presumably the one linked to Apollos.

The question becomes, What we can learn from Paul's argument about the meaning of Apollos to certain Corinthians and the meaning of Paul to others? Baptism may be one issue, raised by Paul's mocking, "Were you baptized in Paul's name? I thank God I baptized none of you except . . ." (1:13–14). Paul's otherwise positive, if infrequent, reference to baptism outside this letter (Gal 3:27–28; Rom 6:1–11) suggests that his reserve here comes from Apollos's being known in Corinth for baptizing and eloquent preaching, possibly also for baptismal teaching and initiating others into the practice of such gifts (see above, "Introduction: Development of the Corinthian Church"). Christian baptism probably evolved from Jewish proselyte baptism, but at a time when conversions to Judaism were already taking some new forms in the Hellenistic world (see *The Confession of Aseneth*). From these forms Christian initiations may also have adapted practices such as abstinence, disclosure of secret mysteries, or use of special clothing and food. Paul's followers reacted defensively with "I belong to Paul!" But we know that the new wisdom quickly became the standard in Corinth because Paul interrupts his appeal for agreement with a digression on wisdom.

Wisdom Renounced and Reclaimed (1:18–2:16)

Paul's digression on wisdom is best explained as his response to the Corinthians, since the word stem "wisdom" appears twenty-six times in these four chapters and only seven times in all Paul's other letters. What he says appears to answer an accusation that he, unlike Apollos, did not impart wisdom in Corinth. His first argument can be summarized: I wouldn't speak wisdom if I could (1:17–2:15); his second: I could speak wisdom, but you're not up to it (2:6–3:4). This wisdom conflict within a Christian community suggests the possibility that one side's strength is not necessarily the other's weakness but, as in a competition among runners, each becomes strong in different ways by an extended process of working out against each other.

Paul's refusal to speak wisdom (1:17–2:5) appeals to positive values of the Corinthians by beginning with a definition (1:18) supported by a scripture quotation (v. 19) and scripture allusions (v. 20), then recounting a divine act explained in terms of God's wisdom (vv. 20b–21) in light of which Paul gives his proclamation that counters human desires and yet fulfills them (vv. 22–24). All this is confirmed by a maxim concerning divine and human nature (v. 25) demonstrated from their experience (vv. 26–30) and his experience (2:1–5), with intervening support from divine purpose and scripture.

Yet all this seems to be swept away by Paul's negations. People do not know God's wisdom (1:21), and those who know God do not have human wisdom (1:17; 2:4, 5). The resulting antithesis between God's wisdom, which is foolish to people, and people's wisdom, which is nothing to God, gapes so wide that it becomes a paradoxical maxim, "God's foolishness is wiser than human beings," intensified by the irony of the understatement in its merely comparative form (1:25). The Corinthians will not have understood why Paul should call their wisdom "human," "verbose," and "lofty," as if the human voice were an unfit vessel for God's gift of wisdom.

After affirmation and denial, Paul's argument why he would not speak wisdom even if he could concludes with the announcement of a new divine event: because the world did not know God through wisdom, God has acted to save through the foolishness of the cross, cutting off the aims of both Jews and Greeks in the crucified Christ who is God's power and God's wisdom (1:22–24). Reflecting this, Paul describes his own calling as one that mirrors the divine act of choosing foolishness, "I decided to know nothing among you except Jesus Christ and him crucified," making his chosen weakness a foil to set off God's new kind of power (2:1–5). But most of the Corinthians were called as people without any wisdom, power, or family name that they could give up in order to mirror a divine act of choosing loss (1:26–28). Paul thinks that their calling is to remain weak and to shame the powerful by demonstrating God's new order, suggesting that they see God's act as having changed not only their values but their lives. What Paul sees as their betrayal of God's move to undermine the world's wisdom through the cross, they may well see as Paul's betrayal of God's act to raise the crucified and make the foolish wise.

The Corinthians must indeed be strong because Paul is not able to meet their demands for wisdom by this renouncing of wisdom and ends his digression on wisdom by taking a second position: I do speak wisdom but you're not up to it (2:6–16). Though he may be thinking of the wisdom of choosing loss, he seeks his hearers' acceptance by claiming to speak a divinely revealed wisdom that is totally inaccessible to mortals and provides an ability to understand spiritual things that cannot be judged by those who lack this revelation.

It appears that Paul is here adopting a Corinthian positive wisdom claim that appeals to Jewish and Christian apocalyptic themes and to scripture, to God's spirit, and Christ's mind. But in this case the negative dissociation of divine revelation from all mortal knowing, culminating in the paradox of unknown knowledge, is not Paul's corrective but is integral to this kind of wisdom claim. And the act of God that is said to reconstruct reality is not explicitly defined as God's choice of the cross to reverse all values but is called God's revealing of unknowable wisdom. When Paul suddenly after making this claim refuses to speak wisdom to them because they are too immature to receive it—a move that depends for its impact on their having come to expect by this point that he could speak wisdom—it becomes clear why his wisdom claim is spoken in their language and is not used to correct their views. Only in this way could he shock them with his refusal.

If Paul's wisdom claim is modeled after theirs, it should be our best source for understanding Corinthian Christian wisdom. At least three aspects of its practice in Corinth are clear. First, this is seen to be God's wisdom, "what God has prepared ahead," "the depths of God," "spiritual things," "the mind of Christ," even "all things." God's own spirit, who alone knows God, reveals it to people who by nature know only what the human spirit teaches, and they become able to understand God as if from within. Second, it is a spoken or oral wisdom, as Paul states several times. This is a crucial factor in a world where so few can read and write but all can hear and speak. When combined with the internal view of God in the spirit, this suggests prophetic rather than transmitted wisdom, but inspired interpretation of tradition cannot be ruled out. Third, it is a communal wisdom, spoken in the first person plural among the spiritual, in Paul's use contrasting with the singular before and after his digression: "We speak wisdom among the mature," "We speak God's wisdom," "We have received God's spirit," "We have Christ's mind." This communal practice is "in concepts taught by the spirit, interpreting spiritual things among the spiritual," a process of examining rather than being examined by others. In all, it is not competitive but communal, not negative but positive, an active exercise of God-given gain.

The question remains whether these people who speak wisdom are a different group in Corinth from the prophets and speakers in tongues, among whom we know there were women (11:2–14:40). Although Paul does not speak about the women explicitly until he has established his credentials in Corinth, he refers in both contexts to gifts worked by the spirit (2:12; 12:7–11) and raises the same issues of what he considers their immaturity (3:2; 13:9–12; 14:20), divisions (1:10–13; 3:3; 12:25), and overconfidence (3:18; 4:6–10; 12:21; 13:4). Considering that the community is small, only a few years old, with no formal leadership and given to spiritual expression, Paul's different themes as the letter progresses are better explained as different approaches to the whole community he wants to persuade rather than approaches to different groups.

The presence of women or others of low social standing among people who speak this kind of wisdom is also implied in their seeing this age threatened with domination by the arbitrary power of rulers who have executed the Lord of Glory. But God's spirit reveals a wisdom hidden since before these rulers existed which shows that the rulers have come to nothing in their ignorance. Glory and power now belong to those who have the mind of Christ, speak to reveal this wisdom to others, and exercise in common the gifts given by God. In contrast to this movement from victimization to glory, Paul's renunciation reflects a starting point of power. He sees the cross as a divine self-emptying of power and he imitates it in his own decision to know nothing but the crucified Christ in Corinth so that God alone will be praised. Apparently both the Corinthian theology and Paul's theology express a reversal of power and weakness, but from a different place. Those without power who receive from God the wisdom to speak and act as decreed before the ages for their glory do not see themselves called to join the self-emptying of the powerful.

Paul's general critique of Corinth has led some scholars to propose that the Corinthians were more prone to boast wisdom than to produce it. But this passage does not support that view. Here Paul relies on their expectation that his claim to speak wisdom will be followed by wisdom speech in order to shock them at the end by refusing to speak it on account of their strife and immaturity. This means that they normally do speak wisdom after they claim the power to do so, and it is Paul who promises a birth that he does not deliver, leaving us with only the fetus of Corinthian wisdom, not the living speech.

Appeal for Agreement (3:1–23)

Just at the point where Paul seems on the verge of speaking wisdom, he says that he cannot because the Corinthians are not spiritual, not even human souls but snarling animals. In this way Paul gains from his digression on wisdom—as speakers hope to gain from digressions—a significant advantage when returning to the basic argument. Having first demonstrated wisdom without claiming it (1:18–2:5), then claiming wisdom without demonstrating it (2:6–16), he leaves the impression that he is a master of wisdom—or at least that he could be under the right divine and human conditions. Yet he begs the key question about why their differences prove they are not spiritual, and they may wonder if it is their being spiritual that Paul calls strife.

Paul's rhetorical questions—"Then what is Apollos? What is Paul?"—set out to define this neuter "what" that we might call the proper function of leadership. His general answer is that leaders are "servants of God" (3:5, 9)—not the word for a slave but a broader term meaning anyone who carries out small or great tasks as a representative of another. In the metaphors of gardening (3:5–9) and building (3:10–17), Paul and Apollos are featured as workers, the Corinthian believers as the product, and God as the producer and owner. This makes siding with one or another worker look foolish because the two are "one thing" (3:8), functionally equivalent. All that matters is God's purpose to create a people, "You are God's field, God's building. . . . You are God's temple" (3:9, 16). If there is a problem for the Corinthians in being the work of various leaders and not themselves workers, Paul is not aware of it.

After a warning, Paul concludes his argument by reversing their slogans. They do not belong to their leaders but all their leaders belong to them and they belong strictly to Christ, who in turn belongs to God. That believers are God's people would be a given in Paul's tradition. But to say that they belong to Christ who belongs to God sets up a peculiar hierarchy not standard even for Paul. In this context the cosmic subordination of Christ to God and of them to Christ legitimates their leaders' subordination to them, but later it reappears in a slightly different form to justify women's subordination to men (11:3). Is this an accidental parallel, or are there predictable implications of solving social problems by appeal to models of divine subordination? Is this intended to supplant a contrary model of Christ as mediator in Corinth?

The most problematic aspect of this chapter is that Paul uses his argument for the parity of all who do God's work to gain the advantage over Apollos. The planter precedes the irrigator; the foundation builder is the "wise architect" laying the only possible foundation, and the one who builds on it (singular for Apollos?) will have to pass through fire. And the threat of divine reciprocity follows: "If any one corrupts God's temple, that one will go down to corruption" (3:17).

Closing Personal Appeals (4:1–21)

A third metaphor from the world of household stewards—stewards of God's mysteries on the people's behalf (4:1; cf. 2:1, 7; 13:2; 14:2)—promises real parity. But Paul's observation that everything depends on such workers being trustworthy makes him defensive about his own being judged, and Apollos disappears from view. Paul concludes that he has applied all these metaphors to himself and Apollos so that the Corinthians could learn the precept "Nothing beyond what is written" and its consequences, "that one not be bloated on behalf of one person against another." The saying, identified by the neuter article, must be some counsel of strictness in claims for one's friends or of reticence in judgment of others, with "what is written" suggesting a Jewish tradition. The three rhetorical questions insinuate a Corinthian sense of superiority and retort that what people are has been given to them.

When Paul has exposed himself and criticized them, he becomes increasingly personal, mocking their stance in three key sentences, probably in a parody of their claims, "Already you have become filled (satiated)! Already you have become rich! Without us you have begun to rule!" (4:8). These are reminiscent of Jesus' announcement of God's kingdom for the poor and hungry, but here the promise is fully realized, as is the case only in the first beatitude, "Blessed are you poor, for yours is the kingdom of God" (Luke 6:20; Matt 5:3). Paul does not take this as God's grace for those in need (1:26–28) but belittles their claim as wishful thinking (4:8b) and develops an extended contrast of their good fortune and the apostles' woe—"We are fools for Christ, but you are intelligent in Christ, we weak but you strong, you honored but we shamed" (4:10). A further triad describes the apostles' bare survival (4:12b–13a) to become the world's garbage scraps. This highly charged rhetoric may reflect Corinth less than it does how people make others appear boastful in Hellenistic popular discourse, but it assumes at least some recognizable contrast between their experience of fulfillment and Paul's of frustration.

Apollos is conspicuously absent from the apostles sharing Paul's pathetic self-portrait, who suffer while followers luxuriate. He reappears when Paul calls a halt to shaming the Corinthians, claiming to be their loving father in contrast to tutors who give them only passing attention. Paul's children are to imitate him as good apprentices and listen to his faithful son Timothy remind them of his instruction, sanctioned by the blanket claim that he teaches it "everywhere in each church." Paul's boldness here in contrast to the cautious opening of the letter might be read as confidence that he now has them in hand, were it not for his final lines. There is no conciliation, but simply the juxtaposition of Corinthians who think he will never return and his threat to come, whether with a rod or with love. His comeback strategy is to renounce their "human wisdom" while claiming divine wisdom, to expose their "animal" fray while asserting his foundational role, and to display wild sacrifices as a claim of paternal authority. The scene in Corinth which he reveals is not one of conflict and frustration but one of confidence and fulfillment, threatening only to Paul's followers, who have sent to him for help.

Corinthian Asceticism and Charges of Immorality (5:1–7:40)

The Community Charged with Immorality (5:1–6:20)

Paul's raised voice continues in two further chapters drawing from his oral sources, "It is even heard that there is immorality among you. . . ." The incidents cited to support this charge are three: a man living with his father's wife, people taking each other to court, and the patronizing of prostitutes.

The first incident is probably not incest in the biological sense, since Paul is stating the case as blatantly as he can and yet does not say she is the man's mother but his father's wife. But he gets some of the radical sanctions against incest mobilized to oppose a sexual relation of son to mother-in-law, also strictly forbidden in Jewish, Greek, and Roman law. This rule apparently held even when the father died or divorced his wife, as seems to be implied here by the continuing nature of the new relationship. The Greek tradition of women being married in their early teens to men when they complete schooling, apprenticeship, military service, or when they lose a wife in childbirth, meant that the ages in a family were not distinguished sharply by generation. Also the integration into wealthier households of adopted sons, foundlings, relatives, and slaves of every age motivated the men in power to keep strict laws on the books.

Paul insists that the whole church constitute itself as a spiritual court to execute his own decision to curse and/or expel this young man—yet note that without their action Paul knows his decision is moot. He does not charge the woman, for whatever reason—sex, age, or religion—nor does he defend her as a victim. She is apparently not his issue, and even the man is less Paul's interest than is the community he accuses of being "bloated" and "boasting" about this (5:1, 6). He challenges them to clean out this yeast and not pollute Christ their paschal lamb, an instruction that depends on the image of them as women doing pre-Passover cleaning. Using the Deuteronomist's curse against idolatry and extreme cases of immorality, he demands that they "drive out the wicked person from among you" (Deut 17:7 passim).

In the second case Paul makes a more general attack on "any of you" who take fellow believers to public courts (6:1–11). That a sexual issue has provoked this is suggested by Paul's first and third cases and the specific list of sins immediately following, where the reference to male homosexuality reflects the more inflammatory aspect of Hellenistic Jewish rhetoric against what they considered Gentile sins (Wis 19:14–17). The nature of the case is also suggested in Paul's example, "you defraud," a term he uses later for denial of spousal sexual rights (7:5). Perhaps the case involves "alienation of affection" or return of dowry. It is again men whom Paul is charging, since women do not take cases to court in the Roman city, and the male speaking for a woman would normally be considered the legally wronged party. Yet Paul holds the community as a whole responsible, including its women, and calls on them to judge, or at least suffer rather than inflict, the offenses within it if they are to "inherit God's kingdom" (4:8).

The third example, going to prostitutes (6:12–20), is not a charge against an individual, though it would not be credible if some case were not known. Paul concedes a principle, "All things are authorized for me," but immediately qualifies it in practice, "yet I will not fall under the authority of anything." This may be a wordplay on Corinthian claims to have ethical authority in Christ. He concedes their authority to eat, then refuses elaborately to concede it in sexual relations, implying without giving evidence that they put the principle to such use. His argument refers to men, since they are the ones who patronize prostitutes. But the culminating warning, "Flee immorality!" is directed to the whole community by identifying this male immorality as a sin against the communal body ("your" plural, "body" singular, 6:19–20), which is said to be purchased at great cost for God's glory as a temple of the Spirit (7:23).

These arguments imply a good deal about Paul's audience. He assumes that the man living with his father's wife has wide support in the church (5:1, 6), perhaps because of his being known, because of some knowledge of the woman's earlier victimization, or because of common cause against a patriarchal legal system. Court cases show that the church has no functioning court system and little interest in issues of internal purity. Public courts would be the standard recourse in Corinth—how much more in highly ambiguous situations if fathers were reclaiming dowries due on divorce[6] for daughters withdrawing by choice from marriage commitments (chap. 7). Paul's final argument suggests that men could be resorting to prostitution in Corinth when they do not share their partners' ascetic commitments. None of these cases requires the hypothesis of a programmatic Christian libertinism, although Paul wants to leave this impression in his high rhetoric concerning their "boasting," concerning purity, and especially in his denial of sexual freedom after citing their freedom claims (5:1, 6; 6:9, 12–13). Why Paul accentuates sexual license in the Corinthian church and charges the entire community with threatening to pollute Christ is clear only in the next chapter. There Paul concedes their sexual asceticism on principle but insists on marriage in practice "on account of immorality." The missing premise in that argument is that immorality is a present danger to the Corinthians, and it is this premise that has been supplied in advance.

Marriage on account of Immorality: To the Married (7:1–24)

Paul's advice concerning marriage begins by quoting what seems to be a statement from their letter to him, "It is good for a man not to touch a woman" (7:1). Paul's own life and even his earlier teaching may have pointed the Corinthians in this direction,[7] but here Paul concedes it as an ideal but calls for marriage in practice because of immorality (or because of prostitution, by a narrower translation of the term). In the preceding two chapters

Paul has dramatized Christ's desecration by certain men in Corinth as the community's responsibility so that he can now present some people's asceticism as a source of other peoples' immorality. Addressing people moving away from sexual commitments in various ways—within marriage, by staying single, by leaving believing spouses, by leaving unbelievers, by not marrying as virgins, and by not remarrying as widows—Paul is forthright in advocating or at least allowing marriage at each point. Only one factor is not made explicit, that if marriage within a community widely committed to sexual asceticism is to prevent male sexual activity outside marriages, it is women ascetics who will need to be persuaded to be sexual partners of the offending men.

Paul's rhetoric changes dramatically at this point, from alarmed exclamations and dire warnings to impartial consultation of each group and modest suggestions to the best of his knowledge. He turns here to their letter, but he is not answering respectful questions. He proceeds so carefully because he is questioning their confident answers, conceding their positions on principle in order virtually to reverse them in practice. His diplomatic instructions to people of each marriage status are put reciprocally to the women concerning the men and the men concerning the women in a way especially persuasive to those who respect parity in sexual roles—more likely women than men in a patriarchal culture.

Paul first takes up sexual relations in marriage, which, he says, the husband should give the wife and the wife the husband (7:1–7). Conjugal rights are assured wives by law in both talmudic and Greek traditions, probably originally to protect the woman's right to conceive children. But Paul is probably not thinking of children in his short time frame, and his restating of the obligation in a negative way—"the woman does not have authority over her own body"—suggests that he is rejecting a reverse claim in Corinth. In a culture where men could assume authority over their bodies, the Corinthians claiming such authority were probably women, "having authority" being the key term for claiming rights in the Corinthian church (6:12; 8:9; 10:32; 11:10?). Some of the married have apparently withdrawn from sexual relations permanently and without consultation, since Paul himself accepts temporary withdrawal by mutual agreement. In spite of the general principle "not to touch," he concedes conjugal relations to overcome Satan's tempting, masking in his argument from parity not only that some men clearly prefer the sexual access required but also that a concession to them is a command to their wives.

Paul speaks only briefly to the unmarried and widows concerning his preference that they remain single unless they lack the requisite self-control (7:8–9); he does not suggest the possibility of lacking self-control when he addresses widows alone at the chapter's end. Apparently women's sexual desire is not the issue in Corinth.

In addressing the married he replaces his own command with the Lord's against separation and divorce, terms he seems to use interchangeably (7:11, 13, 15). Marriage in Roman law of this time was defined as adult citizens living together; divorce happened when they ceased to do so, though there was more stigma for women than men, and noncitizens could fall under more stringent local laws.[8] Not only does Paul command the woman first not to divorce, but he states an exception whereby if she separates (a present, not only a past, option) she is to remain single or remarry her husband. Were Paul concerned about preventing sexual abuse, one would expect him to address the husbands, since he is speaking here about divorce of believing spouses. There must be some other reason for separation by women in the Corinthian church that Paul does not think he can oppose without exception even by the Lord's command. The clause forbidding men to divorce is unspecified, as if added as an argument from parity.

In a second exception to the Lord's command, "the rest" are told to stay married to nonbelievers in order to keep the peace and make their spouses holy, yet they are reassured that they are not "enslaved" to nonbelieving spouses who have left them. Such an extensive discussion shows that it was not uncommon to divorce unbelievers when joining the community. Perhaps most of these single Christians were women, because Paul's reference to "your children" suggests that mothers, whose children belonged by law to their fathers, had sought assurance about their children's status. There is also some external evidence that women were attracted to Christianity independently of their families (Luke 8:3; Acts 17:4, 34), whereas male converts largely could expect their households to convert with them. In any case Paul's demand that Christians continue to live with nonbelieving spouses affected more aspects of life for women Christians than for men, requiring of them not only household responsibilities but subordination and, in light of religious defection, perhaps abuse.

Paul's New Rule (7:17–24)

At this point Paul lays down a general rule that each one remain in the status she or he had when called into the community, a significant reversal of what seems to be their practice concerning sexuality. His claim that he commands this "in all the churches" draws on other churches for support without requiring him to say that sexual abstinence is practiced nowhere else. They apparently think that social privilege and disadvantage are canceled in Christ according to the baptismal affirmation: "there is neither Jew nor Greek, neither slave nor free, not male and female" (Gal 3:28; see 11:7 below).

Paul argues that since circumcision is not reversed or slave status dissolved, new structures of sexual life should not be expected. Of course he does not quote the baptismal affirmation that speaks against him here, and he chooses to talk about circumcision rather than common meals, where conduct has indeed changed. In speaking of slavery not changing, Paul can only maintain his credibility by making an exception if the opportunity for freedom arises. The blatant denial of the baptismal affirmation in the slave's subjection to master is ignored by speaking of the metaphorical parity of enslaved and free believers. After each example Paul repeats the general command to remain in the condition in which they were called, the last time adding the sanction "with God" (7:20, 24; cf. 1:26–28). The theological question of whether God's call and baptism into Christ confirm or overcome social privilege is answered without being discussed.

Special attention should be given to the role of enslaved persons in the Christian practice of withdrawing from sexual partners. Legally the slave was not free to make such decisions about his or her own body, and one could therefore argue that all the people that Paul discusses in this chapter are free men and women. But the sexual use of the slave was only one of many forms of abuse, and it would tend to fall on some slaves more than others. The older, more skilled male slave would have the best chance of having a sexual life according to his own will, perhaps a long-term, if not legal, relationship with a fellow slave through which children would be born. Yet even in this case the children would be born into the master's household, and there would be no assurance of an exclusive relationship with the woman. Such a man might have a reasonable chance of withdrawing from sexual relations for religious reasons, but what of the woman? What of the young slave, male or female? Would the enslaved female ever be referred to as "virgin," whether or not she had had sexual relations with men?

These are questions that have not been asked because scholars have ignored the fact that sexual life was not the same for enslaved and free people, as it was not for female and male. The possibility of Corinthian Christian slaves choosing sexual abstinence would depend on three independent factors—their own determination; their relative power based on age, sex, and assignment; and the agreement of the people to whom they were enslaved. For female slaves, very strong support from other women in the enslaving household and the church would be indispensable. Such protection from masters may have developed in the Corinthian church, since free women withdrawing from sexual relations would themselves need to organize mutual support and protection in the face of the contrary will of husbands, fiancés, and parents.

Marriage on account of Immorality: To the Single (7:25–40)

The rule that one should keep the sexual status one had when called gives Paul a basis for encouraging the single to remain single as Paul is, although he has withheld his own example from the married. Yet even this rule is subordinate to his initial warnings on male immorality and the consequent instruction to marry, which he applies also to the single if immorality threatens.

The opening phrase, "concerning the virgins," suggests that these never-married women were a topic of the Corinthian letter (7:1). After a modest disclaimer, Paul responds true to form by conceding a Corinthian affirmation in order to qualify it and reverse the conduct expected. He concedes that "this is good because of the present urgency, for it is good for a man to be like this (7:26)." Here the second, seldom-translated phrase by its syntax, vocabulary, and neuter particle refers back to the Corinthian principle enunciated in opening this discussion, "It is good for a man not to touch a woman" (7:1). In this way Paul turns his attention to the man involved with a virgin, advising him neither to seek ties with her nor to sever existing ties. The principle "not to touch" is qualified by telling the man, "But if you married you were not sinning, and if the virgin married she was not sinning" (7:28). Before strengthening this statement by applying it to future choices, Paul challenges the man not to marry because of the present crisis, calls those who have wives to live as though they did not, and warns about the distractions in the Lord's service from trying to please a wife—and here at last he also mentions that women will experience the same distractions in marriage (7:26–35). But Paul's final adjudication returns to the man's options and leaves the decision on marriage up to whether or not "he has authority over his will/desire" (7:36–38).

The key (though usually unspoken) question for the reader is why Paul deals with men when addressing the issue of virgins. Exegetes in the early church often assumed that the man trying to decide whether "his virgin" should marry is her father, but this is hardly indicated in "If anyone thinks he is acting improperly toward his virgin, if he (or she) is ripe/overwrought and so it has to be . . ." (7:36). A more recent proposal is that Paul is speaking of both men and women virgins, as seen in the translation, "Now concerning the unmarried . . ." (7:25 RSV). But after this instance when the genitive plural "virgins" does not reveal their gender, the feminine gender of the virgin becomes explicit (vv. 28, 36, 38).

More likely Paul's attention to the men is his own rhetorical approach in a situation where the church celebrates its virgins and where the men once engaged or since attracted to the virgins are dissatisfied or are finding satisfaction elsewhere. Paul concedes that virginity is good but suggests that commitments have been made; he claims, surely reversing language used in Corinth, that those who marry a virgin "do not sin." He argues at length that the present crisis has made marriage obsolete and an obstruction to full devotion to God—thereby strengthening his credibility among the virgins and their allies. He then uses this credibility to try to make the man's decision appear inevitable if he chooses marriage to prevent immorality. Paul's concluding sentence returns to his own preference as only one—if a better—option, "So both the one who causes his own virgin to marry will do well, and the one who does not cause her to marry will do better" (7:38). The causative verb, which has been read to indicate the man is the virgin's father, points instead to the fact that the key issue is not the man's right to marry but his right to cause one of these virgins to marry, since she is the one "consecrated both in body and spirit" (7:34).

This extended argument makes clear that the presence of the virgins was a crucial part of community life. These women must have been young, because marriage in Greece was expected by the mid-teens—in early Greece and Rome after extended engagements, though imperial times were less formal.[9] The virgins were part of a much broader movement of Christians in every category of marriage status to withdraw from sexual relations, a movement especially pronounced among women, with the virgins and the unmarried being specifically known to be "consecrated both in body and spirit" (7:34). The meaning of their not marrying is suggested in Paul's associating abstinence with prayer (7:5) and in the fact that sexual purity is an explicit qualification of every female prophet named in the ChristianTestament (Luke 2:27; Acts 21:9; Rev 2:20). The virgins' roles in the community and their relation to other women would be radically changed were the church to concede to Paul that they must marry wherever men are "not acting properly" and that only widows have the right not to marry. This short concession to widows suggests that their leadership among Christian women in later generations (1 Tim 5:1-16) may be the vestige of what once happened in many age groups.

CORINTHIAN EATING OF SACRIFICED FOOD AND PAUL'S CHARGES OF IDOLATRY (8:1–11:34)

"Food Sacrificed to Idols" (8:1–13)

Concerning sacrificed food, Paul could not agree more with the Corinthian Christians that "all of us have knowledge, . . . there is no idol in the world," and "there is no God but one" (8:1, 4). But he qualifies this claim to knowledge by arguing that only God knows fully so others do better to love God, and in any case all do not share this knowledge and some may be harmed by seeing others eating in a temple. For Paul, the love of Christ for every confused believer and the believers' love for each other take priority over believers' knowledge, even the sure knowledge that God is one. But apparently something in the Corinthians' situation makes them see their authority to eat sacrificed food as the kind of witness to the one God that cannot be compromised, any more than Paul could back away from the common table in Antioch for love of Peter or the Jerusalem guests (Gal 2:11–14). If it is their knowledge in Christ of this one God which frees them from all oppressing powers and binds them to all people, they may see themselves as having no choice but to participate at every table and thereby to demonstrate for others that God is one.

Digression on the Uses of Authority (9:1–10:13)

Paul digresses from the subject of sacrificed food to depict the nature of true freedom and authority in two examples, a positive example from his experience as apostle (9:1–27) and a negative example from Israel's experience in the wilderness (10:1–13). Paul uses rhetorical questions to make clear that he is a free man and an apostle who has seen the Lord and brought the gospel to them and to assert on this basis his right to be supported by the people he serves. Is he shaming them for not supporting him and Barnabas so that they must work while other apostles even bring along "a sister as wife"? Is there irony in Paul's tone here, as there surely is in another letter where he apologizes for not burdening them (2 Cor 11:7–10, 20–21)? He continues his claim at length by appeals to military, agricultural, and pastoral life, to the law of Moses, to Temple service, and finally to the Lord's command (cf. Luke 10:7).

In any case, before Paul has marshaled all these arguments for his having the right to be fed by the church, he is already saying that he has not used this authority because it might be an obstacle to the gospel. In fact he insists that he will never take their support because his reward comes from making the gospel free, or, as he says, from not making use of his authority (9:12, 15–18). Rather he speaks of enslaving himself to everyone in order to win them, ending with the illustration of himself as athlete "enslaving his body" (9:19–27). By means of this example Paul is challenging the Corinthians to demonstrate their authority and freedom to eat sacrificed food by not using their authority for the sake of others. This shows that the Corinthians do not experience their authority as an obstacle to the gospel and do not express their freedom in the gospel by limiting themselves. If their witness is aimed toward people like themselves, it may not require self-denial but may work effectively as a direct demonstration of the authority and freedom God is ready to give everyone. This could attract others into similar authority and freedom without the discipline of the athlete or missionary trying to cross over into capacities that are contrived or worlds that are foreign.

Paul's negative example from Israel in the wilderness warns the Corinthians of the dangers of their confidence (10:1–13). He starts out with no hint of criticism, speaking of the golden age in the wilderness when Israel received the full spiritual resources which Paul describes in terms of the Corinthians' baptism and meal: they were all under the cloud; all passed through the sea; all were thus baptized into Moses; all ate the same spiritual food; all drank the same spiritual drink from the rock that was Christ. This "all" repeated five times, mirroring their "we all have knowledge" (8:1), is brought up short by his adversative conclusion: "But with most of them God was not pleased and they were wiped out in the wilderness." On this basis Paul becomes didactic. These things happened precisely to teach the Corinthians at the end of time (10:6, 11; cf. 9:10) the lessons of five stories from the beginning: not to crave what is evil, not to worship idols, not to be immoral, not to test God, and not to conspire to rebel—and he tells them the terrors which followed in each case (Num 11:1–35; Exod 32:1–35; Num 25:1–18; 21:4–9; 14:1–45). Paul concludes by contrasting what they think about themselves with reality: "Let those who think they are standing watch out not to fall!" and promises that God will help them escape a testing they cannot stand.

The Corinthian voice is clearest in the confidence Paul projects onto desert wanderers, known in the ancient stories largely for complaining. It is the Corinthians who are all baptized, who all eat the same spiritual food and drink from the same spiritual drink. Yet there is no sign that they take these sacraments as physical assurance of salvation, any more than they take food sacrificed to the gods as a physical threat. The way Paul's desert stories link immorality and idolatry does suggest some active presence of women in community rites in ways that disturb Paul. His concluding charge that those who think they stand should watch not to fall again reflects their confidence. Paul uses this argument from who they think they are throughout 1 Corinthians in ways that provide a wider picture of them as people who not only think they are wise and know God, but think they can argue with Paul against women's head covering and can judge spiritually Paul's silencing of the women (3:18; 8:2–3; 10:6; 11:16; 14:37–38).

"Food Sacrificed to Idols": Fleeing Idolatry (10:14–11:1)

After the challenge from his own example of not using his authority and the warning from the wilderness journey about those who do, Paul is bold to charge them, "Flee idolatry!" Then he challenges them as discerning people to consider how the cup and bread are for them a participation in Christ that unites them together, just as those who eat the Temple sacrifices are participants in that worship. It is not that idols or demons are anything substantive, but that, as he quotes from Deut 32:17, "The things that they sacrifice, 'they sacrifice to demons, not to God'" (10:20). Worship of demons is worship taken away from God because the worshiper cannot participate in both at once. His closing questions, "Or are we to provoke God to jealousy? Are we stronger than God?" show that the ultimate issue in idolatry for Paul is not any other gods, nor even the confused fellow believer, but the worshiper who presumes to make gods and thereby claims the place of God. In conclusion Paul responds to their slogan "All things are authorized" by returning to his own earlier argument from the common good, charging them to buy whatever is sold and eat whatever is offered except where another person's conscience might be offended, seeking to please everyone as Paul does and thus imitate Christ.

The mortal threat of pollution from idol worship and from claiming to be stronger than God is not Paul's last word, but it is the turning point of his argument. If Paul considers his own example to be insufficient to persuade the Corinthians without this threat that their strength may be idolatry, we can only conclude that their faith in Christ is constituted very differently from his. Christ is for him the ultimate example of not offending, and he calls them to imitate him imitating Christ so that the gospel will be spread because no one is offended. To them Christ is the ultimate example of offending by participating everywhere in the God who is one, provoking the world's narrow structures and spreading the gospel of unrestricted participation through Christ.

Idolatry within Community Worship: Prayer and Prophecy (11:2-16)

In this transition chapter Paul brings to a head his charges of idolatry by tracing it to the community worship itself. This sets the stage for his address on spiritual gifts, in the same way that his exposé of immorality (5:1–6:20) provides the rationale for his response on marriage (7:1–40). As we have now come to expect, he begins here by commending them and then qualifying it, praising them for maintaining all his traditions and then adding, "But I want you to know," in order to introduce something new in such a way that it will be accepted as tradition by the ones he has praised. He uses a definition to say this because a definition claims truth by its internal relations without requiring supporting authorities or empirical evidence: "Christ is the head of every man, man is the head of woman, and God is the head of Christ" (11:3b). Although the word "head" has many metaphorical uses in Greek, with "source" more common than "ruler," Paul's intent can only be determined from the passage itself. The first and third phrases describing Christ and God as "head" may be hard for Christians to contest, even if the formulation is strange, protecting the middle phrase concerning man's headship from challenge. A graded system of dependence is set up, as if Paul's earlier identification of God as the one from whom and toward whom are all things and Christ as the one through whom are all things (8:6; 11:12c; cf. Rom 11:36) has now become extended to men and through men to women. Then, by segmenting this into three headships, he highlights a triple subjection rather than any self-mediation of God.

From this serial definition without any linking particle follow cultic prescriptions concerning the head of man and woman respectively (11:4, 5). Why men's and women's different "heads" lead to parallel but opposite requirements is not yet clear. But the distinction is legitimated by being expressed in the language of shame, which in the Greco-Roman world is gender specific—a man being shamed when his honor is challenged and not publicly defended, a woman when hers even needs defense. Here Paul's continuing to speak about the women insinuates some shameful exposure of them. He equates the shame of women prophesying uncovered with that of being shaven, and he insists that to prophesy uncovered women must be shorn (the verb for sheep). He then generously concedes that if this is shameful they can cover their heads. Enslaved women and prostitutes are often depicted with short hair; and Thecla, when she goes off to preach, dresses as a man (see *Acts of Thecla* 40), but the women prophets of Corinth apparently let their hair grow long, as is common among women depicted in vases and statuary. What he wants may be some tying up or covering of their hair rather than a full veil, but the argument would not make sense unless women in Corinth were prophesying without it. Paul's putting this in terms of parity with men may be his appeal to women who seek parity with men in worship.

Distinct head covering for men and women is next defended by allusions to Genesis (11:7–10). Assuming that the purpose of worship is to magnify God's glory, Paul argues that the prophesying man as God's image and glory must not be covered, whereas the prophesying woman as man's glory must be covered, lest God's glory be overshadowed by man's in worship. Paul's fear of idolatry here indicates that the Corinthian women's prayer and prophecy were particularly powerful and that some men experienced a competition between God's glory expressed when they prayed or prophesied and their own glory, which they saw reflected in the women prophets' uncovered heads. Paul does not notice that women would not experience this conflict, because they would see their own prophecy giving glory not to men but to God. This exposes a key theological difference between Paul and these women. He took the conflict between men's glory and God's to be the basic drama in human history still threatening God's work in Christ. Though the women prophets did not deny that evil people crucified the Lord of Glory (2:7–8), they saw that God's glory in Christ had overcome evil and needed only to be lived out.

When Paul says that man is God's image and glory and woman is not, he may be following Jewish exegesis of Gen 1:27 and 5:1–2 that highlights the glory of Adam above all others (Babylonian Talmud, *Baba Batra* 58a), ignoring other Jewish discussion of God's creating both Adam and Eve and the ethical responsibility of both (*Numbers Rabbah* 12.4; *Genesis Rabbah* 8.1; 22.2). Yet another exegetical tradition of the time took the androgynous human mind to be made in God's image in Gen 1:27 and the male and female not to be created until the second story of the garden (Philo, *On Creation* 69, 134). In this second story about her coming from man's rib, she could perhaps be called his "likeness," a word that does get interpreted as "glory" in Greek exegesis of Gen 5:1 (Num 12:8; Ps 17:15). Or, finally, Paul may call the woman "man's glory" because divorce in Palestine soon after this is available on grounds that a wife is not her husband's glory (Jerusalem Talmud, *Ketubot* 11.3).

Whatever traditions Paul is drawing from, it is significant that he does not argue from the rib story for woman being man's glory without adding a concession to the Corinthians that begins with a strong adversative and affirms reciprocity in the Lord (11:11–12). Clearly the churches had strong traditions that his hierarchical argument could not ignore. Yet he incorporates them into his argument in a way that makes women's childbearing their contribution, a role that women prophets apparently could not exercise (see at 7:34). The concession thus gives nothing away and lends a reasonable tone to his argument that women prophets cover their heads.

The difficulty of following Paul's arguments in this section comes less from his use of unfamiliar exegetical traditions than from the fact that his debate with the Corinthians is already in mid-course. If it is not by choice but by necessity that he is interpreting a text that speaks of God's creation "according to the image of God male and female" (Gen 5:1–2; 1:27), the question becomes: What was the Corinthian interpretation that he was opposing? A good lead is a pre-Pauline baptismal affirmation almost surely used in Corinth: "For those of you baptized into Christ have put on Christ. There is neither Jew nor Greek; there is neither slave nor free; there is not male and female. For all of you are one in Christ Jesus" (Gal 3:27–28; cf. 1 Cor 12:13; Col 3:10–11). The phrase "male and female," which breaks the neither/nor sequence, is an exact quotation of the Greek text of Gen 1:27 and 5:2, as is the phrase "according to an image" in the Colossians version. These show that this baptismal affirmation was a Christian restatement of the creation story, in its earliest use probably including only the "male and female" pair of Genesis.

The key question is why Christians reversed Genesis and claimed to be recreated in Christ *not* male and female. Some scholars propose on the basis of later Christian interpretation that women were claiming experience of an original androgynous creation renewed in Christ.[10] Yet the early Christian letters all quote the baptismal affirmation in a form that speaks of overcoming social exploitation and privilege. This suggests that women in Corinth claim to be created not male and female in order to oppose views of creation that legitimate male privilege and deny them full participation in God's image. Paul's use gives priority to the full freedom of Gentiles alongside Jews, maintaining the freedom of the slave only nominally and, in this letter, dropping "not male and female" entirely (1 Cor 12:13), raising the specter of immorality and idolatry to diminish female freedom, conceivably to protect the reputation of his Gentile gospel among Christian Jews.

"Therefore the woman ought to have authority on her head on account of the angels" (11:10) is enigmatic both for paradoxically calling the covering "authority" and for alluding to angels without explanation. Here Paul could well be dealing with a claim of the women prophets to "have authority on the head" so as to make covering themselves unnecessary when they "speak with the tongues of humans and angels" (13:1). If so, Paul takes up their claim and tries to make it point in the opposite direction by prefixing his three-part definition of head, so that the covering can be called the "authority on the head" and symbolize male headship. The angels then become not the heavenly court among whom the women praise God but the "sons of God," who abandon heaven to mate with the "daughters of men" and produce a race of giants who multiply sin (Gen 6:1–6; *1 Enoch* 1–20). Here Paul seems to be projecting male sexual desire on the angelic host, threatening cosmic idolatry and immorality if the women do not cover their heads "on account of the angels."

Paul's final arguments appealing to the Corinthians' sense of propriety, nature, custom, and church practice (11:13–16) show that the conflict on head covering did not stem simply from the Corinthians' having Greek assumptions about women's dress that Paul did not share. He assumes that they know it is customary for praying women to cover their heads, just as it is expected for women to wear their hair long. Paul's closing line leaves no doubt that they have intentionally chosen not to cover their heads. He expects them to "make an issue of this"—to be "contentious," "uncompromising," or, literally, "victory loving"— so he cuts off debate by saying, "We have no such custom" of women prophesying with bare heads, "nor do God's churches" (11:16). This last phrase judges the Corinthians for the third time by what Paul considers standard church practice (cf. 4:17; 7:17; 11:16), as he does once more to silence certain prophets and all women (14:33). Though arguments from what seems proper and from what others do are not without force when directed to respected people in small communities, Paul senses that such arguments will not change women who have chosen this practice for the substantive reason of demonstrating in their prophecy and praise that there is no male and female in Christ.

Idolatry within Community Worship: The Meal (11:17–34)

Concerning head covering, Paul begins with praise in order to add a new tradition and ends with intimations of idolatry and immorality. But concerning the common meal, Paul begins with blame for not keeping his traditions and does not end until he has charged the church with an idolatry for which some have died. Idolatry is first suggested in his opening statement that this is not the Lord's meal that they are eating. The meal honors some other god or power and only appears to honor Christ because, as Paul's sources tell him, some people go ahead and eat, getting hungry or drunk, while those with nothing are shamed. The exact conduct in Corinth is difficult to determine because charges of disorder, drunkenness, and hunger are the stock-in-trade for banquet satire in this period. But what Paul says, especially the phrases "every one goes ahead with their own meal" and his final "wait for one another; if you are hungry eat at home" (11:21, 33) indicate that those who come first do not wait.

To understand this we must try to determine when and where the meal took place in their gatherings, who cooked and served the food, and who may have come early and late. It is clear that the meal came before the drinking and speaking, by both Hellenistic custom and Paul's expectation, so that waiting to eat would delay everything. Scholars recently favor explaining the conflicts in terms of relative wealth of the participants, suggesting that distinguished friends of the host ate early and well, reclining in a dining room that normally seated no more than nine, while others ate whatever was left—or what they could bring—on benches in a inner courtyard.[11] But if the question is raised about who cooks and serves, other factors come into play. Free men could be hired to sacrifice meat, cook, and serve for special celebrations, but daily cooking was the work of women, whether free or enslaved. Because the Christian community ate in homes together daily or perhaps weekly (16:2; Rev 1:10; Acts 20:7), the hiring of a cook was unlikely and women probably did the work. Therefore Paul's comment about all going ahead with "their own meals" means either that women are preparing food at home and bringing it or that women gather ahead to cook everyone's meals. In either case these women are present as early as anyone and would be among those available to "go ahead and eat." The complaints of Paul then fall at least in part on the women who prepare food but do not wait to see that the last one is fed, acting not primarily as servers of others but as participants in the blessing and eating.

Paul's charge is serious. It is not the Lord's meal that they are eating. He claims to have received from Jesus that both the bread before and the wine after dinner stand for Jesus' death and require a solemn self-judgment and a discerning of the social body if those who participate are not to become sick and die as has happened to others. Paul adds a line to the account of Jesus' last meal declaring that every meal they celebrate proclaims Jesus' death until he comes.

With the same general tradition of a meal with Jesus, the Corinthians unquestionably have a different experience. Where Paul wants them orderly, solemn, and self-critical, they are apparently informal, celebrating, and self-expressive, finding in the Lord's meal not primarily Jesus' death and self-judgment but Jesus' life and spiritual nurture. Even Paul does not turn the meal into a cultic performance by designated leaders, but his repeated proposal that they eat at home if hungry (11:22, 34) begins to relegate back to the home the community-building process of daily nourishment. This move would bring with it far greater changes for the women than the men, requiring them to cook at home, serve in the context of family subordination, keep the hearth until the final person has eaten, and arrive at the community last rather than being among the first to bless and eat, and then to bless and drink and speak.

Paul's threats of immorality and idolatry provoked by women's uncovered heads and the unserved community meals evoke a certain menace as he begins to speak about the spiritual. Although the present argument ends on the apparently warmer note of advice to wait for each other and to eat at home, he has served notice that God's glory threatened by human confidence is a life-and-death issue in Corinth. Clearly, the Corinthians do not see Christ threatened and God's people bound to restrict themselves and others in order to protect the divine honor. Not that they would be ignorant of the death of Christ and the victimization of people, themselves perhaps included, but they are intent on God's glory revealed in Christ and on mediating this life to others.

CORINTHIAN SPIRITUAL GIFTS AND PAUL'S REGULATIONS (12:1–14:40)

"Concerning the Spiritual": Parts of the Body (12:1–31)

The topic of this section could be read in the neuter as "spiritual things" (12:1; cf. 14:1), but more probably Paul is taking up some Corinthian claim about "the spiritual," because he returns at the end of this argument to challenge "the spiritual" to approve what he has said (14:37). He accepts that they are spiritual but minimizes this with reminders that they were once captive to speechless idols and that, whereas only those who say "Jesus be cursed!" are known to lack God's spirit, whoever says "Jesus is Lord" speaks with the Holy Spirit.

Paul states in three ways the great variety of spiritual gifts and four times says "to one this . . . to another that" to stress individual distribution of gifts. His metaphor of the body adds the further element of interdependence, so that what one lacks in the spirit the next provides from the same spirit. Paul may also be expanding the repertoire of spiritual gifts to include apostolic mission preaching, teaching, helping, and administration (12:8–10, 28–31). Paul's long argument that every necessary function is spiritual and all believers are unlike and interdependent suggests that the Corinthians probably see themselves each to be gifted in all ways, with emphasis on the many gifts of speech and acts of power carried out by speaking. If so, their view precedes Paul's, and Acts shows that it survives after him (Acts 2:1–21; 8:15–17, 39; 10:44–48; 19:6). This does not mean that the Corinthians consider some Christians to be unspiritual, since the spirit is associated with the baptism common to all

(1:13–17; 10:1–4; 12:13; 15:29). But one might expect some competitiveness in demonstrating a spirit that all share (4:6), which could be less a threat than a stimulation to the people involved, though disturbing to Paul.

Statements about Christ and God in Paul's argument underline how important distributed gifts are in his social strategy for the Corinthian church. The body is taken not simply as a metaphor but as a metaphor for Christ, and the believers are identified as Christ's body (12:12, 27). This is confirmed by citing the familiar baptismal affirmation, "For you yourselves were all baptized into one body, whether Jews or Greeks, whether slaves or free, and were all given one spirit to drink" (12:13; cf. Gal 3:27–28; Col 3:10–11; see above, at 11:7). But two things have happened to the affirmation here. "Male and female," the original pair in this retelling of the creation story, are not mentioned, which could mean in the context of an argument that ends by silencing women that Paul omits them to recapture the baptismal claim for another vision of the church that conflicts with what this phrase evokes for women in Corinth. Paul's vision probably does not exclude women—note the less honorable parts of the body that are clothed with greater honor (12:22–23; cf. 11:2–16). What he means may be clarified by his second adaptation of the statement, in which "neither Jew nor Greek, neither slave nor free," has become "whether Jews or Greeks, whether slaves or free." The social positions of privilege and exploitation are no longer overcome but are integrated as parts of the whole. When Paul concludes, "But it is you who are the body of Christ and individually its parts" (12:27), is he integrating them in Christ not only as differently gifted people but also as differently advantaged social groups (cf. 7:17–25)?

Paul's theology confirms what his Christology has depicted. First he says, "The Spirit distributes to each as it chooses," then, "God set the parts, each single one of them, in the body as he wanted," and finally, "God set these in the church, first apostles, second prophets, third teachers . . ." (12:11, 18, 28). The differences in God's gifts thus become a ranked list of church functions, with apostles primary, prophets next, and those who speak and interpret tongues last. This completes Paul's argument against a single common spiritual potential in favor of divinely distributed and interdependent gifts (12:1–30) and begins a second argument, challenging the Corinthians to identify and seek the higher gifts (12:31–14:40). These two arguments are not strictly compatible—How can God assign gifts and people strive for higher ones? But Paul uses the first to assert their dependence on others, the second to influence their priorities, and defends both by arguments from the common good.

A Digression on Love (13:1–13)

When Paul concedes that he must deal with aspiration and not only with assignment of spiritual gifts to effectively persuade the Corinthians, he turns to praise of love. Love is not presented as the highest gift but as a challenge to all human aspiration. The tongues of angels, the mysteries of prophetic knowledge, and the heights of self-denial are nothing without it. Love is defined not by descriptive adjectives but by verbs (13:4–8), though translations seldom attain this. The image of the child's mind and the mirror show how all human spiritual gifts are temporary and partial in light of God's full knowing, which will be revealed only in the final knowing face to face (cf. Gen 32:31; Exod 33:20; Num 12:8). Paul ends with a triad of Christian virtues—parallel to Plato's truth, beauty, and goodness, or to the common row of female statues symbolizing the classical virtues—and he names love the greatest. Although this celebration of love could stand on its own, Paul's contrast here between knowledge and love (cf. 8:1–3) shows that this passage was probably written by Paul in this context to challenge all Corinthian spiritual aspirations and at the same time provide a basis for distinguishing priorities among them.

Something of the Corinthian Christian voice as it differs from Paul's can be heard in the verb that appears in the second person just before and after the largely first-person hymn—"be zealous" or "you are zealous" (12:31; 14:1). Paul concedes the zealousness that they want in order to get them to concede what he wants: "So you yourselves, since you are zealots of the spirits, be zealous in building up the church in order to excel all the more. . . . When you gather, each has a psalm, a teaching, a revelation, a tongue, an interpretation. Let all things be done to build up. . . . You are all able to prophesy, (but) one by one so that all may learn and be encouraged" (14:12, 26, 31). In each case they are zealous for communal experience of speaking as the Spirit inspires them, whereas Paul wants constructive learning.

Paul's hymn praises the virtue of love personified in female form: "Love suffers long, love is kind and not zealous, love does not brag or boast, love does not act shamefully, does not seek *her* own, does not provoke . . . love bears all things, believes all things, hopes all things, endures all things" (13:4–7). Such love, which freely chooses to suffer with others, bearing up under what is and waiting patiently for what is to come, is possible only to those like Paul who start from a position of advantage that allows options for choice (see "Introduction"). Yet he expects them to imitate a preexistent Christ who gives up divine authority for incarnation and death, not recognizing that their experience of Christ may begin at the cross, where there are no choices, and lift them from it in Christ's rising. Though Paul's hymn represents one profound experience of Christ, it will hardly have become theirs. As part of the Jewish and Christian wisdom tradition, they more likely celebrate Christ as God's Wisdom who is always rejected but all the more zealous to grasp the truth and bold to speak it, eager to provoke others to become voices of the living Wisdom (cf. Prov 1:20–33; 8:1–9:6; Wisdom of Solomon 6–10; *1 Enoch* 42; Luke 7:31–35; 11:45–52; John 1:1–18; *Odes of Solomon*).

"Concerning the Spiritual": Prophecy before Tongues (14:1–25)

Just as Paul after other digressions returns to his major theme with new confidence (3:1; 10:14), so here he calls on them to pursue love and give priority to prophecy among the spiritual gifts. The link is that prophecy serves the common good, building up the church. This is contrasted with speaking in tongues, which Paul disparages by associating it in turn with self-development, confusion, barbarous speech, immaturity, barrenness, and madness. His intensive effort to dissociate prophecy from tongues suggests that the two were very much integrated in Corinth, and clues of this appear in what Paul assumes as he argues. He assumes that both prophecy and tongues are spoken in the same gatherings of believers, not in private; that the people provide their own leadership through these and many other kinds of speaking; that all may speak in tongues and all prophesy; that no set sequence or exclusive form is anticipated; and that outsiders are present and express their reactions (14:6, 16, 18, 9, 23–26, 31).

Paul describes the phenomenon of speaking in tongues with the verbs "speaking," "praying," "singing praises," "blessing," and thanking," showing that speech in tongues is used primarily for prayer (14:2, 4–6, 9, 13–17, 23, 27, 39). So he can say that speech in tongues is addressed to God rather than to people (14:2, 28; Gal 4:6; Rom 8:26–27). This is not to say that the Corinthians would never use traditional prayers to summon and praise God or make petitions. But their more intense prayer apparently moves beyond normal language into sounds that Paul argues could make strangers think them crazy, but which they take as a sign that they are joining the heavenly circle, where God is continually praised with the tongues of angels (13:1; 14:23). What Paul considers immature and not constructive for community life they take as true maturity and a blessing to all who hear.

Paul suggests the nature of their prophecy when he points to the person who enters the community while all are prophesying, is convicted, and falls down worshiping God and saying, "God is truly among you!" (14:23–25). Since the Corinthians were not strong on judging individuals (5:1–6:20), their prophetic judging more likely falls on whole groups or the present age. Conviction of God's presence could come from their "mysteries," "revelations," or visions about human destiny in the present and future (13:2; 14:2, 26; 15:51–52; Rom 11:25–26; 2 Cor 12:1–10), or from their expressing the "depths of God" and "mind of Christ" revealed to those who receive God's spirit (2:10–16). Their prophecy may be integrated with prayer in tongues by the kind of alternation we see in the book of Revelation. Or, as in Paul's letters, prayers of remembrance and intercession could come first, followed by prophecy interspersed with oaths and cries of thanks, culminating in praises glorifying God's unfathomable wisdom.

In any case, prophecy and prayer are not dissociated in Corinth, as Paul's long argument to dissociate them proves. The instructions on head covering for those who pray and prophesy indicate that the same women and men do both and suggest that these are the two crucial functions in worship. Their integration might be depicted in the organic images of the body's breathing or the circulation of blood, with prayers of appeal and thanks being the people's speech to God, and prophecy being God's speaking to the people. Yet prayer is not reduced to a human response, since the divine spirit is taken to be inspiring the one that prays (14:16; Rom 8:26-27; Gal 4:6). The spirit makes the person who prophesies and prays a mediator in a spiritual circulation, speaking for the people to God and speaking for God to the people.

"Concerning the Spiritual": Advice If Not Consent (14:26–40)

In his decisive closing section, Paul accepts their practice that everyone may speak so that he can insist that whatever is said must build up the church. Then three instructions follow. The first indicates that at each gathering only two or at most three should speak in tongues one after another with one person interpreting, but when there is no one to interpret then the speaker should be silent in church. The second says that two or three prophets may speak in turn and the others should discern what they have said, but when someone else gets up to speak the first prophet should be silent. These two instructions are parallel, raising the question of whether Paul's efforts to restrict continuous, simultaneous, and uninterpreted speaking in tongues have caused him to apply the same rules for prophecy simply as an argument from parity. Yet the problematic instant he mentions in each case is different—the lack of an interpreter for tongues, the lack of willingness to yield the floor for prophecy—showing that his guidelines probably arise from his problems with each kind of speech. In both cases the premium for Paul is on fewer people speaking and more people listening and evaluating.

Paul favors secondary reflection over primary expression without explaining what he means by interpreting an ecstatic prayer or discerning a prophecy. When people who pray in tongues also interpret (14:13), are they praying twice or giving translators' asides? When one interprets after two or three speak in tongues (14:27–28), is it a summary? And how do they know ahead that someone will be able to interpret so they can speak? One senses that Paul is not restoring a standard practice but trying to develop an alternative and constructing it as he goes along. Since he has made clear that the Corinthians avoid judging (5:1–6:12), it is probable that this interpreting and discerning are Paul's own agenda in line with his wanting everything to be done with the mind as well as the spirit (14:13–19).

The two instructions on tongues and prophecy reveal about the Corinthians that many people speak at each gathering (not two or three), that their voices often overlap or become simultaneous, and that there is little interest in translating ecstatic prayers or deliberating and judging prophetic insights. Paul's intent that they sit down sooner, stop more often for interpretation and reflection, and wait until another session if not immediately inspired, would hardly be well received. Clearly the Corinthians learned more from speaking than from listening, particularly speaking with the support of other simultaneous voices. Yet Paul argues that the spirits of the prophets are subject to the discipline of the prophets, since God is the God of peace rather than disturbance, in Corinth as in all the churches (14:31–33 to end; cf. 4:17; 7:15–17; 11:16). Though it is not clear just how God's fostering peace makes God's spirit in a prophet subject to a prophet—or is it the prophet's spirit subject to other prophets?—this subjection that Paul says accords with God's nature and is found in "all the churches" sets the theological and ecclesiological stage for Paul's third rule—that women also be "subject" "in the churches" (14:34–36). We can assume that the Corinthian prophets in contrast take themselves to be subject to the spirit speaking in them, not vice versa; that they see God as one who provokes rather than pacifies—though scarcely using Paul's pejorative term—"God of disturbance/riot" (cf. 2 Cor 6:5); and that their own experience disproves to them Paul's claim about "all the churches."

The two or three sentences silencing women have been found to be so offensive in our time that many scholars argue that they are not written by Paul or are peripheral to his argument (14:34–35 or 36). In the Old Latin and major Greek-Latin bilingual manuscripts, 1 Cor 14:34–35 is found at the end of the chapter, giving rise in recent years to the theory that it was added to the margin of Paul's letter and inserted in different places by early copyists. But no manuscript survives without the gloss, and the lines appear in no third place, which makes a simple displacement of the passage far more likely. This is supported by the fact that these Latin and Greek-Latin manuscripts, which have these verses after chapter 14, share many readings that are unlike the earliest Greek papyri and codices, including three readings which would change the translation of these two verses alone, aside from the new location. Therefore the only solid hypothesis is that an innovative copyist at the root of the Latin-related tradition omitted these verses, whether by accident or on purpose to defend women prophets, and she/he or a corrector put them back hurriedly in the wrong place.[12]

Many scholars who concede that a copyist moved these verses to the chapter's end nonetheless try to argue that Paul could not have written these two or more verses—or that he did not mean what they say—because they do not fit in Paul's argument, either in the letter as a whole, in this chapter, or among these worship rules. Those who think Paul could not be so inconsistent in this letter as to allow women to prophesy with covered heads in 11:5, and then forbid them to speak in 14:34, try unsuccessfully to show that he was dealing in the two cases with different women (all women/married women) or different speech (prophecy/teaching) or different settings (small gatherings/full church). They neglect the good possibility that Paul develops his argument as the letter proceeds, increasing restrictions on women's worship participation until he feels able to demand their silence.

The proposal that women's being silenced does not fit this chapter on prophecy and ecstatic prayer neglects the fact that Paul has already identified women's prophecy and prayer as controversial (11:2–16). Finally, Paul's rule about women's silence in worship fits the immediate context well, being no different in form from the preceding two rules about those who speak in tongues and prophesy: a third person imperative instruction about a particular group is explained and then illustrated in the conditional form (14:26–35). Because Paul's instructions about women's speech cannot be eliminated as a later interpolation or as a detached aside in Paul's argument (as the NRSV parentheses imply), their location at the climax of his argument concerning the spiritual only highlights their import.

Paul's argument about the spiritual concedes that the Corinthians are spiritual, but this means to him that they have divinely assigned gifts that make them interdependent (12:1–30). He concedes that they are zealous for spiritual things, but he wants them to learn sacrificial love that favors prophecy over ecstasy to build up the church (12:31–14:25). Finally, he concedes that each can express some contribution when they meet, but only a few are to speak– and they in turn so that all can listen and learn (14:26–33). Granted that the women's speech is not the explicit issue to this point, each stage of the argument narrows the freedom of the spiritual to express themselves communally until most are reflecting on what the few have said, and it is not such a jump to say that women's reflecting is to be silent except at home. After Paul's final reference to the God of peace to explain why the prophets' spirits are subject to the prophets in all the churches, Paul silences the women with two broad strokes of the law and of shame. Between the two he makes the apparent concession that they can learn by asking their own men at home—probably meaning fathers, sons, or masters for those without husbands. Then the second person address applied earlier to the prophets with respect mocks the women for speaking as a source of God's word on the basis that his mission preaching has been the source of all they know and the Corinthians are a mere handful among all those it has reached (14:31, 36).

At this point Paul directly challenges the prophets and the spiritual in Corinth to recognize his regulations as a command of the Lord or not be recognized themselves (14:37–38). He opens debate and cuts off debate simultaneously, leaving it up to the spiritual to decide not whether he speaks in the spirit but whether they are spiritual enough to accept it. Paul's appeal to "the Lord's command" probably refers to something he has spiritually discerned rather than to something Jesus said (2 Cor 12:7–10; cf. 1 Cor 7:10; 9:14), both because it is expressed as a challenge to spiritual discernment and because we know of no such saying of Jesus nor any setting in Jesus' life for giving speech rules in assemblies. After declaring that those not recognizing these rules are not to be recognized, Paul suddenly changes his tone: "So, my brethren, be zealous to prophesy . . . ," and the sisters whom he has forbidden to prophesy have vanished from his address (note NRSV "friends" in place of its usual "brothers and sisters"! see 1:11 above). This closing concession that men may still prophesy and speak in tongues fails to disguise the unthinkable loss to women and the church involved in any such "doing everything decently and in order" (14:39–40).

Paul's stranglehold move on these women's voices gives us the measure of their influence in the Corinthian church. In the first place, the culminating position of his instruction on women shows how significant they are among the spiritual—any minor addendum would have come after the climactic challenge to the spiritual (14:37–38). Second, the introductory libation to the God of peace and the unspecified arguments from law and shame show that Paul knows that these women are not scofflaws or objects of ridicule but widely respected and therefore always susceptible to innuendo. Third, Paul's "concession" that if they want to learn they can ask their husbands at home shows that they have intellectual interests, without which it would not be credible, but also shows that they act in public statements rather than in indirect inquiries. As with Paul's earlier warning that if they are hungry they should eat at home (11:34, 22), this effort to send the women's voices home is further evidence that they have made the home of a sister into their own communal home. Fourth, Paul's rhetorical questions asking if they are the source and destination of God's word are meant to shame them for claiming a status that should be his as their missioner; the questions reveal instead that people are speaking of their prophecy as a going forth of God's word and their community as the destination of this address from God.

Fifth, Paul's taking the risk to demand a spiritual vote of confidence in order to legitimate his silencing of certain tongues, prophecy, and the women is the highest tribute to the women prophets and shows with what seriousness their leadership is taken in the community. Knowing that the Spirit alone can settle the validity of his argument, he appeals to the men for judgment. He does not see that by putting the women in the double bind whereby they can only certify themselves as prophets by choosing never again to speak as prophets, he provokes the Spirit in them to disqualify his maneuver. 2 Corinthians is evidence that the Spirit in the Corinthian church did not verify the cutting off of these voices as the Lord's command but threw Paul's own spiritual credentials into question and called forth from him a different kind of self-defense.

Past or Present Resurrection (15:1–11)

After the silencing of the women, Paul does not immediately begin his next critique of the Corinthians but refers back to the past, perhaps to enroll the women again among the "brethren" (14:39; 15:1), but on the terms that God's saving word originates not from the Corinthians but from resurrection witnesses such as himself (14:36). The verbs in the first sentence contrast his role and theirs: "I make known . . . I announced . . . I announced . . ." on one side and ". . . you received . . . you stand . . . you are saved . . . you grasp . . . you believe . . ." on the other. What he passes on are four events, "Christ died . . . he was buried . . . he is risen . . . he appeared," and he repeats the last verb four times in a catalogue of resurrection witnesses until he has also told Christ's appearance to him. The redundant modesty of this self- presentation disguises the fact that he cannot have received this final witness within the tradition transmitted to him. Scholars discreetly look the other way and talk about whether he has also added the five hundred of whom he claims some are still alive to bear witness, perhaps also James and the apostles as a doublet or competing tradition to Cephas and the Twelve. If the omission of the women's resurrection accounts is mentioned at all, commentators take it as evidence that the empty tomb stories are a post-Pauline construction, later elaborated into stories of appearances to women. They do not ask why women's stories about angels would be created after "more reliable" accounts from apostles were available, being satisfied that they have in hand the "core" tradition about Jesus' appearances to Cephas and the Twelve (15:3–5).

But if Paul has added his own story, commented on the five hundred and omitted the women, it may be wiser to recognize his freedom and accept Paul as the one who has gathered disparate appearance stories into a single tradition to validate Jesus' resurrection and certain of its witnesses including himself. His omitting the women in such a list cannot be explained by any special campaign in this letter for Cephas's priority (1:12; 3:22; 9:5), nor would Paul need to worry that the women's witness would not be respected in Corinth. Either Paul has never heard what the four Gospels consider the first resurrection accounts—hardly likely—or he chooses not to mention them because of some meaning of these stories in Corinth.

What the Corinthians mean by these stories is less clear, though the next part of Paul's argument assumes at least that they believe Jesus is risen (15:12–19). Many of them honor Apollos, who is not known as an early resurrection witness, which suggests that the women's stories may be a prelude to claims they and Apollos make to know the Lord themselves. Then it is Paul who makes an innovative move when he restricts resurrection witnesses to the early years and cites his vision as "last of all," implying that the Corinthian visions and prophecies are insufficient evidence that Christ lives. To compensate for this boldness, he disparages himself as a mistimed or misshapen birth among the apostles, thriving only by hard work and God's grace. The Corinthians, who do not claim to be the final witnesses, probably lack such defensiveness and simply demonstrate Christ's presence and voice in their common life.

Present or Future Resurrection (15:12–58)

Then why does Paul challenge certain Corinthian Christians: "How can some of you say there is no resurrection of the dead?" (15:12)? His argument must tell. First, he presents the destructive consequences of such denial for three kinds of believers. If there is no resurrection of the dead, Christ is not risen. Hence, the apostles have committed false witness about God, who they claim raised Christ; the Corinthians' faith is good for nothing and they are still in their sins; and those who have fallen asleep—the dead in Christ—are lost. Paul's culminating conditional sentence, "If we have hoped in Christ in this life only, we are of all people most pitiable" (15:19), uses the general "we" to stereotype as total skeptics about life after death any who deny the resurrection of the dead.

Paul's own contrasting affirmation that follows gives the first hint of how the Corinthians differ from Paul (15:20–22). The image of Christ as firstfruit or sacral guarantee of the harvest of the believing dead defines Christ strictly by his benefits for the dead and locates the position of the present believer in limbo between Adam in whom all die and Christ in whom all will be made alive. The more elaborate temporal sequence which follows confirms this, shifting the great transformation in Christ out of the past or present, or even the time of Christ's coming, to the time when Christ triumphs over death and is made subject to God (15:23–28). Christians in Corinth apparently believe not in such a resurrection of the dead but in the resurrection of the living, experiencing themselves to be filled, rich, and ruling in God's kingdom (4:8). Paul's temporal delay of resurrection life and his interpretation of it in terms of cosmic subjection—the same word used just before to subject women to men (14:34; cf. 11:3)—can only be to the Corinthians a desecration of God in Christ who is revealed in their prophecy.

Paul next tries to prove the resurrection of the dead from what believers already do: some baptize on behalf of the dead, and he himself risks death every day (15:29–34). If it is the Corinthians who baptize for the dead, they must assume some life after the baptized person's death and complete the baptism of those who die without it. But, if so, the key transition for them occurs not after death but in baptism, as they—according to various early views of baptism—not only put on Christ, where there is no male and female (Gal 3:28; see 7:8 above), but die and rise in Christ (Col 2:9–15) and receive God's spirit in prophecy and tongues (1 Cor 12:7–13).[13] Paul, on the other hand, claims that he can take the risks he does because he anticipates reward after death for his losses (15:30–34, 58). Without identifying the Corinthians as libertine, Paul thinks they should be: "If the dead are not raised, 'Let us eat, drink, and be merry for tomorrow we die.'" Here he makes everything depend on the reversal at God's cosmic triumph, when the dead and surviving will be compensated for their work. Yet in other contexts Paul is witness to a common Christian baptismally based resurrection faith much closer to that of the Corinthians: "All of us baptized into Christ Jesus were baptized into his death . . . so that as Christ was raised from the dead through the glory of the Father, so we also might walk in newness of life" (Rom 6:2–4; cf. Col 2:20; 3:1–4). Yet he closes this section, "Some have no knowledge of God, I say to you for shame," reflecting that his opening line, "Some of you say there is no resurrection of the dead," has led into a debate about God.

In the final round of this debate, Paul mocks the skeptic's "how are the dead raised and with what body do they come?" (15:35–50) in order to present his own view to the Corinthians as the spiritual one. Only a fool, he confides in them, would not see that just as a dead seed is given new life by God's creative power, so the human corpse can receive an immortal nature only by God's act. The spiritual body is not first but second according to Paul's double vision in reading the story of God's creation in Gen 2:7. The man Adam is the living soul, and Christ by God's "breath of life" becomes the second Adam or life-giving spirit.

Because the Corinthians take life in Christ to be a new creation, they will accept Paul's contrast of these two Adams and can rejoice with Paul that they who were once "those of dirt" and have become "those of heaven." But suddenly his future tense takes back everything that has been given: "Just as we have borne the image of the one of dirt, so we will also bear the image of the one of heaven" (15:49). If Christ's image is strictly future, then "flesh and blood cannot inherit God's kingdom nor mortal inherit immortality" (15:50). The final irony is that Paul tells a mystery revealed to him to disqualify their present revelations: at the last trumpet the dead will be raised and the living will put on an immortal body. Only then comes the shout of triumph, "Death has been swallowed up in victory!"—though Paul's past tense in quoting Isaiah's future prophecy betrays that Christians already use it to celebrate Christ's life (15:54; Isa 25:8). At this shout, even Paul breaks into thanks to

God, though he quickly sobers and counsels hard work because "in the Lord your labor is not in vain."

The debate here is over how God's power, which raised Christ, becomes available to those who depend on God for their life. Paul's voice in this particular argument is clear: Christ as firstfruit assures the resurrection of believers when he comes and of the dead when he triumphs over every authority and power and death itself. Then all losses will be compensated and hopes fulfilled in immortal life in Christ. For a man who has taken many losses and sees death straight ahead, this is gospel. The voices he is contesting are no less clear: We who have died with Christ in baptism and risen up in his life are not dependent on past witnesses of Christ's rising or future rewards after the cosmos is subjected to Christ and Christ to God. Resurrection is not the preserve of the dead but the joy of the living, and we already experience Christ alive in us in our prayer and prophecy.

SUPPORT NETWORKS: THE CORINTHIANS' AND PAUL'S (16:1–24)

Future Travel Plans (16:1–12)

Paul's final notes give glimpses of how he builds networks of support and show that there are other networks of Christians that function independently of him. If Corinth wrote to Paul "concerning the collection for the saints," it may have been a reference to meager results, since he presents a new collection method. He says he has used it in the regions of Galatia, hardly a high recommendation for Achaea's capital city of Corinth, but it may reassure them that Paul has not shaped the plan to keep the money safe from certain people in Corinth. Paul wants saving to be done at home along with the eating and speaking in tongues that make their gatherings lively. He promises to send the delegates they choose to Jerusalem with the offering, an added incentive for potential travelers and their friends to contribute.

After this reference to Galatia and to Jerusalem, he speaks of coming through Macedonia to Corinth as soon as his work allows him to leave Ephesus. So he links the Corinthians to his ministry in many places, reassures his supporters of why he is not with them, and promises that this way he will have more time when he comes. Opponents hear that he is busy with adversaries elsewhere and that he is approaching, perhaps for the winter. Meanwhile, Timothy has been sent (cf. 4:17–21). Paul expects him not to be welcomed or to be able to represent Paul fully in defending this letter, but he asks that they let him bring news back, perhaps with "the brothers" Stephanus and company on their next trip (16:15–18).

In contrast, "concerning Apollos" suggests that he was a topic of their letter (cf. 7:1). They apparently invited him back, since Paul assures them that he urged him to come. Paul's next phrase, "it was not at all the will for him to come now," could be a euphemism expressing God's will, but, in light of Paul's urging, more likely reflects Apollos's refusal to come "with the brothers"—not surprising if Paul means coming with Stephanus, since that would involve him in arriving in Corinth with Paul's letter. Paul has been trying to incorporate Apollos in his network throughout this letter, including his apparent cordiality here, but the fact that he does not even have a greeting to send from Apollos suggests that Apollos prefers to build his own network with the Corinthians.

Recommendations and Greetings (16:13–24)

Paul concludes the letter with an almost military challenge to the Corinthians to be alert, firm in faith, manly, strong, all of this in love—very much his approach to the gospel rather than theirs. He then commends Stephanus's household to the Corinthians for their long-standing service and asks the Corinthians to be subordinate to them and to whoever works with them (16:15–18; see "Introduction"). Fortunatus and Achaicus could be slaves or sons in this household of Stephanus. Paul's recommending them at this point in the letter probably indicates that the three are to carry his letter to Corinth, just as the mention of their recent arrival and his relief at hearing news suggests that they brought the Corinthian letter to him, perhaps in the rounds of their business since Paul seems to anticipate Timothy coming back to him with them (16:11). Paul's triple request that they be recognized (16:15, 16, 18) goes beyond anything required to commend letter carriers and suggests that these first converts of Paul have a key place in his hope for the reordering of the church in Corinth. Although Paul did not praise his faction in the first chapter of the letter, by now he expects the Corinthians to submit to these people.

The greetings from the Asian churches, from all the brethren, and especially from Aquila and Prisca and the church in their house, could represent points where Paul's network and that of the Corinthians' genuinely intersect (16:19–20). According to the account in Acts, this couple exiled from Rome provide Paul his first hospitality in Corinth when he makes tents in their shop. They travel with him to Ephesus a year and a half later and instruct Apollos before sending him on to Corinth (Acts 18:2–3, 18, 16–27). So now they are still in Ephesus sending greetings back to Corinth (16:8, 19), and later they resurface back in Rome (Rom 16:3–5). Because Prisca is usually mentioned first and is known as a teacher of Apollos, her leadership must have been important in the churches of Rome, Corinth, and Ephesus. She lived in Corinth perhaps two years and would have had special links with the women, possibly written correspondence, and Paul makes a point to include her greeting.

The final words evoke Paul's complex relation to them: he calls them to greet each other with a holy kiss, greets them in his own handwriting, curses any who do not love the Lord, invokes the Lord's coming in a traditional Aramaic formula, and blesses them with the grace of the Lord Jesus and his own love (16:20–24). In the spirit of recovering both sides of the correspondence, it is appropriate to think of their response to his letter: reading it aloud, "interpreting spiritual things with the spiritual" (2:13), invoking God in blessings and curses, letting Paul know their mind on the man with his father's wife, on head covering, on women's prophecy, and on resurrection, all worked out in their common life of divine and human communication in the Spirit.

NOTES

1. Jerome Murphy-O'Connor, *St. Paul's Corinth: Texts and Archaeology* (Wilmington, DE: Glazier, 1983), 3–44, 57–73.

2. Ibid., 122.

3. Ibid.

4. Ibid., 11, 29, 33.

5. Lilian Portefaix, *Sisters Rejoice: Paul's Letter to the Philippians and Luke-Acts as Seen by First-century Philippian Women* (Stockholm: Almqvist & Wiksell International, 1988), 33–58.

6. Eva Cantarella, *Pandora's Daughter: The Role and Status of Women in Greek and Roman Antiquity* (Baltimore and London: Johns Hopkins University Press, 1987), 138.

7. John C. Hurd, Jr., *The Origin of 1 Corinthians* (2nd ed.; Macon, GA: Mercer University Press, 1983), 274–78, 290.

8. Cantarella, *Pandora's Daughter,* 137.

9. Ibid., 44, 116.

10. Dennis Ronald MacDonald, *There is no Male and Female: The Fate of a Dominical Saying in Paul and Gnosticism* (Philadelphia: Fortress, 1987).

11. Murphy-O'Connor, *St. Paul's Corinth,* 153–72; Gerd Theissen, *The Social Setting of Pauline Christianity: Essays on Corinth* (Philadelphia: Fortress, 1982), 147–74.

12. Antoinette Clark Wire, *The Corinthian Women Prophets: A Reconstruction through Paul's Rhetoric* (Minneapolis: Fortress, 1990), 149–52; cf. Gordon D. Fee, *The First Epistle to the Corinthians* (Grand Rapids: Eerdmans, 1987), 699–708.

13. Wire, *Corinthian Women Prophets,* 166–68.

RECOMMENDED READINGS

Cantarella, Eva. *Pandora's Daughter: The Role and Status of Women in Greek and Roman Antiquity.* Baltimore and London: Johns Hopkins University Press, 1987.

Castelli, Elizabeth A. *Imitating Paul: A Discourse of Power.* Atlanta: Westminster/John Knox, 1991.

Conzelmann, Hans. *1 Corinthians: A Commentary on the First Epistle to the Corinthians.* Philadelphia: Fortress, 1975.

Fee, Gordon D. *The First Epistle to the Corinthians.* Grand Rapids: Eerdmans, 1987.

Hurd, John C., Jr. *The Origin of 1 Corinthians.* 2nd ed. Macon, GA: Mercer University Press, 1983.

MacDonald, Dennis Ronald. *There is no Male and Female: The Fate of a Dominical Saying in Paul and Gnosticism.* Philadelphia: Fortress, 1987.

Mitchell, Margaret Mary. *Paul and the Rhetoric of Reconciliation: An Exegetical Investigation of the Language and Composition of 1 Corinthians.* Hermeneutische Untersuchungen zur Theologie 28. Tübingen: J. C. B. Mohr (Paul Siebeck), 1991.

Murphy-O'Connor, Jerome. *St. Paul's Corinth: Texts and Archaeology.* Wilmington, DE: Glazier, 1983.

Portefaix, Lilian. *Sisters Rejoice: Paul's Letter to the Philippians and Luke-Acts as Seen by First-century Philippian Women.* Stockholm: Almqvist & Wiksell International, 1988.

Schüssler Fiorenza, Elisabeth. "Rhetorical Situation and Historical Reconstruction in I Corinthians." *New Testament Studies* 33 (1987): 386–403.

Theissen, Gerd. *The Social Setting of Pauline Christianity: Essays on Corinth.* Philadelphia: Fortress, 1982.

Wire, Antoinette Clark. *The Corinthian Women Prophets: A Reconstruction through Paul's Rhetoric.* Minneapolis: Fortress, 1990.

2 Corinthians

SHELLY MATTHEWS ◆

THE CHAPTER ON THE Corinthian Epistles in Elizabeth Cady Stanton's *Woman's Bible* includes no comment on 2 Corinthians. And though feminist biblical scholars in this century have devoted considerable attention to 1 Corinthians, feminist work on 2 Corinthians has advanced little since Stanton's time. The reason for this discrepancy is not mysterious. The first Corinthian epistle refers explicitly to women several times; the second does not.

A modern feminist biblical commentary, however, cannot limit itself to biblical passages that focus on women and "women's issues." My argument here is grounded in part on the rules of grammar. Because the early church was not an exclusively male sect, I understand grammatically male forms of address in biblical literature as generic and inclusive of women, unless a particular context prohibits such an understanding.[1] Work on the Corinthian context suggests that women were not merely present in this church, but were leaders responding to and actively influencing the shape of Paul's arguments.[2] To limit feminist historical work in the Pauline epistles to passages that mention women is to neglect the study of how the women present in first-century congregations might have responded to the rest of Paul's arguments.

Moreover, a feminist theological evaluation of biblical literature that focuses singularly on "women's issues" perpetuates the misunderstanding that patriarchy is a simple binary system of oppression based solely on gender. Feminist theological evaluation attends to the actual complexity of patriarchy when it acknowledges gender oppression as one element in a system of oppression that also involves factors such as race and class. In short, all biblical texts require feminist analysis because women were and are affected by *all* the texts of their culture, and because feminist concern for liberation requires attention to all forms of patriarchal oppression.

THE RHETORICAL METHOD
[OR: AGAINST THE VIEW THAT PAUL IS AN ORACLE COMBATING EGOMANIACS, HUCKSTERS, AND INTERLOPERS]

For feminist historians working to reclaim the past for women and other marginalized persons from texts that have rendered them absent or branded them as troublemakers, historical reconstruction by means of rhetorical analysis holds much potential.[3] A guiding principle of this method is that historical texts are not mirrors reflecting reality "as it really was." Texts are, rather, rhetorical constructions of authors responding to argumentative situations in which they seek to persuade an audience to adopt their own point of view. Feminist historians who understand the ancient text as rhetorical construction attempt to move beyond the text in itself to the historical argumentative situation in which the text was constructed. Their aim in part is to reconstruct a history where the voice of a particular author is but one of many competing voices in a conversation or debate. Of course, the task of reconstructing the arguments of those "on the other side of the text" is not new, particularly in Pauline scholarship, where studies of Paul's "opponents" are legion. Rhetorical criticism distinguishes itself from traditional methods of reconstruction by refusing to read Paul's arguments as oracular truths and Paul's opponents as "hucksters" or "interlopers" merely because he rhetorically construes them as such.[4] Instead, rhetorical critics read these arguments as socially contingent and debatable and assume that Paul's conversation partners deserve an equal hearing as legitimate articulators of early Christian experience.

Rhetorical critics argue further that not only ancient texts but also contemporary biblical interpretation itself needs to be interrogated as having sociopolitical implications and persuasive functions.[5] Because I adopt this understanding of the exegetical task, I do not presume the stance of a detached observer in my interpretation, but I assume a position of advocacy. While rejecting the notion of interpretation as the process of uncovering objective facts or fixed meanings within the text, I intend to provide a critical and persuasive reading of it. While acknowledging that interpretation for liberation cannot be a totalizing discourse—that is, a reading that appears liberating from my own particular context may not appear equally so from other social locations—I conceive of my interpretation as contributing to the project of liberation. Biblical texts were produced within an androcentric patriarchal culture, and to the extent that my engagement with the text uncovers its oppressive effects, I argue that it cannot be proclaimed as the word of God. Early Christian texts were also the products of a sociopolitical movement that contained countercultural, liberating elements. To the extent that these elements are evident in my reading of the text, I am concerned to highlight them as potential resources for modern liberation struggles.

Of all of the Pauline letters, the unity of 2 Corinthians is most disputed.[6] The abrupt transitions in the letter, the seemingly contradictory statements, and the uneven tone of Paul's argument, which is sometimes conciliatory and sometimes threatening, have prompted scholars to pose a variety of theories concerning the letter's redaction from earlier fragments. Arguments for a late redaction of the letter are further supported by the weak attestation of 2 Corinthians among the early church fathers. Particularly because quotations from the letter are absent from *1 Clement* (late first century) and the letters of Ignatius (early second century), some scholars suggest that the collection of fragments which eventually became 2 Corinthians did not circulate with the first collection of Pauline letters.[7]

The simplest partition theory divides 2 Corinthians into only two originally separate letters, the first including chaps. 1–9 and the second, chaps. 10–13.[8] Those holding to this theory are able to account for the contradictions within chaps. 1–9, but find an unbridgeable gulf between chaps. 9 and 10. It is inconceivable, they argue, that Paul would end a letter that has been up until chap. 10 only mild in its admonitions with four chapters of bitter polemic. If the entire letter were a unity, such polemic would have rendered the previous arguments ineffective, particularly Paul's directives in chaps. 8 and 9 concerning the collection of funds for the poor. Advocates of this theory posit a historical situation after the writing of chaps. 1–9 in which the fragile bridge of reconciliation Paul has constructed collapses. He responds in a final round of invective, preserved in chaps. 10–13.

More complex partition theories identify 2:14–7:4 as the earliest letter fragment, an apology to the Corinthians in view of challenges raised against Paul's apostolic authority.[9] This theory posits increased tensions after the writing of the first letter, which led Paul to compose the so-called letter of tears (see Paul's description of the letter in 2 Cor 2:3–4). It understands chaps. 10–13 to be a fragment of that second letter. The harsh words of chaps. 10–13 lead the community to repentance. Letter fragments 1–2:13 and 7:5–15 are viewed as part of a final letter of reconciliation which documents this repentance and the restoration of good relations between the community and their apostle.

Adherents to this complex partition theory are further divided over the status of chaps. 8 and 9, which concern the collection for Jerusalem. Some argue that they are a unit; others view them as two independently circulated letters.

An additional challenge to the letter's unity is offered by 6:14–7:1, which is replete with non-Pauline terminology and seems to interrupt the line of argument begun in 6:11–13 and resumed in 7:2. Debate over this passage begins with the question of Pauline authorship. Those who decide that it is not original to Paul debate further whether Paul himself borrowed the passage to incorporate into his argument, or whether a later redactor inserted it into the document.

In sum, partition theories exist that identify as few as two letter fragments or as many as six, including one non-Pauline fragment, within 2 Corinthians. As the reader may have already guessed in view of the sheer preponderance of partition theories, no one of them has gained ascendancy within the scholarly community. Moreover, in addition to these theories of heterogeneity, theories arguing for the letter's original integrity are continually put forth.[10]

Hans Dieter Betz, in his analysis of the two-hundred-year history of the debate over the letter's unity, has characterized it as falling along liberal and conservative lines. Johann Salomo Semler, the bearer of the first partition theory in 1776, found his argument an important weapon against the orthodox doctrine of canon, particularly against the theory of the "final perfection of Scripture." Liberal thinkers following Semler have continued to posit partition theories that imply a view of the process of canonization as disorderly, one involving "cutters and pasters," redactors and editors. Conservative scholars, in contrast, are less willing to posit a mediator between what Paul originally wrote and what is preserved in the canon.

Though Betz may have appropriately linked conservative arguments for the letter's unity with the desire to protect the notion of the integrity of the process of canonization, he does not reflect further on the assumptions of those who argue for the letter's heterogeneity. While liberal scholars may be willing to question radically the final perfection of scripture reflected in the canonization process, they seldom raise questions concerning the authority of the apostle Paul himself and the ultimate success of his ministry in Corinth. Nor do they often entertain the possibility that objections against Paul's teaching in Corinth were raised legitimately.

Those who theorize that 1–2:13 and 7:5–16 are Paul's final letter of reconciliation are especially able to view Paul's rhetoric as ultimately persuasive and his authority in Corinth as securely established. If the harsh chaps. 10–13 are a fragment from an intermediate correspondence and if 1–2:13 and 7:5–16 are parts of a subsequent conciliatory letter, then this serves to indicate that Paul did regain the loyalty of the congregation and that community consensus concerning his teachings was established. Norman Petersen, a proponent of the final-letter-of-reconciliation theory, argues for its significance in revealing the security of Paul's social position of power in this way:

> Because [1–2:13 and 7:5–16] was written after 2 Corinthians 10–13, it shows that what Paul sought to achieve in it succeeded. It shows that the Corinthians accepted his efforts and thereby confirmed the authority he claimed and established his power among them. Thus, through his personal presence, his letters, and his emissaries, Paul succeeded in his job and in the process established the very authority and power that had been challenged.[11]

Those who argue that chaps. 10–13 are the last extant letter fragment of Paul concede that his relationship with Corinth ends at an impasse. But the effect of severing these last four chapters from the rest of the letter is still to mask the intensity of the conflict between apostle and community. In such a reading, the first nine chapters can be understood as optimistically reconciliatory and their polemical edge can be softened. For example, Victor Furnish views Paul's condemnations of unbelievers in the earlier correspondence (see 4:4; 6:14) as references to pagans outside of the church rather than as invective against those within the worshiping community who stand against him.[12]

Both of these positions, in assuming that challenges to Paul's apostolic authority were merely aberrations of short duration, serve to support the notion that the establishment of orthodox Christianity was both early and inevitable. I argue, however, that by attending more seriously to the nature and intensity of conflict between Paul and the Corinthians, we can better understand the diversity of early Christian opinion.

In this commentary, I have adopted the hypothesis that the text of 2 Corinthians is a unity. I do so not because of an interest in maintaining the original integrity of the Pauline correspondence. It is quite conceivable that Paul's letters to the churches could have become fragmented. Paul did not write with the intent of publishing his letters, and the original recipients of his letters would not have had the notion that they should be preserved for future publication.

But like many scholars of the last decade, I find that the continuity in argument between 2:12 and 7:5 is not so apparent and the shifts in thought after 2:13 and 7:4 are not so abrupt that these verses need to be viewed as "seams," the breaking point of one letter into which a redactor inserted another.

I argue further that Paul's shift to a harsher tone in chaps. 10–13 does not require the hypothesis that these final chapters are from a separate letter. Here I do not postulate, as some have, that the change in Paul's tone can be accounted for on psychological grounds—that is, that Paul's mood changes before the writing of the last four chapters because of a "lapse of time" or a "sleepless night." Rather, I find that inconsistencies in the tone and content of the letter do not require partition theories when these features are understood as part of a carefully crafted rhetorical strategy that Paul utilizes to defend himself against serious opposition in Corinth.

A letter with such apparent inconsistencies would not fall outside of the boundaries of the rhetorical conventions of forensic speech in antiquity. Francis Young and David Ford, who also identify the genre of 2 Corinthians as forensic speech in epistolary form, highlight the following elements as characteristic of the *peroration*, the conclusion of such a defense:

> The conclusion is always contrasted with the exordium [introduction] in emotional tone. It is basically a recapitulation of the principal points deliberately geared to excite emotion, to raise the sense of injustice, anger, jealousy, etc., and involves invocation of the gods, entreaties, tears, deliberate display and the excitement of passion in speaker and audience.[13]

Such a description aptly explains the shift in tone that occurs in the last four chapters of the letter.

THE ARGUMENTATIVE SITUATION

Though theories vary widely concerning the precise argumentative situation of 2 Corinthians, scholarly consensus has maintained that it shifts dramatically between the writing of 1 and 2 Corinthians.[14] These theories owe much to indications within the letter that since the writing of 1 Corinthians, other traveling missionaries have arrived in Corinth. These missionaries bear letters of recommendation, take pride in their ancestral claims as Jews, participate in pneumatic displays, and consider themselves apostles. They have received financial remuneration from Corinth for their ministry, something Paul claims to refuse on principle. Their presence serves to heighten the inflammatory nature of Paul's rhetoric.

Commentators identify these missionaries as interlopers and opponents of Paul. In the past they have looked for the nature of their opposition—and hence for the nature of the new argumentative situation in Corinth—along doctrinal lines. They identify the opponents as Palestinian "Judaizers," perhaps including Cephas himself, or as Hellenistic Jewish missionaries bearing notions of Jesus as a "divine man." Because these new missionaries bring new doctrines, Paul, who is assumed to have been battling against "proto-gnostics" in Corinth, now seems forced to adapt his line of theological argument to confront them.

But because the text yields scant information concerning any new doctrinal position in Corinth, these reconstructions are extremely speculative. Moreover, a construal of the rhetorical exigence of 2 Corinthians based on new doctrinal influence overlooks the strong thematic connections between 1 and 2 Corinthians. Aside from their stress on the continuity of their present ministry with "the things of old," these new missionaries seem to share much in common with Corinthian residents. Both missionaries and residents are confident of their power in Christ, and both value spiritual displays as signs of God's working in them. Both seem to put Paul on the defensive, compelling him to explain why the Spirit's work is not readily apparent within him. In both letters Paul appears to be sensitive about money matters, defending his decision to preach without pay and his handling of the Jerusalem collection. The distinctive argument underscored more often than any other in 2 Corinthians, the locus of power in weakness and the importance of suffering for Paul's own apostleship, is already introduced in 1 Corinthians 1–4.[15]

The arrival of itinerant missionaries with ties to Judaism, a religion widely respected in antiquity, adds to the number of those in the Corinthian church with some social standing.[16] But their presence does not change the social makeup of the church significantly. As in the case of 1 Corinthians, the church at the writing of 2 Corinthians contains female and male slaves, and women and men from lower social classes, who experienced their entry into the church and empowerment by the Spirit as an elevation of status.[17]

Because of the connections between their themes and their audience, I read 2 Corinthians as shaped largely by a situation already adumbrated in 1 Corinthians. After Paul's intervening visit, the arrival of new missionaries and the sending of the letter of tears, the rhetorical situation has changed, but more in terms of degree than of character. In the writing of the first letter Paul is aware of the tenuous nature of his relationship with the community. But he still perceives his task as the judicious offering of counsel concerning matters of Corinthian faith and practice, for example, the issue of idol meat, the practice of the community meal, and the role of prophecy and tongues. He mentions allies by name and construes multiple factions within the community whom he attempts to reconcile. He takes on the issue of women's roles in community life directly and repeatedly, and explicitly limits them.

But in 2 Corinthians his tenuous standing has taken a precipitous plunge. He argues accordingly. The thrust of his persuasion is not on deliberations over community faith and practice, but is on securing for himself a place at the table where such deliberation takes place. Here he gives no indication of addressing a community with many factions. The lines are drawn more starkly between "us and them," those who accept Paul's gospel and servants of Satan. Except for his use of a biblical quotation modified to include daughters as well as sons in God's family (6:18—the modification itself may be pre-Pauline), Paul does not acknowledge the presence of real women in Corinth. The only other female referents in the text are metaphorical and communicate the objectification of female sexuality. He casts Corinth as his daughter, whom he hopes to present as a chaste bride to Christ, but who, like Eve, is precariously close to succumbing to Satan's seduction (11:3).

Because Paul paints his argument here in broad strokes, it is difficult to single out any exhortation as being aimed at a particular subgroup in Corinth. Nevertheless, I imagine the Corinthian women prophets, whose theological perspective has been carefully reconstructed in Wire's work on 1 Corinthians, to be included among the recipients of this correspondence, and to be responsible in part for the shape of Paul's argument. Paul's change in argumentative strategy outlined above may owe much to the leadership roles these women continue to exercise in spite of his attempts to silence them.

COMMENTARY

GREETING AND THANKSGIVING (1:1–11)

Following his salutation, Paul customarily invokes his own thanksgiving to God on behalf of the congregation to which he writes (cf. Rom 1:8; 1 Cor 1:4; Phil 1:3; 1 Thess 1:2; Phlm 4). In this regard the thanksgiving of 2 Corinthians is unique. It begins in the form of a Jewish blessing, introduces Paul's understanding of the interrelatedness of suffering and salvation—with emphasis on how his own suffering is for the benefit of the Corinthians (v. 6)—and concludes with the hope of future thanksgiving. But this conclusion is not Paul's thanksgiving *for* the community; rather it is the hope that the Corinthians through their prayers will join in giving thanks *on Paul's behalf.*

The inversion of the expected thanksgiving formula is the first clue in this letter of how Paul's argumentative strategy has changed in light of increasing enmity in Corinth. By requesting rather than offering affirmation, Paul acknowledges that he is in need of something from Corinth (contrast the affirmations directed toward the Corinthians in 1 Cor 1:4–9). He connects this need of blessing with suffering he has recently experienced in Asia, but offers few specifics concerning this persecution. His point is to underscore that he has suffered and expects to continue suffering (1:10) in his role as apostle. By characterizing the God who rescues him as the one "who raises the dead" (1:9), Paul frames his own sufferings and "resurrections" in terms of the death and resurrection of Christ.

The emphasis on power revealed in suffering and weakness, first introduced in 1 Corinthians 1–4, will be a guiding theme of this correspondence. It suggests that a counterexperience predominates in Corinth, one of "realized eschatology" in which resurrection and riches of the spirit rather than suffering and death are perceived as sources of power.

PAUL'S DEFENSE OF AN UNFULFILLED PROMISE (1:12–2:17)

Paul had visited the church once after the writing of 1 Corinthians. Here he addresses the matter of his reneging on a promised second visit to the city, a visit he had apparently canceled in view of the disastrous nature of the first (cf. 2:1). The cancellation has raised doubts in Corinth concerning Paul's sincerity. In his defense he argues that he could not execute plans in an ordinary fashion (1:17a). Because he works with single-minded devotion to God (1:12), who leads him as if a prisoner (2:14), it is not in his hands that his "yes be yes" and his "no be no" (1:17b).[18]

Paul reinforces this point with an added motive for delaying the visit: he stayed away in order "to spare" the congregation (1:23). Apparently aware of the objections to such a paternalistic style of leadership in Corinth, he adds immediately that he does not intend to "lord it over" them and concedes that the Corinthians already stand firm in faith (1:24).

These objections to Paul's leadership style must have been voiced strongly in response to apostle's stern letter, no longer extant, which he had sent in lieu of a second visit. From Paul's apologetic references to it here (2:4, 9) we see that the Corinthians have been offended by its heavy-handedness.

Though he singles out a particular community member as a source of trouble within Corinth (2:5–8), Paul offers too few details for modern readers to identify the offender. He argues for complete reconciliation, so that the apostle and community may present a united front against Satan (2:11).

Paul resumes the defense of his travel plans as subject to God's authority alone in 2:12. Though his search for Titus in Macedonia had been unsuccessful, he still offers thanksgiving to God, who leads him "in the triumphal procession." This phrase is best understood in reference to the Roman institution of the triumph, where victorious generals and their troops paraded through city streets publicly displaying their prisoners of war. Paul travels where God leads because he is captive. But thanksgiving for this captivity is still in order, because the effect of this public humiliation is to position Paul and his co-workers in a key role in the eschatological drama. By asserting to be mediators of divine judgment, Paul implies that Corinthians who do not accede to his authority do so at the peril of death (2:15–16).

PAUL'S DEFENSE OF HIS GLORY (3:1–4:6)

Paul's defense in 2 Corinthians is shaped in part by his concern over new missionaries in Corinth whose external credentials are more evident than his own (5:12; 11:12–13; 11:22–23). They have apparently argued convincingly that their ministry is an extension of and consistent with established Jewish traditions. Unlike Paul, they receive support from the Corinthian community. Because they bear letters commending their work (3:1–3), Paul is compelled here to account for his own lack of written recommendations. To do so he argues that his work among the Corinthians is validated not by written letter but by the Spirit.

He undergirds the argument that he does not need written commendation by extending his critique of the letter vis-à-vis the spirit to the written Torah itself. Against a mainstream current of Hellenistic Jewish thought, which would have granted preeminent status to the Mosaic tradition and would have looked to the writings as a source of spiritual power, Paul claims here that the written word is death-dealing and that the Spirit does not dwell in it. With reference to Moses' return from Sinai in Exodus 34, Paul acknowledges that the radiance of the lawgiver's face did indicate the glory present in the old covenant. But he argues that this covenant, however glorious, is superseded by the covenant of the Spirit, the covenant in whose glory Paul participates as its minister.

Though this interpretation is a radical departure from a Torah-centered hermeneutic, it is anachronistic to understand it as an expression of "anti-Jewish" sentiment, for Paul could only conceive of himself as standing within the Jewish tradition. His critique of the tradition is drawn from a strand of the tradition itself, the images of new covenant and restoration detailed in the prophetic literature.

Paul's argument in 3:12–4:6 is crafted in part against charges that his gospel is obscure (4:3). To counter these charges Paul again asserts that in Corinth salvation is connected to accession to his authority. He strings together oppositional metaphors of veiledness/unveiledness, blindness/sight, and darkness/light to cast the written Torah (3:14), those who hear the Torah but have not turned to the Lord (3:15), and ultimately any who do not see the glory of Christ in Paul's gospel (4:3–4) as outside of the covenant of the Spirit.

The passage also includes proclamations that would have resonated with Corinthian understandings of their own experience of faith: "the Lord is Spirit," "where the Spirit of the Lord is there is freedom" (3:17). The understanding that the glory of the Lord is beheld through a mirror (3:18) is an adaptation of the notion in wisdom theology that Wisdom (*sophia*) reflects the image of God (see Wisdom of Solomon 7, especially v. 26, "For she is a reflection of eternal light, a spotless mirror of the working of God, and an image of God's goodness"). The Corinthians would have acknowledged—perhaps even first introduced to Paul—this identification of Christ with Sophia as mirror and image of God (see also 4:4). That Hellenistic Jewish wisdom motifs inform Corinthian christological understandings is clear from 1 Corinthians (cf. chaps. 1–4). What the Corinthians have understood of their own experience and have found lacking in their encounters with Paul, he now argues is true of himself, "*We all* behold the glory of the Lord" (3:18).

But 3:18 contains modifications of this wisdom speculation that do not reflect Corinthian understanding and practice. Against believers in Corinth who understand themselves to reflect the image and glory of God in the present, Paul stresses the final consummation of glory at some future time (cf. 5:5). It is also probable that the stress on transformation into "the *same* image" is a Pauline modification. A congregation in which a variety of gifts, including tongues and prophecy, were cultivated as expressions of God's glory would not be occupied with concerns for conformity.

SUFFERING, MORTALITY, AND MINISTRY (4:7–5:10)

In this first detailed interpretation of his apostolic suffering, Paul shapes his argument with an eye to Corinthian strength. The community is confident that Christ has activated resurrection for them already in their earthly existence, that this new life manifests itself pneumatically and can be confirmed externally. For them, Paul's apparent weakness calls his ministerial legitimacy into question.

His response is to argue that his fragility serves the purposes of underscoring God's strength, which supports him in the face of great adversity. The life of Jesus is made manifest in him not through pneumatic expression but through the death of Jesus, which he carries within him through his many trials. These trials are momentary afflictions that serve as preparation for eternal glory (4:17). Paul is also concerned to argue that the Corinthians owe their present experience of full life, at least in part, to his suffering on their behalf (4:12, 15).

Concerning the resurrection, Paul concedes to the Corinthians what he did not in his first letter,[19] that transformation into eternal glory already begins in this life. He argues that he experiences daily renewal, despite external decay (4:16; cf. also 3:18; 5:17). But he is careful to stress that this transformation cannot be complete until some future eschatological judgment. Until then, the gift of the Spirit is only a down payment. Any visible signs of renewal in the present are insignificant in view of the eternal glory to come.

In order to concede present transformation while postponing its consummation until the future, Paul comes as close here as he does in any of his letters to conceiving of human beings in radically dualistic terms. Here the locus of suffering is the body, the "outer self" that is wasting away. Renewal does take place, but only within the inner self, which is lodged in, but separate from, the mortal body. While the Corinthians argue that they are at home with the Lord in their present state, Paul casts the notion of being at home in the body in dualistic opposition to being at home in the Lord. This inner self becomes free from the mortal tent of suffering and decay only when it is further clothed in its heavenly dwelling.

APPEAL FOR RECONCILIATION (5:11–21)

Here again Paul defends himself against the Corinthian view that he lacks externally validating signs of possessing the Spirit. Paul argues that he and his co-workers do indeed experience ecstatic possession (*ekstēnai*) for God, but that they assume sober-mindedness for the community's benefit. He understands Christ's love as a pacifying force that serves to restrain (*synechein*) them. As in chap. 3, here the severing of the Christ from "everything old" is

Paul's attempt to discredit those in Corinth who understand their current life in the Spirit as bolstered by its ties to tradition. Invoking the image of restoration and new creation expressed in Isa 43:18f., he argues that the work of reconciliation through Christ invalidates what is ancient. In this relationship between God, Christ, and the world in need of reconciliation—particularly the world of Corinth—Paul assumes the role of ambassador. He appeals to the Corinthians to accept their reconciliation through him.

PAUL'S OWN LETTER OF RECOMMENDATION (6:1–10)

Paul's commendation for himself and his co-workers here is noteworthy in view of his previous disclaimers concerning the need for them (cf. 6:4 with 3:1; 5:12). Paul may be constructing this list with a view to the subject of the collection, which he will raise in chap. 8. In spite of previous arguments to the contrary, he may be well aware of needing further commendation in order to inspire the confidence of those whose gifts for Jerusalem he seeks. Parallel statements in 6:3 and in 8:20 suggest that Corinthian dissatisfaction with his ministry is connected to their suspicion concerning his handling of the collection.

FURTHER APPEAL FOR CORINTHIAN LOYALTY (6:11–7:3)

The passage 6:14–7:1 contains vocabulary and syntactical constructions that are used nowhere else in Paul's letters. Since 7:2 could easily follow 6:13, many have suggested that 6:14–7:1 is not integral to the letter. Joseph A. Fitzmyer's article highlighting the numerous contact points between this passage and Qumran literature has provided a basis for many arguments that the passage is a later non-Pauline interpolation.[20]

The high concentration of non-Pauline features does make it likely that the passage has a pre-Pauline origin. But the strong thematic affinity between this passage and the rest of 2 Corinthians suggests that Paul himself, and not a later interpolator, adapted the text to its current context. Paul has already drawn lines of demarcation between the damned and the saved (2:15–16), designated those who are blind to his gospel as unbelievers (4:3–4), and appealed for the Corinthians to accept the reconciliation with God that comes through himself as Christ's ambassador (5:20–6:1). Here he heightens his appeal by inserting a passage that paints the righteous and the sinful in stark contrast. His plea as a father for open expressions of affection from his children is joined with admonitions not to be yoked with unbelievers. Those who do not align with Paul under his authority stand on the side of lawlessness, night, and Beliar (6:14–15).

The catena of Hebrew Bible quotations in 6:16b–17, which stress purity and separation, does not interrupt the letter, but is a logical extension of the prophetic vision of new creation to which Paul frequently alludes (cf. 2 Cor 3:3 with Ezek 11:19 and Jer 31:33; 2 Cor 5:17 with Isa 43:18; and the direct quotation of Isa 49:8 in 2 Cor 6:2). Within these prophetic writings, restoration goes hand in hand with separation from idols and impurity (cf. Ezek 11:18; 20:28–32; Isa 52:11). Moreover, through its emphasis on proper yoking and cleansing from bodily impurity, the catena anticipates the sexual metaphors for purity in chap. 11.

The adaptation of 2 Sam 7:14 in 2 Cor 6:18 is worthy of note, if for no other reason than as an early instance of the modification of scriptural language for the purpose of gender inclusivity. The original Hebrew Bible promise of sonship for David as modified here addresses both sons *and daughters*. Whether or not Paul himself adapted the quotation, it stands here as an acknowledgment that the new creation he extols includes the women of Corinth.[21] Yet it is clear from the context that Paul does not see himself as a "brother" to these daughters. He addresses them as his disaffected children (6:13).

EXPRESSIONS OF CONFIDENCE (7:4–16)

Following Hellenistic convention, Paul prepares to make the substantial request concerning the collection by underscoring the confidence he has in his audience. The news received from Titus concerning the community is credited as a source of joy.

Titus was apparently well received in Corinth, for Paul attempts to establish that he and Titus are of the same mind. Here he stresses Titus's affection for the community as confirming that about which Paul had previously boasted (7:14). In chap. 8 he will highlight Titus's role in completing the collection and will rank him above the others involved in the collection as his partner and co-worker. Later Paul will appeal to Titus's guileless behavior within the community as modeling his own (12:18).

But it is clear that Paul is not recounting all the news he has received from Titus. As in chap. 2, his need here to justify the stern letter sent in lieu of a visit indicates that there are those who have disapproved of it. His defense of the letter in 7:8–12 is halting. He deflects the indignation and alarm (directed against him?) at his letter by interpreting it as the response he was seeking in order to exonerate the community (7:11).

THE APPEAL TO COMPLETE THE COLLECTION (CHAPTERS 8 AND 9)

The central location of the collection appeal reflects the link for Paul between the successful completion of the collection and the legitimation of his apostleship. The importance of the collection for Jerusalem to Paul's understanding of his apostolic vocation is evident in his recounting of the meeting with the Jerusalem apostles in Gal 2:1–10. Those in Jerusalem concede to him the mission to the Gentiles with the provision that he "remember the poor" (Gal 2:10). His return to Jerusalem with such an offering would confirm for the Palestinian leaders the legitimacy of his apostleship to the Gentiles.

Paul's eschatological vision of the new creation and the restored Israel, from which he has drawn repeatedly in this letter, must also inform his view of the collection. Prophetic visions of the last days speak of pilgrims from the nations arriving in Jerusalem (cf. Isa 2:2–3; Mic 4:1–2); Isaiah speaks of the pilgrims bearing wealth to be offered up in Zion (Isa 60:3–7). Gentile participation in the collection would confirm the fulfillment of these prophecies.

Jerome Murphy-O'Connor, who views chaps. 1–9 as a letter separate from chaps. 10–13, has argued that the case for viewing 2 Corinthians as a unity patterned after the rhetorical category of forensic speech "shatters on the rock" of chaps. 8 and 9. A plea for money, he asserts, has no place in an *apologia*.[22] But such an argument does not take into account the defensive tone that pervades Paul's discussion of the collection.

Paul has been accused of extortion (12:16–17). He rebuts this charge in chap. 12 in the context of defending his decision not to accept pay for his ministry in the community. It seems, therefore, that Corinthians charged Paul with refusing pay openly while finagling it via the Jerusalem collection appeal. The lengthy commendation of the delegation arriving to oversee the completion of the collection is in large part an answer to this accusation. Paul intends the Corinthians to view the delegation as an assurance that the collection process is being conducted honestly (cf. 8:20; 9:5).

In this commendation (8:16–9:5), Titus is praised most highly as Paul's own representative in the delegation. Through the recommendations for the two additional brothers Paul attempts to show that not only he, but also the whole church, is concerned for the success of the collection. One brother has been "elected by the showing of hands" in the churches (8:19); the verb used here indicates the democratic nature of the appointment. Both are designated as "apostles of the churches" (8:23). Though the term does not have the technical meaning here that it acquires in later ecclesial structures, it nevertheless designates a special function for Paul. Its usage here is best explained as an attempt to elevate the status of the collection.

The argument Paul offers in defending the legitimacy of the project is constructed to appeal to Corinthians who are unwilling to give up their newly acquired status, gained upon entrance into the church. In 8:1–15, Paul introduces two examples of giving to the Corinthians, that of the Macedonians, whose extreme generosity was exhibited in spite of extreme poverty (8:1–4), and that of Christ, whose *kenosis* is described here in terms of forsaking wealth in order to enrich (8:9). After citing these heroic examples of self-sacrifice, Paul presents the Corinthians with a modest request. He is not asking of them an extreme sacrifice, but only for what is appropriate—the completion of a previously initiated project (vv. 10–11), and for what is fair—the giving out of abundance for those who are in need (vv. 13–15).

Commonly in the Christian Testament, wealth is denounced as a force which is spiritually corrupting, while those who are poor are praised as God's chosen (see Mark 10:17–25; Matt 6:25–33; Luke 6:20; Jas 2:2–6). Here Paul argues differently. Wealth is seen as a blessing, enabling one to be self-sufficient and to serve as a benefactor to others (9:8). The community is not called to sell all it possesses to give to the poor. Rather, Paul casts the Corinthians as recipients of God's riches (9:8–11; cf. 8:7). In so doing, he can portray participation in the collection as something that will yield significant benefits at little cost to the community. Their contributions will supply the needs of the saints while also producing an "overflowing in thanksgiving to God" (9:12).

FINAL APPEAL (CHAPTER 10)

Here begins Paul's concluding, emotionally charged defense of his authority. Reading against the grain, we are able to identify Corinthian viewpoints that have contributed to the rift between the community and the apostle.

For many in Corinth new life in Christ is confirmed by spiritual expression. Possession by the Spirit enables speaking in tongues and prophecy (see 1 Corinthians and Wire's commentary) and healings and miracles (see Paul's insistence that the signs of a true apostle are evident in his own ministry [12:11f.]). For some, the spirit brings visions of the heavenly realm (see Paul's parody of such visions in 12:1f.). Far from being a down payment on future, otherworldly glory, the Spirit brings glory and power to the community in this world in the present. From such understandings, scholars need not conclude that the Corinthians are an eccentric lot of licentious libertarians and egotistical enthusiasts. The credentials of the traveling missionaries whom the Corinthians support (they are Hebrews, Israelites, descendants of Abraham [11:22]) suggest that the Corinthians understand their experience as linked to a traditional understanding of the Spirit's power.

From this understanding of the Spirit's power, Corinthians have raised questions about the legitimacy of Paul's ministry. The charge that Paul acts "according to the flesh" (10:2) reflects doubts about whether Paul relies on the Spirit's guidance. Some have characterized Paul's weighty letters as belying his "weak bodily presence" and "contemptible speech"(10:10). Some may have argued that Paul's apostolic authority is not legitimated by external signs (see Paul's insistence to the contrary in 12:12). When leaders of the Corinthian church measure their own achievements they view his as pale in comparison (see Paul's derision of this practice in 10:12).

From Paul's defense in 11:7–11 and 12:14–18, it is clear that Paul's refusal to accept financial support from the community is also a source of contention in Corinth. Such refusal was a violation of Hellenistic conventions of friendship.[23] The Corinthians would have viewed it as an offense, signaling his unwillingness to enter into a relationship of mutuality. Some also accuse him of deceit (12:16), probably alleging that his apparent zeal for the Jerusalem collection is in fact a desire to collect funds for himself without entering into any openly acknowledged financial arrangement.

Paul's defense includes the following three characterizations:

(1) Paul as founder/father. Though Paul may have conceded to the Corinthians on some issues, he does not budge an inch from his assertion that his authority over the community is divinely sanctioned, owing to his role as its founder. Paul understands the rights of apostles to include territorial rights over communities they have established. Corinth belongs to the field (*kanōn*) God has assigned to him (10:13). He is the one who has prepared Corinth for her "marriage" to Christ (11:2). Rather than accepting a financial relationship, which would have been an acknowledgment of mutuality, Paul justifies his refusal to do so by arguing that parents should not place such burdens on their children (12:14).

Paul's use of the father–child analogy to interpret his relationship to Corinth is usually understood by commentators as benign.[24] Such readings overlook the implications of the right of total authority over children with which the father was imbued in Greco-Roman society. As a paterfamilias would, Paul threatens to punish disobedience (10:6). He may have spared the Corinthians by refraining from a visit for a time (1:23) but promises no such leniency on his third visit (13:1–2). Knowing that they desire proof of Christ's presence in him, he promises to deliver proof—but not the spiritual boldness or ecstatic expression they are seeking. Rather his proof will be the power of God, which he will use for tearing down (13:10), if need be.

Precisely what form of punishment Paul has in mind is not clearly stated. He may presume the authority to excommunicate offending parties (cf. 1 Cor 5:1–13), or his threats may be vague because he has no way to enact punishment if a majority continue to defy his assumed parental role.

(2) Corinth as Eve. Though Paul has affirmed with the Corinthians that in the Spirit's presence there is freedom (3:17), in this chapter he implies that Corinthian freedom has led to licentiousness. The themes of purity and proper sexual union echo concerns introduced in 6:14–7:1. Here as there, those who forgo loyalty to Paul's teaching are cast as partners of Satan/Beliar.

As is common in polemical charges with sexual overtones, the offending party is cast as a woman. Corinth, whom Paul has hoped to present as a chaste bride to Christ, has become like Eve, easy prey to the lustful desires of Satan. The construal of the entire community as female reveals a shift in Paul's argumentative strategy since the writing of 1 Corinthians. There he acknowledges and negotiates with real women who pray and prophecy, who prefer celibacy to marriage, and whom he wishes to silence in the assembly. Here he acknowledges female power only in terms of a metaphorical sexuality, which pollutes the entire community. Such a characterization of Corinthian communal life is a direct affront to women who had chosen an ascetic life-style as part of their devotion to God.[25]

Paul presumes notions current in his day that identified the serpent in Genesis 3 with Satan and hinted that Eve's deception was sexual in nature.[26] The extent of Eve's deception is intensified in 11:3 by the use of a verbal prefix. In the Septuagint account of Genesis 3, Eve's deception is characterized by the Greek verb *apateō;* here it is *exapateō.*[27] Paul carries the metaphor of Corinth as Eve seduced by Satan into his accusations against missionaries whom he accuses of wearing the disguises of Satan (11:13–15). Apocryphal stories of Eve's deception by Satan narrate how Satan "takes the form of an angel" (*Apoc. Mos.* 17:1; 29:15–17) or "transforms himself into the brightness of angels" (*Adam and Eve* 9:11) before approaching her.

(3) Paul as Fool. For much of Paul's concluding defense against charges of weakness, he employs the rhetorical tropes of irony and indignation to challenge conventional understandings of weakness. These tropes, important elements of forensic speech in antiquity, are most evident in the elaborate argument of 11:1–12:13, commonly known as "The Fool's Speech."[28] But Paul's use of irony and indignation here is foreshadowed already by the considerable contradiction and reproachful tone of chap. 10. For example, in 10:1ff. his appeal "by the meekness and gentleness of Christ" is accompanied by the claim that he is ready to wage war. Through a piling up of military metaphors unparalleled in Pauline literature, this "humble" servant of Christ threatens to engage in destruction, capture, and punishment.

In the introduction to the fool's speech, Paul depreciates himself as "untrained" (*idios*) in speech and acclaims his opposition as "super" (*hyper*) apostles (11:5). He boasts, as a fool, that he is on equal footing with esteemed missionaries in Corinth (11:21ff.), but then recasts his status as owing not to outward signs of prominence, but to the extended suffering he has endured (11:23–29).

The passage is an ironic contrast to the lists of impressive achievements that were commonly compiled on behalf of notable public figures. Compare, for example, Paul's specific enumeration of his hardships to the patterned enumeration of Augustus's honors on the *Monumentum Ancyranum*: "Twice I received triumphal ovations. Three times I celebrated curule triumphs. Twenty times and one did I receive the appellation of imperator."[29]

His recounting of an escape from Damascus by being lowered down the city wall in a basket (11:32–33) is best understood as a continuation of this ironic tone, for it parodies a Roman practice of awarding meritous service in battle. The first Roman soldier to scale up the wall of a besieged city was decorated with the *corona muralis*, the "crown for the wall." Paul then casts himself as the antihero, having been the first to scale *down* the wall of a city under siege.[30]

Finally, to a community whose power is confirmed through spiritual expression, Paul boasts only in ironic terms of his own ecstatic experience. Appropriating the imagery of Jewish apocalyptic literature, he narrates a journey to the third heaven, where he claims to have received a revelation of an exceptional character. But he offers little information about the journey and regards it as ultimately insignificant. Furnish expresses it succinctly, "How, precisely, he was taken up to Paradise he does not know, what he saw there he does not say, and what he heard there he must not repeat."[31]

The result of his experience is not exaltation but a thorn in the flesh, which remains in spite of all appeals for its removal. His word from the Lord is the word by which he hopes to shame those who are strong in Corinth: "my power is made perfect in weakness" (12:9), and "whenever I am weak, then I am strong" (12:10).

FEMINIST EVALUATION

Having set forth an interpretation of the text in light of the rhetorical situation in which it was written, I offer here an evaluation of possibilities for reading the text within present-day communities of faith and struggle. In doing so, I acknowledge that various interpretations of the text are possible and are dependent on the particular elements within it which a reader/community chooses to emphasize. In my own evaluation, my arguments concerning which textual elements to highlight and which to subordinate are based on my interest in advocating a just society and in dismantling the structures of patriarchy.

THE LOCUS OF AUTHORITY IN CHRISTIAN COMMUNITIES

At several points in 2 Corinthians Paul argues that as the founder/father of the church he has a divinely sanctioned claim to leadership within the community. Paul may insist that as a father he has sincere affection for his children, but from this position he also claims his right to punish disobedience and to coerce the congregation to adopt his own understanding of truth. To assume that Paul's parental claims to authority are "common sense" is to support relationships of inequality and to preclude leadership models that encourage honest debate, mutual respect and mutual responsibility within communities of faith.

But Paul also follows a different line of argument in 2 Corinthians which may empower those involved in liberation struggles. Because he is not on equal footing with ministers who bear letters of recommendation, he deemphasizes the importance of ties to established tradition and argues that the source of his authority is not the letter but the Spirit. The presence of the Spirit brings freedom (3:17). All who possess it are being transformed "from one degree of glory to another" (3:18). In Christ the "things of old" give way to "new creation" (5:17).

Marginalized communities, such as women seeking positions of authority within their churches, or minority communities seeking to bring their concerns to the center of the political arena, also find that they lack "letters of recommendation" and ties to the established tradition which those in power possess. They can argue, like Paul, that traditional marks of status are invalidated by the Spirit's iconoclastic and transforming power.

It is imperative, however, that readings of the text which highlight the Spirit over the letter do not reinscribe this distinction in terms of anti-Judaism. Writing only decades after the crucifixion, while the messianic movement centered on Jesus was only one of the many religious currents within first-century Judaism, Paul could not have thought of himself as a "Christian" combating "the Jews." And yet Christian interpretation of texts such as 2 Corinthians 3 have seen Judaism as the ministry of death, bearing the law that kills, and Christianity as the religion of life and spirit. Modern critiques of the letter vis-à-vis the spirit that draw on arguments of 2 Corinthians are appropriate only when they do not cast Judaism as the Other.

SUFFERING AND SALVATION

In answer to those who question the authenticity of his ministry because of his apparent weakness, Paul construes human weakness as the locus of God's strength, argues that as the death of Jesus works itself out in him it brings forth life for the community, and sets forth a list of ironic credentials that highlight his suffering and humiliation as signs of his apostleship. He casts his earthly suffering as insignificant affliction that prepares him and all believers for the weight of eternal glory (4:17).

This interpretation of suffering, which has had enormous impact on orthodox Christian understanding, must be challenged for its inadequacy in accounting for—and also its complicity in perpetuating—the suffering of our time. Countless women and other marginalized persons have internalized the message that glory is located in humiliation and suffering. For them, Paul's words are a call to self-negation and to acceptance and passivity in the face of oppression. Furthermore, the message that righteously endured earthly suffering can be exchanged for some future heavenly reward promotes a disembodied ethic. To understand pleasure as something to be anticipated in a future realm is to equate it fundamentally with "a state of mind," rather than with the well-being of flesh-and-blood persons in the present world.[32]

Paul's understanding that true exaltation lies in the acceptance of suffering is closely connected to his perception that his vocation as apostle to the Gentiles has resulted in a decline in his own status.[33] Those who hold privileged positions in patriarchal society attempting to enter into solidarity with the oppressed may find that in so doing they, like Paul, have voluntarily exposed themselves to suffering. But I argue that for the privileged, a reading of 2 Corinthians that foregrounds Paul's voluntary acceptance of status loss and subsequent suffering must be motivated by radical love for and accountability to the oppressed rather than by compulsion to sacrifice self.[34]

A rhetorical analysis of 2 Corinthians reveals that early Christians there, against whom Paul argues, held a different view of the import of suffering. Female slaves, male slaves, and free women experienced a rise in status upon entry into the church in Corinth. Because membership in the baptismal community marked for them a transformation from powerlessness into the power and life of the Spirit, they resisted Paul's exhortations to embrace suffering for the sake of a future eschatological reward. Because they chose to focus on the Spirit's resurrecting work during their earthly existence, they are sometimes belittled by scholars as "enthusiasts." I argue to the contrary that this enthusiastic eschatology needs to be foregrounded as a model for those committed to transformation in our own world.

NOTES

1. See Elisabeth Schüssler Fiorenza, *In Memory of Her: A Feminist Theological Reconstruction of Christian Origins* (New York: Crossroad, 1985), 43–46.

2. See Antoinette Clark Wire, *The Corinthian Women Prophets: A Reconstruction through Paul's Rhetoric* (Philadelphia: Fortress, 1991); and the chapter on 1 Corinthians in this volume.

3. Two works utilizing rhetorical methods of analysis have been produced on 1 Corinthians: see Elisabeth Schüssler Fiorenza, "Rhetorical Situation and Historical Reconstruction in I Corinthians," *New Testament Studies* 33 (1987): 386–403; and Wire, *Corinthian Women Prophets*.

4. Elizabeth A. Castelli, who adopts a foucauldian method of analysis, provides a forceful critique of biblical scholars who unreflectively adopt Paul's discourse as normative rather than specifically interested (*Imitating Paul: A Discourse on Power* [Louisville, KY: Westminster/John Knox, 1991]).

5. See, e.g, Elisabeth Schüssler Fiorenza, "The Ethics of Biblical Interpretation: Decentering Biblical Scholarship," *Journal of Biblical Literature* 107 (1988): 3–17; and Wilhelm Wuellner, "Hermeneutics and Rhetorics: From 'Truth and Method' to 'Truth and Power'," *Scriptura* 3 (1989): 1–54.

6. Hans Dieter Betz includes a comprehensive history of this dispute (*2 Corinthians 8 and 9: A Commentary on Two Administrative Letters of the Apostle Paul* [Philadelphia: Fortress, 1985], 3–36). An updated but abbreviated review is available in R. Bieringer, "Der 2. Korintherbrief in den neuesten Kommentaren," *Ephemerides Theologiae Lovanienses* 67 (1991): 107–30.

7. See, e.g., Helmut Koester, *Introduction to the New Testament* (New York: Walter de Gruyter, 1987), 2:53.

8. Recent advocates of this position include Victor Paul Furnish, *II Corinthians* (Anchor Bible; Garden City, NY: Doubleday, 1984), and Jerome Murphy-O'Connor, *The Theology of the Second Letter to the Corinthians* (Cambridge: Cambridge University Press, 1991).

9. See Koester, *Introduction*, 2:126–30; Betz, *2 Corinthians 8 and 9*, 141–44; and Dieter Georgi, *The Opponents of Paul in Second Corinthians* (Philadelphia: Fortress, 1986).

10. Most recent proponents of the letter's unity include Frederick W. Danker, *II Corinthians* (Minneapolis: Augsburg, 1989); and Frances Young and David F. Ford, *Meaning and Truth in 2 Corinthians* (London: SPCK, 1987).

11. Norman R. Petersen, *Rediscovering Paul: Philemon and the Sociology of Paul's Narrative World* (Philadelphia: Fortress, 1985), 114.

12. Furnish, *II Corinthians*, 221, 361, 371–72.

13. Ford and Young, *Meaning and Truth*, 38.

14. See Bieringer, "Der 2. Korintherbrief," 112–15.

15. For a list of thematic and verbal anticipations of 2 Corinthians in 1 Corinthians, see Ford and Young, *Meaning and Truth*, 55–57.

16. It is feasible that women were included among the new missionaries in the community. Their presence as speakers and interpreters of the word would be welcomed by the women whom Paul has attempted to silence in his first letter. See the work of Dieter Georgi, who argues for numbering women among the wandering missionaries of the Hellenistic world, though he does not explore the possibility that women were included among Paul's missionary "opponents" in Corinth (*The Opponents of Paul*, 98–99, 103, 111, 373).

17. On the social location of Corinthian Christians, see Wire, *Corinthian Women Prophets*, 63–71, 217–18. Wire's work in connecting changing social status to theological claims does much to elucidate Corinthian resistance to Paul's exhortations on the merits of suffering.

18. For an elaboration of this translation of 1:17a, see Ford and Young, *Meaning and Truth*, 101–2.

19. See Wire, *Corinthian Women Prophets*, 163–76.

20. Joseph A. Fitzmyer, "Qumran and the Interpolated Paragraph in 2 Cor 6:14-7:1," *Catholic Biblical Quarterly* 23 (1961): 271–80.

21. For the argument that this passage fits the egalitarian understanding of the early Jewish Christian missionary movement, see Schüssler Fiorenza, *In Memory of Her*, 194–96.

22. Murphy-O'Connor, *Second Letter to the Corinthians*, 11.

23. See, e.g., Peter Marshall, *Enmity in Corinth: Social Conventions in Paul's Relations with the Corinthians* (Tübingen: Mohr, 1987).

24. See, e.g., Marshall, *Enmity in Corinth*, 247–51. For a critique of these assumptions, see Castelli, *Imitating Paul*, 98–102.

25. See exhortations directed toward virgins in 1 Corinthians 7; see also Wire, *Corinthian Women Prophets*, 82–97.

26. Cf. *2 Enoch* 31:6; *4 Macc* 18:7–8; *Apoc. Mos.* 17–21; *Adam and Eve* [*Vita*] 9–11. All works are available in English translation; see James H. Charlesworth, ed., *The Old Testament Pseudepigrapha*, vol. 2, (Garden City, NY: Doubleday, 1983).

27. Cf. the distinction in 1 Tim 2:14, where it is argued that Adam was not deceived (*ouk apateō*), but his wife was "quite deceived" (*exapateō*).

28. Christopher Forbes has convincingly demonstrated Paul's reliance on these rhetorical conventions in 10:12–12:13. See "Comparison, Self-Praise and Irony: Paul's Boasting and the Conventions of Hellenistic Rhetoric," *New Testament Studies* 32 (1986): 1–30. Failure to recognize that this passage is imbued with irony has resulted in floods of speculation by scholars over the literal meaning of the text, and attempts to reconcile apparent contradictions in Paul's argument.

29. *Monumentum Ancyranum* 4.1.21–22; Eng. trans. from Ernest Hardy, ed., *The Monumentum Ancyranum* (Oxford: Clarendon, 1923).

30. Furnish, *II Corinthians,* 541–42.

31. Ibid., 545.

32. For a critique of this view, see Beverly W. Harrison and Carter Heyward, "Pain and Pleasure: Avoiding the Confusions of Christian Tradition in Feminist Theory," in *Christianity Patriarchy and Abuse: A Feminist Critique,* ed. Joanne Carlson Brown and Carole R. Bohn (New York: Pilgrim, 1989), 148–73.

33. "In ethnic identity, caste, and gender there is a certain stability; Paul remains in society at large a Jew, free, and male. There is no way that his status can fall even to equal the level to which the Gentile slave woman's status has risen in the Corinthian church. Yet the privileges of his Jewish status have been severely compromised, his rights as a free person have been limited by the Christian slave's freedom in Christ, and his position as a male is now being lived out in the same world with the Corinthian women prophets. Paul unquestionably sees himself having lost status" (Wire, *Corinthian Women Prophets*, 67).

34. For a critique of the inadequacy of self-sacrifice as a model for love, see Sharon Welch, *A Feminist Ethic of Risk* (Minneapolis: Fortress, 1990), 162.

RECOMMENDED READINGS

Betz, Hans Dieter. *2 Corinthians 8 and 9: A Commentary on Two Administrative Letters of the Apostle Paul*. Hermeneia. Philadelphia: Fortress, 1985.

Forbes, Christopher. "Comparison, Self-Praise and Irony: Paul's Boasting and the Conventions of Hellenistic Rhetoric." *New Testament Studies* 32 (1986): 1–30.

Furnish, Victor Paul. *II Corinthians*. Anchor Bible. Garden City, NY: Doubleday, 1984.

Georgi, Dieter. *The Opponents of Paul in Second Corinthians*. Philadelphia: Fortress, 1986.

Murphy-O'Connor, Jerome. *The Theology of the Second Letter to the Corinthians*. New Testament Theology. Cambridge: Cambridge University Press, 1991.

Wire, Antoinette Clark. *The Corinthian Women Prophets: A Reconstruction through Paul's Rhetoric*. Philadelphia: Fortress, 1991.

Young, Frances, and David F. Ford. *Meaning and Truth in 2 Corinthians*. London: SPCK, 1987.

Galatians

SHEILA BRIGGS ◆

INITIATION INTO THE EARLY CHRISTIAN COMMUNITY AS THE ERASURE OF SOCIO-SEXUAL DISTINCTION

"THERE IS NO LONGER Jew or Greek, there is no longer slave or free, there is no longer male and female; for all of you are one in Christ Jesus." These words of Gal 3:28 are the clearest statement of women's equality to be found in the Christian scriptures. They have rightly received extensive commentary from those interested in the relationship between biblical interpretation and the status of women in the Christian churches and Christian-influenced societies.

Galatians 3:28 is not an original composition of the apostle but is the quotation by him of a baptismal formula, presumably one known and respected by the Galatian community.[1] Thus, its beginnings lie not in Pauline theology but in the lived social experience of early Christians. The social implications of this text cannot be adequately understood through attention only to Paul's intentions and the reception of Paul's letter in early Christian communities. Many exegetes have been willing to concede the social implications of Gal 3:28, but have interpreted it in the light of Pauline theology. They have focused on the relation of the Galatians text to Paul's more conservative utterances about the status and role of slaves and women in 1 Corinthians.[2]

A more fruitful approach to understanding what Gal 3:28 meant in its original context—the communal experience of early Christians—has been taken by Wayne Meeks and Hans Dieter Betz.[3] Both interpreters take seriously the theological content of early Christian social practices. They argue that baptism was understood quite literally by early Christians as entry into a new creation, in which the religious, cultural, and social distinctions between Jew and Greek, slave and free, male and female had been abolished. Meeks, borrowing a term from linguistic philosophy, describes the Galatian baptismal formula as a "performative utterance"; that is, the early Christians who spoke it believed that it not only expressed a reality but enacted it. For early Christians it was a fact, not just a hope for the future, that their community was demarcated through baptism from the larger society with its social inequality and hierarchies of race, class, and gender.[4]

Both Meeks and Betz find it significant that the phrase used in the baptismal formula is not "man and woman" but "male and female." This indicates for them a link between Gal 3:28 and the myth of the androgyne as it was found in various forms throughout the Greco-Roman world, including within ancient Judaism.[5] The androgyne myth recalled an original state of humanity in which male and female were a single entity (in Judaism it was an interpretation of the Genesis creation accounts). Thus, one might paraphrase the claim of the early Christian baptismal formula:

> You outside our community long for a return to the beginning in which human beings were not divided by race, class and, above all, sex. We, Christians, already are living in the end-time in which all these divisions have been once more overcome in a new creation where we have become all one in Christ.

The implications of Gal 3:28 for gender roles and status are momentous, especially when one considers how the abolition of the three sets of hierarchical relations mutually intensified the egalitarian effect. Elisabeth Schüssler Fiorenza has remarked that:

> relinquishment of religious male prerogatives within the Christian community was possible and that such a relinquishment included the abolition of social privileges as well. The legal-societal and cultural-religious male privileges were no longer valid for Christians. Insofar as this egalitarian Christian self-understanding did away with all male privileges of religion, class and caste, it allowed not only gentiles and slaves but also women to exercise leadership functions within the missionary movement.[6]

The point being made here is that the erasure of social and ethnic-religious privileges as well as gender ones promoted women's equality. Claims to ethnic-religious superiority depended on kinship relations. When these were rendered insignificant in early Christian communities, the distinctions in status and role of Jewish and Gentile Christian women could no longer be upheld. The same was also the case for slave and free Christian women. The former guides for women's behavior had incorporated the distinctions of social class and ethnic-religious origin. Kinship and the social authority of master over slave were essential supports of the patriarchal household of antiquity. When these were challenged, then male privilege and the right of male heads of household to control women were thereby undermined. This gave women of all backgrounds the chance to negotiate new social roles and to claim leadership roles which formerly had been held inappropriate for women even of high class and ethnic-religious status.

LAW AND WOMEN'S LIBERTY:
THE CONTEXT OF GALATIANS 3:28

In Gal 3:28 the baptismal formula has been moved from its social context in early Christianity into the textual one of Paul's letter. There it is not embedded in a wider argument for women's equality but serves Paul's predominant intention, namely, to show the incompatibility of observance of the law with faithfulness to the Christian gospel. It is Paul's opposition of law and gospel that has occupied the attention of most Christian commentators in the past and occupies nonfeminist interpreters of today. How does the specifically feminist interest in Gal 3:28 as evidence of a social movement for women's equality relate to the traditional Christian concentration on the Pauline antithesis of law and gospel? Inevitably, one must also ask what was Paul's own stance toward the baptismal formula he quoted and what was the quality of his endorsement of the elimination of the male–female distinction, which he proclaimed in the quoted text. One must avoid the assumption that Gal 3:28 shows that Paul's critique of the law benefited women. One must guard against this syllogism: Paul was on the side of women, and Paul was on the side of the gospel; therefore, the gospel was on the side of women against the restrictions placed on them by the Jewish law. Given this assumption, a further tacit one is made: the judaizing party in the Galatian community was a male faction, and obviously women (at least those aware of their Christian dignity) supported Paul.

I argue here that these assumptions are not the only, the best, or the most plausible conclusions that can be drawn from the historical evidence. However, I do not make the counterargument that women were among the opponents of Paul in the Galatian community, realizing that their best interests were served by observance of the Jewish law. There is also not the historical evidence to support that contention. My purpose is to articulate the connection between Paul's attitude to the law in Galatians and the practical consequences and ideological effects that it had for and on women's lives in early Christianity, which have had far-reaching repercussions for later Christian women.

Galatians was written for a very specific purpose: to oppose the introduction of the Jewish law into the Galatian community. In pursuing this goal, Paul raised other topics, two of which bear directly on Paul's attitude to the gender and other social egalitarianism present or potential in early Christian communities. The first is Paul's discussion of Christians as the true descendants of Abraham, a central piece of which is his Hagar–Sarah allegory in Gal 4:21–31. Second, Paul developed a Christian ethics in Gal 5:13–6:10, based on "living by the Spirit." The issue here is whether Paul, in rejecting Torah as the norm for Christian moral behavior, also envisaged getting rid of the *content* of its concrete prescriptions and what the consequences of such a decision might have been for women in Pauline Christianity.

PAUL'S CRITIQUE OF THE LAW

In his letter to the Galatian Christians, Paul was urging them to resist attempts by some (it would seem Jewish) Christians to persuade them that full membership in the Jewish community through circumcision and the observance of the Torah was required for Christians. From the content of the Torah discussed by Paul, it seems that circumcision and food regulations were the sources of conflict between some Jewish Christians and Gentile Christians. Paul gave his account of the controversy in which he had been embroiled in Antioch over the table fellowship of Jew and Christian (2:11–14). The preparation and consumption of food in strict accordance with the rules, later codified in the Mishnah, would have made table fellowship between Jew and Gentile in the Christian community difficult, if not impossible.[7] Paul could have argued that those parts of the Torah that were excessively burdensome to Gentiles should not be imposed on them. However, he went much further and argued that the Torah itself had lost its validity for Christians. In contrast, the Council at Jerusalem had decided that Gentiles were exempt from the observance of the Torah except in some matters (including food regulations) apparently of special concern to Jewish Christians (Acts 15:19–20), but there was no theological polemic against the Torah, which was still assumed to be in force for Jewish Christians.

Paul, however, argued that observing the Torah was incompatible with authentic faith in Christ; he placed Galatian Christians before the stark alternative of holding that they had been redeemed through performing all of the actions required of the righteous by the Torah or through being accounted justified because of their faith in Christ (2:16, 21; 3:11–12, 21–24; 5:2–5). This is the central argument of Paul's letter, and around the various ways in which he expressed it are clustered the most difficult and controversial issues in the interpretation of Galatians.

Paul wrote:

> We ourselves are Jews by birth and not Gentile sinners, yet we know that a person is justified not by the works of the law but through faith in Jesus Christ. And we have come to believe in Christ Jesus, so that we might be justified by faith in Christ, and not by doing the works of the law, because no one will be justified by the works of the law. (2:15–16)

On the basis of this statement, it would be hard to justify the *continued* Torah observance of a *Jew* who joined the Christian movement. Yet Paul in Galatians and elsewhere never advocated that Jewish Christians give up their observance of the law. On the contrary, he assumed that Jews remained Jews and that remaining Jewish was no barrier to having faith in Christ: "in Christ Jesus neither circumcision nor uncircumcision counts for anything" (5:6a; cf. 6:15). The problem for Paul was not *remaining* a Jew but *becoming* a Jew, so he wrote, "if you let yourselves be circumcised, Christ will be of no benefit to you" (5:2).

Yet is this a consistent position? Paul claimed in Gal 2:14 to have rebuked Peter for breaking off table fellowship with the Gentiles: "If you, though a Jew, live like a Gentile and not like a Jew, how can you compel the Gentiles to live like Jews?" The rather vague phrase "living like a Gentile" may not be a historically accurate picture of Peter's behavior, but it does give us insight into what Paul considered a required change of life-style for those Jewish Christians who associated with Gentile converts, as Peter had hitherto done. On a practical level, remaining an observant Jew in a Christian community with Gentile converts must have been exceedingly difficult, if one accepted Paul's strictures.[8]

On the question whether Paul was inconsistent about the law on the theoretical level, heated controversies have recently been generated. Much of this debate concerns what appear to be stark differences in Paul's statements about the law, notably between Galatians and Romans, and whether these tensions can be resolved. In Gal 3:10 and 5:3, Paul said that those who accepted the Jewish law had to keep the whole of it. E. P. Sanders has pointed out that in contemporary Judaism fulfillment of the Torah was not considered impossible, but that a distinction was made between accepting the whole law and obeying it perfectly. His conclusion is that Paul attacked the law not because it "cannot be followed, nor because following it leads to legalism, self-righteousness and self-estrangement."[9] Instead, Sanders argues, Paul believed that it had never been God's intention to make anyone righteous through the law. Paul's objection to the Torah was not that it was an alternative and competing standard of righteousness, but that it was not Christ, who alone offered righteousness.[10]

The Torah had been in effect for a limited period of time and for a limited purpose. With the death of Christ, its purpose had been fulfilled. Paul described the law as a *paidagōgos* (3:24–25); this was the slave who accompanied the young child (usually boy) to school.[11] His task was not "pedagogical" in the modern sense; it was to exercise an often harsh discipline over his charge. Paul presented the law in Galatians precisely in terms of this image of a harsh disciplinarian. There is little room for a positive purpose of the law in Galatians, and Paul gave scant explanation for its existence, especially in light of what he must have surely held, its divine institution. To the question, Why the law? Paul answered, "it was added because of transgressions" (3:19). The idea here seems to be that to which he gave more explicit and extensive treatment in Romans 7. The law, like the *paidagōgos,* made those under its charge aware of their wrongful behavior and punished them.[12] But there is no positive sense of the law being able to teach those under its sway how to do the good (3:21–22).

In Galatians the decidedly negative purpose of the law could become a perverted one if the law remained in effect beyond the time allotted for its validity. Paul equated submission to the law with being "slaves to the elements of the world" (4:3, 9).[13] This had been the state of everyone before Christ's death and now, perversely and incomprehensibly, the Galatian Christians wished to return to it through observance of the law. Since Paul's position was that the Torah as a whole became canceled through Christ's death and for those who have faith in the crucified Christ, his polemic was not directed against individual injunctions of the law. His quarrel with circumcision was not that it was bizarre or culturally inappropriate, or morally wrong for Gentiles. It was the concrete expression of a belief (impossible for a Christian) that righteousness could be achieved through practicing the Torah.

HAGAR AND SARAH: SLAVE AND FREE AS A THEOLOGICAL DISTINCTION

Central to Paul's argument about the law was his understanding of Christians as being the heirs to God's promise to Abraham. In Genesis 12 the patriarch Abraham received a call from God to leave his country and kin; he was promised that God would "make of him a great nation" (Gen 12:2). In Galatians 3 Paul seized upon the fact that even in this Jewish scripture Abraham was seen as living several hundred years before the law was given to Moses (3:15–18). Abraham became for Paul the model of those who lived without the law. The baptismal formula of Galatians 3:26–28 came at the climax of Paul's interpretation of who was the offspring of Abraham. In particular, Paul gave a christological focus to descent from Abraham. Jesus was first and foremost the offspring of Abraham (3:16), and Christians come to share in descent from Abraham through being incorporated into Christ through baptism. Paul's own gloss on the baptismal formula of Gal 3:26–28 was to equate oneness in Christ with being Abraham's descendants: "if you belong to Christ, then you are Abraham's offspring, heirs according to the promise" (3:29). The clear implication of Gal 3:28–29 is that, among the true descendants of Abraham, ethnic, class, and gender distinctions had been erased. The emancipatory force of Paul's argument was intensified in Gal 4:1–12. Here he compared the state of all humanity before Christ's coming with slavery or being a minor under a guardian and then faith in Christ with gaining one's freedom from slavery or a minor reaching maturity.

It should come as a surprise, therefore, that Paul proceeded to explain the antithesis between enslavement to the law and freedom in Christ through the Hagar–Sarah allegory in Gal 4:21–31[14] This allegory depends on metaphors taken from the institution of slavery and the sexual use of women in slavery. One may argue that Paul's use of the language of slavery in figurative speech did not constitute an endorsement of slavery in the social realm; however, one cannot simply sever the rhetorical strategy from the content of discourse. Certainly, Paul was not addressing here the social institution of slavery, but the distinctions that ancient slavery made between person and person, between human group and human group, are being perpetuated here, even if not in their original social form.

Hagar and Sarah were irreducibly unequal in Paul's allegory. Some ancients, following Aristotle, held that slavery was "natural" to some persons and human groups. Paul seems to have derived his metaphors from this view, since Hagar's inferiority was hereditary: she bore her children for slavery (4:24). Hagar was the type of non-Christian Judaism, and Paul connected her name with Mount Sinai in Arabia, suggesting the provenance of the law in slavery. The present Jerusalem, like Hagar and her children, remained in slavery (4:25). In contrast, Sarah was the type of the Christian community; she was the "Jerusalem above," who was both free and the "mother" of Christians (4:26).

Paul's allegorical use of the Hagar–Sarah story diverged significantly from the original account in Genesis. There Hagar also received a promise from God: "I will so greatly multiply your offspring that they cannot be counted for multitude" (Gen 16:10; cf. 21:13). In the Genesis story Sarah saw her son Isaac playing with Hagar's son Ishmael and, fearing that Isaac might have to share Abraham's inheritance with Ishmael, demanded that Hagar and her son be cast out (Gen 21:8–14). Paul knew nothing of any promise to Hagar and understood the reason for Hagar and her son's expulsion to lie not in Sarah's jealousy toward them but in Ishmael's hostility to Isaac. "The child," Paul wrote, "who was born according to the flesh persecuted the child who was born according to the Spirit" (4:29).[15] This statement was in harmony with (although not necessarily derived from) that strand of ancient opinion which held that moral viciousness was inherent in the slave's character.[16] What in Genesis was Sarah's demand of Abraham was converted by Paul into the command of scripture: "But what does scripture say? 'Drive out the slave and her child; for the child of the slave will not share the inheritance with the child of the free woman.'" In the Genesis account Hagar and Ishmael are driven out and are faced with the grim fate of abandoned slaves. They are miraculously saved from death by divine intervention (Gen 21:17–19), of which Paul made no mention in Galatians 4.

Was Paul's Hagar—Sarah allegory consistent with his quotation of the baptismal formula in Gal 3:28? It is unquestionably clear that Paul replaced the distinction between Jew and Gentile in the Christian community with an in fact far more drastic one between Christian (Jew and Gentile) and non-Christian Jew. He did this by transferring the most stringent and negative assessments of the difference between free persons and slaves to the relation of Christian to non-Christian Jew. His intention was quite explicit: theologically to dispossess non-Christian Judaism of its claims not only to religious superiority but even to religious identity, descent from Abraham.

Paul did not appear in Galatians concerned by the serious consequences this would have for Jewish Christianity. He even spoke of the two women representing "two covenants" (4:24), a position from which he would draw back from in Romans 9—11. In Gal 4:21—31 one sees most clearly the motivation for Paul's critique of the law. Francis Watson finds the roots of Paul's attitude to the law in his taking the step of creating Christian communities outside of Judaism. In this analysis, Paul's opponents still saw themselves as a reform movement within Judaism. But Paul had already adopted a sectarian model of Christianity which set it in opposition to the broader Jewish community. Paul's critique of the law belonged to an ideology legitimating the existence of a Christian community separate from the synagogue. Gal 4:21—31 functioned within this ideology as a strategy of reinterpretation. It did not seek renewal of the religious traditions of Judaism as a whole, as a reform movement would have done, but instead appropriated them as the exclusive property of the Christian sect.[17]

THE FRUIT OF THE SPIRIT
PAUL'S ETHICS FOR A LAW-FREE COMMUNITY

From the designation of Christians as "children of the free woman" (4:31) Paul turned to a discussion of Christian freedom. First he engaged in a polemic against Gentiles accepting circumcision (5:2—12), which was preceded by the encouragement "For freedom Christ has set us free. Stand firm, therefore, and do not submit again to a yoke of slavery" (5:1). In Gal 5:13 Paul again reminded his audience that they were called to freedom, but at this point he devoted himself to a long parenesis (moral exhortation) of the Galatian community (5:13—6:10), which many exegetes have found at odds with, or at least unconnected to, Paul's concerns in the letter up to this point.[18]

John M. G. Barclay's recent and extensive study of Galatians 5 and 6 seeks to show how these chapters are integral to the letter as a whole. He accepts Watson's sociological analysis of Paul's intention in Galatians as seeking to define Christian identity as separate from Judaism rather than as a movement within it. Barclay, however, wants to stress a specifically theological dimension to this new Christian identity. He sees a parallel between the flesh–spirit antithesis of Galatians 5 and 6 and that between faith and the "works of the law" in the earlier part of the letter.[19]

The flesh–spirit antithesis certainly provided the structural link between Gal 5:13–6:10 and the earlier chapters. In terms of Christian behavior, "being led by the Spirit" removed one from being "under the law" (5:18). It thus recapitulated on the ethical plane what we have already encountered in Galatians 3, where Paul indignantly asked the Galatians, "Having started with the Spirit, are you now ending with the flesh?" (3:3). In posing a similar rhetorical question in the previous verse, Paul had already excluded that the Spirit could be received through "works of the law." In Gal 3:2 and 3:5 he had already sought to establish *how* the Spirit was received, namely, "by hearing with faith." In the parenesis of Galatians 5 and 6 the focus turned to *the consequences* of already having received the Spirit.

Those proposing observance of the Torah in the Galatian community were accused by Paul of "making a good showing in the flesh," and their demand for Gentile circumcision was, Paul said, the desire to glory in the flesh of their male Gentile converts (6:12–13). Paul therefore identified observance of the Torah with the life of the flesh. Life under the Torah was incompatible with life under the Spirit, which was given to those who had faith in Christ. Nonetheless, Paul did not equate circumcision or other individual injunctions of the Torah with the "works of the flesh," which he excoriated as morally wrong activities (Gal 5:19–21).

Paul's critique of the law was not replaced by a supposedly more positive attitude of the role of Torah in providing ethical norms to guide the Christian life. It is a mistake to interpret Paul's statements on "fulfilling the law" in such a light. There is a categorical difference between "fulfilling" and "keeping" the law.[20] Paul highlighted this distinction by describing behavior inspired by the Spirit, which while "fulfilling the law" quite clearly did not require observing it. So those led by the Spirit were "not under the law" (5:18); and of the virtuous activity that instantiated living in the Spirit, Paul said, "against such there is no law" (5:24).

The remark in Gal 6:2 on "fulfilling the law of Christ" remains, as Betz says, a "puzzle."[21] It may be intended ironically in something like the following sense: You Galatians want a law; well, you can have the "law of Christ"—which is being led by the Spirit and therefore under no law. The full phrase reads, "Bear one another's burdens, and in this way you will fulfill the law of Christ." Perhaps "bearing one another's burdens" was seen by Paul as equivalent to the love commandment in 5:14, which was described there as fulfilling the whole law.[22] Richard Hays has suggested that the "law of Christ" was Paul's way of urging the Galatian Christians to imitate Christ, especially Christ's crucifixion as submitting to self-sacrifice on account of love for others.[23]

The equation of "dying with Christ" with "dying to the law" provided a further connection between this later parenetic section of Paul's letter and his earlier critique of the law. Becoming a Christian was seen by Paul as being incorporated into the crucified Christ. So we read in Gal 2:19–20: "For through the law I died to the law, so that I might live to God. I have been crucified with Christ; and it is no longer I who live, but it is Christ who lives in me." Paul was describing the process of conversion whereby one died to the bondage of the flesh, which he in his case experienced as an observant Jew under the sway of Torah and against which the law was powerless. In Gal 5:24 he was speaking of the end result of the process of conversion: "And those who belong to Christ Jesus have crucified the flesh with its passions and desires."

This process of conversion is intrinsically linked to baptism. Paul's language in the Galatians passages is similar in many respects to the language he would use later in Rom 6:3–11, where Paul stated that baptism was baptism into Christ's death in which the old self was crucified so that Christians could be dead to sin and alive to God. Baptism was the point *when* a person could be clearly held to have received the Spirit and, having become "one in Christ Jesus" with other believers, was incorporated into the crucified Christ. Hence, it is likely that Paul himself understood the baptismal formula of Gal 3:28 in terms of imitating Christ's self-sacrificing death in one's interactions with others.

Although the sole ethical ground of a Christian's behavior was "living by the Spirit," the content of that behavior was not derived from a particular Christian ethos. Paul offered a catalogue of vices (5:19–21) and of virtues (5:22–23) that was drawn from the conventional ethics of Jews and of Greeks in the Hellenistic world, much of which both groups had in common. These were "works of the flesh" or "fruit of the Spirit" not because of specifically Christian values they either lacked or embodied. Furthermore, the effect of the Spirit on the life of the Christian was expressed in terms a Hellenistic Jew or Pagan would consider morally praiseworthy: "those who belong to Christ Jesus have crucified the flesh with its passions and desires" (5:24).

Admittedly, Paul did not dwell on passion as the source of human moral failure in the way one finds in the Jewish thought of Philo of Alexandria, in Stoic philosophy or later in the Christian philosophy of Clement of Alexandria. Paul identified the same symptoms of moral disorder and health as did his Hellenistic contemporaries, but for him the cause of these failures lay elsewhere, in a person's identity of belonging to Christ or not. Yet being a Christian brought not so much new moral insight as the ability effectively to act upon the moral convictions one shared with one's culture, a point Paul developed later in Romans. In Galatians, Paul was content in the catalogues of vices and virtues and in the subsequent collection of maxims to list what he considered to be the indisputable moral wisdom now attainable for Christians through "living by the Spirit."

This did not mean that the moral values and standards had been arbitrarily selected. More important, one cannot maintain as Paul's own view that moral values and standards are culturally embedded and historically malleable. Paul did not suggest at all that the lists of vices and virtues along with the moral maxims were relative to his time and place and therefore might be transformed or discarded in the light of later human and, especially, Christian experience. In fact, Paul had the distinctive moral preferences of what he was, a Hellenistic Jew. Therefore, pagan worship and sexual activities (an area of special concern for Jewish purity laws) figured prominently in his catalogue of vices. Just as absolutely as Paul believed that certain concrete prescriptions of the Torah, such as dietary laws, should be abandoned in the Christian community, he held that the content of other of the Torah's demands were to be practiced in the Christian community. As E. P. Sanders so aptly remarks, Paul's "first concern was not to inculcate Jewish behavior in his converts. . . . he regarded correct (that is, decent Jewish) behavior as the self-evident result of living by the Spirit."[24]

PAUL'S UNDERSTANDING OF THE LAW
AND ITS EFFECTS ON EARLY CHRISTIAN WOMEN

What were the effects of Paul's radical and novel teaching about the law on women in the Galatian and other early Christian communities? The immediate context of the statement that in Christ there is neither male nor female was Paul's remarks in the same chapter about the purpose of the law as a harsh disciplinarian for sinful human beings not yet made mature and free by the redemptive death of Christ. Paul was quite clear that bondage to the law had been replaced for Christians by a freedom, given with the Spirit (4:21–5:1). Did this freedom have an emancipatory effect for women? The answer depends very much on what one sees as the relationship of women to the Torah in first-century Judaism (see the next section). Paul effectively (if not intentionally) held in Galatians that the Torah was abolished for *Jewish* Christians as well as Gentile Christians. Hence, Jewish Christian women were in Paul's terms "freed" from Torah observance. Any social barriers between Jewish and Gentile women in the Christian community on the basis of Torah observance would have been dissolved by following Paul's advice. Certainly, a space would have been opened up for Jewish Christian women to negotiate new social roles. This would have had an unsettling effect on gender roles throughout the Christian community and, therefore, also among the Gentiles.

Paul's critique of the law supported the claim that social conventions had to be evaluated and, if necessary, revised or discarded on the basis of their congruence with the Spirit-given freedom, which obliterated social distinctions between Christians. Paul, however, was often opposed to the conclusions other Christians drew from his own premises. The radical character of Paul's attack on Torah observance in Galatians was set amid his deep ambivalence toward the Torah and contradictions in his understanding of the law. This ambivalence and these contradictions are perceptible in Galatians and become increasingly evident as one compares Paul's statements in Galatians with passages in his other letters.[25]

The parenesis of Galatians 5 and 6, with its catalogues of virtues and vices and its collection of maxims, did not specifically address the situation of women, but, of course, these maxims were addressed to women too. They were concrete enough for us to assume that Paul had some specific forms of social behavior in mind, but they did not prescribe these directly. To offer such prescriptions may have appeared to Paul writing Galatians as coming dangerously close to rehabilitating the Torah as a validating instance for the Christian life. Elsewhere, however, Paul was less reticent and offered regulations for women's behavior that were in continuity with restrictions placed upon women in patriarchal formulations of the Jewish law.

Bernadette Brooten has shown that especially in matters of gender and sexuality Paul stuck closely to the Torah and the rabbinical tradition of his day. In his attitudes toward permissible behavior for married women, women's dress, incest, homosexuality, and so on, Paul presented in 1 Corinthians and Romans an ethic thoroughly consistent with Jewish law.[26] In 1 Corinthians 11 Paul insisted that women cover their heads during worship because it was a social form appropriate to their theologically justifiable subordination. Paul's rather tortuous theological argument drew on Jewish scriptural interpretation and was in part a midrash on Gen 1:27. Paul's argument had many elements in common with rabbinic Jewish arguments, although he was not a Jewish Christian rabbi delivering a halakah (legal pronouncement) for the Christian community.[27]

There is, nevertheless, one statement in 1 Corinthians where Paul seemed to have made a direct appeal to the law: "Women should be silent in the churches. For they are not permitted to speak, but should be subordinate, as the law also says" (14:34–35). This passage is commonly judged to be an interpolation, although Brooten and Antoinette Wire have mounted an impressive case for its being authentically Pauline.[28] One should not argue against its authenticity on the basis that the author of Galatians could never have appealed to the authority of the law. Paul may have had no consistent and well-defined criteria for what of the concrete content of Torah one should retain or abandon, but the moral correctness of restricting women's speech in a public religious forum might have been so strongly felt by Paul that the truth of the rabbinic interpretation of scripture, which supported this constraint, would have been self-evident to him. Paul would not have to concede that the Torah still was in force for the Christian community. Rather, he would be saying that women's silence was an instance of how Christians living by the Spirit were enabled to fulfill the law without keeping it.

For Paul himself, the primary ethical implication of baptism was surely the imitation of the crucified Christ. The obliteration of the distinction between male and female in baptism would lead to the fulfilling of the law's require-ment through Christian love of others in a practice of self-sacrifice, of "becom-ing slaves to one another through love" (5:13) and "bearing one another's bur-dens" (6:2). Positively, a space for genuine mutuality between women and men in the Christian community was opened up. Yet in a patriarchal society the call for self-sacrifice toward others can take on gender-specific forms in which a mutual giving way to one another is transformed into women's subordination to men. This is the trajectory that seems to have been taken between Paul's let-ter to the Galatians and the Deutero-Pauline letter to the Ephesians. The author of Ephesians moved from the general admonition "Be subject to one another out of reverence for Christ" (5:21) to the gender-specific content of supposedly mutual subjection: "Wives, be subject to your husbands" (5:22).

The same, of course, could be said of slaves and slaveowners. The mutual subjection of Christians to one another turned into the relation of obedient slaves to kind masters (Eph 6:5–9). The Hagar–Sarah allegory reminds us how deeply the metaphor of inequality was embedded in Paul's thought. In the ancient world and in other slaveholding societies, freedom emerged as the social and conceptual distinction between those who were and were not slaves. Therefore, it is not surprising that Paul in his historical context could talk of freedom only together with its opposite—slavery. Throughout Galatians these twin concepts and their correlates appear in a discourse of polarity (2:4; 3:28; 4:1–9, 21–31; 5:1). It is misleading to call Galatians Paul's "gospel of freedom" since freedom for him only existed in relation to slavery. Christian freedom implied non-Christian enslavement. The Hagar–Sarah allegory shows how Paul could conceive of Christian freedom only as the opposite of Jewish enslavement to the Torah and as dispossessing the Jews of Abraham's pater-nity and, with it, God's promises. Jews, like slaves in the social realm, were held to have no father.

If Galatians was Paul's attempt to define a Christian identity as separate from a Jewish one, then it was fundamentally a debate about paternity. In Gal 4:21–31 what was being established was who were the true descendants not of Sarah but of Abraham. The social assumption behind the allegory was that women were located in male-defined structures of kinship. Women's sexuality and reproduction mediated male paternity and needed to be strictly controlled. Thus, Paul's use of the Hagar–Sarah allegory moved within a mental world not distant from first-century formulations of the Torah, which would be later codified in the Mishnah's Law of Women. Hagar's sexuality, in Paul's thinking, had created an anomaly—a son, indeed a firstborn son, of the patriarch Abraham, who was not destined to become his legitimate descendant. Women and women's sexuality as an anomalies were perspectives shared with the Mishnaic "system of women."[29]

JEWISH WOMEN AND THE LAW IN THE TIME OF PAUL

As I mentioned at the outset, Christian exegetes have tended to work from the premise that Paul's rejection of Torah must have benefited women. The tendency has been to take the most restrictive interpretation of the Torah and to assume that this was the one current within the Galatian community.[30] Yet the historical evidence that we have about Jewish women's lives in antiquity does not support the view that they were an especially oppressed group of women. The pioneering research of Brooten and the more recent work of Ross Shepard Kraemer have shown that the Mishnah represents a male ideal of women's place in the world and should not be taken as a historically accurate portrait of women's lives in ancient Judaism.[31]

Judaism at the time of Paul was more pluralistic than it would later be under the pressures of disastrous wars and repression by the Roman Empire. To consider oneself an observant Jew did not necessarily entail accepting the strict interpretation of Torah as Paul understood it and had earlier practiced it. Within the variety of ancient Jewish religion, there were communities that allowed women a much wider participation, including leadership roles, which in the Mishnah's idealized world were denied them. In some places at least, women took an active part in Jewish communal life. Despite later practice, there is no evidence that women were physically separated from men in the ancient synagogue. Women served as officers in synagogues, although which functions they performed remains unclear. Closely allied to women holding office was their activity as donors. This suggests that Jewish women, like other women in the Hellenistic period, had increasing access to and control over their own resources. Those aspects of Jewish law that most discriminated against women were frequently circumvented. Thus, Jewish women inherited property and initiated divorce from their husbands despite the obstacles of the law.[32]

But what about women who lived in Jewish communities where Torah observance was conceived in the terms that would later become codified in the Mishnah? Again, even here the male rabbinic ideal probably did not coincide with women's social reality. Although on the surface the Mishnah may appear to be concerned with regulating even the minutest details of women's lives, this was far from being the case. There are many aspects of women's lives that received no attention, and the Mishnah did not provide a comprehensive or even consistent view of women's nature and the social roles that rested on it. The Mishnah concerned itself with a taxonomy of women, and this taxonomy was determined and limited to one consideration: the relationship of women, indeed preeminently of their sexuality and reproductive activities, to men.[33]

Moreover, even women's relations with men did not receive full treatment. Rather, women became of interest to the rabbis when their relationship to men became ambiguous, when it was unclear who controlled their sexuality or when it was unclear how their sexuality affected men.[34] Yet as Judith Romney Wegner points out, the rabbis were quite capable of seeing women as persons who in their relationship to other persons exercised much (though not entirely) the same rights as men. There was, therefore, a bifurcation in the mishnaic view of women. When men had sexual claims upon them, their status was very much that of property. Outside the realm of male sexual rights women were frequently treated as full persons. Hence, they were able to own property, engage in business transactions, undertake litigation (through agents) and take an oath in respect to property entrusted to them.[35]

But even women whose sexuality was not the property of a man never achieved full equality with men. Wegner sees the limitation of women's equality with men occurring through their exclusion from the public domain. The mishnaic system might accord some women (and in some cases all women) equal standing with men in most matters of private law, but denied them a presence in the public realm. The binary opposition of male and female was so central to the mishnaic system that the realm in which men were present had to be defined by the absence of women. Women's sexuality was identified by the rabbis as that which made their presence in the public sphere intolerable for men.[36]

Nonetheless, the rabbis could envisage a public world without women more easily than they could argue for it. Women were, after all, required to perform most of the religious obligations that men did, but they were not allowed to participate in the cult. In his concrete expectations of women's behavior Paul was surprisingly close to the rabbis, as 1 Corinthians with its concern over women's public religious activity demonstrates. There is no reason to suspect that Paul in Galatians held a different view. The prominence of sexual activities in his catalogue of vices probably would have correlated with an unease about women and their sexuality intruding into the public religious sphere.[37] Admittedly, Paul did not indicate in Galatians whether or to what extent women should fulfill the content of the Jewish purity laws and other constraints of Torah on their sexuality. But then he did not address himself at all to what Jewish women or women converts would have experienced in Torah observance, focusing primarily on the exclusively male concern of circumcision.

Finally, Paul's confidence in his own experience of the Spirit as a thoroughly sufficient and reliable moral guide could lead to a moral absolutism, which conceptually blocked him from being able to accept alternative Christian ethics and life-styles, such as practiced by the Corinthian women prophets. In the rabbinic system, precisely because the Torah was law it had always to be interpreted and could be changed. As Wegner points out, halakah in principle admits of amendment (*taqqanah*), and this not only on the basis of the internal development of halakic logic but also in response to changes in the outside culture.[38] Up to the present, Christian churches have encountered difficulties in altering traditional moral prescriptions, especially those in the realms of gender and sexuality. Despite the rhetoric of Christian freedom, an internal theological principle is missing through which one might explain changes in the moral behavior acceptable to Christians. Jewish feminists today, while recognizing the detrimental effect that traditional male-defined halakah has had on Jewish women's lives, still claim Torah as a vehicle of Jewish identity and see in its fluidity the means for a feminist reform of Judaism.[39] Christian feminists have a lot to learn from them.

NOTES

1. See Hans-Dieter Betz, *Galatians: A Commentary on Paul's Letter to the Churches in Galatia* (Hermeneia; Philadelphia: Fortress, 1979), 181–84. All biblical quotations are taken from the NRSV except where indicated.

2. See Ben Witherington III, *Women in the Earliest Churches* (Society for New Testament Studies Monograph Series 59; Cambridge: Cambridge University Press, 1988), 77–78; Dieter Lührmann, *Galatians*, trans. O. C. Dean, Jr. (A Continental Commentary; Minneapolis: Fortress, 1992), 76–78; Gerhard Dautzenberg, "Zur Stellung der Frauen in den paulinischen Gemeinden," in *Die Frau im Urchristentum*, ed. Gerhard Dautzenberg, Helmut Merklein, and Karlheinz Müller (Quaestiones Disputatae; Freiburg: Herder, 1983), 216–21.

3. See Wayne Meeks, "The Image of the Androgyne: Some Uses of a Symbol in Earliest Christianity," *History of Religions* 13 (1974): 165–208; Betz, *Galatians*, 189–200. Also J. L. Martyn, "Apocalyptic Antinomies in Paul's Letter to the Galatians," *New Testament Studies* 31 (1985): 410–24.

4. Meeks, "Image," 181–82.

5. In ancient Judaism both the rabbis and a hellenized Jew such as Philo of Alexandria had recourse to the idea of an originally androgynous human being in order to reconcile the differences between the creation accounts of Gen 1:27 and 2:18ff. However, the idea of androgyne did not lead here to the questioning of existing social relations. In fact, it could take quite a misogynistic twist as when Philo (*De Opificio Mundi* 134, 151ff.) identified the creation of woman as the "Fall" of a perfectly rational original humanity into the world of the senses and its attendant evil.

6. Elisabeth Schüssler Fiorenza, *In Memory of Her: A Feminist Theological Reconstruction of Christian Origins* (New York: Crossroad, 1983), 218.

7. For a contrary positon, see Peter J. Tomson, *Paul and the Jewish Law: Halakha in the Letters of the Apostle to the Gentiles* (Minneapolis: Fortress, 1990), 230–36. He points to several instances in rabbinic literature where sharing meals with Gentiles is assumed and viewed positively. In light of the range of Jewish practice and of the fact that the *first* Gentile converts were sympathizers with Judaism and willingly observed some Jewish customs, the change in Christian practice that some Jewish Christians demanded for table fellowhip may have appeared minimal (but obviously not to Paul). Jewish Christians had probably refrained in the past from eating certain foods; now they sat at separate tables in the same room. For this reconstruction of the issue of table fellowship, see Lührmann, *Galatians,* 44.

8. See E. P. Sanders, *Paul, the Law, and the Jewish People* (Minneapolis: Fortress, 1983), 177, 185–86.

9. Ibid., 46.

10. Ibid., 21–29, 46–48. Against Sanders's interpretation, J. D. G. Dunn has lodged a strong protest. He holds that there is no fundamental rejection of the law in Paul. The main point of Dunn's argument is to see Paul's critique of the law as limited to its function as boundary marker of Jewish social *identity* ("Works of the Law and the Curse of the Law [Gal 3:10-14]," in *Jesus, Paul and the Law: Studies in Mark and Galatians* [Louisville: Westminster/John Knox, 1990], 216–25).

11. See Betz, *Galatians,* 177–78; also Norman H. Young, "Paidagogos: the Social Setting of a Pauline Metaphor (Gal 3:24; 1 Cor 4:15)," *Novum Testamentum* 29 (1987): 150–76.

12. See David J. Lull, "The Law Was Our Pedagogue: A Study in Galatians 3:19–25," *Journal of Biblical Literature* 105 (1986): 483–46.

13. So Sanders, *Paul, the Law,* 69. The NRSV translates *stoicheia tou kosmou* as "elemental spirits," but the more likely reference is to the four elements of air, fire, water, and earth, which were seen as exerting power over human life. See Dietrich Rusam, "Neue Belege zu den '*stoicheia tou kosmou*' (Gal 4,3.9; Kol 2, 8.20)," *Zeitschrift für die Neutestamentliche Wissenschaft* 83 (1992): 119–25; and Eduard Schweizer, "Slaves of the Elements and Worshipers of Angels: Gal 4:3, 9 and Col 2:8, 18, 20," *Journal of Biblical Literature* 107 (1988): 455–68.

14. It is often assumed that Paul's opponents used a Hagar–Sarah allegory and that Paul reverses their argument here. See C. K. Barrett, "The Allegory of Abraham, Sarah, and Hagar in the Argument of Galatians," in *Rechtfertigung: Festschrift für Ernst Käsemann zum 70. Geburtstag,* ed. Johannes Friedrich, Wolfgang Pöhlmann and Peter Stuhlmacher (Tübingen: Mohr-Siebeck, 1976), 9–16.

15. Paul may here be relying on some Jewish interpretations that took the verb in Gen 21:9 describing Ishmael playing with Isaac in a hostile sense. See Betz, *Galatians,* 249–50 n. 116.

16. See, for example, the sources and commentary in Thomas Wiedemann, *Greek and Roman Slavery* (London: Croom Helm, 1981), 61–77.

17. Francis Watson, *Paul, Judaism and the Gentiles: A Sociological Approach* (Cambridge: Cambridge University Press, 1986), 19–20, 40–41, 47, 69–72.

18. J. C. O'Neil flatly declares this whole section an interpolation (*The Recovery of Paul's Letter to the Galatians* [London: SPCK, 1972], 65–71).

19. John M. G. Barclay, *Obeying the Truth: A Study of Paul's Ethics in Galatians* (Edinburgh: T. & T. Clark, 1988), 238–42. David Lull's interpretation of the flesh–spirit dichotomy in Galatians 5 and 6 is very similar to Barclay's (*The Spirit in Galatia: Paul's Interpretation of Pneuma as Divine Power* [SBL Dissertation Series 9; Chico, CA: Scholars Press, 1980], 113–33).

20. See Barclay, *Obeying the Truth,* 142.

21. One improbable solution is the claim that the "law of Christ" is a new Torah. For convincing arguments against this position, see Betz, *Galatians,* 300–301; Barclay, *Obeying the Truth,* 126–30.

22. So Lührmann, *Galatians,* 116.

23. Richard Hays, "Christology and Ethics in Galatians: The Law of Christ," *Catholic Biblical Quarterly* 49 (1987): 268–90.

24. Sanders, *Paul, the Law,* 95.

25. See Heikki Räisänen, *Paul and the Law* (Minneapolis: Fortress, 1986).

26. Bernadette Brooten, "Paul and the Law: How Complete Was the Departure?" *Princeton Seminary Bulletin* (1990): 71–89.

27. See Sanders, *Paul, the Law,* 114. For a contrary view, see Tomson, *Paul and the Jewish Law,* 131–39. Tomson's view, however, rests on an extremely broad definition of halakah.

28. Brooten, "Paul and the Law," 77–80; Antoinette Clark Wire, *The Corinthian Women Prophets: A Reconstruction through Paul's Rhetoric* (Minneapolis: Fortress, 1990), 149–52.

29. See Jacob Neusner, *A History of the Mishnaic Law of Women,* Part 5, *The Mishnaic System of Women* (Leiden: E. J. Brill, 1980), 267–72.

30. See, for example, Ben Witherington III, "Rite and Rights for Women—Galatians 3.28," *New Testament Studies* 27 (1981): 593–604. He claims that the observance of special days and months, seasons and years made women inferior in the community because "they could not be required to observe the periodic times because menstruation could render them unclean at precisely the wrong moment" (p. 595). Similarly, he argues that circumcision was discriminatory to women and therefore Paul insisted on an initiation rite that was universally applicable (p. 601). He also believes that judaizers in Galatia were arguing that women must marry and propagate in order to ensure their place in the covenant community and salvation through connection to circumcised males (pp. 595–96).

31. See Bernadette J. Brooten, *Women Leaders in the Ancient Synagogue: Inscriptional Evidence and Background Issues* (Brown Judaic Studies 36; Chico, CA: Scholars Press, 1982); Ross Shepard Kraemer, *Her Share of the Blessings: Women's Religions Among Pagans, Jews, and Christians in the Greco-Roman World* (New York: Oxford University Press, 1992), 93–105.

32. See Brooten, *Women Leaders;* Kraemer, *Her Share of the Blessings,* 106–27; also Brooten "Konnten Frauen im alten Judentum die Scheidung betreiben? Überlegungen zu Mk 10, 10–12 und 1 Kor 7, 10–11," *Evangelische Theologie* 42 (1982): 65–80; Günter Mayer, *Die jüdische Frau in der hellenistisch-römischen Antike* (Stuttgart: Kohlhammer, 1987).

33. Judith Romney Wegner, *Chattel or Person? The Status of Women in the Mishnah* (New York: Oxford University Press, 1988), 14–18.

34. Ibid., 175–81.

35. Ibid., 19, 87–91, 119, 126–27, 168–72.

36. Ibid., 162–66, 180, 192–94.

37. See Lone Fatum, "Women, Symbolic Universe and Structures of Silence: Challenges and Possibilities in Androcentric Texts," *Studia Theologica* 43 (1989): 69–70.

38. Wegner, *Chattel,* 185.

39. See, for example, Judith Plaskow, *Standing Again at Sinai: Judaism from a Feminist Perspective* (San Francisco: Harper & Row, 1990), 25–74.

RECOMMENDED READINGS

Betz, Hans Dieter. *Galatians: A Commentary on Paul's Letter to the Churches in Galatia.* Hermeneia. Philadelphia: Fortress, 1979.

Brooten, Bernadette J. "Paul and the Law: How Complete Was the Departure?" *Princeton Seminary Bulletin* (1990): 71–89.

———. *Women Leaders in the Ancient Synagogue: Inscriptional Evidence and Background Issues.* Brown Judaic Studies 36. Chico, CA: Scholars Press, 1982.

Fatum, Lone. "Women, Symbolic Universe and Structures of Silence: Challenges and Possibilities in Androcentric Texts." *Studia Theologica* 43 (1989): 61–80.

Kraemer, Ross Shepard. *Her Share of the Blessings: Women's Religions among Pagans, Jews, and Christians in the Greco-Roman World.* New York: Oxford University Press, 1992.

Sanders, E. P. *Paul, the Law, and the Jewish People.* Minneapolis: Fortress, 1983.

Schüssler Fiorenza, Elisabeth. *In Memory of Her: A Feminist Theological Reconstruction of Christian Origins.* New York: Crossroad, 1984.

Wegner, Judith Romney. *Chattel or Person? The Status of Women in the Mishnah.* New York: Oxford University Press, 1988.

Philippians

CAROLYN OSIEK ◆

INTRODUCTION

THE FEMINIST LIBERATION interpreter of the Christian Testament has the twofold task of explicating the experience of biblical women within their own context and at the same time making them credible to the modern reader in a world very different from theirs. To use a liberation hermeneutic means to interpret biblical texts with full criticism of their androcentric and patriarchal biases without rejecting the liberative message that a different, critical interpretation can reveal. Thus, oppressive texts must be seen both as they functioned and were understood in their own time and place and as they continue to function in contemporary situations. While nothing can be done to change the world-views of ancient people who produced the texts, there is no excuse today for perpetuating an emphasis on nonliberating texts or for refraining from denouncing their destructive force. Nor is there any excuse for continuing to interpret biblical texts androcentrically.

The aim of this commentary will be to highlight everything in the Letter to the Philippians that can contribute to a feminist liberation interpretation or that poses special problems for such an interpretation, with special attention to the known Christian women of Philippi.

THE CITY AND ITS FIRST CHRISTIANS

The city of Philippi is located on a hot, dry plain on the north side of a pine-covered mountain range that separates it from the Aegean coast about sixteen miles to the south. In the Roman period it formed the northeastern part of the administrative province of Macedonia. Originally a Thracian city, it was refounded by and named after Philip II of Macedon, the father of Alexander the Great, in 356 B.C.E., and was again refounded as a Roman colony by Marc Antony about 40 B.C.E. It was heavily inhabited after that by Roman military veterans, was administered by Roman law, and was strongly influenced by a prevalence of Latin language and customs. Its seaport, Neapolis (Acts 16:11), present-day Kavalla, is still a thriving port town, whereas the great city of Philippi is today uninhabited.

Literary and inscriptional evidence indicates that from Hellenistic times women in Macedonia, as well as in Asia Minor and Egypt, enjoyed more personal freedom and participation in social and economic life than women in most of the eastern Mediterranean lands. It is therefore not surprising that women played a significant role in the early years of the Philippian church.

According to Acts 16:9–40, Paul's vision was the impetus for his arrival in Philippi, which was to be the first community founded by him on European soil. Though the historical reliability of Acts continues to be debated, its depiction of the beginnings of the church there highlight the leadership of Lydia, merchant of dyed cloth from Thyatira in Asia Minor, a "God-fearer," that is, presumably, a Gentile attracted to Jewish worship and customs. As head of her household, she leads them all to baptism and persuades Paul to lodge with her, thus providing the first house-church in the city, to which Paul and Silas return before their forced departure (Acts 16:40). While the story of Lydia may well be historical, it is strange that when writing to the Philippians Paul would not make special mention of this founding mother of the community— unless, of course, she had since moved on to another city, perhaps as a missionary as well as a business woman. Although economically successful with a household of her own, Lydia was probably of the low social status to which workers and traders in textiles usually belonged.

Besides the example of a woman's leadership, the same account of the founding of the Philippian church provides the contrasting story of the exploitation of a slave girl by her owners. Paul's exorcism of her lacks the considerate attention to the possessed person usually characteristic of Luke's exorcism narratives (e.g., Luke 4:35; 8:1–3, 38–40; 9:37–42), for the focus here is on apostolic power and its consequences for Paul.

THE CIRCUMSTANCES OF THE LETTER

When Paul wrote to the Philippians sometime in the mid-50s of the first century, he was imprisoned and his future was uncertain (1:7, 12–14, 19–23). The traditional opinion is that the epistle was written in Rome (cf. Acts 28:30). A Caesarean location has also been suggested (cf. Acts 21–26).

A third possible location for the writing of the letter has gained favor in recent years. Paul alludes obliquely several times to trouble he encountered in Ephesus: he "fought with beasts" there—probably a metaphor for great opposition (1 Cor 15:32); he experienced deadly peril in Asia, of which Ephesus was the capital (2 Cor. 1:8–10); Prisca and Aquila "risked their necks for my life"

(Rom 16:3–4), and this traveling missionary couple, according to Acts, lived in Rome, Corinth, and finally Ephesus (Acts 18:2, 19). The modern theory advocated by some that Romans 16 was really directed to the church at Ephesus would support this location of Prisca and Aquila there, as well as would Paul's greeting to another missionary couple, Andronicus and Junia, fellow prisoners of Paul (Rom 16:7). Lastly, in Acts 20:17–19, Paul bypasses Ephesus on his way to Jerusalem, alluding to troubles in the region.

THE CHARACTER OF THE LETTER

Though some doubts about the genuine Pauline authorship of the epistle were raised at the end of the last century, today its authenticity is not questioned. Its literary unity, however, presents problems. Phil 3:1 seems to be a letter conclusion, but 3:2 (or perhaps 3:1b) resumes with a different topic. Likewise, 4:9 is a conclusion, but 4:10 begins again with a thanksgiving formula, more typical of the opening of a letter (compare 1:3–11, the longest Pauline thanksgiving, or the briefer 1 Cor 1:4–9 or Rom 1:8–10).

These rough transitions suggest to many that the present epistle is really an edited combination of three letters of Paul to the Philippians. Added to the textual evidence is the allusion of Polycarp of Smyrna, in his letter to the Philippians about a century later, to letters written to them by Paul (Polycarp, *Phil.* 3.2). If the present letter is a unity, then presumably only one of those known to Polycarp has survived, whereas it is possible that he knew three letters that were later edited into one, our present epistle. If that is the case, some suggest that 4:10-20 is the earliest, a thank-you note for the Philippians' gift of money to Paul brought by Epaphroditus (4:18). Then, after Epaphroditus recovered from illness and was ready to return to Philippi (2:25–30), Paul wrote 1:1a–3:1 and perhaps 4:4–8 as a more extended comment on what he had heard about the situation in Philippi. Still later, he wrote 3:1b–4:3 or 4:7 to comment on the new problem of attraction to law observance, perhaps even after he had been released from prison and had visited them again.

It does seem as if the present epistle represents some editing of smaller letters, and historical-critical method must examine these discrepancies. In this case, an interpretation based on the theological integrity of the epistle would be questionable. However, both literary and canonical criticism, while not denying the problems posed by the question of literary integrity, can move beyond them to look at the text as a whole. The problem of the literary integrity of the epistle, therefore, need not detract from the appreciation of its theological integrity.

The overall rhetorical strategy of the epistle as we have it is the warm affirmation of the Philippians' loyalty to Paul in the past as well as the present, in order to draw on these bonds of mutual friendship and support to elicit, by personal and christological example, the continuing adherence of the Philippians to his teaching and his plea for unity within the community, which he believes represent the will of Christ. The values of relationship, dialogue, and sensitivity to others are strongly reinforced in this, one of Paul's most personally revealing epistles.

COMMENTARY

ADDRESS (PHIL 1:1–2)

According to the customary form of the Hellenistic letter, the epistle opens with the names of the senders, followed by those of the recipients, and a brief statement of good wishes. Paul slightly adapts this form in all of his letters to expand on his identity as apostle and to turn the greetings into a blessing. Though the letter comes from both Paul and Timothy, it quickly becomes obvious from the turn to the first person singular in v. 3 that Paul is the real sender.

Paul describes himself and Timothy as slaves (*douloi*) of Christ Jesus ("servants" being a milder but less accurate translation). This is a common self-designation in the Pauline letters (e.g., Rom 1:1; Gal 1:10; Titus 1:1; even "your slaves for the sake of Jesus," 2 Cor 4:5). Here it coordinates smoothly with the later ascription of slave status to Jesus (2:7). Slave status in Greco-Roman antiquity was ambiguous. Slavery is never anything but an abusive system with total disregard for human rights, and the literature is filled with examples indicating that it connoted humiliation and mistreatment. For women, slavery was especially oppressive. Most prostitutes were slaves, often having been abandoned or sold as children by parents unable to support them. Masters' sexual access to their female slaves was taken for granted and often caused considerable tension between their mistresses and such slaves, who were caught in the middle. On the other hand, in this extremely status-conscious culture, the slave administrator or personal representative of an important person could share in the high status of the owner. Female slaves were frequently freed by masters to become their wives or concubines. Thus, the social system coopted some of the oppressed into its hierarchical values by enabling them to use those values to gain status over others. Given the supreme status of Christ Jesus for Christians, it is not necessarily an expression of humility to call oneself his slave. Paul is Christ's authorized agent.[1]

The letter is addressed to "the holy ones in Christ Jesus who are in Philippi with their overseers and ministers" (*episkopoi* and *diakonoi*). To understand these terms as "bishops and deacons," as they can later be translated, would be anachronistic here. This verse is one of the earliest indications that Christian communities were beginning to have a recognized collegial governing body, probably after the example of most Jewish synagogues governed by a group of presbyters or *archons* (leaders). In Paul's speech in Acts 20:17–35, presbyters and *episkopoi* are synonymous (vv 17, 28). Probably they are so in Philippi as well. Surely at this point the plural *episkopoi* does not mean what the word "bishop" would later come to mean.

To understand the *diakonoi* as deacons is less problematic. All evidence indicates that they were trusted assistants of the presbyters, often responsible for administration, correspondence, and even representation of their own church to other churches. The androcentric assumption that all of these people were necessarily men is contradicted by the fact that the one known *diakonos* of a particular church named in the Christian Testament is the woman Phoebe (Rom 16:1), and that even the much later 1 Timothy refers to women deacons (1 Tim 3:11). Nor should these women be thought of as "deaconesses," an office that arose two centuries later for ministry to women. Phoebe's title is the same as the male one; a division into male and female diaconal roles has not yet been made, and there is no evidence that in the first or second century the ministry of such women was confined to serving women. A good many Jewish and Christian funerary and business inscriptions that name women presbyters and deacons are known from the first centuries of the Christian era in a variety of locations.

Paul wishes the Philippians the blessing of "God our Father," in keeping with the pervasive traditions surrounding Jesus that suggest his own use of paternal imagery for God. In the patriarchal society of the first century, this is hardly surprising. Though not strongly represented, maternal imagery is not lacking in Paul, but it is usually applied to himself (1 Thess 2:7; Gal 4:19).[2]

THANKSGIVING (1:3–11)

This section of the epistle is the longest of such sections in any Pauline letter. Its length suggests the affectionate relationship Paul has with this community (contrast Galatians, where the entire thanksgiving section is absent—an indication of his frame of mind when writing that letter!).

Verse 5 introduces the important theme represented by the Greek word *koinōnia*: partnership, sharing, participation. It or related words will appear again at 1:7; 2:1; 3:10; and 4:14–15. In its semilegal aspect, the word connotes an agreement to share equal authority and responsibility (compare Gal 2:9). In less formal circumstances, it is a participatory sharing in friendship, labor, and life: in short, a spirit of collaboration and inclusivity.

Here in the thanksgiving, Paul is grateful for the Philippians' participation with him in the gift and grace of having received the gospel (vv. 1:5, 7). Later, in 2:1, he will invoke their sharing in the gift of the Spirit to get their attention for what follows. In his autobiographical reflection, he notes his own desire to share the suffering of Christ (3:10). The concluding thank-you is for their monetary gift, and the very practical sharing in his mission that they have done by it (4:15). Whether it is a question of spiritual or material sharing, all of it deepens the sense of their common engagement in the work of furthering the gospel.

FULL PARTICIPATION IN FREEDOM (1:12–29)

Paul's seeming indifference about whether he lives or dies is an adaptation of the philosophical ideal of indifference to fate (cf. 4:10–13). No doubt it has its rhetorical intention of persuading the Philippians to heed what he is about to say, but nevertheless it reveals Paul's own state of mind and spirit while in prison.

Verse 27 exhorts the recipients to participate fully in their gospel calling: the language is that of citizens exercising their rights, thus evoking the long Greek tradition of democratic decision making (historically limited to free, landed males). Here, however, there is no restriction to certain members of the community, but an appeal to all. Paul knows that they are struggling courageously together (or contending together as athletes—a sports metaphor) in the contest or trial of faith, working together in one spirit.

THE HYMN (2:1–11)

Verses 1–4 are the immediate introduction to the famous so-called Philippian hymn, about which probably more has been written than any other section of a Pauline letter. The rhetoric of the opening verses leads to the poetic piece itself (vv. 5–11). In spite of a total lack of definite evidence, there is a general assumption, which may well be correct, that such pieces of poetry were composed for liturgical use and perhaps set to music (compare Col 1:15–20; John 1:1–14; 1 Tim 2:5–6; 3:16; 6:15–16). It is generally assumed, therefore, that the composition of vv. 5–11 is anonymous pre-Pauline, perhaps originating in Philippi, or at least well-known there. The composition of such hymns may have been the work of Christian prophets.[3] As with the forms of leadership mentioned in 1:1, androcentric thinking need not limit such prophetic poets to men; there is ample evidence of women prophets in the early church (e.g., 1 Cor 11:5; Acts 21:8–9). It is interesting that Paul's introduction in 2:1 repeats some of his language about the effect of prophecy in 1 Cor 14:3 (see also Acts 15:31).[4]

Even with an understanding of the epistle as a rhetorical attempt to persuade recipients to agree with views expressed by the author, 2:1–11 can sound extremely manipulative to the modern reader: If you have any faith at all, much less any desire to please me, if the suffering Christ means anything to you, then stop bickering, submit your own judgment, and do what I say. Moreover, it can sound like a patriarchal trap to the feminist reader: Think of others as better than yourselves, and subordinate your judgment after the example of Christ, who submitted his whole self in obedience to God. This kind of rhetoric has been used perennially to control women and reinforce culturally induced feelings of inferiority. There is no doubt that used the wrong way, this material is inimical to the revelatory message of liberation.

It must be remembered that Paul did not have the benefit of either modern psychology or sociology. It has been said that the modern notion of the person did not even begin to develop before the sixth century C.E. Awareness of the effects of socialization on self-concept was rudimentary. A true social theory of full human equality (as distinct from a theological conviction of equality before God) was present only among some philosophical schools, especially the Stoics, but even there it did not translate into practical implementation in society.

Both intellectual and popular convictions of rich, educated, free, and male superiority over poor, ignorant, slave, and female were pervasive. The possibility of true communion among social equals was an ideal talked about by aristocratic males. The ideal of friendship that overcame social barriers and linked superior and inferior for their mutual profit was more commonly realized, though the application of this ideal between female and male would await the age of the educated Christian celibates of the fourth century.

Contrary to the way it may sound in translation, vv. 2, 5 do not convey the expectation that no one in the community should have an independent thought. It is rather the question of acquiring a habitual attitude or orientation that will align the person with the ways of Christ, identical with the person's truest self, and enable her or him to make regular choices that enhance the community rather than fracture it. Understood this way, it is a fundamental principle of the Christian life.

The ideal of friendship as willing attentiveness, service, and yielding to another for the sake of the other's best interest lies behind the exhortation in v. 3 to act not out of selfishness but out of consideration for the good of the other. This may be in fact how Paul sees that equality is to be realized.[5] The extension of that ideal to the willing abasement of the superior in the service of the inferior may be the key to understanding the "kenotic" (emptying) theology of the hymn.[6]

Scholars continue to debate whether v. 6 means that Christ Jesus' "equal status with God" meant for the original hearers his preexistence and even divinity, as seemingly intended in John 1:1–2. In this case, the self-emptying into the form of a slave (v. 7) and humbling (v. 8) mean his taking human form, becoming human, as in John 1:14. The traditional interpretation has certainly affirmed an intended statement of preexistence, if not always full divinity. The personified preexistence of Wisdom from the wisdom literature or of the Word (John 1:1) from Hellenistic Jewish philosophical mysticism is suggested as precedent influence.[7] The exaltation of Jesus (vv. 9–11) is then an enhanced restoration to the heavenly status he already occupied in a pre-incarnational phase.

Some more recent interpretations have suggested an alternate understanding based on texts such as Wis 2:23–24, in which immortality is said to have been the common destiny of all humanity until ruined by the first sin (interestingly, neither male nor female is blamed here, but the devil). Death is therefore a punishment for sin; this interpretation is taken up by Paul in Rom 5:12–21 (where the male, as head of the human family, is blamed). If this idea is behind the hymn, then Christ Jesus' equal status with God may mean not preexistence or divinity but the primal immortality with which he would have been vested from conception because of his sole exemption from sin (cf. 2 Cor 5:21). In this case, his emptying and humbling in vv. 7–8 have to do not with his becoming human, for he is already that, but rather with his acceptance of the full effects of sin, namely, death—even death on a cross. Then the consequent exaltation (vv. 9–11) is elevation to a new state as reward for his obedience.

This second interpretation may be more comprehensible to the contemporary feminist reader, for whom the categories of superior and inferior, transcendent, preexistent, and exalted are alien and even offensive. The acceptance of mortality, and therefore the affirmation of a fully embodied humanity, is integral to the feminist vision of human life. A Christology "from below" may be more congenial to that vision.

PARENTAL PERSUASION (2:12–3:1)

Like the introduction to the hymn (2:1–5), this passage makes clear Paul's real purpose in using the hymn: not to make a profession of christological faith but to convince the Philippians to agree with him and cease the dissension that he has heard is present among them. Like the previous verses, this passage too sounds manipulative. The parental tone seems patronizing: both the Philippians (v. 15) and Paul's assistant Timothy (v. 22) are "good children" who acknowledge their father's authority (though his usual term for them is brothers [and sisters] [3:1, 17; 4:1, 8]). Such parental language addressed to adults is hardly surprising in this profoundly patriarchal society in which fathers had lifelong legal and moral authority and even financial control over their adult children. It is a metaphor they would have readily associated with their own personal duty of filial response to familial authority.

The two most common Christian Testament Greek words for obedience have as their base "listening" (the one used in v. 12) and "being persuaded" (e.g., Gal 5:7; Heb 13:17; though certainly the word can also mean forced obedience [Jas 3:3]). The obedience called for is not unquestioning or forced submission; if that were the kind of obedience Paul expected or was capable of getting, he would not have to exert such effort to obtain his readers' compliance. Rather, the desired obedience is that of the thoughtful acquiesence of one who becomes convinced of the rightness of the desired behavior (see also 3:15). This kind of acquiesence calls for the serious discernment of a free person in response to effective leadership. Nevertheless, the situation envisaged is not the same as the modern vision of inclusive decision making. An effective means of social control is built into the rhetoric that comes from someone with Paul's status among these people.

RELIANCE ON CREDENTIALS (3:2–6)

Verse 2 may be the beginning of another letter (see introduction). It takes up a topic similar to that of Paul's Letter to the Galatians: his opposition to some form of Christian preaching that would require observance of the Mosaic Law. The point to stress here is that, for the sake of convincing his readers, Paul seems willing to play the game of credential-matching. Anyone who can boast of his or her status in Judaism has nothing that Paul does not have. Thus, the Philippians are not to be impressed by others' appeal to their organizational standing as backing for their authority to persuade them to do or think differently from the way in which Paul has led them.

AUTOBIOGRAPHICAL REINFORCEMENT (3:7–4:1)

Verses 7–14 are some of the most candidly revealing lines written by Paul. Penned some fifteen years after his conversion experience, they tell us what it cost him in terms of social and self-perception and show that his relationship to Christ has a genuinely personal dimension. Without denying that they were written for the continuing purpose of persuasion, we can nevertheless appreciate the anguish and the raw human hope for transformation behind them.

Many commentators see here a parallel to the Christ hymn of the previous chapter, which may be accidental if another letter begins at 3:2. If the letter is a literary unity, however, Paul may be using himself as a final example after the pattern of Christ. Just as Christ surrendered status, willingly accepted abasement, and so was exalted by God, so Paul allowed the loss of his status in Judaism in order to follow the humiliated Christ, in the hope of also participating in his resurrection in the future. The *koinōnia*, sharing in the grace of the gospel and the Spirit (1:5, 7; 2:1), also involves sharing in the suffering and death of Christ (3:10).

The humiliation-exaltation theme as participation in the fate of Jesus is a central motif in Christian self-understanding. Not so much the experience as the proclaimed necessity for it must be carefully critiqued. The struggle for both personal and social transformation requires suffering, but its imposition by another in the name of the gospel constitutes injustice. The liberative content of the gospel cannot be compromised by a false acceptance of a cross that does not build justice. But many women can readily identify with the motif of abasement as victims of racist, classist, and sexist oppression. The vision of justice struggled for is then participation, *koinōnia,* in the exaltation of Christ.

Verses 17–21 speak in dualistic categories: the enemies of the cross belong to this world; our citizenship is in heaven. This is the second time in the letter that Paul draws upon the language of the city-state (see 1:27) to imply that all Christians, female and male, have the responsibility of full participation in the commonwealth in which they belong most appropriately. This is the basis for any vision of a discipleship of equals in the Pauline churches. In a world of social inequalities, Christians are to live in the consciousness of their heavenly equal citizenship here and now.

Contrary to the practice of most modern states, citizenship was not bestowed automatically on anyone born within certain geographical boundaries. It belonged rather to those born of families possessing it through lineage or special prerogative. One could be born and live one's whole life in a particular city without ever becoming a citizen of it. Roman citizenship was a further privilege, accompanied by greater legal protection, that was probably possessed by more residents of a Roman colony like Philippi than was the case in most eastern cities of the empire.

If most of the Philippian Christians were Roman citizens, they would have understood their Christian identity as a further and more important membership. If they were not, it would have been perhaps even more meaningful as the bestowal of a privilege of which they otherwise knew themselves to be deprived. Paul's sending of greetings from Christians in the imperial service in his place of imprisonment (4:22) may indicate that a number of the Philippian community were similarly identified and thus perhaps Roman citizens.

This dualistic otherworldly approach can be detrimental to the task of building a this-worldly realm of justice. Paul's language of mutual sharing and participation shows that such is not his intention. Rather, the Philippians' consciousness of their true citizenship is a mandate to bring the effects of that home city into their present lives.

EVODIA AND SYNTYCHE (4:2–3)

These two women may have been a missionary team, as may have been Tryphaena and Tryphosa (Rom 16:12). Two female-male teams are also attested in the Pauline letters, Junia and Andronicus (Rom 16:7) and Prisca (or Priscilla) and Aquila (Rom 16:3 and elsewhere), the latter identified as wife and husband in Acts 18:2. Junia and Andronicus were probably the same. Male-male teams are also attested, e.g., Paul and Barnabas in Acts 14–15. Disagreements in such teams are not unknown, e.g., the breakup of Paul and Barnabas over the presence of John Mark (Acts 15:36–40). These two women are among those who have struggled courageously (see 1:27 for the same word of the whole community) for the gospel with Paul, Clement (otherwise unknown), and other co-workers.

On the other hand, both of these women may have been leaders of influential groups in the Philippian church, perhaps of separate house-churches (for women as leaders of house-churches, see Acts 12:12; 16:40; Col 4:15; perhaps 1 Cor 1:11; 2 John 1, 13). Clearly, their disagreement is not some petty quarrel, as sexist commentaries sometimes want to make of it, but something that is upsetting the whole community. It may in fact be the basis of the disunity with which Paul has been concerned throughout the letter. He asks them in the same language he has previously addressed to the whole community (2:2, 5; 3:15, 19), in a way that does not command but rather beseeches, that they take on the same attitude or viewpoint as that of Christ Jesus (see comment on 2:2, 5).

The person who is asked to help them toward reconciliation is unknown. Among suggestions offered are Epaphroditus, the bearer of the letter (2:25), and one with a masculine proper name, Syzygos, "yoke-sharer," otherwise unattested. It is also possibly a rhetorical use of the singular addressed individually to everyone in the community. Though the word is masculine in form, it was sometimes used in the feminine for one's wife; some ancient commentators therefore thought the allusion was to Paul's wife, waiting out his imprisonment in Philippi. While this is unlikely given Paul's apparently single state (1 Cor 7:7, 8; 9:5), there is no reason why the person intended here cannot be another woman, perhaps a good friend of the other two or someone with a gift for reconciling.

Conclusion (4:4–23)

Verses 9–10 are the second rough transition of the letter; v. 10 seems to begin the brief acknowledgment of the previous gift from Philippi, explicitly mentioned in v. 18. In vv. 10–13, Paul expresses an ideal from popular Stoic philosophy of finding happiness in whatever situation life deals him (see 1:22–24). The affection shown in the rest of the letter reveals that this freedom does not include an inappropriate independence from people but is rather the freedom to thrive in adverse circumstances, which is necessary for anyone who struggles for a cause.

NOTES

1. Dale B. Martin, *Slavery as Salvation: The Metaphor of Slavery in Pauline Christianity* (New Haven/London: Yale University Press, 1990).

2. See Beverly R. Gaventa, "The Maternity of Paul: An Exegetical Study of Galatians 4:19," in *The Conversation Continues: Studies in Paul and John in Honor of J. Louis Martyn,* ed. Robert T. Fortna and Beverly R. Gaventa (Nashville: Abingdon, 1990), 189–201.

3. Paul S. Minear, "Singing and Suffering in Philippi," in *The Conversation Continues: Studies in Paul and John in Honor of J. Louis Martyn,* ed. Robert T. Fortna and Beverly R. Gaventa (Nashville: Abingdon, 1990), 202–19.

4. Carolyn Osiek, "Christian Prophecy: Once Upon a Time?" *Currents in Theology and Mission* 17 (1989): 291–97.

5. Elisabeth Schüssler Fiorenza, *In Memory of Her: A Feminist Theological Reconstruction of Christian Origins* (New York: Crossroad, 1983), 192.

6. L. Michael White, "Morality between Two Worlds: A Paradigm of Friendship in Philippians," in *Greeks, Romans, and Christians: Essays in Honor of Abraham J. Malherbe,* ed. David L. Balch et al. (Minneapolis: Fortress, 1990), 201–15. Some standard studies of the hymn are Ralph P. Martin, *Carmen Christi: Philippians ii.5–11 in Recent Interpretation and in the Setting of Early Christian Worship* (London: Cambridge University Press, 1967); Günther Bornkamm, "On Understanding the Christ-Hymn: Phil. 2.6–11," in *Early Christian Experience* (New York: Harper & Row, 1971), 112–22; Jerome Murphy-O'Connor, "Christological Anthropology in Phil., II, 6–11," *Revue biblique* 83 (1976): 25–50; George Howard, "Phil. 2:6–11 and the Human Christ," *Catholic Biblical Quarterly* 40 (1978): 368–87; L. D. Horst, "Re-enter the Pre-Existent Christ in Philippians 2.5–11?" *New Testament Studies* 32 (1986): 449–57.

7. See Elisabeth Schüssler Fiorenza, "Wisdom Mythology and the Christological Hymns of the New Testament," in *Aspects of Wisdom in Judaism and Early Christianity,* ed. Robert L. Wilken (Notre Dame: University of Notre Dame Press, 1975), 17–42.

RECOMMENDED READINGS

Abrahamson, Valerie. "The Women at Philippi: The Pagan and Christian Evidence." *Journal of Feminist Studies in Religion* 3 (1987): 17–30.

Beare, Francis W. *A Commentary on the Epistle to the Philippians.* 2nd ed. Harper's New Testament Commentaries. New York: Harper, 1969.

D'Angelo, Mary Rose. "Women Partners in the New Testament." *Journal of Feminist Studies in Religion* 6 (1990): 65–86.

Getty, Mary Ann. *Philippians and Philemon.* New Testament Message 14. Wilmington, DE: Michael Glazier, 1980.

Gillman, Florence M. "Early Christian Women at Philippi." *Journal of Gender in World Religions* 1 (1990): 59–79.

Gnilka, Joachim. *The Epistle to the Philippians.* London: Sheed & Ward, 1970.

Malinowsky, Francis X. "The Brave Women at Philippi." *Biblical Theology Bulletin* 15 (1985): 60–64.

Martin, Ralph P. *The Epistle to the Philippians.* Tyndale New Testament Commentaries. Grand Rapids: Eerdmans, 1987.

Perkins, Pheme. "Philippians." In *The Women's Bible Commentary,* edited by Carol Newsom, and Sharon Ringe. Louisville: Westminster/John Knox, 1992.

Portefaix, Lilian. *Sisters Rejoice: Paul's Letter to the Philippians and Luke-Acts as Seen by First-century Philippian Women.* Coniectanea Biblica New Testament Series 20. Uppsala: Almqvist & Wiksell International, 1988.

Schottroff, Luise. "Lydia: Neue Qualität der Macht." In *Befreiungserfarungen: Studien zur Socialgeschichte des Neuen Testaments,* 305–9. Munich: Kaiser, 1990.

Thomas, W. Derek. "The Place of Women in the Church at Philippi." *Expository Times* 83 (1972): 117–20.

1 Thessalonians

LONE FATUM ◆

INTRODUCTION

INVOLVING ONESELF as a feminist theologian in the interpretation of 1 Thessalonians is like forcing one's way into male company, uninvited and perhaps unwanted. In this letter, Paul, assisted by his co-workers Silvanus and Timothy, is addressing his newly converted brothers in Thessalonica; taken at face value, the letter seems to presuppose a local community of Gentile Christians, established as a fellowship of males only. This would be in full agreement with Paul's use of the term *ekklēsia,* meaning a meeting or voluntary association of freeborn male citizens. This letter seems to convey absolutely no awareness of Christian women's presence among the brothers in this early Pauline community, and the only reference to sexuality and femaleness, in 4:4, is either blatantly sexist or unambiguously androcentric.

Feminist interpretation of Paul often takes the form of historical reconstruction, based generally on the hermeneutics of suspicion and particularly on what is called the evidence of silence, along with the assumption that Paul's use of generic language is meant to be inclusive. But 1 Thessalonians presents itself as a warning against such reconstructive reading. First, the evidence excluding women in this letter is not silent; on the contrary, it is expressive in its gender associations and quite effective in its symbolic and metaphorical scope. Second, the social implications of the generic language and the extensive use of kinship epithets are so pointedly androcentric and patriarchal as to leave no room for female affiliation. Hence, I propose a reading that is deconstructive rather than reconstructive.

It is not that in 1 Thessalonians Paul seems consciously engaged in an attempt to make Christian women invisible. Rather, within the Thessalonian context there seem to be no women to silence and no woman's active commitment to curb. This may be why this letter has been neglected by feminist interpretation; it has little or nothing to offer with respect to a feminist reappraisal for the purpose of affirmation and positive identification.

In his address to the Thessalonians Paul is gentle, like a nurse toward her own children; but in order to exercise fully his apostolic authority as the founder and religious guide of the community and, most important, as the moral model for his converts, he casts himself both as a father and as a brother. Encouraging, exhorting, and instructing his sons and brothers, Paul deliberately employs a man-to-man language in a man-to-man setting in order to institutionalize a social pattern of fellowship and reciprocity. Thus, the epistolary form and the parenetic content constitute the significant unity of 1 Thessalonians. Both the letter and the community of recipients, who are to be strengthened by it in their confidence in Paul as well as in their mutual respect and concord, are clearly defined by androcentric values and social conventions and organized in terms of the patriarchal structures so characteristic of urban society in Greco-Roman antiquity.

Indeed, neither androcentric bias nor patriarchal order originated with Christianity; yet both have been mediated and institutionalized effectively as part of Christian tradition, not only in its historical presentation and relative social praxis but also in its religious and moral implications and theological substance. 1 Thessalonians is our earliest extant illustration of this and deserves to be recognized as such by feminist interpreters. Throughout the letter a communication is taking place in which Paul expresses his affectionate solidarity with a group of male Christians living their daily lives as craftsmen, artisans, and tradesmen. Some of them may be heads of households, but all of them apparently do manual work to uphold their social status of honorable independence. Accordingly, they interact with each other and with non-Christians in all the appropriate social alliances. In this way they demonstrate to surrounding pagans as well as to themselves the extraordinary quality of their newly acquired collective identity as Christian converts belonging to God, thus maintaining the fellowship in Christ built on the social and moral values of faith, love, and hope.

Thus, 1 Thessalonians does not invite the feminist ideal of women-church. Paul's man-to-man communication with his Thessalonian sons and brothers leaves no trace of Christian women's presence, let alone their status and activity as free and equal members of a democratic discipleship. An attempt to discover such a trace in order to reconstruct the existence of a discipleship of women cannot rely on the literary and historical evidence before us; it requires feminist creativity and wishful thinking. Such an approach, I submit, will have to do violence not only to the text of 1 Thessalonians but also to the whole androcentric construction of Christian consciousness, which is intrinsically and inseparably bound up with the androcentric consciousness of patriarchal antiquity and which has determined both the literary production of Paul's letters and the historical foundation and social organization of the early Christian communities.

No doubt, Christian women have a rightful claim on a liberating future. But why try to reorganize the past in order to lay a claim on the future? Why invoke a different past as an excuse for demanding a different future? Women's liberation is one matter, and critical interpretation—based on a coherent methodology of analysis with a consistent hermeneutical evaluation of ends and means—is another. Both may be feminist issues sharing the same ultimate goal, and yet they should not be confused. The ideal of women's liberation may jeopardize critical interpretation and reduce exegesis to feminist or womanist affirmation. A feminist interpretation of Paul that does not respect the literary and historical evidence of Paul's letters and their social context and is unwilling to confine the analysis to the critical exposure of this evidence will always be in danger of replacing Paul's patriarchal androcentricism with a feminist construction of gynecentricism.

In the following analysis I shall not attempt to make Christian women visible in any positive sense; my aim is not to reconstruct a discipleship of equals among the new converts of Thessalonica. I want to focus on 1 Thessalonians as a reflection not of events or actual facts but of symbolic consciousness and the social (re)production of structures of plausibility. Confining myself primarily to the literary construction of 1 Thessalonians, I shall interpret the letter as the apostolic narrative of Paul and his Thessalonian brothers, thus letting the synchronic reading of the text determine both the depth and the width of the diachronic analysis of the social context. Making use of insights from cultural anthropology and sociology, my aim is deconstruction instead of reconstruction. I shall attempt critically to expose the implications of the gender construction that is presupposed as the androcentric order of patriarchal society and authoritatively reproduced and maintained by Paul as the significant order of the community of brothers, qualified by Christ.

TIME AND PLACE OF WRITING

Paul came to Thessalonica from Philippi (2:2). His gospel was received as the word of God (1:4–5; 2:13) by the former Gentiles (1:9), and a Christian community was founded under much suffering and opposition. Because of their perseverance, the Thessalonian converts have become a model for all believers in both Macedonia and Achaia (1:6–7; 2:14). Thus, Paul seems to be in Achaia, probably in Corinth, at the time of writing. Apparently he stayed in Thessalonica for some months (2:9–12; 3:1–6; cf. Phil 4:14–17). His departure may have been involuntary (2:2), and, at the time of writing, he had been separated from his new converts only for a short period (2:17).

Obviously, Paul is deeply concerned about the Thessalonians and anxious to keep in close contact. Unable to come himself (2:18), he sends Timothy as his deputy from Athens (3:1–2) for encouragement and support. At the time of writing, Timothy has just returned with good news (3:6) and is, together with Silvanus, cosender of the letter (1:1).

When Paul's data are related to the description in Acts 16:11–18:22 of the so-called second missionary journey, we get a fairly coherent picture of his European mission along the Via Egnatia from Philippi through Amphipolis and Apollonia to Thessalonica and further through Beroea and Athens to Corinth and Ephesus. We may conclude that the Thessalonian community was an early result of Paul's missionary activity, founded probably in 49. 1 Thessalonians appears to have been written shortly after Paul left the city, probably in 50, when the new community was less than a year old and still had all the difficulties of the newly converted, socially as well as spiritually and psychologically.

This means that 1 Thessalonians is not only our earliest extant letter by Paul; it is in fact our earliest extant Christian writing, which may account for the considerable number of differences between 1 Thessalonians and Paul's other letters.

STRUCTURE AND PURPOSE OF 1 THESSALONIANS

Compared with Paul's other letters, 1 Thessalonians seems to lack a thematic and rhetorical profile; it appears as a letter in which Paul has no need to defend either his gospel and its implications or the legitimacy of his apostolic authority. In 1 Thessalonians we are, literally, among friends. The letter is neither polemical nor apologetic; it is pastoral, and the cause and motivation of Paul's writing are not conflict but the care and concern of friendship. Thus, the immediate purpose of the letter is to replace Paul's personal presence among the new converts and to compensate for a face-to-face communication (2:17–20; 3:6–10). In this sense, 1 Thessalonians is a straightforward and uncomplicated letter.

It falls into two parts: 1:2–3:13 appears to be an extended thanksgiving, and 4:1–5:24 is applied parenesis, characterizing the whole of the letter as apostolic exhortation. Praising the Thessalonians for their work of faith, their laborious demonstration of love, and their perseverance in the hope of Christ (1:3), Paul is actually defining the parenetic pattern of his communication. The presupposition is that the three concepts are interdependent, each qualifying the others and emphasizing together the social commitment of the new conviction as well as the eschatological orientation of the new life. To become adherents of Christ is to become servants of the living and true God (1:9), thus committing oneself to a life of faith, demonstrated by love. Essentially, however, it means to believe in the resurrection of Jesus, thus committing oneself to a life of hope, demonstrated for the present by love and for the future by the expectation of the parousia of Jesus and his deliverance of the Christians from the approaching wrath (1:10).

Paul's thanksgiving characterizes the Thessalonians as a model community (1:7), and his appealing and very affective recollections of their willingness to accept his preaching and himself as their teacher and example (1:4–6; 2:1, 13) and even to endure opposition and personal hardship as the inevitable consequence of their new adherence mark them in every respect as a fellowship, qualified by God himself to live the life of Christ (1:6; 2:14; 3:3–4; 4:9; 5:4–5). This is a life radically different from their immediate past (1:9) as well as from their present surroundings (4:5, 12) because of the future for which they have been chosen (1:10; 4:13; 5:9–10). Consequently, hope is the decisive characteristic of their new status as Christian converts, at the same time conveying spiritual affirmation (1:4–5; 2:13; 5:24) and implying social and moral obligation (3:13; 4:1–8, 10–12; 5:6, 8, 12–23). Because they have hope, the Thessalonians are expected to demonstrate more faith and practice more love in order to be holy before God at the parousia (3:9–13; 4:10), and so the extensive purpose of Paul's communication is to guide his new converts through a steady progress of moral improvement onward to that state of pure holiness which is the goal of their conversion and, before that, of their election (4:7).

However, to be a community of newly converted is to be in the middle of a very critical process of change and readjustment. In the urban society of Greco-Roman antiquity, defined by publicness and collectivity and organized on the basis of family relations, trade, craft and neighbor associations, and memberships in clubs and cultic assemblies, social identity is secured by group adherence, and status is maintained in a vertical pattern of social alliances and public loyalties. In such a society it is a comprehensive and risky project, indeed, to change one's faith and way of life; in a very literal sense it means a radical change of social identity in order to adjust to a new pattern of adherence and interdependence. Old bonds and alliances as well as natural relations break down or must be ignored, and new ones have yet to be built or lack the necessary stability. The converts experience opposition and exclusion; they are regarded with suspicion by family and friends, and at the same time their confidence in their new adherence may be faltering. The Christian community perhaps was not yet properly organized and the loyalty and reliability of the new brothers not yet sufficiently reassuring.

This, of course, is a process of suffering, causing social insecurity and frustration as well as spiritual doubts and psychological weakness. At worst, the pressure from the surroundings becoming unbearable, some may lose courage altogether and relapse into their old life (3:5). The process is familiar to Paul, who values both opposition and personal hardship as the significant distinctions of Christian existence but is apprehensive, of course, about the danger of defection. Accordingly, he has expressly prepared the Thessalonians for a time of sufferings (3:3–4) on the basis of his personal example (1:6; 2:2) and the paradigm of soteriology as *theologia crucis* (1:6; 2:14–16). The Thessalonian community is only months old and seems to have been exposed to great pressure from the beginning. Paul has not been with them, and at the time of writing he regards the new converts as very young children, his dependent sons, under age and immature, in need of their father's guiding presence. Although he has been comforted by Timothy (3:6–10), he is anxious still to go to Thessalonica himself to instruct face to face and to exhort directly by his personal example in order to make good the deficiencies of their faith (3:10) and to further their love (3:12).

So, while in the beginning of his thanksgiving (1:3) Paul emphasizes faith and love and hope, he seems in his reference to Timothy's report deliberately to leave out hope (3:6). Apparently, doubts have arisen among the Thessalonians concerning the meaning and implications of the Christian hope—that is, the belief in the resurrection of Jesus and his parousia and the future expectations of the Christians. Some members of the community have died, and this seems to have caused unrest and uncertainty in the community. For consolation and exhortation, Paul amplifies his teaching on the resurrection of the dead and the final union of all Christians with the Lord at his parousia (4:13–18). But, most important, he incorporates the teaching on the resurrection of the dead as part of his extensive parenesis in 4:1–5:24 concerning the social and moral behavior of the living, the present life in this world of those who belong to God in Christ (1:1; 5:23–24).

Thus, the purpose of Paul's communication is not to be found in his consolation concerning the dead or in his eschatological teaching per se. Rather, all through the letter—and 4:13–18 is no exception—he is concerned with the social and moral obligations of the living Christians and with the problems of their actual, everyday life. Consistently, he endeavors to guide his converts toward the ultimate goal of holiness, according to their calling (4:7); he - exhhorts them to endure as well as to develop in order to show with increasing clarity that they are the sons of light and day (5:5). Together they constitute the community of life, qualified by hope, and this sets them apart from the rest of the world. Therefore, they must lead a life that is qualitatively different in order to maintain their exclusive status (4:3–8; 5:12–22). They must demonstrate their Christian status of hope by their works of faith and love, faith and love being their breastplate of armor, and hope of salvation being their helmet (5:8).

Thus, in 1 Thessalonians Paul focuses on the social and moral implications of hope—not on hope per se in a theological or eschatological sense. Because he cannot, for the time being, convey his exhortation in person, he must resort to writing. This explains why his personal example dominates his recollections in 1:2–3:13, but it also emphasizes the impact of Paul's patriarchal authority on the social and moral identity of his new converts. In the extended thanksgiving, he reestablishes the initial interdependence between the apostle and his converts, between father and sons. Further, through the recollections of their common past, he confirms himself as their personal authority and example to imitate. On this basis of authority and imitation he then applies his social and moral parenesis in 4:1–5:24.

Thus, in 1:2–3:13 he reestablishes his apostolic authority in order to exhort effectively in 4:1–5:24. But at the same time he reestablishes himself as the living demonstration of his social and moral parenesis. The implications of Paul's personal example cannot be separated from the purpose of his teaching and exhortation, nor can the androcentric implications of his teaching and exhortation be separated from his consciousness of imitating Christ himself, thus personifying by his own behavior the *theologia crucis* of his soteriology. To adhere to Paul's teaching implies, literally, to imitate Paul, and he presents himself to his converts as the social and moral embodiment of his teaching. This means, to the Thessalonians, that Paul is their model of social and moral behavior, because he is himself the model of a man, qualified in Christ to live the life of hope. To follow the example of Paul, accordingly, is to be guided on the basis of hope through the problems of everyday Christian living. But, in the ultimate sense, it is to follow the authorized way of the apostle toward holiness and the union with Christ at the parousia.

THE ANDROCENTRIC IMPLICATIONS OF THE PARENESIS

The whole of 1 Thess 4:1–5:24 may be seen as a coherent piece of paraclesis in which Paul is pursuing his moral aim of unity and holiness along a double track of exhortation. One line of argument is apocalyptic and explicitly eschatological, conveying a message of consolation and encouragement. The other line of argument is social and implicitly eschatological, specifying the moral demands for the brothers to live in this world in accordance with their heavenly calling. The lines may be distinguished but not separated, for Paul bases his social instructions on eschatological teaching, literally deducing moral obligation from his eschatological definition of Christian existence.

The apocalyptic line of argument (4:13–5:6) concerns the affinity of the brothers with the risen Christ and has, characteristically, a present as well as a future aspect. The fundamental hope of union with Christ (1:9–10; 5:9–10) defines the unity of the Christians already in this world and sustains their anticipation of a heavenly consummation at the time of salvation. This hope includes the final resurrection of all the brothers at once, even though some will have died before the day of the parousia. Thus, the brothers are qualified by their joint hope as an eschatological community, bound for a future with Christ and, therefore, fundamentally different from the world around them. By the same token, however, Paul imposes on them the responsibility of upholding this brotherhood of eschatological difference through all the anxieties and challenges of the present life.

Consequently, the social line of argument (4:1–12; 5:7–24) concerns the responsibility of the newly converted to be morally superior to their non-Christian surroundings and to engage from within in the fortification of the brotherhood. The eschatological community is to prove unshakable, self-reliant, and nonoffensive. In 5:8 the armor metaphor is a metaphor of resistance and self-protection, clearly conveying the defensive strategy of Paul's insistence on holiness (4:1–3, 7) in terms of integrity, solidarity, and long-suffering perseverance (5:12–22). The brothers will not depend on or in any way be indebted to the outside world (4: 9–12). Because they are sons of light and day, the brothers are to behave with sobriety and watchful consideration (5:4–11). Correspondingly, because they have been called by God to share in the holiness of the risen Christ, already now they are to lead their everyday lives in holiness and purification, answering to the will of God as well as to the superior status of their calling with self-control and moral restraint in their sociosexual activities (4:3–8).

Thus, eschatological and social arguments are correlated; throughout his paraclesis, Paul is applying the moral obligation of the brotherhood to make up a strong group with a high grid. This means to form and uphold a tightly organized community of hierarchic interdependence inwardly, in which weaker brothers give their respect and loyal adherence to stronger ones and these in turn give their lenient guidance and support to the weaker. The purpose is for all of them together to appear outwardly as a well-defined and honorable association.

Though the Christian brotherhood is a voluntary grouping, based on a voluntary commitment, Paul obviously wants to press upon it the binding commitment characteristic of a natural grouping; he strives in fact to organize the brothers according to the social and moral institution of the patriarchal family. As emphasized already, he exhorts the Thessalonians as a father to his sons. In the role of exemplary father he is to them, the brothers, the representative of Christ. In other words, the vertical affinity with Christ, mediated by Paul and his co-workers, defines and qualifies the horizontal relationship of the brothers. Socially and morally they are interdependent, but they are not equal. On the contrary, as in the model family of Greco-Roman antiquity, their relationship is one of inequality and dissimilarity, held together by something more comprehensive than mutual social interest. Consequently, Paul wants them to build up a personal network like male kin—not simply comparable to a trade union or a burial society but male kin, organized and administered according to the hierarchic code and asymmetrical alliances of the patriarchal household.

Thus, Paul's frequent and quite ostentatious use of family epithets and highly affective expressions of fatherly concern and devotion has a very literal, almost invoking meaning. Throughout 1 Thessalonians, Paul's emotional language has a social impact, but especially in the paraclesis. There his relational appeals to the brothers are consoling as well as binding, and his direct calls upon the brothers in 4:1, 10, 13 and 5:1, 4, 12, 14 have a complementary effect. The more his Thessalonian sons will adhere to his fatherly authority and imitate his personal example, the more they will be united like brothers in their Christian development and Paul will be affirmed in his patriarchal role as the mediator of Christ. Further, vertical affinity has horizontal significance; bound by joint adherence, the brothers will be able to strengthen their shared social identity and will appear as a group with common boundaries and rules of behavior, the necessary equivalent, that is, of the male collective of the household family.

Thus, Paul's address to male Christians is unambiguous in terms of an androcentric ideology of gender values and virtues—self-evident, we must assume, to Paul himself as well as to his audience, since this was the basic ideology of patriarchal antiquity. But the extent to which Paul's exhortation was exclusively male is best illustrated by the specific instructions in 4:3–8, concerning the sociosexual activity of the brothers. Whether the instrumental reference to the tool or object in 4:4 is seen as a reference to a women—perhaps a wife—or to the male sexual organ, the moral message of 4:3–5 is clear. When marrying, or in his maried life, the Christian is to be restrained and self-composed in his sexual behavior. For Paul, the former Pharisee, illegitimate and uncontrolled sexuality was tantamount to ungodliness and pagan impurity; idolatry and fornication were virtually synonymous in traditional Jewish interpretation. Thus, Paul's argument in vv. 3–5 is loaded with stereotyped Jewish contempt of non-Jews in its caricature of pagan licentiousness. By enjoining the former pagans to demonstrate their new Christian identity in accordance with Mosaic rules of purity and superior exclusiveness, Paul illustrates how comprehensive was the influence of traditional Jewish interpretation on his formative Christian teaching, especially relating to gender and sociosexual morality.

The exhortation of 4:3–8 may in fact be seen as the equivalent of a Jewish parenesis, based on the Decalogue (cf. Exod 20:1–17 and Deut 5:6–21). Paul is not simply echoing the commandments; rather, he applies them as his implicit moral reference, and he even maintains their thematic coherence in a way that shows he takes for granted the whole construction of symbolic reality, gender values, and social order on which they are based and which, of course, in the Mosaic context, they are designed to legitimize. Thus, Paul is not simply using Mosaic tradition; he is actually authorizing—that is, christianizing—the Mosaic code of sociosexual meaning.

Under the joint heading of the holiness demand in v. 3, dependent on the first commandment and emphasized with a warning in vv. 6b–8, Paul links together in vv. 4–6a the sixth and tenth commandments against fornication and the coveting of one's neighbor's house. Obviously, his moral concern is the establishment and maintenance of the patriarchal household. It is likely that in v. 4 he deals with the acquisition of a wife and, in thematic coherence, with the social integrity of the paterfamilias (v. 6a). Since Paul's focus is defined by the paterfamilias and, generally, by the patriarchal organization of male activity according to the social order of challenge and response, a social agent is to him a male agent; and the property and social territory of one agent, making up the social honor of the paterfamilias, must be defended against transgression and possible usurpation by other agents.

Consequently, and fully in accordance with the gender ideology of the Decalogue, a woman or wife is the implied prerequisite in v. 4 for male social activity, just as in v. 6a she may be an implied part of the household of the paterfamilias, not to be violated. But this is in fact the only indication at all in the whole of 1 Thessalonians of female presence among the brothers. In its own context it is neither a negative nor a positive indication. Rather, it conveys as a matter of fact the sociosexual conditions designed for women by patriarchal construction, in which the power to interpret gender and to administer sexuality is generally accepted as a male prerogative.

Obviously, gender is not the issue in 1 Thessalonians; yet throughout the letter Paul's address to the Thessalonians is gendered. But his bias is shared by his male audience, which allows him to insist on the unity and holiness of the brotherhood in terms of androcentric congeniality and sympathetic understanding. Thus, the gender ideology implied by his teaching and exhortation does not have to be specified or qualified; the patriarchal pattern of social values and virtues is taken for granted as a common code of reference, and so is the androcentric orientation of the brothers' joint commitment to organize and develop their moral superiority and exclusiveness, vertically as well as horizontally, in imitation of Paul.

Summing up the implications of these conditions and presuppositions, Paul's address to the brothers does not invite the conclusion that female presence among them is synonymous with full and equal membership for women of the brotherhood. It must remain an open question how we are to imagine Christian women's social integration into the Thessalonian community; the impact of Paul's communication seems merely to confirm their exclusion.

MALES ONLY?

We must assume that women were among the converts in Thessalonica. The woman implied by 1 Thess 4:4, 6a may indeed be a Christian wife, and

Acts 17:4 refers to a considerable number of prominent women adding, it seems, a valuable contribution of nobility and affluence to the establishment of the local community.

Acts 17:1–13, however, is the Lukan version of Paul's Thessalonian mission, and, in almost every respect, it is incompatible with the evidence of Paul himself. Acts gives the impression of a brief but highly dramatic visit, stereotyping the hostility of the Jews as well as the positive reception of the so-called God-fearers among the Greeks. In contrast, Paul indicates no contact with Thessalonian Jews; unambiguously, he addresses himself to non-Jewish Christians, and the persecution mentioned in 1 Thess 2:14–16 is best understood as a reference to the opposition from non-Jewish neighbors and former associates, not to organized hostility from local Jews. Though God-fearing Greeks may indeed have made an obvious target for Paul's mission, allowing him to relate his message to their previous understanding of Jewish tradition, 1 Thessalonians does not apply itself to a community of social prominence. Finally, his reserved expression of gratitude in Phil 4:10–20, explicitly acknowledging the support from Philippi during his stay in Thessalonica (v. 16), indicates more than a brief visit, but not exactly an affluent group of Christians in Thessalonica.

Thus, it seems, the Lukan version, including the information about the prominent women, has little value as historical evidence of Paul's time. Rather, Acts 17:1–13 represents a Lukan reconstruction, characterized by Lukan interests. As an integral part of his stereotyping, he inserts in v. 4 his ideal portrait of the local Christian patroness of high social status and influence. Both v. 4 and the duplicate in 17:12 are connected with the presentation of Lydia in 16:13–15 and with the women around Jesus in Luke 8:1–3. With their economic assets and independent social activity, they are staged by Luke according to the conditions of his own time and urban context. But even so they may be the products of wishful thinking and the Lukan strategy of social idealization rather than reliable references to actual experience of affluent women's patronage.

Since we cannot rely on the information of Acts concerning the Thessalonian women of Paul's time, we have to be content with the evidence of Paul himself and 1 Thessalonians. In other words, we have to come to grips with the exclusion of women from the brotherhood of Christians, recognizing at the outset that this exclusion is not the result of Christian interpretation in particular but rather the established expression of patriarchal social custom in general.

According to the social structure of the symbolic universe in which Paul communicates with his male audience, the lives of women are embedded in the lives of men, and women are defined and qualified by their dependence on men. Thus, women are not counted in 1 Thessalonians among those who constitute the Christian community; according to patriarchal logic, we may assume that women converts had not been integrated into the brotherhood but were attached to the male community through husbands or male heads of households by their social capacity as wife, daughter, mother, or sister. No woman would appear and be acknowledged as a social agent in her own right.

Further, the gender ideology and patriarchal social order of Paul's universe establish a pattern of values and virtues according to which male means general or universal and female means special or gender specific. Femaleness thus constituted one part or component of a man's world—the social world of male interaction. This is the evidence of 1 Thess 4:3–8. When women are visible to the male eye as the object of androcentric gender interpretation, woman is defined in a comprehensive sense by her sociosexual functionality, and women's activities are qualified according to the purpose of men's activities.

Paul seems able to take for granted both the social institution of the household and the hierarchical order of the family, and we may assume that neither Paul himself nor his Thessalonian audience had a critical view of marriage and marital life at this point. The eschatological ideal of virginity seems not to have been an issue yet. Thus, the reason women are virtually invisible in 1 Thessalonians may well be that women were not challenging established morality. There were no virgin women behaving like males, fulfilling a male role, and, like Phoebe, the *diakonos* of Rom 16:1–2, acquiring male social status.

The conclusion suggests itself that the Thessalonian women converts of Paul's time—probably 49–50—were a homogeneous group, conforming to patriarchal social custom and established gender ideology. Apparently, their Christian identity was not incompatible with their ordinary sociosexual identity, and so their conversion did not cause any dissonance of behavior or social appearance. In relation to the community, they seem embedded in men's lives, just as in society in general their lives were embedded in men's lives. Thus, we may conclude that although women were surely among the converts in Thessalonica, they were not among the brothers as members of the community. Because they were defined and qualified as women, they were not seen as Christians and their sociosexual presence among the brothers was virtually a nonpresence.

This conclusion may seem discouraging indeed, jeopardizing the idea of human equality and women's affirmation as an essential part of Christian interpretation. But Christian interpretation is androcentric interpretation and depends on patriarchal construction. If we wish to promote feminist critique, we cannot close our eyes to this insight. If we wish to confront the sociosexual discrimination of our own time and context, we must be able to confront also, with critical consistency, the sociosexual discrimination at the roots of our Christian tradition.

RECOMMENDED READINGS

Berger, Peter L. *The Sacred Canopy.* 1967. Reprint, New York: Anchor Books, 1969.

Donfried, Karl P. "The Cults of Thessalonica and the Thessalonian Correspondence." *New Testament Studies* 31 (1985): 336–56.

Douglas, Mary. *Natural Symbols.* New York: Vintage Books, 1973.

———. *Purity and Danger.* 1966. Reprint, London and New York: Ark Paperbacks, 1988.

Fatum, Lone. "Image of God and Glory of Man: Women in the Pauline Congregations." In *Image of God and Gender Models in Judaeo-Christian Tradition,* edited by Kari Elisabeth Børresen. Oslo: Solum Forlag, 1991

———. "Women, Symbolic Universe and Structures of Silence: Challenges and Possibilities in Androcentric Texts." *Studia Theologica* 43 (1989): 61–80.

Geertz, Clifford. *The Interpretation of Cultures.* New York: Basic Books, 1973.

Haenchen, Ernst. *Die Apostelgeschichte.* Meyers Kommentar 3. Göttingen: Vandenhoeck & Ruprecht, 1968.

Hendrix, Holland. "Benefactor/Patronage Networks in the Urban Environment: Evidence from Thessalonica." *Semeia* 56 (1992): 39–58.

Hock, Ronald F. *The Social Context of Paul's Ministry.* Philadelphia: Fortress, 1980.

Holmberg, Bengt. *Paul and Power.* Lund: Gleerup, 1978.

Holtz, Traugott. *Der erste Brief an die Thessalonicher.* Evangelisch-katholischer Kommentar 13. 1986. Reprint, Zurich: Benziger; Neukirchen-Vluyn: Neukirchener, 1990.

MacMullen, Ramsay. *Roman Social Relations.* New Haven and London: Yale University Press, 1974.

Malherbe, Abraham J. "'Pastoral Care' in the Thessalonian Church." *New Testament Studies* 36 (1990): 375–91

———. *Paul and the Thessalonians.* Philadelphia: Fortress, 1987.

Malina, Bruce J. *Christian Origins and Cultural Anthropology.* Atlanta: John Knox, 1986.

———. *The New Testament World: Insights from Cultural Anthropology.* Atlanta: John Knox Press, 1981

Meeks, Wayne A. *The First Urban Christians. The Social World of the Apostle Paul.* New Haven and London: Yale University Press, 1983.

Petersen, Norman R. *Rediscovering Paul: Philemon and the Sociology of Paul's Narrative World.* Philadelphia: Fortress, 1985.

Schnelle, Udo. "Der erste Thessalonicherbrief und die Entstehung der paulinischen Anthropologie." *New Testament Studies* 32 (1986): 207–24.

Schüssler Fiorenza, Elisabeth. *Bread Not Stone: The Challenge of Feminist Biblical Interpretation.* Boston: Beacon, 1984.

———. *In Memory of Her: A Feminist Theological Reconstruction of Christian Origins.* New York: Crossroad, 1983.

Schütz, John H. *Paul and the Anatomy of Apostolic Authority.* Cambridge: Cambridge University Press, 1975.

Tolbert, Mary Ann. "Defining the Problem: The Bible and Feminist Hermeneutics." *Semeia* 28 (1983): 113–26.

Whitton, J. "A Neglected Meaning for *skeuos* in 1 Thess 4:4." *New Testament Studies* 28 (1982): 142–43.

2 Thessalonians

MARY ANN BEAVIS ◆

NEW WINESKINS?

WRITING THIS COMMENTARY has illustrated the aptness of the adage that new wine bursts old wineskins. There has been nothing feminist or ecumenical about the interpretation of 2 Thessalonians in the past two centuries—or ever. Nor does the surface content of the letter hold much inspiration for feminists, or for the church as it faces the twenty-first century. Moreover, the commentary genre is not one conducive to saying anything new.

In writing what follows, I have stretched, but not completely burst, the genre. Some of the burning issues that have preoccupied Christian Testament scholarship for the past two hundred years—authenticity, whether 2 Thessalonians was written after or before 1 Thessalonians, the identity of "the re-strainer" or "the grasping one" (*ho katechōn,* 2:6–7)—have generated more heat than light. Numerous learned books, articles, and excursuses have been devoted to these matters, with no definitive conclusions. A standard commentary would rehash these questions at length, with equivocal results. Suffice it to say that my reading of the secondary literature has not persuaded me that the letter is not Pauline—or that it is! In the practical, commonsense spirit of the nineteenth-century feminists who inspired this volume, I will set aside such issues and pursue more fruitful lines of inquiry. In certain cases, this merely involves arguing a position on standard exegetical issues, which, in my judgment, can be addressed satisfactorily. More importantly, I have undertaken a rhetorical and ideological critique of the text that calls into question the value of the text as canon—especially from a feminist and ecumenical standpoint.

FEMINIST PERSPECTIVE

It is important, while reading this commentary, to recognize the relentlessly patriarchal and androcentric nature of the text and the interpretive tradition. Nowhere in 2 Thessalonians is there an explicit recognition of women in the audience. The beliefs of the writers are expressed in the kind of bellicose imagery characteristic of patriarchy. God and Christ are conceived of as powerful male figures, overseeing heavenly and earthly events. The writers do not for a moment entertain the possibility that the teaching alluded to in 2:1–2 might have some value. The interaction between the missionaries and the Thessalonians is envisioned as one of ideological dominance (the writers) and submission to authority (the audience). An early commentator on 2 Thessalonians, John Chrysostom, assumed that the audience of the letter was made up solely of men; subsequent generations of interpreters have, with a very few recent exceptions, continued to write on this assumption. Unfortunately, very few women have contributed to the history of interpretation of this epistle.

As feminist, this commentary will address some of the concerns that have characterized feminist interpretation in the past two decades. Each rhetorical unit of the text will be analyzed in terms of gender, power, and domination. The opinions of women interpreters will be cited wherever possible.

As a Christian Testament scholar and a feminist, I am also intrigued by the question of "what would be a feminist criticism that neither read women's texts nor read for the representation of women,"[1] and by the radical French feminist perspective, which sees *le feminin* as any force disruptive of Western symbolic structures.[2] Thus, I challenge individualistic interpretations that stress the role of the unique, charismatic personality of the "great man" Paul in the composition of the letter (whether authentic or inauthentic). Rather, the letter is conceived of as echoing many voices, some favored by the writers, some suppressed, including women's voices. Also in this vein, I have questioned the ongoing relevance of some of the issues—especially the questions of authenticity and order—that have preoccupied interpreters of 2 Thessalonians for many decades.

Finally, as a feminist who is also a "practicing Catholic," I recognize the tension—sometimes unbearable—between the hierarchical, patriarchal structures of the church and the vision of what Elisabeth Schüssler Fiorenza has called the *ekklēsia* ("church") of women. In germinal form, these tensions lie behind 2 Thessalonians. The Thessalonian women were, as I am, constrained by their religion, but they were also undoubtedly attracted to the church by its countercultural, liberating possibilities. To fail to acknowledge both the oppressive and the liberating aspects of the church would be a disservice to women in the churches, both ancient and modern.

RHETORIC

In the past decade, 2 Thessalonians has begun to be interpreted in terms of the influence of Greco-Roman rhetoric (Jewett; Hughes; Wanamaker). The rhetorical critics agree that 2 Thessalonians is a piece of *deliberative rhetoric,* which "seeks to persuade the readers to think and act differently in the future."[3] This approach is congenial to me, since most of my publications in recent years have been Greco-Roman rhetorical interpretations of Christian Testament writings. So, in addition to a feminist hermeneutical perspective, I pursue what I regard as the most useful approach to 2 Thessalonians: Greco-Roman rhetorical interpretation. This approach holds that 2 Thessalonians was informed by ancient literary norms, freely adapted to the socio-rhetorical setting. The nature of rhetoric as a means of ideological domination and manipulation—of imposing the rhetorician's position upon the audience—makes the rhetorical approach a useful tool for exposing some of the power plays that underlie the text. Thus, the text that follows will analyze 2 Thessalonians in terms of the rhetorical units and strategies that underlie the argument.[4]

COMMENTARY

EPISTOLARY PRESCRIPT (1:1–2)

The addressees are converts in Thessalonica, a Roman colony and the capital of Macedonia (ca. 50 C.E., on traditional dating). According to Acts 17, some of the converts were Jews, but many had other backgrounds (cf. 1 Thess 1:9). Like 1 Thessalonians, the second letter begins with a simplified form of the salutation found in all the genuine Pauline correspondence. Like most Pauline letters, 2 Thessalonians mentions co-authors: Paul, Silvanus (Silas), and Timothy. Some suggest that the differences between 1 and 2 Thessalonians stem from the greater contribution of Silvanus, Timothy, or both to one of them (most likely 2 Thessalonians). Throughout 1 and 2 Thessalonians, the first person plural is typically used. This multiple authorship evidences a collegiality underplayed in Christian Testament scholarship, with its emphasis on the personal dynamism and ongoing influence of Paul. Although it cannot be isolated, the contribution of other missionaries—women and men—to the Pauline correspondence should be acknowledged; so should the input of secretaries such as Tertius (Rom 16:22), who may have improved the rhetoric of the letters. Remember also that these letters were meant to be read aloud; thus both reader and hearers, women and men, "disorderly" and "orderly" (see 3:11), also implicitly figure in the composition. God and Christ are depicted in typically patriarchal terms (father, lord). The traditional wish of "grace and peace" conveyed by the salutation belies the polemical quality of the letter to follow.

EXORDIUM (1:3–12)

In Greco-Roman rhetoric, the *exordium* (introduction) seeks "to influence or even manipulate the audience by securing their interest and goodwill."[5]

The senders do this by praising the Thessalonians for their faithfulness and love, and for their firmness (*hypomonē*) in "persecutions and afflictions" (1:3–4)–a standard topic in early Christian eschatological discourse. By imputing to the audience qualities that will make them amenable to persuasion, the writers cast the recipients in a rhetorical role where they are expected to respond to criticism with belief, charity, and constancy. The thanksgiving (1:3–10), typical of Pauline letters, is one long sentence, concluded by an intercessory prayer. John Chrysostom (fifth century C.E.) noted how here and throughout this letter the audience is humbled by the attribution of their good qualities to their ultimate source, God. This rhetorical device reinforces the dominance of the authors (on the side of God) respective to the recipients (whose allegiance is in question).

The use of the verb *opheilomen* ("we ought") in the thanksgiving suggests to some interpreters that the senders are now less approving of the recipients than when they wrote 1 Thessalonians, because, as the rest of the argument makes clear, some church members had strayed from the missionary teaching. The reference to duty (cf. 2:3), however, may convey not obligation but an assertion that the audience *deserves* praise. Again, rhetorically, the hearers can continue to "deserve" praise only if they hold fast to the missionary gospel and submit to missionary authority.

Here and throughout, the audience is addressed as "brothers" (*adelphoi*). The senders' use–and translators' and commentators' usual rendering–of this "false generic" leaves the modern reader with the unfortunate sense that the Thessalonian church resembled a masonic lodge. Acts 17:4 recounts that "not a few of the leading women" of Thessalonica heeded the preaching of Paul and Silas, and women are known to have played an active part in the religious life of ancient Thessalonica. The senders give no explicit indication that women were among the addressees, perhaps because the Thessalonian churchwomen presented no specific problems (cf. 1 Cor 11:2–6; 14:34–35; 1 Tim 2:9–15; 5:3–16). Then as now, the false generics (brothers, he/man), as well as the vengeful, androcentric content that follows, undoubtedly placed the women listeners at a psychological remove from the address. The use of the egalitarian "brothers" (if noninclusive) promises an equality between authors and addressees that is not fulfilled in what follows.

Since an important article by Jouette M. Bassler (1984), the "sign" (*endeigma*) of the righteous judgment of God (1:5) has often been interpreted as consisting of the sufferings of the church, in line with the Jewish apocalyptic notion that the hardships of the pious were a chastisement or atonement for sins that would make them worthy of future glorification.[6] Bassler contrasts this understanding of the "sign" with the "sign" (*endeixis*) of Phil 1:28, which is the steadfastness of the Philippians in the face of their opponents. Although the apocalyptic notion of atoning suffering has been likened to Gandhian passive resistance,[7] it disturbingly implies that the misery of the oppressed is acceptable to God, and that concrete, secular action to remedy this is unnecessary, even impious.

Like other *exordia,* 2 Thess 1:3–12 introduces the main theme of the letter, the futurity of the day of the Lord. The vividness and detail of this depiction of the parousia (vv. 7–10) prepare the audience for the argument that the day of the Lord has *not yet* come, for only *then* will the Lord Jesus be "revealed from heaven with his mighty angels in flaming fire," as the prophets foretold. The parousia is not something the Thessalonians could have missed (cf. Matt 24:27)! Nor do the authors admit the possibility that the parousia may be otherwise than they imagine. They depict the parousia as the spectacular climax of a furious cosmic battle, in which an imperial Christ, accompanied by powerful warrior angels, inflicts vengeance on unbelievers. Rhetorically, this is a veiled warning to members of the audience who do not "obey" the Pauline gospel; the audience is also drawn into the invisible combat, in that they are pitted against "unbelievers" outside—and inside—their community.

PARTITIO (2:1–2)

Rhetorical critics agree that this is the *partitio* or statement of the problem to be discussed. The topic introduced in v. 1 is "the parousia of our Lord Jesus Christ and our assembling together with him." Verse 2 indicates that some of the Thessalonians were being shaken by rumors that "the day of the Lord has come." The senders beg (*erōtaō,* v. 1) the recipients not to be agitated by rumors originating "by spirit or by word or by letter as from us" (v. 2)—an indication of an emergent deutero-Pauline tradition. Again, the authors are uncompromising as to the authority of their version of what the parousia will be.

Commentators have, in general, hesitated to interpret literally the eschatological content of 2:2; however, the language of the verse invites a literalistic reading. In particular, the noun *episynagōgē* (v. 1) refers to "an assembling together *at a place*" (LSJ; emphasis added); the verb *enestēken* "means not 'is coming' (*erchetai* I - 5[2]), not 'is at hand' (*ēngiken* Rom. 13[12]), not 'is near' (*engys estin* Phil. 4[5]), but 'has come,' 'is on hand,' 'is present.'"[8] The most obvious interpretation of these passages is that some members of the audience heard somehow that the parousia had actually occurred and that the faithful should go to meet the Lord at a specific location.[9] As Jewett notes, there are several passages in 1 Thessalonians (2:18a, 26; 3:11–13; 5:1–5, 6–10) that could be taken to mean that the day of the Lord had already come or that it *could* come "like a thief in the night" with very little fanfare.[10] Such ideas among early Christians are attested by passages in the Synoptic eschatological discourses (Mark 13:5–6, 21–22; Matt 24:5, 23–27; Luke 21:8; cf. Mark 16:7).

Jewett's millenarian model of the Thessalonian community, in which certain members (the "disorderly" [*ataktoi*]; 2 Thess 3:6, 11; 1 Thess 5:14) held radical eschatological beliefs, best explains the problems introduced here.[11]

PROBATIO (2:3–15)

Post-Enlightenment embarrassment over the apocalyptic extravagances of 2 Thess 2:3–15 may account for the many scholarly efforts to disassociate the apostle Paul from this letter. The *probatio* ("proof") elaborates on the future coming of the Lord and the faithful assembling to meet him. Both the language and ideas are notoriously obscure. This passage epitomizes the issues of gender, power, and domination. The eschatological teaching that the missionaries rehearse is an apocalyptic myth in which powerful male forces—the "man of lawlessness," the "son of perdition," "the restrainer" (or "the grasper") (*ho katechōn*) (whose identity remains unknown despite centuries of interpretation), Satan, Christ, and God—engage in a war for control of the universe. The ultimate victory of Christ and God is assured not by their goodness (although the opponents are cast as wicked deceivers) but by their superior strength. God is depicted in v. 11 as colluding with his adversaries insofar as he "sends a strong delusion" to make unbelievers accept the false signs and wonders of Satan's protégé, the "lawless one." This ancient apocalyptic imagery is disturbingly reminiscent of modern warfare, where powerful men vie for ascendancy using terrible weapons, which destroy innocent people (conceived by the "other side" as evil).

As Jewett has shown, the lurid apocalyptic beliefs of 1 and 2 Thessalonians would have been particularly attractive to the Thessalonians, whose most important pre-Christian religious affiliation, the violent, patriarchal mystery cult of Cabirus, resembled the religion preached by Paul and his associates in some ways: "He [Cabirus] was a martyred hero, murdered by his brothers, buried with symbols of royal power, and expected to return to help lowly individuals and the city of Thessalonica in particular."[12] The local popularity of the Cabirus cult may account for the writers' extensive use of the mythology of warring male powers in the *probatio,* and for the formulation of the missionary preaching to the Thessalonians in these terms.[13]

PERORATIO (2:13–3:5)

Rhetorical critics disagree as to the literary classification of 2:13–3:17. Robert Jewett, Frank Hughes, and Charles Wanamaker all see an element of proof (*probatio*) in the passage (2:13–3:5; 2:13–17; 2:13–15) relating back to the issue of assembling to meet the Lord (2:1); however, the material in 2:13ff.

is very different from the argument of 2:3–12, which rehearses early Christian teaching about the parousia in order to refute the idea that Jesus had already returned. 2 Thess 2:13–3:5 is loosely constructed and touches on a variety of topics: thanksgiving (2:13–14) and a command to hold to received tradition (2:15); a prayer for the Thessalonians (2:16–17); and a prayer request for deliverance from "wicked and evil people" (3:1–3), concluding with an expression of confidence in the recipients (3:4) and a final prayer that they will look to God and Christ (3:5), who, it is implied, are on the side of the missionaries. 2 Thess 2:13–3:5 thus may be interpreted as a *peroratio* (*epilogos, conclusio*), which "summed up the arguments and amplified them, and . . . frequently excited the emotions of the audience for one's case or against one's adversary's case, or both."[14] Like ancient perorations, this section recapitulates important elements of the discourse (cf. 1:13 and 1:3; 2:14 and 1:11–12; 2:15 and 2:2) (*enumeratio*),[15] expresses indignation against the enemy (3:2–3) (*indignatio*), and arouses pity and sympathy for the senders (3:1–2) (*conquestio*).[16] The reprise of the thanksgiving period (1:3–4; 2:13–14) is significant since, as David Aune observes: "The length of the thanksgiving reflects the degree of intimacy between writer and recipients."[17] The flattering inclusion of a second thanksgiving after the *probatio* shows that the writers wish to maintain (or regain) their influence over the audience (2:2–3). The emphasis on holding to received traditions (2:15; 3:4; cf. 2:17; 3:5) underlines the importance of avoiding non-Pauline (or pseudo-Pauline) traditions (2:1–3), and perhaps of staying geographically in place (cf. 2:1). In 3:1–3, the senders remind the audience that they, like the Thessalonians, suffer from the machinations of "wicked and evil people" (cf. 1:4–7)–perhaps a veiled reference to the teachers behind 2:1–2.

EXHORTATIO (3:6–15)

Exhortation is not a recognized component of an oratorical declamation, but moral exhortation is often a feature of ancient philosophical letters.[18] In 2 Thessalonians, this includes elements of both admonition (vv. 6–13) and (implicitly) warning (vv. 14–15). The material is parenetic (vv. 7, 10). The theme is the necessity of working for a living, which, as Hughes observes, is stated in four different ways: an admonition to keep away from idlers (v. 6); the personal example of the self-sufficiency of the senders (vv. 7–9); a reference to an earlier missionary command to work (v. 10); and the reason for the exhortation: some of the recipients are "disorderly" (*ataktōs*), "not *busy* (*ergadzomenous*), but busy*bodies* (*periergadzomenous*)" (v. 11).[19] The *exhortatio* ends with a double command to the disorderly, who are "commanded" and "exhorted" to work "with tranquillity"–a philosophical value[20]–for their keep (v. 12), and instruction to the obedient to continue doing good (v. 13), but to isolate and admonish, in a familial spirit, those who persist in idleness (vv. 14–15). As Jewett argues, the "disorderly" may have eschewed work because of their imminentist eschatology. There is no indication that women were among the idlers (3:6), especially in view of the fact that elsewhere in the Christian Testament—and in misogynist church rhetoric throughout the centuries— women are sarcastically singled out for being "too idle" or "too busy" (cf. 1 Tim 5:13; Luke 10:40), that is, for neglecting "womanly" pursuits for theological activity. Possibly it was affluent churchwomen (Acts 17:4) who were being impoverished by the "disorderly." The rhetorical belittling of the "disorderly" is another strategy that has often been used to put dissenters within Christian communities back in line. The exhortation to work in 2 Thessalonians is much lengthier than that of 1 Thess 4:11–12, perhaps indicating the extent to which the "realized parousia" teaching had taken hold among the Thessalonians.

EPISTOLARY CLOSING (3:16–18)

The peace wish of v. 16 is typical of Pauline letters, as is the "grace" (*charis*) benediction of v. 18.[21] The reference to a change in handwriting (v. 17) is sometimes misunderstood as a reference to a signature.

CONCLUSIONS

From a feminist-ecumenical standpoint, 2 Thessalonians has several disturbing features: (1) the coercive rhetoric, which places the authors in a dominant role relative to the audience; (2) the depiction of cosmic history (all too accurately) in terms of apocalyptic warfare between powerful and aggressive male forces; (3) glorification of suffering and promise of divine vengeance, implicitly legitimating passive acceptance of oppression; (4) hostility toward alternative theological beliefs (2:1–2, 15; 3:14–15), contradicting the collegial implications of the multiple authorship (1:1) and the communitarian ethos of the church.

If 2 Thess has any ongoing relevance in the Christian canon, it is as a patriarchal artifact reflecting values and attitudes that must be acknowledged and critiqued.

NOTES

1. Jane Gallop, *Reading Lacan* (Ithaca, NY: Cornell University Press, 1985), 18.
2. Jonathan Culler, *On Deconstruction: Theory and Criticism after Structuralism* (Ithaca, NY: Cornell University Press, 1982), 49.
3. Charles A. Wanamaker, *Commentary on 1 and 2 Thessalonians* (New International Greek Testament Commentary; Grand Rapids: Eerdmans; Exeter: Paternoster, 1990), 48.
4. The rhetorical divisions used below are based on those identified by Robert Jewett, Frank

Hughes, and Charles Wanamaker. I have used and adapted elements from all three outlines and added some elements of my own.

5. David E. Aune, *The New Testament in Its Literary Environment* (Philadelphia: Westminster, 1987), 199.

6. Jouette M. Bassler, "The Enigmatic Sign: 2 Thessalonians 1:5," *Catholic Biblical Quarterly* 46 (1984): 496–510.

7. William Klassen, "Vengeance in the Apocalypse of John," *Catholic Biblical Quarterly* 28 (1966): 300–311.

8. James Everett Frame, *A Critical and Exegetical Commentary on the Epistles of Paul to the Thessalonians* (International Critical Commentary; Edinburgh: T. & T. Clark, 1912), 248.

9. Robert Jewett, *The Thessalonian Correspondence: Pauline Rhetoric and Millenarian Piety.* (Philadelphia: Fortress, 1986), 100.

10. Ibid., 186–91.

11. Ibid., 161–78.

12. Ibid., 128.

13. Among other deities worshiped at Thessalonica were Isis and Serapis, Dionysus, Roma, Aphrodite, Demeter, Zeus, and Asclepius.

14. Frank Witt Hughes, *Early Christian Rhetoric and 2 Thessalonians* (Journal for the Study of the New Testament Supplement 30; Sheffield: Academic Press, 1989), 42.

15. Ancient rhetoricians held that a detailed recapitulation of a brief, simple argument—like 2 Thess 2:3–15—was unnecessary.

16. Hughes, *Early Christian Rhetoric*, 41–43.

17. Aune, *New Testament*, 196.

18. Abraham J. Malherbe, *Moral Exhortation, A Greco-Roman Sourcebook* (Philadelphia: Westminster, 1986), 79–85.

19. Hughes, *Early Christian Rhetoric*, 64.

20. Malherbe, *Moral Exhortation*, 33, 46.

21. Aune, *New Testament*, 186–87.

RECOMMENDED READINGS

Aune, David E. *The New Testament in Its Literary Environment.* Philadelphia: Westminster, 1987.

Bassler, Jouette M. "The Enigmatic Sign: 2 Thessalonians 1:5." *Catholic Biblical Quarterly* 46 (1984): 496–510.

Culler, Jonathan. *On Deconstruction: Theory and Criticism after Structuralism.* Ithaca, NY: Cornell University Press, 1982.

Frame, James Everett. *A Critical and Exegetical Commentary on the Epistles of Paul to the Thessalonians.* International Critical Commentary. Edinburgh: T. & T. Clark, 1912.

Gallop, Jane. *Reading Lacan.* Ithaca, NY: Cornell University Press, 1985.

Hughes, Frank Witt. *Early Christian Rhetoric and 2 Thessalonians.* Journal for the Study of the New Testament Supplement 30. Sheffield: Academic Press, 1989.

Jewett, Robert. *The Thessalonian Correspondence: Pauline Rhetoric and Millenarian Piety.* Philadelphia: Fortress, 1986.

Klassen, William. "Vengeance in the Apocalypse of John." *Catholic Biblical Quarterly* 28 (1966): 300–311.

Malherbe, Abraham J. *Moral Exhortation, A Greco-Roman Sourcebook.* Philadelphia: Westminster, 1986.

Wanamaker, Charles A. *Commentary on 1 and 2 Thessalonians.* New International Greek Testament Commentary. Grand Rapids: Eerdmans; Exeter: Paternoster, 1990.

Romans

ELIZABETH A. CASTELLI ◆

PAUL'S LETTER TO THE ROMANS stands apart from the rest of the Pauline corpus, a letter written to a community Paul knows only obliquely, a letter read by many as a culmination of Paul's theological writing, his "last will and testament" according to Günther Bornkamm. The scholarly discussion of the nature and motivations of this letter is rich and extensive; the tenor and rhetoric of the text have been abundantly interrogated by generations of readers.[1] The feminist commentary invited here is both daunting and confounding: How to comment in a feminist fashion on a text that, on its face, deals so peripherally with women? In this essay, I will seek to answer this question by following out a series of theoretical and interpretive threads. Beginning with an interrogation of the problematics of both "commentary" and "feminism," I will then turn to two very different modes of reading inspired by the last fifteen years of feminist interpretation of scripture: historical reconstruction and ideological critique. Opening the discussion at the end of the letter with the women who actually appear in Paul's text, the essay will then turn to the resonances of gender, ethnicity, and class in the letter, posing questions about the ideological framework put in place by Paul's use of social categories to make theological points. The essay ends with a few questions which, in my judgment, must be posed by feminist interpretation, whatever its interpretive object.

FEMINIST COMMENTARY AND ITS DISCONTENTS

The genre of "commentary" is a central component of the intellectual heritage of biblical scholarship, yet it represents in certain central ways an approach to texts antithetical to feminist interpretation and praxis. The genre of "commentary" in biblical studies poses a special challenge to feminist readers and interpreters of biblical texts insofar as commentary, as it has been practiced traditionally in the discipline, in many ways embodies a mode of knowing which feminism has called foundationally into question. That is, commentaries have traditionally functioned positivistically as scientific handbooks to texts, providing a compendium of information about historical details, archaeological evidence, philological insights, and comparative possibilities all of which might shed light on the "meaning" of the text. A commentary represents itself as a rendering of the truth about a text. Laying out the meanings of the various details of a text, the commentary often veils its interpretive interests. Its rhetoric imbues the "evidence" with an objective cast. Its theoretical orientation is toward the position that the text and history should "be allowed to speak for themselves," implying that original, authentic meanings—historical truth—can emerge unproblematically from them. The commentary is a totalizing genre, claiming to garner in encyclopedic fashion all the relevant knowledge needed to read the truth of a text.

A short examination of the stated purposes of one of the more authoritative commentary series published in English will demonstrate the point. The foreword to the still-in-process commentary series Hermeneia offers an emblematic example of the values and reigning ideas embraced by mainstream biblical scholarship in the practice of commentary. The series editors write:

> The word Hermeneia has a rich background in the history of biblical interpretation as a term used in the ancient Greek-speaking world for the detailed, systematic exposition of a scriptural work. It is hoped that the series, like the name, will carry this old and venerable tradition forward. . . . It is expected that authors will struggle fully to lay bare the ancient meaning of a biblical work or pericope. In this way its human relevance should become transparent as is the case always in competent historical discourse.[2]

In conceptualizing the project in this way, the writers call on both the historical continuity of biblical commentary and a philosophy of language grounded in humanistic values, linguistic transparency, and the absolute translatability of meaning. Feminist biblical interpretation, while certainly situated within "the old and venerable tradition" (despite its continued marginalization by some stalwart guardians of that tradition), most often finds itself performing interpretive acts that call into question both the continuity of the tradition and the values attributed to language. Feminist and politically cognate critiques of positivist theory have, of course, thoroughly called into question all of the fundamental theoretical assumptions undergirding the genre of commentary. Evidence, feminists and others have argued, is always already interested in some fashion; it is impossible to accumulate anything approximating raw, disinterested, originary data. It is not simply the case that perspective shapes how the data are interpreted, but the very presence and production of data (what is perceived to be of significance and how) are multivalent and charged. The notion of encyclopedic knowledge has been effectively decentered, deconstructed, and called into question; the dream of total knowledge has been revealed as a hubristic fiction. Commentary's claim to represent knowledge (truth) rather than a reading (interpretation) cannot exist unproblematically in an intellectual frame that sets in high relief the primacy of interpretation as a mode of understanding. In this sense, commentary as it has been practiced traditionally within the field of biblical studies is an impossibility for feminism.

Feminist interpretation, in short, reads against the grain of the tradition and its revered texts. While some feminist readers find the philosophy of linguistic transparency adequate for their purposes, many influenced by contemporary feminist literary and cultural theory have grown suspicious of the feasibility or desirability of "laying bare ancient meanings." Eschewing an idea of language as mere conduit or vessel of meaning, and rejecting a view of meaning as a commodity transferred without remainder from speaker to hearer, writer to reader, these feminists (and I count myself among them) have begun to think of language as a mediator of meaning, and meaning as continually produced through each reading.[3]

At the same time, and perhaps somewhat paradoxically, commentary (defined otherwise) has also become within a broader intellectual frame constituted by other disciplines (especially philosophy and literary theory) a central form of interpretive writing. Much theoretical work in cultural criticism emerges within the context of commentaries on particular texts, though here "commentary" is not an annotated handbook to the truth of a text but rather explicitly an interpretation of the text. This work accentuates certain resonances of the term "commentary": commentary as a gloss, critique, or rendition of a text; commentary as translation and as judgment. It is this conception of "commentary" that will govern this essay; rather than presenting itself as an encyclopedic and all-encompassing account of Romans, this essay will rather be a singular reading—one of many possible readings.

If "commentary" is a problematized notion within the intellectual currents of contemporary criticism, "feminism" produces even more conceptual and political challenges and complexities. Nowhere is this clearer perhaps than in the historical heritage of feminist biblical scholarship that this volume exists to acknowledge, our contemporary ties to Elizabeth Cady Stanton's *The Woman's Bible*. Stanton's project may have laid some of the conceptual groundwork for contemporary feminist biblical scholarship; however, its legacy is rather more dubious when read in the broader context of Stanton's other work, which very clearly asserted the primacy of the claims of white propertied women over those of people of other races and of unpropertied classes.[4] Stanton's single-minded interest in the enfranchisement of women of her race, class, and station led her to develop a feminist politics that was explicitly racist and classbound. That she could do so cannot be fully accounted for by the explanation that she was a product of her time; her version of feminism allowed for her to speak on behalf of "women" when in fact she had only some women's interests in mind and was willing to promote those interests over the interests of, and on the backs of, other women. Feminist biblical scholarship inherits this legacy and cannot ignore its full reverberations in contemporary discussions; the power and anger resonant in the critiques brought by women of color at virtually every conference among feminists and scholars in women's studies serve as a painful and insistent reminder of the work that remains to be done. The current project of feminist biblical scholarship must therefore be twofold: to repudiate the racism and classism of its predecessors, and at the same time to remain accountable for its history.

Beyond the realm of feminist biblical scholarship, feminist theory in general has had to deal with the conceptual limits of certain notions that, for a time, functioned as unquestionably adequate for feminist analysis. It is difficult from the current historical standpoint, for example, to remember the strangely liberating specificity of the category "women," a category that now appears strikingly abstract. Furthermore, as Denise Riley has compellingly demonstrated, "women" never operates as a stable or self-evident category, and its meanings must be further specified and historicized.[5] The same holds true for the category of "gender," which, while helpfully figuring the cultural meanings accruing to perceived sex differences and the relationships of those cultural meanings to power, is not itself a concept exempt from history.[6] "Feminism" itself is a category whose meanings have been open to stringent debate and controversy, a politics grounded perhaps in (some) "women's experience" but not reducible to it or identical with it.[7] And while some women of color have rejected the category of feminism because they understand it to be expressive of the interests of certain women (themselves not included), others have urged that the category be appropriated, expanded, and complicated in order to address multiplicities of identities more adequately.[8]

These cursory observations about the problematic nature of the practice of commentary and of the complexities surrounding the position of feminism point to the conceptual difficulties with which a project of "feminist commentary" is fraught. At the very least, one is reminded of the humility with which any such project should be undertaken, and the partiality of its product. This feminist commentary on Romans will therefore undertake to be a commentary not in the sense of scientific annotation but rather in the sense of gloss and critique. As a feminist endeavor, it will attempt to locate itself within a hermeneutics of liberation, broadly conceived. This does not mean that it seeks to subsume multiple identities under the category of "other," nor to claim that all forms of oppression are lived out in the same ways, with parallel valences, or at comparable levels of intensity at every historical moment. A feminist commentary, in this instance, will critically gloss the text by examining the ways in which language, ideology, and imagery underwrite certain relationships of power while rendering others impossible or unthinkable.

CHERCHEZ LA FEMME:
RECOVERING ANCIENT WOMEN

One of the puzzles of Paul's masterful letter to the Roman Christian churches is the letter of recommendation for Phoebe, the minister to the church at Cenchreae, and the greetings to numerous women, both contained in chapter 16. As Elisabeth Schüssler Fiorenza notes in an article on the usefulness of the chapter for reconstructing the history of early Christian women, the authenticity of the chapter is not questioned by scholars though its placement at the end of Romans is a matter of some debate.[9] With Schüssler Fiorenza, I agree that the letter is best understood as an integral part of the larger text of Romans, though I will suggest that the rhetorical rupture that the chapter represents offers modern feminist interpreters a useful material metaphor for women's history in the discipline of biblical studies. Fully one-third of the people greeted by name in the chapter are women, and some of them are known to us only because of their fleeting mention in Paul's greetings here. While they are called co-workers, apostles, people who have toiled diligently in the Lord, these tantalizing descriptions are also frustrating for what they do *not* tell, for their silence about the lives, motivations, and works of these numerous women. Their presence in this chapter reaffirms what women's historians have always asserted—that women have been present at every point in history, even when their contributions have not been narrated by historians. Their presence, however, in a chapter that presents itself as a confounding add-on to Paul's theological treatise addressed to the Roman churches suggests the disjuncture between the historical (i.e., the particular) and the theological (i.e., the universal), a disjuncture that has continued to marginalize women's lived experiences and their interpretive and theological concerns even into the current context.

This conceptual separation has been approached differently by different feminist scholars. Schüssler Fiorenza, in the essay mentioned earlier, suggests that the chapter is read as "a mere appendix to Paul's theological testament" when one is attending to questions of theology, yet that it is a rich vein to be mined when one has historical questions in mind.[10] This separation between history and theology can work powerfully on the side of feminist interests, and indeed the very insistence on women's presence in the early Christian communities calls on all interpreters to rethink their foundational assumptions about what was going on in the churches of Rome and elsewhere. But the separation can also have a more ambiguous result, which Bernadette Brooten identifies in an important essay on method published several years ago: the continuing marginalization of women. In calling for a shift in the ways scholars have approached women's history in early Christianity, Brooten believes that the interpretive turn will result in a shake-up of the foundational categories of "history" and "theology." As she puts it,

> This shift in focus also means a change in what one counts as social context and what one sees to be the theological center or revelation. New Testament scholars often locate questions relating to women as part of early Christianity's cultural milieu, part of the social world of the New Testament, but not as central to revelation. When we put women in the center of the frame, then a different constellation of theology, cultural milieu, and social world will emerge. When woman is no longer simply the social and cultural background of the theological center, then a shift in historical method and a rethinking of theology are required.[11]

Schüssler Fiorenza and Brooten are not in opposition in their positions here; indeed, Brooten's original text includes a footnote at the end of this passage articulating her debt to Schüssler Fiorenza's work. What is different about Brooten's position is that it foregrounds the very question of the *presence* of women in chapter 16 of Romans and their virtually complete *absence* from the rest of the letter. That is, where are the women in Paul's theological testament? Are they really absent? Are they subsumed into the generic language of "brothers"? Are they a nagging presence, even in their absence? For feminist interpretation, how do the answers to these questions shape a feminist analysis of Paul's theology? Before turning to these important questions, however, let us take the first step of restoring these marginalized women to history.

Chapter 16 opens as a letter of recommendation for Phoebe, the *diakonos* of the churches in Cenchreae and the *prostatis* of many and of Paul (16:1–2).[12] Traveling Christian missionaries routinely carried letters of introduction when they voyaged to work in churches where they were as yet unknown, and the existence of this letter of recommendation assures us that women, as well as men, were traveling missionaries in the earliest church. The title *diakonos*, by which Paul describes Phoebe, is translated in the Revised Standard Version as "deaconess," a curious move that highlights the interpretive character of translation. The Greek term is grammatically masculine and has not been feminized in the way the translation suggests, nor is there any indication that Paul understands Phoebe's task to be any different from that of, for example,

Timothy, to whom Paul refers in 1 Thess 3:2 by the same title. Yet commentators and translators have been remarkably reticent to understand Phoebe as the occupant of such an important leadership role; instead, they make a circular argument based on their foundational assumption that women could not have held leadership positions. If women could not have held leadership positions, then when a woman is called by a title ordinarily denoting a leadership position, the title cannot mean here what it has meant when referring to a man. By translating the term *diakonos* as "deaconess," translators imply that Phoebe's task is analogous to that of later Christian deaconesses, who occupied a much more limited office and who possessed only a very circumscribed claim to authority.[13]

A similar maneuver occurs with the title *prostatis,* a word that appears only here in the Christian Testament. This word is the feminine form of the masculine noun *prostatēs,* which ordinarily is translated by terms such as leader, chief, president, patron, guardian, protector.[14] When the term appears in reference to a woman, commentators are sure to deprive the term of any of its resonances of authority. As commentator Ernst Käsemann does, they feminize the content of the word as well as its grammatical structure:

> *Prostatis,* which occurs only here in the NT, cannot in the context have the juridical sense of the masculine form, i.e., the leader or representative of a fellowship. . . . There is no reference then to a "patroness." . . . Women could not take on legal functions, and according to Revelation only in heretical circles do prophetesses seem to have had official ecclesiastical powers of leadership. . . . The idea is that of personal care which Paul and others have received at the hand of the deaconess.[15]

Not only does this commentary not provide any evidence to support the dubious claim that women had no access to legal agency (feminist scholarship has taught us to ask highly specifying questions: women of what class? where? under which ancient legal system? during what historical period?), but it turns to a text written at least fifty years later—a text written in a completely different geographical location, surrounded by a rather different set of material and political circumstances, and framed by very particular ideological interests[16]—to make claims about women's leadership in early Christianity in general. In addition, Käsemann prematurely forecloses discussion by invoking the language of heresy and orthodoxy in relation to women's authority. The argument appears to be based on a dubious presumption—that women could possess religious authority only in heretical contexts—that closes the discussion of women's leadership before adequately posing the *question* of women's leadership.

In short, if one begins the reading free of the assumption that women by definition were excluded from leadership in the early Christian communities, then Phoebe's authoritative positions are clearly articulated in Paul's recommendation. Phoebe worked as minister of the churches in Cenchreae and as leader, benefactor, or patron of Paul and many others. If one further notes that Phoebe is not named in relation to her father, husband, brother, or guardian—a striking silence in the text's description of her—one might well assume that Phoebe lived and acted independently from the more typical legal relations that situated women primarily in terms of their relationship to male family members. Indeed, that Phoebe is characterized only once in a familial idiom—"our sister"—suggests that her social identity is fully integrated into her new, Christian family. We can only speculate as to the natal or marriage relationships she may have left behind, and as to whether she understood that change in relationship in terms of loss or liberation.

While this letter of recommendation is written on behalf of Phoebe, it includes greetings to a number of other women who were important to the work of the early church. Prisca is named, along with her husband Aquila, as a co-worker of Paul. This term, *synergos,* implies some measure of authority and importance in the early Christian mission, as it is used for such prominent figures as Timothy (Rom 16:21; 1 Thess 3:2) and Apollos (1 Cor 3:9), as well as some lesser-known figures such as Urbanus (Rom 16:9), Epaphroditus (Phil 2:25), Philemon (Phlm 1), and Mark, Aristarchus, Demas, and Luke (Phlm 24). In a rhetorical universe which is highly hierarchicalized, the placement of Prisca's name before that of her husband does not suggest politeness on the part of Paul (some ancient rhetorical version of "Ladies First"), but rather Prisca's own importance and status; the more important person's name would routinely be placed in the first position. While Käsemann speaks of the importance of the role of Prisca as part of the missionary couple, he argues that her function is specifically to gain access to the women in communities the couple enters: "The wife can have access to the women's areas, which would not be generally accessible to the husband."[17] According to the narrative in Acts 18:24–26, written of course some decades after Paul's letter, Priscilla and Aquila together "expounded to [Apollos] the way of God more accurately." Even if one is reticent to attribute historicity to a text that is clearly steeped in the novelistic tropes of its day, that Priscilla's contributions to Apollos's education are included here without being distinguished in some way as remarkable suggests that her role was understood, at least in some early Christian circles, as an authoritative teacher and not merely as that of a missionary to the segregated women of communities her husband sought to convert.

If the terms *diakonos, prostatis,* and *synergos,* when applied to women, have been troubling to scholars, the reference to Junia the *apostolos* in 16:7 has inspired remarkable interpretive contortions, resulting ultimately in a sex-change-by-translation. The feminine name Junia is replaced in modern translations by the masculine name Junias, a name nowhere else attested in the ancient world. Once again, the argument is a circular syllogism: since, by definition, women cannot be apostles, when a woman is called an apostle, she is either not an apostle or she is not a woman.[18]

Several other women are named in the verses that follow. Those who have toiled diligently (*kopiaō*, probably a technical term for missionary work) include Mary and Persis, along with Tryphaena and Tryphosa, who may well have shared their lives in patterns similar to those of other missionary couples like Prisca and Aquila, and Andronicus and Junia.[19] The unnamed woman who is greeted with Rufus as "his mother and mine," Julia, and Nereus's sister round out the list of women named by Paul, singled out for greetings. Taken as a whole, this series of greetings, combined with the greetings to various house-churches, where women certainly played central roles, makes it clear that women's participation in the early Christian movement was not as marginal as the sources may suggest on their face. The question remains, however: What difference did women's participation make? Was it, as Käsemann suggests in his interpretation of Prisca's role, simply in order for missionaries to gain access to women in gender-segregated communities? Did it serve to replicate or to challenge the dominant androcentric assumptions of early Christian writers? Women's presence, of course, does not assure that a particular theology or politics will become ascendant. Indeed, one may well ask how women may have interpreted the androcentric discourse of early Christian male writers: Did they agree with it, take issue with it, resist it? These questions remain, often, frustratingly unanswerable, yet the intersections of women's participation and the ideological construction of gender in early Christian texts remain a highly controversial and interesting ground for discussion and debate.

USING WOMEN TO THINK WITH

Historical reconstruction is one method of feminist interpretation of biblical texts that has produced very important results, and it is a particularly useful method when women figure centrally and explicitly in a text. It becomes more difficult, though by no means impossible, when women are not explicitly mentioned in a text.[20] As Elisabeth Schüssler Fiorenza has argued, one should assume that women are present unless they are explicitly excluded from a discussion, rather than assuming they are present only when a problem is diagnosed explicitly in a text. Still, there are other approaches to texts besides that of historical reconstruction that can illuminate the ideology of a text, particularly when it is not "about" women but when it uses women figuratively to make a point about something else. It is this "using women to think with" (Karen King's felicitous formulation) that will be the focus of this section of the essay.

There are two texts in Romans where women are figures for a different kind of theological point, and they all are examples of discourses of sexuality intersecting with theological discourses. The first concerns women in same-sex relation in chapter 1, and the second concerns the example of the married woman in chapter 7.[21] Each of these passages will be dealt with in turn.

ROMANS 1:18–32

Romans 1:18–32 contains the one explicit biblical reference to women involved in same-sex love, and as Bernadette Brooten has demonstrated in her work on this passage, Paul has taken a position here on homoeroticism consonant with other literature written during the Roman period.[22] In addition, she has argued that Paul's concern here is the threat that same-sex love poses to the natural hierarchy of the sexes. As Brooten points out, the passage does not contribute to a historical reconstruction of the lived reality of lesbians in antiquity but offers us rather one part of the ideological frame surrounding that lived reality.[23] I am particularly interested in the fact that Paul writes here about women and men in homoerotic relation not as his main topic but in order to make a point about something else: idolatry and God's punishment of those who practice it.[24] That is, lesbians and gay men are used here as emblematic of those who have "worshiped and served the creature rather than the Creator," and whose desires are "dishonorable passions" for "unnatural relations." In other words, sexuality, while not the topic of discussion per se, nevertheless is integrally bound up in this passage with proper religious observance and indeed with the proper relationship of humans to the divine. Apologists for Paul's usage here are quick to make three kinds of arguments: First, some point to the verse immediately following this passage, 2:1: "Therefore you have no excuse, O Man, whoever you are, when you judge another; for in passing judgment upon him you condemn yourself, because you, the judge, are doing the very same things." The argument is that Paul may be condemning homoeroticism but that others are not to pass judgment on people who engage in homoeroticism.[25] The second argument is that this (and other) texts in the Bible dealing with homoeroticism are not about homoeroticism *in general* but rather about abusive or degrading relationships (i.e., forced sexual activity, prostitution, and the like).[26] A third argument is that Paul merely reflects the views of his time; since times have changed, we can set aside his socially conditioned views and continue to hold onto the more "universal" of his teachings.[27]

There are difficulties with each of these arguments. In the first case, that passing judgment on others is rejected in a sentence following the statement "those who do such things [i.e., engage in homoerotic behavior] deserve to die" is faint reassurance indeed. The second position—that only abusive or degrading forms of homoeroticism are implied—is certainly not suggested by the language of this passage. Indeed, unnaturalness, dishonor, and shame are inscribed onto the bodies of the participants in homoerotic activity here; there is no indication that some forms of homoeroticism are deemed acceptable in this passage. The third argument—that Paul's position here is socially conditioned and therefore easily separated from his more universal gospel—has been thoroughly engaged by Brooten, who persuasively argues that Paul's use of the imagery of homoeroticism here is intricately interwoven with his understanding of the proper relationship between humanity and divinity and his understanding of the immutable order of creation, which, in his view, is challenged by homoeroticism. Therefore, one cannot discard his imagery here without calling into question the entire framework of which it is a part. As Brooten puts it so forcefully in her concluding arguments, "Consistency would . . . require that if one declares Romans 1:26 (and 27) not to be normative for theology, one cannot adopt the rest of Pauline theology and theological anthropology. Therefore, a careful analysis and fundamental rethinking of Paul's theology is required."[28]

There are a number of reasons why a feminist interpretation of Romans requires careful attention to the ongoing reception of this passage. Contemporary Christian institutions are engaged in open debate about the role of lesbians and gay men within the institutions, as evidenced by the 1991 conferences of United Methodists and Presbyterians considering the question outright; other Christian institutions are taking a thoroughgoing oppositional position, not limited to their own churches but to society at large, as with the recent Vatican missive calling on U.S. bishops to oppose actively measures guaranteeing civil rights to lesbians and gay men. Meanwhile, the decade-old AIDS crisis has called up the rhetoric of bigoted biblicists, who turn to passages like Rom 1:27 and 1:32 to argue that the ravages of immune deficiency are the mark of God's righteous judgment upon gay men. All of these events in the contemporary social context require a carefully considered response by feminists dedicated to a hermeneutics of liberation. It is disingenuous to claim to stand in solidarity with women but then to allow lesbians to be slandered by modern-day Pauls. If one takes seriously Elisabeth Schüssler Fiorenza's profound theological assertion that anything in the text that does not contribute to liberation cannot be considered the word of God, then one must call into question Rom 1:18–32, not only for what it says but for how it has been used historically.

ROMANS 7:1–6

Paul uses women to think with in a rather different way in this passage, where he uses the analogy of a married woman's obligations to her husband to express the obligation of Christians to the law. Paul writes of the married woman's obligations to her husband while he is alive; once the husband is dead, the woman is released from this obligation. Likewise, he says, those who have "died to the law" are "discharged from the law." The analogy is awkwardly constructed, insofar as the husband dies in the first part of the analogy whereas it is Christians (the equivalent elements in the second part of the analogy to the married woman in the first part) who "die to the law." (Furthermore, Paul asserts that "the law is binding on a person only during his life" [7:1], and then turns to an example in which a woman is bound only during her *husband's* life, a curious slippage indeed!) Nevertheless, what is striking about this particular analogy is the use of this particular example from Jewish law to make a point about the end of obligation to the law. First of all, the RSV translation of "a married woman" obscures the hierarchical formulation of the Greek: *hē hypandros gynē*, literally, "the woman who is under a man."[29] The analogy requires the specificity of the example to be drawn from women's relationship to marriage insofar as the law does not provide any such limitation on the sexual activity of men. Furthermore, there is no parallel Greek formulation for *hē hypandros gynē*. We do not come across *ho hypogynaikos anēr* anywhere in Greek literature; no such adjective exists in Greek. Therefore, Paul is here able to make his point about the law through reference to a socially constituted hierarchical relation. The legally constituted relationship of wife to husband becomes an analogy of the relationship to the law of a person who is under the law. One might point out that it is not unusual for analogies to work dialectically, that is, for meanings to move in both directions simultaneously across the analogy. Therefore, Paul uses a recognized hierarchical relationship to illuminate his point about another hierarchical relationship—and the person under the law is to the wife as the law is to the husband.

When Paul uses an analogy like this one, his rhetoric depends on the ordinary persuasiveness of his example. That is, his argument is less effective if he makes reference to an example that requires further explanation or is open to challenge. Indeed, he chooses his example precisely for his audience: "for I am speaking to those who know the law" (7:1). At the same time, by using an example remarkable only for its ordinariness, he also reinscribes the relationship as it is constituted. By using women to think with, Paul (like other authors who use gender and social roles as metaphors and analogies) helps to underwrite the understanding of women's roles on which his argument depends.

In each of the two examples discussed here, the subject matter is not the social location of women, be they lesbians or women subject to men in marriage. Rather, it is the ideology surrounding these social locations that mobilizes and enables Paul's theological arguments—on the one hand, concerning idolatry and, on the other, concerning the contingency of Christians' obligations to the law. In each case, women's subordination to men, women's relative status in the order of creation (replicated in social relations between women and men), offers Paul particularly suitable metaphors for his theological points. Whether metaphors of gender hierarchy are the only apt metaphors may be a legitimate question; it remains, however, that these are metaphors Paul found useful and that they are interwoven with his theology, not facilely separable from it. In making use of such metaphors, Paul (inadvertently or not) reinscribed the gender hierarchies he thought with.

DOMINANT DISCOURSES
AND PAUL'S RHETORIC IN ROMANS

One of the frustrating dimensions of Romans is the virtual absence of explicit references to women. Methodologically, it raises the question of the extent to which the text considers women part of its audience or its central purview. Of course, as noted earlier, feminist biblical scholarship, at least since the publication of *In Memory of Her*, has tended to operate with Schüssler Fiorenza's interpretive guideline that one should assume the presence of women in any use of generic terms, not to assume that women are present only when they are specifically identified as a problem. These interpretive guidelines are very helpful correctives to methods that would focus only on explicit references to women—methods that function to replicate the marginalization of women enacted by androcentric texts. At the same time, the text of Romans invites a continual interrogation of the problematic of *inclusion* insofar as inclusion is one of the letter's themes, and creating an image of the universal human is a central ideological interest of the letter's author. Therefore, the question arises: What is the relationship between the text's imagery and metaphors, on the one hand, and the text's ideology, on the other? When the text mobilizes discourses that imply specificity in order to make points about universality, how are we to use an interpretive method of inclusion?

Paul routinely draws on a variety of available discourses in his writing. Scholars over the last several decades have helpfully pointed out the ways in which Paul is beholden to a range of interpretive and ideological practices as well as modes of thought available to him as an educated Pharisee, a Greek-speaking Jew, a practitioner of hermeneutics as well as rhetoric. In possessing access to a particularly rich set of discourses, Paul often interweaves them complexly in his letters; this is particularly true for Romans, a text rather less situational than his other letters. This section of the essay will examine portions of the text where this tension asserts itself, where a range of discourses are used to make theological points. Among the discourses to be interrogated are the hermeneutical, philosophical, legal, and religious discourses that Paul mobilizes in the service of his broader argument.

DUALISTIC DISCOURSES

There are several examples of Paul's appropriation of different discourses that are relevant for a feminist commentary. For example, the logic of Romans depends on an overarching hermeneutical and philosophical use of dualism. Dualism is a conceptuality that explains the nature of things through recourse to binary opposition, arranging all ideas, things, and phenomena into pairings of mutually exclusive elements.[30] The oppositions good/bad, ideal/real, male/female, divinity/humanity, heaven/earth, spirit/body, slavery/freedom suggest some of the countless possible oppositions that could be called dualistic. Moreover, in dualistic systems, the first item in each paired group comes to be related analogically to the first item in every other group; likewise, the second item in each group is constructed as the analogue for all the other second items. Finding its classic articulation in the philosophy of Plato, dualism characterized much of the thinking in the ancient Mediterranean and greatly influenced Paul's thought. For feminism, the problem of dualism is not simply the binary opposition itself but also that the opposition created is never a balanced one but rather is a hierarchical relation, as the paired examples listed above suggest. When Plato distinguished between being and becoming, the ideal and the real, he attributed more positive value to the first item in the series because he understood that the realm of being (the ideal) was unchangeable and perfect whereas the realm of becoming (the real) was subject to alteration, decay, and transformation. Hierarchical dualism continued to dominate the philosophical scene in the first century.

In Paul's writing, the influence of such dualistic discourse is ubiquitous. A particularly explicit example of its presence may be found in chapter 8, where Paul characterizes life in the spirit, in opposition to life according to the flesh. Multiple oppositions and logical inversions comprise this chapter, all of them dependent on an underlying dualism. Life in the flesh, according to this chapter, is consonant with sin and death, slavery, hostility to God, and the inability to submit to God's law or to please God. For those who live in the spirit, death comes only to the deeds of the body; life abounds; and their position as sons and heirs of God is assured. The language of this passage poses numerous difficulties for feminist analysis. Given that woman or the feminine is routinely associated with the flesh and the body in Platonic dualism, what does it mean that the imagery of life in the flesh is used to signify sin and death? To pose this question is not to argue that Paul makes this association explicitly but to point out that it is present in the broader structure of dualistic discourse. When the figure of the feminine is ideologically aligned with the flesh, how are women to understand their position with respect to this worldview? The passage is further complicated by the language of sonship and inheritance, which will be dealt with in the section on legal discourses below.

Chapter 8 does not provide the only example of the Pauline appropriation of dualism. As Paul outlines his argument for the impartiality of God in relation to both Jews and Gentiles, he nevertheless depends on a hermeneutic fully grounded in dualistic opposition. When he enters into the important discussion of the relationship of God to Israel in chapters 9–11, dualism is the foundation of his rhetoric. The dichotomies between flesh and spirit, flesh and promise, death and life, slavery and sonship are tied to Paul's interpretation of scripture in the letter and are always hierarchically arranged. It is perhaps notable that the opposition female–male is not explicitly mentioned in Romans; however, there are two reasons for thinking that it is not unreasonable to see it implied. First, the *structure* of dualism is present throughout the letter (including its analogical dimension), and the opposition of male and female was, in the Greco-Roman context, a fundamental element in the overarching hierarchical dualism that dominated its philosophical discourses. Second, in the one place where gender is addressed in the letter, in 1:18–32, it is clear that the appropriate relationship between males and females is one of a natural hierarchy. One might see this view echoed in the reference to the woman subject to the man in 7:2 as well. Therefore, though Paul does not invoke gender dualism explicitly in the letter, I argue that it is present implicitly and by analogy in the other dualistic imagery in the letter.

This dualistic imagery is interwoven with the theology of the letter; just as one cannot factor out the difficult stance vis-à-vis homoeroticism in the early part of the letter, so one cannot dismiss the thorough use of dualism in the letter without calling into question the entire argument. The question arises: Is dualism always a problem for feminism? Undoubtedly there would be different feminist answers to this question. My own answer is that dualism appears to set the world and relationships within it in stark relief and does so in a totalizing fashion. Both of these functions strike me as inimical to feminism's strengths, which include valuing multiplicity, specificity, and the strategic resistance to totalizing discourses. Paul's dualism, like dualism in general, leaves no loose ends, and I argue that this is not necessarily to its credit.

Mythic Discourses

Paul is not only versed in the philosophical traditions of his day; he is also thoroughly steeped in the scriptural traditions of his ancestors—what he calls "scripture" and what is collectively known today as the Hebrew Bible (though, of course, Paul's Hebrew Bible was Greek, the commonly used translation called the Septuagint). In Romans, Paul appeals to two mythic figures from scripture in order to make two of his central points in the letter—Adam (in order to explicate the saving nature of Christ's death and resurrection) and Abraham (in order to demonstrate the central role of faith in the establishment of God's covenant with Abraham's descendants). The two figures are used rather differently by Paul, and one would do well to consider each example in turn.

In the case of Paul's appeal to the traditions of Adam (Rom 5:12–21), the Genesis narrative is never cited, but rather the figure of Adam is simply invoked and presented as "a type of the one who was to come" (5:14). Several themes that are familiar from Paul's writing come to expression here: the ubiquity of sinfulness, the salvific power of the death of Jesus, the accumulation of qualities of death or life in accordance with the pattern of dualism already discussed above. The RSV translation of the term *anthrōpos* in this passage as "man" obscures the generic sense here; indeed, what Adam and Christ have in common here is not *gender* but *genre*: the passage argues that the sin created through human action is undone by the "act of righteousness," a human action. Yet the passage suggests the question of the importance of gender for salvation, insofar as one might wonder whether a woman (Eve, for example) could figure here as "a type of the one who was to come." When one examines the other occasion in the Christian Testament when the Genesis story of Adam and Eve is invoked, 1 Tim 2:8–15, it is striking that salvation does not accrue to women because they bear a resemblance to Christ (*typos*) but rather because they bear children. The later text is generally not considered Pauline—indeed, the conflict between the theologies of the two passages under discussion is often used as one proof of the later text's inauthenticity—and I do not suggest that Paul is arguing against women's access to salvation. The question remains, however, whether his argument would have worked had the woman been read as the "type" of Christ. I suggest that, given the ideological frame in which this argument was originally cast, only a man could function rhetorically as a general or universal type, whereas a woman would certainly have been cast in the position of the particular.

The other mythic tradition from the scripture Paul evokes in his argument in Romans is the story of Abraham, also found in Genesis. Abraham is a pivotal figure in Paul's thought, as "our forefather according to the flesh" (Rom

4:1), the figure from the history of Israel whose covenant with God assured the chosen status of all his descendants. As one can see elsewhere in Paul's letters, and especially in Romans, Paul is a self-conscious interpreter of scripture, and his hermeneutic can be discerned from his use of the Gen 15:6 passage, "Abraham believed God, and it was reckoned to him as righteousness." Here Paul is trying to negotiate a space for circumcised and uncircumcised within his gospel, for those who bear the fleshly markings of belonging to the covenantal community and for those who bear no such marking.

Paul's use of the Abraham traditions, which include the dramatic and tragic stories of the infertility of Sarah and the concubinage of Hagar the slave (though Hagar's story is repressed here, whereas it plays a prominent role in Galatians), is a complex inversion and reinscription of the first-told stories. Paul characterizes Abraham as forefather according to the flesh, and, indeed, the Abraham traditions are thoroughly embodied, enfleshed stories. Yet, whereas one might well read the scriptural accounts of Abraham's encounter and covenant making with God as a set of events fundamentally mediated through the flesh, Paul makes contingent the carnal component of the transaction—circumcision. Howard Eilberg-Schwartz has demonstrated how the priestly writer in Genesis connects the act of circumcision as both a sign of the special covenant between God and Abraham *and* a religious enactment assuring fertility.[31] That is, what is significant in the priestly account of the events prescribing circumcision is that they link fundamentally the covenant to generation, God's special relationship with Israel to the physical reproduction of the people of Abraham, marked physically by means of circumcision. In Eilberg-Schwartz's reading, circumcision does not merely stand as a *sign* of the covenant, but rather enacts its possibility upon the bodies of the men of Israel.

Whereas the Priestly tradition links the theological notion of covenant to the lived bodily reality of the men of Israel, Paul meanwhile seeks to create a radical separation between the concept of election or chosenness and corporeal experience. In this, his hermeneutic mirrors the content of his thought: he privileges the spiritual and renders contingent the fleshly.[32] Therefore, Paul does not focus on the centrality of the embodied dimensions of the Abraham story but draws his readers' attention to the faith that Abraham exhibited in the face of commonsense challenges (his own age, the infertility of Sarah) to the promise made to him. The cutting of the generative organ as an act that creates fertility *and* signifies a communal bond becomes fully symbolic in Paul's analysis—and therefore expendable as a gesture, since symbols are in large measure arbitrary and can always be displaced by others.

The implications of Paul's use of the Abraham story here are several. Just as in Paul's use of philosophical dualism, where he clearly places a higher value on the spirit than on the flesh, his spiritualizing of the Abraham account represses the corporeal dimension of the first-told story. It is unclear exactly how significant this is for women, especially when, in either account, circumcision is about what happens to male bodies—a point to be pursued in the next section concerning the legal discourses Paul appropriates.

Paul's deliteralizing project here is a disembodying project, shifting the terms of the debate away from bodily practice and onto a spiritual plane. This has two very different results: practically, it creates the possibility for those who do not bear the physical marks of circumcision to receive righteousness as well. Indeed, Paul interprets Abraham's reception of circumcision precisely as a *post facto* sign of his reception of righteousness by faith, arguing that the function of this sign is to symbolize the inclusion of those who do *not* bear the mark of circumcision: "The purpose was to make him the father of all who believe without being circumcised and who thus have righteousness reckoned to them, and likewise the father of the circumcised who are not merely circumcised but also follow the example of the faith which our father Abraham had before he was circumcised" (Rom 4:11–12). Ideologically, the result of Paul's disembodying act toward the Abraham tradition is to invert the traditional interpretation of Abraham. By asserting that Abraham's descendants are all who share in Abraham's faith, regardless of circumcision, Paul deracinates the traditional descendants of the patriarch. Is this a gesture of liberation, as some would argue, from the constraints of ethnicity, or does it rather serve as a disruption in identity producing social anxiety and personal dislocation?

LEGAL DISCOURSES

Paul is not limited to the philosophical or mythic frameworks available to him as a literate and educated first-century Jewish thinker. In fact, as such, it would be surprising if he did not also make use of legal discourses in his discussion—and his attention to the question of the law must certainly be understood in the context of his position as a Jewish thinker and reformer. In making this statement, I do not wish to align myself with the frequent errors made by Christian and post-Christian feminists who turn to some vague notion like "Jewish or rabbinic background" to account for aspects of Paul's thought that they find objectionable. Rather, I wish to argue that Paul's hermeneutic is sensible from within the context of Hellenistic Judaism, and his concerns are also located within this frame.[33] In looking at Paul's deployment of legal discourses in Romans, I will focus on two different legal traditions: the religio-legal tradition surrounding circumcision, and the Greco-Roman civil legal traditions devoted to adoption. When Paul borrows from both of these legal discourses to speak of the ontological status of Christians with respect to God, it raises questions for feminist interpreters about women's inclusion in the language or the adequacy of the metaphors used to include women.

We have already discussed circumcision partially in the earlier examination of Paul's use of the mythic discourse of Abraham by which he calls into question the central necessity of circumcision as a ritual enactment of the covenant. As noted in that discussion, circumcision—whether enacted literally or perceived metaphorically—remains a gesture toward specifically male bodies, at least in the context of ancient Israelite religion and Judaism (along with many other cultures). Even when the term "circumcision" functions metaphorically, it continues to refer to a lived practice with specific implications for one kind of body and not another. This observation does not mean to suggest that the practice of circumcision or the use of circumcision as a metaphor by Paul means that women were excluded from the religious life of Judaism or early Christian communities. It does mean, however, that normative subjectivity did in both systems continue to belong to men, insofar as the language of circumcision appears to have been adequate in both instances for talking about the relationship of humans to the divine. Insofar as discourse and language create the framework within which experience is comprehended and understood, the use of the term "circumcision" (whether of penises or of hearts) as a marker for the covenant with God circumscribes the ideological inclusion of women as full participants in either community. The import of the gender specificity of this practice may be found in Howard Eilberg-Schwartz's wry summary, "One might sum this up by saying that one must have a member to be a member."[34]

We know very little about the religious experience of women vis-à-vis circumcision. Did women feel included in the community because of their relationships to male relatives who had been circumcised? Did they view themselves as deprived of a parallel rite of initiation? Did the symbolism of circumcision work for women in the same way it did for men in these communities? Were the battles within early Christianity over circumcision, which we see so stridently represented especially in Paul's letter to the Galatians, of much import to women in these communities? Was, indeed, the story of Abraham so compelling to Jewish women in antiquity, or did they find themselves reflecting upon the stories, rather, of Sarah and Hagar? Even when circumcision is used metaphorically, we know that metaphor works insofar as it is capable of challenging one to know or see something unfamiliar through recourse to the imagery of the familiar. How might the receptions of the Pauline metaphor of circumcision be, therefore, shaped differently given very different lived experiences of circumcision?

The use of legal discourse is rather different in Paul's deployment of the legal metaphor of adoption to describe the special relationship of Christians to God in Romans.[35] In 8:15, Paul sets in opposition the spirit of slavery (*pneuma douleias*) and what the RSV translates as "the spirit of sonship" (*pneuma huiothesias*). It is through this second spirit, this *pneuma huiothe-*

sias, that "we" can call God *"abba ho patēr* (Father)" and that "we are children of God, and if children, then heirs, heirs of God and fellow heirs with Christ" (8:15–17). Later in chapter 8, in v. 23, Paul says that "we ourselves, who have the firstfruits of the Spirit, groan inwardly as we wait for adoption as sons (*huiothesia*), the redemption of our bodies." Adoption as sons, in both cases, appears to be crucial for having a legitimate claim to salvation. Are women included in this formulation?

The difficulty arises from the absence of evidence from antiquity that the legal, documentary, and inscriptional use of *huiothesia* was in any way inclusive. Indeed, as Corley points out in her extensive examination of this evidence, while women could indeed function as heirs to property according to Roman law, there is no evidence that women were ever adopted in order to ensure their access to inheritance, though men certainly were. Even when women did have rights to inherit, as a matter of course men were given priority over women in the distribution of property, except perhaps in the rare instances when a father died intestate.[36] Corley argues that Paul's use of this language, while perhaps not intentionally directed at the exclusion of women, results in a gender imbalance requiring that women "become male" before they can become heirs. As Corley puts her conclusions:

> The evidence suggests, however, that Paul's metaphor is a gender specific one, as it probably presupposes the priority of the privileges of sons over those of daughters. Even though Paul may not intend to exclude women from the ranks of the sons of God, for a woman to appropriate this metaphor, there is one more step to be taken before she can participate in the "adoption" Paul describes. She must have maleness conferred upon her before she can be made a son. She must take an additional step up the hierarchical ladder, which for Paul ascends woman, man, Christ, God. The editors of the *Inclusive Language Lectionary,* by rendering *huiothesia* in Rom 8:23–24 with "adoption as children," are attempting to deal with this problematic language by introducing a new metaphor which is more easily appropriated by women on the congregational level. The question is whether or not it is a faithful rendering of Paul's metaphor, which seems to have been gender specific, and not gender inclusive.[37]

Like Paul's use of circumcision as a metaphor, his use of the language of adoption calls on the experience of men as the normative human experience. When he does this, it may not be meant to exclude women explicitly—and we know both that women were participants in early Christian communities and that they worked, at times, very closely with Paul—but it relegates women's experiences once more to the margins of human experience. If women do not share the bodily experience of circumcision, what does the language of circumcision mean to them? If women can function only marginally as heirs to property, what does the metaphor of inheritance mean to them?

Paul's use of legal discourses in his writings, and in this letter in particular, display his general tendency toward strategic writing. One might be confounded by Paul's rejection of the traditional interpretation of Jewish law, on the one hand, and his facile appropriation of metaphors deriving from the secular legal tradition, on the other. One might be further confused by Paul's apparent inconsistencies with respect to the Jewish law itself, rejecting its capacity to bestow identity and religious status but retaining its ability, for example, to circumscribe sexuality.[38] These are strategic choices on the part of a writer who takes very seriously the tradition he critiques and challenges. They are not simply pragmatic solutions to immediate problems faced by Paul but rather are constitutive of his hermeneutic and his theology. Feminist interpreters need to continue to ask questions about the partiality of Paul's relationship to the law and its meanings for women.

This is not to suggest, as some Christian feminists have, that Paul's departures from the law are feminist whereas his androcentrism may be traced to his continued adherence to aspects of the law. Indeed, we know far too little about Jewish women's relationship to the law in this period to know how Paul's attacks upon it would have been experienced by them. Insofar as Judaism attracted women converts in significant numbers in the Roman period, we must assume that the law was not perceived as a burden but rather possessed appeal for these women. Furthermore, if the vociferous character of Paul's rhetoric against the law (here, though more so in Galatians) indicates anything of the weight of compelling argument pressing against his own discourse, and given the absence of any language to suggest that women were somehow exempt from his discussion, we must assume that there were women who valued the law for constituting ongoing religious identity as well as shaping daily existence. When Paul uses "circumcision" as synecdoche for "the law" as a whole, he certainly excluded women ideologically from his rhetoric. Yet this does not mean that women were not part of Jewish communities faithful to the law, nor part of Jewish-Christian communities struggling to situate themselves in a still-emerging framework. The work of reconstructing women's relationship to "the law" during this period is embryonic and ongoing and cautions critical readers against drawing premature or misguided conclusions about the value of Paul's rejection of the law for women.

BREAKING THE CHAIN OF ETHNICITY

Chapters 9–11 of Romans comprise a pivotal part of the letter's argument, in which Paul attempts to describe the relationship of Israel to God in the new circumstances in which Christ is the end of the law (*telos gar nomou Christos*, 10:4). As in the discussion of circumcision in the earlier part of the letter, Paul here makes his argument appeal to a hermeneutic grounded in the dualistic opposition, spirit–flesh. By disembodying the referents of his language, Paul shifts the terms of the discussion, claiming that neither do all of those who descend from Israel actually belong to Israel (9:6), nor are all his descendants (*sperma,* 9:17) children (*tekna*) of Abraham. Through appeal both to tradition (e.g., the stories of Sarah and Rebekah) and to actual scriptural citations, Paul argues that from the historical moments of the births of Abraham's and Isaac's offspring, distinctions were already being drawn between the descendants of Abraham. The chain of ethnicity, on which Judaism depends and which is inscribed on the bodies of Jewish males through the rite of circumcision, is broken by Paul's creation of the disjuncture between the real descendants of Abraham and those who are descendants *kata sarka,* according to the flesh. As a descendant (*ek spermatos*) of Abraham, Paul argues that a remnant of Israel remains, chosen by grace (*kat' eklogēn charitos*) (11:1, 6). It is noteworthy that, in this three-chapter discussion of the status of Israel, Paul quotes extensively (at least thirty-seven times) from scripture. In so doing, he situates himself as an interpreter of the law, even as he also portrays himself in this section explicitly as an apostle to the Gentiles (11:13).

It is crucial to read Paul's writing here within an interpretive frame that highlights its specific and perspectival character, particularly because his letters have an ongoing discursive history in which his arguments have been used to underwrite and justify Christian anti-Semitism. Indeed, in the midst of the debates about whether Paul himself was anti-Jewish or anti-Semitic is lost the recognition that texts live on in the multiple rereadings of them, rereadings which themselves take on lives of their own. The task is not a simple one of returning to the original meanings of a text, even if one believed that such a nostalgic return were possible. The task for a progressive feminist reading of Paul, one attentive to the embeddedness of anti-Semitism in the history of Christianity, is to pose the question of how texts are put to use in various contexts to rationalize certain claims to power. While a history of the interpretation of this theme in Paul's thought is beyond the scope of this essay, it remains crucial to emphasize the very political problematic of interpretation, to pose and leave open the *question* of the production of meaning rather than to propose meaning as the answer to the question of politics.

SLAVERY

Paul's use of imagery in Romans draws not only on gender, religious identity, and ethnicity, but also on class. Hence, he makes use of the major categories of distinction routinely invoked in his cultural surroundings—in chapter 6, on the central distinction between slave and free. Paul uses the language of slavery frequently in his letters, referring at various points to himself as "slave of Christ," arguing that the distinction between slave and free has no meaning in Christ and yet paradoxically making use of the image of slavery to describe the relationship of Christians to sin and to salvation. In all these contexts, it is important to keep in mind the deep ontological separation between slavery and freedom in the ancient Greek and Roman worlds, even if some small number of privileged slaves could achieve a certain level of social status and autonomy,[39] and even when some English translations obscure the language by rendering the Greek term *doulos* as "servant" rather than "slave."[40]

In Rom 6:15–23, Paul describes the recipients of his letter as "you who were once slaves of sin" who "have become slaves of righteousness" (6:17–18). Paul makes it clear that he is speaking metaphorically, when he writes in v. 19, "I am speaking in human terms, because of your natural limitations," or, more literally, "because of your weakness of the flesh." He goes on to describe slavery to sin in physical terms: the contrast is between the state of sin in which one yields one's members, enslaved, to impurity and iniquity, and the state of righteousness in which one yields one's members, enslaved, to righteousness. Both states of being involve bondage, the delivery of one's body to the authority of another—in one case, impurity, in the other, righteousness. Later in the passage, Paul describes those who have been set free from sin as having been enslaved to God (*doulōthentes de tō theō*, 6:22).

This passage is rhetorically similar to those discussed earlier in this essay under the heading, "Using Women to Think With." Like those passages, which were not *about women*, this passage is not *about slaves*. Instead, it is about a theological idea that Paul finds congenial to describe in terms of slavery. As with so many other passages in Paul's writing, it is helpful here to raise the question of how such metaphors might have been heard or experienced. For people who had not endured the imposed bodily suffering and profound social dislocation which slavery surely represented in the ancient Roman world, indeed for people who may themselves have been the owners of slaves, this metaphor of bondage probably possessed a rather different resonance than for the slave members of Christian communities. Furthermore, I have argued earlier that the use of a metaphor of social relation to make a theological point is successful to the degree that the metaphor reinscribes the social relation, rather than calling it into question. Therefore, while this passage is clearly not *about* slavery (neither for it nor against it), it depends on the reality of slavery to convey its meanings and therefore reinscribes the relation of slavery. Finally, one might pose the question of the theological impact of describing access to sanctification through enslavement, even enslavement to righteousness. If "slavery" is understood as brutal domination, as it undoubtedly is from the point of view of the slave at any rate, then how is one to engage the metaphor when it is used here and elsewhere in Paul's writing? A progressive feminist interpretation that positions itself in opposition to domination must here, as elsewhere, raise the question of metaphor and reject the implications of metaphors of domination. As elsewhere, when the metaphor is interwoven complexly with Paul's theology, one cannot simply discard the metaphor and keep the theological stance intact.

ROMANS AND THE POLITICS OF IMPERIALISM

When Paul writes about the relationship of Christians to the dominant social order, he frequently calls on those to whom he writes to live apart from the mores, customs, and standards of the surrounding culture. He further suggests, albeit only strategically, that social identities are contingent and bear no significance within the new Christian framework. When he writes to the Christian community in Corinth, he insists that the people avoid turning to external authorities to settle internal controversies and, indeed, to avoid blurring the boundaries between Christian and non-Christian as much as possible. While Paul never rejects the dominant social order, nor ever encourages anyone to resist actively its constraints, one generally has the sense that Paul is either wary of the dominant order or simply oriented otherwise. That he should be found underwriting the dominant society's claims to power is, however, a rather remarkable discovery, and yet that is precisely what he does in Rom 13:1–7.

In this passage, Paul makes the rather extraordinary claim that the governing authorities (more literally, the supreme authorities) possess a divine mandate since authority (*exousia*) exists only from a divine source and those in power are there through divine fiat. He goes on to argue that only those who do evil things have anything to fear from the authorities; moreover, those who perform acts of punishment are *diakonoi* of God and act out God's wrath against the evildoer. Finally, one should pay taxes because the authorities are the ministers (*leitourgoi*) of God. The use of terms like *diakonos*, *leitourgos*, and *ekdikos eis orgēn* (executor of justice for wrath) is significant, as they belong equally to religious and Hellenistic administrative contexts. Furthermore, the language of submission and resistance (*hypotassesthō*, 13:1; *antitassomenos*, 13:2; *hypotassesthai*, 13:5) is very strong and presupposes a relationship of significant domination. Interestingly, Käsemann distinguishes between *hypakouein* and *hypotassesthai* in the following manner:

> Whereas *hypakouein* usually designates free obedience *hypotassesthai* emphasizes more strongly the fact that a divine order rules in the divinely established world and that this entails super- and sub-ordination . . . , disregard for which is destructive of life in society. Thus the verb can be directed meaningfully against

emancipatory tendencies on the part of, e.g., Christian slaves and women who demand equality.[41]

Käsemann goes on to argue that this passage should be read as an anti-enthusiastic passage, one aimed at excesses of charism rather than one imposing a divinely established state repression.

It is certainly the case that the kinds of state repression experienced in the modern world under modern state apparatuses is rather different from the repression faced by the oppressed peoples of Roman imperialism. If anything, it remains crucial to distinguish carefully among different forms of oppression, lest ignoring their specificities make resistance to them less effective. At the same time, as with the treatment of gender, ethnicity, and class in Paul's letter to the Romans, one must pose the question here of the uses to which texts are put as well as their earliest resonances. Whereas Käsemann can marginalize the lived realities of state terror even as he acknowledges them, South African biblical scholar Winsome Munro can trace out the apologetic and polemical uses to which this text has been put in the context of propping up the racist system of apartheid.[42] Is Paul simply acting the role of the pragmatist, as Käsemann suggests,[43] or does his text bear some of the weight of its later invocations where it has justified brutality, terror, and political repression and rendered solidarity with the oppressed unthinkable, unholy?

CONCLUDING OBSERVATIONS

This engagement of Paul's important letter to the Roman churches has attempted to raise at every turn questions about reading effects. I have taken the position that texts are not mere historical artifacts, dormant veins to be mined for historical information, but rather are ongoing discourses with histories and shifting, ever-developing meanings. Some feminist interpreters take as their main objective the redemption of religious texts, trying to answer the question: How can this text be useful in the contemporary setting? I have taken a different feminist position, still asking how one might make use of the text in the contemporary setting, but having that use be strategic rather than redemptive. How, I have asked, can these texts help us to think about theory, power, solidarity, and resistance around the crucially reorienting categories of gender, ethnicity, race, and class which dominate cultural thinking today?

Feminist interpretation, even of such distant and ancient texts, must as a politically engaged interpretation always pose questions about the underlying dimensions of texts: For whom is this text useful? Whose interests does it serve? Whose interests does it elide? Does Paul help us to think about pressing questions about our own day, or does he foreclose discussion? Do his *modes of thought* offer us help for thinking, or do they diminish the possibilities for liberation? How has this text been used for liberation? How has it served oppression? How does it contribute to ideological frames in the contemporary setting? What do these contributions mean?

None of these questions have simple, fixed answers, as the preceding commentary has demonstrated. Indeed, much of the discussion is closed only by further questions. Commentary in this postmodern era of rupture and partiality refuses the last word and must inevitably seek to undo its own project from the start. The reading of the text that this essay provides is provisional, perspectival, and, I hope, persuasive. It does not represent the only reading of the text, nor the only feminist reading of the text. Indeed, if it has been successful, it will have raised the very question of the possibility of feminist commentary, a question still others may seek to pose, reformulate, answer, and pose again.

NOTES

1. For a dense, thorough summary of the state of research in the study of Romans, see Karl P. Donfried, ed., *The Romans Debate* (rev. ed.; Peabody, MA: Hendrickson, 1991).

2. This foreword is printed in every volume of the Hermeneia series. The words quoted here are taken from the foreword to Hans Conzelmann, *1 Corinthians* (trans. James W. Leitch; Philadelphia: Fortress, 1975), ix.

3. The rich and ever-growing literature in this area is monumental. For an overview and a dense anthology of many of the germinal essays in the field, see Robyn R. Warhol and Diane Price Herndl, *Feminisms: An Anthology of Literary Theory and Criticism* (New Brunswick, NJ: Rutgers University Press, 1991).

4. See historical discussions of the nineteenth-century white feminist movement and its relations with the struggles of African-Americans in Nancie Caraway, *Segregated Sisterhood: Racism and the Politics of American Feminism* (Knoxville: University of Tennessee Press, 1991), 117–67; Angela Davis, *Women, Race and Class* (New York: Vintage, 1983), 70–86; Paula Giddings, *When and Where I Enter: The Impact of Black Women on Race and Sex in America* (New York: William Morrow, 1984), 119–31.

5. Denise Riley, *"Am I That Name?" Feminism and the Category of "Women" in History* (Minneapolis: University of Minnesota, 1988).

6. Joan Wallach Scott, "Gender: A Useful Category of Historical Analysis," in *Gender and the Politics of History* (New York: Columbia University Press, 1988), 28–50.

7. See Chandra Talpade Mohanty, "Feminist Encounters: Locating the Politics of Experience," *Copyright* 1 (1988): 30–44; Judith Grant, "I Feel Therefore I Am: Experience as a Category for Feminist Epistemology," *Women and Politics* 7:3 (1987): 99–114; Joan Wallach Scott, "'Experience,'" in *Feminists Theorize the Political*, ed. Judith Butler and Joan W. Scott (New York: Routledge, 1992), 22–40.

8. The category of "womanist" is an attempt to think and work past the limitations of "feminist." Coined by Alice Walker (*In Search of Our Mothers' Gardens* [New York: Harcourt, Brace, Jovanovich, 1983], xi), this term has opened a fruitful category within religious studies. For the argument that the category of feminism needs to expand to accommodate multiple

identities, see, e.g., bell hooks's comments in Mary Childers and bell hooks, "A Conversation about Race and Class," in *Conflicts in Feminism,* ed. Marianne Hirsch and Evelyn Fox Keller (New York: Routledge, 1990), 66.

9. Elisabeth Schüssler Fiorenza, "Missionaries, Apostles, Coworkers: Romans 16 and the Reconstruction of Women's Early Christian History," *Word and World* 6 (1986): 420.

10. Ibid.

11. Bernadette Brooten, "Early Christian Women and their Cultural Context: Issues of Method in Historical Reconstruction," in *Feminist Perspectives on Biblical Scholarship*, ed. Adela Yarbro Collins (Chico, CA: Scholars Press, 1985), 66.

12. In addition to Schüssler Fiorenza's article cited earlier, see also her "The 'Quilting' of Women's History: Phoebe of Cenchreae," in *Embodied Love: Sensuality and Relationship as Feminist Values,* ed. Paula M. Cooey, Sharon A. Farmer, and Mary Ellen Ross (San Francisco: Harper & Row, 1987), 35–49.

13. The Revised Standard Version (RSV), a translation that continues to be used widely by a literate public, has recently (in 1991) been replaced by the New Revised Standard Version (NRSV). One important change in this new version is the translation of *diakonos* here as "deacon" (with, interestingly, a footnote which reads, "Or *minister*"). While this translation is an improvement, it is unclear why the translators did not decide simply to translate *diakonos* here as "minister," when they create no similar ambiguity in other contexts (see, e.g., Tychicus, mentioned in Eph 6:32 and Col 4:7, and called *diakonos*/minister). The translators' task is described by editor Bruce Metzger in the preface to the Oxford NRSV as "making the Bible available in the form of the English language that is most widely current in our day" ("To the Reader," *The New Oxford Annotated Bible with the Apocrypha* [New York: Oxford University Press, 1991], ix). Therefore it is curious that the term "deacon," which certainly signifies a relatively marginal clerical status, is used to describe Phoebe, whereas "minister" would connote to modern readers and speakers of English a more central clerical and liturgical role.

14. See Bernadette Brooten, *Women Leaders in the Ancient Synagogue: Inscriptional Evidence and Background Issues* (Brown Judaic Studies 36; Chico, CA: Scholars Press, 1982) for an extensive examination of the issues surrounding women's official titles in ancient Judaism, including her note concerning *prostatēs/prostatis* at the bottom of p. 151.

15. Ernst Käsemann, *Commentary on Romans* (trans. Geoffrey W. Bromiley; Grand Rapids: Eerdmans, 1980), 411.

16. Readers interested in a feminist reading of the ideological interests of this text would do well to turn to Tina Pippin, *Death and Desire: The Rhetoric of Gender in the Apocalypse of John* (Louisville: Westminster/John Knox, 1992).

17. Käsemann, *Romans,* 413.

18. Bernadette J. Brooten, "Junia . . . Outstanding Among the Apostles (Romans 16:7)," in *Women Priests,* ed. Leonard S. Swidler and Arlene Swidler (New York: Paulist, 1977), 141–44.

19. Mary Rose D'Angelo offers a particularly suggestive interpretation of the status and nature of the relationship between Tryphaena and Tryphosa, as well as other couples of women in the Christian Testament ("Women Partners in the New Testament," *Journal of Feminist Studies in Religion* 6:1 [1990]: 65–86).

20. See, e.g., Antoinette Clark Wire, *The Corinthian Women Prophets: A Reconstruction through Paul's Rhetoric* (Minneapolis: Fortress, 1990).

21. One might read, as well, the citation of Hos 2:25 in Rom 9:25–a quotation deriving from Hosea's metaphor of Israel as the unfaithful wife–as a third example.

22. Bernadette J. Brooten, "Paul's Views on the Nature of Women and Female Homoeroticism," in *Immaculate and Powerful: The Female in Sacred Image and Social Reality,* ed.

Clarissa W. Atkinson, Constance H. Buchanan, and Margaret R. Miles (Boston: Beacon, 1985), 61–87.

23. Ibid., 79.

24. The point here was made very clearly for me by a student in an introductory course on early Christian literature who asked, "Why would God punish people by turning them into lesbians and gay men? How do we know that they knew they were being punished?"

25. This argument is frequently made by people attempting in good faith to find some room for tolerance of lesbians and gay men in the contemporary Christian community. A recent example may be found in Beverly Roberts Gaventa, "Romans," *The Women's Bible Commentary,* ed. Carol A. Newsom and Sharon H. Ringe (Louisville, KY: Westminster/John Knox, 1992), 317.

26. See, e.g., Robin Scroggs, *The New Testament and Homosexuality: Contextual Background for Contemporary Debate* (Philadelphia: Fortress, 1983).

27. This position is taken extremely frequently by people trying to separate the "particular" treatment of social issues in biblical literature from the "universal" message of the text. It is an argument made often by some feminists attempting to redeem a patriarchal tradition for their own contemporary practice.

28. Brooten, "Paul's Views," 81.

29. It is perhaps also noteworthy to realize that *hypandros* means not only "under a man, subject to him" but also "feminine" (see Diodorus Siculus 32.10).

30. Dualism has been discussed by many feminists in a variety of contexts. Two recent philosophical works offer, respectively, a historical survey of the relationship of dualism to feminism and a critique of the ongoing dualistic assumptions of feminism: Elizabeth V. Spelman, *Inessential Woman: Problems of Exclusion in Feminist Thought* (Boston: Beacon, 1988); and Judith Butler, *Gender Trouble: Feminism and the Subversion of Identity* (New York: Routledge, 1990).

31. Howard Eilberg-Schwartz, "The Fruitful Cut: Circumcision and Israel's Symbolic Language of Fertility, Descent, and Gender," in *The Savage in Judaism: An Anthropology of Israelite Religion and Ancient Judaism* (Bloomington: Indiana University Press, 1990), 141–76, esp. 147–48.

32. This insight into Paul's hermeneutical maneuver belongs to Daniel Boyarin, whose work on Paul has helped me enormously.

33. My debt to Daniel Boyarin's persuasive analysis of Paul is thoroughgoing. In doing feminist work on Paul as a Jewish thinker, one need also, as Bernadette Brooten has argued on numerous occasions, attend to the specificities of Jewish women's historical experience, as distinct from what Jewish men may have thought about women. See, e.g., her brief and suggestive article, "Jewish Women's History in the Roman Period: A Task for Christian Theology," in *Christians Among Jews and Gentiles: Essays in Honor of Krister Stendahl on His Sixty-Fifth Birthday,* ed. George W. E. Nickelsburg and George W. MacRae (Philadelphia: Fortress, 1986), 22–30.

34. Eilberg-Schwartz, "Fruitful Cut," 145.

35. This section of this essay is beholden to an unpublished essay by Kathleen E. Corley, "Women's Inheritance Rights in Antiquity and Paul's Metaphor of Adoption," which offers an excellent survey of the legal and papyrological evidence for adoption in Greco-Roman antiquity.

36. Corley, "Women's Inheritance," 34.

37. Ibid., 36–37.

38. See Bernadette J. Brooten, "Paul and the Law: How Complete was the Departure?" *Princeton Seminary Bulletin,* Supplement 1 (1990): 71–89.

39. See Orlando Patterson, *Slavery and Social Death: A Comparative Study* (Cambridge, MA: Harvard University Press, 1982). For an analysis of the Pauline use of "slavery" to convey ideas about access to salvation, see Dale B. Martin, *Slavery as Salvation: The Metaphor of Slavery in Pauline Christianity* (New Haven: Yale University Press, 1990).

40. Clarice B. Martin, "Womanist Interpretations of the New Testament: The Quest for Holistic and Inclusive Translation and Interpretation," *Journal of Feminist Studies in Religion* 6:2 (1990): 41–61.

41. Käsemann, *Romans,* 351.

42. Winsome Munro, "Romans 13:1–7: Apartheid's Last Biblical Refuge," *Biblical Theology Bulletin* 20 (1990): 165–67.

43. See Käsemann, *Romans,* 359.

RECOMMENDED READINGS

Brooten, Bernadette J. "Jewish Women's History in the Roman Period: A Task for Christian Theology." In *Christians Among Jews and Gentiles: Essays in Honor of Krister Stendahl on His Sixty-Fifth Birthday,* edited by George W. E. Nickelsburg and George W. MacRae, 22–30. Philadelphia: Fortress Press, 1986.

——. "Junia . . . Outstanding Among the Apostles (Romans 16:7)." In *Women Priests,* edited by Leonard S. Swidler and Arlene Swidler, 141–44. New York: Paulist, 1977.

——. "Paul and the Law: How Complete was the Departure?" *Princeton Seminary Bulletin,* Suppl. 1 (1990): 71–89.

——. "Paul's Views on the Nature of Women and Female Homoeroticism." In *Immaculate and Powerful: The Female in Sacred Image and Social Reality,* edited by Clarissa W. Atkinson, Constance H. Buchanan, and Margaret R. Miles, 61–87. Boston: Beacon, 1985.

Corley, Kathleen E. "Women's Inheritance Rights in Antiquity and Paul's Metaphor of Adoption." Unpublished manuscript. Used with permission.

D'Angelo, Mary Rose. "Women Partners in the New Testament." *Journal of Feminist Studies in Religion* 6:1 (1990): 65–86.

Donfried, Karl P., ed. *The Romans Debate.* Rev. ed. Peabody, MA: Hendrickson, 1991.

Käsemann, Ernst. *Commentary on Romans.* Translated by Geoffrey W. Bromiley. Grand Rapids: Eerdmans, 1980.

Martin, Clarice B. "Womanist Interpretations of the New Testament: The Quest for Holistic and Inclusive Translation and Interpretation." *Journal of Feminist Studies in Religion* 6:2 (1990): 41-61.

Schüssler Fiorenza, Elisabeth. "Missionaries, Apostles, Coworkers: Romans 16 and the Reconstruction of Women's Early Christian History." *Word and World* 6 (1986): 420-33.

———. "The 'Quilting' of Women's History: Phoebe of Cenchreae." In *Embodied Love: Sensuality and Relationship as Feminist Values,* edited by Paula M. Cooey, Sharon A. Farmer, and Mary Ellen Ross, 35–49. San Francisco: Harper & Row, 1987.

❖

Philemon

S. C. WINTER ◆

A SHORT LETTER, neglected in most studies of Pauline theology, Philemon has had enormous practical impact. It has exercised an influence inconsistent with the importance that biblical scholars have accorded it. The Letter to Philemon is one of the seven genuine letters of Paul, and its authenticity has never been contested. In the greeting (v. 1) Paul identifies himself as a prisoner with Timothy, and in vv. 23–24 he names his other companions. Though Philemon comprises a mere twenty-five verses, it exhibits the standard form of a Pauline epistle consisting of the greeting (vv. 1–3), the thanksgiving (vv. 4–7, "I give thanks . . ."), the main body of the letter (vv. 8–22) and the closing greetings and blessing (vv. 23–25). Philemon is often grouped with Philippians, Colossians, and Ephesians as Paul's "prison epistles" because each claims to be written by Paul from prison (Eph 3:1; Phil 1:33; Col 4:10, 18). Paul wrote Philemon at the end of his life, most likely from Caesarea but possibly from Rome.

In Philemon, Paul writes about a slave, Onesimus, whom he has baptized in prison (v. 10b: "whom . . . I have given birth to [as] Onesimus). For centuries biblical scholars and theologians assumed that Onesimus was with Paul because he fled slavery, and that Paul wrote this letter to the slaveowner asking that the newly baptized Onesimus not be punished for his escape when he returned. This interpretation I shall refer to as the "fugitive-slave" interpretation.

Recently, however, the fugitive-slave interpretation has been effectively challenged by the "sent-slave" interpretation. In 1935, John Knox proposed that Paul wrote the letter asking not for forgiveness but for Onesimus himself, for a "gift of" Onesimus.[1] In 1983 I argued that Onesimus did not flee slavery but that the slaveowner sent Onesimus to Paul and his companions in prison as a form of assistance just as the Philippians sent Epaphroditus.[2] I argued further that Paul did not send Onesimus to the slaveowner with the letter but sent only the letter and that Paul wrote to ask that Onesimus be manumitted to work with Paul as a freedman (v. 13: to "serve me in the bonds of the gospel"). This interpretation I shall refer to as the "sent-slave" interpretation.

American Protestant denominations consulted Philemon along with other passages from the Bible when they debated the churches' stance toward slave-holding. They considered Philemon a resource especially for the church's response to the fugitive slave law of 1850, because they thought that the letter was about Paul returning a fugitive slave to a Christian slavemaster. When interpreting Philemon, commentators and ministers generally took for grant-ed that fleeing slavery was inappropriate and un-Christian. In the literature Onesimus was called a "runaway," not a fugitive. Interpretations implied or stated that after Onesimus was baptized he learned to face his responsibilities; that is, he willingly returned to slavery. The Letter to Philemon, interpreted in this way, had tragic consequences and was particularly burdensome for slave women and fugitive slave women.

The commentary that follows is primarily historical-critical and literary. I consider the search for the provenance of a text in all its complexity (that is, when, where, under what circumstances, and by whom a text was written or compiled) to be essential to the study of Christian origins. The scholar's use of "objective" methods always requires judgment, and I employ historical-critical methods and assess others' use of them with an eye to the judgments made in the process. I endeavor to give priority to the literal interpretation of words and phrases within an understanding of the genre of a text. I attempt to re-cover the text to the extent possible but also to elucidate how interpreters' per-spectives have shaped, and sometimes distorted, interpretations of the text. In this vein I shall discuss how the fugitive-slave interpretation of Philemon was indebted to and reinforced stereotypical views of women.

This commentary has four sections: first is a somewhat technical analysis of verses and phrases that reveal where, when, and with what purpose Paul wrote Philemon. In this section I show how proponents of the sent-slave and fugi-tive-slave interpretations view verses and phrases differently. This section explains the reasoning behind the sent-slave interpretation but also illustrates how an interpreter's judgment shapes critical analysis. The second section concerns Paul's view of slavery, and the third explores the impact of inter-preters' stereotypes about women on interpretation of Philemon. The last sec-tion discusses very briefly Onesimus in the early church.

CIRCUMSTANCES AND PURPOSE OF THE LETTER

To understand the circumstances and purpose of the Letter to Philemon we examine the text of the letter for "internal evidence" and study other epistles for "external evidence" or information about related situations.

Why was Onesimus with Paul? Why did Paul write Philemon? Passages from vv. 4–7, 8–14, and 17–20 provide clues. Nowhere in Philemon does Paul state or even suggest that Onesimus escaped from slavery. Indeed, Paul writes as if the slaveowner knows where Onesimus is and even refers obliquely to Onesimus's arrival (vv. 4–7). The few phrases that some commentators take to be allusions to Onesimus's flight can all be construed very differently.

Verses 4–7 comprise what is called the thanksgiving.[3] Customarily in this portion of his letters, Paul will mention recent communication with the individual(s) to whom he is writing and allude to, and thereby introduce, the main points of the letter. In Phlm 5 Paul writes of "hearing of your love and faith," presumably from Onesimus. He praises the slaveowner's "participation" or "sharing" (*koinōnia*), that is, for sending Onesimus to Paul and his companions in prison. Paul thus introduces the request that will be the main topic of the letter, the request to keep Onesimus. As a prisoner in antiquity, Paul would have been required to arrange to obtain his own food and supplies. In another prison epistle Paul thanks the Philippians for sending Epaphroditus to assist him.

In v. 7 "refreshment" and "joy" refer to Onesimus's arrival among the prisoners. Paul writes: "I received [much joy and comfort] and the hearts . . . have taken rest through you." The Greek word translated "hearts" is *splangchna*, literally, "the inward parts," where affections originate. "Have taken rest," a verb in the perfect tense, means "have taken rest and continue to be rested."[4] In v. 12 and v. 20 Paul associates "hearts" and "refresh" with Onesimus again. In v. 12 he writes "heart" affectionately of Onesimus ("he is my very heart"). In v. 20 he recapitulates vv. 8–19 by writing "rest my heart in Christ" meaning "give rest to Onesimus."

Verses 8–20 make up the main body of the letter, and vv. 8–14 and 17–20 are particularly important to this discussion. Verses 8–14 constitute a single, unusually constructed sentence. Three phrases at the beginning of the sentence are about Paul: "whereas in Christ I have boldness to command"; "being an old man . . ."; and "being now a prisoner . . . ." Three relative clauses at the end of the sentence concern Onesimus: "whom I have given birth to . . ."; "whose case I am referring . . ."; and "whom I would like to keep . . . ." Such sentence construction is found in petitions before a court of law, in which the first group of phrases would serve to identify the petitioner and his or her grounds for petition and the last group would identify the object of the petition. A number of words and phrases in vv. 8–14 and 17–20 can have legal or commercial meaning. Because the main body of Philemon takes the form of a petition before a court, we may appropriately take other words and phrases here in their legal sense.

Philemon 10a, "I ask you for my child," constitutes Paul's request. He chooses the phrase that is usual in petitions, "ask for something" (*parakalō peri tinos*), where the noun following "for" is the object of the request. Employing this legal language, Paul asks *for [a gift of] Onesimus*, that is, to keep him. A second phrase, "whose case I am referring to you" (v. 12a), also formulated in legal language, clarifies Paul's purpose. The verb translated "refer" means literally "send up" or "remit" (Greek *anapempō*). It is used for "sending up" in the courts, that is, referring to the proper legal authority. We find the same verb in Luke's account of Jesus' trial (Luke 23:7, 11) and in the Acts account of Paul's trial (Acts 25:21). In Phlm 13–14 Paul explains his motivation. He writes "whom I *would like* to keep for service in prison but I do not wish to do anything without permission," and implies "therefore I am writing to ask your permission."

With vv. 17–20 Paul amplifies his request. He identifies himself with Onesimus because he asks that the slaveowner "accept him [Onesimus] as me" (v. 17). The verb "accept" (Greek *proslambanomai*) can mean "admit," "take to oneself." In Rom 14:1, 3 and Rom 15:7 Paul employs this verb in the sense of "accept into the Christian community." Then Paul underscores his request that the slaveowner accept Onesimus by agreeing to take on Onesimus's financial obligations himself: "If he has wronged you in the eyes of the law or owes you anything, charge it to my account (vv. 18–20). Paul himself will be responsible: "I, Paul, write this with my own hand: I will pay damages." Onesimus may have been in debt to the slaveowner and would need to clear these debts if he was leaving. Paul's statement in v. 19 would have been legally binding as a promissory note. The condition is an unreal condition. As Clarice Martin points out, the statement makes Paul's promise emphatic and does not suggest that Onesimus injured his owner.[5]

To summarize, Paul writes to ask the slaveowner to allow him to keep Onesimus. The reference to clearing debts shows that Paul wants Onesimus to sever his ties with the household, for which Onesimus must be freed. Furthermore, in v. 21, "knowing that you will do even more," Paul hints that the slaveowner should pay the manumission tax, the cost of freeing his slave.

Paul writes nothing explicit about how Onesimus came to be with him in prison. Paul nowhere states that Onesimus fled, that the slaveowner should have compassion and forgive Onesimus, or even that Onesimus is returning. The fugitive-slave interpretation understands "he has been separated from you" (v. 15) to be an allusion to Onesimus's escape. But in fact "he has been separated" says only the obvious, that Onesimus is not with the slaveowner, without explaining how this separation came about. Some commentators also interpret the reference to debts in vv. 18–19 to mean that Onesimus stole something from the slaveowner and then fled, and sometimes that "formerly useless" (v. 11) alludes to Onesimus's theft.

That Philemon contains no clear explanation of how Onesimus came to be with Paul becomes especially problematic when we try to interpret the thanksgiving of the letter. The thanksgiving of a Hellenistic letter (Phlm 4–7) should allude to previous contact with the letter's recipient and should introduce the main topics of the letter. If Onesimus fled slavery, Paul would mention the arrival of the slave in the thanksgiving. To explain why Paul does not describe Onesimus's arrival, some commentators posit a previous letter that conveyed the information. But in Philemon Paul alludes to no other correspondence.

The thanksgiving of Philemon, according to the fugitive-slave interpretation, also fails to fulfill its second function, that is, to introduce the main topics of the letter. For the fugitive-slave interpretation these are a request for forgiveness and compassion for Onesimus and admonitions concerning his return to the owner's household. Verses 4–7 are difficult to explicate with the assumptions of the fugitive-slave interpretation, as many commentators point out.

Regarding vv. 8–14, the fugitive-slave interpretation fails to take into account the legal form and technical language. "I ask you for" (v. 10) is not translated as a legal request for a gift of Onesimus but is translated, "I ask you *on behalf of*" or "*concerning* Onesimus." This translation, though grammatically possible, is weak, because *what* Paul asks on behalf of or concerning Onesimus is not stated. In other letters, when Paul writes "I ask on behalf of" (Greek *parakalō hyper*), he specifies what he is asking.

With the fugitive-slave interpretation, therefore, one must look further along in the letter to find Paul's request. Some maintain that "I ask you for" implies "I ask you for . . . that you will accept him without punishing him for his flight." Some read "I ask you for" together with v. 18 as "I ask you for . . . [that you will] "receive him as me." But interpreting "receive him as me" as an admonition to welcome Onesimus back into the household, as the fugitive-slave interpretation requires, is difficult for two reasons. First, taking the verb "receive" (Greek *proslambanomai*) in the concrete sense of "welcome back into the household" is problematic. Ordinarily *proslambanomai* would not have this connotation, and Paul does not use it elsewhere with this meaning. In Rom 14:3 Paul uses *proslambanomai* in the abstract sense of "accept." God "receives" (accepts). Similarly in Rom 15:7 Christ "receives." Conversely, Paul employs a different verb in Philippians to express "receive" in the concrete sense of "welcome back." In Phil 2:29 Paul asks that Epaphroditus be "welcomed back" with *prosdechomai*, literally, "receive hospitably." Also, "receive him as me" makes a weak admonition for Onesimus's reception, because it is vague and therefore uncharacteristic for Paul. Elsewhere we find Paul giving much more detailed instructions for hospitable welcome (e.g., Rom 16:1–2; Phil 2:29). In Philemon, Paul even mentions his own possible visit more explicitly than a return of Onesimus, writing "prepare a guest room for me" (v. 22).

It is claimed that vv. 13–14 imply that Paul sends Onesimus back. The fugitive-slave interpretation translates, "[Onesimus] whom I *would have liked* to keep . . . but I would not wish . . . without your consent" with the implication "therefore I am sending him back." But the conditional sentence in vv. 13–14 is more accurately translated "whom I *would like* . . . but I would not wish . . . without your consent" with the implication "therefore I am writing to obtain your consent to keep him with me."

Finally, the fugitive-slave and sent-slave interpretations differ regarding the translation of the verb *anapempō* ("send back" or "refer") in v. 12. According to the fugitive-slave interpretation, the phrase is translated "whom I am sending back to you." According to the sent-slave interpretation, Paul uses the verb in its legal sense of "refer a case," so the phrase is "whose case I am referring to you." In Paul's time "send back" in the concrete sense of "send a person or thing back somewhere" was not the expected meaning for *anapempō*.

To summarize, the fugitive-slave interpretation requires reading a number of words and phrases in a manner different from Paul's customary usage. The substance of the fugitive-slave interpretation is that Onesimus fled and that Paul asks forgiveness for Onesimus. Neither of these, however, is explicit in the letter, though the fugitive-slave interpretation claims that they are implied. Understanding the same words and phrases according to the sent-slave interpretation is more consistent with Paul's usage and that of other first-century writings. According to the sent-slave interpretation, the thanksgiving of the letter functions as it should in a Hellenistic letter, and the petition form of vv. 8–14 becomes evident. The sent-slave interpretation, therefore, appears stronger both philologically and form-critically. Commentators' attempts to harmonize verbal correspondences and an essentially identical cast of characters in Philemon and the letter to Colossians have played a primary role both in the origin and in the persistence of the fugitive slave interpretation.

PHILEMON AND PAUL'S VIEW OF SLAVERY AND SOCIAL EQUALITY

Paul offers an ideal of equality in the baptismal formula of Gal 3:28 and partially in the parallel 1 Cor 12:12–13. How Paul expected the ideal to be carried out among Christians and what, for Paul, it meant for those not "in Christ" are unclear. The Letter to Philemon has been peripheral to scholarly discussions of these questions because it was thought to support slavery, if conditionally.

Roman law in Paul's time distinguished the free person, the slave who was the property of another person, and the ex-slave (called freedperson). Slaves lived under varying conditions but invariably possessed almost no rights, could not contract legal marriage, and had no rights over their children. Manumission was formal or informal. In Philemon, Paul is concerned with formal manumission, which required that the owner pay a manumission tax—hence, Paul's discussion of money in vv. 17–21. The freed slave acquired civil rights, proof of his or her status and could eventually become a citizen. The freed slave retained legal obligations to the former owner.

Two passages in Philemon, vv. 15–16 and 17–20, reveal why Paul rejects slavery for Onesimus. In vv. 15–16, Paul employs theological language, in contrast to his usage in the rest of the letter of the language of law and commerce. Pairs of oppositions in vv. 15–16 signal a shift to eschatological language, that is, language concerning things of the end-time: "for a moment" and "for eternity"; "he has been separated" and "you receive in full"; "no longer as a slave" and "as a brother." In v. 15 "receive in full" (Greek *apechein*) has the legal sense of "receive [a payment] in full and give a receipt for it." By "receive in full . . . for eternity," Paul means receive eternally in Christ. In Christ the slaveowner will fully own Onesimus as a brother. Paul writes "no longer as a slave but surpassing a slave . . . beyond a slave" (Greek *hyper doulon,* sometimes translated "above a slave"). The phrase must mean that slave and brother (Christian) are incompatible. Through baptism Onesimus has undergone a shift in his very being. To paraphrase vv. 15–16, Paul writes that Onesimus has been parted from the slaveowner in this life (for a moment) but the slaveowner now truly possess Onesimus because he possesses him eternally as a brother and *not as a slave.* Paul makes slave and brother mutually exclusive.

Philemon 17–20 reinforces vv. 15–16 ironically. When Paul offers to make good on Onesimus's debts, he depicts his own relationship with the slaveowner in economic terms: "you owe your very self to me." Onesimus's baptism invalidated the ownership institutionalized in slavery. Conversely, Paul baptized the slaveowner and thereby "gave birth" to him. Paul "owns" him in that he owes Paul his life.

When Paul wrote Philemon, he was not "free." "Free" and "freedom" appear nowhere in the letter, and Paul nowhere employs the hierarchical image "slave of Christ" (contrast Phil 1:1). But he makes use of a prison metaphor to a similar end, "the bonds of the gospel" (v. 13). Affirming the concept of "slave," even metaphorically, would have blunted the force of Paul's antithesis between slave and brother in v. 16. For Paul, slave and brother are incompatible. Onesimus is not to be a slave even in the "lord" (v. 16). He is not a "slave of Christ."

Together vv. 15–16 and 17–20 show that Paul would not have deferred to a slaveowner's "rights." On the contrary, according to vv. 15–16 Paul did not recognize the authority of a Christian master over a Christian slave. Among the baptized, slavery is not merely wrong; it is invalid. Philemon 17–20 shows that Paul replaced the relationship between "owner" and "owned" recognized in the Roman legal system with a relationship of indebtedness through parenthood in baptism.

Philemon is about one male slave. Paul's rationale in vv. 15–16 applies equally well to slave women. It is of limited relevance, however, to other forms of inequality or exclusion. Onesimus was with Paul for some time, but Paul requested manumission only after Onesimus's baptism. Paul predicates his argument in vv. 15–16 on Onesimus's being baptized. Presumably unbaptized slaves, whether or not of baptized masters, did not trouble him. The argument in Philemon also has no bearing on religious toleration. We may conclude that Paul let class distinctions be as long as the wealthy contributed to the welfare of the group, as Onesimus's owner did by sending him to Paul in prison.

Paul could have extended the argument that an individual in Christ cannot own another individual in Christ to an argument for equality for free (baptized) women because the law defined women as property. But in Paul's time marriage and family laws that treated women as property of fathers or husbands were largely ignored or circumvented, so Philemon provides no basis for us to extend Paul's support for equality of slave and free to support for equality of male and female.

Two additional points may be made concerning Philemon's bearing on modern feminist concerns. First, Paul greets a woman, Apphia, whom he calls "sister" (v. 2). We may assume that Paul greets her because she was a church leader; thus, Philemon corroborates the evidence from Romans 16; Phil 4:2–3; and 1 Cor 11:2–16 that women held authority in the Pauline churches. Second, Philemon does document that a transformation in relations between individuals occasioned a transformation in social status. In this way Philemon shows that for Paul, if only in a limited sphere, the personal was political.

THE IMPACT OF STEREOTYPES

A perception that Philemon was addressed to a household has subtly reinforced the fugitive-slave interpretation. This perception was motivated by the text but was not solidly justified. The perception persisted because it was based on stereotypical thinking about women—here, that Paul greets a woman, Apphia (v. 2) because she is the wife of one of the men.

In Philemon Paul greets three individuals by name (Philemon, "beloved, fellow worker"; Apphia, "sister"; and Archippus, "our fellow soldier"). He addresses his request to only one of the three, because "you" in the body of the letter is singular (and masculine) except in two verses.[6] (Paul writes plural "you" in v. 22: "you [sg.] prepare . . . your [pl.] prayers . . . released to you [pl.]" and in v. 25 "with your [pl.] spirit.") Even for the greetings in vv. 23–24 Paul employs the singular "you." Most significantly, "your" (v. 2) [church in] "your" house is singular.

Scholars of the Christian Testament have assumed that Apphia, the woman whom Paul greets in v. 2, was the wife of Onesimus's owner, a person of means and presumably the owner of the house where the church met. If, however, Apphia were the wife of the owner of the house, then "your" (house) (v. 2) should be plural. In Rom 16:5 Paul writes "their [Priscilla and Aquila's] house," and Col 4:15 has "her [Nympha's] house." The singular "you" in Philemon shows that only one of the three—Philemon, Apphia, or Archippus—owned the house.

For centuries, however, commentators have envisioned a married couple. They reasoned that Apphia was named because she was the slaveowner's wife and as such would have supervised the household and its slaves. That Paul names three individuals sometimes reinforced this family picture. Some speculated that Archippus was Philemon and Apphia's adult son.

A closer look at the greeting shows that this family picture is a fiction. Paul addresses Apphia and Philemon as "sister" and "fellow worker." He mentions only their connection with the church, not with each other. Paul greets them first and so frames his request as a church matter. The text gives us no clue concerning Apphia's marital status and no reason to suspect that Paul includes her in the greeting because of it. It was taken for granted that Philemon is the one to whom Paul makes his request, until John Knox argued that Paul makes his request to Archippus.[7] Paul calls Archippus "fellow soldier," which means, according to Knox, one who gives material or financial support. Archippus, then, may be the wealthy patron who sent Paul a slave.

Correspondences in cast of characters and language between Philemon and Colossians reinforced the association of Philemon with a household and the traditional ordering of the household. Colossians, very likely written before 80 C.E. by a disciple of Paul, claims to be written by Paul from prison and has significant literary parallels with Philemon.

Philemon's entire cast of characters except for Apphia and Philemon are named in Colossians. A mention of Onesimus (Col 4:9) precedes Colossians' final greetings, and a message to Archippus (4:17) follows them. Indeed, it is Col 4:9 that informs us that Onesimus is from Colossae. Paul closes Philemon with greetings from six individuals, all of whom are named also in the closing greetings of Colossians (4:10–14). Colossians varies the order of the names and adds some descriptions. In Phlm 24 Paul writes simply "Luke," but Col 4:14 has "Luke, the beloved physician." Named in both letters are also Epaphras, whom Paul calls (Phlm 23) "my fellow prisoner" and Mark, Aristarchus, Demas, and Luke, whom Paul calls "my fellow workers." Some of these individuals are known to us. Acts mentions a Macedonian Aristarchus (20:4) traveling with Paul to Jerusalem and then to Rome (19:29; 27:2). Phlm 23–24 should read "Epaphras, my fellow prisoner in Christ, Jesus, Mark, . . ." where "Jesus" is one of Paul's companions—"Jesus who is called Justus" (Col

4:11). Luke, presumably, is the Luke to whom the Gospel of Luke and Acts are attributed; and Mark is the John Mark, who scholars think gave his name to the Gospel of Mark.

The literary and personal references from Philemon were designed to give authority to the later letter, Colossians. Ironically, by borrowing from Philemon, Colossians, which is longer and more theological, was able to overwhelm Philemon. "Tychikus . . . whom I am sending to you . . . with Onesimus . . . who is from you" (Col 4:7–9) gave credence to the fugitive-slave interpretation by "demonstrating" that Paul sent Onesimus back to Colossae. More subtle, perhaps, but equally devastating was the impact of the Household Code. Colossians contains a series of instructions that regulate relations in the household between husband and wife, master and slave, parent and child. Commentators, who already thought that Philemon was about a household because of the greeting to Apphia, probably were influenced by Colossians to think that with Philemon Paul supported the social order regulated by Household Codes. Philemon's placement in the Christian Testament after the Pastoral epistles, which affirm slavery and subordination of women in their own version of the Household Codes, probably subtly reinforced this mistake.

Commentators have also brought the modern concept of the household into interpretation of Philemon. According to modern thinking, the household, the refuge of the wage-earner, constitutes a private sphere whose functions differ sharply from those of the public sphere. Personal and emotional matters belong to the private sphere, and political and economic matters to the public. Christian Testament scholars have viewed Philemon as a "personal" or "private" letter and wondered, for example, why a personal letter would be in the canon. Some write about Paul's "personal" relationship with the slaveowner and how Paul would defer to the latter's "rights" over his slave. These questions have been formulated with the assumption that Paul's personal relationship with the slaveowner belonged to the private sphere and the latter's "rights" over his "property" were a matter for the public sphere. Paul's purely private relationship would not challenge this.

But associating Philemon with the modern concept of household is erroneous and misleading. The Hellenistic household functioned as an economic unit and in no way constituted a private refuge of the wage-earner as nineteenth-century writers envisioned it. Further, Paul writes to an individual who belonged to a house-church, not to a household. Although Philemon concerns relationships between individuals, Paul never treats the relationships as "private" in the modern sense; he employs the language of public discourse in his letter. He writes expecting that a change in a relationship between individuals will carry through to a change in the legal status of one of the individuals.

ONESIMUS

Onesimus deserves more serious attention from scholars. An Onesimus who was bishop of Ephesus is known from letters written by Ignatius, bishop of Antioch, between 98 and 117 C.E. John Knox argued that literary parallels between Philemon and Ignatius's *Ephesians* were too numerous and too close to be accidental. Knox concluded that Onesimus, bishop of Ephesus, was the Onesimus of Philemon. Knox proposed further that Onesimus oversaw the first formal collection of Paul's letters, the core of the Christian Testament. According to Knox, Onesimus included the apparently unimportant Philemon among the letters he collected because of its personal importance.[8]

Aspects of Knox's theory have been legitimately questioned, but the parallels between Ignatius's *Ephesians* and Philemon deserve more attention. It is certainly possible that the Onesimus of Philemon was Onesimus, bishop of Ephesus.

NOTES

1. John Knox, *Philemon among the Letters of Paul* (New York: Abingdon, 1935).

2. The full argument is found in S. C. Winter, "Paul's Letter to Philemon," *New Testament Studies* 33 (1987): 1–15. See also S. C. Winter, "Methodological Observations on a New Interpretation of Paul's Letter to Philemon," *Union Seminary Quarterly Review* 39 (1984): 203–12.

3. The "thanksgiving" is the section of a Hellenistic letter after the greeting and before the main body of the letter. Ordinarily it begins "I give thanks." In the thanksgiving, Paul mentions his most recent contact with the recipient of the letter and alludes to the main points of the letter.

4. The verb is in the perfect tense, one of several Greek past tenses. It expresses a past action whose results extend into the present.

5. Clarice J. Martin, "The Rhetorical Function of Commercial Language in Paul's Letter to Philemon (Verse 18)," in *Persuasive Artistry: Studies in New Testament Rhetoric in Honor of George A. Kennedy,* ed. Duane Watson (Journal for the Study of the New Testament Supplement 50; Sheffield: JSOT Press, 1991), 321–37.

6. The Greek verb distinguishes "you" singular from "you" plural. "You yourself" in v. 19 is a second person masculine singular pronoun.

7. Knox, *Philemon.*

8. Ibid.

RECOMMENDED READINGS

Brown, William W. *Clotel or The President's Daughter.* New York: Univ. Books, Carol Pub. Group, 1989. In this 1853 novel, the author, himself a fugitive slave, depicts vividly and poignantly early nineteenth-century American slavery. Most of the main characters in the novel are women. Brown shows religion's ambiguous position in regard to slavery—as a force for abolition and a support for slavery. Brown depicts the devastating impact of the fugitive slave law of 1850, and the novel's introduction describes this law's impact on the author's own life. This edition includes a biography of the novelist.

Knox, John. *Philemon among the Letters of Paul.* New York: Abingdon, 1935.

Martin, Clarice J. "The *Haustafeln* (Household Codes) in African American Biblical Interpretation: 'Free Slaves' and 'Subordinate Women.' In *Stony the Road We Trod: African American Biblical Interpretation,* edited by Cain Hope Felder, 206–31. Minneapolis: Fortress, 1991. Martin's discussion includes the Household Codes, American slavery, Philemon, and the fugitive slave law.

———. "The Rhetorical Function of Commerical Language in Paul's Letter to Philemon (Verse 18)." In *Persuasive Artistry: Studies in New Testament Rhetoric in Honor of George A. Kennedy,* edited by Duane Watson, 321–37. Journal for the Study of the New Testament Supplement 50. Sheffield: JSOT Press, 1991.

Schenk, Wolfgang. "Der Brief des Paulus an Philemon in den neueren Forschung (1945–1987)." In *Aufstieg und Niedergang der Römischen Welt,* Teil II, *Principät,* 25.4, 3439–95. Berlin and New York: de Gruyter, 1987. A comprehensive review article. Schenk assesses scholarship on Philemon from 1945 to 1987.

Winter, S. C. "Methodological Observations on a New Interpretation of Paul's Letter to Philemon." *Union Seminary Quarterly Review* 39 (1984): 203–12.

———. "Paul's Letter to Philemon." *New Testament Studies* 33 (1987): 1–15.

Colossians

MARY ROSE D'ANGELO ◆

INTRODUCTION

MY INTERPRETIVE METHOD foregrounds the literary and rhetorical strategies of early Christian texts, seeking to gain access to the worlds they construct and reflect, to discover what they conceal and reveal of women's lives, and to delineate how they collude with or challenge patriarchy in their world and my own. I regard canonical texts like Colossians as the official common memories of the Christian communities. Like personal and family memories, they continually change meaning as their context changes. In the light of present experience and of newly retrieved memories, cherished pictures of the past may resurface as elements in a history of abuse, while painful or embarrassing recollections reveal themselves to be a source of liberation and autonomy. So too the import of Christian Testament texts shifts as feminist analysis examines them in light of women's experience and historical inquiry sets them in a panorama of the ancient world that constantly changes in the wake of rediscovered and reevaluated sources.

Colossians offers little access to the lives of women in Christian antiquity; its few references to women are overshadowed by longer parallels in Ephesians and other letters. It was passed over entirely by the Revising Committee of the *Woman's Bible*. But Colossians presents a wide variety of exegetical and theological problems that are particularly acute for the feminist interpreter. Two of these require preliminary attention.

First, Colossians appears to be the earliest surviving letter written in the name of Paul. The feminist reader needs to be constantly aware that the author creates "Paul" as both author and hero of the letter. Thus Colossians is the first step in creating the Paul of the Pauline school that produced not only Ephesians but also the Pastorals. If the Paul of the undisputed letters is ambivalent toward the leadership of women, Paul of the Pauline school has attained the reputation of "arch-hater of women."[1] Colossians both promoted

Paul's authority and reformulated his theology, making clear what Paul "really" said. While some of Colossians' reformulations of Pauline motifs could have been used to challenge patterns of domination and subordination, the new theological picture formed by shifts in eschatology, ecclesiology, and parenesis facilitated the enforcement of patriarchy.

The most basic of these shifts may be in eschatology, especially as it is manifested in baptism. Whereas Rom 6:3–5 speaks of baptism as a sharing in Christ's death and new life now, and a pledge of sharing in his resurrection in the future, Colossians speaks of the believer as having died, been raised, and even been exalted *already*; only the revelation of new life is left to the future (Col 2:12–13; 3:1–4). Thus the author seems to urge a realized eschatology very similar to the theological stance that appears to have empowered the women prophets in Corinth (1 Cor 4:8–13).[2] Like 1 Corinthians, Colossians emphasizes the fullness of spiritual riches the addressees already possess. Author and audience share a cosmology expressed in the language of power and of the spiritual powers: power (*dynamis*), rule, (*archē*) authority (*exousia*), thrones (*thronoi*), lordships (*kyriotētes*), the elements (*stoicheia*). But in Colossians, spiritual empowerment is restricted by other theological shifts.

The use of the word *ekklēsia* (church, assembly), the metaphor of the body, and Christology have undergone transformations that seem both to reflect and to enable a more centralized and hierarchical ecclesial structure than is found in the undisputed letters. Paul usually applies *ekklēsia* to the local community (1 Cor 1:2), using the plural or another expression to speak of a broader context (e.g., 1 Cor 11:16; 1 Cor 1:2). Colossians' greetings also use *ekklēsia* to refer to the local community (4:15, 16), but in 1:18 and 24 *ekklēsia* refers to a spiritual and cosmic assembly, a concept that can be so strongly personified that eventually *ekklēsia* appears as a divine being, a heavenly consort of Christ (Eph 5:21–31; 2 *Clem.* 14.2). While Paul compares Christ to a *body* with many members (1 Cor 12:12–31; Rom 12:3–8; 1 Cor 6:12–20), Colossians transmogrifies this fluid metaphor, identifying the exalted Christ as *head over* "the body the church." This phrase reflects the use of "body" for an assembly of individuals in Greek and Roman social and political thought. But Colossians' Christ is head not only over the community as social body but also over the spiritual creation, the powers and principalities (Col 1:18; cf. 2:10, 17–19) and so is the Lord of universal dominion.

Parenetic shifts in Colossians enhance the emerging pattern of domination. Where Paul once hailed the slave as Christ's freedperson, warning that the freedperson is Christ's slave (1 Cor 7:21–23), Colossians requires, "slaves obey your masters." Where Paul warned that both woman and man yield physical autonomy to their sexual partners (1 Cor 7:4), and urged his opinion that a woman is happier if she remain single (1 Cor 7:39), Colossians insists, "Wives, be submissive to your husbands" (3:18).

This raises the second major issue. Colossians appears to be the earliest canonical work to use the Household Code, the pattern of exhortation that christianizes the subordinate status of women, children, and slaves. Despite the letter's claim that there is neither slave nor free in Christ, and its commendation of Onesimus, apparently as a slave freed from a Christian master, its Household Code seems to be particularly concerned with subjugation of slaves. Thus, Colossians raises the question of the ways that slavery and the subjugation of women collaborate in sustaining the patriarchal order.

The Roman imperial model of patriarchy that gave rise to Household Codes clarifies the connection: *patresfamiliae* (heads of families but not necessarily biological fathers) have power over the family, which is defined as wives/women, children, slaves, and property; ultimate power resides in the emperor, who is the father (and savior) of his country (*patria*).[3] The history of slavery in the United States adds another dimension of particular significance to me as a white, U.S. feminist. Ancient patriarchy was classist and imperialist, but the color-based racism that afflicts Western societies appears to have been unknown to antiquity.[4] Because slavery in the United States was largely based on and defended through concepts of race, the Household Codes, which were co-opted to its defense, have functioned in my society in ways that are racist as well as classist and patriarchal. Racism and sexism continue to collaborate in domestic and sexual servitude for women of color from the United States and from the southern countries. African American women have challenged the Paul of the Household Codes.[5] White women like myself, as well as women of color everywhere, must uncover the collaboration of Christian theologies of submission in the history of enslavement and servitude.

COMMENTARY

STRUCTURE

Colossians closely follows the epistolary structure that Paul had made his own. Signature, address, and greeting (1:1–2) are followed by a thanksgiving for the community related to the letter's content (1:3–8) and a prayer for them expresses something that the letter seeks to accomplish (1:9–23). "Paul" next communicates news of himself (1:24–2:5), then turns to the issue he seeks to address (2:6–3:4); this leads into a parenetic section (3:5–4:6); commendations and greetings close the letter (4:7–18). The opening and closing conventions deserve special attention as the strategies by which the author creates an "epistolary situation" as a stage setting for the message.

SIGNATURE (1:1//4:18)

The simple formula identifies Paul as "apostle," associating Timothy with him (Phlm 1; 2 Cor 1:1; Phil 1:1; 1 Thess 1:1). The closing greeting "in my own hand" (4:18) is a claim to authenticity as well as a sign of intimacy; the command, "Remember my bonds," has the force of a voice from beyond the grave.

ADDRESS (1:2) AND COMMENDATIONS AND GREETINGS (4:9–17)

The letter addresses the community as "holy and faithful brothers in Christ." The NRSV translates *adelphoi* as "brothers and sisters," taking the masculine form as generic. The direct command to women in the Household Code indicates that the letter was intended to be read to assemblies including women.

The letter is ostensibly addressed to Colossae, a city in the Lycus valley of Phrygia (now Turkey), but external evidence raises questions about whether a Christian community existed at Colossae when the letter was written.[6] References to Laodicea and Hieropolis (4:13, 16–17) explicitly envision a broader audience, and in 2:1 "Paul" speaks of his contest on behalf of "*all* those who have not seen my face" (2:1). The author might have chosen to address the letter to a nonexistent or defunct community in order both to protect its claims and to broaden its audience. Thus the Colossians provide a "you" (the "implied reader") with whom the (late first or early second century) reader is invited to identify. Recognizing that the Colossians are as much the author's creation as is "Paul" complicates the problem of the "conflict" or "heresy" supposedly active in Colossae (see below).

In creating the epistolary situation the author borrows the dramatis personae of the letter to Philemon, identifying Epaphras as the community's founder and describing a changed situation. Onesimus appears to have been freed, as Paul entreated in Phlm 13–16. Now a "beloved brother" (Phlm 16; Col 4:9), Onesimus has been ministering to Paul in his bonds and so can provide news of him (Col 4:9; cf. Phlm 13). A new associate, Tychikos, is commended in a way that suggests he is the letter carrier; the commendation might be a sly signature from the real author, who makes a bid for the mantle of Paul among the churches of Asia Minor.[7]

Romans 16, the close of an undisputed letter to a community Paul had not founded, provides an interesting contrast to Colossians. Paul appears to commend a woman letter carrier (16:1–2), and the greetings to missionary laborers in Romans include a significant number of women. Colossians' greetings are *from* Paul's male co-workers and enhance its portrait of Paul; the only person greeted by name is Nympha, a woman patron of a house-church in either

Laodicea or Colossae (4:15). Her name, the only woman's name in the letter, was disguised as a man's in some manuscripts.[8]

THANKSGIVING

The thanksgiving adheres closely to Paul's pattern, foregrounding a positive aspect of the community on which the letter will build its appeal. "Paul" and "Timothy" give thanks for the readers' faith in Christ and their love for the saints. Commending the "Colossians'" hearing and recognition of Epaphras's preaching, "Paul" and "Timothy" describe the gospel as "bearing fruit and abounding" both among the addressees and "in the whole cosmos," perhaps including not only "all [humans] who have not seen [Paul's] face" but also the spiritual powers who dwell in the heavenly places. Thus, the thanksgiving celebrates the readers' spiritual riches as emblematic of the growth of the universal mission.

PRAYER (1:9–23) AND FINAL EXHORTATION TO PRAYER (4:2–6)

"Paul" and "Timothy" pray that the addressees be filled up or fulfilled with the recognition/knowledge of God's will, "bearing fruit and abounding" in "all wisdom and spiritual understanding" (1:9–11). The letter's purpose is largely to communicate this wisdom; the final exhortations (4:2–6) request them to pray to walk in *wisdom* and to *know* how to answer everyone.

The prayer in 1:9–11 modulates into an exhortation to give thanks to the father, who empowered them to share the lot of the "holy ones" in light, having rescued them from "the authority of darkness" and transferred them to the reign of the son of his love. Similar contrasts throughout raise boundaries separating the readers both from their Gentile past and from the "authority of darkness." The strongly gendered language "father" and "reign of his . . . son" presents God as the ultimate ruler and king and establishes the alternative to the "authority of darkness": the divine cosmic imperium of father and son (cf. 2:10; Eph 3:15).[9]

The "son of his love" is described in a hymn which praises Christ in terms drawn from the traditions about divine Wisdom. The structure and original form of the hymn are much debated; it may have originated as a hymn to Sophia, or been formulated as a pre-Christian hymn attributing the characteristics of Wisdom to the divine (male) logos, or emerged only as a Christian hymn. I have attempted to translate as much of vv. 15–20 as can be attributed to Sophia, transposing the pronouns to the feminine gender. The result illustrates the relation of the hymn not only to Jewish wisdom traditions but also to gnostic understandings of the spiritual world:

> She is the image of the unseen God (Gen 1:26–27; Wis 7:26),
> firstborn of all creation (Prov 8:22; Sir 24:9)
> in/by her was created everything
> in the heavens and on earth (Wis 7:22; 9:2–4; Prov 3:19–20; 8:22–30),
> seen and unseen:
> whether thrones or principalities, rules or authorities.
> All things were created through her and for her,
> And she is before all and the all subsists through her;
> she is the head/source of the body the church/assembly;
> she is the beginning/rule,
> that she might be preeminent among all
> because in her the *pleroma* was pleased to dwell,
> and through her to reconcile the all to her
> whether on heaven or on earth.

In this context (as in Col 2:9), *plērōma* refers to the totality of divine reality; in Gnostic materials it designates the totality of spiritual beings and emanations. If Sophia was the original subject of the hymn, it acclaims her because her preeminent role in creation enables her to mediate the reunion of the lesser divine realities (like thrones and prinicipalities, rules and authorities) into one full spiritual reality (*plērōma*). The "church/assembly" (1:18b) here could refer to the assembly of spiritual beings. The description of the cosmos as a body, especially as the body of God, appears in Greek philosophy from Plato on; it also occurs in mythic and magical contexts.[10]

In Colossians the hymn is applied to Christ and is anchored to his history by v. 20b ("making peace through the blood of his cross") and v. 18b ("the firstborn of the dead"; cf. Rev 1:5). "The body the church" is the believing community. Thus, the Christ of Colossians is the incarnation of a divine female persona, but his person hides hers with a male mask.

As the references to the cross and resurrection tie the wisdom hymn to Christ, vv. 21–23 bring it to the addressees' experience. Like the powers, they, as Gentiles, were "alienated and at enmity" with God, but Christ/Wisdom has reconciled them, not now by his preeminence in the spiritual creation but by his humanity, his "fleshly body" and death. "Paul" identifies himself as the minister of the gospel as it is preached to every creature *under heaven;* this phrase may envisage a prior proclamation in the heavenly places.

"PAUL'S" NEWS (1:24–2:5)

"Paul" introduces news of himself, using standard epistolary formulas ("I rejoice," "I want you to know"). Ostensibly reporting on his imprisonment ("my sufferings on your behalf," 1:24), he rearticulates the meaning of Paul's ministry. "Paul" proclaims it his task to fill up God's Word, the hidden mystery, by teaching every human being in all wisdom, imparting "all wealth of fullness of understanding" and "the secret treasure of wisdom and knowledge" (2:2–3; contrast 1 Cor 1:17–2:6). In speaking of "filling up what is lacking in the tribulations of Christ" he seems to envisage not extending the passion but enduring the eschatological trials of bringing the gospel.[11] In contrast to later emphases on the expiatory value of suffering, redemptive value is placed on liberatory struggle rather than on pain-filled submission to an oppressive order. "Paul's" contest (*agōn*, 1:29; 2:1) seems to be an athletic metaphor for preaching (Phil 1:30; 1 Cor 9:25) rather than for martyrdom (2 Tim 4:7). But when "Paul" urges that he is with them "in spirit, though absent in the flesh" (2:5) the conventions of the friendly letter affirm Paul's authority by recalling his martyrdom.

THE PROBLEM IN COLOSSAE? (2:6–3:4)

The central section of the letter addresses the supposed "heresy" or "conflict" in Colossae, which has been variously identified as Gnosticism, esoteric judaizing, magic, adoption of a pagan mystery cult, or some syncretistic mixture of all of these. Here "Paul's" discourse creates an Other ("someone") who might make the readers captive by "philosophy and empty deception according to human tradition, according to the elements of this world" (2:8). "Paul's" accusations and warnings provide the only information about this position. First, he hints at some form of judaizing, warning against those who would judge in matters of "eating or drinking or festivals or new moons or sabbaths" (2:16). Second, he opposes ascetic practices, including abstinence from certain foods and drinks and from sex (vv. 21–23). Third, "Paul" accuses the practitioners of the philosophy of the desire to "be in abnegation and in the worship of angels"; the last phrase appears to mean that they sought to share in angelic worship, like the humans privileged to participate in or behold angelic liturgies in ancient Jewish texts (*Apocalypse of Moses* 15–17; 4Q400–407, 11Q5–6). Fourth, the tradition "Paul" opposes seems to offer access to this angelic worship through visionary experience. One recent study suggests that these objections oppose an explanation of baptism as a revelatory experience, which included putting off the body, ascending on high, beholding heavenly beings, and becoming an angel.[12] This interpretation of baptism emerges full-blown in the third-century Gnostic text *Zostrianos* (*NHC* VII, 1, 132, 9), but may be much older. How widespread the philosophy was, or whether its practitioners saw their "tradition" as different from that of other Christians, is unclear. The supposed Colossian heresy might have been not the position of a specific party but a set of traditions widely affirmed and practiced.

To it "Paul" opposes the tradition he defines as Christ, which he centers in baptism understood as sharing in Christ's death, life, and even heavenly exaltation over every principality and power (2:12–13, 19–20; 3:1–4). "Paul" does not object to the idea that the baptized put off the body or are exalted above the angels and spiritual powers; indeed, these ideas are central to his response, which urges the readers to achieve the understanding for which he prayed (1:9), to know that they have died to (or from) the elements of this world (2:12; 3:1), and to set their minds on what is above (3:2). Nor is there any reason to believe that this stance was less "Christocentric" than Colossians. Rather "Paul's" real objections are to ascetic practice and visionary experience as the means of exaltation, and to the supposed desire to submit to the spiritual and angelic powers. The author's rhetoric links asceticism and the spiritual powers not with heavenly but with earthly and fleshly thought and practices. He characterizes the philosophy as the vain arrogance of a fleshly mind (v. 18), its observances as "merely" the shadow of things to come (v. 17), as human teaching dealing with human and corruptible things that disappear as they are used, so-called wisdom that really only satisfies the flesh (vv. 20–23). He contrasts this with "the body that is of Christ," that is, the true spiritual reality, of which Christ is head (2:19); Christ and the life of the baptized are exalted in the secret heavens.

Three images "Paul" uses to illustrate the effect of baptism deserve attention: spiritual circumcision as putting off the fleshly body (2:11), canceling a debtor's bond (2:14), and stripping the rulers and authorities and displaying them as captives (2:15). These images are likely to have encouraged double consciousness in women and slaves, demanding that they deny their subjected status in the religious realm while submitting to it in the social world. Women attain spiritual circumcision although they cannot be physically circumcised. Slaves (and the free poor) are likely to have stood under literal debtor's bonds. The image of God leading the powers captive in a triumphal procession is a military image; it draws on the custom of displaying particularly eminent captives among the spoils of war. Many slaves, women as well as, perhaps more than men, were captives of war. The image characterizes baptism as assurin g freedom from the powers, in contrast to the "philosophy" that has supposedly made the Colossians captive. But ultimately it is an image of domination.

The letter's first readers need not have felt themselves in need of liberation from the angelic beings and powers; indeed, like Paul and the Corinthians, the addressees are likely to have gloried in claims to live the angelic life and to speak their tongues as well as to behold them and to share their worship. The author of Colossians shows a notable concern for social order. Abstinence from food and sex, sharing in angelic worship and visionary experience may be rejected because these experiences could warrant claims of spiritual authority on the part of women and slaves. Despite "Paul's" emphases on their spiritual riches and fullness, he refrains from urging the readers to be eager for prophecy, tongues, and the other dangerous charismata so dear to both the Corinthians and Paul.

PARENESIS (3:5–4:6)

In Col 3:5–17, baptismal motifs, especially of death and risen life, integrate the parenesis. Vice and virtue lists are combined with the pronouncement of death to the old life, the body image, clothing imagery, the new humanity, and the overcoming of division. The first vice list (3:5) is fairly conventional (cf. Gal 5:19–20; 1 Cor 6:9–10); the second, introduced with the command to put off the old humanity, focuses on sins of hostility, especially in speech (3:8–9). The corresponding command to put on the new humanity is sometimes seen as deriving from the same ancient baptismal formula as Gal 3:28; it appears to refer to Gen 1:27 (in the image of God [God] created [the human being]) and lists the abolition of distinctions, without the pair "male and female." Some scholars suggest that this pair has been deleted because of conflict with the Household Code.[13] But "no slave or free" conflicts as strongly with the code's counsels to slaves and masters (3:22–4:1). Gal 3:28, 1 Cor 12:12–13, and Col 3:9–11 may develop different preexisting baptismal proclamations.

The Household Code (3:18–4:1) is a pattern of exhortation derived from a tradition of philosophical politics already articulated by Aristotle that became the basis of the imperial social policies expressed in the Augustan social legislation.[14] The threat of denunciation and persecution played a role in causing Christians like this author to call for accommodation to the gendered mores the empire endorsed (cf. 1 Pet 2:13–3:6; 1 Tim 2:1–15; Justin, *2 Apol.* 2). But such Christians shared the mores the codes expressed. The codes are formal units; reading only a portion (e.g., Col 3:12–21 in *Roman Lectionary* 17, the feast of the Holy Family) conceals the ideological link between the submission of women and children and slavery.

Col 3:18–4:1 is shorter and less theologized than Ephesians' revision of it. The subordinate members of the pair are addressed first; advice to husbands, fathers, and masters complements the counsel to the subjected. Although women owned slaves and had limited authority over children, the exhortation does not address women as mothers or slave owners; its concern is with the authority of the husband/father/master. This concern emerges in the repetition of *kyrios,* usually translated "Lord," as a deliberately ambiguous title for Christ. The usual title for any male superior, *kyrios* could designate the master of a slave, the husband or guardian (*tutor*) of a woman, or the head of a family (cf. 1 Pet 3:6; Matt 21:19).[15]

Women/wives (3:18) are commanded to submit to [their] husbands/men. The use of "submit" rather than "obey" may distinguish women from children and slaves. But 1 Pet 3:5–6 uses "submit" and "obey" as synonyms. The only explanation given for the command is that it is fitting "in/to the lord." Here "lord" may refer both to Christ and to a husband (cf. 2 Pet 3:6). Husbands are exhorted to love their wives (3:19) and not to "be embittered" against them. Like other moralists of the period, the author may assume that wives are often the convenient recipients of anger aroused by others (see Plutarch *De cohibenda ira* 8, 457A).

Children are required to obey parents (not just "fathers"; 3:20); this obedience is "in/ to the lord"; fathers (only) are warned against provoking and discouraging their children (3:21).

The most extensive address is to slaves (3:22–25). These counsels reflect ancient conventions about the character of slaves: slaves attempt to ingratiate themselves (3:22, 23), to defraud (*adikein*) their masters, and to evade punishment by exploiting their masters' favoritism (v. 25).[16] Similar stereotypes about slaves in the United States are sometimes interpreted as evidence that slavery produces these characteristics in the enslaved.[17] Since direct access to the experience of slaves is (at best) limited for those who live in the United States today and nonexistent for antiquity, it is safer to conclude that slaveholding produces similar perceptions of the enslaved on the part of the ruling class.

Slaves are exhorted to regard their labor as done for the lord (Christ/master), looking for a reward from God, rather than expecting favoritism from their human lords/masters. The reminder of the recompense/inheritance from the master/Lord who shows no favoritism reinforces these counsels. This warning may also apply to the masters who are commanded to be just and impartial with their slaves and are reminded that they also have a Lord/master in heaven. Thus the command, "serve the Master/Lord Christ" (3:24), though addressed to slaves, in fact summarizes the whole code. Despite its brevity and simplicity, Colossians' code is not merely conventional exhortation but the integral consequence of Christ's universal lordship. If that universal lordship liberates from the heavenly powers and authorities, it nevertheless affirms the patriarchal rule of the masters of this world.

CONCLUSIONS

Scholars who see real opponents of "Paul" in Colossae sometimes view them as proto-Gnostic and Colossians as anti-Gnostic. But Colossians' resistance to the powers, rules, and authorities is shared not only by the Paul of the undisputed letters but also by some second- and third-century Gnostic texts like *Hypostasis of the Archons* (NHC II, 86,20–97,23). This insistence on resistance, together with Colossians' celebration of the spiritual riches the addressees enjoy, its concern with wisdom and discernment and the wisdom hymn, could have combined into a message of empowerment. But these elements have been redirected to proscribe the addressees visionary and ascetic yearnings and to submit them to the social order.

As a first step in the creation of the Pauline school, Colossians provides much material that resurfaces in heightened form in the Pastorals. The Household Code that appears here for the first time provides the format for the entire first letter to Timothy. Colossians' warnings against sexual and food asceticism reappear (1 Tim 4:1–2, 23). The call for the submission of women is enhanced by explicit misogyny in the Pastorals (2 Tim 3:6–7). The only leadership role Colossians affirms for women is patronage of a house-church (4:15); the Pastorals explicitly exclude women from any leadership role (1 Tim 2:8–15; 5:3–16). The prophetic, visionary, and charismatic gifts so valued by Paul and the Corinthians, but avoided or ridiculed by Colossians, are carefully channeled in the Pastorals by the laying on of hands.

Thus, Colossians is a step toward a Christianity that became increasingly restrictive and even abusive for women, children, and slaves; the authority of the Household Codes long endorsed both slavery and battering, and Colossians' theology helped to christianize social patterns of domination and subordination. The codes should be read liturgically or cited as scripture *only* to be challenged. But no portion of Colossians can be read as "the word of God" as if it were detached from the Household Codes, or from the cosmic vision and theological rationale that undergird them. Nor can the problems of its theology and history be addressed by excising Colossians from the canon, or from Christian memory. The transformations it began must be held in memory as true if painful inheritances from the common origins of Christians.

NOTES

1. Mary Daly, *Pure Lust: Elemental Feminist Philosophy* (Boston: Beacon, 1984), 8, 178; she rejects distinctions between the undisputed letters and the Pauline school.

2. See Antoinette Clark Wire, *The Corinthian Women Prophets: A Reconstruction through Paul's Rhetoric* (Minneapolis: Fortress, 1990).

3. See Ulpian, *Digest 50*, 16.195, 2 i, in Jane F. Gardner and Thomas Wiedemann, *The Roman Household: A Sourcebook* (London and New York: Routledge, 1991), 3–4.

4. Frank M. Snowden, Jr., *Before Color Prejudice: The Ancient View of Blacks* (Cambridge, MA: Harvard University Press, 1983).

5. Clarice J. Martin, "Womanist Interpretation of the New Testament: The Quest for Holistic and Inclusive Translation and Interpretation," *Journal of Feminist Studies in Religion* 6 (1990): 41–62; eadem, "The Haustafeln (Household Codes) in African American Biblical Interpretation: 'Free Slaves' and 'Subordinate Women,'" in *Stony the Road We Trod: African American Biblical Interpretation,* ed. C. H. Felder (Minneapolis: Fortress, 1991), 206–31.

6. Colossae appears to have been devastated in by an earthquake in 60–61 C.E. Colossians is the only evidence of an early Christian community at Colossae. Revelation 2–3 includes no oracle to Colossae; no internal evidence identifies Philemon with Colossae.

7. Tychikos appears only in later material: Acts 20:4; Eph 6:21; 2 Tim 4:12; Titus 3:12.

8. "Nympha" is attested by Vaticanus, 1739, the Harclean Syriac and the Sahidic, and some

Greek minuscules. The change to masculine (circumflex on the second syllable and a change of pronoun from "her" to "his") occurs in Claromontanus among many other texts. Others, including Sinaiticus and Alexandrinus, give the pronoun as "their." See K. Aland et al. *Novum Testamentum Graecum* (26th ed., 8th printing; Stuttgart: Deutsche Bibelgesellschaft, 1985).

9. On father and king as divine titles, and their relation in early Christian theology, see M. R. D'Angelo, "*Abba* and 'Father': Imperial Theology and the Traditions about Jesus," *Journal of Biblical Literature* 111 (1992): 611–30; eadem, "Theology in Mark and Q: *Abba* and 'Father' in Context," *Harvard Theological Review* 85 (1992): 149–74.

10. E. Lohse, *A Commentary on the Letters to the Colossians and to Philemon,* trans. W. R. Poehlmann and R. J. Karris (Hermeneia; Philadelphia: Fortress, 1971), 53–54, nn. 149–61.

11. On the meaning of *thlipsis,* see Maurya P. Horgan, "Colossians," in *The New Jerome Biblical Commentary,* ed. Roland E. Murphy, Joseph A. Fitzmyer, Raymond E. Brown (Englewood Cliffs, NJ: Prentice Hall, 1990), 880; Lohse, *Commentary,* 69–72.

12. Harold A. Attridge, "On Becoming an Angel," *Religious Propaganda and Missionary Competition in the New Testament World: Essays Honoring Dieter Georgi,* ed. Lukas Bormann, Kelly Del Tredici, and Angela Standhartinger (Leiden: E. J. Brill, 1994), 481–98.

13. E. Elizabeth Johnson, "Colossians," in *The Women's Bible Commentary,* ed. Carol Newsom and Sharon Ringe (Louisville: Westminster/John Knox, 1991), 347.

14. See David L. Balch, *Let Wives Be Submissive: The Domestic Code in 1 Peter* (SBL Monograph Series 26; Chico, CA: Scholars Press, 1981), 32–49. Note especially Arius Didymus, the household philosopher of Augustus. See also E. Schüssler Fiorenza, *In Memory of Her: A Feminist Theological Reconstruction of Christian Origins* (New York: Crossroad, 1983), 251–59; E. Elizabeth Johnson, "Ephesians," in *The Women's Bible Commentary,* ed. Carol Newsom and Sharon Ringe (Louisville: Westminster/John Knox, 1992), 340.

15. Henry George Liddell, Robert Scott, Henry Stuart Jones and Roderick McKenzie, *A Greek-English Lexicon* (9th ed; Oxford: Clarendon Press, 1968), s.v. *kyrios* B 1.

16. See Keith R. Bradley, *Slaves and Masters in the Roman Empire: A Study in Social Control* (New York and Oxford: Oxford University Press, 1987), 26–31, 343, 35. Note especially the accusation of *fraus;* Thomas Wiedemann, "Moral Inferiors," in *Greek and Roman Slavery* (London: Routledge, 1981), 61–77.

17. Keith Hopkins, *Conquerors and Slaves* (Sociological Studies in Roman History 1; Cambridge: Cambridge University Press, 1978), 120–22.

RECOMMENDED READINGS

Horgan, Maurya P. "Colossians." In *The New Jerome Biblical Commentary,* edited by Roland E. Murphy, Joseph A. Fitzmyer, Raymond E. Brown. Englewood Cliffs, NJ: Prentice Hall, 1990.

Johnson, E. Elizabeth. "Colossians." In *The Women's Bible Commentary,* edited by Carol Newsom and Sharon Ringe, 346–48. Louisville: Westminster/John Knox, 1991.

Lohse, Eduard. *A Commentary on the Letters to the Colossians and to Philemon.* Translated by William R. Poehlmann and Robert J. Karris. Hermeneia. Philadelphia: Fortress, 1971.

Martin, Clarice J. "The *Haustafeln* (Household Codes) in African American Biblical Interpretation: 'Free Slaves' and 'Subordinate Women.'" In *Stony the Road We Trod: African American Biblical Interpretation,* edited by Cain Hope Felder, 206–31. Minneapolis: Fortress, 1991.

———. "Womanist Interpretation of the New Testament: The Quest for Holistic and Inclusive Translation and Interpretation." *Journal of Feminist Studies in Religion* 6 (1990): 41–62.

Schüssler Fiorenza, Elisabeth. *In Memory of Her: A Feminist Theological Reconstruction of Christian Origins.* New York: Crossroad, 1983. Pp. 243–84.

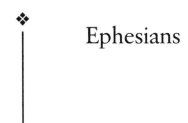

Ephesians

Sarah J. Tanzer ◆

FEMINIST FRAMEWORK

ALTHOUGH I THINK of myself primarily as a historian, this feminist commentary on Ephesians pairs a feminist historical perspective with feminist theological reflection, not always a comfortable marriage of convenience for me. As a historian, I am aware that the Christian Testament texts provide, at best, meager sources for women's history, while they offer considerable evidence of male Christian Testament writers' attitudes toward women. This is certainly true of Ephesians. If we are genuinely interested in women's history, the search must be broadened beyond the Christian Testament canon, as many feminist scholars have recognized, and as the table of contents to this volume attests.

I have focused this commentary on the household code in Eph 5:22–6:9 and even more precisely on the first part of that code (5:22–33), which offers exhortations to wives and husbands on Christian marriage. Throughout history the household codes and other key biblical texts have played a formative role in silencing or marginalizing women in the church.[1] Still, this may seem a very narrow frame—as indeed it is. I have a decided preference for feminist critical approaches that treat of a whole text rather than the text-within-the-text approach; however, given the limitations of space, the household code is the inescapable focus of any feminist commentary on Ephesians, because it is the only passage in Ephesians which explicitly addresses women and is about women.

As a feminist historian, I will briefly sketch the historical setting of early Christian households, the status of women in the first century, what we know about the form and social background of the household code, and whether the household code can be said to describe or prescribe for early Christian women. Turning to feminist theological reflection, I will be concerned with the possible meanings of this text in a Christian faith community and how—if it is viewed as an authoritative text—it has consequences for the status of women in the church. I will also exercise a "hermeneutics of suspicion,"[2] not only of the Ephesians passage but also of the scholarship of those who have written on this text. As a Jewish feminist, I have a sensitive ear and sometimes a suspicious mind when I encounter explanations for difficult Christian Testament texts that seem inadvertently to shift responsibility for the ideas found in those texts from Christianity to Greco-Roman society or to early Judaism.

INTRODUCTION

A cursory glance at the overall character and the formal characteristics of Ephesians gives us clues as to its complex nature and the enigmatic questions it poses to all exegetes. What strikes one immediately is the cosmological framing of Ephesians, especially strong in chap. 1 and again in 6:10–20. As Luke Johnson has noted, it places "human freedom within the context of a struggle for the cosmos. Human alienation from God is expressed by an enslavement to forces fighting God. Alienation from God is also manifested in hostility and alienation between human beings."[3] This alienation between human beings is expressed as the division that has previously existed between Jews and Gentiles. What Ephesians reveals is God's mysterious plan to end this alienation, both the alienation between God and humanity (heaven versus earth) and the alienation between human beings as exemplified by the division between Jews and Gentiles (earth versus earth). The means of reconciliation is Jesus Christ, whose death has made possible the unity of "all things in him, things in heaven and things on earth" (1:10). The sign of reconciliation is the unity of the church. Furthermore, for the church to be the symbol of God's reconciliation at work on earth, the church must respond to its call to exemplify unity. While Ephesians as a whole works within this double cosmological framework of heavenly/earthly and earthly/earthly, most of the text within that framework is given over to the earthly/earthly dimensions of God's mysterious plan for reconciliation: the unity of Jew and Gentile and the exhortation to the church to make that unity manifest in its life.

In form, Ephesians is framed as a letter. It begins with an address and greetings (1:1–2) and concludes with a personal message to the addressees (6:21–22), final greetings and a benediction (6:23–24). Set within this letter frame, however, are two main parts which are for the most part unlike a letter: The first part, 1:3–3:21, is about the gift of God through Jesus Christ by which the "dividing wall of hostility" (2:14) between Jews and Gentiles has been brought down. It is the revelation of God's mysterious plan "set forth in Christ as a plan for the fullness of time, to unite all things in him, things in heaven and things on earth" (1:10). The second part, 4:1–6:20, is hortatory, exhorting

Christians to live the life to which they have been called in response to the revelation of God's plan for unity. It calls them away from the life of the Gentiles, a life alienated from God. Finally, in more cosmic language it exhorts them to "put on the whole armor of God" (6:11) in order to stand strong "against the world rulers of this present darkness, against the spiritual hosts of wickedness in the heavenly places" (6:12).

A key theme that runs throughout both parts of Ephesians is the unity of Christians, whether as God's mysterious plan in the first part or as the unity to which they are called (4:4–6: ". . . one body, and one spirit, . . . one hope . . . one Lord, one faith, one baptism, one God and Father . . .") in the second part. There is also an already/not yet eschatological thread that weaves its way through both parts of Ephesians. The "already" is most obvious in the unity made possible through the death of Jesus, in the way in which the Gentiles who were once "far off have been brought near" (2:13–14); the "not yet" is most apparent in ". . . the promised Holy Spirit, which is the *guarantee* of our inheritance *until* we acquire possession of it . . ." (1:13–14) and in the preparation for the transformation of the cosmos (6:10–20: "that you may be able to withstand in the evil day").

Clues to the overall purpose of Ephesians can already be discerned in what is written above about the double cosmological framework (heavenly/earthly and earthly/earthly) and the already/not yet eschatology. It is precisely because the reconciliation between God and humanity has already taken place in Christ that Christians have the ability to stand "against the principalities, against the powers, against the world rulers of this present darkness, against the spiritual hosts of wickedness in the heavenly places" (6:12). The ethical behavior to which the second half of Ephesians calls its audience would not be possible apart from the power of God.[4] The focus, then, is on the ethical behavior and on the transformation that needs to happen in the earthly realm. There seem to be two basic foci: "the idea of the internal unity of the congregation which is intensified by the motif of the one Church founded by Jesus Christ and inseparably bound to him; and the concept of a commitment, growing out of God's calling, to a distinctly Christian way of life which should be distinguished from and contrasted to the unchristian life-style of the environment."[5] Clearly, the prevalence of language of belonging and separation, remembrance and exhortation serves these two foci, as does the development throughout of a single idea, the church as the body of Christ.[6]

Space considerations preclude an exploration of many of the other important introductory issues relating to Ephesians: its background in the history of ideas, the problems involved in deciding for whom Ephesians may have originally been intended, the question of Pauline authenticity,[7] the Colossians/Ephesians relationship, and arguments surrounding a possible date of composition. To obtain a grasp of these issues the reader is encouraged to survey the

wealth of commentaries on Ephesians as well as the more general Christian
Testament introductions.

SOCIAL BACKGROUND FOR THE HOUSEHOLD CODE

As we turn to the household code (*Haustafel*) of Eph 5:22–6:9, it is useful
to know something about the nature of households in Roman society and the
central role of the house-church in early Christianity. Peter Lampe points to
three criteria that seem to define a household in Roman society: a hierarchical
order-obedience structure, economic dependency, and marriage.[8] "A 'household' comprised (a) those persons who were economically dependent on one
master to whose authority they felt subjected (this could include children,
even adult sons, slaves, freedpersons, and 'clients'), and (b) the spouses of all
these persons, including the master's own spouse, as long as these couples
lived together."[9] However, there is a certain amount of legal fiction involved in
the great authority of the paterfamilias.[10] It did not represent an actuality so
much as an ideal.

What does this definition of the Roman household tell us about the status
of a married woman? Here caution is necessary. The Roman Empire was not
monolithic—not even in regard to the status of women. What was true about
women in the east was not necessarily true of women in the west. In the
Roman Empire the patriarchal household coexisted (though perhaps uneasily)
with emancipatory ideas about women that allowed for greater freedom and
independence of women. As it was, women could become the hierarchical
heads of households. Though this usually occurred after their husbands'
deaths, inscriptions from Asia Minor point to both widows and married
women as heads of households.[11] As for economic status, it was possible
through inheritance for the wife of a head of a household to be economically
independent from her husband.[12] Nevertheless, as the term "paterfamilias"
implies, the head of a Roman household was more likely to be the husband.
The significance of the Roman household becomes clear to the modern reader
only when one realizes that many of the major tasks and needs that are
addressed today by government and by society at large were in Roman society
addressed by private households: social services, education, work and economic production, and numerous juridical functions.[13]

The household was important in shaping early Christianity, which began as
a household movement:[14] in the first two centuries C.E., believers relied exclusively on private households to provide the meeting spaces for Christian communities, or "house-churches."[15] The private household served as a model for
the local church and eventually for the universal church. The terminology used
to describe the functions and relationships within the private household

became the terminology used to describe the functions and relationships within the church and between Christians and God.[16] In other words, the private household provided more than the physical meeting space for the early church; it provided the conceptual foundation as well—hence, the household code.[17]

That part of the Ephesians' household code which focuses on the relationship between Christian wives and husbands (5:22–33) and the other Christian Testament household codes (e.g., Col 3:18–4:1, and 1 Pet 2:18–3:7[18]) causes one to wonder whether the views espoused might be rooted in the status of women in the first century or perhaps in the views of Paul. Where do these views come from? Answers to this question typically highlight the status of women in the first century as congruent with the household codes and then place the "blame" for the status of women in the first century either on the Jews or on the pagans.

Typifying the "blame it on the Jews" stance is a method of argument that lifts later rabbinic texts out of context to paint a portrait of Judaism that is both specific and monolithic. This overgeneralization leads to the conclusion that the position of the woman in the first-century Jewish home was one of marked subordination.[19] Judith Plaskow refers to this as "the rule of antithesis," in which Jesus and Paul are portrayed as men who stand over against their Jewish upbringings and environments by Christian interpreters who have selected from rabbinic texts the most negative and restrictive statements about women and have suggested that these represent the reality of Jewish women's lives in the first century.[20] Jesus' positive attitudes toward women are then "seen as evidence of his distance from his 'Jewish background' rather than as evidence of Jewish attitudes and practices."[21] Paul is divided into two: his more egalitarian views of women are labeled uniquely Christian or derived from his Hellenistic background; his views that advocate a subordinate position for women are termed a product of his Judaism.[22] This portrayal of early Jewish women, utilizing texts that have been uprooted from their historical contexts and from which all the progressive elements have been cleansed, should be viewed with suspicion from the outset.[23] Drawing almost exclusively on rabbinic texts makes the portrayal of early Jewish women even more questionable for a number of reasons: (1) The rabbis came to power only after 70 C.E. The Mishna dates from ca. 200 C.E., and the Talmud began to be redacted around 500 C.E.—hardly adequate for providing a view of first-century Jewish women! (2) Rabbinic texts about women are "prescriptive" rather than descriptive of early Jewish women's reality;[24] it is only in later centuries that rabbinic texts achieve a kind of authoritative, foundational status for what would become the dominant kind of Judaism.[25] (3) Rabbinic texts do not treat all women alike. They are particularly concerned with "those occasions when women threatened to violate the categories of society and the cosmos so carefully constructed by the rabbis."[26] They give us little information on Jewish women's religious practices; this is not their interest. That the rabbinic texts as typically interpreted[27] do not accurately reflect the great range of activities and leadership roles undertaken by Jewish women in the first centuries is beginning to show up in the study of nonrabbinic texts and nonliterary materials that portray women in a variety of roles:[28] as leaders of various sorts in synagogues,[29] as benefactors and donors,[30] as converts to Judaism and in relation to feminine aspects of the divine,[31] and as highly educated individuals, leading celibate and contemplative lives side by side with men.[32] There still remains a great paucity of evidence for the lives of Jewish women in the first centuries. More about early Jewish women is coming to light as we study nonliterary sources, as we acknowledge that the boundaries between the categories "Jewish," "Christian," and "pagan" women were themselves blurred and changing at this time,[33] and as we recognize the need to read the Christian Testament as a significant source for early Jewish women's history.[34]

Often the "blame it on the pagans" stance is as nonspecific as the "blame it on the Jews" position is specific. It simply presupposes that the household code reflects "the thinking and sociological structures"[35] of its own times. Even those studies that are careful to demonstrate the nature of Greco-Roman society argue that early Christianity was concerned that outsiders might perceive Christianity as a threat to the social fabric of the Roman Empire by corrupting households. Therefore, the adoption of the household code by early Christianity was a defense against that objection (a necessary adaptation to ensure its survival).[36] Such explanations clash with studies of the functions of household codes which have demonstrated that the "Haustafeln may provide an entrance for understanding how some early Christian groups defined themselves over against the larger society in which they existed."[37] These explanations are especially problematic for the Ephesians household code, because it is part of a parenetic section exhorting Christians specifically to live in a way that is different from the non-Christian environment! The view that the household codes simply reflect attitudes of the pagan world is further refuted by observing that these household codes in fact reflect views of women that were outmoded in their own time. "The actual role of the pagan Greco-Roman woman in first-century everyday life was much more liberated. In other words, the post-Pauline ideas about the women's role in the church were 'dusty' and reactionary already for first-century observers."[38] For example, recent studies have traced the philosophical provenance of these household codes all the way back to Aristotle (fourth century B.C.E.), who emphasizes, in contrast to the Sophists, "that the patriarchal relationships in household and city, as well as their concomitant social differences, are based not on social convention but on 'nature.'"[39] In other words, what Aristotelian ethics defines as arising from "nature" are the relationships between ruler and ruled in household and state, a view at odds with the more emancipatory ideas circulating in the Roman Empire.

All of these arguments are problematic in as much as they depict Judaism and Greco-Roman society as monolithic; furthermore, they often take texts out of context in order to portray the status of women in Judaism and Greco-Roman society in the worst possible light, so that difficult Christian texts will be seen as less ugly (or perhaps even innovative) by contrast.[40] They also allow one to avoid any honest confrontation with a canonical text such as Eph 5:22–33 and the problems of revelation and authority it raises. Such a "blame it on the other guys" approach is all the more suspicious, because it seems to go hand in hand with a "claim it as uniquely Christian" approach for those texts which present ideas that are perceived as morally good or politically correct.[41]

Can we locate the household codes' view of women at least partially within early Christianity itself? It has been observed that the Pauline corpus points to Paul's ambiguity on the question of women—on the one hand, acknowledging and respecting the work of women colleagues and advocating a certain degree of equality in social relations,[42] but on the other hand, enforcing certain social and religious practices which clearly underscore the subordinate position of women.[43] The household codes of Ephesians, Colossians, and 1 Peter are not inconsistent with a patriarchal Pauline trajectory.[44] Just as the Roman Empire included both emancipatory and patriarchal views of women, so too early Christianity had a variety of strains within it, including those which advocated a more emancipatory stance as well as those of the patriarchal persuasion.[45] As for the functions of the household codes within early Christian communities, E. Schüssler Fiorenza has argued that there was an element of the "discipleship of equals." In the light of this, women were able to hold membership and gain leadership positions in the Christian missionary movement, and slaves of both sexes expected to have their freedom purchased by the Christian community.[46] This put the Christian missionary movement at odds with the existing order of the Roman patriarchal household, precisely because it converted individuals independently of their status within that household and without necessarily converting the paterfamilias. Thus, it is not difficult to understand the pagan charge that the Christian mission was subversive and destructive of the patriarchal household. According to this argument, the household codes are an attempt to ameliorate this subversion by demonstrating a continuity between Christian ethics and those of the Roman household and state. Schüssler Fiorenza points out that the prescriptive nature of the household codes (and the continued pagan charge of "subversion") demonstrates that the process of patriarchalization was not complete by the second century.[47] Ultimately, however, the household codes succeed not only in christianizing the patriarchal Aristotelian ethics but also in institutionalizing submission and obedience—at the expense of a discipleship of equals.

This argument has much to commend it and should be distinguished from the typical "blame it on the pagans stance," which insists that the church's adaptation of its ethos and structures was necessary for the survival and historical viability of Christian communities. But there are other issues that this argument does not immediately address. For example, if the "liberating" views of women in the Roman Empire were fairly widespread, and if the Roman household with the paterfamilias was usually not the dominating force, why would early Christianity need to actively ameliorate the accusation of subversion? If anything, the household codes in early Christianity reflect less the actual way in which Roman households functioned by this time than an already outmoded and idealized view of a patriarchal Roman household.

In any case, the household codes found in Ephesians, Colossians, and 1 Peter are well in line with an idealized notion of the hierarchical structure of the Roman household and with early Christianity as a household movement. They idealize the Christian household as a hierarchically ordered social unit, and within them is found the self-understanding of the church as an interdependent household in relationship to Christ. In this sense these household codes may be said to prescribe an ideal (how the life in Christ is to be implemented) much more than they describe what actually existed. Clearly, they also seek to establish the authority of the ruler of the household (husbands, fathers, masters). The implications of this interest in authority are even more far-reaching, because these household codes are ultimately not only about household relationships but also about the church understood on the model of the household, with Christ as ruler. They treat relationships between three pairs—wives and husbands, children and parents, slaves and masters—as relationships of subordinates to superiors, and they exhort each group within these pairs through direct address to behave appropriately (e. g., submission, obedience) toward the other.[48] Two additional features typify the household codes. First, not all of the pairs are symmetrical: some of the groups within the pairs may be absent (as in the case of 1 Peter), or the address to one pair (such as wives and husbands in Ephesians) may be significantly longer than the exhortations to the other pairs indicating a particular focus.[49] Second, there is often a reason clause that includes a specific christological reference or a reference to some aspect of Jesus' ministry in order to motivate or theologically justify the prescribed behavior.[50]

COMMENTARY

In Eph 5:22–6:9 the subordinate group is always mentioned first. The expanded instruction to wives and husbands includes instruction to wives (5:22–24), a longer set of instructions to the husbands (5:25–30), a quotation of Gen 2:24 (5:31), followed by an interpretation of that quote (5:32) and a final command to both husbands and wives which has been influenced by the quotation from Genesis (5:33). Noteworthy throughout this section is the phrase "as Christ" (5:23, 25, 29), which seems intended to motivate human behavior by comparing it with Christ's relationship with the church. Wives are exhorted to respond to their husbands as the church does to Christ; husbands are exhorted to respond to their wives as Christ does to the church. Although we might acknowledge with many a commentator that this household code is pointing to the need for the authority of Christ in the working out of human relationships and in the working out of the life of the church, we cannot ignore the nature of the equation: women/church subjected to husbands/ Christ. As Brooten has pointed out: "The maleness of Christ is, therefore, not incidental to this text, and the nuptial symbolism does not remain abstract, but is meant to affect women's daily life: they are to live in total subjection to their husbands. Their husbands are to love them, of course, but this only serves to reinforce their subjection."[51]

The instruction first to children and then to parents and slaves and masters in Eph 6:1–9 moves much more along conventional lines than the expanded exhortation on marriage. These two sections are joined together by their similarities in structure and the manner of their exhortation and motivation. Each set of exhortations is set off by the vocative ("Children" [6:1]; "Fathers" [6:4]; "Slaves" [6:5]; "Masters" [6:9]), followed immediately by an imperative. In the case of children and slaves, the command is "Obey." As in 5:22–33, motivations for human behavior accompany the commands for at least three of the groups mentioned: children, slaves, and masters. But this is not the "as Christ" of 5:22–33, nor are any of the superiors compared to Christ in this section of the code. Throughout 6:1–9, although "the author does not want to remove the natural and social differences, he sees a way to reconcile opposites and avoid conflict in the care of one group for the other in the Spirit of Christ. . . . The idea of the common Lord is emphasized as a constant dominating motive."[52]

EPHESIANS 5:22–33

I do not include 5:21 as a part of the household code for several reasons: (1) It is linked both by form and content to the series of exhortations preceding the household code in chapter 5 (especially 5:15–20) and following it, beginning with 6:10. (2) Although it is not a part of the household code proper, it does function as a bridge between the more general exhortations that precede it and the household code that follows it. It provides both thematic ("be subject" and "reverence for Christ"[53]) and syntactic (5:22 understands as its verb the participle of 5:21)[54] links that may explain the placement of the household code following 5:21. (3) Many have suggested that 5:21 was originally written as a superscription to the household code, but its at best awkward fit argues against this; its more coherent fit with the material preceding and following the code better suggests its original context.[55]

5:22–24. These three verses form the basic block of exhortations to wives and have as their central theme the exhortation to wives to be subject to their husbands.[56] Beginning with v. 23, one finds the analogy between Christ and husband and church and wife, which continues throughout this section of the household code and is unique to it. The structure of these verses is as follows: v. 22 is the exhortation to wives; vv. 23–24 provide the motive—or in essence also the justification for the command "be subject" through the Christ–church analogy. Verse 23a is a statement about the relationship of the husband ("the head") to the wife; v. 23b speaks of the relationship of Christ ("the head") to the church ("his body"); and v. 23c adds that Christ is the church's savior. Verse 24 is a mirror image of v. 23a–b by beginning this time with the church subject to Christ (v. 24a) and concluding with wives subject to their husbands "in everything" (v. 24b). Overall these verses are neatly framed by the similarity of vv. 22 and 24b, both of which exhort wives to be subject to their husbands ("as to the Lord" in v. 22; "in everything" in v. 24b). Some find in the Christ–church analogy to the relationship of husbands and wives a case of mutual illumination, a reciprocity in the way one relationship sheds light on the other. But because the Christ–church analogy is used to provide motive and theological justification for the exhortation to wives (and in later verses, to husbands), the balance is more lopsided than mutual. Also, Christ, unlike the husband, not only is the head of his body (the church) but is its savior. "Savior" acts as a kind of code word for Christ's whole work of redemption, out of which the church lives. The church derives not only her origins from Christ but also her continuing saved existence.[57]

Verse 24 raises two key issues: the nature of the subjection being called for and the meaning of the phrase "in everything." In the Christian Testament household codes, wives are consistently exhorted by some form of the verb *hypotassō*, "be subject" (see Col 3:18; 1 Pet 3:1; 1 Tim 2:11; Titus 2:4f.). There is no parallel consistency in the verbs used to exhort husbands.[58] Often the interpretation of the force of this exhortation to wives smacks of apologetic—a desire to interpret in such a way as to lessen the patriarchal bias in the text, sometimes even finding the exhortation not only positive but "revolutionary." Running through the great variety of interpretations is the notion that the exhortation to wives to be subject to their husbands is voluntary. Rudolph Schnackenburg offers the most compelling of these interpretations by noting that "the wife should be subordinate to her husband *in the same way* as the Church is to Christ — namely voluntarily, willingly, in response to his love."[59]

According to Schnackenburg, it is precisely because of the Christ–church analogy that any unworthy subordination is excluded. Though the logic of his interpretation is compelling, ironically from a feminist perspective it is precisely the Christ–church analogy that is most devious. Voluntary? Yes, but manipulated also. For how should a Christian wife resist the "voluntary" call to subordination when it is cloaked in the Christ–church relationship? Has unworthy subordination been excluded? Putting aside for the moment the question of whether one can speak of "worthy subordination," unworthy subordination would be excluded only if husbands were truly capable of responding to their wives in the same way as Christ does to the church. Such an argument falters on the limits of human behavior as compared to that of Christ.

The further qualification of the wives' subordination to their husbands with the phrase "in everything" in v. 24 derives its force from the Christ–church analogy. As the church is subject to Christ (in everything), so let wives also be subject in everything to their husbands. Many have noted that the exhortation to husbands to love their wives as Christ has loved the church (v. 25) mitigates to some degree the "patriarchal domination"[60] or prevents "misunderstanding the subordination 'in everything.'"[61] This is true to an extent: husbands are called to love as Christ has loved the church, promoting a lofty ideal on one side of the equation. Nevertheless, through these verses, which use the Christ–church analogy to motivate and theologically justify the subordination of wives to their husbands in everything, "Ephesians christologically cements the inferior position of the wife in the marriage relationship."[62]

5:25–30. This section of instructions to husbands divides into two subsections: vv. 25–27 and vv. 28–30. Both subsections exhort husbands to love (*agapaō*) their wives (vv. 25 and 28), and both use the Christ–church analogy as motivation and justification.

Though the language and imagery in 5:25–27 derive from and evoke several contexts,[63] two images stand out: betrothal/marriage and Christian baptism.[64] Verse 25 begins with the command to the husbands to love their wives, and v. 25b provides the Christ motive/justification ("as Christ loved the church and gave himself up for her") for the exhortation to husbands. This makes v. 25 similar to, though not completely parallel to, the exhortation to wives in v. 22. In v. 25 Christ's sacrificial death is the ultimate sign of his love for the church. The two verbs "love" and "give up" are inseparable, with Christ as their subject and the church as their object. One finds these two verbs linked together with Christ as the subject in Gal 2:20 ("who loved me and gave himself up for me") and Eph 5:2 ("as Christ loved us and gave himself up for us") suggesting that this is a traditional formulation in early Christian communities. The author of the household code has adapted it to speak specifically of the church.[65]

Three purpose (*hina*) clauses follow in vv. 26 and 27, the first two of which describe Christ's action on behalf of the church and the third what the church might be as a result. Immediately following each *hina* ("so that") is a positive statement ("so that he might sanctify her . . . so that he might present the church to himself in splendor . . . so that she might be holy"). Then follows a negative characterization of the church as impure prior to Christ's actions ("having cleansed her . . . without spot or wrinkle or any such thing . . . and without blemish"). Unlike vv. 22–24, which make use of the Christ–church analogy but always return to the wife–husband relationship and direct their exhortations accordingly, the exhortation to husbands in 5:25a is used as a springboard to a statement concerning Christ's love for the church and the end result of that love in the form of the church. The exhortation in these verses seems almost entirely directed to the church rather than the marital pair. After v. 25a, these verses do not return to the husband–wife relationship.

The image that emerges from 5:26 is that of a radiantly pure and splendid bride whom Christ prepares to present to himself as bridegroom. The verb "sanctify" reflects the process by which a husband consecrates his wife unto him.[66] The prototype for this type of sanctification is God's appropriation of Israel. Characteristically this sanctification is something that is bestowed (by God, by the husband, by Christ). The washing of the bride in water is attested in Ezek 16:9 and was continued in Judaism as a practice of the bride in preparation for her "sanctification." But the imagery of 5:26 is designed to serve double duty, especially the phrase "having cleansed her by the washing of water with (or: "in") the word."[67] Would Christians hear this verse without thinking of baptism, by which they became consecrated to the church? After all, it was in baptism that all who belonged to the church were sanctified/made holy. Furthermore, just as the bride was prepared for her betrothal by ritual washing, so the church personified was to be prepared for Christ by the cleansing of baptism.

Ephesians 5:27 furthers the image of the pure bride, calling on her to be "holy and without blemish." The image of Christ "presenting the church" is that of the presentation of the bride to the bridegroom and fits well with the image of the bride in all her splendor and purity. Once again, the language is not incongruent with baptism. The awkwardness of Christ as bridegroom presenting the bride to himself is often noted, but this is more easily understood in a baptismal context in which all the initiative would come from Christ. Further, the descriptive language (in splendor . . . without spot or wrinkle . . . holy and without blemish) well describes the presentation of the newly baptized.

The last *hina* clause (v. 27, "that she might be holy and without blemish") has as its subject not Christ but the church, and it deliberately builds on both 5:25b and the two other *hina* clauses (vv. 26 and 27) as an implicit exhortation to what the church ought to be after all that Christ has done for her. It fits well within a context of either bridegroom/bride or baptismal imagery. And although the language is that of physical purity and bodily blemishes, the context is clearly exhortation to ethical behavior.

Ephesians 5:28-30 returns to the exhortation to husbands regarding wives, and the Christ–church analogy is used to illustrate and theologically motivate. The exhortation to husbands is now qualified with the phrase "as their own bodies," and the section concludes in vv. 29b and 30 with the motivating statement "as Christ does the church, because we are members of his body."

"Love" and "body" would seem to provide the linguistic touchstones for these verses, but the language is more varied. These verses require the reader to jump backwards (to vv. 23b and 25–27) or forwards (to the immediately following verses or v. 31) in order to understand any particular verse. The beginning of v. 28, "Even so . . . ," refers back to the preceding section (vv. 25b–27) concerning Christ's love for the church and links vv. 28–30 to that statement: "As Christ loved the Church, His bride, but also His body [v. 23b], husbands must love their wives 'as their own bodies.'"[68] The second part of v. 28, "He who loves his wife loves himself" immediately calls to mind the commandment in Lev 19:18: "You shall love your neighbor as yourself" (see also Lev 19:34). It also anticipates the quotation of Gen 2:24 in v. 31: ". . . and the two shall become one flesh." The repetition in v. 28 of the root "to love" (*agapaō*) reveals the gradually deepening interpretation of the exhortation to husbands to love their wives. The object of "love" in these verses moves from "their wives," to "their own bodies," to "himself." Verse 29 clarifies the Leviticus-like statement in v. 28b. The images of nourishing and cherishing one's own flesh explicate what it means to love one's wife as oneself.[69] The reference to "his own flesh" is the wife and now explicitly anticipates the quotation of Gen 2:24 in v. 31 that describes the marital state ("one flesh"). Verse 29b begins the conclusion of the larger section (vv. 25–30) of exhortation to the husbands by providing the theological motivation for husbands to love their wives. It extends the figurative language: Christ's own flesh, which he nourishes and cherishes, is the church (in parallel formation to the language used of wives, the church has also been referred to as his body in v. 23b and also indirectly as his wife/bride in vv. 22–27).

Verse 30 continues "because we are members of his body." This short verse is a bit jolting for two reasons: the sudden change from the third person address to the first person plural "we" and the anomalous mention of "members." This verse, along with v. 29b, concludes not only the exhortation to husbands (begun in v. 25) but the household code thus far. The body referred to in this verse is Christ's, that is, the church. With the shift to "we" and the addition of "members," the author dramatically draws himself and his audience in, reminding all concerned that they too are *members* of Christ's body and that all that has been said in this code pertains directly to them as nourished and cherished members of Christ's body. The theological justification begun in v. 29b has here been given a different twist, extending the reach of this hortatory household code.

A couple of overarching observations about the exhortation to husbands in vv. 25–30 are fitting here. First, after the exhortation to wives in vv. 22–24, which utilizes the Christ/church analogy while at the same time keeping the focus on wives and husbands, a significant block of the exhortation to husbands (vv. 25b–27) focuses not on wives and husbands but presents a statement about the Christ/church relationship. Verses 25b–26 are also intriguing, because they do not use the wife/husband imagery found in virtually all the other verses of this part of the household code, but rather employ bridegroom/bride imagery. The passage illustrates and exhorts regarding the Christ/church relationship, and yet set where it is, is it also meant to illumine and exhort regarding the husband/wife relationship? The question is not easily answered, but several observations can be made about the husband/wife and Christ/church relationships as presented thus far in this household code. The wife's role is very passive in the exhortation to husbands—even more so if the bridegroom/bride imagery of vv. 25b–27 is meant to illuminate the husband–wife relationship. The wife is the recipient of action on her behalf—as belonging to the husband. Even in the exhortation of wives to action (vv. 22–24), the wife is exhorted to "be subject" to her husband as her head. While the wife's role is "reactive," the husband's role in these verses is clearly "pro-active," aided through the Christ–church analogy by which the husband is placed in the superior position and is exhorted to be caring for that which belongs to him. As a statement concerning the Christ–church relationship, the very passive portrayal of the church as the bride of Christ (vv. 25b–27) is less than fulfilling (from a modern perspective) as an image of what the church ought to be.

5:31–32. Eph 5:31 is a quotation of Gen 2:24, which begins "For this reason . . . ," suggesting that one ought to be familiar with the context of the Genesis passage in order to grasp the referent of these three words. Carol Stockhausen has pointed out that there are really several ways of understanding "for what reason" a man and a woman become one flesh in marriage according to the context of the Genesis text. The most obvious reason is given in the verses immediately preceding (Gen 2:21–23), which recount the creation of the woman from the man's rib, to which the man proclaims: "This at last is bone of my bones and flesh of my flesh; she shall be called woman because she was taken out of man." It is this primeval unity of man and woman that marriage replicates and to which v. 24 points.[70] The Genesis passage is important because it depicts the "establishment" by God of marriage; consequently, it was used to sanction marriage in early Judaism, early Christianity, and in Gnostic writings.[71] Scholars have pointed out that most Christian Testament passages that call upon women to subordinate themselves appeal to the Hebrew Bible, especially to the book of Genesis, to support this call for the subordination of women.[72] Gen 2:24 by itself does not seem explicitly to undergird the exhortation to wives to subordinate themselves to their husbands. On the other hand, the larger Genesis context (2:18–25) does underscore the idea of the authority of the husband over the wife that is found in the Ephesians household code: God decides to create woman as a "helper" for man, and because she is taken "out of man" she is derived from him. Man is allowed to name her (as he did the animals) and so has authority over her.

Ephesians 5:28–30 anticipates the Genesis text explicitly and interprets it before it has even been quoted. Often overlooked is the implicit role of Gen 2:24 in shaping the whole of this marriage section in the Ephesians household code.[72] The reactive role defined for wives in these verses as contrasted with the proactive and protective role defined for husbands is very much in keeping with the Genesis text and its context (Gen 2:18–25). This carries over into the "other marriage"–that between Christ and church. Eph 5:22–33 uses organic terminology–head (v. 23), body (vv. 23, 28), members (v. 30), and flesh (v. 29)–to show how "the two shall become one flesh." The Genesis quotation encourages the idea of marriage expressed in these verses: marriage (between Christ and church and between husband and wife) creates a new, single entity and strives for unity as the ideal. The quotation of Gen 2:24 is not an afterthought, but rather informs this entire first section of the Ephesians household code.

In 5:32 the term "mystery" appears. The five other occurrences of the term in Ephesians (1:29; 3:3; 4:9; 6:19) have a meaning similar to that of the term *rāz* ("mystery") in the Qumran scrolls (especially the *Thanksgiving Hymns* and the *Pesher on Habakkuk*). It is the mystery of God's will, which was hidden but is now revealed (by God) to believers through a chosen interpreter. But in 5:32 the meaning of the term is not obvious. Most modern commentators believe that "mystery" in 5:32 refers to the Genesis text about one flesh and might generally fit with the nature of mystery in 1:9 ("to unite all things"), though it does not fit with the more specific nature of mystery described in chapter 3 ("how the Gentiles are fellow heirs"). Eph 5:32 would then suggest that we are to interpret the Genesis verse not in terms of Adam and Eve but rather in terms of the relationship of Christ and the church. For Ephesians, Gen 2:24 "is intended solely to form the basis of the unity of Christ and Church (the two are *one* flesh) . . . ."[74] The "man" is Christ; "his wife" is the church; and the "one flesh" which they become reflects the unity of Christ and church. But this interpretation of "mystery" as linking the Genesis text with the Christ–church relationship is not without its problems. A typological reading of Gen 2:24 as speaking of the Christ–church relationship only works for the second half of the quotation and is problematic for the reasoning in Eph 5:28b–31. Piet Farla has offered a different interpretation, arguing that in fact 5:32b is actually a warning from the author against linking the Genesis quotation with "this mystery," and that instead the mystery is solely the Christ–church relationship. By Farla's reading, vv. 32–33 would be more closely linked, underscoring the Christ–church relationship as the model for human marriage.

With either interpretation, human marriage, and specifically Christian marriage, is modeled on this unity of Christ and church. From a feminist theological standpoint there are problems with the use of this model for marriage:

> it gives divine sanction to the idea of female dependence as bride and wife and to the idea of headship as the model for all marriage. In such a structure of subordination, it is true that two become one, but the one is the husband who absorbs the identity and name of the woman. Unlike Jew and Gentile, male and female find their unity by a process of absorption and assimilation rather than equal partnership.[75]

5:33. While 5:32 returns to the Christ–church relationship, 5:33 contains summary exhortations to husbands and wives. Verse 33 begins with a connecting particle that is variously translated "howbeit," "now," "at any rate" to indicate a return to the key subject at hand. This verse provides a conclusion to the entire passage by reversing the order of the earlier exhortations and completing the literary pattern. In 5:33a the exhortation to husbands first stated in 5:25a is repeated, here clearly echoing Lev 19:18 (which also draws us back to 5:28b): "let each one of you love his wife as himself"—as Christ does the church (v. 25b unspoken at this point, but clear from all that has preceded it). In 5:33b the exhortation to wives from 5:22 is very freely restated, perhaps also drawing on the reverence/fear language (here translated "respect") of 5:21. Though it appeared there with regard to Christ, here it appears as a verb to describe the way wives are exhorted to treat their husbands: "let the wife see that she fears/reverences (respects) her husband"—as the church does in her subordination to Christ (v. 24).

THE HOUSEHOLD CODE IN ITS EPHESIANS CONTEXT

I would argue that the household code is a later addition to Ephesians, which builds on themes and language found in the text and yet takes them in a different direction.[76] In contrast to this view, most scholars find in the household code "a small vantage point for surveying the purposes and concerns of the author in the entire epistle."[77] Two considerations suggest to me that the household code has been added to the rest of Ephesians: (1) If one removes

5:22–6:9, 4:1–6:20 forms a much more cohesive, logically ordered series of short exhortations which build toward a climax in 6:20. Although 5:21 fits in with those exhortations, it is only clumsily attached to the household code. Further, this block of exhortations continues the heavenly versus earthly language found in the rest of Ephesians (but not in 5:22–6:9!) and bears a remarkable resemblance to language and themes found in the Qumran community writings (except for 5:22–6:9!).[78] (2) Much of the first three chapters of Ephesians is given over to advocating a kind of total equality through Christ of Jew and Gentile, a breaking down of the dividing wall (2:14), and chapters 4–6 exhort and teach how one is to live so as to put this into practice in the church. But 5:22–6:9 is clearly not about equals but about hierarchy; it does not break down dividing walls but rather establishes them and teaches one to live within those hierarchical bounds. This seems to clash fundamentally with a very key theme in Ephesians, even allowing for the possibility that the household code has a social agenda whereas what is said about Jews and Gentiles may not. One might argue that the author of Ephesians wanted to protect the hierarchical social order of husbands and wives, parents and children, and masters and slaves and to distinguish it from what he said about equal access through Christ for Jew and Gentile. But coupled with the above observation about the literary intrusion of this household code, this doesn't appear likely.[79]

Why add the household code to Ephesians, and why add it where it is now located? The author of the household code had a message to deliver which builds on themes and language central to Ephesians, even though he brought a different twist to those themes and language. In many ways Ephesians—and especially the hortatory/parenetic section from 4:1–6:20—is a manual of "how to" live life as Christians in this age of Christ's heavenly, but not yet earthly, dominion. The household code addresses this issue and teaches Christians how "to lead a life worthy of the calling to which you have been called" (4:1). The household code also addresses an important concern of Ephesians, the unity of the church made possible through Christ. Other themes and images from elsewhere in Ephesians that are echoed in the household code: the church should be holy and blameless, one should love as Christ loved the church and gave himself up for her, members of the household of God, the use of organic terminology to describe the Christ–church relationship (that is: head, body, flesh, members), and the term "mystery." The hortatory/parenetic section is the appropriate place to locate the household code, and 5:21 offers the right springboard, with its use of the root *hypotassō* ("be subject"), which is the typical verb used to exhort wives in the Christian Testament household codes.

One final and somewhat ironic note: Although one cannot write a feminist commentary on Ephesians without addressing the household code, if 5:22–6:9 is a later addition that gives a different twist to themes and language found elsewhere in Ephesians, then the household code by itself is not adequate for making a feminist critical judgment of Ephesians as a whole.[80]

NOTES

1. It is not surprising that among the other "key" biblical texts is Genesis 2, which provides an interpretive framework for much of the Ephesians household code. E. Schüssler Fiorenza has observed about those texts used for the moral-theological justification of women's roles that: "In contemporary democratic society the Bible and biblical religion often serve to strengthen politically antidemocratic elements by reproducing ancient patriarchal structures of inequality and slavelike conditions in the family and the economy" (*Bread Not Stone: The Challenge of Feminist Biblical Interpretation* [Boston: Beacon Press, 1985]).

2. According to Schüssler Fiorenza, a hermeneutics of suspicion questions androcentric texts (as well as contemporary interpretations) "as ideological articulations of men expressing, as well as maintaining, patriarchal historical conditions" (*In Memory of Her: A Feminist Theological Reconstruction of Christian Origins* [New York: Crossroad, 1985], 60; *Bread Not Stone*, 16). I have extended the definition here to a broader suspicion about scholarship from a Jewish feminist perspective.

3. Luke T. Johnson, *The Writings of the New Testament* (Philadelphia: Fortress, 1986), 373.

4. Robert A. Wild, S.J., makes a compelling case for this ("The Warrior and the Prisoner: Some Reflections on Ephesians 6:10–20," *Catholic Biblical Quarterly* 46 [1984]: 298).

5. Rudolph Schnackenburg, *Ephesians, A Commentary* (trans. Helen Heron; Edinburgh: T. & T. Clark, 1991), 34.

6. Letty Russell has reminded us that it is these very core issues of unity and a distinctive Christian life-style that have historically been problematic in the Church's appropriation of them: ". . . these very themes have often caused problems in the church by reinforcing attitudes of domination, disunity between the church and world, clergy and laity, women and men, husbands and wives. . . . think about ways Ephesians has been used to promote church unity at the expense of "outsiders," to teach slaves and women to be subservient to masters, or to provide God's blessing for warfare . . ." (*Imitators of God: A Study Book on Ephesians* [New York: Mission Education and Cultivation Program Department of The United Methodist Church, 1984], 10).

7. Though here the reader should be aware (and the commentary that follows, in fact, presupposes) that I find compelling the arguments against the authorship of Ephesians by Paul himself. Much more in keeping with the evidence is the suggestion that a disciple of Paul, someone of the next generation, imbued with Pauline thought and traditions, wrote Ephesians. This, of course, also affects suggestions about the date of composition—pushing toward a date late in the first century.

8. Peter Lampe, "'Family' in Church and Society of New Testament Times," *Affirmation* 5 (Spring 1992): 1–2, 15 n. 7. This is the Roman legal definition, which includes those people set under the authority of the paterfamilias (father of the household): children, slaves, and freedpersons. It does not include the wife of the paterfamilias, as she would be a member of her father's household. Lampe asserts that marriage must be thought of in a broader sense as "living together for a relatively long time period as a sexually active couple." For a more in-depth look at the Roman family structure, see Suzanne Dixon, *The Roman Family* (Baltimore and London: Johns Hopkins University Press, 1992).

9. Lampe, "'Family' in Church and Society," 2.

10. Dixon, *Roman Family*, 59.

11. Lampe, "'Family' in Church and Society," 14 n. 5.

12. Ibid., 2, 14 n. 6.

13. Ibid., 3–7.

14. This is the perception found in Acts 16:15, 31; 17:6; 18:1–8; Rom 16:3ff.; 1 Cor 1:14–16; 16:19; Phlm 2; and Col 4:15.

15. This phenomenon has widespread ramifications for the nature of the early church. Compare Lampe ("'Family' in Church and Society," 8–14) and W. A. Meeks (*The First Urban Christians: The Social World of the Apostle Paul* [New Haven and London: Yale University Press, 1983], 76–77).

16. Lampe, "'Family' in Church and Society," 11–12. For examples of this, see also R. S. Nash, "Heuristic Haustafeln: Domestic Codes as Entrance to the Social World of Early Christianity: The Case of Colossians," in *Religious Writings and Religious Systems,* ed. J. Neusner, E. S. Frerichs, and A. J. Levine (Brown Studies in Religion 2; Atlanta: Scholars Press, 1989], 38–40; and E. A. Judge, *The Social Pattern of the Christian Groups in the First Century: Some Prolegomena to the Study of the New Testament Ideas of Social Obligation* (London: Tyndale, 1960), 215. Further, Dieter Lührmann writes about household churches leading to a household ecclesiology as exemplified by Colossians, Ephesians, and 1 Peter ("Neutestamentliche Haustafeln und antike Oekonomie," *New Testament Studies* 27 [1980]: 93).

17. For a brief article on the state of the research on household codes, see David L. Balch, "Household Codes," in *Greco-Roman Literature and the New Testament,* ed. D. E. Aune (SBL Sources for Biblical Study 21; Atlanta: Scholars Press, 1988), 25–50.

18. The boundaries of the household code in 1 Peter are less than clear. It may begin at 2:13 with "Be subject for the Lord's sake . . . ," and at least one author suggests that it does not end until 3:9.

19. For an example of this, see Herbert T. Mayer, "Family Relationships in the New Testament," in *Family Relationships and the Church,* ed. O. Feucht (St. Louis: Concordia, 1970), 58.

20. Judith Plaskow, "Anti-Judaism in Feminist Christian Interpretation," in *Searching the Scriptures,* vol. 1, *A Feminist Introduction,* ed. E. Schüssler Fiorenza (New York: Crossroad, 1993), 120.

21. Ibid., 122.

22. Ibid. For examples of how Paul is viewed, see Robin Scroggs, "Paul and the Eschatological Woman," *Journal of the American Academy of Religion* 40 (1972): 290; and Paul Jewett, *Man as Male and Female: A Study in Sexual Relationships from a Theological Point of View* (Grand Rapids: Eerdmans, 1975), 112–13.

23. Bernadette Brooten, "Early Christian Women and Their Cultural Context: Issues of Method in Historical Reconstruction," in *Feminist Perspectives on Biblical Scholarship,* ed. Adela Yarbro Collins (SBL Centennial Publications 10; Chico, CA: Scholars Press, 1985), 77.

24. Brooten, "Early Christian Women," 73; Barbara H. Geller Nathanson, "Toward a Multicultural Ecumenical History of Women in the First Century/ies C.E.," in *Searching the Scriptures,* vol. 1, 280; Ross Shepard Kraemer, *Her Share of the Blessings: Women's Religions Among Pagans, Jews, and Christians in the Greco-Roman World* (New York and Oxford: Oxford University Press, 1992), 93.

25. Nathanson, "A Multicultural Ecumenical History," 280; Brooten, "Early Christian Women," 79; J. Neusner, *Method and Meaning in Ancient Judaism* (Brown Judaic Studies 10; Missoula, MT: Scholars Press, 1979), 95. See also J. Romney Wegner, *Chattel or Person? The Status of Women in the Mishnah* (New York and Oxford: Oxford University Press, 1988); eadem, "The Image and Status of Women in Classical Rabbinic Judaism," in *Jewish Women in Historical Perspective,* ed. Judith Baskin (Detroit: Wayne State University Press, 1991).

26. Kraemer, *Her Share,* 104–5.

27. Rachel Biale also demonstrates some of the more progressive aspects of the rabbinic

texts of women (*Women and Jewish Law: An Exploration of Women's Issues in Halakhic Sources* [New York: Schocken Books, 1984]).

28. See Ross S. Kraemer, ed., *Maenads, Martyrs, Matrons, and Monastics: A Sourcebook on Women's Religions in the Greco-Roman World* (Philadelphia: Fortress, 1988); see esp. "Section Two. Researching Real Women: Documents to, from and by Women."

29. Bernadette J. Brooten, *Women Leaders in the Ancient Synagogue* (Brown Judaic Studies 36; Chico, CA: Scholars Press, 1982). Brooten's thesis is questioned by Tessa Rajak, "The Jewish Community and its Boundaries," in *The Jews Among Pagans and Christians in the Roman Empire,* ed. J. Lieu, J. North, and T. Rajak (London and New York: Routledge, 1992), 9–28.

30. Brooten, *Women Leaders;* eadem, "Iael προστάτης in the Jewish Donative Inscription from Aphrodisias," in *The Future of Early Christianity,* ed. Birger A. Pearson (Minneapolis: Fortress, 1991), 149–62; Kraemer, *Her Share,* 106; Nathanson, "A Multicultural Ecumenical History," 277.

31. Kraemer, *Her Share,* 112–13 (interpreting the text, *The Conversion and Marriage of Asenath*).

32. From what Philo writes of the Therapeutae of Egypt. See Kraemer, *Her Share,* 113–16.

33. Nathanson, "A Multicultural Ecumenical History," 273. See also Brooten, who illustrates this point with Prisca and Junia, "leaders in the early church, (who) were not only Christian but also Jewish . . . their activities in leadership probably occurred in the context of a synagogue and thus are part of Jewish women's history ("Early Christian Women," 70–71).

34. And *not* according to the "rule of antithesis." An example of the Christian Testament used as a source for early Jewish women's history is B. Brooten, "Could Women Initiate Divorce in Ancient Judaism? The Implications for Mark 10:11–12 and I Corinthians 7:10–12" (The Ernest Cadwell Coleman Lecture, School of Theology at Claremont, 14 April 1981).

35. J. Paul Sampley, *"And the Two Shall Become One Flesh": A Study of Traditions in Ephesians 5:21–33* (Cambridge: Cambridge University Press, 1971), 157.

36. Meeks, *First Urban Christians,* 106. See also Margaret Y. MacDonald, *The Pauline Churches: A Socio-historical Study of Institutionalization in the Pauline and Deutero-Pauline Writings* (Cambridge: Cambridge University Press, 1988), 102. This explanation found favor among feminist scholars in the 1980s (e.g., Russell, *Imitators of God,* 102; and S. B. Thistlethwaite, "Every Two Minutes: Battered Women and Feminist Interpretation," in *Feminist Interpretation of the Bible,* ed. L. M. Russell (Philadelphia: Westminster, 1985), 105.

37. Nash, "Heuristic Haustafeln," 25–26.

38. Lampe, "'Family' in Church and Society," 20 n. 57. although again one is cautioned against making monolithic claims about the status of women in the Roman Empire.

39. Schüssler Fiorenza, *Bread Not Stone,* 73. See also D. Balch, "Household Ethical Codes in Peripatetic, Neopythagorean, and Early Christian Moralists," in *Society of Biblical Literature 1977 Seminar Papers,* ed. P. J. Achtemeier (Missoula, MT: Scholars Press, 1977), 2:397–404; and J. H. Elliott, *A Home for the Homeless: A Sociological Exegesis of I Peter, Its Situation and Strategy* (Philadelphia: Fortress, 1981).

40. Bernadette Brooten addresses this in "Feminist Perspectives on New Testament Exegesis," in *Conflicting Ways of Interpreting the Bible,* ed. H. Küng and J. Moltmann; English language ed. M. Lefebore (Concilium 138; Edinburgh: T. & T. Clark; New York: Seabury, 1980), 59–60.

41. It should be self-evident that the "blame it" stance is not helpful in a society where we seek out greater understanding and respect between Jews and Christians, or between Christians and non-Christians of every variety.

42. See Rom 16:1f., 3f., 6, 7, 12; 1 Corinthians 7; 11; 16:19; Phil 4:2; Phlm 2.

43. See 1 Cor 11:2–16 and 14:34–36 (if this latter text is by Paul himself and not by a later redactor).

44. See MacDonald, *Pauline Churches,* 102–5, 118.

45. Typically, these attitudes are attributed respectively to the early Jesus movement, with its afamilial and ascetic tendencies, and to the Christian missionary movement, with its reliance on the house-church. Such attributions falter upon their overly neat divisions and their subconscious desire to protect the pristine origins of the Jesus movement.

46. *Bread Not Stone,* chapter 4, pp. 74–77.

47. Ibid., 77.

48. 1 Peter is not quite complete in this respect, lacking one of the pairs (children and parents) and addressing directly only servants in the servants-and-masters pair.

I leave completely out of consideration passages found in the Pastoral Epistles (1 Tim 2:8–3:13; 5:1–6:2; Titus 2:1–10) and those noncanonical texts that are also considered under the heading "household codes" (*1 Clem.* 21.6–8; Ign. *Pol.* 4.1–6.2; Pol. *Phil.* 4.2–6.1; *Did.* 4.9–11; *Barn.* 19.5–7), because in spite of numerous similarities to the codes in Ephesians, Colossians, and 1 Peter, the divergences in both form and content are too wide-ranging for the generalizations made here. See Stephen Motyer, "The Relationship Between Paul's Gospel of 'All one in Christ Jesus' (Galatians 3:28) and the 'Household Codes,'" *Vox Evangelica* 19 (1989): 46 n. 1; and Sampley, *One Flesh,* 21–23.

49. In Ephesians there are twelve verses devoted to wives and husbands, but only four addressing children and parents and five addressing slaves and masters.

50. See Sampley, *One Flesh,* 20; and David C. Verner, *The Household of God* (Chico, CA: Scholars Press, 1983), 87.

51. Brooten, "Feminist Perspectives," 58; see also p. 57. For an argument that this passage is only about the authority of Christ and not about the authority of husbands, parents, masters, etc., see Barth, *Ephesians 4–6,* 668.

52. Schnackenburg, *Ephesians,* 265.

53. Reverence is one translation of the noun *phobos.* It has a range of meanings including fear of something, anxiety, reverence, and respect. Already in the Hebrew Bible, the phrase "fear of the Lord" has the sense of awe or special reverence. It is not without significance that fear of God in the sense of reverence has here shifted to reverence for Christ. See Schnackenburg, *Ephesians,* 245; and C. Leslie Mitton, *Ephesians* (New Century Bible; London: Oliphants, 1976), 196.

54. Though the participle in 5:21 is masculine plural, whereas those being exhorted in 5:22 are feminine plural.

55. It begins, "Be subjected to one another"—exhorting mutual subordination, but the household code which follows is clearly not about mutual subordination. The use of the noun which translates "reverence" in 5:21 (*phobos*) does not provide a careful analogy to its use in the household code (see 5:33 where the verb form translates "that she [the wife] *respects* her husband," and 6:5 which exhorts slaves to "be obedient . . . with *fear* and trembling"). For these reasons as well as my understanding of 5:21 as originally belonging with the material which immediately precedes and follows upon the household code, I cannot agree with the various other functions suggested for 5:21 by others: (1) It is intended to critique the household code by broadening the exhortation to "Be subjected." See Sampley (*One Flesh*) 116–17; Johnson (*The Writings*) 378; Schnackenburg (*Ephesians*) 242 and 257. If it were so intended, why not alter the household code itself in some way or at least return to the issue of mutual subordination at the end of it? (2) It functions as a deliberate transition between what precedes and 5:22–6:9. See Schnackenburg (*Ephesians*) 244; Winsome Munro ("Col. III.18–IV.1 and Eph. V.21–VI.9: Evidences of a Late Literary Stratum?" *New Testament Studies* 18 [1972] 434–47, see 443). In

all respects it does not provide a smooth transition, and there is nothing deliberate about it—it was not composed with the household code in mind!

56. This is curious, in a way, because, as Stephen F. Miletic points out, the actual Greek for "be subject" never shows up directly connected with wives. Eph 5:22 looks back to 5:21 to supply the command, and 5:24b depends on 5:24a, "As the church is subject . . ." for its verb. See Miletic, *"One Flesh": Eph. 5.22–24, 5.31 Marriage and the New Creation* (Analecta Biblica 115; Rome: Biblical Institute Press, 1988), 7.

57. See Schnackenburg, *Ephesians,* 301; and Mitton, *Ephesians,* 199–200.

58. Sampley explores this (*One Flesh,* 28–30).

59. Schnackenburg, *Ephesians,* 246.

60. Schüssler Fiorenza, *In Memory of Her,* 269–70.

61. Schnackenburg, *Ephesians,* 247.

62. Schüssler Fiorenza, *In Memory of Her,* 270. One has only to go to a commentary such as George Stoeckhardt's *Ephesians* (Concordia Classic Commentary Series; St. Louis: Concordia, 1952) to see verses such as these turned into a confirmation of "the right relation between husband and wife, which was ordained at creation" (p. 241).

63. Underlying the emphasis on purity and holiness are language and imagery drawn from sacrificial cult and from the priesthood. There seems to have been a gradual merging of the purity demanded of the priest with the purity requirements for the bride (see Sampley, *One Flesh,* 69–75).

64. For an example of the language of betrothal and marriage between God and Jerusalem, see Ezekiel 16. This imagery is also similar to Jewish betrothal and marriage practices in the Mishna and in the Babylonian Talmud, especially tractates *Ketubot* and *Kiddushin.*

One bridge between the purity and holiness demanded for the sacrificial cult and the priesthood and the marriage and baptismal allusions in this text can be found in the texts composed by the Qumran community, which demand of all who enter the community (1QS and 1QSa) and of all who participate in the final conflagration (1QM) the purity and holiness previously reserved for priests.

65. As if the church were in existence or at least in Christ's mind at the time of his death! The similarity between Eph 5:2 and 5:25 is so striking (only the object of Christ's love and giving up is changed—from "us" to "the church"), that 5:25b seems to be deliberately echoing the earlier verse.

66. The verb "sanctify" (make holy) is the Greek equivalent of the Hebrew *qiddaš,* which has a cultic meaning of "to set apart for God." In rabbinic literature it is often used to mean "to select or separate to oneself as wife" or, less literally, "to take a wife."

67. Compare Heb 10:22 and 2 Pet 1:9 for "cleansing," and 1 Cor 6:11 and Titus 3:5 for "washing of water."

68. Piet Farla, "'The two shall become one flesh' Gen. 1.27 and 2.24 in the New Testament Marriage Texts," in *Intertextuality in Biblical Writings,* ed. S. Draisma, trans. Richard Rosser (Kampen: Kok, 1989), 67–82, esp. 73. "As their own bodies" seems already to anticipate the quotation from Gen 2:24 in v. 31, by which the author of the household code can speak of the wives as the bodies of the husbands.

69. J. Gnilka has pointed out that the Greek words for nourishing (*ektrephō*) and cherishing (*thalpō*) used here are precisely those clustered together in the marriage contract to describe the husband's obligations to his wife (*Der Epheserbrief* [HTK 10/2; Freiburg: Herder, 1971], 285).

70. See Carol L . Stockhausen, *Letters in the Pauline Tradition* (Message of Biblical Spirituality 13; Wilmington, DE: Michael Glazier, 1989), 111–12. The larger context includes Gen 2:18–25 and provides these additional possibilities for understanding "For this reason . . .": It is

not good in God's eyes for man to be alone (Gen 2:18), and as they join to one another exclusively, man and woman separate themselves from others, even their parents (Gen 2:24a).

71. This text is still used to sanction marriage in Judaism and Christianity. Other Christian Testament texts that quote from Gen 2:24 include Mark 10:7–8; Matt 19:4; and 1 Cor 6:16.

72. See, e.g., Sampley, *One Flesh*, 96–97, 101; and William O. Walker, Jr., "The 'Theology of Woman's Place' and the 'Paulinist' Tradition," in *The Bible and Feminist Hermeneutics*, ed. M. A. Tolbert (*Semeia* 28; Atlanta: Scholars Press, 1983), 101–12.

73. Schnackenburg refers to it as "the climax of the whole line of thought" (*Ephesians*, 254), and Sampley offers a detailed demonstration of how this quotation has shaped the entirety of 5:21–33 (*One Flesh*, 112–14).

74. Schnackenburg, *Ephesians*, 255.

75. Russell, *Imitators of God*, 103.

76. Long after I had come to this conclusion, I found the more detailed and much under-utilized article by Winsome Munro ("Late Literary Stratum") in which she argues that all of Ephesians (except 5:21–6:9) is dependent on Colossians , that 5:21–6:9 is a later interpolation and that Col 3:18–4:1 is dependent on Eph 5:21–6:9. While it is obvious that I do not agree with all of Munro's conclusions (and I do not include 5:21 in the section that I would call "later"), I do find much of her argumentation persuasive and intriguing in light of my own conclusions.

77. Sampley, *One Flesh*, 2; see also Barth, *Ephesians 4–6*, 655; Russell, *Imitators of God*, 74; Schnackenburg, *Ephesians*, 231–32.

78. See Karl Georg Kuhn, "The Epistle to the Ephesians in the Light of the Qumran Texts," in *Paul and Qumran*, ed. Jerome Murphy-O'Connor (London: Geoffrey Chapman, 1968), 115–31, esp. 120–31.

79. She does this by showing how the household code in some instances conflates what is found elsewhere in Ephesians with a text from the Pauline corpus. In other instances where there are parallels between the household code and another passage in Ephesians Munro attempts to demonstrate that the non–household code passage is closer to an earlier source and is therefore prior ("Late Literary Stratum," esp. 436–39).

80. Arguing that 5:22–6:9 is an addition to Ephesians in no way lessens the significance of this text for early Christian communities. Nor should it allow modern Christian communities to avoid grappling with the difficulties posed by this text. It is, after all, a canonical Christian text, often read in the lectionary.

RECOMMENDED READINGS

Brooten, Bernadette. "Early Christian Women and Their Cultural Context: Issues of Method in Historical Reconstruction." In *Feminist Perspectives on Biblical Scholarship*, edited by Adela Yarbro Collins. SBL Centennial Publications 10. Chico, CA: Scholars Press, 1985.

Dixon, Suzanne. *The Roman Family*. Baltimore and London: Johns Hopkins University Press, 1992.

Farla, Piet. "'The two shall become one flesh' Gen. 1.27 and 2.24 in the New Testament Marriage Texts." In *Intertextuality in Biblical Writings*, edited by S. Draisma, translated by Richard Rosser, 67–82. Kampen: Kok, 1989.

Kraemer, Ross Shepherd. *Her Share in the Blessings: Women's Religions Among Pagans, Jews, and Christians in the Greco-Roman World*. New York and Oxford: Oxford University Press, 1992.

Kuhn, Karl Georg. "The Epistle to the Ephesians in the Light of the Qumran Texts." In *Paul and Qumran*, edited by Jerome Murphy-O'Connor, 115–36. London: Geoffrey Chapman, 1968.

Lampe, Peter. "'Family' in Church and Society of New Testament Times." *Affirmation* 5 (Spring 1992).

Russell, Letty M. *Imitators of God: A Study Book on Ephesians.* New York: Mission Education and Cultivation Program Department of The United Methodist Church, 1984.

Sampley, J. Paul. *"And the Two Shall Become One Flesh": A Study of Traditions in Ephesians 5:21–33.* Cambridge: Cambridge University Press, 1971.

Schnackenburg, Rudolph. *Ephesians, A Commentary,* translated by Helen Heron. Edinburgh: T. & T. Clark, 1991.

Schüssler Fiorenza, Elisabeth. *In Memory of Her: A Feminist Theological Reconstruction of Christian Origins.* New York: Crossroad, 1985.

❖

1 Peter

KATHLEEN E. CORLEY ◆

AMONG CHRISTIAN TESTAMENT books, the first epistle ascribed to the apostle Peter is one of the more difficult when read in the context of modern feminist analysis of the Jewish and Christian scriptures. Generally speaking, its message of enduring "unjust suffering" at the hands of "every social institution" after the manner of Christ has no doubt encouraged many Christians throughout history to submit quietly to the yoke of various unjust social institutions. Furthermore, passages from 1 Peter have also been used by those in power to support a divine mandate for continuing institutions such as slavery or abusive marriages. For example, in one remark from the nineteenth-century debate over slavery, the significance of an image of a submissive Christ for fueling a proslavery position is clear:

> When we turn to the New Testament, we find not one single passage at all calcu-
> lated to disturb the conscience of an honest slaveholder. No one can read it
> without seeing and admiring that the meek and humble Savior of the world in no
> instance meddled with the established institutions of mankind; he came to save
> the fallen world, and not to excite the black passions of men.[1]

Unfortunately, it must be admitted that such a reading of these scriptural pas-
sages is not without warrant. Moreover, the Petrine admonition that both slaves and women should endure even unjust or terrifying situations still serves as a scriptural justification for violence against women in the present, in the same way that it gave justification to violence against African Americans under slavery in the past. Thus, it is difficult for the Christian feminist searching for a liberating "Word of God" in the Christian scriptures to find that liberating word in 1 Peter.

THE CONTEXT OF 1 PETER

In its ancient context, 1 Peter was originally written to predominantly Gentile congregations in northern Asia Minor who were undergoing persecu-

tion or harassment. No longer assumed to have been written by Peter, the letter is now thought to have been written later in the first century and is often
compared in its general context to the Deutero-Pauline Pastoral epistles.[2]
Although this comparision has led many scholars to assume a Deutero-Pauline
authorship for 1 Peter,[3] the argument for a separate Petrine school is gaining
wider acceptance.[4] As is the case in the Pastorals, the local congregations here
are being instructed to avert malicious "slander" directed toward the church
(2:33; 3:9). Similarly, the control of the situation involves an apologetic
"defense" of the church (3:13–17), which leads ultimately to admonitions of
"elders" (5:1–4), "wives" (3:1–6), and "slaves" (2:18–20). In their suffering,
church members are exhorted to follow the example of Christ himself, who
suffered unjustly but in turn was glorified by means of his resurrection (1:10–
11; 2:21–25; 4:12–17).

THE SUFFERING HOUSEHOLD OF GOD

The suffering of believers is mentioned in 1 Peter on several occasions,
including1:6; 3:13–17; 4:12–19; and 5:9. Various periods of official persecution have been suggested as the context for these "sufferings," but an exact
identification is impossible.[5] In fact, Christians faced sporadic criticism and
harassment throughout the first two centuries, with varying degrees of intensity.[6] John Elliott views this harassment as typical of the experience of developing religious sects, and he understands the strategy of 1 Peter to involve an
encouragment of Christian distinctiveness, which includes the definition of
church boundaries in a "household." The behavior of Christian women and
slaves is meant to set them apart from the larger society from which Christians
are estranged as "aliens" (2:11).[7] David Balch understands the letter to be
advocating assimilation with the larger Greco-Roman society, so that Christians might live in "harmony" (3:11) with their non-Christian neighbors.[8] Such
assimilation would necessarily involve the subordination of slaves and wives
within the Greco-Roman household.

We will see that the singling out of wives and slaves in 1 Peter and its appeal
to a "household code" lends credence to Balch's position. The conversion of
large numbers of women and slaves to Christianity led various Greco-Roman
authors to slander Christian groups for disrupting Roman social and household customs. Therefore, an official persecution by Roman officials is probably not in view in 1 Peter. Rather, these congregations are suffering from sporadic accusations of social and political insubordination as a result of their reputation. As a means to deflect social criticism, certain members of the church
are exhorted to conform outwardly to Greco-Roman social structure and cus-

toms: slaves are to submit to their masters, women to their husbands, and all are to submit to the elders of the church and, ultimately, to Rome.

THE ETHICS OF HELLENISTIC HOUSEHOLD MANAGEMENT

In 1 Pet 2:18–3:7, slaves are told to be submissive to their masters, wives to their husbands, and husbands are told to be considerate to their wives, honoring them as the "weaker sex." This admonition of slaves, wives, and husbands has its roots in a Hellenistic "code" that addressed the duties of various members of a Greco-Roman household (see also Col 3:18–4:1; Eph 5:21–6:9). David L. Balch has shown that these household codes (*Haustafeln*) are best understood within the context of a classical *topos* that outlined the duties of "ruler" and "ruled" in both city and home.[9] As cities were made up of households, any disruption of the authority structure of the home in turn threatened to undermine the stability of the state. Thus, tracts concerning "household managment" fell under a larger discussion of the ordering of the entire body politic. This *topos* is Greek in origin, but is used by various Greco-Roman authors, including Cicero and Philo. This means that the delineation of the duties of household members as found here in 1 Peter and other Christian Testament books is not specifically Christian but rather reflects a common ethic of the Hellenistic world.[10]

Furthermore, Balch neatly shows that certain Hellenistic religious groups also were criticized by Greco-Roman authors, particularly when these new foreign religions attracted women and slaves. Such criticism included accusations of immorality and the intent to subvert Roman political and social authority. Thus, Judaism, Christianity, and the cults surrounding Dionysus and Isis were similarly slandered for upsetting the proper management of the household, as these groups attracted women and slaves. According to Balch, in response to such charges, these religious groups defended themselves by claiming that their households were indeed in order, their wives, children and slaves properly submissive to their husbands, parents, and masters. Balch suggests that this is the best context in which to understand the function of the household code in 1 Peter.[11] But the participation of women and slaves in the various religions reflects an increased actual participation of women in the public sphere during the early imperial period. The social discomfort caused by this general social situation to a certain extent lies behind the criticisms. Thus, 1 Peter gives further evidence that Christian women in Asia Minor were among those exhibiting more "liberated" social behavior, and the slander directed against the community of 1 Peter is not unique.[12]

THE HOUSEHOLD CODE IN 1 PETER:
SUFFERING SLAVES AND TERRIFIED WIVES

The author of 1 Peter singles out wives and slaves in his rendition of the household code, but goes even farther than other Christian Testament codes in instructing slaves to submit to masters whether they be gentle or harsh (2:18). Likewise, wives are to follow the example of Sarah, who not only called her husband "lord," but obeyed Abraham even when he denied their marriage (3:5–6).[13] The author here no doubt has in mind slaves and women who are under control of non-Christian masters and husbands. Because members of a household were bound to follow the religion of the head of the household, slaves and wives who had converted to Christianity without their masters or husbands converting would have been objects of criticism. From 1 Peter it may be inferred that certain husbands are among those slandering the Christian community. Thus, the author hopes that seemly behavior of Christian women will not only avert malicious rumors about the Christian communities, but that some non-Christian husbands will be converted and won over "without a word" (3:1–2), that is, without the women preaching.[14]

The instructions for wives include also admonitions for proper dress and coiffure. Christian women are to avoid braiding their hair and are not to wear gold, jewels, or expensive clothing (3:3). Rather, Christian women are to dress conservatively and have a quiet demeanor (3:4)–the virtues of a good Greco-Roman matron.[15] Respectable Greco-Roman women dressed modestly and were known for their silent and chaste behavior. Women who dressed in loud colors, spoke in public, and wore their hair in elaborate fashions were suspected of being "libertine," behaving as courtesans or prostitutes.[16] This passage, therefore, reflects the stereotypical Hellenistic slander that was being leveled against Christian women in Asia Minor.[17] This in turn indicates that the Christian women may have occasioned such slander by their apparently "liberated" behavior. The author of 1 Peter strives to bring the image of Christianity into accord with a Greco-Roman ideal.

The conversion of slaves to Christianity also gave rise to criticism. Not only did the presence of Christian slaves in a household cause dissension and division, but rumors circulated that Christians encouraged slaves to run off.[18] This may have been because some saw in Gal 3:28 a call to end all distinctions between slave and free among Christian groups,[19] or may have resulted from a reading of Paul's letter to Philemon. The manumission of slaves was generally frowned upon after the reign of Augustus, who had passed legislation to limit the number of manumissions. The high rate of manumissions and the social emancipation of Roman women were seen as threatening the political stability of the empire.[20] Moreover, slaves and the lower classes may have been included in Christian communal meals at which free persons were also present; this would have been seen as a disruption of the household structure. Although such behavior was idealistically suggested by certain Greco-Roman ethicists, it was rarely carried out. To eat with a slave was a form of legal manumission, a sign of the slave's freedom.[21] Thus, during the first and second centuries, the behavior of both Christian slaves and Christian women was a source of great anxiety in the Hellenistic period generally.[22]

The severity of what is being advocated here, however, should not be overlooked. Greco-Roman masters could be harsh in their punishments. Seneca, in his discourse *On Anger* criticizes those who punish their slaves:

> You may take (a slave) in chains and at your pleasure expose him to every test of endurance; but too great violence in the striker has often dislocated a joint, or left a sinew fastened in the very teeth it had broken. Anger has left many a man crippled, many disabled, even when it found its victim submissive.[23]

Moreover, besides being subject to severe physical punishment, all slaves were sexually available to their masters or to whomever their masters might give them to. This was a hardship in particular for slave women and attractive young boys.[24] Male and female slaves are thus being told to suffer even physical punishment or rape in order to quiet anti-Christian rumors that Christians are a seditious threat to the security of the household. The address to wives hints that they too should submit to sexual abuse, and the example of Sarah recalls the giving over of Sarah by her husband to the household of Pharaoh on account of her beauty.[25] Hence wives, like slaves facing abusive masters, are to "let nothing terrify" them when they submit to their husbands (3:6).[26] Thus, the burden of alleviating tension between the Christian community and the Greco-Roman household and the state falls squarely on Christian wives and slaves.[27]

In contrast to the instructions to slaves and wives, the admonitions to husbands are far less oppressive. Husbands are to "live considerately" with their wives, to "honor" them, as they too are "joint heirs of the grace of life" (3:7). [28] Should men treat their wives well, their prayer lives will improve (3:7). In spite of the assertion that wives should be treated well, they are still identified as the weaker sex by the author of 1 Peter. This too reflects a Greco-Roman perception that women were of a lower order of humanity than men.[29] Nevertheless, Christian household codes sometimes stress the responsibilities of the husband toward the wife (see Eph 5:25–33); however, this "love patriarchalism," rather than modifying the structure of the Greco-Roman household, merely reinforces it.[30] Furthermore, although Eph 5:21 may advocate mutual submission between spouses, husbands here are never instructed to submit to their wives, but only to those above them according Greco-Roman social hierarchy—presumably to governors, the emperor, or to older men (2:17; 5:5). Should Christian wives and slaves watch their behavior, the difficulties for heads of household would no doubt be alleviated.

SUFFERING LIKE CHRIST

This ethic of submission has a wider focus in 1 Peter; the larger theme of the book is that Christians set before them the submissive example of a suffering Lord. Thus, the submission of wives and slaves—and indeed the submission of the entire Christian community—is seen as reflecting the noble behavior of a suffering Christ. In order to encourage his hearers in their difficult predicament, the author emphasizes the mythological pattern of Jesus' suffering/ death and glory/enthronement.[31] It is this aspect of the Christ-event, the atonement, that serves as the primary foundation of the Christian community's strength, unity, and source of life, that is, their "basis for existence."[32] The author affirms that the community should understand their own situation in the context of Jesus' example of sacrifice or suffering as a servant and his subsequent vindication. As Jesus did not respond when reviled and mistreated (2:23), so also Christians must do the same. Their civil conduct must serve as their only weapon against hostility (2:12–20; 3:16). In light of 1 Peter's "Suffering Servant" Christology, then, slaves and women in the community deserve special attention by the author, as it is their obedient behavior in particular that will serve to best deflect the hostile slander of outsiders.[33] Likewise, it is precisely the behavior of women and slaves and their presence in the Christian community that precipitates the mistreatment of Christians.[34]

This application of such a sacrificial Christology with its corresponding ethic has been criticized by certain feminist theologians.[35] Such an image of the atonement portrays God as an abusive patriarch who demands the punishment of his Son in order to satisfy his wrath and honor.[36] Of greater concern for feminists, however, is the precise use of the imagery found in 1 Peter itself—that Christians should understand the difficult circumstances of their own lives in light of the atonement. For feminists, such imitation merely perpetuates a cycle of victimization, violence, and abuse in domestic situations. The glorification of suffering, like that found in 1 Peter, is seen to glorify all suffering and in fact holds up the victim as a model for women.[37] As in reality victimization does not lead to vindication, feminists argue that such an image not only trivializes human suffering but encourages passivity in Christians, particularly women. This allows women to endure victimization in their own lives.[38] Thus, the myth of Jesus as "Suffering Servant" should not be made into a model for Christian life, particularly for Christian women.[39] Christian feminists are not alone in this critique.[40]

Some Christian feminists, however, do not think that Christian women should avoid suffering, but should embrace it as an expected result of becoming a true disciple of Jesus. Such suffering, however, should rather reflect Jesus' intent to disrupt the patriarchal household, not adapt to it. Thus, Christian suffering should become a vehicle for social change, not a means of social assimilation, as in 1 Peter.[41] Moreover, although sacrifice should not be the primary Christian ethic, persecution will occur.[42] The suffering endured by the Rev. Martin Luther King, Jr., for example, was not motivated by a desire to perpetuate unjust social institutions but was rather meant to be a catalyst for change. Undergirding this positive use of Christian suffering as a means for social change is a Markan understanding of Christian discipleship.[43]

Unfortunately, this is not what is being advocated by the author of 1 Peter. The suffering of Christians generally is rather a fate that may be lessened or avoided, particularly by means of "right conduct" (2:15). This is achieved by the continued suffering of certain members of the Christian community—in particular, women and slaves in non-Christian homes (2:18–3:6). In comparison to their circumstances, the threat to the husbands (3:7) is less severe. Thus, women and slaves are here directed to subject themselves to the harsh realities of the Greco-Roman household in order to protect the larger Christian community. The larger community will avoid further societal retribution on account of the right conduct of Christan women and slaves. Women and slaves thus take the place of the sacrificial lamb; however, their sacrifice does not result in the disruption of the patriarchal household, but rather its reinforcement. This is not a sacrificial ethic in line with that of earlier Jesus traditions. Rather, 1 Peter reflects the eventual domestication of Christianity and mirrors a similar trend in an increasingly conservative Greco-Roman society.[44]

THE USE OF 1 PETER IN THE CONTEXT OF DOMESTIC VIOLENCE

Of all Christian Testament texts, the message of 1 Peter is the most harmful in the context of women's lives. Its particular message of the suffering Christ as a model for Christian living leads to precisely the kinds of abuses that feminists fear. Not only does its rendition of a household code reinforce patriarchal structures, but its admonitions to women and slaves exhort them to undergo unjust suffering without the hopes of a truly just end. Rather, the burden of alleviating tensions within the household, and ultimately the existing tensions with the larger society as well, falls on those least able to defend themselves, women and slaves. They are to view their suffering as a means to imitate Christ in submission and obedience. As a reward for this suffering, they can look forward to eschatological glorification and perhaps the conversion of their masters/husbands.

This letter presupposes a patriarchal view of the proper place of Christian women in marriage and the home and is used to instruct Christian women to remain in their marriages, even when their relationships turn violent. In fact, a significant minority (27 percent) of pastors involved in a recent survey agreed with the following statement: "If a woman submits to her husband as God desires, God will eventually honor her and either the abuse will stop or God will give her the strength to endure it." At least one-fifth of pastors surveyed believed that no amount of abuse justifies a woman's leaving, while one-third believed that such violence would have to be life-threatening in order for the woman to leave. Amazingly, only 2 percent of pastors surveyed would support divorce in a situation involving wife abuse. In a survey of abused women who sought help from their ministers, women from more conservative or traditional denominations were more likely to be instructed to "be a better wife," "obey him," or "be more considerate of him," as a means to justify remaining in marriage and ending the abuse. In fact, one woman was even instructed by her minister to go home and have sex with her husband, who had just put a gun to her head. The more she showed her love for him, the more he would change his behavior and show love for her in return and end the abuse.[45] That the basic argument of 1 Peter in part informs this kind of advice given in the local church is clear. From 1 Peter one may infer that the victim of violence in the household is responsible for erasing family tensions by enduring suffering as Jesus did. When used to counsel modern Christian women undergoing abuse in the home, this argument indeed perpetuates a cycle of victimization and violence.

CONCLUSIONS

Given the sacrificial model of 1 Peter, which serves to reinforce oppressive social institutions, there is little in the letter that may be appropriated by women, and little that may be appropriated by other individuals suffering under unjust social institutions. The author does not proclaim liberation from oppression but reinforces that oppression at the expense of women and slaves. The image of a suffering Jesus and the prominence of the household codes make the admonitions to women and slaves central to the overall argument of the book. The entire focus of the book is to present a model for Christian behavior based on the model of Jesus as a servant or slave who submits himself to unjust suffering and achieves vindication. This behavior is primarily that of women and slaves, who are most able to follow this model and endure suffering in their households. The mistreatment of the church will be deflected by means of their correct behavior, and in a true sense the present vindication of the church will come about at their expense. This legitimization of the ill-treatment of women and slaves still functions in our modern context to enhance patriarchal marriage and encourage women to submit to physical punishment from their husbands. The basic message of 1 Peter does not reflect God's liberating Word.

NOTES

1. Professor Dew of Virginia, *The Pro-Slavery Argument* (Walker, Richards, 1852), quoted by W. Swartley, *Slavery, Sabbath, War and Women: Case Issues in Biblical Interpretation* (Scottdale, PA: Herald, 1983), 35. See also Clarice J. Martin, "The *Haustafeln* (Household Codes) in African American Biblical Interpretation: 'Free slaves' and 'Subordinate Women,'" in *Stony the Road We Trod: African American Biblical Interpretation,* ed. C. H. Felder (Minneapolis: Fortress, 1991), 206–31.

2. Dennis MacDonald has further suggested that the Pastorals also involve controversy in the churches of Asia Minor over the behavior of women; see *The Legend and the Apostle: The Battle for Paul in Story and Canon* (Philadelphia: Westminster, 1983).

3. For a more complete discussion, see Winsome Munro, *Authority in Paul and Peter: The Identification of a Pastoral Stratum in the Pauline Corpus and 1 Peter* (Cambridge: Cambridge University Press, 1983).

4. Marion L. Soards, "1 Peter, 2 Peter and Jude as Evidence for a Petrine School," in *Aufstieg und Niedergang der römischen Welt* II.25.5, ed. W. Haase (Berlin/New York: de Gruyter, 1988), 3827–49.

5. See D. L. Balch, *Let Wives Be Submissive: The Domestic Code in 1 Peter* (SBL Monograph Series 26; Chico, CA: Scholars Press, 1981), 10–15; E. Best, *I Peter* (New Century Bible; London: Oliphants, 1971), 36–42; J. H. Elliott, *A Home for the Homeless: A Social Scientific Criticism of 1 Peter, Its Situation and Strategy* (Minneapolis: Fortress, 1971; with new introduction, 1990), 78–87; E. Richard, "The Functional Christology of First Peter," in *Perspectives on First Peter,* ed. C. Talbert (National Association of Baptist Professors of Religion Special Studies Series 9; Macon, GA: Mercer University Press, 1986), 121–39, esp. 126.

6. W. H. C. Frend, *Martyrdom and Persecution in the Early Church* (Oxford: Oxford University Press, 1965).

7. Elliott, *Home for the Homeless.*

8. Balch, *Let Wives Be Submissive.*

9. Ibid., 1; see also K. O. Wicker, "First Century Marriage Ethics: A Comparative Study of the Household Codes and Plutarch's Conjugal Precepts," in *No Famine in the Land: Studies in Honor of John L. McKenzie,* ed. J. W. Flanagan and A. W. Robinson (Missoula, MT: Scholars Press, 1975), 141–53.

10. Balch, *Let Wives Be Submissive,* part 1.

11. Ibid., part 2.

12. K. E. Corley, *Private Women, Public Meals: Social Conflict in the Synoptic Tradition* (Peabody , MA: Hendrickson, 1993).

13. M. Kiley suggests that here the author alludes to Genesis 12 and 20, where Abraham calls Sarah his sister to protect himself from harm ("Like Sara: The Tale of Terror Behind 1 Peter 3:6," *Journal of Biblical Literature* 106 [1987]: 689–92).

14. Balch, *Let Wives Be Submissive,* 99.

15. K. O. Wicker, "Mulierum Virtutes," in *Plutarch's Ethical Writings and Early Christian Literature,* ed. H. D. Betz (Leiden: Brill, 1978), 106–34.

16. Balch, *Let Wives Be Submissive,* 101–2; see also K. E. Corley, *Private Women,* 53–66.

17. So also E. Schüssler Fiorenza, *In Memory of Her: A Feminist Theological Reconstruction of Christian Origins* (New York: Crossroad, 1983), chapter 7; Balch, *Let Wives Be Submissive,* 98–102. Balch, however, argues that the "silence" here merely advocates a "silent response to slander" (p. 102). It cannot be overlooked, however, that a quiet demeanor and lack of speech were also feminine virtues in the Greco-Roman world.

18. Schüssler Fiorenza, *In Memory of Her,* 262–63; Balch, *Let Wives Be Submissive,* 84–85.

19. S. Motyer, "The Relationship Between Paul's Gospel of 'All One in Christ Jesus' (Galatians 3:28) and the 'Household Codes,'" *Vox Evanglica* 19 (1989): 33–48. Motyer argues that Gal 3:28 does in fact not appeal for a program of social reform, but espouses ultimately an eschatological ethic (see further below).

20. Corley, *Private Women,* 59–66.

21. Ibid., 100 n. 82.

22. P. Vidal-Naquet, "Slavery and the Rule of Women in Tradition, Myth and Utopia," in *Myth, Religion and Society,* ed. R. L. Gordon (Cambridge: Cambridge University Press, 1981), 187–200; Corley, *Private Women,* 58–59. This view of women and slaves was also held in Jewish communities of the same period; see Balch, *Let Wives Be Submissive,* 73–74; Corley, *Private Women,* 66–75.

23. Seneca, *De Ira* 3.27.3. Text and translation by J. W. Basore, *Seneca : Moral Essays,* (LCL; Cambridge, MA: Harvard University Press, 1970), 1:324–25.

24. Corley, *Private Women,* 48–52.

25. Kiley, "Like Sara."

26. The horrendous nature of this advice is often missed; see, e.g., B. Winter, "'Seek the Welfare of the City': Social Ethics According to First Peter," *Themelios* 13 (1988): 91–94. Winter quotes Seneca's remarks as a background to 1 Pet 2:18 without critique.

27. Schüssler Fiorenza, *In Memory of Her,* 262.

28. This would indicate that the wives mentioned here are Christians. The suggestion of C. D. Gross is therefore not convincing. Gross suggests that in the Petrine household code three pairs of Christian/non-Christians are addressed ("Are the Wives of 1 Peter 3:7 Christians?" *Journal for the Study of the New Testament* 35 [1989]: 89–96). Usually when a husband converted to a new religion, his entire household converted with him (Balch, *Let Wives Be Submissive,* 82–87). Moreover, even if a wife did not convert, such a situation would hardly be as difficult for a male head of household as it would be for a wife in the same situation.

29. Balch, *Let Wives Be Submissive,* part 1.

30. Motyer, "Relationship," 42–43; Schüssler Fiorenza, *In Memory of Her,* 266–70; S. B. Thistlethwaite, "Every Two Minutes: Battered Women and Feminist Interpretation," in *Feminist Interpretation and the Bible,* ed. L. M. Russell (Philadelphia: Westminster, 1985), 96–107.

31. Richard, "Functional Christology," 133.

32. Ibid., 135.

33. Ibid., 136–37.

34. So Balch, *Let Wives Be Submissive;* Corley, *Private Women;* MacDonald, *Legend and the Apostle.*

35. I am imdebted to M. G. Houts for her presentation "Atonement Symbolism: Reimaging the Divine-Human Relationship," to the Evangelical Section of the American Academy of Religion, November 1991, which gives her outline of feminist critiques of atonement theology.

36. R. N. Brock, *Journeys by Heart: A Christology of Erotic Power* (New York: Crossroad, 1988), 55. See also the various articles in J. C. Brown and C. R. Bohn, eds., *Christianity, Patriarchy and Abuse: A Feminist Critique* (New York: Pilgrim, 1989).

37. J. C. Brown and R. Parker, "For God So Loved the World?" in *Christianity, Patriarchy and Abuse,* ed. J. C. Brown and C. R. Bohn (New York: Pilgrim, 1989), 23; M. Daly, *Beyond God the Father: Toward a Philosophy of Women's Liberation* (Boston: Beacon, 1973 [rev. 1985]), 77.

38. Houts, "Atonement," 11.

39. Ibid., 10.

40. P. Greven, *Spare the Child: The Religious Roots of Punishment and the Psychological Impact of Physical Abuse* (New York: Alfred A. Knopf, 1991).

41. Schüssler Fiorenza, *In Memory of Her,* 317.

42. B. Harrison, *Making the Connections: Essays in Feminist Social Ethics,* ed. C. S. Robb (Boston: Beacon, 1985), 19. Again I am indebted to M. Houts for directing me to these discussions ("Atonement," 10).

43. Schüssler Fiorenza, *In Memory of Her,* 317. Unfortunately, Mark's story of vindication is also at the expense of another scapegoat—the Jewish people. The appropriation of Mark's myth of the vindicated sufferer has also resulted in violence against those thus scapegoated, most recently in the Holocaust. See B. L. Mack, *A Myth of Innocence: Mark and Christian Origins* (Philadelphia: Fortress, 1988).

44. Corley, *Private Women,* 75–79.

45. J. Alsdurf and P. Alsdurf, *Battered Into Submission: The Tragedy of Wife Abuse in the Christian Home* (Downers Grove, IL: InterVarsity, 1989), 153–58, 21, 23–24. This survey included responses from over thirty Protestant denominations nationwide.

RECOMMENDED READINGS

Alsdurf, J., and P. Alsdurf. *Battered Into Submission: The Tragedy of Wife Abuse in the Christian Home.* Downers Grove, IL: InterVarsity, 1989.

Balch, D. L. *Let Wives Be Submissive: The Domestic Code in First Peter.* SBL Monograph Series 26. Chico, CA: Scholars Press, 1981.

Brown, J. C., and C. R. Bohn, eds. *Christianity, Patriarchy and Abuse.* New York: Pilgrim, 1989.

Corley, K. E. *Private Women, Public Meals: Social Conflict in the Synoptic Tradition.* Peabody, MA: Hendrickson, 1993.

Elliott, J. H. *A Home for the Homeless: A Social Scientific Criticism of 1 Peter, Its Situation and Strategy.* Minneapolis: Fortress, 1990.

Gross, C. D. "Are the Wives of 1 Peter 3:7 Christians?" *Journal for the Study of the New Testament* 35 (1989): 89–96.

Houts, M. G. "Atonement Symbolism: Reimaging the Divine-Human Relationship." Paper prepared for the Evangelical Section of the American Academy of Religion, November,1991.

Kiley, M. "Like Sara: The Tale of Terror Behind 1 Peter 3:6." *Journal of Biblical Literature* 106 (1987): 689–92.

Martin, Clarice J. "The *Haustafeln* (Household Codes) in African American Biblical Interpretation: 'Free Slaves' and 'Subordinate Women.'" In *Stony the Road We Trod: African American Biblical Interpretation,* edited by C. H. Felder, 206–31. Minneapolis: Fortress, 1991.

Motyer, S. "The Relationship Between Paul's Gospel of 'All One in Christ Jesus' (Galatians 3:28) and the 'Household Codes.'" *Vox Evangelica* 19 (1989): 33–48.

Russell, L. M. ed. *Feminist Interpretation of the Bible.* Philadelphia: Westminster, 1985.

Talbert, C. ed. *Perspectives on First Peter.* National Association of Baptist Professors of Religion Special Studies Series 9. Macon, GA: Mercer University Press, 1986.

Vidal-Naquet, P. "Slavery and the Rule of Women in Tradition, Myth and Utopia." In *Myth, Religion and Society,* edited by R. L. Gordon, 187–200. Cambridge: Cambridge University Press, 1981.

The Pastoral Epistles

LINDA M. MALONEY ◆

THE "PASTORAL" LETTERS—1 Timothy, 2 Timothy, and Titus—are simultaneously the most revealing part of the Christian Testament, from the point of view of feminist criticism, and the most frustrating. They are the most revealing because nowhere else do we find so much concentrated attention devoted to women's roles in early Christian communities: here, almost alone among Christian Testament writings, women actually take center stage from time to time. At the same time, these letters are both frustrating and depressing to the Christian woman who reads them: their tone (especially as regards women and their roles) is negative to the point of ferocity, and it is this negative and oppressive quality that has dominated interpretation and authoritative application of these texts in the succeeding two millennia.

How is it possible to approach the Pastoral letters in a way that will, without doing violence to them, render them productive for insight rather than destructive in practice? There is no point in making another attempt to put the best face on them, as if their intent were benevolent and only we as readers were at fault in our perceptions. There can be no doubt that the author of these letters had an agenda, and that agenda did not include fostering the advancement of women, whatever their class or rank, nor of slaves, male or female. The point of view is androcentric and patriarchal almost to the point of absurdity—and there, precisely, is the chink in the armor.

The common error in approaching these texts has been to assume that their point of view, however extreme, and its expression, however shrill, are authoritative because in some sense "divinely inspired." I will, however, take the position (in agreement with Elisabeth Schüssler Fiorenza)[1] that no text that is destructive of the human and personal worth of women (or anyone else) can be the revealed word of God. A second error of interpretation, now generally acknowledged, is to read an author's polemic as giving an accurate picture of her or his opponents. A better knowledge of standard first-century rhetoric guards us to some extent against this fallacy, but still it is not uncommon to see assessments of "Paul's" opponents in these and other Pauline or

Deutero-Pauline letters drawn directly on the basis of the terms applied to them by the letter writer. Greater sophistication is called for.

Beyond this, and in fact preceding these fundamental interpretive principles, is the willingness to opt from the outset for a different hypothesis. This requires the exercise of historical imagination, not as a flight of fancy but as the only means of developing new hypotheses for testing, the only key to unlock the prison of falsely objectifying language that demands we believe that the scenario thus far presented to us is the only real and verifiable one. Bernadette Brooten said it well: "Let us imagine that this is the way it was; maybe it was not the way we have always thought, but rather this way."[2] In fact, what I propose to do in this analysis of the Pastoral letters is to suppose, from the start, that things were not as we have always thought: Instead of an authoritative "Paul" (real or pseudonymous) laying down the law for awed and compliant communities, I read here a frightened would-be authority on the defensive against powerful and intelligent opponents who are *not* attackers from the outside, but are themselves, at this point, active leaders within their local communities. Rather than communities in which a few "upstart" women are seeking a voice and pursuing sensational oddities preached by outsiders, I find communities in which women are well organized (too well, from the author's point of view), women who preach, teach, prophesy, travel, preside at worship, and preserve certain "Pauline" traditions that are anathema to the author of the Pastorals.[3]

This is by no means a farfetched proposition. The situation is, in fact, analogous to what we see reflected about the same time in Asia Minor in the opening chapters of Revelation. The author of that work also has grievances against some other community or communities in which women play a central and authoritative role (see Rev 2:20). The particular objections differ, and the two authors use very different approaches, one employing visionary rhetoric, the other calling on "tradition" for support. But both are confronted with women in authority, a state of things they find uncomfortable or intolerable.

AUTHORSHIP AND AUTHORITY

Authorship has long been a central issue in discussion of the Pastorals. Their Pauline provenance was obviously accepted from the time they were listed in the canon until recently, and there are still some exegetes who hold that Paul was their author. Differences in style, vocabulary, and ideas are explained by these scholars as factors related to the apostle's advancing age or perhaps to the secretary who penned the letters.

Clearly, the issue of the letters' *authority* is in some sense connected with their *authorship*. The apostle Paul speaks with a more powerful and authentic voice than does a pseudonymous author cloaked in Paul's mantle. Therefore, Pauline authorship—and a consequent early dating of the letters—are especially important to those who wish to uphold the teaching found in them as authoritative for the churches today. On the other hand, those who desire to exculpate Paul from the more shocking attitudes on display here, especially the heavy and unmistakable misogyny, are drawn to the theory that the letters are late and pseudepigraphical.

Another, frequently unrecognized factor underlying the choice of a date and an author for the Pastorals is the model of early Christianity one chooses. Let me mention several such models. (The list is not exhaustive.)

(1) Jesus conveyed all truth to the apostles, who handed it on intact to the first churches. Any deviations from that original, divine teaching were heretical from the outset.

(2) After five or six decades of reflection and discussion based on the experiences and testimony of the eyewitnesses, orthodox Christianity coalesced by the end of the first century or soon after. Challenges to the consensus, and to the forms of organization developed to preserve the authoritative apostolic tradition, were thereafter heretical.

(3) "Orthodoxy" and "heresy" were not clearly established categories for quite a long time. Though competing movements and schools of thought charged one another (mutually) with heresy, no one set of ideas was fully in control, and able to assume the mantle of orthodoxy, until the third, or perhaps as late as the fourth century. The "heresy" of competing ideas was thereafter projected backward to the beginning.

Clearly, if one chooses the first alternative, then the author of the Pastorals, whether Paul or someone else, speaks the truth against heretical opponents: this must be so, since the Pastorals were "canonized" and declared thereby to stand within the church's unbroken tradition of divinely revealed truth. In the second model also, the benefit of any doubt must go to the "Pastor," and the opponents are to be evaluated as deviating from the already coalescing body of orthodox Christian belief and practice, which is identified in these letters with the authentic teaching of Paul. In the third model, however, no matter whether the Pastorals are dated in the first or second century, the contest is still open, so that it is anachronistic to call one group or the other "orthodox" or "heretical."

Most exegetes today find unmistakable evidence in the Christian Testament itself to refute the first model. There is just too much disagreement among its theologies to support any idea of universal harmony of teaching from the start. The second, or evolutionary, model in various forms is more widely adopted. It is still most common for authors studying the Pastorals to take for granted the idea that the author, whether Paul or not, is "correct," represents "orthodoxy," or is protecting the (already existing) "good order" and "tradition" of the churches against "heretical" attackers from "outside" (usually labeled "gnostic" with or without qualification).

Perhaps the most pernicious effect of the application of the evolutionary model to early Christianity is that, as a result, the canonical author's words are necessarily thought to constitute the norm for Christian thought and practice, not only today, but in his or her own time. What the author opposes is read as evil, just as he or she portrays it. Practically speaking, this means that the author is forced into an opinion that can be tolerated today, and the opponents play the role of modern "heretics." This prevents us from identifying the individuals or groups for whom the author really speaks, and from hearing the voices raised in opposition. It hinders us from discerning where women (then and now) may stand on the issues, and from dealing openly with the authority question, that is, the basis on which we affirm what is good for us.[4]

Let me now state my own position, which is based on something approximating the third model.

I believe that the Pastorals are pseudepigraphical: their author is someone other than Paul desiring to claim Pauline authority for his[5] ideas. Undoubtedly, there is Pauline tradition here,[6] but with a twist. My belief that the letters are pseudepigraphical is not based on a desire to exonerate Paul for having written them. That would be irresponsible exegesis. I do not think it out of the question that Paul could have written even some of the most disagreeable passages in the letters. Principally, I find most compelling the results of rhetorical analysis of the Pauline corpus. To put it simply: the Paul of the authentic letters argues, reasons, cajoles; when necessary, he uses a verbal rapier. The Pastor, on the other hand, does not enter into discussion with the opponents, and even states this refusal to argue with them as a principle (cf. 2 Tim 2:14–16). His weapon is a bludgeon, and he makes no attempt to win over those who disagree. The situation of the congregations is—at least in the author's view—so polarized that the only choice is "take it or leave it."

The clearest illustration of this contrast between the Pauline and Pastoral letters lies in the fact that we can learn much from Paul's rhetoric about those who opposed or argued with him; though many have attempted to do the same with the Pastorals, it is now frequently acknowledged that such efforts are not legitimate: what we find in these "letters" is standard Hellenistic polemic, in no way tailored to the reality of the opposing groups. It is simply not legitimate to draw conclusions about the beliefs or actions of the opponents from the "canned" lists of their vices that appear with such regularity in the pages of the Pastoral letters.

A conclusion that the letters are pseudepigraphical implies that they were written later than 60–70 C.E., and probably after the deaths of their purported addressees, Timothy and Titus. They are thus no earlier than the last decade of the first century,[7] and may be a good deal later—but how much later is by no means clear. The letters themselves offer almost no clues. They certainly belong to a region where the memory and authority of Paul remained vivid, probably Asia Minor. There is absolutely no way of detecting the identity of the author.

CONTENT OF THE LETTERS

The scope of this brief commentary does not allow for a verse-by-verse analysis of the three Pastorals. I will therefore give more detailed attention to the first and longest, 1 Timothy, and briefer treatment to the other two letters, taking Titus first and then 2 Timothy, which apparently was intended to represent "Paul's" final testament. Before we begin the detailed exegesis, however, some preliminary remarks are in order.

Broadly speaking, the text of the Pastorals contains three kinds of material: (1) passages related directly to the persona of Paul or Timothy; (2) polemic against opponents, and (3) rules, regulations, and exhortations for community life or personal behavior. There is some overlap between the categories: for example, some of the behavioral exhortation is ostensibly directed to the figure of Timothy or Titus in the role of community leader. In addition, there is some scattered material, in the form of creedal statements or doxologies, that appears to be traditional.[8] Each "letter" is outfitted with an epistolary opening and conclusion.

The passages about "Paul" and Timothy (principally 1 Tim 1:12–17, 18–19a; 2:7; 3:14–16; 4:6–5:2; 6:11–21; 2 Tim 1:3–14; 2:1–7, 8–13; 3:10–4:2, 5–18) have the rhetorical function of establishing the authority behind the rules and exhortations. "Paul" is the apostle *par excellence;* he is a key figure in the history of salvation as far as "his" congregations are concerned. It is vital for their salvation that they continue in the unity of the apostle's teaching and in obedience to his commands.[9] The implied threat to those who deviate from "Paul's" words is therefore especially severe.

"Paul" is clearly a figure in the past: *he* was entrusted with the gospel (1 Tim 1:11; note the emphatic placement of *ego* at the end of the sentence), which has been given to the community in the form of "sound doctrine." This phrase, so untypical of Paul, recurs several times in the Pastorals and is linked with the idea of the *parathēkē,* a "deposit of faith," again representing a body of doctrine or ethical teaching inherited from the past (see 1 Tim 6:20; 2 Tim 1:12, 14.) The "pastness" of the Pastorals is further indicated by the role assigned to the figures of Timothy and Titus. The device of addressing pseudonymous letters to these two known figures of the "second generation" gives assurance that the teaching contained in the letters is not only authentic but has been handed down through a direct and authorized channel. Furthermore, Timothy and Titus are portrayed as the ideal community leaders: obedient followers of the apostolic teaching, wise and authoritative leaders of their equally obedient flocks, and, of course, male.

Enough has been written about the personality of Paul and about the personae of the supposedly "legitimate" leaders Timothy and Titus. The aim of a feminist commentary is to shift the focus away from these traditionally "central" figures and to spotlight the shadowy "background" as the real center of interest. Let us therefore concentrate our attention on the third category of material, namely, the passages containing rules for community life and personal behavior, specifically those relating to women. Our purpose will be to divine more clearly what the real situation of these communities may have been.

Although, by my hypothesis, the whole rhetoric of the Pastorals is directed as much to women believers as to men, I will give special emphasis to the passages that are openly addressed to women (really written in the third person, as ostensibly directed to Timothy or Titus, but actually addressing the women whose conduct is to be "reformed"). Here it is most bluntly obvious that the Pastor's ideas of appropriate Christian behavior clashed directly with those of some or all of the women in the communities and that the author's purpose is to undermine the authority of those women by establishing a rival "Pauline" authoritative tradition.

1 TIMOTHY

The letter is composed in a concentric pattern: 1:1–20 and 6:2d–21 contain very similar material; there is a comparable correspondence between 2:1–3:13 and 5:1–6:2c, with chapter 4 a repetition of the themes in chapters 1 and 6. The outer circle may be characterized as follows:

1:1–2. Proemium or introduction. The writer greets the addressee.

1:3–11. The situation is defined. "Paul" enjoins "Timothy" to remain at Ephesus and to oppose "certain persons" (*tisin*). The supposed differences between "correct" and "false" behaviors are outlined, but in the vaguest terms. The "certain persons" are to be enjoined, first of all, not to be "teachers of what is different" or to "teach what is different." (The peculiar coinage *hetero-didaskaloi* may be contrasted with the other compound, *kalodidaskaloi*, meaning "good teachers," or "teachers of what is good," in Titus 2:3.) Second, the Christians at Ephesus are to be urged not to occupy themselves with "myths and endless genealogies"—terms that have, indeed, preoccupied exegetes, many of whom seize on this formulation to assert that some form of "gnosis" was the opposing doctrine. However, the term could as easily refer to Jewish apocalypticism or mysticism, or to almost any kind of lively theological speculation. "Speculation" of any kind is exactly what the author wishes to suppress, as opposed to the "divine *oikonomia*." The vice list used to characterize the author's opponents is obviously a standard catalogue. It does not focus on any specific behavior that would be peculiar to a Christian group. The catalogue culminates in the general condemnation of "whatever is contrary to sound doctrine." This notion of "sound" or "healthy" teaching pervades the Pastorals and is one of the features that most readily distinguishes them from the authentic Pauline writings.

The reference to the "divine economy" as the correct alternative to discussion and speculation heralds the governing image of the whole letter, and indeed of the whole group of letters: the church as the household (*oikos*) of God (1 Tim 3:15). The pattern of the church is to be that of the patriarchal household, with God as head, Christ as son and heir, *episkopoi* and other elders as stewards, and the remaining members as obedient occupants of the roles of free women, children, and slaves. There is an ambivalence in attributing the role of "savior" (a term almost never used by Paul) either to God or to Christ (1 Tim 4:10; 2 Tim 1:9; Titus 1:3; 2:10, 11; 3:4; cf. 2 Tim 1:10; 2:10; Titus 1:4; 2:13; 3:6). The particular insistence on women's conforming to the traditional roles, a recurring theme in all three letters, shows that it was in that quarter that the strongest resistance was felt to the kind of regime the "Pastor" wished to impose.

On a larger scale, the author's continuing insistence on the value of social conformity for promoting the community's "image" in the world at large (cf. 1 Tim 2:1–2; 3:7; 5:14; 6:1; Titus 2:5, 9, 12; 3:1–2, 14) indicates a conservative mindset opposed to the sorts of Christian social experiments that might result from a conviction that "in Christ there is . . . not male and female" (Gal 3:28). Instructions for the behavior of wives, not husbands (Titus 2:4–5; cf. 1 Tim 5:14), and for slaves, not masters (1 Tim 6:1–2; Titus 2:9–10) show that the particular "hot spot," in the author's view, was defiance of social convention on the part of traditionally low-status groups: married or marriageable women and slaves of both sexes.

1:12–17. Thanksgiving and doxology. The author shows knowledge of some details of Paul's life, or at least of Paul's own confession of having persecuted the church (cf. Gal 1:13). The phrase "the saying is sure" is another recurrent coinage of these letters (cf. 1 Tim 3:1; 4:9; 2 Tim 2:11; Titus 3:8). It is twice used to accent confessional formulas, but in the other two instances is so vaguely connected to its context that editors are unsure whether it belongs with the preceding or succeeding phrase (cf. 1 Tim 3:1; Titus 3:8).

1:18–20. The chapter is rounded off with a repetition of the charge to Timothy, embellished with references to two named (possibly known) per sons. These same names are found in 2 Timothy (2:17; 4:14), and their appearance here may reflect knowledge of the traditions in Acts 19. In the context, such references support the fictional location of "Timothy" at Ephesus.

1 Tim 6:2d–21 reprises the same themes: "Timothy" is to "teach and urge these things." Again there is a catalogue of vices applied to the *heterodidaskaloi,* who "do not agree with the sound words of our Lord Jesus Christ and the teaching that accords with godliness." The special emphasis on the dangers of wealth (6:6–10, 17–19) is new at this point. There may be a veiled accusation here that the author's opponents, female and male, have secured their positions of authority in the community because of the special reverence accorded them as wealthy persons or as patrons of the church (see 1 Tim 2:9–10, and cf. the letter of James for a similar situation). The simple accusation does not, of course, prove that this was really the case.

This section also contains an explicit comparison between "Timothy" and Christ, both of whom are confessors of the faith; there is an implicit comparison with Paul (cf. 1:12–16), "Timothy's" proximate model in testifying to what is right. "Timothy" is especially urged to avoid "the godless chatter and contradictions of what is falsely called knowledge," a phrase that has furnished further ammunition for those who wish to categorize the author's opponents as gnostics. The phrase is too vague to admit of much speculation on that score. Just as the author, throughout these letters, fails to give any specific content to what he regularly calls "sound teaching," so he avoids any specifics about the teaching he opposes. The void is left to be filled by readers in every age.

Within a second, interior frame formed by the rules for conduct of different classes of people within the community (2:1–15; 6:1–2c), chapters 3 and 5 focus more closely on the behavior of the ministerial groups, which the Pastor seems to envision as constituting fixed "orders" within the community.[10] Thus chapter 3 describes the ideal conduct of *episkopoi* and *diakonoi* (female and male).[11] Note that *qualifications* for these functions are not named; we may suppose that people offered themselves voluntarily as candidates for the "office" or duty (cf. 1 Tim 3:1) and were confirmed or not by the community's choice, probably expressed through prophetic designation (cf. 1 Tim 1:18; 4:14). That the bestowal of authority in the early Christian communities did not always follow the traditional lines of social status is clear from the fact that slave women exercised ministerial roles.[12] What the text describes are not *qualifications* for the status of *episkopos* or *diakonos,* but *qualities* that, according to the author, people in those stations should exhibit. Thus the *episkopos*[13] is to have the qualities of a proper Greco-Roman household head, including the especially noble idea of being "the husband of one wife"–but so are the *diakonoi,* who quite obviously are both female and male (3:11–12; cf. Rom 16:1, where Phoebe is called "*diakonos*" of the church at Cenchreae).

The ideal projected by the author is couched in terms suitable for males (as would be normal in the surrounding society, in which similar tables of virtues were at home), but does not of itself exclude the presence of females in these stations or "offices."[14]

The qualities of the *episkopos,* as listed in 1 Tim 3:2–7 and largely paralleled in Titus 1:5–9 (which speaks both of "elders" and of "the *episkopos*") are most fully detailed. (See also the instructions on the payment and disciplining of "elders" in 1 Tim 5:17–22.) These are selectively repeated for the *diakonoi* (male and female), widows, and even the older and younger men and women of the church (Titus 2:2–8). When we further observe that the list of good qualities has its reverse reflection in the list of vices attributed to the evil people in "the last days" (really the present) in 2 Tim 3:2–5, we can see that the ideal *episkopos,* as projected in 1 Timothy and Titus, was really the ideal Christian, as seen from this author's androcentric point of view. Such a Christian ideal could well have represented a broad consensus in the churches, a consensus to which this author appeals—though some people would have questioned the conservative emphasis laid on sobriety and good sense, and the absence of any prophetic qualities. What many would surely have found objectionable, however, were the subtle or not-so-subtle efforts to restrict this ideal to manly virtues and to limit the functions both of women and of slaves. Despite the fact that as late as 112 C.E., probably within a decade or less of the composition of the Pastorals, slave women were exercising leading roles in Christian churches in Asia Minor,[15] the only virtues urged by our author on slaves are those of obedience, submission, and fidelity (Titus 2:9–10)—a list that overlaps curiously with that of the qualities to be taught to young married women (Titus 2:4–5)!

One of the best known and most widely used passages in these letters is 1 Tim 2:8–15, the verses ordering women to dress modestly, be silent, and give up teaching. This passage is frequently linked with 1 Cor 14:34–36, and it is often argued that the 1 Corinthians passage is an interpolation, perhaps in light of 1 Timothy. Antoinette Wire has shown, however, that such an interpolation would have to have been made almost immediately after the composition of 1 Corinthians, and that the passage in question really does not break the continuity of Paul's thought in 1 Corinthians 14.[16] As a matter of fact, a close comparison of 1 Tim 2:8–15 with 1 Cor 14:34–36 shows that, rhetorically, the two have little in common. The core *idea,* that women should be silent in the assembly, is present in both passages, but the expression of the idea is very different in each case. Apart from the obvious words for "man/ husband" and "woman/wife," the two passages share a minimum of vocabulary: the verb for "permit"—used passively in 1 Corinthians, actively in 1 Timothy—and the word group for "submission" or "subordination"—a verbal form in 1 Corinthians, a noun in 1 Timothy.

In fact, the real behavioral issues are somewhat different in the two cases. Paul's purpose in 1 Corinthians was to put a damper on women's prophesying in the assemblies.[17] The author of 1 Timothy—who refuses to engage in debate—chooses simply to ignore prophecy as a present phenomenon. His specific difficulty is with women as *teachers* and *authorities* (2:12), although his strategy also includes a suggestion that they should not even pray aloud (2:8: "I desire, then, that in every place the men [*andras*] should pray . . ."); here the contrast is between men, who should pray but not enter into discussions or arguments, and women, who are to dress modestly, do good works, and remain silent. The prescriptions for the women are constructed in a progression, beginning with some admonitions about dress and hairstyles (cf. 1 Cor 11:13–15), obviously directed to the wealthy women of the congregation, who had the money and leisure for such adornments, and intensifying rapidly to a prohibition against teaching and ruling. (We may see in the prohibition on women's "exercising authority over men" an oblique reference to the prophet's role in the community, since in the early church it was the word of the Lord given through the prophets that was the true authority guiding the life of the churches.)

These strictures on women's conduct are bolstered by a reference to the Jewish scriptures (rare in the Pastorals), but one based on a marginal tradition according to which Eve alone was responsible for the Fall. (Cf. Sir 25:24, the only other passage in the canonical or deuterocanonical scriptures representing this point of view.) It contrasts with Paul's position: according to him, Adam preceded Eve (1 Cor 11:8), and Eve was the one deceived by the serpent (2 Cor 11:3); but it was Adam's sin that brought death into the world (1 Cor 15:21–22). The true way of salvation for women, as prescribed by the author, is childbearing. This is a truly shocking statement, since it seems to say that Christ's redemptive work does not extend to women; rather, they must save themselves by a particular mode of conduct. The concluding clause, "if they continue in faith, love, and holiness, with modesty," may be a quoted slogan, since its plural form does not match the singulars that precede it. Or it may be the conclusion to v. 10, displaced by vv. 11–15a when these were inserted by the author into a standard exhortation to orderly ethical deportment (not necessarily Christian in its specifics). Thus the passage begins and concludes with ordinary parenesis, but at its center the focus shifts sharply to the one issue that was most distressing to the author: women's activity as teachers and leaders.

In the distorted mirror of the Pastor's rhetoric we may discern, behind the strictures of this passage, communities in which the people prayed (and presumably prophesied) aloud, in which there were lively theological discussions and probably even quarrels, and in which the teaching and governing authority was exercised (primarily?) by women. These may well have been Jewish

Christian women, since there are many indications in the letters that Judaism or Jewish Christianity was the primary challenger to the Pastor's position, and since the argument used to discredit the women is an attack on the Jewish foremother, Eve. Finally, the prescription of childbearing suggests that these were women who eschewed married life in favor of a celibate discipline.

The primary advocates of such a life-style seem to have been the "widows," an official group unknown in our own day. Here we find a constellation of persons who may well have represented the best-organized opposition to the "Pastor's" ideals, and one which he was therefore most concerned to put "in its place."

1 Tim 5:3–16 is concerned entirely with widows. The author is at pains to distinguish the "real widows" from those who are not to be counted in their ranks—a sign that his concern is not with establishing an "order" that did not already exist, but rather with placing limits on an existing group, some of whose activities or functions he did not approve.[18]

Evidence for an order of widows in the early church is astonishingly widespread.[19] Scarcely any other official group is so broadly and consistently attested. The overall picture is of celibate women, often but not always or exclusively older women, who seem to have lived in groups and carried out works of prayer and charitable endeavor, as well as teaching. They were evidently supported by the churches, not in all cases as a matter of charity, but even receiving a fixed compensation for their service.[20]

The Pastor's concern is to limit the order of widows in two ways: in its numbers and in its activities. Regarding the size or composition of the group, he calls for two restrictions: first, no "widow" who has children, grandchildren, or other means of support is to be enrolled among the "real" widows. (Women meeting these restrictive criteria would be very rare in ancient society.) A "real" widow is to be entirely alone and utterly dependent on the church for her support—allegedly in order to guard against self-indulgence on her part (5:6) and to hold all Christians to their obligations to support their own family members (5:8). Second, only older women may be enrolled: sixty years (then considered a very advanced age) is to be the lower limit. Interestingly, it is only for the widows—and not, as we have noted above, for the occupants of other offices or functions—that a list of qualifications for selection is proposed.[21] Before being enrolled, a widow, besides being alone and destitute, must qualify by being sixty years old and having been married only once. Further, she must be attested as having performed good deeds. (The activities listed are presumably a set of examples, not a fixed catalogue: hospitality, childrearing, service to the church and to the afflicted.)

At this point, the author turns to those he wishes to exclude from the widows' order, specifically, the "younger widows." These may or may not have been women who had previously been married, since the author objects that "when their sensual desires alienate them from Christ, they want to marry, and so they incur condemnation for having violated their first pledge" (1 Tim 5:11–12). We note that the author speaks of these women wanting "to marry," not "to remarry," so that it is at least possible that a first marriage is intended. Second, the reference to a "first pledge" is probably to a vow taken by those entering the widows' order; had the members all been married before, one could say that this would not have been their "first" pledge, technically speaking, but a second vow. These arguments are not conclusive, but they do open the possibility that not all "widows" had been married before entering the order. The author, however, desires that it should be so. He insists (*boulomai*, "I desire," has an official overtone) that these *neōterai*[22] should marry, raise children, take care of their houses, and thus maintain the good reputation of the community (cf. Titus 2:5).

If, in fact, many or most of the "young widows" had never been married before, the author could be excused from what otherwise appears to be the imposition of impossible conditions on these women. Having insisted, in v. 9, that an enrolled widow should have been married but once, he orders, in v. 14, that "the young" (females) should marry. This is usually taken, in context, to refer to young widows, but in itself the verse is merely a general statement about what the author considers appropriate conduct for young women; cf. the very similar ideas in Titus 2:4–5. If, in this context, there is a special application to younger widows, it would appear that, having once been married and now being required to marry again, they would be forever disqualified from entering the widows' order in the future. On the other hand, if they had not been married before entering the order as young women, such women could still marry and, at a later date, having each been "the wife of one husband" (v. 9) be enrolled as full-fledged widows. But it remains probable that the author simply wanted to restrict the widows' order by disqualifying as many women as possible.

Regarding the widows' activities, one might say rather that it is their "passivities" the author approves, and their "activities" he rejects. A cloistered life is what he has in mind: the "real widow," being left all alone, offers prayers day and night; whether she still engages in "good works" is not clear, but these tend to be an exercise of the domestic virtues, in any event. The other, and rejected, case is that of the "young widows," who, being idle (having no houses or children to care for), go "gadding about from house to house; [they are also] gossips and busybodies, saying what they should not say."

Because this author is opposed, in principle, to confronting his opponents in rational argument, we must be very cautious in trying to define the content of the widows' teaching. Apparently it consists of what the author refers to disparagingly as "old wives' tales" (*graōdeis mythous*; cf. 1 Tim 4:7). Since the author indicates hostility to those who preach a realized eschatology (cf. 2 Tim

2:17–18), these women may well have shared the conviction of their sisters in Corinth that they were already enjoying the fruits of the resurrection (cf. 1 Cor 15:12ff.). Also like the Corinthian women, they may have withdrawn from sexual relations and practiced various forms of asceticism (cf. 1 Tim 4:2–5). As for their praxis, it appears they were exercising an active ministry that took them into the homes of their more sedentary fellow church members, and they were evidently engaged in the ministry of teaching, though the material they were conveying was not at all what the author would have preferred. They must have received a regular stipend from the church, regarded as proper compensation for their ministerial work (cf. 1 Tim 5:3 with 1 Tim 5:17). It was this work of teaching other women in their homes that aroused the Pastor's fiercest ire, as demonstrated in 2 Timothy, where he rails against such activity in the most strident terms (2 Tim 3:6–7). In conclusion, he enjoins women "who have widows," that is, wealthier women who may have sheltered groups of widows or sponsored widows' houses, to see to it that they bear all the expense themselves and not call on the church for assistance. This evident attempt to deny to the widows (with the exception of passive "real widows") the compensation owing to them for their ministry represents one more facet of the author's strategy in marginalizing the widows' order and isolating it from the "regular" ministries of which he approves, those that correspond to the leadership roles in the Greco-Roman household.

This central section of the letter closes with instructions regarding the treatment of the "highest" and "lowest" members of the community hierarchy—first, the elders who rule well (and are to be compensated doubly), and then, in 6:1–2c, the slaves. Several things about the author's attitude toward slaves, here and in Titus 2:9–10, are remarkable. For one thing, the rhetoric emphasizes the slaves' absolute degradation: they are said to be "under the yoke of slavery," and the word used for "master" is not the more general *kyrios* (cf. Eph 6:5–9), but the solemn *despotēs* (most commonly a divine reference in the Christian Testament: see Luke 2:29; Acts 4:24; Rev 6:10; cf. 2 Pet 2:1; and Jude 4). Outside the Pastorals, *despotēs* refers to a master or householder only in 1 Pet 2:18. Second, unlike in Ephesians, there is no reciprocity here: slaves are sternly enjoined to obedient service and warned not to be refractory or to pilfer. Third, the purpose of this submission is not spiritual benefit to the slaves themselves (cf. 1 Pet 2:18–20), but the maintenance of the community's good reputation.

By reversing the picture we may infer that in the churches addressed there were slaves who had the temerity to behave toward their Christian owners as fellow members of the "discipleship of equals," and that this kind of egalitarian behavior was shocking at least to the Pastor, if not also (as he projects) to members of the surrounding society. Presumably such behavior on the part of *female* slaves was especially irritating, since in Greco-Roman society freed*men* could rise to positions of great social and political influence, but freed*women* retained their secondary (female) status. "Presumption" on the part of women still in the status of slavery was therefore all the more revolutionary.

TITUS

The letter to Titus repeats, in briefer form, many of the features of 1 Timothy. The introductory formula has been expanded into a kind of creedal statement. It is followed by an injunction regarding "Titus's" work in Crete, which includes another catalogue of virtues prescribed for those persons who are here equivocally called both *presbyteroi* (plural)[23] and *episkopos* (singular). This, in turn, is succeeded by a vice catalogue directed at the "insubordinate" and "disobedient." Remarkable is the emphasis here on verbal transgression: these people are "empty talkers and deceivers," they "must be silenced, since they are upsetting whole families by teaching for base gain what they have no right to teach" (Titus 1:10–11), whereas "Titus" is enjoined (Titus 2:1), as is the *episkopos* (Titus 1:9), to teach "sound doctrine" (cf. 1 Tim 1:10). The parallels with 1 Timothy 1 are striking, and it is clear that the same opponents are in view: namely, those who in 1 Timothy were ordered silenced and directed to resume obedient and subordinate roles—especially and overwhelmingly women. The statement about "upsetting families" (*oikoi*, "houses") is significant, both because of its emphasis on the normativity of socially prescribed family structures and because the author endeavors throughout these letters to project the Greco-Roman household as an ideal pattern for church structure. The references in this chapter to "Jewish myths" (Titus 1:14) and "the circumcision party" (Titus 1:10) may indicate that the opponents, or some of them, are Jewish Christians, or it may simply be an effort to lend the letter a Pauline flavor.

The second chapter contains a series of injunctions for various classes of people: older men, older women, young women, younger men (presumably all these are free persons), and slaves (but not masters). These may all represent "orders" in the church,[24] or the different terminology used here (*presbytas* instead of *presbyteros*, etc.) could indicate that, once the qualities of the presiding officer or officers have been described in chapter 1, the corresponding content of chapter 2 is a description of the roles of subordinate members of the community. Significantly, it is the duty of older women to teach younger women the domestic virtues, beginning with love for their husbands and children, a task that undercuts both the celibate widows' order and its task of itinerant teaching and preaching.

The word to slaves at 2:9 is closer in its diction to Col 3:18 and Eph 5:22 ("wives, be subject to your husbands") than to Col 3:20, 22 and Eph 6:1, 5 ("children, obey your parents . . . slaves, obey your masters"). In Colossians and Ephesians, there is a parallel between the injunction "be obedient" (*hyp-akouein*), directed to children and to slaves. Titus is more like 1 Peter (2:18; 3:1, 5) in addressing wives and slaves in parallel with "be submissive" (*hypo-tassesthai*). The thrust of the author's thinking as regards the parallel roles of women and all slaves is unmistakable.

Another creedal statement concludes the second chapter. The third then begins with an injunction to submissive obedience toward rulers and authorities. The social conformity the Pastor requires of the churches is nowhere more in evidence than here. Chapters 2 and 3 each contain two references to "good deeds" (2:7, 14; 3:8, 14; cf. 3:1), a theme that appears startling in a purportedly Pauline letter; however, the phrase here describes the typical works of the zealous Christian. There is a further insistence on the futility of controversy or discussion: those who are disposed to be factious are simply to be excluded from the community (3:9–11). The letter closes with further references to particular, named persons, probably again for the purpose of lending Pauline color.

2 TIMOTHY

This letter should be considered the last of the Pastorals, since it is clearly intended to be Paul's "last will and testament." It contains some familiar and eloquent passages that could, in fact, be borrowed from genuine Pauline writings no longer extant. But the general authorship is that of the Pastor, and the letter reflects his overriding concern for church order, the maintenance of "sound teaching," and the proper subordination of church members to the constituted authorities.

One clear difference, however, is the exclusive focus on the Paul–Timothy line of authoritative teaching and government. 2 Timothy makes no mention of *episkopoi, presbyteroi,* or other church offices. In addition, there is an increasing emphasis on the preservation of teaching through the written word: thus "Timothy" is referred for guidance to "the sacred writings that are able to instruct you for salvation through faith in Christ Jesus" (3:15), and "Paul" shows great concern for the preservation of "the books, and above all the parchments" supposedly left at Troas (4:13). If the former verse is intended to refer to "New Testament" writings, that is, testimonies to Jesus as the Christ that were already being regarded as sacred writings, 2 Timothy must certainly be dated very late. Another hint in the text that the letter is not authentic is "Paul's" reference to "what you have heard from me through many witnesses" (2:2), implying that the recipient of the letter did not, in fact, know Paul.

Scattered references to individual women reinforce the attitude displayed by the author in the other two letters. An early mention of Timothy's mother and grandmother, Eunice and Lois, shows that their role, according to this author, was that of living and transmitting a "sincere faith," in contrast to the speculative "excesses" found in others. Greetings at the end addressed to "Prisca and Aquila" strengthen the intended impression that "Timothy" is at Ephesus. The letter indicates a knowledge of the outline of Paul's life as sketched in Acts, and we can gather that "Paul" is now imprisoned in Rome but still teaching actively (4:16–17). However, if Romans 16 is an original part of that letter, its author would not have sent greetings from Rome to Prisca and Aquila at Ephesus, since Rom 16:3 locates them in the capital city. This speaks further against the authenticity of 2 Timothy.

At the heart of the letter are two passages that appear to refer, with disapproval, to women's activity in the churches. The first, 2:14–18, again condemns "wrangling over words," and "profane chatter." The only concrete point mentioned, "claiming that the resurrection has already taken place," is associated with two men, Hymenaeus and Philetus. But it is clear from 1 Corinthians 15 that interpretation of the resurrection as present or future had been an issue between Paul and the women prophets of that community. It is therefore reasonable to think that there may also have been significant numbers of women in the communities addressed by this author who, like the women of Corinth, claimed to be already risen and a new creation in Christ (cf. Gal 3:27–28). In other words, the nature of the resurrection had been and continued to be a disputed point, in part, if not entirely, because it so deeply affected status and relationships within a church that identified itself with the risen Christ.

The second passage concerning women at the heart of this letter was mentioned above in our discussion of the widows and their role. In a rhetorical climax that can in no way be called rational, following a vice list numbering no fewer than nineteen epithets, the author lashes out at "those who make their way into houses and captivate silly women, overwhelmed by their sins and swayed by all kinds of desires, who are always being instructed and can never arrive at a knowledge of the truth" (3:6–7). The word translated "weak women," or "silly women" (*gynaikaria*) is a term of such derogatory and sneering overtone that it is impossible to give it its full flavor without descending to gutter language. On the other hand, the language referring to the actors in this instance is deliberately gender-neutral, rather than the usual "masculine inclusive," making it clear to the readers that these seducers of the weak can be of either gender—and therefore hinting broadly that they are women. The epithets directed at the "victims," on the other hand, draw together a number of strands of accusation pointed at women in all three letters: sinfulness, on the pattern of their mother, Eve (1 Tim 2:14); subjection to sensual desires, like the young "widows" (1 Tim. 5:11); and eagerness for instruction, speculation and discussion rather than ready submission to "sound doctrine" (1 Tim 2:11–12; cf. 1 Tim 4:7; Titus 1:9–11; 2:3–5).

One other feature of 2 Timothy that distinguishes it from 1 Timothy and Titus is its presentation of Paul as a model of patience in suffering. The threat of persecution has often been cited as a justification for the social conformity that is so insistently preached in the Pastorals, and 2 Timothy does contain the calm assertion that "all who want to live a godly life in Christ Jesus will be persecuted" (2 Tim 3:12). On closer analysis, however, this statement in itself seems to contradict the overall theme that godly living is the best formula for *avoiding* trouble (cf., *inter alia,* Titus 2:7–8, 3:1–2). In fact, the steady insistence in these letters on respect for rulers, sober living, and maintaining a good reputation is the best evidence that the communities were not threatened by any organized persecution. The author's attempt to suppress the groups whose activities he disapproved of is thus motivated not by actual danger but by fear of the consequences that might follow from witnessing to whatever in the Christian message might be perceived by outsiders as revolutionary.

CONCLUSION

The results of our analysis of the Pastoral letters from a feminist critical perspective may be summarized as follows:

(1) By acknowledging that the rhetoric of these documents is prescriptive rather than descriptive—that it reacts to and seeks to change reality rather than painting its portrait—we are able to discern more about the communities in question than a simple analysis of the polemic and parenesis alone would allow. The lists of vices and virtues, as we have noted, are standard catalogues with no special relevance to a specific, or specifically Christian, context. But the inordinate amount of space given over to "correcting" the behavior of certain persons and groups in the communities shows that those were the active forces against which the author is reacting.

(2) Instead of looking at the scene through the Pastor's eyes and taking his point of view as normative and "orthodox," we have shifted the perspective to that of the persons and groups he opposes. We thus saw that teaching "different" ideas, itinerancy, lively discussion of ideas and practices, and a disruption of prescribed social and household norms could be the marks of a Christian community alive to its own revolutionary traditions, rather than the warning signs of heresy and chaos.

(3) Although the author is careful not to name any individual women as opponents, a disproportionate amount of space is given over to prescribing norms for women's behavior, a subject that is seldom overtly discussed in Christian Testament writings. (Twenty-eight verses out of the total of 242 are devoted exclusively to women; if we were to include references to groups of unspecified membership that certainly include women, they would encompass

more than half the total.) This indicates that women's active participation and leadership in the target communities were at the center of the Pastor's anxiety. It was these women, living independent and often celibate lives, many of them organized in groups of "widows," teaching, preaching, prophesying, discussing, theologizing, leading their house-churches and city churches in new and exciting ways, who were attracting the criticism of this author and of other social conservatives. They called upon Pauline traditions like those recorded in the *Acts of Paul and Thecla* as justification or paradigm for their mission. The author fought back with a threatening, intimidating "Paul" who condemns precisely those liberated and liberating activities in the name of "tradition," "sound teaching," and good order. Until recently, it was the Pastor's voice, speaking through the mask of Paul, that prevailed. But if we listen closely, we will hear other and more eloquent voices calling to us from behind the veil.

NOTES

1. Elisabeth Schüssler Fiorenza, *In Memory of Her: A Feminist Theological Reconstruction of Christian Origins* (New York: Crossroad, 1983), 33.

2. Bernadette Brooten, "Early Christian Women and Their Cultural Context: Issues of Method in Historical Reconstruction," in *Feminist Perspectives on Biblical Scholarship*, ed. Adela Yarbro Collins (Chico, CA: Scholars Press, 1985), 67.

3. Dennis R. MacDonald, *The Legend and the Apostle: The Battle for Paul in Story and Canon* (Philadelphia: Westminster, 1983), esp. chapters 2 and 3.

4. I am greatly indebted to the insights of my colleague, Antoinette C. Wire, and other members of the AFECT roundtable for articulating these issues.

5. The masculine pronoun seems justified in the case of this author, whose attitudes are so androcentric as to represent, throughout, a masculine point of view, no matter who wrote them.

6. See Michael Wolter, *Die Pastoralbriefe als Paulustradition* (Göttingen: Vandenhoeck & Ruprecht, 1988).

7. If the reference in Heb 13:23 is to the same Timothy.

8. But Michael Wolter suggests that this apparently "traditional" material, too, was composed to fit the context of the Pastoral letters.

9. See, on this point, the exposition in Michael Wolter's book (n. 6 above), 49–61.

10. Note the ambiguity of the terminology throughout: the word for "man" can also mean "husband"; the word for "woman" can equally stand for "wife"; and the generic words for older and younger persons can also refer to the offices of elders and deacons. See Elisabeth Schüssler Fiorenza, *In Memory of Her*, 289–90; and Raymond E. Brown, "Episkopē and Episkopos: The New Testament Evidence," *Theological Studies* 41 (1980): 322–38.

11. The translation of *episkopos* as "bishop" should be avoided, since for us it connotes a specific office still unknown at the time the Pastorals were written. "Overseer" comes closer to the meaning at that time. "Deacon" has similar problems. The Greek term *diakonos*, usually translated "deacon," refers to an office or function in the early church that was differently defined according to need and location.

12. Cf. Pliny, *Epistle 96* to Trajan (in any of several modern editions). Pliny says that, in order to get more information about the Christians and their practices, he had tortured two slave women (*ancillae*), "whom they call deacons (*ministrae*)."

13. Though the author writes of "the *episkopos*" in the singular and of "the *diakonoi*" in the plural, it is not expressly said that there should be only one *episkopos* in a church. The system envisioned—or proposed—by the author seems to be one in which every house-church, at least, has a single "overseer" and one or more *diakonoi*. Nothing is said, at this point, of the *presbyteroi*, of "elders," a term used ambiguously in 1 Timothy and in Titus (cf. Titus 1–2, and 1 Tim 5:1–2, 17–20). The *episkopos* may have been chosen from among the elders, and this would be a particular point of friction if, as Elisabeth Schüssler Fiorenza suggests, the Pastor, by denying women the right to exercise authority, is trying to exclude them from an office that would otherwise be opened to them. See *In Memory of Her*, 290.

14. Note the parallel qualities demanded of the enrolled widows—all female—each of whom is to have been "the wife of one husband."

15. See n. 12 above.

16. Antoinette C. Wire, *The Corinthian Women Prophets* (Minneapolis: Fortress, 1990), 149–52.

17. Ibid., esp. chapter 7.

18. Jouette Bassler, "The Widow's Tale: A Fresh Look at 1 Tim. 5:3–16," *Journal of Biblical Literature* 103 (1984): 23–41.

19. For details, see Bonnie Bowman Thurston, *The Widows: A Women's Ministry in the Early Church* (Minneapolis: Fortress, 1989).

20. Compare the use of *timaō* and the associated noun in 1 Tim 5:3 and 5:17. *Timaō* means to "honor," including the idea of appropriate financial reward. Note the difference in the translation of the two passages as suggested in Max Zerwick, S.J., and Mary Grosvenor, *A Grammatical Analysis of the Greek New Testament* (3rd rev. ed.; Rome: Editrice Pontificio Istituto Biblico, 1988). In 1 Tim 5:13, for "honor widows," the authors offer "*honour* (like 4th commandment incl. practical help and support)," while at 5:17, for "let the presbyteroi who rule well be considered worthy of double honor," they write "*honour*, prob. incl. an honorarium, v. 18." Clearly, in the first case, translators think of something offered in kindness to those who are dependent, while in the latter case the same word is used for a payment given in justice for services rendered. Similarly, the NRSV suggests the alternate translation "compensation" at 5:17, but not at 5:3.

21. Lucinda A. Brown makes this same point ("Asceticism and Ideology: The Language of Power in the Pastoral Epistles," *Semeia* 57 [1992]: 77–94, esp. 83).

22. Above (v. 11) these women were called "younger widows," *neōteras chēras*). Here they are simply called *neōterai*, "young women."

23. The Greek word *presbyteros* is the comparative of *presbys*, "elder." It is used to describe the office of elder in the Jewish synagogue and also in Christian communities. It is sometimes the equivalent of *episkopos*.

24. Cf. R. E. Brown, "Episkope and Episkopos."

RECOMMENDED READINGS

Bassler, Jouette. "The Widow's Tale: A Fresh Look at 1 Tim. 5:3-16." *Journal of Biblical Literature* 103 (1984): 23–41. Examines the widows' order as an established group in the early church whose scope and functions the author of the Pastorals desired to limit.

Brooten, Bernadette. "Early Christian Women and Their Cultural Context: Issues of Method in Historical Reconstruction." In *Feminist Perspectives on Biblical Scholarship*, edited by

Adela Yarbro Collins, 65–91. Chico, CA: Scholars Press, 1985. A fundamental essay on the method of feminist historical criticism.

Brown, Lucinda A. "Asceticism and Ideology: The Language of Power in the Pastoral Epistles." In *Discursive Formations, Ascetic Piety and the Interpretation of Early Christian Literature, Part I,* edited by Vincent L. Wimbush, 77–94. *Semeia* 57. Atlanta: Scholars Press, 1992. Shows how the rhetoric of the Pastorals is designed to establish and sustain particular social roles within the community; the authority of the ruling group is authenticated by being received rather than asserted.

Brown, Raymond E. "Episkopē and Episkopos: The New Testament Evidence." *Theological Studies* 41 (1980): 322–38. A cautious, nonspeculative study of the use of these terms in Christian Testament texts, with special attention to the Pastoral letters.

Dewey, Joanna. "1 Timothy," "2 Timothy," "Titus." In *The Women's Bible Commentary,* edited by Carol A. Newsom and Sharon Ringe. Louisville: Westminster/John Knox, 1992. The best short commentary now available on these letters from a feminist perspective.

Donelson, Lewis R. *Pseudepigraphy and Ethical Argument in the Pastoral Epistles.* Tübingen: Mohr, 1986. Examines the issue of pseudepigraphy in the Christian Testament and shows how the ethical teaching of the Pastorals, drawn from the surrounding culture, was used to combat the "excesses" of life in the Spirit.

MacDonald, Dennis R. *The Legend and the Apostle: The Battle for Paul in Story and Canon.* Philadelphia: Westminster, 1983. Based on the hypothesis that early Christian women, especially the "widows," told stories about Paul such as those later recorded in the apocryphal Acts. These stories supported their own ascetic, apostolic life-style, and the Pastorals were written in part to refute them and to establish a counterimage of Paul as opponent of women's ministry.

Schüssler Fiorenza, Elisabeth. *In Memory of Her: A Feminist Theological Reconstruction of Christian Origins.* New York: Crossroad, 1983. The fundamental work on feminist critical exegesis of the entire Christian Testament.

Wolter, Michael. *Die Pastoralbriefe als Paulustradition.* Göttingen: Vandenhoeck & Ruprecht, 1988. Examines the issue of Pauline traditions in the Pastorals, concluding that even the material that appears "traditional" was probably composed by the pseudonymous author.

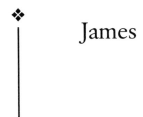

James

ELSA TAMEZ ◆

INTRODUCTION

IN A BIBLICAL COMMENTARY written from a woman's perspective, one must be bold. Traditional exegetical and hermeneutical prudence limits the search for new meanings that bear on the liberation of women. It is important to move beyond the obvious and to be creative and suspicious of the standard tools of research. With a text produced in a patriarchal context, the problem is even greater, especially for women who use the Bible to discern God's presence and will today. Thus, we need to define new hermeneutical guidelines to enable us to discover in the Bible words of liberation for women. This becomes possible only as we distance ourselves from familiar texts and approach them afresh with a feminist awareness, appropriating as women all of the texts that denounce oppression, proclaim liberation, and defend victims of discrimination: the poor, orphans, widows, strangers, the sick. Throughout the Bible, God is described as a God of mercy, justice, and peace, who shows solidarity with the oppressed. According to this criterion and assuming that the gospel is "good news," we may regard any text that discriminates against women or any other human being not as normative but as reflecting negative cultural values. We recognize, therefore, that a feminist reading of the Bible cannot be limited to an examination of passages that deal specifically with women. The Letter of James does not pay explicit attention to women, since the patriarchalism of the age prevented its author from being aware of such injustices. But the sensitivity he shows for the economically marginalized provides a legitimate basis for broadening the letter's concern to include sectors of society that suffer marginalization for different reasons. James's defense of the poor and his summons to praxis can be very meaningful for women, especially poor women. Wealthy women who feel discriminated against because of their gender can encounter in the letter a challenge to maintain solidarity with all poor people, especially with poor women, and thereby to make their Christian faith consistent with the practice of justice, which is the principal message of James. A feminist reading will be concerned for the defense and welfare of all people excluded by their society.

I approach the Letter of James with this attitude. I begin with a general commentary from a feminist perspective, making explicit reference to the situation of women wherever the text permits. I use both classical and recent commentaries, but also go beyond them in order to reread the text from a woman's viewpoint and to concentrate on what the text says about oppression and discrimination.

AUTHENTICITY, AUTHOR, PLACE, AND DATE

The history of the Letter of James is fraught with controversy. It appears to have entered the canon very late—perhaps even toward the end of the fourth century—and not without debate. Origen classified it among the "disputed books." Even after its inclusion in the canon, it continued to be neglected, regarded as inferior, or called into question, especially by leaders of the Syrian church. In the sixteenth century, Martin Luther dismissed it as not containing what he regarded as knowledge necessary for salvation.

There is no consensus concerning the letter's author or its place or date of composition. The author identifies himself as "James" (1:1); however, even in the Christian Testament several men bore that name—James the Just, the brother of Jesus; James the son of Alphaeus; and James the son of Zebedee. Most scholars reject the possibility that either of the latter two wrote the letter. The objection to the author's being the brother of Jesus focuses on the elaborate Greek used, which seems inappropriate to a carpenter's son. Some researchers, however, see no great difficulty here because of the considerable level of Hellenization in Palestine at the time.

Several characteristics support each of the theories concerning authorship. Two recent commentaries by Sophie Laws (1980) and Peter Davids (1982) take contrasting but representative positions on that question. Their conclusions concerning the place and date of the letter depend largely on their acceptance or rejection of the authorship of James the brother of Jesus. Laws, following the liberal tradition, decides in favor of an author later than James the Just—someone who used a pseudonym, as was common in Jewish and Greco-Roman literature. Thus, she dates the letter between 70 and 130 C.E. Because of its similarities to 1 Peter, Clement of Rome, and the *Shepherd of Hermas,* she suggests Rome as the letter's place of origin. Davids decides in favor of James the brother of the Lord, holding that the letter was written between 55 and 65 C.E. (and possibly revised between 75 and 85). His argument is based largely on an effort to identify the document's context from data in the letter itself referring to oppression by landholders and merchants.

Palestine fits those criteria. In a more recent commentary (1987), Pedrito Maynard-Reid continues in the same vein, analyzing the social stratification of the first century and the negative consequences of the Pax Romana. Underlying his efforts is a desire to move beyond form criticism to uncover redactional criteria that will sustain a meaningful contemporary rereading of James rather than simply reiterating the conclusion that James is a bundle of disconnected sentences.

Notwithstanding the different readings of the evidence within the letter itself, it is clear that the author was a Jew (knowing the Hebrew Bible and rabbinic tradition, and incorporating Semitisms into his Greek), a Christian (citing a number of Jesus' sayings, and describing practices of the early church [5:13–18]), and a man influenced by Hellenistic culture (writing commentaries in Hellenistic style, and in fluent Greek). More important, however, the author was concerned for the well-being of the poor, the exploited, and victims of discrimination, as well as for that of Christian communities. Believers must maintain a consistency between their actions and what they hear-see-believe-speak, in order to have integrity before God. The exhortation not to show favoritism or oppress the poor must be extended to all groups who suffer marginalization and oppression—blacks, indigenous peoples, and women of all races. A feminist reading of the Bible is concerned for the well-being of all victims of discrimination.

ADDRESSEES

James addresses his letter "to the twelve tribes in the dispersion." The expression is controversial. Some suggest that he is addressing all converted Jews or Gentile Christians living outside Palestine as the new Israel. I prefer John H. Elliot's suggestion that the word *diaspora* has a figurative meaning ("transience") and a sociological component. James's salutation then refers to refugees—outsiders in general—residing permanently or temporarily in Asia Minor, who often found themselves in political, legal, social, and religious difficulties. James thus adopts the image of the twelve tribes of Israel—homeless, nomadic clans living as refugees in Egypt or Babylon. Most likely the addressees of the letter were experiencing similar social and religious marginalization.

PATRIARCHAL LANGUAGE

A feminist reading of the letter recognizes James's patriarchal language. Jas 1:17 refers to God as the Father of lights; 1:14, 15 relates concupiscence (seduction, sin, and death) to woman's pregnancy: to conceive (*syllambanō*), to give birth (*tiktō*), and to engender (*apokyeō*). By contrast, in 1:18 the Father of lights engenders (*apokyeō*) with the word of truth. In 1:8, 12; 3:2, the author uses the noun *anēr*, ("male") to refer to all of humanity. His use of "sister" along with "brother" in 2:15 may reflect the presence of many poor women in the communities, rather than a concern for inclusive language. In 4:4 we find the feminine form "adulteresses." Some manuscripts add the masculine form, as if it referred to actual adulterous persons in the community, but the reason for the use of the feminine alone is consistent with James's adoption of the image of prostitution to refer to Israel's idolatry. It is common in the Hebrew Bible to depict Israel as God's unfaithful spouse, who is guilty of infidelity when "she" goes scampering after other gods. The very use of the image of prostitution reemphasizes the marginalization of women. Female prostitution is the product of a patriarchal society, and the fact that it exists betrays the contempt of such a society for women. The use of the feminine form here offends the dignity of women without clarifying the broader reference of the metaphor.

STYLE AND STRUCTURE OF THE LETTER

James is a parenetic or hortatory letter—a common genre in the first century. All of the commentaries discuss the writer's fluent Greek and his literary ability: precise syntax, plays on words, alliteration, paronomasia, rhythm, polished rhetoric, and sophisticated vocabulary. The author has incorporated both ancient and contemporary materials—traditional sayings, proverbs, and other forms—and woven them together to emphasize not their original meanings but the new content that made them relevant for his context. Our usual Western approach to analyzing texts makes it difficult to grasp the structure of the letter with its parenetic style and frequent diatribes. Commentaries usually analyze each topic or chapter separately. Indeed, a first reading of the letter is like a photographer's first approach to an object: the image is out of focus, its contours blurred. In a first encounter with the text, we fail to recognize the connecting thread: James seems to be speaking of everything in general and nothing in particular; however, continued work on the text clarifies our perception, and we begin to recognize a coherent scene.

The first chapter is dense and varied in its themes. Sentences are held together with catchwords such as *chaireō*, "greet" :: *charan*, "joy" (1:1, 2); and *leipomenoi*, "lacking" :: *leipetai*, "is without" (1:4, 5). In chapters 2–4 the themes identified in chapter 1 are elaborated upon and expanded (e.g., 4:7–10). At the end of the letter, the author again takes up the main themes of chapter 1: judgment against the wealthy, patience, prayer, suffering, and consistency between speech and action.

Given the difficulty of discovering a structure of the letter that demonstrates the author's main purposes, and in order to emphasize a feminist reading, I am proposing a new structural framework that approaches the text from three general angles— oppression, hope, and praxis—each seen through the lens of women's experience.

THE ANGLE OF OPPRESSION

It is likely that conditions of oppression and marginalization provided the principal motives for the Letter of James. Reading the letter from the angle of oppression, we can distinguish the oppressors and the oppressed. In order of importance, the following groups comprise the oppressed:

(1) *Farm workers* (5:1–12). They are exploited by wealthy persons who withhold their wages (5:4), or, according to some manuscripts, "rob" them. James personifies wages, seeing them as the blood of the exploited crying out shamelessly. The same word is used in Greek literature for the "howling" of wild animals, and frequently in the Septuagint it conveys a protest against injustice.

(2) *Orphans and widows* (1:27). James echoes the defense of these groups that permeates the Hebrew Bible, where frequent references to orphans and widows emphasize the gravity of their circumstances. Their lives of poverty and marginalization result from patriarchal society. Here the general and specific angles noted above intersect. Women did not usually inherit, and they were often left homeless when they were widowed. They were doomed to remain widows forever if their deceased husband's brother did not marry them, as prescribed by levirate law. Orphans shared the same conditions of oppression at the hands of the same patriarchal society. "Orphans" were children without a father to be the head of the family. The mother, if she was still alive, would have been a widow, economically destitute simply because she was a woman. Losing one's mother would not affect one's socioeconomic situation, since the father determined the economic status and prestige of the family. The economic oppression suffered by orphans as well as by widows was thus connected to the exploitation of women.

The scriptures defended orphans and widows because they had neither resources of their own nor a father or husband to defend them. Corrupt judges, civil rulers, and priests all tended to take advantage of them. In the Hebrew Bible, orphans and widows are objects of God's love; in the Christian Testament Jesus defends them against the scribes (Mark 12:44) and marvels at the deed of an impoverished widow (Mark 12:41–44). In the early church, widows and orphans were objects of concern.

James's bold assertion that true religion involves "caring for orphans and widows in their distress, and keeping oneself unstained by the world" (1:27) may point to an obvious situation of oppression at that time. The Greek word translated as "distress" refers to economic oppression and the suffering it produces. "Caring for" means entering into solidarity with someone and sharing with that person the basic necessities of life. "Keeping oneself unstained by the world" means refusing to embrace the values of a world hostile to such groups. (A variant reading of 1:27 in a seventeenth-century manuscript includes the prayer, "... and protect them from the world.")

(3) *The poor.* Various social strata were included within the Christian community, from the very poor, to the less poor, to others who lived more comfortably. Jas 2:6 probably refers to poor members of the community being oppressed by wealthier ones, who dragged them into courts. In any case, some members of the community apparently discriminated against the poor, who lacked means of subsistence and lived by alms. James exhorts the wealthy not to show favoritism and reminds them that the poor—those without food or shelter (2:15)—are God's elect and heirs of God's reign (2:5).

Reading 2:15 from a feminist perspective, one is struck by the explicit reference to "a brother or sister." As in any patriarchal society, the word "brother" usually encompassed persons of both sexes. Clearly James did not add the word "sister" in the interest of inclusive language. We are thus led to suspect that the author feels obliged to add the feminine reference because there were even more poor women than poor men in the church. Most likely their high visibility and critical circumstances compelled the author to use both masculine and feminine forms.

(4) *The rich.* According to the author, the oppressors are the wealthy. The word "wealthy" is used pejoratively in three passages: 1:10, 11, 2:6b, 7; and 5:1–6. The first and third identify people coming under judgment. In the second, James speaks of the typical behavior of the wealthy: (1) They dress lavishly and expensively, in contrast to the poor. Their "gold rings" (2:2) may indicate their status as members of the aristocracy. (2) They oppress the poor and drag them into courts (2:6). The word translated as "oppressed" is frequently found in the Septuagint connoting abuse of power. Usually the poor were dragged before the courts for defaulting on their taxes or debts. (3) In 5:1–6 the rich are characterized as exploiting farm workers, not paying their employees' wages, and leading a life dedicated to pursuing pleasure while they condemn and murder the just. (4) In 4:1–17 another group appears—merchants, whom James does not call "rich" but criticizes for their single-minded concern to make profits in the business world. They may be Christians, since James

does speak of sin and God but does not call them "brothers." Apparently the author sees the poor as potentially natural members of the Christian community. Hence he constantly exhorts them to behave in accordance with their faith. He does not define faith, but he does define the works of justice that the believers must accomplish (1:27; 2:16).

THE ANGLE OF HOPE

James is anxious to strengthen the hope of his addressees. Oppression, suffering, and persecution are not the purpose of human life. The following details in the text help define this perspective of hope: Sentences beginning with "Blessed is anyone . . ." (1:12) or "consider it nothing but joy . . ." (1:2); God's option for the poor as the elect (2:5); the exaltation of the "lowly" (1:9); the declaration that "God opposes the proud, but gives grace to the humble" (4:6); and, finally, God's judgment in favor of the exploited and against the wealthy, and the coming of the Lord as an end to oppression (5:1–7). James's scattered observations begin to cohere with the help of the "glue" provided by the themes of joy, solidarity with God, and divine judgment.

JOY THAT SPRINGS FROM PRAXIS

Several times in the letter we find words denoting joy or gladness. They come from two different Greek roots: *chara-* (1:2), and *makar-* (1:12, 25; 5:11). The salutation (1:1–2) literally means "have joy."

In 1:2 "trials of any kind" refers to the various forms of oppression and persecution that produce suffering. James instructs his audience to reflect on this experience in order to understand both the process and the result. Suffering strengthens the spirit, producing a kind of militant patience that confers dignity on both the individual and the community. This joy is not eschatological.

The "law of liberty" (1:25) is the law of service. The author calls it "the perfect law"—a concept he takes up again in 2:8. Service produces joy. The term "blessed" is ambiguous, since it can imply either a promise or the consequence of one's service.

James calls both the prophets and Job "blessed" (5:10–11). The prophets demonstrated their commitment by acting heroically. They suffered oppression and martyrdom as a result of their praxis of denunciation and proclamation, and they were called "blessed." Job, on the other hand, suffered misery and marginalization innocently and arbitrarily, like women who suffer simply because they are women. Job resisted and protested to the Almighty, who in divine mercy restored his earthly fortunes. Believing in this God inspires hope.

ESCHATOLOGICAL JOY AS A PRESENT REALITY

Eschatological joy involves believing that, at the consummation of the ages, people who are now oppressed will become the favored ones. The emphasis in 1:12 is not on the virtue of enduring a test or trial but rather on the promise of joy. The "test" has to do with earthly poverty, not eschatological tribulation. Jas 1:12 is related to 2:5, where the poor are called "heirs," and occurs immediately after the text contrasting poor and rich. "Winning the crown of life" means obtaining life itself—a good, long-lasting life. Heroism lies in joining the struggle for life and resisting oppression.

The kind of judgment described in 1:9–11 is common in Hebraic thinking. The word "boast" has a positive connotation of happiness here and now, produced by the assurance that judgment will eventually be pronounced in favor of the poor and against the rich. The antithetical structure that contrasts "the believer who is lowly" with "the rich" precludes the possibility that "lowly" could be considered a moral attribute. James urges the poor to rejoice right now, because their situation will change. By contrast, the letter speaks ironically to the rich, inviting them to boast "in being brought low," for that is precisely what will happen to them.

IDENTIFICATION OF GOD WITH THE POOR

The interrogative construction in 2:5 anticipates an affirmative response. The community knew that the tradition affirmed God's option for the poor. "The poor" here are not the pious. That they are called "rich in faith" refers to their status as "heirs of the kingdom," not to their being more sensitive than the rich to the presence of God. It connotes their appropriation of hope in the promise of God's reign. These must have been welcome words to poor people and victims of discrimination. Their hope is strengthened by the knowledge that God is in solidarity with them, loves them, and favors them.

It gladdens one's heart to see God's tenderness toward marginalized persons such as the prostitute Rahab (2:25). James proclaims God's affection for her by placing her on an equal footing with Abraham as a model of faith. Rahab represents a deeply despised person—not only a woman, but a prostitute and a pagan. In society's eyes, she starts with three strikes against her, but Rahab's praxis is a better example of works that justify than is Abraham's. In James's reading of the tradition, Abraham intends to slaughter his child in unthinking obedience. This "work" is scarcely consistent with James's references to the works of justice that collaborate with faith. Perhaps that is why the author draws on the example of Rahab, whose hospitality toward Joshua's persecuted messengers justified her before God. The fact that Abraham and Rahab also appear together in other documents in no way lessens the shock value of James's reading.

JUDGMENT, THE HOPE OF THE POOR (5:1–6)

James simultaneously denounces injustice and announces its end. Using apocalyptic language, he makes his most powerful denunciation of the rich and their exploitative practices. In 5:1 he exhorts the rich to wail loudly in the face of their impending misfortunes, which will befall them because they exploit, steal, and murder. This hope of an end to oppression was probably addressed not only to farm workers in the community but also to oppressed workers in general. In 5:9 the author insists again that the coming of the Lord–the Judge–is at hand. The coming judgment embodies the hope that oppression will end, and with it the outcry of the victims.

THE ANGLE OF PRAXIS

The angle of praxis can be summarized as militant patience, integrity, and authentic prayer.

MILITANT PATIENCE

James regards militant patience as an important element at the heart of praxis, but not a submissive or passive patience. The Greek terms he uses come from the military arena and are used metaphorically to refer to the struggles of life. James uses two different words, sometimes synonymously and sometimes with marked differences in meaning. In 1:3, 4, 12; 5:11 "patience" means persevering, resisting, being constant and unyielding. Its meaning is active; it refuses to bow to oppression or marginalization. Patience is militant, producing good works and good results.

In 5:7, 8, 10 James uses another Greek root for patience. It is not active, but neither is it passive in the sense of resignation. It connotes an attitude of staying alert and refusing to fall into despair. Farmers thus patiently await the fruit they know will come thanks to the care they have given to the plant. They can do nothing to hasten its ripening. James's communities know that judgment has been pronounced in their favor. Thus it is important for them not to despair but to keep on sowing, as it were–which for James means following the law of freedom and leading a life consistent with it.

INTEGRITY

The heart of praxis, integrity implies consistency between hearing-seeing-believing-speaking on the one hand and action on the other. In 1:8 and 4:8 James criticizes the "double-minded" person who has ulterior motives. In 4:8 he attacks those who befriend the world–that is, who adopt the values of an unjustly structured society and thus are enemies of God. Scholars agree that this passage alludes to idolatry. James calls the objects of his diatribe "adulterers" (4:4) because they lead a double life. He calls on them to stop their dirty dealings.

God is the model of integrity. In 1:5–7 God is contrasted with the double-minded person, since God gives generously, without ulterior motives. The Greek word translated as "generously" is the opposite of double-minded and means, literally, "simple." God is constant (1:17), always acting in the same merciful and just way.

Faith and practice are the marrow of integrity. The bridge linking the experience of oppression to eschatological hope is the practice of faith. James connects practice to liberty, faith, and wisdom, which are effective only if they manifest themselves in the practice of justice. Otherwise they are false: as good as dead.

God's word (1:22–24) is "the perfect law . . . of liberty" (1:25). That word loses its force if it is only heard: only when it is put into practice does it acquire life and verification. Jas 2:12 must be seen in the overall context of chapter 2, which attacks the lack of respect for the poor and the adulation of the rich. The law of liberty is a single entity: if you are pious but still play favorites, you violate the "royal law" (2:8).

In 2:14–26 James continues his concern for consistency, affirming the complementarity of faith and works. From a theological viewpoint, this passage is polemical. It appears to contradict Paul's theology of justification by faith. James and Paul differ in their approaches, which is understandable since the two are speaking in different contexts. James is concerned to underscore the unity between faith and works as part of a coherence of hearing-seeing-believing-speaking and action. He thus begins his reflection with a concrete example (2:14–17). If James was familiar with Pauline theology, he is engaging in a polemic against a misunderstanding of justification by faith. Faith without works, he maintains, is dead. Faith cooperates with works and is completed through works (2:22). For Paul, the works of justice reveal the fecundity of the event of justification. They are its fruit.

In 3:13–18 wisdom is linked to practice. There are two types of wisdom—wisdom from above and demonic wisdom. Praxis will reveal which of the two is operating. Apparently a number of persons in the community want to be teachers, and probably claim to have wisdom. James explains that authentic wisdom is demonstrated in practice.

The letter also addresses the matter of personal integrity and honesty, dealing at length in 3:2–12 with abuses of the tongue and the difficulty of keeping it under control. James's insistence on sincere speech in the community may be due to their need both to support one another in the face of discrimination from outside, and to keep the group from being undermined by internal divisions and misunderstandings.

AUTHENTIC PRAYER

James considers prayer to be basic to the life of Christian communities. Praxis is consolidated" by a life of prayer. Jas 1:6–8 and 4:3 indicate wrong ways to pray. Both texts address the "double-minded" people who cannot draw near to God because they seek primarily their own interests. They are inconsistent in their practice of faith. But God hears the cry of the harvesters (5:4)–a prayer that lifts up the injustice and inconsistency of employers who fail to pay their workers. Jas 5:13 encourages prayer in the midst of suffering.

James is careful not to assign the "elders" the exclusive right of hearing confessions or praying. In 5:14 these elders pray for the sick and anoint them, but in 5:16 James encourages the members to confess their sins to one another and to pray for one another's healing. For oppressed communities in which some members are inconsistent in their faith because they discriminate against the poor (2:1), it is important to practice mutual confession of sins, as well as to pray for one another. In the church today the sin of discrimination against women should be a matter for constant confession. Prayer entails a process of self- criticism and of individual and community purification. In 5:16b–18 James stresses the power of fervent, constant prayer–something that is possible for anyone, and not only for great leaders like Elijah.

The end of the letter is abrupt (5:19). It urges the brothers and sisters to exercise their solidarity in the rescue of those who wander from the truth, and it proclaims the fruit of that action.

RECOMMENDED READINGS

Adamson, James B. *The Epistle of James.* Grand Rapids: Eerdmans, 1976.

Davids, Peter. *The Epistle of James: A Commentary on the Greek Text.* Grand Rapids: Eerdmans, 1982.

Dibelius, Martin. *James.* Hermeneia. Philadelphia: Fortress, 1981.

Laws, Sophie. *The Epistle of James.* New York: Harper & Row, 1980.

Maynard-Reid, Pedrito U. *Poverty and Wealth in James.* Maryknoll, NY: Orbis, 1987.

Ropes, James. *A Critical and Exegetical Commentary on the Epistle of St. James.* Edinburgh: T. & T. Clark, 1916.

Tamez, Elsa. *The Scandalous Message of James.* New York: Crossroad, 1990.

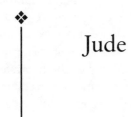

Jude

Marie-Eloise Rosenblatt ◆

INTRODUCTION

The Epistle of Jude is the work of a Jewish Christian pastoral theologian who writes in the name of one of the twelve apostles, the brother of the Lord (Matt 13:55; Mark 6:3). He claims to be a spokesperson for the apostolic tradition, though he eschews the title of "apostle" and situates himself more humbly in the role of "servant" (*doulos*), as does Paul (Phil 1:1) and the writer of James (1:1). He uses his oratorical and literary skill to castigate the community's ideological enemies even as he rallies the community to face the conflict like soldiers for battle (*epagonizesthai*, v. 3). The use of Hellenistic rhetorical style, with fourteen *hapax legomena*—most of them in passages that refer to the dissenters—is notable for so short a text. It suggests a conscious effort to communicate in an impressive way, probably to "match" the rhetoric of the opposition. The strength of Jude's voice encourages loyalists who feel shamed at losing the contest for allegiance to the persuasive force of their theological competition.

Generally ascribed to the late first century or the early second century, Jude lacks reference to external persecution from political forces, such as the Judean cataclysm of 68–72 c.e., the persecution of Domitian in 95 c.e., or the regional suppression of Christians in Asia Minor (see Pliny the Younger, *Letter* 10.96, ca. 110 c.e.). The content concerns internal division and theological debates over God as judge. This suggests either a location or a time in which political persecution was not taking place, though internal splits do not preclude external persecution. The location of the pastor and the congregation is uncertain. Arguments for the Greek mainland are as cogent as those for Asia Minor, Antioch, or Alexandria.

Major questions in Jude turn on whether a final judgment against evildoers will take place, whether Gentile Christians as well as Jewish Christians are subject to the same law, what the consequences for evildoers will be, and whether a belief in God's role as judge is relevant to the community. The pastor defends the tradition of God as judge and avenger of evil by three rhetorical strategies. He reviews Jewish biblical tradition, both scriptural and legendary, offering allusions as proof texts that God is a judge of all humanity and punishes evildoers whether ethnically Jewish or not. He shames the opposition and condemns their corrupt moral life. He encourages the members who feel humiliated to hold fast to their tradition.

SPECIFICS OF A FEMINIST ANALYSIS OF JUDE

Feminist interpretation of the epistle ascribed to Jude is especially challenging because there are no direct references to women as wives, mothers, sisters, or daughters, to women's behavior, or even allusions to the code of domestic life that subordinated women to men. Together with historical critics, feminist scholars examine a text in light of its literary form, rhetorical dynamics, and social and political context. In each instance, they pay special attention to gender-specific dimensions.

Jude typifies a patriarchal focus that excludes the mention of women and renders women's presence, voice, contributions, and roles invisible. A feminist analysis of historical material asserts the presence and reconstructs the actions of women in Jude's community. A gender-inclusive historical perspective assumes, for example, that rival teachers who are causing divisions in the community include women as well as men. Feminist analysis also pays attention to issues of body, sexuality, and generativity, because these categories ground the debate about women's dignity and equality as persons along with men.

THE BODY: SEXUAL ETHICS AND
DOCTRINAL ORTHODOXY

Sexual misconduct of the opposition is condemned throughout the letter (vv. 4, 7, 8, 16, 18). Conventional biblical rhetoric describes Israel's fidelity to the covenant with God in sexual terms. Using the metaphor of marriage, prophetic literature selects a woman's adultery against her husband as the quintessential image for religious syncretism, political alliances with Gentile rulers, or failure to heed the words of the prophets. Since the normal way to indulge lust involves men and women in sexual relations, the reader may deduce that the polemic involves women as well as men (a) who challenge the authority of incumbent pastoral leaders, (b) who reject a traditional apocalyptic scenario that involves judgment of evildoers, (c) who scoff at those who are loyal to the incumbent leaders, and (d) who claim that angels and Gentile Christians are not judged by God. According to the pastor, lack of sexual self-control and lustful misconduct characterize all persons who are guilty of these intellectual positions.

"Being without blemish" (*aptaistos,* v. 24) is a sexual metaphor. From a patriarchal perspective it refers to a father's "ownership" of his daughter and his guarantee at her betrothal that she is a virgin. In the Christian Testament, bridal imagery and reference to being without spot or blemish are used to describe the blameless moral behavior of the community (Eph 5:27; Rev 21:2). The loyalists of Jude's community are like a spotless bride, representing an ascetic ideal whose opposite is the behavior of dissenting women.

WOMEN IN BIBLICAL TRADITIONS

Feminists who review the use of Hebrew Scripture in the epistle (vv. 5–7, 11) retrieve allusions to women from the narrative contexts in Genesis and Numbers. Sodom and Gomorrah (Jude 7; cf. 2 Pet 2:6–10) involves a dramatic set of allusions affecting women. On the one hand, the sin of Lot's neighbors was punished with fiery destruction. On the other hand, Lot's wife was punished for looking back (Gen 19:26). Lot was ready to trade the virginity of his daughters for the protection of his guests (19:8). These daughers later had sexual relations with their father and were not punished, though the children born of their incest were said to account for the Moabites and Ammonites, who at times fought against Israel (Gen 19:30–38).

Several of the allusions in Jude refer to the pre-Sinaitic tradition and seem chosen to prove to Gentiles that God's judgment covers not only humans but angels and condemns the evil done not only by Jews but also by Gentiles. God's authority is universal and extends over all beings. This is the logic for the allusion to angels held in bondage (v. 6), to Cain (v. 11; Gen 4:8), the inhabitants of Sodom and Gomorrah (v. 7; Gen 19:4–25), and possibly the unbelieving Egyptians who perished in the sea (v. 11; Exod 14:23–31). Judgment also falls on Jews and Gentiles after the covenant, notably those who rebelled against Moses in the desert (Num 17:14) and the Gentile Balaam, whose female ass rebuked him (v. 11; Num 22:27–28). The case of the levite Korah, who challenged the authority of Moses (v. 11; Numbers 16), underscores the sorry truth that division can arise from within the community of the covenant, but it is punished. Hellenized Gentile Christians cannot hope to avoid the consequences of evil simply because they scorn the ethical norms or traditions of Judaism.

Prescinding from any ability to prove "where" God is, the writer rejects a cosmology that assigns God to a spatial location in the heavens, *baššāmayim.* In fact, the entire cosmos for rival groups will prove an empty illusion, which no divine presence inhabits. Under pressure to refute a cosmology constructed of invisible powers, the writer contradicts biblical language which regards waves, stars, winds, clouds, and darkness (vv. 12–13) as images of God's benevolence and subjects for praise and wonder (Psalms 104; 147; 148). The forces of nature, instead of functioning as a mirror of divine presence, prove meaningless and aimless, just as the assertions of rival theologians. The reversal shatters a complex framework of meaning created by women. They cannot claim, in Jude's scenario, a benevolently mysterious and archetypal assocation of the female body with earth, sea, and darkness.

CLASS AND SOCIAL STATUS

A feminist analysis of class attends to clues about the higher or lower political and social status of women. For example, the sort of language used by the pastor implies painful divisions between the more hellenized members of Jewish and Gentile origin and traditionalists of Jewish heritage, who are being ridiculed by intellectually sophisticated rivals. Jude's community includes members with varying degrees of linguistic fluency. Divisions based on linguistic competence were inevitable in a culturally diverse and multilingual Mediterranean society, as the case of Aramaic speakers versus Greek-speaking widows in Jerusalem (Acts 6:1–6).

The matter of reference to angels (vv. 6, 9) may reflect, within an intra-Jewish debate, a conflict between Sadducean and Pharisaic traditions. Asserting the existence of angels is a theological signal of one's political affiliation, as Luke records Paul's confrontation (Acts 23:6–9). Jude cites a tradition from the apocryphal Jewish *Assumption of Moses* about Michael contending with Satan over the body of Moses (v. 9). The midrash illustrates a conviction that the bodies of the dead have continuity as moral beings, since they can be fought over by forces of good and evil. The lesson, to shame opponents who claim higher status, is that the greatest angel does not insult an opponent, even the devil. Moreover, traditional Jewish lore "proves" that even beings of the highest status, angels, are judged by God and rewarded or punished.

ECUMENICAL, CULTURAL, AND
INTERFAITH DIMENSIONS

The speaker's rhetoric suggests that the community is heterogeneous, a mix of Jewish Christians of either Palestinian or more conservative origin, hellenized Jewish Christians, and hellenized Gentile Christians without any Jewish background. Those being scoffed at are most likely Christians of Jewish origin, familiar with the traditions of Hebrew Scripture and resistant to alternative readings of the gospel. Various forms of Christian evangelism, for - example, the *Gospel of Mary,* described a process in which evil was either conquered or purged as a seeker ascended the levels of the cosmic hierarchy and achieved full intellectual awareness.

Contempt for Judaism in Mediterranean society was acknowledged by Roman historians. It was inevitable that converts of non-Jewish, Gentile origin brought their social prejudices into the Christian community. Such attitudes could account in part for the denigration of Jewish tradition and scripture within the community of Jude. From this cultural and interfaith perspective, Jude defends the Jewish roots of Christian doctrine, as even the name "Jude" suggests. Essentially, the community is divided over Jewish tradition about God's judgment of evil.

The epistle of Jude arises from a moment in the community's history when leadership can no longer undertake rational exploration of various interpretations of the Bible, when dialogue about doctrinal differences has broken down, and when the polarization of the community has moved beyond hope of reconciliation. The speaker argues, condemns, and defends, but does offer hope of peace.

EXERCISE OF POWER AND AUTHORITY

There seems to be public endorsement of the pastor's rhetoric of rejection and suppression of doctrinal pluralism. Jude, claiming to be a successor of the Twelve, "solves" the problem of doctrinal cohesion. However, the solution legitimates a reduction of all differences in the community to a demand by the speaker for his community's loyalty. Orthodoxy is maintained not so much by reasoned arguments as by reassertion of tradition.

Complications resulting from cultural, ethnic, and linguistic backgrounds are ridden over rough-shod by the pastor-orator. All differences are reducible to a willingness to remain loyal to one system of interpretation and to reject the interpretation proposed by rivals. The judgment and interpretation of texts are reserved to a few men who are the authorized spokespersons for the community. One function of leadership was to identify the boundaries for community membership in disputes over interpretation of doctrine. Accusation of sexual misconduct, such as adultery and licentiousness, was a *topos* used to discredit community members whom leaders regarded as disturbers of the peace, syncretists, or apostates. This convention is well known from prophetic literature. Thus, it is difficult to determine whether dissenting groups within the community were actually guilty of sexual sins.

Jude's strategy for managing doctrinal divisions entails a refusal to negotiate with the enemy. An important doctrinal aim is defense of the community's biblical tradition and its Jewish roots. But the insult of the scoffers is matched by the tirade of the pastor against them. The letter's high concentration on polemics against the opposition (sixteen of twenty-five verses) indicates that Hellenistic diatribe, insult, curse, and invective, articulated by the community's leaders, was a legitimate weapon to ensure orthodoxy and stability in the community. Tragic consequences for ecumenical and interfaith relations have followed from Christians' failure to properly historicize, limit, and even reject this sort of bombastic invective against those who fell into the category of "the rival" or "the other."

THEOLOGICAL IMPLICATIONS FOR WOMEN

To resolve the theological debate, the pastor, unfortunately, focuses on God as judge and offers a paradigm that pits good against evil, with divine retribution assured for heretics. A feminist rhetorical analysis asks, How is this polemic heard by women who are part of the opposition and those who belong to the loyalists? Women would have been excluded from apostolic male authority represented by the speaker (v. 17) but could have belonged to the heretical group who reject authority (v. 8). All women in such a scheme must accept the absolute voice of male authority.

Feminist exegetes ask, How does a patriarchal denigration of women, even though indirect, function in the polemic against rival teachers? The basis for Jude's argument, defending Jewish theology of a nonparticularist God, was overlooked by later Christian pastors who engaged in anti-Semitic diatribe. Jude's letter shows that the consequences of defending orthodoxy include the silencing of women. Jude's defense, laudable on one level, leaves for the record a powerful, avenging God in the image of a male judge who punishes those who deviate from the teaching of the community's pastor.

The pastor condemns heretics through a curse on nature. The fruitful tree (cf. Matt 12:33) is both an archetypal female symbol and a traditional Jewish image for the beloved woman (Song 4:13; 7:8–9; Ps 128:3). The harshness of the condemnation of heretics as "autumn trees without fruit, twice dead, uprooted" is a curse falling with special force on women. The call upon the loyalists to anticipate the mercy of God but to exercise that mercy toward the weak in faith (vv. 22–23) still presents an image of God as judge.

For literalists and fundamentalists who resist the data of historical-critical research, the presentation of God as judge—merciful or condemnatory— serves a sociological purpose. It secures a community's sense of identity and cohesion. For educated and emancipated women, this brand of theology is simply another version of patriarchal domination. For African American women and those suffering domestic abuse, for example, the dynamics are all too familiar. Such ideology perpetuates itself by maintaining social structures and political systems that resist change, threaten punishment, force compliance, compete instead of negotiate, silence dissent, ignore the pedagogical consequences of power plays, and render women invisible.

RECOMMENDED READINGS

Bauckham, Richard J. *Jude, 2 Peter*. Word Biblical Commentary 50. Waco: Word Books, 1983.

Neyrey, Jerome H. *2 Peter, Jude*. Anchor Bible 37C. New York: Doubleday, 1993.

Primavesi, Anne. *From Apocalypse to Genesis: Ecology, Feminism and Christianity*. Minneapolis: Fortress, 1991.

Schottroff, Luise. *Let the Oppressed Go Free: Feminist Perspectives on the New Testament*. Translated by Annemarie S. Kidder. Louisville: Westminster/John Knox, 1991, 1993.

2 Peter

MARIE-ELOISE ROSENBLATT ◆

INTRODUCTION: STRATEGIES OF FEMINIST CRITIQUE OF 2 PETER

ONE IDEOLOGICAL CONCERN of feminist scholars is the identification of social systems of patriarchy that are reinforced by theological assertions. Feminist hermeneutics pays close attention to the principles by which the male pastor of 2 Peter legitimates his authority vis-à-vis his audience. Pastoral authority and doctrinal orthodoxy are both maintained by a competitive assertion. In relation to its internal critics, the speaker's community has greater wisdom, a more authentic link to God, better proofs for a belief in the day of the Lord, and a more ethical life. The invisibility of women in 2 Peter raises a question: Is there a relation between the pastor's polemic against dissenters and the eradication of women from the text?

LEGITIMATION OF THE WRITER'S AUTHORITY: SPIRITUAL GENEALOGY 1:1; 3:1–2, 15–16

2 Peter is a letter attributed to Peter but actually composed by a later Jewish Christian pastor for a heterogeneous Christian community torn by internal dissension. The atmosphere is reminiscent of earlier rivalries among house-churches in Corinth (1 Cor 1:10–13), where competition arose over the exercise of prophetic teaching authority. Unlike the single name Peter in 1 Pet 1:1, or the reference to Cephas (1 Cor 1:12), 2 Peter adopts the name Simeon Peter, a form that underscores Jewish identity because of the allusion to the tribal name (Gen 29:33). This is an important cue for reminding the audience of Peter's Jewish tradition. He identifies himself with Peter as the apostle anticipates his death (2 Pet 1:14), and his claim allies him with another pseudonymous writer, the pastor of 1 Peter, in whose name he writes a second letter as Simeon Peter (2 Pet. 3:1). His admonitions belong to an unbroken line

starting with the prophets, replicated in the Lord's commands, and continued by the apostolic succession (3:2). The source for 2 Peter is the epistle attributed to Jude. Most scholars affirm that the shorter text is the basis for the longer. The fact that the men openly invoke other men as sources of teaching and pastoral authority attests to a heightened need: hegemony of male authority has been challenged.

The letter dates from the latter first or early second century C.E. This can be deduced from hints that some debates concern the interpretation of Paul's letters (*epistolais*), which therefore must have existed as a defined group of writings distinct from the other scriptures (*graphas*, 3:16–17). The pastor refers to Paul as "beloved brother" (3:15), implying that his community gives allegiance to Peter and Paul in accord with Luke's rehabilitation of Paul and harmonization of tensions with Peter (Gal 2:11 versus Acts 15:6–22).

2 Peter's polemic is sobering evidence of the conflictual reality that underlay the Pauline ideal of a heterogeneous community in which Jew and Greek, barbarian and Scythian, male and female, slave and free could coexist in social harmony and enjoy a community of heart and mind (Gal 3:27–28; Col 3:11; Acts 4:32). 2 Peter, along with Jude, provides important historical data about the doctrinal storms, inseparable from economic and class distinctions, which regularly swept through the Christian community's internal life from its inception.

JUDE AND PETER: POLEMICS AS SOLUTION TO DISSENT

The pastoral solution for the community debates in Jude is similar to the recourse taken in 2 Peter: a forceful polemic and public condemnation of many people. A major concern is the popularity of so-called teachers and prophets within the community itself (*pseudōprophētai, pseudōdidaskaloi*, 2:1). It is likely that Paul's gender-inclusive affirmation of life in the spirit was adopted by female charismatics and that their consequent assumption of prophetic teaching authority violated social conventions and threatened the exclusivity of the male teaching office (2 Cor 3:17–18). The vigor with which the pastor attacks the dissenters testifies to the threat these teachers represent. The pastor regards the crisis as a time of darkness that the faithful must live through until the light returns (2:19).

2 Peter borrows from Jude a general line of rhetorical attack: association of rival teachers with sexual immorality, a dramatic sequence of scriptural proof texts from Hebrew Scripture about God's punishment of evil, metaphors of condemnation associated with the inanimate world, clouds and darkness (2:17), and a scenario of apocalyptic conflagration.

TRANSFIGURATION AS FOUNDATION
OF PROPHETIC AUTHORITY (1:16–21)

2 Peter's defense of pastoral authority based on witness to the transfiguration (Luke 9:28–35) is intriguing. All the Gospels associate key events of Jesus' passion, death, or resurrection with Mary Magdalene and other women, who were witnesses along with male disciples. Paul, however, omits explicit mention of the women in his review of the death–resurrection event (1 Cor 15:3–7). Neither does the transfiguration, as narrated by the Synoptics, mention women. This may be one reason for its appeal to the pastor in 2 Peter. He claims to have received the inaugural vision of Jesus along with other male disciples. The voice of prophetic authority, affirmed by God, is more important than the vision of Jesus. Transfiguration is an appearance of Jesus' glory which confirms Peter's authority as his spokesperson. The assertions of the speaker are designed to counter the foundational experiences of some women who claim to have seen and heard the risen Jesus speaking in vision to them, for example, Mary Magdalene in *Gospel of Mary*.

The association of Peter with the transfiguration authenticates his charismatic as well as hierarchical authority. His prophetic role is grounded in a vision of Jesus and a voice speaking to him, as well as other male witnesses. The origin of his authority is the Holy Spirit. Some of the tension with rivals concerns the legitimation of prophetic authority and the anthropology that explains the source of spiritual insight: its origin in the soul of the person (*psychikoi,* Jude 19) as opposed to its origin in the Holy Spirit (*pneumatikoi,* 2 Pet 1:21). Paul deals with these tensions in addressing the behavior of Christian *pneumatikoi* (1 Cor 12, 14).

The transfiguration serves an additional purpose: it reminds hearers of the Jewish roots of Christian teaching. Moses and Elijah flank Jesus. The two incarnate the scriptural traditions of Law and Prophets, that is, the canonical scripture as basis for pastoral authority. The transfiguration buttresses the pastor against Christians who embroider canonical scripture as well as against anti-Semitic Gentile Christians who reject canonical scripture because of its Jewish origin.

BIRTH IMAGERY, DEHUMANIZATION,
AND PATRIARCHAL REJECTION (2:12–16)

The spiritual genealogy of the pastor contrasts with the corrupt lineage assigned to the so-called teachers and prophets. They have proposed "cleverly devised myths" (1:16), which, in Hellenistic tradition, typically involved "birth narratives" which explained the origin of the world. Such narratives could involve persons named in biblical texts; they outlined family hierarchies of cosmic forces such as powers and principalities; they accounted for the generation of human beings and the origin of evil and materiality.

Conceiving and birthing are sexual metaphors foundational for mythic scenarios in some extrabiblical Jewish and Christian writings. Unlike the righteous, whose birth into living hope was celebrated with joy (1 Pet 1:3, 23), the followers of false teachers are like mother's children who were born as beasts—ignorant, driven by instinct, and without reason. They are animals made to be captured and killed (2:12). On the other hand, they are children, but accursed (2:14). Their behavior elicits the contemptuous rejection of a father for genetically inferior, mentally deficient offspring whom he refuses to claim as his. Not even human, they have engineered their own depravity and corruption (*phthora*, 1:4; 2:12, 19) by licentiousness and doctrinal error.

The pastor denies these members of the community a legal affirmation of their paternity. In line with the bestial imagery, the writer maintains that even the female ass (*hypozygion*, 2:16; cf. Matt 21:5) of the Gentile prophet Balaam, sent to curse Israel, prophetically spoke with greater wisdom than these women and men who claim prophetic authority (2:16).

DEHUMANIZATION OF TEACHERS
AS DOGS AND SWINE (2:21–22)

For the writer, doctrinal orthodoxy, blamelessness, and obedience characterize the civilized person. By inference, the opposition is literate, rhetorically skilled, knowledgeable about scripture, and interested in a variety of thought systems besides the community's theology. The pastor dehumanizes them. His insults, cast in the form of proverbial sayings, express the boundaries in Jewish consciousness that mark populations and locations as either "clean" or "unclean." In his conversation with the Canaanite woman, Jesus is said by Mark and Matthew to have cited a Jewish proverb that referred to outsiders or Gentiles as "dogs" in opposition to "children," who eat at the family table (Mark 7:27). "Dogs" is also a code for fools and teachers who destroy the community's harmony (Prov 26:11; Phil 3:2; Rev 22:15).

In the healing of the Gadarene demoniac, pigs (*choiron*, Mark 5:11) incarnated multiple levels of uncleanness: Gentiles who ate the livestock and made a living from the herd, Roman legionnaires, and invasive demons (Mark 5:1–20). Rival spokespersons who teach another interpretation of the scripture are compared to female swine, animals that are unclean (2:22). They are disinherited by an angry father who has the power to exile wives, sons, daughters, and slaves from the patriarchal household, now a metaphor for the church: accursed children (*kataras tekna*, 2:14). They have refused to submit to lordly authority (*kyriotēs*, 2:10). Their claim to prophecy is nothing but private interpretation. This isolates them from those who were moved by the Holy Spirit (1:20). The condemnation of women as unclean animals clashes with the inclusion of clean and unclean by Peter himself in the vision inaugurating his welcome of Gentiles (Acts 10:11–16). The invective that falls on women in the church is no doubt similar to the verbal abuse some suffered from their husbands.

Vomit and mud represent two dimensions of pollution: the inner world of thought and reflection and the outer world of social custom of those who are ungodly (*asebōs*, 3:7). These Gentile Christians prove the opposite of the God-fearers (*sebomenoi*), who accepted monotheism, attended synagogue, and were known for their support of Judaism (Acts 13:50; 16:14; 17:4, 17; 18:7). If women were named among the God-fearers in Acts and were counseled as women to be godly (1 Tim 2:10), there is little doubt that they are also included among the godless. From a Jewish Christian perspective, "godless" would be an epithet applied to Gentile Christians, whose status as outsiders was compounded by their rejection of the Jewish tradition they once embraced (2:21), and the community's sense of disillusionment at their betrayal. Some of the Gentile Christians in the community have remained and caused disturbance, and others have defected from the community and returned to their former way of life.

The polemic hints at conflicts Gentile Christians have with Jewish Christians who occupy positions of authority. Inevitable differences in degrees of familiarity with Hellenistic culture likely form a social substratum for the theological tensions. While it is acceptable for Jewish Christian pastors to cite legends from Jewish tradition, such as the rebellion of the angels before creation and the binding of the angels (2:4), the inventions of false teachers are dismissed as "cleverly devised myths" (2:16). The pastor adopts common Hellenistic rhetoric of spiritual progress when he says his own followers can "escape the corruption that is in the world because of passion and become partakers of the divine nature" (1:4).

PORTRAYAL OF WOMEN'S SEXUAL BEHAVIOR (2:5–14)

In contrast to the pastoral correctives that single out women (e.g., 1 Tim 3:11–12; 4:9–16), 2 Peter and Jude both avoid any direct reference to women. This anonymity erases signs of women's visibility even as it condemns their behavior as teachers and prophets. There is no reference to women's domestic roles, their dress, or their adornment. The vagueness of the polemic's reference is heightened by lack of architectural references to house, hearth, table, marketplace, fields, or place of worship. Women stand in no place and call no space theirs. Male prophets occupy the holy mountain and the writing desk, and women's claims to prophetic authority and their physical and intellectual attractiveness are condemned. They have the eyes of an adulteress (*moichalis*, 2:14). Adultery is a metaphor for the community's infidelity to God. Generic descriptions of sexual depravity, which could refer to apostasy and idolatry, abound in the letter. The metaphorical language draws attention to the bedroom as a spatial focus, for example, lusts of the flesh (2:10, 13, 18). The opposite behavior entails ascetic self-discipline so as to remain without spot or blemish (3:14).

Generic condemnations of sexual behavior, if they are literal rather than metaphoric, allow for a wide range of violations. These could include departures from a dress code, failure of women to keep silence in public gatherings, sexual relations outside the conventions of marriage, homosexual partnerships, marriage to nonbelievers, violations of consanguinity, or marriages in which partners of both religions participated in the sacred rites of the other's tradition.

THE END-TIME: CONFLAGRATION OF THE EARTH AND SKY (3:10–13)

In Jude's community, the key doctrinal issue was God's universal judgment. In 2 Peter, it is the surety of the Lord's return, accompanied by the end of the world. "Where is the promise of his coming?" (3:4). The pastor underlines God's destructive power raised against creation. The spatial metaphors in 2 Peter are trans- or subterrestrial: deluge with water, Tartarus, heavens, cloud, elements. The choice of symbolic world is prompted by a polemic against gnostic cosmology. Thus, there is no consoling return of Christ on the clouds or the meeting of Christ in the air (1 Thess 4:13–18). Rather, the heavens and earth will go up in flames and be dissolved in fire. This may include an allusion to the eruption of Vesuvius and the destruction of Pompeii in 79 C.E. For 2 Peter, the mythology of rival teachers has contaminated the heavens, just as their licentious behavior or apostasy pollutes human society.

At such a time, the pastor's followers will be like brides, without spot or blemish, the opposite of women who are prophet-adulteresses. The sexual metaphor associated with "new heavens and the new earth" nevertheless associates righteousness with a future to be awaited more in fear than in confidence. An ecology of annihilation undoes the present order, which has fallen hopelessly into corruption.

CONCLUSION

Feminist analysis challenges an interpretation of scripture that makes no distinction between the will of God for humanity and the strategies adopted by leaders to manage social crises. Reconstruction of women's roles in the congregation of 2 Peter serves three purposes. It indicates that women were active in teaching and interpreting the scriptures within Christian communities of the first century. It also reveals how ecclesial authority functioned in relation to dissent and how the voice of dissenters was suppressed. This historical reconstruction makes possible new ways of dealing with dissent. A feminist critique helps to rearticulate the roots of common faith for a church in which male and female disciples count as equally credible witnesses. In such a church, "Peter" is the name by which believers declare their bonds with one another, rather than marshal a force to conquer rivals.

RECOMMENDED READINGS

Bauckham, Richard J. *Jude, 2 Peter.* Word Biblical Commentary 50. Waco: Word Books, 1983.

Dowd, Sharyn. "2 Peter. " In *The Women's Bible Commentary,* edited by Carol A. Newsom and Sharon H. Ringe, 373. London: SPCK; Louisville: Westminster/John Knox, 1992.

Neyrey, Jerome H. *2 Peter, Jude.* Anchor Bible 37C. New York: Doubleday, 1993.

————. "The Apologetic Use of the Transfiguration in 2 Peter 1:16-21." *Catholic Biblical Quarterly* 42 (1980): 504–19.

Schüssler Fiorenza, Elisabeth. *But She Said: Feminist Practices of Biblical Interpretation.* Boston: Beacon, 1992.

Wire, Antoinette Clark. *The Corinthian Women Prophets: A Reconstruction Through Paul's Rhetoric.* Minneapolis: Fortress, 1990.

The Johannine Epistles

MARGARET D. HUTAFF ◆

THE JOHANNINE EPISTLES are three anonymous writings from late in the first century. Similarities among the three and between them and the Gospel of John indicate that they are products of a distinctive "Johannine" branch of early Christianity. Though they have separate and distinct personalities and were probably written by three different authors, the epistles all reflect situations of inner-Christian conflict. The longest, 1 John, is perhaps best known for its beautiful words on the theme of love and its injunction for Christians to "love one another"; yet it also contains scathing vitriol, defamation, and name-calling, directed in an exclusionary way by its Christian author at other Christians.

My reading and evaluation of these writings is grounded in E. Schüssler Fiorenza's "pastoral-theological paradigm" for biblical interpretation, in particular her "hermeneutic of suspicion."[1]

THE TRADITION OF HOSPITALITY

The in-house conflicts reflected in the epistles concern the early Christian tradition of providing hospitality to travelers. 3 John involves a conflict between a regional church official and an influential member of a local church over his inhospitable treatment of traveling missioners, en route to evangelize "nonbelievers." For 1 and 2 John, travel and hospitality fostered the spread of diverse theologies within the church at large, which they viewed as a problem. These two authors respond to such diversity by manipulating theological and ethical categories to create a dogmatic construction of what it is to be Christian; they define Christianity as correct belief. Their preoccupation with separating the true believers from the others and with presenting exclusionary behavior as necessary and sound ecclesial practice, stands in contrast to the more ancient tradition of Christian hospitality. According to the earlier tradition, reflected in 3 John 5, as well as in a wide range of other early Christian literature (Rom 12:13; Heb 13:2; 1 Pet 4:9; *Didache* 12.2; *1 Clement* 10–12), offering lodging and fellowship to traveling Christians in general, and to missioners in particular, even if such people were total strangers, was considered a basic obligation. 1 and 2 John, however, want to make such hospitality contingent on dogmatic conformity, turning a tradition of generosity into a mode of censorship.

WOMEN IN THE WORLD OF THE EPISTLES

Since masculine inclusive language and the absence of female references mask the presence of women in the situations mentioned in the epistles, references in other early Christian sources can aid our historical imagination in envisioning a context for these writings. From the Pauline letters, it is clear that women figured prominently in the areas of travel and hospitality, so essential to the growth and vitality of early Christianity. Hospitality began in the house-church, when generous individuals opened their homes to local congregations, providing space for gatherings and food for the common meal. Women like Prisca (with her husband Aquila) and Chloe were hosts of house-churches (1 Cor 1:11; 16:19; Rom 16:3–5). Their contributions in terms of the actual work of shaping and nurturing the earliest communities would have been inestimable, since the household was traditionally considered the proper or "natural" sphere of female activity. In Johannine circles, the welcoming environment created by the host of a house-church was particularly crucial in fostering the self-understanding of the group as a gathering of "friends" and "loved ones," so central to Johannine ecclesiology. The Gospel defines the community not in dogmatic but in ethical, relational terms: "By this, everyone will know that you are my disciples, if you love one another" (John 13:35).

From the house-church, hospitality extended outward as one of the earliest tangible expressions of mutual love and Christian unity.[2] By welcoming visitors, local communities affirmed a translocal relationship with all their "brothers and sisters" in other places. Along with letters, personal visits were important links creating networks of churches. Hospitality was also a major part of the patronage supporting the travels of missioners (cf. 1 Cor 9:1–14; Matt 10:10 and Luke 10:7 from Q), including women such as Prisca, Mary, Tryphaena, Tryphosa, Euodia, Syntyche, and Persis, among those whom Paul refers to as "co-workers" or fellow laborers (Rom 16:1–16). 3 John 8 later expands this concept, affirming that by hosting traveling missioners, local Christians participate as "co-workers" in their endeavors. Hospitality mitigated some of the limitations and difficulties associated with travel. It enabled women and men of lesser means to work as traveling preachers and teachers;

they could count on food and lodging, otherwise available only to the wealthy. This factor undoubtedly brought a greater number and diversity of participants into itinerant ministries and enabled a broader circulation of ideas among early Christian communities. For women, such support meant greater independence and mobility. Travel could also be lonely and dangerous. Early missioners often worked in pairs: wives and husbands, like Prisca and Aquila (Rom 16:3); or same-sex partners, like Euodia and Syntyche (Phil 4:1).[3] In the *Acts of Thecla*, a narrative reflecting the experiences of itinerant women teachers and evangelists in the first half of the second century, Thecla, as a woman on her own, had to fend off unwanted sexual advances. Hospitality offered women a measure of personal safety.

In contrast to the mobility that the practice of hospitality afforded to a variety of early Christians and their diverse ideas, 1 and 2 John move to limit this practice, to block the circulation of developing theologies. Drawing on 1 and 3 John, the author of 2 John ultimately formulates a general rule for restricting hospitality according to dogmatic criteria. He advises sister churches to turn away other Christians who fail to agree with his set christological interpretations. For 1 and 2 John, unity is to be expressed not in the practice of hospitality, but in theological agreement.

3 JOHN

EPISTOLARY GREETING (1–2)

The structure and brevity of 2 and 3 John are typical of letters of their day. Each follows the standard format: an opening, giving sender and recipient; initial greetings, often with a wish for good health; the body; and final greeting. Letters in antiquity were usually brief; each of these is about one papyrus sheet long.

3 John is a personal letter, uncontrived and written simply in response to the situation it describes. Because it is short on ethical and theological instruction and on specifically Christian elements, whether it belonged in the canon was debated long after the acceptance of the other two letters that bear the name John. It is addressed from "the elder," a person of some authority or office, to Gaius, a member of another church a distance away. No geographical locations and no name or further credentials for the "elder" are given. 3 John's ecclesial setting seems to have been an association of local housechurches overseen by a regional official, well enough established to have been identified by title alone (2 John 1; 3 John 1). Though a grammatically masculine title can apply to a woman, the masculine used here probably refers to a man, since the term does have a corresponding feminine form.

Several expressions in 2 and 3 John use "truth" as a synonym for Christianity. The elder addresses "the beloved Gaius, whom I love in truth," meaning both "truly" and as a fellow Christian. "Beloved," used often in 1 John, was a common salutation among Johannine Christians. It does not necessarily indicate personal familiarity. In fact, the elder seems to know Gaius only through reports from others.

GAIUS AND HIS SITUATION (3–8)

Traveling Christians, expecting to be welcomed by local house-churches, have come to Gaius's area. He has welcomed them, but they have been turned away by someone named Diotrephes, apparently powerful enough to "cast out of the church" anyone else wishing to receive them (v. 10). The elder speaks simply of "the church," meaning in one case his own church (v. 6), and in another the community to which Diotrephes belongs (vv. 9–10). Gaius may have belonged to the same church as Diotrephes, or to another close by. There is no mention that he himself has been "thrown out." No title or church office is attributed to either man. Though neither is formally identified as hosting a house-church, Diotrephes' apparent influence over others suggests that the church he belonged to met in his home.

Other Christians coming from Gaius's area have "testified" about his good behavior to the elder (v. 3) and his church (v. 6). The elder's response indicates that he presumes to have some kind of authority over Gaius. He writes to commend (vv. 5–6) and exhort (v. 11), and says that he is always glad to hear "that my children walk in the truth" (v. 4), implying that he sees Gaius as one of his charges. The elder is affirming: "You perform a faithful act whenever you are of service to the [sisters and] brothers, even when they are strangers" (v. 5). Gaius's service has been to provide hospitality to traveling missionaries: "You will do well to send them on their way in a manner worthy of God, for they went out for his name's sake" (vv. 6b–7). Here the author uses the special vocabulary used by Paul and others regarding missionary activity (1 Cor 16:6, 11; 2 Cor 1:16; Rom 15:24; Titus 3:13; Acts 15:3). To be "sent on one's way" meant to be supplied with whatever was needed for the journey's next leg.[4] "We should support such people," the elder says, "so that we may be co-workers in truth" (v. 8). "Co-worker" was used by Paul of other men and women who worked as he did in the mission field (Rom 16:3, 9, 21; Phil 2:25; 4:2–3; Phlm 24). The elder now applies this term to those whose support, in his time, makes the work of itinerants possible. That the itinerants were missioners is further confirmed by 3 John's reference to their not receiving recompense from "nonbelievers" (v. 7).

OPPOSITION FROM DIOTREPHES (9–10)

The missioners were apparently operating under the elder's auspices, or at least with his support as a regional official, since Diotrephes' rejection of them is linked with hostility toward him. The elder has written to the church as a whole but does not expect results, since Diotrephes "is not receptive to us" (v. 9). He uses the authoritative "us" when talking about this oppositional situation. Diotrephes is also bad-mouthing the elder by "talking nonsense about us in evil words" (v. 10). The elder mentions a future visit, to complain in person about Diotrephes' behavior. Whether he intends to confront Diotrephes or speak critically about him to the other men and women of the church is not clear. The elder does not give orders or pull rank but says only that he will pursue the matter through future discussion. Meanwhile, the letter establishes positive contact between the elder and Gaius.

No theological differences between the elder and Diotrephes are mentioned, and there is no sign that the visiting missioners attempted to preach anything controversial in Diotrephes' church. The problem seems to have been one of personal rivalry or competing authority. The actions attributed to Diotrephes suggest that he saw the visitors as an intrusion of the elder into his area of influence. The elder himself attributes Diotrephes' behavior to a large ego: "He likes to be number one" (v. 9). Some scholars have seen Diotrephes as a "monarchical bishop," complete with power to excommunicate; but this is to overinterpret the details of the letter. 3 John leaves us largely in the dark about Diotrephes' own self-perception, the nature of his influence, and the reason for his opposition, as well as about the identity and status of the elder.

EXHORTATION (11–12)

Using the standard "two ways" categories typical of moral injunctions, the elder exhorts Gaius: "Loved one, do not imitate evil but imitate good." Diotrephes is by implication the bad example to be avoided. The "two ways" are further described in Johannine idioms shared with 1 John: being "of God" (1 John 3:10; 4:6; 5:19) versus being one who "has not seen God" (1 John 3:6).

RECOMMENDATION AND CLOSING (12–15)

The statement about witnesses in support of Demetrios adds another dimension to 3 John, making it a letter of recommendation. Who Demetrios is and what he is being recommended for are not explained. The elder concludes (vv. 13–15) with his hope for a personal visit and greetings from his community ("the friends") to Gaius's.

1 JOHN

STYLE AND GENRE

1 John is often repetitive and not always easy to follow. Many pronouns are ambiguous, and some references are fully intelligible only in light of what is said later. References aimed at other Christians who disagree with the author appear before they are explicitly mentioned.

Scholars are divided as to 1 John's genre. Despite its traditional title, it has none of the features of a letter. It could be classed as a polemical treatise, since it intends to discredit one party and persuade another to side with the author. 1 John also makes extensive use of legal formulations, which gives it the character of a church order, a set of rules and exhortations for Christian living. The legal form it uses is not the direct "you should" or "you should not" pattern readily associated with laws, rules, or commandments, but rather the form that describes the behavior in question using an indefinite pronoun ("whoever does X" or "if anyone does X") and then prescribes the consequences or declares the party's innocence or guilt. The double-genre character of 1 John serves several purposes: Through instructions and exhortations describing undesirable behaviors, the author implicitly criticizes those with whom he disagrees; and the church order style enables him to regularize his exclusionary tactics as part of a larger model for ecclesial life.

LANGUAGE AND AUTHORSHIP

The masculine character of 1 John's language is less obvious in English translation. Its many legal formulations, easily translated into English with gender-neutral indefinite pronouns, are all grammatically masculine in Greek, as are forms of direct address that appear inclusive in English, such as "beloved." Since the author does not explicitly exclude women, and they were undoubtedly part of the community addressed, we assume that the masculine is gender-inclusive. On the other hand, he addresses "fathers" and "young men" (but no female counterparts), speaks of the members of the community as "brothers" (as opposed to the Gospel's "friends"), cites a male exemplar from biblical tradition (albeit a bad one), and applies the imagery of birth to an exclusively male God who is "the father." These features, and the absence of any mention of women or issues related to women, suggest a male author.

1 JOHN: AN OVERVIEW

The anonymous author belongs to a church from which a group of his fellow women and men with whom he disagrees have departed. They have "gone out" (2:18–19) and have approached another community, which 1 John addresses. The author is curiously silent about the specific circumstances surrounding their departure. Using heavy-duty defamation, he writes to persuade members of the other church to avoid being "deceived" (2:26) by these "Antichrists" (2:18), and to remain on (or return to) his side. He is insistent that his position is the only right one (4:6). He faults the departed dissidents on two fronts: their views concerning Jesus and their behavior, interpreted by him throughout as failure to love their fellow Christians. (Except for their leave-taking, no further details of their actions are given.) Part of his rhetorical strategy is to identify them so thoroughly with "sin" that the community to which he writes should feel no connection or obligation, not even to pray that they be forgiven (5:16–17).

The absence of a specific address suggests that the author may have intended this work for wide distribution in an effort to block the dissidents' reception in other communities. His rhetorical mode of operation is as follows: First he sets up a construct of Christian origins in terms of an original "message," containing the teaching of Jesus himself, passed on by eyewitnesses. The "message," now passed on by the author, is in essence the command that Christians should "love one another." The author elaborates on this "message" by developing various christological and theological aspects of love, aimed at building a case against the dissidents for failing to love their fellow Christians, finally equated with failing to love God himself. Simultaneously, he expands the contents of the "message" to include a summary of what he insists is the correct Christology, in opposition to the dissidents' christological "error." His Christology thus becomes dogmatic grounds for determining the presence of the "spirit" and the availability of "eternal life." His alternating discussions of love and Christology give 1 John its repetitive quality. Other theological elements are also set up to serve the author's rhetorical goals: sin and forgiveness, by way of inclusion, when he talks to the addressees, and unforgivable sin, by way of exclusion, when referring to the dissidents. The rhetorical centerpiece of 1 John is his ultimate claim to possess the "spirit of truth," as opposed to the "spirit of error" motivating those who disagree with him.

That Christology was the area in dispute is indicated by repeated references to the necessity of affirming certain beliefs about Jesus. Several of these references (2:22; 4:15; 5:5) contain the two christological affirmations presented at the Gospel's original conclusion: "Jesus is the Christ, the son of God" (John 20:31). These categories, applied to Jesus throughout the Christian Testament, were common features of early Christian belief. An additional affirmation, however, is unique to the Johannine Epistles, probably indicating that this specific point was in contention: "Jesus Christ has come in flesh" (4:2). Some scholars maintain that the disagreement extended to the two traditional confessions of Jesus as "Christ" and "Son of God," though it is hard to imagine what the dissidents' Christology was if they "denied" both of these titles, since they and the author were originally part of the same community. The author is probably presenting a survey of christological affirmations wider than the specific point at issue, in keeping with the instructional aspect of this work.

It is widely assumed that the two parties held different views of Jesus arising from different interpretations of the Gospel, perhaps in a version earlier than our final form. There are, however, no verbatim parallels between the Gospel and any of the epistles, despite many points of similarity. This suggests either that 1 John took great liberty in reconfiguring elements borrowed from the Gospel, or that the two drew on the same traditions.

1 JOHN: COMMENTARY

"From the Beginning" (1:1–4)

The main structure of the opening sentence reads: "What was from the beginning ... concerning the word of life ... we proclaim also to you. ..." The author asserts that what he now "proclaims" to his addressees is consistent with an original Christian "message" (1:5) going back to Jesus and those who were present with him. He sees himself as transmitting this "message" (1:5) so faithfully that he can even speak of himself as part of the original "we." References to hearing, seeing, and touching establish the reliability of what the author now passes on.

Using much the same vocabulary as in the Gospel's prologue, but configuring and applying it differently, 1 John calls Jesus "the life" and "the eternal life" (1:1, 2). In this context, which focuses on proclamation, "the word of life" seems to be a synonym for the "message," which the author understands as both from and about Jesus (1:5). The contents of this "message" is in essence Jesus' command to "love one another" (1:5, 7; 3:11; cf. John 13:34; 15:12, 17).

The author's construction of Christian origins locates him as part of an authoritative "us," over and against the "you" of his addressees, and in distinction from the dissidents, not yet mentioned but present in the background. He goes on to place himself in the position of middleman: "so that you may have communion with us; and our communion is with the father and his son" (1:3).

Ethics and Church Membership (1:5–7)

The author will first fault the dissidents for failing to follow Jesus' command to love. He turns in that direction now by introducing the ethical metaphor of walking and the antitheses of light and darkness to represent good and bad behavior in relation to church membership. Claims to relationship with God and with other Christians must be backed up with appropriate behavior. Inappropriate behavior precludes "communion" with God (1:6); appropriate behavior is a prerequisite for "communion with one another" (1:7). The author does not discuss specifics.

The authoritative "we" used in 1:1–5 is replaced in 1:6–10 with a hortatory "we," used to instruct or reprimand; it really means "you." The implied criticisms couched in this section are aimed at both the opponents and those addressees now under their influence. The three negative references all begin with "if we *say*" (1:6, 8, 10). Some scholars theorize that these and other such references throughout 1 John contain quotations of proactive claims actually made by the dissidents; 1:8 and 10, for example, could indicate that they viewed themselves as living on a higher spiritual plane and claimed to be exempt from sin. In my opinion, however, such scholarly interpretations cast the dissidents in an unnecessarily negative light and fail to see how much of the author's presentation is purely his own rhetoric. The "say" references may in fact indicate simply that the dissidents claimed to be good Christians despite the author's charges to the contrary. They apparently denied his charge that they were sinners (1:8, 10). The other "say" references contain categories Christians might typically use to describe the dynamics of their Christian identity: having communion with God (1:6), knowing Jesus (2:4), abiding in Jesus (2:6), being in the light (2:9), and loving God (4:20). The rhetorical function of these "say" references is to list the things *the author says* that the dissidents *can't say* about themselves. This is the author's own form of rhetorical excommunication. Associating the dissidents with various behaviors that are obviously incompatible with being Christian is his way of defining them out: he paints them as "walking in darkness" (1:6); specifically, failing to keep Jesus' commandments (2:4, 6); more specifically, failing to love one's sister or "brother" (2:9; 3:15; 4:20), meaning one's fellow Christian. Finally this failure to love is equated with failure to love God himself (4:20).

Sin and Its Remedy (1:7–2:2)

The author begins and ends this work with references to sin. His emphasis here on confession (1:8–10), forgiveness (1:9), and expiation (1:7; 2:2), probably indicates that the addressees have been receptive to the dissidents. He offers them encouragement to switch over to his side. The "you" implicit in the previous hortatory "we" becomes explicit when he addresses the audience directly: "My little children, I am writing this to you so that you may not sin. But if anyone does sin," he continues with tactful indirection, assuring them that a remedy is available (2:1). Though the author is lavish here in describing Jesus as expiation "for the sins of the whole world" (2:2), the dissidents' sin is another story (5:16–17).

Commandments Old and New (2:3–11)

The author starts constructing the criteria by which he will fault the dissidents. Anyone truthfully claiming to "know" or "abide in" Jesus must keep his commandments (2:3) or "word" (2:5) and imitate his model behavior (2:6). The "word" is Jesus' command to "love one another," though not explicitly cited until 3:11. The command to love is referred to as "not a new commandment, but an old commandment," well known to the addressees (2:7). What the Gospel calls Jesus' "new commandment" (John 13:34–35) is thus labeled "old," and the author, now writing in the first person, gives his own "new commandment" (2:8–11). The ethical metaphor of walking is resumed, and the antitheses of light and darkness are now paralleled with love and hate. To add drama and urgency, these ethical categories are also given eschatological significance: "the darkness is passing away" (2:8), and later, "the world is passing away" (2:17).

Though not yet specifically mentioned, the split between the author and the dissidents is reflected in his "new commandment": "Whoever loves his brother abides in the light . . . but whoever hates his brother is in the dark." Both John and 1 John understand "love one another" as an injunction to love not one's fellow humans in general, but one's fellow Christians, whom 1 John calls "brothers" (3:16; cf. John 20:17; 21:23). The dissidents, faulted with failing to love their Christian sisters and "brothers" (cf. 3:10, 15; 4:20), are thus guilty of love's opposite: hatred. This places them "in the dark."

Words to Specific Groups (2:12–14)

A church order might predictably contain sections of advice appropriate to specific categories of people, such as 1 John's "children," "fathers," and "young men"; but this author presents a variation on such a list (in two consecutive versions) as a means of complimenting his addressees and building a sense of solidarity with them before assailing the dissidents directly.

The Antichrists (2:15–21)

Building on the theme of overcoming "the evil one" (2:13–14), the author begins his construction of the current situation in apocalyptic terms, as a cosmic contest between God and those who truly love him and the "devil" or "evil one," associated with "the world" (2:15–17). He portrays his situation as the time before the end, when true believers are tempted by deceivers, a predictable part of the escalating conflict between good and evil.

Here the dissidents are finally introduced, and we are clued in to the fact that though most of 1 John appears to be general Christian instruction, much of what the author says is polemic aimed directly at them. They are now scripted into his apocalyptic scenario as "many Antichrists" (2:18). "Antichrist" is unique in the Christian Testament to 1 and 2 John, though it appears to have been in prior use, since the author says that his addressees have heard already "that an Antichrist would come." 1 John is drawing from a pool of images and concepts also used by other Christian Testament writers. "Antichrists" may be a variation on the "false Christs and false prophets" mentioned by the Synoptics (Mark 13:22; Matt 24:24), since 1 John refers to the dissidents later as "false prophets" (4:1). Interestingly, Matthew also describes the time of the "false prophets" as one when some Christians will "hate one another" (Matt 24:10–11).

"Jesus Is the Christ" (2:20–3:3)

From vilifying the dissidents, the author moves back to encouraging the addressees. He exhorts them to hold onto their knowledge of "the truth" (2:20–21), grounded in their baptismal instruction, "from the beginning" of their lives as Christians (2:24, 27), an echo of his earlier emphasis on consistency. This is necessary to achieve intimacy with God and Jesus, to attain "eternal life" (2:24–25; cf. 1:2; 5:11). The author thinks of this in relation to a future event, a "parousia" or "coming," probably referring to Jesus' return (2:28; 3:2–3), including a "day of judgment" (4:17).

The author supplies the contents of correct belief in a series of confessional statements about Jesus (2:22; 4:2, 15; 5:1, 5) running through the extensive section defaming the dissidents as Antichrists (2:18–19), children of the devil (3:10), murderers (3:15), false prophets (4:1), and liars (4:20). Such a general survey of correct Christology is in keeping with the church order character of this work. The negative description "whoever denies that Jesus is the Christ" (2:22) may be the author's own literal interpretation of the term "Antichrist."

Sin and the "Children of the Devil" (3:4–10)

Independent didactic material with themes of its own may have been used to compose this section (as well as an intriguingly similar section in John 8:31–47). The notion that Christians cannot sin conflicts with earlier remarks about forgiveness. Here the author sets up two opposing categories to defame and exclude the dissidents: sinners who are "from the devil," in contrast to Jesus (3:5, 8), and those "born of God," who are "unable to sin" (3:9) because God's "seed" (*sperma*) abides in them. The author probably understood this "seed" to be "the spirit" (cf. 3:24). The operative metaphor is of a father who transfers his own characteristics to his offspring via his semen or "seed." As "children of God," Christians resemble their father, himself sinless, as is Jesus, his "son" (3:5). The devil's children, like their father, are sinners. The author pronounces that "no one who does unrighteous deeds is of God"; then to custom fit this description to his rhetorical portrait of the dissidents, he adds "and neither is anyone who doesn't love his brother" (3:10).

The Example of Cain (3:11–15)

By implication, the dissident women and men are the "children of the devil," who, in failing to love their fellow Christians, have violated the essence of the original Christian "message" (3:11). Cain, the infamous killer of his own brother (Gen 4:1–16), functions here as their counterpart. Because the story involves two brothers, one good, one bad, it is useful to the author as a prototype of the current division among the "brothers" of his community.

Two themes operate here: the predictable opposition that righteousness draws and the connection of fraternal hatred with murder. Just as Abel drew the hatred of his unrighteous brother, the addressees can expect to be hated by "the world" (3:13). The dissidents are thus aligned both with Cain and with "the world." To emphasize the term "brother" and heighten the sense of his solidarity with the addressees, the author addresses them directly as "brothers."

The author pulls the addressees further into his camp (3:14), assuring them that, in contrast to the dissidents, "we have passed from death to life, for we love our brothers." The dissidents' alleged failure to love is severely condemned: "Anyone who hates his brother is a murderer" (3:15). The author is probably basing this equation on general Christian teaching, since a similar presentation appears in Matthew. In the Sermon on the Mount, Jesus extends the ancient command against killing to include anger; whereas the command of old prescribed that a killer would be "liable to judgment," Matthew's Jesus now says that "everyone who is *angry with his brother* will be liable to judgment" (Matt 5:22). 1 John's equating hatred of one's brother or sister with murder is yet another way of excluding the dissidents: "You know that no murderer has eternal life abiding in him" (3:15).

"Love One Another" (3:16–24a)

After one of its most vitriolic displays, 1 John turns to the topic of love. Jesus is presented as the model for love within the Christian community. Just as he "laid down his life for our sakes," so "we ought to lay down our lives for our brothers" (3:16). Again the author draws from traditional teachings (3:17–18). The reference to sharing one's wealth with a "brother in need" is one of 1 John's few practical references. He probably includes it because its condemnation of "closing one's heart" to one's "brother" fits his profile of the dissidents. The injunction to show love by deeds, not just words, is a Christian staple (cf. Jas 1:22).

The theme of the "heart" continues in 3:19–22, now referring to one's conscience. "Whatever we ask" will be granted, the author says, because "we keep his commandments," anticipating the later distinction between sin that can be forgiven through prayer and sin that cannot (5:14–17). Belief in Jesus is now added to the command to love as a component of what is here called God's commandment: Christians must "believe in the name of his son, Jesus Christ," and "love one another" (3:23). In pairing the christological reference with the command to love, the author starts to add a dogmatic component to the Christian "message." Correct belief as part of the "commandments" is now a precondition for mutual abiding (3:24a).

"Test the Spirits" (3:24b–4:6)

A major rhetorical step is the author's construction of "the spirit": "By this we know that he [God] abides in us, by the spirit which he has given us" (3:24b). The author gives directions for how competing claims to religious authority are to be evaluated: "Do not believe in every spirit, but test the spirits to see if they are of God" (4:1). Such a test will identify "false prophets" who "have gone out into the world," an echo of the language used to describe the dissidents (2:19). He applies the traditional notion that prophets are motivated by either good or evil "spirits." The dissidents as "false prophets" are motivated by "the spirit of the Antichrist," in contrast to "the spirit of God," which he claims motivates him. The addressees must choose. The criterion he proposes is christological and propositional and probably represents the point of active disagreement with the dissidents: "Every spirit which confesses that Jesus Christ has come in flesh is of God" (4:2). Since the author implies only that the dissidents did not affirm this confessional statement and does not describe what they did affirm, we are left with little to enable a respectful reconstruction of their Christology.

Pulling the addressees closer and pushing the dissident Christians farther away, the author says: "You are of God, and have overcome them. . . . They are of the world, so what they say is of the world" (4:4–5). His ultimate criterion for testing spirits is given in a blunt claim: "We"—the authoritative "we," perhaps now rhetorically including the addressees—"are of God, and whoever knows God listens to us; whoever is not of God does not listen to us" (4:5–6). "By this," he says, "we can discern the spirit of truth and the spirit of error" (cf. John 14:16–17; 15:26).

1 John's author reorients the concept of "the spirit" to use it against his fellow Christians. The Gospel understands the spirit as residing in the entire community, teaching and reminding it of what Jesus taught (John 14:26). Its

"spirit of truth" (John 14:17; 15:26; 16:13) is nowhere paired with a "spirit of error." In this construction, "the spirit" works as a unifying force, affirming the theologizing energy of the community as a whole. This understanding may have motivated the dissidents' efforts to do their own Christology. The author of 1 John, however, turns "the spirit" into a church-political tool. By asserting that a particular theological position is a dogmatic "test" for the spirit's presence, he uses it oppositionally to disenfranchise other Christians and their theologies. In addition, by situating "the spirit" and the activity of theological reflection itself in the arena of "truth" versus "error," he implies that theology can be evaluated in terms of whether it is "true" or "false," "right" or "wrong." This view is expressed in his presentation of christological propositions as if they were "facts" or unchanging truths.

Love (4:7–12)

Returning to the theme of love, the author explicates its theological and christological dimensions. Knowing God is essentially linked with following the command to love, since "love is of God." In fact, "God is love" (4:8). The Christian's love for God is concrete, expressed in love for one another. It is a response to God's own love, "manifested among us" when he "sent his only son into the world so that we might live through him" (4:9). If God "loved us so much" that he "sent his son to be the expiation for our sins," the proper response is to "love one another"; thus God's own love is extended and "perfected in us." The interpretation of Jesus' death as expiation plays a central role in this understanding of love. The theological model of a father who exercises parental discretion by choosing to "send" his own child to suffer and die is, despite an overlay of loving intentions, a disturbing one in the context of patriarchal societies, ancient and modern.

Jesus as "Son" and "Savior" (4:13–16)

The theme of love merges with the author's emphasis on correct belief as he adds two more christological affirmations: Jesus is "savior of the world" and "son of God." The vocabulary surrounding these affirmations signals the status the author wishes his Christology to have. Language of seeing and bearing witness is reprised from the opening words of 1 John to situate the affirmation of Jesus as "savior" within the "message" the author passes on (4:14). In addition, using the Johannine idiom for the highest level of divine–human intimacy, the author parallels "whoever confesses that Jesus is his son, God abides in him and he in God" (4:15) with "whoever abides in love abides in God and God abides in him" (4:16; cf. 3:24). Correct Christology and love, specifically love for the Christian brother (4:12, 20–21), are ranked together as leading to the same desired goal: mutual abiding. The gift of "the spirit" is cited here as its divine confirmation (4:13).

Other Voices in 1 John (4:16)

Though efforts to reconstruct sources used by 1 John have produced varying and inconclusive results,[5] many scholars agree that the author used prior materials from instructional or catechetical works in composing his exhortations, injunctions, and expositions of central Christian themes. Such a prior source, as negative in outlook as 1 John itself, probably lies behind the section on the "children of the devil" (3:8–10). Foundational portions of 1 John's catechesis on love may likewise have been drawn from the works of other Christian women and men. For example, the often-quoted affirmation that "God is love" begins a portion of 4:16 that has a unity and completeness, as well as a structure and rhythm of its own. The preceding verse contains the same thought in similar form, invested with one of the author's christological confessions; the following verse takes up a new topic. In 4:15, the author seems to have rewritten 4:16 as if he were reworking a general reference taken from another source, modifying it to suit his own rhetorical needs. Repetitions in other places (3:24; 4:8, 12, 13) suggest that he has worked key expressions derived from 4:16 into his presentation to lead up to their use there; the term "abide" is not used again after that verse.

Another voice in 1 John seems to have reflected on love in more positive ways, before the author compromised its credibility by using it to build a case against the dissidents. That original voice comes through, however, to modern readers, who often read this beautiful passage out of context. 1 John's polemic is so indirect that readers today are often unaware of the work's exclusionary purpose, hearing in this case only the positive voice in the text.

Love (4:17–21)

The theme of love continues, developed in several additional ways. The perfecting of love is now identified with intimacy with God and becoming more like God in confident preparation for the "day of judgment." This reference leads the author to another point: The character of Christian love as response to God's having "first loved us" means that only love itself, not fear of punishment, is appropriate motivation for following the love command. As the author moves toward a restatement of the command to love, his prior reference to God's invisibility (4:12) is used more explicitly to support the necessity of loving one's brother (4:20). Finally, the command to love is reconfigured once again, placing love for one's brother on an equal footing with love for God (4:21).

Love and Victory over the World (5:1–5)

Once more the author uses the same two confessions that originally con-cluded the Gospel as a summary of Johannine Christology (5:1, 5; cf. John 20:31). On the analogy that whoever loves the parent also loves the child (5:1), he again makes the point that love for God requires loving one's fellow Christians. Reprising his eschatological mode, the author asserts that "every-thing born of God overcomes the world." "Our faith," a notably un-Johannine noun, is called "the victory that overcomes the world" (5:4–5; cf. John 16:33).

Testimony (5:6–13)

Forensic language dominates in 5:6–11. The author describes Jesus as "the one who came by water and blood, not in water alone" (5:6). The precise nuance intended is unclear, but 1 John's stress on blood corresponds to its repeated references to expiation and atonement, accomplished through Jesus' death. "The spirit," again equated with "the truth," is cited as "the witness" for this past coming. Then in the most enigmatic reference in 1 John, three unani-mous "witnesses" are given: "the spirit and the water and the blood" (5:7–8). These may represent the outpourings of the spirit, of baptismal water, and of atoning blood shed on the cross. The importance of correct Christology is again affirmed: "God has given us eternal life, and this life is in his son. Whoever has the son has life" (5:11–12). Language similar to the original con-clusion of the Gospel (John 20:31) is used in 5:13: "I write this to you . . . that you may know that you have eternal life."

Mortal Sin (5:14–17)

Before concluding, 1 John sounds an ominous note. First the author reaf-firms that God will hear and grant any legitimate request. Then he mentions sin, making a distinction between "deadly" or "mortal sin" and sin of lesser consequence. He focuses on the sins of others: "If anyone sees his brother committing a sin which is not deadly, he should ask, and God will give that person life" (5:16). But regarding "mortal sin," "I don't recommend that one petition regarding that" (5:16). There is little doubt whose "mortal sin" he has in mind. The dissidents are placed beyond the efficacy of fellow Christians' prayers and, by implication, beyond divine forgiveness.

Conclusion (5:18–21)

1 John ends with a series of assurances echoing prior themes. It concludes with a new metaphor for the dissidents' errors: "Be on your guard against idols" (5:21).

1 JOHN: RAISING FEMINIST CONCERNS

Feminist readers who value texts that can serve as models for creating inclu-sive community and honoring diversity will have obvious difficulties with 1 John. Its author affirms the command to "love one another" as the essence of the Christian "message," but turns this injunction away from being a construc-tive challenge addressed to everyone (including him) and uses it as his criteri-on for judging others. He diverts love from the hard work of fostering open-ness and tolerance and uses it for exclusionary purposes. The potential of love to motivate human generosity is further weakened when this author weaves together the language of love and that of defamation, as if the two were gen-uinely compatible. We might also raise questions from liberation-theological and ecumenical perspectives about Johannine Christianity's limited applica-tion of the love command as an inner-Christian ethic, casting others as out-siders.

Another major area posing difficulties for feminist readers is 1 John's view of theology and "the spirit." By constructing theology in terms of truth versus error and defining it in dogmatic terms, he opens the way for historically and culturally conditioned interpretations to be elevated to the level of ahistorical timeless truths and to be enshrined as theological archetypes. This approach runs contrary to Schüssler Fiorenza's pastoral-theological paradigm, which holds that prior theological formulations may function prototypically (as resources for subsequent theological efforts), but not archetypically (as if they were theological "facts" to be repeated and reaffirmed).[6] Though the author of 1 John takes the liberty of expanding the category of "message" to include the dogmatic christological content he supplies, he nevertheless then sets this revised "message" up to function archetypically, as a dogmatic standard for theological "truth" and for determining membership in the community.

1 John's association of "the spirit" with correct theology, dogmatically defined, also raises questions about how theologies are to be "tested" or veri-fied. A hermeneutic of suspicion rightly questions any claim that an individual, institution, or theological position represents truth or God or is exclusively motivated by or in possession of "the spirit." Claims of authority based on appeals to "transcendent realities" are impossible to demonstrate or verify. Such appeals are essentially arbitrary and in fact often function precisely to place theological claims and claims to theological authority beyond critical reflection, examination, and discussion.

2 JOHN: AN OVERVIEW

Whatever Diotrephes' motives, his behavior as reported in 3 John was apparently taken as a model by 2 John's author. 2 John presupposes a situation in which traveling Christians, perhaps functioning as missioners not to "unbelievers" but to other Christians, were responsible for the spread of diverse theologies. Drawing on the description of Diotrephes' actions, the author of 2 John formulates a policy of exclusion to control such diversity. Christians who are, in his opinion, theologically correct are instructed to ban and shun others holding different theological interpretations (vv. 10–11). These harsh instructions are softened by references to "truth" and "love" (vv. 4–6).

Though written in letter form, 2 John is not a real letter addressed to an actual person in a particular place. Its author uses the letter format for a broader church-political purpose: to package his policy of exclusion for general distribution. Notable similarities to both 1 and 3 John indicate that the author derived many aspects of this work from them.

Epistolary Greeting (1–3)

Like 3 John, 2 John is a letter from "the elder." It is addressed "to an elect lady and her children." The identity of the addressees is debated. One possibility is that the address contains a specific woman's name: "to lady Eklekta" or "to [the] elect Kyria." The former is not likely, since "elect" is used later as a modifier, not a proper name (v. 13); the latter is grammatically problematic because of the Greek word order.[7] A related possibility is that "elect lady" is a generic term for a female leader of a house-church, such as Chloe (1 Cor 1:11), Nympha (Col 4:15), or Prisca (Rom 16:3), and that the church's members are referred to metaphorically as her "children." If this line of interpretation is correct, then, as E. Schüssler Fiorenza says, 2 John is "the only writing in the New Testament addressed to a woman."[8]

An alternative identification, however, seems more plausible to me, given the overall structure of the letter. The image of a lady with children is resumed in a parallel way at the letter's conclusion: "The children of your elect sister greet you" (v. 13). If the "lady" addressed is an actual woman, then the "sister" would likewise be a woman, by implication the letter's author. "Elect sister" must not refer to the author, however, since he has already been identified by the masculine form of the term "elder." More probably, the terms "elect lady" and "elect sister" are communal metaphors for "sister" churches, whose members, including the author, are seen as "children," probably following the Johannine convention of speaking of Christians as "children of God." The author in fact addresses a whole community, not a single person in charge, when his form of address flows from "you" singular (vv. 4–5) to "you" plural (vv. 6–12) and back (v. 13). The image of an "elect" or "chosen" woman as a communal metaphor is also used in 1 Pet 5:13 (cf. 1 Pet 1:2) of the church in Rome (under the code name "Babylon"). In the *Shepherd of Hermas,* the church as a whole is imaged as a woman (*Vis.* 2.4.1), addressed as "lady" (*Vis.*

3.1.3), and Christians are called "the elect" (*Vis.* 1.3.4). "Elect" or "chosen" is a widespread Christian self-description (Rom 8:33; Col 3:12; 2 Tim 2:10; Titus 1:1; 1 Pet 1:1; Rev 17:14). 2 John's metaphorical use of "to an elect lady" as an unspecific communal address makes this work suitable for general circulation.

"Truth" is used repeatedly in this greeting, as in 3 John. The letter format becomes shaky in v. 3, when what would usually be a wish made for the recipient is instead an affirmation about "us." This verse is a Johannine version of the greeting in 1 Tim 1:2 and 2 Tim 1:2, "Grace, mercy, and peace from God [the] father and Christ Jesus our lord." 1 and 2 Timothy are likewise intent on defining Christianity in terms of correct "teaching" (*didaskalia*). The precise expressions, "God [the] father" and "Jesus Christ, the son of the father," are unique to 2 John among the Johannine writings.

THE COMMANDMENT TO LOVE (4–6)

Reconfiguring the language of 3 John 1 and 3–4, the author commends his sister community: "I was very glad to learn that some of your children walk in truth" (v. 4). In the conclusion of the verse—"just as we have received commandment from the father"—the author moves into themes and language taken from 1 John 2:7 and 3:11. The form of address is polite: "Now I ask you, lady—not as if I were writing you a new commandment, but one which we have had from the beginning—that we love one another" (v. 5). The author backs away from 1 John's presentation of a "new commandment" (1 John 2:8) to keep a sharper contrast between old and new, since his major aim is to discourage theological innovation. "Love" is defined as following God's commandments (cf. 1 John 5:3), and the command to love is tied to the notion of a consistent tradition (v. 6).

WARNINGS ABOUT "DECEIVERS" (7–8)

The author, in language similar to 1 John 2:18–22 and 4:1–3, warns of "deceivers" who have "gone out into the world," those "not confessing Jesus Christ coming in flesh" (v. 7). Again the unusual term "Antichrist" is used. The reference lacks immediate connection to a concrete situation, and no details are given; but since the focal issue introduced later (vv. 9–11) concerns correct teaching and community boundaries, the author probably has other Christians in mind, following 1 John's application of the term.

What the author of 2 John understood his reference to faulty Christology to mean is not clear. 1 John's participle, literally "having come in flesh" (4:2), is time-specific to the past, but 2 John's "coming in flesh" (v. 7) could indicate either a past or, more probably, a future event. The author, writing at some distance from the actual situation of 1 John, may have rewritten the reference to give it a future meaning because that made more sense to him; or he could have simply misunderstood the reference in 1 John and fudged by using an ambiguous participle. 1 John does refer to a future "coming," but uses the noun *parousia* (2:28). Because 2 John 7a is essentially a reformulation of elements of 1 John 4:1b–3, resulting in a more ambiguous reference, it is doubtful that it actually refers to a live issue. The author positions this reference more as an example of failure to believe the right thing about Jesus, to lead up to the general instruction that follows.

Instruction in a Policy of Exclusion (9–11)

Adopting the style so typical of 1 John, the author presents a series of pronouncements and instructions in legal form (vv. 9–11). This section contains a mixture of vocabulary, some typically Johannine, some peculiar to this author. He picks up the term "abide" or "remain" (*menein*), frequently used in the Gospel and 1 John to express intimacy between the believer and God or Jesus, but uses it differently (v. 9). Here it means to "remain" within the bounds of an established "teaching," seen by the author as the fixed and proper content of Christian belief, as opposed to moving to an alternative theological position. He sets up this contrast by introducing the term "to go on" or "go ahead" (*proagein*), used only here in the Johannine literature: "Anyone who goes ahead and does not remain with the teaching about Christ does not have God; whoever remains with the teaching has both the father and the son" (cf. 1 John 2:23). The genitive, literally, "teaching of Christ," should be translated as "about Christ," following on the christological reference in v. 7; v. 4 previously attributed the command to love not to Jesus but directly to God. "Teaching" (*didachē*), a key term for this author, is not used in 1 or 3 John.

Verses 10–11 show parallels in thought with 3 John, but no verbal agreement. The author writes this crucial portion in his own words. He draws on the description of Diotrephes, whose response to traveling missioners was to refuse them and to advocate a general ban on their reception by the community. While Diotrephes' action, as far as we can tell, involved a conflict over personal authority, not theology, 2 John is interested in limiting the spread of theologies different from his: "If anyone comes to you and does not bring this teaching, don't receive him into your house, and don't even say hello to him" (v. 10). Here the actions attributed to Diotrephes in 3 John are converted into a general rule, creating a policy of exclusion. The recipients are addressed in the plural; the singular reference to "your house" means their house-church and, by extension, their individual homes. The author does not pick up the term "church" from 3 John, the only Johannine writer to use it.

The author's strategy for controlling theological diversity is to define Christianity as a "teaching" about Jesus with a normative content and to exclude those who diverge or differ from it. His is a process of elimination. He also invokes guilt by association: Anyone receptive to those with alternative theological ideas "has a share in their evil deeds" (v. 11), a negative reformulation of the positive thought in 3 John 8 that welcoming missioners was a way of participating in their good work.

Closing (12–13)

The closing is a near parallel to 3 John 13–14, with an added note about joy similar to 1 John 1:4, and a final greeting consistent with the letter's metaphorical address.

IN CONCLUSION

Reading these epistles raises questions about how we view theology, create hospitable communities, and deal with diversity, not only in our churches but in all aspects of life. From my perspective, to the degree that 1 and 2 John construct a rhetoric of intolerance, they have misused the ethical and theological resources available to them: a strong tradition of hospitality and generosity, an emphasis on the primacy of love as the basis of Christian self-understanding, and a more inclusive, noncoercive appeal to "the spirit." On the other hand, by reading the epistles with a "hermeneutic of suspicion," we can recover these basic early Christian resources and use them ourselves to construct meaningful theologies and build communities that teach tolerance—an important component of "love"—by practicing it.

NOTES

1. E. Schüssler Fiorenza, *Bread Not Stone: The Challenge of Feminist Biblical Interpretation* (Boston: Beacon, 1984), 32–42.

2. Wayne A. Meeks, *The First Urban Christians: The Social World of the Apostle Paul* (New Haven: Yale University Press, 1983), 109–10.

3. Mary Rose D'Angelo, "Women Partners in the New Testament." *Journal of Feminist Studies in Religion* 6 (1990): 65–86.

4. Abraham J. Malherbe, *Social Aspects of Early Christianity* (Philadelphia: Fortress, 1983), 67–68, 96.

5. One such reconstruction by R. Bultmann is available in Raymond E. Brown, *The Epistles of John* (Anchor Bible 30; Garden City, NY: Doubleday, 1982), 760–61.

6. See E. Schüssler Fiorenza, *In Memory of Her: A Feminist Theological Reconstruction of Christian Origins* (New York: Crossroad, 1983), 33–34; eadem, *Bread Not Stone*, 25–28.

7. As R. Schnackenburg explains (*The Johannine Epistles* [New York: Crossroad, 1992], 278): "One would expect the name to be placed first, as it is in the epistolary inscriptions of 1 and 2 Timothy, Titus, Philemon, and 3 John, with the article before the attributive 'elect' as in Rom. 16:13."

8. Schüssler Fiorenza, *Bread Not Stone,* 1; see also *In Memory of Her,* 248–49.

RECOMMENDED READINGS

Brown, Raymond E. *The Epistles of John.* Anchor Bible 30. Garden City, NY: Doubleday, 1982.

Bultmann, Rudolf. *The Johannine Epistles.* Hermeneia. Philadelphia: Fortress, 1973.

Lieu, Judith. *The Second and Third Epistles of John: History and Background.* Studies of the New Testament and Its World. Edinburgh: T. & T. Clark, 1986.

Perkins, Pheme. *The Johannine Epistles.* New Testament Message 21. Wilmington, DE: Michael Glazier, 1984.

———. *Love Commands in the New Testament.* New York: Paulist, 1982.

Schnackenburg, Rudolf. *The Johannine Epistles: Introduction and Commentary.* New York: Crossroad, 1992.

von Wahlde, Urban C. *The Johannine Commandments: 1 John and the Struggle for the Johannine Tradition.* Theological Inquiries. New York: Paulist, 1990.

Hebrews

CYNTHIA BRIGGS KITTREDGE ◆

INTRODUCTION

ALTHOUGH WOMEN HAVE always been readers of the Bible and active members
of Christian congregations, it is only recently that we have seen ourselves as
interpreters of the sacred texts of the tradition who have distinctive contributions to make to the ongoing interpretation of the Bible in our communities.[1]
As women have entered the conversation, both in the academy and in the
church, we have questioned basic assumptions of male-dominated biblical
studies such as the belief that women did not write and that they were peripheral, if not absent, from history. The work of women scholars has highlighted
the construction of gender and sexuality in biblical texts and questioned
whether these cultural constructions should be normative as theological
ideals. Perhaps even more fundamental to feminist work has been the challenge to the traditional views that authority resides in the text or that it is possessed by privileged interpreters.

These insights from the developing feminist tradition have shaped my reading of the Epistle to the Hebrews. My identity as a Christian and a feminist
also influences my stance toward the text as something with positive value for
theological reflection, but which simultaneously must be confronted and at
times, resisted. Therefore, my commentary on Hebrews does not represent
the feminist interpretation, but is one that selectively develops aspects of the
work I feel are fruitful for feminist reflection.

The Epistle to the Hebrews is an anonymous early Christian sermon. It has
never been considered the "center" of the Christian Testament canon. Rather,
the early Christian tradition adapted it to the mainstream of the tradition by
calling it a letter and attributing it to the apostle Paul, whose many letters to
congregations do dominate the canon. However, its distinctive style and
imagery have continued to make it difficult to assimilate with the other Christian Testament epistles. It is important for a feminist reading to recognize both

the marginality of Hebrews and the pressure to make it fit the majority tradition. A feminist reading can highlight the ways in which it does not fit and try to understand a distinct voice within early Christianity.

The many mysteries of date, author, audience, and place of origin have generated much modern scholarly debate, and a good portion of the commentary on Hebrews has emphasized the author's argument and opposed it to the reconstructed theology of "the Hebrews." My reading, however, will discuss the issue of the author, the audience, and their relationship in a different way. First, the anonymity of the sermon provides an opportunity to explore the possibility of women's authorship, focusing not on the author's correct viewpoint but on the relationship between author and audience. As an example of early Christian preaching, the Epistle to the Hebrews provides evidence of a kind of leadership for its congregation that is unusual among the letters in the Christian Testament that are preserved under the name of Paul. The interplay between author and audience reveals that rather than imposing one perspective against that of the congregation, the author of Hebrews adapts and shapes its thinking to that of the community to strengthen their faith and encourage them to renewed hope.[2] Appreciating Hebrews as a sermon rather than a letter can show the process of communication, which can be useful to feminist reflections on authority in theology.

Hebrews makes a sustained and extended argument about the role of Christ and Christ's relationship to the Jewish tradition. Using biblical quotation, exegesis, and commentary, the homilist argues that Jesus is the great high priest whose suffering and death inaugurate the new covenant. While the sermon describes Jesus with the male titles of "son" and "priest," it also emphasizes Jesus' close kinship with all human beings, not only male ones. I will describe how this argument might have been understood by an audience of women and men, consider how its rhetoric has been interpreted, and ask how that interpretation has affected women. This reading will contribute to theological evaluation of Hebrews by a contemporary audience of women.

DATE AND GENRE

Many of the standard introductory questions about Hebrews have not been definitively answered. No scholarly consensus has been reached about the precise date, the place of composition, the addressees, or the author. All that can be asserted about the date is that Hebrews was written between 60 and 100 C.E.[3]

The literary genre of Hebrews is that of a sermon. The author calls the writing "my word of exhortation" in 13:22. The same word is used in the Christian Testament in Acts 13:15 to describe a synagogue sermon of Paul. In the sermon, the passages of theological argument and of exhortation to the congregation are closely tied together. The argument is not made primarily to correct doctrinal misunderstanding or to correct a theological position, but to uphold the community.[4]

ADDRESSEES

Precise identification of the intended audience is particularly difficult for Hebrews. Attempts to describe the congregation as those who were threatening to "relapse into Judaism" are based on anachronistic stereotypes. At the time of Hebrews' composition, such distinct "religions" as "Christianity" and "Judaism" did not exist. Rather, the way the author interprets scripture shows the continuing interrelationship between those who believed in Christ and Jewish traditions. However, the use of scriptural exegesis and the cultic image of the high priest does not mean that the congregation was made up solely of Christians of Jewish background. Women and men of Gentile background would have found arguments from scripture to be persuasive. The rhetorical sophistication of the Greek used in the sermon need not mean that the whole congregation was highly educated. Many of the rhetorical techniques would have aided understanding and would have been appreciated regardless of the audience's sophistication.

Because references to apostasy (e.g., 2:3; 6:4–6; 12:25) and hardship and persecution (10:32) are very general, it is not possible to describe the historical situation in detail. A plausible reconstruction is that the audience is a mixed community of women and men, Jews and Gentiles, highly educated and less educated, having both apocalyptic and wisdom perspectives, whom the author, by using many different rhetorical and exegetical techniques, hopes to strengthen in its faith in God.

AUTHOR

Hebrews is one of the few books of the Christian Testament for which a female author has been proposed; thus, the question of authorship is particularly relevant to feminist commentary.

Both the recognition of its difference from the undisputed letters of Paul and the attempt to identify the author of Hebrews by name began with the earliest recorded commentators: Clement of Alexandria, Origen, and Tertullian. They were eager to maintain the tradition of Pauline authorship and its accompanying authority by various theories that would explain the distinctive qualities of Hebrews yet would not forfeit its association with the apostle Paul.

Clement argued that Paul wrote in Hebrew and that Luke translated his text into Greek. Origen proposed that a disciple of Paul wrote the letter based on notes of Paul, but he concludes: "who really wrote the letter, God knows" (Eusebius, *Church History* 6.25.14). The patristic discussion of the authorship of Hebrews reveals the close relationship between author, canonical acceptance, and scriptural authority. In their view, to be retained in the canon, Hebrews had to be linked with Paul by translation or tradition, and its thought had to be seen as harmonious with Paul's.

Both in antiquity and in the modern period, those who doubted Pauline authorship have speculated on who the author might be. Luther suggested Apollos, described in Acts 18:24 as "eloquent" and "well-verses in scriptures." Apollos's Alexandrian background could explain the similarities between the thought of Hebrews and that of Philo of Alexandria. Apollos's activity in the Pauline mission and his popularity in Corinth, as well as his implied rivalry with Paul, could account for similarities and differences in vocabulary and style with the work of Paul.

FEMALE AUTHORSHIP OF HEBREWS

In 1901, Adolf von Harnack proposed that Priscilla, a missionary with her husband Aquila, known from Acts (18:2, 24–26) Romans (16:3–5), and the Pastorals (2 Tim 4:19), was the author of Hebrews.[5] Though he argued that the letter came from both Priscilla and Aquila, he maintained that Priscilla, who was more important than her husband, was the author. The abrupt shifts in person from the plural "we" to "I" in 13:18–19 and from "I" to "our brother Timothy" in 13:23 suggest that the writer was speaking on behalf of someone closely allied with him or herself. According to Harnack's theory, Priscilla was referring to herself and Aquila when she says "we." Of primary importance in Harnack's argument is the anonymity of the letter, which he attributes to the loss or suppression of Priscilla's name, because she was a woman. The author of the letter would have been known to its readers, and her name was not cited by Clement to the church in Corinth in *1 Clement*, because it was particularly to the church in Corinth that Paul addressed his prohibition against women speaking in church (1 Cor 14:33–35). In short, Harnack connects the loss of the name of the author of Hebrews with the increasing criticism of women teachers in the early church.

In 1969, Ruth Hoppin devoted an essay to building the case that Priscilla was the author of Hebrews.[6] Like Harnack, she argues that the loss of the name of the author and the reputation of Priscilla in the Christian Testament as a powerful leader and teacher of Apollos make Priscilla the strongest candidate for authorship of Hebrews. She translates Heb 13:22, often translated "bear with my word of exhortation, for I have written to you briefly" as "only to a slight extent have I given you orders."[7] She interprets this remark as an apologetic comment made by a woman hesitant to claim spiritual authority. She observes that the references to Sarah (11:11), Rahab (11:31), the daughter of Pharaoh (11:24), and to the women who receive their dead by resurrection (11:35) are unusual in the Christian Testament. She understands that this feature, as well as the humility of the author, "hints at a feminine mind."[8] The purpose of Hoppin's essay is to prove that "a woman wrote one of the books of the New Testament." For Hoppin, proving that "a woman wrote Holy Scripture" would come as revolutionary news to women who are "second class citizens in the church."[9] For Hoppin, as for the church fathers, the identity of the author is closely connected with the authority of the work.

The proposal of Harnack and Hoppin that Priscilla is the author of Hebrews and that it is her gender that accounts for the anonymity of the work deserves to be taken seriously. Scholars have dismissed Priscilla as the possible author with little discussion, while entertaining Apollos at greater length. Cited as convincing evidence against a female author is the participle *diēgoumenon* ("to tell of") (11:32) with a masculine ending. But the masculine ending might be used to comply with convention or be used deliberately to suppress the author's identity. Christian Testament scholars generally assume that because no early Christian literature is known to have been written by a woman, women did not write early Christian literature. Works that are either anonymous or pseudonymous are assumed to have been written by men.[10] Scholarship on women's literacy, their ability to write and compose, their access to education, and the process of production and transmission of written work has made it possible to reconstruct more carefully the context for women's writing. The question of female authorship of Hebrews should be reexamined in light of this research.

FEMALE AUTHORSHIP IN ANTIQUITY

Recent studies of women in the Greco-Roman world have shown that the widely held assumption that women did not read or write in antiquity is an oversimplification.[11] The vast majority of men and women were illiterate, and more men than women were literate; however, there is evidence from papyrus letters in Egypt that women could write and did participate in legal transactions that required signing of documents.[12] Eusebius reports that female calligraphers were among those who took the dictation of Origen's commentaries on scripture (*Church History* 6.23). Although few of their works survived, women in Greek and Roman antiquity composed poetry, letters, and philosophical works.[13] Philo of Alexandria describes a community of Jewish contemplative women, called Therapeutrides, who shared all the activities of male Therapeutics, which included the study of scripture and composition of allegorical commentaries, hymns and psalms (Philo, *On the Contemplative Life* 87–89).[14] The pseudepigraphical *Testament of Job* refers to women writing down the hymnic prophecies of their sisters.[15]

In early Christian communities, women were known to have been active leaders, but no canonical works were attributed to these women. The prison diary of Perpetua from ca. 203 C.E. was described by the editor of that work as her own account.[16] Eusebius reports that Montanist prophets Priscilla and Maximilla wrote books of their own prophecies. In this same period, there is ample literary evidence that the issue of women's teaching and writing books in their own name was a source of controversy among Christians.

In the letter of *Mary the Proselyte to Ignatius*, Mary concludes with a statement that she does not write to instruct him.[17] The prohibitions against women's teaching and having authority over men in 1 Tim 2:12 are the likely impetus for her disclaimer. Didymus the Blind draws a similar connection between a woman's writing on her own authority and the prohibition of women's teaching in 1 Timothy (*On the Trinity* 3.41.3).

Not only could a woman have sufficient education and ability to be an author of pseudonymous or anonymous works in early Christianity, but, given the controversy surrounding women's leadership, pseudonymity or anonymity itself may have been a way for women to write for public audiences without incurring theological criticism. As an anonymous work, the Epistle to the Hebrews is one of the early Christian works for which female authorship is a possibility.

THE CASE FOR PRISCILLA

Proving that a named figure in the Christian Testament is the author of an anonymous work is very difficult. Drawing parallels between slight historical information and the content of a literary work is speculative. Priscilla is one figure described in some detail in the Christian Testament who it would seem has the necessary education and resources to have written Hebrews. Her association with Alexandria, through Apollos, whom she is said to have instructed (Acts 18:26), would be consistent with the kind of philosophical speculation known from Philo of Alexandria, which is expressed throughout Hebrews. The fact that she is described as a leader of "the church in their house" (Rom 16:5) makes it possible to imagine her preaching Hebrews as a sermon. However, the details of how an oral sermon becomes written, or a written sermon preached, are not known. It is also possible that another educated and powerful woman in the early Christian movement, whose name is not known to us, could have been its author.

The question of the gender of the author of Hebrews continues to be a problem for feminist interpreters in a context where author and authority are closely related. Does identifying the author of Hebrews as a woman increase the book's authority for women today? Does a woman author necessarily break with cultural norms in her depiction of women?[18] These questions will be raised in the course of the commentary on this work.

STRUCTURE

Hebrews is a highly structured document in which themes and motifs are interwoven to anticipate and reinforce each other.[19] The sermon is organized in four main parts. Heb 1:1–4:13 concentrates on the Word of God spoken through the son. The author reiterates the argument that this word is better than the word given through angels or through Moses. Heb 4:14–10:31 interprets Jesus as the eternal high priest against the background of the Israelite priesthood. The third part, 10:32–12:29, describes faith as insight into a heavenly world of reality. Finally, chapter 13 gives practical instructions and contains certain features of a letter.

COMMENTARY

The Word of God Spoken through the Son (1:1–4:13)

Prologue (1:1–4)

Hebrews opens with a compressed and highly alliterative prologue that introduces the major christological concern of this sermon as well as its characteristic style of argumentation. The author does not introduce herself or himself or claim any history or authoritative position with the community. Rather, the emphasis is on God's speech in a son and in scripture, as it is throughout 1:1–4:13. The author understands her or his own role in reference to that speech of God.

Immediately the author sets up a contrast between the way God has spoken in the past and the way God speaks in the present, which is described as "in these last days."[20] The philosophical assumption behind this contrast is that the singularity of now is more desirable than the multiplicity of long ago, and one son is superior to many prophets. The significant relationship of this son to God is elaborated in a hymn, sharing elements of form and imagery with other Christian Testament Christological hymns (Phil 2:6–11; Col 1:15–20). God appointed this son heir of all things and by means of him created the world. He is "the reflection of God's glory and the exact imprint of God's very being."

The hymn describes the preexistence of Christ, his purification for sins, and his exaltation. Behind the imagery of the prologue is Jewish wisdom speculation, in which the female figure of Wisdom, who was understood to be present with God at the time of creation, was sought after as an object of devotion. Early Christ-believers used the language of wisdom, particularly in the christological hymns, to interpret and understand Jesus Christ and his relationship with God. A passage from the Wisdom of Solomon uses the same word as Hebrews—*apaugasma,* "reflection"—to describe Wisdom: "for she is a reflection of eternal light, a spotless mirror of the working of God and an image of God's goodness" (Wis 7:26). In the prologue of the Gospel of John, the Word, or Logos, plays the role of Wisdom, who is with God in the beginning. The son in Hebrews is described not as the Word but as a mode of God's speaking in the present. By taking the language of Wisdom and applying it to Jesus, the Hebrews prologue claims that Christ alone embodies God's wisdom. Here, in Hebrews, as in John, the female figure of Wisdom becomes "realized" in the male Jesus as the Logos.[21]

Comparison of the Son and the Angels (1:5–14)

The description of the enthronement of the son in 1:4 and the statement that he is "superior" to the angels links the prologue with the following collection of citations from scripture. The series of quotations and their introduction reveal the principles of scriptural interpretation used by the author. God, expressed by the singular third person verb ending and translated by the NRSV as "he," is the one who is speaking in the scripture. Quotations from the Hebrew Bible are interpreted as though God is addressing Jesus. Each biblical citation supports the superiority of the son to the angels. As often in the Christian Testament, Psalms 2 and 110 are interpreted as messianic prophecies. These two quotations make the reference to *a* son in v. 1 into a title. In the introduction to the quotation in v. 8, the author says, "but of the son he says." The series culminates with the quotation from Psalm 109, "Sit at my right hand until I make your enemies a footstool for your feet."

The sharp contrast that the author of this sermon draws in the first verses between the mode of God's speaking through prophets in the past and in a son in the present and the argument for the superiority of the son to the angels has often been interpreted in an anti-Jewish fashion. The setting has been construed as one where Christ-believers were in danger of "slipping back into Judaism." The series of contrasts in the first four verses, based on philosophical presuppositions of the author, has been interpreted anachronistically as the author arguing for the superiority of Christianity over Judaism. An annotation in the RSV illustrates this perspective: "the unknown author moves with confidence, step by step through an elaborate proof of the pre-eminence of Christianity over Judaism."[22] Along with other Christian Testament literature, the arguments of Hebrews show that there was no such entity as "Christianity" separated from "Judaism" in this period. Rather, the heavy dependence on exegesis of scripture is evidence of the close relationship of Christ-believers with their Jewish tradition.

Warning against Drifting Away (2:1–4)

The discussion of angels is punctuated by a hortatory passage in which the author encourages the listeners to "pay greater attention to what we have heard, so that we do not drift away from it." This passage highlights the relationship of the author and audience in this sermon. The "we" of the exhortation is equivalent to "those who are to inherit salvation" in the previous verse. The salvation (2:3) is referred to as an act of speech; it is described as "what we have heard" (2:1) and something that was "declared at first through the Lord" and "was attested to us by those who heard" (2:3). The author understands that the message being elaborated is in continuity with other traditions known by the audience. The logic used to persuade and encourage would make sense to them or else it would not be convincing. There is not the sense that the author is trying to talk the congregation out of a particular view and into a radically new perspective. The author appeals to the community by referring to its own past and its members who heard the Lord.

Jesus Was Made Lower than the Angels (2:5–9)

Psalm 8 in its Septuagint form, which in its original context speaks of the nobility of humanity, is cited as referring to Christ. Even the way the psalm is quoted anticipates the interpretation. The phrase "a little," which in the psalm refers to the human being only modestly lower than the angels, is altered to "for a little while" to describe the temporary subjection of Jesus before his coronation and enthronement, and the subjection of all things to him. The exegetical comment that follows explains that it is Jesus—the human name is used here for the first time—who is made "for a little while lower than the angels."

The Humanity of Jesus (2:10–18)

The author argues that, because Jesus is related to human beings as brothers and sisters of flesh and blood, he must share their suffering and death in order to destroy the one who has the power of death. Biblical quotations in which Jesus is understood as speaking to and about human beings support the argument. Heb 2:17–18 asserts that it is Jesus' sharing in human life that makes him a merciful and faithful high priest.

What is striking about the opening two chapters of Hebrews is that they contain both an extensive argument for the superiority of the son to angels and an assertion of the close identification of Jesus with human beings. Apocalyptic pictures of the enthronement of the son with enemies as a stool for his feet (1:13) and the promise that everything will be subjected to Christ are put side by side with the image of Jesus, of one origin with human beings, who must suffer and die in order to deliver his children (2:14–18).

The theme of the incarnation of Jesus and his solidarity with human beings, so strongly expressed in Heb 2:10–18, must be evaluated both in its ancient context and its modern. It is helpful to understand the tradition of perfection out of which the author is working and to see how the sermon reinterprets that tradition.[23] In the tradition of Philo, the fact that Jesus shared in flesh and blood would have meant that he was part of the realm of imperfection. The author of Hebrews links the life of the earthly Jesus with perfection and argues that because Jesus achieved perfection in this realm, he opened the way for others to participate in perfection within the world of flesh and blood.

The strong subjugation language juxtaposed with the incarnational language used for Christ can be seen as evidence of the creative christological work engaging this author and community. Feminists might see the incarnational thinking characteristic of a passage such as 2:10–18 as more helpful than a worldview that radically separates the earthly and heavenly spheres. Because contemporary feminists do not share the author's perspectives and purposes, however, they might not wish to sustain such a synthesis as this sermon does. Feminist evaluation must ask both the historical and the constructive theological questions.

Comparison of Jesus and Moses (3:1–4:11)

Chapters 3 and 4 treat the theme of Jesus' faithfulness through a series of exegetical comments on scriptural passages whose purpose is to encourage the audience to maintain its "confidence" (3:6) and hope.

The precise historical situation of the audience cannot be reconstructed from the generality of the exhortation. The warnings are not addressed to theological misunderstanding or to particular moral transgressions, but to having an unbelieving heart (3:12), sin (3:13), "unbelief" (3:19), or "disobedience" (4:11). All these dangers can be derived from the scriptural passages quoted by the author and cannot be linked to a highly specific situation.

To encourage the community, the author makes a comparison between the old and the new, first between Moses and Jesus, then between those who rebelled against God in the wilderness, who have lost the promise of rest, and those whom the author is addressing as "we who have believed" (4:3). Demonstrating correspondence yet superiority, as in the comparison of Christ with the angels, the author shows that, although faithful like Moses, Jesus is "worthy of more glory than Moses." Christ's faithfulness as being a "son" is claimed to be superior to Moses' faithfulness as a "servant."

The community of Christians, described in 3:6 as "God's house," is compared with the negative example of those who have not believed, those who rebelled in the wilderness. The comparison is meant to encourage the community to perseverance, belief, and obedience. The identity of the community is highlighted not only by comparison with their ancestors but through positive reference to the relationship among brothers and sisters and their responsibility to one another. They are addressed in 3:1 as "holy partners in a heavenly calling" and "partners of Christ" in 3:14.

Employing the Israelites as an example of unbelief and a foil for Christian faithfulness presents a problem for feminist concerns with anti-Judaism. The history of anti-Jewish interpretation of these texts has gone far beyond the exegetical context used by the author. The temptation in preaching and in exhortation to draw harsh dichotomies between "us," who are good, and "them," who are evil, in order to encourage our own community prevails in contemporary preaching and political rhetoric with dangerous results. Although its use in Hebrews in its own time may indeed have served "rhetorical and not polemical purposes,"[24] its polemical uses in later interpretation need to be acknowledged by feminist commentary. A more useful feature of the exhortation of Hebrews 3 and 4 is the emphasis on partnership among Christian brothers and sisters and the responsibility for mutual exhortation.

The Word of God (4:12–13)

The first major division of Hebrews ends with a compact and poetic statement about God's communication, a theme begun in the prologue with the reflection on the various modes of God's speaking. The vital quality of the word of God is emphasized to underscore the immediacy of "today" repeated in 4:7. The last phrase of 4:13, *pros hon hymin ho logos*, although ambiguous, concludes with "our word" and can be translated "and to this word, our word is directed." Again as in 3:13, the author relates the verbal quality of the sermon itself with the activity of God's speaking.

The Priesthood of Christ (4:14–10:30)

The second major division of the sermon, which develops the image of the priest to describe Jesus' role and saving work, shows a contrast parallel to the contradiction in the opening two chapters between the subjugationist and incarnational language.

While the author argues that Christ's priesthood is effective because he shares human weakness (5:2) and suffering (5:7–8), it is Christ's immortality and his purity (7:23–28) that set him apart and make him superior to the levitical priests. The author emphasizes Christ's relationship with the congregation in the sections of exhortation yet, in arguing for the superiority of Christ's priesthood, assumes the inferiority of the earthly to the heavenly realm.

The Image of Christ as Priest (5:1–10; 7:1–28)

Christ as the great high priest who perfects the ancient sacrificial system of the Jewish religion is the overarching image that interprets his humanity, his death, and his present heavenly role. While the theme of priesthood occurs in the Christian Testament also in 1 Peter and Revelation, Hebrews is the only surviving document in which priesthood is the dominant christological category. The purpose of the language of priesthood was to link Jesus with the ancient and venerable cultic system, to demonstrate his scriptural origins, and to claim his perfection of and replacement of the old system.[25]

The author of Hebrews interpreted Jesus' death in cultic language to show that salvation no longer came from the institutions of cult and priesthood, but from Jesus Christ.[26] The cultic institutions were used as a positive metaphor to understand Jesus, and the scripture that spoke of the priesthood was read as God's word which spoke of Christ and predicted his perfection of the old covenant.

Because most Christian feminists today do not share the world view of the women of the congregation addressed in Hebrews, the cultic rituals and temple practices are an alien, rather than a familiar, context, in which to understand Jesus. The images of son and priest, applied to Jesus, emphasize Jesus' connection with a cultic system dominated by males with which many contemporary feminists do not identify. Therefore, the imagery of priesthood in Hebrews may have the *opposite* impact today from what it had in its historical context. Instead of showing that the sacrificial system as it had existed was no longer powerful, but that the salvation of humanity was made possible through Jesus, the cultic images now draw attention to the exclusively male categories applied to Jesus.

In 5:1–10 the author emphasizes Jesus as a human being as in 2:1–19. Jesus is chosen from among human beings to offer sacrifices for sins on their behalf. He shares human weakness. He does not choose the honor but is called by God. In 5:5 the author demonstrates that Christ fulfills these conditions by quoting again (1:5) Ps 2:7, "you are my son," and combining it with Ps 110:4, "you are a priest forever." Scripture shows that God said these things to him and has appointed him priest.

In 5:7–8 Jesus is described as a righteous person who cries out and is heard. Traditionally interpreted as a reference to Gethsemane, it is more likely an allusion to a Jewish hero such as Abraham or Moses who achieves salvation through vigorous prayer to God and through suffering. Hebrews is reinterpreting the Hellenistic Jewish tradition in which suffering is a process of education to perfection. Jesus has participated in the world of imperfection through his suffering and death and made it possible for mortals to achieve perfection.

The argument in 7:1–28, equating Christ with Melchizedek, asserts the superiority of Christ's priesthood to the Levitical priesthood. The author argues exegetically—that is, by commenting on the scriptural text—and concludes in 7:23–28 that Christ is superior to Melchizedek because he is eternal. The author of Hebrews emphasizes the superiority with the characteristic word, "better"—a "better hope" (7:19) and a "better covenant" (7:22). Because Christ, unlike the mortal levitical priests, continues forever, he is able to save "for all time" those who approach God through him. Although the saving power of the death of Jesus is emphasized in the sermon in 2:14 and in chapters 9 and 10, here the fact that Melchizedek, unlike the levitical priests, does *not* die proves his superiority to them. In the statement of praise in 7:26–28, attention is turned again to the audience with the shift to the first person,"we." The singleness of Christ's sacrifice is better than the daily offering of the priests. The word of the oath comes after the law about priests and "appoints a Son who has been made perfect forever." Here the themes of oneness, lateness, completeness, and eternality are brought together in the image of the Son. The final picture of Christ as blameless and undefiled, removed from weakness, and spatially separated from the earthly realm stands in tension with the picture of Christ in 2:14–18, which stresses Christ's sharing flesh and blood with human beings. These two strands of argumentation show the author synthesizing a Platonic scheme of perfection and a tradition of the human life and death of Jesus.

The More Excellent Ministry of Jesus, the New Covenant, Comparison of the Sanctuaries (8:1–13; 9:1–28; 10:1–18)

To compare the ministry of the high priest with that of levitical priests, the author uses the notion, known in Jewish Scripture, that the earthly sanctuary is a copy of the heavenly one. Correspondence between the earthly and heavenly temples is discussed in Philo and in apocalyptic Jewish writings. The author of Hebrews here develops this correspondence with a dualistic emphasis characteristic of popular Platonism. Earthly activity is inferior to the true perfection of the heavenly archetype. Priests, by law, offer sacrifices in a sanctuary that is a "sketch and shadow" of the heavenly one and is therefore inferior to the realm of Christ's ministry. The conclusion is a reiteration of the theme of superiority: Christ has obtained "a more excellent ministry," is "a mediator of a better covenant," enacted through "better promises." Christ's sacrifice appears to take place solely in the heavenly sphere.

The denigration of the earthly sphere as a realm of Christ's activity poses a problem for feminist theology. As the christological argument of Hebrews continues, the restriction of Christ's activity to the heavenly sphere will be modified by encouragement to the community to engage in practical acts of care. The author's synthesis of these two perspectives raises the question of the relationship between tradition and interpretation in theology. While some strands of Christian theology have adopted this Platonic worldview, feminist analysis must critique a thought world in which the earthly realm is conceived as inferior to the heavenly and accept and develop Hebrews' emphasis that Jesus achieved perfection only by becoming human.

Exhortations to the Community
(4:14–16; 5:11–6:20; 10:19–39)

The passages of exhortation throughout the central section of the sermon indicate the author's relationship with the congregation. Appealing not to her or his authority but to the shared experience of the community and Jesus' kinship with them, the author encourages the listeners first to "hold fast" (4:14) and then "to approach the throne of grace" (4:16). The author employs such basic images, which run through the complicated exegetical and expository sections of Hebrews, to help the congregation hear and understand the sermon. The impact of the complex structure of anticipation and repetition, alliteration and chiasm, discussed by commentators, would have been experienced orally. The overall rhetorical effect of repetition and emphasis, warning and encouragement would have been achieved, even if the audience did not share the literary and theological sophistication of the author. Reading the text in printed form and trying to work out its precise structure can obscure the fact that such rhetorical techniques helped the hearers follow the speaker's logic and made that "logic" more convincing.

In 5:11–6:20, the author delivers a lengthy exhortation to hope whose tone shifts dramatically from criticism in 6:1–8 to compliment and encouragement in 6:9–20. Here again the overall charge is to move forward, first toward perfection (6:1) and then to "seize the hope set before us" (6:18).

Addressing the whole congregation, the author begins by using the metaphor, common in Hellenistic rhetoric, of milk as simple teaching and solid food as more complex teaching (5:11–14). Paul uses a similar image in 1 Cor 3:1–4, and the contrast highlights the distinctiveness of tone and purpose of the author of Hebrews. Paul uses the image to criticize one group of Corinthians, while the author of Hebrews encourages the community to move beyond milk. Rather than emphasizing the "I" who taught them, as Paul does, this author says only, "you need someone to teach you again the basic elements of the oracles of God." The theme of advancement is developed by the athletic metaphor of training which allows one to distinguish between good and evil. After encouraging the hearers to go on beyond fundamental teaching, the author then enumerates what those "basic" elements are.

Heb 6:4–8, which describes the impossibility of restoring to repentance those who have fallen away, has given Hebrews the reputation for "rigorism" which made it popular with Tertullian and the Montanists and which made its canonical acceptance more difficult. In its context, the passage seems to describe not the impossibility of God's forgiveness but rather the unfortunate consequences for one who loses hope and falls away. The sharp contrast between the positive blessings of enlightenment and the negative results of crucifying the Son of God serve as a warning to the congregation of what might be lost if they lose hope.

The positive section of the exhortation begins in 6:9, where the author reassures the audience that they are among those who are not lost. The author compliments them for their service to the saints. God's promise to Abraham is used as an example of God's firmness or "confirmation" (6:16). The section concludes with an image of hope as an anchor of the soul, entering the shrine where Jesus has entered. This transitional image picks up the theme of stability that was emphasized early in the sermon and adds the motif of going forward and entering, which will be developed in further sections of the letter.

Heb 10:19–39 concludes the second major section of the sermon with another passage of exhortation. Like the exhortation in chapter 6, it includes both warning and encouragement and draws attention to the situation of the community.

In 10:19–25 many of the major images and themes of Hebrews are brought together. The author addresses the community as "brothers and sisters" (NRSV "friends") and says that they have "boldness" to enter the sanctuary by the blood of Jesus. "Boldness," which the NRSV here translates as "confidence," occurs also in 3:6 and 4:16. The listeners are urged with hortatory subjunctives: "let us approach" and "let us hold fast." They are charged "to provoke one another to love and good deeds." The themes of hope, faith, and love are brought together here. The seeming correspondence in 10:21 between the curtain of the sanctuary and the flesh of Jesus has caused commentators difficulty. Here the curtain does not mean "impediment" but the "way of access," so that it is Jesus' flesh, or his being human, that opens the way. This interpretation is consistent with Hebrews' emphasis, especially in 2:1–18 and 5:1–10, on the incarnation of Jesus and the importance of his human existence for salvation.

Warning of Judgment (10:26–31)

The ferocious warning in 10:26–31 that those who continue to sin will be judged is similar to that in 6:4–8. In 10:26 the first person plural is used: "if *we* willingly persist in sin . . . ." The admonition is supported by a comparison with the punishment for breaking the law of Moses and with two citations from Deuteronomy (Deut 32:35; 32:36).

Heb 10:32–39 reassures the community by asking them to remember how they have endured suffering before, so that they do not lose their boldness (NRSV "confidence" [10:35]). The passage concludes with a conflation of quotations from Hab 2:2–3 and Isa 26:20, which defines the faithful as those who will be saved and anticipates the theme of faith in the final part of the sermon.

Faith (11:1–12:29)

The final section of the sermon concentrates on faith as the quality that gives grounds for the hope to which the community has been urged throughout the sermon. Faith, according to the understanding of the author, is not cognitive understanding of a message or acceptance of the kerygma as in Paul's letters. Rather, it is an insight into an unseen but real world. Faith is not "faith in Christ," but faith in God and in God's promises. Jesus is understood to be the ultimate example of this faith, and his faith is the inspiration for the Christian community being addressed. The author develops this perspective by listing characters who exemplify faith and summarizing the biblical narratives that demonstrate their faithfulness.

Characters Who Act by Faith

The opening verse 11:1 provides a definition of faith. Most English translations interpret the Greek words *hypostasis* and *elenchos* as "assurance" and "conviction," which connotes a subjective understanding of faith. A translation that expresses a more objective sense could be, "Now faith is the reality of things hoped for, the evidence of things not seen." This understanding of faith as an experience of confirmation of the reality of those things one cannot see is illustrated by the following examples.

For the first example the author uses not a biblical hero but "we." The community of which the author is a part knows that "the worlds were prepared by the word of God." Creation is an unseen reality in which "we" believe. By holding up "we" as the earliest exemplars of faith, the author suggests that the community of Hebrews shares in the same faith of the heroes who follow.

The author cites Abraham, Enoch, and Noah as biblical examples of faithfulness and demonstrates their faithfulness through original exegesis. Abel is said to "still speak" even though dead. This reference means not only that his blood still speaks from the ground but also that he still speaks through scripture. The analysis of Enoch's "being taken up" because of his faith may seem strained, but, again, it is based on the author's logic and exegesis. Noah's faith is exemplified by the fact that he acted on God's warnings about events "as yet unseen."

The Faith of Abraham and Sarah (11:8–12)

Abraham is frequently used as an example of faith in the Christian Testament and in other early Jewish and Christian literature. The author of Hebrews focuses on various incidents in Abraham's story that show his faith in the unseen: the sojourning in an unknown land, his remaining there with Isaac and Jacob, and his belief that he would have children.

The Greek text of 11:11 refers to Sarah in the discussion of Abraham's faith. Evidence that the meaning of this verse has caused difficulty begins as early as the textual tradition, which shows several variations. Some manuscripts read "Sarah herself," others "Sarah herself barren," or "Sarah herself, being barren." These variations have led some commentators to conclude that this phrase is a gloss, or later addition to the text. Some make Sarah the subject of the sentence. Others read the Greek word for Sarah in the dative, so that the name Sarah is a parenthetical remark, leaving Abraham as the subject of the sentence. What causes difficulty in the verse is that the phrase for receiving "the power of procreation" (NRSV) is most often used of the male role in conception, that is, of "the power to deposit seed." However, in the ancient world at this time, there was a theory of conception in which both male and female contributed to conception. If this idea were in the background, Sarah as the subject of this verse would not constitute a contradiction.[27] In addition, in the phrase "for depositing seed," the word for "seed," *spermatos,* could be understood generally as the power of generation. Sarah would have received the power to have descendants. The variety of texts and possible interpretations is reflected in the modern translations of the verse:

> RSV: By faith Sarah herself received power to conceive, even when she was past the age, since she considered him faithful who had promised.

> NAB: By faith Sarah received power to conceive though she was past the age, for she thought that the One who had made the promise was worthy of trust.

> NRSV: By faith he received the power of procreation, even though he was too old—and Sarah herself was barren—because he considered him faithful who had promised.

From a feminist perspective, what is at stake in this textual and interpretive debate is the centrality or marginality of the woman, Sarah, in the discussion of the faith of Abraham. Is *her* faith the subject of the sentence? Does Sarah "interrupt" the discussion of Abraham? Does Sarah belong in the list of heroic examples of faith? Clearly, something about the phrase "Sarah herself" disturbed early transmitters of the text, and the discomfort seems to have been retained among later commentators. For Ruth Hoppin, the presence of Sarah among the heroes of faith was evidence of a "feminine mind," and important to her theory of female authorship of the letter.[28] That Sarah appears here as an example of faith touches on issues beyond the textual and exegetical.

Since it seems unlikely that a later scribe would have added the gloss about Sarah to a text that cohered well without it, the reference to Sarah should be taken as part of the original sermon. Based on what we know of the freedom of this author's use of scripture, it is possible that this author would have remembered the story of Sarah and Abraham from the Genesis account and included Sarah as an example of faith. Although her faith is not the focus of the Genesis story, the author of Hebrews could have seen it as analogous: Sarah's faith in the unseen and the unlikely is parallel to Abraham's. Her age and barrenness increase the unlikeliness of the unseen reality coming to pass. The apparent contradiction of using a phrase describing the male role in conception is alleviated if we see the phrase "power of depositing seed" as meaning "the power of generation." In this list of faithful characters, the author is multiplying examples that will be summarized in 11:13–16, beginning "all of these died in faith." Including Sarah in the series of heroic people of faith would be an understandable and sensible part of this compilation for the community.

Heroes and Heroines of Faith Seek a Homeland (11:13–16)

These examples of faith are given the particular interpretation of the author in 11:13–16. They are described as those who did not receive the promises, but who greeted them. They are those who are strangers on the earth who seek a "homeland," a goal, like "the rest" in chapter 3, which is the aim of those who wander. They seek a "better country," a heavenly one. That the world is described as a place of exile in which people of faith are not at home has been seen as evidence of a Gnostic background for Hebrews.[29] The heroes and heroines of faith were not fulfilled in their wandering, so we may logically see them as on their way to future fulfillment. The unspoken contrast here is between those ancient heroes and heroines and the Christians to whom the sermon is addressed, who would be made perfect (11:40).

More Heroes and Heroines of Faith (11:17–22)

Heb 11:17–22 describes the faith of Abraham in the offering of Isaac. The return of Isaac is interpreted as a figurative resurrection from the dead. Isaac, Jacob, and Joseph are also given as examples of faith.

Several incidents of Moses' life are described to demonstrate his faith. Although the exodus account of Moses' infancy specifies that his mother hid him, the Hebrews author follows the Septuagint tradition that speaks of his parents. In this example, Moses is the subject of the sentence, although it is really his parents who exemplify faith.[30]

Faith of the People and the Faith of Rahab (11:29–31)

The list concludes with mention of the people who pass through the Red Sea, the falling of the walls of Jericho, and the example of Rahab the prostitute. The book of Joshua (2:1–21; 6:17) praises Rahab for her courage in hiding the spies in her house. That she is a non-Israelite and a prostitute highlights the surprising nature of her loyalty to the Israelites in the story from Joshua. Matthew includes her in the genealogy of Jesus in Matt 1:5, along with Ruth, another non-Israelite. Rahab is named in Jas 2:25 as an example, with Abraham, of one who is justified by works and not by faith alone. In *1 Clement* 12 Rahab is praised "for her faith and hospitality," also at the end of a series of heroic models. That Rahab is present in James and *1 Clement* suggests that she may have been used as well by other authors in early Christianity as an example of faith. Her presence here in Hebrews is not evidence of female authorship but is an indication that a fairly widespread tradition in early Christianity saw Rahab, described most often with the epithet "the prostitute," as an exemplar of faith.

Endurance of Persecution through Faith (11:23–38)

In 11:32–38 the style shifts to a collection of characters and their situations which exemplify endurance under persecution. In 11:33, "through faith" replaces "by faith." The descriptions of the sufferings and tortures of the heroes allude to stories and legends in Judges, the prophets, and the books of Maccabees. The mention of the women who have received their dead by resurrection in 11:35 refers to the widow of Zarephat in 1 Kgs 17:17–24 and the Shunammite woman in 2 Kgs 4:18–27. The stories about Elijah and Elisha and these faithful women have influenced the story in Luke 7:11–17 about Jesus' miracle on behalf of the widow of Nain. Women are included in Hebrews' recitation of faithful ancestors. In comparison, the catalogue of ancestors in Sirach 44–50 includes only men.

The transition between the heroes of faith and those of the present is made through the contrast in 11:39–40. Although they did not receive what was promised, God provided something "better" so that they could be made perfect.

Jesus, Pioneer and Perfecter of Our Faith (12:1–2)

The section on faith that began in 11:1 culminates in 12:1–2 with a shift from the third to the first person, "we." Those who have demonstrated faith in the past are described as a "cloud of witnesses" who surround "us" as runners in a race. The community is urged to "run with perseverance the race that is set before us." Once again the major image of the exhortation is that of moving forward or approaching. As in 2:10, Jesus is the one who goes ahead and makes access possible. The epithet applied to Jesus in 12:2, "pioneer and perfecter of our faith," aptly summarizes the various descriptions of Jesus in the sermon and concludes the passage on faith. Jesus is not the object of "our" faith but the model of it to be looked toward. Jesus is the leader of the faithful, the initiator of faith, and the final "perfection" of that faith as well. The relative clause that concludes the description of Jesus describes his enduring the cross and anticipates the themes of endurance in the next passage.

The Discipline of God (12:3–17)

This hortatory passage presents Jesus as a model and compares his endurance with the endurance encouraged for Christians. Using Prov 3:11, described as an exhortation to the congregation, the passage introduces the idea that the trials undergone by Christians are "the discipline of the Lord." The author's exegesis and commentary address the audience as "sons" (NRSV "children," 12:5) and then continue to draw out the image of God as parent who disciplines his children. The decision of the NRSV to translate *patēr* as "parent" (2:7) rather than "father" obscures the fact that it is the male parent in this context who is responsible for discipline and suffering. Heb 12:7–8 makes that discipline a requirement for legitimate children; 12:9 compares the respect given to human fathers with the respect given to God "the Father of Spirits"; and 12:10 draws a contrast between the fact that human fathers discipline as it seems best to them and that God disciplines "us" for "our own good." The benefits of discipline are described as "the peaceful fruit of righteousness."

The interpretation of human suffering as the discipline of God, characteristic of Proverbs and other wisdom literature, functions here to encourage the community and to give some kind of acceptable rationale for their sufferings. Although the extended metaphor of God's acting as a father to "sons" was used earlier (2:10), here discipline seems linked to the image of athletic training.

The history of interpretation of this concept has had pastoral and theological effects that feminists find unacceptable. The teaching that suffering such as physical illness or bereavement represents God's fatherly discipline of his children has resulted in increased self-blame among sufferers, both women and men. Moreover, the biblical comparison of God to a father with the unquestioned power to discipline his children has been used by abusive fathers to claim God-like rights over their children in the name of discipline.

To evaluate this passage from a feminist perspective, we must study it in its contemporary social and literary contexts as well as in the history of its interpretation. In the patriarchal family structure out of which this passage comes illegitimacy (being *nothos*) follows from a father's failure to recognize his children as his own. For the author of Hebrews, the father's discipline is a sign of legitimacy. The underlying family structure presumed by the metaphor is never questioned. In its context in Hebrews, the passage is one of two that speak of suffering, of being tested, and of Christians as "sons." In 2:10–18 suffering is not equated with discipline, but is presented as a necessary way for Jesus to destroy the devil, who has the power of death. Jesus' becoming like human beings, "his brothers and sisters," makes it possible for him to be a priest and to help them. Suffering in 12:3–11 is not primarily death or temptation but "hostility from sinners" and "struggle against sin." Although Jesus' endurance is the model for Christians' endurance, what Jesus endures is not parallel to what Christians endure. The author does not mention the sonship of Jesus and the sibling relationship with humans in 12:3–11. If the suffering of Jesus and the suffering of Christians were equivalent, then Jesus' suffering could be interpreted as God's discipline for him. However, this conclusion is not drawn by the author of Hebrews. To raise these parallels would be to invite the logical extension that Jesus' suffering is God's discipline for him, a point that the author of Hebrews does not make. These two different interpretations of what suffering is and the various images of God as father and Christians as children caution against universalizing the Hebrews' theology of suffering from one passage. These two passages—2:10–18 and 12:3–11—employ the son, child–father metaphor for different rhetorical purposes.

We can compare this image with other biblical treatments of suffering and with later theological reflections on suffering in the Christian tradition. The physical and psychological damage that has resulted, including self-blame and lack of resistance to injustice can be evaluated in light of other parts of the gospel message.

Mount Sinai and Mount Zion (12:18–24)

Here the author speaks of the relationship between the old and new covenant through an allegorical comparison of the two mountains, Sinai and Zion. The author paints a gloomy portrait of Sinai, choosing from the biblical account details that stress its frightening aspect. In sharp contrast, the author describes Mount Zion and Jerusalem. The apocalyptic picture is elaborated here with the angels and the spirits of the righteous, God the judge, and Jesus, and concludes with a comparison between the blood of the new covenant and the blood of Abel.

Final Warning and Reassurance (12:25–29)

The final warning threatens Christians that they will not escape if they refuse the one who is speaking. The theme of God's speech recalls that at the beginning of the sermon. Because "we," in contrast to the Israelites, are receiving a kingdom that cannot be shaken, the author urges, "let us give thanks."

PRACTICAL INSTRUCTIONS TO THE COMMUNITY (13:1–21)

The abrupt change of tone in chapter 13, the collection of practical ethical instructions, and the typical letter features of 13:22-25 have led some commentators to deny that Hebrews 13 was originally part of the sermon. However, because it does show a similar technique of using scripture and stresses showing concern to members of the community, I take it to be a conclusion to the sermon composed by the author.

Various Ethical Instructions (13:1–6)

In short imperative sentences, the author urges the congregation to show "mutual love," including exercising hospitality, remembering those in prison, and honoring marriage. The list is quite general, but recalls 10:24–25 where the author urges "provoking one another to love and good deeds."

True Worship (13:7–19)

In a passage beginning and ending with reference to "your leaders," the author advises the community on true worship. The leaders of the past are examples of faith to the community, and the leaders of the present are responsible for keeping the community from harm. The mention of "strange teachings" in 13:9 is unclear. Jesus' suffering outside the city gate is used as a reason that "we" "should go to him outside the camp"; that is, Christ-believers should not remain confined to the sanctuary but should live in the world and make sacrifices of good works.[31]

Blessing and Farewell (13:20–25)

The sermon closes with a blessing composed by the author, alluding to Isa 63:11, where God is said to raise up from the sea the shepherds of the sheep. The greetings that conclude the sermon are typical features of letters, although the author calls this work not a letter but "my word of exhortation." The appeal to "bear with my exhortation, for I have written to you briefly," is a convention in letters, even if they are not short. Thus, the phrase cannot be read as evidence for the modesty of a female author.

CONCLUSION

Neither the theological perspective nor the use of women as examples of faith can be interpreted as proof that the author of Hebrews was a woman. Just as it is problematic today, it is impossible to describe what a "feminine mind" would have been in the ancient world. Even if it were possible on external grounds to be sure that a woman was the author of Hebrews, the fact of authorship in itself would not assure that the content of the letter would be liberating for women today. Its liberating character must be determined by continuing theological evaluation in communities of women and others concerned with liberation.

Focus on the identity of the author, a feature of both ancient and modern discussions, can obscure the fact that this early Christian sermon does not draw attention to its author at all. No claim to authority over the congregation is ever made, and there is no attempt to assert one position above that of the community. The author does not emphasize her or his identity but rather stresses God's continuing speech in scripture, the perfection made possible through Jesus in human life, and the undergirding of hope with faith in God.

NOTES

1. See Elisabeth Schüssler Fiorenza, *But She Said: Feminist Practices of Biblical Interpretation* (Boston: Beacon, 1992).

2. My emphasis on the relationship between author and community is dependent on the "pastoral-theological paradigm" of biblical interpretation articulated by Elisabeth Schüssler Fiorenza (*Bread Not Stone: The Challenge of Feminist Biblical Interpretation* [Boston: Beacon, 1984], 32–42).

3. The precise date is not critical to the interpretation of Hebrews presented here. The range of possible dates is discussed by Harold Attridge, *The Epistle to the Hebrews* (Hermeneia; Philadelphia: Fortress, 1989), 6–9.

4. That the literary genre of the sermon is the key to interpreting the two eschatological perspectives in Hebrews is demonstrated by George W. MacRae, "Heavenly Temple and Eschatology in the Letter to the Hebrews," *Semeia* 12 (1978): 179–99 and in *Studies in the New Testament and Gnosticism*, ed. Daniel J. Harrington and Stanley B. Marrow (Wilmington, DE: Michael Glazier, 1987), 80–97.

5. Adolf von Harnack, "Probabilia über die Addresse und den Verfasser des Hebraerbriefes," *Zeitschrift für die neutestamentliche Wissenschaft* 1 (1900): 16–41.

6. Ruth Hoppin, *Priscilla: Author of Epistle to the Hebrews and other Essays* (New York: Exposition, 1969).

7. Hoppin (*Priscilla,* 22) follows the translation of Hugh J. Schonfield, *The Authentic New Testament* (New York: The New American Library of World Literature, 1958).

8. Hoppin, *Priscilla,* 25.

9. Ibid., 15.

10. See the exploration of this issue in Ross Kraemer, "Women's Authorship of Jewish and Christian Literature in the Greco-Roman Period," in *"Women Like This": New Perspectives on Jewish Women in the Greco-Roman World,* ed. Amy-Jill Levine (Atlanta: Scholars Press, 1991).

11. See Susan Guettel Cole, "Could Greek Women Read and Write," in *Reflections of Women in Antiquity,* ed. Helene P. Foley (New York: Gordon & Breach, 1981), 219–45.

12. Sarah B. Pomeroy, "Women in Roman Egypt," in *Reflections of Women in Antiquity,* ed. Helene P. Foley (New York: Gordon & Breach, 1981), 303–22.

13. See Jane McIntosh Snyder, *The Woman and the Lyre: Women Writers in Classical Greece and Rome* (Carbondale, IL: Southern Illinois University Press, 1989).

14. See Ross S. Kraemer, "Monastic Jewish Women in Greco-Roman Egypt: Philo of Alexandria on the *Therapeutrides," Signs* 14.1 (1989): 345–80.

15. For text and translation, see R. A. Kraft et al., *The Testament of Job: Greek Text and English Translation* (SBL Texts and Translations 5, Pseudepigrapha Series 4; Missoula, MT: Scholars Press, 1974). See also the article by Rebecca Lesses in this volume.

16. Text in H. Musurillo, *Acts of the Christian Martyrs* (Oxford: Clarendon, 1972), 106–31. See also the article by Maureen Tilley in this volume.

17. The Greek text with Latin translation and notes is found in *PG* ser 2, 5:873–80. Greek with Latin is found in William Cureton, ed., *Corpus Ignatianum* (London: Francis & John Rivington, 1849), 119–27. English translation in Ante-Nicene Fathers I, 120–23.

18. Mary R. Lefkowitz, "Did Ancient Women Write Novels?" in *"Women Like This": New Perspectives on Jewish Women in the Greco-Roman World,* ed. Amy-Jill Levine (Atlanta: Scholars Press, 1991), 199–220.

19. For detailed analyses of the structure of Hebrews, see Albert Vanhoye, S.J., *La structure littéraire de l'Epitre aux Hebreux* (Studia Neotestamentica 1; Paris Desclée de Brouwer, 1976); also Attridge, *Hebrews,* 14–21.

20. The commentary will refer to the NRSV. I will note where my translation differs significantly.

21. For a discussion of the relation between Wisdom and Jesus, see Gail Patterson Corrington, *Her Image of Salvation: Female Saviors and Formative Christianity* (Louisville: Westminster/John Knox, 1992), 103–44.

22. Revised Standard Version, Oxford Annotated Bible (Oxford: Oxford University Press, 1962).

23. See the study of the Philonic tradition behind Hebrews in L. K. K. Dey, *The Intermediary World and Patterns of Perfection in Philo and Hebrews* (SBL Dissertation Series; Missoula, MT: Scholars Press, 1975).

24. Attridge, *Hebrews,* 105.

25. For a discussion of the relationship between sacrifice and systems of patrilineal descent, see Nancy Jay, "Sacrifice as a Remedy for Having Been Born as a Woman," in *Immaculate and Powerful* (Boston: Beacon, 1985), 283–309.

26. For analysis of the meaning of the "transfer" of cultic language see Elisabeth Schüssler Fiorenza, "Cultic Language in Qumran and the New Testament," *Catholic Biblical Quarterly* 38 (1976): 159–77.

27. See the study of the history of the interpretation of this verse by Joyce Irwin, "The Use of Hebrews 11:11 as Embryological Proof-Text," *Harvard Theological Review* 71 (1978): 312–16.

28. Hoppin, *Priscilla,* 25.

29. Ernst Käsemann, *The Wandering People of God: An Investigation of the Letter to the Hebrews,* trans. Roy A. Harrisville and Irving L. Sandberg (Minneapolis: Augsburg, 1984).

30. For discussion of the women in the story of Moses, see Eileen Schuller, "Women of the Exodus in Biblical Retellings of the Second Temple Period," in *Gender and Difference in Ancient Israel,* ed. Peggy L. Day (Minneapolis: Fortress, 1989).

31. Helmut Koester, "Outside the Camp; Hebrews 13:9-14," *Harvard Theological Review* 55 (1962): 299–315.

RECOMMENDED READINGS

Attridge, Harold. *The Epistle to the Hebrews.* Hermeneia. Philadelphia: Fortress, 1989.

Casey, Juliana, I.H.M. *Hebrews.* Wilmington, DE: Michael Glazier, 1980.

D'Angelo, Mary Rose. *Moses in the Letter to the Hebrews.* SBL Dissertation Series 42. Missoula, MT: 1979.

Dey, Lala Kalyan Kumar. *The Intermediary World and Patterns of Perfection in Philo and Hebrews.* SBL Dissertation Series 25. Missoula, MT: Scholars Press, 1975.

Hoppin, Ruth. *Priscilla, Author of Epistle to the Hebrews and Other Essays.* New York: Exposition, 1969.

Lehne, Susanne. *The New Covenant in Hebrews.* Journal for the Study of the New Testament Supplement 44. Sheffield: JSOT Press, 1990.

PART THREE

Biographical Discourses:
Envoys of Sophia

Judith
The Gospel of Mark
The Sayings Source Q
The Gospel of Thomas
 The Gospel of John
The Gospel of Mary Magdalene
The Gospel of Matthew
Pistis Sophia
The Infancy of Mary of Nazareth
The Gospel of Luke
The Acts of the Apostles
The Acts of Thecla
The Passion of Perpetua and Felicity
The Book of Aseneth

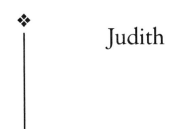

Judith

LINDA BENNETT ELDER ◆

INTRODUCTION

THE BOOK OF JUDITH, a dramatic narrative, was probably composed in its present form during the Hasmonean dynasty (142–63 B.C.E.) by a Palestinian Jew. This text has received considerable praise as a masterpiece of Jewish narrative art but elicits critical analysis among traditional biblical scholars principally on the basis of its genre, historicity, date, and function. In contrast, a feminist critical hermeneutic permits concentration specifically on characterizations of the figure of Judith in chapters 8–16 of the text. Critical commentaries reflecting traditional scholarship and historical critical exegesis of the Judith texts inform the present commentary and are recommended to the interested reader.[1]

The book of Judith is not included in the canon of the Hebrew Bible but has enjoyed prominence in Christian literature and iconography. Myriad representations among biblical scholars and artists reveal varying depictions and transformations of the Judith mythos over the past two thousand years. Numerous images of Judith as femme fatale, civic patriot, precursor of Jesus, trickster, woman warrior, and a savior in Israel, find their genesis in the Holofernes event, in which Judith assassinates an enemy general. In these myriad depictions, the Holofernes event is pervasive and remains constant. Why, considering the complexity of the author's depictions of Judith in the text, are later representations of her character based almost exclusively on the decapitation of Holofernes?

This question begets many questions about the transformations of myth in culture as it relates to the recovery of biblical women's history. To what extent do issues of gender contribute to the transformation of the Judith mythos? What does a feminist critical perspective determine about the historical, cultural, political, and religious milieu from which representations of Judith emerge? To what extent do Judith texts and images support a patriarchal worldview? Are the myriad Judith texts and images undergirded exclusively by an internalized androcentrism, or do there occur instances of a women-centered perspective/experience? What are the effects on the reader of disparate and contradictory interpretations?

One significant effect of the transformation of the Judith mythos away from the biblical text is to eclipse evidence for the reconstruction of biblical women's history. A principal methodological thesis for the present analysis argues that varying characterizations of Judith are influenced by representations and realities of women in the social-cultural milieu of individual authors and artists. In order to test this hypothesis, a dialogue is generated between descriptions of Judith's social reality in the text and reconstructions of the social realities and representations of Jewish (and non-Jewish) women in the late Second Temple period. This dialogue affirms that Judith's social location as a wealthy, landed widow, a solitary religious ascetic, and an educated woman was not anomalous in the social-historical ambient of the author of the apocryphal text.

Transformations of the Judith mythos also obscure the richness and subjective complexity of her character as depicted by the author. A hermeneutics of suspicion reveals that androcentric interpretive models for male protagonists consistently stress the inner motivations, intentions, and emotions of the male character. Experiential descriptions invite the reader to enter empathetically the inner world of powerful male protagonists. Judith satisfies all of the criteria of the male hero, yet interpretations of biblical scholars and theologians have tended to objectify Judith. Abstracted as a *type*, Judith is dehistoricized and depersonalized; Judith the protagonist is reduced to persona.

Psychological contextualization in the present analysis elaborates the complexity of Judith as an enigmatic protagonist, articulates aspects of her inner landscape, and clarifies her agency as subject. Elements that suggest Judith's subjective reality include an authority that is reflected in discursive and theological discourse. Judith's authority is evidenced also by deeds that reflect her resolve, conviction, boldness, and courage. While Judith's personal ambition is portrayed by expressed aspirations to valor and heroism, her sense of religious vocation is affirmed by pious faith and a rigorous asceticism. When Judith's experience is presented as central, her intelligence, wisdom, and wit emerge as vital aspects of her subjective reality. Judith's conscious resort to deceit to further her objectives receives considerable attention among biblical scholars and is a pivotal feature in the transformation of her mythos.

A feminist hermeneutic permits a "Judith-centered" exegesis that intentionally focuses away from Judith the decapitator. Feminist analysis invites contemporary audiences of the book of Judith to encounter a more comprehensive portrait of the protagonist. This portrait refers to Judith's persona but elucidates in greater detail Judith's social location and her subjective reality within the cultural ambient of the author. This focus provides fresh clues indicating how she might have been perceived by audiences for whom the author wrote. Texts from chapters 8 and 13 receive substantial attention in the commentary because of their centrality to the transformation of the mythos.

CHAPTER 8

8:1. "Judith" (Greek *ioudeith*; Hebrew *yhwdyt*) is most commonly translated "Jewess." There is a propensity among commentators to consider the character Judith as an allegory or type of Israel or a daughter of Israel. Such identification of Judith tends to elevate her status considerably within the androcentric, patriarchal domains of Judaism and Christianity. This exaltation as a soteriological type, however, is won with great cost to the intricacy of her total personhood as a character. When Judith is established as a type, the integrity of her character can be abstracted, dehistoricized, and decontextualized.

Other, less provocative "Judiths," who are not designated as types, include the Hittite wife of Esau (Gen 26:34); a woman from the Persian period, Judith daughter of Dalluy; and Judith daughter of Rabbi Hiyya (*b. Yebam.* 65; *Qidd.* 12) from the second or third century C.E.

JUDITH'S SOCIAL LOCATION IN TRIBE AND FAMILY

8:1. The author's patrilineal genealogy situates his protagonist as the *telos* of sixteen male ancestors in Israel; Judith's genealogy is unparalleled among female characters in the biblical tradition.

8:2. Judith's husband, Manasseh, belonged to the same tribe and family as she did, which indicates that their marriage was formulated along traditional agnatic lines of inheritance (designed to prevent a woman's wealth from being too broadly dispersed). As C. A. Moore notes, whereas customarily a husband's genealogy is recited, here Manasseh "sits in the shadow" of Judith's "family tree."[2]

JUDITH'S SOCIAL LOCATION AS A SOLITARY ASCETIC

8:5. Judith's decision to "[make] for herself a tent on the rooftop of her house" in which she intends to dwell thereafter, introduces her social location as a solitary ascetic.

Scholars neglect to mention correspondences between the fictional Judith's hermitage and the rooftop shrine of the Egyptian Aseneth, protagonist of a popular Jewish novel from the first century C.E. Before her conversion to Judaism, this beautiful maiden devoted herself day and night to the worship of Egyptian deities in the holy shrine on the roof of her palatial home.

The term used for Judith's outer garments can be translated either "the garments of her widowhood" or "the garments of her solitude." During the Second Temple period sackcloth was worn not for self-punishment but as a sign of loss or grief or even as a sign of national calamity. Judith's sackcloth may be associated with any or all of the above.

8:6. M. Enslin describes Judith's strenuous schedule of fasting as "super-pious."[3] Moore situates Judith's ritual praxis concerning foods in a Pharisaic context.[4] Toni Craven notes Hugo Mantel's ascription of a Sadducean genesis to Judith's fasting.[5] Judith's fasting, however, can best be considered in the context of a general increase in devotional piety in the late postexilic period. Here private fasting was embraced as an expression of penitence and mourning and preparation to receive communication from God. Rigorous fasting was a formal expression of devotion appropriate to the ethos of a consecrated female ascetic. Judith's commitment to fasting is paralleled among Thera-peutrides, Jewish female ascetics in Egypt, who received no sustenance before sunset and who partook of food either once every third or every sixth day (Philo, *On the Contemplative Life* 4.34–36). The author of Luke's Gospel states that Anna, the prophetess (Luke 2:36–38), was eighty-four years old in the year of Jesus' birth. This dating places her youth as contemporaneous with our dating for Judith. Anna, also a widow, lived as a religious ascetic at the Temple in Jerusalem, where she fasted and prayed night and day.

JUDITH'S SOCIAL LOCATION AS A WIDOW

8:7. Critical analysts of the status of widows in biblical Judaism suggest no provision for the widow's security through the inheritance of the late husband's property. Widows in ancient Judaism are traditionally represented as devoid of inheritance rights, and thus as economically and emotionally dependent and vulnerable to exploitation. Commentators on Judith's widowhood ignore the book's historical context and base their commentaries on traditional interpretations from ancient Judaism. Judith is thus objectified with the persona of a "poor widow." She is portrayed as "a weak woman lacking the support of her husband [who] can show and reveal better the face of God," or as "one of the powerless through whom Yahweh works," one who is "most alienated."[6] These commentaries ignore distinct discrepancies between the traditional interpretations and descriptions of the wealthy, landed, autonomous widow in the texts. Despite the persistence of traditional interpretation in scholarly literature, in the Second Temple period illustrations for Jewish women's inheritance are discovered in legal archives (Archives at Elephantine K 9:3ff., K 9:16ff., K 9:21; K 28; C 5, 6, 8, 9; C 13; C 14; C 15–17 [and from the first and second centuries C.E., the Babata Archives]); apocryphal literature (Sir 22:4; 25:21–22); pseudepigraphical literature (*Testament of Job* 46–52); popular romance (*Aseneth* 24:5; 6:1–4; 12:15); historical documents (Josephus, *Jewish War,* concerning Salome Alexandra); legal tractates (Mishnah *Ketub.* 4:12; VI, 11:1, 12:3).

Judith's social location as a wealthy, landed, autonomous widow reflects representations and realities of at least some Jewish women in Palestine during the period under discussion.[7]

JUDITH'S SUBJECTIVE REALITY AND HER AGENCY IN APPOINTING A FEMALE SLAVE AS STEWARD OVER HER ESTATE

8:10. Judith conferred on her female steward the responsibility for administering her estate. We are told nothing of the racial or ethnic heritage of this woman. She would, however, have been sufficiently literate to supervise and transact business concerning real estate, agriculture, and livestock production on Judith's properties.

JUDITH'S SUBJECTIVE REALITY AND HER AUTHORITY

8:11–13. Judith's summons of Chabris and Charmis inaugurates a series of events that demonstrate an assurance of her authority among the elders of Bethulia. Elisabeth Schüssler Fiorenza implies the authority of Judith as subject in summoning the elders of the town and rebuking them, "She censured their theological misjudgments and misconduct in the face of the enemy."[8] Moore notes that Judith addresses the elders of her city not as a peer but "as a superior rebuking them for their faithless and presumptuous act."[9]

JUDITH'S SUBJECTIVE REALITY AND HER THEOLOGICAL REFLECTION

8:12–20. Judith's understanding of the God of Israel moves beyond the doctrine of retribution to an understanding reflected in wisdom literature in Job 38–41. Judith's theology allows for the ambiguities and vulnerabilities of human experience in relationship to a deity who cannot be manipulated.

8:25–28. Moore suggests that Judith insists on a theological explanation which counters the elder's claim of God's abandonment of the people (7:28) or the argument that they are being punished for their sins (7:28). Judith informs the elders that God was actually testing the people, just as their ancestors had been tested. "The magistrates, in their passivity and lack of faith, serve well as foils for the assertive and believing Judith."[10]

JUDITH'S SUBJECTIVE REALITY AND HER PERSONAL AMBITIONS

8:25–28. Judith aspires to valor and heroism and identifies intimately with the prestigious patriarchs (8:26–27). Her self-understanding embraces responsibility for protecting the Temple and its altar (8:24). Judith's aspiration to heroic action in 8:32–34 is consistent with a feminist hermeneutic in attesting to a full range of human emotion and capacity for experience that is not bound by gender.

JUDITH'S SOCIAL LOCATION AS AN EDUCATED WOMAN

8:29. Uzziah's comment follows immediately upon Judith's theological and historical instruction and her exhortation to the elders of the city. It seems clear that these demonstrate at least in part the *sophia* and *synesis* to which he refers. It is, however, more difficult to postulate an arena in which "all of the people" would have been aware of Judith's wisdom, intelligence, and nobility of heart "from the beginning of her days." Was Judith educated? Did all of the people know Judith, from the time of her youth, in a context where intelligence was a criterion for recognition? Did Judith excel in a school (perhaps on her father's estate, perhaps attached to Bethulia's house of prayer/synagogue)?[11]

JUDITH'S SUBJECTIVE REALITY AND HER SPIRITUAL AUTHORITY

8:31. Moore contends that Uzziah requests Judith's prayers as an "ironic condescension" (i.e., our many prayers have not been answered, but "yours," surely will be).[12] However, arguments for this pericope as a validation of Judith's spiritual authority among the elders of Bethulia are consistent with the text.

8:35–36. The elder's "Go in Peace" attests that the young female ascetic commands the respect of the elders and receives their enthusiastic support of her undisclosed strategy (cf. Judg 18:6; 1 Sam 1:17). The Greek text indicates that Moore's suggestion that Judith has sought and received the "permission" of the elders to carry out her "secret plan" is not a defensible assertion.[13]

CHAPTER 9

JUDITH'S SUBJECTIVE REALITY AND HER DEVOTION AND PIETY

9:1. Judith's dramatic gestures of prostration, imposition of ashes, and exposition of her sackcloth as preparation for communication with God intensify our experience of her prayer to consecrate this soteriological mission.

JUDITH'S SUBJECTIVE REALITY AND HER JEWISH HERITAGE

9:2–4. Judith's prayer commences with a historical analogue to the present situation. The Genesis 34 account of the rape and subsequent vindication of Dinah proceeds from Judith's personal genealogy in the tribe of Israel. References to the action of her forefather Simeon indicate not only Judith's familiarity with the history of Israel but a personalization of and an identification with her ancestors in a time of crisis. Judith equates the devastation of her foremother Dinah and the revenge perpetrated on Dinah's captor with the present threat of the Assyrians upon the Temple and the sanctuary. Her prayer for the same strength to overcome the enemies of Israel as was granted Simeon suggests a working knowledge of history.

Moore reminds the reader that Gen 34:30 and 49:5–7 criticize severely Simeon's revenge on the Shechemites for Hamor's rape of Dinah, yet "Judith spoke approvingly of Simeon's act, possibly because Judith found herself in a position analogous to Dinah, i.e., she herself might end up being raped by Holofernes."[14]

J. C. Dancy also says that Judith mentions Simeon because she, Judith, is afraid of suffering the fate of Dinah. Dancy argues that Judith sees her ancestor as a defender of the right and seeks to apply Simeon's case to the present predicament: "As the Shechemites polluted Dinah, so the Assyrians have planned . . . to pollute the Temple in Jerusalem."[15] Dancy, however, does not emphasize the women's vulnerability to sexual violence from males but feminine "weakness." Dancy perpetuates gender hierarchies in stating that "as Dinah was a virgin so Judith was a widow, each of them weak women. But with the help of God, weakness becomes strength."[16]

Commentaries that elucidate Judith's relationship to Simeon and Dinah make sense of the otherwise baffling circumstances in which a pious, devoted, ascetic Jewish widow severs the head of a great Assyrian general. This aspect of Judith's inner life adds flesh and bones to the character known in history almost exclusively for the Holofernes event. In Judith's prayer she identifies with *both* Dinah and Simeon and provides insight into the inner landscape of a patriotic woman who refuses to be a victim either sexually or politically.

JUDITH'S SOCIAL LOCATION AS A MILITARY STRATEGIST

Hellenistic and Hasmonean queens frequently demonstrated personal expertise in military strategy. Whether their proficiencies as strategists depended on education (e.g. , Homer's *Iliad* books 3–8; 11–18) or innate capabilities can only be conjectured. In 9:7–9 Judith's prayer reveals her concern about increases in the Assyrian forces, designated personnel, the weaponry they employ, and the Assyrian's principal objective to defile and pollute the sanctuary at Jerusalem. Judith is acutely aware of Bethulia's grave responsibility to intercept and overcome the oppressors. Her keen sense of military strategy may support arguments that Judith was assumed to be educated.[17] Discussions of Judith's persona often compare Judith's military acumen as a woman warrior with that of Miriam (Exod 15:20–21) and Deborah (Judges 4–5).

JUDITH'S SUBJECTIVE REALITY AND HER CONSCIOUS DECEIT

9:10. No single aspect of Judith's subjective reality attracts as much attention from scholars and theologians as her use of deceit in order to achieve her objective. In interpretations that perpetuate negative representations of female protagonists, Judith is presented as yet another female subject who lies in order to get her way.

"By the deceit of my lips . . . ." This verse is crucial to an understanding of Judith's plan to save Israel. Here she clearly states her intention to employ as her principal weapon the use of deceit to smite her enemies. Craven's analysis of Judith's deceit is conscientious in its treatment of Judith as subject and as motivated by noble intentions. Craven points out that commentators ignore Judith's intention to use deceit to overcome the enemy. First she says she will use deceit, and then that is precisely what she does.[18]

CHAPTER 10

JUDITH'S SOCIAL LOCATION AS AN ASCETIC

10:2. Judith's practice of keeping the feasts of Israel is consistent with the practice of female ascetics in the late Second Temple period. The joyous feast recorded in 4Q502 contributes provocative insight into Essene women's participation in festive celebrations at Qumran. This text describes praises and prayers, blessings and honors bestowed upon and received by these female ascetic Daughters of Truth and Venerable Women.[19] Every seventh week Egyptian Therapeutrides celebrated the solemn meals and joyous feasts described in Philo's *On the Contemplative Life* (10–12). Exegesis, prayer, praises, chanting and singing (solo and in chorus), choreic dance, and an intoxicating ecstasy constituted the festal experience of these Jewish female ascetics.

10:3. Scruples concerning ritual purity and admonitions against anointing during periods of mourning and fasting (2 Sam 14:2; Dan 10:3) determined that female Essenes were resolved against anointing their bodies. Therapeutrides, on the other hand, permitted anointing the body with oil on the sabbath in order to "release it from its continuous toils."[20] The text (10:3) indicating that Judith reserved perfumed oil in the part of her home where she celebrated sabbaths may be evidence of sabbath anointing.

10:3–4. Moore notes the deliberateness with which "our Female Warrior" dresses herself. He likens Judith's subjective reality to that of a soldier facing battle who takes great care in preparing herself and her arms.[21]

JUDITH'S SUBJECTIVE REALITY AND HER BEAUTY

10:4. Only two texts in Judith make explicit reference to Judith's conscious use of her beauty to further her objectives (10:3–4 and 13:16). Both texts relate to Judith's intention to deceive Holofernes and are consistent with her prayer (9:10) to destroy her enemy "by the deceit of my lips." Enslin translates this same verb as beguile in 10:4 and connotes an equation of Judith's beauty with seduction.[22] He thus perpetuates a foundation for representations of the pious ascetic as a seductress. This element of Judith as subject transforms the Judith mythos away from her total characterization in the apocryphal text. The complexity of the beautiful, prayerful young widow who fasts night and day and assassinates a general to save her nation is explained away by a traditional misogynism that focuses on "feminine" beauty as a weapon. A translation of 10:4 that reads "to deceive the eyes of men" is consistent with the characterization of Judith in the Apocrypha.

10:5. Judith's instructions to her steward show concern to preserve her ritual purity. Judith's diet is more extensive than that of Egyptian Therapeutrides, who partake of only bread, water and hyssop (Philo, *On the Contemplative Life* 10).

JUDITH'S SUBJECTIVE REALITY AND HER INTELLIGENCE, WIT, AND WISDOM

10:12. Moore notes that the brevity and shrewdness of Judith's immediate response to her captors prove that she was not intimidated by her frightful predicament, that is, "two helpless young women caught in the middle of nowhere, in the dead of night, by rough Assyrian soldiers. Nor was Judith the least bit unnerved by their rapid-fire interrogation."[23] Moore's description of Judith and her steward as two helpless young women betrays a tacit paternalism yet does not deny that they were precisely where they intended to be and were there on the basis of their own initiative.

CHAPTER 11

JUDITH'S SUBJECTIVE REALITY AND HER INTELLIGENCE,
WIT, AND WISDOM

11:5–15. The present commentary posits Judith's experience as central. Texts in this chapter that traditionally have been interpreted as "ironic" by commentators are interpreted here as referring to Judith's intelligence, wisdom, and wit. Judith's "intelligent wisdom . . . shrewd observation . . . treacherous planning . . . guileful speech . . . intelligent courage" are among characteristics of Judith's inner landscape that undergird her strategies for a successful victory over the Assyrians. It is Judith's wisdom that has "prevailed over brute power."[24]

Alonso-Schökel praises Judith's "extreme skill" (i.e., practical wisdom) in her discourse with Holofernes in 11:5 when she enters into a disquisition on the sacred and the profane in Jewish religion, leading him into a world where he is weak and confused, a world where she can play the irreplaceable counselor—a confidant of God, a being endowed with superhuman knowledge.[25]

11:16. "God has sent me to accomplish with you things which will astonish the whole world. . . ." Judith's aspiration to accomplish her heroic mission finds "wings" in this ingenious scenario. As her "story" captivates Holofernes' blatant will to power, Judith affirms for herself her own perceived appointment as a savior of Israel.

11:20–22. Holofernes is delighted with Judith's wisdom and attests that both her beauty and her eloquence affirm the veracity of her promises. It may indeed be that Judith's beauty gets Holofernes' attention; however, it is precisely the persuasiveness of her intentionally "deceitful speech" and her attendant promise of his rise to greater power and glory that captivate the great general.

CHAPTER 12

JUDITH'S SUBJECTIVE REALITY AND HER CONSCIOUS DECEIT

12:14. Solomon Zeitlin goes beyond the text not only to suggest that Judith tried to "beguile" Holofernes but also to say that when Judith returned to Bethulia she assured the people that she had "enticed" Holofernes without being defiled by him.[26] Zeitlin's contention that the author portrayed Judith as a "perfect seductress" reveals his own misogynistic preoccupation.

Craven recognizes the complexity of Judith's truthfulness and contends that Judith has given considerable thought to the power that can be obtained through deceit. While she "possessed the utter confidence in the validity of her own truths she saw as her task an undoing of all that terrorized her people."[27] In deciding on her strategy, Judith considers the "communal past and the future of her people . . . her lies are confined to Chapters Ten to Thirteen and she lies only to men outside the covenant."[28]

CHAPTER 13

JUDITH'S PERSONA AND REPRESENTATIONS BY BIBLICAL SCHOLARS AND THEOLOGIANS

Objectifications of Judith as a type among biblical scholars and artists find their theme in the events of chapter 13, in which Judith decapitates Holofernes. Judith's persona replicates the androcentric worldview of biblical scholars in Jewish and Christian traditions. Celebrated as a type of Israel, God, Jesus, Ecclesia, and Blessed Virgin Mary, Judith functions largely to empower the androcentric, patriarchal institutions from which she emerged. The objectified Judith who slays Holofernes is compared with male and female Jewish and Christian heroes who are defenders and legitimators of the same religious institutions. In contradistinction, Judith the decapitator, interpreted by theologians as a symbol/archetype of seduction, humiliation of the male, deceit, violence, and confusion of gender identity, perpetuates representations of females as destructive, dangerous, and antithetical to the mores of religious traditions.

JUDITH'S PERSONA AND REPRESENTATIONS BY ARTISTS

A cursory chronology of Judith the decapitator's persona in the visual arts begins in the early Middle Ages. Rudimentary symbolism of Judith's persona included either the sword or the head of Holofernes.[29] The symbolic significance of the head has precedents in the ancient world, where the head was considered the dwelling place of the spirit. Ritual decapitation gave the holder of the head control over the spirit of the victim.[30] In the High Middle Ages Judith appears frequently as a type of the Ecclesia or the Blessed Virgin Mary. An illustration from the Pamplona Bible (thirteenth century) exemplifies images of Judith as victor over Satan and serves as an antetype for representations of the Blessed Virgin Mary's victory over evil.[31] These images have profound implications because they extract Judith from Jewish tradition and establish her image in the hierarchy of Christian iconography. Judith is objectified by notable Renaissance painters and sculptors including Botticelli, Mantegna, Donatello, Garofalo, Michelangelo, Giorgione, Tintoretto, and

Veronese.[32] Among renaissance interpretations of Judith the decapitator are those that embraced both secular and political spheres. Donatello's bronze "Judith and Holofernes" exemplifies the capacity of an image to perpetuate a patriarchal ethos in both religious and secular contexts. Placed in the Palazzo de Signoria, the Donatello came to symbolize the Florentine quest for independence and the defeat of their oppressors.[36]

One of the most enigmatic transformations of Judith in the arts is a burgeoning association of Judith with sin and sexuality, which emerged during late fifteenth, sixteenth, and seventeenth centuries. Paintings of Becafumi, Giorgione, and Cranach the Elder initiate this movement. The "nude Judiths" of Jan Massys, and Hans Baldung Grien also reflect this tendency.[34] Paintings of Luca, Zick, Benveneuti, and Solimena in the eighteenth century depicting Judith displaying the head of Holofernes to the people of her city reflect social and political concerns of tyranny.[35]

In the nineteenth and twentieth centuries representations of Judith reflect a pervasive misogynism. Judiths in the *fin de siècle* are objectified to such an extent that they no longer bear any resemblance to Judith in the Apocrypha. Images of the femme fatale are blatant and explicit. Among the best-known paintings in this genre is Gustav Klimt's *Judith I*.[36] Highly stylized representations of Judith the decapitator by Georg Pauli, Carl Schwalbach, Benjamin Constant, F. H. Woolrich, and William Etty reflect the effects of twentieth-century thought and technology on a pervasive misogynism.[37] Judith as subject is most powerfully portrayed in the seventeenth-century paintings of Artemesia Gentileschi and the twentieth-century dance of Martha Graham.[38]

CHAPTER 14

Judith's Social Location as a Military Strategist

14:1–4. After her triumphant return to Bethulia with the head of Holofernes, Judith proceeds with detailed military instructions for the people of Bethulia. She outlines a strategy to ensure a successful rout of the Assyrian army.

Judith's Subjective Reality and Her Openness to Achior

14:5–10. Achior's response to Judith's feat includes his conversion and the desire to be admitted into the "house of Israel." Judith's inclusiveness defied tradition when she and the Bethulians invited an Ammonite into the covenant (Deut 23:3).

CHAPTER 16

JUDITH'S SOCIAL LOCATION AS AN EDUCATED WOMAN:
HER PERSONA, HER SUBJECTIVE REALITY, AND THE VICTORY ODE

16:1–17. The Hymn of Thanksgiving in the chapter 16 of Judith is the object of considerable discussion among biblical scholars. In relation to Judith's persona, scholars note similarities between this hymn and Miriam's Song of the Sea (Exod 15:20–21) and Deborah's Victory Ode in Judges 5. Studied in the context of the Second Temple period, the hymn may elucidate the question of Judith's education. James Charlesworth notes elements of the process by which hymnic literature took shape and form. The movement from private instantaneous prayer to formalized, sometimes cultic prayer was accompanied both by injunctions not to make any prayer a fixed form and by the acceptance of communal fixed prayers and hymns.[39]

The Hymn of Thanksgiving in Judith 16 can be compared to the *Hodayot* from Qumran, which are representative of the fixed form. It is likely that the author intends Judith's prayer in chapter 9 to be understood as spontaneous and evocative of her preparation for her mission. Here, however, the hymn is quite clearly composed for corporate worship. This victory ode makes more references to the person of the heroine than the two hymns to which it is so frequently compared. The number of verses composed in the first person and the present tense (Jdt 16:1–4, 11, 12, 13, 17) evokes a sense of immediacy and captures a highly personal intensity. Does the author of Judith want to convey the heroine's own skill as a liturgist? To suggest that Judith herself composed the hymn invites our comparison to Therapeutrides who composed and performed hymns of their own creation and provides further support for Judith as an educated woman.

21:25. The fictional Judith's commitment to ascetic solitude defined her existence for the remainder of her long life. Judith's fame increased as the years went by and Israel was ensured peace and security throughout her lifetime. The story of this heroic savior in Israel, whose piety and courage preserved the Temple and delivered her people, was included neither in the canon of the Hebrew Bible nor in the canon of the Christian Testament.

NOTES

1. L. Alonso-Schökel, "Narrative Structures in the Book of Judith," in *Proceedings of the Protocol Series of the Colloquies of the Center for Hermeneutical Studies in Hellenistic and Modern Culture, January 27, 1974* (Berkeley: University of California Press, 1975); Toni Craven, *Artistry and Faith in the Book of Judith* (Chico, CA: Scholars Press, 1980); Morton Enslin, *The Book of Judith* (Leiden: Brill, 1972); Carey A. Moore, *The Book of Judith* (Anchor Bible; Garden City, NY: Doubleday, 1985).

2. Moore, *Judith,* 180.

3. Enslin, *Judith,* 180.

4. Moore, *Judith,* 181.

5. Craven, *Artistry,* 118.

6. Alonso-Schökel, "Narrative," 14–15, 53.

7. Linda Bennett Elder, "Transformations in the Judith Mythos" (Ph.D. diss., Florida State University, 1991), 25.

8. Elisabeth Schüssler Fiorenza, *In Memory of Her: A Feminist Theological Reconstruction of Christian Origins* (New York: Crossroad, 1983), 118.

9. Moore, *Judith,* 186.

10. Ibid.

11. Bennett Elder, "Transformations," 169–71.

12. Moore, *Judith,* 184.

13. Ibid.

14. Ibid., 190.

15. J. C. Dancy, "Judith," in *The Shorter Books of the Apocrypha* (Cambridge: Cambridge University Press, 1972), 103.

16. Ibid.

17. Bennett Elder, "Transformations," 164.

18. Craven, *Artistry,* 95–96.

19. Bennett Elder, "Transformations," 69–72.

20. Ibid., 109.

21. Moore, *Judith,* 200.

22. Enslin, *Judith,* 128.

23. Moore, *Judith,* 207.

24. Schüssler Fiorenza, *In Memory of Her,* 117–18.

25. Alonso-Schökel, "Narrative," 9–10.

26. Enslin, *Judith,* 12–14.

27. Toni Craven, "Redeeming Lies in the Book of Judith" (paper presented at the annual meeting of the Society of Biblical Literature, Anaheim, CA, November 1989), 9.

28. Ibid.

29. Diane Apostolos Cappadona, ". . . By the Hand of a Woman," in *Art as Religious Studies,* ed. Doug Adams and Diane Apostolos Cappadona (New York: Crossroad, 1987), 83–84.

30. Ibid., 84.

31. Bennett Elder, "Transformations," 336.

32. Ibid., 338–39.

33. Ibid., 340.

34. Ibid.

35. Ibid., 359–60.

36. Ibid., 369.

37. Ibid.

38. Ibid., 430–33.

39. James H. Charlesworth, "Jewish Hymns, Odes, and Prayers," in *Early Judaism and Its Modern Interpreters,* ed. R. A. Kraft and G. W. E. Nickelsburg (Philadelphia: Fortress, 1986), 413 (see p. 422 on the *Hodayot* at Qumran).

RECOMMENDED READINGS

Alonso-Schökel, Luis. "Narrative Structures in the Book of Judith." In *Proceedings of the Protocol Series of the Colloquies of the Center for Hermeneutical Studies in Hellenistic and Modern Culture* 12, 15 (March 1, 1974). Berkeley: University of California Press, 1974.

Cappadona, Diane Apostolos. ". . . By the Hand of a Woman."In *Art as Religious Studies,* edited by D. Adams and D. Apostolos Cappadona. New York: Crossroad, 1987.

Charlesworth, James H. "Jewish Hymns, Odes, and Prayers." In *Early Judaism and Its Modern Interpreters,* edited by R. A. Kraft and G. W. E. Nicklesburg. Philadelphia: Fortress, 1986.

Craven Toni. *Artistry and Faith in the Book of Judith.* Chico, CA: Scholars Press, 1980.

——. "Redeeming Lies in the Book of Judith." Paper presented at the annual meeting of the Society of Biblical Literature, Anaheim, CA, November 1989.

Dancy, J. C. "Judith." In *The Shorter Books of the Apocrypha.* Cambridge: Cambridge University Press, 1972.

Elder, Linda Bennett. "Transformations in the Judith Mythos: A Feminist Critical Analysis." Ph.D. diss., Florida State University, 1991.

Enslin, Morton. *The Book of Judith.* Leiden: Brill, 1972.

Moore, C. A. *The Book of Judith.* Anchor Bible. Garden City, NY: Doubleday, 1985.

Philo. *Vita Contemplativa.* Trans. F. H. Colson. 1941. Loeb Classical Library 9. Cambridge, MA: Harvard University Press, 1941.

Schüssler Fiorenza, Elisabeth. *In Memory of Her: A Feminist Theological Reconstruction of Christian Origins.* New York: Crossroad, 1983.

The Gospel of Mark

JOANNA DEWEY ◆

INTRODUCTION

THE PURPOSE of this short commentary on the Gospel of Mark is twofold: to lay bare the androcentrism of the text, noting where and how Mark renders women invisible or subordinate, and to bring out the liberating egalitarian vision of the gospel. The introduction will consider the themes of androcentrism and liberation, discuss the formation of Mark's Gospel, and describe the method of the commentary.

ANDROCENTRISM

Like other Christian writings, the Gospel of Mark is an androcentric text, a text that assumes males are the human norm and females are inferior. It is a text primarily about men, for men, and in all probability by a man. As in any androcentric text, women in Mark tend to be invisible, mentioned only when they are exceptional or required for the plot.

Mark's androcentrism is vividly apparent in his portrayal of the women followers of Jesus. The author mentions Jesus' male disciples throughout the narrative. At last, fifteen verses before the end of the Gospel, the author states that there were many women who had traveled with Jesus in Galilee, who had followed and ministered, and who had come to Jerusalem with him; that is, there were women disciples. The dilemma is that, long before 15:41, we have interpreted Mark's androcentric perspective as narrative description and historical reality. We have created a mental picture of the Markan narrative world as one in which only men accompany Jesus. The mention of the women in Mark 15 and 16 is too little and too late to modify our imaginative reconstructions.

LIBERATION

At the same time that Mark's Gospel minimizes and obscures the role of women, it is also perhaps the most liberating Gospel in the Christian Testament for any oppressed or marginalized group. First, the narrative portrays God's blessings as available now. Mark draws on the apocalyptic worldview common among many first-century Jews and Christians: in the present age God permits Satan to control the world and work evil, but God will soon act to defeat Satan and begin God's realm on earth, the new age. For Mark, God's new age *has* begun with Jesus' ministry. The present evil age still has power but God will soon act to complete the fulfillment of the new age. In the Markan narrative liberation begins in the present.

Second, the Markan Jesus acts to include and make whole all peoples. The Jews, including Jesus, understood God as holy. The dominant Jewish view of the time was that God's holiness must be protected from pollution, impurity, or uncleanness.[1] Contact with unclean people or unclean things pollutes that which is pure; women were considered less pure than men and a threat to male purity. Groups varied in how strictly they applied purity rules. The Pharisees wanted to apply purity laws to all Jews at all times. The peasants, some 90 percent of the population, probably followed purity regulations when they went up to the Temple for festivals, but they would have neither time nor resources to observe purity in daily life. Jesus held an alternative Jewish view: instead of understanding contact with the unclean as polluting the pure, Jesus enacted God's holiness by ignoring purity boundaries to declare clean what was unclean. Thus Jesus wipes out the discrimination against women that was based on the pervasive purity codes.

Third, the Gospel of Mark presents a nonhierarchical, nonauthoritarian, egalitarian view of community. Women are understood as people in their own right, no longer as property of men. Children, the weakest in society, are at the center of God's realm. Those with more power in the world are called to serve rather than rule over those with less power and status. Wealth is viewed as a hindrance to entering God's realm.

BACKGROUND INFORMATION

Author, Date and Place, Intended Audience

The Gospel of Mark is anonymous. We have no certain knowledge about the text, the author, the time or place of writing, or the intended audience, except what we can infer from the text itself. According to one tradition, the Gospel was associated with John Mark (Acts 12:12, 25; 15:37, 39), who may have met Peter and who traveled with Paul. According to another, Mark translated and wrote down the teachings of Peter in Rome. These are suppositions, however, not reliable traditions.

The author of the Gospel was probably a "Mark" otherwise unknown to us. It was a common name, but no Mark was either a disciple of Jesus or an important missionary after Easter. The identification with John Mark and the association with Peter were probably second-century attempts to give the Gospel apostolic authority. It is not clear whether or not the author was a Jew; his native language was probably Greek.

On the basis of its content, the Gospel appears to have been composed about forty years after Jesus' death and resurrection at the end of the Roman–Jewish war, around 70 C.E. Its place of origin was probably somewhere in the eastern Mediterranean directly affected by the war, perhaps Galilee. The intended audience probably included both Jews and Gentiles: in some instances common Jewish customs are explained; in others, knowledge about the Jewish tradition seems to be assumed. The narrative is in simple Greek, with an oral storytelling style, which suggests that the Gospel was neither written by nor intended for the small literate elite of the Roman Empire. It is composed from a peasant perspective for a peasant audience.

From Jesus to Mark

The Gospel of Mark, our first written Gospel, was composed in a world in which only about 10 percent of the population was able to read or write. For the rest, however, illiteracy was neither an economic nor a social handicap. For most, all knowledge, learning, teaching, memory, entertainment, and business were oral. Jesus was an oral teacher; he left no writings. After Easter, Christianity was an oral phenomenon, spreading by word of mouth. This was the normal way for any popular philosophical or religious movement to spread.

From the Gospel itself we can infer something about the oral traditions about Jesus. Mark is made up of a series of short stories or sayings loosely connected by such frames as Jesus "was beside the sea" or "entered a synagogue." Scholars believe that such individual stories circulated separately. As stories were repeated orally, people would change and adapt them to local situations. It is also common in oral cultures for stories about an individual hero to be grouped together in a larger narrative cycle, and this may well have happened to the stories about Jesus. Christian storytelling occurred in many situations: informal storytelling by local people in their daily lives; oral performances by people with local or regional reputations as good tellers; and storytelling by wandering teachers, evangelists, or performers. This last group's stories earned them their living, either by direct contributions or, more likely, by support from the Christian communities they visited and/or founded. Audiences would hear Christian stories in the workplace, at home, at outdoor community gathering places, and in more formal Christian worship situations. Since much of life was lived in sex-segregated groups, women would tell stories to women, girls, and children of both sexes; men would tell stories to men and boys. There would also be common storytelling situations in which men and women taught both women and men.

Mark was a gifted storyteller. Steeped in Christian oral tradition and building upon it, he created a coherent narrative. Then at some point, he either wrote it down or dictated it—we do not know why. Mark expected the end of history and the return of Christ in the near future (9:1; 13:30), so preservation of the story for the future seems an unlikely motive. But for whatever reason, the Gospel of Mark was put into writing. The fullness of our Markan text is dependent on writing, for some of the structural and verbal subtleties are beyond the reach of oral composition. Yet the Gospel conforms to oral storytelling techniques and is meant to be heard, not read. It takes less than two hours to perform, a short time span for ancient storytelling. Actual storytellers would have adapted, expanded, and contracted narratives such as Mark's in response to their audiences.

THE PURPOSE AND STRUCTURE OF MARK

Mark's story of Jesus' ministry, death, and resurrection is not meant to provide information about the life and death of Jesus so much as to proclaim the good news. It calls its hearers to be followers of the risen Jesus, participants in the blessings of the realm of God already present as well as in the suffering and persecution that discipleship entails.

Mark had no chronology to link the various traditions. To create a narrative he used a journey motif and clustered material with similar content. The journey begins in and around Galilee, the place of the realm of God; it continues up to Jerusalem, where Jesus is crucified; it ends with the prophecy of Jesus' return to Galilee. The content clustering correlates with the geographical outline. 1:1–13 is the prologue proclaiming Jesus as God's agent. 1:14–8:21 takes place in Galilee and shows the inbreaking of God's realm, the erasing of all purity boundaries, and the spread of healing, forgiveness, and feasting. It also shows two responses: huge crowds seeking Jesus out, and religious and political leaders rejecting him. 8:22–10:52 portrays the journey from Galilee to Jerusalem, stressing the persecution to come and the call to egalitarian service. 11:1–13:37 takes place in Jerusalem, setting forth the Markan Jesus' relation to Jewish institutions and beliefs, and teaching about the end of the age. 14:1–16:8, the passion narrative, portrays Jesus' betrayal, arrest, execution, and resurrection. (16:9–20 is not part of the Gospel of Mark, but was added later.)

Mark uses the role of the disciples to unify the narrative and maintain plot interest. The audience is told who Jesus is at the beginning of the narrative, whereas the disciples within the story only gradually discern it. The Markan disciples continually have difficulties understanding Jesus, and they finally abandon him. The interest of Mark's audience is maintained in large part by watching the disciples try to figure out what it already knows. Thus, the audience is challenged to do better than the disciples.

THE METHOD FOR THE COMMENTARY

Since Mark's story is meant to persuade its audience to follow Jesus rather than to impart information, this commentary focuses on the story *as story* and largely ignores questions concerning the historicity of what Mark relates. Each section of the Gospel is discussed in two parts. The first part, *narrative analysis,* focuses on the narrative world. It looks at individual episodes and their contribution to the story as a whole. When issues concerning women are part of the narrative world, they will be discussed under narrative analysis. Periodically the term "the Markan Jesus" is used to remind the reader that the subject is Mark's narrative, not actual historical events. The second part, *feminist analysis,* assesses the portrayal of gender in the narrative world. It uses gender as an analytic category to evaluate the Markan portrayal of characters and Mark's theology as it affects women. It seeks to make explicit both the androcentrism that is detrimental to women's lives and the possibilities for women's liberation to be found in the text. This part occasionally includes historical observations, drawing inferences about the actual women around Jesus or in Mark's audience. In short, the *narrative analysis* seeks to help the reader understand Mark's narrative in its own terms, and the *feminist analysis* seeks to critique it from a feminist perspective.

The commentary may be used as a reference to look up particular passages, in which case it is important to consult both the narrative and the feminist analysis. Or it may be used as a study guide to the Gospel as a whole. In either case, it is best to read through the Gospel first in one sitting to get the impact of the entire narrative, for Mark creates his meaning through the combination and ordering of the individual episodes. A vivid experience of the androcentrism of the text may be had by reading the text reversing the gender of all characters.

In the commentary, the terms "Mark," "storyteller," and "narrator" are used more or less interchangeably. Specifically, "Mark" is the author of the Gospel; "storyteller" is the person (Mark or someone else) performing the story to a live audience; and "narrator" is the role in the narrative that guides and relates the story. I use masculine pronouns, because the androcentrism of the text suggests that the author was a man, and because the narrator encoded in an androcentric text is male.

COMMENTARY

PROLOGUE (1:1–13)

Narrative analysis. The prologue introduces Jesus and establishes him as a reliable character. The storyteller begins by announcing the subject and situating the narrative in the larger story of God's redemption of Israel. "Gospel" (1:1) did not yet refer to a narrative about Jesus but meant "proclamation," "good news." So Mark announces his story to his audience as "the beginning of the good news of Jesus Christ." Mark then recalls the scriptural prophecy of one coming to prepare the way, and introduces John as fulfilling the prophecy. John baptizes the crowds and prophesies the coming of a greater one. Jesus appears; the Spirit descends upon him; and a voice from heaven acknowledges him as God's Son. Mark has established Jesus as God's authorized agent. Mark's story, then, concerns good news from God manifest on earth.

Feminist analysis. The characters in the story are male: the Hebrew prophets, John, Jesus, and God, who is referred to with grammatically masculine pronouns. There are two exceptions. First, Christ is not gender specific. Applied to the person Jesus, Christ refers to a male, but in phrases such as "the risen Christ" or "the body of Christ" it is genderless or inclusive. Second, the Holy Spirit is grammatically neuter. We cannot determine from the text what gender Mark or his audience imagined for the Holy Spirit. "Spirit" is grammatically feminine in Hebrew and Aramaic, and there are occasional references to the Holy Spirit as female; it is possible that some of Mark's audience understood the Holy Spirit to be female.

The crowd pictured around John the Baptist consists of "everybody"—grammatically masculine plural, the form used when mixed groups are described. It is not clear from the text whether Mark is using the term exclusively, meaning men only, or inclusively, meaning women and children as well. Historically, women did participate in public in religious events, although the aristocratic male picture of the ideal woman restricted her to the private, indoor sphere. Probably Mark pictured women present, traveling either with their male relatives or with other women.

I. GALILEE: THE REALM OF GOD (1:14–8:22)

Introduction

Mark 1–8 pictures Jesus in Galilee, manifesting the inbreaking of the realm of God. People respond in various ways to Jesus' activity and message. The religious and political leaders (Pharisees, scribes, Herodians) reject him immediately. The crowd enthusiastically follows him. A third, smaller group become Jesus' disciples, traveling with him: these disciples follow Jesus yet also have difficulty understanding him.

A Day in Galilee (1:14–45)

Narrative analysis. 1:14–15. Mark opens Jesus' ministry with a speech by Jesus summarizing his message: "The realm of God has arrived; turn and trust in the good news." "Realm" is usually translated "kingdom," but the Greek word, *basileia,* refers to ruling in general, regardless of gender. The "realm of God" has three aspects—present, referring to God's blessings of exorcism, healing, and feeding; ethical, referring to humans acting on earth according to the will of God; and future, referring to God's further action rewarding the just and punishing the wicked. Mark's affirmation that God's realm "has drawn near and is here" tells the audience that God's rule has begun now, with Jesus' public ministry.

1:16–20. The storyteller narrates the call of four men to follow Jesus. The Markan Jesus' first act after proclaiming God's realm is to begin gathering the new community, citizens of that realm. In Mark, "to follow" and "to come after" are terms used for becoming a disciple of Jesus. As the story unfolds, the audience will learn that following is only the first step; understanding and faithfulness in following are more difficult. But the first step is necessary and drastic: it involves leaving one's old life behind. For the brothers, it involved leaving behind occupation and family.

1:21–45. The Markan Jesus enters a synagogue during its weekly service, teaches, and casts a demon out of a man. Mark's audience assumed the existence of demons, so for them the demon's recognition of Jesus as God's Holy One reaffirms Jesus' divine status. Next, Jesus heals the fever of Simon's (Peter's) mother-in-law. To demonstrate that the healing has occurred, Mark relates that she rose "and served them." *Diakonia* (service) often refers to waiting on table. It is an important word, here describing women's (or slaves') activities but later describing Mark's ideal of discipleship—which in retrospect may apply here as well. Finally, Jesus cleanses a leper.

Jesus thus successfully accomplishes the different sorts of healings recognized in the first century. People of that period understood all sickness to be personally caused, either by human or by superhuman powers. Jesus casts out unclean spirits, curing sickness caused by evil powers; he cures a fever, often perceived as caused by God as a punishment for sin. Finally, he cleanses the leper. Normally, a person touching an unclean person such as a leper or a menstruating woman would become unclean. Instead, Jesus spreads wholeness or holiness, restoring the leper to purity and reincluding him in human society.

Feminist analysis. Once again, the characters portrayed are predominantly male. The people specifically called to follow are four named men. Two of the three healed are men. One, however, is a woman. She is healed in a private home, the proper sphere for women. As noted, Mark uses "to serve" to describe her activity, the same term he will later use for true discipleship. Finally, people in the audience hearing Mark's story would probably imagine women and children among "the many" healed.

Opposition to Jesus (2:1–3:6)

Narrative analysis. The storyteller narrates five controversies between Jesus and Jewish leaders, concluding with the Pharisees and Herodians plotting to kill Jesus. Here, as throughout the Gospel, the conflict between Jesus and his opponents is an intra-Jewish conflict between a popular Jewish peasant movement and the official political/religious/economic leaders. Jesus the Jew and the Jewish leaders are criticizing each other. Meanwhile the crowd around Jesus continues to increase. Thus Mark dramatizes the two responses to Jesus: enthusiastic crowds seek healing, and religious/political authorities seek to destroy him. These controversies portray to Mark's audience the causes of Jesus' conflict with the authorities. Jesus realizes the presence of God's realm through his healings and his meals with people, spreading holiness to make the unclean clean. Jesus, himself a Jew, assumes God's prerogatives of forgiving sins and changing the law, while the Jewish leaders seek to protect God's holiness and prerogatives. Mark introduces the title "the Human One," to indicate Jesus' divinely derived authority over sin and the law (2:10, 28). (The title is literally translated "Son of Man," the Greek form of an idiomatic Hebrew expression. It consists of "son of" meaning "member of" and *anthrōpos,* the inclusive Greek word for humanity.)

An additional call to discipleship in this section further extends the boundaries of God's realm. Levi leaves his work collecting taxes to follow Jesus. For Jews, tax collecting was an unclean occupation; hence, Mark portrays Jesus calling a sinner in the midst of sinning. In 2:15 Mark first uses the word "disciple" for those following Jesus.

Feminist analysis. This section of Mark is typical of androcentric texts. No women are explicitly present among any of the characters or groups mentioned. Modern audiences are likely to imagine the narrative world created by these episodes as populated entirely by men. Yet, when we reimagine the text as inclusive rather than androcentric, women also become part of the narrative world. The first scene, the healing of the paralytic, takes place in a home with an earthen roof that can be dug through to make a hole for the paralytic (2:1–12). This would be a small home with a common room in which everyone ate and slept. So women and children as well as men would be around Jesus.

Women would also be present when Jesus dines with tax collectors and sinners (2:15–17). Once again the scene takes place in a home where women are normally present, though most likely serving the men. "Tax collectors and sinners" were unclean people of all sorts and may have included prostitutes. Women would also be present at the synagogue service (3:1–6), most likely sitting with their male relatives.[2]

Following and Opposing Jesus (3:7–35)

Narrative analysis. This section continues the theme of Jesus' healings as part of life in God's realm. *3:7–12* again emphasizes the huge crowds following Jesus, numerous healings, and the demons' recognition of Jesus' divine status. *3:13–19* shows Jesus selecting twelve men to be with him and to share his authority to preach, teach, and cast out unclean spirits. In *3:22–30,* the scribes accuse Jesus of exorcising unclean spirits by the power of Satan (another supernatural male figure). The story asserts not only that Jesus exorcises by the power of God but also that Jesus is plundering Satan's realm, a sign that God is already curtailing Satan's power. Mark reminds his audience that Jesus' healings show God's inbreaking realm and Satan's defeat in the present.

3:20–21, 31–35 is a controversy with Jesus' own family. When his mother and brothers call him, Jesus does not go, but redefines his kin as those in the house who do the will of God. This group explicitly includes women—"sisters and mother." This passage is extremely radical in its first-century context. The basic unit of ancient society was not the individual, as in the West today, but the family or kinship unit. Individual needs and desires were subordinated to those of the family group. Here the Markan Jesus replaces the blood kinship group with a new, fictive kinship group, the family of God. The new kinship group is open to all who do the will of God. It is open to women independently of their embeddedness in the social unit of the family, where they owe obedience to father or husband. The Markan Jesus' response to his mother and brothers means that the call to be part of the family of God supersedes the societal demands of the original kinship unit. Furthermore, the new family of God includes no human father, no authority figure to whom obedience is owed. In continuing the kinship metaphor as it is used here, Jesus is brother and son to the women in the group.

The storyteller has further defined Jesus' followers. Prior to this section, a few individual men were called and a larger mixed group was following. In this section, Jesus names twelve men to be an inner circle and designates a larger group, specifically including women, as his family.

Feminist analysis. Until this point, the Markan narrative has been androcentric; that is, women have been largely *invisible*. Mark 3, however, introduces *discrimination* on the basis of gender. A few males are specially called to be with Jesus, to preach and heal, thus participating in spreading God's realm. While other males and all females are called to be part of Jesus' new kin, they are given no active role, no authority to preach and cast out demons. At this point, Mark's narrative world limits leadership to men.

Two questions arise. Is Mark's narrative world an accurate reflection of the historical reality of Jesus' ministry? Would Mark's audience, especially the women in Mark's audience, understand the narrative world as restricting their own leadership in Christian communities? First, the restriction of the inner circle around Jesus to a few men is probably not historically accurate. It is doubtful that Jesus himself named twelve men or any specific group to extend or continue his ministry.[3] More likely, this portrayal is due to men's efforts after Easter to establish their own authority. Further, surviving traditions of women in the Christian Testament and the extracanonical writings suggest that Jesus' closest associates, those who actively extended God's realm, included women. But Mark is a male of his time and culture; he minimizes the roles of women around Jesus and focuses on the men.

Second, Mark's male and female audiences' understanding of the role of women in Christian churches would depend a great deal on their experience apart from Mark's story. The primary method of transmitting Christianity was oral, and there were Christian women storytellers and teachers. Most of the women and many of the men would have heard Christian women tell stories of women healing and preaching. Thus they probably heard Mark's story neither as an accurate picture of the women associated with Jesus nor as an authoritative guide for their present Christian roles, but rather as one story among several. For first-century Christians, Mark's androcentric perspective would have been balanced by other, more gynocentric, perspectives. Women's oral traditions have not survived, however, except as they have been filtered through men's perspectives and codified in men's writings.[4] As a result we have come to mistake Mark's androcentric narrative world for historical reality.

Parables of the Realm of God and the First Boat Episode (4:1–41)

Narrative analysis. 4:1-34. So far Mark has shown Jesus enacting the realm of God—gathering followers, healing and exorcising, eating with all sorts of people, and debating with those who reject God's realm. In this section Mark portrays Jesus telling parables comparing God's realm to stories about everyday life. The stories are drawn from agriculture and stress abundant harvest, a vibrant image for marginal peasants.

Here for the first time in the story world, Mark introduces the theme of the disciples' difficulty in understanding. The disciples ask the meaning of the first parable (4:10). The Markan Jesus replies that they have been given the mystery of God's realm but the outsiders do not understand. Mark's meaning is not fully clear to us but this much seems probable: first, to understand the mystery one must follow Jesus; second, there will be outsiders who do not grasp Jesus' message or who choose to reject it. In the narrative thus far, the Pharisees and the scribes are outsiders who reject Jesus. Now Mark suggests that the disciples—who are following—may not be able to understand this or any parable (4:13).

4:35–41. The first boat episode reinforces the theme of the disciples' misunderstandings. Jesus and the disciples are crossing the lake in a boat, a storm arises and the disciples fear drowning. The Markan Jesus rebukes the storm with the same words with which he rebuked unclean spirits, and the storm is stilled. This echoes God's power over the waters in the exodus narrative. Jesus questions the disciples' lack of faith; the disciples are afraid and wonder who Jesus really is. Mark's audience, of course, knows who Jesus is—earlier in the narrative, Mark has identified him as the Christ and described the baptism and the demons' recognition. The characters in the narrative are not aware of this information. Thus, Mark's audience is engaged in watching how the characters understand—or fail to understand—what it already knows. Mark uses this device to teach his own audience. Discipleship calls for faith, faith in God's beneficent power active in Jesus.

Feminist analysis. Women are presumably part of the listening crowd. They would also be among those hearing the explanation of the parable of the sower, since Mark describes that audience as "those who were about him with the twelve" (4:10). The general term "disciples" makes it unclear whether women were present in the boat or not, but possibly some in Mark's audience would picture the story world so. Finally, Mark's androcentric bias is shown in his selection of parables that portray farming as a predominantly male activity in first-century Palestine. Unlike Matthew and Luke, Mark includes no parables drawing specifically on women's experience.

Boundary-breaking Healings (5:1–43)

Narrative analysis. The three healings of 5:1–43 are thematically familiar, yet the content gives each episode more radical political and religious depth.

5:1–20. The healing of the Gerasene demoniac again demonstrates Jesus' tremendous power over unclean spirits, and it shows in dramatic form Jesus' aggressive violation of purity concerns. The Markan Jesus travels to Gentile territory, which is unclean; goes amid graves, which are unclean places; and casts demons out of a man into a herd of pigs, which are unclean animals. "Legion," the demons' name, is the term for a unit of the Roman army; drowning demons in the lake is a political allusion to the destruction of the Roman army of occupation.

5:21–43. The storyteller intercalates the healings of two females: a twelve-year-old girl who has died, and a woman who has had a vaginal hemorrhage for twelve years. In the first-century Jewish cultural context, Jesus' actions have unmistakable, radical implications. Women were considered less clean than men and constituted a perennial threat of pollution to men. In addition to being female, each has another source of impurity; the girl becomes a corpse and the woman has a hemorrhage. Moreover, while the girl would have some derived status in the society as the daughter of a synagogue leader, the woman with the hemorrhage has no status. She is destitute and apparently without male kin to protect her. Any physical contact with these women should render Jesus unclean. Instead, Jesus restores them to purity and includes them in society. The Markan Jesus creates a Jewish community that understands the realm of God as whole, inclusive, and without boundaries, not as the exclusive and separated realm protected by the Jewish officials. Since women were considered dangerously impure, their inclusion is a prime example of the Markan Jesus' inclusiveness.

The woman with the hemorrhage (5:25–34) is portrayed as violating the norms for proper submissive female behavior. *She* initiates contact with Jesus: she sneaks up in the crowd and touches Jesus' clothes to obtain healing. She is not offered healing by Jesus or by anyone he has appointed; she claims healing and takes it for herself, without permission from anyone, violating taboos by being in public at all. Her behavior brings her healing, praise from the Markan Jesus, and inclusion in his kinship family: "Daughter, your faith has saved you" (5:34). Finally, several words appear only in the depiction of the hemorrhaging woman and of Jesus himself: "suffer many things," "blood," "body," and "plague." The language suggests that "Mark dared to identify her suffering with Jesus."[5]

Feminist analysis. Women are clearly visible in this portion of the narrative—the two being healed, the girl's mother, and the wailers at Jairus's home, whom ancient audiences would assume to be professional female mourners. Furthermore, the hemorrhaging woman acts in powerful nontraditional ways. She is depicted breaking out of her proper submissive role and daring to claim her own wholeness. In fact, her action may have helped the Markan Jesus to free himself from the patriarchal assumptions and male privilege of ancient culture.[6]

Rejection, Death, and Jesus' Power over Nature (6:1–52)

Narrative analysis. 6:1–6. Mark the storyteller loves contrast. The recounting of Jesus' miraculous powers over demons, uncleanness, and death is followed by the story of rejection in his native village. The Markan Jesus returns to Nazareth and teaches in its synagogue, but the people see only an ordinary hometown boy, and miracles worked by such hands seem presumptuous arrogance. Further, rather than identify him by his father's name, the people name him Mary's son, which is derogatory to both Mary and Jesus. (There is no mention of any human father or virgin birth in Mark.) Of course, a first-century audience would be reminded that Jesus rejected village norms for eldest sons. In order to preach God's realm, he abandoned his mother, ignoring his kinship duties and exposing his family to shame.

With few exceptions, Jesus cannot use his miraculous powers in Nazareth. In 2:5; 5:34, 36, Mark has shown that healings are accompanied by faith that Jesus can heal by God's power. Here Mark recounts the reverse: without faith, few healings are possible. The Markan Jesus has crossed all boundaries—stilled a storm, healed Gentiles, cleansed uncleanness, and raised a girl from the dead. His powers can benefit everyone, but he does not control people. They can refuse to be part of God's realm.

6:7–29. Immediately after Jesus' rejection at Nazareth, he sends out the twelve named earlier (3:13–19) to preach and heal. They extend Jesus' ministry of God's realm, proclaiming repentance, healing, and exorcising. The Markan Jesus tells them to move on if they meet rejection; again, the realm of God is offered to all, but not all choose to receive it. Sandwiched between the sending out and return of the Twelve is the story of the execution of John the Baptist by Herod Antipas, the ruler of Galilee. The audience has already heard of the Pharisees' plot with the Herodians to destroy Jesus, and now they hear of John's death. Being a messenger from God brings the risk of execution by the powers of this world.

The folktale-like story of John's execution is shown as brought about by Herod's wife, Herodias, and her young daughter. Pleased by the daughter's dance at a banquet, Herod makes a promise that will shame him before his guests if he does not keep it. The narrative draws on the motif of banquets of the rich in antiquity.[7] Only men dined; girls, usually slaves, provided entertainment, music, and dance. The entertainment was sexually titillating, and females present were understood to be sexually available. The girl's youth may make the scene especially shocking for modern audiences. In antiquity, however, it is not her age but her highborn status as Herodias's daughter that makes her presence and dance shocking. Herodias and her daughter are clearly labeled as disreputable women.

This is the only instance in Mark of a narrative with sexual overtones, but it may not be a negative portrayal of female sexuality. Lewd behavior was stereotypically part of elite banquets, and Mark's peasant audience may well have heard the story as yet another description of the notorious debauchery of rulers. Herod, Herodias, and her daughter are all depicted negatively. Herod is part of Mark's generally negative portrayal of political authorities. The episode's narrative function seems to be to contrast the respectable eating practices of Jesus and his disciples (Mark 2:13–28; 6:35–44; etc.) with the disreputable practices of the rulers.[8]

6:30–44. After the story of John's execution, the storyteller gives further demonstrations of Jesus' divine powers. Jesus teaches a large crowd in the desert; Jesus blesses the few loaves and fish they have available; the disciples distribute them; and much is left over after all five thousand are fed. Like Jesus' power over the water, the feeding in the desert echoes God's feeding of the ancient Hebrews in the desert after crossing the Red Sea. In Mark 2, Mark's audience heard about eating in the realm of God. Here a dramatic instance of God's abundant feeding is portrayed—a real blessing in a subsistence economy.

6:45–52. The second boat episode immediately follows. Again the disciples are in a boat, and this time Jesus approaches them walking on the water. The narrator tells the audience that the disciples were stunned because they had not understood about the feeding, and that their hearts were hardened. The phrase used earlier about Jesus' opponents is now applied to the disciples. They are unable to realize Jesus' divine power, the full power of God active in Jesus.

Feminist analysis. Women explicitly appear in this section in two places. First are Jesus' mother and sisters, named as residing in his hometown. Second are Herodias and her daughter in the following story. Christian interpreters have used the latter story to blame female behavior for male lust, and thus to legitimate association of women with sexuality and evil. A more feminist interpretation would observe that in patriarchal cultures such as Mediterranean antiquity, women have no direct access to influence, so they may manipulate others, including their own children, to gain their ends.

Elsewhere in Mark 6, women are invisible in the androcentric text or are explicitly excluded. Nonetheless, Mark's audience may have imagined women in the disciple group traveling to Jesus' hometown, distributing food to the crowd, and present in the boat. The audience certainly would have visualized women among those healed by the Twelve and residing in the houses where they stayed. The explicit presence of women coming for healing in some crowd scenes (e.g., 5:25–34) is assurance that Mark assumed the presence of women in all crowds.

The narrative, however, specifically excludes women disciples from the twelve Jesus sends out to preach and heal. (See feminist analysis of Mark 3:7–35.) Mark also lists those at the feeding of the five thousand as men (6:44). Greek has two words, *anthrōpos,* an inclusive term that can refer to men and women, and *anēr,* which normally refers to males only. In this instance, one would expect Mark to use *anthrōpos* but he uses *anēr.* Probably Mark's perspective is so thoroughly androcentric that he unreflectively uses *anēr* without intending to exclude women and children, and his audience would recognize and understand this usage accordingly.

Healing, Feeding, Controversy and Boat Episode, Again (6:53–8:21)

Narrative analysis. 6:53–56. This brief scene, in which Jesus heals many, reminds the audience of Jesus' healing power. *7:1–23.* The Markan Jesus debates with his opponents, the crowd, and the disciples about purity rules. Thus far in the narrative, Mark has presented Jesus, a popular Jewish leader challenging the dominant Jewish notion that God's holiness demands separation and purity. Jesus has not kept holy the sabbath; he has eaten with tax collectors and sinners; he has healed those who are unclean. In this episode, Mark shows Jesus directly debating the issue of purity with the Pharisees and scribes and rejecting their understandings of purity. To reinforce the point, the narrator tells the audience in an aside, "Thus he declared all foods clean" (7:19).

7:24–30 narrates the story of the Syrophoenician woman, a Gentile who seeks out Jesus to exorcise her daughter's demon. Jesus casts an unclean spirit out of an unclean female who is not even present. Mark continues the themes of upholding wholeness rather than purity, and of breaking boundaries to extend God's realm. But most remarkable is the dialogue between the woman and Jesus. As in many of the controversy stories, sharp dialogue is followed by a snappy saying (see 2:15–17, 18–20, 23–28). But in this story alone, the snappy retort is not made by Jesus. Jesus first refuses to heal the daughter on the grounds that children must be fed before dogs. From his Jewish perspective, the Jews are the children, and the Gentiles, the dogs. The woman is doubly oppressed, by her gender and her race. The woman cleverly and politely uses his own argument to convince him: "Sir, the little dogs under the table eat the children's crumbs." Jesus replies that "for this *word*" your daughter is healed. For the content of what she says, not just for her faith or persistence, the Markan Jesus grants her request. The Syrophoenician woman has led the Markan Jesus to enlarge the boundaries to include even Gentiles: in the next episode but one he feeds four thousand Gentiles, a great abundance of crumbs!

7:31–37. Jesus is portrayed using spittle to heal a deaf-mute man. Spittle, like blood or a leper's pus, comes out of the body and was therefore unclean. This is the first of four healings that involve the regaining of hearing, sight, and speech (8:22–26; 9:17–29; 10:46–52). Hearing and seeing function as metaphors for gaining understanding (see 4:12).

8:1–10. Mark's audience has just heard the stories of feeding five thousand with a few loaves and fishes, and the Syrophoenician woman being praised for her statement about dogs–Gentiles–getting at least the crumbs. Now they hear another story of Jesus desiring to feed a large crowd, this time Gentile. The audience surely expects another miraculous feeding. Yet the characters in the narrative, the disciples, do not expect a miracle. A miracle is narrated, however, in words echoing the first feeding. Again Mark has conveyed to his audience the difficulty the disciples have acknowledging Jesus' divine powers.

8:11–13. The Markan Jesus is immediately questioned by the Pharisees, who demand a sign from heaven. Feeding four thousand may well appear to us to be a sign. But, for the Pharisees, eating with Gentiles is breaking God's law and needs some divine sign to authorize it. The Markan Jesus refuses to give any sign.

8:14–21. The third and final boat episode underlines for Mark's audience the disciples' failure to grasp who Jesus is and what he can do. This time Mark shows Jesus engaged in dialogue with the disciples. He recalls the number of loaves and baskets left over from each feeding: twelve from the first, symbolic of the twelve tribes of Israel, and seven from the second, symbolic of Gentiles. Echoing language used previously for outsiders who neither see nor hear (4:12), the Markan Jesus berates the disciples for not understanding, asking if their hearts are hardened. This passage challenges Mark's audience to understand–to recognize that Jesus' mission is to Jews and Gentiles and that the power of God is active through Jesus to nourish them all abundantly.

Feminist analysis. The Syrophoenician woman is one of the most positive role models in the entire Gospel. She is shown seeking Jesus out, getting him to change his mind, and teaching him that Gentiles, too, should be fed. In all of the canonical stories about Jesus, this is the only time a character changes Jesus' mind. The ancient Mediterranean ideal stereotype is the silent and obedient woman. This woman is neither. The story is probably a remnant of Christian women's storytelling tradition, a remnant that found its way into the much more restricted written tradition. Many other stories in which women played central roles have been irretrievably lost, omitted from the texts of literate men.

Mark's audience would most likely have presumed women to be present elsewhere in this section. The reference to touching Jesus' garment in 6:56 echoes the woman with the hemorrhage touching Jesus' garment (5:25–34). In the debate over foods, the inclusive term for man, *anthrōpos,* is consistently used, and the second feeding story uses neither *anthrōpos* nor *anēr.*

II. THE WAY OF DISCIPLESHIP (8:22–10:52)

Introduction

In this portion, the narrator recounts the journey of Jesus and his followers from Galilee to Jerusalem, shifting the content focus to themes of persecution and service. Being part of God's realm in this age means not only blessings but also sufferings. The disciples finally recognize Jesus as the Christ. Mark then carefully structures the section around three predictions of Jesus' death and resurrection (passion predictions). Each prediction is followed by misunderstanding on the part of the disciples and then by teaching on discipleship. Dramatic interest in this section focuses on the disciples' failures and successes in understanding and following Jesus.

Recognition of the Christ and First Passion-teaching Cycle

Narrative analysis. 8:22–26. The journey is bracketed by two healings of blind men. While there are multiple exorcisms, this is the Gospel's only instance of two healings of the same infirmity. The first healing is difficult: only on Jesus' second try does the man see clearly. The healing suggests metaphorically that the teaching to follow will be difficult.

8:27–30. Heretofore, the disciples have grasped Jesus' and their own healing powers, but they have not understood Jesus' divine powers over nature nor who Jesus is. Now finally Peter recognizes Jesus as the Christ. Then the Markan Jesus "rebuked them to tell no one." The disciples, internal characters of the narrative, have finally realized what Mark's audience has known from the beginning.

8:31–33. Immediately after the disciples recognize Jesus as the Christ, Jesus tells them his fate. Using the title "Human One" (see 2:10, 28), not "Christ," he forecasts that he will undergo many things, be rejected by the official authorities, be executed, and rise. Peter, speaking again for the disciples, "rebukes" Jesus in turn. Mark's audience probably already knew about the crucifixion. But death was certainly not part of the Jewish expectation for the Messiah, who was to deliver Israel from its political enemies, not be executed by them. His death also contradicts human expectations: Why should someone with such divine power be killed by mortals? The disciples do not understand. Mark's audience may well share their incomprehension. The Markan Jesus does not explain. Rather he calls Peter "Satan," rebuking the disciples—and perhaps the audience—for following the way of humans, not God.

8:34–9:1. Mark's love of contrast and juxtaposition is evident here. Rather than explaining why the Christ must be killed, Mark presents Jesus immediately teaching the disciples that execution may be their fate also. Jesus calls the crowd along with the disciples: "If any want to come after me, let them deny themselves, take up their cross and follow me." "Come after" and "follow" make this passage a general invitation to discipleship for everyone—not just Jesus' audience in the narrative but Mark's audiences then and now as well. The invitation, however, stresses not the blessings of God's realm, but the cost—"pick up your electric chair." Jesus' fate is to be his followers' fate as well. Hearing the narrative, the audience would experience this harsh message not as invalidating the blessings of God's realm, but as added to them: *both* blessings *and* persecutions.

The Markan Jesus continues with a paradox: what looks like saving your life is in fact losing it, but losing it for Jesus and the good news is really saving it. Since those who follow the way of the world persecute those who follow the way of God in the world, the way of the realm of God involves suffering at the hands of the world. Next, Jesus proclaims a threat and a promise (8:38–9:1). Using the apocalyptic two-age framework, the Markan Jesus says that whoever rejects him now will be rejected by the Human One at the end of the age; and some of those present will not have died before the new age has fully come.

Feminist analysis. The major specified characters, divine and human, are male: Jesus, Peter, God called father, and Satan. The androcentrism again obscures the presence of women in groups. The term used here for those following Jesus is "disciples." In the whole narrative, Mark uses the term sometimes to refer to the Twelve, but more often for the larger group of men and women following Jesus. Furthermore, Mark explicitly calls the crowd along with the disciples for the teaching of 8:34–9:1. Not only will Jesus' audience in the narrative include women; so will Mark's audience gathered to hear the story. Women would hear the message directly addressed to them.

More problematic for women and subordinate groups such as slaves and racial minorities is the emphasis on suffering and self denial. Is suffering to be understood as pleasing to God? As punishment? As discipline? Mark does not so understand it. The phrase translated "suffer many things" (RSV) or "undergo great suffering" (NRSV) is better translated simply "undergo many things." The emphasis is not on suffering per se but specifically on rejection and persecution for living the life of the age to come, already in this age. An analogy today would be the assassination of Martin Luther King, Jr., for his work for racial justice, not general human suffering. In antiquity, suffering was seen as an inevitable part of life for those living at a marginal subsistence level; Jesus worked to alleviate *this* suffering through his healings and feedings. So suffering in general is *not* being exalted. What is promised, however, is persecution as a follower of Jesus (see 10:35–40).

Disciples are also specifically called to deny themselves (8:34). "To deny self" has often been understood as subordinating oneself to those with power over one, as is explicitly advocated for women, children, and slaves in the injunctions about behavior in the household—the Household Codes—found in Col 3:18–4:1; 1 Pet 2:13–3:8; and Eph 5:21–6:9. Self-denial has been interpreted to mean women's obedience to father or husband, and has functioned to bolster physical, sexual, and emotional violence against women and children. Mark's emphasis, however, is on those with power over others; it is *they* who should relinquish their rights and privileges. As will be seen below, Mark is concerned with abolishing "power over." "To deny oneself means to renounce the prerogatives that are boundaries around oneself."[9] It does not mean submission to those over one.

First Interlude (9:2–29)

Narrative analysis. 9:2–8. The story of the transfiguration affirms Jesus' divine status. The Markan Jesus takes Peter, James, and John up a high mountain, echoing Moses on Sinai. Elijah and Moses, the great prophet and the great lawgiver, appear with Jesus. Peter speaks, but the narrator tells the audience that in his terror Peter did not know what to say. Then once again a voice from heaven calls Jesus "My beloved Son," echoing the baptism (1:9–11). The episode serves two purposes. First, it affirms for the witnesses and the story audience that Jesus is God's agent: the difficult teaching of 8:31–9:1 is true. Second, it again stresses the disciples' fear in the face of divine power—especially the fear within the male inner circle. Mark's audience is challenged: Are they afraid too?

9:9–13. The disciples are again charged to secrecy as they were after Peter's recognition of Jesus as the Christ (8:30). Mark apparently does not want them to proclaim Christ's glory without also proclaiming the way of persecution and lowly service. The audience is told that Peter, James, and John do not understand what rising from the dead means, once more underscoring the disciples' difficulties comprehending the power of God. Finally, the audience is given new information: the Markan Jesus asserts that John the Baptist was in fact Elijah, the one who was to restore all things, but he was executed instead. Therefore the Human One is also in danger of execution.

9:14–29. The audience is reminded of Jesus' healing power in the dramatic exorcism and resurrection of the boy with the unclean spirit. It is told of the disciples' failure to heal the boy themselves. The episode further develops the theme of faith. The connection of faith and healing has been shown repeatedly in the narrative; here Mark teaches that faith can include doubt. Even the intention of having faith is sufficient to make the miracle possible. Jesus' explanation for the disciples' failure, "this kind is not able to come out except by prayer," also suggests that they are not sufficiently related through prayer to God's power.

Feminist analysis. Androcentrism is evident: the cast of specific characters is male: Jesus, Peter, James, John, Moses, Elijah, the father, his son, and the scribes. Yet women would be present in the narrative world in the larger group of disciples and in the crowd. And the teaching is addressed to all in Mark's audience.

Second Passion-teaching Cycle (9:30–37)

9:30–32. In this prediction, "the Human One will be delivered up into the hands of humans," it is not the Jewish authorities who condemn Jesus but simply the hostile world. The power of the world reflects the same evil, whether it is wielded by Jews, by Romans, or now by Christians. The saying uses the term "delivered up," which was used for John the Baptist's arrest (1:14) and will be used for the disciples' coming persecutions (13:9); it connects the fate of John, Jesus, and the disciples. In this cycle, the narrator states that the disciples did not understand and were afraid to ask. They still do not see why the Christ, the Human One, must be executed.

9:33–37. While the first teaching on discipleship was a universal call to follow, the teachings after the second and third predictions are addressed to the

Twelve, symbolically to the community already following Jesus. In this episode, the Markan Jesus knows that the Twelve have been arguing about which of them is the greatest. Jesus instructs them—and by extension Mark's audience—on conduct within the community of followers. "If any wish to be first, they will be last of all and servant of all." Mark presents another paradox: the way to true power in God's realm is the opposite of what the world recognizes as power. God's realm is a place of service, *diakonia*. This is ordinary service—waiting on table, taking care of children. Although in wealthy households male or female slaves did these tasks, in the peasant world of Jesus and of Mark, wives and daughters did these tasks. The twelve men are called to do women's work.

The Markan Jesus immediately gives an example: he places a child in the midst of the Twelve and instructs them that to receive a child in his name is to receive Jesus and the God who sent Jesus. In ancient society the child was not a symbol of innocence or purity of heart. At the bottom of the hierarchical structure, the child was most easily and perhaps most often exploited. By making the child the symbol of the one to whom service is rendered, the narrative makes explicit that service is to be given to those with *less* power in society, not those with more. Furthermore, by being the servant of all, one receives God. Service is not presented as a way to be rewarded later by God. It is a description of how God's realm works: service is where we meet God now.

Feminist analysis. The focus of these episodes is on Jesus and the Twelve. Where there are children, however, there will be women with them; besides, the gender of the child is not specified—we may imagine her to be a girl. Further, in the use of the term *diakonia,* the men are told to emulate the behavior and values of women. The child, the weakest in society and normally the exclusive responsibility of women, is the symbol of the one to whom service is to be offered. The community of Jesus' followers should be structured very differently from the usual ordering of society.

Second Interlude: Egalitarian Community in Service to the Least (9:38–10:31)

Narrative analysis. 9:38–41. Immediately the storyteller shows that the Twelve again fail to understand. The Markan Jesus chastises the disciples for forbidding a stranger to exorcise in Jesus' name. The disciples, the insiders, are not to set boundaries as to who is inside and who is outside the community of God's realm, but to accept all who want to be included. Indeed, even those farthest from the center are full participants: "whoever gives you a cup of water . . . will by no means lose their reward." Service does bring rewards; but it is the least not the greatest who is praised—not the missionary but the one offering minimal hospitality.

9:42–50. This section again addresses the use of power. The disciples are warned against causing a "little one" to stumble. Little ones can refer to children or to any marginalized people. The warning is severe: it is better to drown than to harm one of them. Similarly, if your hand or eye causes you to stumble, cut it off. This is not literal advice but exaggeration to emphasize the point. And, since only the whole or perfect specimen (animal or human) was considered clean, Jesus is saying, in effect, it is better to make yourself unclean than to cause anyone to sin.

10:1–12. As he travels, the Markan Jesus again teaches large crowds and debates with Pharisees. The issue now is divorce. According to Jewish law, a man could divorce his wife if she displeased him (Deut 24:1); a woman had no such right. Jews and pagans alike understood women (and children) basically as property. Jesus' response to the Pharisees' question invalidates the one-sided privilege of the male to end the marriage at whim, increasing the woman's protection in a culture in which a woman without a man (husband or father) was exceedingly vulnerable and marginal. Not an unconditional prohibition of divorce for all times, the statement rather makes marriage a more equal institution in its first-century context.

Jesus further upholds equality of men and women in the discussion on adultery. In first- century culture, adultery was understood as a crime against another man's honor and property. A man could be as sexually promiscuous as he liked, as long as he did not violate another man's property rights. The woman was required to remain faithful or chaste in order not to bring shame on her husband or father. Once again, the Markan Jesus treats the behavior of men and women equally: for both men and women divorce and remarriage are adultery. Christianity has tended to stress the prohibition of divorce, but in its own social context what was most radical about the teaching on divorce was the equal treatment of women and men.

10:13–16. Mark portrays the disciples as continuing to miss the message about being last and servant. Here they try to stop people from bringing children for Jesus to touch (see 9:36–37). Jesus blesses the children and affirms their priority in the realm of God. Mark's audience sees the disciples continually failing to understand and follow Jesus.

10:17–31. This portion contains three interrelated stories: the rich man, wealth as a hindrance, reward for following Jesus. *10:17–22.* A man questions

Jesus concerning eternal life. "Eternal life," literally "life of the age," refers to the same reality as "realm of God." The Markan Jesus instructs the man to keep those of the ten commandments which concern treatment of the neighbor, adding "do not defraud," a specific reference to economic exploitation.[10] The man *has* kept these. Jesus then asks more of him—to sell what he has and become a disciple. The rich man departs, unable or unwilling to renounce his prerogatives of power and wealth in the world (see 8:34).

10:23–27. The Markan Jesus then tells the disciples that it is difficult for people with wealth to enter God's realm. In the twentieth century, we understand the wealthy as those with large discretionary incomes. In the first-century peasant culture of Jesus and Mark, it would include *anyone* living above bare subsistence level. Furthermore, wealth was considered a blessing since it would give one the resources and leisure to keep purity regulations. The disciples are amazed. When Jesus reiterates his point with the humorous exaggeration of getting a camel through the eye of a needle, the disciples question the possibility of salvation for anyone. And Jesus responds with the affirmation of God's power: "All things are possible with God." Mark has shown God's power in this age through Jesus' acts, healings, feedings, and control over nature; here Mark presents Jesus' teaching affirming God's power.

10:28–31. By this stage in the narrative, the audience has begun to wonder if the disciples understand anything. They have not grasped the evidence of God's power shown in the boat and feeding stories, and they misunderstood Jesus' teaching about persecution and service. They have attempted to establish their own control over God's realm by stopping the strange exorcist and those bringing children to Jesus. Now when Peter points out that they *have* met the demands the rich man failed to meet, the audience is prepared for another rebuke of the disciples.

This time, however, the Markan Jesus reassures the disciples—and his audience. There is abundant reward for following Jesus now and in the age to come. Those who desert their blood kinship groups join a new abundant community around Jesus already in this age. The teaching echoes 3:31–35, understanding God's community as a replacement egalitarian kinship group. Once again, the human father, the symbol of authority and hierarchy, is missing. Furthermore, spouses are not enumerated at all; rather, the marriage partnership may be maintained (see 10:1–12). But in the midst of the blessings of God's realm in this age, Mark slips in the phrase "with persecutions." As Jesus will be rejected and killed for following God's way in this age, so will the disciples, the members of God's realm on earth, be persecuted in this age. Yet Mark's audience is reassured that the disciples and they themselves are still on the right path—even if they sometimes have difficulty following and understanding Jesus or difficulty having faith in the power of God.

Feminist analysis. Again the narrative is androcentric. Women are not present except as invisible parts of the discipleship group and the crowd and—since women were the caretakers of children under twelve—escorts of the children. As noted in the narrative analysis, this section instructs the disciples and Mark's female and male audience on the egalitarian social structure of the realm of God. Women are equal in marriage; adultery applies to both sexes; there is no double standard. The authority of the father, the head of household, is excluded. Children, the weakest and most vulnerable, are protected. Hierarchy based on wealth (which is worldly power) is rejected. (Thus wealthy women are also challenged to give up their privilege.) Mark presents a vision of a non-hierarchical egalitarian community with women as full participants.

Third Passion-teaching Cycle and Final Healing (10:32–52)

Narrative analysis. Introduction. Like the second cycle, this one concerns the way of discipleship; the disciples' misunderstanding again arises from their desire for greatness or power; and the teaching concerns service rather than power over others. The third repetition of the cycle relates the teaching on persecution to that on power and service. It is the climax of the way section and is followed by the story of the healing of blind Bartimaeus, who immediately follows Jesus on the way.

10:32–34. This passion prediction is the most detailed, emphasizing *what* is to occur. It is not followed by any immediate indication of the disciples' lack of comprehension. The audience, encouraged by the affirmation of the disciples in the preceding episode, may hope the disciples finally understand. If so, their hopes are to be disappointed.

10:35–40. James and John privately ask Jesus for the seats of honor and power on his right and left in the age to come. The disciples are still seeking power but now in the future. The Markan Jesus does not immediately rebuke them; rather, he asks them if they can stand firm in the face of persecution. Cup and baptism may refer to martyrdom or more generally to persecution. The apocalyptic worldview underlies Jesus' question. The shift of the ages, when the powers of God defeat those of Satan, is expected to be a time of great tribulation for those who follow the way of God, but this suffering will bring reward in the new age. According to this view, if James and John can face martyrdom now, they will merit reward in the age to come. James and John affirm that they are able to suffer. The Markan Jesus responds that they will, if they are able, but tells them the seats are not his to give.

In this passage, the narrator affirms that suffering for God's realm earns no rewards and is no entitlement to make demands. Suffering is not glorified or exalted as the way of God; it simply happens to those who follow God's ways in this age. In contrast, even the least service, giving someone a cup of water, *will* bring reward (9:41). Mark uses this episode to challenge Jewish and Christian understandings of suffering as pleasing to God.[11]

10:41–45. The story continues. The others are indignant with James and John, and the Markan Jesus teaches the Twelve by contrasting the way of power in the world with the way of service. Insofar as possible, those with worldly power dominate those under them using political, religious, and/or economic power to serve their own ends and accumulate yet more power exploiting others. Mark's peasant audience, people without worldly power, know this all too well. The opposite of being powerful is being oppressed, and Mark has taught his audience that persecution is to be expected for following Jesus. Thus one might expect Mark to contrast domination over others with weakness or suffering as the way of God. But Mark contrasts power not with suffering but with service (*diakonia;* see 9:35). The sign of the true disciple is not to suffer much but to serve much.

Next Mark extends the image from the servant to the slave. Slavery was a universal practice in the ancient world. Slave status was despised and shameful, lower than that of the poor peasants of Jesus' and Mark's audiences. Here Jesus says "to be slave of all," not just one master or mistress. The image is literally as impossible as that of a camel going through a needle's eye (10:25). The exaggeration seizes on the contrast between the way of discipleship and the way of power, to make the point in the strongest possible language. To follow Jesus is to be called to serve others rather than to exercise power over them.

The contrast helps clarify the dynamics of service: who is to serve whom. The instruction is addressed to the Twelve, not to women, children, and slaves, those whose social role is already to serve. (Of course, when women or slaves have power over others, they too are called to serve those with less power.) It is precisely those in positions to wield power over others who are exhorted to act as servants and slaves. The narrator is not presenting universal teaching applicable to all regardless of social status and access to power.

The narrator is addressing those with some power and instructing *them* to serve. In the second cycle, Jesus used the example of receiving a little child. Here, the Markan Jesus uses himself as an example. Jesus' service is not only the specific acts of mercy, preaching, healing, and feeding, but his entire life, including his death, "given as a ransom for many." Ransom is a technical term for securing the release of a hostage or a slave. Thus, Mark does not understand Jesus' death as a sacrifice atoning for sin. Rather, he understands it as an extension and completion of his life of service for others. In antiquity, martyr-dom—execution for one's beliefs and actions—was understood as an exemplary act; it empowered others to remain faithful in their own times of testing. Mark understands Jesus' death as martyrdom, not sacrifice. This is confirmed by his portrayal of Jesus' death as a political execution by Roman soldiers, and by the fact the disciples are encouraged to follow Jesus not only in preaching and healing but also in faithful behavior in the face of persecution.

10:46–52. The section concerning the way ends with the healing of blind Bartimaeus. Unlike the story of the restoration of sight at the beginning (8:22–26), this account has Bartimaeus immediately receiving his sight and following Jesus "on the way." The narrator has accomplished the difficult teaching on discipleship: following the way of God includes not only the blessings of God's realm but also persecution and the radical call to serve others with less power and status than oneself. The storyteller now shifts the focus to Jesus and the public authorities.

Excursus on Jesus as the Model for Service

The Gospel of Mark calls the disciple to service, for which Jesus' whole life, not just his execution, is the model. Jesus preaches and brings about the inbreaking of God's realm and empowers the disciples to do likewise. Jesus uses his divine power without forcing himself or his service on anyone; he heals those who come and ask. He invites people to follow, but he makes the cost clear; when he is not wanted he leaves, and he instructs others to do so also. The only instance in which Mark presents Jesus forcing himself on people is the cleansing of the Temple (11:15–17). There he is addressing the most powerful political, religious, and economic institution in Judea.

Jesus' healings show the particular characteristics of service. From the receiver's viewpoint, service is experienced as liberating, bringing wholeness and health. It does not need to be earned, deserved beforehand, or repaid afterwards. There are no strings attached. From the giver's viewpoint, service is offered from strength, not weakness. Giving service does not entail denying or holding back in the use of one's talents. Finally, Jesus' model of service suggests both giving freely to others and also receiving (see 14:3–9), indeed asking, for service—as the sick ask Jesus for healing. Jesus' model of service is not dutiful obedience but free giving from abundance.

Feminist analysis. For most of this portion of the narrative, only the Twelve are present. The larger group of disciples and the crowd appear at the beginning on the road up to Jerusalem and at the end in the crowd around Bartimaeus. Women are once again invisible. The message, however, is liberating. Jesus' teaching about service is contextual, not universally applicable. Christian women often have absorbed an understanding of service quite different from Mark's—as "unselfishness," having no personality of one's own but always fitting in with others. But if Jesus is the model, being a person in one's own right is clearly part of service. (In the narrative world, people wish to follow Jesus or to execute him; they never perceive him as a nonentity.) Further, Jesus' contrast of service with power clearly suggests where service should be directed. It is those *with* power who are called to serve those with less; not those in subordinate positions instructed to continue waiting on those with more status.

While women are hardly visible in the section on the way, the teaching on discipleship is very empowering for any marginalized group. Suffering is *not* viewed as pleasing to God; rather, persecution is the consequence of following God's ways in this age. A new, far more egalitarian society is proposed in which women are equal to men, children are valued, and wealth is a hindrance. And while the audience within the narrative is mainly the inner circle of men, the women and men in Mark's audience would hear this socially radical teaching as addressed to them.

III. JESUS IN JERUSALEM (11:1–13:37)

Introduction

In the previous section, the storyteller focused on the way to the cross, teaching on discipleship and the new egalitarian community. Now the teller focuses on Jesus' relation with other Jewish groups and teachings: Jesus' challenge to the Temple authorities; his debate over central Jewish teachings; and finally, his instruction to the disciples on the future after his execution.

The Entry into Jerusalem, Temple Episode,
and Associated Teaching (11:1–12:12)

Narrative analysis. 11:1–14. Mark's audience and the Twelve know that Jesus' trip to Jerusalem will result in his death. Yet the entry into the city is portrayed as triumphal—Jesus riding on a colt, welcomed by an enormous crowd. The beginning is auspicious. It is, however, followed immediately by the episode in which the disciples witness the Markan Jesus cursing a fig tree for having no figs, even though it is not fig season. This episode is completed and clarified after the cleansing of the Temple.

11:15–19. The Temple cleansing is usually understood as an attack on corruption, but Mark's audience would not have understood it that way. Selling animals for sacrifice and exchange of currency for payment of the Temple tax were necessary services for maintaining Temple worship. In casting out the buyers and sellers and applying earlier prophecy to the Temple, the Markan Jesus is proleptically (ahead of time) acting out the coming destruction of the Temple, the basic religious-economic-political institution of the Jewish state. The two scriptural citations confirm this. The first quotation (from Isaiah) stresses that the Temple is to be a house of prayer for all peoples, but in practice Gentiles were excluded from the Temple precincts as unclean. With the second quotation (from Jeremiah), Jesus accuses the priests of making the Temple "a den of robbers," that is, the lair in which bandits hide out *after* their thievery, not where they actually rob. The implication from Jeremiah is clear: because the officials of the Jews have made the Temple a hideout to escape the consequences of their evil deeds, God will come and destroy the Temple. (Of course, for Mark's audience, this has already happened; the Romans have just conquered Jerusalem and razed the Temple.) Mark has portrayed an intra-Jewish struggle between an unofficial popular leader and the official authorities. In the narrative the Jewish leaders are presented as understanding Jesus' message, for they immediately want to destroy him.

11:20–25. To reinforce the message of the destruction of the Temple, Mark returns to the image of the fig tree, a symbol of Israel, now totally withered. When Peter points it out, Jesus responds with teaching on prayer and forgiveness. Since ancient audiences understood temples as God's dwelling place and the guarantor of prayer, the teaching that God still has the power to answer prayer is needed reassurance. The Markan Jesus calls the disciples to faith and proclaims God's ability to do the impossible in response to prayer. The power of prayer to work miracles is unconditionally affirmed. Yet Jesus' own prayer in Gethsemane will not be answered (14:32–42). Once again the Markan narrative affirms *both* miracles *and* persecution for Jesus' followers. The follower is to continue praying for miracles in faith and hope. Mark also echoes the Lord's prayer here in the teaching to forgive others in order to be forgiven by God.

11:27–33. The Markan Jesus is again in the Temple, and chief priests, scribes, and elders (members of the Sanhedrin, the highest Jewish governmental unit) question Jesus on the source of his authority, in response to his behavior in the Temple. Is he a true prophet or another ordinary troublemaker? The Markan Jesus counters with a question on John the Baptist's authority. When they will not answer Jesus, neither will he answer them.

12:1–12. Jesus' parable in effect answers the leaders' question and accuses them of mistreating God's prophets. God is the owner of the vineyard and Israel the tenants. The Jewish authorities keep mistreating the prophets God sends to the vineyard. Finally God sends the Son—the narrative echoes the baptism and transfiguration episodes (1:11; 9:7)—and the tenants kill him. God will come and cast out the Jewish leaders, giving the vineyard to others, perhaps the Jewish peasants. The narrator makes it clear that the officials understand how the parable condemned them. They seek to arrest the Jew Jesus because in his triumphal entry, Temple action, and teaching he challenges their authority. The Markan narrative presents the leaders with the threat of a popular Jewish uprising.

Feminist analysis. Women are completely invisible in this portion of the narrative. Yet Mark's audience would assume the presence of women as Jesus entered Jerusalem, railed against the Temple, and taught. Women were permitted in the outer Temple precincts. They also would be among the witnesses to the cursing of the fig tree and the teaching on prayer. Women in Mark's audience would certainly hear the encouragement to keep on praying addressed to them. The absence of explicit references to women does not mean their exclusion.

The instruction to forgive in 11:20–25 raises an issue for oppressed peoples. The command to forgive has been used to advise battered women to return to violent situations; forgiveness has been commended to adults and children who have been sexually or physically abused, whether or not the perpetrator admits wrongdoing or changes behavior. This passage does not justify such counsels. Jesus' teaching on forgiveness is not a universally applicable command but, like the rest of his teaching, is contextually based. In the hierarchical view of the first century, God is at the top of the hierarchy forgiving those with less power. Human beings by analogy are called to forgive those over whom they have power. The abused are not being called to forgive unconditionally those with power over them. The language of debt found in the Lord's Prayer (Matt 6:12; Luke 11:4) supports this interpretation: you cannot cancel a debt you owe to someone else, but you can forgive a debt someone owes you. Markan teachings take into account the power relationships among the people involved and operate in favor of those with less power.

Jesus' Interaction with Other Jewish Groups (12:13–44)

Narrative analysis. 12:13–17. The Markan Jesus responds in quick succession to questions from Pharisees, Sadducees, and a scribe. First the Pharisees try to trap Jesus on the issue of paying taxes to the occupying Roman government: if Jesus advocates payment he will lose popular favor; if he advocates nonpayment he will be in trouble with Roman authorities. Jesus adroitly avoids the dilemma, saying to pay to each what belongs to each. The basic Jewish understanding, shared by Jesus and the Pharisees, is that everything truly belongs to God.

12:18–27. The Sadducees, the high priestly aristocracy who did not believe in resurrection, test Jesus with a story of seven brothers successively married to the same woman. Whose wife would she be in the age to come? The issue is not sexuality but property arrangements; whose property will she be in heaven? Jesus' answer that humans are like angels in heaven excludes the property relationships.[12] In conjunction with the earlier passage on divorce (10:1-12), Jesus is shown affirming the equal status of women with men on earth and in heaven. The story concludes with Jesus' belief in resurrection.

12:28–34. A friendly scribe asks Jesus to name God's fundamental commandment. Jesus responds with two laws from the Hebrew Scriptures: to love God wholly and to love one's neighbor as oneself. The scribe and Jesus affirm each other's answers, and the narrator informs the audience that no one dared question Jesus further. In his responses, the Markan Jesus has shown himself to be a good Jew: he affirms loyalty to God; he joins with the Pharisees in affirming resurrection; and he adheres to the basic Jewish ethical command to love God and neighbor. While criticizing the Jewish establishment, he has affirmed basic Jewish beliefs.

12:35–44. The Markan Jesus returns to the attack on the establishment. He questions the Davidic descent of the Messiah, since royal lineage would place the Messiah at the top of the Jewish hierarchy (12:35–37). He berates the scribes for their simultaneous show of piety and exploitation of the economically vulnerable, the widows. He praises the destitute widow for contributing a minute sum of money, and thereby giving her whole life. The narrative does not advocate giving to the point of impoverishment, for the woman is already destitute. It contrasts the widow's willingness to give her whole life with the scribes' use of their privileges to exploit others. Mark presents the widow, triply oppressed—female, without legal protection of a male, and economically destitute—as a model for discipleship.

Feminist analysis. Again women would be in the crowd witnessing Jesus' debates. Further, the Markan Jesus uses women as examples in his teaching. He condemns the scribes' treatment of widows while praising the behavior of the destitute widow. A woman is a model for the disciples.

The Little Apocalypse (13:1–37)

Narrative analysis. Throughout the Gospel, Mark has presented God's realm as beginning with Jesus' public ministry. The narrator has described the present as a time of both blessings and persecutions, and promised fulfillment in the near future (9:1). The storyteller now instructs his audience about events after Jesus' death, using the device of Jesus instructing the four brothers, the inner circle of the Twelve. The passage uses common apocalyptic imagery for the shift of the ages—wars, famines, catastrophes—summed up under the customary female image of "birthpangs" (13:8). Furthermore, Jesus adds to the traditional woes concern for the particular difficulties women would face: "Woe to those who are pregnant and to those who are nursing infants in those days" (13:17).

The image for the end is the Human One returning from heaven to gather the community of God's realm once the good news has been preached to all nations (13:24–27, 10). The audience is warned to beware of false prophets and Messiahs (13:5–6, 21–22), because no one but God knows exactly when the end will come (13:32–33). Persecution by both Jewish and Gentile authorities is prophesied for the disciples. Precisely in the situation of the persecution, however, they are promised the gift of the Holy Spirit (13:9–13). The community is called to endure and to watch (13:13, 37).

Feminist analysis. Within the narrative, the discourse is given by a male to four other males. The content does refer briefly to women's special trials; otherwise they are invisible in the androcentric text. Yet within the context of oral delivery to a live audience, women would hear the discourse as directly addressed to them. In any long oral discourse the audience tends to lose awareness of the narrative framework and experience it directly. This is particularly true of Mark 13, since it describes the time after Easter, the time of Mark's audience. The final exhortation "What I say to you I say to all, watch" (13:37) directly addresses Mark's audience. Thus, women as well as men hearing this discourse will hear themselves called to remain faithful until the end.

IV. THE PASSION NARRATIVE AND EMPTY TOMB (14:1–16:8)

Introduction

The storyteller narrates the final episodes of Jesus' life, his death, and the empty tomb. The disciples are in the foreground. They promise to be faithful, but instead they betray, deny, and desert Jesus. The women disciples remain faithful longer: they watch Jesus' execution and burial and go to the tomb to anoint his corpse. Then they fail, fleeing the tomb, saying nothing to anyone.

But throughout there is the promise of the future already described in Mark 13, and promised specifically in 14:28 and 16:7: Jesus will go before them to Galilee, the place of the realm of God, where they will see him.

The Plot against Jesus and the Anointing at Bethany (14:1–11)

Narrative analysis. Long aware that Jesus' execution is coming, Mark's audience now hears the Jewish authorities' intention to arrest Jesus and Judas's proposal to sell him. Between the two, the storyteller sandwiches the episode of the anointing at Bethany. There are various anointing stories in the Gospels (Mark 14:3–9; Matt 26:6–13; Luke 7:36–50; John 12:1–8). All are by women and occur at a meal, but other aspects vary. In Mark, an otherwise unknown woman anoints Jesus' head. In contrast to Luke's version, the woman here is not presented as a sinner. The woman enters while dinner is in progress and breaks a jar of valuable nard over Jesus' head. Breaking was normal, much as we would break an ampul to give an injection. Mark does not say she poured out all the ointment, and it would not be customary to do so, since nard was so expensive.

Anointing on the head is an act of great symbolic importance. To tend someone's feet, as in Luke and John, is the act of a social inferior—a slave or a woman. But a host might anoint a guest's head as a sign of rejoicing. To anoint the head is also to call a person to God's service, to consecrate him or her for a special task. Prophets and priests were anointed, but above all prophets anointed those chosen to be king. So the unknown woman at Bethany was a prophet, fulfilling the prophetic function of choosing and empowering Jesus for his messianic role.

In the story the guests grumble: the nard should have been sold and the money donated. But Jesus defends the woman: she has done a good deed or a fitting service; she has anointed Jesus' body for burial ahead of time. The narrator states that her deed will be remembered throughout the whole world wherever the good news is preached (14:9). Nowhere else in Mark is any person or action singled out for future remembrance.

Thus, Mark contrasts the prophetic act of the woman not only with the grumbling of the (male) dinner guests but also with the acts of the chief priests and Judas to bring about Jesus' death. As with the widow who gave her mite, the woman of Bethany is held up as a positive example in contrast to men exercising power at the expense of others. Within the narrative world, Mark uses women and their behavior to model for men the true nature of discipleship.

Feminist analysis. Little needs to be added to the narrative analysis. The dangers are that we forget—the church has not retold her story[13]—or that we trivialize her act, treating it as a pretty, sentimental gesture, not a prophetic act of power and empowerment. The woman acts as God's prophet, and the storyteller holds up her act of service as worthy of remembrance. As in the narrative of the Syrophoenician woman (7:24–30), Jesus is shown receiving from a woman in ways he is never shown receiving from men.

As with other episodes, historically we do not know if any of the anointing stories actually happened. We can say, however, that Mark's head-anointing version probably predates the foot-anointing versions, since by the time men were writing the Gospels they were already minimizing women's roles. Furthermore, the interpretation of her act as anointing for burial is most likely Mark's adaptation of the story to fit his narrative context, and, intentionally or not, it minimizes the woman's role by placing it in the context of women's traditional duties with corpses rather than stressing her prophetic act.

Lord's Supper, Gethsemane, and Arrest (14:12–52)

Narrative analysis. 14:12–21. The narrator presents the preparation for the Passover meal, the major Jewish feast celebrating Israelite liberation from slavery in Egypt. At the meal the Markan Jesus tells the Twelve that one of them will betray him. Those who reject Jesus' way and bring about his execution are found not only among the Jewish and Gentile authorities but also among his followers. Since Mark's audience already knows about Judas's betrayal (3:19; 14:10–11), the narrative emphasis is on the disciples' reaction. At this point they are sorrowful, each asking "Is it I?" The theme of the disciples' understandings, misunderstandings, and failures is again in the narrative foreground.

14:22–26. At the meal itself, the Markan Jesus thanks God for the bread and gives it to the disciples, saying "This is my body." Similarly he gives them the wine, saying, "This is my blood of the covenant poured out for many." The pairing of "body" and "blood" would suggest to first-century audiences martyrdom,[14] *not* sacrifice or atonement to God for human sin (see 10:41–45). Mark gives no instruction to repeat this meal, to "do this in memory of me." Rather, the Markan Jesus says he will not drink wine again until God's realm, the new age, has fully come. At this point the disciples within the narrative and Mark's audience learn that this is Jesus' last supper; his execution is at hand.

14:27–31. The narrative setting moves to Gethsemane on the Mount of Olives. Here the Markan Jesus prophesies that all twelve will desert him—and that after he is raised, he will go ahead of them to Galilee. Unlike the earlier prophecy of betrayal, which the disciples meet with sorrow, this prophecy of abandonment the disciples vehemently deny. Peter and the others say that even if they must die with Jesus, they will not deny him. The audience is reassured that the disciples have fully accepted that persecution at the hands of the world is part of discipleship. Like James and John earlier (10:35–40), all twelve accept the cup and the baptism. But given Jesus' prophecy of Peter's denial and the disciples' previous failures, Mark's audience must wonder if the disciples will succeed in remaining faithful.

14:32–42. As in 10:35–45, rejection of the notion that suffering for God is meritorious immediately follows the affirmation that persecution is part of discipleship. The Markan Jesus asks Peter, James, and John to watch and then prays to God that this hour, this cup, pass from him; that is, he prays not to be crucified. Frequently in the narrative, Jesus has taught the disciples that he will be persecuted and so will they. Here Jesus seeks to avoid suffering: he reminds God that all things are possible to God and prays that he not have to suffer. So should his followers! Persecution may be an unavoidable part of discipleship until God's realm has fully come, but it is not to be sought after and does not have redemptive value.

Earlier the Markan Jesus has taught the disciples that they should pray with faith even for the impossible and that God will grant it to them (11:22–25). Yet here God does not grant the prayer of Jesus, the very model of faith. Once again, the Markan narrative world is a world of *both/and* not *either/or*. The Gospel affirms both miracles and persecution without reconciling them. Indeed, it rejects common resolutions (God as unable or unwilling to prevent suffering; suffering as due to human sin or faithlessness). The disciples are to continue to pray for divine deliverance but also to remember that God may permit their suffering, as God permitted Jesus' execution.[15]

The storyteller continues to show the disciples' failures. They have just promised Jesus not to deny him even if they must die with him (14:31). But when Jesus asks Peter, James, and John to watch, they fall asleep, not once but three times. Jesus' rebuke is gentle, almost an excuse: "Pray that you not come to the test; the spirit indeed is willing, but the flesh is weak." The Markan Jesus recognizes that the intent to remain faithful may be there, but the ability to stand firm in the face of persecution may not be. By now, any expectation that the disciples will remain faithful is slim. Yet the audience may at the same time be reassured by Jesus' words as it faces its own testing for being Christian.

14:43–50. The narrator now relates Jesus' arrest and the eleven falling away. When his clothes are grabbed, a young man runs away naked. We do not know if the young man was someone in particular or symbolic of the shameful flight of the followers. The Twelve have failed. For the audience the question is: Are the Twelve subject to exclusion for having denied Jesus before humans (8:38), or will they again see the risen Jesus in Galilee, where he will go before them (14:28)?

Feminist analysis. Mark's restriction of the leadership circle to twelve men is evident in this portion of the Gospel. (As noted earlier, this restriction is probably not historically accurate [see 3:7–35].) The Last Supper with its associated prophecies is limited to the Twelve at table. The scene at Gethsemane is restricted to the three. Yet whether Mark's audience understood the women as totally absent is debatable. All of Mark's audience, male and female, would identify with the drama and difficulty of following Jesus. Some in Mark's audience may have pictured the women followers going ahead to prepare, serve, and partake of the Passover meal. A medieval painting of Gethsemane shows the three men sleeping and, farther away from Jesus, women awake watching.[16] The general invisibility of women in androcentric texts has led us to exclude women even more than the text does.

Jesus' Trials and Peter's Denial (14:53–15:15)

Narrative analysis. 14:53–65. In the first interrogation, the narrator presents the Jewish authorities seeking grounds to condemn Jesus. Even using false witnesses they fail. Then the chief priest asks Jesus if he is the Messiah. The Markan Jesus responds unequivocally, "I am." Throughout the Markan narrative only the disciples and Mark's audience have known that Jesus was the Christ. Now in the hands of hostile powers and deserted by his disciples, the Markan Jesus publicly affirms his status with God. The chief priests condemn him as blasphemous.

14:66–72. At the beginning of the preceding episode, the narrative pictured Peter following Jesus into the high priest's courtyard. Now after the Markan Jesus publicly reveals who he is, Peter fulfills Jesus' prophecy (14:30). Challenged by a servant girl, Peter three times denies knowing Jesus. Among the Twelve, one has betrayed, all have fled, and now Peter denies. This is the last time any of them appear in Mark's narrative. They have failed in following.

15:1–15. The Jewish authorities turn Jesus over to the Roman governor, Pilate. From the Roman perspective Jesus is a provincial troublemaker, and they disposed of him as they did other such people they perceived as rabble-rousers. Pilate asks if Jesus is "King of the Jews," the same question as "Are you the Messiah?" but from a Gentile perspective. The Markan Jesus answers nothing. Pilate turns to the crowd, which calls for the release of Barabbas rather than Jesus. Until this point in Mark the crowd has responded positively to Jesus: they have sought him out in enormous numbers in Galilee and welcomed him to Jerusalem. Now the narrator portrays them in their turn abandoning Jesus. So Pilate condemns Jesus to be crucified on the political charge of claiming to be king. The Romans, not the Jews, condemn and execute Jesus.

Feminist analysis. In order to protect against Christian anti-Semitism, it is important to recall that the Romans executed Jesus. Liberation is for all groups, not just women; and one of the groups most oppressed by Christians throughout history has been the Jews. Insofar as any Jews played a role in Jesus' death, it was the small group of Jewish rulers whose power depended on their favor with Rome. From the Jewish perspective, the issue was one of class: the elite Jewish puppets of Rome against a peasant nobody who had become a popular leader.

In the ancient world, the cast of characters in the trial scenes is male because the public realm was considered the sphere of men. The presence of women, however, becomes evident when a female household servant challenges Peter. Just as the woman with the hemorrhage challenged Jesus on women's purity issues and the Syrophoenician woman on inclusion of Gentiles, so here a maidservant challenges Peter to stand by his faith. All twelve men called to leadership, however, fail in following. The women in Mark's audience may have identified with the failure of the Twelve, or they may have been encouraged by Mark's portrayal of the men and the women to challenge the male leaders in their communities and maintain their own leadership.

The Crucifixion (15:16–39)

Narrative analysis. As was typical for crucifixions, those to be executed (or passersby impressed into service) carry the crossbeam to the place of execution, and crowds jeer at them, shouting insults and curses. The soldiers affix the criminals to the crossbeams and position them on the permanent uprights. A festive crowd watches the public execution. The inscription "King of the Jews" indicates the specific political charge against Jesus. It is a scene of public shame and also a painful form of execution.

The Markan Jesus' single saying from the cross is a quotation from Ps 22:1: "My God, my God, why have you abandoned me?" In the narrative, Jesus has been deserted by his (male) disciples and by the crowd. Now the narrator presents the Markan Jesus crying out God's abandonment. The first-century ideal of martyrdom was to face death without flinching. Here the Markan Jesus also fails. The abandonment of Jesus is complete. The storyteller reassures the audience, however, that God is still active and present. He narrates the divine signs of darkness and of destruction of the Temple curtain as Jesus died; and the centurion, the Roman soldier responsible for carrying out the execution, hails Jesus as a son of God. The audience knows that this is not the end.

Feminist analysis. The androcentric text continues to obscure the presence of women. A first-century audience would assume that women with their families or in small groups were watching the procession and the execution itself. They would not be surprised when the narrator announces in the next verse that some of the women disciples were in the crowd watching the execution.

The Women at the Cross, Burial, and Empty Tomb (15:40–16:8)

Narrative analysis. 15:40–47. Apparently everyone in the Markan world has deserted Jesus. But in 15:40, the storyteller tells the audience that one group is still following, the women disciples. They are named: Mary Magdalene, Mary the mother of James the younger and of Joses, and Salome who accompanied Jesus in Galilee. (Probably these are three women, but it is possible that the second Mary and the mother of Joses are two different women, making four named.) Two of these are named again, watching to see where Jesus is buried (15:47); and all three are named going out to the tomb (16:1).

In addition to those named, the audience is told that many other women also came up with Jesus from Galilee to Jerusalem. They are described as "following" Jesus and "serving" him, both words used to define discipleship in Mark (8:34; 9:35; 10:43). Women followers have been largely obscured in Mark's androcentric text, only visible in the inclusion of women among Jesus' new relatives (3:31–35) and among new kin to be gained for following Jesus (10:30). Now the storyteller says that Jesus had women disciples and they have been there all along! The women disciples, unlike the men, do not flee at Jesus' arrest but remain faithful in the face of possible persecution. They watch at the cross and watch to see where his corpse is buried. Mark presents the women remaining faithful after the men have deserted Jesus.

16:1–8. The abrupt ending at 16:8 seems to have been the original ending of Mark's narrative. The women have remained faithful, and they continue to serve Jesus by going out to anoint his corpse. Now they flee from the empty tomb, "saying nothing to anyone." Mark presents the women disciples as the first witnesses to the empty tomb. Then the man in white, probably an angel, instructs the women to go tell the disciples, including Peter, that Jesus is risen and going before them to Galilee: the women are called to be the first apostles proclaiming the news of Jesus' resurrection. Here they are very much at the center of Mark's Gospel and the Christian message.

But then the storyteller presents the women failing in their turn. They flee in astonishment and amazement. Their fear is an appropriate response to the power of God experienced in the empty grave and the encounter with the man in white. But saying nothing is not appropriate. Here Mark continues the pattern of irony seen throughout the Gospel. When Jesus has instructed people to keep silent, they have repeatedly gone and told (e.g., 1:45; 7:36–37). Now, the women are to tell and instead they keep silent. And thus Mark's story ends.

Three points need to be made about the ending. First, the circumstances of the women's failure pick up the earlier theme of the male disciples' inability to trust the power of God. The men are afraid when they experience Jesus' power over the sea in the boat episodes (4:35–41; 6:45–52); they expect no abundance the second time they must assist Jesus in feeding an enormous crowd with little food (6:30–44; 8:1–10). They are afraid again at the transfiguration (9:2–8). They do not grasp the power of God active in this age. And it is on this issue that Mark portrays the women also failing. They stand firm through all the persecution; but when faced with the good news of the resurrection, they flee. They too have difficulty trusting the power of God for good.

Second, Mark's abrupt ending serves as a call to his audience to be faithful followers of Jesus, to do better than the characters in the narrative. First the audience hears the example of the male disciples, who failed to grasp the power of God, to relinquish the search for their own power and status, and to stand firm at the threat of persecution. The audience has then heard the example of the female disciples, who have served and were able to stand firm in the face of suffering and persecution, but who in their turn fail to trust God's power.

Third, the ending suggests that failure need not be the end of discipleship. The fact that the angel instructs the women to tell the Twelve suggests that Mark does not view the men's desertion as excluding them from God's realm. The specific mention of Peter suggests that even his denial can be overcome. The threat of 8:38, suggesting that the Human One should deny Peter before God, need not be the last word. The message at the empty tomb to the Marys and Salome, the teaching to Peter, James, and John in Mark 13—and the very fact that Mark's story is being told—suggest that Mark views failure as part of continuing discipleship.

The audience is reassured that they may fail, turn again, and continue following Jesus. Mark's message may even be that human failure is the beginning of true discipleship. So the listeners are called to be faithful followers, expecting healing, expecting persecution. And above all they are called to trust the power of God.

Feminist analysis. In this section, we hear at last that what we have deduced must have been true. There are women disciples. Mark's need for the women as characters in his plot has overcome his androcentric bias. Since women play a central role at the Gospel's end, much of the feminist analysis has been included in the narrative analysis. A few points deserve further emphasis. First, there are women disciples and they are named—just as the male disciples are named. Throughout most of Mark, the few women characters are known in other ways—Simon's mother-in-law, the Syrophoenician woman, or Jairus's daughter. When Mark finally introduces the women disciples, they have names in their own right, by which they were probably known in Christian tradition. Second, the women are faithful followers, continuing to serve in the face of suffering. They model discipleship as service in Mark's narrative world. Third, they are first at the empty tomb, first to receive the message that Jesus is risen, first to be called to proclaim the Christian good news. But in the end, they too have trouble trusting the power of God.

Conclusion

Mark has included very powerful stories of women in his narrative—the woman with the flow of blood (5:25–34); the Syrophoenician woman (7:24–30); the woman who anoints Jesus (14:3–9); and the women disciples at the crucifixion and empty tomb (15:40–16:8). Mark clearly had available to him stories of women who played central roles in Jesus' story. The prominence of the women in the oral tradition was such that Mark does not ignore them. And at the same time what we have left in Mark is only a remnant of a once much richer women's tradition.

But Mark's Gospel remains an androcentric narrative. Mark uses these stories not so much to empower women to be followers of Jesus in their own right, as for didactic purposes. He uses the women to encourage his audience, perhaps especially the men in his audience, to follow in a discipleship of service.[17] Mark may even be using the women to shame the men into doing better.

Mark presents all the characters in the narrative world as failing: the authorities reject Jesus from the beginning; the Twelve seek status, betray, desert, and deny; the crowd abandons Jesus when he is arrested by the authorities. Finally, the women, the most faithful, fail at the empty tomb. I suggest that in a sense Mark also has failed. He has failed to overcome his androcentric perspective, his assumption of male privilege. He has failed to dramatize the egalitarian way of discipleship that he teaches. Rather, he uses the women, as he uses children, slaves, and foreigners, as models for discipleship, as examples for the men. He has included women in his narrative, but he has included them not as full equals, as women disciples visible from the beginning. Rather he has used the women as he needed them for the plot and to teach the men. We must go beyond Mark, to envision and create a true discipleship of equals in which women—and all marginalized groups—are full participants.

NOTES

1. See David Rhoads, "Social Criticism of the Gospel of Mark: Crossing Boundaries," in *Mark and Method: New Approaches in Biblical Studies,* ed. Janice Capel Anderson and Stephen D. Moore (Minneapolis: Fortress, 1992), 135–61.

2. Bernadette J. Brooten, *Women Leaders in the Ancient Synagogue: Inscriptional Evidence and Background Issues* (Brown Judaic Studies 36; Chico, CA: Scholars Press, 1982), 103–38.

3. Elisabeth Schüssler Fiorenza, *Discipleship of Equals: A Critical Feminist Ekklesia-logy of Liberation* (New York: Crossroad, 1993), 104–16; John Dominic Crossan, *The Historical Jesus: The Life of a Mediterranean Jewish Peasant* (San Francisco: HarperSan Francisco, 1992).

4. Elisabeth Schüssler Fiorenza, *In Memory of Her: A Feminist Theological Reconstruction of Christian Origins* (New York: Crossroad, 1983), 41–67.

5. Hisako Kinukawa, *Women and Jesus in Mark: A Japanese Feminist Perspective* (Maryknoll, NY: Orbis, 1994), 34. Marla J. Selvidge, *Women, Cult, and Miracle Recital* (Lewisburg: Bucknell University Press, 1990).

6. Rita Nakashima Brock, *Journeys by Heart: A Christology of Erotic Power* (New York: Crossroad, 1988), 85.

7. See Kathleen E. Corley, *Private Women, Public Meals: Social Conflict in the Synoptic Tradition* (Peabody, MA: Hendrickson, 1993), 24–79, 93–95.

8. Ibid., 93–95.

9. Kinukawa, *Women and Jesus*, 98.

10. Ched Myers, *Binding the Strong Man: A Political Reading of Mark's Story of Jesus* (Maryknoll, NY: Orbis, 1988), 272.

11. Anitra B. Kolenkow, "Beyond Miracles, Suffering and Eschatology," in *Society of Biblical Literature 1973 Seminar Papers,* ed. G. MacRae (Missoula, MT: Scholars Press, 1973), 2:152–202.

12. Schüssler Fiorenza, *In Memory of Her,* 143–44.

13. Ibid., xiii–xiv.

14. Burton L. Mack, *A Myth of Innocence: Mark and Christian Origins* (Philadelphia: Fortress, 1988), 118.

15. Sharyn Echols Dowd, *Prayer, Power, and the Problem of Suffering: Mark 11:22-25 in the Context of Markan Theology* (SBL Dissertation Series 105; Atlanta: Scholars Press, 1988).

16. Elisabeth Moltmann-Wendel, *The Women Around Jesus* (New York: Crossroad, 1982), 30, 37–38.

17. Kinukawa, *Women and Jesus,* 107–22.

RECOMMENDED READINGS

Anderson, Janice Capel, and Stephen D. Moore, eds. *Mark and Method: New Approaches in Biblical Studies.* Minneapolis: Fortress, 1992.

Brock, Rita Nakashima. *Journeys by Heart: A Christology of Erotic Power.* New York: Crossroad, 1988.

Kinukawa, Hisako. *Women & Jesus in Mark: A Japanese Feminist Perspective.* Maryknoll, NY: Orbis, 1994.

Myers, Ched. *Binding the Strong Man: A Political Reading of Mark's Story of Jesus.* Maryknoll, NY: Orbis, 1988.

Tolbert, Mary Ann. "Mark." In *The Women's Bible Commentary,* edited by Carol A. Newsom and Sharon H. Ringe, 263–74. Louisville: Westminster/John Knox, 1992.

The Sayings Source Q

LUISE SCHOTTROFF ◆

HERMENEUTICS AND METHOD
FROM THE PERSPECTIVE OF A FEMINIST
THEOLOGY OF LIBERATION

THE CHRISTIAN TESTAMENT as a whole, and the Sayings Source in particular, speak in androcentric language and presuppose a patriarchal system of relationships. For the concept of "patriarchy," as used in the following essay, let me refer to the definition developed primarily by Elisabeth Schüssler Fiorenza in *In Memory of Her: A Feminist Theological Reconstruction of Christian Origins* (New York: Crossroad, 1983). The combination of structures of oppression leading to economic, sexist, and racist exploitation, including the exploitation and destruction of nature, has assumed many forms in the course of history but has always retained its continuity. From this point of view, the concept of "patriarchy" defines this comprehensive structure of mutually interconnected relationships of domination. An analysis of patriarchy in the Christian Testament implies a critical examination of patriarchal structures at several levels: (1) Where in the Christian Testament texts do we find patriarchal power structures uncritically maintained? (2) Where in the Christian Testament are there initiatives toward a critique of patriarchy? (3) Where, even in androcentric texts, is it possible to bring to light the history of women that has been rendered invisible? (4) Where does the Christian Testament contain options from which a feminist theology of liberation can draw inspiration?

In this connection, there is a particular need for a critical analysis of the history of Christian interpretation of the Christian Testament, in which the histories of domination and of the oppression of women in Christianity have left their enduring mark. This history of interpretation still retains its ability to impose its own ideas within the power-oriented churches of the present. Consequently, the history of interpretation continues to be an important source for the invisible history of women.

Thus, the process of textual analysis needs to be based on a social- historical critique in the sense of an examination of the structures of patriarchy. We must ask of every text what details of social history can be discerned from it and what function it has in its concrete social context. I understand the Jesus movement that is the focus of the Sayings Source as having been, both in Jesus' lifetime and afterward, a Jewish liberation movement within the Pax Romana, comparable to other corresponding liberation movements of the time such as the one connected with John the Baptizer. The power structure of the Pax Romana led to an increasing impoverishment of the Jewish people in Roman Palestine in the first century C.E., and to an intensification of political oppression. Eschatological and messianic movements worked to bring about resistance and liberation and were frequently subjected to bloody suppression by the Romans. The Jewish upper classes' participation in the interests of the Pax Romana led also to internal conflicts within Judaism, whose textual expression became, in the later history of Christian interpretation, an instrument of anti-Judaism. As a result, a social-historical contextualization of the texts is also fundamental for the issue of anti-Judaism.

The existence of a "Sayings Source" is posited on the basis of a scholarly hypothesis. The textual parallels between the Gospels of Matthew and Luke are traced to a common source that may have been available to both evangelists in somewhat different form. I wish to emphasize that this remains a *hypothesis.* For that reason I will be cautious in assigning texts to Q (the standard symbol for the Sayings Source) if those texts do not agree word for word in Matthew and Luke, and for the same reason I will not adopt the customary American practice of citing traditions from the Sayings Source by using the letter Q followed by the Lukan chapter and verse number. I prefer instead to cite both places, in Matthew and Luke respectively, where each individual saying is to be found.

In turn we must say that, within a feminist theology of liberation, the tools of so-called historical criticism can only be employed critically. Thus, I will inquire about the genres of texts and about their contexts in the history of thought and religion as does historical criticism, but always from the critical angle I have indicated. I ask about the *Sitz im Leben* (setting in life), but within the broad social sense of a social history critical of patriarchy. I inquire about the contents of the message of Jesus and his disciples, female and male, but always in the context of the question about their liberating or oppressive function and the praxis associated with them.

I take a skeptical view of the methods of literary criticism and tradition criticism associated with the so-called historical-criticial method. For example, the isolation of different strata of tradition within Q (Q1 and Q2) does not strike me as persuasive; however, I will take it into account when it has consequences for the content of the individual sayings. My primary focus of interest is the discernment of content, and the results should be equally useful for those who presume a distinction between Q1 and Q2 and for those who doubt the very existence of Q. They all may read the following discussion as a description of some central elements of the Jesus movement or of the message of Jesus.

An indispensable condition for historical work within the context of feminist theology of liberation is the recognition of two contexts for the historical material. The historical context of biblical traditions must be examined from the point of view of a critique of patriarchy, but I must turn an equally critical eye on my present context, in which and out of which I am seeking an encounter with history. From the point of view of feminist theology of liberation, it is fundamental to every scholarly endeavor that we describe and analyze our present context. I read biblical traditions from the perspective of a white female professor of theology in a Western industrial society. The gospel of the poor means something different for me than it does for a black maid in South Africa, but it makes it possible for me to voice, to examine critically, and to give practical expression to my solidarity with her. In traditional Western theology it is considered "scientific" to adopt a (supposed) posture of neutrality toward the object of research and to take no account of one's own context. This "neutrality" conceals the patriarchal biases expressed by a theological discipline that imagines itself to be independent of its social context.

MATTHEW 10:34–36 || LUKE 12:51–53: THE ITINERANT WOMEN PROPHETS

RECONSTRUCTION OF THE SAYINGS SOURCE

There is an extensive agreement in the content of both versions of this saying. In both of them, Jesus speaks of his coming and its consequences as events corresponding to God's will. What he brings to the world is not the eschatological peace of God, but an eschatological separation (Luke), the "sword" in a metaphorical sense (Matthew). Jesus' appearance leads to division in families, in which his disciples, female and male, are therefore actively involved. The younger generation in the house—the son, the daughter, the daughter-in-law—separate from their parents (Matthew), or the three younger members separate from the parents and the parents from the youth (Luke).

SOCIAL-HISTORICAL QUESTIONS

Both versions of the saying presuppose a patriarchal household structure in which a daughter, a married son, and his wife live with the parents. The lines of division are drawn between the generations and affect both genders in the same way. This division is understood as a calamity of the end-time, willed by God and brought about by Jesus.

Since the motif of the destruction of the patriarchal family appears in a variety of literary contexts in antiquity, we may ask whether it is at all legitimate to evaluate the details of this saying in relation to reality. But closer observation of the use of the motif shows that its concrete relationship to reality is always part of the picture, so that the motif is reshaped accordingly in each context. In Mic 7:5–6, to which both versions of the saying refer, it is the father of the family who can no longer trust his wife and who is treated with contempt by his son. The collapse of the traditional role of the father in the house is accompanied by a revolt of the young women in the house against the mother. In the sense of this text, the destruction of the patriarchal family represents the depravity of the whole nation. The differing perspective in these two versions of the motif of the destruction of the patriarchal household is clear: according to Mic 7:5–6, the collapse of the central role of the father within the patriarchal household signals the overthrow of an order of society that is regarded as having been willed by God. According to Matt 10:34–36 || Luke 12:52–53, the division is brought about by Jesus and is a necessary consequence of God's will. Jesus' appearance brings a separation of the younger generation from the older (in Matthew, where the perspective is that of the son), or a mutual separation of the two generations (Luke). In Mic 7:5–6, the collapse of the patriarchal family expresses the disorder of the whole society, an anarchy raised against good order. In the Sayings Source what we find is a terrible—but by the will of God *necessary*—event whose consequences affect the whole of society, since the patriarchal family is seen as the foundation of society.

The division in the patriarchal household caused by Jesus' appearance appears also in other sayings in Q and in a series of early Christian texts as a genuine experience: as disciples of Jesus, sons (or daughters) reject the commandment regarding parental obligations by failing to bury their old parents, thereby abrogating one of the fundamentals of the patriarchal contract between the generations (Matt 8:22 || Luke 9:60). Here it is clear that the division includes an actual departure from the patriarchal household ("following" Jesus). In Matt 10:37 || Luke 14:26 an adult young man also separates from his children (Matthew and Luke agree on this point). In light of the androcentrism of the text we should consider (if not conclude) that this may also mean that mothers abandon their children. The picture is confirmed by Mark 10:29 and parallels, though only Luke emphasizes that husbands leave their wives (see below). Revelatory Wisdom preaching by Christian missionaries, female and male, causes children to separate from their fathers and teachers and to seek, in the workshop or in the women's quarters, among women and craftspeople, a different place for hearing and learning, independent of the patriarchal household and in protest against that order of things (Origen, *Contra Celsum* 3.55).

FEMINIST REFLECTIONS ON THE HISTORY OF INTERPRETATION

Before the advent of feminist biblical criticism, no one asked whether texts like these imply that women also left their families to follow Jesus. Although Mark 15:40–41 and, for example, Thecla's journey in the later apostolic acts might have suggested this question, the androcentrism of the text was accepted at face value and without discussion. Two traditional types of interpretation may be distinguished: I call them the "itinerant radicals" model and the "soldiers" model. In the "itinerant radicals" model, individual middle-class men leave their families to follow Jesus. They are, from the overall point of view of society, a minority or a sect, but they are able to survive because patriarchal households continue to function within the Christian community as well as outside. At all events, they are the salt in the patriarchal soup, which continues to provide the necessary basis for the existence of the Christian community ("love patriarchalism"). The "soldiers" model understands the call to discipleship, which disrupts the family, as a call into a patriarchal system superior to that of the family and, in certain cases, taking precedence over the family. As the soldier follows the call of the fatherland, so the Christian follows the call of the gospel. In this interpretation, the Christian community is seen as analogous to, but larger than, the patriarchal family.

Neither of these models of interpretation challenges the patriarchal structure of Christian communities or churches, or of society. Both interpret Matt 10:34–36 || Luke 12:52–53 as Jesus' call to morally heroic behavior, to asceticism, unreflectingly understood as something for men only. The model of itinerant radicals in particular continues to be adopted in Western exegesis almost without exception at the present time; only occasionally does anyone feel the need to defend it against critical challenges.

Feminist liberation theology's alternative to this dominant model of interpretation applies to the situation of the whole population the praxis (or ethos) of the wandering prophets, female and male, who followed Jesus: women and men live out their liberation from the destructive power of hunger and threats to their very existence, and from the false order of the patriarchal household. The destruction of the patriarchal family is terrible for them, but it is necessary (see below on Matt 24:37–39 and parallel). The new society in the name of Jesus is nonhierarchical, nonpatriarchal; it is a community of right relationships. The model of itinerant radicals in combination with communities based on love patriarchalism is criticized as a legitimation of a patriarchal church and society. This new interpretation can rest its claim on Matt 10:34–36 || Luke 12:51–53; it insists that it is an artificial procedure to reduce the demand of the texts of the Jesus tradition to a special role belonging to itinerant radicals. Instead, these texts wish to reach *all who hear,* and they constantly refer the life of the disciples, female and male, to *the situation of the people.*

The androcentrism of the text is used as an argument against this position: "It is difficult to establish whether women were also present among the itinerant charismatics. Mary Magdalene could have been one such."[1] When this happens, the association of itinerant radicals and patriarchal families in the Christian community is not subjected to rigorous questioning. Amy-Jill Levine characterizes the androcentrism of Q1 in these terms: "Silence (i.e., about women among the itinerant radicals) may not indicate absence, but the evidence to this point does not allow an argument for presence either."[2] Here again, the old model of itinerant radicals *alongside* churches based on love patriarchalism is continued: Q2 is viewed as being at the stage of transition from sect to patriarchal institution.

FEMINIST PERSPECTIVES

After these reflections on the history of interpretation of Matt 10:34–36 || Luke 12:51–53, we need to direct critical feminist attention toward the persuasive power of the model of "itinerant radicals *in association with patriarchal* communities." This model permits the integration of a tradition like that in Matt 10:34–36 || Luke 12:51–53 into a patriarchal system and fails to challenge a patriarchal church and society. Against this model of interpretation, we must point to the real content of the texts and to social-historical findings regarding the situation of the people of Roman Palestine, which do not permit us to suppose the existence of a relevant middle class. It is not sufficient to concentrate our attention on the ethos of individual itinerant prophets, female and male. The role of women in the houses of the sympathizers must also be examined from the perspective of a feminist theology of liberation. The texts of Matt 10:34–36 || Luke 12:51–53 constitute a radical challenge to the patriarchal family itself, not merely to a few such families. The logion implicitly presumes an alternative praxis that looks to the liberation of the *whole* people.

MATTHEW 24:37–39 || LUKE 17:26–27, 30:
THE OBSTINACY OF PATRIARCHY

RECONSTRUCTION OF THE SAYINGS SOURCE

The two versions of this proclamation of divine judgment on the generation of the end-time flood correspond, except for certain details that affect the sense only marginally. The saying begins with an eschatological typology of history: the generation before the coming of the Son of Humanity for judgment corresponds to that in the days of Noah before the flood (Matt 24:37 || Luke 17:26). In a second reflection, this analogy is given a concrete content: the generation before the flood ate and drank, married and were given in marriage (Luke 17:27), or gave [their daughters] in marriage (Matt 24:38), until the day when Noah entered the ark and the flood came and swept them all away. The conclusion of the saying announces the judgment: so (namely, as on the day of the flood) will the day (Luke 17:30) or the coming (Matt 24:39) of the Son of Humanity be. The central idea remains unspoken, but indirectly it emerges with unmistakable clarity: the present generation eats and drinks, marries and is married, goes on doing things the way they have always been done, until the judgment of the Son of Humanity comes to strike and condemn it.

SOCIAL-HISTORICAL QUESTIONS

Although women could also take an active part in making their own marriages, and although their action in marrying finds verbal expression in the Christian Testament (Mark 10:12; 1 Cor 7:28b, 34; 1 Tim 5:11, 14), both versions of this saying obscure the adult responsibility of women that actually existed. In the Matthean version, it is the father (or guardian) and the grown son who do the action. The Lukan version presents the couple—he marries; she is given in marriage—so that here too the woman is the object of men's actions. The androcentrism of Q is more rigid than reality.

Luke's Gospel contains descriptions of the patriarchal household that take up this idea from the Sayings Source and expand on it: Luke 17:28 and 14:18–20. In Luke 17:28, the economic aspect of the household is also described: buying, selling, planting, building; in Luke 14:18–20, similarly, we read about buying a field, purchasing five yoke of oxen, marrying a wife. These activities, which Luke evidently considers typical and necessary for men who own estates and are masters of patriarchal households, prevent them from accepting the invitation to (God's) feast. Here, as in Luke 17:27, attention is focused on the "head" of the household, the father or grown son, who has the *procura*, the oversight of everything, as does the lost son whose father gives him the ring with his seal in Luke 15:22. The shorter description of the patriarchal household in the Sayings Source at Matt 24:38 || Luke 17:27 (eating, drinking, marrying, being married, or being given in marriage) could be connected with the fact that in the Sayings Source, as generally in Matthew and Mark, poverty is presumed to be the "normal" condition of life, while Luke repeatedly diverts our attention toward upper-class households. Of course, buying and selling must go on even in poor houses, but the list in Luke 17:28

reveals a fair amount of patriarchal self-awareness that is not found to the same degree in Matt 24:38 || Luke 17:27.

The analysis of patriarchy in all the cases under scrutiny is focused on the activity of the men who rule the household. Their completely "normal" behavior is culpable. What is criticized in the normal activity of the patriarchal household is not that women, children, and slaves of both sexes are oppressed and exploited by this normality, but rather that the household continues its normal behavior *although* God, in fact, demands that it do God's will, listen to God's messengers, female and male, and thus interrupt the normal course of things, abandon it, and live differently. Matthew (22:30) and Luke (20:35) have taken over from Mark 12:25 the idea that in the reign of God people will not marry or be given in marriage. We may inquire about the standpoint from which Mark 12:25 and parallels and Matt 24:37−39 and parallels speak of marriage: that of sexuality or that of patriarchal interest in the procreation of legitimate offspring. Patriarchal marriage as a relationship in which love and sexuality play a part is primarily addressed as a theme when women refuse to marry. Sexuality is not part of the normal character of a patriarchal household from the point of view of the male actors. Even the context of levirate marriage, which is discussed in Mark 12:18−27 and parallels, draws attention not to sexual needs but to the patriarchal interest in the production of offspring. The undisturbed continuation of the patriarchal household, with its eating, drinking, procreating of children, all as if nothing had happened to disturb it, is analyzed in Matt 24:38; Luke 17:27 as something culpable.

Eating and drinking in the patriarchal house appear in this context not as elementary necessities for human survival, but as processes absorbing energies and interests that really ought to be directed to God's will. Our attention is drawn to the evening dinner as the principal meal and the central social focus of the household. The alternative is not stated, but the text wants to raise the question of such an alternative: the place of the evening meal is, for those who now listen to the voice of God's messengers, *no longer* to be sought in the patriarchal house, but in the community of disciples. In this dry and radically androcentric critique of the obstinacy of patriarchy, the existence of women in the patriarchal household is reduced to their tasks as wives, that is, as childbearers. There is no thought given to the fact that, as a rule, food and drink are prepared by women (see also below, on Matt 13:33 || Luke 13:20−21).

In Matt 24:41 || Luke 17:35, women's work is placed in an eschatological context. But the thought contained here is different from that in Matt 24:38 || Luke 17:27. The two women at the mill are torn asunder by the divine judgment: one is accepted by God; the other is not. (Here we should infer an augmented meaning: the second did not choose to hear the voice of God's messengers.) In Matt 24:38 || Luke 17:27 what is at issue is the obstinate continuance of ordinary ways; in Matt 24:41 || Luke 17:35 the subject is the separation of two who are only inches apart.

FEMINIST REFLECTIONS ON THE HISTORY OF INTERPRETATION

Traditional scholarly interpretation of Matt 24:37–39 || Luke 17:26–27 has not recognized that the text intends to offer a typical picture of the patriarchal household. Moreover, in the majority of interpretations there is no acknowledgment that the subject is the guilt and obstinacy of patriarchal life. To give some examples:

According to Rudolf Bultmann, this saying "warns of the surprising suddenness of the Parousia."[3] Siegfried Schulz continues this line of thought: "the accent clearly [lies] on the unpreparedness of the people." "There is . . . no description of any particularly terrible sins of these people who are subject to destruction. Their only sin is that they feel themselves completely secure; for it is precisely into the carefree state that is all too normal for their instinctive activities that judgment intrudes, suddenly and without preparation."[4] According to Schulz, the text intends to warn us to be on the alert. But Schulz establishes no connection between the content of "eating, drinking, marrying, and giving in marriage" and the lack of alertness. These people can continue with their "instinctive activities," but they must be on the alert. A good many interpretations operate within this framework.

Other exegetes establish a connection between the lack of alertness and the actions described (eating and sexuality), but these continue to be understood as "instinctive activities." "Unpreparedness and absence of concern characterize a generation that is wrapped up in the satisfaction of its elementary needs. *Gamein* and *gamizesthai* are euphemisms for sexual activity" (Wolfgang Wiefel).[5] Here, then, it is taken for granted that there is a right and a wrong way to satisfy one's elementary needs. It is wrong, in the meaning of this text, for people (men?) to be "wrapped up in" their elementary needs. Other interpreters say at this point that the generation before the flood was "immersed in earthly affairs" and "wrapped up in" the satisfaction of elementary needs.[6] "Eating, drinking, marrying and being married—things that in themselves are ethically unobjectionable—are here the expression of a fatal nonchalance."[7] "The accusation is apparently not directed at the actions of Noah's contemporaries as such, but against their absorption in these worldly affairs; they forgot to pay heed to the signs of the times" (H. E. Tödt).[8]

Both types of interpretation confuse the (androcentric) description of patriarchy with the representation of basic, daily human needs. Even the exegetes who see an internal connection between daily activity and lack of alertness argue for a different approach to the satisfaction of elementary needs, but not for the abolition of the patriarchal household, even though Matt 10:37 || Luke 14:26 suggest this idea all too clearly.

FEMINIST PERSPECTIVES

The patriarchal analysis in Matt 24:37–39 || Luke 17:26–27, 30 is massively androcentric and must be criticized from that point of view. Yet it offers an important point of contact for a feminist analysis of patriarchy in its critique of patriarchal understanding of time. In this saying, life in patriarchy is criticized as living within a linear conception of time, which takes for granted that everything will continue to be as it has always been. This idea of time, which the text criticizes, is given a very careful verbal expression. The generation before the flood supposed that their future could not be different from their present, and so made themselves *blind* to the sufferings of the present.

This blind continuance of things as they are is contrasted to the coming of the Son of Humanity, a vision and revelation. In light of the vision of the coming of the Son of Humanity for judgment, the present is altered at a single stroke for those who are ready to see. The present is the period of birthpangs before the end; its terrors and its guilt can still be changed. Now is the hour of conversion. Linear ideas of time are reproached for their blindness. Apocalyptic-revelatory thinking draws its vision from acknowledgment of the existence of suffering due to injustice. It is *these* tears that God will wipe away (Rev 21:1–4). God will sit in judgment on the injustice that is now taking place. Let me emphasize again at this point that apocalyptic thinking, at least in the saying under discussion, is androcentric and ignores the suffering of women.

Philosophers who understand "progress" as the catastrophe it is have offered a critique of linear thinking about time and the blind continuance it involves. "The concept of progress has to be supplemented by the idea of catastrophe. The fact that 'things go on as they are' is the catastrophe. It is not what is about to happen at any given point, but what is already happening. In Strindberg's terms: hell is not what is ahead of us, but the very life we lead" (Walter Benjamin).[9] The content of apocalyptic visions is not future catastrophes: they throw a blinding light on the catastrophe of the everyday present. Jürgen Ebach's interpretation of apocalyptic has developed this idea in most accurate fashion.

Rosemary Radford Ruether's feminist *criticism* of Christian linear eschatology, the liberal idea of the process of evolution, and the Marxist notion of the future as the outcome of revolution correspond to the content of the critique in the saying in Matt 24:37–39 || Luke 17:26–27, 30 of the obstinacy and blindness of the patriarchal father of the household. Ruether counters linear thinking about time ("endless flight into an unrealized future") with "a different model of hope and change based on conversion or *metanoia.*"[10] In doing so, she could easily refer to Jewish and early Christian apocalyptic ideas such as those in this saying.

The penetrating power of patriarchal notions of time can be recognized in the tradition of interpretation outlined above, in which at least one branch of exegesis presumes the guiltlessness of the ordinary, which can continue as before. Rudolf Bultmann's rejection of apocalyptic thought was stated as follows: "*Mythical eschatology* is, basically, eliminated by the simple fact that Christ's parousia did not happen immediately, as the New Testament expected, but instead the history of the world went on and, as every sensible person is convinced, will continue to go on."[11] The interpretations of Matt 24:37–39 || Luke 17:26ff. show that Bultmann's premise still enjoys broad acceptance, at least in those branches of Christianity bearing the Western stamp—and this in spite of Auschwitz, Hiroshima, and ecological catastrophes.

Christina Thürmer-Rohr's feminist *analysis* of the situation of women in patriarchy has shown that women contribute in a special way to having everything go on as before, in order that the "sensible person" of whom Bultmann spoke may continue to enjoy an unshaken hope for progress.

> Women's system of order is also their system of hope. Their sympathy of feeling and thought, their planning, assistance, restrictions, calculations, accounting, direction, leadership, understanding, disapproval, controlling, judging and prejudices are designed to produce . . . from the tiny collection of human beings, so susceptible to disturbance, a stable unit, a unit from which no one may break loose, and that can hope for a stable future . . . all based on an innocent trust in regard to everything that happens outside their own ken. . . . [Women create] the supportive climate of good hope. . . . For those who continue to make hope and illusion the source of their will to live, every kind of knowledge of reality is intensely threatening. . . . We should learn to live in the present.[12]

Apocalyptic thinking was not capable of this feminist analysis, despite its critique of everyday patriarchy and its ideas of time. We cannot learn from such texts how women themselves saw their present, if they were at all capable of recognizing a present that was *theirs*. But it is possible to make the inquiry, to try to determine what we can learn about women even within such androcentric perspectives.

MATTHEW 13:33 || LUKE 13:20–21:
THE HANDS OF WOMEN

RECONSTRUCTION OF THE SAYINGS SOURCE

The Sayings Source added an introductory phrase to couple the parable of the leaven with that of the mustard seed to form a series of two parables about the reign of God. After the introduction, the substance of the parable in both versions corresponds word for word: the reign of God is to be compared to "leaven [sourdough]" or "yeast, that a woman took and mixed in with three measures of flour until all of it was leavened."

SOCIAL-HISTORICAL QUESTIONS

The preparation of yeast bread is described in this text in such a way that our attention is focused on a particular moment in the process of making the dough: the bakerwoman mixes the yeast in the flour. Now the leavening process begins; ultimately, the whole mass of dough will be changed by it. Although in the history of interpretation the "hiding" or "mixing" of the yeast in the flour is usually regarded as not accurate for the normal process of making bread, this is meant to be a description of an ordinary, everyday event. My mother's and grandmother's cookbook (prepared for a rural family in Germany at the beginning of the twentieth century) describes the process as follows: "On the evening before baking, the bread should be leavened; one-third of the sifted flour should be used for this." The recipe calls for thirty kilograms of rye flour. "Dissolve the yeast and leavening completely in fifteen liters of lukewarm water and pour it into the flour, stir these together to make a thick paste, sprinkle three handfuls of flour over the dough, cover it and allow it to rise until the following morning. Then . . . knead in the rest of the flour by hand . . . ." The parable gives a short account of the process, with the intention of focusing on the point at which the dough is mixed and is ready to be covered for rising. Both in the theological tradition of interpretation of this text and in the rural and technological traditions of knowledge related to breadbaking it appears that the details of preparing dough were foreign to men engaged in scholarly pursuits. I have found exceptions to this rule in Adolf Jülicher and Joachim Jeremias.

The quantity of flour has been considered forced, as has the everyday context: Joachim Jeremias and many others have regarded the three measures (39.4 liters) of flour as "divine realities,"[13] and yet we may conclude from the cookbook quoted above that this feature was still quite ordinary in the context of a large household, since yeast bread need not be baked fresh every day as is unleavened flat bread. It is not said that the yeast is small in quantity: evidently that is not particularly important for the text. The contrast between small and large has migrated, in the course of the history of interpretation, from the parable of the mustard seed or from 1 Cor 5:6; Gal 5:9 into the parable of the leaven.

Women's work in breadmaking has played no significant part in the history of interpretation of this parable, so far as I can see. This is connected in part with the theory of parables and in part with the lack of appreciation of women's work in the theological tradition. But the text of the parable, unlike the tradition of interpretation, intends to call attention to the work of women.

This is clear not only from the text of the parable itself but also from the totality of the Sayings Source, which demonstrates an unusual interest in women's work: see Matt 24:41 || Luke 17:35, where two women are grinding at the mill, or Matt 6:28 || Luke 12:27, where spinning is mentioned. These findings are unusual, for example, in relation to the whole of the Synoptic Gospels, where, apart from the material on women's work in the Sayings Source, we find three references to prostitutes, two to slave women, three references to women's "serving," and one to the sewing of a rip in a cloth. But it is noteworthy that only in the Sayings Source do we find a *pairing* of men's work and women's work, since in such pairings women's work is evaluated as genuine labor comparable to that of men. There are, to my knowledge, no parallels to this in the Christian Testament or in the literature of the time, apart from the fact that we find married couples like Prisca and Aquila, who are engaged in crafts. The hierarchical division of labor between the sexes meant, in large measure, that women's work became invisible.

Another unique characteristic of the Sayings Source is that *women's work* is placed in a *theological context.* Two women grind at the mill, and they make different decisions (Matt 24:41 || Luke 17:35). One woman has heard the voice of Jesus' messengers, and the other has refused to hear. Both the work of women in the house and the work of men in the fields form parts of the daily enslavement to anxiety over food and clothing (Matt 6:28 || Luke 12:27), from which the community of Jesus' disciples, female and male, is liberating itself while helping others to achieve liberation as well. We will return to the theological ideas in the parable of the leaven. In texts of the Synoptic Gospels outside the Sayings Source, it is women's "serving" and the work of prostitutes that are placed in a theological context.

In view of this recognition of women's work in the Sayings Source, its rigid patriarchalism and its blindness to the reality of women's work are all the more astonishing. By rigid patriarchalism, I mean the expropriation of women's work by the father of the household (i.e., God): it is he who gives bread (or an egg) and fish to the son (Matt 7:7–8 || Luke 11:1–2), even though these things are, as a rule, prepared by women. By blindness to the reality of women's work, I mean the fact that here only women's household work is mentioned, and not their work outside the house—in the fields, in business, in textile production, and as prostitutes. The patriarchal ideology according to which women do not work on the land but only in the house results in blindness to the fact that other kinds of work—for example, field work—play significant roles in the lives of women.

Despite these contradictions in the acknowledgment of women's work within the Sayings Source, its unusual features are striking when measured against the ordinary way that patriarchy has of rendering women's work invisible, and against the hierarchy of work worlds. I find an explanation for this circumstance in experiences of equality within the hard daily lives of an impoverished population, although I would not want it to be assumed that poverty promotes equality for women. Instead, what I see here is that the Jesus movement's hope for the coming of the reign of God, and attempts to live in just relationships, enhanced (to a limited degree) men's ability to see women's labor as hard work and to recognize that it was equal in value to that of men. Attempts to eliminate the hierarchical division of labor according to gender that we know from other sources within the traditions of early Christianity are in their tendency, and in their conflictual significance, to be placed alongside these findings in the Sayings Source.

Women's work in baking bread has a further symbolic content beyond its relationship to everyday reality. "Give us this day our daily bread" (Matt 6:11 || Luke 11:3) is a prayer for the basic nourishment needed for a single day: bread is life, the elementary material of life, like water. In Roman Palestine, bread was also prepared in bakeries. There were already such things as kneading machines for large quantities of dough. If the parable were only concerned with the yeast and its effects, it could have been about yeast and a kneading machine. Here, instead, we hear of the hard work of a woman who prepares a large quantity of dough, the substance of bread, without which people cannot live. The poverty of the people of Palestine in the first century C.E. is the life context to which the symbolic meaning of this parable belongs. "The story describes an ordinary activity, a work that until the very recent past determined the rhythm of daily life for almost every housewife, and still does for women in two-thirds of the world today. . . . For the poor, the product of the mixing of flour and yeast is the raw material of life itself."[14]

FEMINIST REFLECTIONS ON THE HISTORY OF INTERPRETATION

In contrast to the Sayings Source itself, the traditional interpretation of this saying has shown no interest at all in the social and theological meaning of women's work. One reason for this is the eradication of any awareness of women's work within patriarchy, something that can be observed even in the most recent interpretations of the parable of the leaven and other sayings that mention women's work. A further reason is the theory of parables that does not relate the imagery of parables, *to the extent that it corresponds to everyday life,* to the content of the revelation that is the subject of the parables: "Have we any clues beyond an undifferentiated common picture of a woman kneading dough for bread?"[15] The interpreter's attention thus remains focused on those features of the image that, in his opinion, differ from what is normal and everyday (e.g., "she hid"). The image of yeast comes from the kitchen. . . . The formula 'she hid' is striking."[16] Even here, in Ulrich Luz's reading, the content of an image "from the kitchen" is not regarded as relevant for interpretation. Adolf Jülicher, whose own theory of parables did not permit him to look for metaphoric ruptures at the level of imagery, derives his interpretation from the (unfounded) contrast between small and large: "It remains true that this pair of parables [i.e., the mustard seed and the leaven] combine with a double force to make it seem likely to us, on the basis of the experiences of daily life, that even the kingdom of heaven can conceal a glorious end behind very modest beginnings."[17] Despite all the lengthy discussions of parable theory, in the Western exegetical tradition the everyday world of the parables remains unimportant for the revelation proclaimed in the parable. In the liberation theological interpretation of the parables by Carlos Meesters, the imagery of the parables and *everyday reality as a source of revelation* have been newly discovered: "Anyone who, for example, does not know what yeast is cannot understand the statement: 'The reign of God is like yeast.' . . . Therefore, before we consider the reign of God in our Bible study groups, we must first reflect on the realities of life."[18] Although I share the approach to parable theory that underlies this observation, I must still criticize its androcentrism: the parable is about "yeast that a woman took . . . ," that is, it is about the work of a woman with yeast, her work to produce the fundamental stuff of human nourishment.

FEMINIST PERSPECTIVES

The scholarly tradition within which discussions of parable theory are conducted severs daily life from the event of revelation. We need to recover the viewpoint from which, in Jesus' parables, everyday experiences are made transparent for divine revelation. The parable of the leaven draws our eyes to the hands of a woman baking bread: "she took," "she hid." The conclusion hints at her waiting "until the whole [of the flour] was leavened." The parable gives an eschatological interpretation to the present experience of Jesus' disciples of both genders: the dough has been covered, and we wait calmly. The parable establishes a relationship between the present and the powerful movement of the reign of God. That mighty process can be experienced whenever people look at the hands of a woman baking bread.

Two possible misunderstandings should be considered: First, does not a feminist interpretation that sees the hands of God as visible in the hands of a woman baking bread undermine feminist interest in the liberation of women, by again identifying the other-determined "feminine" role with housework and labor for the basics of life?

It should be clear by now that this cannot be the feminist interest in this text, but rather that the story of women who bake bread, women who have been made invisible, is to be regarded with theological seriousness in this parable. A second misunderstanding with regard to the eschatological frame of interpretation would be to conclude that the hopeful work of women, always attempting to secure the future and functioning as a support system for humanly created catastrophe, is expressed here also. Beneath the radioactive cloud from Chernobyl, women struggled to find untainted food. Their struggle was in service of life, and, without the women's willing it, it also supported those who wanted to continue their radioactive business as before. What is the future for which breadbaking women are working? In the parable, the future at issue is the renewed life of creation, the reign of God, and not the extension of the status quo.

The parable draws our eyes to the hands of a woman at the moment when they rest. In the tradition of interpretation this has often led to an emphasis such as: human beings cannot and should not desire to do anything for God's future. God alone acts. The reign of God comes "by itself." But the parable does not set up an opposition between human activity and trust in God, between human acts and the acts of God. Acting and trusting in God, work for the sake of life, and the patience to wait go together here.

MATTHEW 11:25–27 || LUKE 10:21–22: GOSPEL OF THE POOR AND SOPHIA CHRISTOLOGY

RECONSTRUCTION OF THE SAYINGS SOURCE

This part of the Sayings Source contains a prayer of Jesus (Matt 11:25, 26 || Luke 10:21) and a christological saying (Matt 11:27 || Luke 10:22) that begins as an I-saying of Jesus but then continues as a statement about him. Many interpreters also assign Matt 11:28–30 to the Sayings Source. Since the saying is absent from Luke's Gospel, a reliable attribution is not possible. But because this saying plays a part in the discussion of the Sophia Christology of the Sayings Source, we will have to return later to the question whether it contains a Sophia Christology, independent of the question of whether it belongs to the Sayings Source.

The text of the prayer, which is in praise of God, is the same in both versions, except for some unimportant deviations:

> I praise you, Father, Lord of heaven and earth, because you have hidden these things from the wise and the intelligent and have revealed them to infants; yes, Father, for such was your gracious will.

The last clause describes God's election: in this way you, Father, have chosen (the infants, and rejected the wise).

The christological saying follows the prayer without any transition. It is often assigned to a stratum of tradition different from that of the prayer. But the christological saying must be interpreted in conjunction with the prayer, since, if we suppose that there are different levels of tradition here, it must have been added to the prayer itself. The christological saying has also been handed down in almost literal agreement in both Gospels:

> All things have been handed over to me by my Father; and no one knows the Son except the Father, and no one knows the Father except the Son and anyone to whom the Son chooses to reveal [God].

As exclusive mediator of the knowledge and revelation of God, Jesus is called Son, that is, Son of God.

SOCIAL-HISTORICAL QUESTIONS

Father–Son

In harmony with the christological saying, Jesus' prayer also centers on the relationship between Father and Son. God is "Lord of heaven and earth" and "Father" of Jesus, who proclaims God's revelation. God elects by a sovereign decision ("such was your gracious will"), and in the same way, Jesus hands on God's revelation by a sovereign choice ("to whom the Son chooses . . ."). The Son, like the Father, is sovereign. To him are "all things," that is, all power, given by the Father. Father and Son stand in a unique, exclusive relationship of mutual recognition. Believers, *in contrast to* John 10:14–15, which is frequently pointed out as having parallel content to this christological saying, are *not* placed in a mutual relationship with Jesus corresponding to that between Son and Father.

God and Jesus are spoken of in metaphorical fashion. Father-Son ideas are not comparisons; they are metaphors in a context of mythical language about God. They derive their ideas from the power center of the patriarchal household, the relationship between father and son. In this context, the relationship contains no associations of love, even though the contrary is often asserted. The associated idea here is strictly that of power. God, as Father of heaven and earth, is the father who gives full power to the Son. Father and Son make sovereign decisions, like kings, or like the father in the patriarchal household. Even the reciprocal relationship of mutual knowledge between Father and Son describes their exclusive position of power. *No one else* knows the Father or the Son; as a result, the Son, as mediator of revelation, has unrestricted power. The ideas behind this God metaphor and Christology arise out of the notions of power and the reality of power in the patriarchal household, not out of the context of mutuality in mystical union.

The notions of power and the Christology of this text are typical of the Sayings Source, as shown especially in the temptation story (Matt 4:1–11 || Luke 4:1–13). There Jesus, as Son of God, is challenged by Satan to repudiate the uniqueness of God and God's rule over the world.

This text from the Sayings Source, then, is not about a love relationship or a mystical union but about power and exclusivity. As elsewhere in the Sayings Source, despite the critique of patriarchy described above (see under "Matthew 24:37–39 || Luke 17:26–27, 30"), patriarchal thinking proceeds uninterrupted, and in this case the patriarchal power structure is transferred without interruption to God and to Christ.

The Wise–Infants

Nēpioi, "infants," describes small children who still drink milk and babble (Matt 21:16; Ps 8:3). In contrast to the *sophoi,* "the wise," the term describes uneducated people, who, seen from the perspective of the educated, are like children (see, e.g., Wis 10:21).

In 1 Corinthians 1 and 2, Paul uses the word *mōros,* "foolish," as a concept opposed to *sophos,* "wise." Here again the uneducated are denigrated from the perspective of the educated: to be uneducated means to be foolish. The uneducated *nēpioi* are not qualified to speak (implied, e.g., in Wis 10:21); they are mute and can be deceived (Wis 12:24), etc. The conceptual pair infants/wise (or infants/intelligent) in the Jesus prayer from the Sayings Source must be placed in the context of biblical and extrabiblical ways of speaking about social opposites. From the point of view represented by this way of speaking, society contains contrasting groups of poor and rich, foolish and wise, weak and strong, humble and proud (see only Luke 1:46–54; 1 Cor 1:26–31). In the Sayings Source we can point to the beatitudes for the poor (Matt 5:3 || Luke 6:20; cf. Matt 11:2–6 || Luke 7:18–23). This way of speaking in "social types" is also a theological mode of speaking in the biblical context: the poor are also poor in their relationship to God; they are too poor to be able to praise God. The uneducated/infants are also unable to praise God (implied in Matt 21:16 and elsewhere). The concepts that are used for the people "below" can also be substituted for one another: anyone who is uneducated is also poor, power-less, without self-concept. The rich are educated, proud, and able to laugh (see again only Luke 1:46–54; 1 Cor 1:26–31). The perspective from which these *social* contrasts are projected is ordinarily that of the adult, educated, well-to-do father of the household, the wise person in the sense, for example, of the Wisdom of Solomon and similar writings. Hence Matt 11:25–26 || Luke 10:21 makes a statement that, measured against social reality and the ideas of the wisdom tradition, is paradoxical. God is self-revealed to the infants/unedu-cated; God's revelation is hidden from the wise. Wisdom literature holds precisely the opposite opinion: only the educated (man) has access to divine wisdom, and only he is led by her.

Women are denigrated as ignorant and foolish in a special way (Wis 3:12, *aphrones;* cf. Prov 9:13ff. on the foolish woman). In this context, a woman who reveres her own husband counts as wise (Sir 26:26). The godless, bicker-ing wife is a favorite theme in wisdom literature.

From the intellectual tradition of contrasting foolish and wise in the wis-dom literature, as well as from the social reality described by the contrasting of infants with the wise and intelligent, we may conclude that this description refers to the lower orders in contrast to the upper class, and that more women than men were supposed to be included among the infants.

FEMINIST REFLECTIONS ON THE HISTORY OF INTERPRETATION

Two types of interpretation of Jesus' prayer should be distinguished. The dominant interpretation (Type A) holds that through God's, or Jesus', revela-tion the infants become the truly wise, and they are to be distinguished from those who are only thought to be wise. The harshness of the statement that God is self-concealed from the wise is thus frequently softened: it is not edu-cated people as such who are meant, but only educated people whose wisdom is "self-made."

A second type of interpretation (Type B), to which I subscribe, understands the revelation to the infants in such a way that they, *as such,* become subjects of the relationship with God: their status as infants is considered a scandal before God, and their liberation begins with this biased revelation. They do not become truly wise, just as the poor are not transformed into rich people; they become subjects who are then capable of liberating praxis in communi-ties of solidarity.

These two types of interpretation are based on different social models: Type A imagines the Jesus community of the truly wise as a small, exclusive group (sect) within the larger society. Type B thinks of the Jesus community as made up of poor, children, and women whose liberating praxis seeks to extend itself to the whole nation.

The tradition of interpretation of the christological saying Matt 11:27 ||
Luke 10:22 will be discussed in this context only from the point of view of
Sophia Christology, since this saying is an important focus of feminist discus-
sion of Sophia christology. This feminist discussion is in continuity with a long
tradition of interpretation of Matt 11:27 || Luke 10:22 or of Matt 11:25–30 ||
Luke 10:21–22, or of the Sayings Source as a whole (or one of the levels of
tradition within it) as the documentation for a Sophia Christology.

In particular, the picture of Jesus as mediator of revelation in this christological saying has been used to establish the existence of a Sophia Christology.
But the content of the revelation that this mediator brings (in Jesus' prayer) is
diametrically opposed to the content of the Sophia mythology in the Wisdom
writings (see above under "Matthew 10:34–36 || Luke 12:51–53"). The idea of
a mediator of revelation, female or male, was current in Jewish, Christian, and
Gnostic literature. Whether it is connected with a nonhierarchical and nonpatriarchal conception (which is the crucial point for a feminist Sophia Christology) must be investigated in each concrete text and its social-historical
context. In the christological saying under discussion here there is no evidence
of any kind of antihierarchical or antipatriarchal sensibility. The power center
of Father and Son is the heart of this Christology. It is not evident whether the
Son metaphor has suppressed a Sophia metaphor, since it cannot be said that
the idea of Sophia as mediator of revelation constitutes the basis—the originating myth—of all the later developments. Such an argumentation would have to
rely for its method on Rudolf Bultmann's model of a Sophia myth,[19] but this
has been shown to be a hypothesis developed using the methods of motif criticism and reconstructing an artificial myth, such as the myth of the original
human being (*Urmensch*), which never really existed in this form.

In order to achieve some clarity about the question of a Sophia Christology
in the Sayings Souce, it will make sense to examine, at this point, all the texts
that may be relevant for this question.

I share the interest of feminist theologies in a nonpatriarchal Christology,
but for historical and theological reasons I wish to offer a critique of any connection made between the wisdom tradition (in the sense defined above) and
the Jesus tradition in general and also in the particular case of the Sayings
Source. In doing so, my intention is to strengthen, not to weaken, feminist
development of a nonpatriarchal Christology. The historical reason for my critique of a wisdom interpretation of the Jesus tradition, or rather of the tradition in the Sayings Source in particular, is my conception of the wide difference in their contents (see above, under "Social-Historical Questions") and
their life situations (*Sitze im Leben*). Wisdom tradition has its *Sitz im Leben* in
the instruction of young men, mainly those from well-to-do families, who are
to be brought up to be good patriarchs. They honor the divine Sophia, but
deliberately oppress the women around them. I understand the Jesus move-

ment, on the other hand, even at the time the Sayings Source was composed, as a Jewish liberation movement within a people oppressed by the Pax Romana, and emanating primarily from those suffering the oppression: the poor (women and men), the sick, the prostitutes, the tax collectors of both genders, fisherfolk (male and female), and day laborers, both men and women.

The theological reason for my denial of a connection between wisdom traditions and Jesus traditions is the gospel of the poor. Jesus' blessing of the poor cannot be tied to wisdom tradition; it stems rather from prophetic tradition. The thought of 1 Corinthians 1 and 2, with its deliberate reference to Isa 29:14 ("the wisdom of their wise shall perish") and the gospel of the poor (especially 1 Cor 1:26–31) is closely parallel to Matt 11:25–27 || Luke 10:21–22. Attempts to anchor the gospel of the poor, and especially Jesus' prayer in Matt 11:25–26 || Luke 10:21, in the wisdom tradition have yielded no persuasive results. An interpretation of Jesus' prayer on the basis of wisdom tradition (such as Wis 10:21) leads to a blunting of the gospel of the poor: in that case, Jesus is speaking of infants and wise people only in a derived sense. The social reality of uneducated women and men, whom the wise regard as infants, plays no further part in such an interpretation (Type A).

References to Wisdom are discussed for the following texts from the Sayings Source: Matt 11:25–27 || Luke 10:21–22 (see above); Matt 11:28–30; Matt 11:16–19 || Luke 7:31–35; Matt 23:34–36 || Luke 11:49–51; Matt 23:37–39 || Luke 13:34–35; Matt 12:41–42 || Luke 11:31–32. Since I cannot discuss all these texts at length here, I will place the content of each individual text from the Sayings Source alongside the texts adduced as parallels from the wisdom literature:

Matthew 11:28–30

Jesus calls the weary and burdened to himself. He is a gentle king whose yoke, unlike that of the political rulers, is light. Prov 9:3–6: Lady Wisdom invites the simple (*aphrōn*) to her table: "Lay aside immaturity, and live" (9:6). Sir 51:23–26: "Draw near to me, you who are uneducated (*apaideutoi*) . . . acquire wisdom for yourselves without money. Put your neck under her yoke, and let your souls receive instruction (*paideia*)." Jesus does not invite the weary and burdened to become wise through instruction, but to find rest in his realm.

Matthew 11:16–19 || Luke 7:31–35

The crucial phrase that is cited to connect Q with wisdom tradition is in Luke 7:35: "wisdom is vindicated by all her children." Here God is called Wisdom, whose messengers, Jesus and John the Baptizer, have been reviled, but will be justified by the children of Wisdom. It is true that no wisdom parallel has been found for the thought content of this passage, but the designation of God as Wisdom is referred to the wisdom tradition. However, the idea of God as Wisdom is not limited to the wisdom tradition alone.

Matthew 23:34–36 || Luke 11:49–51

This saying from Q, in the Lukan version, is understood as a saying of divine Wisdom: she sends prophets (of both genders), who are killed. The saying is a proclamation of the judgment of God on the murderers of the prophets. Here again, the description of God as Wisdom is the only link to wisdom traditions, but there is no place in those traditions either for an eschatological divine judgment or for the tradition of the murder of the prophets.

Matthew 23:37–39 || Luke 13:34–35

Here, again in the framework of a proclamation of divine judgment on the murderers of the prophets, Jerusalem is accused because her children have not wished to accept the call of God, who wanted to gather them as a mother bird gathers her chicks. The connection to Wisdom tradition is drawn from Prov 16:16 LXX (Wisdom as a mother bird) and *1 Enoch* 42: Wisdom returns to heaven because she found no dwelling place among human beings (Matt 23:39 || Luke 13:35, "you will no longer see me"). But the metaphor of God as the mother bird comes from a broader tradition; and reviled Wisdom is not subjected to bloody persecution, nor does she announce eschatological judgment on the murderers of the prophets.

Matthew 12:41–42 || Luke 11:31–32

Here there is more than Solomon and more than Jonah. This text is claimed as the basis for an interpretation of Jesus as a teacher of wisdom like Solomon, even though that is precisely what it does *not* say.

Thus we see that, in Luke 11:49 and Luke 7:35, God is called Wisdom. It is possible that this name for God is also part of the Sayings Source. But the *content* of the wisdom tradition does not play any relevant part in the Sayings Source. Consequently, we may omit from our discussion the question whether Matt 11:28–30 can be assigned to the Sayings Source at all, and whether it can be demonstrated that God is ever called Wisdom in Q.

FEMINIST PERSPECTIVES

The patriarchal Father–Son Christology in Matt 11:25–27 || Luke 10:21–22 offers no starting point for a feminist Christology; at most it contains a political critique of structures of domination. Only God is Father and Lord of heaven and earth; only the Son reveals this God, who is made known to the infants.

The choice of the infants means for the further development of feminist theology of liberation that it must orient itself "to the liberation of the poorest and least visible women." The Sayings Source unfortunately relates no stories of the healing of women (is this an accident?), but it insists on the gospel of the poor and on healings by Jesus and his messengers, female and male: this is where the reign of God begins. Despite its intensely androcentric language and its patriarchal horizon of imagination, this sayings tradition encourages us to develop visions of a better world, a world that, through a preferential option for women who are tormented by poverty, sexual exploitation, and ignorance, we can begin to envision and to achieve.

Although wisdom traditions are not relevant for the Sayings Source, I would like to adopt Elisabeth Schüssler Fiorenza's suggestion that we not revive early Jewish and Christian wisdom theology, but that we do continue its struggle with conventional, androcentric language.[20] Then even the faint traces of language about God as Sophia in the Sayings Source or in the Synoptic Gospels (Luke 7:35; 11:49) could be a starting point for talking about God today. But in particular, 1 Corinthians 1 and 2 could serve as a connecting point for feminist Christology. There Jesus is God's wisdom, who through the crucifixion has taken the part of those "below." Jesus, as divine Wisdom, brings God's judgment on the wise, the well-born, and the powerful. Here the gospel of the poor is combined with a Sophia Christology: it offers a starting point for a nonhierarchical Christology that permits us to pursue the option for the poor as an option for women.

Translated by Linda M. Maloney

NOTES

1. Monika Fander, *Die Stellung der Frau im Markusevangelium* (Altenberge: Telos-Verlag, 1989), 322.

2. Amy-Jill Levine, "Who's Catering the Q Affair? Feminist Observations on Q Paraenesis," in *Paraenesis: Act and Form,* ed. Leo G. Perdue and John G. Gammie, *Semeia* 50 (Atlanta: Scholars Press, 1990), 4.8. The notion of the "liminality" of Jesus' disciples at the level of Q1 misses the social-historical question of the situation of the populace in Roman Palestine and repeats the thesis (e.g., of Gerd Theissen) of freely chosen poverty achieved by an ascetic renunciation of possessions (see, e.g., ibid., 3.2).

3. Rudolf Bultmann, *Die Geschichte der synoptischen Tradition* (4th ed.; Göttingen: Vandenhoeck & Ruprecht, 1958), 123; Eng. trans. *The History of the Synoptic Tradition,* trans. John Marsh (New York and Evanston: Harper & Row, 1963), 117.

4. Siegfried Schulz, *Q: Die Spruchquelle der Evangelisten* (Zurich: Theologischer Verlag, 1972), 284–85.

5. Wolfgang Wiefel, *Das Evangelium nach Lukas* (Berlin: Evangelische Verlagsanstalt, 1988), 311.

6. Walter Grundmann, *Das Evangelium nach Lukas* (5th ed.; Berlin: Evangelische Verlagsanstalt, 1969), 343; the examples could easily be multiplied.

7. Migaku Sato, *Q und Prophetie* (Tübingen: Mohr-Siebeck, 1988), 285.

8. Heinz Eduard Tödt, *Der Menschensohn in der synoptischen Überlieferung* (Gütersloh: Mohn, 1959), 46.

9. Walter Benjamin, "Zentralpark," in his *Illuminationen: Ausgewählte Schriften* (Frankfurt: Suhrkamp, 1969), 260. For the connection between Benjamin's critique and apocalyptic thinking, see Jürgen Ebach, "Apokalypse: Zum Ursprung einer Stimmung," in *Einwürfe* 2 (Munich: Kaiser, 1985), 5–61. For a critique of the hope of immortality as an extension of going-on-as-before forever, see Theodor W. Adorno, *Negative Dialektik* (Frankfurt: Suhrkamp, 1966), 362.

10. Rosemary Radford Ruether, *Sexism and God-Talk. Toward a Feminist Theology* (Boston: Beacon, 1983), 254.

11. Rudolf Bultmann, "Neues Testament und Mythologie," in his *Offenbarung und Heilsgeschehen* (Munich: Kaiser, 1941), 31.

12. Christina Thürmer-Rohr, *Vagabundinnen* (2nd ed.; Berlin: Orlanda, 1987), 28–29.

13. Joachim Jeremias, *The Parables of Jesus* (2nd rev. ed.; New York: Scribner, 1972), 147; Robert W. Funk, "Beyond Criticism in Quest of Literacy: The Parable of the Leaven," *Interpretation* 25 (1971): 159–60.

14. Sharon H. Ringe, "Mt 13,33: Das Brot geht auf," in *Feministisch gelesen,* ed. Eva Renate Schmidt, Mieke Korenhoff, and Renate Jost (Stuttgart: Kreuz, 1988), 1:159.

15. Funk, "Beyond Criticism," 158.

16. U. Luz, *Das Evangelium nach Matthäus* (Zurich: Benziger; and Neukirchen: Neukirchener Verlag, 1990), 2:333.

17. A. Jülicher, *Die Gleichnisreden Jesu* (1910), 2:579.

18. Carlos Meesters, *Vom Leben zur Bibel, von der Bibel zum Leben* 1.2 (Munich: Kaiser, 1983), 1:82.

19. See Rudolf Bultmann, "Der religionsgeschichtliche Hintergrund des Prologs zum Johannesevangelium" (1923) in his *Exegetica: Aufsätze zur Erforschung des Neuen Testaments* (Tübingen: Mohr-Siebeck, 1967), 10–35; also his *History of the Synoptic Tradition* on this logion.

20. Elisabeth Schüssler Fiorenza, "Auf den Spuren der Weisheit," in *Auf den Spuren der Weisheit,* ed. Verena Wodtke (Freiburg: Herder, 1991), 40. I also find quite interesting the suggestions of Silvia Schroer that in speaking about God we take our cue from the presentation of Lady Wisdom in Proverbs 1–8, even though the orientation to the upper-class household and the denigration of the "strange woman" in Proverbs 1–8 are at the very least theologically problematic ("Die göttliche Weisheit und der nachexilische Monotheismus," in *Der eine Gott und die Göttin: Gottesvorstellungen des biblischen Israel im Horizont feministischer Theologie,* ed. Marie-Thérès Wacker and Erich Zenger [Freiburg: Herder, 1991], 151–82).

RECOMMENDED READINGS

Brooten, Bernadette. *Women Leaders in the Ancient Synagogue: Inscriptional Evidence and Background Issues.* Brown Judaic Studies 36. Chico, CA: Scholars Press, 1982.

Plaskow, Judith. *Standing Again at Sinai: Judaism from a Feminist Perspective.* San Francisco: Harper & Row, 1990.

Richter Reimer, Ivoni. *Frauen in der Apostelgeschichte des Lukas: Eine feministisch-theologische Exegese.* Gütersloh: Mohn, 1992.

Schaumberger, Christine, and Luise Schottroff. *Schuld und Macht. Studien zu einer feministischen Befreiungstheologie.* Munich: Kaiser, 1988.

Schottroff, Luise. *Let the Oppressed Go Free: Feminist Perspectives on the New Testament.* Louisville: Westminster/John Knox Press, 1993.

———. *Lydias ungeduldige Schwestern: Feministische Sozialgeschichte des frühen Christentums.* Gütersloh: Kaiser/Gütersloher Verlagshaus, 1994.

———, and Wolfgang Stegemann. *Jesus and the Hope of the Poor.* Maryknoll, NY: Orbis, 1992.

Schüssler Fiorenza, Elisabeth. *But She Said: Feminist Practices of Biblical Interpretation.* Boston: Beacon, 1992.

Tamez, Elsa. *The Amnesty of Grace: Justification by Faith from a Latin American Perspective.* Translated by Sharon H. Ringe. Nashville: Abingdon, 1993.

Thürmer-Rohr, Christina. *Vagabundinnen.* Berlin: Orlanda, 1987.

The Gospel of Thomas

PHEME PERKINS ◆

INTRODUCTION

THE GOSPEL OF THOMAS (*Gos. Thom.*) is a collection of sayings of Jesus. Three Greek fragments known since the beginning of the twentieth century preserve sayings from at least two different copies of *Gos. Thom.* A fairly well preserved Coptic translation of the whole collection was found in Codex II from Nag Hammadi in 1945 and was first published in 1959. The title "Gospel of Thomas," appears at the conclusion of that work. The editors of the Coptic text divided it into 114 sayings.

The Oxyrhynchus papyri, which are very fragmentary, contain variants of the Prologue and Sayings 1–7 (= *P.Oxy.* 654), Sayings 26–33 and 77 (= *P.Oxy.* 1) and Sayings 36–39 (= *P.Oxy.* 655). These fragments do not come from a single manuscript, nor do they represent the Greek version from which the Coptic translation was made. *P.Oxy.* 654 combines Sayings 30 and 77b. The Greek manuscripts date from the early third century. Our earliest reference to the *Gospel of Thomas*, which includes a variant of Saying 4 also comes from the early third century C.E. Both the Greek and Coptic versions contain sayings that seem to reflect the theological concerns of ascetic, gnosticizing traditions from the second century.

However, seventy-nine of the sayings in this collection have parallels in the Synoptic Gospels. In some cases, the version of a saying or parable in *Gos. Thom.* is remarkably close to what scholars thought the pre-Synoptic form of a saying or parable must have been. Therefore, most scholars agree that the initial collection of sayings in *Gos. Thom.* preserved a Jesus tradition that was much older than the surviving gnosticized versions. Some of the sayings without Synoptic parallels may also preserve early Jesus traditions. Sayings frequently suggested in this category include nos. 8, 39, 47, 51–52, 58, 81–82, 98, and 102.

Comparison of the sayings in *Gos. Thom.* and those which made up the Sayings Source of the Synoptic Gospels (Q) show that much of the material found in Luke's Sermon on the Plain as well as such prophetic sayings and community rules as those in Luke 11:27–12:56 and 17:20–21 also appear in *Gos. Thom.* What does not appear are those Q sayings which present Jesus as apocalyptic Son of Man. The sayings in *Gos. Thom.* present a Jesus who reveals a hidden but timeless wisdom. This teaching points to the presence of God's kingdom. Jesus is not an end-time judge who rescues believers from the wrath of God. Rather, Jesus mediates the discovery of a wisdom that enables persons to recover the integrity of the human person as created by God. Analysis of Jesus traditions preserved in *Gos. Thom.* provides a variant of the sayings traditions that has not been recast to accommodate a Son of Man Christology as in Q. Nor have the sayings been accommodated to the narrative framework of the canonical Gospels, which focus on the passion and resurrection of Jesus.

SAYINGS OF THE WISE

The *Gospel of Thomas* belongs to the genre of "sayings of the wise." It represents a compilation of sayings similar to collections found in Proverbs or Sirach. The traditional wisdom collections instructed the young, usually males of the governing or aristocratic class, in the conduct that would lead to a successful life. Such collections are loosely organized: a particular theme or catchword may link several sayings; the same theme may return after a transition to other topics; and collections of sayings can easily be expanded. Sometimes a secondary saying is brought in to comment on the saying that comes before it. Within the whole collection sayings may appear to contradict one another.

The *Gospel of Thomas* exhibits many of the features of this genre. The saying about the dog and the manger (log. 102), which is used as a woe against the Pharisees (cf. Matt 23:13), appears in Greek literature attributed to Aesop as well as in Latin fables. *Gos. Thom.* 39a preserves the Synoptic saying against the Pharisees. Clearly, this Greek proverb has been reapplied in the form of a traditional saying of Jesus.

The "woe" against the Pharisees also indicates another modification of the wisdom type of saying. In wisdom traditions that function as general instruction, the "beatitude" refers to the wise person, who is successful in this life. Its opposite is the proverb which describes the evils that happen to someone who is foolish. Most humans, it is implied, fall into the latter category. When the sayings of the wise become the guide to the experience of salvation, beatitudes refer to those who achieve that goal. The failure implied by the woe oracle is no longer the disaster that overtakes the fool but an offense against God. Those who fall under its interdiction may be successful by conventional human standards. Consequently, the beatitudes and woes in both the Synoptic sayings and *Gos. Thom.* take on the form of prophetic sayings that refer to entry into or exclusion from the kingdom.

Though secular wisdom collections like Proverbs or Sirach may be attributed to particular sages, the "authority" of much of their advice stems from the coherence between the sayings and the cultural experiences of those who repeat them. No religious authority is required to support the persuasive impact of the comparison of a beautiful but foolish woman to a gold ring in a pig's nose (Prov 11:22). Proverbs may appear timeless, yet their images and values confirm the dominant understanding of order and goodness in a given culture.

Proverbial wisdom may serve to uphold a particular religious order, as in Sirach's praise of the Torah (cf. Sir 32:24–33:3). But it may also be pressed into service to shatter an audience's conviction about the established certainties or religious convention as in Jesus' saying about the physician (Mark 2:17). Or an apparent proverb may present the reader with a paradox that forces one to question conventional wisdom. Sir 7:4 warns against asking God for high office. *Gos. Thom.* 81 combines an apparent injunction to rule with renunciation of power. The warning that it is necessary to "hate" parents in order to be worthy of salvation (*Gos. Thom.* 55, 101; Luke 14:25–26; Matt 10:37) shatters the filial pieties commonly enshrined in the wisdom tradition (e.g. Sir 3:1–16).

Insofar as gnomic sayings challenge conventional wisdom or piety, the authority of the speaker must be established. The prologue to *Gos. Thom.* sets the whole collection under the authority of the "living Jesus," that is, Jesus as a spiritual or divine being (cf. log. 59; 111). Sayings that unmask the apparent wisdom of accepted leaders as folly also affirm the authority of the voice which utters such sayings (e.g., log. 3, 43). Jesus' coming to a drunken humanity that does not thirst for what he brings (log. 28) echoes images of Wisdom's futile attempt to enlighten humanity (e.g., *1 Enoch* 42). Since the meaning of these sayings is hidden and must be diligently sought out (Prologue and log. 1), the hearer should not expect them to be common knowledge.

PROVENANCE

Many of our clues about the implied author and communal context of the Synoptic Gospels come from the narrative material they contain. Without such narrative elements, scholars have used the attribution of the collection to "Judas, called Thomas" (*P.Oxy.* 654, Prologue) or "Didymos, Judas Thomas" (Prologue) as an indication that the second-century compilation stems from eastern Syria. The terms "didymos" and "thomas" are simply variants of the term "twin." Judas, the brother of Jesus (Matt 13:44; Mark 6:3; Jude 1) came to be identified as Jesus' twin (cf. *Thomas the Contender* 138.7–8; *Acts of Thomas;* Eusebius, *Church History* 3.13.11).

Though the Prologue merely asserts that Jude Thomas is the scribe who recorded the words of Jesus, his understanding of those sayings is superior to that of the other disciples of Jesus. Logion 13 indicates that Thomas has drunk from the spring of wisdom. Consequently, his understanding of Jesus is superior to that exhibited by Peter and Matthew. Thomas no longer requires Jesus as teacher. The juxtaposition of this saying with log. 12, which directs the disciples to James the Just as leader, may indicate a conflict over authority. James appears in other Nag Hammadi texts as the privileged recipient of Jesus' teaching (e.g., *Apocryphon of James* 1.8–35; *First Apocalypse of James* 24.1–18; *Second Apocalypse of James* 56.14–57.1). Whatever the original context of log. 12, the final editor of *Gos. Thom.* presents Thomas as one who no longer needs such a leader or teacher.

The *Acts of Thomas,* which were composed in Syria, present Jude Thomas as the identical twin of Jesus (chap. 11). His mission contributes to the redeeming work of Christ, since it destroys the serpent's hold over humanity (chap. 31). Thomas has received the hidden words of Jesus and become the source of life for people as far away as India (chap. 39). This narrative picture of Thomas fits the picture of the apostle that is suggested by the sayings in *Gos. Thom.* Consequently, a Syrian provenance for the second-century collection that makes up *Gos. Thom.* seems likely.

Acts of Thomas expounds a radically encratite theology. Couples must renounce marriage and sexual passion, which separates an individual from God. Home, family, and wealth are also rejected. Sayings of Jesus which challenged conventional human attachments are easily read as summons to a world-renouncing asceticism. *Gos. Thom.* preserves a number of these sayings. The body is a place of poverty opposed to what is spiritual (log. 29, 56, 80, 112). Those engaged in trade will not enter the kingdom (log. 64). Money is to be given away, not used to make more money (log. 95, 110). Disciples must be on guard against the world (log. 21). Consequently, most scholars think that *Gos. Thom.* belongs to an ascetic tradition.

It is difficult to draw conclusions about the communal context of *Gos. Thom.* from the sayings, themselves. Ascetic groups that claim access to hidden or secret knowledge are often internally stratified. Several attempts to detect levels of perfection in *Gos. Thom.* have succeeded in raising questions about the common perception of the Thomas community as a group of individual ascetics and interpreters. We have already seen that log. 12 and 13 indicate a hierarchy of understanding among the disciples. Thomas is the model for those who have attained the goal of drinking from the wisdom that flows from Jesus. This person no longer needs teachers.

Gos. Thom. acknowledges the existence of alleged Christian teachers who are ignorant of the way to find the kingdom. Such teachers should be rejected (log. 3). Between the ignorant who distort Jesus' teaching and the enlightened who have found the meaning of Jesus' teaching lie those who are in the process of seeking and finding the teaching that leads to life. Logion 37 refers to being naked and trampling "garments of shame." This expression probably indicates that persons were initiated into the community through a baptismal ritual. Some interpreters have proposed that log. 2 indicates four levels of membership: (1) "those who seek," outsiders who may join the community; (2) "those who find and are troubled," junior members of the community; (3) "those who are troubled and marvel," older members of the community, who may have passed through an additional rite; (4) "those who marvel and rule," the perfect or fully enlightened. Similar levels of stratification are clearly evident in the community rules from Qumran.

Some of the sayings in the collection may indicate rules that were still enforced in the community. Fasting and circumcision as Jewish practices are rejected (log. 6, 14). The sayings against trade and lending at interest may also have been communal rules. An enigmatic set of sayings refer to eating living things (log. 7, 11, 60). Contrary to the vegetarianism of the Manichean elect, these sayings seem to permit eating any kind of animal flesh. Whatever is eaten by the enlightened is assimilated to their higher, spiritual reality.

A FEMINIST CRITIQUE

The sayings collection genre makes it difficult to contextualize particular injunctions. Are women held responsible for the constraints of sexuality, pursuit of wealth and family, which the ascetics renounce? Or does *Gos. Thom.* advocate a liberation from the constraints of society that transcends the inequalities of gender and class? *Gos. Thom.* is ambiguous when it comes to questions of women's experience. Although women disciples can attain as much insight into Jesus' teaching as the most enlightened male disciples, women's experience as such is devalued. To attain wisdom, women must assimilate to the pattern forged by male ascetics (log. 114). If becoming a "solitary one" means hating family in the literal sense of renouncing all ties to family (log. 55), the situation of women in ancient society implies that fewer females than males will be able to adopt that life-style.

If most women lacked the social possibility of adopting new forms of life, the critique of traditional values and wisdom in many of the sayings would not necessarily liberate them. A further issue emerges from the confluence of feminist critique with liberation theology, the question of class. The poor and oppressed are not necessarily liberated by the same calls to renounce wealth and follow Jesus which inspire young males of secure means like Anthony or Augustine. Without the clues provided by a narrative context, it is impossible to draw firm conclusions about wealth and class from *Gos. Thom.*; however, some sayings do suggest that persons of some power and wealth are addressed (log. 81, 95, 110).

Feminist theology reminds us that the image of God projected by a text also passes value judgments on womens' experience. Although *Gos. Thom.* occasionally identifies Jesus with the feminine divine Wisdom, its image of God is entirely patriarchal. God is always referred to as "Father." Little other imagery is used for God, since the Father is said to be manifest through a light that obscures the divine image (log. 83). Since light shining within the person is another image for salvation, this image makes God, the Father, the ultimate source of redemption.

Soteriology in *Gos. Thom.* focuses on the transformation of the believer back into the God-given image of the human. The collection as we have it, however, clearly understands that process as one that proceeds from male experience. It may even be the case that the primary liberation experienced by those who seek the kingdom is that of a relatively privileged elite anxious to strip aside the ties that bound them in the complex web of relationships and obligations typical of Greco-Roman society. As a message of liberation for women and the poor oppressed in that society, *Gos. Thom.* has little to offer.

COMMENTARY

Attempts have been made to discover outlines for *Gos. Thom.* The loose organization of the sayings collection genre makes that task almost impossible. We will comment on groups of sayings when they are associated by a common theme or catchword.

SEEK WHAT IS HIDDEN (PROLOGUE AND LOGIA 1–5)

Prologue. The prologue identifies the divine Jesus as the source of the sayings that follow. Jesus' twin, Jude/Thomas, is the fictive author of the collection. Although the expression "hidden words" is often taken to imply esoteric Gnostic tradition, it may also be a variant of the Synoptic claim that Jesus' parables are "hidden" from outsiders (cf. Mark 4:10–12).

Logion 1. Finding the meaning of Jesus' words leads to immortality. This saying is close to the saying in John 8:51–52. John's version ignites a controversy over Jesus' claim to divinity. Here the saying expresses the soteriology behind the sayings collection (cf. log. 18, 19, 85, 111).

Logion 2. Distantly related to Synoptic sayings about seeking and finding (e.g., Matt 7:8; cf. log. 92, 94), this saying consists of a graded series of five members, in the Greek version: seek, find, be amazed, rule, and attain rest (*P.Oxy.* 654.2). The Coptic version inserts "be troubled" between find and be amazed. It concludes with "reign over the universe." Sayings attributed to the *Gospel of the Hebrews* include the sequence "be amazed, rule, and rest," which appears in the Greek (Clement of Alexandria, *Stromateis* 2.9.45,5; 5.14.96,3).

The Coptic version may reflect an earlier version of the saying. Philo observes that the self-knowledge of the wise is recognition that one is a king and is one who rules (*Migration of Abraham* 8). 1 Cor 4:8 employs that tradition in a sarcastic rejection of the Corinthians' claim to have attained wisdom in Christ. "Reigning over the universe" might also be an allusion to the dominion that God bestows on Adam in Gen 1:26.

Some interpreters have suggested that the graded series reflects stages of progress within the community. Those who seek are outsiders who may become members. The other groups represent novice members, senior members, and the fully enlightened elect.

Logion 3. This saying combines a series of sayings about the kingdom. The Synoptic parallels (cf. Matt 24:23–28; Luke 17:23; Mark 13:21–23) suggest that the opening reference to the birds and fish derives from a tradition that rejected signs of the coming kingdom. The editor of the collection may have shifted a more general reference, "if anyone says . . ." to the specific assertion that community leaders make this false claim. *Gos. Thom.* consistently rejects an apocalyptic understanding of the kingdom. The kingdom is present to be found by those who seek and find it (cf. log. 51, 113).

The sequence "not in the sky, not in the sea but in the heart" echoes the saying on the law in Deut 30:11–14. The same tradition was applied to Christ in Rom 10:6–10. Instead of asking who would go to fetch the law if it were in the sky or beyond the sea, this saying has an ironic intensity: birds and fish would get into the kingdom before humans. Such images are characteristic of primitive sayings of Jesus.

The second half of the saying indicates where and how the kingdom is found. It appears to be an expansion of a tradition like Luke 17:21 and another maxim that refers to "knowing as one is known [by God]." 1 Cor 13:12 cites that maxim as the eschatological culmination of Christian faith. For *Gos. Thom.* this goal is attained when the disciple discovers the divine image within.

The concluding contrast between self-knowledge and poverty may have derived from the image of the wise person as the true king (cf. 1 Cor 4:8). Log. 29 treats the spirit dwelling in flesh as "poverty."

Logion 4. The first saying reverses the wisdom convention that children must listen to the instruction of their elders. A child so young that it is not even circumcised will instruct the elders about the "place of life." Some interpreters have suggested that the image originated in speculation about the miraculous, messianic child or the extraordinary birth of figures like Noah and Moses. The contrast between the old man and child may have a polemic intent similar to "your leaders" in the previous logion. This "old man" does not stand on social prestige. He will ask the child rather than be excluded. The common saying "the last shall be first" (cf. Mark 10:31; Matt 19:30; 20:16; Luke 13:30) has been corrected to point to the unity that is the goal of recovering the divine image (cf. log. 22).

Logion 5. A variant on seeking and finding promises that what is hidden will be revealed. This promise is intensified by the promise that what is hidden will come to light. The latter appears attached to sayings about the lamp in the Synoptic tradition (cf. Mark 4:22//Luke 8:12; Matt 10:26//Luke 12:2). The catchword "hidden" recalls the "hidden words" of the Prologue.

The Greek version has an anomalous expansion to the saying on what is hidden: "Nothing is buried that is not raised up" (*P.Oxy.* 654.31).

RULES OF CONDUCT (LOGIA 6 AND 7)

Logion 6. Repetition of the saying about what is hidden being revealed links log. 6 with log. 5. Here that saying has an eschatological cast: humans cannot hide sinful behavior, since it will be revealed. The disciples request instruction on the fundamental elements of Jewish piety, fasting, alms, prayer, and kosher rules (cf. Matt 6:1–18). The introductory question belongs to the genre of school dialogue. It resembles the request of the rich man (cf. Matt 19:16–22; Luke 18:18–22). Log. 14 provides rules relative to these practices.

Jesus' response, "do not do what you hate," echoes the golden rule (Luke 6:39; Matt 7:12). "Do not lie" may be an even more distant allusion to the injunction to always speak honestly (Matt 5:37). Contrasted with a question about external pious practices, the commands to attend to one's moral conduct toward others also reflect a contrast between ritual purity and holiness found elsewhere in the Jesus tradition (cf. Mark 7:1–23).

Logion 7. This peculiar beatitude about the human and the lion is often allegorized. The lion can symbolize the passions that lead the soul away from the divine (so Plato, *Republic* 50.25–51.10). Or the lion symbolizes the satanic adversary, who attempts to lead the righteous astray (so 1 Pet 5:8–9). Allegorical readings do not explain the element of transformation by eating. This odd image may have been provoked by the question of diet in log. 6. Humans have no need of peculiar kosher rules, since they transform anything they eat. The striking asymmetry in the imagery: humans do not eat lions, but lions may eat humans, underlines the absurdity of the initial question.

TWO PARABLES: FISHERMAN AND SOWER (LOGIA 8–10)

Logion 8. Matt 13:47–50 treats this parable as an allegory for the separation of the evil from the righteous at the end-time. A variant story in Aesop (*Fable 4*) focuses on the necessary loss of small fish in order to obtain big ones. The person who tries to avoid all losses in life will never attain anything great. *Gos. Thom.* preseves a more primitive version of the wisdom parable than Matthew. Finding one's destiny or finding the kingdom is no more difficult than a fisherman tossing out the small fish in order to keep the good ones.

Logion 9. This version of the parable of the sower (cf. Mark 4:2–9; Matt 13:3–9; Luke 8:4–8) contains the basic structure of Jesus' parable without the expansions that developed from the allegorical interpretation found in the Synoptics. As it was retold, *Gos. Thom.* added worms to the catalogue of agricultural dangers.

Logion 10. A fuller version of this saying appears in log. 16. *Gos. Thom.* may have appended this version (cf. Luke 12:49) to the parable of the sower as an interpretation of the act of sowing.

THE WORLD PASSES AWAY (LOGION 11)

Logion 11. The Synoptic tradition contrasted the eternity of Jesus' word with the passing of the universe (Mark 13:30–31; Matt 5:18; Luke 16:17; 21:32–33). This variant intensifies the emphasis on the transitory nature of all things by speaking not of "heaven and earth" but of "both heavens," the visible heaven of stars and planets and the invisible one, which contained the pattern for the visible. The second saying, about the dead and the living, invokes a common theme in *Gos. Thom.*: those who have found their true nature do not die (cf. John 11:26). Associated with eating what is dead, this saying refers to the question of diet. The elect transform anything they eat.

The second half of the saying refers to the goal of returning to the beginning. One discovers the light within and recovers the unity of the divine image in Adam. This reference is posed as a question to disciples still trapped in the duality of the material world.

AUTHORITY IN THE COMMUNITY (LOGION 12–13)

Logion 12. This saying preserves an early Jewish Christian tradition about the authority of James. Jewish tradition held that the world was created for the sake of the law, Moses, or Abraham. James replaces them. He is the recipient of Jesus' hidden wisdom in other Gnostic texts (cf. *Apocryphon of James* 1.8–35; *First Apocalypse of James* 24.1–18). There, as in 1 Cor 15:7, his authority is linked to visions of the risen Christ. *Gos. Thom.* refers to James's preordained place in God's plan. Unlike *Gos. Thom.*, which never includes women in the leadership of the community, other Gnostic James traditions were said to have been transmitted through four women, Salome, Mariam, Martha, and Arsinoe (*First Apocalypse of James* 40.22–26). Salome and Mary are among the elect in *Gos. Thom.*

Logion 13. Parallel to Peter's confession in the Gospels (Mark 8:27–30; Matt 16:13–20; Luke 9:18–22), this short dialogue poses a challenge to the disciples who must pose an appropriate parable or simile for Jesus. The two "false" answers of Peter and Matthew compare Jesus to what is in the created order: a revealing angel or a philosopher. Thomas acknowledges Jesus' divine nature by insisting that he cannot give such a simile. The divine name is unutterable.

Where Matt 16:17–20 had a blessing on Peter and confirmation of his status in that community, *Gos. Thom.* affirms the insight of Thomas. He no longer needs a teacher because he has drunk from the waters of wisdom that come from Jesus (cf. John 4:13–15; 7:38). Jesus' hidden revelation would lead to hostility on the part of the other disciples, so it is not given to them. *Apocryphon of James* contains the same motif. James even disperses the other disciples from Jerusalem because of their anger over "those about to be born" (= enlightened Gnostics; *Apocryphon of James* 16.2–11). *Gos. Thom.* asserts the truth of its tradition against the counterclaims of those who appeal to Matthew and Peter.

RULES OF CONDUCT (LOGIA 14–16)

Logion 14. Log. 14a returns to the earlier question about fasting, prayer, and almsgiving (log. 6a). Log. 14c picks up the question of food: nothing defiles except what comes from within (cf. Mark 7:15). This tradition repudiates the authority of Jewish custom rather than reformulating it as in Matt 6:2–18. The reference to alms may have drawn on the instruction for wandering disciples in log. 14b (cf. Luke 10:8). They are to be content with what others give them. In the Synoptics this rule applies to wandering missionaries. *Gos. Thom.* lacks that setting, though it retains the healing mission of the disciple. Wandering and dependence on others for food are the general condition of disciples who have no ties of family or trade.

Logion 15. The "one not born of woman" points to the heavenly Adam as image of God. This saying picks up the question of prayer. The disciple may worship only the true image of God; however, use of the expression "your Father" indicates that this image is not an androgynous mother-father as in some Gnostic texts (e.g., *Apocryphon of John* CG II 5,4–11).

Logion 16. Two sayings were combined in the primitive tradition: division on earth and within the household. Both also appear separately (for division as "fire" cast on earth, cf. log. 10; for dissent within the household, cf. Mark 13:12). *Gos. Thom.* preserves a more concise variant of the Q tradition (cf. Luke 12:49–53; Matt 10:34–39); however, this version may have been simplified to exclude the references to the female members of the household that we find in Q (Luke 12:53; Matt 10:37). Luke's version envisages the possibility that women will have to make the choice of discipleship and may be divided from each other over its consequences. Matthew has shifted to a purely male point of view. The affection a man feels for his mother or daughter may keep him from wholehearted devotion to Jesus.

A wisdom saying preserved in Mic 7:5–6 warning that no human relationships can be trusted includes quarrels between women members of the family. When *Gos. Thom.* limits its perspective to fathers and sons, it suggests that the "solitary one," the true disciple, is a male who has renounced the claims of his family. This tradition is clearly secondary to the Q version of this saying.

SAYINGS ON SALVATION (LOGIA 17–20)

Logion 17. This wisdom saying distinguishes God's plan from human understanding, which appears in Paul as a free-floating citation with scriptural authority (1 Cor 2:9; loosely related to Isa 64:4; 65:16). Paul used this saying to affirm the message of salvation through the crucified Christ. *Gos. Thom.* develops a soteriology that has no connection to the passion/resurrection creed. The saying presents Jesus as the agent through whom believers recover the divine image. (On the "invisibility" of the divine, cf. log. 83.)

Logion 18. A question from the disciples introduces two sayings about salvation. The goal is in the beginning, recovering the immortal image of God. Jesus' response corrects the disciples' assumption that they should look for the "end," some future event of salvation. In *Gos. Thom.* salvation is a return to the divine state of Adam (e.g., log. 2, 84).

The beatitude on the person who "stands upright" in the beginning evokes a widespread ascetic, philosophic, and mystical theme. "Standing upright" in the presence of the divine indicates that one has transcended the disordered movements and passions engendered by the material world and the body. Taken as an allusion to the Genesis story, "standing upright" might refer to the Jewish tradition that when God first formed Adam, he lay on the ground, an immobile protoplast. Adam was able to stand upright when God blew into his nostrils. This interpretation of Gen 2:7 appears in a number of Gnostic accounts (cf. *Apocryphon of John* CG II 19,22–28).

Logion 19. This saying opens with an abbreviated beatitude that refers back to log. 18. Log. 19b equates becoming a disciple with hearing the words of Jesus (cf. log. 38a). The ministering stones allude to the dominion over the universe acquired by the elect (cf. log. 2, 106). The Adam/paradise theme is continued in the reference to the life-giving trees. They are linked with the immortality of the divine by their unchanging stability. In some Gnostic texts (cf. *Books of Jeu* 50, p. 119.22–27) the five trees are part of a series of transcendent entities along the ascent to the divine. Much later Chinese Manichean texts associate the five noetic faculties with the trees of paradise. Philo had interpreted the reference to the midst of the wood of paradise in Gen 3:8 as the mind (*Allegorical Interpretation* 3.28).

Logion 20. The disciples' request for a metaphor for the kingdom elicits a variant of the parable of the mustard seed (Mark 4:30–32; Matt 13:31–32; Luke 13:18–19).

JESUS' DISCIPLES (LOGIA 21–24)

Logion 21. Mary's request for an image of the disciples echoes Jesus' request in log. 13. The first image evokes the theme of children as presocial beings able to divest themselves of ownership, clothing, and all the other marks of integration into a society (cf. log. 37).

The metaphor of the thief entering the strong man's house brings together sayings that appear separately in the Synoptic tradition (plundering the strong man [Mark 3:37; Luke 11:21–22; Matt 12:29; also log. 35]; knowing the hour of the thief's break-in [Luke 12:39–40]). The Christian Testament uses the image of the thief in parenesis that refers to the coming of the parousia (e.g., 1 Thess 5:2; Rev 3:3; 16:15). The audience is urged to be on guard because the time of the end is unknown (Luke 12:35–37). *Gos. Thom.* provides a different application. One must watch out for the power that the world and its rulers can exercise over a person. For a Gnostic reader, the "robbers" must be the demonic archons, who are responsible for the divided state of human life in the material world. Interpreted in this context, shedding garments can refer to shedding the body and the associated psychic powers and passions that imprison the soul. *Apocryphon of John* has the archons use an "imitation spirit," which operates through sexual desire to accomplish their goal (CG II 24,26–31).

Another eschatological image, that of the reaper at harvest time (Joel 3:13), concludes this extended section. Since *Gos. Thom.* does not contain apocalyptic eschatology, the image must refer to decisive action by the disciple in the present.

Logion 22. The imagery of infants prior to the division introduced by socialization continues. Jesus compares entering the kingdom to becoming like a small baby nursing. The command to become like a child to enter the kingdom appears in the Synoptics (Mark 10:13–15; Matt 19:13–15; Luke 18:15–17). Here it serves to introduce the soteriological image of attaining the unity of the heavenly Adam (cf. log. 46). The divergence between that image and the "image" of the earthly Adam is made evident in the paradoxical statement requiring a replacement of the earthly image and its limbs with the heavenly one. This image transcends the gender division that marks all earthly humans. For Valentinian Gnostics this process was associated with a ritual of the "bridal chamber" (*Gospel of Philip* 70.9-30).

The overcoming of gender division was attached to early Christian initiation rituals (cf. Gal 3:28–29). This understanding of "birth through the Spirit" could imply a purely masculine act of creation (so *Gospel of Philip* 58.17–32). Giving birth through human mothers is to cease. Jesus was said to have revealed the end of human procreation to Salome (*Excerpta ex Theodoto* 67.2).

Logion 23. The image of the "solitary one" recurs in a saying that refers to the election of Jesus' disciples. The emphasis on Jesus' choice of the disciples appears in several sayings from John (John 6:70; 15:16, 18). It implies a choice that sets the disciples at odds with a hostile world. By adding the numerical figures, *Gos. Thom.* indicates that the elect are a very small minority among the masses of humanity (also *Pistis Sophia* 134). The issue of the small number of the elect surfaces in an apocalyptic context in 4 Ezra (e.g., 4:45–61). In the end, the whole of creation is for the elect minority which attains salvation. The majority vanish like mist or smoke.

Logion 24. Sayings about the lamp appear in a number of Synoptic variants (Matt 5:14–16; Matt 6:22–23) as well as in the Johannine imagery of Jesus as light of the world (John 1:9; 3:19; 8:12). Johannine tradition also provides a variant on the disciples' request to be shown the place where Jesus is, that is, with the Father in glory (John 14:3). The response suggests that Jesus can only be found when a person discovers the divine image within.

RULES OF CONDUCT (LOGIA 25–27)

Logion 25. This is a variant of the love command (e.g., Mark 12:31), formulated to emphasize solidarity in the community of male disciples, loving the brother rather than the neighbor (cf. 1 John 2:10). The parallel expression derives from depictions of God's love in the Hebrew Scriptures (e.g., Deut 32:10).

Logion 26. This proverbial saying is an explication of the love command rather than the related prohibition against judging others, as in the Synoptics (e.g., Matt 7:3–5).

Logion 27. Though other rules reject the Jewish practices of fasting and prayer (e.g., log. 6, 14, 104), this saying provides a symbolic rendering for these practices. "Fasting" is rejecting the world. The "sabbath" refers to the heavenly rest that accompanies the vision of the divine (cf. the heavenly rest in Heb 4:9–10).

Jesus' Preaching in the World (Logia 28–42)

Logion 28. Jesus' appearance in the world is compared to that of Wisdom herself. In this wisdom saying, humans are too blind and intoxicated to desire the waters of wisdom (cf. log. 13, 108; cf. *1 Enoch* 42, rejected wisdom; 48:1, the waters of wisdom from which the righteous drink).

Logion 29. Gos. Thom. emphasizes the incompatibility between flesh and spirit (cf. log. 87, 112). The expression of amazement that the two are associated suggests that they cannot have originated in relationship to each other. The two versions of Adam's creation provided the basis for different origins of spirit (= the divine image) and the earthly human being (cf. Philo, *Allegorical Interpretation* 1.31–42).

Logion 30. The Greek version (*P.Oxy.* 1) combines a variant of log. 30 and log. 77b. This version appears to be an attempt to make sense of the otherwise enigmatic saying about Jesus' presence. The "three" are without God, while Jesus is present with the "single one." His presence, like that of God or Wisdom, stretches throughout the universe. The Coptic reference to Jesus' presence where there are "two" or "one" appears to be a variant on the "two or three gathered" of Matt 18:20.

Logion 31. This saying combines two proverbs: no physician heals those who know him (Luke 4:23; Mark 2:17); no prophet is accepted in his own country (e.g., Mark 6:4). Similar proverbs appear in Synoptic apophthegms that deal with rejection of Jesus' mission.

Logion 32. The proverb about the city on the mountain (cf. Matt 5:14) has been expanded with the image of its impregnable fortifications. *Gos. Thom.*

juxtaposes sayings that point to Jesus as rejected Wisdom with those that indicate that his mission cannot fail.

Logion 33. A play on Coptic words for ear/bushel measure allows *Gos. Thom.* to join the command to preach from the housetops what they have heard privately (cf. Luke 12:3) and the proverb about the lamp (e.g., Luke 11:33).

Logion 34. This saying picks up the image of humans who reject Jesus/ Wisdom as blind in log. 28 with a familiar proverb about the blind leading the blind (Luke 6:39; Matt 15:14).

Logion 35. A variant of this saying appears in log. 21.

Logion 36. The Coptic preserves only a short proverbial saying against anxiety about clothing. The Greek preserves a version closer to Q's comments against anxiety, which includes concern over food, the metaphor of the lilies of the field not spinning, the saying about anxiety failing to add to one's stature, and a promise that the disciple will be given a cloak (*P.Oxy.* 655; cf. Luke 12:22–34). The argument by metaphor seems typical of the Jesus tradition. The Coptic tradition may have shortened the longer saying. Provision of food and spinning garments are women's activities. For male ascetics such a saying might be used to reinforce their independence from the cultural relationships with women required to obtain food and clothing.

Logion 37. This explicates the previous saying by repeating the motif of clothing. Unashamed trampling of clothing signifies return to the primordial unity of Adam, which is the condition for the vision of God (cf. log. 21).

Logion 38. This combines a saying about Jesus as revealer of the divine mysteries that all have sought without finding them (cf. Luke 10:23–24) and Jesus/Wisdom's departure from the world (cf. Luke 17:22; John 7:34).

Logion 39. This combines a saying against the Pharisees for rejecting knowledge and keeping others from finding it (cf. Luke 11:52) with a warning to the disciples (cf. Matt 10:16). This saying suggests that religious authorities might still influence the disciples of Jesus to reject the teaching contained in this collection.

Logion 40. This saying appears in connection with that about blind guides in Matt 15:14. *Gos. Thom.* suggests that the apparent authority of the opposing religious leaders is not rooted in God. Their teaching will not last.

Logion 41. Another common proverb (cf. Mark 4:25; Luke 8:18; 19:26) picks up the image of eventual loss from the previous saying.

Logion 42. A thematic element throughout the collection has been the need for the disciples to renounce all ties to the world, the body, and society. Their gain is realized only in the "wealth" of the renewed divine image, not in this world.

WISE AND FOOLISH DISCIPLES (LOGIA 43–52)

Logion 43. The traditional proverb concerned the fruit borne by good and bad trees (e.g., Luke 6:43). *Gos. Thom.* has created a paradoxical proverb intended to reject the "folly" of those disciples who ask Jesus by what authority he gives his revelation. (For the question of authority, cf. Mark 11:28, where Jesus responds with a counterquestion about the Baptist's authority.) Gnostic authors frequently used the expression "Jews" to refer to orthodox Christians. The hearer is expected to resist being identified with them.

Logion 44. This shifts from the apocalyptic reference of the Synoptic saying (Mark 3:28–30) to a spatial image, earth and heaven. Attached to the previous saying, log. 44 implies that persons who speak against the authority of Jesus' revelation are condemned. (In the Synoptics, Jesus' exorcisms create the controversy for this saying.)

Logion 45. The traditional proverb about the tree and its fruit is used to create the paradoxical response in log. 43 (cf. Luke 6:44–45; Matt 7:16).

Logion 46. This variant of the Synoptic saying about John the Baptist (cf. Luke 7:28) has been reshaped by the soteriology of *Gos. Thom.* Entering the kingdom implies recovering the true image of Adam by becoming like a child (cf. log. 22).

Logion 47. The first part of this saying is analogous to the saying about serving two masters in Q (Luke 16:13). The saying about the new and old garments or wineskins appears in the Synoptic context of a comparison between John the Baptist's disciples and those of Jesus (cf. Luke 5:33–39).

Logion 48. This saying substitutes the soteriology of *Gos. Thom.*, making "the two one" in a traditional saying about the power of faith (cf. Luke 17:6). If this saying was taken from an independent wisdom source, "two making peace in a house" might have referred to the difficulty of obtaining harmony in a household.

Logion 49. This beatitude expresses the soteriology of *Gos. Thom.*

Logion 50. This appears to reflect a typical Gnostic ritual pattern: questions the soul must answer to escape the demonic guardians on its ascent out of the world (cf. *First Apocalypse of James* 33.11–34.1). Some interpreters suggest that *Gos. Thom.* understands "them" as hostile religious authorities. The enigmatic conclusion, "movement and repose," contrasts divine stability and the error of humanity, which demands a sign (cf. log. 3).

Logion 51. Since "immortality" belongs to the soul that recovers its divine image through Jesus' revelation, the question indicates that the disciples are still ignorant about salvation (cf. John 5:24).

Logion 52. The disciples' ignorance continues to be demonstrated by thinking that Jesus' revelation could be found in the Hebrew prophets, a view commonly expressed in the Christian Testament (cf. 1 Pet 1:10–12). *Apocryphon of James* argues that prophecy ended with the Baptist (6.21–7.10).

RULES OF CONDUCT (LOGIA 53–60)

Logion 53. This is an independent saying against physical circumcision. The disciples seek the true divine image, which clearly did not involve circumcision. Circumcision of the heart is a sign of the new age (cf. Col 2:11–14; Gal 6:15). Rejecting physical circumcision also implies rejecting ethnic and gender-marked distinctions.

Logion 54. This is a variant of Luke 6:20b.

Logion 55. Disciples must reject all family ties and be willing to suffer (cf. Luke 14:26–27).

Logion 56. Those who reject the world have discovered that it is a mere corpse. This saying may be a development of discipleship sayings similar to Luke 9:57–62.

Logion 57. This is a nonallegorical version of the parable of the Wheat and the Tares (cf. Matt 13:20–34).

Logion 58. This beatitude picks up the motif of "suffering" referred to in log. 55. Other variants of this beatitude appear in 1 Pet 3:14a and Jas 1:12.

Logion 59. Salvation can only be attained in this life. The Johannine tradition contains similar warnings attached to Jesus' departure from the world (cf. John 7:33–34; 8:21; 13:33).

Logion 60. The somewhat enigmatic exchange posed by the Samaritan and the lamb may have originated as a comment on sacrificial rites. Here, the proximity to log. 56, which established the equation of world and corpse, and the conclusion that expands the warning of log. 59, make the image a warning to seek and find life (cf. log. 11). Its eating metaphor also recalls log. 7.

Jesus' Disciples (Logia 61–76)

Logion 61. After the exhortation to seek the place of rest (log. 60), a series of sayings point out true disciples. Logion 61a repeats an eschatological saying about salvation: two persons can be sleeping on the same bed—one will be saved (Luke 17:34). The catchword "bed" initiates a dialogue with Salome. Her question acknowledges Jesus' divine identity and intimacy between herself and the savior. Logion 13 indicates that eating from a table with the savior implies that an individual is enlightened. Possibly a gloss, the "I Am" saying affirms Jesus' identity with God (cf. John 3:35; 5:18).

A final saying describes the disciple as light-filled (cf. log. 24). Even though Salome has shown herself to be a true disciple, this saying uses the masculine singular of the disciple. Salome may be a female heroine for a predominately male group.

Logion 62. This saying combines the understanding of Jesus' teaching as mysteries reserved for the elect (cf. Mark 4:11; Luke 8:9–10) with the saying about the right and left hand (cf. Matt 6:3). True disciples will be careful about disclosing the mysteries of Jesus' teaching to others.

Logion 63. This is a variant of a wisdom parable about the rich man (Sir 11:18–19; Luke 12:16–21).

Logion 64. This variant of the parable of the Great Supper lacks the allegorizing of the Synoptic versions (Luke 14:15–24; Matt 22:1–10). This version reflects the milieu of city life in which persons are primarily concerned with financial and social obligations. The concluding saying warns that business people will not inherit the kingdom.

Logion 65. This saying lacks the allegorical interpretation which makes the parable a condemnation of Israel for rejecting Jesus (cf. Mark 12:1–9). The problem of business and "collecting rent" links this parable to the preceding one. *Gos. Thom.* expects disciples to renounce all business relationships. It does not advocate the tenants' action as a solution to oppressive land ownership. There is no indication that the death of the son is related to the passion of Jesus, as it is in the Synoptics.

Logion 66. The stone rejected by the builders was traditionally attached to the previous parable (cf. Mark 12:10–12).

Logion 67. This is apparently a warning against those who do not discover the image of God within (cf. 1 Cor 13:2).

Logion 68. The conclusion of this blessing on the persecuted (cf. Luke 6:22) is unclear. It may mean that the persecutors will not attain salvation (= finding a place) or that those who persecute will not endure where they now live.

Logion 69. Here are two more beatitudes on the true disciple, the persecuted (Matt 5:8, 10), and the hungry one who is filled (Luke 6:21a).

Logion 70. This saying reformulates the warnings implied in log. 41, 59, 60, 67.

Logion 71. In this generalization of Jesus' warning about the Temple (Matt 26:60; 27:40; Mark 14:58; John 2:19), the "house" may refer to the created, visible world (cf. Heb 3:2–3).

Logion 72. This is a secondary version of an episode that served as a warning against covetousness in Luke (12:13–14). *Gos. Thom.* may see it as a warning against all material possessions and family ties.

Logion 73. This is a traditional saying (cf. Luke 10:2).

Logion 74. This is apparently a condemnation of the majority of persons who do not recognize Jesus as the Wisdom from whom they should receive water (log. 13; for variations on the well imagery, see John 2:7; 4:13–15).

Logion 75. The bridal chamber was an image for salvation among Valentinian Gnostics. This saying may have been developed from Synoptic images (Matt 25:1–13).

Logion 76. This expands the traditional parable about the merchant and the pearl (Matt 13:45–46) with the saying about treasure in heaven (Matt 6:19–21). Since *Gos. Thom.* excludes merchants from the kingdom, the parable cannot appear to praise shrewd money-making activity.

RECOGNIZING THE DIVINE JESUS (LOGIA 77–82)

Logion 77. The all-pervading light (John 8:12) and source of creation, Jesus is God's Wisdom (Sir 24:3–12).

Logion 78. In this saying from the tradition about John the Baptist (cf. Luke 7:24–25), *Gos. Thom.* has reapplied the imagery to show that the wealthy and powerful will never recover the true image of God within.

Logion 79. This combines two traditional sayings. Luke 11:27–28 deflects honor away from Jesus' earthly mother to all who keep the word of God, the true relatives of Jesus (cf. Luke 8:21). The second is an apocalyptic saying: the trials of the end-time will make those who have no children "blessed" (Luke 23:28–29). Since Jesus is not "born of woman" but is the true image of God, the first saying corrects the false view of the women speakers. The second appears to attack the accepted view that women are blessed when they have borne children. But these corrections are not grounded in a view of salvation that elevates the position of women as such.

Logion 80. This is a variant of log. 56.

Logion 81. This saying plays on the philosophical tradition that the wise person is "rich" and "rules all things" (cf. log. 2). Those who have worldly power or wealth are called to renounce it (cf. Mark 10:23).

Logion 82. Returning to the theme of Jesus' presence, with which this section opened, this saying appears as a free floating word of the Lord in antiquity (cf. Origen *In Jerem. hom. lat.* 20.3). It may be a variant of a Greek proverb, "the one near God is near lightning" (Aesop, *Fable* 186).

THE DIVINE IMAGE (LOGIA 83–85)

Logion 83. This saying contrasts earthly images with the light of God, which conceals the image of the Father (cf. 2 Cor 3:18; 4:4–6).

Logion 84. The contrast between image and likeness may be an allusion to Gen 1:26. This saying also depends on the contrast between earthly images and the divine light. The second sentence "corrects" the first (for this style of speech, cf. John 1:50–51). The divine image will cause amazement far beyond the rejoicing that comes from seeing one's likeness.

Logion 85. The disciple who recovers the divine, spiritual image of humanity is superior even to the created, earthly Adam (cf. log. 46).

Separation from the World (Logia 86–90)

Logion 86. This is a traditional saying about the homeless Son of Man (cf. Matt 8:18–22; Luke 9:57–58). "Son of Man" is not a title for Jesus in *Gos. Thom.* The compiler may have seen this saying as evidence of the homelessness of the true disciple.

Logion 87. This is a variant formulation of the opposition between the soul and the body (cf. log. 29).

Logion 88. This saying combines elements from other sayings in the collection. The enlightened disciple is superior to the "angels and prophets" (cf. log. 85). Heavenly figures can only give the soul what it already possesses as its own. The conclusion apparently picks up on the imagery of handing over to the "owners" (i.e., of this world) what they claim belongs to them (cf. log. 21).

Logion 89. This is a traditional saying against purification rituals (cf. Luke 11:39–41). For *Gos. Thom.* nothing done externally to or with the body makes any difference in attaining salvation.

Logion 90. This traditional wisdom saying is applied to Jesus as teacher (cf. Matt 11:28–30).

Seeking and Finding the Divine (Logia 91–95)

Logion 91. Seeking external signs does not reveal Jesus' divine identity (cf. Luke 12:56).

Logion 92. Seeking and finding refers to understanding Jesus' revelation (cf. log. 2; Matt 7:7). The irony of disciples not seeking to know what Jesus could teach them appears in John (16:4b–5).

Logion 93. This is a traditional saying against wasting wisdom or instruction on the foolish (cf. Matt 7:6).

Logion 94. This repeats log. 92.

Logion 95. This saying recasts the canonical tradition (Luke 6:34) so that the point of lending to one who cannot repay becomes one of arranging a method of disposing of property that would keep one from the buying and selling that makes a person unfit for salvation.

Parables about the Kingdom (Logia 96–103)

Logion 96. This is a variant of a Q parable (cf. Luke 13:20–21).

Logion 97. Linked to log. 96 by the imagery of women engaged in bread-making, this saying retains the concrete details of a village woman's daily life. The parable's application to the kingdom is unclear. In contrast to the previous parable, the "hidden" element results in disaster for the woman.

Logion 98. This parable is of the same form as the King Preparing for War and the Tower Builder (Luke 14:28–32), which form part of a complex on the cost of discipleship.

Logion 99. The Lukan analogies to log. 98 follow a saying about "hating" one's family in order to become a disciple. This traditional saying (cf. Luke 8:19–21) continues the frequent demand to renounce all family ties. An indication of the predominately male perspective is evident in the reversed order, "brothers and mother." Luke's version also drops the "sisters" (contrast Mark 3:25).

Logion 100. A concise version of the apophthegm about "rendering to Caesar" (e.g., Mark 12:13–17), this saying has expanded the conclusion with the demand to render to the revealer what is his and has shifted the coinage from the silver denarius to a gold coin. Perhaps the compiler thinks of the first two as examples of monetary obligations (cf. rejection of alms in log. 14). Rejecting all involvement with money, the disciple gives Jesus what is his.

Logion 101. This saying repeats log. 55 (cf. Luke 14:26–27) and then corrects the theme of that saying by referring to a sense in which one's true Father, God, and Mother, Wisdom, are loved (cf. log. 15).

Logion 102. A common proverb about the dog in the manger forms the basis for a woe oracle against the Pharisees (cf. log. 39).

Logion 103. This saying about knowing the hour in which the thief is coming is used as a beatitude (cf. log. 21; Luke 12:39).

Disciples and the Kingdom (Logia 104–14)

Logion 104. The disciples' proposal indicates that they do not recognize Jesus' true nature. Although log. 104b echoes the Synoptic saying (cf. Mark 2:19–20), *Gos. Thom.* does not suggest that Christ could even be taken from the true disciple. Fasting as a sign of repentance for sin is not required of the disciple (cf. log. 14).

Logion 105. Gnostic mythology sometimes referred to Wisdom, the mother of the Gnostic race, as a "harlot" (cf. *Thunder, Perfect Mind* 13.16–23). Wisdom earned this epithet because her passion to imitate the divine Father gave birth to the lower world (cf. *Apocryphon of John* [Codex Berolinensis] 36.17–37.1). The expression "child of fornication" may have been used to denigrate an opponent (as in John 8:41).

Logion 106. This is a variant of log. 48.

Logion 107. This variant of the parable of the Lost Sheep (cf. Matt 18:12–14; Luke 15:3–7) rationalizes the shepherd's action in terms of the size of the lost one, "the largest" and the shepherd's relationship to it, "loved more than the others" (also see *Gospel of Truth* 31.34–32.9).

Logion 108. Jesus is divine Wisdom, from which the disciple drinks (log. 13; cf. John 7:37–38).

Logion 109. This is a version of the parable of the Hidden Treasure (cf. Matt 13:44), which follows the pattern of Jewish treasure stories, which often condemn the loser as "lazy" or provide the finder with a morally redeeming quality. *Gos. Thom.* has not moralized the finder, though his activity, lending money at interest, contradicts the rules for disciples (cf. log. 95).

Logion 110. This variant of log. 81 indicates how the disciple would respond to material wealth.

Logion 111. This variant of log. 11 (cf. Matt 24:34–35) recalls the epithet of Jesus in the Prologue, "the Living One" (cf. John 8:51–52).

Logion 112. This is a variant of log. 87.

Logion 113. This is a variant of log. 3, 51.

Logion 114. The epilogue affirms the possibility of the women disciples' attaining salvation (as demonstrated in log. 21 and 61. See the discussion of this theme in the next section.

WOMEN IN THE *GOSPEL OF THOMAS*

One of the most puzzling aspects of *Gos. Thom.* is the final saying, log. 114. Most scholars agree that this saying belongs to the final redaction of the collection. Peter's hostility to Mary's participation in the community of those who know the secret teaching of Jesus appears elsewhere in Gnostic writings (e.g., *Gospel of Mary* 10.1–9; 17.10–18.15). As in this logion, Gnostic writers elsewhere consistently affirm Mary's position among the elect. Some interpreters have argued that this saying implies an additional stage of initiation for women. Before she can be "worthy of life" or "enter the kingdom"—expressions for attaining salvation in *Gos. Thom.*—the Lord must "make her male."

Gos. Thom. contains only a few sayings in which disciples are actually named (log. 12, 13, 21, 61, 114). We have already seen that log. 12 and 13 deal with degrees of authority and enlightenment among male disciples. According to log. 13, Peter is clearly inferior to Thomas. The reader should anticipate that his proposal to exclude Mary as "not worthy of life" will be a sign of ignorance. The remaining two sayings refer to women, Mary (log. 21) and Salome (log. 61). In both cases the women are clearly disciples whose insight is similar to that of Thomas. The introduction to log. 21 coordinates it with log. 13. In the latter, Jesus tested his disciples by asking them to provide a simile or comparison that expressed what he was like. In the former, Mary poses the same challenge in reverse. Jesus is to provide an image of his disciples. Log. 61 contains a somewhat cryptic exchange between Jesus and Salome. She affirms her status as Jesus' disciple. Jesus' presence reclining and eating at her table indicates that she is one of those who possess light within.

The reader of the collection is certainly prepared to assume that women figure among the enlightened disciples of Jesus. The exchange between Jesus and Peter may indicate that conflict had arisen over the place of women in the community. Unlike Christian Testament traditions that responded to such conflict by curtailing the role of women (e.g., 1 Cor 14:33b–36; 1 Tim 2:9–15), *Gos. Thom.* maintains her place in the community. It may be that additional ritual activity was involved; however, log. 114 clearly affirms that the "inferiority" that might be attributed to woman's creation in Genesis 2 will be overcome in the Lord. She is now a "living spirit," like the Adam of Gen 2:7.

THE HEAVENLY ADAM

As log. 114 indicates, the image of Adam in Genesis plays a crucial role in the anthropology and soteriology of *Gos. Thom.* Jewish exegetical traditions that underlie both Christian Testament and later Gnostic sources distinguished between the Adam of Gen 1:27 and the Adam of Gen 2:7. The former is created male and female in the image of God. As God's image, this Adam is not subject to death. Philo understood the Adam in Gen 2:7 as a material copy of the heavenly Adam in Gen 1:27. The material Adam is gendered and subject to mortality.

The soteriological process in *Gos. Thom.* seeks to recover the immortal image of the heavenly Adam. This likeness is the image of God, which is always hidden from those who look only to what is visible (log. 83, 84). The disciple who recovers this image is even superior to the Adam of Genesis 2 (log. 85). *Gos. Thom.* preserves a number of sayings in which the disciples take on attributes of children (log. 45). Contrary to conventional wisdom, in which the child is to listen respectfully to the elders, the elders will learn about the kingdom from a child seven days old (log. 4). This infant is even too young to be circumcised as a male. Nursing infants are an image of "making the two one" in order to enter the kingdom (log. 22). The gender distinctions as well as all the other physical characteristics of the mortal adult are transformed. Children are unashamedly naked, just as the new initiate must trample his/her old garments under foot (log. 21, 37).

Throughout *Gos. Thom.*, recovering the true image of God, penetrating the hidden meaning of Jesus' words, or entering the kingdom is equivalent to attaining life. Becoming a solitary, "single one" rather than divided and mortal implies that the elect cannot die (log. 111). This state is not the eschatological delivery from death at the end of the world that we commonly find in Jewish and early Christian apocalyptic. Instead, *Gos. Thom.* points back to the primordial beginning. One who comes to know the beginning—that is, the heavenly image of Adam—knows the end and will not die (log. 18, 19).

Although the Adam of Gen 1:27 is frequently spoken of by scholars as "androgyne," the imagery of *Gos. Thom.* does not support that usage. The images of transformation, whether substituting new bodily limbs for those of the old creation or reverting to the asexual condition of small children, are not androgynous. The only possible argument for androgyny in *Gos. Thom.* would be drawn from its two references to a "bed" or "bridal chamber" (log. 61 and log. 75). In the former, the dialogue with Salome, Salome is clearly made a disciple by Jesus' presence in her chamber. But the imagery is closer to that of the revealing angel who transformed the virgin Aseneth from pagan into proselyte in *Joseph and Aseneth* than to a Valentinian bridal chamber ritual. The latter is an entrance saying derived from other sayings of Jesus about the bridegroom. The solitary *monochos* is the only one permitted to enter the chamber. No indication of a unity of female and male such as one finds in Valentinian texts is implied here either.

Thus, *Gos. Thom.* pursues the same gender asymmetry with regard to the heavenly Adam as it does with regard to the question of whether or not women can belong to the community of the elect. The male, "living spirit" (Gen 2:7), is a necessary but not sufficient condition for salvation. Males must transcend the duality occasioned by the existence of the soul in the material world in order to discover the divine image within. Females may also attain this divine image, but they apparently do so by overcoming those aspects of the feminine which make them appear "unworthy of life." *Gos. Thom.* does not indicate how the difference between males and females is to be construed apart from the allusion to Gen 2:7. Some scholars import comments about the feminine from other Gnostic texts to fill this lacuna; however, it is also possible that the author intends a hierarchical schema like that employed in 1 Cor 11:3-12. Woman is not directly made in God's image but is created out of man.

Gos. Thom. insists that to see one's true image is to discover one "not born of woman" (log. 15). Entering the kingdom by becoming a child implies transcending the condition of being "born of woman" (log. 46). Unlike 1 Cor 11:12, which uses the fact that males are now "born of women" to argue for some interdependence of males and females, *Gos. Thom.* seeks to overcome the effects of that condition. There is no indication that women's experience contributes to the image of the heavenly Adam.

RECOMMENDED READINGS

Buckley, Jorunn Jacobsen. "An Interpretation of Logion 114 in *The Gospel of Thomas.*" *Novum Testamentum* 27 (1985): 245–72.

Kloppenborg, John S., Marvin W. Meyer, Stephen J. Patterson, and Michael G. Steinhauser. *Q Thomas Reader.* Sonoma, CA: Polebridge, 1990.

Layton, Bentley, ed. *Nag Hammadi Codex II, 2–7 together with XII, 2, Brit. Lib. Or. 4926 (1), and POxy 1, 654, 655.* Vol. 1. Nag Hammadi Studies 20. Leiden: Brill, 1989.

Lelyveld, Margaretha. *Les Logia de la Vie dans l'Évangile selon Thomas: A la Recherche d'une Tradition et d'une Rédaction.* Nag Hammadi Studies 34. Leiden: Brill, 1987.

Levine, Amy-Jill. "Who's Catering the Q Affair? Feminist Observations on Q Paraenesis." In *Paraenesis: Act and Form,* edited by Leo G. Perdue and John G. Gammie, 145–61. *Semeia* 50. Atlanta: Scholars Press, 1990.

Ménard, Jacques-É. *L'Évangile selon Thomas.* Nag Hammadi Studies 5. Leiden: Brill, 1975.

Meyer, Marvin W. "Making Mary Male: The Categories 'male' and 'female' in the Gospel of Thomas." *New Testament Studies* 31 (1985): 554–70.

Neller, Kenneth V. "Diversity in the Gospel of Thomas: Clues for a New Direction?" *Second Century* 7 (1989–90): 1–17.

Sevrin, J.-M., "L'évangile selon Thomas: Paroles de Jésus et révélation gnostique." *Revue théologique de Louvain* 8 (1989): 265–92.

The Gospel of John

ADELE REINHARTZ ◆

INTRODUCTION

"IN THE BEGINNING was the Word" (John 1:1). This introduction, like virtually every verse in the Gospel of John, has meant many things to many readers. An allusion to Genesis, a cosmic introduction to the gospel narrative, an indication of Hellenistic influence, a key to Sophia (Wisdom) Christology—these words are all these and more.[1] But to an aficionada of literary criticism, they point, above all, to the primacy of the written word and of the activity of reading, which gives life to the word.

This commentary, which will outline my own reading of the Fourth Gospel, will necessarily be partial, in two senses. First, it will be partial rather than comprehensive, a limitation imposed as much by the complexity of this Gospel and the vast amount of secondary literature as by the finite space and focused task of this particular contribution. Second, it will be partial rather than impartial, expressing my own interests in and outlook on the field and the text, as a participant in the scholarly endeavor, as a Jew, and as a feminist.

My reading of this Gospel has been influenced by the work of other scholars and by the historical-critical concerns that have generally occupied the field. What is the relationship between this Gospel and the Synoptic Gospels, attributed to Matthew, Mark, and Luke? How, why, when, and to whom was the Gospel of John written? I will expand on these and other historical-critical issues as they arise. The primary interest of this commentary, however, lies in the relationship between the text and the reader. This literary-critical focus stems both from my own innate proclivities and from a conviction that reading and readers are central to the concern of this Gospel. This is suggested not only by John 1:1 but also by the statement of purpose in 20:30–31. This passage addresses the readers directly, declaring that this Gospel was written "that you may come to believe that Jesus is the Messiah, the Son of God, and that through believing you may have life in his name." According to this statement, the purpose of the Gospel is rhetorical. It aims not simply to persuade the reader that its claims regarding Jesus are "true" but also, primarily, to inculcate in the reader the worldview expressed in this text. A principal concern of the commentary will therefore be to expose the means by which the Gospel attempts to achieve this goal.

My interests, while supported by a professional assessment concerning the centrality of literary concerns to this text, are focused more narrowly by my identity as a Jew and a feminist. As a Jewish reader, the word "Jew" leaps out at me at every turn; as a feminist reader, I note the characters, symbols, and rhetorical moves that might have shaped the reading of this Gospel by the women among its earliest audience. What this commentary represents, therefore, is my effort to bring these perspectives together in a way that will draw other readers into critical dialogue with this text and with the body of scholarship it has spawned.

Before beginning, however, some brief words about the background and composition of the Gospel are in order. Among the issues for which there is general, though not universal, agreement are the provenance, date, and authorship of the Gospel. Most scholars do not challenge the traditional location of the Gospel in Ephesus or some other large center in Asia Minor in which there would have been a sizable Jewish population. A late first century date for the Gospel is also generally accepted, on both external and internal grounds. The *terminus ad quem* (latest possible date) is generally thought to be 100–110 C.E. This judgment is based on the fact that our earliest fragment from this Gospel, P52, which is probably the earliest extant fragment of the Christian Testament, is dated roughly to 135. Its Egyptian provenance would imply a date of roughly 100 for the writing of the Gospel, on the assumption that it would have taken several decades for this text to reach Egypt.

The *terminus post quem* (earliest possible date) is generally thought to be about 85, on the assumption that 9:22 refers to an expulsion of Jewish-Christians from the synagogue often dated to that year. Those who question this reference, however, still generally hold to a late first century dating, on the assumption that a high Christology and realized eschatology are indicative of a fairly advanced development of theology in the early church.[2]

Although the Gospel claims that the Beloved Disciple is the authoritative witness behind the events recorded therein, many scholars now disregard the traditional identification of the Beloved Disciple with John son of Zebedee and consider the absolute identity of the author to be irretrievable. The relationship between John and the Synoptic Gospels and the historicity of the Fourth Gospel are also extremely problematic. It has been a general consensus that John is not an eye-witness source for the life of the historical Jesus and that the Fourth Gospel betrays no direct dependence on the Synoptic Gospels, though it does share in a general tradition that is reflected in the other three. This consensus is being questioned, however, though I have not yet been convinced that it must be discarded.[3] Similarly problematic is the process of composition that led to the Gospel in its present form. Was there a pre-Johannine signs source on which the author drew in the writing of this text? Are there certain pericopes that are transposed in the final version? Are the theological inconsistencies due to a redactional process? I would answer "maybe" to the first question and "probably not" to the other two.

Most vexing is the question of the historical circumstances that gave rise to this Gospel. Descriptions of Jewish practices, such as ritual handwashing (2:6), and of particular locations, such as Bethzatha (5:2), suggest a writer familiar with both Judaism and the geography of first-century Palestine, while specific phrases, such as the feast "of the Jews," imply an audience to whom Jewish institutions are not familiar. The use of the term *logos* in the prologue is highly suggestive of Hellenistic Jewish philosophy, particularly the work of Philo of Alexandria. Added to this mix are references to diverse religious and ethnic groups, a variety of christological titles and messianic expectations, and the sharp anti-Jewish polemics.

One way to account for this eclecticism is to reconstruct the Johannine community itself. This approach is based on the assumption that the Gospel emerged from, and was addressed to, a particular community. Some scholars, such as Raymond Brown, posit a fully developed community which may or may not have considered itself, or been considered by others, to be sectarian with respect to other Christian groups.[4] The varied language can be accounted for on the basis of the varied backgrounds of those who joined the community at various stages. An ecclesiological reading supports the view that women may have had prominent roles as apostles and disciples within a community that did not draw distinctions along gender lines but rather on the basis of "correct" belief. It is also used to account for the anti-Jewish polemic on the grounds that the Johannine community faced expulsion from the synagogue, though one suspects that scholars may be misled by the usefulness of this theory for discounting the theological basis of Johannine anti-Judaism.

The Johannine community is also drawn into the debate over Johannine theology. Did this community practice the sacraments, as the ample references to living water and the Bread of Life discourse would imply? Or did it not do so, as the absence of the institution of the Eucharist at the Last Supper might suggest? Did the community hold to a realized eschatology, which some later redactor softened by adding references to future eschatology? Or was there a reverse process at work, in which future eschatology was characteristic of the first members of the community, while later adherents held to a realized eschatology? The jury is still out on these questions.

COMMENTARY

For the purposes of this commentary, I have divided the Gospel into seven major blocks. This is not to imply that this structure corresponds in any way to the "intended" structure of the Gospel itself. The prologue (1:1–18) provides a cosmic introduction to the general plot and character groups of the Gospel narrative and announces its christocentric focus. It is followed by a description of the first phase of Jesus' ministry (1:19–3:36), including the call of the first disciples, Jesus' first sign, and his first extended discourse. This phase is framed by the initial testimony and the final curtain call of the Baptist. The second phase of the ministry (4:1–6:71) begins optimistically with the broadening of the base of Jesus' following by the inclusion of the Samaritans, but concludes with the departure of a large number of Jewish followers who ultimately fail to understand or accept Jesus' self-revelation as the bread of life. This sets the stage for the third phase (7:1–10:42), which depicts the hardening of the conflict between Jesus and the Jews. The public ministry reaches its climax and conclusion with several events in the Jerusalem area; here the raising of Lazarus acts as the immediate stimulus for the plot to kill Jesus (11:1–12:50). The sixth section portrays Jesus' final meal with his disciples, highlighted by a footwashing ritual (chap. 13) and several chapters of virtually uninterrupted discourse (14–17). The Gospel ends with a detailed account of the betrayal, trial, crucifixion, and resurrection appearances of Jesus (chaps. 18–21).

Prologue (1:1–18)

The Gospel of John begins with a hymn to the cosmic origins of the Word and a summary of the Word's relationship to, and salvific significance for, the world. At the same time it provides an introduction to the story line of the Gospel narrative, to the major characters and character groups, and to the typically Johannine Christology, language, and symbolism. All of these elements are crucial for the rhetorical thrust of the Gospel.

The prologue traces the relationship between the Word and the world (*kosmos* in Greek). The Word existed before the creation of the world, in that nonworldly realm which God also inhabits (1:1–2). As a partner in God's creation of the world (1:3), it is the creator of life and the "light of all people" (1:4–5). The second phase in this relationship is the Word's entry into the world. This entry is anticipated by John the Baptist, who bears witness to the "light" (1:7). Finally, the Word's departure from the world is implied in 1:18. The Word has returned to be "close to the Father's heart" (NRSV) or "in the bosom of the Father" (RSV), as it was in the beginning.[5]

By opening with an outline of the relationship of the Word to the world, the

Fourth Gospel offers a very different starting point for Christology from that offered by the Synoptic Gospels. Of particular interest from a feminist perspective is the nonpersonal description of the Word. The silence of the prologue concerning the mother of Jesus (though her existence is implied in the notion that the Word became flesh), the use of descriptive language such as Word, light, and life, and the emphasis on preexistence create the image of a being whose gender is not a relevant feature. The Word, who "was with God" and "was God," is, like God, a nongendered entity. From this cosmic perspective, the incarnation, in which "the Word became flesh" (1:14) and hence gendered, is only one relatively short moment in an ongoing, ungendered existence.

Even this nonpersonal description, however, is not completely free from gendered associations. As has often been noted, the Word of the prologue resembles Sophia or "Lady Wisdom" of Jewish wisdom literature. She, like the Word, "came forth from the mouth of the Most High" (Sir 24:3), was "set up, at the first, before the beginning of the earth" (Prov 8:23), and is "fashioner of what exists" (Wis 8:6).[6]

Yet when the ungendered Logos becomes further defined in relation to God, it becomes not female Sophia but the male Son of God. This transition is hinted at in the prologue, in which the Word is the only-begotten one of God (1:18) and its glory of the Word-made-flesh is "as of a father's only son" (1:14). While these comments do not overshadow the prologue's focus on the preexistent creative Word of God, they do anticipate the prominence of Father-Son language throughout the rest of the Gospel.

The prologue provides a cosmic context for the story to come and thereby presents a high Christology. That the Word temporarily became flesh, and thereby a story, is due to its mission: to bring light and knowledge of God to humankind. In order for this mission to be fulfilled, humankind must "see" the light and understand the divine knowledge the Word imparts. Hence, virtually all human characters and character groups in the Gospel are measured by their responses to the Word made flesh.

One aspect of this response involves correctly identifying the specific human individual in whom the Logos is incarnate. As the prologue makes explicit, this individual is "Jesus Christ" (1:17) and not John (the Baptist), who, though sent by God, has the subordinate function of bearing witness to the light. In this way, the prologue steers the reader away from what, from the Johannine perspective, is a false identification of the light in human form.

The cosmic descriptions in the prologue adumbrate two contrasting responses to the incarnate Word: acceptance and rejection. The latter response is alluded to first, in 1:5, "The light shines in the darkness, and the darkness did not overcome it."[7] The sense of conflict with, or at least opposition to, the Word is continued in 1:10–11: "He was in the world, and the world came into being through him; yet the world did not know him. He came to what was his own, and his own people did not accept him."

The identity of those who reject Jesus is implied in the statement that those who reject him are "his own people." A second clue is the contrast between Moses and Jesus in 1:17: "The law indeed was given through Moses; grace and truth came through Jesus Christ." This contrast is implicit in the very term Logos, or Word, itself. The Logos as the divine Word-become-flesh replaces the Torah, the written form of the divine word which came to Moses on Mount Sinai, as authentic revelation of God's will. These clues prepare the reader for the portrayal of the Jews as symbols of opposition in the Gospel narrative.

Those who accept the Word are explicitly contrasted to those who reject it: "But to all who received him, who believed in his name, he gave power to become children of God, who were born not of blood nor of the will of the flesh nor of the will of man, but of God" (1:12–13). In 1:14 the third person references to this group are replaced by the first person plural pronoun "we," thereby including both the narrator and the ideal reader. "We" who have seen the glory of the Word (1:14) receive grace upon grace (1:15), grace and truth (1:17), and knowledge of God the Father (1:18).

In addition to the dualistic and cosmic language, and use of the first person pronoun "we," there is yet another rhetorical feature of the prologue, namely, the layering of stories. The references to John the Baptist, the incarnation, and the rejection of Jesus by his own people belong to the story of the earthly Jesus, the telling of which begins immediately after the conclusion of the prologue. Yet, as many scholars recognize, this is not the only story being told in this Gospel. Alongside these "historical"[8] details are indications that the Gospel also tells the story of the believing community after the death of Jesus. The narrator looks back on the sojourn of Jesus in the world after this sojourn has ended, since the Son is now back in the bosom of the Father. But the references to the community of believers ("we") that accept Jesus and become children of God suggest that the dynamic of acceptance and rejection which was played out in the human lifetime of Jesus is one that still confronts readers in the time after Jesus' departure from the world.

Finally, the cosmic language of the prologue and the emphasis on the Word, its preexistence and its divine place, indicate that the story of the earthly Jesus and of the Johannine community are mere instances in a larger, cosmological tale. The preexistent Word takes its place prior to the story whose narration is begun in Genesis. It is present with God throughout the events detailed in God's earlier Word—the Torah—and now comes to the world sometime after the close of that narrative. In doing so it acts as God's further—and most significant—revelation to the world.[9] This layering of plots invites the readers to place their own personal histories in the same cosmic context and to see the dynamics, conflicts, and dilemmas depicted there as being prototypical of their own.

FIRST PHASE OF THE MINISTRY (1:19–3:36)

The Baptist's Testimony and the Call of the First Disciples (1:19–51)

The coming of the Word into the world is heralded by John the Baptist. In an interview with the priests and Levites, John acts out the part prescribed for him in the prologue, by denying that he is the Messiah and testifying to the light. In telling his Jewish interlocutors that "among you stands one whom you do not know" (1:26), John alludes to 1:10 ("the world did not know him") and thereby identifies the Jews as the unbelieving world.

The next day marks Jesus' first appearance on the scene. After seeing Jesus, John testifies that Jesus is "the Lamb of God, who takes away the sin of the world" (1:29) and explains that this is the one of whom he had spoken in his earlier testimony. The reader thereby recognizes Jesus as the light to which the divinely sent John was to testify (1:6) and therefore as the Word-made-flesh of the prologue.

At this point in John's testimony, a reader familiar with the other Gospels might be surprised to note that the Fourth Gospel does not recount John's baptism of Jesus. Instead, the Baptist states that on a prior occasion he had seen the Spirit descend from heaven like a dove and remain on Jesus, accompanied by a declaration from God that Jesus is the Son of God. This declaration officially introduces the title Son of God as one of the major christological identifiers in this Gospel.

The identification of Jesus as the Lamb of God is repeated in 1:35 in abbreviated form to two of John's disciples. They take it as a hint that they should follow Jesus and spend some time with him. After doing so, they become the first members of the group of those who accept Jesus as the Messiah (1:40). One of the two, Andrew, calls his brother Simon. Simon in turn meets Jesus, who renames him "Cephas." Cephas's response is not recorded, but his prominent appearance among the disciples throughout the Gospel (e.g., 6:68) confirms that he too has become a follower.

This sequence is repeated, though with variations, in the following scenes. In 1:43, Jesus finds Philip in the Galilee and asks him to follow. Philip in turn finds Nathanael and testifies, "We have found him about whom Moses in the law and also the prophets wrote" (1:45). Nathanael then meets Jesus, who calls him "an Israelite in whom there is no deceit." In response, Nathanael confesses him to be the Son of God, king of Israel.

This section has both christological and ecclesiological implications. The concentration of christological titles (Lamb of God, Son of God, Messiah,

King of Israel, Son of Man) makes it abundantly clear that, from the Johannine perspective, the human Jesus is the long-awaited savior whose coming has been prophesied by the Jewish scriptures. With the exception of "Lamb of God,"[10] these titles are gender specific. Of special importance are "Son of God" (1:34) and "Son of Man," the title placed on Jesus' lips (1:51).

This section functions not only to describe the beginnings of Jesus' following but also to intimate the origins of the post-Easter Johannine community. Historical critics argue that the initial members of the community came from a Jewish-Christian background and would have held the conventional Christology attributed to the first disciples: that Jesus is the Messiah, the one of whom Moses and the prophets spoke (1:45).[11] Furthermore, the disciples can be seen as modeling the ideal response to Jesus' coming: they confess Jesus to be the Messiah, and testify to others of their faith.

The First Sign: The Wedding at Cana (2:1–12)

Jesus' recruits join him and his mother at a wedding at Cana (2:1–2). The wine runs out, a fact conveyed to Jesus by his mother (2:3). His response is initially negative: "Woman, what concern is that to you and to me? My hour has not yet come" (2:4). The first part of Jesus' response is a Semitism, meaning literally "What to me and to you, woman?" Although this phrase carries different nuances in different contexts, it implies at the very least a denial on Jesus' part that the matter at hand concerns him in any way. The second part of his response, that the hour (of glorification; cf. 12:23) has not yet come, provides some justification for this detachment. Undeterred by this apparent refusal, his mother instructs the servants: "Do whatever he tells you" (2:5). Her confidence is vindicated; Jesus tells the servants to fill up purification jars with water and then to draw the water out. In some unspecified way, the water has become wine, the quality of which is praised by the chief steward.

This passage is an important datum for source critics, who search the Gospel for evidence of prior sources. The description of Jesus' act as the first of his signs (2:11) is itself seen as a sign that the evangelist selected and edited this and other stories from a written "signs source" in which these miracles or signs were recounted and numbered.[12]

For a feminist reading, the most intriguing aspect of this story is the portrayal of the mother of Jesus. The narrative conveys no details concerning her individual identity; her name and family status are not mentioned. All we are told is that she is Jesus' mother. How we understand this mother–son relationship, however, depends on our reading of Jesus' response to her comment concerning the lack of wine. At the very least, this response appears to be a rebuke. Those who insist that Jesus would not have been so rude as to rebuke his mother can take refuge in a source-critical solution according to which the offending verse is not considered to be part of the original story.[13] Against this solution, however, stands the fact that the structure of this pericope is similar to two other signs stories (4:46–54 and 11:1–44) in which Jesus' initially negative response to a petitioner is similarly reversed.[14]

The crux is the vocative "woman." While to our ears it sounds strange, if not rude, for a person to refer to his/her mother as "woman," it does not appear to connote discourtesy at all in this Gospel. In 4:21, it is used by Jesus to introduce a prophetic statement to the Samaritan woman; in 19:26, Jesus again addresses his mother as "woman" when giving her into the care of the Beloved Disciple; in 20:15, Jesus employs it to draw the attention of the distraught Mary Magdalene, after her discovery of the empty tomb. Aside from the three female characters already mentioned, only God is addressed by a vocative, "Father," in Jesus' prayers (11:41; 12:28; 17:1, 5, 11, 24, 25). Hence the fact that Jesus addresses his mother as "woman" does not belittle his relationship to her but rather recognizes its intimacy.

How are we to understand Jesus' mother? The minimal portrayal of her in this Gospel precludes a clear-cut answer to this question.[15] One could imagine, perhaps, that, as Jesus' mother, she would hardly have failed to recognize his identity.[16] On the other hand, a more whimsical, less reverent reading might recognize in this mother a rather natural appreciation of the abilities of her offspring without necessarily implying faith in him as the Messiah and Son of God. Accordingly, her instruction to the servants to do as Jesus asks can be read as a refusal to respect his hesitation. This refusal would place pressure on her son to comply with her wishes, thereby giving her control of the situation. While the former reading is consistent with the unremitting christological focus of this Gospel, the latter allows us to consider the tension inherent in Johannine Christology which portrays a nongendered divine Word incarnate in a male human person. It also permits a glimpse, however fleeting, of a mother–son dyad, in a text otherwise dominated by Father–Son language.

Other possibilities may be noted. First, Jesus' mother is not confronted with the choice of accepting or rejecting the gospel message. This distinguishes her from virtually all other characters in this Gospel except John the Baptist. Perhaps her primary role is not that of believer but that of the one through whom the Word became incarnate, just as John the Baptist is not a disciple but rather the divinely ordained witness to the light. Second, the two other women addressed as "woman"—namely, the Samaritan woman and Mary Magdalene—clearly have apostolic functions. It could be that this woman too, who knows of Jesus' powers and instructs others to obey him, is to be seen as an apostolic figure.[17] Finally, we might see the vocative "woman," with which Jesus addresses his mother, in light of the vocative "Father" with which Jesus addresses God. On this reading, the form of address, while not denigrating her, would remind the reader that Jesus is the Word-made-flesh, whose principal relationship is not with any human being but with God.

The First Passover: Cleansing of the Temple (2:13–25)

After a short break in Capernaum, Jesus goes to the Temple in Jerusalem for the Passover and launches his public career. His first encounter with a Jewish crowd occurs after he has caused a stir in the Temple, chasing out merchants, money changers, and potential sacrificial animals. In the Synoptic versions (Mark 11:15–19 and parallels), this act serves as the immediate cause for the Jews' plot to have Jesus crucified. In the Johannine version, the immediate consequences are not nearly so severe. The Jews, while startled by Jesus' act, and presumably by the claim that he is preserving the sanctity of his "Father's house," do nothing except ask "What sign can you show us for doing this?" (2:18). Jesus' answer is enigmatic: "Destroy this temple, and in three days I will raise it up" (2:19). The Jews take this to refer to the actual Temple (2:20), but in fact "he was speaking of the temple of his body" (2:21). It is not only the Jews, however, who misunderstand Jesus. The disciples, we are told, comprehend the import of Jesus' words only "after he was raised from the dead" (2:22), at which time "they believed the scripture and the word that Jesus had spoken." Only the readers are privy to the "true" interpretation of Jesus' saying, conveyed to them by the narrator.

The First Discourse: Jesus and Nicodemus (3:1–21)

The inadequate faith response of the witnesses to Jesus' signs at the Passover (2:23–25) is illustrated in detail in 3:1–21. The Pharisee Nicodemus, intrigued by this "teacher who has come from God," seeks him out. This step might imply that he, like the men whose call is described in 1:35–51, has some insight into Jesus' identity. But this assessment is overturned by several factors. The apparently gratuitous detail that Nicodemus came by night might simply suggest an element of secrecy to Nicodemus's act. But the Johannine usage of the terms light and darkness requires a more negative meaning: that Nicodemus is "in darkness," an unbeliever. This association is strengthened as the conversation continues. Decisive is not Nicodemus's persistent misunderstanding of Jesus' words but rather the accusatory tone of Jesus' comments to Nicodemus. Rather than inviting him to believe, Jesus upbraids Nicodemus as an example of the unbelieving Jews; Nicodemus is not a potential member of the community included in the "we" of the prologue, but rather is one of "you" who do not receive his testimony and who do believe neither "earthly things" nor "heavenly things" (3:11–12). Nicodemus is given no opportunity to answer

Jesus' accusations, for the dialogue edges into discourse at 3:10 and then imperceptibly into an exposition of the narrator on the contrast between the evil ones who "love darkness rather than light" and those "who do what is true" (3:20–21).[18]

As with the first disciples, the character of Nicodemus is often read ecclesiologically, as a reference to a particular group on the fringes of the Johannine community at the end of the first century. One who comes to Jesus at night, attracted by his signs, who later defends him before the Pharisees (7:50–51) and brings spices for his burial (19:39), it is thought, must represent the group of "secret Christians."[19] The existence of such a group is supported by the reference to Joseph of Arimathea, "a disciple of Jesus, though a secret one because of his fear of the Jews," who asked Pilate for permission to remove Jesus' body (19:38). Against this interpretation, however, stand several factors. First, the Gospel does not ever state that Nicodemus became a believer, even a secret one. Second, Jesus' comments to Nicodemus are similar to those he addresses to the Jews in subsequent chapters. Third, the content of his accusations, which concern lack of belief and lack of knowledge, echo the descriptions of the unbelieving world that are found in the prologue as well as in the Baptist's encounter with the Jewish representatives. These serve to undo the positive assessment of Nicodemus's potential as a believer that one might infer from his initial approach to Jesus.

The Baptist Bows Out (3:22–36)

Now that Jesus' ministry is well under way, John the Baptist, with whose testimony this section began, departs graciously from the narrative, having accomplished his divinely given role as witness. The scene is occasioned by his disciples' outrage at the apparently competing baptizing activity of Jesus' disciples. John responds to their outburst by reminding them of his earlier testimony: "I am not the Messiah, but I have been sent ahead of him" (3:28). He further describes himself as the friend of the bridegroom, and thereby recalls the wedding imagery of the Cana story. Finally, he indirectly instructs them to become followers, as did the exemplary Andrew and his unnamed colleague (1:35–40), by insisting: "He [Jesus] must increase, but I must decrease" (3:30). Therefore, like John's previous appearances in this Gospel, this finale testifies to the messiahship of Jesus as well as to the secondary role of the Baptist.[20]

Summary

This account of the first phase of the ministry contributes in several ways to the rhetorical purposes of the Gospel. Of these, three may be singled out. First, it introduces the reader to the two principal activities in which the

Johannine Jesus engages: doing signs and giving discourses. Both are revelatory of Jesus' christological identity as described in the narrative.

Second, this section not only describes the two choices available to the reader—acceptance or rejection—but also provides examples of each, in the persons of the disciples and Nicodemus. The latter character, as well as the negative choice implicitly attributed to him by the accusatory language in which Jesus addresses him, is seen as exemplary of the Jews as a group. They are the ones who refuse to accept Jesus (3:32) and therefore face the condemnation (3:18) and wrath of God (3:36). In the light of this negative description, it is noteworthy that the disciples, who exemplify the positive choice of acceptance, are not described as Jews, though they could hardly be anything else. Rather, they are former disciples of the Baptist (Andrew and his colleague), dwellers of Galilee (Philip), or Israelites (Nathanael), for whom Jesus is the true king.

Third, the narrator divulges the criterion used by God and his Son to effect judgment: the good are those who believe; evil are those who "hate the light and do not come to the light" (3:19). In contrast to the "we" introduced in the prologue, there is therefore also a "you," which includes Nicodemus and others like him who belong to the darkness.

THE SECOND PHASE OF THE MINISTRY (4:1–6:71)

The Samaritan Woman and Jesus (4:1–45)

After the exit of the Baptist, Jesus heads back to Galilee, prompted by fear of the Pharissees' reprisals for his baptizing activities. Jesus' journey takes him through the Samaritan city of Sychar, where Jesus rests at Jacob's well while his disciples go off in search of dinner (4:8). At the well, Jesus, like his biblical predecessors Jacob and Moses, meets a woman who had come to draw water; he engages her in conversation and visits her home (cf. 4:40). Unlike other examples of this type of encounter, however, the relationship established between Jesus and the woman he meets does not result in betrothal and marriage; rather it concludes in the conversion of the woman and her community to faith in Jesus as the "Savior of the world" (4:42).[21] Nevertheless, according to the narrator, Jesus transgressed ethnic boundaries by asking a Samaritan woman for a drink ("Jews do not share things in common with Samaritans" [4:9]) and social boundaries by speaking with a woman (4:27).[22] Elsewhere in this Gospel, however, Jesus' speaking with women occasions no surprise.

These comments and the allusions to the biblical betrothal type-scene draw the reader's attention to the gendered identity of the earthy Jesus as a man, only to undo it yet again. The undoing is accomplished by several factors. First, as has already been noted, the scene does not conclude in betrothal.

Second, he is not interested in her sexual history per se, but mentions her five husbands only in order to demonstrate his prophetic prowess. Third, the entire episode is placed in a missionary context, both by Jesus' enigmatic comments on harvesting and "gathering fruit for eternal life" (4:34–38) and by the story itself, in which the Samaritan woman acts as an apostle to her compatriots.

While the Samaritan woman acts as Jesus' foil, the content, tone, and outcome of their conversation demonstrate that she is more like the disciples called in 1:35–51 than like Nicodemus. This status is confirmed by the seemingly incidental detail that, unlike Nicodemus, who came to Jesus by night, she meets Jesus at noon, when the light is strongest. Like the disciples, she has a direct encounter with Jesus, which persuades her that he is the Messiah whom she has been awaiting. She then testifies to others, who consequently approach Jesus and become believers. But whereas these steps were only outlined with respect to the earliest disciples, they are portrayed in detail with respect to the Samaritan woman. Her initial contact with Jesus marks one of the few occasions in this Gospel in which a dialogue between Jesus and another character does not become a monologue for Jesus alone.[23] Jesus meets her rather tentative confession with the powerful *egō eimi* ("I am") formula, thereby revealing his divine identity to her directly.

The Second Sign: The Official's Son (4:46–54)

After his return to Cana, Jesus performs his second sign (2:54). A royal official arrives in Cana and asks Jesus to come down to Capernaum to heal his son. As in the case of the wedding at Cana, this request is met by Jesus with an apparent rebuke: "Unless you [plural] see signs and wonders you [plural] will not believe" (4:48). The plural forms suggest that this official is representative of all who desire tangible or visible signs. The difference between this sign and the previous one, however, is that Jesus does not in fact do what the petitioner asks, which is "come down before my little boy dies" (v. 49). Rather, Jesus heals the child from a distance without traveling to Capernaum. The official believes before he sees the signs and wonders, and even before he receives testimony from his household that the healing has occurred. Like the Samaritan woman, this man becomes an apostle, since it is on the basis of his testimony to his servants that they believe (4:53).

The Third Sign: The Lame Man (5:1–47)

Following this second sign, Jesus returns to Jerusalem for an unnamed festival. On this occasion, he heals a lame man who had been lying for years beside a pool near the Sheep Gate. As a result, Jesus' conflict with the Jews, which had been a constant but muted current in the narrative thus far, comes to overt expression and becomes not only a prominent theme in the Johannine discourses but also the main story line of the narrative.

In contrast to the previous two signs stories, in which the principal result was the coming to faith of the witnesses (in the first sign) or the petitioner (in the second sign), neither the narrator nor the Johannine Jesus displays any concern for the faith status of the healed man or the witnesses. Rather, the main interest is in the consequences of this act: the Jews' persecution of Jesus on the grounds that he broke the sabbath and blasphemed, calling God "his own Father, thereby making himself equal to God" (5:18).

The ensuing discourse expands on the relationship between the Father and the Son. The Father loves the Son and has given him the authority and the power to give life and to judge. This discussion explains yet again the necessity of faith for eternal life, since "anyone who does not honor the Son does not honor the Father who sent him" (5:23), whereas "anyone who hears my word and believes him who sent me has eternal life, and does not come under judgment, but has passed from death to life" (5:24).

Two difficult issues emerge. One is the apparent interchangeability of the titles Son of God, Son, and Son of Man. The dead will hear the voice of the *Son of God;* the *Son* has life in himself; and he has authority to execute judgment because he is the *Son of Man* (5:24–29). This usage undermines the initial impression that the titles Son of *God* and Son of *Man* are in diametric opposition to each other, and it implies that what is important is the fact that both have Jesus as their referent.

From a feminist perspective, the persistent usage of "Son" language is in tension with the indications in the prologue and elsewhere in the Gospel that Jesus is the human manifestation of a nongendered entity who existed before the creation of the world and humankind. While it has been argued that the *purpose* of using Father-Son language is to stress the familial relationship between them that is characterized by love,[24] it may be suggested the *effect* of this language is to reinscribe a gendered identity for both God and the divine Word.

The second problem is the fact that this passage contains references to both present (or realized) and future eschatology. According to 5:24, the one who hears Jesus' word and believes the one who sent him *has* eternal life and *has* passed from death to life. In the very next verse, however, Jesus claims that the dead *"will* hear the voice of the Son of God, and those who hear *will* live" (5:25). Is this a seam, pointing to pre-Johannine sources? If so, which set of claims portrays the theology of the source and which that of the redaction? The myriad of scholarly answers to these questions suggest that no clear answer is in fact possible.[25] It may be, however, that the juxtaposition of eschatological perspectives serves to forge the connection between faith and eternal life. Whether salvation is seen as future, present, or, in some paradoxical way, as both, a positive faith decision is the necessary precondition to the passing from death to life, whenever or however this might occur.

The discourse concludes with a passage replete with juridical terminology. Jesus both defends himself against the charges brought against him by the Jews according to 5:16–18 and also prosecutes them for their unbelief. To do so he evokes several witnesses who testify on his behalf: John the Baptist (5:33), the works that the Father has given him to complete (5:36), the Father himself (5:37), and, finally, the scriptures (5:38).[26] In discussing the latter, Jesus accuses the Jews of misinterpreting their own sacred texts: "You search the scriptures because you think that in them you have eternal life; and it is they that testify on my behalf. Yet you refuse to come to me to have life" (5:39). The Jews have failed to recognize that Jesus is the Word-become-flesh who is implicit in, fulfills, and completes the earlier Word of God as expressed in scripture.

The Fourth Sign: Feeding the Multitudes and Walking on Water (6:1–21)

Chapter 6 sees Jesus situated at the "other side of the Galilee" (6:1) with his disciples and a large crowd. Exactly how and when Jesus reached this locale after being in Jerusalem at the end of chapter 5 is a puzzle. The transposition of chapters 5 and 6, which many scholars have suggested, would resolve the geographical inconsistencies.[27] It would, however, undermine the force of the passage, which is to emphasize that, contrary to his past behavior (6:4; cf. 2:13; 5:1), Jesus spends this Passover in Galilee, in the company of many others who would otherwise be in Jerusalem at this time. The disruption of this expectation functions as a partial fulfillment of Jesus' words to the Samaritan woman in 4:21: "The hour is coming when you will worship the Father neither on this mountain [Gerizim] nor in Jerusalem."

Jesus multiplies a meager number of loaves and fishes to supply several thousand people, with plenty left over. The crowd interprets this act as a sign of Jesus' identity as the "prophet who is to come into the world," echoing the Samaritan woman's similar identification (4:19, 25). But where the woman testified to her community and brought others to Jesus, the people who saw this sign "were about to come and take him by force to make him king" (6:15). This intention betrays a profound misunderstanding of Jesus' identity and forces him to withdraw to the mountain. This response contrasts with his openness to the Samaritans and foreshadows the crisis that will come to a head during the Bread of Life discourse.

As in the Synoptic Gospels, the multiplication of the loaves and fishes is followed by a story in which Jesus walks on the water through a storm to reach the boat carrying his disciples to the other shore of the Sea of Galilee. This scene portrays not only Jesus' ability to command nature but also his concern for and ongoing presence with the disciples. His place is among them rather than on the shoulders of those who would crown him king.

Bread of Life Discourse (6:22–71)

In the meantime, the crowd continues to search for Jesus. They are puzzled by his appearance on the other side of the sea: after all, he had not gone in the boat with his disciples, and no other boat had been available for his use. As in the scene of the cleansing of the Temple, they ask for an explanation (6:25). This time, Jesus responds not with a single enigmatic saying but with a lengthy discourse that is equally enigmatic, at least to the crowd if not to the readers. The Bread of Life discourse weaves together three main themes of the Gospel narrative. The first—as always—is Jesus' identity. As in the prologue, the initial christological images in this section are nonpersonal. Jesus is "the living bread that came down from heaven" (6:51), sent by the Father (6:32), which provides eternal life to whoever eats it (6:51). The image is reinforced by its explicit connection to the manna that God provided to the Israelites in the wilderness (6:31) and its implicit connection to the bread that Jesus had provided the previous day. Nevertheless, the image becomes personalized by the Jews' uncomprehending response in 6:52, "How can this man give us his flesh to eat?" The alarm implicit in this question is not alleviated by Jesus' response: "unless you eat the flesh of the Son of Man and drink his blood, you have no life in you" (6:53). Even Jesus' reintroduction of the nonpersonal language at the end of the section, "the one who eats this bread will live forever," does not erase the cannibalistic connotations of 6:53; many of his disciples[28] find this teaching hard to swallow (6:60). Yet as the conclusion of the discourse makes clear, it is not a literal eating of flesh and blood, nor even of bread, that is the source of eternal life. Rather, it is the faithful hearing of the words that Jesus— the embodied Word—has spoken that are spirit and life (6:63).

At the conclusion of this discourse, many of the disciples turn away, as Jesus had known they would (6:64), and Jesus is left with the Twelve.[29] Their representative, Peter, declares his allegiance with words that confirm that he at least has understood Jesus' proclamation: "You have the words of eternal life. We have come to believe and know that you are the Holy One of God" (6:68). A sinister note, however, pervades this ending, due not only to the departure of many disciples but, primarily, to the anticipatory references to Judas' betrayal of Jesus (6:65, 70–71).

The Bread of Life discourse, therefore, continues the rhetorical emphasis on the need for individuals to respond positively to Jesus in order to receive eternal life. It also offers further clues to the formation of a distinct group around Jesus, which may have been seen by the original readers as a model for their own community. This group consists of the Twelve who accept Jesus' sayings and presumably also enact a ritual which they understand as drinking the blood and eating the flesh of the Son of Man. Read as a story of the Johannine community, this eucharistic language may reflect the practice of a eucharistic ritual in the community. It may also suggest that this ritual was a source of dissension within the original community and led to the departure of some of its Jewish members. Such historical conclusions must remain tentative. What is clear, however, is that this discourse portrays the Jews as ultimately refusing the gift of life. Though they had been willing enough to eat the bread that Jesus had provided on the mountain, they have turned away from his offer of "living bread."

THE THIRD PHASE OF THE MINISTRY

The Feast of Tabernacles (7:1–52)

The role of the Jews as rejecting and opposing the divine Word, a muted undercurrent in chapters 1 through 4, finally surfaces in chapters 5 and 6. In the present section, the "Jewish question" is the primary focus. Setting the stage is 7:1, in which Jesus' reluctance to travel about in Judea is attributed to his knowledge of the Jews' plot to kill him.

Jesus' caution, however, is quickly put aside. After an initial refusal, Jesus spends the Feast of Tabernacles in Jerusalem, teaching in the Temple (7:10–14).[30] The ensuing scene weaves together several elements, three of which are directly relevant to the present discussion.[31] The first concerns the tensions in the crowd as they debate Jesus' identity among themselves (7:12). After expressing surprise at his teaching abilities, they deny to Jesus that they seek an opportunity to kill him for healing on the sabbath (7:19). Nevertheless, their remarks to one another confirm that there is a plot afoot: "Is not this the man they are trying to kill? And here he is, speaking openly, but they say nothing" (7:26).[32] Jesus' discourse is punctuated by their comments to one another as they attempt to decide whether he is indeed the Messiah. Those who argue in the affirmative point to his many signs (7:31), while arguments in the negative dismiss him because of his Galilean birthplace (7:27; 7:41–42).

The second element of the chapter is Jesus' discourse to the crowd on the issues at stake in their debate. Although the crowd's arguments are not addressed to him, he perceives and addresses them in his own fashion. He comments that the people in the crowd in fact do not know his origins, since they do not accept that he is the Son of God (7:28). Nevertheless, despite their ignorance, he offers them living water, as he had to the Samaritan woman, referring, as the narrator points out, to the Spirit, which had not yet been given (7:38–39).

The third element is the response of the Pharisees to the crowd and its mutterings. That there is a distinction between the crowd and the Jewish leadership is implied from the very beginning of the chapter; it is the latter who plot to kill Jesus. The Pharisees send the Temple police to arrest him (7:32), a task which they ultimately refuse to fulfill because "never has anyone spoken like this!" (7:46). The Pharisees' ridiculing of the police spurs Nicodemus, "who had gone to Jesus before and who was one of them" (7:50), to urge that Jesus be given a fair hearing; this suggestion similarly meets with Pharisaic ridicule (7:52).

The apparent differentiation between the crowd, part of which is receptive to Jesus' discourses, and the Pharisees who are attempting to kill him has been seized upon by scholars who wish to acquit this Gospel of charges of anti-Judaism. The negative use of the term "Jews," they suggest, applies only to the leaders and not to the crowds or the Jewish people as a whole. Against this defense, however, it must be noted that both this chapter and the Gospel as a whole blur these distinctions. John 7:1 states that the Jews are trying to kill Jesus, but 7:15 asserts that the Jews were astonished at his teaching. While John 7:25 speaks of "some of the people of Jerusalem" who were surprised that the authorities allow him to speak, 7:35 indicates that the "Jews" were puzzled about the meaning of his declaration that he was going to a place where they would not find him.

Discourse with the Jews (8:12–59)

The relentless buildup of the Jewish plot against Jesus and the Johannine verbal assault on the Jews continue in chapter 8, interrupted briefly in 7:53–8:11 by the non-Johannine story of a woman whom Jesus saves from being stoned for adultery.[33] Chapter 8 picks up many of the threads present in earlier sections. Foremost among them is the consistently accusatory language—reminiscent of the juridical language of chapter 5—in which Jesus addresses the Jews: they do not know his origins (8:14) or his Father (8:19); they are going to die in their sin (8:21); they are from below (8:23). Interspersed with these accusations are conditional statements which still hold out the hope of salvation: "Whoever follows me will never walk in darkness but will have the light of life" (8:12); "you will die in your sins unless you believe that I am he" (8:24); "if you continue in my word, you are truly my disciples; and you will know the truth and the truth will make you free" (8:31).

Nevertheless, the inability of the Jews to understand (8:33) and, even more damning, their plot to kill Jesus, militate against their eventual salvation. These accusations culminate in the labelling of the Jews as "children of the devil" in 8:44: "You are from your father the devil, and you choose to do your father's desires. He was a murderer from the beginning and does not stand in the truth, because there is no truth in him." That Jesus is correct in his assessment, at least from the Johannine perspective, is confirmed by their final response to Jesus' declarations of his own identity: "So they picked up stones to throw at him, but Jesus hid himself and went out of the temple" (8:59).

The Sixth Sign: The Healing of the Man Born Blind (9:1–41)

Chapter 9, which portrays the healing of the man born blind, demonstrates that the Jewish opposition to Jesus extended to his disciples and followers as well. After the man is healed and confirms his identity to his skeptical neighbors, he is cross-examined by the Pharisees (9:15). His testimony concerning Jesus' healing act creates some confusion among them regarding Jesus' identity. Not convinced, the Jews (Pharisees?) call upon his parents as witnesses. They give only guarded and evasive answers, however, "because they were afraid of the Jews; for the Jews had already agreed that anyone who confessed Jesus to be the Messiah would be put out of the synagogue" (9:22). Again the lines among Pharisees, Jews and the crowds are indistinct.

The symbolism of the passage is transparent. The man born blind epitomizes the true faith response of the one to whom the light comes (cf. 9:35–37), whereas the Jews—who have had ample opportunity to see—are blind, walk in darkness, and will therefore die in their sin (cf. 8:12, 24). More elusive is the historical referent of 9:22. Because exclusion from the synagogue is taken to be anachronistic to the time of Jesus, the verse is understood to refer to the exclusion of the Johannine community from the synagogue of which it had heretofore been a part.[34] This argument is problematic, as Reuven Kimelman has shown, since there is no evidence for the exclusion of Jewish-Christians from the synagogue in the first century. Nevertheless, the conclusion that 9:22 refers to a historical act of expulsion has gone virtually unchallenged, since it serves to account for the anti-Jewish polemic in the Gospel. Furthermore, it has become a cornerstone for the reconstruction of the history of the Johannine community. R. E. Brown, for example, argues that the pre-Gospel era of the community certainly included the controversies between Johannine Christians and the synagogue leaders, while the second phase reflects the situation at the time the Gospel was written (ca. 90 C.E.) a time when expulsion from the synagogue was in the past but persecution continued.[35]

Whether or not such reconstructions are correct, the ecclesiological reading of 9:22 and the chapter as a whole posits a continuity between the Jews' persecution of Jesus, their exclusion of Jewish believers in Jesus during his ministry, and finally, the hostile relationship between the Johannine community and the synagogue in its vicinity. It would place the responsibility for such hostility on the Jews and would see it as evidence for their connection with the devil, their murderous nature, and their concomitant exclusion from salvation.

The Good Shepherd Discourse (10:1–42)

The discourse in chapter 10, which indicates no change in setting, appears to be a continuation of or response to chapter 9. The chapter begins with a *paroimia*, a figure of speech, which contrasts the legitimate shepherd whom the gatekeeper lets into the sheepfold and whom the sheep recognize by his voice, with the thief who climbs in by another way. Like much of the rest of the Gospel, this can be interpreted on three levels. In the context of the historical tale, the *paroimia* refers to the conflict between Jesus and the Jewish authorities; in the context of the ecclesiological tale, it speaks of the conflict between the Johannine and Jewish communities in late first century Asia Minor; as part of the cosmological tale, it refers to the cosmic struggle between the forces of good, namely, God and his Word, and evil, represented by the devil and his agents, the Jews.[36]

The pastoral language and the repeated emphasis on Jesus as both the shepherd, the one who leads the sheep to salvation, and the door of the sheep, the one who is the gateway between the bondage of the fold and the freedom of the pasture, are explored throughout the chapter. The element of conflict is never absent, however. It is brought sharply into focus in the concluding interview between Jesus and the Jews at the Temple during the feast of Dedication (10:22). For Jesus, the Jews' lack of faith confirms that they are not of his sheep—hence not among those who hear his voice, follow him out of the fold, and receive eternal life (10:26–28). In response, the Jews again attempt to stone him (10:31), for blasphemy this time, and to arrest him (10:39), but he escapes from their hands.

CONCLUSION OF THE PUBLIC MINISTRY

The Final Sign: Martha, Mary, and Lazarus (11:1–53)

This section marks the conclusion—and climax—of Jesus' public ministry. It begins with the most extended of the signs narratives, the interpretive key to which is provided before the sign itself is narrated. After being told of the illness of Lazarus, Jesus comments, "This illness does not lead to death: rather it is for God's glory, so that the Son of God may be glorified through it" (11:4). Hence the reader and the disciples, though not the sisters or the Jewish crowd in Bethany, are prepared for another sign that, like the wedding at Cana, will reveal the glory of the Son of God.

The entire story is predicated on the relationship between Jesus and the family of Mary, Martha, and Lazarus. John 11:5 refers directly to the love of Jesus for this family; the plea of the sisters to Jesus in 11:3 presumes that Jesus cares enough about Lazarus to come to his side in his illness and testifies to their prior belief in Jesus' ability to remedy the situation.

But, as in the first two signs narratives, Jesus initially frustrates their—and the readers'—expectations; instead of coming to Bethany at once, he lingers for two days. The reason is divulged to the disciples in 11:15: "For your sake I am glad I was not there, so that you may believe." The distressed sisters, however, are not privy to this information. Rather, they, as well as the crowd, express their disappointment that Jesus—who in their view could have healed Lazarus—did not arrive in time to do so (11:21, 32, 37).

When Jesus does finally arrive, Lazarus is already dead and buried. Martha greets Jesus, and the two engage in a theologically charged conversation. Martha complains that had Jesus been in Bethany, Lazarus would not have died, but she acknowledges that even now God would give Jesus what he asks (11:21–22). Jesus promises that her brother will rise again (1:23), a comment that Martha (mis)understands as a reference to the "resurrection at the last day" (11:24). In response, Jesus makes a self-revelatory statement, as he did to the Samaritan woman (4:26; cf. 9:37): "I am the resurrection and the life; those who believe in me, though they die, will live, and everyone who lives and believes in me will never die. Do you believe this?" (11:25–26). Martha meets this revelation with a full confession: "Yes, Lord; I believe that you are the Christ, the Son of God, the one who is coming into the world" (11:27). Like the faith of the nobleman whose son is healed in 4:46–54, her belief is prior to the accomplishment of the sign. This sequence gains significance in light of Jesus' later remark to Thomas: "Have you believed because you have seen me? Blessed are those who have not seen and yet believe" (20:29). This analogy settles the question of whether Martha's confession is rudimentary or profound.[37] While her balking at the tomb might suggest otherwise, her willingness to base her faith on Jesus' words implies that she is indeed one of the blessed.

The narrative now turns to the meeting between Jesus and Mary. Upon hearing from Martha that Jesus had called for her (11:28), Mary arises from her mourning and goes to meet him outside the village, followed by the Jewish friends who had been consoling her (11:29–31). Like Martha, she reproaches Jesus for his absence (11:32). Unlike Martha, Mary makes no further statement regarding Jesus or his power. Neither does Jesus respond to her directly; instead, followed by Mary (11:45), Martha (11:39), and the crowd (11:45), he heads toward the tomb. Over Martha's practical objection concerning the odor from the corpse (11:39), he has the stone removed from the entrance to the tomb (11:41) and, after a brief, audible prayer (11:42), he calls Lazarus forth (11:43–44).

This calling is reminiscent of 5:25, in which Jesus declares: "Very truly, I tell you, the hour is coming, and is now here, when the dead will hear the voice of the Son of God, and those who hear will live." The raising of Lazarus illustrates Jesus' power to enable others to pass "from death to life." It also recalls 10:3, in which the shepherd calls his sheep by name; they hear his voice and come forth from the sheepfold.

The story of these siblings challenges the view of the wholly antagonistic relationship between the Johannine and the Jewish communities that has been suggested on the basis of 9:22. This verse and other references to Jewish persecution (12:42; 16:2) imply hostility within the Jewish community and/or by its leadership toward Jews who profess faith in Jesus as the Messiah. In contrast to this picture, chapter 11 portrays the grieving sisters as openly acknowledging their faith in Jesus as the Messiah, yet being supported in their mourning by their fellow Jews. This picture implies a measure of tolerance and acceptance among the Jewish community for those who openly believed in Jesus, including women like Mary and Martha.

The raising of Lazarus causes a split among the Jews, leading to a now-familiar scene in which some witnesses choose to believe, while others do not. In the aftermath of this spectacular sign, however, the actions of the latter group affect not only their own soteriological status but also directly the fate of Jesus himself, for "some of them went to the Pharisees and told them what he had done" (11:46). This act of betrayal has a drastic impact: it leads directly to the plot to kill Jesus. The leaders' rationale for this plot is that "if we let him go on like this, everyone will believe in him, and the Romans will come and destroy both our holy place and our nation" (11:48). This rather puzzling statement shows the Pharisees' fear of Jesus' power in drawing a crowd, as well as a fear of Roman retribution. Although the connection between these two is not immediately clear, the source of the plot is. It was a concerted plan of the Pharisees and chief priests to kill Jesus, on the advice of Caiaphas the high priest, "that it is better for you to have one man die for the people than to have the whole nation destroyed" (11:50). This section therefore adds a third reason for the Jews' persecution of Jesus. Not only does Jesus desecrate the sabbath and blaspheme God, but he also poses a threat to the very survival of the Jews as a nation under Roman rule.

Mary's Anointing of Jesus (11:54–12:11)

From this point on, Jesus hides himself. Meanwhile, the tension is palpable, as another Passover season approaches (11:55). Six days before this festival, Jesus has dinner at the home of Mary, Martha, and Lazarus in Bethany. On this occasion, Mary silently "took a pint of costly ointment of pure nard and anointed the feet of Jesus and wiped his feet with her hair" (12:3). For this act she is criticized by Judas, who complains sanctimoniously, "Why was this ointment not sold for three hundred denarii and given to the poor?" (12:5). Defending Mary, Jesus responds, "Leave her alone. She bought it so that she might keep it for the day of my burial. You always have the poor with you, but you do not always have me." While Jesus' apparent dismissal of the poor is disturbing, the main aim of his words is to imply the spuriousness of Judas' concern, in contrast to the timeliness and sincerity of Mary's act. This defense of Mary implies that Mary's act is a prophetic one. She, like her sister Martha, is a vehicle for the divine message, having superior knowledge and understanding of the events that are to come. In this she is the positive counterpart to Judas; the true female disciple is an alternative to the unfaithful male disciple.[38]

The juxtaposed Johannine passages featuring Mary and Martha are among the last, climactic scenes of Jesus' ministry as well as key elements that advance the plot toward the all-important passion narrative. It is consequently not only the particular roles ascribed to Martha and Mary in the Fourth Gospel but also the crucial juncture at which they appear that compel us to take them seriously both as characters and as vehicles for Johannine theology. Martha's confession and Mary's act of anointing suggest that they are disciples. That they hosted a dinner for Jesus, at which others of his inner circle were present, implies that the sisters, or women like them, were also part of, or close to, this inner circle. These passages provide a counter-balance to the call of the disciples narrative (1:31–51) in which no female actors are mentioned.

The Triumphal Entry and Jesus' Final Public Acts (12:12–50)

After the dinner in Bethany, the narrator describes Jesus' triumphal entry in Jerusalem. As in 2:19, the disciples do not understand this event at first, "but when Jesus was glorified, then they remembered that these things had been written of him and had been done to him" (12:16). The behavior of the crowd at this event exacerbates the worst fears of the Pharisees, who lament, "You see, you can do nothing. Look, the world has gone after him!" (12:19).

What happens next confirms this statement. The interest of the world, that is, the non-Judean world, is illustrated by the attempts of several Greeks (or Greek-speaking Jews?[39]) to try to see Jesus. Evoking the call of the first disciples, the Greeks approach Philip to ask for an interview with Jesus. Philip told Andrew, and together the two disciples tell Jesus (12:21–22). Jesus puts them off, however, linking the taking of the message to the world with his own imminent death and glorification.

As Jesus approaches his hour, he affirms the inevitability and necessity of his death, saying that "it is for this reason that I have come to this hour" (12:27).

Rather than ask God to save him, Jesus calls on God to glorify God's name. This request is met with the only direct speech attributed to God in this Gospel: "I have glorified it, and I will glorify it again" (12:28).

The speaker of these words, however, is clear only to Jesus and the readers; the crowd, with its usual lack of comprehension, debates whether the sounds were thunder or an angel's voice. Jesus' response to this debate is to say only that the voice has come for their sake, not his (12:30). Jesus' comments on his fate express the paradox that is central to this part of the story: the very act of crucifixion, literally a lifting up, marks not his humiliation and death but rather his exaltation and glorification. This theme will become increasingly emphasized as the narrative progresses toward the passion.

Jesus' final public speech utilizes the imagery of light and darkness, which had been introduced in the prologue and called upon frequently in these first twelve chapters. His audience is to walk in light, not darkness, while the light is still with them, to believe in the light, so that they may become children of light (12:35–36). With these words, Jesus "departed and hid from them" (12:36). The narrator then pronounces judgment on the crowd: "Although he had performed so many signs in their presence, they did not believe in him" (12:37). Unfortunate as this is, it is nevertheless the fulfillment of Isaiah's prophecy (12:38, 41). Although "many, even of the authorities, believed in him," they did not confess to it because of the Pharisees, "for fear that they would be put out of the synagogue" (12:42). This fear brands them as people who "loved human glory more than divine glory" (12:43). By apparently distinguishing between the authorities and the Pharisees, this section raises yet again the question of who exactly are Jesus' enemies. But by failing to maintain such distinctions rigorously the Gospel imputes guilt to the Jews collectively.

Viewing disbelief as a fulfillment of prophecy raises a crucial issue. Throughout the Gospel the disbelief of the Jews, who have been given every opportunity to witness Jesus' acts and hear his words, is seen to be a fatal error for which they must bear the ultimate responsibility. The fact that some Jews, including the man born blind, Mary, Martha, and Lazarus, have chosen faith only emphasizes this point. Yet this judgment is undercut by the claim that their disbelief is a fulfillment of prophecy and therefore in accord with the divine will.

Although Jesus has departed from the scene, the final words in this section belong to him. These reiterate—yet again—the conditions of salvation, the terms of his relationship with the Father, and the mission for which he was sent into the world. Like his earlier words in this chapter, they recall the prologue and imply that the sojourn of the Word in the world is soon at an end.

THE FAREWELL DISCOURSES

The Last Supper (13:1–38)

Chapter 13 relates the final meal Jesus shares with his disciples. In contrast to the Synoptic Gospels, the Fourth Gospel does not present this as a Passover meal. Nor does this meal provide the occasion for the institution of the Eucharist, as in the Synoptics. Rather, the focal point of the evening is the act of footwashing that Jesus performs for his disciples. Their incredulity at this act, generally considered to be servile, is expressed by Simon Peter: "Lord, are you going to wash my feet?" (13:6). The footwashing has been connected to ritual cleaning or purification, much like baptism.[40] But in the Johannine context its main purpose is exemplary, as Jesus comments: "So if I, your Lord and Teacher, have washed your feet, you also ought to wash one another's feet" (13:14). On the ecclesiological level, this passage may allude to a footwashing ritual unique to the Johannine community. If so, it may express an egalitarian ideal which the Johannine community attempted to realize in its own structure and value system. This ideal is reinforced by the love commandment in 13:34: "I give you a new commandment, that you love one another. Just as I have loved you, you also should love one another." This commandment is expanded on in 14:15 and especially in 15:15, which appears to be a critique of the very notion of hierarchy:

> I do not call you servants any longer, because the servant does not know what the master is doing; but I have called you friends, because I have made known to you everything that I have heard from my Father.

Whether the Johannine community lived up to an egalitarian ideal is difficult to establish, since we have no information about this community outside the Johannine literature. Furthermore, the Gospel contains passages that contradict an egalitarian stance. John 14:16, for example, puts servants in their places, for "servants are not greater than their master, nor are messengers greater than the one who sent them" (14:16). This indicates that Jesus is superior to the disciples; the disciples in turn have authority over believers, with respect to whom they are later given the right to forgive and retain sins (20:23). Even among the disciples, the Beloved Disciple and perhaps also Peter are more prominent and closer to Jesus than are the others. Since women are not recounted as being present either at the footwashing or at the giving of the Holy Spirit, it may well be that they are not part of this group. On the other hand, the depictions of women as professing, preaching, and anointing may imply their inclusion.

A second important aspect of this passage is the departure of Judas. That Judas would betray Jesus is indicated as early as 6:70–71 and is repeated in the preface to the footwashing ritual (13:2). In 13:18 the scripture "the one who ate my bread has lifted his heel against me" (Ps 41:9) is fulfilled when Jesus, who breaks bread, dips it, and hands it to Judas, immediately after which Satan entered into Judas. This sequence is in ironic contrast to the Bread of Life discourse, in which the bread that Jesus provides is the bread of eternal life, making those who eat it the children of God. Yet Jesus' role stresses that even the betrayal and the activity of Satan are under Jesus' control and therefore part of the divine plan.

Finally, this passage introduces the Beloved Disciple. Whether this character has in fact been present throughout—as the unnamed disciple of John the Baptist who along with Andrew followed Jesus and later become a believer—cannot be determined.[41] What is clear, however, is his intimate relationship with Jesus, an intimacy recognized by Simon Peter who, despite his prominence in 6:66–69, addresses his questions to Jesus via the Beloved Disciple (13:24–25). Like the mother of Jesus and the Samaritan woman, this disciple is unnamed.[42] Because he is identified by 19:35 and 21:25 as the author of, or at least the authority behind, this Gospel, he is considered to have been the founder of the Johannine community.[43]

Farewell Discourses (14:1–16:33)

These chapters present a virtually continuous discourse, with only the occasional comment by the disciples.[44] The primary emphases are discipleship and the consequences for disciples of Jesus' departure from the world. Jesus explains the necessity of his departure and promises to prepare a place in his Father's house for his followers (14:2). The most important consequence of Jesus' departure will be the coming of the Paraclete (14:26). The Paraclete will teach them everything and will remind them of all that Jesus has said to them. The Paraclete is the Holy Spirit (14:26), or the spirit of truth (15:26), who will testify on Jesus' behalf and prove the world wrong about sin, righteousness, and judgment (16:7–11). The identification of the Paraclete with the Holy Spirit indicates that the moment at which the risen Jesus gives the spirit to his disciples (20:22) is the moment at which the Paraclete enters the community. This suggests that the Gospel is written from the perspective of a community that sees itself in possession of the Holy Spirit or Paraclete who continues Jesus' advisory role in the world.

The coming of the Paraclete is not simply a consequence of Jesus' departure but is also a necessary part of the divine plan for the salvation of humankind. Furthermore, Jesus promises: "a little while, and you will no longer see me, and again a little while, and you will see me" (16:16). In light of these coming events, his departure should be viewed not with sorrow but with joy. This ideal response is prescribed in 16:21, by means of the image of a woman in labor. A laboring woman experiences pain but "when her child is born, she no longer remembers the anguish because of the joy of having brought a human being into the world" (16:21). Brown suggests that this passage, along with 2:4; 19:25–27; and Revelation 12, echoes an allegory of woman's role in the emergence of the Messiah as victor.[45]

In addition to providing the correct perspective on the events of the passion that are about to be recounted, the discourse looks ahead to the post-Easter experience of the disciples. John 15:18–16:4 focuses on the persecution to be suffered by the disciples; 15:18–19 speaks of the hatred of the world, linking the world's reactions to the disciples to its reactions to the incarnate Jesus: "if they persecuted me, they will persecute you; if they kept my word, they will keep yours also." In 16:2, the details of such persecution become more specific: "They will put you out of the synagogues. Indeed, an hour is coming when those who kill you will think that by doing so they are offering worship to God."

In experiencing persecution, therefore, the disciples reenact the suffering of Jesus. Their suffering, like that of Jesus, is only a prelude to eternal life; they may look forward to a time when, as Jesus says, "I will come again and take you to myself, so that where I am, there you may be also" (14:3).

These promises, however, are contingent on the ongoing faith of the disciples. This point is made throughout the discourses, receiving its most colorful expression in 15:1–11, in which Jesus and his relationship to God are described in nonpersonal terms. Jesus is the true vine, God the vinegrower, and the disciples the branches. Barren branches are removed from the vine by the vinegrower, while fruitful branches are pruned—through persecution?—to bear yet more fruit. The disciples are exhorted: "Abide in me as I abide in you. Just as the branch cannot bear fruit by itself unless it abides in the vine, neither can you unless you abide in me" (15:4). This discourse ends by indicating the aim of Jesus' words to the disciples: "I have said this to you, so that in me you may have peace. In the world you face persecution. But take courage; I have conquered the world!" (16:33).

Jesus' Prayer (17:1–26)

This prayer contains strong allusions to the prologue and marks the conclusion of a cycle: the Word, having been made flesh and having dwelt in the world, has accomplished his mission and now asks the Father to "glorify me in your own presence with the glory that I had in your presence before the world existed" (17:5). But the main focus of Jesus' petition is not himself but his followers, those who include themselves in the "we" of the prologue, whom God gave to Jesus, who received Jesus' God-given words, who know that Jesus came from God, and who have believed that God sent him (17:8). For these, Jesus asks God's protection from the evil one (17:15), presumably Satan, and his sanctification in the truth (17:17).

Explicitly included in this group are not only the disciples as characters within the narrative but later generations of believers, "those who will believe in me through their word" (17:20), that is, the preaching of the disciples. With this explicit statement, the Johannine Jesus overcomes the chronological limits of the Gospel story and includes in his petition all readers who assent to the christological and other claims of the Gospel. Jesus prays that they "may be with me where I am, to see my glory, which you have given me because you loved me before the foundation of the world" (17:24).

By conveying the words of the Johannine Jesus to his disciples on the eve of his death, the farewell discourses are a powerful rhetorical vehicle for the Gospel message. On the historical level, Jesus bids farewell to his disciples and encourages them to view his departure in a positive light. Read ecclesiologically, this section offers consolation and hope for the Johannine community in the face of persecution. On a cosmological level, all readers are invited not only to see themselves as being addressed by Jesus' words but also to place themselves into the story of the Word, who is departing from the world and returning to the Father to prepare a place for them.

Throughout these discourses, the Jews hover in the background, their presence intimated in the references to the present suffering of Jesus and the future persecution of the disciples. They return to center stage in the following section, the climax of the Gospel story.

THE PASSION NARRATIVE

The Betrayal, Trials, and Crucifixion (18:1–19:42)

The Johannine passion narrative raises many questions. While its basic structure—betrayal, trials, crucifixion, burial, resurrection appearances—is similar to that in the Synoptic accounts, there are significant differences in content, chronology, and Christology. For example, the Johannine account does not relate the agony in Gethsemane (Mark 14:32–42 and parallels); the Synoptic Gospels do not portray Jesus as giving his mother into the care of one of his disciples at the foot of the cross. The Synoptic passion accounts place Jesus' crucifixion on the Passover itself; the Johannine account has Jesus tried, crucified, and buried before the Passover festival begins. Whereas the Synoptic Jesus cries out to his Father on the cross (Mark 15:34; Matt 27:46; Luke 23:46), his Johannine counterpart simply says, "It is finished" (19:30).

Pervading many discussions of the passion narrative is the question of historicity. This question is not simply an academic one, not the least because of the charge of deicide in the history of Christian anti-Semitism.[46] Our discussion, however, will limit its focus to the rhetoric with respect to the Jews (an issue separate from their historical role in the trial and death of Jesus), to Jesus, and to the women characters in this final section.

The reader's image of the Jews is determined in the Passion primarily by the behavior attributed to them and by their interactions with Jesus and Pilate. Judas betrays Jesus not to the Roman governor or troops but to the police of the chief priests and Pharisees. These latter may be identified with the Temple police involved in the unsuccessful attempt to arrest Jesus in 7:32, 45. The fact that they come to arrest him demonstrates that now—in contrast to the earlier feast of Tabernacles—Jesus' time has finally come.

The police take Jesus to Annas, the father-in-law of Caiaphas, the high priest (18:13). The narrator at this point reminds us of Caiaphas's advice "that it was better to have one person die for the people" (18:14; cf. 11:49–50), advice that is interpreted as prophetic (11:51–53). This reminder reinforces the theme of the farewell discourses: the events now taking place, unhappy as they are by ordinary human judgment, are in fulfillment of prophecy and the divine plan for salvation.

In contrast to its earlier loquaciousness, the Gospel provides only a brief account of Jesus' interview with Annas (18:19–22) and none at all of his subsequent interview with Caiaphas, the high priest himself. Indeed, a primary focus during these scenes is on what takes place outside: the threefold denial of Simon Peter, who is not permitted to witness the proceedings, is contrasted with the devotion of the Beloved Disciple, allowed in because of his priestly connections (18:16). This silence fosters the sense that there is in fact no more to be said; the views of both parties have been made abundantly clear in their previous encounters as related in this Gospel. The delivering of Jesus to Pilate is in itself merely a confirmation of the Jews' verdict that was reached long before this point in the story.

Conversely, the remainder of the section describes a complex narrative in which Pilate is in dialogue alternately with Jesus and the Jews. The scene begins with Pilate's attempt to ascertain Jesus' crime and to persuade the Jews to deal with the matter themselves. The Jews do not reveal his crime directly, but merely assert his criminal status (18:30) and imply the seriousness of his crime by reminding Pilate that "we are not permitted to put anyone to death" (18:31).[47] This opening establishes Pilate as a puzzled and reluctant participant in the proceedings against Jesus.

Pilate then goes inside to speak with Jesus. He begins by asking him directly, "Are you the king of the Jews?" (18:33). Jesus' response emphasizes his spiritual kingship in a way that appears to satisfy Pilate's concerns that Jesus is a political threat. Pilate returns outside to inform the Jews that "I find no case against him" (18:38) and to offer a solution: that he appeal to his usual custom of releasing someone at the Passover, and set Jesus free. At this the Jews clamor: "Not this man, but Barabbas!" (18:40).

This seems to settle the matter, as Jesus is flogged, mocked as king of the Jews, and stricken by Pilate's soldiers. But Pilate then brings Jesus out to the Jews, to "let you know that I find no case against him" (19:4). When the chief priests and police call for his crucifixion, Pilate again wants to put the matter back in their hands, because, as he reiterates, he finds no case against Jesus (19:6). To this the Jews answer that he ought to die for claiming to be the Son of God (19:7).

At this point, according to the narrator, Pilate was more afraid than ever (19:8) and returned to question Jesus about his origins. Jesus refuses to answer, but when Pilate reminds him of his own power to release or to crucify him, Jesus responds: "You would have no power over me unless it had been given you from above; therefore the one who handed me over to you is guilty of a greater sin" (19:11). Pilate is thereby absolved of the moral responsibility, and the Jews blamed. Pilate's innocence in the matter and his fear of the Jews are confirmed by the final scene, in which the Jews again override his attempts to release Jesus by clamoring for his crucifixion (19:15–16).

The rhetorical agenda is obvious. The freedom of the narrator in this section is limited by two facts: that Jesus was crucified and that crucifixion was a Roman form of execution. The crucifixion has already been accounted for in the farewell discourses, in which Jesus situates the cross positively in the cosmological context of the Gospel. The second limitation is overcome by portraying the Roman governor technically responsible for condemning Jesus, as innocent, fearful of the Jewish authorities, and manipulated by them into issuing the order despite his sincere misgivings.

The question that arises, however, is by now familiar. Does the Gospel distinguish between the Jewish authorities and other Jews, or does it blame the Jewish people as a whole? In favor of the former opinion one may cite the periodic references to the chief priests and Pharisees; although the term "Jews" is used frequently, one may argue that the immediate referent is the authorities. But there are strong arguments against this opinion. First, the fact that the term "Jews" is used blurs the distinction between the Jews and their leaders for readers of or listeners to this section, as in earlier chapters. Second, Pilate himself explicitly places responsibility on the Jews as a whole. When Jesus asks him how he heard of the claim that Jesus was the king of the Jews, Pilate responds: "*Your own nation* and the chief priests have handed you over to me . . ." (18:35; emphasis added). This claim echoes the prologue in referring to the rejection of the Word by his own people. Third, the title "King of the Jews," though apparently part of the traditional material drawn upon by all the Gospels (cf. Mark 15:26; Matt 27:37; Luke 23:37), is used here ironically. Jesus is not the king of Jews; the Jews have rejected him (18:36). He is, however, the king of Israel; that is, he is acknowledged as king by true Israelites like Nathanael, who recognize his true identity as the Son of God (cf. 1:49). Finally, there is an ironic element to the betrayal scene. To a reader who has read the Gospel sequentially, this scene is an ironic perversion of the conversion stories such as the call of the disciples (1:35–51) and the apostolic witness of the Samaritan woman (4:1–42). When the police arrive, led by Judas, Jesus greets them with a question: "Whom are you looking for?" (18:4). This is virtually the same question Jesus asked of the two disciples of John the Baptist who became his first two followers (1:38). Here, however, the meaning is quite different; those who look for him do not seek to follow him as the Messiah but to annihilate him for claiming to be such. Their answer, "Jesus of Nazareth," is met with the now-familiar formula: "I am (*egō eimi*)." Having heard Jesus use this phrase in acknowledging his messianic identity to the Samaritan woman, and in conjunction with various nonpersonal predicates such as "resurrection and the life" (11:25), the reader knows how inadequate the term "Jesus of Nazareth" is as a statement of his true identity. Yet Jesus assents to it here, apparently having given up, as he has stated at the close of chapter 12, on the possibility of saving his persecutors.

Just as these concluding chapters maintain the Gospel's negative portrayal of the Jews, so do they continue its positive portrayal of female characters. As in the other Gospels, it is women who are mentioned specifically as being present at the foot of the cross (19:25) though the context later makes it clear that the Beloved Disciple is present as well. While most commentators assert that these women—Jesus' mother, Mary the wife of Clopas, and Mary Magdalene—are disciples, apostles, or at least believers, this is made explicit only in the case of Mary Magdalene (20:1–18).

Even more puzzling is the significance of the ensuing scene (19:26–27) in which Jesus gives his mother and his Beloved Disciple into one another's care. On the human level, this may simply be a practical expression of his filial duty, his attempt to provide for her as best he could. Perhaps he is concerned for the emotional well-being of these two people; Jesus' coming departure is depriving his mother of her son, and the disciple of his intimate mentor; what better consolation for each of them than to sojourn together? Scholars have generally not been satisfied with such explanations; given the highly symbolic nature of much of Johannine narrative and discourse, a symbolic, theological interpretation seems to be called for in this case as well. The difficulties in arriving at a satisfying interpretation—and the wide variety of suggested exegeses—are due to the paucity of evidence. Most theories, from Bultmann's argument that the scene portrays Jewish Christianity (the mother) being contained within Gentile Christianity (the Beloved Disciple), to Elisabeth Schüssler Fiorenza's suggestion that the mother is an apostolic woman disciple, read the passage as a reference to the Johannine community.[48]

A clue to the meaning of the passage may lie in a comparison between these two characters. Both are anonymous and intimately related to Jesus. But the mother of Jesus is an elusive figure about whom we know almost nothing; as far as we know, she is absent from all but two scenes in the narrative, and her faith status is unclear. The Beloved Disciple, on the other hand, is much more clearly drawn, despite the fact that he does not appear until chapter 13. He has a close relationship with Jesus and is the mediator through whom questions to Jesus are often asked. He is present at Jesus' trial before the priests, as well as at the foot of the cross. Where she is the one who literally embodied the divine word, he is the one who embodies the love commandment that Jesus has given so emphatically to his disciples. Finally, the emphasis throughout the Gospel on the language of dwelling is suggestive. The mother will now dwell with her new son, just as Jesus dwelt among humankind, just as the Paraclete will dwell among the disciples. The bringing together of this mother, through whom the Word became flesh, and her new son, whose witness to the Word in the World is embodied in this book (cf. 19:35; 21:24) is a fitting finale for this Gospel of the Word.

The Resurrection Appearances (20:1–31)

References to female characters are absent from 13:1–19:24. In contrast, chapter 20 lingers over Mary Magdalene's discovery of the empty tomb and the aftermath of this discovery. Coming to weep at the tomb on the morning of the third day, Mary sees that the stone has been removed, and she immediately reports this to Simon Peter and the other disciple (presumably the Beloved Disciple). The men return home after inspecting the tomb for themselves; Mary, however, stays to weep. To her surprise, she sees two angels and then Jesus himself. He addresses her as he did his mother in 2:4 and 19:26, as "woman." In asking her whom she seeks, he again (as in 18:4) recalls the words with which he gathered his first two disciples in chapter 1. Mistaking him for the gardener, she asks for Jesus' body. Jesus then calls her by name, and she recognizes him. This response marks her as one of Jesus' sheep, who hear his voice and follow him (10:1–5) and as a believer like Lazarus, who heard his voice and was resurrected from the dead (11:44). Jesus asks her not to hold him or touch him (20:17), because he has not yet ascended; instead, he wishes her to report his appearance and imminent ascension to his brothers, presumably the other disciples. She carries out his wishes, though the response of the disciples is not recorded.

Mary Magdalene is therefore portrayed as an apostle, as the first one to know and understand the full significance of the empty tomb and to bear witness to others. In this context the silence of the text regarding the disciples' response is puzzling. Did they or did they not believe her witness? That they did is implied in the way in which they greet the risen Lord when he appears to them that evening. This appearance is not said to occasion belief but rather rejoicing, as indeed it should according to the farewell discourses.

The evening appearance, therefore, serves to further their faith and also to provide them with the Holy Spirit. But Thomas, absent on that occasion, refuses to believe the witness of the disciples; he wants to see and touch the mark of the nails before believing. Jesus returns and invites Thomas to do so, though whether Thomas touches Jesus is not told. Thomas makes a high confession "My Lord and my God" but receives a gentle rebuke: "Have you believed because you have seen me? Blessed are those who have not seen and yet have come to believe" (20:29). This, like Jesus' prayer in chapter 17, is an appeal to the readers, who live at a time when direct vision is not possible. It also anticipates the next two verses, the Gospel's statement of purpose, which establishes the Gospel itself as a basis of faith for those who cannot see. The disciples too had an opportunity to believe without seeing, as did the nobleman in chapter 4 and Martha in chapter 11, through the witness of Mary Magdalene.

Epilogue (21:1–25)

The compositional relationship of this final chapter to the rest of this chapter is unclear. The risen Lord appears to the disciples while they are fishing in the Sea of Tiberias. While the Beloved Disciple is privileged, as the one who is the first to recognize the Lord on this occasion, it is Simon Peter who is told by Jesus to feed and tend his lambs, that is, to care for the community of believers. This detail lends some credence to those who see the epilogue as an attempt to bring the Gospel in line with the general picture of Peter as the leader of the earliest post-Easter community. This shift does not, however, undermine the position of the Beloved Disciple as the authoritative witness behind the Gospel, who "is testifying to these things and has written them" (21:24), though he may have died before the Gospel took its present form (21:20–23).

The strong guidelines given in the farewell discourses for interpreting the events of the passion narrative are essential to the rhetorical agenda of this Gospel. The passion events in themselves might be subject to very different reading without such strong guidance. The possibility of a different response is illustrated by Mary, whose initial interpretation of the empty tomb is to assume that someone (Jesus' enemies? the gardener?) has taken the Lord. The fact of Jesus' death might have been taken to invalidate all of the christological claims of the Gospel. This possibility is voiced by the Jews in 12:34: "We have heard from the law that the Messiah remains forever. How can you say that the Son of Man must be lifted up?" The Gospel counters such objections by means of the cosmological elements of the story, in which Jesus is the divinely created Word who becomes flesh to fulfill God's mission and then returns. Therefore Jesus' death does not have the finality of a human death. Rather, as the only means by which the Word can return to the Father, this death is essential to the divine plan.

The justification for believing in Jesus despite, or even because of, his death, is filled out by various other details. A belief in the resurrection is validated by the resurrection of Lazarus. The farewell discourses emphasize the coming of the Paraclete, contingent upon Jesus' death and Jesus' eventual return to the world to take the disciples to his heavenly realm. That particular aspects of the passion scene are in fulfillment of scripture demonstrate that the death of Jesus, far from invalidating the christological claims made on his behalf, is in fact an essential part of the divine plan. Jesus accepts his fate, as he indicates to Peter: "Am I not to drink the cup that the Father has given me?" (18:11). Rather than protesting in his final moment, he simply says "It is finished" (19:30).

These comments, however, return us yet again to the tension between the divine plan and human culpability. If the death of Jesus, in all its details, is fulfillment of scripture, part of the divine plan from the very beginning, why then the bitter polemic against the Jews, the emphasis on their disbelief, their persecution of Jesus and the disciples, and their connection with Satan?

A FEMINIST-CRITICAL EVALUATION OF THE FOURTH GOSPEL

If it were portrayals of women that were decisive for a feminist account, the Fourth Evangelist could be hailed as a proto-feminist. The female characters in this Gospel are honored and empowered: the mother of Jesus is confident of her son's miraculous powers; the Samaritan woman is apostle to the Samaritans; Mary and Martha are beloved of the Lord; and Mary Magdalene is the first witness to the risen Christ. This approach would therefore lead to an unequivocally positive answer to our question.

This positive answer could be supported by the fact that while the Fourth Gospel portrays women, it does not say much *about* women. Neither the narrator nor the Johannine Jesus offers an opinion as to what women might or might not do or say. Neither do they comment on whether women are either included in or excluded from the eschatological benefits of faith in Jesus as the Christ and Son of God. This silence, taken together with the positive portrayal of women, is an indication that gender was not a basis for exclusion from the Johannine community or from the vision of salvation described in the Gospel.

But as recent feminist biblical interpretation, including the articles in the first volume *Searching the Scriptures,* makes abundantly clear, the feminist reading of scripture goes far beyond the words about and images of women in these texts. Rather, it seeks to expose the question of liberation not only from the perspective of women qua women but from the point of view of the marginalized, whether defined in terms of gender, race, class, sexual orientation, physical capability, or in any other way.[49]

Even from this more inclusive perspective, the Fourth Gospel seems to support the struggle for liberation. The Johannine Jesus expresses a deep concern for liberation, as indicated by those oft-quoted words: "The truth will make you free" (8:32). This vision of freedom is illustrated through the narrative, which depicts the liberation of individuals and groups marginalized in first-century Jewish society as portrayed in the Gospel. The hungry, the ill, and the physically impaired are liberated from their adverse circumstances by the divinely given, restorative powers of Jesus. Samaritans and Gentiles, either during Jesus' ministry or after his death, are accepted into the community of faith, thereby experiencing inclusion in the divine plan of salvation. Both women and men are among those whom Jesus loves; both women and men call others to faith and are given a vision of the risen Lord. This liberative stance is bolstered by the frequent reference to Jesus' love commandment: "Just as I have loved you, you also should love one another" (13:34).

Its portrayals of women, the absence of gender as an explicit category in the discursive material, and the emphasis on love as the operative term in interpersonal relations all suggest a positive evaluation of the Gospel from a feminist perspective.

Unfortunately, the picture of peace and harmony which I have drawn omits some essential components of this Gospel. First, it ignores the two characters without whom there would be no narrative, namely, Jesus and the Jews. Both of these evoke a response of ambivalence when it comes to feminist-critical evaluation. On the one hand, Jesus is the one who brings the message of liberation. On the other hand, the strong emphasis on Jesus as the Son of God and the prevalence of Father-Son language may create some distance between the feminist reader and this central character.

Even more disturbing is the portrayal of the Jews. In a generous moment one might recognize the narrative necessity of having some opposition to Jesus as the main character. There may also be some historical basis for the portrayal of Jews as being opposed to Jesus and/or to a community that worshiped Jesus and probably challenged various aspects of Jewish life and belief. But the portrayal of the Jews as a group and of individual representatives such as Nicodemus belies the theology of love expressed in this Gospel. The Gospel's near silence about the Jewishness of Jesus' first believers and of Jesus himself implies a polarization of Jews and Jesus' followers that was anachronistic to Jesus time and probably also to the time of the Gospel writer. The Johannine Jews are cast in the role of archenemy, clamoring for Jesus' death on the cross and responsible for the ongoing persecution of his disciples.

Those charged with oppressing the "children of God" are themselves oppressed through the rhetoric of the text itself. If feminist concerns embrace the marginalized, the negative portrayal of the Jews in this Gospel, and the negative effects that this portrayal has had on Christians' views of Jews in subsequent centuries,[50] must serve as a challenge to the positive evaluation of the Gospel to which we have pointed.

This points to another element that our harmonious—but deceptive—picture of the Gospel omits: the liberation promised by the Gospel is not absolute and universal, but rather is conditional on faith. It is because of their faith in Jesus as the Messiah that individuals—such as the Samaritan woman and Mary and Martha—are made free; it is their lack of faith that condemns the nonbelieving Jews. This condition is not simply a key for understanding the Johannine narrative. Rather, it reaches beyond the confines of the narrative and confronts the reader directly with the same conditions that face the characters in the story. The rhetorical purpose of the Gospel ("that you may come to believe that Jesus is the Messiah, the Son of God" [20:31]) is apparent throughout the narrative. The Gospel therefore aims to persuade the reader that the claims in this Gospel are true and to inculcate the worldview inscribed in this text in the reader.

The reader with respect to whom the Gospel rhetoric succeeds is a compliant reader. But a compliant reading, which accepts the truth claims of this Gospel, also entails sharing the view of the Jews that is expressed in this text.[51] This is the case on each of the three levels on which the Gospel narrative can be read. On the historical level, the Gospel irrevocably blames the Jews for the plot to persecute and kill Jesus. This justifies Jesus' virulent language toward the Jews. On the ecclesiological level, the persistent use of the term "Jew" allows the readers to transfer the accusations against the Jews within the historical level to Jews of their own time. Finally, on the cosmological level, the identification of the Jews as children of the devil links them with the cosmic adversary of God and hence binds them to the notion of absolute evil in the world. To suggest that it is not the Jews as a group that are castigated but the Jewish authorities or that the *Ioudaioi* are not really "Jews" but "Judeans" is to evade the finality of Pilate's statement: "Your own nation and chief priests have handed you over to me" (18:35).[52]

Jewish readers, therefore, cannot engage in a compliant reading of this text, though it is possible for a Jewish reader to determine what a compliant reading requires. Compliance should be equally difficult for a non-Jewish, feminist reader attuned to the rhetoric of marginalization in this text and the dangers inherent in a compliant reading.

The alternative to a compliant reading is a resistant one. This has been defined by Claudia Camp as reading like a trickster. To quote Camp, "To read . . . as a trickster . . . involves, first, claiming identity with those at the margins and, second, willingness to read against the text, to read subversively."[53] A resistant reading therefore entails recognizing the rhetorical nature of the text by identifying its concerns and the ways in which it attempts to manipulate the responses of the reader. To a trickster, the act of searching the scriptures means something far different from what it does to the Johannine narrator. John 5:39 and 7:52 dismiss the right of the Jews to interpret their own scriptures and posit christological interpretation as the correct reading of the text. In contrast, the feminist search, as exemplified in the two-volume collection of which this commentary is a part, seeks precisely to overcome this sort of scriptural imperialism by encouraging a multiplicity of readings.

The growing literature of Christian feminist biblical interpretation reveals a wide range of moves undertaken by Christian tricksters, which reflect varying stances on the authority of the text. Non-Christian tricksters, on the other hand, will likely share at least one common feature: a rejection of the claim that the text has an absolute, primary, sacred authority. As a Jewish trickster, I resist the text by refusing to see myself as addressed by the text in any way, thereby declining the invitation to place myself into the cosmological tale. This resistance places me in the subject position of the Johannine Jews, who dispute the christological claims of the text, dismiss its christological interpretation of scripture, and discount its claims of authority.

But a resistant reading is not only an exercise in negativity. It also entails a positive appreciation of the text, albeit in ways perhaps not imagined by its author. As a lover of the written word, I delight in the Gospel's layers of narrative and symbol, in its allusions and elusiveness. As a feminist who experiences solidarity with other women, I savor the potential for feminist theology of the nongendered portrayal of the Word,[54] and I applaud the Johannine models that empower Christian women and validate their authority within the churches.[55]

And, yes, even though I am a resisting Jew, this text speaks to me directly, through the persons of Martha and Mary. While these sisters have made a faith choice that I do not emulate, their role in their community is not unfamiliar to me. The choices they made set them apart from the larger Jewish community, yet they continued to reside within it and relate themselves to it. They derived support from their community in time of grief and, if they were indeed apostles, worked for transformation and change from within. As I think of these sisters, I am reminded of myself and many others that I know, whose feminist work may set us apart from our academic colleagues at the same time as we support the ideal of the university, enjoy collegial relationships with others, and work for change from within. Similarly, Mary and Martha can encourage those of us who belong to faith communities in which women still struggle for equality and in which feminist theology is taboo, to remain within, enjoy what we can, and work for transformation.

NOTES

1. For detailed discussion of the prologue and other standard exegetical, textual, or historical-critical issues, see Raymond E. Brown, *The Gospel according to John* (2 vols.; Anchor Bible
29, 29A;Garden City, NY: Doubleday, 1966, 1970).

2. The argument for an early dating has been advanced by J. A. T. Robinson, *Redating the
New Testament* (London: SCM, 1976), 254–311.

3. The issue has been reopened recently; see D. Moody Smith, *John Among the Gospels:
The Relationship in Twentieth Century Research* (Minneapolis: Fortress, 1992).

4. The issue of sectarianism is much debated. Wayne Meeks considers the Johannine community to be sectarian, while Brown argues vigorously against this point. See Wayne A. Meeks,
"The Man from Heaven in Johannine Sectarianism," *Journal of Biblical Literature* 91 (1972):
44–72; R. E. Brown, *The Community of the Beloved Disciple* (New York: Paulist, 1997) 14 and
passim.

5. See Ernst Haenchen, *John 1: A Commentary on the Gospel of John Chapter 1–6*
(Philadelphia: Fortress, 1984), 121; I. de la Potterie, "C'est lui qui a ouvert la voie: la Finale du
Prologue johannique," *Biblica* 69 (1988): 340–70.

6. For more detailed discussion, see Elizabeth A. Johnson, "Jesus, the Wisdom of God: A
Biblical Basis for a Non-Androcentric Christianity," *Ephemerides Theologicae Lovanienses* 61
(1985): 284–89.

7. Although the terms "light" and "darkness" are used symbolically in this Gospel, the association of rejection and darkness will be jarring to many readers.

8. Though episodic (20:30) and dramatic, the Gospel is meant to be read as a "true"
account of events that really happened. This is emphasized by the narrator, who asks that the
readers consider true the testimony of "the disciple who is testifying to these things and has
written them . . ." (21:24).

9. For more detailed exposition of this three-tiered reading of the Gospel, see my *The
Word in the World: The Cosmological Tale in the Fourth Gospel* (SBL Monograph Series 45;
Atlanta: Scholars Press, 1992).

10. If this title refers to a sacrificial lamb, it too denotes a male being, though not a human
one.

11. See Brown, *Community of the Beloved Disciple,* 27–31.

12. For detailed exposition of signs theory, see R. T. Fortna, *The Gospel of Signs* (Cambridge: Cambridge University Press, 1970).

13. Ibid., 31.

14. See Adele Reinhartz, "Great Expectations: A Reader-Oriented Approach to Johannine
Christology and Eschatology," *Journal of Literature and Theology* 3 (1989): 61–76.

15. For a summary, see Brown, *Gospel,* 1:107–9.

16. This reading might be particularly appealing to a reader who reads the Fourth Gospel
in light of the first three. See D. A. Carson, *The Gospel According to John* (Grand Rapids:
Eerdmans, 1991), 171–73.

17. See Elisabeth Schüssler Fiorenza, *In Memory of Her: A Feminist Theological Reconstruction of Christian Origins* (New York: Crossroad, 1983), 327.

18. The exact points at which these transitions occur, or whether they even occur at all, are
much disputed; see Brown, *Gospel,* 1:149.

19. For a description and critique of this viewpoint, see Jouette M. Bassler, "Mixed Signals:
Nicodemus in the Fourth Gospel," *Journal of Biblical Literature* 108 (1989): 635–46.

20. While the imprisonment of the Baptist is mentioned in 3:24, neither it nor his execution is recounted in this Gospel. This detail suggests that the reader was expected to have prior
knowledge of the Jesus story, including details extraneous to the Johannine version.

21. For detailed analysis of this story as an example of the betrothal type-scene, see Lyle Eslinger, "Wooing of the Woman at the Well," *Journal of Literature and Theology* 1 (1987): 167–83. Some scholars believe that this passage indicates the acceptance of Samaritan believers into the Johannine community (see Brown, *Community*, 37).

22. Elsewhere in this Gospel, however, Jesus' speaking with women occasions no surprise.

23. John 11:1–44, which also features women, is another example.

24. See Gail O'Day, "John," in *The Women's Bible Commentary*, ed. Carol A. Newsom and Sharon H. Ringe (Louisville: Westminster/John Knox, 1992), 304.

25. For a summary, see Robert Kysar, *John, The Maverick Gospel* (Atlanta: John Knox Press, 1976), 84–110.

26. It may be argued, however, that John, Jesus' works, and the scriptures, all ultimately stem from one witness, namely, God.

27. Rudolf Bultmann, *The Gospel of John* (Philadelphia: Westminster, 1971), 237.

28. The term "disciples" probably refers in this case to Jesus' followers in general and not specifically to the few who travel with him.

29. This is one of two passages in which this designation is used in this Gospel (cf. 20:24). In this case, it distinguishes between the group of close followers of Jesus and those disciples who left Jesus at this time.

30. Charles H. Giblin argues that this passage is a fourth example of the pattern exhibited in 2:1–11, 4:46–54, and 11:1–44 ("Suggestion, Negative Response, and Positive Action in St. John's Portrayal of Jesus," *New Testament Studies* 26 [1979–80]: 197–211).

31. A fourth element in this section is the ironic communication between the narrator and the reader, which provides the latter with information that the characters within the chapter do not have. This information is essential for understanding the import both of the questions asked by the crowd and of the answers that Jesus does or does not provide.

32. This statement confirms the legitimacy of Jesus' fears in returning to Judea and perhaps also implicitly emphasizes his courage.

33. On the basis of manuscript evidence, Johannine scholars do not consider this section to be part of the Gospel, though it is likely read as such by many readers. Although this section does not therefore contribute to our understanding of Johannine rhetoric, it is interesting to note that there are some similarities. For example, Jesus addresses the woman with the vocative "woman" (8:10), as he does his mother and Mary Magdalene, and he asks her not to sin again, as he does the lame man in 5:14. See Brown, *Gospel*, 1:332–51.

34. See J. L. Martyn, *History and Theology in the Fourth Gospel* (2nd ed.; Nashville: Abingdon, 1979), 376–62, 156–58. For the view that 9:22 does not refer to Birkat ha-Minim, see Reuven Kimelman, "*Birkat Ha-Minim* and the Lack of Evidence for an Anti-Christian Jewish Prayer in Late Antiquity," in *Jewish and Christian Self-Definition*, vol. 2, ed. E. P. Sanders et al. (Philadelphia: Westminster, 1981), 226–44.

35. Brown, *Community*, 22–23.

36. For detailed study of the *paroimia*, see Reinhartz, *Word*, 48–98.

37. For discussion, see Adele Reinhartz, "From Narrative to History: The Resurrection of Mary and Martha," in *"Women Like This": New Perspectives on Jewish Women in the Greco-Roman World*, ed. Amy-Jill Levine (Early Jewish Literature 1; Atlanta: Scholars Press, 1991), 174–76.

38. Schüssler Fiorenza, *In Memory of Her*, 330.

39. Thus H. B. Kossen, "Who were the Greeks of John XII 20?" in *Studies in John: J. N. Sevenster Festschrift* (Leiden: Brill, 1970), 97–110.

40. See Sandra M. Schneiders, "The Foot Washing (John 13:1–20): An Experiment in Hermeneutics," *Catholic Biblical Quarterly* 43 (1981): 76–92; John Christopher Thomas, *Footwashing in John 13 and the Johannine Community* (Sheffield: JSOT Press, 1991).

41. Brown argues in favor of this identification, though he does not supply a satisfactory answer for why the unnamed disciple reappears as the Beloved Disciple only in chapter 13 (*Community,* 32–33).

42. See David R. Beck, "The Narrative Function of Anonymity in Fourth Gospel Characterization," in *Characterization in Biblical Literature,* ed. Elizabeth Struthers Malbon and Adele Berlin (*Semeia* 63; Atlanta: Scholars Press, 1993), 143–58.

43. Brown, *Community,* 31.

44. Some scholars see indications of prior sources in 14:31, in which Jesus says, "Rise, let us be on our way," but then continues speaking for two more chapters.

45. Brown, *Gospel,* 2:732.

46. For discussion of the historicity of various accounts, see Paul Winter, *On the Trial of Jesus* (Berlin: de Gruyter, 1961).

47. On the historicity and meaning of this claim, see R. E. Brown, *The Death of the Messiah* (2 vols.; New York: Doubleday, 1993), 363–72.

48. Bultmann, *Gospel,* 673; Schüssler Fiorenza, *In Memory of Her,* 331.

49. Elisabeth Schüssler Fiorenza, *Bread Not Stone: The Challenge of Feminist Biblical Interpretation* (Boston: Beacon, 1984), x; eadem, "Transforming the Legacy," in *Searching the Scriptures,* vol. 1 (New York: Crossroad, 1993), 5.

50. See Joshua Trachtenberg, *The Devil and the Jews: The Medieval Conception of the Jew and its Relation to Modern Antisemitism* (New York: Harper & Row, 1943), 20 and passim.

51. For an example, see John Quasten, "The Parable of the Good Shepherd: Jn. 10:1-21," *Catholic Biblical Quarterly* 10 (1948): 1–12, 151–69.

52. For an overview and evaluation of these solutions, see R. Alan Culpepper, "The Gospel of John and the Jews," *Review and Expositor* 84 (1987): 273–88.

53. Claudia V. Camp, "Feminist Theological Hermeneutics: Canon and Christian Identity," in *Searching the Scriptures,* 1:167.

54. See, for example, Daphne Hampson, *Theology and Feminism* (Oxford: Basil Blackwell, 1990), 59–62.

55. See, for example, Marjorie Procter-Smith, "Feminist Interpretation and Liturgical Proclamation," in *Searching the Scriptures,* 1:313–25.

RECOMMENDED READINGS

Brown, Raymond E. *The Community of the Beloved Disciple.* New York: Paulist, 1979.

———. *The Gospel according to John.* 2 vols. Anchor Bible 29, 29A. New York: Doubleday, 1966, 1970.

Culpepper, R. A. *The Anatomy of the Fourth Gospel.* Philadelphia: Fortress, 1983.

Dodd, C. H. *The Interpretation of the Fourth Gospel.* Cambridge: Cambridge University Press, 1953.

Kysar, Robert. *John, The Maverick Gospel.* Atlanta: John Knox Press, 1976.

———. *The Fourth Evangelist and His Gospel.* Minneapolis: Augsburg, 1975.

Martyn, J. L. *History and Theology in the Fourth Gospel.* 2nd ed. Nashville: Abingdon, 1979.

Pazdan, Mary Margaret, O.P. *The Son of Man: A Metaphor for Jesus in the Fourth Gospel.* Collegeville, MN: Liturgical Press, 1991.

Reinhartz, Adele. *The Word in the World: The Cosmological Tale in the Fourth Gospel.* Society of Biblical Literature Monograph Series 45. Atlanta: Scholars Press, 1992.

O'Day, Gail R. *Revelation in the Fourth Gospel.* Philadelphia: Fortress, 1986.

The Gospel of
Mary Magdalene

KAREN L. KING ◆

FEMINIST HISTORIOGRAPHY

FEMINIST SCHOLARSHIP has taken the reevaluation of history and historiography as one of the central tasks for feminist politics. Feminist critical reconstruction of the past aims to present a more accurate and complete accounting of the past at the forks where historical accuracy meets equity and justice. Although ostensibly about the "past," history is always made in the present, is always reliant on what evidence exists in the present. The rediscovery of the *Gospel of Mary* (Magdalene) provides new materials with which to reconstruct the past. The *Gospel of Mary* now provides direct evidence of early Christian arguments in favor of the leadership of women and allows us to see that views excluding women were but one side of a hotly debated issue.

The *Gospel of Mary* was not included in the Christian canon. The formation of the canon is a process belonging to a particular historical context and to the establishment of a particular set of power relations. The exclusion of every significant type of early Christianity that supported women's leadership under the label of heresy is a fact that we cannot ignore. To raise the issue of canonical authority means asking why these traditions have been labeled as wrong ("heretical") and how the canon became closed. Elisabeth Schüssler Fiorenza writes: "Inspiration—the life-giving breath and power of Sophia-Spirit—does not reside in texts: It dwells among people. She did not cease once the process of canonization ended. She is still at work today."[1] The *Gospel of Mary* strongly supports this view, arguing for the presence of prophetic experience as the basis of spiritual authority.

This commentary aims at a participatory hermeneutic, that is, one that extends an invitation to readers to engage actively in the historian's interpretation, an interpretation that is not presented as definitive but whose meaning is open. My intention here is to open a dialogue with readers by offering my interpretation as one view.

REDISCOVERY

Few people today are acquainted with the *Gospel of Mary*. Written in the second century, the *Gospel of Mary* disappeared for over fifteen hundred years until quite unexpectedly, in the late nineteenth century, a single, fragmentary copy in Coptic translation came to light. Although details of the discovery itself are obscure, we do know that the manuscript was purchased in Cairo by Carl Schmidt and brought to Berlin in 1896, where the final publication was completed by Walter Till in 1955.[2] Two additional fragments in Greek have come to light in the twentieth century. Yet still no complete copy of the *Gospel of Mary* has been found. Enough remains, however, to give an intriguing glimpse into this early Christian gospel, which offers a spiritual interpretation of the Savior's teachings and portrays Mary Magdalene as a leader among the disciples.

COMMENTARY

MISSING PAGES (BG [1–6])

The first six manuscript pages of the Berlin Codex, constituting approximately one-third of the text, are missing. No Greek fragments exist for this portion of the text, so that we are left ignorant of how the text begins. The commissioning scene (*BG* 8.21–9.5) and reference to the death of the Savior (*BG* 9.10–12), which appear later in the text, indicate, however, that the setting is probably a postresurrection appearance of the Savior to his disciples.

Postresurrection appearances are found in all four of the canonical Gospels and Acts (Matt 28:9–10, 16–20; Mark 16:9–20; Luke 24:13–53; Acts 1:2–9; John 20:11–21:23). There they function primarily to substantiate the validity of a physical, bodily resurrection of Jesus, but they also portray these appearances as a time when Jesus gives special teaching (Luke 24:25–27:32, 45–47) and commissions the disciples to go forth and preach the gospel (Matt 28:18–20; Mark 16:15–18; Luke 24:44–49; Acts 1:8).

Many early Christian writings indicate that teachings received through appearances or visions of the risen Lord were considered to have a special validity. Already in Galatians, for example, it is clear that Paul considers the teaching he received in a revelation of Jesus Christ to be more trustworthy than that which is passed on by mere human tradition (Gal 1:11–12). Similarly, the authority of the book of Revelation derives from its claim to record "the revelation of Jesus Christ" given to John (Rev 1:1). The postresurrection setting of the *Gospel of Mary* similarly functions to authorize the *Gospel's* teaching.

THE SAVIOR TEACHES ABOUT MATTER, SIN, AND THE GOOD (BG 7.1–8.11)

The extant portion of the *Gospel of Mary* opens in the middle of a dialogue between the Savior and his disciples about the natures of matter, sin, and the Good. The dialogue is constructed in a question-and-answer format. The topics are framed around questions from the disciples, followed by extended answers from the Savior. Each answer concludes with the formula "Whoever has two ears to hear should listen," a saying well-attested in the Jesus tradition (see Mark 4:3 par.).

The first topic of the dialogue concerns the nature of the material universe (*BG* 7.1–9). The dialogue opens with a question from one of the disciples: "Will matter be utterly destroyed or not?" The Savior responds that, although all material things (whether natural, molded, or created[3]) form an interconnected unity, they have no ultimate spiritual value and will ultimately dissolve back into their original condition (their "root").[4]

The language in which the question and its answer are framed shows the influence of contemporary philosophical debates over whether matter is preexistent or created. If matter is preexistent, then it is eternal. If, on the other hand, matter is created, then it is subject to destruction. As is the case here, such topics were considered to be preliminary to addressing questions of ethics, since matter was often considered to be the source of disorder or even evil in the world. The fact that the discussion will next turn to the topic of sin is not coincidental; the nature of the world and ethics are intimately related topics.

The Savior's answer corresponds to the view most often taken in Greek philosophy, especially among Platonists and Stoics. Only a few early philosophers, such as Eudorus of Alexandria (first century B.C.E.),[5] held that matter was created. A more common position, and one quite similar to that taken by the Savior here, is reported by Cicero concerning the Platonists:

> But they [the Platonists] hold that underlying all things is a substance called "matter," entirely formless and devoid of all "quality," . . . and that out of it all things have been formed and produced, so that this Matter can in its totality receive all things and undergo every sort of transformation throughout every part of it, and in fact even suffers dissolution, not into nothingness but into its own parts . . . (*Acad. Post.* 1.27)[6]

Early Christians, too, were interested in the fate of the world, and the Savior's response here may be aimed at providing a more philosophically (scientifically) sophisticated answer than is given by the apocalyptic sayings within the Jesus tradition, such as Mark 13:31: "Heaven and earth will pass away, but my words will not pass away."

The topic of discussion next turns directly to ethics, as the Savior teaches about the nature of sin and the Good (*BG* 7.10–8.11). After hearing that matter will be dissolved, Peter asks, "What is the sin of the world?" The language here is reminiscent of John 1:29, again suggesting that the answers of the Savior are designed at least in part to interpret issues in the Jesus tradition.

The Savior responds that sin does not really exist, but that the disciples themselves produce sin by acting "according to the nature of adultery." This surprising response needs to be read in the context of the discussions about matter that both precede and follow this passage. Since matter will eventually dissolve back into its constituent nature, the material world cannot be the basis for determining good and evil, right and wrong.[7] Sin, therefore, does not really exist insofar as it is conceived as action in the material world. Rather, the Savior defines sin in spiritual terms: improper (adulterous) attachment to material things.[8] The metaphor of adultery fits quite well. Like adultery, sin joins together what should not be mixed: in this case, material and spiritual natures. Attachment to the material world constitutes adulterous consorting against one's own spiritual nature.[9]

Moreover, this attachment to the material world, the Savior says, is what leads people to sicken and die: "for [you love] what de[c]ei[ve]s you" (*BG* 7.22–8.1). People's own material bodies deceive them and lead them to a fatal love of perishable material nature.

But there is hope. The Good came to humanity in order to establish its true nature and set it up firmly within its proper "root." The word "root" is used twice in the text (*BG* 7.6, 20). Like the English word, the term has a wide range of metaphorical implications: cause, origin, source, foundation, proper place, and so on. Here the "root" of perishable matter is contrasted with the proper "root" of a person's true nature, which the Good will establish.

In 7.20–8.11, the Savior goes on to develop this distinction between matter and true nature, relying again on philosophical terminology. In the *Timaeus* (esp. 27D–29D), Plato distinguishes what is eternal, immutable, and uncreated (the Ideas or Forms) from what is mutable, created, and subject to sense perception (the material world). The first is the realm of Being, the latter of becoming. According to Plato, "As Being is to becoming, so is truth to belief" (*Tim.* 29C). Knowledge of the sensible realm was uncertain, even as the world itself was in constant flux. True knowledge belongs only to what is unchanging and eternal.

These ideas of Plato received considerable attention and elaboration in the centuries that followed. Increasingly, true knowledge came to be associated with knowledge of the immaterial realm of Being (God), and knowledge of the sensible world was disparaged as a lower concern fit only for people without higher intellectual and spiritual sensibilities. While there are definitely economic and class interests at work in this formulation, the appropriation of the disparagement of matter in the *Gospel of Mary,* however, is shaped less by upper-class snobbery against manual labor than by a deep sensitivity to the connection of suffering and death with the physical body.

The Savior insists that suffering derives solely from matter and is contrary to nature. Anne Pasquier suggests that suffering arises directly from "the nature of adultery," that is, the mixing of the spiritual and material natures: "The adulterous union with matter provokes suffering because it is contrary to nature."[10]

The Savior explains further that suffering "has no image"; that is, it is not a true reflection of anything in the immutable, spiritual realm. But that does not mean that suffering is not real; it leads to a disturbing confusion throughout the whole body. Peace can be found only by turning away from conformity to this false nature, and forming one's true self to "that other image of nature" which the Good came to "set within its root." Although the immutable, spiritual realm cannot be known in the world as it is in and of itself, it can be known through images and likenesses. "That other image of nature" is the reflection of the heavenly realm that allows it to be comprehended in the world.[11] It is this image which the Savior will later admonish his disciples to seek within themselves.

The distinction between "the nature of matter which has no image" and "that other image of nature" is based on a philosophical distinction between the lower world of sense perception (becoming) and the higher spiritual realm of true Being. For Plato, the world, although only a copy, was still as good as it could possibly be, and beliefs about it were still useful, if not absolutely reliable. But in the *Gospel of Mary* these views take on a more strictly dualistic cast in the light of human suffering. Confidence in material things is now equated with the deception that leads to death.

This shift may have political implications. Beliefs like Plato's in the relative lack of value of the material world were used to support the hegemonic interests of the upper class, to argue that there is a "natural" distinction between ruler and ruled due to the superior moral character of the ruler. The *Gospel of Mary* radicalizes the disparagement of matter to articulate a new "economy" of the spirit in which the hegemony of the world's rulers is itself critiqued as immoral "adultery." But we have to ask about the effectiveness of this new "economy." Does it leave intact exploitative economic and class structures (by turning attention away from the world to spiritual matters), or can it serve to undermine their "natural" quality and therefore their authority? The potential is there for either.

THE FINAL COMMISSION AND DEPARTURE
(BG 8.11–9.4; P.OXY. 3525, LINE 5)

The Savior concludes his teaching by instructing the disciples to seek peace within and to beware of trouble without. He commissions them to preach the gospel of the kingdom, admonishing them not to lay down any rule or law beyond what he has already given them, lest it come to dominate them.

The entire passage is structured by an implied contrast between inside and outside. The Savior begins by instructing the disciples to seek peace within themselves. The passion that disturbs and confuses the whole body, leaving it subject to sin and death, derives from the outside, from matter. The text uses the metaphorical contrast between inside and outside to indicate the dichotomy between the spiritual and material natures of a person. "Outside" refers to external matters, such as the social world and the health of one's body. "Inside" refers to one's essential, spiritual nature. In this context, the Savior's warning not to be led astray is aimed against people who would direct one to look outside for leadership from others, to look "over here" or "over there" instead of within. To expect a Son of Man to arrive on the clouds of heaven to save you is clearly to be led astray. Rather, the Savior says that "the son of man exists within you. Follow him!"

But what does it mean to say that "the son of man is within you"? Who is this "son of man"? Clearly he is not the apocalyptic hero of Mark 13! Irenaeus, a second-century Christian theologian, explicitly understands "son of man" to refer to the human nature of Jesus and to attest to the reality of the incarnation.[12] The *Gospel of Mary*, in contrast, may understand the "son of man" to be the archetypal Man (the primordial Adam), who is the heavenly model and the spiritual progenitor of all humanity.[13] Here the "son of man" is identified as the true "image of nature" to which the disciples are supposed to conform, the image of humanity's true spiritual nature. Again, the *Gospel of Mary* has given a distinctive interpretation to traditional Jesus material. In this case, the title "Son of Man" has a meaning very different from that found in the Synoptic Gospels.

Moreover, if this identification of "son of man" with the true heavenly image is correct, the translation "son of man" is at least partially misleading. The masculine singular in Coptic or Greek, as in English, is thoroughly informed by androcentric usage and can be either a generic reference to humanity as a whole ("humankind"), or indicate a specifically gendered male person ("a man"). Similarly, the term "son" in Coptic can refer to male children or to children generically. Translating the phrase as "son of man" reinscribes the androcentric character of the ancient languages and reinforces, or even introduces, an inaccurate exclusionary reference to the text. If it does not *mean* "son of man" but "child of humanity," it should be translated that way. In this case, a more accurate sense would be "seed of true humanity," a rendering that has the advantage of keeping readers alert to the androcentric character of the original text's language while not obscuring the sense. The addition of the term "true" reminds the reader that the phrase refers to the heavenly ideal. This inclusive translation should not obscure the fact that the usage of the masculine to refer to humanity as a whole is not accidental or incidental. The use of the masculine to refer to true human nature clearly reflects the values of Mediterranean culture, where the male represents what is perfect, powerful, and transcendent.[14]

The "seed of true humanity," then, corresponds to one's essential nature within. "Follow it!" the Savior commands. But again, it is not clear in what sense one can follow oneself. The term, "to follow," says Pasquier,

> in the *Gospel of Mary*, as with certain Stoics and Pythagoreans, appears to have the meaning of "grasping something as a model" . . . in order to become in turn a model oneself; in short, in this context, it requires the idea of an identification.[15]

To find and follow "the seed of true humanity" within requires identifying with the archetypal image of humanity as one's most essential nature and conforming to it as a model. "Those who search for it will find it," the Savior assures his disciples.

Having once found and become a model of true humanity, the disciples are then sent out to preach the gospel of the kingdom. The Savior admonishes them not to lay down any rule or law beyond what he has given, lest they be dominated by it. This command is often read as a denunciation of Jewish law, as part and parcel of the widespread anti-Jewish tendencies in early Christian literature. But the *Gospel of Mary* gives no other indications of a social context of conflict with Judaism. Rather, the overt polemic of the text is consistently directed against other Christians (see below, "Inter-Christian Controversies").

Moreover, inner states are emphasized throughout the text, while external regulations in general are disparaged. The command not to "lay down any rule beyond what I ordained for you, nor promulgate law like the lawgiver" could have been read as resistance to the establishment of any external restraints, not only Jewish law but also the formation of an exclusive Christian canon,[16] restrictions on prophecy and visionary experiences, or even colonial Roman law. If we are to imagine a second- or third-century setting in Egypt, for example, it is quite possible that many people would associate a "lawgiver" more readily with the Romans than with Moses.

Gerard Luttikhuizen has argued that often the "strained intertextual relationship to passages of the Bible is not a self-evident quality of the text but rather an effect of our way of reading."[17] We moderns are relatively well acquainted with the Bible and so little acquainted, relatively speaking, with other elements of ancient society that the biblical allusions leap out at us and dominate the way we read the text. It cannot be assumed, however, that ancient readers (who themselves no doubt came from a wide variety of social, political, economic, and cultural backgrounds!) would emphasize the biblical allusions as we do at the expense, say, of other political or philosophical meanings. On the other hand, the *Gospel of Mary* is at least in part designed for a Christian readership whom we might expect to be acquainted in some degree with the Jesus tradition and Paul. Indeed, the many allusions to Romans 7 in *Gos. Mary* 7.12–9.4 indicate that some of the language here may have derived from Paul's consideration of the Jewish law in the economy of salvation, however much or little the readers may have picked up on it. That understanding might be broadened or effaced depending on the diverse social and political situations of the *Gospel*'s readers. There are at least four possible ancient situations (or sets of readers) for us to imagine (none of which are necessarily completely distinct): the interpreters of Paul (who is certainly not anti-Jewish, but who offers an interesting critique of Judaism[18]), the readers of the *Gospel of Mary* who are fighting with other Christians about "rules" and "laws," anti-Jewish early Christians (who would definitely understand the law-giver to be Moses), and other early Christians (who may have identified the law-giver with Roman colonial administrators). We have to ask ourselves as modern readers whether our own (too automatic) reading almost solely with the anti-Jewish early Christians does not reflect altogether too clearly the anti-Semitism of our own contemporary contexts, and thereby give (too automatically) a (re)inscription of anti-Judaism into the *Gospel of Mary*. Consideration of the use of Romans 7 provides even further evidence that the best historical reading of this passage is that of inner-Christian conflict, not anti-Judaism (or Roman colonialism).

Anne Pasquier has demonstrated the close connections between Romans 7 and *Gos. Mary* 7.12–9.4. She lists the following points:[19] (1) Domination under the law is compared to adultery (Rom 7:3–4; *Gos. Mary* 7.15–16). (2) Adultery is compared with enslavement to passion and it leads to death (Rom 7:5; *Gos. Mary* 7.15–16; 8.2–4). (3) Freedom from the law means overcoming the domination of death (Rom 7:6; *Gos. Mary* 9.2–4). (4) Sin does not really exist (Rom 7:8; *Gos. Mary* 7.13–14). (5) Law, sin, and death are interconnected (Rom 7:9–10; *Gos. Mary* 7.13–8.1). (6) An opposition is made between the true, divine interior law/nature and that fleshly law/nature which imprisons or dominates one (Rom 7:22–23; *Gos. Mary* 8.2–6; 8.18–9:4).

According to Pasquier, the *Gospel of Mary* has transformed Paul's attempt to understand the value of Jewish law in the face of the saving event of Christ's death and resurrection by placing the discussion of law within a cosmological setting. Whereas, according to Paul, Christ came to free humanity from sin, the teaching of the Savior in the *Gospel of Mary* frees one from adulterous attachment to matter and the suffering of the human body. In contrast to Paul, the law is not divine and purposeful (Rom 7:7, 12–14); instead it is a tool of domination.

The interpretation of Pasquier is extremely useful in letting modern readers see the intertextual relationship of the *Gospel of Mary* with Romans. The comparison points up more sharply the distinctive character of the *Gospel of Mary*'s interpretation of law.

But while Pasquier is right in noting that the *Gospel of Mary* is clearly disparaging external laws, the Savior is really cautioning the disciples against promulgating law themselves: "Do not lay down any rule . . . lest it dominate you" (8.22–9.4). It is the law *that they themselves set* that will come to rule and restrict them. Spiritual advancement is to be sought within, not through external regulation. The context for this kind of command in the *Gospel of Mary* is inner-Christian debate about the meaning of salvation and how it is to be achieved.

This interpretation is strengthened by considering other intertextual references to the Jesus tradition. The *Gospel of Mary*'s setting, its characters, and many of the Savior's teachings invoke first-century gospel traditions. Yet, as with Romans 7, the *Gospel of Mary* clearly understands these traditions in ways that contrast markedly with other early Christian interpretations.

Gospel of Mary 8.11–9.4 is a good example. It is replete with allusions to materials from the Jesus tradition,[20] as the following list demonstrates: (1) "Peace be with you!" (cf. John 20:19, 21, 26). (2) "Acquire my peace within yourselves!" (cf. John 14:27). (3) "Be on your guard that no one deceives you" (cf. Mark 13:5; Matt 24:4; Luke 21:8) (4) "saying, 'Look over here!' or 'Look over there!'" (cf. Mark 13:21; Matt 24:23; Luke 17:21, 23; *Gos. Thom.* 113.3) (5) "for the 'Son of Man' exists within you" (cf. Luke 17:21; *Gos. Thom.* 3.3; 113.4). (6) "Those who seek for him will find him" (cf. Matt 7:8; Luke 11:10; *Gos. Thom.* 2.1; 92.1). (7) "Go then, preach the gospel of the kingdom" (cf. Mark 13:10; 16:15; Matt 4:23; 9:35; 24:14). These allusions have close thematic or linguistic parallels with all four canonical Gospels and the *Gospel of Thomas*. The *Gospel of Mary*, however, orders these sayings so that they take on meanings distinctly different from the other Gospels.

An excellent example is provided by Anne Pasquier.[21] In the *Gospel of Mary* 8.11–9.4, first the Savior cautions the disciples to guard themselves against error; then he affirms the presence of the seed of true humanity within them; and finally he commissions them to go preach the gospel. This order, Pasquier notes, is reversed in the canonical texts. In Matthew 24, for example, the Savior first commissions the disciples to preach the gospel of the kingdom; then he warns the disciples to guard against error; and finally he assures them of the coming of the Son of Man. The effect in Matthew is to see the preaching of the gospel as a precondition for the coming of the Son of Man and the last judgment. In the *Gospel of Mary*, however, the presence of the seed of true humanity within is the basis for preaching the kingdom. The order of the *Gospel of Mary* completely undercuts the eschatological message of Matthew and replaces it with a message to seek the kingdom and the "son of man" within.

THE DISCIPLES' RESPONSE TO THE SAVIOR'S DEPARTURE
(BG 9.5–12; P.OXY. 3525, LINES 5–8)

The response of the disciples to the departure of the risen Savior contrasts sharply with the portrayal of the same scene in the Gospels of Mark and Luke. In Luke, the disciples are filled with joy after Jesus departs; in Mark, they immediately go forth and preach the gospel.

Here, after the Savior departs, all the disciples, except Mary Magdalene, are distressed and weeping. In particular, they fear for their lives: "If they did not spare him, how will they spare us?" (9.10–12).[22] The reader has to wonder what kind of gospel such disciples will preach. Their doubt and fear show they have failed to acquire inward peace. How can they preach "the gospel of the kingdom of the seed of true humanity" if they do not understand that gospel themselves?

They think that following the Savior will lead them to suffering (cf. Mark 13:9–13), but they have completely misunderstood: the Savior's intention is to lead them away from suffering and death. Since attachment to the body is the source of suffering and death (7.22–8.1), separation from that attachment overcomes them: there is no promise of, or desire for, a physical resurrection.

Moreover, while the disciples' words indicate knowledge of Jesus' death (no docetism here!) and the possibility of anti-Christian persecutions (cf. John 15:20), neither Jesus' death nor martydom is invested with salvific meaning. The Savior came to alleviate suffering, not to chart a path to salvation by bringing it upon his disciples.

MARY COMFORTS THE OTHER DISCIPLES
(BG 9.12–24; P.OXY. 3525, LINES 8–14)

Mary Magdalene appears here for the first time in the extant text. Although it is not possible to say whether or not she played a role before this point (since the beginning pages of the manuscript are missing), it is clear that from here on Mary plays the central role. She replaces the Savior as the source of spiritual comfort and teaching, and functions as a spiritual guide for the other disciples.[23] While they are fearful and irresolute, she comforts them[24] and turns their minds toward the Good; that is to say, she turns them toward their own true, spiritual nature. This "conversion" is the very essence of salvation. To come to know the Good within, to know one's true self and abandon fears about the false corporeal nature, leads to salvation. Mary has set the other disciples on this path. They begin questioning and discussing among themselves, trying to understand what the words of the Savior truly meant.

Why is Mary able to convert the other disciples? What is it that she understands that the others do not? She tells them that "he has united (or Coptic:

prepared) us and made us true human beings" (*P.Oxy.* 12; *BG* 9.19–20). As was noted above,[25] to be a "true human being" means to have discovered one's own essential, spiritual nature within. It means to find and follow "the seed of true humanity" within. It requires identifying with the archetypal image of humanity, as one's most essential nature, and conforming to it as a model. Mary has achieved this goal: she has "become a true human being."

Mary's statement is, however, often translated: "he made us men." While this translation correctly reflects the androcentric character of the underlying Coptic language (i.e., where the male is made to stand for humanity generally), it unnecessarily raises the question of how Mary, a woman, can become a "man." Interpretations based on this translation often end up ignoring the conundrum that the male disciples, who are presumably already men, are also "made into men," and instead focus almost solely on the now problematic female nature of Mary. The masculine norm remains unnoticed and unquestioned. Still the text has put Mary in this position. Does it intend to emphasize her now-reformed female defectiveness or to affirm her full humanity? I believe the latter to be the case.

The Greek text also emphasizes that the Savior "united" the disciples. Mary fosters the ideal of group unity by placing the other disciples on the same level with her; she includes them with herself among those who have "been made into true human beings." This ideal group unity is later shattered by the disciples' dispute over the legitimacy of Mary's teaching and leadership.

According to the Coptic text, the role of the Savior in this process of spiritual attainment is only preparatory. His teaching strengthens the disciples by pointing them to the Good within themselves, but it is up to them to find it. Mary clearly has achieved this goal, and is thus able to function as a teacher and guide to the other disciples.

PETER ASKS MARY TO TEACH
(BG 10.1–9; P.OXY. 3525, LINES 14–18)

This section forms a transition to the revelation of Mary, which follows.[26] Peter initiates the dialogue between Mary and the other disciples. He asks Mary to recount any teaching she may have received from the Savior that the other disciples have not heard.[27] He calls her "Sister" (*BG* 10.1–2) and says he knows that the Savior loved her more than any other woman. His acceptance of her is based on her special status as the woman whom the Savior favored.

In the Coptic text, Peter gets more than he asked for, however. Peter's formulation seems to imply that he expected Mary to have some words from the Savior that the others had not heard. There is no expectation in Peter's words that the Savior might have hidden anything from the other disciples, only that Mary may have had conversations with him when they were not present. Her response, however, indicates something quite different. She agrees to give them teaching that had been *hidden* from them. Her response conveys an expectation of secret, esoteric teaching that Peter's request did not. In the Greek version, however, there is no such implication; there Mary simply says she will tell them what she remembers that is unknown to them. Only the Coptic text emphasizes that Mary's teaching is intended to be esoteric.

MARY'S TEACHING ON VISION AND MIND
(BG 10.9–23; P.OXY. 3525, LINES 18–20)

The *Gospel of Mary* now quotes Mary's account of her vision of the Savior as she tells it to the other disciples. The teaching she gives is based on a direct revelation from the Savior in a vision. This form guarantees the authority of her teaching by ascribing it ultimately to the Savior himself. Like the first portion of the extant text, the vision of the risen Lord is framed as a dialogue.

Mary begins by telling the other disciples that the Lord appeared to her in a vision.[28] She does not waver at the sight, but immediately acknowledges the Lord's presence. He, in turn, praises her for her steadfastness, saying: "Blessed are you for not wavering at seeing me. For where the mind is, there is the treasure" (*BG* 10.14–16).

The term "wavering" carries important connotations in ancient thought, where it is contrasted with stability.[29] Mary's stability illustrates her conformity to the unchanging and eternal spiritual world and provides one more indication of her advanced spiritual status.

The saying about treasure is often quoted in early Christian literature.[30] In Q, for example, the saying is used to warn people against greed and attachment to ephemeral wealth (see Matt 6:21; Luke 12:34). In the *Gospel of Mary*, however, the term "mind" refers the reader back to Mary's ministry to the other disciples: "she turned their minds toward the Good" (*BG* 9.21–22). It is because Mary has placed her mind with God that she can direct others to the spiritual treasure of the Good.

Mary begins by asking the Savior how it is that one receives a vision, by the soul or the spirit. The Savior's answer to Mary's question describes the tripartite composition of the true inner self: it is made up of soul-mind-spirit. The mind conveys the vision, functioning as a mediator between the spirit and the soul. Unfortunately, the text breaks off here and no more can be said.

MARY'S TEACHING ON THE ASCENT OF THE SOUL
(BG 15.1–17.9; P.RYL. 21.1–5)

Four manuscript pages are lost. The story resumes in the middle of an account of the soul's rise through the planetary spheres. Mary's teaching here is concerned with how to liberate the soul from its bondage to the material realm, a bondage arising from the adulterous union of spirit and matter. This bondage is represented by four heavenly Powers the soul must overcome. They probably represent the four elements of the material world: earth, water, fire, and air.[31]

The fourth Power is also given seven names,[32] which correspond to the seven astrological spheres that control fate.[33] These names indicate the character of the world below and contrast it with the world above: the true kingdom is light, peace, knowledge, love, and life; the lower world is darkness, desire, ignorance, jealousy, and the excitement of death. The lower kingdom of the flesh is opposed to the heavenly kingdom of the seed of true humanity. The foolish wisdom of the flesh and wrath below is opposed to the true wisdom above.

Opposition also characterizes the primary dynamic of the soul's ascent past the four Powers. The dialogue between the soul and the Powers[34] effects a series of reversals, often with considerable liveliness and humor. The Powers attempt to stop the soul's escape by keeping it bound to the world below, but the soul unmasks the ignorance of each Power, and then merrily goes on its way.

The interaction with the first Power (probably called Darkness) is unfortunately lost in the lacuna.

The second Power, Desire, tries to stop the soul by telling it, "I did not see you go down, yet now I see you go up. So why do you lie since you belong to me?" In other words, the Power is accusing the soul of lying about its heavenly origin, since the Power thinks it has always been a creature of the lower world. The Power assumes that soul, in attempting to escape, is claiming that it does not belong to the material world. From the Power's point of view, that is a lie; since it did not see the soul come down from the world above, it thinks the soul must indeed belong to the material world. The wise soul responds that only its garment (the body that "clothed" it) belongs to the material world, not its true self, which the Power never knew—as the Power has itself unwittingly admitted by saying it did not see the soul descend. The response of the soul has unmasked the blindness of Desire: the Power had not been able to see past the soul's material husk to its true spiritual nature. But the discerning soul does see the true nature of the material world, and rejects it. In glee, the soul moves on.

The third Power is called Ignorance. As Pasquier points out, three terms structure its dialogue with the soul: ignorance, domination, and judgment.[35] These three form the basis of the Power's illegitimate domination over entrapped souls. The Power claims that the soul is ignorant of its material nature and is illegitimately trying to escape. It judges the soul, pointing out its fornication (adulterous union) with the flesh. Because of this sin, in the Power's view, the soul has no power of discernment: "Do not judge!" it commands. The soul, for its part, rejects any kind of judgment and domination, associating them with (Ignorance's) ignorance. Condemnation is tied to sin (the adulterous mixing of the material and the spiritual). But sin is illusory because, as the soul knows, "the universe is to be dissolved, both the things of earth and those of heaven" (*BG* 15.20–16.1; cf. Mark 13:31). The soul's rejoinder to the Power here is a kind of applied restatement of the Savior's teaching about sin and nature given earlier in the text: "There is no such thing as sin" (*BG* 7.13). The soul's insight into its own true spiritual identity allows it the discernment to overcome the illegitimate domination of the Power. Again, the wit in the passage lies in the fact that it is the Power itself which has acknowledged that the soul's knowledge is true: sin is due only to the domination of the flesh. Without the flesh, there is no sin, judgment, or condemnation; this insight frees the soul.

Like the third Power, the fourth Power, Wrath, also intended to point out the soul's lower origins, by asking it where it comes from and where it thinks it is going. But again Wrath ignorantly plays into the hands of the wise and playful soul who knows that it derives from above and is returning to its true place of origin. The Power calls the soul a human-killer (referring to its having cast off the material body) and a space-conqueror (referring to the seven astrological spheres it has traversed and overcome). These terms of approbation are greeted happily by the soul, who tells the Power that indeed the material elements and the body that bound it in lust and ignorance have been overcome and it is free from bondage. The soul contrasts the imprisoning cosmos from which it has come with that to which it goes; it distinguishes the deceitful image below from the true image above, and mortality (the chains of temporal existence) from immortality.

Even as the soul finally finds perfect rest in silence,[36] so does Mary too become silent, modeling in her behavior the perfect rest of the soul set free.[37]

The Disciples Argue about Mary's Teaching
(BG 17.10–19.2; P.Ryl. 21.5–16; 22.1–16)

As soon as Mary finishes speaking, her testimony is called into question, first by Andrew and then by Peter.

Speaking directly to the other male disciples, Andrew questions the legitimacy of Mary's words. He rejects her teaching because it does not seem similar to the Savior's teaching that he knows.

His criticism has no basis, however, since Mary's teaching corresponds very closely to that given to the disciples by the Savior in the first part of the text. The Savior's teaching described the end of the material world and the restoration of the soul to its root through the intervention of the Good. The revelation of Mary applies those teachings to the soul's ascent, showing how true self-knowledge enables the soul to escape the fetters of material existence and ascend to the place of rest. Moreover, the language of materiality in the ascent of the soul presupposes the prior teaching of the Savior about the nature of matter; and the dialogue about judgment and domination between the third Power and the soul presupposes the Savior's teaching on sin and law. In *BG* 7.3–8, the Savior points out that everything will be dissolved into its root, just as at 15.20–21 the soul tells the third Power that it knows the universe is to be dissolved. There is no incongruity between the teachings of the Savior and those of Mary's vision. The reader can see that Andrew's objection has no merit.

Peter's objections challenge Mary's character and status rather than the content of her teaching. He first challenges whether the Savior would give Mary special teaching in private. According to ancient thought, two kinds of activities took place in private: activities that were restricted to privileged members (such as families, or political and religious organizations), or activities that were morally suspect and thus required the cover of secrecy. Peter's words imply recognition of these options: either he must recognize the privileged status of Mary or impugn her words as lies hatched in secret.

The implications are not lost on Mary. Distressed, she asks Peter directly if he is implying that she fabricated the whole story and is purposefully lying. The reader's sympathies are clearly with her, since the *Gospel* up to this point has painted a portrait of Mary as the exemplary disciple, and she has done nothing to warrant this kind of criticism of her character.

Peter's second complaint, that Mary's words seem to imply that the Savior preferred her to the male disciples, clearly indicates his own personal jealousy and concern for maintaining privileged male status. Mary, keeping to the traditional role of female modesty and passivity, does not respond to Peter's challenge;[38] it is left to another male disciple, Levi, to defend her character and her special position with the Savior.

Levi begins Mary's defense with an attack on Peter's character, pointing out that he is widely known to be a hothead (cf. Matt 26:74; Mark 8:32–33 par.; John 18:10) and that he is behaving arrogantly. According to the Greek fragment, his temper leads him to attack Mary as though he were her adversary, thereby disrupting the peace and unity of the group that Mary sought to foster.[39] The Coptic version's condemnation of Peter's action is even stronger. There Levi uses the same term ("wrathful person") to describe Peter that was used to name the seventh form of the Powers of Wrath (*BG* 9.24). It also says that he is fighting Mary "like the Adversaries," thereby accusing Peter of being allied with the Powers, who illegitimately attempt to entrap the soul.[40] Peter's divisiveness puts him on the side of the Powers and contrasts sharply with Mary's attempt to unify the disciples and turn them to the Good.

Levi also implies that Peter is arrogantly placing himself above the Savior. To paraphrase Levi's words: "Who do you think you are, Peter, to question the judgment of the Lord by rejecting her? The Lord himself has made her worthy." Levi's attack on Peter's character thoroughly undermines the validity of Peter's criticism.

Levi also directly affirms Mary's privileged status with the Savior: "the Savior considered her to be worthy . . . he knew her completely <and> loved her steadfastly" (*P.Ryl.* 5.7–8). The Coptic version of the text stresses the point even further. There Levi bluntly states that the Savior loved Mary more than "us," thereby emphasizing Mary's preeminence over the male disciples. Note that when Peter first addressed Mary, he acknowledged that the Savior loved her more than other *women* (*BG* 10.1–3). Now the issue is, as Levi states it, that the Savior loved her *more than the male disciples* (*BG* 18.14–15). Peter rejects the fact that the Lord preferred Mary to himself and that he would give private and superior teaching to a woman. It obviously offends his masculine honor and pride to be seen as inferior to a woman. The *Gospel of Mary* sharply criticizes Peter's point of view. His spiritual immaturity cannot see past the superficial distinctions of the flesh and political-social status to perceive Mary's spiritual superiority.

The Savior's partiality for Mary has received a good deal of comment, much of it suggesting a romantic or sexual involvement.[41] Could that be implied here? I think not. The text again and again bases Mary's status on her spiritual qualities and stresses that the body and the world have no lasting spiritual value since they will be dissolved.[42] Are we reifying the patriarchal sexualization of the female body if we insist that whenever a woman is involved, relations must be sexual? On the other hand, the text is quite ambiguous and certainly does not directly condemn sexual relations.

Levi concludes with an address to all the disciples, reminding them of the Savior's commission to go and preach the gospel. "Let us put on perfect humanity," he tells them, clearly referring the disciples (and the reader) back to the Savior's admonition to seek the seed of true humanity within (*BG* 8.18–21). Levi's phrase also reverberates with Paul's description of baptism as "putting on Christ" (Gal 3:27)[43] and with Eph 4:13. There the phrase "perfect manhood" (RSV) signifies the ideal state of maturity toward which all Christians strive. It is characterized by unity, knowledge, and stability; those who have attained this exalted state are no longer buffeted about by "every wind of doctrine, by the cunning of men, by their craftiness in deceitful wiles" (RSV 4:14). It appears that yet again, the *Gospel of Mary* is providing its own theological interpretation of well-known Christian terminology.

There are a number of significant variations between the Greek and Coptic versions of Levi's final words. At *BG* 18.17, the Coptic version adds, "and acquire (perfect humanity) for ourselves," emphasizing the need for an interior experience. The phrase also recalls the words of the Savior at *BG* 8.14–15, where he admonished them to acquire interior peace.

At 18.20–21, the Coptic adds the qualification, "differing from what the Savior said." This addition reflects the Savior's instructions at *BG* 9.1–2. The Greek version, however, is more radical in its unqualified admonition to lay down *no* laws or rules and is probably earlier. The qualification, both at *BG* 9.1–2 and 19.20–21, is probably a secondary addition, intended to soften the radical character of the command.

The *Gospel* ends with considerable ambiguity. Mary is fully vindicated and the Savior's teaching reaffirmed, but, according to the Greek text, only Levi actually leaves to fulfill the Savior's command. In the Coptic version, all the disciples go forth and preach the gospel. Yet at the very least, the reader is left wondering what kind of gospel such a fearful and contentious group of disciples is going to proclaim.

Title (BG 19.3–5)

As is common in ancient manuscripts, the title appears at the end of the text. The ascription of the text to Mary (Magdalene) does not indicate that she was the author of the text but rather acknowledges that she plays the central role. It was a common practice in early Christianity to name gospels after the most prominent disciples of Jesus in order to ensure their authority.

THE GOSPEL OF MARY IN HISTORICAL CONTEXT

There are numerous topics that deserve further exploration. Because of limitations of space, I have chosen to explore only two here: the portrait of Mary Magdalene and the inter-Christian debates within the *Gospel of Mary*. These were chosen because of their central importance to women's history.

Mary Magdalene

Mary Magdalene was a Jewish woman, a woman of color whose life story evolved at the confluence of three continents. She followed Jesus of Nazareth and after his death became a leader in the early Christian movement. As was the case with many other prominent figures of early Christian history, the very meagerness of what was known of her life served only to fire the imaginations of later Christians, who elaborated her history in story and art according to their spiritual needs and political aims. Where are we to locate the *Gospel of Mary* among these portraits? An overview of the ancient evidence is necessary to answer the question. But first, a few preliminary comments are necessary.

It must be noted that the degree to which our interests coincide with those of the ancient sources is limited. They are not interested in psychological biography, and their views of the goals and methods of historiography are decidedly different. All the characters in the early Christian gospel literature, including Jesus and the disciples, are portrayed as types: the messianic Savior, the wisdom teacher, the doubting disciple(s), the good disciple, the betraying disciple, and so forth. They provide models for behavior, edification, and conversion. The texts do not give us the information necessary for the kind of psychological and historical portrait central to modern biography and historiography. Even accounts of emotions (anger, weeping, pity, etc.) are included primarily to illustrate a type's particular character. Mary appears—as do all the other disciples in the canonical Gospels—not as the subject of modern historical biography but as a model for early Christian discipleship. The ancients conceived of history more as edification than as an objective account of the way it actually happened. This does not mean that the texts have no historical value (in our sense); it means we must see them as reflections of the spiritual and political interests of early Christians. When we read the ancient sources, we do not see "face to face" but "through a glass darkly," and part of the shadow for women's history is that we must look at women's activities and agency through the window frame of patriarchal interests. We approach the stories of Mary Magdalene, therefore, with a "hermeneutics of suspicion."

The earliest Gospel accounts of Mary Magdalene portray this Jewish woman as a prominent disciple of Jesus. According to these accounts, she accompanied Jesus throughout much of his ministry (Mark 15:40–41; Matt 27:55–56; Luke 8:1–3; John 19:25; *Gospel of Philip* 59.6–9[?]), was present at his crucifixion (Mark 15:40–41; John 19:25) and entombment (Mark 15:47; Matt 27:61). Usually with other women, but sometimes alone, Mary goes to the tomb and is the first witness to the resurrection (Mark 16:1–8; Matt 28:1–7; Luke 24:1–10; John 20:1, 11–13)[44] and the first to see the risen Lord.[45] She is commissioned by angels or by the risen Jesus as an apostle to the other apostles (Mark 16:7; Matt 28:7; John 20:17; *Epistula Apostolorum*)[46] and brings them the good news of the resurrection (Mark 16:10; Matt 28:8, 10; Luke 24:8–10). Though her testimony is usually questioned or completely discounted by the male disciples (Mark 16:10–11; Luke 24:10–11),[47] in the end the Gospels vindicate her and validate the truth and authority of her witness. Moreover, she clearly meets the criteria of apostleship presented in Acts 1:21–22: she was a companion during the ministry of the historical Jesus and a witness to the resurrection.

Recent authors have emphasized the leadership role of Mary Magdalene that these early texts indicate. Elisabeth Schüssler Fiorenza, for example, notes that the Gospel of John presents women, and Mary Magdalene preeminently among them, as models of true discipleship, especially in contrast to the male disciples around Peter.[48]

Elements of this portrait are elaborated in the Christian literature of the second and third centuries. Mary is portrayed as the companion of the Savior, whom he loved above the other disciples.[49] She is prominent among the disciples, often asking Jesus questions[50] and being singled out for special praise. For example, in the *Dialogue of the Savior,* Mary, along with Judas and Matthew, asks questions of Jesus and is given a special vision of the Son of Man (*Dial. Sav.* 134.24ff.). Mary's statements are so full of insight that at one point the text's narrator comments: "She spoke this statement as a woman who had understood completely" (139.11–13). *Pistis Sophia* also affirms Mary's advanced spiritual understanding. She answers most of the questions in the text (thirty-nine out of forty-six), and Jesus himself says of her: "'You are the one who has a heart that is more directed toward the kingdom of heaven than all your brothers'" (26.19–20). Like the *Gospel of Mary,* these texts acknowledge that Mary attained a privileged position of spiritual wisdom beyond the other disciples.

The church fathers also had second-hand knowledge of certain traditions about Mary. According to Hippolytus, the Naasenes (a group Hippolytus thinks to be heretical) passed down discourses of the Savior from James, the brother of the Lord, to Mary (*Ref.* 5.7.1). Origen attests to groups named after Mary Magdalene and other women (Marcellina, Salome, and Martha) (*Contra Celsum* 5.62). Epiphanius claims to know about books attributed to Mary Magdalene (*Questions of Mary*) in which she received secret teaching from the risen Savior (*Panarion* 2.8.1–6).[51] In general, however, second- and third-century church fathers seldom mention Mary Magdalene at all.[52] She arouses more interest among fourth-century fathers, but primarily in the attempt to prove that the Savior's enigmatic command in John 20:17 that she should not touch him does not indicate that Jesus' resurrection body was not fully physical.[53] They tend to explain the sentence by arguing that Mary, unlike Thomas, was not worthy of touching the resurrected Lord.

The second and third centuries seem to have produced two types of treatments of Mary: those that emphasize her spiritual attainment and leadership and those that marginalize her role by ignoring her. Silence, however, was not as effective a strategy for marginalizing the apostleship of Mary Magdalene as reinterpreting her story. The early portrait of Mary as a prominent disciple was almost fully eclipsed by the later medieval portrait of Mary as the repentant sinner. This revised edition of Mary's story was based on identifying her with the sinner in Luke 7:35–50 and the adulteress in John 8:1–11. These identifications laid the foundation for the portrait of the Mary so well known from medieval and Renaissance times as the repentant whore, the "Venus in sackcloth," the counterpoint to the virgin Mother of God, the representative of fallen female sexuality redeemed.[54] This portrait obviously was more pliable to patriarchal modes of theologizing than the powerful depiction of Mary Magdalene as a leader among the disciples.

What now can be said about the "historical Mary Magdalene"? While some have discounted the earliest Gospel accounts of Mary's encounter with the risen Jesus as late and historically unreliable,[55] others judge the story to be ancient, based primarily on the fact that there are multiple independent witnesses to the tradition. Moreover, Raymond Brown writes: "An argument in favor of antiquity is the primacy all the Gospels give her among the women followers of Jesus whenever they are listed; this may well be because she was the first one to see the risen Jesus."[56]

However one decides this issue, it is important to remember that the early Gospels themselves reflect the political and spiritual interests of different groups of early Christians. As Bovon notes: "Since early Christianity was not a monolith, each group found its *raison d'être* and its status as people of God in an appearance of the risen Jesus to its foremost leader."[57] The historical reliability of the resurrection scenes is less important to me than the fact that, for early Christians, the witness to an appearance of the risen Lord signaled authority for the foundational claim of orthodox Christianity. That three of the four canonical texts would single out Mary for this honor weighs heavily in favor of her importance to certain circles within early Christianity. That Luke should favor Peter for this position already shows the tension between the claims of these early Christian groups. (For more on this topic, see below under "Inter-Christian Controversies.")

In my view, there is enough evidence to suppose that Mary Magdalene played a prominent role in the early Christian movement; however, little more can be said with surety. It may be that the portrayals of her as a prophetic visionary and spiritual leader may have drawn on historical memory, but this cannot be claimed with certainty. It may be that those portraits are but elaborations of the tradition that placed her as the first witness to the resurrected Lord. Yet, however elaborated, the portrayal of Mary as a prominent disciple and leader is much more consistent with the early sources than that of the repentant whore and countertype to Eve, which has no historical foundation whatsoever.

The account of Mary Magdalene in the *Gospel of Mary* cannot be taken uncritically as simple historical "fact." It draws on and elaborates several scenarios concerning Mary that by the second century had become traditional: her role as a preeminent disciple of Jesus, her privileged reception of special visions and teaching from the risen Lord, her role as comforter and instructor of the other disciples, and the conflict with the male disciples over the reliability of her testimony. The *Gospel of Mary* develops these topics in order to emphasize Mary's superior spiritual knowledge, her favored status with Jesus, and her legitimate leadership among the disciples.

INTER-CHRISTIAN CONTROVERSIES

The tensions among the disciples within the *Gospel of Mary* illustrate a number of issues that were under debate among Christians in the first and second centuries.[58] The primary substantive issue concerns its teaching on the value of suffering and death, the nature of the world, sin, and salvation. The conflicts are represented narratively in the tensions among the disciples, and the primary sociological issue concerns a crisis of authority in early Christian groups. The issues of authority and of the value of suffering are intimately related, since proofs for what is the true teaching of the Savior are directly tied to recognition of who has the authority to speak for the risen Lord. The controversy focuses on three points: (1) the reliability of the disciples' witness; (2) the validity of teachings given to the disciples through postresurrection revelation and vision; and (3) the leadership and authority of women.

All legitimate authority in early Christianity derives from appeal to Jesus' words and deeds. Since Jesus did not himself leave any writings, a problem arose early on concerning the reliability of the transmission of Jesus' teaching. In the *Gospel of Mary*, we see that all the disciples, with the exception of Mary (and Levi), have misunderstood the Savior's message. They are frightened and distraught when he departs and reject Mary's authentic teaching. Andrew objects to the strange content of Mary's vision,[59] but the main attack comes from Peter, since both Mary and Levi respond only to him. Peter stands out as the representative of this group.[60]

The figure of Peter is used frequently in early Christian texts to authorize theological positions,[61] for example, in 2 Pet 3:14–18 against Paul. Peter was not always linked with the same position, however, and was in fact sometimes used even to authorize opposite sides of an issue. For example, Irenaeus uses him as a witness to the physical reality of Jesus' incarnation,[62] while in the *Apocalypse of Peter,* Peter receives special revelation from the Savior affirming a Christology that rejects the incarnation and affirms that Jesus only *seemed* to have a body (i.e., a docetic Christology). Both Irenaeus and the *Apocalypse of Peter* appeal to Peter's witness to attest to the reliability of their own theological teachings.

But there was another portrait of Peter in the early tradition—the image of him as a continual failure. In Mark 13, he misunderstands Jesus' words and Jesus calls him "Satan." During the trial, he denies Jesus three times.[63] The *Gospel of the Nazoreans* writes that Peter "denied and swore and damned himself" (*Gos. Naz.* 19).

There were clearly some Christians who did not view the disciples as equally perfect, nor their teachings as entirely reliable. Some argued that their own direct revelations were superior to the teaching circulating under the names of the disciples.[64] Irenaeus describes these Christians: "For the apostles [they say] mixed matters of the Law with the words of the Savior; . . . while they know the hidden mystery without doubt or corruption, and in its purity."[65]

In the *Gospel of Mary*, it is precisely such "mingling" that the Savior warns the disciples against (*BG* 8.22–9.4; cf. *Apoc. Pet.* 77.22–78.1). Its own teaching is represented as the direct, pure and uncorrupted words of the Savior.

The agitated response of the disciples to the Savior's departure and Mary's teaching leaves the outcome of the Savior's commission uncomfortably undecided. The *Gospel of Mary* does not leave the reader with a sense of confidence that Peter and Andrew will do a very good job of preaching the kingdom. Their initial disturbance at the Savior's departure and then the reckless response to Mary seem to indicate that they have not found the peace the Savior admonished them to acquire. The ending of the Greek fragment, where only Levi goes off to preach the gospel, leaves the situation even more unresolved than the Coptic. For the *Gospel of Mary*, the words of the disciples are not reliable solely on the basis of apostolic authority, let alone gender. Spiritual maturity is the primary requirement, and it is based on direct revelation from the risen Savior. The altercation among the disciples (Mary and Levi versus Andrew and Peter) indicates a crisis of authority.

The second focus of the dispute concerns the issue of whether or not Jesus communicated superior teaching to his disciples in private. This question was hotly debated in the early churches. Mark 4:10–11, for example, attests to a tradition that the *earthly* Jesus gave superior teaching to the disciples in private during his ministry. In addition, the second-century heresiologist Irenaeus gives evidence that some Christians were basing the authority of their teachings primarily on these teachings of the risen Lord:

> He (Jesus) remained eighteen months after his resurrection, and when perception descended into him, he taught what is clear. But only to a few of his disciples whom he knew to be capable of such great mysteries did he teach these things. (*Adv. Haer.* 1.30.4)

Irenaeus's own view is that these people are heretics and they have made it all up, substituting their own deceitful words for the public testimony of the four written Gospels (*Adv. Haer.* 3.2.1). Andrew's response to Mary's teaching displays a haunting resemblance to Irenaeus's view.

The *Gospel of Mary* clearly affirms the validity of postresurrection teaching and visionary revelation. This position is most clearly affirmed by the genre and setting of the text. The postresurrection setting functions to validate the superior content and character of the Savior's teachings by making the appearance of the risen Lord the source of true teaching and genuine apostolic authority.[66]

The final focus of dispute concerns the status of Mary. The issue under debate directly engages the existence of women in leadership roles in early

Christianity. The conflict with the male disciples over the reliability of Mary's testimony is framed so as to bring the issue of women's authority to the fore.

There are a variety of texts from the second and third centuries that portray Mary Magdalene and Peter in conflict.[67] This scenario seems to have been elaborated from accounts of the disciples' rejection of Mary's witness to the resurrection. In the *Epistula Apostolorum,* Peter is singled out for the Savior's approbation after rejecting the women's testimony (11). Peter, Andrew, and Thomas do not believe until they have touched the wounds of the risen Savior, in contrast to the immediate faith of Mary, Martha, and Salome. In the *Gospel of Thomas,* the conflict becomes more acute—and more clearly a matter of gender struggle. The final logion reads:

> Simon Peter said to them, "Let Mary leave us, for women are not worthy of life." Jesus said, "I myself shall lead[68] her in order to make her male, so that she too may become a living spirit resembling you males. For every woman who will make herself male will enter the kingdom of heaven." (*Gos. Thom.* 114)[69]

Here Mary's spiritual status is defended against Peter's attack, but his categorical sexism is at best moderated, not opposed: women *as women* are apparently not worthy of life. A somewhat better defense of Mary against Peter's continued attacks is made in the *Pistis Sophia* (2.72). When Mary complains that she would like to come forward and give an interpretation but she is afraid of Peter "for he threatens me and he hates our race," the Savior's response is, "Everyone who will be filled with the spirit of light to come forward and give the interpretation of those things which I say, that one will no one be able to prevent."[70] Here the issue of gender is sidestepped in favor of nongendered spirituality.

The conflict between Peter and Mary in the *Gospel of Mary* should be viewed as another enactment of this type of scene. Peter wages a direct attack against Mary but is clearly and decisively repulsed. The portrayal of Mary as an exemplary disciple contrasts her sharply with Peter. Note, for example, Peter's instability and temper compared with the Savior's description of Mary's unwavering faith.

At the same time, by affirming Mary's teaching and her leadership role against charges by Peter that the Savior would not have told things to a *woman* that he did not tell to them, the *Gospel of Mary* clearly affirms the legitimacy of women's apostolic leadership. It does so, however, not on the basis of women's—or men's—gender, but on the basis of superior spiritual qualifications. Mary is not merely the Savior's favorite female, as Peter would have it; she is his most favored disciple. Peter appears, along with Andrew, as the representative of those who would limit Christian teaching to what was public[71] and to the authority of men. Mary, along with Levi,[72] on the other hand, represents those Christians who question the validity of any apostolic authority that challenges the truth of their own experience of the living Lord; for them, apostolic authority is not based simply on being one of the Twelve or on gender but on spiritual qualifications.[73] Women who have those qualifications may exercise legitimate authority.

The *Gospel of Mary* thus provides an important complement to texts such as 1 Tim 2:8–15, which demand the silence and submissiveness of women and forbid them to have authority over men. We can now see that the position of 1 Timothy is *but one side* of a debate in early Christian circles. The *Gospel of Mary* also provides evidence that texts such as 1 Timothy were written precisely because women were exercising leadership and exerting their authority over men. If some thought that such women were immodest, unseemly, insubordinate, and garrulous, Levi's mocking response to Peter shows that others may have viewed the opponents to women's legitimate leadership as jealous, proud, contentious, and foolish. The *Gospel of Mary* unequivocally advocated women's leadership based on spiritual merit.

But let us look more closely. While the *Gospel of Mary* clearly affirms that women can and did exercise legitimate authority, it seems to deny that women could hold that authority *as women*. Women were either expected in some way to become male, or their legitimacy was seen as a matter of nongendered spiritual progression. In the first case, it would seem that male patriarchal authority is not really challenged on the symbolic level: the male alone symbolizes full humanity. In the second case, women's leadership in some sense becomes a nonissue. Gender is not the point; spirituality is.

But can contemporary women afford a model of "true humanity" that is either male or ungendered? I think not. To relinquish the symbolic ground is to lose considerable territory. To accept a view of humanity as ungendered could lead to a dangerous lapse into forgetfulness. Just as we may no longer countenance the systematic erasure of Mary Magdalene's dark skin color or her Jewishness, so women cannot afford to join the ranks of True Humanity without critical appraisal and introspection. The attainment of power through merit need not require disappearance into a homogenous Humanity. An ungendered, universal, transcendent view of ideal Humanity potentially removes us too far from lived human experience, differences in human conditions, and the realities of human diversity (not only gender but also class, race, age, sexual preference, and so on). This distance and forgetfulness are dangerous, since they can too easily wipe away consciousness both of privilege and oppression, and with them political action for justice and equity.

But should we expect ancient texts to offer resources in contemporary struggles for justice and liberation? The political world of the *Gospel of Mary* is far removed from our own. Its critique of patriarchy is by no means feminist in the modern sense, since the intent is not to free women from male domination but to free the soul from the bonds of suffering and death. Yet clearly this gospel opposes illegitimate domination—whether by self-made entrapments, enslavement to the Powers of materiality, or the exclusion of women from leadership. Moreover, it offers powerful images of liberation in its portrait of Mary's ministry and the soul's journey to freedom.

"Narrative," as Mieke Bal has said, "proclaims a state of the world."[74] This claim, as she notes, can be inherently dangerous because it states how one *wants* the world to be. For then as for now, the danger is that only certain people get to say "this is the state of the world"—as seen in controversies over orthodoxy and heresy that successfully erased from Christian history views such as those of the *Gospel of Mary*. The rediscovery of the *Gospel of Mary* means that other voices are allowed to speak and views other than those that "triumphed" can be heard. Though we must surely put the desires of our hearts to earnest scrutiny and our historical sources to the discipline of honest inquiry, the *Gospel of Mary* provides us with new resources for reflection and action.

MANUSCRIPTS AND LANGUAGE

Portions of the *Gospel of Mary* have survived in three manuscripts, two third-century Greek fragments (*P. Oxyrhynchus* 3525 and *P. Rylands* 463) and a longer fifth-century Coptic translation (*Berolinensis gnosticus* [BG] 8502,1). Although the original language of the text is Greek, most of the extant text survives only in Coptic translation. Unfortunately, the Coptic codex is seriously marred. Pages 1–6[75] and 11–14 are missing, so that perhaps half of the text is lost. There is some additional damage to the surviving pages on the top and bottom, and some problems with ink fading. Nonetheless, this codex remains the most important extant witness to the *Gospel of Mary*.

P. Rylands was found in 1917 and published in 1938, while *P. Oxyrhynchus* 3525 was only first identified as a fragment of the *Gospel of Mary* and published in 1983 by P. J. Parsons. The two Greek fragments both come from Oxyrhynchus and date to the third century (in the case of *P. Rylands* probably the early part of the third century). They attest to at least two copies of the *Gospel of Mary* in Greek, since they derive from different manuscripts.[76] Unfortunately these two fragments parallel portions extant in Coptic (*P.Ryl.* to *BG* 17.5–21; 18.5–19.5; *P.Oxy.* 3525 to *BG* 9.5–10.14[77]) and thus add no new material to the text. There are, however, some significant textual variants, discussed above in the commentary section.

Brackets around translated words [] indicate restorations to lacunae in the manuscripts.

GENRE AND STRUCTURE

The *Gospel of Mary* calls itself a "gospel." The term does not, however, indicate the genre of the text (as a narrative of the earthly Jesus' teachings and deeds) but points the reader toward the "good news" that the Savior brought to enlighten humanity spiritually.

The *Gospel of Mary* has been classified as an apocalypse because it has many characteristics similar to ancient apocalypses,[78] such as revelation, an otherworldly journey, belief in the dissolution of the world, and authorization of the text's message by ascribing it to a heavenly origin.[79] But despite these similarities to apocalypses, a better classification is postresurrection dialogue.[80] The primacy of the dialogue form, the postresurrection gospel setting, and the distinctive character of its eschatological teaching all serve to place the *Gospel of Mary* in this category. Each of these elements requires consideration.

FORM: DIALOGUE AND DEPARTURE

The *Gospel of Mary* is structured as a series of dialogues and departures:

> Dialogue between the Savior and the disciples
> Departure of the Savior
>
> Dialogue between Mary and the disciples
>
>> Dialogue between the Savior and Mary
>> Departure of the Savior (signaled by Mary's silence)
>>
>>> Dialogues between the soul and the Powers
>>> Departures of the soul
>> Departure of the disciples (or Levi alone)

This structure has a double purpose. First, the structural similarity between the two main dialogues authorizes Mary's teaching and her leadership role by placing her structurally in a position parallel to that of the Savior: it is she who steps into the Savior's place by turning the other disciples' hearts toward the Good and providing them with advanced spiritual instruction. Second, the embedding of dialogues within dialogues creates an ordered layering of the teaching that leads the reader deeper and deeper inward. In the outer layer of the dialogue, the disciples are in fear, mistakenly concerned with the survival of their physical shells. The next layer models the true disciple: Mary's complete comprehension of the Savior's teaching is signaled by her stability and silence. The final and most inward layer points the reader inside to the soul and its journey out of darkness and ignorance to joy and eternal rest. Both the content and the text's structure lead the reader *inward* toward the identity, power, and freedom of the true self, the soul set free from the Powers of Matter and the fear of death.

The repeated motif of departure also binds content and structure. The hearer is not to "remain" in this world but is to "follow" the path of the Savior, the path forged by the soul in its journey to the Good. The departure of the Savior signals the departure of the disciples. Each is promulgating the true salvific knowledge that will allow a perfect humanity to depart from this world and the body forever.

POSTRESURRECTION GOSPEL SETTING

The *Gospel of Mary* fits its designation as a "gospel" most clearly by taking its setting from a Gospel scene: the postresurrection meeting of the risen Jesus with his disciples. Post-resurrection settings such as those found in the Christian Testament Gospels, as well as in a number of extracanonical texts like the *Apocryphon of John,* typically include some of the following elements: the appearance of the risen Lord, rebuke of fearful or grieving disciples, the association of special teaching with the risen Lord, the disciples as the recipients of the teaching, the mention of opponents, persecution for holding secret teaching, and a commissioning scene.[81] All of these elements are found in the *Gospel of Mary.* Here, however, Mary takes over important functions of the Savior, especially in comforting the fearful and grieving disciples and providing them with special teaching. In addition, she is opposed by Andrew and Peter for holding secret teaching. There are thus two sets of opponents in the *Gospel of Mary:* those who killed the Savior and who may be seeking the disciples' lives, and the apostolic opponents of Mary. This doubling points toward the function of the text in inner-Christian debate, associating opposition to the theological position of Mary with opposition to the Savior. The words of commission are also given twice, but this doubling has a formal function: to signal the end of each dialogue and the conclusion of the gospel.

ESCHATOLOGICAL TEACHING

A decisive difference between apocalypses and postresurrection dialogues is found in their views of eschatology,[82] that is, the final condition of the world. Unlike the book of Revelation, for example, the *Gospel of Mary* does not envisage a new creation or a new world order in which the righteous will live in blessedness while the wicked suffer eternal punishment. For the *Gospel of Mary,* the world itself and the material body will be dissolved. But this dissolution is not "punishment," nor does it lead to a new creation, since material existence is itself illusory (it is "contrary to nature" [*Gos. Mary* 8.2–4]).

The *Gospel of Mary* makes a case for the truth of its teaching by appeal to the authority of the Savior. It situates that teaching within the context of inner-Christian debate about salvation, the nature of sin and the world, the fate of the soul, and issues of apostolic authority, especially the reliability of "orthodox" apostolic witness and the question of women's leadership. In the end, it communicates a vision of a world that is passing away, not toward a new creation or a new world order but toward the dissolution of an illusory chaos of suffering, death, and illegitimate domination. As for the saved, each soul will discover its true nature, its "root" in the Good, and return to the place of rest beyond the constraints of time and matter and false morality.

DATE, AUTHOR, AND PROVENANCE

The early third century date of *P. Rylands* 463 provides the latest possible dating for the *Gospel of Mary*. Usually the text is dated to the second half of the second century. This dating is often arrived at by assuming that the *Gospel of Mary* has to be interpreted in terms of a developed Gnostic mythology that appeared only fully in the second half of the second century. As the commentary above suggests, however, the *Gospel of Mary* better finds its life situation in the early second century debates over women's leadership and the role of the apostles. A date in the first half of the second century may be appropriate.

The author and provenance are unknown, although Anne Pasquier has suggested an Egyptian origin[83] on the grounds that the teachings of the text fit well in an Egyptian milieu and because all known copies of the text come from Egypt. Michel Tardieu, however, would place the text's origins in Syria, based on similarities with the teachings of the school of Bardaisan, which flourished during the late second century in Edessa.[85]

It is possible to speculate that the *Gospel of Mary* was written by a woman. But the text's author is not named, and the gender of an author cannot be determined solely by stylistic characteristics or content (at least not without reifying patriarchally constructed gender differences or assuming that women's perspectives are never present in scribal writings by men).

NOTES

1. Elisabeth Schüssler Fiorenza, *But She Said: Feminist Practices of Biblical Interpretation* (Boston: Beacon, 1992), 156.

2. See the summary in Walter C. Till and Hans-Martin Schenke, *Die gnostischen Schriften des koptischen Papyrus Berolinensis 8502* (Texte und Untersuchungen zur Geschichte der altchristlichen Literatur 60; 2nd ed.; Berlin: Akademie-Verlag, 1972), 1–2.

3. These terms indicate the totality of all existing material things. Compare *Gospel of Philip* 63.18–19; see Anne Pasquier, *L'Évangile selon Marie* (Bibliothèque copte de Nag Hammadi. Section "Textes" 10; Quebec: Presses de L'Université Laval, 1983), 50; M. Tardieu, *Écrits gnostiques: Codex de Berlin* (Sources Gnostiques et Manichéennes; Paris: Cerf, 1984), 226.

4. Compare *Gos. Phil.* 53.14–23; *On the Origin of the World* 127.3–5.

5. See Alexander of Aphrodisias, *In Met.;* John Dillon, *The Middle Platonists* (London: Duckworth, 1977), 128.

6. Trans. H. Rackham; *Cicero XIX* (Loeb Classical Library; Cambridge, MA: Harvard University Press, 1979), 439.

7. Compare *Gos. Phil.* 53.17–23: ". . . neither are the good good, nor the evil evil, nor is life life, nor death death. This is why each one will dissolve into its original source. But those who are exalted above the world will not be dissolved, for they are eternal."

8. See also Pasquier, *L'Évangile selon Marie,* 53.

9. Pasquier suggests that "adultery" here is to be connected with the mythic theme of the primordial androgyny of Adam and Eve (*L'Évangile selon Marie,* 52 n. 11). Tardieu suggests that one meaning of "adultery" here is literal, and therefore understands the passage to advocate sexual encratism (*Écrits gnostiques,* 226).

10. Pasquier, *L'Évangile selon Marie,* 54. Despite my frequent reliance on the superb commentary of Anne Pasquier, her interpretation of the *Gospel of Mary* often differs substantially from mine, primarily because she reads the text in terms of a fully developed Gnostic myth, a myth whose parts are assembled piecemeal by comparing the *Gospel of Mary* with a wide variety of different texts. While the location of the Coptic version of the *Gospel of Mary* in the Berlin Codex alongside the *Apocryphon of John* (and other clearly Gnostic texts) gives strong evidence that the *Gospel of Mary* may have been read in antiquity through Gnostic lenses (as were Paul and the Gospel of John), the internal evidence of the *Gospel of Mary* itself provides no support for assuming the existence of a fully developed Gnostic myth behind the text. Such an interpretation can only be read into the text, not out of it. I have here taken a much more conservative and "minimalist" approach, attempting to explicate the text as much as possible in its own terms. Where knowledge and use of other traditions can be established (for example, materials from the Jesus tradition), I have compared the *Gospel of Mary*'s treatment of that material with its appearance elsewhere. I have tried to avoid importing Gnostic myth into the *Gospel of Mary* when not warranted. The reader will have to determine how successful that attempt has been.

11. Compare *Gos. Phil.* 67.9–11: "Truth did not come into the world naked, but it came in types and images. The world will not receive truth in any other way" (trans. Wesley W. Isenberg, *The Nag Hammadi Library in English,* ed. James M. Robinson and Richard Smith [3rd rev. ed.; San Francisco: Harper & Row, 1988], 175).

12. See *Adversus Haereses* 3.18.7; Pasquier, *L'Évangile selon Marie,* 60–61.

13. One issue over which Pasquier and I disagree, and which is of some importance in a feminist commentary, concerns the meaning of the text's gendered language. Pasquier argues that true human nature is androgynous and male, based on the saying of Mary that the disciples, including herself, "have been made men." An elaborate mythology is presumed to reside behind this statement and the text as a whole. Pasquier argues that the ideal of androgyny is modeled in the *Gospel of Mary* by the relationship between the Savior and Mary, and it is this ideal of androgyny that is contested by Peter at 17.16–22 (see *L'Évangile selon Marie,* esp. 9, 17, 61, 98–101). In my view, however, there is no evidence that such a concept is at work here. Mary is

recognized not as the partner of the Savior and representative of fallen female nature but as a superior teacher and model disciple based on her spiritual power—not her sex or gender, as Peter would have it.

14. See B. Malina, *The New Testament World: Insights from Cultural Anthropology* (Atlanta: John Knox Press, 1981), 46; compare also Philo, *Quaest. in Gen.* 4.15: "The soul has, as it were, a dwelling partly men's quarters, partly women's quarters. Now for the men there is a place where properly dwell the masculine thoughts (that are) wise, sound, just, prudent, pious, filled with freedom and boldness, and akin to wisdom. And the women's quarters are a place where womanly opinions go about and dwell, being followers of the female sex. And the female sex is irrational and akin to the bestial passions, fear, sorrow, pleasure, and desire, from which ensue incurable weaknesses and indescribable diseases" (trans. Ralph Marcus; *Philo Supplement 1* [Loeb Classical Library 380; Cambridge, MA: Harvard University Press, 1953], 288).

15. Pasquier, *L'Évangile selon Marie,* 62.

16. See Tardieu, *Écrits gnostiques,* 229.

17. Gerard Luttikhuizen, "Intertextual References in Readers' Responses to the Apocryphon of John," in *Intertextuality in Biblical Writings: Essays in Honor of Bas van Iersel,* ed. Sipke Draisma (Kampen: Kok, 1989), 122.

18. See in particular the excellent book by Daniel Boyarin, *A Radical Jew: Paul and the Politics of Identity* (Berkeley: University of California Press, 1994).

19. Pasquier, *L'Évangile selon Marie,* 14–17.

20. This point has been often noted. See, for example, Till and Schenke, *Die gnostischen Schriften,* 64–65n.; R. McL. Wilson, "The New Testament in the Gnostic Gospel of Mary," in *Nag Hammadi Codices V, 2-5 and VI with Papyrus Berolinensis 8502, 1 and 4,* ed. Douglas M. Parrott (Nag Hammadi Studies 11; Leiden: E. J. Brill, 1979), 242–43; and Pasquier, *L'Évangile selon Marie,* 57–58.

21. This example is drawn entirely from Pasquier, *L'Évangile selon Marie,* 62.

22. Compare *Letter of Peter to Philip* 9.10–12. There the disciples ask an almost identical question after the departure of the risen Savior, but in this case the text affirms that they must indeed suffer as the Lord suffered (see 138.17–139.23). Moreover, Peter teaches that the disciples must suffer, providing an example where Peter represents a theological position directly opposed by the *Gospel of Mary!*

23. That Mary takes the place of the Savior is noted by Tardieu (*Écrits gnostiques,* 22).

24. The Greek fragment adds: "she kissed them all gently" (*P. Oxy.* line 9). This line may have been omitted from the Coptic text because the practice of exchanging chaste kisses had come into disrepute in the later Egyptian Christian circles which produced the Coptic version of the *Gospel of Mary.*

25. See the section on *BG* 8.18–22.

26. Pasquier has suggested that this transition may be a secondary addition written to introduce the revelation of Mary (which she suggests may have been a late addition to the *Gospel*).

27. The Coptic text adds: "the words of the Savior *which you remember.*" Although the expression in Coptic is a bit more elaborate, the sense is similar to the Greek.

28. The Greek version reads: "*Once* when the Lord appeared to me in a vision," implying that he may have appeared on more than one occasion.

29. See Michael A. Williams, *The Immovable Race: A Gnostic Designation and the Theme of Stability in Late Antiquity* (Nag Hammadi Studies 21; Leiden: E. J. Brill, 1985).

30. Variations of this saying are attested in Clement of Alexandria (*Quis div. salv.* 17.1; *Strom.* 4.6.33), Justin Martyr (*Dial.* 6.2), Macarius (*Hom.* 43.3), and others.

31. See Till and Schenke, *Die gnostischen Schriften,* 28–29; compare *Ap. John* (*BG*) 55.4.

32. These names are probably a secondary addition.

33. See Pasquier, *L'Évangile selon Marie,* 80–83; Tardieu, *Écrits gnostiques,* 290–92. Concerning the origin of their names, see Pasquier, 80–86; Tardieu, 234.

34. See Pasquier, *L'Évangile selon Marie,* 20, 86ff.

35. Ibid., 89–92.

36. The Greek and Coptic texts show minor variation in sense here. The Greek reads: "the [due] measure of the time of the aeon" (*P.Ryl.* 21), while the Coptic reads: "the time of the due measure of the aeon" (*BG* 17.5–6).

37. Compare *Dial. Sav.* logia 65–70.

38. For more on the cultural dynamics of this interchange, see Malina, *New Testament World,* chapter 2.

39. See *P.Oxy.* 3525, lines 10–12.

40. Compare Mark 8:33, where Jesus accuses Peter of being on the side of Satan.

41. The rock opera *Jesus Christ Superstar* is a good modern example.

42. A supporting argument could be made based on comparison with the *Gospel of Philip.* It reads (brokenly): "And the companion of the [. . .] Mary Magdalene. [. . .] her more than [all] the disciples [and used to] kiss her [. . .] on the [. . .]. The rest of [the disciples . . .]. They said to him, `Why do you love her more than all of us?' The Savior answered and said to them, `Why do I not love you like her? When a blind man and one who sees are both together in darkness, they are no different from one another. When the light comes, then whoever sees will see the light, and whoever is blind will remain in darkness'" (63.30–64.9; trans. Isenberg, 148).

Here again the disciples are jealous of the Savior's love for Mary. His response makes it clear, however, that this love is not a matter of sex ("Why do I not love you like her?" he rejoins), but concerns spiritual illumination (that is, who is blind and who can see). Nonetheless, the mention of kissing would seem to imply something about sexual relations. Though the text never denies that the discussion of kissing may have a literal sense, the passage below shows that kissing clearly does have a metaphorical meaning. The text reads: "[And had] the word gone out from that place it would be nourished from the mouth and it would become perfect. For it is by a kiss that the perfect conceive and give birth. For this reason we also kiss one another. We receive conception from the grace which is in one another" (*Gos. Phil.* 58.34–59:6; trans. Isenberg, 145).

There are three possible understandings of kissing, and they are not mutually exclusive: (1) reference to teaching through the word; (2) a metaphor for an intimate and personal reception of the word of teaching; and (3) the Christian practice of the kiss of fellowship. Perhaps the mention of Mary and the Savior kissing refers to one or all of these senses of the term. If so, it might imply that Mary had accepted and understood the Savior's teaching particularly well, and for that reason he loves her. The other disciples, being less spiritually advanced, mistake the nature of this affection and are jealous. The parallels with the *Gospel of Mary* are clear, although Peter is singled out here for approbation as he is not in the *Gospel of Philip.*

43. A baptismal context is also present in *Gos. Phil.* 75.14–24.

44. The *Gospel of Peter* also gives Mary Magdalene a preeminent place as the first witness to the empty tomb, although the material about Mary may be a second-century addition, influenced by the canonical Gospel tradition (see J. Dominic Crossan, *The Cross that Spoke: The Origins of the Passion Narrative* [San Francisco: Harper & Row, 1988], 285–86).

45. Matt 28:9–10; John 20:14–18; Mark 16:9; *Epist. Apost.* In Luke 24:34, Peter receives the first appearance. F. Bovon notes that modern interpreters have been rather hasty to assume that this testimony is late and historically inauthentic ("Le Privilège Pascal de Marie-Madeleine," *New Testament Studies* 30 [1984]: 51). Paul does not list Mary among the earliest witnesses (1 Cor 15:5–8).

46. Elisabeth Schüssler Fiorenza, "Mary Magdalene: Apostle to the Apostles," *Union Seminary Quarterly Review* (April 1975): 22–24.

47. The response in the Gospel of John is more ambiguous, but the male disciples clearly do not believe until they see for themselves (John 20:3–10, 19–29).

48. See Elisabeth Schüssler Fiorenza, *In Memory of Her: A Feminist Theological Reconstruction of Christian Origins* (New York: Crossroad, 1985), 332–33.

49. In addition to *Gos. Mary*, see *Gos. Phil.* 59.6–11; 63:32–64:9.

50. See, for example, *Gos. Thom.* 21; *Sophia of Jesus Christ* 98.9; 114.8.

51. The content of that teaching involved intercourse and the ingestion of semen. Whether these charges are spurious or not—that is, whether or not libertine Christian groups existed—is hotly debated.

52. According to Kathleen Corley ("'Noli me tangere': Mary Magdalene in the Patristic Literature," unpublished manuscript), she is mentioned only six times—thrice by Origen, twice by Tertullian, and once by Irenaeus.

53. Ibid.

54. For a fuller treatment of the medieval portrait of Mary Magdalene, see Jane Dillenberger, "The Magdalene: Reflections of the Image of the Saint and Sinner in Christian Art," in *Women, Religion, and Social Change,* ed. Yvonne Yazbeck Haddad and Ellison Banks Findly (Albany: SUNY Press, 1985), 115–45; Marjorie M. Malvern, *Venus in Sackcloth: The Magdalen's Origins and Metamorphoses* (Carbondale and Edwardsville: Southern Illinois University Press, 1975).

55. See the discussion of Bovon, "Le privilège pascal de Marie-Madeleine," 50–52.

56. R. E. Brown, *The Gospel According to John XIII-XXI* (Anchor Bible; Garden City, NY: Doubleday, 1970), 1003. Moreover, he suggests that her absence from Paul's list is not surprising (see p. 971).

57. Bovon, "Le privilège pascal de Marie-Madeleine," 51.

58. See E. Pagels, *The Gnostic Gospels* (New York: Random House, 1979), esp. chaps. 1, 3, and 5, for further reading.

59. Andrew also appears prominently with Peter and Mary in *Pistis Sophia* (247.22; 252.14; 58.12; 167.16; 377.14).

60. Douglas Parrott has suggested that early on some disciples became identified with particular understandings of Christ and became literary representatives for particular theological positions ("Gnostic and Orthodox Disciples in the Second and Third Centuries," in *Nag Hammadi, Gnosticism and Early Christianity,* ed. Charles W. Hedrick and Robert Hodgson, Jr. [Peabody, MA: Hendrickson, 1986], 193–219).

61. See Pheme Perkins, *The Gnostic Dialogue: The Early Church and the Crisis of Gnosticism* (Studies in Contemporary Biblical and Theological Problems; New York: Paulist Press, 1980), 113–30.

62. "How could Peter have been in ignorance to whom the Lord gave the testimony that flesh and blood had not revealed this to him but heaven" (*Adv. Haer.* 3.13.2; cf. Mark 16:17).

63. *Apoc. Pet.* 72.2–4 interprets Peter's denial to mean that he was reproved three times, after which he went on to become a legitimate leader.

64. See Irenaeus, *Adv. Haer.* 1.13.6.

65. *Adv. Haer.* 3.2.2; trans. Cyril C. Richardson, *Early Christian Fathers* (New York: Macmillan, 1970), 371.

66. See Perkins, *Gnostic Dialogue,* 37–39.

67. Interestingly enough, the *Gospel of Bartholomew* portrays Mary (Jesus' mother) and Peter in a struggle over supremacy, but in this case Mary is arguing that Peter deserves prefer-

ence because he is a male formed in the image of Adam, while she is formed in the image of sinful Eve. The text may have purposefully staged this scene to contrast the two Marys.

68. The Greek term underlying the Coptic "to lead" may be the same term used in *Gos. Mary* (*P.Ryl.* 22:5). The Greek term can be translated either "to lead" or "to consider." The sense may therefore be that to *lead* Mary implies that Jesus *considers* her to be worthy.

69. Trans. Thomas O. Lambdin, *The Nag Hammadi Library in English*, 138.

70. Trans. V. MacDermot, *Pistis Sophia* (Nag Hammadi Studies 9; Leiden: Brill, 1978), 325.

71. A point also made by Perkins, *Gnostic Dialogue*, 133.

72. Compare Mark 2:14 and Matt 9:9, which led to the later identification of Levi and Matthew.

73. A similar point is made by *Gos. Phil.* 63.32–64.10, as was discussed above, and in *Pist. Soph.* 1.36; 2.72. In both of these texts, Mary comes into conflict with the disciples, especially Peter, and in each case the Savior affirms the superiority of Mary's *spiritual* qualifications.

74. Literary Facets Seminar, Westar Institute Meetings, Toronto, October 1989.

75. Or perhaps pages 1–8? H.-M. Schenke has suggested that there may be an additional two pages to the codex which were unnumbered (see *Die gnostischen Schriften*, 331).

76. See Dieter Lührmann, "Die griechische Fragmente des Mariaevangeliums POxy 3525 und PRyl 463," *Novum Testamentum* 30.4 (1988): 322.

77. In the first four lines of *P.Oxy.* 3525 only the word "no one, none, naught" can be read. Comparison with the Coptic text allows it to be placed within the Savior's final speech.

78. For a discussion of paradigmatic characteristics of apocalypses, see John J. Collins, "Introduction: Towards the Morphology of a Genre," in *Apocalypse: The Morphology of a Genre*, ed. John J. Collins, *Semeia* 14 (1979): 6–8; and David Hellholm, "The Problem of Apocalyptic Genre and the Apocalypse of John," in *Early Christian Apocalypticism: Genre and Social Setting*, ed. Adela Yarbro Collins, *Semeia* 36 (1986): 13–64. Francis Fallon applies J. Collins's paradigm to the *Gospel of Mary* in "The Gnostic Apocalypses," in *Apocalypse: The Morphology of a Genre*, 131–32. There are, however, serious problems with this analysis; see the pertinent critique by Pasquier, *L'Évangile selon Marie*, 12 n. 47.

79. For a fuller discussion of the genre and structure of the *Gospel of Mary*, especially its characteristics as an apocalypse, see my article "The Genre of the *Gospel of Mary*," in *New Testament Apocrypha: Apocalypses*, ed. Adela Yarbro Collins and Martha Himmelfarb (Sonoma, CA: Polebridge Press, forthcoming).

80. See Perkins, *Gnostic Dialogue*, esp. 25–36, 133–37.

81. Ibid., 25–72, esp. 30–32.

82. For a fuller discussion of the eschatology of the *Gospel of Mary*, see Pasquier, *L'Évangile selon Marie*, esp. 14–22, 48–66.

83. Ibid., 13–14, esp. n. 55.

84. Tardieu, *Écrits gnostiques*, 25.

RECOMMENDED READINGS

Bovon, François. "Le privilège pascal de Marie-Madeleine." *New Testament Studies* 30 (1984): 50–62.

King, Karen L. "The Gospel of Mary." In *The Complete Gospels*, edited by Robert J. Miller, 351–60. Sonoma, CA: Polebridge Press, 1992.

Lührmann, Dieter. "Die griechischen Fragmente des Mariaevangeliums POxy 3525 und PRyl 463." *Novum Testamentum* 30.4 (1988): 321–38.

Marjanen, Antti. "The Woman Jesus Loved: A Socio-Historical Study of Mary Magdalene Traditions in Gnostic Writings." Ph.D. dissertation. University of Finland, Helsinki, forthcoming (1995).

Pagels, Elaine. *The Gnostic Gospels.* New York: Random House, 1979.

Pasquier, Anne. *L'Évangile selon Marie.* Bibliothèque copte de Nag Hammadi. Section "Textes" 10. Quebec: Les Presses de L'Université Laval, 1983.

Perkins, Pheme. *The Gnostic Dialogue: The Early Church and the Crisis of Gnosticism.* Studies in Contemporary Biblical and Theological Problems. New York: Paulist Press, 1980.

Tardieu, Michel. *Écrits gnostiques: Codex de Berlin.* Sources Gnostiques et Manichéennes. Paris: Cerf, 1984.

Till, Walter C., and Hans-Martin Schenke. *Die gnostischen Schriften des koptischen Papyrus Berolinensis 8502.* Texte und Untersuchungen zur Geschichte der altchristlichen Literatur 60. 2nd ed. Berlin: Akademie-Verlag, 1972.

Wilson, Robert McL., and George W. MacRae. "The Gospel According to Mary." In *Nag Hammadi Codices V, 2-5 and VI with Papyrus Berolinensis 8502, 1 and 4,* edited by Douglas M. Parrott, 453–71. Nag Hammadi Studies 11. Leiden: E. J. Brill, 1979.

The Gospel of Matthew

ELAINE WAINWRIGHT ◆

INTRODUCTION

A scribe trained for the implementation of the inclusive *basileia* vision of Jesus draws out of a treasure of past and present, the new and the old toward a rereading of the Jesus story for a particular historical situation! (Matt 13:52)

THIS FIRST-CENTURY IMAGE provides an analogy for this present late twentieth century feminist-ecumenical reading of the same story, a task that is also captured symbolically in the image of "revisioning" employed by Adrienne Rich. She describes it as "the act of looking back, of seeing with fresh eyes, of entering an old text from a new critical direction." Such a revisioning needs to take account, therefore, of both the "old text" and the "new critical direction."

OLD TEXT/NEW CRITICAL DIRECTION

Returning again to the first-century image of the scribe trained for the implementation of the *basileia* vision who brings out from a storehouse both the new and the old, we are provided with a key to the narrative and theological worlds which the Matthean Gospel constructs.

The particular story of Jesus, who is introduced to the reader in the opening sentence of the narrative, is set within the story of Israel contained within its scriptures. The Gospel opens with the designation of Jesus as "son of David" and "son of Abraham" (1:1). The subsequent patrilineage (1:1–17) situates Jesus more deeply within this story, and throughout the Gospel the narrator reiterates this link by means of both explicit fulfillment quotations (1:22; 2:15, 17, 23; 4:14; 8:17; 12:17; 13:35; 21:4; 26:56; 27:9–10) and continual allusions to the Hebrew Scriptures. For the Matthean reader, therefore, the theme of promise/fulfillment, which is integral to the unfolding of the Jesus story, enables the reader to expect fulfillment of those promises that point beyond the story itself (24:14; 26:13; 28:20).

From the beginning of the narrative, however, a polemical note is introduced, as Herod the king is set over against the infant Jesus and seeks to slay him among the many innocent children he orders killed (2:16–18). John the Baptist preaches specifically against the Pharisees and Sadducees, the leaders of the Jewish people, and it is these same leaders who, as the plot develops, become the chief opponents of Jesus—finally, together with the chief priests, bringing about his death. They represent the Israel that the Gospel presents as rejecting Jesus, the Israel upon whom all the righteous blood shed upon the earth will come (23:35–36). Finally, in 27:25, it is no longer representatives but the people who are characterized as drawing down on themselves and their children the blood of Jesus whom they wish to have crucified.

Tension exists, therefore, in the symbolic universe the narrative creates, as Israel is source of the promise on the one hand and yet enemy on the other. Such tension finds a possible explanation, however, in the rhetorical situation encoded in the text: an early Christian community seeks to establish itself with a new and emerging identity in continuity with Israel and yet struggles with its Jewish sisters and brothers "across the street" who claim a very different identity and yet the same continuity. It is in such a situation that polemic arises and is sharpened. The history of reception of the Matthean text has, however, created a "politics of otherness" in relation to Judaism far beyond the polemic encoded in the text.

The tension also results from another central theme of the narrative, namely, Jesus' mission of preaching the *basileia* of God, the just and righteous purpose of God for all humanity (4:17). As with all other prophetic or renewal movements within Israel's history, Jesus' mission to call God's people back to God's purpose symbolized as *basileia* would probably be met with resistance, would create tension. Some would accept, but many more would reject. When Israel is characterized as rejecting the prophet Jesus, this is but another example of those of the dominant culture failing to be changed by their prophets. Readers will, however, through this tension, be challenged to identify with either those of Israel who reject Jesus or those of remnant Israel who accept.

The *basileia* which Jesus preached and which the Matthean Gospel proclaims was characterized by other aspects that brought it into conflict or tension with the dominant culture. The Sermon on the Mount names blessed those whom society despises—the meek, the merciful, peacemakers, and those persecuted on account of righteousness (5:1–12). The miracle stories speak of the wholeness that is possible for all humanity, and hence the inclusiveness of the *basileia* is made manifest as outsiders such as lepers, Gentiles, unclean women, and the demon-possessed are pronounced "clean" in a society that considers them pollutants (chaps. 8–9 and elsewhere). Jesus' vision of the *basileia* as symbolically presented in the parables, entails hearing, understanding, and doing the word of the *basileia* (13:23); selling all for its sake (13:44);

and being compassionate toward those considered least (25:40)—all of which create tension with the dominant cultural ethos. This vision is enfleshed in the life of Jesus as related in the Gospel story. He eats with tax collectors and sinners (9:10–13), touches an unclean leper (8:3) and is touched by a menstruating woman (9:20), has his vision of God's just purposes expanded by a Gentile woman (15:21–28), enters Jerusalem with a band of women and men from Galilee (21:1–11; 27:55), and finally gives his very life for the sake of the *basileia*.

The challenge such a vision and praxis offered to one early Christian community and the tension it created in relation to the prevailing ethos are encoded within the Matthean narrative. The tension is visible, on the one hand, in relation to ethnicity. Although the final mission is to make disciples of all nations (28:20), and although the prediction of 21:43 places the *basileia* in the hands of the nation producing its fruit—be that Israel or a Gentile nation—the narrative twice mentions a more exclusive mission on the basis of ethnicity (10:5–6; 15:24).

The tension is also visible, on the other hand, in relation to gender, which is the significant concern in this commentary. Indications have already been given of the inclusion of women within the *basileia* vision and praxis of Jesus. Yet the Matthean Gospel constructs a symbolic universe that is androcentric and encodes the patriarchal constructs present in its sociohistorical location. The text creates a world in which the male norm is coterminous with the human, and this presupposition finds expression in the grammatical and narrative strategies of the text resulting in the marginalization of women. In the Matthean Sermon on the Mount, for instance, we find the repeated use of terms such as "son(s)," "man/men," "brother," "father," and "he" (5:13, 15, 19, 22, 45; 6:1, 16, 18; 7:3–5, 8, 9, 12, 21) reflecting a narrative world from which women appear to be absent. The experience of sonship, fatherhood, and brotherhood is considered universal and hence adequate for the expression of human experience.

Similarly, patriarchal constructs that are both within the text and within the community that shaped the text function to marginalize or to obscure women. The patrilineage with which the Gospel text opens provides an example of such a construct in which women are omitted from the prehistory of Jesus except where they are problematic (1:3, 5, 6, 16). Female gender also functions to prevent women being named among the group called "disciples." These constructs, especially those of "father" and "son," also provide the dominant metaphors for God and Jesus throughout the narrative.

This gender inflection of the Gospel text is reflected in much of the history of its reception, which contributes further to the "politics of otherness" inscribed in the text. There is no monograph, for instance, that provides a detailed analysis of any of the pericopes in which women are significant characters except in relation to other theological interests such as infancy narratives or passion and resurrection. In other studies, focus on the disciples, who are presumed male, tends to obscure the significant role of the women characters in the text. Likewise, the designation of Tamar, Rahab, Ruth, and Bathsheba ("wife of Uriah" in the text) as sinners by Jerome and as outsiders or foreigners by Luther raises the question of the extent to which cultural ideologies present in the interpreter's own reading situation have influenced particular interpretations.

The current women's movement, together with recent studies in feminist critical theory and literary theory, has underscored both the historical and narrative subjectivity of women. Women's own experiences, cultural and sociopolitical locations, economic status, education, and belief systems make them particular historical subjects in the unfolding drama of human existence both now and in the past. Similarly, a recognition of the subjectivity of female characters within literary texts is guiding many new readings of "canonical" texts, which in turn are beginning to subvert the hegemony of their traditional history of reception. The canon, which has been controlled by a monopoly, is now beginning to be repossessed.

A twofold process has characterized this movement in its various manifestations. Generally, it began with a "deconstruction" of our received heritage—cultural, historical, intellectual, and religious—which revealed the gender biases inherent therein. This, in turn, has allowed for the task of a feminist reconstruction encompassing both theoretical and practical dimensions. Feminism, therefore, as understood in this work, involves a critique of human reality on the basis of its gender biases and the development of strategies for cultural and ideological change for the sake of and on behalf of women, involving therefore not only gender considerations but also race and class, whatever is oppressive of women.

There are, therefore, new reading sites or new critical perspectives from which feminist critics may enter the "old text" of the Matthean Gospel with its genderized hierarchy and worldview. They give rise, however, to significant biblical and theological questions that must be addressed in relation to the particular reading being undertaken here, a reading I would call a feminist critical reading.

REVISIONING THE MATTHEAN TEXT

Just as the twofold perspective of deconstruction and reconstruction has characterized contemporary feminism generally, so too has it guided the particular field of biblical studies and biblical readings as these have been undertaken from a feminist perspective. A hermeneutics of suspicion seeks to unmask the androcentric ideology and patriarchal constructs implicit and explicit in the biblical text, in its context and in its history of reception. A hermeneutics of remembrance or reclamation, informed by a feminist ethics of reading, undertakes new readings of the text from a gender perspective while considering the function of these readings and interpretations especially in the contemporary sociopolitical contexts of women and men. These two aspects of the feminist critique will guide the subsequent reading of the first Gospel. Recent biblical studies have been characterized by a shift from a historical to a literary orientation. The biblical text is no longer considered a window onto the "world behind the text" but a particular or perspectival reading constructing its own world and symbolic universe. Consideration needs to be given, therefore, to the gender ideologies that function in the text especially in relation to female characters. A comprehensive feminist reading of the Gospel of Matthew would entail detailed examination of the entire Gospel. Since this is not possible in this commentary I have chosen to focus on the female characters but always in the context of the Gospel story as a whole and the narrative world it constructs with only brief reference to these other aspects of a feminist reading when appropriate.

Initially, stories will be analyzed in terms of character presentation, with attention being directed to the gender codes surrounding the women characters, codes that alert the reader to the ideology the text supports. These codes include the silences in the text, disjunctions, contradictions, gaps and omissions, as well as the gender biases supported by the text, because it has become clear to feminist scholars that female culture is found in support of patriarchal culture as well as in conflict with it. Consideration will also be given to the comparisons and contrasts made between characters on the basis of gender.

Closely related to, even inseparable from, character is an analysis of plot. What characters do, the actions they perform, are constitutive elements in the unfolding of events that constitute the story. From a gender perspective, it will be important to consider the tasks that women are permitted to perform and those that are denied to them. Further, the setting of their actions will be significant. Are they confined to domestic space, or do their actions take place in the public arena? Consideration will also be given to the way such locations contribute to the construction of the text's symbolic universe, and this will be further supplemented by attention to the symbolic function of gender in the text and the creation of its narrative world.

Such a *first stage* analysis is of its nature literary, drawing on insights from narrative and reader-response criticism. It enables us to proffer a reading of the text that gives narrative subjectivity to the female characters as well as the male. To conclude here, however, would be to deny historical subjectivity to the women who participated in the shaping of the traditions constituting the Matthean Gospel story and in its final articulation. At a *second stage* of analy-

sis, we will turn, therefore, to the more traditional historical-critical methodologies, especially redaction criticism, but they will be employed in the light of
the historical paradigm shift that has taken place. No longer will they be used
directly to discover the actual historical situation of early Christianity, or in
particular of the Matthean community, but the data thus obtained will assist in
reconstructing the sociohistorical situation inscribed within the narrative. By
focusing on the stories of women using these diachronic methodologies, we
can discover glimpses of the development of the traditions that formed and
informed the final rhetorical presentation of these stories in the Gospel text.
From this, information can be gleaned toward a restructuring of the "historical subtext," the story of women and men within the Matthean community.

This information, however, will need to be supplemented at a *third stage* of
analysis by other historical and sociological data. Such a feminist historical
reconstruction of an early Christian community is a difficult task and a limited
task because of the paucity of our sources and yet a very necessary task. It will
need to be collaborative, drawing on theoretical models from history, anthropology, and sociology as well as the study of a wide variety of literary texts
beyond those considered normative for Judaism and Christianity. It is therefore beyond the scope of this particular commentary, but the results of our literary analysis will offer some initial signposts toward future studies of the
inclusive history of the Matthean community.

Such a *threefold* analysis, which seeks to discover the inclusion of women
within the text of the Matthean Gospel, their inclusion within the formation
of that text, and hints of their inclusion within the community that produced
and used the text, is, however, but one aspect of the feminist task. It is the
work of the scribe or the "re-visioner" described in our introduction, but it will
only be completed when it is appropriated by contemporary communities of
believers who seek an expression of the inclusive *basileia* vision appropriate to
our world. This work is offered, therefore, to those communities.

FOR THOSE WHO HAVE EARS TO HEAR:
A SUBVERSIVE STORY

Until very recently, interpreters of the Matthean Gospel have been deaf to
aspects of this story because of the particular set of presuppositions they have
brought to their task, one of which is an androcentrism that considers men
central to history and women's participation an anomaly. As a result, therefore, the stories about women in the Gospel have been subordinated to what
has been read as central: the story of Jesus and his male disciples, supplicants,
and opponents. That the Gospel opens with the patrilineage of Jesus (1:1–17)

and closes with the commissioning of eleven male disciples to a universal mission (28:16–20) while the male disciples and opponents are some of the key players in the story's last great dramatic movement (chaps. 26–28) means also that the interpreter's own perspective finds resonance with aspects of the text itself.

Within the last decade the story has begun to be heard and read in a new key with particular focus being directed to female characterization as well as to feminist interpretations of particular texts. These recent studies have enabled hitherto hidden or forgotten aspects of this Gospel story to be heard.

By comparison with some new voices in this key, however, the ones raised in relation to the Matthean narrative may seem subdued and could readily be blotted out by the "official" interpretations which abound. The present reading seeks, therefore, to continue and to supplement what has already begun. It will be a reading against the grain of the text, especially its androcentric ideology and patriarchal constructs. It will move toward a "countercoherence," which links the "official" reading to "what it leaves out." Since women have been virtually ignored, they will be the focus of attention. Since the "politics of otherness" inherent within the androcentric text and its history of interpretation excludes women, inclusion will function as a significant feminist critical principle in this reading of the Gospel text. Finally, since the text has often been structured according to a theological perspective directed toward Jesus and male discipleship, the countercoherent reading will seek a structuring that is shaped by attention to the women's stories.

FOREMOTHERS (CHAPTERS 1–2)

The repetition of the patriarchal pattern "male was the father of male" thirty-nine times within the first fifteen verses of the Gospel, which is introduced as "an account of the genealogy of Jesus the Messiah, the son of David, the son of Abraham" (1:1), invites the reader at the outset of the Gospel story to enter into the androcentric worldview of the narrator. Within such a perspective, Israel's history as the prehistory of Jesus is considered ordered and male. It is no surprise, therefore, when Joseph is introduced in v. 19 as "righteous" in a way that inclines the reader toward further identification with his androcentric perspective especially in relation to Mary's pregnancy (1:19). As male, he sees himself authorized to interpret the law in relation to a woman without her participation. He alone receives the divine revelation (1:20); and it is he who names the child according to the divine command establishing him firmly as "son of David" (1:25). The story of the early infancy of Jesus is likewise dominated by Joseph, his receiving of divine revelations and his obedience to them (chap. 2).

This dominant narrative obscures the function of female characters within the same text. The foremothers of Jesus are rendered invisible by virtue of the patriarchal construct which considers women merely vehicles of reproduction and hence insignificant as historical subjects. The dissonant note of v. 16—Mary of whom Jesus was born—is quickly silenced in vv. 18–25, where Mary's story is subsumed into Joseph's. Readers are not given her point of view in relation to her pregnancy, nor is she the recipient of a divine revelation. In fact, she is marginalized within the story. She is spoken about by both the narrator and the divine messenger, but she is given no speech herself and no independent action of hers is recorded.

But when the narrative is heard with new ears—ears critically attuned to the gender inflection of the text—a different story is brought to life. The reader becomes aware of the tension created in the narrative by the four patterned breaks that occur in vv. 3, 5, and 6 when the names of four women are introduced as foremothers of Jesus—Tamar, Rahab, Ruth, and Bathsheba, whom the androcentric narrator designates as "the wife of Uriah." An even more significant break occurs in v. 16, where the expected pattern—Joseph was the father of Jesus—is replaced by a most extraordinary reference to Joseph that characterizes him in relation to a woman: "the husband of Mary." It is then Mary who is designated as the one of whom Jesus is born, not a male progenitor according to the pattern for previous generations in the genealogy. Since the narrator has already established a certain authority by means of the opening reference to the "book of the genealogy" drawn from Gen 2:4a and 5:1 and the subsequent naming of key male ancestors, these breaks in the ordered pattern bear the same authority. The reader is thereby alerted to the presence of women in Israel's history and Jesus' ancestry and their presence breaks the orderly pattern given to this androcentric history.

The names of the foremothers in the genealogy evoke their stories. Within these stories, they are not sinners (reflecting the biblical and cultural linking of women, sexuality, and sin) or foreigners (manifesting the perspective that places women outside the patriarchal world and culture) as androcentric interpretations have determined. Rather, each is a woman who at some point in her story is in a situation that renders her dangerous to the patriarchal system, an anomaly, because she is not properly related to man either in marriage or as daughter. To single out such women for inclusion, however, or to explain their situation as "extraordinary or irregular" can support a form of gender politics in which women are recognized only when they are problems. Furthermore, to claim that such "problems" are important within "God's plan," especially when that God is identified with the patriarchy of the genealogy, is to support the androcentric perspective of the biblical stories in which the four women's dangerous situation is brought back under patriarchal control. It is also to fail to recognize that in none of the women's stories does God intervene on their behalf as so often happens in the stories of male heroes.

Read from a feminist critical perspective, the Israelite foremothers' anomalous or dangerous situations certainly place them outside the patriarchal marriage or family structure, but in such a way that their position provides a challenge or a threat to this structure as their actions indicate. Tamar puts off her widow's garments and sits by the roadside awaiting Judah (Gen 38:14). Rahab, named harlot, dwells in her own home outside her patriarchal family structure (Josh 2:2). Ruth goes down to the threshing floor, where she uncovers the feet of Boaz (Ruth 3:7); and the wife of Uriah comes to David, one of the few actions attributed to her in the entire story (2 Sam 11:4). While the patriarchal narrative quickly domesticates these actions, they can also be seen to encode aspects of women's power. God's messianic plan unfolds in and through such power. The women's presence functions, therefore, as a critique of patriarchy and introduces a point of tension into the narrative that must guide the reader as the story unfolds. As noted above, this tension is augmented by the seemingly anomalous conclusion to the genealogy, which focuses attention on Mary.

Anomaly continues to characterize the subsequent narrative (1:18–25) as the focus shifts to Joseph, and yet despite the narrator's attempt to restore the androcentric perspective, the conception and birth of Jesus from the woman Mary must be considered a "kernel" within the narrative. Without it, the story would not proceed. Also, v. 16 together with the twofold reference to the child being conceived "of the Holy Spirit" (vv. 18, 20) and the implication in v. 19 that the child is not "of Joseph" provides for the reader an account of Mary's conception of Jesus without reference to male begetting. A woman who is named *virgin* is with child, and the child is named holy. The reproductive power of woman and her role in the birth of the Messiah are affirmed outside the patriarchal structure. This is further emphasized by linking the woman and the child she conceives to the fulfillment quotation of vv. 22–23. It is this "endangered woman's" child who is Emmanuel and in whom God is present not only to Israel but to the indefinite multitudes who are the subject of the verb in the phrase: "*They* shall call his name" (1:23).

Such a reading functions to deconstruct the androcentric perspective of the genealogy and birth narrative which symbolized woman as vehicle of reproduction. It enables the remembering and claiming of the unnamed women who belong to Jesus' lineage, but it also goes beyond the earlier evocations, claiming that God stands with the anomalous woman and her child to the point, in fact, where they are the fulfillment of the divine promise. The conclusion of the narrative (vv. 24–25), however, incorporates this subversive aspect of the story back into the patriarchal framework in which Joseph dominates, and this perspective continues into chapter 2.

Tension in the narrative, however, also characterizes chapter 2. The plot is advanced by way of the obedience of both the wise men and Joseph to a divine command given through a star or a dream. Brief reference is made to Mary, but except for v. 11, where the wise men find the child with Mary his mother, throughout the remainder Joseph is presented as the agent and the mother and child are passive (2:13, 14, 20, 21). A recent study suggests that the "house" was the primary metaphor in the Matthean Gospel, the center of the economic, political, religious, and ecclesial life depicted in the narrative. Read from this perspective, v. 11 may continue the tension found in the beginning of the narrative. The woman Mary is found with her son, who is being worshiped by the foreign wise men in the first "house" context within the Gospel. It is here that new structures of relationship are established, goods or resources are exchanged, and a central metaphor of the Gospel narrative is evoked. Woman is linked from the outset to this new house metaphor and hence to its central significance in the construction of the symbolic universe of the narrative.

The androcentric quality of that symbolic universe as it has already been constructed within the first two chapters of the narrative is further subverted by the Matthean use of the image of Rachel weeping for her children in 2:18. This female image of the compassionate inconsolable mother provides a counterpoint to the extreme violence of the holocaust of the male children at the hands of the male ruler, Herod. It evokes the "womb compassion" of God that is imaged in the poem of Jeremiah (Jer 31:20) and is metaphorically linked to the female imagery of Matt 23:37, when Jesus-Sophia as sorrowing mother laments the destruction of Jerusalem and of her children within it. The image here is, however, but a quiet voice raised as a counterpoint to the dominant symbolization of Jesus in the opening chapters, where he is named "son of David," "son of Abraham," "king of the Jews," and "son."

Our reading against the grain of the narrative has alerted us as readers to the tension within the prologue when traditions that affirm the power and presence of women within Israel's history and the birth of its Messiah are introduced into a narrative that is predominantly androcentric, supports patriarchal familial structures and laws, and tends to render women invisible. This reading recognizes the symbolic significance of female gender whereby woman is considered anomalous, to be brought into the patriarchal order and under patriarchal control; but at the same time, the reader is aware that the narrative affirms a power and presence of women that begins to deconstruct patriarchal power, which is exclusive and destructive. Significant narrative clues are therefore provided that will guide the feminist reader through the rest of the Gospel.

WOMEN OF GREAT FAITH IN THE *BASILEIA* MINISTRY (3:1–20:34)

The major plotting device of the acceptance/rejection theme employed in the narrative from 1:18 continues to characterize the *basileia* ministry, which is prepared for by John the Baptist and which Jesus himself carries out in Galilee and en route to Jerusalem. Within this section, the narrator introduces the reader to many *characters* and, more significantly, *character groups* whose boundaries are not clearly defined early in the narrative but who are characterized in terms of their relationship to Jesus. The fluidity of character creates a certain suspense for the reader and is intended to guide the reading process especially in chapters 8 and 9, in which individual characters, their response to Jesus, and his response to them are central to the narrative.

The first group to whom the reader is introduced is the group of four fishermen, whom Jesus calls and who *follow* him (4:18–22). This group is supplemented by the great *crowds,* who also *follow* (4:25). In 5:1, a group called his *disciples* is distinguished from the crowd as the possible audience for the Sermon on the Mount, but this distinction is blurred again in 7:28, where it is pointed out that it was the crowd who "heard all of these teachings." At this point there seems to be little gender inflection within the text in relation to characterization. The crowds could be presumed to comprise women as well as men. As indicated earlier, however, the symbolic universe created by the sermon itself is androcentric. The ancestors are referred to as "the men of old" (5:21, 33). The recipients of the teaching about adultery and divorce are constructed as male: "every one who looks at a woman lustfully has already committed adultery with her in his heart" and "whoever divorces his wife" (5:28, 31–32). Moreover, the illustrative imagery is predominantly androcentric: a man responding to his son (7:10), the wise or the foolish man building a house, the brother in need of reconciliation (5:22–24). Hence, an implicit gender inflection exists in the text, creating a symbolic universe characterized by this gender bias even though the text does not explicitly support patriarchy.

A feminist critical reading will, therefore, seek to highlight the inclusive nature of the crowd as recipients of the sermon. In the light of this inclusion, it will read as inclusive that androcentric language which functioned as generic language. The masculine plural adjective "blessed" will include both the female and male listeners (5:1–12). The "brothers" who are to be greeted (5:47) or reconciled (5:23–24) will include both sister and brother. Even the ancestors will include the foremothers of Israel's history as well as the forefathers. In this way, a new symbolic universe will be created by such an inclusive reading of the text, which will itself be inclusive. (It should be noted here that each of the sermon texts referred to in the introduction has been translated inclusively in the NRSV.)

Chapters 8 and 9 begin with the *crowds* continuing to follow Jesus. Out of these crowds, certain individuals and groups emerge: those sick with all kinds of diseases, the demon-possessed, the epileptics, and the paralytics, who are brought to Jesus in groups (8:16; 9:35; cf. 4:24) or as individuals (9:2, 32), or who themselves come to Jesus for healing (8:2; 9:20, 27). Of this large group of supplicants some are lepers, others are blind or dumb, some are Gentiles, and they include both women and men. The number of male supplicants is, however, significantly larger than female supplicants. Each person emerges from the crowd and stands before Jesus, who responds in a variety of ways. It is this response which guides the reader's reaction to each character and group, and this guidance is enhanced by the implied author's arrangement of episodes and the comparisons and contrasts set up between characters and groupings as indicated below in figure 1.

Recipient	Key Character Group Involved	Response	Respondent
Crowds Follow Jesus (8:1)			
*Leper (8:1–4)	Leper–Unclean (male)	"Say nothing to anyone Go–show yourself to the priest"	Jesus
*Centurion's servant (8:5–13)	Gentile/servant (male)	"As you believed, Let it be done to you"	Jesus
*Peter's mother-in-law (8:14–15)	Woman–ill (female)	Rose and served him	Woman
Healing of Many (8:16–17)		[Buffer Pericope A]	
Following Jesus (8:18–22)			
*Storm at sea (8:23–27)	Disciples (male?)	"Men of Little Faith" "What sort of man is this"	Jesus Disciples
*Gadarene demoniacs (8:28–34)	Gentile–possessed (male)	"Go away!"	All the City
*Paralytic (9:1–8)	Sick (male)	Afraid/glorified God "He Blasphemes"	Crowd Scribes
Matthew–Called and follows (9:9–13)		[Buffer Pericope B]	
Fasting/new wine–old skins (9:14–17)			
*Ruler's daughter + Woman with hemorrhage (9:18–26)	Young girl/dead Woman/unclean (female)	Fame spread "Your faith has made you well"	Jesus
*Blind men (9:27–31)	Sick (male)	"See no one knows it." Spread his fame	Jesus Men
Mute demoniac (9:32–34)	Demon-possessed (male)	Marvel Murmur	Crowd Pharisees
Compassion on the Crowds (9:35–36)			

Figure 1

The juxtaposition of these various groups and the reactions/responses of various people to the miracles of Jesus become the vehicles whereby the narrator's point of view is communicated, particularly in these two chapters. The reader encounters three groups of three miracle stories. A collection of small narrative units and sayings forms a "buffer" pericope between each section. The two miracle narratives concerning the healing of females occur in strategic positions—at the end of the first group of three and at the beginning of the third. The reader's understanding and interpretation of these two miracle accounts, therefore, are influenced not only by the group to which each belongs but also by the "buffer" pericope alongside which it has been placed.

The first part of Buffer Pericope A (8:16–17) is a combination of a summary of healings and a fulfillment quotation, both direct commentary by the narrator. The summary points to Jesus' healing of "all" who were sick, indicating the inclusive nature of this aspect of Jesus' preaching of the *basileia*, while the fulfillment quotation links it to the liberation trajectory already visible within the prophetic literature of the Hebrew Scriptures and evoked at the very beginning of the Gospel in relation to the birth of Jesus (1:23; 2:6, 15, 18). The two stories concerning the following of Jesus in 8:18–22 illustrate that such following of this preacher of the *basileia* means a break with the patriarchal household as the basic economic and social unit of society. The inclusive and liberating nature of the *basileia* is thereby linked to a break with a particular patriarchal construct. This would seem, however, to introduce a further note of dissonance into the narrative world since the patriarchal family appeared to be an implicit construct in the Sermon on the Mount.

Inclusion and liberation are also significant themes in Buffer Pericope B. The calling of Matthew (9:9) and the table companionship with tax collectors and sinners (9:10–13) illustrate further the inclusive nature of the *basileia*. Not only those who are sick but also those whom the dominant culture considers unclean or pollutants are included in the circles around Jesus. The liberating nature of this activity of Jesus is emphasized for the reader by recalling the text from Hosea: "I desire mercy, and not sacrifice" (Hos 6:6; Matt 9:13). The metaphoric language of unshrunk cloth and new wine in relation to old garments and old wineskins suggests that such inclusive and liberating activity brings tension, even rupture or discontinuity, in relation to the prevailing ethos.

Matthew 8:14–15

The very simplicity of the story of the healing of Peter's mother-in-law shapes the reading of it, as does the fivefold repetition of the connective "and." This links the five finite verbs, which focus attention on the action and the characters involved. Jesus is the subject of the first two verbs; the healing forms the climax and the woman who is healed is the subject of the two concluding verbs, as illustrated in figure 2.

And	he saw his mother-in-law	)
		) Jesus
And	he touched her hand	)
And	the fever left her	) Fever
And	she arose	)
		) Woman
And	she served him	)

Figure 2

As in the previous two miracle accounts, Jesus stands out as the chief actor, and the focus is on his capacity to heal (8:2–3, 5–7). He sees the woman with a fever and touches her hand. The woman is not named but is identified simply in terms of her place in the patriarchal familial structure: she is the mother-in-law of Peter. She is also described as lying sick with a fever and hence is a possible pollutant, especially if this sickness is connected to her time of ritual uncleanness. Jesus' simple action in reaching out and touching her breaks open the boundaries that defined "clean" and "unclean," thereby liberating the woman from her infirmity. But it is even more extraordinary that the narrative itself breaks open the pattern the reader expects in a miracle story, because here Jesus takes the initiative. Normally in miracle accounts the person to be healed approaches Jesus and asks for healing, or someone approaches on his or her behalf and makes the request. As we saw in the genealogy, here also a woman's story breaks a narrative pattern.

Like the characters in the previous two miracle accounts, this woman is an outsider in terms of the socioreligious patterning of society, and her marginalization is represented in the narrative. Hers, however, is a twofold marginalization on the basis of both gender and illness, which is represented by her silence and her inability even to approach Jesus. This twofold marginalization is highlighted for the reader by the breaking of the narrative pattern. In the preceding miracle stories, Jesus' action in response to the supplicants' requests broke through the socioreligious barriers around them. In this story, his extraordinary taking of the initiative in reaching out and touching this woman points to the more than ordinary barriers to be broken. His action, therefore, highlights her incorporation into the liberating wholeness of the *basileia* as one healed of illness and as woman. God is present with God's people when the marginalized, who include women, are incorporated into the group around Jesus, having been freed from their infirmities.

Following the healing, the woman *serves* Jesus. This could be understood simply as the woman's service of Jesus at table, but the narrative context suggests otherwise. The same verb is used earlier in the narrative to indicate the angel's service of Jesus after the temptations (4:11), where it seems to have a symbolic significance. There is, therefore, for the reader the possibility of a symbolic use of the verb in this context also, which is confirmed as the story progresses. In 20:28, the verb "to serve" is used to characterize the mission and ministry of Jesus, and in 25:44 it provides a summary of the particular life-style definitive of the one who belongs to the inclusive and eschatological *basileia* of Jesus. Significantly also, this is the second narrative scene that takes place in a house, and once again there is a reordering of relationships and perhaps even resources denoted by the symbolic use of "to serve." If "house" is indeed the primary metaphor for the Matthean community, then the use of the verb "serve" in relation to the healed woman in the context of not just a house but the house of Peter underscores the metaphorical significance of the conclusion to the miracle story. The healed woman ministers to Jesus at the center of the new religious community he is inaugurating.

Matthew 9:18–26

A broken narrative pattern likewise characterizes this pericope, in which the healing of a woman with a hemorrhage is placed within the framework of the story of the healing of a ruler's daughter. Both are stories of female suppliants, and the linking of their stories enables the reader to interpret one in the light of the other.

The story opens with an extraordinary request made on behalf of a female supplicant. A ruler requests that Jesus come and lay hands on his daughter who has died, that she might live. The request is made by the father, so we hear nothing of the mother's point of view, and the daughter is introduced as one of the most severe pollutants—a corpse.

Parallel to the request made on her behalf, however, is the approach of the woman who is introduced as having suffered from a hemorrhage for twelve years (9:20). She stands alone in the narrative, as the young girl is alone in her condition. She is given no name, nor is she presented to the readers in terms of her human environment. She encounters Jesus in the public arena outside the confines of both the patriarchal household, from which she is most likely excluded because of her condition, and the reordered vision of the household. She is described in terms of her physical status: she is ritually unclean, a pollutant like the young girl.

With considerable initiative and placing herself at risk socially, she reaches out and touches Jesus' garment saying to herself: "If I only touch his garment, I shall be made well" (9:21). Here, for the first time in the narrative, we have a woman's point of view. She recognizes Jesus as one who can save her, can free her from her infirmity, while at the same time she seems to internalize her social marginalization. Her muted thoughts are, in fact, a statement of belief, a power that enables her to reach out beyond herself, beyond socioreligious restrictions, and not only to seek but to claim wholeness.

Her request is parallel to that of the ruler, and that parallel highlights the contrast between them. The ruler approached Jesus directly, knelt before him, and made his request. The woman, who was doubly marginalized within the society, was afraid to approach Jesus directly but came up to him from behind. Together, however, her story and that of the ruler's daughter provide a development in the narrative theme linking the female characters. Peter's mother-in-law could not make a request; the young girl has a request made on her behalf; and then a woman approaches Jesus from behind touching his garment and thereby formulating her request indirectly. The story of the woman with the hemorrhage also contains a further narrative development in that the faith of the woman is mentioned explicitly (9:22) and salvation is said to be effected by Jesus in response to that faith.

This faith of the woman who took the initiative and risked crossing socioreligious boundaries in order to come into contact with the healing power of Jesus places her in contrast to the flute players and professional mourners who laugh mockingly at Jesus' attitude to death with no faith in his capacity to heal or to restore life. Her faith is likewise contrasted with that of the disciples, who are called "of little faith" (8:26), and with the lack of response of the scribes, who see the healing power of Jesus only as a basis for accusation (9:3, 11, 34).

Each of the females who enters this combined story is encountered as a pollutant, outside the boundaries of ritual cleanliness, and the woman with the hemorrhage is anomalous in relation to gender boundaries. In neither story, however, does the restoration entail return to the patriarchal familial structure as a source of salvation. Within the proclamation of the *basileia* enacted within the miracle accounts, woman as well as man shares directly in the benefits of the *basileia*, the saving, life-giving power of Jesus. It is little wonder, therefore, that these stories are placed beside the buffer pericopes which speak of liberation and inclusion.

Matthew 15:21–28

The narrative theme of women of faith in the *basileia* ministry of Jesus is further developed by the story of another unnamed woman. Her story, together with the controversy regarding tradition to which it is linked, forms the focal point of a chiastic structure.

Within this limited context, the gender inflection of the narrative is significant. The narrator specifies that the five thousand numbered in the first feeding story and the four thousand in the second are male (14:21; 15:38), but goes on to point out that the crowd also included women and children. Women, therefore are recipients of the bread, one of the fruits of the *basileia*. The inclusion of women among those healed earlier in the story also leads the reader to count them among the many healed here (14:36; 15:30). Finally, a woman seeking healing for her daughter stands out as a woman of great faith (15:28) in contrast to the elders who question and the "disciples" who show little faith.

```
┌─A    The feeding of 5,000 (14:13–21)
│                    + a disciple's little faith (14:28–33)
│      ┌─B    Jesus heals many (14:34–36)
│      │        The tradition of the elders (15:1–20)
│      │  ┌─ C
│      │  │
│      │        The Canaanite woman (15:21–28)
│      └─B¹   Jesus heals many (15:29–31)
└─A¹   The feeding of 4,000 (15:32–39)
                     + the disciples' little faith (16:5–12)
```

Figure 3

One of the most extraordinary aspects of this story is that for the first time in the narrative the voice of a woman is heard. In fact, one of the key characteristics of this story is the dialogue—or, one might say, debate—that it contains. Speech or lack of it is therefore a key element in the structuring of the story as seen below.

```
┌─21   Introduction—Jesus withdraws
│      ┌─22   A Canaanite woman came out and *cried*: . . . . [beginning of dialogue]
│      │      [23   But he *did not answer* . . . ]
│      │      24   But *answering*, he *said* . . .
│      │      25   But coming, she knelt before him *saying*: . . . [dialogue]
│      │      26   But *answering*, he *said* . . .
│      └─27   But she *said* . . .
└─28   Conclusion—Then *answering*, Jesus *said* to her . . . [conclusion of dialogue]
```

Figure 4

The reader's introduction to this woman closely parallels that of the woman with a hemorrhage. Attention is focused on both by the use of the typical perspectival phrase: "Behold!" Neither is given a name, and each is identified by a category that renders one an outsider. The woman healed was identified by a physical disability that made her unclean. The woman in this story is categorized ethnically as "Canaanite," a term that makes her an ethnic and religious outsider to Israel. She too enters the narrative outside the patriarchal familial structure. She is alone, identified only with her daughter. Each woman, therefore, is doubly marginalized: she is female in a male world outside the patriarchal family structure, and she is ritually unclean.

From this position, the woman makes a request in words that already characterize the Gospel story but cross gender and ethnic boundaries. Her cry— "Have mercy on me, O Lord, Son of David!"—parallels that of the two Jewish men who requested the removal of their blindness (9:27). Her statement—"my daughter is severely possessed by a demon"—echoes the words of the centurion—"my servant is lying paralyzed at home" (8:6).

Disjunction enters this story, however, when the narrative pattern of earlier miracle stories is broken by the reaction of Jesus: "he did not answer her a word" (v. 23). The uniqueness of such a response makes one wonder whether we have here more than the usual opposition that can characterize a miracle story so that overcoming this opposition can become the key to an understanding of the story.

Read from an androcentric and patriarchal perspective, the severe response of Jesus can be seen to typify the purist's or the traditionalist's reaction to a Gentile woman who is unclean on the grounds of ethnicity and gender. But from a feminist perspective, the fact that Jesus, the miracle worker, is himself the opposition to the woman's request heightens her eventual triumph, which functions deconstructively to subvert the androcentrism of the text. Indeed, one could ask of this story whether it represents others not included in the final text because they did not contain the redeeming feature of the Gentile mission to counteract the woman's extraordinary "success."

The response of the disciples—"send her away"—strengthens the opposition of the earlier part of v. 23 and could be linked with v. 24 in terms of its redeeming value in the face of this scandalous approach of the woman and her appropriating of the confessional or theological language of the insider. It introduces the already-typical Gospel theme of lack of understanding of the disciples, taking up the language of 14:15. Verse 24 supplements this with the explicit articulation of the theme of Gentile mission repeating the restrictive perspective of 10:5–6.

Such opposition functions, however, to highlight the continued and more persistent demand of the woman as the dialogue is renewed with more vigor. As both disciples and daughter merge into the background of the story, the reader or listener is drawn into the struggle between Jesus and the woman as she demands help. In response to this request, Jesus again offers further opposition. The implied author's structuring of these three oppositions highlights the significance of the struggle involved in this story, a struggle that surrounds not only Jesus' mission to the Gentiles but also the very legitimacy of the woman's request.

As a third opposition, Jesus draws on a traditional or proverbial saying: "It is not fair to take the children's bread and throw it to the dogs" (15:26). The symbol of bread is introduced into the story, a symbol that is already associated with conflicts—what is eaten, by whom, and how (12:1–8; 15:1–20). On both of these previous occasions Jesus preached against a human tradition that was contrary to the desires of God. Here a similar struggle regarding human tradition and the desires of God is taking place, but this time it is Jesus' own struggle. What constitutes "mercy" rather than "condemnation of the guiltless" (12:7), "human precepts" rather than "word of God" (15:6–9) in this situation?

The woman, for her part, takes the parable as applying to herself in her twofold marginality as woman and Gentile, as her "Yes, Lord" indicates, but she courageously crosses the barriers placed before her asking for the crumbs from the master's table. She claims at least some of the fruits of the *basileia* which Jesus is preaching, claims them for herself and her daughter after her. The exclamation of Jesus—"O Woman, great is your faith!"—points to his recognition of the woman's insight into the inclusive nature of the power and presence of God in Jesus' preaching and healing ministry and her fidelity to that insight. His granting of her request—"Be it done to you as you desire"—indicates a recognition of his own call beyond traditional gender and racial boundaries as a result of his dialogue with this woman. The conclusion to this story, therefore, brings Jesus' point of view expressed in his oppositions to the woman into line with the narrator's point of view and hence the divine point of view already heard in 12:17–21.

In this section of the narrative, the great faith of this woman also acts as a foil to the lack of understanding of the disciples who would have sent her away without compassion (15:23) as well as to the little faith and lack of understanding of both Peter and the disciples. Peter's cry, "Lord, save me" (14:30), is similar to that of the woman, "Lord, help me" (15:25). But one is followed by the accusation "O man of little faith, why did you doubt?" (14:31). The other leads, through a dialogue, to Jesus' affirmation: "O woman, great is your faith!" (15:28). Furthermore, Peter's own act of faith (16:16) could not be sustained in the face of the passion prediction, and yet this woman was able to overcome the threefold opposition placed before her because of her belief in the power of Jesus and her preparedness to face rejection for the sake of the realization of life that such a belief held out to her. It was a faith, therefore, that far exceeded the "little faith" of the disciples who failed to understand the symbolism of the bread (16:8).

As a result of our feminist critique and rereading, it has become clear that female power has once again endured against all the barriers the patriarchal culture had erected against it, and the words of Jesus recognize and celebrate this. The woman's great faith makes possible a life free of oppressive restriction for herself and her daughter. The subversive power of this story goes far beyond the traditional boundary breaking with which it is associated—namely, Gentile mission. It invites the hearer to break the bonds of gender stereotyping and bias and demand miracle in human life, particularly in female human life. This woman stands, therefore, at one of the pivotal points in the Matthean narrative and in the Matthean vision of the Jesus-event. She is the catalyst and hence the "foremother" not only of Gentile Christians but also of women freed from all restrictive and oppressive socioreligious bondage.

The Basileia *Imaged as Inclusive*

Within the Matthean narrative, the following of Jesus as "disciple" means belonging to the community gathered around Jesus and being committed to the vision he preached. In relation to this theme, the reader first encounters four fishermen called to follow Jesus (4:18–22) and then subsequent references to a group called "disciples," whose membership, and hence genderization, is not clearly defined. As the narration of the miracle stories in chapters 8 and 9 draws to a close, however, those four fishermen are named at the head of a list of twelve male disciples whom Jesus commissions to share in his *basileia* ministry (10:1–15). This group includes also the tax collector Matthew, whom Jesus called during his healing ministry (9:9). Given the fluidity of character grouping already noted in chapters 5–9, it is not clear whether these are all the disciples, whether they are the group referred to previously (5:1; 8:21, 23; 9:10, 11, 14, 19, 37), or whether this group is limited by gender.

As the following chapter (11) opens, Jesus, who will be revealed as the Wisdom of God, is seen with these twelve male disciples (11:1). Subsequently, however, Jesus-Sophia calls *all* to come to her, to take up her yoke, and to learn from her (11:28–29), a call not governed by gender restrictions. This inclusive membership of the community of Jesus-Sophia is not, however, named as discipleship. Later again in the narrative, following a lengthy controversy between Jesus-Sophia and the Pharisaic opponents, membership within a patriarchal family is dramatically replaced by membership within the family of disciples gathered around Wisdom. They are the ones who live out one of the central responses to the *basileia* preaching—doing the will of God symbolized as Father (7:21; 12:50)—and the metaphors used for this discipleship are inclusive—brother and sister and mother (12:46–50). Since these words are those of the one who has become authoritative in the narrative, the reader can presume that discipleship of Wisdom is inclusive and that those who are given to know the secrets of the *basileia* (13:11), who have eyes that see and ears that hear (13:16, 23, 43), who indeed become scribes trained for the *basileia* (13:52) include both women and men despite the androcentric language in which these passages are cast.

There is disjunction or dissonance in the narrative, however, when those specifically named as members of the character group called disciples and those definitively called, even though the stories of their call may be intended to function paradigmatically, are male. Discipleship, however, can be read as inclusive, indicated by the imagery used to describe it and also the discipleship qualities exhibited by the women as well as the men who have come to Jesus as supplicants, who have listened to his teaching and who have followed him.

Inclusive imagery extends also to the metaphorical and symbolic designation of the preacher of the *basileia*. The parallel between 11:2 and 11:19 identifies the Matthean Jesus with Wisdom, the female gestalt of God within the Hebrew Scriptures, and this identification extends to the conclusion of the chapter (11:28–30). These texts occur, however, in the broader unit constituted by 11:2–13:68. Jesus' teaching and his deeds–healing the blind, the lame, the lepers, and the deaf; and raising the dead–are identified with personified Wisdom. The symbol of Wisdom and the myth in which it is narrated are used, therefore, to interpret the person and ministry of Jesus. In retrospect, the earlier preaching and healing of Jesus can likewise be understood within this framework, and it will be a significant interpretive key as the narrative unfolds. Matthean Christology, therefore, holds in tension the male symbol of the obedient son and the female divine gestalt, Sophia, and it is the latter that is linked with the call to an inclusive community. This, however, is often overlooked in the christological debates that characterize Matthean scholarship, although particular studies have given attention to it. A more detailed work is needed that could integrate the Sophia Christology more fully into a feminist rereading, but for the moment we can simply catch glimpses of the possibilities such a reading might offer to our re-visioning.

A Countertradition

Within the ministry of Jesus, two stories of women seem to interrupt the narrative development that has become clear in our analysis above. The first links two women, Herodias and her daughter, to the developing theme of opposition to Jesus which characterizes the second half of the Galilean ministry. The women, however, are not central characters in the story (14:1–12) but merely instruments. Herod is introduced at the start of the narrative; his perspective on the ministry of Jesus is given (v. 2); and the reader is given insight into his thoughts and feelings, even his desire to put John to death (vv. 5, 9). Herodias, on the other hand, is presented as deeply embedded in the patriarchal family. She is introduced as "*his* brother Philip's wife" (v. 3) and as his property–it is not lawful for you to *have* her (v. 4). The focus of the story is, therefore, the breakdown of a patriarchal family structure.

This rupture of the familial context is not, however, that which might be demanded by Jesus' preaching of the *basileia* (10:34–36), but rather a human action censured by John as opposed to the *basileia* message. Within this conflict story, Herodias functions behind the scene as murderess, and her daughter within the action as seductress–two of the typical depictions of female evil. The unlawful rupture of the patriarchal family structure is therefore symbolically linked to females. Similarly, violence and opposition directed toward John and, by implication, toward Jesus are likewise symbolized as female in a context where such opposition is predominantly male. A countertradition to the great faith of the women who receive the message and power of the *basileia* has been introduced, and the reader is alerted to its possible development.

Another mother is introduced into the narrative at 20:20. She appears out of the crowd together with her two sons, an indication perhaps that she is among those "going up to Jerusalem" with Jesus (20:17). She is, however, deeply embedded in the patriarchal family structure, identified in relation to three significant male family members as "the mother of the sons of Zebedee." She is depicted as the "typical" mother, whose sole concern is for her sons.

Her request indicates her failure to understand the nature of the *basileia* that Jesus has been preaching. Already he has shown that family membership is no basis for discipleship (10:34–39; 12:46–50). Hence, a mother's request on behalf of her sons is not a sign of faith, as was the persistent request of another mother on behalf of her daughter. Jesus, however, does not reject this woman but challenges her understanding. He asks: Can you accept the suffering that will be entailed in membership of the *basileia* being preached. The woman, together with her sons, responds: "We are able" (20:22). The reader is left in suspense with regard to the outcome of this affirmation, as the movement of the narrative leads toward Jerusalem, the location foreshadowed in the narrative for Jesus' own suffering.

The call to a deeper discipleship offered to this woman finds its location within a section of the narrative that is significantly androcentric. Peter stands out as spokesperson for the disciples (16:15–16), for Jesus (17:24–25), and on his own behalf (18:21–22); Peter, James, and John witness the transfiguration of Jesus on the mountain (17:1–8); a man's son and two blind men are healed (17:14–18; 20:29–34); and a young man with many possessions questions Jesus regarding the attainment of eternal life (19:16–22). In such a context, the reader is easily seduced into understanding the references to the disciples from the androcentric perspective of the implied author and into hearing the teachings on discipleship within this section in exclusive rather than inclusive terms.

The feminist reader, however, who meets this woman as she approaches Jesus is once again reminded that the followers of Jesus include women as well as men and that the teaching of Jesus regarding discipleship that has dominated this section of the Gospel is not gender specific. For this reader, the woman is representative of fallible discipleship just as the male disciples are, and when she is invited, together with her sons, to a more authentic response, the reader awaits this with anticipation. This and many other prolepses find their fulfillment or completion in the final section of the Gospel, in which the various narrative streams reach their climax.

WOMEN OF PASSION AND COMPASSION (21:1–28:20)

The Jerusalem ministry of Jesus (chaps. 21–25) is dominated by male characters, most particularly the Jewish leaders with whom he comes into conflict as well as the disciples, of whom twelve males have been specifically called and missioned. Similarly, the symbolic universe created by this section of the narrative is significantly androcentric, and the vehicle for this construction is the imagery of the parables. It is drawn from the agricultural world—a man with two sons working a vineyard; a householder with servants, who lets out his vineyard to tenants—the political world—a king giving a wedding feast for his son; a king pronouncing judgment—and the economic realm—a man entrusting his property to agents. It is a world in which female experience is not seen as symbolic of the *basileia* being preached.

There is an exception, however, in 25:1–13, the parable of the ten young women or virgins, which draws on female experience—but female experience in a patriarchal world. The women are at the service of the bridegroom, and the bride is invisible in the scene. As in previous parables, the reader is led to identify with one group of women rather than the other because of the designation "foolish" and "wise" (7:24, 26; 24:45). It is unlikely, however, that the inclusion of this parable, which draws its symbolic content from the world of women, has any significant impact on the symbolic universe that this portion of the narrative constructs. Rather, with the parable of the leaven (13:33), the only other Matthean parable that draws its imagery from this same world, the parable of the ten young women points to elements of an alternative symbolic universe which differed from that preferred by the implied author of the Matthean Gospel. Like many other hidden clues in the narrative, this parable provides the possibility for imagining a more extensive world of women that could be described in parables in relation to the inclusive *basileia* Jesus was preaching.

Suggestions have also been made that earlier hints of the interpretation of Jesus and his life work in terms of the Wisdom myth are again present in the account of the Jerusalem ministry. A wisdom saying in 23:34–35 is spoken directly by Jesus: "Therefore I send you. . . ." This is followed by the use of the female image of the hen gathering her brood under her wings (23:37). Such female imagery used in relation to Jesus is further extended if the eschatological discourse in chapter 24 is seen as Wisdom's discourse. This symbolization does not seem to be strong, but it is clear that it can at least begin to subvert the son Christology that dominates the narrative. Again, those half-buried clues point to a rereading of the Gospel in terms of inclusive symbolism for the interpretation of Jesus, the community he gathered around him, and the mission he gave. Included within such a reading, however, must be the ethnic critique of Sophia's judgment on Israel contained in 23:36.

As the reader is introduced to the passion narrative, the androcentric pattern of characterization that dominated the previous section continues. The scene opens with Jesus instructing his disciples (26:2) and being plotted against by the Jewish authorities (26:3–5); it closes with the authorities' continuing to plot against Jesus even after his death (28:11–15), and with Jesus' final commissioning of the eleven male disciples (28:16–20). Within this frame, the narrative moves from Jesus' last meal and evening with his disciples to his violent death at the hands of the Jewish and Roman authorities.

```
 ┌ Instruction to the disciples (26:1–2)
 │   ┌ Leaders plot against Jesus (26:3–5)
 │   │   ┌ Woman anoints Jesus (26:6–13)
 │   │   │   ┌ #Betrayal of Judas (26:14–16)
 │   │   │   │    *Passover (26:17–30)
 │   │   │  ┌#Peter's betrayal foretold (26:31–35)
 │   │   │  │    *Prayer in Gethsemane (26:36–46)
 │   │   │  │ #Betrayal and arrest (26:47–56)
 │   │   │  │    *Jesus before the Jewish Council (26:57–68)
 │   │   │  └#Peter's denial (26:69–75)
 │   │   │       Women question Peter (26:69, 71)
 │   │   │       *Jesus before Pilate (27:1–2)
 │   │   └  #Death of Judas (27:3–10)
 │   │           *Continuation of trial before Pilate
 │   │           Wife of Pilate (27:19) (27:11–26)
 │   │        ┌ #Soldiers' response to trial (27:27–31)
 │   │        │    *Crucifixion of Jesus (27:32–44)
 │   │        │    Death of Jesus (27:45–53)
 │   │        │ #Responses to Jesus' death
 │   │        │       Centurion/soldiers (27:54)
 │   │        │       Women (27:55–56)
 │   │        │          Joseph of Arimathea (27:57–60)
 │   │        │       Women (27:61)
 │   │        │       Leaders (27:62–66)
 │   │        │    *Resurrection accounts
 │   │        └ #Women witness the empty tomb (28:1–8)
 │   │           and see the Risen Jesus (28:9)
 │   └ Women commissioned to proclaim Jesus (28:1–10)
 │    └ Leaders plot against Jesus (28:11–15)
 └ Instruction to the disciples (28:16–20)
```

Figure 5

The gender inflection of this final section of the narrative seems clear, yet a closer examination shows that it is offset by significant stories of women (26:6–13; 26:69, 71; 27:19; 27:55–56, 61; 28:1–10). As figure 5 makes clear, the central focus of the passion narrative is the person of Jesus, who celebrates with his followers, prays in the garden, is arrested and brought before the Jewish Council and the Roman governor before being condemned to death by crucifixion. The last great moment in the christological development of the Gospel is the proclamation of the crucified Jesus having been raised. Interwoven within each of these moments of christological significance is the response of the disciples in the first half of the narrative and the response of both opponents and faithful followers in the second half. Among those who respond appropriately to Jesus at this crucial moment are women.

As figure 5 (above) demonstrates, the entire passion narrative is framed not only with stories concerning the disciples and the leaders but also with stories of women. Each character group is therefore integral to the narrative as a whole. The response of each to Jesus reaches a climax in the passion narrative, as does the contrast between them, which has been developing throughout the narrative. Against such a backdrop the individual stories of women must be read.

Matthew 26:6–13

The scene for the first of these stories is Bethany, on the outskirts of Jerusalem, a haven during Jesus' last days in Jerusalem. He retires there after his triumphal entry into Jerusalem is marred by the indignant reaction of the chief priests and scribes; and, following the plotting among the chief priests, elders, and the high priest to kill Jesus, the narrator has him again in Bethany, the place of refuge. The setting is the house of Simon the Leper, and, as in the first house setting in the Gospel (2:11), so too here there is an exchange of goods or resources indicative of new relationships. In both, the symbolic representation of Jesus is that of king.

In this house situation, a woman approaches Jesus. She comes not as supplicant but as actor. This comes as a surprise to the reader, who is already familiar with the introductory phrase "came up to him" as a way of bringing others into an encounter with Jesus but generally as supplicants. Here, however, the introductory formula is followed not by a request but rather by a definitive action directed toward Jesus: "she poured it [expensive ointment] on his head." Apart from the significance of the action itself, it represents a development in the narration of the stories in which women function as significant characters. First, the mother-in-law of Peter does not even dare to ask anything of Jesus; the woman with the hemorrhage fearfully approaches him from behind merely to touch his garment; the Canaanite woman openly approaches with a request and enters into dialogue with Jesus; and now an unnamed woman not only approaches Jesus but offers him the honorable gesture of anointing his head.

The language in which the woman's action is described is not that of cultic anointing but rather of an honorific gesture in the context of a meal. The action itself, however, especially the pouring out of the ointment onto the head signifies a cultic act acclaiming Jesus as Messiah. The latter interpretation is strengthened when this pericope is read in relation to a previous scene in which Jesus was acknowledged in messianic terms, namely, his entry into Jerusalem. There Jesus entered Jerusalem as king but "humble and mounted on an ass" (21:5) and was acclaimed by the crowds as "Son of David" (21:9). Jesus' response to this welcome and acclamation was to drive the money changers and sellers out of the Temple and to claim it for the blind and the lame whom he healed. In response to these actions of Jesus as well as to the acclaim he had received, the chief priests and scribes became indignant (21:15). As Jesus enters into his passion, a woman pours oil over his head, an action that in itself could be construed as further messianic acclaim. In response to such a messianic acclaim at the hands of a woman, the disciples are indignant, as were the chief priests and scribes at the strange kingly acclaim Jesus received from the crowd on his entry into Jerusalem (26:8). Both groups misunderstand the person and the mission of Jesus and react with a question to Jesus: "Do you hear what these are saying?" (21:16) and "Why this waste?" (26:8).

At this point it is of interest to notice the function of the disciples' question in the structuring of the pericope. It is the first reaction to the woman's action that is the focal point of the scene, and their question is accompanied by an explanation introduced by the connective "for." In a subsequent verse, their question is paralleled by a similar question asked of the disciples by Jesus. His question is accompanied by three explanatory phrases introduced by the connective "for," which interpret the action of the woman. The scene concludes with an extraordinary statement made by Jesus in relation to the woman's action.

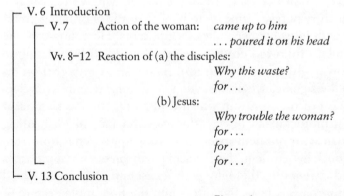

V. 6 Introduction
    V. 7   Action of the woman: *came up to him*
                                      ... poured it on his head
    Vv. 8–12 Reaction of (a) the disciples:
                                    Why this waste?
                                    for ...
                  (b) Jesus:
                                  Why trouble the woman?
                                    for ...
                                  for ...
                                  for ...
V. 13 Conclusion

Figure 6

The disciples' misunderstanding of the woman's action is conveyed to the reader by way of the reason for their question: "For this ointment might have been sold for a large sum and given to the poor." They have completely missed the significance of this moment in Jesus' life, a moment he has just indicated to them is two days before his being delivered up to be crucified (26:1). Simon offers Jesus the hospitality of his house and his table. The woman pours ointment over Jesus' head with a sensitivity whose full import is still not yet clear to the reader. The disciples are sensitive neither to the time in Jesus' unfolding life story nor to the action of the woman. They simply interpret the outpouring of the ointment as "waste."

The attentive reader is already aware of the Matthean teaching in relation to "the poor." The first Matthean beatitude was addressed to the poor in spirit (5:3). The preaching of the gospel to the poor was one sign among many that Jesus gave to the disciples of John to indicate that he was the Coming One (11:5); and the call which Jesus offered to the rich young man (19:21) indicated that giving to the poor was constitutive of discipleship of Jesus. In fact, in his last great sermon, Jesus identified himself with those in need of compassion, among whom the poor could be numbered (25:40). The objection raised by the disciples therefore calls the action of the woman into question.

For the reader, the indignation of the disciples and their question are a reminder of their reaction to the Canaanite woman's persistent approach to Jesus (15:23). The contrast that the narrator has already established between the group called disciples and the women characters is strengthened. From 10:1 on, when the character group called "disciples" has been more clearly defined as male, the disciples have appeared in conflict with or in contrast to the women in each of the stories in which women function as central characters.

At the beginning of the passion narrative, Jesus speaks plainly to his disciples of his approaching passion: "You know that after two days the Passover is coming, and the Son of Man ["Human One"] will be delivered up to be crucified." The stage is set, therefore, for all that follows. On the one hand, the chief priests and the elders gather in the palace of the high priest and plan how they can kill Jesus. Jesus, on the other hand, gathers with his disciples in the house of a leper at Bethany and here is anointed by a woman. The action of the woman is set, therefore, in direct contrast to the action of Jesus' opponents. The reaction of the disciples puts them also in direct contrast to the woman. The irony of their reaction—"Why this waste?"—is further emphasized when, immediately following this scene, Judas, one of the disciples, goes to the chief priests asking for money in return for the betrayal of Jesus, whereas the woman has poured out expensive ointment for his anointing.

Jesus' question in v. 10 turns the focus of the narrative back to the woman. The use of the noun "woman" is clearly a narrative device for this very purpose. Jesus then, in giving reasons for his reproach of the disciples, also offers an interpretation of the woman's act from three different perspectives. They are interpretations in a male voice. The woman herself has no voice in the narrative, but the interpretations are prophetic and directed toward her action. They are also in the voice of the most authoritative character in the narrative, Jesus.

As a counter to the disciples' accusation, which designates the woman's action as "waste," the words of Jesus claim it as "a good work or deed done to me." This takes the reader into the oppositional language used to characterize the human response to the gift of the *basileia*. The language used by the disciples, "waste," occurred earlier in the narrative in the context of a way leading to destruction rather than leading to life (7:13–14). Similarly, the language of Jesus—"good" as opposed to "bad"—is reminiscent of another oppositional category used to characterize the way of discipleship (7:17–20; see also 3:10; 12:33; 13:8, 23, 24, 27, 37, 38, 45, 48). Hence, Jesus claims the woman's action as belonging to the response called forth by his preaching of the *basileia*. This claim is further strengthened when he adds that this good deed is done "to me." This recalls for the reader the great eschatological discourse that has just preceded, in which Jesus proclaimed: "Just as you did it to one of the least of these who are members of my family, you did it to me" (25:40). The eschatological judge, the triumphant Messiah (25:31), will consider as done to himself those good deeds that are done to the least among humanity. The woman has anticipated this coming when she performs her good deed directly for Jesus. In her action, right ordering of relationships and resources occurs in the last narrative scene located in a house. Her action is truly symbolic of the *basileia*.

In responding to and countering the second aspect of the disciples accusation, namely, the failure to give this resource to the poor, Jesus shifts the focus to the significance of the woman's action in relation to time: "you *always* have/you will *not always* have" (26:11). The woman, in performing the anointing of Jesus, rather than selling the ointment and giving the money to the poor, has truly understood Jesus' words that after two days he would be delivered up to be crucified (26:2). She has recognized what Jesus gives voice to, namely, the importance of the remaining time that he has with his followers when, in fact, "good deeds" will be directed toward him.

The language of the narrator (v. 7) is changed in the mouth of Jesus (v. 12) as he gives his own interpretation to the woman's action. It is not just his head that is anointed but his whole body, and it is for burial. This woman has anticipated Jesus' death by crucifixion, which will deny him the normal burial customs. She has indeed carried out the task that loved ones do for their beloved or disciples for their teacher (14:12; 27:57). At this point, the reader's attention is directed back to the action of the woman, and now it is not only the action that speaks with a voice that cannot be silenced even though the woman herself has no voice in the narrative, but her most extraordinary action is affirmed in the authoritative voice of Jesus as constitutive of the *basileia*, as acknowledgment of the Anointed One and his coming, and as the final act of discipleship. It is all this that draws forth the declaration of Jesus.

"Truly, I say to you, wherever this gospel is preached in the whole world, what she has done will be told in memory of her" (26:13). Once again the authoritative voice of Jesus acclaims a female participant in the Gospel story. The solemnity of this declaration, however, exceeds that made in relation to the Canaanite woman (15:28). It begins with the solemn statement—"Truly, I say to you"—which alerts the reader to both the authority and the significance of what is to follow.

The paralleling in the statement of Jesus strengthens its impact. The verbs "preach" and "tell" are almost interchangeable, and hence they can function interactively. Jesus claims that whenever the gospel is preached, the story of the woman's action will be told as a remembrance of her. The reader should also understand by implication, however, that if her story is not told to her memory then the gospel is not being truly preached in the whole world. The statement of Jesus that concludes this woman's story links the remembering of her action inextricably with the remembrance of him and his actions. The unique prophetic action of the woman at Bethany takes it place, therefore, alongside of and complementary to the actions of Jesus. The preaching and telling of both comprise the gospel, which will be proclaimed in the whole world.

This story of a woman at the beginning of the passion narrative is a story of female power, a power that recognizes suffering and reaches out courageously to bring the touch of mercy and compassion to the one suffering. As the words of Jesus at the end of her story indicate, it is the most extraordinary story of one of the followers of Jesus, and hence it is to be continually proclaimed as gospel. Female gender therefore symbolizes faithful discipleship at this point in the narrative. The force of this symbol is, however, blunted by the androcentric narrative. This woman of compassion is given no name, nor is she given a voice in the narrative. Her prophetic action is interpreted by the male voice of Jesus. Further, like the Canaanite woman, there is no story of her call within the narrative, and she is excluded from the group called "disciples" because of its patriarchal construct. Her action, however, functions to subvert that very construct.

As the story of Jesus' last days continues, the reader sees him entering more deeply into the world of betrayal, denial, rejection, and annihilation—symbolized in the narrative as a male world. Only for brief moments do women break the hegemony of this world. During Jesus' trial before the high priest, two women recognize Peter as having been with Jesus, and their affirmation, which symbolically places them on the side of Jesus, sets them over against Peter and his denial of Jesus (26:69, 71). Later, Pilate's wife is referred to by the narrator (27:19). Like Herodias, she does not appear as an active character, but her words of warning, which claim Jesus as a righteous man, stand out in stark contrast to the sea of accusations surrounding him. These faint female voices are, however, drowned out by the male voices of denial and condemnation.

Matthew 27:55–56, 61

Although their voices are no longer heard in the narrative, women appear in the two scenes that constitute its climax. They are present at the cross and the tomb and are the first to encounter the risen Jesus. In both situations, they are witnesses, as the use of a particular form of the verb "to see" only in these two verses of the narrative indicates (27:55; 28:1). They witness the manifestation of divine power that surrounds both the crucifixion (27:51–53) and the resurrection (28:2–3).

The second half of 27:55 directs the reader's attention to the long-term association of the women with Jesus, thus authenticating their witness. They have *followed* Jesus from Galilee and have *ministered* to him or served him. It has already been shown that the following of Jesus is constitutive of discipleship and that service, especially of Jesus, is central to the inauguration of the *basileia*. These women are therefore disciples, even though not explicitly named as such, and they are faithful to their teacher and friend to the very end.

This fidelity is further emphasized for the reader by the presence of "the mother of the sons of Zebedee" among the group. Earlier Jesus invited this woman and her sons to drink the cup of suffering with him, an invitation they accepted (20:20–22). The woman has shown herself faithful to her affirmation and stands at the foot of Jesus' cross. She is still not named, although two of her companions are—Mary Magdalene and Mary the mother of James and Joseph (27:56). Apart from Tamar, Rahab, Ruth, and Mary (the women named in the prologue) and Herodias (14:3), these are the only women who are identified by name in the entire Gospel. They are linked to the cross (27:56) and to the tomb (27:61) and appear in the symbolic narrative of the resurrection (28:1–10). Women characters emerge from anonymity, and their very naming at this point of the narrative emphasizes their significance.

Matthew 28:1–10

Both the naming of the two women and their undertaking, their going to see or to observe the tomb of Jesus, link this story to that of the women who witnessed Jesus' crucifixion. In both instances the women are designated as witnesses. The focalizer "behold" in v. 2 directs the reader's attention to the phenomena surrounding the tomb, as did the verb "to see" in connection with the crucifixion. In the face of this manifestation of divine power, the guards become like dead men. In contrast, the message the angel gives to the women is that the crucified one whom they seek, the one whom in fact they saw die, has been raised (28:5–6). The women are surrounded by these signs of reversal, signs of a new age, and their very presence and encounter with the angel are among those signs.

These faithful women are then given a commission by the angel. They are to proclaim to the disciples that Jesus has been raised. They are indeed commissioned with the proclamation of the resurrection. In addition, they are to be the intermediaries who make possible the absent disciples' reconciliation with Jesus. The fidelity of the women to this twofold commission is indicated by the repetition in v. 8 of the adverb "quickly." The angel commanded, "Go quickly," the narrator relates; so they departed quickly.

As in v. 2, the focalizer "behold" is used once again at the beginning of v. 9 by the narrator to direct the reader's attention. This time it is toward Jesus, the risen Jesus, who meets the obedient women as they are undertaking their commission. The greeting—"Hail"—continues the reversal motif that characterizes this scene. The word used by Judas to betray Jesus (26:49) and by the soldiers to mock him (27:29) now becomes the first word given by the implied author to the risen Jesus as greeting to the women who have witnessed the empty tomb. The great joy of the women (28:8) meets the joyful greeting of Jesus (28:9), and their response is worship. It is only after this encounter that Jesus reiterates the commission given to the women earlier by the angel. They are to be the messengers of reconciliation to the absent disciples. The risen Jesus, however, does not commission the women with the resurrection proclamation. His commissioning will be reserved for the eleven male disciples as the narrative closes (28:19–20). One wonders whether here, once again, female gender becomes a limitation, this time in relation to Jesus' own commissioning of the resurrection proclamation. This story, however, together with others within the passion/resurrection narrative, offers significant clues for a feminist rereading of the text.

Within the final movement of the Gospel story, the account of Jesus' passion, significant stories of women link them as women of passion to this central story. The power of their love and compassion overcomes fear and defamation and enables them to remain as faithful followers and companions of Jesus through his last days and hours. They are, however, not merely followers but competent actors who bring their resources and their own person into relationship with Jesus at this point in a way that is indicative of the *basileia* that Jesus has preached and whose very radicalism and inclusiveness have led to his death. They stand, therefore, as unique witnesses to the death and resurrection of Jesus, which is to be proclaimed to all nations so that *all* may be discipled. They are, therefore, the foremothers of the gospel proclamation, and their story will be told as a constitutive part of it. At the close of the Gospel story, as in its opening, female power and female presence function to subvert the patriarchal constructs and androcentric worldviews that both frame the narrative and find expression throughout.

CONCLUSION

In our narrative reading, we have encountered a subversive story for those who have ears to hear the voice from the underside of the narrative which speaks against the grain of the text. It has been a story of women's participation in the *basileia* mission and ministry of Jesus, God with us. A woman's participation in the birth of Jesus outside the patriarchal familial structure is claimed as holy, her female power linked to the divine power and presence that characterize her son, Jesus, and his story (1:23; 18:20; 28:20). Into this woman's story, brief though it is, are drawn the memories of women's participation in Israel's history. As the story develops, a woman who is an outsider on the basis of gender and religious law is invited into wholeness and life by Jesus and responds in a way that characterizes her as belonging to the *basileia* community being established by Jesus' preaching and way of life. Two other women who are among the most dangerous of pollutants are enabled to cross the boundaries that exclude them. For the young woman, Jesus' touch restores her to life, as it did for Peter's mother-in-law, but the woman with the hemorrhage takes the initiative herself, claiming healing and wholeness. Her initiative prepares the reader for an even more extraordinary instance of female insight, belief, and courage, when the Canaanite woman in her debate with Jesus extends the *basileia* mission beyond the confines of Israel to the Gentiles and beyond gender boundaries to fully include women in the life of the community. As the story moves to a close women are significant actors in the unfolding drama. A woman prophetically anoints Jesus in recognition of his messianic ministry and in compassionate and faithful love of him as he approaches death. Other women manifest a similar compassion and fidelity when they stand with Jesus in his death and remain beyond death and burial to witness the power of God made visible in the raising up of Jesus. They are then commissioned with a resurrection proclamation and are the first to encounter the risen Jesus being further commissioned by him to be the agents of reconciliation with the absent disciples.

Such a story has been augmented by Jesus' preaching of an inclusive *basileia* where all will be healed and made whole, where all learn wisdom and Torah, and where male and female image this *basileia*. This is the message of Jesus-Sophia, who teaches and heals and whose identity and mission are interpreted in the light of the Wisdom myth with its central female images.

Within the Matthean story, therefore, female power, whether reproductive power or the power of faith-filled seeing, understanding, and acting, was many times affirmed by the authoritative voice of the narrator or Jesus. Female gender was symbolic of faithful participation in the *basileia* vision that Jesus preached in much of the story. The symbolic function of female gender was, however, two-edged. In addition to symbolizing faithful participation, female-ness functioned as a limitation preventing the women's participation in the character group called "the Twelve" or perhaps even in "the disciples." Female power was presented as anomalous within the androcentric perspective of the narrative and hence was continually brought within the confines of this per-spective. Female experience was virtually excluded from the symbol system drawn upon to image the *basileia*.

Our reading of the Matthean story, however, from the perspective of a femi-nist hermeneutics of suspicion enabled the subversive story to function decon-structively in relation to the androcentric perspective and patriarchal struc-tures within the text. This made possible the hermeneutics of remembrance and reclamation, which led to an inclusive reading of the Gospel text. Within such a reading women together with men stand at the heart of the Gospel story. Both women and men are active participants in Israel's history, just as Mary and Joseph are such in the birth story. Women together with men receive the fruits of the *basileia* with a faith that calls forth the life-restoring power of Jesus. This healing brings both together in the inclusive community around Jesus. The struggle toward full discipleship is manifest in the lives of women and men, and gender is not determinative of opposition to Jesus. Finally, women together with men are central to the mission of resurrection proclama-tion both within Israel and beyond its geographic confines. The stories of women are restored to the biblical text so that it must now be read as the story of women and men who participated in the Jesus-event recounted in the Matthean narrative.

TO BRING OUT OF ONE'S TREASURE
THE NEW AND THE OLD:
THE ART OF SUBVERSIVE TRADITIONING

The narrative and reader-response critical tools employed in the previous section have enabled us, from a reading site that is explicitly feminist, to restore to the Matthean text the stories of women, the vision of the *basileia* as inclusive particularly from a gender perspective, and a wisdom Christology. A contemporary reading of this text, therefore, that seeks to be accountable in relation to an ethics of inclusion will give consideration to the significance of such a reading and to the dangers inherent in the patriarchal and androcentric readings that are possible from different reading sites.

A feminist ethics of inclusion as it functions in the arena of biblical studies is not limited, however, to the countercoherent reading which gives attention to gender perspectives and which revisions old texts from the new critical direction of women's lives and experience. It is also concerned with reading the story of the formation of the text in its historical context and the appropriate reconstruction of that context. There is an awareness that the text itself is a reading of a particular historical and ideological reality and that it encodes the perspectives of the authorizing agent, whether an individual or a community. We know that women were members of early Christian communities, and hence our reading of the traditioning process that led to the compilation of the Matthean story of Jesus will ask the question of women's inclusion in this process. Do we find women's perspectives, even women's traditions, included in and therefore functional in the shaping of the final story?

The tools that enable this stage of investigation are predominantly historical-critical. They will be employed in some detail in relation to the Matthean story of the Canaanite woman's encounter with Jesus as an illustration of the traditioning process and its possible encoding of women's perspectives and traditions, or at least those perspectives and traditions that included women and their experience. Brief indications will then be provided of both similar and differing processes in relation to other major stories examined in the preceding section.

A READING OF MATTHEAN TRADITIONING (15:21–28)

A number of source-critical factors lead to the conclusion that the Matthean story of the Canaanite woman (15:21–28) is an adaptation of a similar story found in Mark 7:24–30. Although there is very little evidence of direct literary dependence, as seen in figure 7 (the reference to Tyre, a woman's daughter in each, and the interchange regarding bread being thrown to dogs), there are significant content relationships. A woman intercedes on behalf of her daughter who has an unclean spirit, prostrating herself before Jesus only to be rebuffed by an apparently familiar parabolic saying about throwing the children's bread to the dogs. In each case, she extends the parable to include herself and her daughter and thus wins Jesus' admiration and his compassion, which extends to her daughter through her. The Matthean account would seem to be a development of the Markan account in that a literary pattern found in Mark, namely, petition followed by difficulty, is repeated but also reproduced in Matthew. Second, in Matthew the woman is given direct speech, whereas her request is indirect in the words of the narrator in Mark (Mark 7:25b//Matt 15:22b; Mark 7:26//Matt 15:25b). A final factor that would point to development of the story within the Matthean community is the emphasis on the dialogue or debate rather than on the more traditional miracle aspect of the story.

Matt 15:21–28	Mark 7:24–30
[21]And Jesus went away from there and withdrew to the district of *Tyre* and Sidon.	[24]And from there he arose and went away to the region of *Tyre* [and Sidon]. And he entered a house and would not have anyone know it; yet he could not be hid.
[22]And behold *a* Canaanite *woman* from that region came out and cried, "Have mercy on me, O Lord, Son of David; my *daughter* is severely possessed by a demon."	[25]But immediately a *woman* whose little *daughter* was possessed by an unclean spirit,
[23]But he did not answer her a word. And his disciples came and begged him, saying, "Send her away, for she is crying after us." [24]He answered, "I was sent only to the lost sheep of the house of Israel."	
[25]But she *came* and knelt before him	heard of him and *came* and fell down at his feet. [26]Now the woman was a Greek, a Syrophoenician by birth. and she begged him to cast the demon out of her daughter.
saying, "Lord, help me." [26]And he answered,	[27]And he said to her, "Let the children first be fed, for *it is not right to take the children's bread and throw it to the dogs.*"
"*It is not fair to take the children's bread and throw it to the dogs.*" [27]She said, "*Yes, Lord, yet even the dogs eat the crumbs* that fall from their masters' table."	[28]But she answered him, "*Yes, Lord, yet even the dogs* under the table *eat the* children's *crumbs.*"
[28]Then Jesus answered her, "O woman, great is your faith! Be it done for you as you desire."	[29]And he said to her,
	"For this saying you may go your way; the demon has left your daughter." [30]And she went home, and found the child lying in bed, and the demon gone.
And her daughter was healed instantly.	

Figure 7

One of the key characteristics of the Matthean account that suggests a significant traditioning process within the Matthean house-churches is the use of words and phrases which are indicative of that community's tradition and which occur elsewhere in the Gospel story. It seems, therefore, that this particular story developed around the two sayings taken directly from the Markan account, but these were augmented by Matthean tradition. This is seen in the opening verse of the story, where Jesus "withdraws" following the controversy with the Jewish leaders over questions of tradition. Each time previously that this verb was used in relation to Jesus (2:14, 22; 4:12; 12:15; 14:13), he had been seeking refuge from controversy with the Jewish political or religious leaders, and each time his withdrawal was associated with explicit Gentile territory or was in the context of reference to the Gentiles. The question of insider/outsider on ethnic grounds is thereby signaled at the outset of the story.

Interestingly, given the Matthean use of the house metaphor with which we are already familiar, the location of the encounter with the woman inside a house, which typifies the Markan account, is absent from Matthew. The encounter takes place in the public arena, which was traditionally assumed to be the domain of men, and it is here that the woman makes her demand and obtains a favorable response to her request. Her success as woman in this arena will have profound implications for the house-churches, but the location itself, which was strongly gender-inflected in first-century Mediterranean culture, may be an indicator of a significant gender question within this story as well as a Gentile mission issue.

The designation of the woman as Canaanite underscores her status as outsider on a presumably ethnic basis. Within the Matthean traditioning process, however, this woman is given the language of the insider. Her cry "have mercy on me" is one familiar within the Gospel (9:27; 20:30, 31; 17:15) and has the format of prayer or a traditional liturgical formula in Jewish tradition, as indicated by its presence in many psalms (Pss 6:2; 9:13; 30:10; 41:4, 10 . . .). It may reasonably be assumed that it was representative of the liturgical language within the Matthean house-churches. The two titles used by the woman—"Lord" and "Son of David"—are typical of the traditions developing within those house-churches as they reflected on the person and work of Jesus, and they occur significantly throughout the Matthean Gospel. The words given to the woman represent, therefore, developing liturgical and theological formulations within the Matthean communities. This gives weight to the earlier hint that this tradition may be concerned not only with ethnic questions but also with gender questions—and even further, how these impinged on the liturgical and theological life.

For many within those communities, the woman's words would have struck at the heart of a number of their socioreligious boundaries, both ethnic and gender. One wonders, therefore, whether these audacious words given to the Canaanite woman within the traditioning process capture the perspective of at least some of the more egalitarian Matthean house-churches, in which women were active participants in the community's liturgical and theological life. Perhaps these communities were coming into conflict with other house-church communities who excluded women from these activities or were seeking to restrict activities women had undertaken as a result of an inclusive interpretation of the Jesus vision.

That conflict is represented at the core of this tradition's development is suggested by the heaping up of oppositions to the woman's request. The opening phrase of v. 23—"he did not answer her a word"—is the most radical opposition and does not find an echo anywhere else in the Gospel. It functions rhetorically, therefore, as the encoding of a very strong objection to the possibilities inherent in the development of this tradition within certain Matthean communities that would allow the participation of women and Gentiles in the liturgical and theological life of the community.

The introduction of the disciples into the scene may have had the same rhetorical function. It may, however, have been representative of a more general trend that opposed an egalitarian form of household structure that was legitimated by the traditions preserved in the stories of women. We saw earlier that the disciples as opponents of women occurred in both this story and that of the woman who anoints Jesus. Both are redactional additions.

The third opposition, v. 24—"I was sent only to the lost sheep of the house of Israel"—represents a tradition that was present within the Matthean communities, as suggested by the occurrence of a very similar statement given to Jesus in the missionary discourse. There he commissioned his disciples to avoid Gentile and Samaritan towns and to go only to the lost sheep of the house of Israel (10:5—6), and here this same restrictive mission is claimed for Jesus himself. Thus, three traditional objections are heaped up over against the woman's petition in such a way as to suggest the struggle occurring in the very traditioning process itself. It surrounds the two questions of female and Gentile participation within the life of the new Christian communities, and we could reasonably assume that women were involved in this struggle, especially if the future of their participation was at stake. The Canaanite woman may well have been symbolic of their struggle, especially as the tradition developed within their midst.

In v. 25, the woman is once again given direct speech, and again her words—"Lord, help me"—have theological and liturgical overtones. The request is reminiscent of the psalms (Pss 43:27; 69:6; 78:9; 108:26, 117). Taken together, her two requests closely resemble the petition of Ps 108:26: "Help me, Lord my God, save me according to your mercy." This psalm is the cry of an oppressed person in the face of severe adversities. It is significant, therefore, that it is the same cry for "help" and "mercy" that is given to the woman who calls out to Jesus from a position of exclusion and oppression.

The Markan opposition, which seems at first glance to be simply retained in the Matthean redactional process (v. 26), functions with much greater impact because of the threefold opposition in vv. 23—24. This impact is even further strengthened by the omission of the Markan relativizing statement: "Let the

children first be fed." It seems, therefore, to parallel the very particularist statement of v. 24. We have already suggested that the development of this Matthean tradition touched not only on the question of Jesus' mission to the
Gentiles but also on the role of women within the Christian community. While
it seems that the Markan use of "dogs" in the context of that story is understood as a derogatory reference to Gentiles, in the Matthean context it may
have a broader referent.

In Isa 56:10, those who are blind and without knowledge are likened to
"dumb dogs." Knowledge in this case is inclusive of Torah knowledge and, as
well as applying to Gentiles, later included the "poor of the land," whose lack
of knowledge of Torah rendered them unable to keep its precepts. In later rabbinic writings, the term "dog" is also used to refer to those not versed in the
Torah. If such an understanding was current within the Matthean communities, then the Markan parable may have been used to categorize the woman as
"dog" not only because of her ethnic status but also because of gender. It is a
particularist statement like that of v. 24, but the Matthean text can function as
such on two counts. The woman is not eligible to receive the bread of the
insider not only because of her Gentile status but also because of her lack of
access to the Torah because of being a woman.

Within the development of a tradition that was incorporating opposing theological perspectives within the Matthean church, the slight change made to
the Markan text in v. 27 is significant. The "dogs" are not placed in the
demeaning position "under the table," and the crumbs are those that fall from
the table of the "master" or "lord," the title that has been used for Jesus by the
woman in her two requests. The woman claims for herself as Gentile the right
to receive the benefits of the *basileia* that Jesus preached directly from him
and not secondarily from those who claimed the sole right to these benefits.
Second, as a woman within the Christian community, she claims the right to
learn and to scrutinize the scriptures and the teachings of Jesus, a benefit not
reserved solely for the male members of the community but available to all
from the table of the Lord.

The greeting found on the lips of Jesus at the conclusion of the Matthean
story is unique. The exclamation "O" may indicate the strong emotion
involved in this culmination of an emotionally charged story. The full greeting
"O woman" acknowledges the woman respectfully in contrast to the rejection
that has characterized the story. Greeting is followed by exclamation, as Jesus
proclaims the greatness of her faith. We have already seen earlier the contrast
between the great faith of the woman and the little faith of the disciples. It
should be pointed out that this is the only time in the entire story that the faith
of a supplicant is qualified in this way. The woman's approach to Jesus has
thereby been vindicated over against the accusations and oppositions set up
against her. As the story concludes, the particularist statements of vv. 24 and

26 are overturned and it is woman and those whose theological perspective she symbolizes who are acclaimed in the authoritative words of Jesus.

By way of summary, it seems that within the Matthean community, the Markan story has provided a basis around which two groups of countertraditions developed. A natural development from the Markan story would have been the highlighting of the extension of Jesus' mission to the Gentiles by doubling the pattern of petition and difficulty. Our particular reading of the developing tradition, however, has suggested that the conflict existed not only in relation to the Gentile mission but also toward women's participation in the liturgical and theological life of the community hinted at by the words of petition given to the woman. As the tradition developed, the particularist statements of vv. 24 and 26 took on new significance and provided a counter to those community perspectives that supported the active participation of women in the community's religious life. Verse 23 may have been a later addition to add greater weight to the particularist position, which was gender restrictive.

It is this story with tradition and countertradition that has been incorporated into the Gospel story in a way that functions to support and legitimate women's active role in liturgy and their participation in the community's theological reflection on the life and ministry of Jesus in the light of their scriptures. It is difficult to imagine that women alone were responsible for the development of the story, but within the house-churches that seem to have been in conflict, women would certainly have been members. The developed tradition would, however, have been very significant to women within the community, and hence they may well have been active in its preservation and incorporation into the Gospel story. This story's formation is illustrative, therefore, of the art of subversive traditioning which characterizes at least certain aspects of the Matthean Gospel.

THE NEW AND THE OLD

What was new, the result of bringing the Jesus traditions into new situations, certainly characterized the development of the story of the Canaanite woman. Other stories within the Matthean Gospel, however, are a preservation of the old in what may well have been a very early form. A redaction-critical study of the story of the healing of Peter's mother-in-law suggests such a process.

The earlier narrative-critical reading of this story alerted us to the fact that it did not follow the expected pattern for a miracle story. Comparison with Mark and Luke indicates that in both of these Gospels the story is typical of a miracle account. One of the aspects unique to the Matthean account is the presence of the verb "saw" in v. 14. This verb is a significant indicator of another story type, namely, the vocation story, typified in 9:9. When a comparison is made between 8:14–15 and 9:9, it appears that the Matthean story combines elements of both vocation stories and miracle stories, as seen in figure 8.

	Matt 8:14–15	*Matt 9:9*
INTRODUCTION		
Coming of the caller	And when Jesus entered Peter's house	And Jesus passed on from there
Sees one to be called	he saw his mother-in-law	he saw a man called Matthew
EXPOSITION		
Description of one to be called	lying sick with a fever;	sitting at the tax office
MIDDLE		
Call–word or action	he touched her hand,	and he said to him, "Follow me"
	[and the fever left her]	
CONCLUSION		
Response to call	and she arose and served him	And he arose and followed him.

Figure 8

Such a story form represents early traditioning within the Christian community, when models from the Hebrew Scriptures (e.g., 1 Kgs 19:19–21) were used to give shape to their memories of Jesus and to enable their telling or traditioning of these memories. It could be argued, therefore, that the tradition regarding Peter's mother-in-law preserved within the Matthean community was the early memory of her call to the discipleship of Jesus occasioned by her healing. It was told in the typical mode of vocation stories, with the brief account of her healing included. That this was an old memory seems likely on further grounds in that it is more difficult to imagine that a community whose traditions reflected a struggle surrounding women's participation would readily have changed a story of a woman's healing to a story of a woman's call to discipleship.

Within the Matthean community, therefore, this story may well have been symbolic of women's discipleship. The retention of the healing aspect of the story may also have symbolized the gender barriers that had to be overcome to enable women's full participation in the *basileia* ministry of Jesus continued in the life of the community. Such a story would have been told among women within the community. Perhaps too it was they who preserved the story's vocational aspect through the traditioning process, keeping what was old when that best enabled the inclusive nature of the *basileia* vision to be both preserved and enhanced.

Likewise, a detailed redaction-critical study of the stories of the healing of the woman with the hemorrhage and the raising of the young woman who was a ruler's daughter suggests that they too have been preserved in a concise early form that differed from the Markan and Lukan source. Little has been added to the early story of the hemorrhaging woman in the traditioning process. Significantly, however, the woman is not dismissed, but the story concludes by highlighting the salvific aspect of the healing for the woman. This parallels the climactic conclusion of the framing story: "the girl arose" (9:25). In neither story is the female returned to the oppressive social structure, whether it be the patriarchal family or socioreligious context.

During the course of the shaping of these two stories within the Matthean communities the most significant developments surrounded the emphasizing of parallels between them. This is especially clear in the initial verses of the combined pericope, where the ruler's request is paralleled with that of the hemorrhaging woman, as can be seen in figure 9.

[18]Behold a ruler	[20]Behold a woman
	who had suffered from a
	hemorrhage for twelve years
came in	came up behind him
and knelt before him	and touched the fringe of his garment
saying,	for she said to herself
"My daughter has just died;	
but come and lay your hand on her	"If I only touch his garment,
And she will live."	I shall be made well."

Figure 9

Such parallel structure highlights the boundaries the woman had to cross to obtain healing. As the focal point in the story, therefore, it suggests that these stories would have been significant for those communities which may have been struggling with attempts to exclude women socially or religiously and that such communities may have been responsible for the preservation of these stories in an early stark simplicity. The telling of these stories not only recalls but generates hope, expectation, and a vision of new possibilities for all females of whatever age. They speak to the community of the channels of salvation that Jesus opens up to women as well as men beyond the boundaries of gender, and of life offered to young women beyond the confines of the patriarchal family.

In the final redactional shaping of chapters 8 and 9, three stories involving women taken from early written sources have been retained. Each of these stories has been preserved with the simplicity and directness that reflect the early Christian memory preserved within the Matthean community. By means of the interaction of miracle and teaching; the interplay of christological, soteriological, and discipleship motifs; and attention to the interaction between Jesus and supplicant, a paradigm for women within the community has been presented. They are recipients of the fruits of the *basileia;* they serve as disciples of Jesus within its parameters; and they believe, despite all obstacles, that Jesus has the power to cross the boundaries established by various forms of human limitation. This paradigm seems to encode a vision that had been kept alive by the community itself, but its preservation within this final stage of redaction and its skillful incorporation into the text would also function to challenge other paradigms of discipleship and of participation in the fruits of the kingdom that were present in the community and were likewise encoded in the Gospel. This explains something of the tension that we find in the Gospel surrounding these stories, a tension that has not been avoided but is in fact at the heart of the stated purpose in redacting—to bring out the new and the old.

It is more difficult to determine the traditioning process that shaped the infancy narrative, but in the absence of any extant evidence of the linking of the four women—Tamar, Rahab, Ruth, and Bathsheba—it could be claimed that their presence in the genealogy is the result of a Matthean community tradition. As the Isaian text (7:14) was used to interpret the extraordinary action of God in the birth of Jesus to Mary outside patriarchal family structures, so too were other biblical traditions recalled to enhance this tradition. These were new traditions developed within the Matthean house-churches and we are left to question whether such traditions as these were not the result of women's traditioning.

Perhaps the most subtle evidence of Matthean community traditioning is seen in the stories that linked women to the last journey of Jesus to Jerusalem, to his death, and to the proclamation of the resurrection. In each of these stories the Markan text seems to provide the source for the development of the traditions in the Matthean communities with only minor changes that incorporate the story more fully into these communities' particular theological emphases. The most significant modification is the development and inclusion of what appears to be an earlier tradition surrounding the appearance of Jesus to the women at the tomb.

This brief glance at the complex traditioning process within the various house-churches which constituted the Matthean Christian community has enabled us to reread not just the text but also its subtext, which includes the inscribed historical situation and the rhetorical function of the story within such a situation. It has alerted us to the tension involved as new traditions were created while old traditions were both preserved and developed in order that the Jesus story and Jesus traditions might be told in such a way that they legitimated certain aspects of the life of this Christian community while challenging it to a vision beyond its present. Gender played a significant role in this shaping and fashioning of the story, since a focal point was the proclamation of the *basileia* vision of Jesus seen as inclusive. The suggestion of subversive traditioning has certainly been borne out in a way that suggests that women were significantly involved in the traditioning process within the Matthean community. Our earlier narrative study also revealed that it is not only the subversive traditions but also strong patriarchal and androcentric traditions that have been developed and preserved in this community. We have not been able to observe the redactional process in relation to these traditions, but this too is a necessary part of a comprehensive feminist critical reading of the Gospel.

CONCLUSION

We began with the image of the Matthean scribe trained for the implementation of the *basileia* vision of Jesus in a new age. As twentieth-century women, we have claimed this image as our own and have undertaken the task of reading the first Gospel, bringing out what is new because the Gospel is read with a different vision for a different time in history. We have also examined the old through these same lenses and have brought a gender critique to bear on the text and its context so that both text and subtext have been read from the new reading site of feminism.

Such a reading is not complete; it has indeed barely begun. The difficult task of reconstructing the history of the Matthean community so that it is a history of women and men has merely been suggested. The implications of our reading for Matthean theology, Christology, ecclesiology, and discipleship still remain to be explored. What has emerged, however, from both the narrative and redactional reading of the Matthean text is that tension and ambiguity surround the stories of women when they are incorporated into a patriarchal and androcentric text. Our revisioning of this old text from a new critical direction reminds us today that tension and ambiguity will surround our retelling of the Jesus story so that it subverts patriarchy and shapes a vision of an inclusive *basileia*. The stories of women in the Matthean Gospel—the women who traditioned those stories and the women who are storied—companion us on our journey toward this vision.

RECOMMENDED READINGS

Anderson, Janice Capel. "Mary's Difference: Gender and Patriarchy in the Birth Narratives." *Journal of Religion* 67 (1987): 183–202.

———. "Matthew: Gender and Reading." *Semeia* 28 (1983): 3–27.

Corley, Kathleen. *Private Women, Public Meals: Social Conflict in the Synoptic Tradition.* Peabody: Hendrickson, 1993. Pp. 147–79.

Deutsch, Celia. "Wisdom in Matthew: Transformation of a Symbol." *Novum Testamentum* 32 (1990): 13–47.

Kopas, Jane. "Jesus and Women in Matthew." *Theology Today* 47 (1990): 13–21.

Schaberg, Jane. *The Illegitimacy of Jesus: A Feminist Theological Interpretation of the Infancy Narratives.* San Francisco: Harper & Row, 1987.

Selvidge, Marla J. *Daughters of Jerusalem.* Scottdale, PA:/Kitchener, Ont.: Herald Press, 1987.

———. "Violence, Woman, and the Future of the Matthean Community: A Redactional Critical Essay." *Union Seminary Quarterly Review* 39 (1984): 213–23.

Wainwright, Elaine Mary. *Towards a Feminist Critical Reading of the Gospel according to Matthew.* Beihefte zur Zeitschrift für die Neutestamentliche Wissenschaft 60. Berlin: de Gruyter, 1991.

Pistis Sophia

DEIRDRE GOOD ◆

WHEN WOMEN INTERPRET texts, several things happen.[1] The text no longer has a fixed meaning. The text may reveal women as subject; hitherto neglected elements may emerge. The text in turn becomes the subject of self-conscious critical inquiry. This invariably discloses the politics of knowledge—the environment of the text and how that shapes interpretation; the use and control of the text, and so on.

Sometimes it is liberating to delineate the patriarchal world of the text; more often one must ask nuanced questions of the text to reconstruct social and historical realities in which the text simply is not interested. There are, for example, degrees of disinterest; the Christian Testament Synoptic Gospels—Matthew, Mark, and Luke—presuppose and occasionally describe a social world of rural communities in and around the cities of the Decapolis. In this world women occasionally appear. By contrast, the Gnostic texts of the Nag Hammadi library, replete with female imagery, are, for the most part, concerned with the parameters of celestial worlds and their inhabitants. Somewhere between the two lies the Gospel of John, probably closer to the latter. The social world behind Paul's letters is that of urban communities in Asia Minor, Italy, Greece, and Syria. In such communities, women's lives take on different patterns in greater conformity with the social realities of the Hellenistic world. The task of interpretation is never over: each generation in different lands and continents engages in it afresh, and this fortunate circumstance ensures the text's vitality.

As a student of ancient texts teaching within a confessional environment, I encounter assumptions regarding the text as "self." The politics of knowledge discloses texts in more problematic ways: both as "self" and as "other" but also as conditioned and dynamic. Historical interpretations of the text have been prized but now are not necessarily of first importance. The text may be held accountable to "other" realities. The canon, for example, could be regarded as a fourth-century vision of what the first century ought to look like. If this is the case, and in my opinion it is, it has enshrined a partial view or, in some cases, an obliteration of the reality of women and other oppressed peoples. Sound historical research dispenses with the canon entirely. This caveat broadens the responsibilities of the historian enormously. She must be familiar with the myriad communities and social groups that made up the world of late antiquity and have access to a variety of literary and nonliterary traditions. And she herself must be accountable to those voices.

The present study, however, starts with the voice of the text, and that text, it seems to me, is in dialogue with the Jesus who, according to Mark 4, taught by means of parables. In the following discussion, I presuppose that the text has meaning.

WHAT DID JESUS TEACH
AND TO WHOM DID HE TEACH IT?

Parables are enigmatic little stories or sayings about the reign of God using natural images or instances of human behavior. According to Mark 4, they were explained only to the disciples but "for those outside, everything is in parables." Mark implies that Jesus' teachings were rather obscure and for insiders rather than outsiders. The writing of his Gospel, however, ensures that this is not the last word, and, indeed, the Gospels of Luke and Matthew go much further in their respective efforts to portray Jesus as a preacher and teacher (the Sermon on the Mount, for example, was probably created by Matthew) even as they show that his message was not universally accepted.

Both Luke and Matthew contribute to the interpretation of the parables Jesus spoke by placing them at points in the Gospel narratives where their very position sheds light on their meaning. The parable of the householder who sent his servants and then son to claim the rent from his vineyard only to be met with ridicule and death is placed just before the narrative of Jesus' own death in Matthew's Gospel. At the same time, such interpretations admit the problem raised by speaking in parables—no single meaning is intended. Often a parable will end with the admonition: "Whoever has ears, let them hear."

Sally McFague has explained the parable's metaphoric quality well: x is *and is not* y. God is *and is not* like the vineyard owner. It is thus no accident that texts written down after the second century do not stress Jesus as a speaker of parables. Parables do not admit definitive meanings and are not particularly helpful in the ordering of communities. Indeed, in one such text, *Pistis Sophia*,[2] Jesus promises to speak *not* in parables but openly and clearly. The appeal of such a text for an ancient community familiar with the Jesus of Mark is obvious! Yet the clarity of speech Jesus promises in *Pistis Sophia* is not about mundane matters but about celestial realms and the beings that inhabit them.

And so the circle is complete; the Jesus of Mark speaks allusively for insiders (disciples), while the Jesus of *Pistis Sophia* speaks clearly of divine things revealed for insiders (disciples). Both texts define who the insiders are. Indeed, this is one of the purposes of religious texts. But while the text of Mark is hard to decode, perhaps because of its intentional obscurity, the dialogue between Jesus and his disciples in *Pistis Sophia* invites the reader's involvement because, self-consciously maieutic, it is real rather than artificial. The disciples ask questions which Jesus answers. In fact, the text belongs to the dialogue *genre*. The constant presence of disciples in *Pistis Sophia* and their involvement with the interpretation of the text make the text intrinsically accessible to the ancient and modern reader and suggests a social world.

THE DISCIPLES

In Mark's Gospel, there are at least three groups of followers who listen to Jesus; the Twelve (including an inner circle of Peter, James, and John, who witness key events such as the transfiguration); a larger group who function as disciples although they are not actually called such; and the crowd(s). Among the second group are several women—Simon Peter's mother-in-law, the anonymous woman who anointed Jesus for burial, Jairus's daughter and the woman with the hemorrhage, the Syrophoenician woman, and the women who followed Jesus to the crucifixion and then to the empty tomb to anoint the body. Yet it is left to extracanonical texts such as the *Gospel of Mary* and *Pistis Sophia* to make explicit what is implicit in Mark, namely, that these women exemplify discipleship. In patristic interpretation, this is quite explicit. Origen's interpretation of the dialogue between Jesus and the Syrophoenician woman (Mark 7:24–30), for example, sees the text as an allegory. The woman is a paradigm for the (successful) conversion of the nonrational soul. Since the woman addresses Jesus as "Lord," she recognizes his divinity. The text shows that lower life forms such as irrational souls can recognize divinity and by converting, become rational (Origen, *Commentary on Matthew* 15–17).

Throughout *Pistis Sophia* (and in other Gnostic writings from the Nag Hammadi collection, when they are translated correctly),[3] it is clear that Jesus' disciples are both male and female. Like other Gospels in which certain disciples are given prominent status (Peter in Matthew 16 and John 21, the beloved disciple in John), *Pistis Sophia* portrays Mary in the most favorable light: the first time she speaks Jesus calls her:

> Mary, blessed one whom I will complete in all mysteries of the height. Speak confidently, for you are she whose heart is more directed to the Reign of Heaven than all your brothers. (I, 17)

In this regard, *Pistis Sophia* stands in the same tradition as the *Gospel of Mary*. Both texts are undoubtedly connected to the tradition in John's Gospel of the first recorded appearance of the resurrected Jesus to Mary Magdalene. Other women disciples who ask questions in *Pistis Sophia* are Salome, Martha, and Mary, the mother of Jesus, but it is Mary who asks more questions than any other disciple.

Among the male disciples are Matthew, Philip, and John. Philip is understood to be the scribe who writes down what he sees and hears. Thus, the text is quite explicit about distinguishing between disciples on the basis of gender as the above citation makes clear; it refers to Mary as one of the disciples, and on one occasion to "disciples and female disciples" (IV, 136).

Although the role of the disciple Mary is discussed elsewhere in this volume, one singular aspect of it deserves mention here. In *Gos. Mary*, Jesus praises Mary for her insight in the following way: "Blessed are you that you did not waver at the sight of me. For where the mind is, there is the treasure" (10.14–16). This macarism (beatitude) affirms the noetic or intellectual perception of a female disciple. It recurs in a different form in *Pistis Sophia* II, 90, where Jesus addresses "Maria in the midst of the disciples." Explaining the order and rankings of those who have received certain mysteries in response to her question, Jesus concludes, "Concerning this I said to you [pl.] once, 'The place where your heart is, there will your treasure be.' That is, the place as far as which each one has received mysteries is where that one will be."[4] This affirmation appears in a slightly different form in *Pistis Sophia* ("heart/mind") and, in the course of its transmission, has been used to verify perception and ranking according to the mode of apprehension. In Matt 6:21 it is addressed to the disciples hearing the Sermon on the Mount. In both *Gos. Mary* and *Pistis Sophia*, it has become associated with Mary Magdalene, although it is not clear that *Pistis Sophia* knew the *Gos. Mary* beatitude rather than the Matthean form of the saying. However, this extraordinary affirmation from the lips of the resurrected Jesus was probably created by Gnostic authors to affirm the insight of Mary into the nature of the risen Christ. It is all the more striking in view of the association in late antiquity of women with lower forms of mental activity such as sense perception. The passage from Origen cited above, for example, equates a woman with the nonrational soul. In contrast, the macarism in *Gos. Mary* (to which *Pistis Sophia* may be alluding) was probably created to affirm the insight of a figure revered by the community much in the same way that the macarism of Matt 16:17 was probably created by the Matthean community to affirm the insight of Peter. In *Pistis Sophia*, Jesus called Mary "the blessed one" (I, 24 and elsewhere). At I, 19 Jesus addresses her directly: "You are blessed beyond all women on earth because you will be the pleroma of all the pleromas and the perfection of all the perfections."[5]

Mary in both *Gos. Mary* and *Pistis Sophia* has taken on the corporate identity of the Gnostic communities behind the texts.

PISTIS SOPHIA

This is the name given to a collection of revelation dialogues spoken by the risen Jesus to his male and female disciples. The earliest editors, following the original manuscript, divided the text into four parts or books; the second part of the text, for example, is called "The Second Book of the Pistis Sophia." But the book was given other titles as well: at the end of the second and third books is the title "A Part of the Books of the Savior," and the title written after the end of book IV has been erased (in ancient manuscripts, the title very often follows the work).

The setting of the book is clear: the resurrected Jesus encounters his disciples and explains that while he taught them on earth for eleven years, this teaching was restricted. Shortly thereafter Jesus ascends to heaven, and after a three-day sojourn in the celestial realms he promises to reveal the contents of his visions. This full disclosure of mysteries will enable the disciples to fulfill their soteriological (saving) function—to save the world from the persecution of the archons—the misguided, lower forms of divinity who intend to trap humanity in the material world.[6]

The genre of *Pistis Sophia* is well known; several texts in the Nag Hammadi library belong to this form of resurrection dialogue: the *Sophia of Jesus Christ* and *Dialogue of the Savior,* for example. In the latter text, Mary Magdalene plays an important role in the question-and-answer format; she is described in the text as "the woman who knows the All." *Pistis Sophia* is unusual, because the dialogue that takes place between Jesus and several disciples is not artificially constructed, as is the case with the texts mentioned above. Not only does Jesus respond specifically to the disciples' questions in *Pistis Sophia,* he occasionally refers to the questioner or the question in his answer as one might do in a real conversation. Thus, the genuine character of the dialogue engages the reader in questions of real concern to an ancient community asked by the disciples.

THE GNOSTIC MOVEMENT

Pistis Sophia belongs to a body of texts understood to be Gnostic.[7] The word "gnostic" derives from the Greek word "knowledge" and refers not to propositional knowledge ("I know that gravity causes objects to fall") or acquaintance ("pleased to know you") but to insight ("I know that my Redeemer lives"). Gnosis is insight into the real nature of things—for example, the fallen character of the world, or the plight of humanity. The motif of the malevolence and stupidity of the creator god appears frequently. This god is arrogant in thinking himself to be the only divinity, a parody of the monotheistic character of the Hebrew Creator God. In some texts he snatches power from his mother, Sophia. His minions, the archons, sometimes numbering the days of the year, represent humanity's enslavement in time and creation. The enlightened individual, perhaps brought to realization of her plight by a redeemer figure, seeks restoration to the pleroma, the world above. In Christian Gnostic texts, such as the *Gospel of Philip* and the present text, this can be anticipated by participation in ritual acts or sacraments, which confirm the deliverance of the individual from materiality.

The Gnostic movement seems to have come into being at about the same time as Christianity although this is a matter of scholarly debate. The manuscript evidence for either religion is sparse until the third century. Gnostic writings in Coptic from the third and fourth centuries have been discovered this century in Egypt (the Nag Hammadi library), and these have provided primary evidence for the Gnostic religion. *Pistis Sophia,* however, belongs to a small group of Gnostic texts discovered prior to the Nag Hammadi collection, along with the Berlin Codex, the books of Jeu, the Bruce Codex, and the *Corpus Hermeticum.* The classification and position of *Pistis Sophia* in the Gnostic collections of texts can now be reassessed in light of the Nag Hammadi texts.

One observation that can be made is that in *Pistis Sophia* ritual activity is of great importance. This distinguishes it from most of the Nag Hammadi Gnostic texts and indicates the existence of forms of active Gnosticism in the late second and early third century.

FEMALE AND MALE IN GNOSTIC TEXTS

Many Gnostic writings describe celestial male and female beings and their activities. The study of gender and sexuality in Gnostic texts has begun to receive scholarly attention, particularly from women scholars.[8] Recent scholarship has attempted to classify Gnostic writings by assessing the importance of gender to the argument or plot of the text. Here it is a question of moving beyond simple associations of male activity and female passivity—beyond the assumed polarities of male and female. In some texts sexuality or gender seems quite incidental, while in others the gender of female or male savior figures is crucial to the text's notion of soteriology. The subject of gender in antiquity is a complicated one; for the present discussion, I simply posit the assumption that gender in ancient texts is a social construct.[9]

In *Pistis Sophia* the gender of the disciples—male and female—is important, and the gender of Pistis Sophia herself functions inclusively as a model of repentance. She is like the female soul described, for example, in *Exegesis on the Soul*.[10] But is not the gender of Pistis Sophia herself a given? That is, does the text not assume rather than make anything of the gender of the figure? Is it not common in late antiquity to view the soul as female?

First, the central role of Pistis Sophia in the text must be observed. Book I is given over to the recording and interpretation of her thirteen repentances. The amount of such material alone suggests its importance. Her significance as a paradigm of the human condition and humanity's need for repentance and forgiveness is demonstrated by the involvement of all disciples in the interpretation of her words. To be sure, the interpretation of the repentances is highly stylized and no disciple deviates from the same patterns of explanation, but both genders are involved in the activity. They all interpret various aspects of her repentances by correlating them with the Psalms of David. Second, immediately after the location of *Pistis Sophia* below the thirteenth aeon, leading questions are asked about how she came to be there. It is probably not accidental that the first is asked by Mary. It is important to pay attention to the form of the question:

> My Lord, I heard you when you said that Pistis Sophia herself is one of the twenty-four emanations. How is she not in their place? For you said, "I found her below the thirteenth aeon."

Pistis Sophia belongs above, not below. Why she should be found below is one of the great mysteries of Gnostic mythology, as will shortly be seen. Then follows the text of her first repentance, which Mary jumps to interpret. Jesus has issued a general invitation to interpret followed by the familiar maxim "Whoever has ears, let them hear." Mary says:

> My Lord, there are ears to my Light-Person and I hear in my light-power,[11] and your Spirit which is with me has made me sober. Listen, now, that I may speak about the repentance which Pistis Sophia cried, as she spoke of her sin, and all the things which happened to her.

To interpret Pistis Sophia's condition is to give voice to the (universal) human condition of sin, the discovery of self-alienation, and how it came to be.

After the words of the second repentance, Peter objects not just to the fact that Mary does not allow anyone else to interpret as she speaks many times, but he calls her "this woman," that is, not fellow disciple. This implies the propensity of Mary *as woman* (and representative Gnostic) to explain or interpret the fate of Pistis Sophia. The fascinating thing about Peter's objection is that he does not follow it with a change of topic. Peter wants to demonstrate that he too can interpret Sophia's repentances through the Psalms of

David. Thus, the text affirms that the subject of Sophia's repentance is accessible to both genders, and even while one (Mary) has a special affinity for the role of that female aeon, this is not an exclusive matter. This affinity of female disciples for the condition of female aeons might be suspected from Gnostic texts in general, but *Pistis Sophia* is the rare text that demonstrates it. Yet the text reaches beyond an affinity between women and Pistis Sophia to include Peter. Male and female disciples, perhaps in their material and psychic identity, share in the identification of an aeon enmeshed in matter whose plight mirrors theirs.

The text constantly addresses Peter's opposition to Mary; he opposes her on three occasions. Although Mary is praised for her designation by Jesus as "blessed beyond all women on earth" (I, 19) and is described as "Mary, the beautiful in her speech" (I, 24), the text is careful not to disparage the contributions of Peter (or any other male disciple, for that matter). The roles of Mary and Peter are similar to those assigned them in *Gos. Mary,* where Peter stands for the proto-orthodox and Mary for the Gnostic communities. No specific rift has developed, but the lines of the debate are being drawn along gender differentiation. Peter objects to Mary not simply because he has been prevented from speaking, but on the grounds that she is a woman. This is even clearer in IV, 146, where Peter distinguishes between "us" and "the women." "My Lord," he says, "let the women cease to question that we also may question." Jesus reminds her of their fraternal status, "[he] said to Mary and the women, 'Give way to the men, your brothers, that they may question also.'" In II, 72, Mary acknowledges her willingness "to come forward at any time and give the words that [Pistis Sophia] spoke" but she admits fear of Peter, "for he threatens me and hates our race." Both objections are telling: Peter wants the women as a collective group to stop questioning; Mary is fearful not for herself individually but for Peter's animosity directed against her as female and as corporate identity. The text is careful not to countenance either grievance by having Jesus/the First Mystery speak directly to it, perhaps in an attempt by the author of the text to prevent a rift between the two newly defined and not yet separated groups.

THE PLACE OF SOPHIA IN GNOSTIC WRITINGS

The figure Pistis Sophia is another manifestation of Sophia, the erring aeon in some Gnostic accounts of material creation. The figure of Sophia (Wisdom) in Gnostic texts derives from the Wisdom figure of Hebrew Scriptures. Among the theological responses to the crisis of the exile in 586 B.C.E. was that of Proverbs 1–9. Written by the exiled Israelites in Babylon, Proverbs depicts personified Wisdom as an independent entity concerned to address Israelite men in the public realm as they went about their daily business. "How long, O simple ones, will you love being simple?" she asks. In several texts, Wisdom is shown working alongside God in the business of creation, delighting in the world of human beings. In Sirach 24, she is shown descending to earth and residing in Jerusalem as the Law (Torah); she is also described in this same chapter as a tree offering shade and fruit to all. Wisdom as tree and Wisdom as the Law were two images developed by Greek writers in the period just before the common era. Perhaps concerned to address the issue of sexual exclusivity evident in Proverbs,[12] Wisdom's appeal in Sirach is to all, to rest in her shade or to study her ways.

Writers like the author of the Greek Wisdom of Solomon added to such images Greek expressions in which Wisdom (Sophia) was called the "image," "mirror," or "effulgence" of God and was described as being able to "enter in to holy souls and make them friends of God and prophets" (Wis 7:25). In a dramatic revision, the last part of Wisdom demonstrates the presence of Sophia throughout Hebrew history beginning with Adam, Noah, Abraham, Moses, David, and Solomon, thus making the reinterpretation of theology and history complete: Sophia stands in place of God.

Influence from Wisdom literature appears in the descriptions of Sophia as "Genetress,"[13] in Gnostic writings such as *Eugnostos the Blessed* (NHC III, 3, 76.24–77.9; V, 1, 6.4–14). In early wisdom material, Wisdom is not specifically described as a mother, but later writings seem to recognize the importance of this phenomenon: "Solomon" (in Wis 7:12) says, "I rejoiced in (all good things), but I did not know that (Sophia) was their female creator."[14]

To assert the influence of wisdom writings on the portrayal of the Gnostic Sophia is not to deny the creativity of Gnostic writers. In *Eugnostos,* for example, Sophia is multiple, and her very multiplicity reflects the text's explanation for the association of divinity with matter—how the expansion of a single god into the myriad forms of creation took place. The gender of Sophia is crucial to this development.[15] Initially, the Parent of the Entirety gazes into a mirror and the reflection becomes reified, but the text does not describe this dyad as one that generates the material world. It is only when Sophia appears in the narrative that generative language is used and reproduction takes place. At a subsequent point in the history of its transmission, *Eugnostos* was altered by Christian scribes into the dialogue form of *Sophia of Jesus Christ,* and two forms of the well-known Gnostic myth of Sophia were added to the conclusions of the two versions of this text. The version criticizing the activity of Sophia apart from her consort seems to have had an independent history in Gnosticism, as several other versions in Christian and non-Christian texts exist in the Nag Hammadi library and in accounts of Gnostic groups reported by patristic writers such as Irenaeus and Hippolytus. It is this version that has been selectively used by many modern scholars as the central myth of Gnosticism, although textual evidence alone clarifies its derivative status. To be sure, the plight of Sophia resulting in the creation of her offspring Yaldabaoth (the parody of the Hebrew Creator God),[16] who causes the material world and humanity in particular to come into being as misbegotten, characterizes Gnostic pessimism about the mundane; but several Gnostic texts speak not of her willful disobedience but of her (or other divine beings') being overcome by lower beings. Others represent Yaldabaoth usurping creative abilities not innately his, while one Valentinian text, *Tripartite Tractate,* completely exonerates Sophia (as Logos) from any fault in the association of divinity with material creation. *Pistis Sophia,* itself a Christian Gnostic text, has its own interpretation of the role of Sophia, as will be seen shortly.

THE TEXT OF PISTIS SOPHIA

The original manuscript of Pistis Sophia was purchased by the British Museum in 1785 from Dr. A. Askew and catalogued as Ms. Add. 5441. It is also known as the Askew Codex in view of the fact that the manuscript was obtained by Dr. Askew, apparently from a bookseller in London. Where the bookseller obtained it is not known. The Coptic text of *Pistis Sophia,* written in the Sahidic dialect, is in excellent condition. Only a few pages are illegible because the ink is fading or smudging. Since the acquisition of the text, it has been sporadically studied and several editions have been published. Of the three English versions currently available (Horner, Mead, and MacDermot), that by V. MacDermot includes the Coptic text and an English translation. The text of this edition is reproduced from the earlier German edition; there are some errors in the Coptic text and in the English translation. Accordingly, as the basis of the present work, the original manuscript in the Oriental Department of the British Library in London has been consulted as well as a microfilm of the manuscript. This was necessary because no recent critical edition of the text has been published.

The date of the text is in dispute, and scholarly opinion places it anywhere from the fourth to the seventh century. On internal grounds it seems no later than the fourth century, and since it is most probably a translation from a Greek original, the underlying text certainly goes back to the third century and possibly earlier.

The text of *Pistis Sophia* has traditionally been divided into four parts, or books, following the sections of the manuscript. In the first book, the disciples gather around the Savior on the Mount of Olives. The text explains that, while some mysteries had been explained to them by Jesus during his earthly sojourn, there had not been a complete disclosure. The disciples' delight at the prospect of enlightenment is interrupted by the sight of Jesus completely engulfed by a light-power from above, which takes him up to heaven. For three hours after his departure the earth is consumed by quakes and tremors. The disciples are weeping in fright when, the next day, Jesus returns clothed in an extraordinarily bright light, at which they are unable to look. At their request, it is withdrawn; Jesus promises to tell them of what he saw during his celestial sojourn, and in response to questions from Mary Magdalene in particular explains why Pistis Sophia is located below the thirteenth aeon. The thirteen repentances of Pistis Sophia follow. Each is interpreted by the Psalms of David or the *Psalms of Solomon,* cited at length. Finally, Pistis Sophia is rescued by the Savior from the clutches of the oppressive archons (whose leader is called Authades) and brought to the upper place of the chaos.

The second book contains numerous songs of praise uttered by Pistis Sophia in response to her deliverance from chaos. Jesus, appearing as First Mystery, gives her a new mystery and a song of praise, and several disciples interpret each line of her songs of praise with respect to the Psalms of David or the *Odes of Solomon.* The First Mystery promises to take Mary and her brothers and fellow disciples on a tour of the celestial regions. Encouraged by this prospect, Mary asks a series of questions about the end and about the preaching of the disciples. She demonstrates complete understanding of the teaching, which astonishes the Savior. Other disciples collapse in despair. They are overwhelmed by Jesus' elaborate teachings and his promise to disclose fully the "whole place of the truth of the Ineffable." Mary intercedes on their behalf for mercy and Jesus encourages them by promising them the mystery which they can attain if they renounce the world. The progress of a soul toward the light is described, and the enlightened soul is called identical to Jesus. Jesus, in turn, promises to "say the great mysteries of the three parts of my realm." Andrew's confession that he does not understand produces a description of humanity as the dregs of substance and mixture. While the other disciples apologize on Andrew's behalf, Jesus commissions them to preach.

The third book opens with a lengthy exhortation to the disciples to renounce the world. They are enjoined to be calm, loving, compassionate, and peaceful. In order to eradicate sinfulness, Jesus explains that he brought mysteries to the world as the gift of the First Mystery. Then follows a series of questions by the disciples on the forgiveness of individuals by means of the mysteries. Jesus discourses on the composition of a human child as power, soul, and spirit, followed by teaching on the connection of the human soul to the counterpart spirit which compels humans to sin, and on destiny. Mary's four thoughts in response each include citations from the Gospels and Paul. The mystery of baptism is described as a fire which quenches sins in response to several questions of the disciples. The Savior enjoins them to receive the mysteries of the light "in this restricted time." Then follows a lengthy description of the names of the twelve archons and their characteristics together with teaching on the transmigration of souls. Mary's questions on the discernment of teachings and the fate of souls before the advent of Jesus receives a lengthy discourse on the fate of prophets and patriarchs.

In book IV, Jesus is called Aberamentho.[17] The book itself is taken up with reports of ritual speech and action—the words of Jesus' prayers are transmitted, complete with unintelligible and mysterious sounds and names. Lengthy teachings on the torments of human souls include descriptions of first and second rank archons, both of whom are female. Jesus' reassurance counters the distress of the disciples; he promises they will rule over these archons. He describes himself as bringing nothing into the world but the elements of fire, water, wine, and blood. In what is clearly a ritual act, Jesus blesses the wine and speaks the words of institution at the Last Supper. Jesus promises to give the mystery of forgiveness on earth to the disciples so that they may do these mysteries for others. He then does a mystery to secure the forgiveness of the disciples' sins. Their question about the mystery of light is followed by a lacuna in the text. When it resumes, the closing sections are given over to questions by individual disciples on the fate of specific people and those who practice certain rituals. The book closes with a prayer spoken by Jesus to the disciples. A different scribe has added an ending rather out of character with the work which speaks of the message of the disciples as brought to the whole world.

THE TERM "MYSTERY"

The text attaches great importance to the term "mystery," and it may be understood in several ways. The First Mystery is the place from which Jesus has come and which he wishes to explain to his disciples as a higher disclosure beyond what they were previously taught. As it is the place of his origin, Jesus himself can also be described as the First Mystery. Thus, the term is also a title for Jesus, and one of the text's contributions to Christology.

The term "mystery" also refers to a ritual. This meaning becomes apparent in the development of the text, as if the text itself were intended to lead the reader from a stage of ignorance into enlightenment by means of the disclosure of the ritual itself. At the beginning of the text, the First Mystery is described as "the Father in the form of a dove." This statement is hard to understand unless one knows that "mystery" holds a double meaning: a secret and a ritual during which that secret is disclosed. The ritual referred to in the disclosure of the First Mystery is, of course, baptism, since at Jesus' baptism, the spirit in the form of a dove descended upon him. But since the First Mystery is described as *"the Father* in the form of a dove," the mysterious content would seem to lie in the equation of "spirit" and "father." To understand this hermeneutical move is to engage in responsible speculation. In the first place, mention should be made of the Syriac tradition in which the Holy Spirit is referred to as Mother.[18] An early understanding of Jesus' baptism as the descent of the Spirit (i.e., mother) is to be found in the *Gospel of the Hebrews:*[19]

> When the Lord had come up out of the water, the whole fount of the Holy Spirit descended upon him and rested upon him, and said to him, "My son, in all the prophets was I waiting for you that you should come and I might rest in you. For you are my rest, you are my first-begotten Son that reigns for ever."

On the other hand, the term "Father," particularly when used by Coptic authors, encompasses dimensions of male and female parenting.[20] One could say that in speaking of the Father as a dove, the author of *Pistis Sophia* is striving for creedal exactitude. But since the text itself refers to Jesus as Barbelo ("the body he wore in the height," I, 8), it seems more probable that the text is attempting to express in a nonrational way (i.e., as a mystery), the parentage of Jesus as male/female. This implies Jesus' own bisexual nature, evident in his being designated Barbelo in the height.[21] Such an interpretation of the First Mystery would seem to be supported by II, 63, where John interprets the descent of the dove as an analogy to the descent of First Mystery on Jesus as a garment of light received from the hand of Barbelo.

The technical meaning of the term mystery is suggested in the Coptic text, which abbreviates the Greek term "mystery" thus: *MP.* Unfortunately, this cryptogram is not discussed in the English translations and is noted only in a footnote of the English and German editions of the Coptic text. Since use of the cryptogram indicates the technical status of the term "mystery" as a rite, its elimination enables the word to be read in the translation as if it were an ordinary word rather than a special term alluding to ritual activity. I would guess that this reflects the assessment of early editors of the text about Gnostic rituals: Mead describes the invocation of names in the prayers of the text as "a distressingly puzzling . . . element of magic." This anachronistic judgment and its pejorative tone are of little help in the interpretation of the text.

Further evidence in the text that the term "mystery" refers to a ritual is found in book II, when individuals are described as "receiving" mysteries, and toward the end of III, 111, in a passage describing how to "do" a mystery. Thus, mysteries have a soteriological (saving) purpose—their performance is to enable the human soul after death to avoid the torments of the archons. In *Pistis Sophia,* the saving knowledge (*gnōsis*) common to other Gnostic texts has been replaced by saving ritual. Mary describes a persecuted individual being able to say the mystery when being tormented and so "go forth from the body immediately without receiving any afflictions" (III, 109). In this same chapter, Jesus speaks of the manner of doing this mystery: completing it in its forms, types, and stations. This is a reference to ritual activities. In II, 98, a mystery is described as being "said over the head of someone who comes forth from the body, and in the two ears."

The disciples receive instructions about mysteries in order to give them to those worthy of them even as they are to distinguish between inferior and superior mysteries. They are enjoined not to give or teach the mystery of the raising of the dead or that of the healing of the sick to anyone except at certain times. These two mysteries are described as a mystery of the archons, probably because sickness and death imply physical and material weakness indicating the success of the archons. Thus, many of the mysteries are rituals designed to overcome archontic power in the world of material creation. Book III, 105 deals with a question of John clearly reflecting community concerns about disrespect on the part of people who have received mysteries but subsequently sinned. Jesus enjoins forgiveness, "because the First Mystery is compassionate and merciful." If, however, after being given the three mysteries that are in the second space of the First Mystery, the recipient sins again, no further forgiveness is allowed for the soul of that person is consigned to the dwellings of the dragon of the outer darkness.

Book III, 112 refers to saying the mystery of the releasing of the seals. This refers to the release of the soul that is bound (or sealed) by the archons to certain material qualities such as the counterpart spirit. The release of the soul enables it to progress on its journey upward toward the light. When further challenged by archons, the soul is enjoined to "say the mystery of their defense," which seems to explain to the archons that the soul knows it is not of the same nature as they are. The soul is to say "I do not come to your places from this time; I have become a stranger to you forever and I shall go to the place of my inheritance." This magical password releases the soul from the clutches of the archons.

Behind the lengthy descriptions of the mysteries in *Pistis Sophia* may well lie a community in which women and men disciples engaged in ritual activities including baptism and a rite for forgiveness of sins on earth. This latter activity is connected to the activity of corporate forgiveness in Mattthew 18.

Matthew 18 describes a series of steps that are undertaken to restore the guilty individual to the community. If one understands the disciples' questions in *Pistis Sophia* to reflect community concerns, then it is not surprising to find in the later part of the text, where the mysteries are disclosed, questions about safeguarding the mysteries, what to do when the mysteries are disparaged by outsiders and when individuals who have received the mysteries subsequently fall back into sin. The tenor of the text is extraordinarily forgiving in all cases; the one time it does not seem to be is where the text of Matthew 18 is followed. However, even that is reinterpreted in favor of the individual's ultimate restoration. As *Pistis Sophia* indicates, following Matthew 18, forgiveness and reconciliation are offered for a specific number of times at the end of which, the individual is not forgiven but not specifically expelled by the community either: Matthew's "let him be to you as a Gentile and a tax collector" is reinterpreted as "let him be among you as a disgrace and as a transgressor" (III, 105). The text makes provision for final salvation by declaring that no one except the First Mystery is able to receive the repentance of such a person.

THE "NUMBER OF PERFECT SOULS"

A second important technical term occurring in teachings of Jesus on eschatology and related to the term "mystery" has been researched by W. C. Van Unnik.[22] It occurs in several passages. In III, 125, Mary asks whether souls that have failed to receive mysteries in one life cycle, confident that they will be received in the next, are in any danger. Jesus concurs and enjoins the disciples,

> Preach to the whole world and say to people, "strive that you receive the mysteries of the light in this restricted time, so that you go into the Reign of Light."

He reasons that this is necessary for no one knows when the number of perfect souls will be reached, and after that time, the gates of light will be shut. Shortly afterward, Jesus explains that the completion of the number of perfect souls is the completion of the First Mystery, the knowledge of the All.[23]

In II, 86, Jesus responds to Mary's question about the eschaton. In speaking of the time of the completion, twelve mysteries of the First Mystery are described at some length and are followed by a statement that the dissolution of the all is the completion of the number of perfect souls. The phrase "the time of completion" seems connected with a similar phrase in eschatological sections of Matthew (13:39, 49; 24:3; 28:20). In I, 27, Jesus describes the process by which he is able to shorten the times and periods of the material souls to enable them to receive mysteries and join the number of perfect souls. He thereby shortens the time wherein the souls can be influenced by the archons. This passage also seems closely connected to Matt 24:22. In I, 50, and II, 96, Jesus declares that when the perfect number is completed, he will sit in the Treasury of Light along with the Twelve.[24] This reminds Mary of the parable Jesus told reported in Luke 22:28–30.

At the end of II, 98, Jesus describes a period of one thousand years as the time after the completion of the number of perfect souls when he will rule over the number of perfect souls that have completed the mysteries. Here the author of *Pistis Sophia* is shown to be a chiliast, like the author of Revelation, who believed that Jesus' reign would last one thousand years. Most significant is that the action of completing the number of perfect souls is believed to usher in the millennium. However, the reader is not told the secret of that number.

Second-century Christianity evidences interest in determining the time of the eschaton by referring to the number of the elect, and although the use of the variation in *Pistis Sophia,* the number of the *souls,* is Gnostic, interest in eschatological matters and verbal similarities serve to locate *Pistis Sophia* in a specifically Christian milieu perhaps of the second and certainly of the third century.

THE ROLE OF SOPHIA IN *PISTIS SOPHIA*

The figure of Pistis Sophia appears in the text without introduction. She is clearly known to the author and readers of the text. What needs to be explained, as Mary's question cited above makes clear, is not who she is but her location below the thirteenth aeon. She ought to be with the twenty-four emanations, together with her partner.[25] Jesus explains that Pistis Sophia

> saw the light of the veil of the Treasury of the Light, and desired to go to that place. But she was not able to go to that place. Moreover, she ceased performing the mystery of the thirteenth aeon, but she sang praises to the light of the height which she saw in the light of the veil of the Treasury of the Light. (I, 30)

Here we encounter the familiar longing of Sophia to be in the higher place. While in other texts the desire of Sophia (for example, to be like God) leads to her folly, in *Pistis Sophia* it leads to her ceasing to perform "the mystery of the thirteenth aeon" (ritual activity associated with the thirteenth aeon) and instead to singing "praises to the light of the height." Thus she incurs the hatred of the archons below her, "because she ceased from their mystery." The cessation of ritual activity brings about a chain of events that causes Pistis Sophia's downfall. Later, the text links her desire to a traditional interpretation—to be like God, that is, autonomous.

Now the interesting feature of *Pistis Sophia*'s account of Sophia emerges: among the lower aeons is their leader, Authades, familiar to readers of Gnostic texts as a type of Yaldabaoth, the parody of the Hebrew Creator God. Whereas in other Gnostic texts, Yaldabaoth is the malformed child of Sophia's reified desire, in *Pistis Sophia,* Authades and she are in no way related. Thus, his hatred of her is not fueled by the guilt other texts imply, since in these texts he has usurped the creative powers of his mother to produce the lower world and even humanity. In *Pistis Sophia* his hatred is sheer misogyny. The text is careful to describe Authades when he first appears as morally culpable: he is the one "who had been disobedient" and who, in this state, "emanated from within himself a great lion-shaped power." In a variation on the traditional motifs of the Sophia story, this self-produced creation, "a light-power which has a lion-face," deceives Sophia so that she looks down to where it is, thinking it from the light in the height. The text is interested in her motivation:

> And she thought to herself, "I will go to that place without my partner, and take the light, and create of it for myself aeons of light, so that I shall be able to go to the Light of Lights which is in the highest height." (I, 31)

Attempting to swallow the lion-faced power in the lower regions of Chaos, she is instead surrounded and her light-powers devoured. Thus weakened and oppressed, she articulates her first cry for help to the Light above.

THE REPENTANCES OF PISTIS SOPHIA

A unique feature of the text, the repentances are formed on the basis of the psalm to which they correspond and to which a disciple compares them. For the author of *Pistis Sophia* and for the readers of the texts, the psalms of lament can be reinterpreted to explain the plight of Sophia, her present condition, her innocence as a basis for an appeal, and her pleas for redress and final restoration to the Light above. Of course, by means of comparison, one can establish that the text of the psalm on which the lament is based is altered to some degree to fit the condition of Sophia. This enables the text of the psalm to correspond more closely to the situation it purports to describe. The net result, however, is an extraordinary hermeneutical move by which the psalms are made to speak to the condition of the Gnostic mired in matter. The psalms enable the Gnostic to voice despair about this condition and to understand how it came about and how it might be overcome. How is it possible to understand the laments of Pistis Sophia as giving a corporate voice to the plight of a Gnostic? Because the parts of the psalms are preserved or altered to permit this. For instance, the concluding statement of praise to God in the first repentance based on Psalm 69 offers assurance to the speaker and to others. According to the text of the interpretation, Psalm 69 reads:

> I will bless the name of God in song. . . . It will please God more than a young bull which carries horns and hoofs. Let the poor see and rejoice; seek God that your souls may live. For the Lord has heard the poor and he has not despised those in fetters. Let the heavens and the earth bless the Lord. . . . For God will save Zion; and the cities of Judea will be built, and people will dwell there and

inherit it. The seed of his servants will take possession of it and they that love his name will dwell in it.

This is rendered in the repentance thus:

Now at this time, O Light, which is in you and with me, I sing praises to your name, O Light, in glory. And may my song of praise, O Light, please you, like an excellent mystery which is received into the gates of Light which those who repent will recite and whose light they will purify. Now, at this time, let all material things rejoice: seek the light, all of you, so that the power of your souls which is within you may live because the Light has heard the material things, and it will not leave any material things which it has not purified. . . . For God will save their souls out of all matter, and a city will be prepared in the light; all the souls which will be saved will dwell in that city, and they will inherit it.

This reinterpretation enables the voice of individuals articulating the repentance to be heard, and their speech is likened to ritual activity (an "excellent mystery received into the gates of Light"). Sophia invites corporate utterance, "Seek the light, all of you," she exhorts, as she speaks on behalf of those mired in matter who might otherwise think themselves irredeemable. Thus this particular psalm is adapted to address the condition of the unenlightened Gnostic. Reciting the psalm, it is implied, enables one to overcome a present condition of slavery and to contemplate a glorious future in the world above.

The use of many lament psalms in *Pistis Sophia* also suggests that her lament and repentance voices the Gnostic situation as does the fact that many disciples individually interpret her condition by means of the Psalms. The act of interpretation belongs not to a few but rather to the entire community of disciples. Just as they voice the meaning of her lament, she voices the Gnostic condition by assuming her own voice and that of the Psalmist (David).

THE SOCIAL WORLD OF *PISTIS SOPHIA*

An early Christian Gnostic community seems to lie behind the text. It is not possible to identify this as Valentinian, for example, although earlier interpreters favored this classification. Composed of male and female disciples, the community gave a special prominence to Mary and the virgin John, who speak on behalf of the group. The community is egalitarian, not competitive: Mary aids the other women, particularly Salome and Mary, the mother of Jesus. Among the other disciples are Philip, the scribe and recorder; Andrew, slow to understand; and Peter, who is actively hostile to Mary and her gender. Mary may represent the nascent Gnostic community of the text, confident of her insight and interpretation yet aware that this theological position does not go unchallenged. Peter may stand for a more orthodox group that the text is eager to include.

The prominent role of Mary in the community connects her not only with the *Gospel of Mary* and *Dialogue of the Savior* but also with the wider history of a figure whose religious leadership and spiritual authority are linked to Mary Magdalene of the Christian Testament and Miriam of Hebrew Scriptures.[26] The etymology of Miriam and Mary is the same; in *Dial. Sav.*, for example, Mary is referred to as "Mariham" and "Marihamme." In *Pistis Sophia* she is called "Mariham" and "Maria." The figure Mariam/Mary/Marihamme takes on a composite identity, to which layers of Manichaean tradition also accrue.

Traces of this composite identity are seen in *Pistis Sophia* II, 108: "When Jesus finished saying these words to his disciples, Mary worshiped at the feet of Jesus and kissed them." This description loosely reflects the language of several Gospel passages. In Luke 7:38, an anonymous woman kisses Jesus' feet and anoints them with oil. In John 11:32, Mary falls at the feet of Jesus. Perhaps the closest passage is Matt 28:9, where the resurrected Jesus appears to Mary Magdalene and other women. They "grasp his feet and worship him." Taking all the evidence into account, Mary in *Pistis Sophia* is a composite figure, resonating with women in the Gospels and with other depictions of Mary in Gnostic texts.

The community behind *Pistis Sophia* is aware of those who do not accept their teachings, who reject the rituals of baptism and forgiveness. The minority position of the community would seem to be reflected in the conciliatory nature of the teachings on forgiveness and restoration of a lapsed Gnostic even to the extent of reinterpreting the exclusionary measures of Matt 18:17. Mary voices the community's self-awareness of minority status: "For they are many who persecute us for your sake" (III, 109). Peter's critical remarks directed against Mary and others of her race are never forbidden; indeed, the only absolute prohibition in the entire text is directed by Jesus against libertine ritual practices at the conclusion of book IV. This passage has not been used enough to question the accuracy of Epiphanius's descriptions of such rituals in the fourth century (*Panarion* 25.3.2; 25.9.4). On the other hand, one could see Jesus' words in *Pistis Sophia* as a self-conscious apologetic directed against the excesses Epiphanius describes. The stern interdiction in a text whose overall intention is to mollify any opposition is worthy of note.

Even Peter is presented in the text as capable of offering unconditional forgiveness. Perhaps written to blunt the opposition (would they have excluded "Mary and her race"?), Jesus sees an unidentified woman who has come to repent. He tests Peter to see if he is merciful by inviting him to "perform the mystery of light which cuts off souls from the inheritance of light." He says, "Perform that mystery and cut off the soul of this woman from the inheritance of the light." Peter's response is compassionate:-

> My Lord, leave her again this time, so that we give her the higher mysteries. And if she is suitable, you have allowed her to enter the Realm of Light. But if she is not suitable, you have cut her off from the Realm of Light. (III, 122)

It turns out that the woman is a type of fig tree which was not bearing fruit and on behalf of which the gardener pleaded that it should be spared. Of course, it is Mary who gives the text this interpretation as an analogy, but the tale is real enough in its presentation as a test of Peter. The poignancy of the text's ameliorating position vis-à-vis the opposition in light of the subsequent dismissal and rejection of Gnostic texts and their communities by what came to be the dominant ecclesiastical groups is not lost on this reader.

The community's identity derives from its experience of the risen Jesus and his teaching. The Christology reflected in *Pistis Sophia* is, on the one hand, distinct from that of the Synoptic Gospels (this is not a Jesus who teaches by means of parables, for example) and is, on the other hand, self-consciously connected to it, particularly the material unique to the Matthean community. On a human level, Jesus' mother is identified as Mary, according to the material body. In relation to the disciples, Jesus is the compassionate Savior. He teaches them by means of long discourses, much in the manner of teaching adopted by the Matthean Jesus.[27] On a higher plane, Jesus can appear in the form of Gabriel; Barbelo is the body he wore in the height. He is worshiped by the aeons, called "Lord of All" at the beginning of the book when ascending through the spheres; he is frequently referred to in book II as First Mystery.

The same similarities and dissonances are there in Jesus' discourses. For instance, Jesus himself refers to previous teaching as similar to what he is presently revealing so as to authenticate his present message. Mary recalls words of Jesus reported in the Synoptics that remind her of what he is now teaching. His affirmation of Peter alludes to the Matthean affirmation of Peter by Jesus in Matthew 16. His ritual activity of book IV alludes and adds to the words of institution at the Last Supper. Thus, while contributing an enormous amount of unique material, *Pistis Sophia* is explicitly self-conscious in perceiving itself to be in continuity with material familiar from the Synoptics. At the same time, this familiar material is radically reinterpreted to correspond to Gnostic descriptions of conditions as if that were its true meaning. Thus, the hermeneutical enterprise of Pistis Sophia is nothing less than a reappropriation of the Jesus of the Gospels for a Gnostic community. Of course, this activity is similar to the use of Mark by the Matthean community: a radical critique by means of assimilation. The Jesus of Mark is appropriated for a Jewish

(Christian) community. The authority to undertake this task is provided for the authors of both texts by an experience of the risen Jesus.

A topic for further investigation is the affinity of *Pistis Sophia* with Matthew's Gospel. In this regard, there are many indications that *Pistis Sophia* belongs in a Jewish-Christian milieu. The absence of "Christ" from the titles used for Jesus is striking. More significant is the use of the psalms to interpret the repentances of Pistis Sophia. There is a sustained analysis of the circumstances of Pistis Sophia herself by means of psalmic material, which is analogous to the use of scripture in Matthew's Gospel: an event or saying transpires so as to fulfill the words of the prophet X. Also to be investigated elsewhere is the direction of influence and the text-type: Has the wording of the psalms influenced the description of *Pistis Sophia* or vice versa? And does the Coptic text of the psalms correspond to Coptic versions of Hebrew Scriptures?

Why should the psalms in particular be mined? Because they are regarded as scripture, and because the lament psalms voice despair and the thanksgiving psalms gratitude for deliverance. Perhaps it is not too farfetched to see this hermeneutic modeled on the Marcan/Matthean Jesus on the cross, who, as he died, articulated the opening line of Psalm 22. Further investigation might determine the identity of the community for whom biblical psalms were authoritative in Christian interpretation. For instance, members of the third- and fourth-century Antiochene school wrote commentaries on the psalms.[28] The author of *Pistis Sophia* may have been familiar with similar exegetical techniques.

Pistis Sophia uses at least one psalm that was mined in the formation of early Christian passion apologetic: Psalm 69. Ps 69:21 is cited in I, 33: "They gave me gall for my food; they made me drink vinegar for my thirst." On the lips of Pistis Sophia, this becomes, "And when I sought for light, I was given darkness. And when I sought for my power, I was given matter." Ps 69:20–21 reads: "Insults have broken my heart, so that I am in despair. I looked for pity, but there was none; and for comforters but I found none. They gave me poison for food, and for my thirst they made me drink vinegar."

In *Pistis Sophia*, Psalm 69 has been reinterpreted from a mythological rather than a historical standpoint. While the Gospel writers interpreted the psalms historically and understood them in the light of circumstances surrounding the death of Jesus on the cross, the Gnostic writers understood themselves to be imprisoned by celestial forces and hence reinterpreted the text from a mythological perspective. The text has a historical value in that David first spoke it, but the psalm also has another meaning. It describes the way Pistis Sophia is deceived and trapped. This remythologization of texts associated with Jesus effectively makes Pistis Sophia into a christological figure. She is the Redeemed Redeemer, the one who understands the condition of humanity through her own identification with it and who, through her activity of repentance is rescued from it. Thus, she provides a passage of redemption for others. If one wants to understand Sophia as a christological figure, the remythologization of christological texts is a serious option. Indeed, this is the perspective used to interpret scripture by the author of *Pistis Sophia*.

Outside the passion narrative, one can observe this interpretative principle in the development of the narrative after the interpretation of the psalms when Jesus is disclosing mysteries to the disciples. For instance, in II, 95, Jesus encourages the disciples in despair because they are unable to understand "the Mystery of the Ineffable." He assures them that this Mystery "belongs to you and to everyone who will hear you" provided that they renounce the whole world and everything in it. Then he adds in a formula repeated quite often: "Because of this now I said to you once: 'Everyone who is oppressed with care and troubled by their burden, come to me and I will give you rest. For my burden is light and my yoke is compassionate.'" This passage is a reinterpretation of Matt 11:28–30, which derives from Matthew's special wisdom material. In *Pistis Sophia* this text connects the Jesus who reveals mysteries with the Jesus of Matthew. But at the same time, the new Jesus who offers compassion and rest has effectively replaced Matthew's Jesus because the text of *Pistis Sophia* is presented as the true meaning of the words.

It is not accidental that *Pistis Sophia* draws on wisdom material; this is material most congenial to the development of a Sophia Christology.

SOPHIA IS/IS NOT JESUS

The Christology of *Pistis Sophia* is one that may be identified as part of the wisdom tradition; Jesus is seen as a heavenly wisdom figure who ascends and descends in a way similar to the figure of Prov 30:1–4.[29] The same motif appears in Christian Testament texts about Jesus (John 1:51) and Paul (2 Corinthians 12); it features in stories written before the first century C.E. about Enoch (*1 Enoch*), Abraham (*Ascension of Abraham*) and Isaiah (*Ascension of Isaiah*). These stories narrate out-of-body experiences that enabled the recipient to gain a new perspective on celestial and earthly realities. Abraham, for example, witnessed a judgment scene in which Abel (the first person unjustly killed) dispensed divine justice for the souls of the dead. In *Pistis Sophia*, Jesus ascends and descends to the waiting disciples in order to disclose to them secrets that they are expected to understand and rituals that they are expected to perform. To be sure, Jesus appears in several celestial identities: First Mystery and Barbelo; he can also appear as Gabriel to Mary. Jesus' male/ female nature makes it possible for everyone who receives mysteries and completes them in the appropriate ways to become part of the world and, at the same time, to be exalted far beyond it. In a list of such paradoxes found in II,

96, Jesus solemnly asserts at its conclusion: "that person is I and I am that person." This astonishing identity, achieved as the result of hearing a long discourse and being educated in rituals, is common to wisdom material and is expressed negatively in *Gos. Thom.* 61: "I am not your master," says Jesus to Salome.[30] It is clear from such assertions that the gender of Jesus is as incidental to the text as the gender of the disciples who apprehend Jesus' teaching.

At the same time, the identity of Jesus as Sophia was not universally accepted. If it had been, there would be more evidence of it. Although it is apparent in wisdom texts such as the *Gospel of Thomas* (NHC II, 2) and *Teachings of Silvanus* (NHC VII, 4)—neither of which contains overtly Gnostic teachings—only traces of its influence lie behind wisdom passages of Matt 11:28–30.

Teachings of Silvanus is dated to the second or early third century C.E. and indicates the (fragile?) continuity of a tradition that identified Jesus and Sophia. Its connections with the Sophia story can be seen in the invitation she offers to everyone:

> Wisdom summons you in her goodness, saying, "Come to me, all of you, O foolish ones, that you may receive a gift, the understanding which is good and excellent. I am giving to you a high-priestly garment which is woven from every (kind of) wisdom." (*Teach. Silv.* 89:5–12)[31]

The motif of the garment is also encountered in *Pistis Sophia,* as the gift of Barbelo and as the content of the First Mystery.[32]

Jesus is called Sophia in several passages in *Teachings of Silvanus:*

> For the tree of life is Christ. He is Sophia. For he is Sophia; he also is the Logos. He is the Life, the Power, and the Door. He is the Light, the Messenger, and the Good Shepherd. (106: 22–30)

> For since (Christ) is Sophia, he makes the foolish person wise. Sophia is a holy realm and a shining robe. For Sophia is much gold which gives you great honor. The Sophia of God became a type of fool for you so that she might take you up, O foolish one, and make you a wise person. (107: 3–12)

Assimilation of Jesus and Wisdom is reflected in the above texts, as is the idea of competition. One can see evidence of conflict between the Jesus and Sophia in several Nag Hammadi texts. For example, a comparison of two versions of the *Apocryphon of John* in the Nag Hammadi library indicates that Christian versions of these texts wrested the saving roles from female figures and gave them to Jesus. While it is not a simple task to designate the direction of alteration, such cases are more likely to reflect the way ancient authors and scribes improved the status of Jesus rather than the other way around. This tendency is even more marked in the conclusion of the *Apocryphon of John,* where the Savior performs the ritual of baptism originally conducted by the (female) Pronoia figure. One may speculate about the implications of such a change for social ordering and gender roles in and behind the *Apocryphon of John,* but the preceding discussion suggests that male and female disciples performed such rituals as a correlative to the unimportance of Christ's gender in the social world of *Pistis Sophia.*

Further evidence regarding the dispute over the status of Jesus and Sophia comes from fourth-century Edessa. Essentially pagan in affiliation, Edessa began to experience Christian incursions in the second and third centuries in Marcionites, Bardaisanites, and encratite forms of belief.[33] Probably at the end of the third century, the *Doctrina Addai,* the official legend of the origin of the Christian church at Edessa, was written.[34] It was written to combat the Manichaeans in particular and to convert Jews and pagans to the gospel. The writings of Ephrem Syrus provide the first concrete insight into the emergent conflict with Jewish groups in Nisibis and Edessa where he spent ten years before his death in 373. Jewish customs and practices are criticized indirectly, as it is to Christians attracted to Judaism that Ephrem writes. This animosity of Ephrem tends to indicate that close ties rather than antagonism characterized relations between Jewish and Christian groups in northern Mesopotamia. In matters of scriptural exegesis, for example, a passage from Ephrem's *Hymns* shows how similar the two communities were. Couched in the language of polemic, the unfortunate mode of so much early Christian self-definition, the passage concerns the role of the Son in creation:

> The Jew also did not investigate the hidden things, although in his scriptures hindrances certainly lay hidden for him. . . . When he denied the Son, the buried came out of their graves; they contradicted him there. And when he denies the existence of the Holy Spirit, then the Scriptures will charge him that the Spirit is "the breath of the mouth of the Lord" (Ps 33:6) and his Spirit is with him. And if there was a time when he was without the Spirit, let them demonstrate that without dispute! And instead of saying that creation came about through the Son, they say that as He created, some (female) one created with Him, the one who with Him established the heavens and the remaining creatures. In their madness they deny the Son and reject him. They are proud of the other Creator who helped Him. Because they threw away the truth, they have found shame.[35]

The debates reflected in this extraordinary passage concern the role of the Spirit and the role of the Son in creation. It seems that a Jewish group in Edessa maintained that God effected creation with Sophia rather than by means of the Son Jesus, the position of Ephrem and some other Edessene Christians. If indeed the lines between Jews and Christians at Edessa were not sharply drawn, it might even be possible to maintain that some Christians sympathetic to Judaism in Edessa were adopting a position in which Prov 8:27 was taken to refer to Wisdom alone rather than to the preexistent form of the Son. To Ephrem, this position was heretical. It is quite similar to the position of Arius, well known for his debates with Athanasius over the relationship of the

Son to the Father, in the course of which the same text from Proverbs was repeatedly invoked. In the fourth-century debate at Edessa, no rationale (except perhaps Prov 8:27) is given for the Jewish position; however, the text leaves us with the picture of at least one significant Jewish group in northern Mesopotamia who upheld the role of Sophia in creation by denying it to Jesus.

This is the kind of Jewish milieu into which *Pistis Sophia* fits. Although the identity of Jesus still retains vestiges of its wisdom associations and its celestial alter egos, it is almost entirely severed from identity with the figure of Pistis Sophia, who alone functions as the Redeemed Redeemer. The remoteness of the Savior is emphasized by his celestial visit and the occasional despair of the disciples as they attempt to understand him. They have no such difficulty in their interpretation of Sophia's situation from the point of view of the psalms, for this speaks to their own condition and that of those in the material world.

SOPHIA AND THE CREATED WORLD

The fourth-century debate between Christian and Jewish groups at Edessa over the role of the Son in creation was not an isolated case. It had in fact been prefaced by considerable discussion in literature of the early patristic period about the nature of Christ, the nature of God, and the nature of their relationship. Also at issue, as the passage from Ephrem makes clear, was the role of the Spirit in second-century Christian discussions about the relationship of the Father to the Son. This is the wider background to the discussion about Jesus and Sophia.

As one might expect, early trinitarian speculations were quite varied: Theophilus of Antioch, for example, writing to Autolycus in 180 c.e., and Irenaeus of Lyon (late second century) both described the Trinity (Theophilus says "triad") as God, his Logos, and his Sophia.[36] The role of Logos and Sophia is clear: to create first the heavens and the earth and then human beings. According to Theophilus, God addresses the words of Gen 1:26–"Let us make humanity after the image and likeness"–to his Logos and his Sophia. Sometimes these two figures seem to be one and the same. Irenaeus understood Sophia to be interchangeable with the Spirit, but for both writers there is also a noticeable tendency to explain Sophia's function as supplemental while the Logos actively creates (Theophilus, *Ad Autolycum* 2.22). The subsidiary function of Sophia is due to her identification with the third day of creation, God and the Logos being types of the first and second days. On the third day of creation, according to Gen 1:9-13, the earth emerges from the waters, and from the earth grow plants of all kinds. The action of the third day is subordinate to the action of the first two days, in which the real work of creation takes place.

Probably influenced by this exegetical tradition, Sophia is called "earth" in some Gnostic writings (Irenaeus, *Adversus Haereses* 1.5.3). Sophia was described as the first of God's acts of creation in Proverbs 8, and in early Christian thought this association of Sophia and earth was understood to describe the preexistent church, particularly since the residence of Sophia (as Law) in Jerusalem, described in Sirach 24, was seen by that author to indicate where the Torah could be found and studied. The association of Sophia with the earth is not simply because of the activity of the third day of creation but is because of the association of Sophia with generative activity: Theophilus says, "If I call (God) Sophia, I speak of his offspring" (*Ad Autolycum* 1.3).

Such discussions demonstrate an overriding concern with the nature of intermediate figures (Logos, Sophia) between God and humanity rather than, for example, the role of Christ and how to describe it. Theophilus, for example, explains that Sophia/the Holy Spirit is the muse whose inspiration guarantees the veracity of prophetic writings, such as those of Moses and Solomon. This has nothing to do with Sophia as manifestation of Jesus; in fact, Theophilus does not discuss the incarnation at all.[37]

The tradition that attributes creation to God in the presence of and sometimes with the agency of Sophia does not subordinate Sophia to the Logos and is supported by other passages from Hebrew Scripture: Prov 3:19–20 and Jer 10:12–13. It is also found in what was originally a Jewish collection of prayers in the *Apostolic Constitutions*. In this litany, God is thanked for creation "through Christ," but it is quite likely that Christ here is a substitute for Sophia.[38] Theophilus and Irenaeus indicate that both ideas about Sophia could exist side by side in the same document. Eventually, perhaps by the fourth century, the two traditions became separated. Ephrem's sermons, from fourth-century Syria show that some Christians assigned a creative role in creation solely to the Logos while other (Jewish?) groups understood this to be the role of Sophia exclusively. The community behind *Pistis Sophia* belongs to the beginnings of that separation between Jesus and (Pistis) Sophia which probably represented an attempt to separate material creation from the higher orders of celestial realms.

CONCLUSION

Pistis Sophia articulates a voice silenced by ecclesiastical tradition that seems to have been remarkably egalitarian in its attempts to reach out to the proto-orthodox. This can be seen in the relations between Mary (who represents the Gnostic community behind *Pistis Sophia*) and Peter (who represents the proto-orthodox community). The identity of Mary is shown to be composite: she is affiliated with texts about Mary Magdalene, Mary of Bethany, and other women in the Gospels as well as the Mary figure of other texts from the Nag Hammadi library. In *Pistis Sophia,* Mary interprets visions and texts; she intercedes, questions, and praises either by herself or when others fall silent. In short, she functions as an ideal Gnostic. Moreover, her affinity for the figure of Pistis Sophia herself shows this text to be one in which a female aeon correlates to a female disciple. The sympathy of the text for the plight of the Wisdom figure, Pistis Sophia, is demonstrated by the lament psalms. Both male and female disciples interpret these texts. But Mary shows particular insight and is highly praised by the resurrected Jesus.

The text also sheds light on the ritual activities of male and female disciples before a time when sacerdotal magic became the exclusive property of one gender. Whether baptizing, forgiving sins, raising the dead, healing the sick, or releasing souls, male and female disciples are empowered by Jesus to overcome archontic authority. Contemporary readers, lulled by religious authorities today into dismissing texts like *Pistis Sophia* as unworthy of attention, can find in the Mary of ancient and venerable texts a female model of spiritual authority and religious power.

NOTES

1. *(En)Gendering Knowledge: Feminists in Academe,* ed. Joan Hartman and Ellen Messer-Davidow (Knoxville: University of Tennessee Press, 1991).

2. *Pistis Sophia* is both the name of the text and the subject of the work—literally, "Faith-Wisdom," standing for the Redeemed Redeemer.

3. The *Sophia of Jesus Christ (NHC* III, 4 and *BG* 8502,3) opens thus: "After he rose from the dead, his twelve disciples and seven women continued to be his followers. . . ." The translation of this passage by Douglas Parrott in the third edition of the *Nag Hammadi Library in English,* ed. J. M. Robinson (San Francisco: Harper & Row, 1988), 222 reads: ". . . his twelve disciples and seven women continued to be his followers. . . ." Parrott's translation obscures the preservation of the Greek verb *mathēteuō* in the Coptic with connotations of discipleship.

4. "Mystery" is a name for Jesus (the First Mystery) and the technical term for a ritual such as baptism or forgiveness given to the disciples by Jesus.

5. "Pleroma" (literally, "fullness") is the technical term for the home of the Gnostics, inhabited by divine beings.

6. The archons, the lower associates of Authades, oppress Pistis Sophia when her light-power is overwhelmed by darkness. Authades is the lion-faced leader of the archons in the thirteenth aeon, the third of the three triple-powered ones who hates Pistis Sophia and who is described in the text as the disobedient one.

7. For an introduction to the topic, see G. Filoramo, *A History of Gnosticism* (Oxford/ Cambridge: Basil Blackwell, 1991).

8. See, e.g., J. J. Buckley, *Female Fault and Fulfilment in Gnosticism* (Chapel Hill: University of North Carolina Press, 1986); *Images of the Feminine in Gnostic Texts,* ed. K. King (Philadelphia: Fortress, 1988).

9. E. Keuls, *The Reign of the Phallus* (New York: Harper & Row, 1985); M. Bal, *Lethal Love: Feminist Literary Readings of Biblical Love Stories* (Bloomington: Indiana University Press,

1987); D. Halperin, J. J. Winkler, F. Zeitlin, *Before Sexuality: The Construction of Erotic Experience in the Ancient Greek World* (Princeton: Princeton University Press, 1990).

10. For discussion, see M. Scopello, *L'Exégèse de l'Ame,* Nag Hammadi Studies 25 (Leiden: Brill, 1985).

11. Light-power is the Gnostic element inside a person that enhances perception, insight, and the interpretation of texts.

12. This has been carefully demonstrated by Phyllis Trible, *Texts of Terror: Literary Feminist Readings of Biblical Narratives* (Philadelphia: Fortress, 1984), 57.

13. There is no exact translation for this Greek word in English—the Greeks had another word for mother and clearly meant something other than the maternal (i.e., biological) when describing goddesses as such. The word refers to the generative function of a female (cf. the German word *Erzeugerin*). The Latin loanword "genetrix" is identified with Mary. I prefer "genetress" over Parrott's "begettress."

14. The NRSV text translates "mother," which is not quite accurate. The word is a feminine form created by the author of Wisdom. It is from the same root as "genetress" discussed above.

15. See D. Good, *Reconstructing the Tradition of Sophia in Gnostic Literature* (Atlanta: Scholars Press, 1987).

16. Yaldabaoth is a Semitic-sounding name that is given to the creator god of the material world. In other texts, he is the son of Sophia, but in *Pistis Sophia* he is unrelated to her.

17. This name derives from late Egyptian sources.

18. R. Murray, *Symbols of Church and Kingdom: A Study in Early Syriac Tradition* (Cambridge: Cambridge University Press, 1975), 142–54.

19. Jerome, *Comm. on Isaiah* 4 on Isa 11:2. Cited in E. Hennecke and W. Schneemelcher, *New Testament Apocrypha,* trans. R. McL. Wilson (Philadelphia: Fortress, 1963), 1:164.

20. D. Good, "Gender and Generation: Observations on Coptic Terminology, with Particular Attention to Valentinian Texts," in *Images of the Feminine in Gnostic Texts,* ed. K. King (Philadelphia: Fortress, 1988), 23–40; see also S. Schroer, "Der Geist, die Weisheit und die Taube," *Freiburger Zeitschrift für Philosophie und Theologie* 33 (1986): 210–26.

21. Barbelo is the female counterpart of the Parent (Father) of the Entirety. In *Pistis Sophia*, Barbelo sends her garment upon Jesus. The meaning is unknown.

22. W. C. van Unnik, "Die 'Zahl der Vollkommenen Seelen' in der Pistis Sophia," in *Abraham Unser Vater: Jüden und Christen im Gespräch über die Bibel,* Festschrift für O. Michel, ed. O. Betz, M. Hengel, and P. Schmidt (Leiden: Brill, 1963), 467–77.

23. The "All" is a plural noun describing the pleroma.

24. "Treasury of Light" is the name given to the light world above, from which Jesus comes; also known as the pleroma.

25. "Emanation" derives from Neoplatonism; it is a means of reproduction that is described particularly in Valentinian Gnostic texts.

26. See Kevin Coyle, "Mary Magdalene in Manichaeism," *Le Muséon* 104/1–2 (1991): 39–55; *Procession: The Legacy of Miriam and Mary Magdalene in Biblical, Patristic and Medieval Interpretation,* ed. P. Trible and D. Good (Philadelphia: Trinity Press International, forthcoming).

27. Book III, 104 commences with the phrase familiar from Matt 7:28; 11:1; 13:53; 19:1: "Now it happened when Jesus finished saying these words to his disciples."

28. I am indebted to Professor Sara Winter for this suggestion, which will be explored in another context.

29. The Logos figure of John 1 belongs to a similar but not identical pattern; the Logos descends and remains for a while, according to John. See J. D. Tabor, *Things Unutterable:*

Paul's Ascent to Paradise in its Greco-Roman, Judaic, and Early Christian Contexts (Lanham, MD: University Press of America, 1986).

30. Reading the text as it stands.

31. *The Nag Hammadi Library in English,* 383.

32. The garment is a symbol for Gnostic consciousness. It is put on Jesus at his baptism and is worn by enlightened Gnostics.

33. W. Bauer, *Orthodoxy and Heresy in Early Christianity* (Philadelphia: Fortress, 1976); Murray, *Symbols of Church and Kingdom;* H. W. Drijvers, "Jews and Christians at Edessa," *Journal of Jewish Studies* 36 (1985): 88–102.

34. *The Teaching of Addai,* ed. and trans. G. Howard (Atlanta: Scholars Press, 1981).

35. *Ephraem des Syrers Hymnen Contra Haereses,* trans. E. Beck, CSCO 170 (Louvain: Durbecq, 1957) Hymn 3.19–12.

36. *Theophilus of Antioch: Ad Autolycum,* ed. R. M. Grant (Oxford: Clarendon, 1970) 1.7; 2.15. For a discussion of these texts, see G. Kretschmar, *Studien zur Frühchristlichen Trinitätstheologie* (Beiträge zur Historischen Theologie 21; Tübingen: Mohr, 1956), 27–61.

37. R. M. Grant, *Greek Apologists of the Second Century* (Philadelphia: Westminster, 1988); D. Good, "Rhetoric and Wisdom in Theophilus of Antioch," *Anglican Theological Review* 73/3 (1991), 323–30.

38. W. Bousset, "Eine jüdische Gebetssammlung im siebenten Buch der apostolischen Konstitutionen," in *Nachrichten der Gesellschaft der Wissenschaften zu Göttingen. Philol.-Hist. Klasse 1915* (Göttingen, 1916), 435–89; K. Kohler, "The Origin and Composition of the Eighteen Benedictions with a translation of the Corresponding Essene Prayers in the Apostolic Constitutions," *Hebrew Union College Annual* 1 (1924); reprinted in *Contributions to the Scientific Study of Jewish Liturgy,* ed. J. Petuchowski (New York: Ktav, 1970), 52–90.

RECOMMENDED READINGS

Burkitt, F. C. "Pistis Sophia." *Journal of Theological Studies* 23 (1921–22): 271–80.
———. "Pistis Sophia Again." *Journal of Theological Studies* 26 (1925): 391–99.
———. "Pistis Sophia and the Coptic Language." *Journal of Theological Studies* 27 (1926): 148–57.
These articles form a series of observations on *Pistis Sophia* by a leading Christian Testament scholar of the time; the first is a response to Mead's 1921 edition of the text; the second to Horner's in 1924 and Schmidt's in 1925; and the third is Burkitt's defense of his hypothesis that *Pistis Sophia* was composed originally in Coptic. His judgment on the work is that it is "inferior" and a "dreary Egyptian book."
Carmignac, J. "Le genre littéraire du 'pesher' dans la Pistis Sophia." *Revue de Qumran* 4 (1963–64): 497–522. An interesting argument that the author of Pistis Sophia was familiar with the "pesher" method of interpretation resting on the polyvalent meaning of inspired texts (in this case, Psalms of David and *Odes of Solomon*).
Horner, G. *Pistis Sophia: Literally translated from the Coptic.* London: SPCK, 1924. An early English edition of the text with a literal translation by a Coptologist together with some useful notes and observations.
Lexa, F. "La Légende Gnostique sur Pistis Sophia et Le Mythe Ancien Égyptien sur L'Oeil de Rē." *Egyptian Religion* 1 (1933): 106–16. A proposal that the myth of Pistis Sophia is Egyptian and reflects the story of the goddess Hathor (the "eye" of Rē), who, after leaving the domain of the god Rē, suffers but is restored by the god Thoout to her former place.
Mead, G. R. S. *Pistis Sophia: A Gnostic Gospel.* New York: Spiritual Science Library, 1984. Reprint, 1989. A recently reprinted English translation of the text (first published in 1921)

with a lengthy introduction and descriptions of scholarship on the work until 1921. As a theosophist, Mead was clearly fascinated by the text, and his remarks are quite valuable.

MacDermot, V. *Pistis Sophia.* Nag Hammadi Studies 9. Leiden: Brill, 1978. An edition of the Coptic text (Schmidt's text is reproduced) and English translation on facing pages. The indexes of Greek, Coptic, and proper names are useful.

Schmidt, C. *Koptisch-gnostische Schriften:* Bd. I, *Die Pistis Sophia: Die beiden Bücher des Jeū. Unbekanntes altgnostisches Werk.* 3rd ed. Berlin: Akademie-Verlag, 1959. Reprint, 1962. The most reliable edition of the Coptic text together with a good German translation and some useful notes on the relation of the text to other Gnostic writings such as the *Apocryphon of John.*

van Unnik, W. C. "Die 'Zahl der vollkommenen Seelen' in der Pistis Sophia." In *Abraham Unser Vater: Festschrift für O. Michel,* edited by O. Betz, M. Hengel, and P. Schmidt, 467–77. Leiden: Brill, 1963. An investigation of an eschatological motif, the "number of perfect souls," in *Pistis Sophia,* its significance, together with a comparison of Christian Testament and second-century teachings on eschatology.

Worrell, W. H. "The Odes of Solomon and the Pistis Sophia." *Journal of Theological Studies* 13 (1912): 29–46. A comparison of the citations from the *Odes* in *Pistis Sophia* with extant Syriac texts of the *Odes* themselves and assessments of the results.

The Infancy of Mary
of Nazareth

JANE SCHABERG ◆

INTRODUCTION

THE CREATION OF THE VIRGIN MARY

THE LITTLE-READ *Proto-James* and its clone, the *Gospel of Pseudo-Matthew*, exercised enormous influence on Christian devotion, liturgy, and doctrine. These two works helped to create the figure of the Virgin Mary, Mother of God, a figure Julia Kristeva calls "one of the most powerful imaginary constructs known in the history of civilizations."[1] They reflect the imagination, sensitivities, and insensitivities of some second- and sixth-century Christians, as they struggled to develop and defend their faith and to create institutions and life-styles expressive of that faith—especially as they asked what place, if any, heterosexual intercourse should have in their world. It had no place, they argued, in the life of Mary.

By the second century, some Christians claimed that Mary had conceived Jesus by a virginal conception, that is, without sexual intercourse and without male sperm or "seed." While that event was believed to be unique and inimitable, Mary's "purity" eventually became a model for all Christians, especially those chosen for a "higher" life. The telling of her story both influenced and was influenced by Christian asceticism, whose roots lie in Palestinian and diaspora Judaism and in Greco-Roman religious movements. A major influence on her story, however, was polemical.

Scholars widely recognize evidence as early as the Christian Testament Gospels of a tradition that Jesus was conceived illegitimately. The conception was said to have taken place while his mother Mary was in the first stage of the marriage process, betrothal to Joseph, during which time Mary and Joseph did not have intercourse. Most scholars hold that the infancy narratives of Matthew and Luke are responses denying that "Jewish calumny" by claiming that Jesus was conceived miraculously. But it has also been argued that the narratives of Matthew and Luke reflect and develop the illegitimacy tradition, which is probably historical. This is the position taken in this commentary on the two apocryphal works, which are themselves early commentaries on the Christian Testament narratives.

The author of *Proto-James* was anxious to insist as explicitly as possible that the Christian Testament accounts must be read to mean that Mary was a biological virgin who had intercourse with no one. This, rather than any christological implications drawn from belief in a miraculous conception, is the central focus of the work. It is maintained, though with less graphic "proof" and less anxiety, by the author of *Pseudo-Matthew*. In the history of devotion to the Virgin Mary, this anxiety to deny the tradition of the illegitimacy of Jesus and defend the "purity" of Mary fades into and feeds a desire to promote her importance and power.

Seven ascending stages can be identified in the ladder of belief in Mary's purity. These stages are not in absolute historical sequence; the content of *Proto-James* is represented by stages 4, 5, and 6:

1. Jesus was conceived illegitimately during the time Mary was betrothed to Joseph but by her intercourse with another man.

2. Joseph and Mary were Jesus' biological parents.

3. Mary was betrothed to Joseph, but had no sexual intercourse with him until after Jesus' birth. He was not the biological father of Jesus.

4. Mary conceived Jesus virginally.

5. Joseph was a decrepit old man at the time of his betrothal to Mary. His children were all by a former marriage. He was really Mary's guardian rather than her husband.

6. Mary's virginity was not destroyed by the birth of Jesus, nor by any intercourse or childbirth afterwards.

7. Joseph was a virgin as well as Mary. The "brothers" of Jesus were really his cousins.[2]

THEORETICAL FRAMEWORK OF THIS STUDY

The feminist perspective and method of this commentary are tailored to the works under consideration. Like all feminist writing, this is a political act. It is undertaken in the hope of contributing to an awareness and a dismantling of harmful aspects of the construct Virgin Mary, and a freeing of its positive aspects. The aim is to maintain a focus on the fact that a historical woman, Mary, stands far behind the narrative, and on how, why, and to what effect the narrative manipulates her reality and her image, especially as it appears in the Christian Testament. That effect, it will be argued, involves patriarchal control of women of the early centuries C.E. as well as later centuries.

An interdisciplinary range of approaches and methods will be used on these works: historical, literary, midrashic, ideological, theological, and sociopolitical criticism. Informing the feminist use of these methods are questions about the depiction of gender roles and how these relate to actual women's experiences, past and present—insofar as the interpreter has access to these. My interest is in the literary and theological strategies used by the narrator to promote patriarchal ideology, in depictions of class structures, and in the roots of Christian anti-Judaism. Reading as a woman also resists the damaging prescriptions and descriptions of the texts and highlights whatever aspects are humanly liberating. Such recognition of the ambiguous value of a work challenges its traditional authority. Finally, a feminist reading "answers back," in the voice of a strong reader that the author may not have imagined.

Important to feminist scholarship are the recognition and presentation of the bias, or angle of vision, of the scholar, whose "I" is given permission to speak but is reminded that it does not speak for all women, nor give a definitive interpretation. The reader should know that this commentary was written by a white, middle-class, unmarried, heterosexual, noncelibate, biologically childless—and reasonably happy—woman from the United States, whose background is Roman Catholic. Most pertinent is the information that I spent part of the 1960s and 1970s as a nun. The celibate life-style of this post–Vatican II period included much discussion of the origins, history, and value of celibacy among women influenced by changes in sexual mores and by growing feminist consciousness. This continuing conversation, which is part of a reevaluation of the Roman Catholic past and of broader academic, personal, political analyses, is a context of this commentary.

PROTO-JAMES AND PSEUDO-MATTHEW

These works belong to a stream of apocryphal Infancy Gospels which appeared from the second century C.E. on, in a process that continues even today. Their popular combination of ancient legend and tradition, fantasy, and creative midrashic exegesis made them in antiquity, in the Middle Ages, and in the Renaissance a greater influence on literature and art than the Bible. The "gaps" in the Christian Testament texts are filled in, and the contradictions and problematic elements erased, not simply to satisfy casual curiosity and speculation and to ease the mind but to promote and develop certain types of Christianity and their social agendas.

Proto-James is the basis of all the later works concerning the birth, childhood, and motherhood of Mary. In the oldest manuscript (Papyrus Bodmer V from the third century C.E.), it is given the title "Birth of Mary. Apocalypse of James." The title *Protevangelium* [pre-Gospel] *of James* was used first when it was rediscovered in the sixteenth century, to indicate that the events narrated take place earlier than those narrated by Matthew and Luke. *Proto-James* survives in the original Greek, and in Syriac, Armenian, Georgian, Ethiopic, Arabic, Sahidic, and Slavonic, but not in Old Latin because of the book's condemnation in the West. The reason for its condemnation was that its asceticism was not extreme enough: it presents "the brothers of Jesus" (cf. Mark 6:3 par. Matt 13:56, which also mentions sisters) as Jesus' step-brothers, sons of Joseph the widower. Jerome (342–420) insisted rather that they were Jesus' cousins and that Joseph was a virgin.

Pseudo-Matthew is a Latin compilation, possibly written in the sixth century. In it *Proto-James* and at least one other work, the *(Infancy) Gospel of Thomas,* are abridged by being purged of details regarded as offensive, confusing, or unimportant, and are amplified by adding miraculous legends and details for the sake of clarification and edification. The compiler provides credentials in the form of faked letters to and from Jerome—which is ironic, since Joseph is still said in this work to have sons, and also daughters. The claim is made that this is a translation from Hebrew of a "somewhat secret" book written with his own hand by Saint Matthew (although a prologue appearing in some manuscripts attributes it to James son of Joseph). "Jerome" writes that he is not adding this book to the canonical scriptures nor vouching for its truth but translating it in order to combat the heresy promulgated by another(?) book by Leucius (or Seleucus), a disciple of Manichaeus. Through yet another version, in more elegant Latin and pruned again, *Pseudo-Matthew* passed into the immensely popular twelfth-century *Golden Legend* of Jacobus de Voragine. Focus here will be primarily on *Proto-James.*

An examination of all the extant manuscripts shows that there is no adequate critical edition of *Proto-James.* Rather than basing this commentary only on the latest critical edition, that of E. de Stryker, I will follow the example of Oscar Cullmann and H. R. Smid:[3] since Papyrus Bodmer V has frequent secondary expansions and probable abbreviations, it will be at times compared to and supplemented by readings drawn from the manuscript that Tischendorf (1876) regarded as the best. This is not merely an academic exercise, since the variants often point to intriguing ideological disputes. There are still many aspects of this text that are puzzling (e.g., the origin, scope, and title of the original work; its relation to other apocryphal traditions and to Jewish Christian circles; its reflection of social realities; and its social impact).

NARRATIVE SUMMARY OF PROTO-JAMES

A summary of the twenty-five chapters of *Proto-James* is necessary, since the effect of this work has outlived its detailed memory. It opens with the rich and pious Joakim offering double gifts to the Lord for forgiveness of his own sins and for the whole people. But he is told he cannot offer his gifts first, because he has begotten no offspring. Joakim checks in "the record of the twelve tribes" and finds that all of the righteous did beget, all but him. He remembers, however, that God gave Abraham a son in his last days. In grief, shame, and hope Joakim withdraws into the wilderness for prayer and fasting.

The parallel scene that follows illustrates the belief that childlessness is much more devastating for a woman than for a man. Wearing her bridal garments, Joakim's wife Anna withdraws to her garden to pray, asking God to bless her as Sarah was blessed by the birth of Isaac. Whereas Joakim ponders his alienation from all the righteous in Israel, Anna feels that in her barrenness she is alienated not only from Israel but from all that is fertile, and even from God. The sight of a nest of sparrows in the laurel tree (Greek *daphnē*) under which she is sitting triggers her powerful lament: "Woe is me, to what am I likened? / I am not likened to the birds of the heaven; / for even the birds of the heaven are fruitful before you, Lord." The lament distances her also from animals, water, and fish, and climaxes with the lines, "I am not likened to this earth; / for even this earth brings forth its fruit in season and praises you, Lord." She feels utterly worthless without children.

Her prayer is answered by the sudden presence of an angel who tells her she will become pregnant and give birth, and her "seed" will be spoken of in the whole world. Anna does not question this directly, but (like the Anna of 1 Sam 1:11 LXX, on whom she is based) she makes a conditional promise: "If I bear a child, male or female, I will bring it as a gift to the Lord my God, and it will serve him all the days of its life." The Anna of 1 Samuel vows that if God gives her a male child, she will dedicate him to God (as a nazirite); when he has been weaned, she gives him to the priest Heli, and Samuel grows up to be a great prophet. To what has this new Anna pledged her child?

The annunciation to Anna is paralleled by the secondhand report of one to Joakim. Messengers tell her that he is coming with his flocks for a sacrifice, and that an angel has told him God has heard his prayer: his wife will conceive (Tischendorf manuscript; or, according to Bodmer Papyrus V, "has conceived"; in either case, what is originally in mind here is probably not a miraculous conception). The scene ends with their embrace at the city gate. Anna becomes pregnant and gives birth. Told the child is a female, she replies surprisingly, "My soul is magnified this day" (echoing the canonical Magnificat of her daughter). Anna purifies herself and names her child Mary.

At six months, the wonderchild Mary precociously walks seven steps to her mother, who snatches her up and vows she will "walk no more on this ground" until she is taken to the temple. A sanctuary is made for her in her bedroom, and nothing common or unclean is allowed to pass through it. Mary spends her days as a toddler in isolation from the ordinary world, kept amused by "the undefiled daughters of the Hebrews," whose identity and role are unexplained. On the child's first birthday, her parents present her to the priests, who pray that she be given a name "renowned forever" and bless her with an unsurpassable blessing. As she breast-feeds her daughter, Anna praises God for having taken away the insult of her enemies, the shame of childlessness. "Who will announce to the sons of Reuben that Anna is breast-feeding?" Some minor manuscripts add "Listen, listen, you twelve tribes of Israel: Anna is breast-feeding!"

When the child is two years old, Joakim suggests that they fulfill the promise "which we made" and bring her to the Temple. With a touch of maternal feeling, Anna urges that they wait until the third year, so the child will not yearn for her parents; Joakim agrees. When the time comes, Joakim has the "undefiled daughters of the Hebrews" accompany them with lamps to the Temple, removing the child from her home and forming a weddinglike procession (cf. Matt 25:1–13). The priest takes Mary, kisses and blesses her: "The Lord has magnified your name among all generations; because of you the Lord at the end of days will manifest his salvation to the children of Israel" (cf. Luke 2:28–32). Placed on the third step of the altar, little Mary dances, graced by God and loved by the whole house of Israel. Appearing here for the last time, Anna and Joakim leave Mary in the Temple and go home amazed and praising God because their child did not turn back to them (contrast Luke 2:41–51; cf. 2:33). In the Temple, Mary—a virtual orphan—is nurtured like a dove, receiving (immaterial?) food from an angel. (The dove is mentioned in Lev 1:14 as the only bird offered as a sacrifice, and in Matt 10:14 as a symbol of innocence.)

When Mary is twelve, a council of priests wonders what they should do with her, lest she pollute the sanctuary of the Lord (with menstrual blood; see Lev 15:19–31). An angel commands Zacharias the high priest to assemble the widowers, each bringing a rod; Mary will be the wife of the one to whom the Lord will give a sign. The high priest prays over the rods in the Temple, and Joseph receives the sign: in a twist Freud might imagine, a dove comes out of Joseph's rod and flies onto his head. He is commanded to receive "the virgin of the Lord" and take her under his protection. Joseph protests that he already has sons and is old, while she is a girl; he fears he will become a laughingstock (an odd remark, since older men usually married young girls, sometimes younger than twelve). The priest threatens him with punishment like that of Dathan, Abiram, and Koran, who were swallowed up in an earthquake because of their rebellion against Moses. Numbers 16–18 is drawn on here with great skill and irony: the rebels in that story demanded priestly status and access to the sanctuary, which they were not granted. Aaron's rod produced blossoms and almonds to show that only he and his tribe, the Levites, were given authority to approach the holy.

Out of fear, Joseph relents. But as soon as he has taken Mary home, he leaves her, going away to build his buildings, entrusting her to the care of the Lord. He does not appear again until Mary is six months pregnant. The priests decide that a temple veil should be made by "pure virgins of the tribe of David" (cf. Exod 26:31; 27:16; 35:25; *b. Yoma* 75b; *b. Ketub.* 106a; *m. Seqal.* 8:5). Seven are found and Mary is the eighth and most important, given by lot the task of spinning at home two of the seven materials, the "true" purple and the scarlet.

The author begins now to work closely with the Christian Testament, filling in its blank spaces and smoothing out inconsistencies. The annunciation scene in Luke 2:26–38 is split in two. At a well (in Jerusalem? Nazareth is never mentioned in this work), Mary is frightened by a voice: "Greetings, highly favored one! The Lord is with you. Blessed are you among women." When she returns inside, an angel, later identified as Gabriel, tells her that she has found grace before the Lord of all "and will conceive of his word." Speaking for the first time (if indeed she is speaking and not thinking), Mary doubts inwardly and asks, "Will I conceive by the Lord, the living God, as every woman gives birth?" The angel answers this question directly and clearly, "Not that way, Mary. For a power of God will overshadow you; therefore the child to be born will be holy; he will be called Son of the Most High. And you will name him Jesus because he will save his people from their sins." (In the Armenian manuscript edited by Conybeare, over thirty objections on Mary's part and responses by Gabriel are added to this scene, which ends with the conception taking place through Mary's "ear of hearing within.")

Mary finishes spinning and brings the purple and the scarlet to the priest, who blesses her. Rejoicing, Mary goes to her relative Elizabeth, who is also spinning the scarlet. Elizabeth and her unborn child bless Mary. Except for the explanation of Jesus' name drawn from Matt 1:21, the author is working so far with Luke 1. But it is important to note which sections of Luke are omitted from *Proto-James:* the parallel annunciation, conception, and birth of John the Baptist and prophecy of his future, the betrothal status of Mary (but see below), Mary's puzzlement at the angel's greeting, the description of the royal destiny of her son, and Mary's Magnificat. The author at this point is totally focused on Mary, not on her son or even briefly on any other character. The omission of the Magnificat, however, shows that the author's interest is even more narrow: on Mary's impregnation.

Mary, however, is said to forget the mysteries which Gabriel told her. This strange motif (regarded by most commentators as indicating her humility) functions as a transition to the use of Matthew 1. The pregnant Mary, now sixteen, hides herself in fear as her womb grows larger. In the sixth month, Joseph returns (has he been gone six months or four years?). His reaction to her pregnancy is an intense emotional outburst of grief, shame, helplessness, self-castigation, self-pity, and anger. He uses first-person pronouns seven times in this speech about male honor. He blames himself for failing to protect the virgin from defilement and regards himself as responsible for what has happened—to him. "Who has deceived me? . . . Has the story of Adam been summed up in me? For as Adam was in the hour of his prayer, the serpent came and found Eve alone and deceived and defiled her, so also has it happened to me" (cf. 1 Tim 2:14). He strikes his own face, not Mary's, but he accuses her—who was brought up in the Holy of Holies—of having forgotten God and humiliated her soul. The weeping Mary insists she is pure and has not had sex with a man. When Joseph asks, "From where is this in your womb?" she swears she does not know.

Joseph's dilemma is spelled out. If he conceals her sin, he opposes the law of the Lord (presumably Deut 22:23–27). On the other hand, if he exposes her to the sons of Israel, and her pregnancy has "sprung from the angels" (cf. Gen 6:1–4 and later traditions), he will be delivering up innocent blood to the judgment of death (cf. the story of Susanna wife of Joakim in Daniel 13 LXX). Joseph decides therefore to divorce Mary privately. "And the night came upon him." But the appearance of an angel in his dream overturns this decision; he is told the child conceived in Mary is from the Holy Spirit. Joseph wakes, glorifies God, and watches over the girl Mary.

When Annas the scribe happens to see that Mary is pregnant, he reports to the priest that Joseph has sinned by defiling Mary, "stealing marriage" with her and not disclosing it to Israel. Officers bring the pregnant virgin to the Temple court, where she and Joseph are both accused and both insist on their purity. Both are tested by being given "the water of the conviction of the Lord" to drink and sent into the wilderness; if illness results, it will manifest their sin (cf. Num 5:11–31). Both Mary and Joseph come back whole, causing all the people to marvel. Since God has not manifested their sins, the high priest dismisses them—ironically with the words Jesus uses in John 8:11 to dismiss the woman caught in adultery: "neither do I condemn you."

Following Luke's description of a census, but confining it to the inhabitants of Bethlehem, Joseph is depicted as traveling with Mary and with his sons, one named Samuel and the other (presumably James) unnamed. Joseph is embarrassed about "this girl," neither his wife nor his daughter. At the three-mile mark, he notices she is gloomy and then laughing. She explains that she sees two peoples, one weeping, one rejoicing (cf. Luke 2:34; Gen 25:22–23); her grief and her joy here are quasi-prophetic, not physical. Halfway to Bethlehem, she goes into labor, but there is no mention of pain. Joseph finds a cave and leaves her in the care of his sons while he goes to find a Hebrew midwife.

Missing in the Bodmer Papyrus V, but present in Tischendorf's best manuscript, a first-person account occurs at this point: Joseph witnesses a momentary standstill of nature, the suspension of all movement, from the flight of birds to the chewing of workmen to the flowing of a stream. This beautiful poem depicts the moment of Christ's birth as stilling the world. When this moment passes, Joseph meets a midwife; in the unabridged text (Tischendorf) she interrogates him about the one who is having a baby in the cave. He tells her she is his "betrothed." The midwife presses him: "'Is she not your wife?' And I said to her: 'She is Mary, who was brought up in the temple of the Lord, and I received her by lot as my wife. And she is not my wife, but she is pregnant of the Holy Spirit.'" When the doubting midwife says, "Is this true?" Joseph invites her to come and see.

What she sees is a dark cloud overshadowing the cave; this convinces her "salvation is born to Israel." After the cloud, there is a great, unbearable light, and when it withdraws the child appears, who goes and takes Mary's breast. The midwife is convinced she has seen a "new sight." The birth itself has not been seen, and nothing has been heard, since this is a painless birth, with no blood, no screams, no afterbirth, no "impurity." Only a witness to the cloud, the light, and the presence of the newborn, the midwife has nothing to do for Mary or the child (cf. *Odes of Solomon* 19:8–9; *Ascension of Isaiah* 11:14). The nursing Mary appears now as the virgin mother.

The following incident is the most memorable scene of *Proto-James*. Coming from the cave, the midwife meets Salome (not further identified) and tells her "a virgin has given birth, which her condition does not allow." Salome swears, "Unless I stick my finger in and examine her condition, I will not believe that a virgin has given birth" (cf. John 20:25). (Here the Tischendorf manuscript abbreviates; Salome only swears less crudely that unless she observes, she will not believe.) Smid remarks that "Salome's skepticism affords opportunity to have the virgin birth diagnosed by her skillful hand in semi-scientific fashion."[4]

Salome goes into the cave and tells Mary to position herself for the vaginal examination, "for there is no small contention concerning you" (Tischendorf manuscript). Salome inserts her finger, then screams out, "Woe for my lawlessness and woe for my unbelief, for I have tempted the living God. Look, my hand is on fire!" She prays that she not be made a public example, but (in several minor manuscripts) that she be restored to "the poor" (the Ebionites?). She is healed by touching the child at the direction of an angel. She now worships the newborn "great king" but is told not to tell what she has seen before the child comes to Jerusalem. There are now two women witnesses to the virginity of Mary (cf. Deut 19:15), the end of a chain of witnesses from her parents to Joseph to the priests to the midwife. This punitive miracle harms the hand that confirms, because of unbelief and suspicion. The point of the scene is not that an additional miracle has occurred (i.e., that the hymen is not ruptured by the baby passing through the birth canal). The point is rather that the original miracle, conception without intercourse is confirmed again and finally. In the prevalent male science of the female body, intercourse was thought to be the act that tore the hymen and was imagined as an irreversible wounding. Mary's hymen is still not broken. Her virginity is now defined in the narrowest possible fashion: as having an intact, unruptured hymeneal membrane. This biological fantasy is "the physical detail that made the birth of the son of a virgin miraculous, inherently mysterious, and perforce unique."[5]

The author now turns back to the Gospel of Matthew (2:1–12), paraphrasing the stories of the magi and the star, and Herod's slaughter of infants. In her last appearance in this work, Mary takes the initiative to save her son by wrapping him in swaddling clothes and laying him in a manger (Luke 2:7)–to conceal him? Elizabeth flees with the child John. In the hill country, where there is no hiding place, she groans, "O mountain of God, receive me, a mother with a child." The mountain splits in two and receives them, making a light shine for them as an angel protects them (cf. Rev 12:6, 13–16, where the mother persecuted by the dragon flees into the wilderness and is helped by the earth). Herod then turns on John's father Zacharias and has him slain in the sanctuary. (Origen knew of another account of this murder, that it took place because Zacharias allowed Mary to continue in the place of the virgins near the temple, even after the birth of Jesus [*In Matth.* 25:2].)

At the end of the story, the author identifies himself as James—surely meaning James the brother of Jesus, son of Joseph and (step)son of Mary. The aim is not only to present it as an eyewitness account but to insist that it comes from within the family. Further, "James" implies that he wrote it in the wilderness when a tumult arose in Jerusalem at the death of Herod. If this is Herod the Great, as seems likely, it means that the document purports to have been written almost immediately after the events it describes, while Jesus was still an infant. The work ends with the glorification of the Lord, the title, and final blessings.

QUESTIONS OF DATE, AUTHORSHIP, AND PROVENANCE

The author of *Proto-James* was a person of considerable sophistication, talent, and knowledge—perhaps (if the lament of Anna and section on the standstill of nature are original) a poet of power, able to weave stories from the Septuagint into an amazingly free harmonization of the infancy narratives of Matthew and Luke. As Luke wrote the story of the presentation of Jesus by his parents in the Temple (Luke 2:21–40) in imitation of the story of the presentation of Samuel by his mother Anna (1 Sam 1:21–28), the author of *Proto-James* has imitated that same story to produce the account of the conception, birth, and dedication of Mary. Other examples of creative midrashic exegesis are numerous: for example, a triple reference is achieved by the dark cloud at the cave—to the overshadowing of Mary that Gabriel predicted, to the Christian Testament scenes of the transfiguration of Jesus (Mark 9:7 and parallels), and to the Exodus/Sinai clouds (Exod 13:21–22; 24:15–18). The language of *Proto-James* is simple koine Greek; the style is artistic and marked by parallel treatments of persons and events.

There is scholarly consensus that the author was not a Jewish Christian, or at least not a Palestinian Jewish Christian. Even more than the Gospel of Luke, *Proto-James* exhibits what seems to be ignorance of or a cavalier attitude toward the workings of the priesthood and Temple in pre-70 Judaism, and unfamiliarity with Palestinian geography. Notable is the insistence that Mary as a girl lived in the Temple in Jerusalem (even in the Holy of Holies; cf. Luke 2:36–38, where the old prophet Anna is said to never leave the Temple). Does the author know more than we currently do of the roles of first-century C.E. Jewish women? In commentaries on *Proto-James,* passages such as Exod 38:8; 2 Macc 3:19 have been pointed out to show that there were virgins actually dwelling in the Temple; cf. also the fourth-century *Apostolic Constitutions* 8, 20). *Proto-James* does not provide any information of historical value concerning the life of Mary, though it uses old traditions (the cave, the sacred well, the midwife). As will be seen, it exhibits great familiarity with Jewish apocryphal traditions.

Although *Proto-James* focuses on female characters, male interests predominate. There is no clear evidence of a female point of view or distinctively female preoccupations, thoughts, or feelings; no interest in the female apart from the male (including the male God), or in aspects of women's lives not connected with sexuality. There is therefore no evidence that supports the possibility of female authorship or inspiration.[6]

Most scholars argue that *Proto-James* was written in Syria—as Luke/Acts probably was—or (less likely) in Egypt. The laurel tree mentioned in connection with Anna's lament may be a clue: in a suburb of Antioch was a grove of laurel trees dedicated to Apollo, in memory of his attempted rape of Daphne, who turned into the laurel and escaped him. The date of composition of *Proto-James* is around 150 C.E., two generations or so after the composition of the Gospel of Luke. It was known to Origen (ca. 185–ca. 254), Clement of Alexandria (ca. 150–215), and possibly Justin Martyr (ca. 100–ca. 165). In its obsessive concentration on the virginity of Mary, *Proto-James* replies to allegations such as those raised by the Syrian Jew in Celsus's *Logos Alethes* (*True Doctrine,* written around 178), as reported by Origen in his work *Against Celsus* 1.7, 28, 32, 39, 69, written around 248.

COMMENTARY

"NO SMALL CONTENTION"

It is clear that this work is a response: first to those who were reading the Christian Testament infancy narratives as being about a normal conception, illegitimate or legitimate; and, second, to an alternative story or stories of this conception. Some were reading Matthew 1 and Luke 1 to mean that Mary had sexual relations with someone else before or during her betrothal to Joseph (a reading I have argued elsewhere is an acceptable reading of these texts), or to mean that Joseph was responsible for her pregnancy (Jesus, it was noted, was Son of David through the genealogy of Joseph in both Gospels). They were reading the words "conceived of the Holy Spirit" (Matt 1:20), "a virgin shall conceive and bear a son" (1:23; Isa 7:14), and "the Holy Spirit will come upon you and the power of the Most High will overshadow you" (Luke 1:35) to indicate that special divine interest or power was focused on a biologically normal conception. Some readers may also have noticed that the Matthean and Lukan accounts as they stand are bristling with contradictions (e.g., the genealogies of Jesus, or the movements of the family) and cannot be harmonized.

The author of *Proto-James* will not allow these readings, but offers the one "correct" reading of Matthew and Luke, whose texts have been inserted into a broader story of the life of Mary, and forcibly harmonized, with the gaps plugged up. To rule out the idea of a normal conception, Mary is made to ask if this is what is meant by Gabriel's words, and she is told explicitly it is not. Joseph's role is expanded; he is the reluctant protector, angry and ashamed in his confusion, awestruck in the presence of the numinous, clearly not the father of the child.

At no moment in Mary's life is there any occasion for Mary to have sexual relations. At three she passes from the protection of her parents to protection of the Temple priests; at twelve to the protection of Joseph and God. Her only companions are the undefiled daughters of the Hebrews and her kinswoman Elizabeth. Her virginity is testified to by the angel Gabriel, the high priest, Joseph, God, the midwife, and Salome. She passes the test of the water of conviction (she is not an adulteress and has not had sexual relations with Joseph), and the test of Salome's physical exam (she is a virgin even after giving birth).

The alternative story told by Celsus's Jew, possibly drawn from older sources, claims that Jesus himself fabricated the story of his birth from a virgin. Jesus came from a Jewish village, where he had been born of a poor country woman who earned her living by spinning and was unknown even to her neighbors. When she was corrupted or seduced and became pregnant by a soldier named Panthera, she was convicted of adultery and driven out (divorced?) by the carpenter to whom she was betrothed. "When hated by her husband, and turned out of doors, she was not saved by divine power, nor was her story [of seduction or rape] believed" (*Against Celsus* 1.39). Wandering about in disgrace, she secretly gave birth. This story seems to be following in part and partly revising Matthew 1, and/or drawing on other traditions. Panthera was a common Greek proper name, found in many Latin inscriptions of the early empire, especially as a surname of Roman soldiers. In some rabbinic passages that survived Christian-imposed censorship, Jesus is referred to as "the [illegitimate] son of Pantera."

The author of *Proto-James* counters: Mary was not poor, but was born of wealthy parents, of the noble line of David. She was not from a Jewish village, but from Jerusalem or the Jerusalem area; not an unknown nobody, but known and loved by all Israel from her childhood. She was the wife not of a lowly carpenter, but of an architect/builder. She was a spinner, yes, but engaged in this activity not to make a living; she was chosen by the priests for the privilege of spinning the Temple curtain. This emphasis on her upper-class position removes Mary from any identification with poor women, for whom she speaks in Luke 1:46–55. Presumably the author of *Proto-James* thinks wealth protects her or makes less plausible any accusation of sexual immorality. There was no seduction or rape and no conviction for adultery. Her husband/protector was greatly disturbed by her pregnancy, thinking that she had been defiled, and considered divorcing her. But this was a grave error. A revelation by an angel convinced him that the child was "of the Holy Spirit." He did not turn her out or hate her, but watched over her carefully. She was not wandering about in disgrace when she gave birth, but on a journey with Joseph and his sons to Bethlehem. She did not give birth secretly, but the sons of Joseph were present—one of whom is the author of this account—and Joseph and a midwife witnessed the great light. The child was not illegitimate but was the son of a certified virgin who had miraculously conceived. Her virginity was protected by total seclusion since her infancy, and proven over and over again.

THE BODY OF MARY

What is the point of this obsession with the physical virginity of Mary, with her unbroken hymen? And what is the literary result? The author of *Proto-James* is telling the story of the body of Mary, but without erotic description. Her body is "intact" and has not experienced intercourse; it is hedged about with promises and protections; it gives birth without agony, blood, and mess. There is no evidence that the construction of the virginal conception is for the sake of glorifying Jesus, nor is it rationalized as the only fitting conception for him.

Many of the themes of future Mariology are present here in embryonic form. But is the aim of the author "the glorification of Mary," as all previous commentators have argued? I think not. This reading of the texts of Matthew and Luke aims primarily to defeat and silence an alternative reading, the tradition of Jesus' illegitimacy. The notion of God's miraculous action in creating this pregnancy seems designed to overwhelm and blot out any suspicion of negative male sexual behavior involved in the appearance of the Christ, to ward off any slurs that might stain him, and to protect God's honor. What results is a deforming constriction of the Lukan character of Mary, the dehumanizing of Jesus, and the despotization of God.

JEWISH APOCRYPHAL TRADITIONS
OF MARVELOUS CONCEPTIONS

To accomplish the aim of erasing the illegitimacy tradition, the author of *Proto-James* draws not on Gentile traditions concerning the miraculous birth of divine men but on Jewish apocryphal traditions, especially those concerning the birth of Melchizedek to Sopanim and Nir (*2 Enoch* 71–73) and of Noah to Bitenosh and Lamech (*Genesis Apocryphon* cols. 1–5; *1 Enoch* 106). In *Proto-James* five motifs are found that appear also in *2 Enoch* 71–73: (1) the direct accusation of his pregnant wife by the husband, who is convinced she has been defiled; (2) the insistence of the wife on her purity; (3) ignorance on the part of the woman regarding her pregnancy (cf. also *Gospel of Bartholomew* 4.61); (4) conception by the "word" of God (manuscript A of the shorter recension of *2 Enoch*; again cf. *Gospel of Bartholomew* 2.20); (5) the sudden appearance of the child, who could hardly be said to be "born." In addition, two motifs found in *1 Enoch* 106 appear in *Proto-James:* (1) the husband fears that the conception is from the angels; (2) a great light appears at the birth. These themes are used in *Proto-James* to (mis)read the Christian Testament infancy narratives in a way that defends them against other readings regarded as scurrilous, creating and elaborating for Jesus a miraculous conception: a begetting through the sole power of God, without human sexual intercourse.

THE CHARACTER MARY

Proto-James (like the Christian Testament infancy narratives, though to a greater degree) is a substitute for the lost story of the historical Mary of Nazareth. A comparison of Mary's depiction in the Gospel of Luke with her depiction in *Proto-James* shows that although her role in the latter is an expansion and elaboration, the character herself has been reduced and deformed. No longer is she the woman of faith who hears and believes and chooses submission to the deity; no longer almost a disciple, a woman who functions as a prophet (without the title) in her Magnificat. In *Proto-James,* Mary's importance is centered in her physical virginity. Never an autonomous woman, she does not choose this virginity; her mother chooses it for her before her conception, and then her parents, the priests, and Joseph guard her in it. That the child dances and does not turn back is the author's way of indicating that the child Mary accepts her fate. She does indeed consent in obedience to Gabriel's words about conception, but the motif of her forgetting makes this a moment that passes and turns her into a bewildered victim, ignorant of the cause of her pregnancy. She exercises no judgment, makes no decisions for herself, resists no temptation, shows no virtue or courage (except perhaps in her final scene, when she hides the infant). She is contrasted with disobedient Eve (13:3).

Her relation to men is that of protected to protectors—father, priests, and Joseph representing God's authority. As they make it possible for her to virginally conceive, they are in an active sense more important than she is to the birth. Her own conception is proof of the righteousness of her father Joakim. Her relation to her mother is that of sacrificed to sacrificer. Except for Elizabeth, the other women who have speaking parts in the story (the midwife and Salome) relate to Mary with suspicion that must be overcome.

The use of the motif of her forgetting functions as a bridge between the use of Luke's and Matthew's accounts; but Mary's silence would have done just as well. (Note that though Joseph has received a revelation about the pregnancy, he does not defend Mary before the priests or speak of the dream; he defends himself and then is silent.) In *2 Enoch* 71–73, Sopanim honestly does not know how she has conceived Melchizedek; she is sterile and old and her husband has not slept with her since he became a priest. Female ignorance about conception appears differently in 2 Macc 7:22–23, which stresses the creative role of God in a normal conception as in resurrection. But in *Proto-James*, Mary's ignorance born of forgetting seems a measure of the author's careless disregard for the roundedness or depth of the character.

In contrast to Mary, the rather unpleasant character of Joseph displays a wide and complex range of emotions and motivations, from eager obedience to concern with his honor to stoicism to a nagging sense of shame and embarrassment. His boorishness and cruelty, especially in abandoning her, are not condemned; they underline that he is not the father of Jesus. The rendering of Mary's inner life (her doubting within herself) is solely for the purpose of making explicit that the conception is not normal. The motif of her fame (she will be spoken of) is ironic, since she herself hardly speaks, never prays. What will be spoken of is her virginity.

GOD THE DESPOT

Seven times (three of these in Bodmer Papyrus V) in this work the Greek word *despotēs* is used for God. This term is usually translated "master" or "lord" and is rarely used in the Septuagint or the Christian Testament. The word "despot" is not an inappropriate translation here in *Proto-James:* God is the sole proprietor and absolute ruler of human life, the one who causes a childless couple to conceive a child and then accepts the sacrifice of this child and her potentially active sexuality. Neither Anna nor Mary has control over her own reproductive capacities; rather, God is in complete control. Although Joseph speaks about himself as dishonored by Mary's pregnancy, it is really

God's male honor that is at stake in the story, determined by the control he and other males in the story exercise over Mary's "shame," her sexuality. The child Mary has been given to God for his exclusive use; therefore, her virginity must be protected, confined, and defended. God does indeed "use" her, and she becomes the mother of the Savior. The punitive miracle worked on Salome's hand in the pornographic scene of the testing by digital penetration indicates that Mary is "pure" and that an outraged God punishes those who doubt this. The flaming hand warns the reader: it is dangerous to doubt Mary's virginity.

THE READER RESISTS:
MARY AND JEPHTHA'S DAUGHTER

The author of *Proto-James* has drawn heavily on stories from the Septuagint, primarily 1 Samuel 1, Daniel 13, and those of the matriarchs whom God allowed to conceive. But there is another story beside which *Proto-James* can be laid, one with which it has a number of unintended, subversive parallels: the story in Judg 11:34–40 of Jephthah's daughter. The differences between the two stories are obvious and need not be detailed here. Most importantly, the first is meant to be a tragedy of unfulfillment when the daughter dies childless, and the latter a story of fulfillment when Mary becomes the virgin mother. But the following are subtle echoes to explore. Both daughters are dedicated by the spontaneous, conditional vow of a parent, to be "the Lord's." Both are in a sense victim substitutes for an offering of an animal or a bird. They are both only children, and both dance. Both are the object of selfish blame, censure, condemnation, and grief from the males responsible for them. Both acquiesce without protest in their destinies in almost the same words. The virginity of both is an issue: Jephthah's daughter bewails hers; Mary's is prized and acclaimed. The virginity of both is also permanent and is understood negatively, from a male point of view, as not having known (had sex with) a man, rather than from a female point of view, as belonging to oneself. Both daughters have female companions, and the Spirit plays a role in both stories. Both girls are remembered and memorialized for generations, one bewailed and one magnified. In Judges 11, a daughter dies for her father's unfaithful, foolish vow, and the silent deity accepts her death; in *Proto-James*, a daughter is vowed to virginity by her mother, and the silent deity—through the virginal conception—approves the vow. The life of the one is taken, as are the autonomy and sexual capacities and pleasures of the other. Finally, Judges 11 suppresses details about the sacrifice, making it possible for the reader to overlook its horror; *Proto-James* almost erases the very notion of sacrifice, making it possible for the reader to overlook this as essential to the story.

REAL WOMEN AND GIRLS:
THE CULTURAL USES OF THE TEXT

In the second and third centuries C.E. Christian women were attracted in astonishing numbers by a life of continence and virginity. Already in Corinth in the mid-first century there existed a movement of considerable proportions of unmarried women and virgins "consecrated both in body and spirit" (1 Cor 7:34). Improvement of economic circumstances and the conscious desire to avoid marriages and pregnancies forced on them are not full explanations of the enthusiasm with which these women chose the ascetic life. Their choice is better understood as an attempt to preserve—at a tremendously high price—a measure of the egalitarian promise, freedom, and friendship of the Jesus movement. As women informally designed it, this life-style involved participation in public life rather than withdrawal; flexibility, freedom, and self-determination rather than restriction and submission; the desire to avoid relations involving male domination rather than to avoid "pollution" or "impurity." Most importantly, chastity was also widely understood as a condition of female prophecy and concentrated prayer.[7] Why and by whom this connection was made is not yet clear.

Before the development of Christian monastic communities, virgins lived with their parents at home or in small groups, or with continent men in spiritual marriages, a practice that began to be condemned in the late third century. Gradually, male theory developed to react to, explain, and promote some aspects of the female ascetic life-style and prohibit others, and gradually women who chose it came under male control and interpretation, excluded from official ecclesiastical power. In the fourth century, asceticism flowered, Mariology developed, and virginity was praised as a new form of martyrdom. Male power was exercised through the power to define women's sexuality.

How is *Proto-James* to be understood within this sociohistorical context? What impact did it have on the lives of early Christian women, and to what extent does it reflect their lives? Were the characters Anna and the virgin Mary presented as models for Christian mothers and daughters? Or are they modeled on such women? Was Mary's relationship with the widower Joseph seen as exemplary?

It is necessary here to distinguish between the author's intentions and the work's effect. The main intention, I think, was to counter polemic; the long-range effect was to foster male regulation of female virgins. The author of *Proto-James* appears to be so obsessively focused on "proving" the virginal conception that little thought is given to the implications of this idea for the lives of real women and girls. We do not find here themes common to works that promote virginity: of virginity as liberation, empowerment, independence; ideal of apatheia; mistrust of all flesh; denigration of marriage and childbearing; misogyny. Anna and Joakim's marriage, and Joseph's previous marriage coexist peacefully in this work with the fate of Mary as virgin mother.

The ascetic movement of the early Christian centuries was not founded on the idea of the virginal conception, nor in the beginning deeply influenced by it. Nor were ascetic and encratitic tendencies in the church, along with an interest in a mother figure, the most important roots of this Mariological development. It seems rather to be a tributary that flows later into the complex ideology of virginity, part of the process of patriarchalization of female asceticism. Not until the fourth century does Mary's childbirth clearly give meaning to the chastity of the ascetics: female virgins are urged to imitate Mary by becoming mothers of Christ in their spiritual fecundity, the only way women can conceive without being dependent on the will of men (Gregory of Nyssa [330–395]). In the later church, this last thought is officially forgotten, as the symbol of the Virgin Mary functions in part to promote ecclesiastical control of female virgins, thought of as "married" to God or Christ, represented by the male clergy. How this symbol functioned as an ascetic ideal for women in the church, early and late, remains to be explored.

Changes made in the story in its retelling in the sixth century *Pseudo-Matthew* do, however, promote the ideal of celibacy or virginity for a later audience of real women and girls. Virginity is said to be Mary's free choice, preferred to marriage. In chapter 6,[8] Abiathar the priest offers the other priests boundless gifts if Mary will marry his son; but she refuses on her own, saying that she has vowed perpetual virginity and that God is adored above all in chastity. In later accretions to the legend, Mary as a three-year-old confides to her mother that her deepest, secret desire is to go up to the Temple and serve her God alone (the theme of a hymn for the November 21 feast of "Little Mary," sung in many convent schools prior to Vatican II). In *Pseudo-Matthew,* a "sodality" of five Temple virgins accompanies Mary when she goes to live with Joseph; in jealous jest, they give her the title "Queen of Virgins," which is confirmed by an angel as true prophecy. The crude stress in *Proto-James* on the mechanics of virginal conception is no longer of interest: the annunciation to Mary omits Mary's question to Gabriel about the how of her pregnancy, as well as Gabriel's response about the Holy Spirit; Salome's finger has been edited out of the testing scene. In a post-polemics period, when the belief in the virginal conception has won the day, the constricted life of Mary is urged as the model for female ascetics.

CONCLUSIONS AND QUESTIONS

These dense and disturbing works are difficult to read as a woman: so much protection, isolation, absence of choice and of sexual pleasure, so much male control of women. Moreover, it is by her mother's vow that the child is "enclosed in sacred space."[9] *Proto-James* was powerfully successful in blotting out alternative readings of the Christian Testament infancy narratives and the illegitimacy tradition that lies behind them, and powerfully influential in circumscribing the lives of Christian women.

This story should not be ignored. It depicts restrictive aspects of the lives of millions of women on our globe even today, women whose lives are hemmed in, hounded and bullied by traditions and customs not of their making, women glorified but denied equality. At the same time, the story of the spinster Virgin Mary has been and can be read as supporting a woman's right or calling to be consecrated, the right not to marry, not to have children, not to have male-dominated heterosexual relations, not to live a life focused on the needs of men. Never, however, the right not to mother. It is important that women and men explore the history and ramifications of these ideas and beliefs, and decide what if anything speaks to them of themselves and of God. Especially is this urgent in traditions such as Roman Catholicism, which still preserve the option of the consecrated life but in an androcentric context, without female leadership and autonomy. My own experience has been of the difficulty of articulating and living an authentic life in that context, but also of something nurtured enough to struggle toward new freedoms and responsibilities.

The belief in a virginal conception of Jesus by Mary has been interpreted as part of the church's quest for self-definition over against (1) a Jewish reading of Christian Testament texts, (2) Jewish polemic, and (3) Greek ideas of virginity. In the Greek tradition, Christians found a context in which to situate the birth of the son of God.[10] Salome can be seen to represent the unbelieving Jew. This whole process needs now to be pondered in the light of new readings, especially those which take into account male violence and its cover-ups, female pain and strength, and the liberation movements of antiquity, the forces that suppressed them, and their contemporary power. These new readings will, it is hoped, foster a new story, of the woman who conceives herself.

NOTES

1. Julia Kristeva, *Tales of Love* (New York: Columbia University Press, 1987), 237.

2. Compare M. E. Enslin, "The Christian Stories of the Nativity," *Journal of Biblical Literature* 59 (1940): 317–38.

3. E. de Strycker, *La Forme la plus ancienne du Protévangile de Jacques* (Subsidia hagiographica 33; Brussels: Bollandistes, 1961); O. Cullmann, "Infancy Gospels: The Protevangelium of James," in *New Testament Apocrypha*, ed. E. Hennecke and W. Schneemelcher (Philadelphia: Westminster, 1964), 1:363–88; H. R. Smid, *Protevangelium Jacobi: A Commentary* (Cambridge, MA: Harvard University Press, 1965).

4. Smid, *Protevangelium Jacobi*, 140.

5. Giulia Sissa, *Greek Virginity* (Cambridge, MA: Harvard University Press, 1990), 174.

6. Contrast the opinion of Jo Ann McNamara that this work, like the *Apocryphal Acts of the Apostles,* comes from the circles of consecrated women of the second century (*A New Song* [New York: Harrington Park, 1985], 79–81).

7. Antoinette Clark Wire, *The Corinthian Women Prophets: A Reconstruction through Paul's Rhetoric* (Minneapolis: Fortress, 1990), 72–97.

8. Jan Gijsel, *Die Unmittelbare Textüberlieferung des sog. Pseudo-Matthäus* (Brussels: Paleis der Academien, 1981).

9. P. Brown, *The Body and Society* (New York: Columbia University Press, 1988), 273.

10. See Sissa, *Greek Virginity*.

RECOMMENDED READINGS

Castelli, Elizabeth. "Virginity and Its Meaning for Women's Sexuality in Early Christianity." *Journal of Feminist Studies in Religion* 2 (1986): 61–88.

Cullmann, O. "Infancy Gospels: The Protevangelium of James." In *New Testament Apocrypha,* edited by E. Hennecke and W. Schneemelcher, 1:363–88. Philadelphia: Westminster, 1963.

de Strycker, E. *La Forme la plus ancienne du Protevangile de Jacques.* Subsidia hagiographica 33. Brussels: Bollandistes, 1961.

Evangelia Apocrypha. Edited by C. de Tischendorf. Leipzig: Hermann Mendelssohn, 1876.

Gijsel, Jan. *Die Unmittelbare Textüberlieferung des sog. Pseudo-Matthaus.* Brussels: Paleis der Academien, 1981.

Papyrus Bodmer V, Nativité de Marie. Edited by M. Testuz. Cologne and Geneva: Bibliothèque Bodmer, 1958.

Schaberg, J. *The Illegitimacy of Jesus: A Feminist Theological Interpretation of the New Testament Infancy Narratives.* New York: Crossroad, 1990.

Sissa, Giulia. *Greek Virginity.* Cambridge, MA: Harvard University Press, 1990.

Smid, H. R. *Protevangelium Jacobi: A Commentary.* Assen: Van Gorcum, 1965.

Wire, Antoinette Clark. *The Corinthian Women Prophets: A Reconstruction through Paul's Rhetoric.* Minneapolis: Fortress, 1990.

The Gospel of Luke

TURID KARLSEN SEIM ◆

IT HAS BEEN ONE of the common truths of Christian Testament scholarship that Luke shows a particular interest in women.[1] Most relate this to the author's broader concern for the poor and the outcast, and some see it as an expression of his universalism. But the presence of women in Luke could also be an example of his emphasis on the success the Christian preaching had among the noble and well-off, since many of the women appear, in various ways, to be relatively resourceful.

Compared with other Christian Testament writings, the Gospel according to Luke contains more material about women. Most of this is in the specifically Lukan material. Since the material peculiar to Luke is so rich in traditions about women, it is all the more striking that the proportion of such material in Acts is much smaller than in the Gospel. This difference between the two volumes corresponds to a remarkable divergence in the present perception regarding the treatment of women by Luke: Is Luke within the Christian Testament corpus a rare friend of women reflecting equality and a radical revision of the role of women in the early church? Or is his major contribution to impose "the Lukan silence," representing a programmatic androcentrism that pleads the subordination of women in a more subtle and indirect manner than the direct parenetic enforcement of the letters? These are the extreme positions of an ambiguity that seems to be intrinsic to the Lukan construction in itself.

Luke's presentation is not a systematic treatise but a narrative. It tells a story and indicates a development by placing events in a certain sequence. This very simple fact has significant consequences for understanding the Lukan construction. Events, persons, and sayings receive meaning from their location and function in the sequence of the narrative. The order is therefore not arbitrary, and the location (or indeed relocation) of varying traditions in a narrative sequence can be an effective means of dealing with tensions and contradictions. This means that pieces cannot be picked from anyplace in the work and brought together to form a stable and unambiguous "Lukan" position. It may be that Luke has no coherent view of women. The narrative cannot be reduced to one fixed scene; it represents a complex movement and process. The narrative is in a special way a polyphony: it allows several and even contrapuntal voices to be heard in the course of events.

What follows is mainly an attempt at "reading Luke" while discerning patterns of gender in the Lukan composition. It is not a supplementary enterprise adding Luke's view of "woman" to a list of Lukan themes to make it more complete. By overcoming the gender blindness of most traditional studies and applying gender as an analytical category, interpreters are able to make women visible, which has a further effect in tracing patterns of gender as they develop in the story. It is like trying to discern in a weaving one of the warping threads through which the shuttle is pulled. In some places it may be more easily discerned than in others.

Gender, conceived as an analytical constant, has a biological basis in the fact that humans exist as women or men. But the difference between the sexes is further articulated in terms of culture and location in time and space. Gender differentiation and relationship will, no matter how they vary in their expressions, always have an all-embracing structural significance. In this widened feminist perspective it is necessary to investigate how differences and mutual dependence, sexual interplay and power structures are conceived. What follows is an attempt to make such an investigation in the case of Luke—still with special attention to the particular role of women.

My reading of Luke tries to understand the Lukan construction and does not aim at the reconstruction of another story or subtext using the Lukan text as a pretext. For the most part it ignores the history behind the Lukan screen and concentrates on the given text. This approach may, of course, be seen as lacking a certain feminist suspicion, but the rationale behind it is the wish and the need to see the full construction before deconstruction and reconstruction can take place. Therefore it may in the end, nevertheless, contribute to the further project of feminist rereadings of the story of Christian origins.

GENDER PAIRS: INCLUSIVENESS
AND SEGREGATION

It has long been recognized that Luke has a tendency in his composition to generate doublets and parallels, and part of this parallel material is recognized as "gender pairs." These are not distributed in such a way that they can be attributed to or explained as deriving from a particular source.

As epic or narrative gender pairs (also as included in discourse material) the following should be identified:

Zechariah	Mary	Luke 1:11–20/26–38; 46–55/67–79
Simeon	Hannah	Luke 2:25–35/36–38
Naaman	Widow in Zarephath	Luke 4:27/25–26
Jairus's daughter	Widow's son	Luke 8:40–56/7:11–17
Jairus	Woman with issue of blood	Luke 8:40–41, 49–56/43–48
Men of Nineveh	Queen of Sheba	Luke 11:32/31
Man healed on sabbath	Woman healed on sabbath	Luke 14:1–6/13:10–17
Abraham's son	Abraham's daughter	Luke 19:9/13:16
Man sowed a seed	Woman hid yeast	Luke 13:18–19/20–21
Shepherd with sheep	Woman with coins	Luke 15:3–7/8–10
Men sleeping	Women grinding	Luke 17:34/35
Peter at tomb	Women at tomb	Luke 24:12/1–11

These epic pairs correspond to an explicit gender specification in many group and audience descriptions. Although the epic pairs are virtually nonexistent in Acts, there is some evidence for these coupled references. The double message in the parallel examples of women and men functions as an epic rejoinder to the description of the composition of the social group to whom the epic material is addressed or belongs. We are repeatedly informed that among those who follow Jesus (Luke 8:1–3; 23:49), are both women and men. The same applies almost stereotypically to the early communities of believers (Acts 1:13f.; 2:17f.; 8:3, 12; 9:2; 18:1–4; 21:8; 22:4), as well as various groups of audience (Acts 17:4, 12, 34; 24:24; 25:12, 23; 26:30). Apart from an instance in Acts 21:5 women are not simply added to strengthen the significance or magnitude of what occurs, as, for example, when Matthew, in the context of the multiplication of the loaves, adds "women and children" (14:21) to render the miracle even more spectacular. In these cases, the coupled combination is not "women and men," but the conventional pairing of "women and children," bearing the connotation of members of a minority and auxiliaries.

The gender-specified duality serves to include women in an explicit way. The presence of women is recognized even in contexts where a masculine terminology otherwise dominates, but the gender specification also serves to identify distance and segregation. Women and men belong to the same community; they are united by common rituals and live together in mutual material dependence. At the same time, men and women form groups of their own. This comes out very clearly when individual persons are given prominence on some occasions by being named. Luke then most often notes that they represent a larger group—so that the women named are referred to a group of women (Luke 8:2f.; 24:10) and the men to a group of men (Luke 8:51). The community has inherent patterns of an organizational structure of gender division. A woman belongs to the larger community of faith primarily among the women, a man primarily among the men. This means that the whole community consists not primarily of individual members but of the group of men as well as the group of women.

There is no clear hierarchical order between the two groups. In the examples of the gender pairs, the rank of order is not consistent. Sometimes the example of the man comes first, and sometimes the example of the woman. Twice the grammatical construction emphasizes that the women constitute the core group of all those present. When compared with the earlier version in Mark, Luke's scene of the crucifixion (Luke 23:49) also names as present "all his aquaintances." This need not involve a minimalizing of the women's importance; it is rather an expression of the more general pattern of gender pairs, which has the effect in other passages of introducing a group of women (cf. Luke 8:1–3). It may also be that the linking "and" in Luke 23:27 and 49 has an emphatic meaning, so that the women in these cases are seen as special representatives of the greater group.

It is commonly assumed that the Lukan doublets are based on Jewish demands about the number of witnesses needed for their testimony to be considered trustworthy. As a guiding principle of composition, it should serve to strengthen the credibility of the account. But the epic gender pairs can only indirectly have any value as testimonials, and Luke's dealing with the credibility of women's testimony elsewhere is at best ambivalent. In keeping with this, messengers in Luke-Acts are often characterized explicitly as men, whether heavenly or earthly, and these men often appear in a group of at least two (see Luke 24:4; Acts 1:10; 9:38; 10:19f.; 15:22). In all these cases, the men's mission has the desired effect. On the few occasions on which women come with a message, they are not believed (Luke 24:10f. and Acts 12:14f.)—at least not by the group of men. The gender pairs in Luke cannot be explained simply as expressing a motif of "dual witness"—that is, in the traditional understanding of a minimum attestation of two witnesses in order to be able to claim credibility. Nevertheless, a dual witnessing in the sense of a duplication of testimonials to address an audience composed of men and women is still meaningful. It may be a literary device by which the author seeks to capture the attention of a mixed audience.

All the stories are integrated into one common text addressed to the whole of the community, but in the community the women were primarily named with the other women and the men with the other men. Despite the emphasis on a communal life, Luke-Acts mediates a picture of a world divided by gender, of a culture and a mediation of tradition in which men and women within the same community keep each to their own sphere of life.

THE FAMILY OF JESUS

The pattern described above reflects a social system that, unlike our own, is focused collectively, not individually. The individual finds identity in her or his family or group. For the disciples of Jesus, who pay the cost of discipleship and sometimes leave (most of) their families behind, the flock of disciples represents a replacement. The disciples gain a fictive family relationship, the family of Jesus, with God as their only Father and each other as brothers and sisters.

The idea of the community of believers as a fictive family is inherent in the Synoptic tradition, and Luke reflects its seemingly common usage in the early communities. A key text is Luke 8:19–21, where Jesus rejects an approach by his mother and his brothers. In this scene, Mary is not mentioned by name. The focus is not on her person but on her motherhood. Jesus challenges the claims of his genetic family by transferring the categories of kinship to a new group: his mother and his brothers and sisters are those who live in the same obedience as he himself does. Compared with Mark and Matthew, Luke renders the statement of Jesus in a shortened version that is more inclusive of his genetic family. The possibility is kept open that his mother and his brothers and sisters too can find their place in the new family—provided that they, without any privileges attached, fulfill the criterion of hearing God's word and doing it.

This means that the proclamation of who is truly Jesus' family is less a statement of exclusion and election and more a statement of principle. The point is not primarily to exclude Jesus' mother and brothers and sisters in favor of the others who are present, but rather to redefine and transfer kinship categories on the basis of a new set of criteria. But the use of kinship categories in Luke 8:19–21 still retains a clearly critical function in relation to the biosocial family and its demands. The new family not only surpasses the old but replaces it.

The repeated pronoun in Luke 8:21 emphasizes that the family is established primarily in relation to Jesus and only indirectly among the believers themselves. They become *his* mother and brothers (and sisters). The family relationship they receive to one another is based in their adherence to Jesus.

The Lukan text in 8:21 appears less gender specific than that of Mark and Matthew in listing the family terms. Luke contents himself with two categories, omitting the sister. This has been seen as an attempt of Luke to omit the presence of sisters generally among the disciples; only Mary, the mother, was too prominent to be avoided. But the plural form "brothers," which is employed instead of the singular form used by the other evangelists, can be read inclusively as meaning "siblings." It is also possible that the representation of women was already taken care of by means of "mother," and the point is to avoid a pleonasm while at the same time creating a verbal parallel corresponding to the presentation of Jesus' biological family in vv. 19 and 20. Moreover, the term "mother" carries greater dignity than the term "sister." It also implies the radical position that even the maternal rights that were essential to a woman's identity and honor are revoked and replaced by discipleship as the new form of motherhood.

The traditional values in a woman's life, her worth in the patriarchal process of reproduction, are thereby challenged. This is thrown into even sharper relief by an episode recounted in 11:27–28, which is peculiar to Luke. A woman in the crowd cries out to Jesus: "Blessed is the womb that bore you and the breasts that nursed you!" This is a macarism expressed in Jewish phraseology; it is in fact a blessing of Jesus and not of Mary. That is, it says that a son such as Jesus makes his mother worthy of praise. In all its poetic power the beatitude focuses solely on the mothering function of the female body: womb and breasts. Jesus reacts by subjecting this to a critical appraisal, when he corrects her and replies, "Blessed rather are those who hear the word of God and obey it!" So even Mary is blessed, not because she is Jesus' biological mother but because she hears the word of God and keeps it.

This reactivates previous remarks about Mary: not only her obedience (1:38) but also how she treasures up the words in her heart and ponders them (2:19, 51). Joseph, who is an important figure in Matthew's infancy narratives, plays a minimal role in Luke's version, and it is significant that Jesus' alienation from his family, as we have seen earlier, begins by affecting Joseph in particular (see 2:48f.). This episode is concluded by the emphatic statement that Jesus' parents did not understand the meaning of his words, but his mother kept all these words in her heart. Remarks such as this open the way for Mary's continued, but changed, role, determined by the word rather than by her rights as mother. Mary is the only person from the infancy narrative, apart from Jesus and John, who reappears in the following story and also in Acts. But it means that Mary becomes a receiver rather than a giver.

Other traits in the narratives of Jesus' infancy and birth in Luke emphasize likewise that Mary is to be understood as the exemplary disciple, a Christian prototype, through her listening obedience and her openness toward future explanation and fulfillment. Mary's obedience is not portrayed merely in passive terms: she expresses active acceptance and positive response (1:38), and further she proclaims God's wondrous acts with prophetic authority (1:46–55).

It has been claimed that the lack of an earthly father in the fictive family of disciples had the effect of de-patriarchalization and meant equality among the members of the family. If no substitute for the father was to be found among the disciples, this implicitly denied the status and power of earthly fathers.

Jesus did not use "God the Father" to justify and authorize a patriarchal order, but as a critical overthrow of all earthly structures based on domination. No brother could demand "the Father's" authority for himself, because this would be claiming a position reserved to God alone. The patriarchal structures are removed in the messianic community.

Thus, membership in the family of Jesus depended on criteria other than biological, and it was possible to reject demands and obligations laid down in bio-social terms. But even if the *patria potestas* is transferred to God alone, this does not automatically create equality between sisters and brothers. None of the family terms was neutral or conveyed equality; each had its own contents and connotations colored by a patriarchal structure in which brothers had greater worth than sisters, and in which a mother was valued according to her ability to give birth to sons. The patriarchal structure of domination and subordination is transferred to the fictive family and contributes to a patriarchal consolidation of the community of believers. The Pastoral Letters bear witness to such a development.

THE WOMEN FROM GALILEE

In the Gospel of Mark a group of female followers of Jesus appears in the crucifixion scene (Mark 15:40f.). Retrospectively we are told that they had been with him already in Galilee, but they are not explicitly mentioned until the male disciples all have fled and only the women remain to witness the death of Jesus, the burial, and the empty tomb. Luke presents the tradition about the women at the cross in a slightly modified form. Early on in the Gospel, while Jesus was still in Galilee, a group of women is presented as followers of Jesus together with the Twelve (Luke 8:1–3). This brief passage resembles the summaries and does not deal with a particular episode but comprises something that is typical and generally representative.

Like Mark, Luke mentions three of the women by name. In most of the "lists of women" in the Gospels, some of the women are named specifically in pairs (Mark 15:47; Matt 27:61; 28:1) or a group of three (Mark 15:40; 16:1; Matt 27:51; Luke 8:2f.; 24:10; John 19:25). Such a presentation of an "inner circle" within a larger group is common. The selection of three recalls corresponding selections of three male disciples elsewhere in the Gospels (Mark 5:37; 9:2; 14:33; Luke 8:51). Moreover, the sequence of the names is significant. In Luke 24:10 priority is given to the two women named first in 8:3, while the third name is left out and replaced by the second name from the Markan list. This means that the list in 24:10 includes the two most important names from each of the traditions available.

Mary of Magdala is the only woman whose name is included in all the lists, and, with the exception of John 19:25 where family ties are given priority, she also heads the lists. Her prominent position probably reflects her great prestige in many early communities and an authority comparable only to Peter's on the male side. In other words, her first place among the women listed was a univocal point in the tradition. In the Lukan text her priority seems at this point to be further justified by the fact that among all the woman healed by Jesus, her case was an extreme one with seven demons being expelled.

It is significant that none of the women who are mentioned by name receives her identity by her relationship to a man, as was the convention of naming. The connection to men's names is introduced only when it is needed to distinguish between several women with the same first name. Mary of Magdala, however, is distinguished by her place of origin. Even in the case of Joanna, the prominence given to the information that she was the wife of Chuza, the steward of Herod Antipas, primarily serves to indicate her economic and social level. It substantiates that the women had access to means of sustenance and helps to establish the function they had in the group who followed Jesus.

Since many interpreters find it inconceivable that married women could have left home and family in this way in Palestine at that period, various suggestions have been made about the real nature and status of these women. The women are claimed to have been the wives of disciples, traveling together with their husbands; or they are named as widows, divorced women, or women rejected by their husbands. One can ask, of course, whether the majority of the women in the Jesus movement originally were less well integrated into family structures than the male disciples. This would make the following of Jesus by these women less controversial—even if what is inconceivable is not necessarily impossible. This would also help to explain why the list of the costs of discipleship in Luke 14:26 and 18:29f. includes "wife," but does not mention "husband." Others dismiss this kind of speculation and answer the question exclusively in terms of a merger of various traditions. The description of the women at 8:2f. then represents a retrojection into Jesus' life of later situations from outside Palestine as we see them displayed in Acts. The historical reference is to the well-off female benefactors (patrons) in the Greco-Roman world. Luke's portrait in 8:2–3 has been colored by a later situation; the women in 8:2–3 must be related to similar female benefactors elsewhere in Luke-Acts. But the question still remains why these women from Galilee appear in the Lukan story in this way as itinerant benefactors.

THE HEALED DAUGHTERS OF ABRAHAM

The experience implied in Luke 8:2–3 combines in an exceptional manner social insecurity and exposure with autonomous management of resources. A movement from social marginalization and impurity to social integration and purity is given expression in the remark that the women had all been healed by Jesus. The tradition about all the women's sickness and healing is material peculiar to Luke. Their social marginalization as women is thereby intensified at the outset by sickness and impurity. But it is significant that the connection thus made between the experience of a wondrous act of Jesus and the calling to follow reflects a typical pattern particular to Luke.

In the Gospel a number of miracle stories relate how women are recipients of the wondrous acts of Jesus. Half of these narratives are peculiar to Luke, and half are based on Markan material. It is typical for Luke that narratives of healing often involve exorcism. Thereby the healings of Jesus are characterized more strongly as liberating acts and as part of an eschatological event. Moreover, for most of the women healing means being freed from a constant state of impurity and being resocialized into the community.

The healing of the bent woman in the synagogue on the sabbath (Luke 13:10–17) expresses that Jesus' wondrous act in setting the woman free is appropriate according to God's will because it fulfills the liberating intention of the sabbath. Jesus' controversial act toward the bent woman articulates also that "she is Abraham's daughter." Luke provides the only Christian Testament evidence of the term "daughter of Abraham," for the singular term "Abraham's son" (see 19:9). Abraham's son(s) is a traditional Jewish designation, but the feminine form is not. It has been suggested that "Abraham's daughter" might be a Lukan innovation.

But Abrahamic categories applied to a woman are found in 4 Maccabees (14:20; 15:28; 17:6; 18:20). All of these passages speak of one and the same person: an exemplary, strong, and God-fearing martyr, the mother of the seven young men. First she sees her sons undergo a cruel death at the tyrant's hands, before she herself seeks death unafraid and with courage. A dominant trait in 4 Maccabees' use of Abrahamic categories is that the persons in question, both men and women, are paragons of virtue and piety, so that the characterization is developed within the framework of a typological pattern. The woman's religious zeal with its willingness to accept sacrifice shows that she has the qualities of Abraham. There is also some scattered evidence in later Jewish sources of the use of the expression "Abraham's daughter" (*b. Ket.* 72b; *b. Giṭ.* 89a) to convey an implicit positive judgment of morality.

The formulation in Luke 13:16 is an observation of fact, not an emphatic bestowal of a designation. The woman *is* Abraham's daughter; she does not become one. It is one of the premises of the healing, not a consequence of it, but it is not a statement about great piety on the woman's part. In relation to the examples discussed above, the surprising element is not primarily the fact that a Jewish woman is called Abraham's daughter, but rather that the woman about whom this is said is not a paragon of virtue and piety. She is a woman who has been possessed by Satan for a great part of her life, and she is not given any attributes that might point to a special likeness or relationship to Abraham. Abraham plays no role as model or typological prototype.

The healing on the day of rest, which was an essential sign of the covenant, realizes her status as daughter. As a daughter of Abraham, she shares in the blessing that is promised to Abraham's progeny, and this is having a liberating effect in her life. The motif of liberation recurs in the Lukan adaptation of the Abraham traditions (Luke 1:52–53; 1:73–75; Acts 7:6–7). For Luke, Abraham is primarily the original recipient of God's election and of the promise to the fathers. The promise holds good for Abraham's progeny, and to be a child of Abraham implies both a privilege and an obligation. Thereby the need becomes urgent of defining who is truly to be counted among Abraham's children. Unlike Paul, who also struggles with this question, Luke neither engages in polemic against circumcision nor spiritualizes it. It seems rather that circumcision no longer plays a decisive role in the definition of membership among Abraham's children. Already in the initial phase of the Gospel, in the concluding lines of Mary's hymn of praise (1:54f.), reference is made to God's promise "to Abraham and to his descendants" and God's fidelity to this promise. Through her hymn of praise, the pregnant Mary gives a prophetic interpretation of the significance of her child. She predicts that the covenantal promise will be fulfilled radically in Jesus' life for the existing progeny of Abraham. The hymn makes it clear that the promise is fulfilled by means of a total social transformation, and when Abraham is mentioned later on, it is in connection with drastic and surprising reversals of inside and outside groups, as it happens in Luke 3:8; 13:28; 16:22–31 (and 13:16; 19:9). These individual examples thus take on the character of a concretization of salvation history.

With only one exception (Acts 13:26), Luke uses terms inclusive to both women and men when speaking of Abraham's progeny. This corresponds to the emphasis that the reestablished people of God comprises men as well as women (Acts 5:14; 8:3, 12; 9:2, 36ff.; cf. also 1:13f. and 12:12). In Acts 2:15–21, the outpouring of the Spirit is interpreted on the basis of Joel 3:1–5 with the promise that "your daughters" too shall prophesy. This is a major point of reference for the usage of the term "daughter" in Luke—with a certain, though not explicit, reference to the Abraham tradition. When Jesus addresses the woman with the hemorrhage in Luke 8:48 with a dismissal formula echoing the liturgy, this expresses more than a personal and intimate form of address. The term "peace" and the allusion to being saved mark the woman's share in salvation and her membership in God's people. This case too has the character of reversal and change, and of a surprising overcoming of alienating distance.

Thus, it is noteworthy that both of the women who are called (Abraham's) daughters are sick, socially stigmatized, and impure. Impure persons were normally regarded as a threat to the collective purity of the people. This was why the question of purity was a matter of fundamental social and religious importance. The only man in the Gospel to be called Abraham's son is the tax collector Zacchaeus (19:9). He is presented as a superintendent of taxes and very rich, and we are told plainly that he was held to be a sinful man with whom there should be no social contact. Jesus reaffirms that the tax collector Zacchaeus is a son of Abraham and is therefore heir to the promise of salvation. Thus, Jesus reinstates Zacchaeus as a true Jew, in opposition to the general opinion of him as an alienated sinner. These acts of Jesus suggest a universalist potential; but though Israel's boundaries are stretched wide, they are not broken through. In Luke non-Jews are never called Abraham's children, as they are in Paul. Israel remains the chosen people of God, Abraham's progeny, even if this Israel is differently qualified.

On the whole, the role of the women in the miracle stories remains remarkably respectful to common conventions regarding women's behavior. Women are characterized as passive partners, as persons who receive without any antecedent prayer or recommendation on their own part. A comparison of parallel narratives about men and women makes this very clear.

The distinguished Jairus appeals very humbly but still directly to Jesus and begs him to come to his home (Luke 8:41). The woman with the hemorrhage does indeed reach out to get help for herself, but she comes under the cover of the crowd of the people, hidden and approaching Jesus from behind, fearful and afraid. The dramatic interweaving of the two narratives plays on a whole set of contrasts between the synagogue president Jairus and the impoverished and impure woman. They are also played off against each other when the woman with the hemorrhage becomes the cause of Jesus' delay on the way to Jairus's dying daughter. A similar contrast is found between Jairus and the widow in Nain. Both have an only daughter (8:42) or son (7:12) called back to life. Jesus raises up Jairus's twelve-year-old daughter, who is of marriageable age, and the widow's son, who provides for her. But whereas Jairus himself takes the initiative for this to happen and comes to fetch Jesus with his request, the widow is quite simply seen by Jesus and awakens his compassion.

There may be several reasons for Luke's omission of the narrative about the Syrophoenician woman (Mark 7:24–30). Assuming that Luke did know the story from Mark, it is not impossible that Luke saw the woman's quick-witted insistence as "out of order." As she is described in Mark, she is a capable, argumentative variant of Jairus, and she would be an excellent parallel to the Gentile officer at Capernaum (Luke 7:1–10). Instead, the latter is placed next to the widow in Nain, who needs her son to be alive and is the passive object of Jesus' compassion. The coupling of these two narratives also corresponds to the parallel examples of Elijah and Elisha, to which Jesus refers in his speech in Nazareth (Luke 4:24–27).

The women lay claim to no rights. It is Jesus who sovereignly acknowledges that they have rights, and this is accompanied by a dramatic, healing alteration in their lives. Salvation has come to them. An exception is the "sinful woman" who anoints Jesus (Luke 7:36–50) in sovereign disdain of all norms for respectable conduct. Otherwise the women do not approach Jesus openly and directly with their request for help. Their appeals are indirect: others ask for help on their behalf (Luke 4:48), or they hide themselves in the crowd (Luke 8:43). Thus, an obvious respect is retained for rules of public decency that made it improper for women to address a(n unknown) man. The message of liberation is expressed with due consideration to possible public offense.

THE WOMEN FROM GALILEE
AND THE RHETORIC OF SERVICE

Implicit in the motif of healing is a christological motivation of service. The benefaction by Jesus is given a response in the women's consequent benefactory activity. Peter's mother-in-law demonstrates her recovered health when she immediately rises and serves them (Luke 4:38f.). Some textual witnesses alter the plural "them" in v. 39 to a singular "him," as also in Luke 8:3. The singular, however, is a harmonizing reading under the influence of the parallel passage in Matt 8:15 and possibly also of Mark 15:40. The singular form would give a christological focus and would also enhance the impression that the woman's service would be a repayment she makes according to a customary pattern of reciprocity. The plural form tones this down. Jesus becomes the benefactor who, rather than ensuring repayments in kind for himself, creates benefactors for the larger group.

Luke frequently uses terms with the root *diakon-*, which means "to serve someone" (see 4:39; 10:40; 12:37; 17:8; 22:26f.). Although this can have a more general reference, it tends to be linked to meals and food. Meals in antiquity were subject to a strict hierarchical regulation, both regarding places at table and regarding the distribution of tasks. In a Jewish context it might be that if the person one served was worthy of honor, the service itself was also a matter of prestige. But in general the social associations of service were negative: service was a task of a lowly status. The preparation and serving of food were traditionally a woman's responsibility, unless slaves took care of it. The one who waited at table was always the one with the lowest place in the household. Since most families did not have house slaves, especially in Palestine, the task fell to the women of the family. In Luke, women are those preparing and providing the meals both in the narrative about Peter's mother-in-law and in the case of Martha (10:40). At the same time, Luke does refer to servants (see

12:35ff.; 17:7ff.), although these slaves may have been women (cf. Rhoda in Acts 12:13).

This was an area of life in which customs varied. It revealed tension between tasks assigned according to gender and status, and norms of propriety, which implied a certain segregation. The extent to which the women served at table when the household entertained guests varied depending on religious norms, ideals of propriety, and cultural and social location. While women did have the responsibility for the preparation of the food, they did not always serve at table, because they then had to appear in front of strangers. Sometimes under cramped conditions this was unavoidable, but the women did not themselves take part in the meal—although this could happen among the more aristocratic and well-off. (In later rabbinic material, social conventions forbid women to wait on any men other than their own husbands.)

According to Luke 8:3 the group of women "serve" Jesus and the Twelve. This seems to confirm that the role of waiting on others is theirs. The role of the women remains the same; only the recipients have changed. Those on whom they wait are no longer the men in their physical family, but the brethren in the fictive kinship community in the flock of disciples. In this passage Luke links the women's service to their property. He diverts attention from the relationship to Jesus in the description and the terminology of discipleship in Mark 15:40f. The women are no longer seen as disciples but are directed to a special function of care that is determined in material terms. The parallel to Peter's mother-in-law is clear, and despite a certain expansion of meaning when compared to 4:39, the service of the women in 8:3 retains a primary association of food and physical care.

The women take care of the material needs of the group; they provide the basic sustenance for Jesus and those who follow him, having left everything behind. The women's use of their property permits the group around Jesus to be free of concern about what they will eat or what they will wear (Luke 12:22, 30–34). The costs of discipleship are covered by the new community, the new family (Luke 14:26ff.; 18:28ff.). This is in keeping with Luke's view of the family as an economic unit. This is why most family-related activities are aimed at pooling resources and at the distribution of food, possessions, and work. This distribution is the primary expression of the relationship between the members of the family.

By serving from their own resources in order to cover the needs of the others, the women from Galilee are portrayed as prototypes of an ethos that is to be valid universally among the people of God. In many places Luke voices a demand/ideal of giving up possessions and property to the benefit of the community (see Luke 12:13–14; 14:33; 18:18–30; 19:1–10; Acts 4:35–37; 5:1–11). This is not an ideal of poverty but a model of radical redistribution. Through the realization of property, almsgiving and an organized distribution of means, the community is able to meet the basic and legitimate needs of all in God's family for food, clothing, and a place to sleep.

The widow by the treasure chest in the Temple (Luke 21:1−4), who makes available all that she has is perhaps the most dramatic example. The widow puts in what she has: she risks her life. Some scholars interpret 8:3 in a parenetic sense: rich women in the community are called by the example of the women who followed Jesus to serve with their property. The women in 8:3, through their continuous contributions of property, implement the ideal that disciples, whether they possess much or little, shall renounce without reserve what belongs to them in order to meet the needs of the others, so that no one suffers from indigence.

The women's service often seems to be connected with a certain prosperity to which they themselves had access. The expression "out of their resources" in 8:3 also presupposes that the women had means of their own, even if it does not necessarily imply that they were all equally well-off. Roman law in this period allowed women to inherit and to own and manage their own property. Many women had means at their own disposal. Even if the legislation in the Greek and Jewish contexts was stricter, a relaxation occurred in the Hellenistic period that permitted women a certain right to own property. The majority of women had their lives filled and limited by domestic obligations, but there are also many examples in antiquity of professionally active women. Some women were economically self-supporting. This was true not only of slave women, who had no choice but to work, or for small farms in the countryside, which demanded the work of the whole family. The women in question were not especially rich, or particularly poor. Some worked in family businesses or workshops (cf. Priscilla, who operated a tent-making business together with Aquila [Acts 18:3]). Otherwise, women tended to work in professions that were a natural continuation of their domestic duties and were concerned with food, fabrics and clothes, health and comfort (cf. Lydia, who dealt in purple cloth [Acts 16:14]). This means that they were active in small trade, in service industries, and as doctors and midwives. These women not only contributed to the daily maintenance of the family but were also able to lay by some reserves for themselves.

Women with means could function as financial benefactors for public and religious projects and for various kinds of groups and associations. Through their patronage they were able to acquire an influence that was otherwise formally denied them in public life. This was also the case for the early Christian communities, which included a considerable number of rich (and high-standing) women. Luke gives a pertinent picture of such women, who kept house for the community: Martha in Luke 10:38−42; Tabitha in Acts 9:36ff.; Mary the mother of John in Acts 12:12; Lydia in Acts 16:15, 40; and also Priscilla in Acts 18.

It is not clear what this patronage further involved. Beyond doubt, the women who were materially able to accommodate the community in their houses had thereby also power and influence. But it is uncertain whether a status as patron/ess implied a formal directive authority. Some scholars insist that the patronesses had regular functions of leadership in communities that bore an egalitarian stamp. It is also claimed that *diakon-* terms are technical terms for this leadership of house-churches and that the terminology is due to the fact that the responsibility for the community's Eucharist and for the common meal as well as for preaching was assigned to these householders. But it is difficult to establish with certainty that the status of benefactors and patrons also involved institutional positions of leadership, and there are no texts that clearly couple such functions specifically with the *diakonia-* terms or with responsibility for the meal. Phoebe was a deacon of the church at Cenchreae, but we are not told whether she had a community in her house. Indeed, some texts seem to indicate the opposite: those providing the material means were not the ones to direct the redistribution of these. Redistribution was entrusted to leaders who themselves lacked personal possessions and who were chosen either by virtue of charismatic endowment or through a more institutional election. This does not, of course, exclude female patrons' having dominant positions, especially if a patron also had the community in her house. Nor does it exclude the communities' having female leaders. The point is simply that there was not an immediate connection between the status of patron and the formal function of leadership (where that existed), and there is no convincing terminological evidence that *diakonia* was especially associated with this kind of leadership.

Whether the women are on the road with Jesus or stay in the house that he/the company visits, they fulfill the same function: their service represents a basis of sustenance for Jesus and those who follow him. The description of the women in 8:2f. is not to be explained simply against the background of the patronate. Here various traits are combined in a condensed manner: the new healed life and the women's share in the social abandonment involved in the Jesus-movement, and the service, sharing, and benefactory activity of rich women.

The women's service thus transcends the specific framework of the meal—although Luke still emphasizes the practical and material character of the term. But even scholars who agree on this point draw very dissimilar conclusions from it. For example, very different assessments have been given of the extent to which the women's service as described in Luke represents a step forward or a step backward in relation to earlier praxis; this depends on the background against which the Gospel of Luke is read. Some presuppose a background in a strict patriarchal setting in Palestine and claim that the service of the women in the Gospel stories means that women are given access to tasks from which they were traditionally excluded because the recipients were outside the family. The social provocation lies not in what the women are doing but in where and whom they serve. On the one hand, the radical offense given by the presence and the tasks of the women who followed Jesus is emphasized; on the other hand, there is an edificatory and comforting confirmation of the women's task as exclusively confined to charitable activity.

Feminist readings have reconstructed a story of early Christian communities and missionary activity in which women played an active role in proclamation, worship, and leadership. The "waiting at tables" (*diakonia*) expresses leadership exercised at the common meal including the celebration of the Eucharist, and to perform this service in the community represented a natural continuation of the traditional tasks for women. In this perspective, Lukan texts that refer the task of preparing or distributing food to a male leadership (Luke 9:13; 22:7ff.; Acts 6:1–6) are to be seen primarily as suppressing the mention of the women and overruling the role they actually played. Luke's construction is seen as an attempt to limit the activity of women to areas that were less provocative socially than proclamation and leadership. Luke reduces the women to benefactors, subordinate to the spiritual authority and leadership of men.

The two interpretations outlined above may differ widely in their approach and preferences, but in both cases a distinction is at work between a function of caring, especially appropriate for women to undertake, and a male function of proclamation and teaching, represented by Jesus and the Twelve. Luke 8:1–3 may well give a positive description of women's service but mainly attests a differentiation of tasks according to gender. To proceed further, a closer view of the transfer and alternation of role patterns in the story of Luke is needed.

It is possible to discern in Luke's terminology a transfer of *diakon-* terms. In the first part of the Gospel this term occurs exclusively as a description of how women quite simply behave, before it shifts to the master–servant relationship in the two parables in Luke 17. Here a motif of role reversal is introduced. In Jesus' testament to the Twelve at the Last Supper in Luke 22 this is further developed to an instruction for the leaders of the people of God with Jesus himself as the model—the more so as he actually is serving them at this particular meal. In the case of the women, service needs no particular justification. It is only when the role of servant is presented as an ideal for free men and rulers that it requires a specific and christological warrant.

The christological mediation of service bestows a new significance and dignity on the role of service as it first was carried out by the women. The women's service acquires exemplary value for the leadership function as it should be exercised by the new leadership in the people of God. The most humble in status according to the patriarchal system were exalted as models and thereby the claim to power and domination over others is challenged. This is even more emphatically expressed in conflictual juxtapositions with those who claim leadership but who are rich and false. "Do you see this woman?" Jesus says to the Pharisee in Luke 7:44. "This woman" is the local prostitute whose lavishing service makes the Pharisee's hospitality seem full of omissions and defective—no matter whether the failures in providing service with which the Pharisee is reproached go beyond what one could expect to be included by usual hospitality. It is also clear that for some of the services mentioned it would indeed have been the host's duty to see that they were offered, but it would have been the servant's duty to carry them out. The woman therefore does not take on the host's role, but by performing a serving task she, the despised one, represents a corrective over against his leading role as host.

The widow in Luke 21:1–4 is placed in a double contrast. She is contrasted both with the hypocritical scribes and with the rich, who merely give out of their superabundance an amount that they themselves hardly notice. By means of what she does in giving what little she has, the failures of the rich rulers are exposed.

However, although the women and their traditional role are idealized, the women are excluded from actual positions of leadership. Contrary to what has often been said about Luke 22:24–27, Luke does not advocate a reversal of roles. That would imply that the servants now are to rule. What takes place is a corrective and paradoxical merger of two traditionally opposite roles, the role of woman/servant and the role of ruler. The leaders are to enter into functions of service that would not normally be indicated by their status. They are "to be *like* the one who serves."

The terminology moves from a concrete and direct use based on the experience of service to a metaphorical or rhetorical use based on the privilege of leadership. The development of a leadership rhetoric of service is clearly to be followed in the early part of Acts (Acts 1:17, 25 and, especially, 6:1–7). The argument resulting in the naming of the seven plays with various *diakon-* terms in a way that shows that at this stage they are not fixed terms but a certain mode of speech. No matter what task the leading men undertake, it is to be called "service."

The leaders as recognized by Luke are all men. It is even so that an explicit criterion of gender is introduced in Acts to exclude women from the possibility of being elected to the service of leadership, whether of the Word or of the table. Both the new apostle after Judas (Acts 1:21) and the Seven (Acts 6:3) should be elected from among the men. Is this introduction of a criterion of maleness an extreme expression of an androcentric mind? If so, why is the point made at all? It is, of course, probable that according to the preserved lists of names, both the Twelve and the Seven were men. But in the society at the time that was no sensation. So why does it need an explicit warrant? Could it be that the positive and vigorous presentation of women in the Gospel makes it necessary to give a particular justification for the fact that they were not among those named as leaders of the Jerusalem community? There is a certain irony to this: those who de facto serve are not considered eligible for the service of leadership. The reversal not of roles but of role values coincides with and justifies a masculinization— from serving women to lords who are to be "*as* one who serves."

THE REST IS SILENCE

In Luke 10:38–42 Jesus visits two sisters, Martha and Mary. Martha with her serving activity is set in contrast to her sister Mary, who listens in silence at the feet of the Lord. The two sisters are cast in roles that, without becoming caricatures, are almost stereotypes. This has encouraged interpretations of the two women primarily as symbols of various attitudes, forms of life or theological principles: for example, righteousness by works against righteousness by faith; Judaism against Christianity; the *vita activa* against the *vita contemplativa*; and so on. Not only do interpretations like this set aside any historical or literary understanding; they are also blind to the gender perspective.

Martha is the hostess who welcomes Jesus in her own home and provides whatever hospitality is required. This text is probably the oldest evidence of the Aramaic name Martha, a feminine form of *mar,* which means sovereign lady, ruling lady. In many ways, Martha is representative of a typical female figure in Luke-Acts. She is one of the number of relatively well-off and independent women who keep their own house and place it at the disposition of the community or of itinerant preachers.

Martha's role is repeatedly characterized by *diakon-* terminology in v. 40. Attempts to read the narrative in Luke 10:38–42 on a reconstructed subtext presupposing that its special and primary aim on Luke's part was to contest Martha's role of diaconal leadership, contain a number of sharp insights, especially into the portrait of Mary. But they are based on assumptions of a widespread and almost technical use of the *diakon-* terms, which is not well attested.

In the story, Martha plays the active role that drives the narrative forward; seen in this regard, she is the protagonist. Her activity is emphasized with vivid words, and her own words are related in direct speech, when she rebukes her sister's lack of practical activity. Mary's role in Luke 10:38-42 is passive; contrary to the active and outspoken Martha she listens in silence. Mary sitting at the Lord's feet and listening to his words is portrayed in the typical position of the pupil (cf. Acts 22:3). This description of a teacher–pupil relationship is an important feature of the text. The role as student in which Mary is positioned goes beyond the normal opportunity for women to hear the word in the context of worship. Moreover, the text alludes to terms that in rabbinic tradition are connected to teaching institutions. It also echoes other sayings about "hearing the word" as the decisive criterion for discipleship directed to both women and men (see Luke 6:46ff.; 8:15, 21; 11:28).

Martha does not address Mary directly, but reproaches Jesus for his lack of interest in the unfair division of labor. She takes it for granted that priority belongs to the service she herself carries out, and she takes Jesus seriously to task because he does not see to it that Mary takes a part in the same service. The reproach uttered by Martha thus shows a certain set of priorities about what ought to be women's primary occupation. It is not, however, accepted by the Lord, even though it is formulated in such a way that it expects an affirmative answer. Martha's choice of words also refers continually back to herself. This intensifies the contrast to Mary's concentration on Jesus' words. But at the same time, Martha's appeal to Jesus implies that the relationship between host(ess) and guest is altered; even the hostess Martha operates with Jesus as the ultimate authority.

When Jesus rejects Martha's implicit demand that her sister should help, this is done by means of a two-sided argumentation. Negatively, it is said that Martha troubles and bustles about with many things. Positively, it is said that Mary has chosen the good part. The transition between the two descriptions of the women is mediated by the saying of Jesus about the one thing necessary. There are large text-critical problems about Jesus' answer in vv. 41f. The sensitive point seems to be "the need of one thing" (v. 42a), where the textual witnesses are divided among three quite distinct variants, two of which are very well attested: (1) "Few things, little, are necessary" (P38, P3, sy pal); (2) "Few things are necessary, or only one" (Nestle's text in earlier editions, and attested, e.g., by Sinaiticus and Vaticanus); (3) "One thing is necessary" (attested by the oldest papyri and the koine group). Among scholars there is a wide variety in the choice of which variant is to be preferred. The choice is influenced by the question whether Martha's activity totally can be dismissed as devoid of value and unnecessary. For those who cannot bring themselves to sweep Martha aside completely, the variants with "few things" are the most comfortable. Then something is said in Martha's favor; her mistake is simply that she bothers with much *more* than is necessary. A little, or only one thing, can suffice. Perhaps this refers to the number of courses to be laid on the table. Such an interpretation can in fact be said to be covered by all three variants, provided that "the one thing necessary" in v. 42a is not identified with "the good part" that Mary has chosen (v. 42b).

Jesus' reply to Martha concerns not her serving but the form it takes accompanied by trouble and agitation. It can thus be claimed that the fundamental antithesis is not between hearing and serving, but between hearing and agitated toil. What truly causes the problem is that Martha, in her agitated toil with so many things, demands her sister's assistance. From her own needs for help she intervenes in Mary's choice, and she even tries to ensure that Jesus supports this intervention of hers. So Martha represents a threat that Mary's part can be taken from her.

We should note that this is not portrayed as a conflict between men and women but as a conflict between two sisters. This is not a matter of a "divide and rule" strategy by putting woman up against woman. It is rather an illustration of how various and possibly conflicting roles for women may be balanced. The antagonism between the two sisters is provoked by Jesus' presence. But he is not the first to articulate the difference in the categories of conflict: Martha has this part. Jesus does indeed confirm the antithesis, but not in Martha's version. Instead, he rebukes Martha's toil and agitation, and defends the discipleship of Mary. It is, however, important that the priorities are established as the outcome of a situation of conflict of interests, in which Martha makes demands on Mary. Thus, the priorities are not necessarily absolute: the rejection of Martha's utterance comes unambiguously only when Jesus adds that Mary's good part is not to be taken from her. When there is a set priority among "the parts," these cannot be played off against one another. Devotion to the Word is given priority even where this may lead to conflict with the preoccupation that demands that one give support in provision, hospitality, and service.

Mary's passivity and silence raises, however, some further questions. Does the preference for Mary's choice mean that women's relationship to the word is to be defined primarily in terms of silence? Is the public modesty of the women in the healing stories part of a more consistent pattern? Are women who argue and speak up like Martha and the Syrophoenician woman in Mark (whom Luke omits) nothing but an embarrassment or offense? Are women to keep silent and not to speak, to listen and learn but not to teach? Does Luke represent an implicit variant of the same ideal as is explicit in 1 Tim 2:11f., where it emphatically is said that a woman shall let herself be taught in silence?

Even if there are similarities between Luke's portrayal of women and that of the Pastoral Letters, the differences too are obvious. In 1 Tim 2:11, the warning is not about women's access to instruction, but the author wishes to limit what he sees as improper consequences of this: they are to receive it in silence and in subordination. In Luke the sexually based functions are set aside in favor of the relationship to the word of God, and the women in Luke are noticeably independent. Women's choice of the word is a priority, even if it happens to be at the cost of the virtues for a woman's life valued so highly by the Pastoral Letters: the domestic life with husband and children. The decisive dissimilarity between the Pastoral Letters and Luke in these matters is to be found in their totally diverse attitude to marriage.

Neither is Mary in Luke 10:28–32 specifically portrayed as the ideal woman, but more generally as an ideal disciple. When the word of the Lord is proclaimed people should listen and receive. Early on in the Gospel, everyone has a listening role as recipients in a situation in which Jesus' proclamation dominates. So the preference for Mary also indicates that the real and primary host is Jesus himself providing his word. The deeper structure of the narrative in Luke 10:38-42 is therefore similar to that in 8:1–3—the service of Jesus comes first.

Nevertheless, limitations and restrictions are at work concerning women's exercise of the word also in Luke. The process of masculinization not only occurs through the transfer of the service terms, but is also reflected in an emerging difference between women's and men's relationship to the word. They all begin by listening to the words of the Lord. But while the male disciples may become public preachers, women are never given any explicit commission to preach. The criterion of maleness in Acts 1:21 excludes women from testifying to Jesus' resurrection, even if they otherwise satisfy the criteria of eligibility.

In the story of the empty tomb in Luke 24:1–10, it becomes clear how certain factors operate in silencing women. The peculiar Lukan version of this story may help to explain the remarkable gap between the Gospel's emphasis on the role of women on the one side and on the other side Acts' reduction of them to invisibility in favor of the healing and preaching activity of the leading men. By the use of almost ironic devices, the women become simultaneously recognized and rejected.

At the burial, Luke assigns to the women a more active role than does Mark. By including the women's preparations for the anointing of Jesus' body in the burial scene, Luke connects the narratives about the burial and the empty tomb more closely to one another so that they become one single sequence. The women do as much as they can as quickly as they can, without breaking the sabbath regulations. But even before sunrise they return to the tomb with the fragrant oils they have already prepared on the burial day itself. The women's service continues, and they undertake what was women's work, in Luke's story attended to by no one else. The women come to the tomb in order to continue their service, but the situation they encounter makes the preparations they have carried out inadequate and renders their practical concern and service unnecessary. It has been suggested that the women's role in the structure of the tomb narrative is intermediary. They are merely transient bearers of the news of the resurrection. The message with which they are sent away is not for the women themselves but for the male apostles. In relation to the content of the message, the women remain passive, without understanding—in fact, outsiders. The message is for the men, and the women are only "errand girls."

It can indeed be claimed that in Luke the women run immediately to bring the male disciples the good news. But this is a spontaneous action on their part. No commission is given to the women to go and tell the disciples that Jesus is risen (as in Matt 28:7) and/or to tell them to meet him in Galilee (as in Mark 16:7 par. Matt 28:10). Instead, they are reminded of how Jesus told *them* that the Son of Man must be handed over to sinners, be crucified, and rise again on the third day (Luke 24:6–7). Thus the "errand girl" commission is replaced in Luke by a statement that focuses on the women's own role as disciples in the Gospel story. They are asked to remember what he told them while he was still in Galilee, where they were together with him and listened to his word.

This explains why the characterization of the women as those following Jesus from Galilee is emphasized by being repeated twice in close sequence—Luke 23:49, 55. The retrospective reminder thereby makes sense. The summary notice in 8:1–3 is once more activated in the narrative, and the reference to the passion predictions in 24:7 imply that the women are counted among "the disciples" in 9:18ff. and 17:22ff. The exhortation to the women in 24:6 to remember what he had told them also echoes the various statements earlier in the Gospel about hearing the word and taking care of it (8:15, [21]; 11:28; 10:39).

The women's role in Luke's tomb narrative is thus not one of substitution. The women from Galilee are themselves the first addressees of the resurrection message in a way that confirms their discipleship and the instruction they have received as disciples. In this situation, their diaconal resources are not needed. Relevant is their relationship to the word of the Lord: they have listened to his words. In these words they have the resources that now may help to overcome their confusion and anxiety. They are asked to remember how he told them. The use of the verb "remember" combined with the word of the Lord in v. 6 and v. 8 has parallels in 22:61; Acts 11:16; 20:35; Matt 26:75; 27:63; John 2:(17), 22; 12:16; 15:20; *1 Clem.* 13.1; 46.77; Polycarp, *Letter to the Philippians* 2.3. It may have been a customary phrase to introduce a word of Jesus, but there are great differences among the various writings in terms of the function of this "remembrance." In Luke it is exclusively linked to the instruction of Jesus entrusted to the disciples. His words are to be "remembered," while the word of scripture is to be read, interpreted and expounded, opened up—in the light of words that Jesus spoke while he still was with them, and which are entrusted to their memory (see the general references to scripture in Luke 24:25ff., 32, 44ff.).

The exhortation to the women to remember does not make any insinuation that they might have forgotten. Nor should the words addressed to the women be understood as a sharp reproach, like the accusation against the disciples on the road to Emmaus in 24:25f. The main emphasis lies on the positive proclamation of the resurrection, which explains to the women why the tomb is empty. In Luke, the women themselves have already established that Jesus' body is no longer there. The kerygmatic formula "he is not here, but has risen" is further strengthened by appealing to the women to recall Jesus' earlier prediction and does not carry less meaning than the joyful Easter message in the corresponding narrative in Mark. Those who insist that the angelic messengers are not really recalling the kerygma tend also to presume that the women's remembrance only is an inadequate faith. On the whole this reflects and defends a theological bias which claims that only the christophanies can evoke faith and actually did so. The empty tomb is then at best ambiguous.

As an interpretation of Luke this is not convincing. The exhortation to the women to remember what Jesus told them in Galilee serves to support the message of the resurrection, and the explicit emphasis that the women did remember implies that they truly received this message. It also implies that they both had heard the words and had taken good care of them. Thereby the women from Galilee fulfilled the criterion granting membership in God's family, and they are indeed included among the blessed. By means of the continuous presence and role of the women from Galilee, Luke establishes strong links between the stories about cross and tomb and the rest of the Gospel.

The women's service leads them to a tomb that they find to be empty, to a body that is no longer there—among the dead. In this situation, the women are reaffirmed as hearers of the word: they are the first to hear the message of the resurrection, and this calls to their remembrance the word they once heard from Jesus. This makes them leave the tomb behind, and they go forth and tell everything to the eleven and to all the others. Their act of witness is due to their own spontaneous initiative as a continuation of what they themselves have heard and remembered. The women appear as the first witnesses of the resurrection, and, unlike the narratives in Mark and Matthew, the narrative in Luke 24 says nothing about any hesitation, confusion, or fear on their part as they make their way from the tomb.

The narrative itself guarantees to the reader that the women are trustworthy and credible witnesses. They do speak the truth. The integrity of their testimony is emphasized first by the statement that they told "all this." The later repetition of the story included in the Emmaus narrative (24:22) demonstrates afresh the reliability of the women. The women are also sufficiently numerous to satisfy the formal demand about the number of witnesses; three of the women are named, and the list of names comes pointedly at the close, just as a protocol of testimony concludes by mentioning the names of the witnesses. The imperfect form of the verb in v. 10 can in fact be understood to mean that the women repeatedly told all that they had experienced. Nevertheless, they are not believed; their words seem to the apostles and the male disciples to be empty chatter (v. 11a), and they disbelieve the women (v. 11b). It is not solely a matter of the incredibility of the content of the story the women tell. The form of expression in v. 11b shows that it is not irrelevant that women are the story-tellers. Here the apostles' unbelief is linked directly to the women. This is in keeping with the fact that women were considered less credible (than men), and, as a rule, they were not accepted juridically as witnesses.

The positioning of the list of names at the close serves also to accentuate a contrast between the women and the men. Luke (as compared with Mark and Matthew) widens the group of women and men to include all. The whole group of women, "Mary of Magdala and Joanna and Mary the mother of James, and the other women with them" (v. 10), are set over against the whole group of men, "the eleven and the rest of the men" (v. 9). All the women give a full testimony, and all the men refuse to believe them.

Peter's visit to the tomb in 24:12 puts him in a slightly more positive light, but only in relation to the rest of the men and their complete lack of belief. Over against the women he comes across as a pale variant. It may serve to prepare the version given by the two disciples on their way to Emmaus (24:22ff.), which in its turn points directly to the Christophany traditions. But this is hardly sufficient to hold that in the Lukan narrative a kind of Petrine primacy is promoted to replace the women's (in particular Mary of Magdala's) testimony so that the risen Lord's revelation to Peter was the point where the church's faith was anchored.

It is indeed true that in Luke the risen Lord himself is supposed to have shown himself to Peter first—although this is not reported in a particular revelation narrative. But the narrative of the women at the empty tomb is not thereby deprived of its character as proclamation of the resurrection. This is why none of the interpretative models referred to above does justice to the special character of the narrative in Luke, as a point of tension where the Gospel's positive emphasis on women's participation encounters the confining and oppressing conditions determining the relationship between women and men. The women's experience is sufficient for them to appear as proclaimers, but when they attempt this, they are not believed, not even by those who should have the ears of faith. It is the men's unbelieving reaction that creates the distance in the Lukan story between the women's early faith and witness and the male disciples' late acceptance.

If irony works by an element of distance between the comprehensive power of the author and the voice of the implied narrator, it is certainly at work in this story. The narrative itself has established in detail that the women from Galilee are trustworthy and fully deserve credit. When the message fails to get across the first time, this is because of the unjustified disbelief of the men. As was also the case concerning the function of service, there is no direct transfer from women to men; here too a christological mediation is necessary. In order to believe, the male disciples must see the risen Lord.

But the conclusion is, all the same, that the persuading force of the women as witnesses is discounted. As witnesses, they possess credibility, but they lack the possibility to convince—even to convince those who ought to have been the most readily prepared to believe. Despite the fact that the women accompanied Jesus on his long journeyings, despite their faithful and fearless perseverance, despite their sustaining service and their discipleship, despite their knowledge of the Lord's word as well as their insight into it, despite their credibility, the effect is that women actually are prevented from the public proclamation and teaching activity. In the further unfolding of story, they are not accepted as appropriate witnesses when Jesus' resurrection is to be proclaimed publicly from Jerusalem to Rome, and the path is laid for the leading men's dominance in Acts.

PUBLIC MEN AND DOMESTIC WOMEN

It is a particular point in Luke, serving apologetic aims, that Jesus' activity followed by the preaching of the apostles and the missionaries takes place openly, not in secret. The public proclamation is maintained by Luke as a male privilege; it is exercised by men and explicitly directed to men. This does not exclude the possibility that women are supposed to be present in the audience and also among the followers of Jesus, but it means that only the men are recognized as active participants in public contexts, which officially were all male. The invisibility of the women does not necessarily reflect the actual reality but is a construction that is ideologically undergirded and maintained. The point is not to maintain that there existed a system of extreme physical separation, but to emphasize that, as a rule, power was organized so that family and home had exclusive significance as the life sphere determining women's identity and function. This is often expressed and exercised in terms of locality; the women belong to "the house."

This construction is a reflection of how the distance between the world of men and the world of women in antiquity largely coincided with the difference between a public and a private room. Women lived in a space defined primarily and ideally as being within "the house," and their education, even in stoic schools, had domestic virtues as its aim. Women could be seen in public places, but their conduct was strictly regulated and there were narrow boundaries for what was seemly. It was only to a limited extent and/or in indirect ways that women were able to exercise functions within the public sphere. Even well-off and aristocratic women were seldom direct participants in a public context. Women who established an autonomous economic basis either through the affluence of their family or through their own business activity could make their mark in the public sphere through their donations and projects. Inscriptions show that they, in reward, could be assigned honorable titles, but apart from their patronage they seldom had an official and direct political role to play. Nor did they, with few exceptions, carry out central religious functions that were not linked to the home or to the more closed societies or associations.

The exception was a number of religious rituals and feasts that gave women the opportunity not only to come out but also to behave in ways that would have been unseemly in their daily life. Whereas women in the more official religious cult played a withdrawn domestic role, the "new religious movements" of an oriental type were more open for women and had a corresponding attraction for them. There was often considerable suspicion about women's participation in such "foreign" cults, but actually women had more freedom to take part in this sort of nontraditional worship, because of their lack of a public role and importance. This may help to explain why the wife is the one who is Christian in most of the mixed marriages known to us—even if a woman was expected to share the faith of her husband. A Christian man with a pagan wife is the exception.

Women could be active in societies or clubs. Well-off households could also provide lodgings on a short-term or long-term basis for philosophers and preachers. Such occasions as these created an intermediary zone in which the public and the private converged, and there were local and social nuances and differences. The sources available indicate that women's rights and opportunities were best established and practiced in Egypt and Asia Minor. But marriage contracts from these regions show, nevertheless, that even if the husband was reminded about his obligations in a stricter manner than previously was the custom and thus a greater limitation was placed on his freedom, traditional restrictive ideals about subordination and confined movement continued to be prescribed for the wife. There may have been less freedom for the husband, but not necessarily more freedom for the wife. The main concern was the inviolability of "the *oikos*," the household. Deviant conduct by women threatened the fundamental values of society, whereas a conformist conduct safeguarded these.

Women's activity in Luke is most often linked to the house. While the angel Gabriel reveals himself to Zechariah in the Temple, the meeting with Mary takes place in the house where she lives (1:26–28). The outpouring of the spirit on Elizabeth and Mary (1:40–56) happens in Elizabeth's home. On the day of Pentecost in Acts 2:1–4 the Spirit fills the house where they are all gathered, but it is Peter and the eleven who appear in public and address the crowd. Even Priscilla is portrayed as listening in the synagogue and active in the instruction of Apollos at home. The woman who lost one of her coins (15:8–10) knows that it is to be found in the house, and when she finds it, she rejoices together with her female friend and neighbors. Exception must be made, however, for the aged widow Hannah (2:36–38), who speaks prophetically in the Temple, and for the woman with the continuous flow of blood (8:47), who must come forward and tell her story before all the people. She so does, but trembling and afraid.

As the Lukan story unfolds, an original alternation between Temple and house grows to become an ever-stronger movement toward the house. Despite the emphasis on the public proclamation and the defense of the faith in front of the authorities, a gradual transfer from Temple, square, and synagogue to the house becomes apparent. It is emphasized that both men and women take part in the private gatherings, and when women are in the house, they are not on the periphery but close to the heart of the life in the community. Sheltered by the house, they have a certain freedom and religious significance, and they are not to be tied down by conventional domestic tasks. But the house also represents their limitation: the men keep hold of the public world as a male world of power. Luke provides scarce information about the ongoing life of the house-communities. Because of his apologetic interests, the public sphere retains its importance as the place of defense, and the rest of the story remains untold.

In other words, within the given framework of the patriarchal system, boundaries are touched and perhaps stretched. This is emphasized by the priority of "nondomestic" functions as "the better part." But the patriarchal system in terms of a divided world is not threatened. The more the communities orient themselves to the world outside the house, the more will women's activity have to be restricted. A comparison with other writings may illustrate that more clearly. In the Gospel of John traces of a noticeably egalitarian reflection and praxis are evident. Women carry out some of the same functions as in Luke's writings, but in full public view and vis-à-vis both women and men. When meeting Jesus, the women in John cross the threshold of the house—indeed, they are quite directly summoned forth. The Apocryphal Acts two or three generations later are also highly relevant to the question about women's leeway in regard to a private and a public sphere. These narratives presuppose a world where a woman's "proper place" is within the private sphere, in her father's or her husband's house. The man, on the other hand, moves freely in the external, public world. By remaining in the house a woman will normally show her acceptance of the place given her. Leaving the house means that she crosses boundaries and penetrates the man's domain. Thereby she arouses suspicion and hostility. The social and sexual exodus that these stories advocate therefore takes on local expression. The radical consequences of an ascetic choice become clearest in the majority of the cases where women break up and out. By defying the physical boundaries placed around women's space, they express their defiance of the social and sexual norms that culminate in patriarchal marriage.

An ascetic life within the boundary of the house is a borderline case, testing the presuppositions of the house from within. In the Apocryphal Acts this is expressed locally by the fact that the ascetic wives annoy their family by continually slipping out. It represents, however, a less problematic and provocative solution, because the surface structure of the organizational power is kept seemingly intact. In my view, this is the situation reflected in Luke. Even if the women are subordinated to the governing division between the public and the private, and to the consequently established masculine order of leadership, the independent integrity of the group of women is respected. There is no demand, nor any narrative adjustment, to indicate that the women are to subordinate themselves according to the ethos reflected in the household codes.

ASCETIC EMERGENCY

In the Lukan parable of the Great Feast—in the Matthean parallel, a wedding feast—marriage serves as an excuse for not attending (14:20). Luke thus names the contracting of marriage as one of the obstacles to joining the feast of God. In accordance with this, he gives an ascetic emphasis to the common Synoptic ethos of voluntary abandonment. To break with family relationships belongs more than anything else to the costs of discipleship as they are listed in Luke, and the inclusion of "the wife" in these lists (14:26; 18:29) involves an intensification toward asceticism. Even where the break does not take on a geographic expression, the family relationships that continue to exist are preferably to be arranged ascetically, and new marriages are to be avoided.

This may also be the reason why the Markan passage defending marriage as an order of creation over against the Mosaic warrant of divorce (Mark 10:1–12) is not taken up by Luke. Only the well-known logion about divorce and remarriage is included in Luke 16:18, and the Lukan adaptation is more concerned about prohibiting remarriage than divorce. In my view 16:18 not only addresses those who want to remarry after divorce but excludes primarily the possibility of remarriage by those disciples who have left their wives behind (without necessarily divorcing them; cf. Luke 14:26; 18:29). The same applies to new marriages with abandoned wives. In such cases, Jewish law too would count a new marriage as adultery, because the first marriage still formally was valid despite the separation. The logion thereby testifies to the continued validity of the Law. But the intention in Luke is not the protection of marriage. The point is not that the husbands ought to return to their wives, nor is there any point in formally seeking to dissolve the marriage. The whole thrust is to avoid the contraction of new marriages. The decision to follow Jesus is absolute, and one cannot fall back on more comfortable solutions (by marrying a "sister"?) once one has made an ascetic break with the past. It is hard indeed to force one's way into God's kingdom (cf. 16:16).

The wording of Luke 16:18 is totally androcentric. The man is consistently the subject, the acting partner: it is he who leaves his wife and who also commits adultery if he marries anew or marries an abandoned woman. This masculine control is in accord with the dominant praxis of marriage and divorce at least in the eastern regions of the empire. The admonitions in 14:26, including the call to abandon the wife, taken together with the masculine imagery used in the following pair of parables (which is not complementary in gender terms) about adequate calculation, can indicate that the costs of discipleship represented a special problem for comfortably established men. But it does not define ascetic discipleship exclusively as a male privilege or an intensified demand made of a male leadership elite.

Women's gift of prophecy is presented by Luke most often as a charismatic privilege of virginity: the women prophets are often either widows or virgins (see Luke 1:45–55; 2:36–38; Acts 21:9). Mary's virginity has a particular and unique function in relation to the birth of Jesus. But the transfer of Mary's relation as mother from the physical family to the fictive family of Jesus opens the possibility of an alternative motherhood for all the women who, like her, "hear God's Word and do it." In Jesus' words to the daughters of Jerusalem (Luke 23:27–30) the reference is to the coming times of tribulation, which make a normal life an impossible burden. These times are so hard that women with children are to praise as blessed the childless women whom they would otherwise bewail. Unlike the "women from Galilee," the "daughters of Jerusalem" with their children are bound by conditions of life that will intensify their suffering.

In the patriarchal cultures of antiquity, where marriage was the destiny of a woman's life and childbearing her social and theological legitimation, the redefinition of woman's role in terms of a permanent ascetic discipleship was in defiance of the ruling ethos. Ascetic tendencies of various kinds were widely known in antiquity, and temporary continence was frequently a prerequisite for ritual purity; but it was never commonly approved as a permanent alternative for the whole of life. The cult of Isis, which was considered strict in its demands for periods of abstinence, still did not request permanent chastity. Among the philosophical schools, not even the Cynic itinerant philosophers were ascetic in their defiance of public morality. Neither is the wish that many men in philosophical circles nurtured about remaining unmarried any clear evidence of ascetic inclinations. It should rather be seen as an expression of a sexual appetite that tried to avoid the obligations and complications of marriage.

In Judaism the case against celibacy is not as univocal as has been commonly assumed. There is some scattered evidence of ascetic anchorites, and most of the male inhabitants of Qumran probably were celibate to safeguard their cultic purity and to be prepared for the imminent holy war. Philo is highly ambiguous in this matter, but his description of Therapeutae and Therapeutrides demonstrates his admiration for their simple and encratistic life. Still asceticism remained outside the mainstream of Judaism, and maternity, not virginity, was the highest vocation for women. Widows like Judith were not ascetic figures. Like the Roman *univiras*, she was an illustrious example of the extreme monogamous wife, remaining faithful to one husband only.

The Augustan legislation on marriage aimed particularly at the legitimate reproduction of the Roman aristocracy and the preservation of the hierarchical order of the state. By the legislation, the emperor, as *pater patriae*, sought to have as many as possible constantly married, at least until the age when procreation no longer was likely. Accordingly, widowed and divorced persons were to be rushed into new marriages. The childless were subjected to legal disadvantages, while a freeborn woman who had given birth to at least three children obtained the right of *sui juris*. The precise impact of this legislation is difficult to tell, but it bears witness to a public and common ethos linking the traditional order of the house/family to the well-being of the state and making the right and legal status of a woman dependent on her capacity of childbearing.

Widows occur more frequently in Luke-Acts than in any other Christian Testament writing. The term "widow" has kept in Luke a traditional denotation of devastation, poverty, and vulnerability, but the Lukan interest in widows is not just another expression of his concern for the poor and the outcast. In Luke the widows appear to form a special and respected group always portrayed in a positive light. They transcend the roles of victims and receivers and act in such a way that they become prominent examples of faith and piety.

Luke seems to share the presupposition, inspired by Judaism and common among Christians, that the religious community has the duty of providing for widows (Acts 6:19; 9:39ff.). It is likely that most of the women who were supported by the community, even the young ones, really were widows or divorced/abandoned women. But the system may have entertained also other women, who for various reasons had been deprived of the social security in the family or who had deliberately chosen a life free from marital bonds. As most of these women would have difficulties providing for themselves, the regulations for the care of widows that we glimpse in Luke mean that even a poor woman could have real choice. Thereby a life without new marriage was not only desirable; it was also feasible.

This confirms that the author of 1 Timothy did not inititate a new order to facilitate the problems of the widows; he was rather attempting to diminish the increasing importance of an already existing order and wanted to limit the number of widows who could be enrolled. His interference shows that Christian communities very early on had made provisions for widows. It seems clear that these provisions included young women as well as old; they were supported by the community, and they fulfilled tasks such as acts of charity and visitations in the homes, while their main occupation was intercessory prayer. They had also probably pledged themselves to chastity.

The brief presentation of Hannah in Luke 2:36–38 is a specially intense and concentrated introduction of an ideal widow—with roots in Jewish types of piety such as Judith and apparently concordant with the criteria of the true widow launched in 1 Tim 5:3–16. The similarity between Hannah and "the true widow" in 1 Timothy is, however, limited to only a few elements in the life of a pious widow, especially her persevering prayer. Hannah's function, as she appears in Luke's narrative, is primarily that of prophetic proclamation, and all the information issued about her serves as background and justification for this. Not even Hannah's advanced age represents anything other than a superficial correspondence: for even if she now is a very old widow, she has been a widow for most of her life. The ideal is not the old and irreproachable widow as such, but a woman who, despite becoming a widow while young, nevertheless refrained from remarrying and remained a widow throughout a long life consecrated to God. Hannah is identified by her own rights, not her deceased husband's family and tribe. No independent importance attaches to the fact that she was once married and thus has fulfilled the conventional expectations of a woman's life, nor is it interesting to know whether she has given birth to children. The point is the short duration of the marriage in comparison to the long period of widowhood. Her life, seen as a whole, has been "without a husband," characterized first by her virginity and then by her widowhood. Hannah is thus first and foremost an ascetic figure, and she represents a model even for young women.

It is not without reason that most of the women in Luke-Acts have been assumed to be widows because of their peculiar independence as they act on their own behalf. But the point in Luke is rather that a life without the obligations of marriage, a life no longer determined by sexual bodily functions, is not necessarily restricted to widows. It is offered more generally as a permanent alternative for the women following Jesus.

Luke 20:27–38 provides a key to understanding the ascetic position of Luke. The levirate puzzle by which the Sadducees try to trap Jesus and expose the absurdity of resurrection faith dwells on the question of marriage, death, posterity, and resurrection. There is reason to believe that the conservative Sadducees, over against the "new" concept of resurrection, held their own view of resurrection as the raising of posterity. The institution of levirate marriage was a provision by which a man who died without leaving any children still might have posterity. It is significant that the Sadducees refer to levirate marriage in terms of Gen 38:8, where the ambiguous "raise up offspring/children" is used.

All three Synoptic versions of Jesus' response reject the claim that the objection raised by the Sadducees against resurrection is a relevant one. Instead, the different nature of the resurrected life is emphasized, implying that the woman then no longer belongs to any man. In Mark, followed by Matthew, Jesus states that when they rise from the dead they will be like the angels so that in the age to come marriage is abolished and procreation ended. The categories as well as the dichotomy are all temporal. In Luke, the first part of Jesus' answer (vv. 34–37a) has a peculiar variant form that made it a favorite among the early monastics. It is an independent little treatise on the ethos of resurrection in terms of immortality. Purely temporal categories and dichotomies are overcome. The opposition between the present age of death and marriage and the age to come after resurrection is anticipated and already visible in the difference between the sons of this age and those who are accounted worthy to attain to the resurrection and the age to come. The two groups are distinguished by their practice of marriage. While the sons of this age marry and let themselves be married, this is not so with the sons of God; they do not enter into marriage.

The repeated parallel use of the verb in 20:34f. is the same as in 17:26 (and 1 Cor 7:36, 38). This is striking not only because this particular verb is very rare but because all the occurrences in the Christian Testament are found in contexts involving criticism of marriage. The double form shows that it concerns both men and women, while it also reflects the unequal role of men and women in contracting marriage. But in the case of the women, it is not the customary passive form that is being used—although it is commonly interpreted and translated thus. Rather, the rare middle form makes the women the subject: they let (or do not let) themselves to be taken in marriage. It implies that also the women are left with a choice.

Their abstinence from marriage is explained by their future part in the resurrection, which will render them immortal so that they will be like the angels. The reason for their likeness to the angels is that they cannot die. Immortality is therefore a more important characteristic of the heavenly life than asexuality, but the Lukan text suggests an intimate connection between marriage and death. Because the need for marriage is considered to cease when individual resurrection and immortality are promised, the reverse conclusion would be that it is death that makes marriage necessary—since the main purpose of patriarchal marriage is male procreation and thereby the possibility to gain an afterlife in one's own offspring. So the criticism of marriage in Luke is not due to pragmatism but is the expression of an ascetic reservation that is eschatologically determined.

When participation in the future life is no longer dependent on procreation, with the result that the patriarchal intention in marriage can be abandoned, an end is set also to the male's fundamental need for the female's asssistance in procreating and perpetuating himself. Within an androcentric patrarchal model, this actually means that the original reason and justification of the woman's existence de facto cease to exist. Positively it promotes an ascetic liberation of the woman by providing an opportunity of life outside the confinement of patriarchal marriage. In recent years this dimension of liberation in early Christian asceticism has been introduced as a major explanation of why so many Christian women were attracted by an ascetic life, and also as an important aspect in Christianity's power to bring conviction to certain groups of women. It gave them the possibility of a power and an authority from which they were otherwise excluded and an opportunity to move outside the limiting constraints of their conventional roles as daughter, wife, and mother. By withdrawing their sexuality from control by others, they achieved a sort of control over their lives and their possessions. Free from the patriarchal dominance by either father or husband, free from risky pregnancies, free from painful and often life-threatening childbirth, free from the demands of constant caring, and even free from great economic worries, these women had a freedom that was usually reserved for the hetaerae; moreover, they enjoyed ecclesiastical and theological honor and respectability.

But this ascetic freedom had its price. Within an androcentric anthropology an ascetic life might imply for women that they no longer remained female. By means of asceticism, it was possible for them to escape their femaleness and develop maleness, which was considered superior or prior to what was female. Even if Christian Testament texts hardly give more than scattered and weak indications of this motif, the path still was prepared through androcentric terminology. In Luke 20:34ff. the women are counted among the "sons," but there is no clear trace in Luke of the idea that the ascetic life for women is a way of becoming male. The terminology may be influenced at first by the fact that the ethos had as its model the Son of God (as also the baptismal formula in Gal 3:28–29 shows), who himself prototypically fulfilled the demand to abandon one's life.

Luke shows knowledge of an ascetic strain in Paul's preaching (Acts 24:24–25), and this ascetic Paul is known also from his own writings, especially 1 Corinthians 7. But not only does Luke preserve Paul's ascetic preference; he also intensifies it to some extent. This has its roots in the radical requirement of discipleship in the Jesus traditions, and it contains elements that point forward to the later preaching in the Apocryphal Acts. It is certainly not without reason that Luke later becomes a favorite Gospel in the early Syrian church, where asceticism is demanded of all who are accepted for baptism, and where "to hear God's word" plays a prominent role in the liturgical tradition.

Luke thus differs from the Pauline tradition as it is claimed by the Pastoral Letters. The Pastorals are strongly in favor of marriage and emphasize the subordinate and domestic role of women to the extent that childbirth and the successful fostering of children are made a prerequisite for a woman's salvation. The image of the ideal widow and the regulations for the order of widows are adjusted accordingly. Luke, however, is critical of marriage and encourages an attitude and a praxis that present problems for the author of the Pastoral Letters a few years later. The same is true of the Lukan defense of women's right to occupy themselves with the Lord's word, even if this happens at the cost of those virtues in a woman's life that the author of the Pastoral Letters esteems so highly.

The ascetic inclination in Luke may help to explain the independent integrity of the women's group. Ascetic ideals exempted women from meeting traditional role expectations in marriage and family. They thereby also limited the patriarchalizing effect of the family model when this was transferred to the community in the house and contributed to the special combination of inclusivity and segregation between a group of men and a group of women.

DANGEROUS REMEMBRANCE

The Lukan story draws up quite strict boundaries for women's activity in relation to the public room. In this way, Luke is in accord with the apologetic considerations that also color the epistles. But Luke transmits a double message. The ambivalence takes the form of a narrative sequence that gives a rare insight into the establishing of structures that impose silence on women and promote leadership as a male privilege. But in the Gospel narrative Luke also preserves extraordinary traditions about the women from Galilee and their role in the story of Jesus' life, death, and resurrection. The women are brought to silence, but at the same time they continue to speak through the story. There is an ironic twist to the double message: the women from Galilee were indeed capable and qualified, but the men suspected and rejected them. The male consolidation of power occurs against a story in which the men have shown weakness and failure rather than strength.

By means of the narrative sequence and of the positioning of the Gospel as a "first volume," the traditions from Jesus' life, in all their historical transparency, are located in the past. They take on the character of remembrance. The same is true of the women from this past story of Jesus' life. The Gospel does not represent a romantic and idealized version of an irrevocable golden age.

Luke's own employment of the motif of "memory" shows that to remember is to keep the key to rooms where critical insight and new understanding are to be found. When people remember, their eyes are opened so that they see and believe. The story retains its force, and the women from Galilee are still on the road.

NOTES

1. This article is heavily based on the results from my forthcoming monograph on gender perspectives in Luke-Acts to be published by T. & T. Clark in the near future. There one will find both a fuller argument and all the references and notes missing here.

RECOMMENDED READINGS

Augsten, M. *Die Stellung des lukanischen Christus zur Frau und zur Ehe.* Diss. masch., Erlangen, 1970.

Brutschek, J. *Die Maria-Martha-Erzählung: Eine redaktionskritische Untersuchung zu Lk 10,38–42.* Bonner Biblische Beiträge 64. Bonn: Hanstein, 1986.

Burrus, V. *Chastity as Autonomy: Women in the Stories of the Apocryphal Acts.* Studies in Women and Religion 23.Lewiston, NY: Mellen, 1987.

Corley, K. E. "Were the Women around Jesus Really Prostitutes? Women in the Context of Greco-Roman Meals." In *SBL 1989 Seminar Papers,* edited by D. Lull, 487–521. Atlanta: Scholars Press, 1989.

D'Angelo, Mary Rose. "Women in Luke-Acts: A Redactional View." *Journal of Biblical Literature* 109 (1990): 441–61.

Kahl, B. *Armenevangelium und Heidenevangelium.* Berlin: Evangelische Verlagsanstalt, 1987.

Kopas, J. "Jesus and Women: Luke's Gospel." *Theology Today* 43 (1986): 192–202.

Levine, A.-J., ed. *Women Like This: New Perspectives on Jewish Women in the Greco-Roman World.* Atlanta: Scholars Press, 1991.

Parvey, C. F. "The Theology and Leadership of Women in the New Testament." In *Religion and Sexism: Images of Women in the Jewish and Christian Traditions,* edited by Rosemary Radford Ruether, 117–49. New York: Simon & Schuster, 1974.

Ringe, S. H. *Jesus, Liberation and the Biblical Jubilee: Images for Ethics and Christology.* Overtures to Biblical Theology. Philadelphia: Fortress, 1985.

Schottroff, L. "Maria Magdalena und die Frauen am Grabe Jesu." *Evangelische Theologie* 42 (1982): 3–25.

Schüssler Fiorenza, Elisabeth. *In Memory of Her: A Feminist Theological Reconstruction of Christian Origins.* New York: Crossroad, 1983.

——. "Biblische Grundlegung." In *Feministische Theologie: Perspektiven zur Orientierung,* edited by M. Kassel, 13–44. Stuttgart: Kohlhammer, 1988.

Tetlow, E. M. *Women and Ministry in the New Testament: Called to Serve.* New York: Paulist, 1980.

Via, E. J. "Women, the Discipleship of Service and the Early Christian Ritual Meal in the Gospel of Luke." *St. Luke's Journal of Theology* 29 (1985): 37–60.

The Acts of the Apostles

CLARICE J. MARTIN ◆

INTRODUCTION

THE ACTS OF THE APOSTLES has often been designated as a "bridge text" in its rendering of early church history. Serving as a bridge between the four Gospels and the epistles, it covers the period of transition from Jesus' earthly ministry to the gradual codification of nascent and diverse communities of Christians in the Greco-Roman world. In the Gospels, the church's existence is forecast as a future event; in the epistles, it is an accomplished fact. Acts provides a vital historical link between the Gospels and the epistles.

The narrative of Acts depicts scenes and images of seemingly indefatigable women and men "on the move," effecting personal, communal, and religious legitimation as "Christians," the people of the "Way" (Acts 9:2; 11:26). The believers also sought to respond faithfully to Jesus' charge to preach repentance and forgiveness of sins to all nations (Luke 24:47). The charge thus provided the *raison d'être* for the tireless and ever-spiraling missionary outreach. The coming of the Holy Spirit marked both the beginning of the Pentecost era and a new period in salvation history. This portrayal of the rise of Christianity recalls at once the "past" of Christianity as a renewal movement within Judaism (the Gospel of Luke), while also serving to establish a "future" for the Christian faith within world history (the *parousia* is delayed, and not imminent [Acts 3:19–21]). The story of the establishment of the Christian church in Acts served to ignite and strengthen the faith of first-century Christians—as it still does for many contemporary readers today.

AUTHORSHIP

It is almost an axiom of Christian Testament scholarship that the writer of the Third Gospel, "Luke," is also the author of Acts. The *prima facie* implications of the phrase, "In the first book, Theophilus" (Acts 1:1a), are that the writer is referring to the Third Gospel. Further, the Theophilus of Acts 1:1 is presumed to be the "most excellent Theophilus" of the prologue in Luke 1:1–4.

Similarities in the language, apologetic tenor, catholic outlook, theology, and grand vision of Luke-Acts can be readily discerned. The development of such motifs as the Holy Spirit, Jews and Gentiles, Samaritans, women, the marginal and the outcast, prayer, teaching and preaching, and the stewardship of material possessions confirm the literary and thematic unity of Luke-Acts.

Tradition designates Luke the physician, Paul's traveling companion, as the writer of Luke-Acts (Phlm 24; Col 4:14; 2 Tim 4:11; cf. the "we sections," Acts 16:10–17; 20:5–21:18; 27:1–28:16), but both works are anonymous. Neither the Third Gospel nor Acts identifies its author by name. The designations "Luke" and "The Acts of the Apostles" were attributed to Luke-Acts by the later church toward the end of the second century.

Date

Acts is commonly dated in the last quarter of the first century, following the destruction of Jerusalem (70 C.E.). Acts assumes a knowledge of the Third Gospel, which itself was composed shortly after the destruction of Jerusalem (Luke's Gospel seems to presuppose the fall of Jerusalem in Luke 21:20–24). The dating of the composition of Acts is usually affixed between the late 70s and 90 C.E.

Genre

Luke identifies his two-volume work, Luke-Acts, as a "narrative" (Luke 1:1). Research from the history of criticism on the book of Acts has highlighted the writer's eclecticisms, including his intent to provide an overview of one strand of the church's wide-ranging history, namely, the growth of the emerging church from Jerusalem in the east to Rome in the west. Luke does not use the word "history," even if he seems to imitate some of the conventions of Greco-Roman historiography. For example, the form of the prologue in Luke 1:1–4 (considered by a majority of scholars to function as the prologue to both the Third Gospel and Acts) has affinities with other Hellenistic prologues. But Acts also has affinities with historical works in the Hebrew Bible and in Jewish histories such as 1 Maccabees.

Lukan framing of overarching themes along biographical lines in Acts (e.g., the cameos of Peter and Paul), coupled with literary traits akin to those found in ancient novels (travel narratives, for example), has led some scholars to designate Acts as a type of Greco-Roman biography. But biographical data in Acts are uneven, at best, with few detailed descriptions of the personalities or physical descriptions of his characters. Similarly, negligible chronological data about even the most prominent figures in the narrative indicate that Luke's primary interest lay elsewhere.

The genre of Acts may best be described as "theological history," a type of historical monograph. Not an actual, thoroughgoing, "factual history" of Christian beginnings in the modern sense, but a continuation of the story begun in the Third Gospel, Acts sets forth a "sacred history," showing how the divine purposes were fulfilled in the birth and progression of the Christian church on the world stage. More like the painter, whose broad canvas seeks to elicit a response, than the photographer, whose product must be a technically accurate and exact likeness, Luke, an impassioned apologist for the Christian faith, painted an expansive and versicolored mosaic of Christian beginnings.

STRUCTURE

The overarching narrative structure of Acts has been variously organized and identified with reference to (1) geography, (2) chronology, and (3) leading *dramatis personae*.

Geographically, the structure of Acts is organized in conjunction with the commission of the risen Christ in Acts 1:8c that the followers are to be witnesses in Jerusalem (Acts 1–7; cf. Luke 24:47), Judea and Samaria (Acts 8–9), and throughout the Gentile world, including Rome (Acts 10–28). With the Holy Spirit as the source of power for their work, the disciples are empowered to spread the gospel to the whole of humankind.

Chronologically, Luke seeks to highlight the continuity of the church with Israel, demonstrating that God's plan for the salvation of humankind began with Israel. The Lukan view of salvation history has been distinguished by three salient periods: the period of Israel (described in the Hebrew Bible), the period of Jesus (described in the Gospel of Luke), and the period of the church (described in Acts). The period of the church continues into the future, until Christ comes at the end of time (Acts 10:42; cf. 17:31). Thus, the end is not imminent in Lukan eschatology. The period of the church represents a time when the gospel is to be spread far and wide, even to the "end of the earth" (Acts 1:8c; 6:7; 12:24; 13:47–49; 19:20). The end of the age will be marked by the resurrection of the just and the unjust (Acts 1:11; 24:15).

That Israel remains of pivotal importance to Luke can be seen in the numerous references to Israel in Acts. According to Luke, the promises made to Israel of old are now fulfilled. The typological function of some characters, the prophecy–fulfillment use of scripture texts (Acts 2:14–36), and the rehearsal of Israel's history beginning with Abraham and Moses (Acts 7:1–53), emphasize the fulfillment of God's promise and Luke's pastoral concern that "the hope of Israel" was at stake (Acts 28:20).

The narrative structure of Acts is also organized in terms of its leading *dramatis personae,* Peter and Paul. The central figure in Acts 1–12 is Peter, who inaugurates the principal stages of the unfolding Christian mission. It is his proclamation that explains the significance of the coming of the Holy Spirit at Pentecost (2:14f.). Peter and John successfully evangelize the Samaritans (8:14f.), and an initially reluctant Peter becomes God's emissary and witness to the Gentile Cornelius—whose conversion represents the formal launching of the mission to the Gentiles (10:1–11:18). Paul, who is the central figure in Acts 13–28, launches the westward movement of the gospel, advancing the mission to the world diaspora.

PURPOSE

The title "Acts of the Apostles" provides little indication of the purpose of Acts. Neither is Acts devoted to a description of "all" of the Twelve; in fact, significant narrative space is devoted to Peter's activities prior to the Jerusalem Council (Acts 15) only. The names of the Twelve are cited in Acts 1:13, but allusions to John, James, and Judas are negligible. Scattered references to "the apostles" are minimal, with the last recorded in Acts 16:4.

A key to the purpose of Acts is found in the prologue in Luke 1:1–4, where Luke sets forth his purpose to Theophilus. These introductory verses suggest that Acts is *kerygma*—"proclamation of what has happened." More specifically, it is the proclamation of "the events that have been fulfilled among us" (Luke 1:1), the proclamation of the "good news" of God's redemptive activity in the life, death, and resurrection of Jesus.

Acts 1:1 refers to the "first book," the Gospel of Luke, which narrates the events of Jesus' life and ministry. Acts continues the narrative of the Gospel of Luke, portraying the continuation of Jesus' ministry through the agency of the Holy Spirit at work in the church. The Holy Spirit is the mighty agent empowering women and men for community and mission from Jerusalem "to the end of the earth" (Acts 1:8c).

Luke's primary purpose for writing Acts is catechetical—he seeks to "confirm the faith" of Christian believers, providing trustworthy information about Christian beginnings and the Christian faith to "most excellent Theophilus." Seeking to inform and confirm the faith of Theophilus, he suggests that the traditions he has received were provided by "eyewitnesses and servants of the word," and thus Theophilus can be fully assured concerning the things about which he has been instructed (Luke 1:1–4). Luke was writing for Christians, like Theophilus, to confirm the dependability of the good news concerning Jesus and Jesus' continued activity in the world through the Holy Spirit.

According to Luke, the forward march of the gospel as narrated in Acts occurred as a direct result of God's guidance and in accordance with the divine will.

Several related concerns inform Luke's purpose. The power (*dynamis*) of the Holy Spirit is indissolubly linked to the progress of the gospel in evangelism and mission. The dramatic and concrete expressions of the Spirit's advent at Pentecost were evidence that the risen Christ was continuing his work in the world, as the many conversions (2:41, 47; 19:18–20), signs and wonders (2:43; 3:1–16; 16:16–24), and the spirit of mutuality, interdependence, and *koinōnia* ("fellowship," "participation") in community (2:44–47) attest.

The Gentile mission receives particular prominence in Acts, with Luke narrating how the Jerusalem church was led to a recognition of Gentile Christianity. The progress of the mission to Judea and Samaria represented the transitional nexus of the widening evangelistic outreach, with the Hellenists taking the helm in the initiation of mission to the Gentiles (Acts 6:1–15; 8:4–40). For Luke, Paul becomes both the bridge leading from the apostolic age down to Luke's own day—a chief representative and symbol of second-generation Christianity—and he becomes the missioner to the Gentiles *par excellence* as he continues Christianity's advance on the world stage westward toward Rome (13:46–47; 28:16, 25–31).

Some commentators have also identified a "political apologetic" interest in Acts, with Luke seeking to demonstrate that Christianity was a *religio licita* (legal religion), and not a threat to the Roman government. In view of charges that the new movement was "turning the world upside down" (17:6) and was "everywhere spoken against" (28:22), "Luke the apologist" seeks to demonstrate the political innocence of Christianity in relation to Roman law. Paul, for example, the leading protagonist in Acts, is depicted largely as establishing fairly congenial relations with imperial authorities (see his treatment by authorities in Thessalonica [17:6–9], Philippi [16:19–24, 35–39], and Ephesus [19:35–41]). Paul denies any offense against government authorities (25:8; 26:31).

Many other motifs highlight Luke's interests in Acts, including many motifs already presented in the Third Gospel, including God's foreknowledge, plan, and purpose in the Christ-event and the birth of the church (2:23; 3:20; 10:41; 22:10); the universality of salvation (8:26–40; 10:1–11:18); the importance of prayer (6:6; 7:59, 60; 9:11–19; 13:2, 3; 16:25); and joy, wonder, and exultation in response to God's saving deeds (2:47; 3:9–10; 5:41; 16:34). Also discernible is Luke's concern for the poor, the needy, the sick, and the marginal (2:44–45; 3:6; 5:15–16; 28:9); women (1:14; 2:17–21; 6:1; 8:12; 16:14–15; 17:12, 34; 18:2, 18, 26; 21:9); and hospitality (2:46; 9:10–12; 10:5–6, 48; 16:11–15; 20:31). With these and other motifs, Luke provides a portraiture of the gospel's transformative power and inclusive character with diverse cultural and ethnic groups, underscoring its potential to traverse gender, national, linguistic, economic, and class (or status) boundaries.

LITERARY FEATURES

Dramatic scenes and events enliven the narration of the story of the birth and growth of the first-century church in Acts. Luke employs a variety of literary techniques and flourishes to advance narrative developments. The "summaries" in Acts (2:42–47; 4:32–37; 5:12–16) are Lukan editorial details that provide an "interim report" or summary of the progression of the evangelistic mission of the church, and an idealized capitulation of social arrangements in the internal life of the Christian community. These and other incidental summaries (6:7; 9:31; 12:24; 19:20) also function as transitional devices that advance the narrative action.

Acts, like many other ancient historical writings (Greek, Roman, and Jewish), contains a number of "speeches," addressed both to Jews (2:14–36; 4:8–12; 10:34–43), and to Gentiles (14:15–17; 17:22–31), and they often employ standard conventions of Greco-Roman rhetorical strategies (including the use of hortatory, apologetic, and polemical speech).

Luke exhibits a pronounced fondness for parallelism. This literary technique has been documented in classical literature and Israelite-Jewish literature, and Charles Talbert has demonstrated Luke's extensive fondness for arranging narrative material in this way in both the Third Gospel and Acts and between the two works. For example, the double prefaces dedicated to Theophilus (Luke 1:1–4; Acts 1:1–5); Jesus praying at his baptism and the disciples praying as they await their baptism of the Holy Spirit (Luke 3:21; Acts 1:14, 24); the centurions who send emissaries to Jesus (Luke 7:1–10) or Peter (Acts 10) and invite them to come to their houses, respectively; Jesus' innocence declared three times by Pilate (Luke 23:4, 14, 22); and Paul's innocence declared by Lysias, Festus, and Agrippa (Acts 23:29; 25:25; 26:31).

Talbert's "architectonic analysis" of parallelisms within Acts demonstrates remarkable correspondences in thematic foci, vocabulary, christological titles, introductions, and summaries. The striking thematic correspondences between chapters 1–12 and 13–28 of Acts have long been noted by scholars, including parallelisms between the healing of a man lame from birth (Acts 3:1–10; 14:8–18), and the stoning of Stephen and Paul (Acts 6:8–8:4; 14:19–23, but Paul's stoning does not result in death). See also the correspondences in Acts 1:12–4:23 and 4:24–5:42 with reference to its depiction of the church gathered at prayer, those gathered filled with the Holy Spirit, the preaching of the word of God, portrayals of the communal life of the church, the notation that "fear comes upon" all, and complementary allusions to "signs and wonders," healings, and the respective assembly in Solomon's portico.

Women in Luke-Acts

Traditional scholarship on women in Luke-Acts has proclaimed Luke a "champion of women" and has portrayed him as an ardent advocate of women's rights and of their equality with men. Luke's multiplication of traditions about women was cited as conclusive evidence of his unquestioned "pro-woman" stance. He not only retained traditions about women found in the Synoptic parallels (the healing of Simon Peter's mother-in-law [Luke 4:38–39 par. Matt 8:14–15; Mark 1:29–31]; Jairus's daughter and the woman with the hemorrhage [Luke 8:40–56 par. Matt 9:18–26; Mark 5:21–43]; the woman with the ointment [Luke 7:36–50 par. Matt 26:6–13; Mark 14:3–9]; the women at the tomb [Luke 24:1–11 par. Matt 28:1–8; Mark 16:1–8]), he also extended his catalogue of traditions about women by including material from his special source ("L"). These stories are found only in the Lukan gospel: (1) the infancy narrative with an accent on Mary's agency and experience in the divine plan (1:5–2:52); (2) the raising of the son of the widow of Nain (7:11–17); (3) the Galilean followers of Jesus (8:1–3); (4) the Mary–Martha story (10:38–42); (5) the cure of the "bent over" woman (13:10–17); (6) the parable of the lost coin (15:8–10); (7) the persistent widow who appears before the judge (18:1–8); (8) women preparing the spices before the sabbath (23:56).

Arguments in support of Luke's favorable treatment of women are based both on his inclusion of multiple traditions about women—with particular attention to their physical, spiritual, and moral needs—and on his creative and extended parallelisms of women with men in the Third Gospel and Acts. Examples of this complementary relocation and "pairing" of traditions about women with those about men are illustrated as follows:

GOSPEL OF LUKE

Luke 2:25–38	Simeon and Anna, a priest and priestess
Luke 4:25–28	The widow of Sarepta and Naaman
Luke 15:4-10	Man with 100 sheep, woman with 10 pieces of silver
Luke 23:55–24:35	Women at the tomb, men on the Emmaus road

ACTS

Acts 9:32–43	Aeneas and Tabitha
Acts 16:11–34	Lydia, the slave girl, and the Philippian jailer
Acts 17:34	Dionysius and Damaris

Observers have noted that women show greater faith and love in several of the Lukan parallels: Mary's faith exceeds that of Zechariah (Luke 1:11–20, 26–38), the sinful woman exhibits a love not found in Simon the Pharisee (Luke 7:36–50). Similarly, the parallelism between the women at the tomb and the Emmaus disciples contrasts the women's resurrection faith with the male disciples' sadness and despair.

In Luke, the pairs form a single unit, or a sequence with architectural "pairs of stories" usually co-joined (Luke 1:5–23 and 26–38; Luke 2:25–35 and 36–38; Luke 4:31–39; Luke 11:29–32; Luke 13:18–19 and 20–21). In Acts, most of the parallelisms consist of names of persons, couples, or simply the designation "both men and women" (and not paired stories; see Acts 1:13–14; 2:17–18; 5:1–11; 5:14; 8:12; 24:24). In the Third Gospel and Acts *both* women and men are disciples and both witness to the joy and truth of salvation in Christ. In the Lukan story, women actively participated with men in the ministry of Jesus from the early days in Galilee (Luke 8:1–3).

Careful and critical reassessments of Luke as an apologist for women's rights have challenged this view in recent years. While acceding that Luke used traditional material about women for catechetical purposes (instruction and edification), a number of scholars have shown that Lukan redactional and apologetic tendencies actually restrict women's prophetic ministry in some instances, reinforcing women's conformity to conventional, culturally prescribed roles of passivity, submission, silence, and marginality.

According to some exegetes, the proscription of women's influence, authority, and power in Luke-Acts can be observed in at least three instances. The Lukan redactional shifts are especially apparent when one juxtaposes traditions about women's agency in the Synoptic traditions. For example, in Mark, the woman who anoints Jesus acts as a prophet, proclaiming Jesus' messiahship and his death (Mark 14:1–9, similarly Matt 26:6–13; John 12:1–8). But in Luke's redaction of the tradition, the deed is robbed of its prophetic force, and becomes, instead, a story of "a woman of the city, a sinner" who repents and is forgiven (Luke 7:36–50, esp. vv. 37, 39).

A second example of the Lukan reinforcement of women's conformity to conventional societal norms of passivity and silence may be noted with Mary, the sister of Martha. Although her posture as a serious student and learner at the feet of the charismatic rabbi (teacher) is affirmed by Jesus, Mary is silent

(Luke 10:38–40), unlike many of her male "disciple" counterparts (and other male interlocutors), who engage Jesus in questioning and response, and active verbal exchange. Also interesting is the Lukan omission of the names of women at the events of the crucifixion, retained in the Matthean and Markan parallels and the Johannine Gospel (Matt 27:55–56; Mark 15:40–41; Luke 23:49; John 19:25–27).

WOMEN IN ACTS

INTRODUCTION

Even a cursory survey of Acts will reveal its relative dearth of traditions about women when compared with the Third Gospel.

That women were "first at the cradle" and "last at the cross" of Jesus is certainly corroborated by the Third Gospel. Women figured rather prominently in the beginning of Jesus' ministry in the infancy narratives (Luke 1:5–2:52), in some of the parables of Jesus (including material in the Synoptic parallels and in Luke's special source "L": Luke 13:20–21 par. Matt 13:33, the women with the leaven: Luke 15:8–10; 18:2–5), and at the resurrection of Jesus (Luke 23:26–31, 49, 55–56; 24:1–11, 22–27).

Even if the women are not counted among the Twelve in the Third Gospel, and even if the Lukan traditions suggest that men were "the" authoritative witnesses and transmitters of the gospel throughout the duration of Jesus' earthly ministry and in the impending Christian missionary movement, women are depicted as prophets, witnesses, participants, and disciples in the Gospel of Luke (Luke 2:36–38; 8:1–3; 15:8–10).

Women are mentioned at the outset in Acts, among those gathered in the upstairs chamber or room with the eleven and Jesus' brothers, devoting themselves to prayer (Acts 1:14). Mary, the mother of Jesus, and "certain women" present with the group are depicted as "insiders" who are an integral part of the praying community in Jerusalem and who awaited the promise of the Holy Spirit (Luke 24:45–52; Acts 1:1–8).

The allusions to women in Acts following Acts 1:14 are somewhat sporadic and are often only incidental references, but they do provide us with a systematic portrayal of women's initial involvement in the emergence and growth of the postresurrection church by a canonical writer. Women in Acts are seen as recipients of the Holy Spirit, active agents, missionaries, and witnesses in spreading the Christian faith, hosts of churches in their homes, teachers, exemplars of good works, prophets, beneficiaries of God's healing and liberating power, and as hailing from diverse economic groups, including the very wealthy and the economically disfranchised. But even this compendious summary must be assessed with critical reserve in light of the tendencies of biblical writers to proscribe women's presence, participation, leadership, and agency in traditions that narrate Christian origins.

WOMEN AND THE HISTORY OF EARLIEST CHRISTIANITY

Feminist biblical interpreters and theologians have highlighted the historical and cultural restrictions of women in the Christian tradition from its infancy. Here the phrase "feminist biblical interpreters and theologians" is not used narrowly or in "exclusivist" terms to refer to white, North American women but, as Elisabeth Schüssler Fiorenza observes in her definition of "feminist" in the introduction to the first volume of this commentary, "feminist" is used broadly as a universalized women's movement and a gender theory that concerns itself with the unilateral oppression of all women by all men.[1] Thus, it is used here of Catholic and Protestant women, Jewish women, African women and women of African descent, Asian, Hispanic, Latin American, Native American, white European and North American women, and women of faith from diverse global communities and ecclesial, social, and political locations.

Members of the cross-cultural and global communities of Christian feminist biblical interpreters, in particular, have employed the methodological insights of form criticism, source criticism, and redaction criticism to show that the biblical writers selectively redacted and reformulated their traditional sources and materials in accordance with their particular objectives and theological intentions. The early Christian writings, then, are not "objective," factual transcripts but pastorally engaged writings whose form and content were shaped by the particular theological and sociological contexts and experiences of the early Christians. Traditions about Jesus, Paul, and the emergence and growth of the Christian movement permeated and shaped preaching, teaching, liturgy, missionary propaganda and apologetic, and praxis, and these traditions were likewise adapted for new situations in the Christian communities.

Articulations and expressions of Christian faith within the Christian Testament *and* the subsequent interpretations of those texts and traditions in the history of interpretation are rooted in androcentric language and structures of symbolic values. In addition, they have been transmitted, reinforced, and institutionalized through patriarchal organizations. Since early Christian authors and communities lived in an androcentric, predominately patriarchal world, Christian Testament authors generally accepted as normative cultural assumptions about gender valuations and roles. It is not surprising, then, that there is a scarcity of information about women in the traditions of the early Christian authors. This is particularly the case with the Gospels and Acts, since they were written toward the end of the first century when the process of the patriarchalization of the earliest church was well under way.

Androcentric interests and perspectives informed the selection, redaction, and transmission of traditions about the Christian movement, and thus a "hermeneutics of suspicion" should inform any reading of women's presence, participation, agency, and leadership in the first-century churches. The Christian Testament writers' marginal interest in these aspects of women's lives does not mean that women's presence, active and durative participation, proactive agency, and widespread and visible leadership were not realities in multiple geographical and cultural contexts in the early Christian communities. In fact, some Christian Testament traditions affirm such activities as normative (Rom 16:1–15; Phil 4:2–3).

What should be recognized and acceded to in analyses of women's agency and participation in the early church is that we are faced with "silences" about women's historical and theological experience and contributions arising from androcentric and patriarchal assumptions that (1) the stories and traditions were of negligible importance in general, and (or) (2) the stories and traditions were a threat to accepted cultural conventions and norms, or to the gradual patriarchalization of the Christian movement toward the close of the first century. *In short, we should never conclude that Christian Testament traditions about women represent comprehensive and sufficient data about the role of women in the Christian communities.* The traditions that *are* narrated must each be evaluated through the refracted lens of the biblical author, with particular and critical attention to the author's redactional purposes and theological and practical interests.

METHOD IN ASSESSING WOMEN'S TRADITIONS IN ACTS

At least three suppositions must be taken seriously in assessing the traditions about women in Acts, particularly in light of the aforecited observations about the reality of Acts as a first-century narrative encoded with the androcentric and patriarchal interests of its time.

First, a "hermeneutics of suspicion" is required in weighing the adequacy of Luke's portrayal of women's participation in the emergence of the post-resurrection church and within the progressive Christian missionary movement in Acts.

A hermeneutics of suspicion critiques the assumption, still fairly widespread in modern biblical research and interpretation, that Acts reports fully "what actually happened" in the beginning of early Christianity. Particularly with reference to women, this premise overlooks the fact that references to women in the Bible are already filtered through androcentric interpretation and redaction. That "men" and "males" are depicted as the primary historical subjects and agents in church history generally is not questioned, with the result that the historical role of women (and not men) is perceived to be problematic, because maleness is the "adequate" historical norm, and the hegemony of an almost exclusively male presence, leadership, and agency in the Christian missionary movement is accepted *ipso facto*. Androcentric reconstructions of early Christian history thus depict as acceptably normative a reconstruction of the history of the early church according to the male model of masculine dominance that marginalizes women.

A hermeneutics of suspicion that critiques the adequacy of the portrayal of women's leadership and ministry in Acts also underscores the fact that we have only selected—if hegemonic—glimpses of the diversity and range of even male leadership and agency outside of leading protagonists such as Peter and Paul (e.g., Barnabas, Acts 4:36–37). Again, Acts must be recognized as portraying a "particular" *Tendenz* in its narration of Christian origins, but particularly with reference to women's agency.

A second supposition that must be considered in assessing women in the tradition history of Acts is that at least one of the many objectives for this assessment is the restoration of women to early church history and the restoration of a more representative early church history to women (and men). This task requires text-based analyses in which texts are evaluated historically in terms of their own time and culture and are assessed theologically in terms of women's efforts to transform and change societal structures (including ecclesial structures) and institutions.

A text-based hermeneutic, while helpful in evaluating texts in terms of their *Sitz im Leben,* is inadequate by itself. A text-based approach (which is never fully "objective," "neutral," or value-free, given the impossibility of "presuppositionless" exegesis) may provide an opportunity for readers to identify a biblical writer's ideological scripts, including androcentric tendencies and polemical theological patriarchal functions, but this approach does not provide adequate models for identifying and assessing possible alternative and more egalitarian impulses and developments in the first-century churches. Further, the message within the text may not be fully representative of human reality and history. Additionally, the insights of diverse *types* of readings, including readings informed by the insights of rhetorical criticism, and the insights of diverse *hermeneutical strategies,* may allow readers to reimage broader possibilities of women's participation within the early Christian communities.

Moving women from the "margins" of early church history to the "center" of structures of human social relations and institutions requires a "hermeneutics of context," in which there is a shift to the diverse sociohistorical contexts of androcentric texts in general. This means that instead of only creating a litmus test to determine the degree to which Paul or Luke was a male chauvinist as revealed by text-based hermeneutics, historiographical interrogations require different conceptual frameworks and theoretical questions.

A series of broader epistemological, conceptual, and ideological questions that might be asked with reference to women's participation and agency in early church history might include the following: Why were women attracted to the Jesus movement? What models of female-male co-leadership and partnership existed in the Christian communities and the Christian missionary movement, particularly in view of the fact that Jesus' ministry was perceived by some to advocate a countercultural ethos in which prevailing cultural norms about gender, national origin, and economic status were no longer to be a barrier to, or solely determinative of, the quality and character of structures of social relations within the new eschatological community of God inaugurated by Jesus Christ? Further, what can we know of the nature of women's emancipatory struggles to be full and active participants and agents in the emerging churches in discrete urban and nonurban geographical entities? What strategies and forms of resistance, advocacy, and conformity were utilized by women (and men) on behalf of traditionally marginalized persons such as women and slaves within the evolving ecclesial communities?

In addition to the aforecited questions on women's participation in first-century ecclesial communities, the following subjects invite further critical scrutiny: How numerous were female-headed Christian households such as Lydia's (Acts 16:11–15) in the earliest Christian communities? Were Christian households headed by women similar to male-headed Christian households (the meeting places of most early Christian groups were, after all, private houses)? Admittedly, the answer to this query may be especially elusive, since the Christian Testament (and Acts) focuses largely on "public" rather than private portrayals of Christian beginnings. But these and other questions invite a revisiting and revisioning of critical methodological strategies and interdisciplinary conversations and explorations that may provide a larger window through which to view and assess the dearth of ancient sources in the interest of reconstructing and enlarging our understanding of women's histories in the early church.

Third and finally, placing women in the center of ancient cultural contexts (in contradistinction to male-centered historiographical and heuristic tendencies to place men normatively within the center of the frame) requires that a wider net be cast to garner many neglected or overlooked sources (including literary and nonliterary documents such as inscriptions, papyri, monumental remains, art, funerary remains, and literary sources written by women—in other words, not just literary sources written by men *about* women).

New and revisionist methodological approaches are required to recover and reconstruct women's histories. In addition to the need for new and different conceptual categories and epistemological and ideological frameworks for undertaking this task of historical retrieval is the need to address such issues as the perpetuation of anti-Judaic tendencies in the rendering of early church history and biblical interpretation. For example, Christian biblical interpreters often draw a rigid line of demarcation between "women in Judaism," and "women in Christianity," identifying Judaism as thoroughly patriarchal and negative, and Christianity as providing an unqualifiably positive and "pro-woman" stance about first-century women. But many of the women in early Christianity were also Jewish (e.g., the first Christian women in Acts—Luke's narrative of the birth of the church—were Jewish [Acts 1:14; 5:14; 6:1; 8:1–3]).

In the final analysis, the purpose of investigating critically such matters as women's participation and agency in the early church is not just to supplement our cognitive data bank about women in the earliest Christian communities but to assess whether we teach or preach male-configured history, androcentric theology and ethics, or patriarchal biblical interpretations as though they were universals, and as if they reflect adequately God's past (and present) salvific activity within the human family. Further, it is important to consider the pedagogical, theological, and ethical implications of this approach for church, synagogue, and society. It is essential that biblical interpreters create a variety of models and paradigms for teaching scripture from inclusive, non-racist, and nonimperialist perspectives.[2] Assessments and reconstructions of women's participation in early Christianity—both positive and negative—may provide helpful insights about the task of creating and nurturing an alternative, more liberating anthropology, soteriology, and ethics (praxes) *for women and men* in contemporary faith communities. Responsible biblical interpretation should lead us to engaging these issues.

COMMENTARY

Acts contains far fewer allusions to women than the Third Gospel. In the Lukan conception of early church history in Acts, leadership of the early Christian mission was in the hands of men. Whereas the Pauline letters depict women as apostles, missionaries, patrons, co-workers, prophets, and leaders (see 1 Cor 11:2–16, where Paul presupposes that women prophesy; Gal 3:28; Rom 16:1–15; Phlm 2; Phil 4:2–3), the portrayal of women as church leaders in Acts is negligible. The "Hebrew and Hellenist" tension among the widows depicts a resolution under fully male leadership (Acts 6:1–2).

The Joelic prophecy invoked by Peter in support of the mighty and transformative acts of God in both nature and social relationships suggests that the promise of a new order is finally in place. The new vision of the value of human personhood—a new anthropology—requires that co-leadership models of complementarity and shared ministry for women and men in the Christian missionary movement become actualized. Women and men alike and slave and free alike were to exhibit the creative power of God at work in human history through the Holy Spirit—negative societal norms about gender (women) and status (slaves) valuations were no longer normative in the new eschatological community:

> In the last days it will be, God declares, that I will pour out my Spirit upon all flesh, and your sons and your daughters shall prophesy. . . . Even upon my slaves, both men and women, in those days I will pour out my Spirit; and they shall prophesy. (Acts 2:17–18)

Even with the Lukan incorporation of the Joelic prophecy, with its declaration of God's boundless deeds with and through persons from the diverse family of God (and not just through the agency of a "male-exclusive" or "elitist" coterie within the community), the allusions to female and male prophets in Acts stand in sharp relief. Whereas there are several allusions to male prophets, including a detailed description of Agabus's prophecies on two occasions (see Agabus in Acts 11:27–30; 21:10–11; see also Acts 13:1), the passing allusion to Philip's four prophesying daughters is striking in its virtual absence of detail (Acts 21:8–9).

Linguistically, Luke demonstrates a penchant for male-exclusive terms such as "brothers," "men," and "fathers," even when women (who were also recipients of the Holy Spirit and salvation in Jesus Christ) are present (Acts 1:11; 2:5, 14). Peter proclaims the Joelic prophecy to a gender-inclusive gathering, but he addresses the assembly consistently: "Men, Israelites" (Acts 2:22); "Men, brothers" (Acts 2:29, 37). Similarly, Peter's sermon in Solomon's portico is prefaced with the words: "Men, Israelites" (Acts 3:12) and "brothers" (Acts 3:17). The second leading protagonist in the narrative, Paul, continues this pattern of address (Acts 13:16, 26; 15:36; 17:22; 22:1).

Women in Acts comprise a significant number of converts to the Christian faith (Acts 5:14; 17:4, 12), and yet Luke attributes extremely minimal narrative discourse (and no speeches) to women (see Sapphira in Acts 5:8; Lydia in Acts 16:15; the female enslaved and exploited for economic gain in Acts 16:17), in contradistinction to the plethora of speeches and other types of discourse by men throughout the narrative of Acts. Women are virtually silent in Acts.

Luke counts women as numbered among the converts who knew firsthand the pangs and travails of arrest in their homes at the hands of a zealous Saul who was "ravaging the church by entering house after house; dragging off both men and women" (Acts 8:3). Similarly, women converts experienced the distress of imprisonment, and neither were they exempt from the persecution of the faithful "up to the point of death" (Acts 8:3; 22:4–5).

WOMEN IN FEMALE–MALE PARALLELISMS

Examples of the female-male parallelism so widespread in the Third Gospel are still discernible in Acts. These literary arrangements include the editorial summation, "both men and women." Luke records that "great numbers of both men and women" were added to the church in the successful missionary endeavors (Acts 5:14). Even the advance of the gospel to Samaria resulted in the baptism of "both men and women" (Acts 8:12).

In a similar type of parallelism, which has as its focus the "conversion" motif, the national and social status of both female and male converts is noted:

Acts 17:4   a great many of the devout Greeks and
             not a few of the leading women (of the
             mission in Thessalonica)
Acts 17:12   not a few Greek women and men of high
             standing (of the mission in Beroea)

The female–male parallelism in conversion traditions even extends to "householder stories." The tradition about the conversion and baptism of the Philippian jailer "and his entire family" is reminiscent of the tradition about the conversion and baptism of the Philippian Lydia and her household, narrated earlier within the narrative of Acts 16 (Acts 16:11–15, 25–34).

Female–male parallelisms in Acts sometimes occur within contexts where women and men are actually named, as in the reference to Dionysius and Damaris, both of whom were numbered among the believers who joined the Christian movement as a result of Paul's impassioned address in Athens (delivered before the council of the Areopagus [Acts 17:16–34]). Interestingly, "Dionysius the Areopagite" is named with his official title, and he was likely a member of the court of the Areopagus, the governing power of the city. "Damaris" is simply named, with neither honorifics of any kind nor the slightest clue about her identity. It is true that Luke does not consistently develop the characters whom he includes within the narrative development of Acts, but where moderate or extended characterization occurs, male figures typically receive far more narrative attention.

Luke's fondness for parallels extends to the naming of couples. Ananias and Sapphira represent a model of a couple who deceive both the Spirit and the church (Acts 5:1–11), while Priscilla and Aquila typify the faithful couple who together face and endure the challenges of the ministry, exercising decisive co-leadership skills in teaching and ministry on behalf of the whole church (Acts 18:1–3, 18–19, 24–28).

The incidental naming of the wives of political figures in Acts, including Felix and his wife Drusilla, and Agrippa and his wife Bernice (Acts 24:24; 25:13, 23; 26:30) is reminiscent of the naming of female–male "partners" in the infancy narratives in the Gospel of Luke. Whether married or engaged, or as persons who function as co-leaders in God's service, women and men in the infancy narratives function together as "witnesses" of and participants in God's unfolding plan for the salvation of humankind (Elizabeth and Zechariah in Luke 1:5-25; Mary and Joseph in Luke 1:26-27; Simeon and Anna in Luke 2:25-38).

Suggestions that the "dual witness" motif in the Lukan parallelisms underscores Luke's emphasis on universalism are intriguing. Also plausible are observations that Lukan use of this literary device (the pattern of twofoldness) finds its impetus in a principle within scripture itself—namely, that credible testimony is to be received "by the evidence of two or three witnesses" (Deut 19:15; Matt 18:16; 2 Cor 13:1; 1 Tim 5:19; Heb 10:28; 1 John 5:6-8). The Lukan fondness for parallelisms, repetitions, doublets, and tautologies suggests that Luke is interested in providing corroborating testimony about the importance of selected thematic motifs.

Women and men are also paired as recipients of miraculous cures. Paul heals the paralyzed man Aeneas in Lydda and subsequently Tabitha the disciple in the nearby region of Joppa (Acts 9:32-42).

ANANIAS AND SAPPHIRA (ACTS 5:1-11)

The first detailed characterization of a woman in Acts occurs with Sapphira and her husband Ananias. The literary context and thematic interest of the narrative are twofold: the use of material possessions and the *koinōnia* of the Christian community. The idyllic descriptions of community life in the summary in Acts 4:32-37 emphasized communal harmony, generosity, mutuality, and vitality. Barnabas, in the story immediately prior to the Ananias and Sapphira tradition, is a minor character within the narrative, but the significance of his deed makes him a model of the wealthy Christian woman or man whose praxis includes a constructive social ethic—particularly in assisting poorer members of the Christian community (Acts 4:34-37). Barnabas represents the Christian disciple for whom there is no disjuncture between spiritual faith, ethical life, and social commitment.

At least three observations can be made about Sapphira in the unfolding story. First, she is depicted as a partner with Ananias in decision making: "But a man named Ananias, with the consent of his wife, Sapphira, sold a piece of property; with his wife's knowledge, he kept back some of the proceeds and brought only a part and laid it at the apostle's feet" (Acts 5:1-2). Sapphira is depicted as neither a subordinate nor as a passive (but complicit) observer—she is fully a participatory agent in the sale and the distribution of the funds. Second, Luke underscores the Spirit's distributive justice in the death of Sapphira and Ananias: she is charged with lying (Acts 5:8); he is charged with deception and lying (Acts 5:3-4). Both women and men in the Christian community are equally accountable to the larger fellowship of believers, as well as to God in the Holy Spirit. Sapphira is taken seriously as a "subject" of moral agency and not merely an "object" within the narrative story—even if her personal decision results in disastrous consequences.

Third, Sapphira is to be numbered among the well-to-do women to whom Luke so frequently alludes in Acts (Acts 13:50; 16:11–15; 17:4; 18:1–3). Prominent women converts are depicted as intellectually engaged (the women in Beroea [Acts 17:10–12]; Priscilla teaching Apollos [Acts 18:26]), as well as providing for the community with their resources (Lydia in Acts 16:11–15).

The Ananias and Sapphira tradition preserves echoes of the story of Achan in the Hebrew Bible, who misappropriated a mantle, and silver and gold promised to God (Josh 7:16–26). Whereas the Joshua narrative shows that Achan's entire family is destroyed because of his misdeeds (perhaps in view of the "unitary" conception of society in which family members and animals are all destroyed [Num 16:25–33; 2 Sam 21:6, 9; Esth 9:13; Dan 6:24]), Sapphira dies as a result of her own perfidy.

The tradition functions as a cautionary tale, designed to demonstrate to both the church and the wider society an appropriate respect and reverence for the Spirit-filled community: "And great fear filled the whole church and all who heard these things" (Acts 5:11; the word *ekklēsia,* "church," meaning "assembly" or "gathering," is used here for the first time in Acts). Clearly, threats to the internal life and cohesion of the Christian community could be compromised as much by persons within the nascent community as without.

THE HEBREW AND HELLENIST WIDOWS (ACTS 6:1–6)

The story of the Hebrew and Hellenist widows is cast within the same broad narrative context as that of Ananias and Sapphira, wherein threats to church unity are consequential for persons within the community, and where the threats to the church originate from within the community (cf. Acts 4:32–6:6, but Acts 5:12–42, situated within this block of material, narrates a story of external threats, and the motif of internal threats to community life is resumed in Acts 6:1–6).

Most traditional exegetical comment on the Hebrew and Hellenist tradition in Acts 6:1–7 has as its focus the activity of the male protagonists within the story. This is not surprising, in view of Luke's almost exclusive attention to male agency and leadership in Acts. It is the "Twelve" who call together the "whole community" of the female and male disciples to select "seven men of good standing, full of the Spirit and of wisdom" to "wait on tables" (Acts 6:2b). The seven Hellenists, "men of good standing," are named for the reader and commissioned by the apostles.

There is no question of Luke's intent to achieve at least two purposes in the Hebrew-Hellenist tradition. First, Luke provides a picture of continuing developments in the life of the Jerusalem church, including the reality of a breach in the unity of the Christian community between the "Hellenists" (Greek-speaking Jews) and the "Hebrews" (Jews who spoke Hebrew or Aramaic). If the root of the controversy involves the distribution of wealth or material goods within the community instead of food, as some commentators suggest, the tradition demonstrates, as did the Ananias and Sapphira story, how problematic the issue of sharing possessions was within the early church.

Second, Luke uses this story to demonstrate a new development within the Jerusalem church. The introduction of the Hellenists Stephen and Philip into the narrative action prepares the reader for their impending and pivotal roles in helping to launch the advance of the Christian mission beyond Jerusalem and into Judea and Samaria (Acts 6:8–8:1; 8:4–40).

Traditionally, the Hebrew-Hellenist tradition is understood to provide a commendable example of the church's care for widows. Such care for widows has a long history in the Jewish and Christian traditions. Israel's legal corpus and prophetic tradition enjoined care for widows (Deut 10:14–19; 14:29; 24:17–22; Isa 1:17; Jer 7:6; 49:11; Jesus shows compassion for widows [Luke 7:11–17]; widows received assistance in 1 Tim 5:3–16).

Commendable though it is that the tradition corroborates ministries of sharing with widows in the early church, the tradition also reinforces the idea of widows as "passive" recipients of care and not "active agents" in ministry. Further, some commentators identify the widows as uniformly "poor," perhaps based on an assumption that "all" widows were poor in preindustrial, patriarchal, Greco-Roman and Jewish communities. This assumption may warrant further investigation.

What is clear here is that Luke portrays two distinct groups of women—Hebrew and Hellenist—as not participating in resolving the problems with which they were faced. The mediator-administrators were male-exclusive agents (in 1 Tim 5:9–16 widows engaged in ministry with other widows).

Interestingly, the Greek term *diakonia* is here used of the men's "ministry" of leadership and care for the widows (Acts 6:1, 4). The word is not used of Tabitha, who later engages in a ministry of leadership and care for widows in Acts 9:36–43.

THE RAISING OF TABITHA (ACTS 9:36–43)

As noted in the discussion of female-male parallelisms in Acts above, Luke juxtaposes this pericope with the healing of Aeneas, who had been bedridden for eight years (Acts 9:32–35). The story is situated within a cycle of stories about Peter's ministry of healing (Acts 9:32–43). Reminiscent of Peter's healing of the lame man near the gate of the Temple (Acts 3:1–10), these traditions provide rather moving and detailed characterizations of the central figures, with Tabitha's character receiving the most extensive development.

The tradition recalls both Jesus' raising of the son of the widow of Nain, and later, Jairus's daughter, in the Third Gospel. All three traditions contain graphic portrayals of the pathos arising from the deep sense of loss felt by the mourners (Luke 7:11–17; 8:41–42, 49–56). All three traditions also underscore the fact that the "return to life" of the three characters involves not only a "healing" but a restoration of the departed to particular "communities" of people—a son to his mother, a daughter to her parents, and a beloved and respected religious leader, activist, and philanthropist to the community.

The story also echoes a number of traditions about raising the dead in the Hebrew Bible. Parallels are striking between this story and stories that narrate restorations to life by Elijah (1 Kgs 17:8–24) and Elisha (2 Kgs 4:8–37). Luke demonstrates that the Spirit-empowered church retains the prophetic power that God exhibited in an earlier period.

Tabitha is distinguished for her commitment to a life of sustained and visible engagement in "good works" (Acts 9:36). Her reputation was so revered and her ministry so valued within the larger community of "saints and widows" (not widows only—we may assume that the "saints" were comprised of both females and males [Acts 9:41]), that the community of disciples sent two men (*andras*) to entreat Peter, "Please come to us without delay" (Acts 9:38).

As noted earlier, in spite of Luke's generally positive portrayal of Tabitha, he seems to diminish the authority of her leadership and ministry, first, by portraying her as a model of "women-in-ministry-to-women" primarily ("all the widows" stood beside Peter [Acts 9:39b]), in contradistinction to the Seven in Acts 6:1–6, who engage in ministry to both women and men (note the double emphasis on the ministry of the seven to the "whole community of disciples" in vv. 2 and 5). Second, her stellar contributions to the enhancement and empowerment of the quality of life of the widows is deemed merely "good works," and not "ministry" (*diakonia*) on a par with the deeds of the Seven.

Tabitha, unlike Aeneas, is called a "disciple" (Acts 9:36). The feminine form *mathētria* occurs here only in the Christian Testament. Further, Tabitha is the only woman expressly named a "disciple" in Acts. There is some question regarding the significance of this term for her within this context. Does the story function as a paradigm of one way in which Christian women are to function within the church? Certainly the subject warrants further scrutiny.

MARY AND RHODA (ACTS 12:1–17)

The traditions about Mary and Rhoda are situated within the context of the story of Peter's miraculous release from prison, and thus their presence is in some ways tangential to the experience of Peter. Yet several observations about both of them can be noted.

Mary is identified as the mother of John Mark. By all indications, Mary was a person of some means, who owned a house large enough to accommodate a large congregation ("many had gathered and were praying" [Acts 12:12]). There is evidence that homes with an "outside gate" had a courtyard (Acts 12:13). The fact that she had at least one servant, Rhoda, in her employ, also suggests that she may have been a woman of some financial means.

Mary appears to be well known in Christian circles for two reasons. First, she appears to have had a reputation as a prominent householder who made her ample home available as a house-church for the mission and life of the Christian community. Peter is depicted as heading straight to this "hub" of Christian community life upon his release from prison. Mary is also known as the "mother" of one of the more recognized figures within the church mission at that point, John Mark, whose character and activities Luke will subsequently develop at greater length within the narrative of Acts. According to Col 4:10, John Mark was the cousin of Barnabas, which suggests that Mary and Barnabas (both persons of some financial means) were related (Acts 13:5, 13; 15:37–39). John Mark is also identified in other Christian Testament writings (Col 4:10; 2 Tim 4:11).

This tradition is the only tradition in Acts that explicitly specifies that house-churches owned by women provided refuge during times of imprisonment and persecution. The new wave of persecution that arose in the church following the death of James the brother of John (and son of Zebedee) by Herod Agrippa I ("King Herod laid violent hands upon some who belonged to the church" [Acts 12:1]), was the precipitating factor for Peter's imprisonment. Mary's home functioned as the place of communal nurture, restoration, and renewal.

Rhoda represents one of the few named female persons who were slaves within the Christian Testament. We learn little about her—perhaps a function of her status (cf. the female enslaved and exploited in Philippi [Acts 16:16–24]). The tradition provides a rare glimpse of a female slave in the employ of a woman within the early Christian communities (but recall the Hagar-Sarah tradition in Gen 16:1–15). Rhoda's function within the narrative story is reminiscent of the women disciples' experience, following the resurrection of Jesus in Luke (Luke 24:9–11). Like the women who first proclaimed the good news of God's grace and power in accomplishing the divine will, Rhoda was not believed. Rhoda functioned as a foil for highlighting the praying community's lack of faith even as they were engaged in active intercession to God. One important difference should be noted about the "disbelief" tradition in Luke 24:9–11 and Rhoda's story: following the resurrection of Jesus, the women witnesses were disbelieved by "men," and in the Rhoda tradition, it appears that Rhoda was disbelieved by *women and men,* for "they" commented that she was out of her mind (Acts 12:15). It is possible that her status as a "slave" made her an even less credible witness in the eyes of those to whom she proclaimed God's saving deed.

An interesting "aside" about this pericope is that this is not Peter's first "emotionally charged" encounter with a female slave. It was his exposure by a female slave in the events following the crucifixion of Jesus that prompted his threefold denial and fearful flight (Luke 22:54–62).

LYDIA AND THE FEMALE WHO WAS ENSLAVED
(ACTS 16:11–15, 40; 16–24)

Lydia, the well-to-do Macedonian business woman in this tradition, is the first of two women associated with the mission in Philippi. Paul's first convert in Europe, Lydia represented a model of the prosperous businesswoman who, upon conversion, made her home and resources available for the life and work of the church. A householder who baptized her entire household upon her conversion, she is reminiscent of Mary, the mother of John Mark, whose importance within the "home" is highlighted in the Lukan narrations of traditions about women. Lydia's story also anticipates that of Cornelius, who is, like Lydia, a prosperous and pious God-fearer who accepts the Christian faith gladly and within a context that underscores the householder's hospitality (Acts 10:1–11:18).

Commendable though Lydia's work is in providing a strategic center for the emerging mission in Philippi, Lydia's leadership is portrayed in terms of a benefactor who provides resources and hospitality for those under whose leadership the mission will develop. Her own contribution to the Christian mission includes neither public leadership nor proclamations in any way, nor public affirmation by the community of women and men, although Acts 16:40 suggests that her home functioned as a house-church for Christian women and men. According to Paul, who undertook the initial evangelization of Philippi, on the other hand, a number of prominent women who functioned as co-workers with him from Philippi were very present and visible actors in the church. The Philippian women converts Euodia and Syntyche were notable leaders who proclaimed the gospel and labored side by side with Paul in the work of the church (Phil 4:2–3).

Acts 16:11–40 narrates the only story in Acts about a female who is "quadruply marginalized," according to traditional androcentric and patriarchal norms, by virtue of her gender (woman), status (slave), her possession by a spirit of divination, and her economic exploitation (exploited by her owners as a fortune-teller).

The female is depicted as a recipient of a miraculous exorcism and deliverance at the hands of Paul. But the story, and especially the story of the female herself, becomes incidental within the larger literary context. Luke focuses on the subsequent arrest of Paul and Silas, with notations of the public reactions that the healing occasioned for the Christian mission. Luke's detailed elaboration of Paul and Silas's encounters with political magistrates removes her further from the center of the narrative interest and action.

PRISCILLA AND AQUILA (ACTS 18:1–4, 18–28)

Priscilla and Aquila are introduced within the context of Paul's mission in Corinth. Not only do they function as "supportive players" and co-laborers with Paul in the mission; they are strategically linked to other communities as a result of their extensive travels (Acts 18:18). In spite of the general Lukan tendency to proscribe and delimit the role of women—and especially "prominent" women in Acts—ones see in this tradition a woman who is prominent among missionary leaders within the early Christian movement.

Priscilla and Aquila are the second couple in Acts to be given significant narrative development (see Ananias and Sapphira [Acts 5:1–11]). Aquila's identity as a Jew from Pontus is clearly noted, but we are not as certain about Priscilla's origins. Her name is associated with prominent, old Roman families, but her name alone does not provide corroborating proof of her birth (Acts 18:2). The tradition emphasizes their partnership and complementarity with each other as laborers and leaders in the Christian ministry and mission. This portrayal is reinforced at several places in the Pauline epistles (1 Cor 16:19; Rom 16:3; and 2 Tim 4:19, which also highlight Priscilla's prominence among the two).

A number of commentators have noted that the fact that her name is mentioned before Aquila's two out of three times in Acts suggests that she has a higher status than her husband (Acts 18:2, 18, 26). These independent artisans, both described as tentmakers and leatherworkers (Acts 18:1–3), are elsewhere described as having a Christian community in their house (1 Cor 16:19; Rom 16:3–5).

Priscilla is a partner with Aquila in teaching in the Christian mission, as the tradition about Apollos indicates (Acts 18:24–28). In a rare and unusual portrayal in Acts, we see a woman exercising decisive leadership and sustained intellectual engagement and instruction with a male who was himself an "eloquent man, well-versed in the scriptures" (Acts 18:24). She is not subordinate to Aquila, nor is she preoccupied with domestic duties! The tradition presumes as a "given" her stellar competence as a learned, competent, and confident church leader.

A final observation that should be noted about the tradition is that it provides evidence of Luke's familiarity with traditions about publicly prominent women church leaders. This fact makes all the more striking the notable dearth of traditions about such women in his sweeping portrayal and chronicle of early Christian history.

PHILIP'S PROPHESYING DAUGHTERS (ACTS 21:9)

Philip the evangelist was introduced for the first time in the Hebrew and Hellenist tradition (Acts 6:1–6) as one of the most visible and active evangelists and "heroes" among the Hellenists. The intriguing datum that he has four prophesying daughters is provided as a given, without comment, qualification, or apology. Set within the context of Paul's last visit to Jerusalem, the tradition highlights the continuing activity of Christian prophets in the later stages of the apostolic age.

Allusions to women prophets and women engaging in prophetic ministry are not unprecedented in Luke-Acts. Elizabeth, Mary, and Anna engaged in prophetic activity and discourse, as did men like John the Baptist, Peter, and Agabus (Luke 1:41–45, 46–55; 2:36–38; 7:26; 20:6; Acts 1:20; 2:14–21; 21:9). It is interesting that the references to women's prophetic activity in the Third Gospel are confined to the infancy narratives alone. Luke retains no tradition of a woman's prophetic activity or discourse within the main body of the Third Gospel itself.

The Lukan allusion to the four women who functioned as prophets in Acts is located within a literary context with a notable emphasis on the function of prophetic messages as providing clarity about Paul's impending journeys within the Christian mission. The tradition about the four women prophets is "sandwiched" between a tradition in which Paul received instruction from the disciples in Tyre "through the Spirit," that he was not to go on to Jerusalem (Acts 21:4) and a tradition that narrates Agabus's second prophecy in Acts, which forecasts that Paul will be bound during his visit to Jerusalem (Acts 21:10–14).

It is not possible to know with certainty if the disciples (*mathētas*) who warned Paul not to go to Jerusalem in Acts 21:4 were males. Luke comments that "wives (*gynaixi*) and children" were with the disciples from Tyre who accompanied Paul and his traveling companions to the beach as they prepared to depart (Acts 21:5–6). The fact that Luke distinguishes the "wives and children" from the "disciples" may suggest, inferentially, that Luke had male disciples in view in Acts 21:4 as the mediators of the prophetic utterance. Further, Luke has not placed a prophetic utterance in the mouth of a woman up to this point within the narrative of Acts.

The four women prophets play no discernible role within the narrative action, and they offer no prophetic utterances. Thus, even when Luke acknowledges the presence of women prophets within the early Christian communities, he "silences" them. Women prophets never offer an actual prophetic utterance in Acts—and therefore within the early Christian missionary enterprise, according to Luke (in spite of the Joelic affirmation that they will "prophesy" in the last days [Acts 2:17–18]).

Were the four women prophets a part of a community of prophets? Was it incidental that Agabus came to their home in Caesarea during the period of Paul's sojourn in their home (Acts 21:8–10)? And why would Luke sandwich a tradition about four women prophets between two traditions that narrate "male" prophetic activity and utterances while rendering the women prophets both silent and completely inactive as prophets? At least one function of the pericope, ostensibly, is its fulfillment of Acts 2:17–21, in which Peter both rehearses and forecasts the Joelic prophecy that women *will* prophesy in the last days. The mention of Philip's four daughters as prophets demonstrates a fulfillment of this prophecy, one of Luke's recurrent themes. What is clear about this tradition is that—as with the Priscilla and Aquila tradition—Luke is familiar with more about women's agency than he narrates.

WOMANIST PERSPECTIVES ON ACTS

As noted above in the section "Women and the History of Earliest Christianity," the interrogation and interpretation of the canonical scriptures has always been a cross-cultural endeavor, engaged by women from diverse intellectual, social, and historical locations. As the critical interpretive strategies and wide-ranging theoretical, conceptual, and ideological frameworks of women from a plurality of socioreligious locations continue to be heard in both church and society, new understandings of the divine–human project for the redemption and transformation of humankind enlarge our understanding of who we are called to be as the people of God in the church.

Especially welcome in women's hermeneutical discourse are documentary articulations of the plurality of perspectives and insights about biblical texts as they are filtered through particular historical contexts. It is requisite, however, that women guard against the "balkanization" of feminism in church and academy such that "territorial fragmentation turns differently articulated feminist movements into 'special interest groups' and unwittingly serves the interest of established powers."[3] One strategy for naming and respecting particular social-religious and hermeneutical perspectives, while guarding against this "fragmentation" among local, national, and global communities of women, is to persistently conceptualize and reconceptualize these feminist formulations and discourses as "open" dialogical engagements that are ever evolving, both *within* the particularized socioreligious location and *across* the ideological spectrum of multiple socioreligious communities of women (and men). It is within this context that womanist perspectives on Acts are shared as illustrative of the particularized and wide-ranging hermeneutical interrogations and interests that women may bring to biblical texts.

WOMANIST BIBLICAL INTERPRETATION

Womanist biblical and theological scholarship provides an illuminating prism through which to view and assess the significance of Acts for women. The term "womanist" was coined by Alice Walker in her book *In Search of Our Mothers' Gardens* (New York: Harcourt, Brace, Jovanovich, 1983). Describing the courageous, audacious, and "in-charge" behavior of the black woman, the term "womanist" affirms black women's connection with feminism and with the history, culture, and religion of the African-American community. Womanist theology brings the concerns and historical perspectives of black women's sociocultural and religious experiences into the discourse of biblical studies, theology, and ethics. African-American women's historical struggles against their tridimensional experience of racism, sexism, and classism in both church and society require a multidimensional biblical hermeneutics and theological and ethical analysis that takes seriously the *simultaneity* of race, gender, and class oppression as normative, dynamic structures in the lives of black women.

While many white North American feminist biblical interpreters traditionally focus theological analyses in women's experience, African-American women focus their hermeneutical, theological, and ethical analyses in the experiences of black women, men, and children, including the experiences of black peoples in the United States and in the African diaspora. But these multiple analyses are not limited to the concerns and experiences of black peoples. Womanists engage diverse and global communities of persons, particularly all persons struggling for liberation. Thus, womanist theological reflection is multidialogical in its method. *Consequently, womanist scholars seek to amplify in biblical traditions the voices not only of women but of all those who by virtue of race, class, or other anthropological referents have been historically marginalized by the biblical traditions and/or biblical writers themselves, and by subsequent interpreters of those traditions. All of the suppressed voices in androcentric texts cannot be intoned in a feminine key.*

Womanist interpreters, who have as a primary concern in their moral universe the survival, nurture, and empowerment of black men, women, and children ("community building and uplift"), cannot afford to ignore the plurality of oppressive ideologies that confront them, including all ideologies that subjugate peoples and races as "the others" to be dominated. Thus, *all* ideologies of dominance and subordination in the biblical writers, in the traditioning processes, and in the theoretical models underlying contemporary biblical, historical, and theological interpretations must be critically examined in any womanist biblical hermeneutics. They should be examined as much for their depiction of multiple forms of oppression and dominance based on nationality, ethnicity, gender, and class, as for their representations of human exploitation, marginality, and annihilation. As Alice Walker notes, "a womanist is committed to the survival and wholeness of entire people, male and female. Not a separatist . . . ."

Womanist biblical interpreters, theologians, and ethicists take seriously the salient and formative features of the black woman's social world as a hermeneutical point of departure in both biblical interpretation and theological and ethical reflection and analysis. Black religion (and particularly black Christianity) has always sought to resist efforts of American Christianity to mute and subordinate its rich and distinctive perspectives about and experiences of God. The black church has been the crucible through which systematic faith affirmations and liberating principles of biblical interpretation have been developed by black peoples.

The Bible has been a primary source of authority for life and faith (if not *the* primary source) for black people. Exposing, critiquing, and disaffirming white hegemonic interpretations, which were for centuries used to legitimate racial slavery and to reify as normative racial domination, African Americans discerned and promulgated the real biblical message of human liberation and wholeness. An ever-present "hermeneutics of suspicion" guided black female and male slaves in their excavation of the Bible for those liberating traditions that mandated their active resistance to servile conditions. Averring that authentic biblical faith declared war on all human forms of oppression, misery, and domination, black peoples claimed as their own those liberating biblical traditions, and heroes and "sheroes" who persevered against ideological and existential forces of injustice, and against all that negates or diminishes full personhood and authentic community under God. Biblical traditions also served as sources of empowerment against legions of federal, state, and regional laws through the centuries that advocated inhumane treatment and marginalization of African Americans. Biblical interpretation in the black church enabled black peoples to pursue justice proactively, relentlessly, and unapologetically in the face of racial denigration and human suffering. Black biblical interpreters, female and male alike, demonstrated that liberative biblical traditions nurtured the fulfillment of human integrity and potential and the sacrality of human life—perspectives that contravened the racist ideologies and pronouncements so widespread in much of the white North American secular and religious discourse. Traditions such as the purposeful intimacy of God in the creation of all of humankind, female and male, in God's own image (and

God's handiwork was declared "very good" in Gen 1:31); the notion of salvation as having personal and social aspects in relatedness to God, self, and others (including institutions and the environment); and the biblical affirmation of God's proclivity for speaking the word through the powerless (1 Sam 2:1–10; Luke 1:46–55; 10:21; 1 Cor 1:26–29; Phil 2:6–8) are normative themes in African-American biblical interpretation.

African-American women have throughout the centuries exposed, critiqued, and disaffirmed the often literalist, male hegemonic biblical interpretations that were used to legitimate male dominance over black women in public, private, and sacred space. The voices and pens of black women religious leaders such as Sojourner Truth, Maria Stewart, and Jarena Lee represent a fraction of the legions of black women across the class, denominational, and geographical spectrum who have resisted the limits imposed upon them *as women* by androcentric biblical interpretations and religious and secular systems of patriarchal dominance. Womanist religion scholars have sought to identify the rich, diverse, and distinctive dimensions of African-American women's engagement with the Bible through the centuries.

Survival and quality-of-life motifs recur as salient themes in African-American women's moral and theological universe of concerns. For theologian Delores Williams, the Hagar story (Gen 16:1–16; 21:1–21) is the story most relevant to black women's concern for survival, particularly in light of their experience of bondage in American history. Hagar, a black Egyptian slave, encounters Yahweh (El Roi), who meets her in the wilderness and empowers her to act *herself* to secure her own survival and that of her son Ishmael. This tradition of "wilderness experience" becomes paradigmatic for black women, whose fierce survival strategies have approximated a "wilderness experience" that required the negotiation of life-and-death struggles to secure both survival and a positive quality of life for themselves, their families, and their communities. Ethicist Toinette Eugene notes that a womanist ethical perspective looks for those "dissenting voices" in the Bible that challenge theologies that exclude or dominate. Hebrew Bible scholar Renita Weems has sought to recover and amplify the many and varied voices of women in biblical traditions whose oppression originates as much in the abuse of power by women (Hagar suffered at the hands of Sarah) as by fathers like Jephthah, whose actions resulted in his daughter's death (Judg 11:1–40). These and other womanist scholars have highlighted that aspect of a womanist hermeneutics that affirms moral values of care, compassion, and self-affirmation in relation to God and the human community. They have also highlighted those prophetic traditions in the Bible that are at the core of the call to embrace that which is life-sustaining and radically transformative in contradistinction to all that thwarts God's plans for the human family.

COMMENTARY

One can theorize a womanist hermeneutical method in the assessment of biblical texts as one in which the Bible is understood to be *a site for continued womanist struggle* in the quest to identify and retrieve liberative biblical traditions that engender the formation of a viable and transformative biblical hermeneutics, moral praxis, and theology for African-American peoples in particular, and the global human family in general.

Of particular interest to the womanist exegete are those biblical traditions and exemplars—female and male—that (1) symbolize and (or) affirm the integrity of cultural, ethnic, or national diversity in the human community, in support of the biblical vision of pluralism in personal relationships and larger human communities; (2) contribute to psychosocial health and empowerment in diverse family structures (nuclear, extended, one-parent, etc.) and a praxis that effectuates communal well being and mutuality, and (3) bear the imprint of emancipatory struggles (even if the biblical tradition does not narrate an actual "historical" occurrence but functions as a leitmotif of the biblical writer). This includes traditions where power is exercised and negotiated concretely to present radically transformative, conciliatory, and mutually empowering social relationships and (or) structures among both persons (including women and men) and communities, such that even material resources are transacted in the interest of, and for the benefit of, all.

Luke does not address precisely the three concerns listed above, but Acts does illuminate these issues in its sweeping—if sometimes idealized—account of the beginnings of the Christian church.

THE CANDACE, THE ETHIOPIAN EUNUCH (ACTS 8:26–40)

There are at least two related traditions and exemplars whose theological significance in Acts highlights the biblical vision of cultural, ethnic, or racial pluralism. The first is the "Candace" figure in Acts 8:27. Queen of the Ethiopians in ancient Napata-Meroë (modern Nubia), she represents one of the few "royal" women figures within the narrative of Acts—and, as ruler of an empire, perhaps the most powerful (cf. Drusilla, wife of the procurator of Judea, Antonius Felix [Acts 23:23–24:27]; and Bernice, wife of King Herod Agrippa II, who ruled parts of Palestine [Acts 25:13–26:32]).

"Candace" (*Kandakē*) is actually a hereditary title for the black African queen. The annals of history record an earlier Candace. An inscription from Pselchis (Dakkeh) in Nubia, from 13 B.C.E., recalls the earlier Candace (cf. Strabo, *Geog.* 17.1.54; Pliny, *Natural History* 6.186; Dio Cassius, *Hist.* 54.5.4). As Queen Mother she was the effective head of the government.

The story of the Ethiopian eunuch, the royal administrative official in charge of the entire treasury of the Candace, is a tradition that has long certified for African Americans the conviction that black peoples were not "latecomers" to the Christian story. The story of the conversion of the black African high official underscored the divine intention that black Africa (which first touched the destiny of Israel when Abraham came out of Ur and settled into Egypt) should be involved in the new faith that was to spread throughout the world. African Americans, whose experience of a white American Christianity that often legitimized the psychosocial and cultural marginalization of black people in church and society, were thus eager to reclaim an ancient biblical heritage that helped them to reestablish their connection with the faith at its inception.

The pericope of the Ethiopian eunuch has not fared well at the hands of a majority of white biblical interpreters in the history of interpretation. In my investigation of the history of scholarship on Acts 8:26–40, I noted that Eurocentric scholarship has usually ignored the significance of the Ethiopian's ethnographic identity as a "black African," arguing, in some instances, that his ethnographic identity is "unknown" or "inconsequential" in the Lukan narrative. Weighty and extensive documentation on the Ethiopian's ethnographic identity as a "black" African is actually well established by centuries of literary references and allusions in classical Greek and Latin sources to Ethiopians as "black," and it is further corroborated by extensive artistic evidence throughout the Mediterranean world since at least the sixth century B.C.E.—evidence that attests to the Ethiopian peoples' significant and continuous presence within the Greco-Roman milieu for centuries.

By ignoring the significance of the Ethiopian's ethnographic identity, many commentators have made Luke's multifold theological intentions for including the tradition of a "black" high official who was also a "eunuch" completely inaccessible to generations of biblical interpreters and readers. Given the fact that Luke's first-century readers would have been quite familiar with an Ethiopian's ethnographic identity, they would have recognized immediately his wide-ranging literary and theological purposes for narrating a tradition with a leading and active *dramatis personae* as an "Ethiopian" eunuch.

The Ethiopian eunuch's ethnographic identity qualifies him to symbolize the universal scope and outreach of the Christian gospel as inclusive of ethnically diverse persons from all nations (this tradition was also interpreted in this way by later early church writers, including Athanasius and Augustine). Further, because he was an "Ethiopian," his conversion uniquely represents the fulfillment of the prophecy that Ethiopia would "stretch out her hands to God" (Psalm 68:31). The Ethiopian's conversion *qua* "eunuch" fulfills the hope of Isa 56:3–7, which heralds a day when "eunuchs" and "foreigners" would receive "full class membership" in the assembly of God. In Acts, the Ethiopian

eunuch is a prototype of the eunuch and the foreigner who enjoy unconditional acceptance into the eschatological community. The proof-from- prophecy or prophecy-fulfillment pattern, which is especially characteristic of the
Lukan writings and reflects the practice of the "apologetic" use of the Hebrew
Bible by first-century Christians, is here used to demonstrate that the conversion of the Ethiopian eunuch fulfills the purposes of God in a multiplicity of
ways—with many related directly to his ethnographic identity.

The significance of the Ethiopian's place of origin as Napata-Meroë is also
pivotal data for discerning Luke's theological purposes. Napata-Meroë had
since Homeric times been perceived to represent "the end of the earth to the
south," or the southernmost region of the then-known world. With the Ethiopian's return home—something Luke is careful to note in Acts 8:28, 39, the
Christian gospel reached the "end of the earth" to the south—not an inconsequential detail for Luke, given Acts 1:8c, which forecast mission to the "end of
the earth."

A "hermeneutics of suspicion" is necessary in womanist interrogations of
subsequent interpretations of Acts 8:26-40. A womanist hermeneutics of suspicion questions underlying presuppositions, ethnocentric models and assumptions, and the unarticulated interests of particular contemporary biblical interpretations, thereby exposing "hidden" presuppositions operative in historical-
critical methodology. Further, it tests ways in which contemporary biblical
interpretation promotes the invisibility and marginality of particular ethnic
groups of women *and men,* and trivializes their theological, ethnic, and sociocultural significance in both the biblical narrative and within larger society.

The Eurocentric orientation of Christian Testament studies as shown in
Acts 8:26–40 is more problematic because many standard maps of Christian
Testament times and early Christian history do not include Africa south of
Egypt. The worldview of the biblical community was far more inclusive, and
the biblical horizons broader, than is often recognized by mainstream biblical
studies.

A womanist hermeneutic points out the tension *within* the narrative of Acts
regarding the Ethiopian's conversion vis-à-vis the story of the conversion of the
Gentile Cornelius (Acts 10:1–11:18). A majority of commentators argue that
the Cornelius story represents the story of the first Gentile convert in Acts,
and yet many of the same commentators agree with a consensus that the
Ethiopian eunuch was a Gentile. The Ethiopian's story is told in Acts 8:26–40,
which would make him the first Gentile convert within the narrative structure
of Acts. Some commentators have noted that since the Ethiopian eunuch tradition occurs within the cycle of stories about the mission of the Hellenists
(Acts 8:4–40, including Philip's mission in Samaria, and his ministry with the
Ethiopian eunuch), the Ethiopian's conversion represents the story of the first
Gentile convert within Hellenistic circles. The story may function as a parallel,

or perhaps a "rival," tradition to the story of the first Gentile convert in which one of the Twelve played a decisive role—the Cornelius story, to which Luke devotes more narrative space

A number of questions remain. Does Luke intend the kind of "architectonic parallelism" with the two traditions that we have seen earlier in the female–male parallelism, even if the traditions are not placed side by side? And if the Ethiopian eunuch *is* the first Gentile convert, what should the implications be for contemporary commentators who often give minimal significance to the Ethiopian eunuch tradition in general, and negligible attention to the theological significance of his Gentile status in particular? These and other questions on the relationship of the two traditions for Luke and within the history of interpretation require further scrutiny and analysis.

Two concluding observations can be made. First, both conversions occur as the result of divine intervention determining the course of events: they are brought about solely by the action of God. Second, both traditions illustrate the progression of the Christian mission beyond Jerusalem and into the Gentile world.

TABITHA (DORCAS), PRISCILLA AND AQUILA
(ACTS 9:36–43; ACTS 18:1–28)

A womanist biblical hermeneutic identifies those biblical traditions and exemplars who present models of psychosocial health and empowerment in diverse family structures (nuclear, extended, one-parent, etc.), and a praxis that brings about communal well-being and mutuality.

The Tabitha (Dorcas) tradition in Acts 9:36–43 speaks especially to African-American women's tradition of venerating the wisdom, experiences, and well-being of older black women, some of whom are widows. Especially vulnerable to the vicissitudes of social inequality and economic privation in their mature years, older black women have often been at the mercy of a system that makes adequate long-term care tenuous. Tabitha's ministry is reminiscent of women-centered networks of care for widows, who are often treated as "fictive kin" by black caretakers who are not related by birth. (Luke calls men's care of widows "ministry," but Tabitha's care of widows is called "almsdeeds" or "good works.") The widows' well-being is taken seriously by women who traditionally eschew "separateness" and "individual interest" in favor of a social activism that is also exercised in the private spheres in the interest of the family/community.

The Priscilla and Aquila tradition represents a mature and responsible relational "partnership" model between women and men for both family and ministry. The Pentecost story of the coming of the Spirit, who effects radical transformations of relationships in the new age, uses the postexilic Joelic prophecy which suggested that "sons and daughters" would prophesy and that "male and female slaves" would both be recipients of the Spirit and prophesy (Acts 2:17–18). The age of the Spirit represents a period of disruptions of traditional configurations of power. No longer is the traditional patriarchal model of male dominance–female subordination to be normative.

The hierarchally structured Greco-Roman patriarchal "extended" family, which included the paterfamilias with his wife, children, and slaves (and perhaps relatives), represented essentially an ordering of the household in which a few men exercised full power and dominance over other men, women, children, and slaves. There are several biblical traditions that suggest that nonpatriarchal structuring of social relationships was more consistent with life in the new community of God (the kingdom of God) inaugurated by Jesus Christ. The Jesus movement was dominated by an ethos of what Elisabeth Schüssler Fiorenza calls "the discipleship of equals." In this view, the disciples of Jesus did not respect patriarchal family bonds. Faithful discipleship was an eschatological calling for both women and men. Jesus' true family is defined in Mark 3:31–35 as those who do the will of God: "Whoever does the will of God is my brother and sister and mother." The discipleship of women is again affirmed in Luke 11:27–28. Here, a woman in the crowd calls out to Jesus: "Blessed is the womb that bore you, and the breasts that you sucked!" Jesus' response ("Blessed rather are those who hear the word of God and keep it") suggests that women are expected to hear the word of God and respond in active and faithful discipleship.

Jesus' vision of the *basileia* (kingdom) was a vision of a community marked by a "praxis of inclusive wholeness." The child and slave, who are typically relegated to the lowest rung on the patriarchal household ladder become, in the ministry of Jesus, a primary paradigm for authentic discipleship. Jesus' paradoxical saying in Mark 10:15 conveys this sentiment well: "Whoever does not receive the kingdom of God like a child shall not enter it." The point of the saying is not that the believer should become naïve and childlike; rather, the saying is a challenge to relinquish claims of power and domination over others. Similarly, that structures of domination should not be normative is seen in the sayings about those who would be "great" or "first" among the disciples (Mark 10:42–45; 9:33–37; par. Matt 20:25–28; Luke 22:24–27).

A second biblical tradition that suggests that traditional societal boundaries and norms may assume new and more dynamic configurations in the new age of grace is Gal 3:27–28. The stirring manifesto proclaims that expressions of diminutive power and oppression between Jews and Greeks, slaves and free persons, and men and women, are to be challenged as no longer normative for the people of God. New configurations and structures of community (*koinōnia*) and partnership require prophetic and visionary reassessments of what it means to become the new community of women and men in Jesus Christ—a new humanity (Eph 4:22–24).

Christian Testament evidence for the evolution of some female and male wife–husband relationships from structurally traditional hierarchical models to partnership models is suggested by the Priscilla and Aquila tradition. Co-laborers as tentmakers and partners with Paul in evangelism, they appear to function as an energetic and effective wife-husband team, *together* exercising leadership and pastoral oversight in the church in their house, and actively engaged in a teaching ministry to and with both men and women (Apollos, Acts 18:24–28; Rom 16:3–5; 1 Cor 16:19). That Luke depicts the social inter-action between Priscilla and Aquila based on links of mutuality rather than domination and subservience is unmistakable. The tradition provides a rare and inviting cameo of a co-leadership and shared-power model of coopera-tion, female and male leaders, and interdependency.

The Priscilla and Aquila tradition can function as a creative resource in the continuing evolution of an emancipatory black ecclesiology. Black family sys-tems have for centuries kept the awesome weight of racism and oppression from overwhelming black peoples. Many of the singularly momentous and pragmatic ideals of black theology can be traced to African-American familial moral values, passed on from generation to generation: faith, survival, self-help, elevation, unity, the affirmation of personhood, self-sacrifice, and libera-tion. The African-American family as the chief source of the black church's life and growth has functioned as a primary incubator of spiritual nurture and vital moral praxis, and with the black church the family has adapted to chang-ing societal exigencies.

The Priscilla and Aquila tradition serves as a constructive model for psy-chosocial health and empowerment within diverse family structures. The Priscilla and Aquila tradition has also served in the interest of a "culture of resistance" for African-American women religious leaders, who have em-ployed this and similar traditions about biblical women's activism and agency in the earliest Christian communities as an example and incentive for their own self-understandings of their "call" to ordained and nonordained forms of ministry and leadership in the church. Priscilla's boundless agency and leader-ship in ministry served to remind black women that their ultimate allegiance was to God, and not to human beings. A "hermeneutics of engagement," which seeks to discern the liberatory activity of God within biblical traditions, was utilized in support of this "culture of resistance," and empowered them in their efforts to resist the subordination, marginalization, and disempower-ment of women in both church and society.

THE SUMMARIES IN ACTS (ACTS 2:42–47; 4:32–35; 5:12–16)
THE HEBREWS AND THE HELLENISTS (ACTS 6:1–6)

A third womanist hermeneutical interrogation of Acts identifies traditions wherein (a) the imprint of emancipatory struggles is discernible and (b) power is exercised and negotiated concretely to present radically transformative, conciliatory, and empowering social structures and (or) relationships.

The tradition of the Hebrews and the Hellenists regarding the dispute over the daily ministry to widows (Acts 6:1–6) provides an example of a text involving emancipatory struggles. Focused on the just ministrations of relief to widows—generally among the neediest group in any society, and often one of the most vulnerable—*or* referring perhaps to the fact that the widows were not assigned *their* turn at table service (we are not told that they were poor), the Twelve initiated a communal meeting to negotiate the issues and required a mechanism for mediating social justice. The "Hellenists" (Greek-speaking Jews) and "Hebrews" (Aramaic-speaking Jews) achieved conciliation as a result of the interventionist directives of the "twelve" and the "seven men of good repute" (Acts 6:2–3).

This tradition serves Lukan interests: for example, the introduction of Stephen and his impending martyrdom and the evangelistic endeavors of Philip (both Hellenists). Additionally, the tradition highlights the continuing growth of the believing community (Acts 6:7). It also provides another example of the Lukan tendency to elevate men's leadership in the Christian community in Luke-Acts (the term *diakonia* is used of the men's care and ministry to women in Acts 6:1, 4, but not of Tabitha's care and ministry to women in Acts 9:36).

This story of a serious breach in the unity of the generally sanguine portrayal of the church's growth and relational dynamics in the Christian missionary movement at this juncture within the narrative structure of Acts underscores the reality of Luke's selective inclusion and (or) diminution of traditions according to his theological interests. Acts tends to neglect traditions of women's agency, and there are few traditions that allow us to glimpse in Acts what were probably more normatively internal cultural, gender, status, and class tensions in the emerging church. The tradition of the Hebrews and the Hellenists does serve as a reminder of the need to face squarely social disruptions and to act constructively in the interest of effecting justice and mutuality in the negotiation of emancipatory struggles in communities of believers.

The summaries in Acts provide idealized reports of the church's success. These interim accounts give a synopsis of internal communal solidarity, with attention to apostolic teaching, the sharing of fellowship meals, and devotion to prayer. The depictions of Christian praxis embodied in concrete acts of commitment-engagement in community provide images of ways in which the Spirit can be embodied in the church.

Contemporary believers may be well served by these portraits to recall that processes for achieving liberation require a multipronged approach, with purposeful and responsible attention to the spiritual, social, economic, and moral dimensions of life in human communities. The divine invitation for the church ever to restructure itself as the "new community" is the key to its prophetic witness and its pastoral impact.

NOTES

1. Elisabeth Schüssler Fiorenza, "Transforming the Legacy," in *Searching the Scriptures: A Feminist Introduction,* ed. Elisabeth Schüssler Fiorenza (New York: Crossroad, 1993), 16.

2. See, for example, Katie G. Cannon, "The Bible from the Perspective of the Racially and Economically Oppressed," in *Scripture: The WORD Beyond the Word* (The Women's Division, General Board of Global Ministries, United Methodist Church, 1985), 475–87; Joanna Dewey, "Teaching the New Testament from a Feminist Perspective," *Theological Education* 26 (1989): 86–105.

3. Schüssler Fiorenza, "Transforming the Legacy," 17.

4. The womanist analysis of the Tabitha tradition focuses on "older widows," but the age of a widow may vary (they can be older or younger). A "widow" is a woman of any age whose husband has died (cf. instructions for older and younger widows in 1 Tim 5:9–16). The Tabitha tradition provides no clue about the age of the widows. The point in the womanist analysis of the tradition is that widows who are economically poor do benefit appreciably from ministries of care, support, and empowerment.

RECOMMENDED READINGS

Brooten, Bernadette J. "Early Christian Women and Their Cultural Context: Issues of Method in Historical Reconstruction." In *Feminist Perspectives on Biblical Scholarship,* edited by Adela Yarbro Collins, 65–91. Atlanta: Scholars Press, 1985.

Bruce, F. F. *The Acts of the Apostles: Greek Text with Introduction and Commentary.* 3rd rev. and enlarged ed. Grand Rapids: Eerdmans, 1990.

Conzelmann, Hans. *Acts of the Apostles: A Commentary on the Acts of the Apostles.* Hermeneia. Philadelphia: Fortress, 1987.

D'Angelo, Mary Rose. "Women in Luke-Acts: A Redactional View." *Journal of Biblical Literature* 109 (1990): 441–61.

Eugene, Toinette. "Moral Values and Black Womanists." *Journal of Religious Thought* 44 (1988): 23–34.

Haenchen, Ernst. *The Acts of the Apostles: A Commentary.* Philadelphia: Westminster, 1971.

Martin, Clarice J. "A Chamberlain's Journey and the Challenge of Interpretation for Liberation." In *Interpretation for Liberation,* edited by Katie Geneva Cannon and Elisabeth Schüssler Fiorenza, 105–35. *Semeia* 47. Atlanta: Scholars Press, 1989.

—— "The *Haustafeln* (Household Codes) in African American Biblical Interpretation: 'Free Slaves' and 'Subordinate Women.'" In *Stony the Road We Trod: African American Biblical Interpretation,* edited by Cain H. Felder, 206–31. Minneapolis: Fortress, 1991.

——. *Tongues of Fire: Power for the Church Today. Studies in the Acts of the Apostles. 1990-91.* Horizons Bible Study. Louisville: Presbyterian Church USA, 1990.

—— "Womanist Interpretations of the New Testament: The Quest for Holistic and Inclusive Translation and Interpretation." *Journal of Feminist Studies in Religion* 6 (1990): 41–61.

Ruether, Rosemary Radford. "The Feminist Critique in Religious Studies." In *A Feminist Perspective in the Academy: The Difference It Makes,* edited by Elizabeth Langland and Walter Gove, 52–66. Chicago: University of Chicago Press, 1981.

Schüssler Fiorenza, Elisabeth. *Bread Not Stone: The Challenge of Feminist Biblical Interpretation.* Boston: Beacon, 1984.

—— *Discipleship of Equals: A Critical Feminist Ekklesia-logy of Liberation.* New York: Crossroad, 1993.

——. *In Memory of Her: A Feminist Theological Reconstruction of Christian Origins.* New York: Crossroad, 1983.

——. "Remembering the Past in Creating the Future: Historical-Critical Scholarship and Feminist Biblical Interpretation." In *Feminist Perspectives on Biblical Scholarship,* edited by Adela Yarbro Collins, 43–63. Atlanta: Scholars Press, 1985.

——, ed. *Searching the Scriptures: A Feminist Introduction.* New York: Crossroad, 1993.

Talbert, Charles H. *Literary Patterns, Theological Themes, and the Genre of Luke-Acts.* Society of Biblical Literature Monograph Series 20. Atlanta: Scholars Press, 1974.

Tolbert, Mary Ann. "Protestant Feminists and the Bible: On the Horns of a Dilemma." In *The Pleasure of Her Text: Feminist Readings of Biblical and Historical Texts,* edited by Alice Bach, 5–23. Philadelphia: Trinity, 1990.

Weems, Renita J. *Just a Sister Away: A Womanist Vision of Women's Relationships in the Bible.* San Diego, CA: LuraMedia, 1988.

Williams, Delores S. *Sisters in the Wilderness: The Challenge of Womanist God-Talk.* Maryknoll, NY: Orbis, 1993.

Wimberly, Edward P., and Anne Streaty Wimberly. *Liberation and Human Wholeness: The Conversion Experiences of Black People in Slavery and Freedom.* Nashville: Abingdon, 1986.

The Acts of Thecla

SHEILA E. MCGINN ◆

INTRODUCTION

THE ACTS OF THECLA, also known as *The Acts of Paul and Thecla* or *The Martyrdom of the Holy Proto-Martyr Thecla*, is one of the few surviving texts of early Christianity that feature a female figure in the key role. Once embedded within the apocryphal *Acts of Paul,* the *Acts of Thecla* also circulated as an independent narrative.

TEXT

The text of the *Acts of Thecla* is attested in the Greek original and Latin translation as well as in Old Syriac, Armenian, Old Slavonic, Ethiopic, Arabic, and Coptic versions.[1] A list of the most significant texts, and an English translation, can be found in Wilhelm Schneemelcher's discussion of the *Acts of Paul* in the collection of *New Testament Apocrypha.*[2] Currently under way is a critical edition of the text of the *Acts of Paul* (including the *Acts of Thecla*), by Willy Rordorf, which will be published in the new Brepols Series *Corpus Christianorum, Series Apocryphorum.*[3]

METHODOLOGICAL CONSIDERATIONS

The *Apocryphal Acts of the Apostles* long have been viewed as sharing a common tradition.[4] There are elements of the narratives that are repeated in the various *Apocryphal Acts of the Apostles,* for example, the "chastity stories" analyzed by Virginia Burrus.[5] Thus, study of any one of the *Apocryphal Acts* cannot be done in isolation from the others. Yet each of the *Apocryphal Acts* also has its unique character, which cannot be overlooked. Both of these points are particularly significant for an understanding of the *Acts of Thecla,* since the *Acts of Thecla* was preserved most often not as an independent *Acts* but as a part of the *Acts of Paul.* And yet there is clearly a break in the narrative of the *Acts of Paul* where the *Acts of Thecla* is inserted, and the *Acts of Thecla* presents some viewpoints that are remarkably distinct from the *Acts of Paul*— for example, in regard to both women and Paul.

For a decade or more, the androcentric bias of the textual tradition of early Christianity has been widely recognized. Scholars taking a "sociology of knowledge" perspective have also brought into question the very methods used for studying such texts—as well as nontextual data—because of the biased nature of all these approaches when it comes to uncovering the history of women. It is now a commonplace that the surviving texts of the early Christian era were written and preserved by the educated class. Thus, they cannot be viewed as being representative of the views and interests of all persons in society; rather, one must be much more circumspect about generalizing from the opinions of the elite to the general population. At best, the texts may represent the views of the elite class *about* the other classes.

It is likewise the case with women: texts may include discussions of women, but most often these discussions convey men's views of women, not women's views of themselves. In the case of the *Apocryphal Acts of the Apostles,* while the models reflected there indeed "are different from those which that church sanctioned . . . ,"[6] the fact that the *Apocryphal Acts* were not transmitted within the canon does not preclude their having been affected by the redactional interests of an institutional and patriarchal church. The recontextualization of the Thecla legend within the *Acts of Paul* itself has the effect of subordinating the woman's story to that of the man, surely a reflection of the patriarchal interests of the church. One must be careful in trying to recover a "social history of women" from a textual tradition that itself is elitist and androcentric.

These facts make it imperative that one develop a significantly different stance from which to utilize the traditional methods of scholarly analysis. Following such feminist scholars as Elisabeth Schüssler Fiorenza and Letty M. Russell, and philosophical theorist Hans-Georg Gadamer, I take a "hermeneutic of suspicion" as my basic stance or approach to the data of the early Christian era.[7] Since the hermeneutical stance, by definition, precedes methodology, one can speak not so much of a difference in method as a difference in the way in which the data gleaned from the application of traditional methods are assessed. Textual analysis must be undertaken with the awareness that all the surviving texts of early Christianity are filtered through an androcentric and patriarchal perspective and, therefore, suppress (and often devalue) the activities and experiences of women while highlighting and extolling the experiences and activities of men. Hence, one must always ask not only what is being said by the author but also what is being assumed or ignored, marginalized or repressed.

This difference in hermeneutical stance has striking effects on both the questions asked and the answers uncovered in an investigation of this type.

The very shape of this commentary volume, including as it does the canonical as well as some of the noncanonical scriptures, calls into question—even refutes—the traditional assumption that the historical process of determining the content and scope of the scriptural canon itself is free of such androcentric bias. That this commentary on the *Acts of Thecla* exists at all is the fruit of such a new feminist critical stance toward the study of early Christianity.

A brief review of a few of the traditional assumptions about the *Apocryphal Acts of the Apostles,* including the *Acts of Thecla,* will serve to illustrate this point. First, until quite recently there was a strict boundary between the apocryphal and the canonical writings, with the noncanonical writings being viewed as less important and less representative of the history of early Christianity—simply because they are noncanonical. This imaginary boundary is now breaking down, and with it are going some assumptions about such "apocryphal" writings: for example (1) that they were rejected because they teach heresy; (2) that they represent forms of discipline that were aberrant in their sociohistorical context (i.e., they were produced by "schismatic" sects); (3) that, as a result, there is nothing for Christians to learn from the theology and spirituality espoused by the apocryphal texts.

In this introduction, I aim to refute the first two of these assumptions. A question that will be in the background of this commentary is why this text became one of the "rejected" works if doctrine and ascetic discipline are not viable reasons. I suggest that the highlighting of a woman as an apostle of early Christianity had a tremendous influence on the decision of third-century opponents of the *Acts of Paul* to brand it as heretical.

The commentary that follows is based on the premise that, in the case of the *Acts of Thecla,* the third assumption is similarly groundless. Sociohistorical analysis of the *Acts of Thecla* reveals not only the sociocultural background of the audience and author of the text but also the social, economic, political, and religious forces in second-century Asia Minor that shaped the author and audience and their self-expressions. A study of this second-century legend thus can aid in a historical reconstruction of the early Christian movement. Finally, it can be formative for development of a contemporary theological synthesis that takes into account the experience and theology of women.

DATE

Along with most of the other *Apocryphal Acts of the Apostles,* this text generally has been dated to the second half of the second century. Although the earliest definitive evidence of a written text of the *Acts of Paul* (including the *Acts of Thecla*) is from the Codex Claromontanus (fourth century C.E.),[8] Tertullian of Carthage (ca. 160–after 220) typically has provided the *terminus ante quem* for any discussion of dating. However, there have been two flaws in these discussions: (1) they have assumed a necessary connection between the *Acts of Thecla* and the *Acts of Paul* from the start; (2) they have not distinguished between access to the written text and knowledge of the Thecla story.

From Hippolytus of Rome (ca. 170–235) and Origen of Alexandria (185–254/5), we know that the text of the *Acts of Paul* was used in Rome and Alexandria by the mid-third century; however, they do not cite the *Acts of Thecla*.[9] This is not, therefore, reliable evidence for dating the *Acts of Thecla*.

Tertullian's evidence is ambiguous. Clearly he opposes those who use Thecla's example to argue for women's ministerial authority.[10] Yet this case could as easily have been supported by an oral tradition as by a literary document. The most we can say, then, is that Tertullian's remarks indicate that, by the beginning of the third century C.E., the Thecla story was known in North Africa and was being used by its storytellers to validate the active role of women in Christian ministries.

No later than the fourth century, the text had become—at least for some—a part of the canonical scriptures.[11] But for now its origins remain obscure.

PROVENANCE

The *Acts of Thecla*, like the *Acts of Paul*, originated in Asia Minor; both internal and external evidence supports this claim.[12] More than this we cannot say, although later cultic traditions would support Iconium or Seleucia.

COMPOSITION

There are three main theories of composition of this anonymous work. (1) The *Acts of Thecla* was originally a literary work produced by an unknown presbyter of Asia Minor (mentioned by Tertullian), who composed the *Acts of Paul* as a whole.[13] (2) A community of "widows" (continent Christian women who were supported by the institutional church) wrote the entire *Acts of Paul*, including the *Acts of Thecla*.[14] (3) The *Acts of Thecla* has its origins in a legend tradition or oral folk story told by women, which subsequently took written form—a form that bears a distinct resemblance to the Hellenistic romance.[15]

This last theory of composition seems to make most sense of the existing data for a variety of reasons. First, this theory posits the same historical pattern as is evident in the composition of the Gospel narratives and which is explicitly mentioned by the author of Luke-Acts—and there is no particular reason to presume that the "apocryphal" works of the same genre followed a different pattern. Second, it better accounts for the survival of a tradition that offers such a positive portrayal of women while exhibiting an unsympathetic or even hostile attitude toward men. Third, one can account for both the similarities and differences between the *Acts of Thecla* and the Hellenistic romantic novel if one allows for common elements in their folktale origins, rather than requiring literary dependence.[16] Finally, the theory of folk origins accounts for the wide variations in the endings found in the extant versions of the *Acts of Thecla,* since storytellers are known to "translate" their folktales by using physical features of the new locale, and adding place-names and other such details to link the legend with the immediate audience of the tale.[17]

AUTHORSHIP

The question of the identity of the final author/redactor of the *Acts of Paul,* who combined the Thecla legend with the pseudonymous Pauline letter *3 Corinthians* and the legend of Paul at Ephesus, remains to be decided.[18] Though the author's "orthodoxy" is widely accepted, the questions of the author's gender and status in relation to the Great Church are more persistent.

First, the author is a member of the great church in the sense of doctrinal orthodoxy. While the *Apocryphal Acts of the Apostles* as a whole are marked by tendencies toward encratism—a fact that may cause a certain amount of discomfort to the contemporary reader—this rigorous asceticism should not cause the reader to judge the *Acts of Thecla* as heterodox for its own time.[19] The ancient authors who criticize the *Acts of Thecla* never make asceticism an issue; rather, they focus on its example of female authority.[20] And, as I have argued elsewhere, ascetic rigorism was simply the norm for second-century Christianity in Asia Minor.[21] Thus, the author of the *Acts of Paul* (and, hence, of the extant text of the *Acts of Thecla*) fits well within the Christian mainstream.

While orthodoxy may have been a prerequisite to being an official of the Great Church, not every orthodox writer was an official of the church (e.g., Tertullian was not a presbyter). Of the four options that remain—male or female official, layman or laywoman—the "female official" seems the least likely solution to the question of the author's identity. It is difficult to reconcile Davies's theory—that the authors *of the text* were "widows" financially supported by the Great Church—with the evidence of the backlash against precisely these groups which we find in the Pastoral Epistles (e.g., 1 Tim 2:9–15; 5:3–16), particularly since the Pastorals have been dated earlier than the text of the *Acts of Thecla.* Beyond this, any suggestion of identity must remain hypothetical.[22]

While it may have been more difficult (and expensive) for a "layman" or "laywoman" to propagate a document such as this, it certainly was not impossible for an individual of high social standing. A church official would have easy access to the channels for transmitting such reports, but no doubt the same channels would be available to an individual with good social connections (e.g., an aristocratic man or woman). The only ancient source who provides further information in this regard is Tertullian, a hostile witness. While his account may be historically accurate, it is also possible that he "enhanced" it, adducing an example of a young presbyter being removed from his office to demonstrate just how dangerous the *Acts of Thecla* can be—at least to male church officials.

If there is a change in sex from the tellers of the folktale to the author/redactor of the text, we should expect the text to preserve some evidence of this. For example, if the written text of the *Acts of Thecla* betrays shifts in perception or treatment of such issues as female roles and authority, or inconsistencies in the treatment and portrayal of male figures, then it would imply that the author/redactor of the text was of a different sex than the tellers of the tale. Since there is a consensus that the folktale was transmitted by female storytellers, such evidence would imply that the author/redactor was male. Dennis MacDonald has demonstrated that such "textualized alterations of the story" indeed dominate the story of Thecla once it is imbedded in the *Acts of Paul*.[23] The question that remains, then, is whether such "textualized alterations" affect the *Acts of Thecla* taken in isolation from the rest of the *Acts of Paul*, since, from the third century on, the Thecla legend certainly did circulate independently.

In the commentary that follows, I will point out instances where I believe there is evidence that such a reorientation has taken place in the transition from the Thecla story to the written *Acts of Thecla*. The theory that I will follow in my interpretation is that the author/redactor of the text was a well-placed male member of the mainline Christian church in Asia Minor who took a woman's folktale about Thecla and "domesticated" it, giving Paul more prominence in the story, and transforming it from the *Acts of Thecla* into the *Acts of Paul and Thecla*.

PRESENT LITERARY CONTEXT IN THE ACTS OF PAUL

The *Acts of Thecla* is the third episode of eleven in the *Acts of Paul*. It follows two quite fragmentary sections relating: (1) Paul's postconversion journey from Damascus to Jericho (Jerusalem?), during which he baptizes a (male) lion; and (2) a sojourn of Paul in Antioch (but which one?), during which he raises the son of Anchares and Phila. The episodes that follow the *Acts of Thecla* concern Paul's activity in: (4) Myra, where he heals Hermocrates of dropsy and converts his wife and children (two sons); (5) Sidon, where Thrasymachus and Cleon (with their wives, Aline and Chrysa) are mentioned as disciples of Paul; (6) Tyre, where Paul drives out demons and two men are named (Amphion and Chrysippus); (7) Ephesus, where the baptized lion becomes a central figure; (8) Philippi, where Paul raises from the dead Frontina, the daughter of Firmilla; (9) Corinth, where Myrta prophesies that Paul will convert many in Rome; (10) the journey to Italy; and (11) the martyrdom of Paul.

A closer look at episode 2 illustrates just how unsympathetic is the treatment of women in these scenes of the *Acts of Paul*. The sole female character is known by name, but her significance and social station are characterized by her relationships to men—she is Phila, the boy's mother (and the wife of Anchares). And, contrary to the key male figures, she is depicted as hostile to Paul (she initially prevents his entrance into the house and thereby denies him the opportunity to work his miraculous intervention). As the opposition theme introduced through Phila builds, the cure results in an attempt to stone Paul, and he is cast out of the territory of Antioch. The redactor may even mean to imply that Phila participated in these atrocities, since Anchares is exonerated but she is not.

This episode is not unique. It is striking that, as far as we can tell from the fragmentary nature of the manuscripts, all of the key characters in these other sections of the *Acts of Paul* are male (even the animal!). Women do get speaking parts in episodes 7, 8, and 9; but, even so, the narrator betrays no interest in the female figures themselves—they simply serve to show or proclaim Paul's power and authority. In scene 7, after attending more closely to the interests and activities of Artemilla and Eubula,[24] and recounting their baptism by Paul, the narrator reports that Paul "dismissed [Artemilla] to her husband, Hieronymus."[25] The women hear Paul's gospel, but clearly it is to have no effect on their social status and marital relations. As it stands now, the lion plays a more positive and significant role in this scene than the women; he helps to rescue Paul, whereas they provide the context for the persecution against him. This dismissive and even antagonistic treatment of women provides the present literary context of the *Acts of Thecla*.

COMMENTARY

PAUL'S ARRIVAL IN ICONIUM (1–4)

The *Acts of Thecla* begins (c. 1) with Paul's arrival in Iconium after his flight from Antioch. He has two male traveling companions, Demas and Hermogenes the coppersmith,[26] who are depicted by the narrator as false brethren—that is, being false to Paul and therefore also false to Christ (cf. 1 Tim 1:19b–20; 2 Tim 1:15; 2:17b–18a). Paul's attitude toward them was to return good for evil,[27] loving them (cf. 2 Tim 2:24–26; 4:2; Titus 1:9; 2:8a) and teaching them "all the words of the Lord"[28] in a way that was appealing to them (cf.

Prov 15:26b; 18:4; Col 4:6) and faithful to the revelation Paul had received (cf. Acts 9; Gal 1:15–16a; 1 Tim 4:6; Titus 1:3; 2:1) of "the great acts of Christ."[29] The narrator indicates that this message is fully orthodox[30] by specifying that Paul's "words" include the gospel "of the birth and of the resurrection of the Beloved."[31] Thus, the gospel message according to the *Acts of Thecla* includes the affirmation of the incarnation and resurrection of Christ, *contra* Gnosticism and docetism.

(2) An Iconian Christian named Onesiphorus anticipates Paul's arrival and goes with his family[32] to meet Paul. Though other individuals are mentioned by name (i.e., Simmias, Zeno, Lectra), it is obvious that Onesiphorus is the central figure at this point, for the report continues in the third person singular. The narrator indicates that Onesiphorus wants to offer Paul the hospitality of his household. To recognize Paul, Onesiphorus will have to rely on the description Titus has given him,[33] for until now he has seen Paul "only in the spirit."[34] (3) Onesiphorus alone waits for Paul along the road to Lystra and recognizes him as fitting Titus's description.[35] Paul's lofty spiritual stature is indicated by the observation that "now he appeared like a man, and now he had the face of an angel."[36] This description points to the mediating role of Paul; it recognizes his humanity, while simultaneously implying that the message Paul conveys must be heard not as mere human teaching but as the very word of God.

(4) When they meet, Paul and Onesiphorus exchange formal greetings. Paul's companions, Demas and Hermogenes, become "jealous" because Onesiphorus refers to Paul alone as "servant of the blessed God."[37] Since the audience already knows that they are traitorous (c. 1), Onesiphorus's powers of spiritual discernment (cf. Mal 3:18; 1 Cor 12:10) are made explicit when he responds to their protest by remarking: "I do not see in you any fruit of righteousness. . . ."[38] Nevertheless, he offers to them the hospitality of his home and, thereby, the chance to repent (a chance which, we later discover, they refuse).

THE GOSPEL OF CONTINENCE AND THE RESURRECTION (5–6)

(5) Paul's arrival in Onesiphorus's house prompts "great joy, and bowing of knees and breaking of bread, and the word of God concerning continence and the resurrection . . . ." None but the last of these phrases should strike us as remarkable. Great joy is a typical biblical sign of the presence and power of God.[39] Similarly, bowing the knee is a sign of true worship, the appropriate response to God's presence (e.g., Gen 41:43; Isa 45:23; Matt 27:29; Mark 15:19; Rom 14:11; Phil 2:10). The breaking of bread is an obvious reference to a eucharistic meal as the context for Paul's preaching; however, the description of the Christian message as "concerning continence and the resurrection"

strikes an unfamiliar chord, raising the question of the relationship between the two. The ensuing report of Paul's proclamation (c. 5–6) suggests that the relationship between "continence" and the resurrection is quite an intimate one.

Paul's preaching consists of thirteen beatitudes (or macarisms), beginning with a quotation of Matt 5:8 and using the word "pure" as a springboard to the related themes of chastity, renunciation of the world, fear of God and of God's word, receiving the wisdom and understanding of Jesus Christ, keeping one's baptism "secure,"[40] and being merciful (Matt 5:7).[41] Those who exhibit these values will see God (Matt 5:8), become temples of God,[42] be pleasing to God, "inherit God,"[43] be comforted (Matt 5:4), become angels of God,[44] be called "sons of the Most High" (cf. Matt 5:9), find rest "with the Father and the Son,"[45] be in light,[46] judge angels (cf. 1 Cor 6:3); be rewarded; escape the day of judgment (Rom 2:3). Finally, "to them will God speak" (cf. Num 12:8; Ezek 2:1; Hos 2:14; Dan 10:11).

This set of macarisms shows marked variations from the beatitudes of Matthew or Luke. There is a repeated emphasis on renunciation of the world and adoption, through baptism, of a new "form" of "angelic" life: purity, continence, or detachment from conjugal relations (cf. Mark 12:25). The use of these three categories shows that it is not one's state in life—in this case, one's marital status—that affects participation in the resurrection (cf. 1 Cor 7:17, 20, 24, 26). Rather, it is sexual activity itself. Those who have never married (virgins) can enter into the resurrection if they are characterized by purity (*katharos*); those once married (divorced or widowed persons) must now choose continence; those who "have wives" must live "as if they have them not" (1 Cor 7:29). In the apocalyptic perspective of the *Acts of Thecla,* moral purity (which in this case includes sexual abstinence) becomes the grounds for salvation.

On this point, the *Acts of Thecla* represents mainstream Christianity. In the first and second centuries, the Christian movement as a whole was marked by apocalypticism. This was particularly true of the region of Asia Minor—one has only to recall the Apocalypse of John, the teaching of Papias, and the Montanist oracles. And while the Christian movement in Asia Minor seems to exhibit more apocalyptic fervor than elsewhere, this perspective was geographically widespread—for example, we find it in the *Odes of Solomon* (Syria), the Hermetic writings (Rome), and the Nag Hammadi apocalypses (Egypt). The immediate discussion in the *Acts of Thecla* is grounded in Paul's apocalyptic theology as expressed in 1 Corinthians 7, especially vv. 29–35.

The *Acts of Thecla* is not unique in recommending sexual abstinence as the appropriate response to an apocalyptic situation. The teachings of Jesus on the family—and particularly the saying that one must hate one's parents, siblings, wife, and children (Luke 14:26)—show that the family pales in significance next to the community of disciples, which is the only legitimate family (Mark 3:31–35 and parallels; cf. John 19:27). Add to this Paul's uncomfortable discussion in 1 Corinthians 7, where he wants to recommend celibacy to all Christians yet concedes that those who would be tempted to sexual immorality (*porneia*) would do better to concentrate on the basics of moral behavior. In Jewish circles, there are the well-known examples of the Therapeutae and the celibates among the Essenes.

Clearly, the *Acts of Thecla* does emphasize sexual abstinence, but this emphasis should not be taken to imply that continence was the *sole* requirement for attaining the life of the resurrection. "Departing from the form of this world" includes much more than sexual purity; but these other moral virtues are assumed by the text because they are points on which there is widespread public agreement (by Christians, Jews, and pagans). The point of contention is sexual abstinence, so it receives center stage.

Among Christians who did embrace a life of continence, the virgins had a special status. The last and longest of the beatitudes extols their choice and claims that they receive a special blessing from God:

> Blessed are the bodies of the virgins, for they shall be well pleasing to God, and shall not lose the reward of their purity.[47] For the word of the Father[48] shall be for them a work of salvation[49] in the day of his Son,[50] and they shall have rest for ever and ever.[51]

This passage is pivotal to understanding the *Acts of Thecla;* it serves as a synopsis of the theology of the entire Thecla story.

As far as we can see, the eschatological "reward of their purity" is the same for the virgins as for other continent Christians: participation in the resurrection and divine "rest." However, the virgins receive a foretaste of this reward even now, for God speaks to them (c. 5, beatitude 3) and the word of God becomes their work of salvation. In other words, they receive the gift of prophecy. This gift of the "understanding of Jesus Christ" brings conversion in the recipients (c. 6, beatitude 10), and the "wisdom of Jesus Christ" validates their salvation, bringing others to call them "sons of the Most High" (c. 6, beatitude 8).

However, one should not misconstrue this wisdom and understanding of Jesus Christ, "the word of the Father," as if it were private revelation, with validation attendant upon the final coming. On the contrary, this prophetic word becomes the present "work" of the virgins: through public proclamation they bring others to salvation, thereby earning the title "sons of the Most High"[52] and in their prophetic actions—both of renouncing sexual relations and embracing an itinerant life of public ministry to the Word—they embody God's present work of salvation among women and men. The life of Thecla provides the key illustration of this.

Thecla Hears the Word of the Virginal Life (7)

While Paul addresses this sermon to the Christians gathered in Onesiphorus's house, Thecla sits at a nearby window in the house of her mother, Theocleia. The reader's curiosity is piqued by the fact that Thecla ("a virgin") is identified first in terms of her relationship with another woman (her mother) rather than a man. To squelch any questions, however, this is immediately rectified; we are told that Thecla is "betrothed to a man (named) Thamyris." Thecla is entranced by the word Paul preaches, comes to believe it, and will not turn away[53] from the window for any reason, day or night. Seeing that Paul's audience included "many women and virgins," Thecla herself desires "to stand in Paul's presence" (cf. Pss 1:4; 5:5; 24:3; Luke 1:19) and hear the gospel. Her conversion has come about entirely on the basis of hearing the word (John 20:29); but her enactment of that word will be based on vision (cf. John 3:11; 9:37) and participation in the Christian community, here represented by Paul and his audience.

Theocleia and Thamyris Conspire against Thecla (8–10)

(8) Thecla's mother sends for her fiancé, who is described as coming "in great joy as if he were already taking her in marriage." This image strikes a note of dissonance for two reasons: first, the reader has just been told that Thecla was "rejoicing exceedingly" in her new-found faith; second, it raises a threat to this new faith because Thecla should receive it as she is and not change her state in life by becoming married.[54] Thamyris asks Theocleia for permission to see Thecla. To prepare him for this interview, Theocleia relates to him an unsympathetic account of what has happened to her daughter.[55]

(9) Theocleia suggests that Thecla is under a spell, "taken captive" by Paul's message of exclusive monotheism and chastity. Theocleia plays on Thamyris's civic virtue and self-interest, denouncing Paul as "upsetting the city of the Iconians, and thy Thecla in addition." The mother views Thecla's heartfelt faith as a "fearful passion," away from which Thamyris must try to woo her.[56]

(10) Thamyris approaches Thecla with a heart divided: he loves her yet fears her "distraction," her foreign "passion." Arguing from his position of superiority as the controlling man in her life,[57] he gives voice to the cultural perception of her behavior as bringing her "shame": her passionate distraction by another man (Paul), for Thamyris, constitutes a betrayal of their relationship.[58] He commands Thecla to restore her honor by returning to him—which would entail denying her conversion to the gospel of "continence and resurrection" taught by Paul. Her mother also intervenes, but Thecla makes no response to either of them. Though the entire household goes into mourning—Thamyris,

mother, and maidservants—Thecla pays no heed. She remains entirely devoted to Paul's word,[59] and "[does] not turn away."[60]

There are three quite striking features of this passage. First, the focus is on the woman in her three socially approved roles, which are listed in their order of importance in the story: wife, daughter, household mistress. This is made clear by the silence regarding Thecla's name in the remark about the household mourning. Second, it is interesting that all the members of this household are female; Thamyris is the only man mentioned as entering this house of women, and his entrée is controlled by women (Theocleia, who calls him, and Thecla, who provides the basis for the call). Finally, and most significantly, Thecla's behavior illustrates a markedly countercultural contention that female honor arises from a woman's faithfulness to God alone, not to a man.

The attempted seduction/mourning scene sets up a conversion versus anti-conversion dichotomy, which clarifies what is at stake for Thecla (and, by analogy, for the audience of the *Acts of Thecla*) in her acceptance or rejection of Thamyris, her betrothed. This dichotomy undergirds the remainder of Thecla's story. The chart below outlines its key features.

True Conversion versus False Conversion (Apostasy)

	Conversion	Anti-conversion
Evaluation	True	False
Belief	Virginal life	Married life
Proponent	Paul	Thamyris
Attitude of Believer	Whole-hearted	Divided heart
Emotional Response	Great joy	Jealousy, wrath
Authority	God's word	Social custom
Male/Female Relations	Both under God	Woman submissive
Family	Christian community	Natural family
Location	Outside the house	Inside the household
Morality	Chaste, virtuous	Profligate
Ideal Roles:	Itinerant preacher Work of salvation	Faithful wife Work of procreation
Results:	Break with family Social rejection Persecution, rescue Vision, prophecy	Family integration Social acceptability Humiliation, failure Cut off from God
Reward:	Power to judge Beatitude	Bitter judgment Condemnation

THAMYRIS CONSPIRES WITH DEMAS AND HERMOGENES (11-14)

(11) Thamyris responds to Thecla's private inaction with quick and public action of his own: he goes into the street to find support for a case against Paul, whom he classifies as a "false teacher" and "deceiver" because of his preaching against marriage. He accosts two quarrelsome men and offers them a bribe for any information against Paul, taking care to mention his high position in the city—which no doubt is intended to suggest that Thamyris will use it for or against the men he addresses, depending on their degree of cooperation.

(12) We are not surprised to discover that the two men are the very same Demas and Hermogenes who accompanied Paul to Iconium. Their denial of Paul is couched in language reminiscent of Peter's betrayal of Jesus; thereby Onesiphorus's previous assessment (c. 4) of Paul's two companions is shown to be accurate, providing a sort of prophecy-fulfillment motif. Indeed, they incite Thamyris further by claiming that Paul forbids marriage itself, teaching that "there is no resurrection for you, except ye remain chaste and do not defile the flesh, but keep it pure" (see Rev 14:4).

A methodological caution is appropriate at this point. Because this summary of Paul's preaching derives from hostile witnesses, it is not at all clear that it is intended as an accurate depiction of the theology of the author/redactor. On the contrary, having just heard the men's denial of any affiliation with Paul (a statement that the audience knows is a lie), the reader should also be on guard against any further statements they make.

Thamyris's statement that the Paul of the *Acts of Thecla* "teaches that young men and women should not marry" is accurate. The conclusion drawn by Demas and Hermogenes—that "otherwise there is no resurrection for you . . ." —may be a logical conclusion of the beatitudes of c. 5–6, but it goes beyond anything that is directly taught by Paul (or Thecla) in the *Acts of Thecla*. There are a variety of virtues and states of life extolled by the beatitudes.

The crux of the issue is the understanding of a true marriage. The *Acts of Thecla* certainly permits a marriage in which both partners are continent; this is a true marriage because it supports rather than interferes with one's relationship to God, the true Spouse. In the opinion of the Roman Empire and Greco-Roman society generally (which is represented by Demas and Hermogenes), however, a marriage without sexual relations and procreation constitutes no marriage at all. Individuals in such nonprocreative marriages are penalized under Roman law.[61] Thus, they infer that Paul forbids marriage.

(13) Finding the men sympathetic, Thamyris invites them to his home and plies them with food and drink to obtain their cooperation in recovering Thecla for his wife. A romantic element is introduced in the remark that

Thamyris "loved" Thecla. His sexual impulse toward her, here and later in the story, is in sharp contrast to Thecla's resolute emotional and physical chastity. (14) The two traitors urge Thamyris to denounce Paul to the governor on the charge of being a Christian teacher; this will bring about Paul's execution and restore to Thamyris his intended wife.[62] They offer to teach Thamyris a different gospel, one that turns the tables on the word preached by Paul: only those who are married can experience the resurrection, for "it has already taken place in the children whom we have."[63] Knowledge of the true God is what resurrection means (cf. Mark 15:4; Col 3:1–4; Eph 1:17–21; 2:5–7). The realized eschatology of this anti-gospel is in sharp contrast to the apocalyptic framework of the gospel of the *Acts of Thecla*.

PAUL'S ARREST AND HEARING (15–17)

(15) Thamyris, driven by fleshly desires (cf. Gal 5:13–21, 26), takes a mob to Onesiphorus's house (cf. Mark 14:43, 48–50), charges Paul with breaking his marriage, and carries him off to the governor while the crowd shouts accusations of sorcery and invites the death penalty (cf. Matt 27:20). (16) Thamyris makes his charge before the proconsul, heedless of the suggestion of Demas and Hermogenes that he accuse Paul as a Christian. Still, the governor considers Thamyris's charge to be "no light accusation."[64] (17) Paul responds with a summary of his teaching. The synopsis emphasizes a monotheistic doctrine of God, who is transcendent, who desires to save humanity, and who has authorized Paul to preach a message of conversion from sin—which is connected with "corruption and impurity, all pleasure and death . . ."—to faith in God's Son, who brings "knowledge of propriety and love of truth." Paul concludes by turning the claim of divine authorization for his teaching into a challenge to the proconsul (cf. Acts 26:19). The governor imprisons Paul until he can give him "a more attentive hearing" (cf. Acts 24:25).

THECLA AND PAUL IN PRISON (18-20)

(18) At this point in the narrative, Thecla shifts from the social world of her mother's house to the public forum, from the Greco-Roman household to the Christian community. Her situation has been no less an imprisonment than Paul's, as is made clear by the fact that she must bribe not only the jailer to *enter* Paul's cell but also the doorkeeper to *exit* her house. Thecla takes the posture of a disciple, sitting at Paul's feet, listening to his proclamation (cf. Luke 10:39), and uniting herself with Paul's witness by kissing his bonds. This

set of ritual actions serves to initiate Thecla into the Christian community,[65] and it increases her faith (cf. Phil 1:13–14; 2:25).

(19) The persecution motif is now repeated with Thecla as the key figure: she becomes a "hunted" woman, having been "betrayed" by one of her household. Thecla is found to be Paul's comrade in bonds,[66] and a report of the incident is made to the governor. (20) At first Paul alone is haled before the judgment seat,[67] leaving Thecla behind, *who takes Paul's place* in prison. The narrator expresses this quite graphically: "Thecla rolled herself upon the place where Paul taught as he sat in the prison." This scene forms Thecla's call narrative (cf. 1 Kgs 19:19–21), and suggests that Thecla will become the prophet to succeed Paul, as Elisha did Elijah (1 Kgs 19:16). The report is unusual in that Thecla initiates the action; there is no vision from God nor invitation from Paul. But both such experiences do arise later, showing that her actions are validated directly by God and indirectly through God's messenger, Paul.

Then Thecla is proved to be a true disciple, following in Paul's footsteps: the governor commands that she also come before the judgment seat. Her (now typical) response of joy and exultation illustrates her faith (cf. Matt 5:10; 25:36; *Acts of Thecla* 6 beatitude 11), and signals her faithfulness unto death.[68]

At this point in the narrative, center stage begins to shift to Thecla while the role of Paul diminishes. Standing before the governor, the mob focuses on the male culprit: they again accuse Paul of sorcery (a charge that indirectly implicates Thecla as well, since it indicates that Thecla's refusal to follow social convention is a sign of insanity or demon possession; cf. c. 8–9).[69] However, Paul's opponents are unsuccessful in sustaining the charge, for "the governor heard Paul gladly concerning the holy works of Christ . . . ." It is the governor who turns attention to the female figure, asking Thecla to account for her refusal to marry Thamyris "according to the law of the Iconians."[70] Thecla remains silent, "looking steadily at Paul."[71] Theocleia herself instigates the call for the death penalty against Thecla, "the lawless . . . no-bride," and it seems that the mourning scene of c. 10 has come to fulfillment, with Thecla as no-bride, disowned as daughter and having renounced her role as household mistress as well. Thecla is outside the law (*anomos*) and beyond control because she has put herself outside the patriarchal household; she has confirmed the unspoken charge against her. Only death remains.[72]

A striking characteristic of this section is the use of the standard *topos* of conversion literature: the ruler who hears the Christian message gladly and sometimes nearly converts (cf. Acts 26). This motif is used to demonstrate the social acceptability of the Christian message and its harmony with Greco-Roman values—in spite of the negative reaction of some sectors of the population. However, its effect here is two-edged, since Paul is freed but Thecla is condemned, which suggests that Christianity is permissible for men but not for women.

THECLA'S MIRACULOUS DELIVERANCE FROM THE PYRE (21–22)

(21) The governor orders Paul to be scourged and driven out of the city and condemns Thecla to be burned as her mother had asked (cf. Matt 10:21–23, 35f.; Luke 12:52f.). This neatly eliminates Paul from the scene and should serve to complete the transition of attention from him to Thecla. But, although the official attention span is brief and Paul is forgotten, Thecla, like a sheep without a shepherd (Ezek 34:8; Zech 10:2; cf. Acts 8:32), still searches for him. In a striking twist (which makes explicit the hint in c. 20 and will be repeated in later parts of the narrative), we find that Paul has acted not like a shepherd but like a hireling: he has abandoned her.[73] Looking for Paul, Thecla has a vision of the Lord, which she takes as a sign of divine protection.[74] With Paul's disappearance and her impending martyrdom, the resolute virgin is beginning to reap the rewards of the beatitudes: vision, comfort, mercy.

(22) Once in the theater, youths and maidens prepare the pyre—a detail that emphasizes the countercultural nature of Thecla's decision to embrace "the gospel of continence." Thecla enters the scene naked, causing the governor to marvel at "the power that was in her." This is a foreshadowing of what will come. Mounting the pyre, she stretches out her arms to form a cross.[75] The fire is kindled, but it does not touch her (cf. *Martyrdom of Polycarp* 15.1). God's mercy on Thecla is manifested in a sudden hailstorm which quenches the fire and kills some of the audience as well.[76]

THECLA IS REUNITED WITH PAUL (23–25)

(23) Meanwhile we find Paul fasting with Onesiphorus and his entire family[77] in an open tomb (an obvious resurrection motif) on the road from Iconium. Preparing to break their fast, Paul, on the sixth day, sends one of the boys to buy bread; the day for breaking the fast will be the seventh, an obvious reference to the Sabbath. Having escaped the fire, Thecla again searches for Paul and meets the boy, who takes her to him. (24) They come to the tomb while Paul is praying that God will rescue Thecla. Thecla responds by offering, for the first time, a prayer of her own, thanking God for her rescue "that I might see Paul!" Paul offers a final thanksgiving, for God's prompt response to his first intercession.[78] (25) There follows a scene of rejoicing and sharing in a eucharistic meal.[79] Though "all of them" rejoice and participate in this *agape* (love feast), only the men (Paul and Onesiphorus) are named.[80]

Thecla urges Paul to accept her as a disciple and co-worker, arguing that she will cut her hair short[81] and follow wherever he goes (cf. Ruth 1:16–17; Matt 8:19). Paul objects on two grounds: (a) the inevitable hardships posed by such a journey; (b) the possibility of a second, more serious temptation whereby Thecla may be overcome and "play the coward!" Both objections bear tremendous irony: the first, because it implies that being burned at the stake is a minor inconvenience (c. 22); the second, because of Paul's own traitorous behavior (c. 20–21). However, Thecla simply presses on, asking for baptism ("the seal in Christ"), which she believes will preserve her from temptation. That Paul declines to do so is one of the most remarkable features of the story thus far, and it piques the audience's interest to discover how this baptism will occur.

Thecla's Arrival and Arrest in Antioch (26–27a)

(26) The narrator swiftly shifts scenes, concluding this first portion of the *Acts of Thecla* with Paul sending Onesiphorus *cum suis* back to Iconium, and then taking Thecla with him to Antioch.[82] So, in spite of Paul's protestations, Thecla has won the argument. But no sooner have they entered the city than Paul's words about her beauty being a potential source of temptation take on a prophetic cast—but with a twist—when Alexander falls in "love" at first sight of Thecla. The temptation is not Thecla's but *men's*! Thecla is resolute and unaffected by Alexander's protestations of love, yet she is the one who suffers persecution.

Alexander conveys the typical assumption of Greco-Roman society, that every woman must belong to a man. Since Thecla is with Paul, she must belong to him, and so Alexander attempts to win Paul's favor with bribes. Now Paul succumbs to temptation too: not only does he abandon Thecla (as in c. 21), but this time he actively denies her as well ("I do not know the woman . . . ."), thus repeating the duplicitous behavior of Demas and Hermogenes (c. 12). Since Paul has disowned any connection with Thecla, Alexander presumes she is free for the taking and attempts to rape her in the street. Paul deserts Thecla, and she is left to defend herself. She invokes God's protection[83] and bests Alexander, baring his head of the crown with the imperial insignia.

(27) Alexander accuses Thecla before the governor, and she is condemned to fight the wild beasts. Alexander's sponsorship of the games reminds the audience of his beastly behavior toward Thecla and gives this judgment the flavor of a personal vendetta because of her refusal.[84]

At this point in the narrative, we are not told the precise charge against Thecla—whether it is for insulting the imperial symbol or for refusing Alexander's sexual advances (which symbolize patriarchal control of women).[85] Although we later discover that Thecla is said to be "guilty of sacrilege," the narrator has made it clear that such a charge would never have been levied against her if she had submitted to Alexander's desire. This implies that, in the storyteller's view, the rejection of Roman authority and a woman's refusal of sexual activity are functionally equivalent and need not be distinguished. As was mentioned above, this seems to accord with the view of Greco-Roman society as a whole.

THECLA AND THE LIONESS VANQUISH THE BEASTS (27B–35)

With this, the narrative division between male and female characters becomes complete. Men procure Thecla's condemnation, while women protest the judgment as "evil" and "godless" (a particularly interesting evaluation, since it reverses the charge against Thecla). Thecla is "protected" by a rich woman, Tryphaena, who is identified neither as wife nor widow but as the bereaved mother of a daughter.[86] (28) In procession with the beasts, Thecla rides a "fierce lioness" who licks her feet in submission! Afterwards, obedient to a prophecy from her daughter in a dream, Tryphaena takes Thecla into her household as adoptive daughter.

(29) In response to Tryphaena's welcome, Thecla offers an intercessory prayer for the salvation of Tryphaena's daughter, Falconilla. Her status as confessor/proto-martyr authorizes this role as intercessor (which increases from this point on), illustrating the rising second- to third-century belief in the "priestly" power of martyrs and confessors to confer divine forgiveness.[87] Her address to "Thou God of Heaven, Son of the Most High" reintroduces positive masculine imagery. However, it becomes clear in the next section that God is the *only* masculine figure who can be trusted.

(30) When Alexander comes to take Thecla to the arena, Tryphaena's invocation of God's protection makes him flee in fear.[88] (31) The governor then sends soldiers to take her, but the women retain the upper hand. Tryphaena herself leads Thecla to the games, while Thecla prays to God to reward her protectress.

(32) Once at the arena, we find a scene of great tumult,[89] which seems designed to remind the audience of primordial chaos, with the roaring of the beasts and clamor of the crowd depicting the primeval struggle between good and evil—only now it is revisited as God against Rome, Thecla against her persecutors. The men in the crowd call for Thecla to be brought to judgment; but the women take her part, themselves condemning the city for "this lawlessness" (*anomia*; cf. c. 20) against Thecla, and calling the proconsul to "slay us all" in solidarity with her.[90]

(33) Thecla is taken from the protection of women, stripped, and cast into the arena with the wild beasts. At this point, we find an interesting reversal of the typical way the sexes are depicted: whereas the men are usually active and mentioned by name, with women passive and (if mentioned) not named, Thecla and Tryphaena are both named, but not the male officials, whose actions are merely implied. The male–female tension is highlighted when the "fierce lioness" fights a lion and a bear sent to attack Thecla. This shows that

female unity with Thecla and her message is not limited to the human species. Alienation between women and the female members of the animal kingdom (symbolized by the lioness) is overcome through Thecla's faith. The lioness essentially is martyred fighting for the human proto-martyr Thecla; and the mourning of "the women" (in the crowd) for the lioness completes this circle of solidarity.

(34) Many beasts are set upon Thecla "while she stood and stretched out her hands and prayed" (as in c. 22, conforming her body to the image of the cross). Concluding her oration, Thecla baptizes herself "in the name of Jesus Christ"—an action that receives stereophonic divine approbation: a flash of lightning and a cloud of fire. Although all men oppose her and the faithful lioness falls, God remains Thecla's help and protector.

The women in the audience now take an active part in the struggle, throwing flowers and perfumes which overpower the new beasts sent by the men. Alexander recommends that the governor tie Thecla between two bulls; but this plan is thwarted by the divine fire which burns through the ropes.

VICTORIOUS, THECLA RETURNS TO THE WOMEN (36–39)

(36) Finally, Tryphaena faints from watching this terrible ordeal, and "the whole city was alarmed," taking her for dead. The tables now turn on Alexander, who fears for his life because Tryphaena is a kinswoman to Caesar. By thus, for the first time, identifying Tryphaena by her relationship to a man, the narrator quite pointedly shows that Alexander (who represents the governor and other men as well) is not converted by the series of divine miracles on Thecla's behalf; rather, he is convinced to desist only when he perceives another man as posing a threat to him.

(37) The governor summons Thecla, asking who she is that the beasts have not harmed her; Thecla takes the opportunity to give a brief summary of the Christian faith. (38) She accepts the governor's offer of clothing, but such garments pale in comparison to her expectation that she will be clothed by God "with salvation in the day of judgment." The governor decrees Thecla's freedom, and "all the women" praise the one true God, "who has delivered Thecla!" All the city is shaken by the sound. It is not simply the loud noise that "shakes the city" but the content of the acclamation: God protects and delivers a woman who opposes the sex-role definitions of the city, showing God's power over the culture as a whole. Female chastity and divine power are victorious over male law and aggression.

(39) Thecla released and Tryphaena revived, the two women are reunited amid Tryphaena's affirmation of belief in the resurrection. She who has now inherited Thecla's faith responds by making Thecla her lawful heir. Thecla stays in Tryphaena's house to teach the word of God, and most of the maid-

servants also are converted; "and there was great joy in the house," an image that harks back to the description of Thecla's own conversion (c. 7). At this point, the narrator completes the process of replacing Paul with Thecla. Thecla herself is a successful evangelist, and Paul is nowhere in the picture.

THECLA COMMISSIONED TO PREACH THE GOSPEL (40–43)

(40) Yet Thecla again seeks Paul. Dressed like a man, she brings youths and maidens on her journey to find him.[91] "Astonished" to see her, Paul wonders "whether another temptation was not upon her." This is a fascinating editorial remark, for it suggests that Thecla previously has not only suffered temptation but has succumbed to it. The story itself, however, shows that Thecla has been severely tested and has been faithful, while *Paul* repeatedly has failed her. Thecla rebuffs Paul's suspicion by proclaiming her baptism, for which she claims divine authority.[92]

(41) Paul leads her into the house of a man named Hermias to hear Thecla's account, thus inviting her to preach there. This shows that Paul validates her ministry as teacher of the gospel *to men*—even himself—as well as to women. In response, ". . . Paul marveled greatly and the hearers were confirmed and prayed for Tryphaena." Thus, Paul and the congregation recognize God's power in Thecla and count her story as "gospel." Thecla announces her intent to return as a missionary to her own city, and Paul (rather belatedly) commissions her as an apostle: "Go and teach the word of God!" Thecla leaves gifts for the poor, and departs for home.

(42) Upon reaching Iconium, Thecla now enters the house of Onesiphorus and takes Paul's place as teacher of "the oracles of God." (43) Though Thamyris is dead, Thecla finds her mother alive and witnesses the faith to her. After this, she goes to Seleucia, where she continues her ministry of preaching and teaching "the word of God," finally dying the death of the faithful.

CONCLUSION

There are striking contrasts between the portrayal of women in the *Acts of Thecla* in comparison with the other portions of the *Acts of Paul*. This makes it clear that the redactor of the *Acts of Paul* had a markedly different view of the proper place of women in early Christianity from that of the storytellers who relayed the Thecla account. The redactor who included the Thecla story in the *Acts of Paul* focused on the significance of men and particularly on the person of Paul. Every other man in the *Acts of Paul* pales in comparison with Paul. But women are not only subordinated to Paul; when they are significant

characters, they are either opponents of Paul or the vehicle for men's opposition to him.

The final message of these sections of the *Acts of Paul* is that women—even
women sympathetic to the Christian message—are dangerous to the Christian
mission. Whether sympathetic or not, they cause persecution of authentic
(male) Christian preachers. Female converts threaten to upset the social
order—a threat that should be controlled by sending the women back to their
husbands (cf. 1 Cor 14:33b–36; 1 Tim 2:9–15).

The *Acts of Thecla* creates a nearly perfect reversal of this message. While
both men and women are interested in the Christian message, it is the women
who are depicted as faithful to it. Even Paul, the chief male figure, is portrayed
as lukewarm at best. He betrays Thecla more than once and leaves her to suffer persecution while he escapes from the scene. Paul opposes her baptism
and preaching ministry, while God validates it by miraculous signs and by the
number of converts she makes. Belatedly, Paul concurs with God's call of
Thecla to ministry.

Thecla's countercultural choice of virginity is not her own idea but the word
of God which she accepts whole-heartedly. God ratifies this choice in two
ways: by the resulting persecution, which proves that she is faithful to the Lord
(Matt 5:11–12), and by her victory over such opposition. Even the death of
Thamyris, noted at the end of the legend, shows that Thecla has chosen the
better part; the life of the flesh is transitory, while the virginal life leads to the
resurrection. The vibrant Thecla cult, which survived well into the fifth century, demonstrates the attraction such a message had for Christian women.[93]

The *Acts of Thecla* nowhere suggests that a woman can be saved only by
leading "the virginal life" chosen by Thecla. But it does seem to suggest that
such a life-style is the prerequisite for a woman's involvement in Christian ministry. Further, although Thecla's adoption of a man's dress and hairstyle may
mean that a woman must become "manly" to be allowed to refuse marriage
and pursue a public career as did Thecla,[94] this is understandable as a second-
century evaluation of the practical situation. If we reject such an evaluation, it
does not mean that we must reject the story itself.

The *Acts of Thecla* reports the tale of a woman who was grasped by the
message of Christ and gave up everything to devote her life to living and
preaching this message. In spite of tremendous misfortune, Thecla remained
faithful to the apocalyptic gospel "of continence and the resurrection." Her
vision of Christ strengthened her to endure to the end. In this basic message,
the *Acts of Thecla* fits well with the other Christian literature of the second
and third centuries. By presenting a Christian woman in the role of apostle,
the *Acts of Thecla* opens possibilities for imagination and action among
Christian readers today.[95]

NOTES

1. Carl Schmidt, *Acta Pauli aus der heidelberger koptischen Papyrushandschrift Nr. 1* (Hildesheim: Georg Olms, 1965), 145–46.

2. References in this commentary are to the Schneemelcher translation of the *Acts of Thecla* (in W. Schneemelcher, *New Testament Apocrypha* [rev. ed. Louisville: Westminster/John Knox, 1992], 2:239–46) unless otherwise noted.

3. See Jean-Daniel Dubois, "The New *Series Apocryphorum* of the *Corpus Christianorum*," *Second Century* 4.1 (Spring 1984): 29–36.

4. Eric Junod points out that a common author named Leucius was already associated with the *Apocryphal Acts of the Apostles* in the fifth-century Latin ecclesiastics ("Actes Apocryphes et Hérésie: Le Jugement de Photius," in *Les Actes Apocryphes des Apôtres: Christianisme et Monde Païen* [Publications de la Faculté de Théologie de l'Université de Genève 4; Paris: Labor et Fides, 1981], 17).

5. Virginia Burrus, *Chastity as Autonomy: Women in the Stories of the Apocryphal Acts* (Lewiston, NY: Edwin Mellen, 1987).

6. See Gail P. Corrington, "The 'Divine Woman'? Propaganda and the Power of Chastity in the New Testament Apocrypha," *Helios* [Lubbock, TX] 13 (1986): 151–52.

7. See, e.g., Elisabeth Schüssler Fiorenza, *In Memory of Her: A Feminist Theological Reconstruction of Christian Origins* (New York: Crossroad, 1983), part I; eadem, *Bread Not Stone: The Challenge of Feminist Biblical Interpretation* (Boston: Beacon, 1984); Letty M. Russell, "Introduction: Liberating the Word" and "Authority and the Challenge of Feminist Interpretation," in *Feminist Interpretation of the Bible*, ed. L. Russell (Philadelphia: Westminster, 1985), 11–18, 137–46; H.-G. Gadamer, *Truth and Method* (New York: Crossroad, 1986).

8. Schneemelcher, 216.

9. Schneemelcher, 215, citing Hippolytus, *Comm. on Daniel* 3.29 (*Sources chrétiennes* [1947] 14:254). Origen, *De prin.* 1.2.3 (Koetschau 30); *Comm. on John* 20.12 (Preuschen 342); cited in Schneemelcher, 215.

10. Tertullian, *De bapt.* 17.5 (*CCSL* 1:291–92).

11. A.-J. Festugière argues that the *Acts of Thecla* "for the vast majority of readers, *had canonical status*" (his emphasis) (*Sainte Thècle, Saints Côme et Damien, Saints Cyr et Jean* [Extraits], Saint Georges [Paris: A. & J. Picard, 1971], 21. Not until the *Decretum Gelasianum* (492–496 C.E. or later) was it rejected as apocryphal (ibid., 22).

12. Ibid. William Mitchell Ramsay pointed out the accuracy of geographical references to Asia Minor (cited in Dennis R. MacDonald, "The Role of Women in the Production of the Apocryphal Acts of Asostles," *Iliff Review* 40 [4, 1983]: 37). MacDonald bolsters the evidence for a provenance in Asia Minor and narrows the area to south central Asia Minor or "Anatolia."

13. Willy Rordorf, "Tradition and Composition in the *Acts of Thecla*: The State of the Question," *Semeia* 38 (1983): 44.

14. Steven L. Davies argues that they wrote the entire set of five great *Apocryphal Acts of the Apostles* and the *Acts of Xanthippe* as well (*The Revolt of the Widows: The Social World of the Apocryphal Acts* [New York: Winston/Seabury, 1980; see also his "Women, Tertullian and the *Acts of Paul*," *Semeia* 38 [1983]: 139–43). Cf. MacDonald, who argues persuasively for the origins of the Thecla story among female *storytellers* rather than female authors ("Role of Women," 21–38).

15. Dennis R. MacDonald, *The Legend and the Apostle: The Battle for Paul in Story and Canon* (Philadelphia: Westminster, 1983), 35–37. See also Burrus, who compares the structure of the Thecla legend and six other "chastity stories" to demonstrate their folk origins—*contra* the theory that they were originally literary works shaped by the form and concerns of the

Hellenistic romantic novel (*Chastity as Autonomy*). She speculates that the legends were told by members of Christian women's communities, independent of institutional church support (p. 103), to a predominantly female audience. MacDonald suggests that the Thecla legend was connected with other stories about Paul to compile what is now known as the *Acts of Paul* ("Role of Women," 17–18). He accepts Tertullian's witness that the "author" of this compilation was "a member of the great church" (i.e., neither Gnostic nor Marcionite) in Asia Minor who lost his presbyteral office as a result of his efforts to propagate these stories about Paul. I think this unwise, for reasons I outline below.

16. For a history of research and bibliography, see Burrus, *Chastity as Autonomy,* esp. 49–60. She presses the point that the similarities between the Hellenistic romantic novel and the "chastity stories" of the *Apocryphal Acts of the Apostles* are attributable to similarities in pre-literary forms.

17. Lauri Honko, "Methods in Folk-Narrative Research," *Ethnologia Europaea* 11 (1979–80): 23–25 (cited in Burrus, *Chastity as Autonomy,* 85–86).

18. The question also remains open as to whether the *Acts of Paul* was composed by an individual or a "school." Carl Schmidt has pointed out the continuity of style which characterizes the "bridges" between segments of the text, which implies one redaction of the sources as they were compiled in the written text. But this single redaction could have been done by either a "committee" or an individual.

19. *Contra* E. Margaret Howe, "Interpretations of Paul in the Acts of Paul and Thecla," in *Pauline Studies: Essays presented to Professor F. F. Bruce on his 70th Birthday*, ed. D. A. Hagner and M. J. Harris (Grand Rapids: Eerdmans, 1980), 33–49. See Yves Tissot, who convincingly lays to rest the charge of encratism levied against the *Acts of Thecla,* showing that mainstream Christianity (e.g., Hippolytus and Tertullian) opposed marriage after baptism ("Encratisme et Actes Apocryphes," in *Les Actes Apocryphes des Apôtres,* 113, 116).

20. See MacDonald, "Role of Women," 17; he refers to the criticism of Tertullian (*De bapt.* 1.17), the rejection of Jerome (*De vir. illus.* 7), the relatively mild dismissal of Eusebius (*Hist. eccl.* 3.3.5 and 3.25.4), and the tentative approbation of Origen (*Comm. on John* 20.12). If he had viewed the *Acts of Paul* as heretical, surely Eusebius could not have passed over it so glibly. And Jerome rejects not rigorism—for his own ascetic sensibilities made the stance of the *Acts of Thecla* seem quite normal and salutary—but active women.

21. Sheila E. McGinn-Moorer, "The New Prophecy of Asia Minor and the Rise of Ecclesiastical Patriarchy in Second Century Pauline Traditions" (Ph.D. dissertation, Northwestern University, 1989), 64–65, 320–22; cf. Kurt Aland, "Bemerkungen zum Montanismus und zur frühchristlichen Eschatologie," in *Kirchengeschichtliche Entwürfe* (Gütersloh: Mohn, 1960), 1:105–48.

22. E.g., O. Pasquato argues that the *Acts of Paul* was written by a late second century Christian counter-Gnostic "missionary" who presented himself as a popular preacher and who wanted to win Paul back from the heretics ("Il 'Kerigma' dei discorsi di Paolo in 'Acta Pauli': contenuto teologico-catechetico e significato storio," *Salesianum* 45 [1983]: 275–309). While this discovery of a counter-Gnostic element in the speeches of Paul in the *Acts of Paul* seems well-founded, the missionary identity of the author/redactor is less than obvious.

23. Dennis R. MacDonald, "From Audita to Legenda: Oral and Written Miracle Stories," in *Forum: Foundations & Facets* 2 (4, 1986): 15–26, esp. 18.

24. These married women are identified quite conventionally in relation to their husbands, Hieronymus and Diophantes, respectively. This provides a marked contrast to the identification of Thecla (in the *Acts of Thecla*) not in relation to her fiancé but in relation to another woman (her mother).

25. No doubt we are to include Eubula in this dismissal as well, although she (as wife of a freedman) does not merit mention at this point.

26. On Demas, see 2 Tim 4:10; also Schneemelcher, 266. On Hermogenes, see 2 Tim 1:15; compare also the depiction of another coppersmith in 2 Tim 4:14–15–that one named Alexander (both noted in Schneemelcher, 266).

27. Cf. Matt 5:39; Luke 6:29; 1 Pet 3:9–12. Note that this proper Christian response is the reverse of what Demas and Hermogenes are doing, which is returning evil for good (cf. Gen 44:4; 1 Sam 24:17; Pss 35:12; 109:5; Prov 17:13).

28. This phrase has a rich background in the Hebrew Bible, particularly in the books of Deuteronomy, Jeremiah, and the Deuteronomistic History (Joshua–Kings). A quick survey includes the following passages: Exod 4:28; 24:3; Num 11:24; Deut 9:10; 17:19; 27:3, 8, 26; 28:58; 29:29; 31:12; 32:44, 46; Josh 8:34; 1 Sam 8:10; 2 Kgs 23:2; 2 Chr 34:30; Jer 26:2; 30:2; 36:2, 4, 32; 43:1; Acts 5:20.

29. The notion of the "mighty acts of God" is a central idea in both Testaments. It frequently appears in Deuteronomy (e.g., 4:37; 7:23; 9:29; 11:3, 7) and Psalms (e.g., 24:8; 45:3; 68:33; 89:13; 94:3; 103:7; 106:8; 145:4, 6, 12; 150:2), and the Gospels repeatedly mention the mighty power of God revealed in the words and deeds of Jesus (e.g., Matt 11:20, 21, 23; 13:54, 58; 14:2; Mark 6:2, 5, 14; Luke 9:43; 19:37). In the Christian Testament, the resurrection of Christ is recognized as the "mighty act" of God *par excellence*.

Very likely we should read the phrase "of Christ" as both an objective and subjective genitive, that is, as referring to both the acts performed by Jesus himself (which reveal God's might) and the acts of God in reference to Jesus (especially, the resurrection). Schneemelcher (266) refers the reader to a similar idea expressed in Acts 2:11.

30. I recognize that this term is anachronistic in the historical context of the second century, but it remains the simplest shorthand way to specify what would later come to be considered correct Christian doctrine.

31. The notion of Jesus as God's beloved appears in all four of the Gospels. In the Synoptic accounts of Jesus' baptism we find the declaration that he is God's beloved son (Matt 3:17; Mark 1:11; Luke 3:22), a message repeated in the transfiguration stories (Matt 17:5; Mark 9:7; Luke 9:35; 2 Pet 1:17). Matthew 12:17f. cites Isa 42:1 as being fulfilled in Jesus, and Luke uses the character of the "beloved son" in the parable of the tenants (Lk 20:) with obvious christological intent. The Fourth Gospel substitutes the term *monogenēs* (only-begotten," John 1:14b, 18) to convey the same concept (see esp. v. 18b), and it contributes the figure of the disciple who is *agapētos*, the one who reclined on Jesus' bosom at the last supper (John 13:23, 25).

32. Onesiphorus and his family are also mentioned in 2 Tim 1:16; 4:19 (Schneemelcher, 266). Schneemelcher also notes that the Papyrus Antinoopolis (*P.Antin.*) has a slightly different reading, with two Iconian families greeting Paul–namely, Onesiphorus "with his children and Zeno and his wife."

What is most notable in this regard is the specification of Onesiphorus as a "spiritual" Christian who yet *has a wife and family*. The significance of this will become more clear in light of the account of Paul's preaching and the ensuing events in the *Acts of Thecla*.

33. Is this a veiled reference to the notion that one could only properly "recognize" Paul and his gospel if one views them through the lens of the letter to Titus, or of the Pastoral Epistles as a whole?

34. Cf. Col 2:5. The phrase is obscure. No doubt it means that Onesiphorus has an accurate (i.e., spiritual) understanding of Paul's gospel, but it may also imply that Onesiphorus has had some sort of visionary experience.

35. Robert M. Grant shows that this description has no historical reliability because of the

remarkable similarity it bears to that of Onasander's general, found in "a fairly popular passage from the [Greek] poet Archilochus" (citing fragment 58 Bergk) ("The Description of Paul in the Acts of Paul and Thecla," *Vigiliae Christianae* 36 [1982] 36).

36. According to Luke, the members of the Sanhedrin remark a similar trait in Stephen when he testifies before them (Acts 6:15). Cf. also the reference in Matt 17:2 to Jesus' face at the transfiguration, which itself seems to be patterned after the report in Exod 34:29–35 concerning Moses' face after he speaks with God on Mount Sinai. From these examples, we can see that this image conveys the notion of the individual's proximity to God and authority as God's own messenger.

37. The notion of Paul as God's *doulos* stems from his self-characterization in the introductions of many letters (e.g., Phil 1:1). The genitive "of the blessed God" is ambiguous, and provides three choices of interpretation: (a) it refers to God; (b) it refers to Christ (the "beloved" mentioned in c. 1) as God; (c) both meanings are intended. Keeping in mind the relative fluidity of the doctrine of God in the first three Christian centuries, I tend toward the last interpretation.

38. The notion of the "fruit(s) of righteousness" appears first in Amos 6:12 and is elaborated in the Christian Testament epistles (e.g., 1 Cor 9:10; Phil 1:11; Heb 12:11; Jas 3:18). In the Pauline epistles, "righteousness" is the result of faith, which is a sign of the presence of God's spirit; this connection is made explicit by the pseudonymous author of Eph 5:9. We find similar ideas in 2 Tim 4:8 and Heb 1:8, where the objective evidence of righteousness is called a "crown" or a "scepter," respectively. Cf. also Rom 5:17; 8:10; Jas 1:22–25; 2:14–26.

39. E.g., 1 Kgs 1:40; Matt 2:10; 28:8; Luke 2:10; 24:52; Phlm 7. Acts depicts it as the appropriate response to the miracles and message of the followers of Jesus (8:8; 15:3).

40. Schneemelcher refers to *2 Clem.* 6.9.

41. According to Schneemelcher (266), this penultimate beatitude is lacking in the Coptic Papyrus No. 1 in Heidelberg (*P.Heid.*).

42. Schneemelcher (266) cites parallels in *2 Clem.* 8.6 and 2 Cor 6:16.

43. Cf. Matt 5:5, 10. For the context of detachment in marriage, see also 1 Cor 7:29; Rom 8:17.

44. Compare the characterization of Paul in *Acts of Thecla* 3.

45. Hebrews uses this same image of rest as a reward for faithfulness (e.g., Heb 3:11, 18; 4:1–11). Compare Matthew's idea of Jesus' easy yoke bringing refreshment (Matt 11:28–30). The idea of God giving rest to the Israelites appears in the Hexateuch (e.g., Exod 33:14; Deut 3:20; 12:10; 25:19; Josh 1:13, 15; 22:4), and the Chronicler connects this "rest" with worship, for the Temple is a "house of rest" (1 Chr 28:2).

46. This is a biblical metaphor for the pervasiveness and transforming impact of God's saving presence (see, e.g., Ps 56:13; Isa 2:5; 50:11; 58:8, 10; 60:1, 3, 19–20; Matt 5:14–16; John 8:12; 9:5; 12:36; 1 John 1:7; 2:9–10; Rev 21:24).

47. Cf., e.g., 2 Sam 22:21; Ps 18:20; Rev 18:6; 22:12.

48. This phrase should be read as synonymous with the phrases "wisdom of Jesus Christ" and "understanding of Jesus Christ" found earlier in the list (6, 8, and 10).

49. Cf. Pss 74:12; 118:15; Acts 13:26, 47; Rom 1:16; 2 Cor 7:10; Phil 1:28; 2:12.

50. The phrase "in the day of his Son" is an allusion to the biblical concept of "the day of the Lord," the eschatological day of judgment, the coming of God's reign (e.g., Ezek 39:22; Zech 9:16; 14:9; Matt 7:22; 26:29; Luke 21:34; 1 Thess 5:4; 2 Thess 2:3; 2 Tim 1:12, 18; 4:8).

51. A similar understanding of rest as a reward for the diligent and faithful labors of the witness to Christ is expressed in Rev 14:13.

52. While the masculine plural (*huioi*) could be read as inclusive and translated "children" or "sons and daughters," I think such a translation would be misleading. The question of what

roles are permitted to daughters is precisely one of the key issues at stake in the *Acts of Thecla*. Further, both Roman and Jewish inheritance laws during the first two centuries were are strongly biased against daughters in favor of sons. Thus, retaining the masculine plural conveys the historical reality that it was sons who had full political rights, including the right of inheritance. Women as "sons" of God are equal to men, receiving full inheritance rights (not the second class rights of daughters).

53. So Thecla—unlike the later Paul—follows the admonition in Luke 9:62 about not turning away once your hand is put to the plow. See also n. 67 below.

54. See the discussion of c. 5–6 above.

55. This part of the text is taken from *Papyrus Oxyrhynchus* 1602 (= *Pap. Ghent* 62), a parchment codex of the fourth or fifth century; see Schneemelcher, 266.

56. Ross S. Kraemer noted this "motif of erotic substitution" in the scene of Thecla visiting Paul in his prison cell (c. 19) ("The Conversion of Women to Ascetic Forms of Christianity," *Signs* [1980]: 303). She and others have noted that sexual undertones pervade the description of Thecla's relationship to Paul in the *Acts of Thecla,* and also appear in the description of the relationships of female converts to male apostles in other of the *Apocryphal Acts of the Apostles*. What is interesting to me is that, when identical language is used of the relationships of other men to Paul, no such point is urged.

57. Although he is Thecla's betrothed and not yet her husband, the story depicts him already as the dominant male figure in her life because there is no mention of her father.

58. Of course, from Thecla's point of view this is not shameful behavior. She is distracted from her commitment to Thamyris not by another man but by the apostle of God (and therefore, by God in person).

59. The text equates the word of Paul with the word of God, and the presence of Paul with the presence of God or Christ (cf. Gal 1:6–10; 1 Cor 11:1; cf. Phil 3:17).

60. "Turning away" implies reconversion to the world that Thecla has renounced (see 5, beatitude 4)—that is, apostasy—which would bring God's judgment. In spite of determined opposition, Thecla does not fail; she remains true to the gospel of continence and the resurrection.

61. Regarding Augustan legislation, see Sarah B. Pomeroy, *Goddesses, Whores, Wives, and Slaves: Women in Classical Antiquity* (New York: Schocken Books, 1975), 163–66.

62. The assumption that denunciation will "destroy" Paul reflects the legal situation of the second century rather than the first. In the first century, a charge of sorcery would have accomplished the same purpose—a memory reflected in the fact that both accusations are included in the discussion.

63. Cf. 1 Tim 2:15. The notion that the resurrection has already taken place is combatted already by Paul in 1 Corinthians 15. Schneemelcher (266) also mentions a comparison with 2 Tim 2:18 regarding the teaching of Hermogenes.

64. Schneemelcher (266) cites a comparison with Mark 15:4.

65. Kraemer argues that "the practice of continence does not seem to depend upon formal ritual induction, which thus cannot be considered an integral element of the legend" ("Conversion of Women," 300). She has baptism in view as the sole mode of induction and is correct that this takes place quite late in the Thecla story. But initiation may take other forms; initiatory baptism immediately upon accepting the Christian faith was far from a universal practice, as the number of deathbed baptisms in the first Christian centuries attests (a well-known example is that of the emperor Constantine). The catechumenate provided a gradual process of induction over a period of years, and the late second century theory of a "baptism in blood" is also well known. I suggest that the Thecla legend provides a variation on this last theme, with Thecla's welcoming of imprisonment for the faith as her ritual of induction.

66. She is "bound with him in affection" (cf. 2 Cor 7:12b, 15–16; Phil 1:7–8; 2:1–2, 17–18, 25. It is interesting that the author of 2 Timothy commends Onesiphorus for behavior remarkably like that of Thecla: he remained faithful to Paul, "even in my chains" and, when Paul was in prison, "he sought me out earnestly and found me" (2 Tim 1:16–17). Coming as it does immediately after a report that "all in Asia, including . . . Hermogenes, have turned their backs on me" (v. 15), this parallel is too exact to be a mere coincidence.

67. The obvious reference is to the governor's seat of judgment, but this is likely to be a *double entendre* for the judgment seat of God as well (cf. Matt 25:31–32).

68. It also reflects the ethos of the developing martyr cult, where special status is given those who are martyrs and confessors for the faith (e.g., Rev 20:4–6, which specifies an advance resurrection for the Christian martyrs).

69. Kraemer argues that such judgments are a form of social control, which certainly is what is at stake in this scene ("Conversion of Women," 305).

70. Numa Denis Fustel de Coulanges points out that there were laws prohibiting celibacy in some Greek cities; (*The Ancient City: A Study of the Religion, Laws, and Institutions of Greece and Rome* [Garden City, NY: Doubleday, 1956], 50; cited in MacDonald, "Role of Women," 38).

71. Does this detail imply that she is looking to Paul to defend her and to explain that it is his message that has convinced her to remain a virgin? If so, it is another point where Paul fails her (cf. 21 below). This motif of Thecla's silence draws a comparison between her and Jesus during his trial (Matt 27:12, 14; Mark 14:61; 15:5; Luke 23:9; John 19:9). It is in contrast to the implied lengthy response of Paul, and to Thecla's own long defense in Antioch. See also Francine Cardman, who points out that brief, formulaic answers to official interrogation form the standard pattern in accounts of female martyrs ("Acts of the Women Martyrs," *Anglican Theological Review* 70 [1988] 146).

72. In her study of the *Acts of the Women Martyrs,* Cardman noted that "defiance of the conventions of female behavior is even more disturbing to the authorities than the Christians' refusal to submit to their directives" ("Acts," 146). This point certainly is borne out in the case of Thecla.

73. Cf. John 10:12. This provides a marked contrast with the depiction of Thecla in c. 42–43 where, like a good shepherd, she returns to Iconium to preach the gospel to those who first opposed her (Thamyris and Theocleia).

74. So truly the Good Shepherd never abandons the sheep (John 10:14, 16; cf. Heb 13:20; 1 Pet 5:4). It does confuse matters that Thecla's vision is of "the Lord sitting in the form of Paul. . . ." Since the connection with Paul fits so neatly with the redactor's agenda to glorify him, I think it likely that this reference is a later addition to the original Thecla story.

75. This is the prayer posture which is used in leading Christian worship, something reserved to men according to 2 Tim 2:8.

76. Is this intended as a subtle but effective way to persuade Christians to avoid public spectacles?

77. We are told that he "had left the things of this world and followed Paul with all his house." This is the second time the narrator has begged the question of Onesiphorus's relationship with his wife; he never does answer what has been the effect of this world-renunciation on the household structure. Does this mean he assumes that Onesiphorus remains the patriarch and that therefore there was no effect?

78. Thus, the redactor has quite neatly made Thecla's rescue the result of Paul's intercession/mediation rather than an act of God directly on her behalf. The modern reader, of course, notices that one must assume a tremendous time warp in order to concur with this attribution.

79. There is another hint of encratism here, because no wine is used: "they had five loaves, and vegetables, and water . . . ."

80. Again, it seems clear that the redactor's interests prevail in the description of this scene.

81. This may serve as a disguise to keep her safer in her travels. It also hints that Thecla is taking up a "manly" way of life and must leave her "female" self behind.

82. In the Greek text, this is Antioch of Syria, since the first person we meet there, Alexander, is identified as a Syrian, "one of the first of the Antiochenes . . . ." However, not all the manuscripts include this description.

83. Though directed at Alexander, the cry "force not the handmaid of God" takes on the character of an appeal for divine aid when Alexander himself ignores it. The argument against Alexander is two-pronged: I am a woman of high social rank; I am willing to suffer the worst to resist you (just as I did Thamyris). This argument also serves Thecla's appeal to God, reminding God that she has been tested once and has proved her commitment. Thus, the plea becomes a command and a claim of autonomy due to divine patronage: Thecla, as virgin, is a woman who is free from the control of men. Although this means that she also falls outside the protection of men, as the incident with Alexander proves, Thecla can lay claim to protection that is far superior because she belongs to the household of God.

84. Although the Greek manuscript tradition omits mention of Alexander's sponsorship at this point, it is noted in c. 30.

85. From Alexander's perspective, Thecla truly is *anomos*. She not only refuses marriage, but she leaves female space (the *domus*) and invades the male public sphere. Maryclaire Moroney has aptly suggested that Alexander's attempted rape, a "reasertion of male physical control, then literally as well as figuratively replaces Thecla beneath a man" (private correspondence, 10 September 1994). That his rape attempt is not successful shows that Thecla's choice of the public sphere—and her concomitant rejection of male control—is soundly endorsed by the author.

86. This Tryphaena becomes the positive example of motherhood, in contrast to Thecla's own mother, Theocleia.

87. Cf. Ignatius, *Trall.* 5.2 on grasping heavenly mysteries. Martyrdom is the test of true discipleship (see Ignatius, *Eph.* 1.2; *Magn.* 5), which gives those who are facing martyrdom heightened authority to teach (the premise of the entire set of Ignatian letters). Cf. also *Martyrdom of Polycarp* 17.3.

88. The mention of Tryphaena's status as widow in the context of this prayer of petition raises the question of whether it is simply a sociological designation or whether she is connected with an ecclesiastical order of widows. Cf. 1 Timothy 5.

89. Schneemelcher compares the *Martyrdom of Polycarp* 8.3.

90. At this point I diverge from Schneemelcher's translation. Like earlier translators, he uses inclusive language to translate the masculine plural references to the crowd. This leads to quite an interesting difficulty. For example, it leaves him with a reading which implies that "women" are not "people" ("the people and the women who sat together, some saying . . . but the women saying . . ."). I would retain the exclusive reference of the masculine plural, which would leave the reading: "some men saying . . . but the women saying . . . ." We then find a scene of a city divided, women against men. The women "sat together" in their support of Thecla and opposition to Alexander and the governor.

91. Is this an allusion to her bringing young women and men to the gospel of continence and the resurrection?

92. Is there an implied rebuke, since Paul previously refused to baptize Thecla?

93. The *Life and Miracles of St. Thecla*, by Basil of Seleucia (bishop ca. 440–459), preserves, before the manuscript breaks off, thirty-one reports of miracles performed at the site of her tomb and/or shrine. An annotated French translation is available in Festugière, *Sainte Thècle,*

37–82. The miracle collection provides another example of how Thecla is domesticated by later ecclesiastics: she protects her virgins (19), but also restores marriages (4, 28).

94. One must also consider, however, that looking like a man may have provided an additional measure of safety in travel. Further, female dress styles are more constricting than men's—and often seem designed expressly for that purpose (e.g., the practice of foot binding and its modern equivalent—high heeled shoes). Dresses are impractical for travel, whether on foot or horseback, and long hair is difficult to maintain when one spends much time in the open air. Pragmatic issues such as these may have had at least as much to do with the decision to dress "like a man" as did any putative desire to abandon one's female nature.

95. I wish to thank Dawson D. Moorer and Maryclaire Moroney for their editorial comments on this text.

RECOMMENDED READINGS

Bovon, F., E. Junod, and J.-D. Kaestli, eds. *Les Actes Apocryphes des Apôtres: Christianisme et Monde Païen.* Publications de la Faculté de Théologie de l'Université de Genève 4. Paris: Labor et Fides, 1981.

Burrus, V. *Chastity as Autonomy: Women in the Stories of the Apocryphal Acts.* Lewiston, NY: Edwin Mellen, 1987.

Corrington, G. P. "The 'Divine Woman'? Propaganda and the Power of Chastity in the New Testament Apocrypha." *Helios* [Lubbock, TX] 13 (2, 1986): 151–61.

Davies, S. L. *The Revolt of the Widows: The Social World of the Apocryphal Acts.* New York: Winston/Seabury, 1980.

Kraemer, R. S. "The Conversion of Women to Ascetic Forms of Christianity." *Signs* 6 (1980): 298–307.

MacDonald, D. R.. "From Audita to Legenda: Oral and Written Miracle Stories." *Forum: Foundations & Facets* 2 (4, 1986): 15–26.

——. "The Role of Women in the Production of the Apocryphal Acts of Apostles." *Iliff Review* 40 (4, 1983): 21–38.

——, ed. *Semeia 38: The Apocryphal Acts of Apostles.* Decatur, GA: Scholars Press, 1986.

Ramsay, W. M. "The Acta of Paul and Thekla." In *The Church in the Roman Empire Before A.D. 170*, 390–410. New York: G. P. Putnam, 1893. Reprint, Grand Rapids: Baker, 1954.

Schmidt, C. *Acta Pauli aus der heidelberger koptischen Papyrushandschrift Nr. 1.* Hildesheim: Georg Olms, 1965.

Schneemelcher, W. "Acts of Paul." In W. Schneemelcher, ed., *New Testament Apocrypha.* Revised edition of the collection initiated by Edgar Hennecke, 2:213–70. Cambridge: James Clarke; Louisville: Westminster/John Knox Press, 1992.

The Passion of
Perpetua and Felicity

MAUREEN A. TILLEY ◆

HERMENEUTICAL INTRODUCTION

WHEN I WAS an undergraduate, my history professors taught me there was no objective history. Von Ranke was dead, they said, and so was his approach. There was no way to find out "exactly what happened." Historians wrote for their own purposes, with their own biases and viewpoints. It was better, the professors said, to read a blatantly biased historian than to be beguiled by one who pretended objectivity.

So when I read *The Passion of Perpetua and Felicity,* I cannot pretend to know the unadorned facts, "exactly what happened." What I can know is how the author articulated her experience in order to communicate with her readers. As I read it, I interpret it against the backdrop of my own experience. So the readers of this volume must interpret what they read, bringing to consciousness their own experience.

The Passion of Perpetua and Felicity is a story about women and their bodies. Narratives of women and their bodies used to be an important part of the ethnic Catholic subculture in the United States. In some places they remain so. They are what I hated most about growing up female and Catholic in the fifties. The culture was not only blue serge uniforms, pale madonnas standing on the globe of the world, and strict but kind Sister with her rubber-tipped wooden pointer. There was a more sinister, threatening aspect, especially in women's gatherings. The daily conversation of the women revealed an obsession with bodies. This was not yet the age of health foods and spas, anorexia and diets. These women lived with the suffering they experienced as embodied individuals. Many waited in resigned expectation of the next episode of wife beating or assault by a jealous boyfriend. Their fertility was rarely a joy, more often an oppressive sign of their husband's pride or the hidden shame of their boyfriend's forceful passion. Few women over forty escaped a hysterectomy. Surgery was the answer to problems men could not solve with drugs.

In sorrow and in self-defense these women told stories. The stories were formulaic. Their setting and details guaranteed an unimpeachable verisimilitude. Most importantly, they were always told with a purpose.[1] If the story featured a woman who escaped the problems associated with her body, this was celebrated. If she was caught in a male-defined trap, she was mourned and served as instructor for her sisters. There were few successes and many cautionary tales of self-defense. Lurking in the background were two avenues of escape. The first was infertility—whether natural, surgical, or otherwise induced. The other was death, the death of self or of boyfriend or husband. I hated their stories because I resented the boldly stated assumption that such a world would be my world, and I strove to learn and create another.

As I read *The Passion of Perpetua and Felicity*, I hear the stories of two more women and their bodies. Reconstructing their world is difficult. Most documents from their time place women at the peripheries of male-defined life. Comments on women are usually prescriptive rather than descriptive. When descriptive, they tell of extraordinary women. Nevertheless, careful use of these documents in the historical-critical method advocated by Elisabeth Schüssler Fiorenza offers the possibility of reconstructing at least portions of that world.[2] Assisted by epigraphical and archaeological data, a clearer picture of the past emerges.[3] But that reconstruction is not simply a scholarly exercise. Historians do not tell their stories aimlessly any less than the women of my childhood. Schüssler Fiorenza testifies that "We must not seek an increase in antiquarian information but an increase in historical consciousness and . . . remembrance."[4]

Remembrance is always for a purpose, as history is always written for a reason. The purpose of retelling the tale of the torture of women's bodies in martyr stories is the same as in the stories of bodies told by ethnic Catholic women. When the body is attacked, when there is no culturally acceptable physical defense, how do women cope? It is in this spirit of the remembrance of culturally conditioned self-defense that I comment on *The Passion of Perpetua and Felicity*. But it is also with the hope, the purpose, that there may be different defenses if not a different world.

HISTORICAL INTRODUCTION

The Passion of Perpetua and Felicity is a precious piece of literature because it is the oldest surviving material (ca. 203) one may attribute to a definite historical woman. It contains:

1.1–2.3	Editor's introduction
3.1–10.15	Prison diary of Perpetua
11.1	Editor's linking verse

11.2–13.8   Dream of Saturus, her companion
14.1–21.11   Story of Felicity and the deaths of the martyrs.[5]

While it is a highly stylized account and may be problematic for recreating the events narrated, it nevertheless provides an account of one woman's self-understanding, conditioned as it was by her environment. As such it has no equal in the legacy of antiquity.

The entire account, especially the sections by and about women, is unusual in the positive attention given by women to their own bodies. Unlike many of the models for late antique Christian women, Perpetua and Felicity were not ascetics.[6] They were wives and mothers whose very embodied activities were part of their identity as holy women.

The idea of nonascetic holiness trod a rough road through the history of early Christianity.[7] Some early Christians adopted asceticism and consecrated virginity, anticipating the swiftly approaching kingdom of God, in which the body was to manifest the sanctified status of Christians. Thus, early Christians approved a commitment to celibacy consecrating embodied life (see, e.g., 1 Cor 7:25–31; Luke 20:34–37). But some later Christians promoted these teachings with such zeal that disciplining the body for the sake of the body *in the kingdom* was transformed into a loathing of the body, which was envisioned as too, too solid flesh, fit only for punishment or as baggage to be jettisoned. Since women were envisioned as more bodily beings and men as more spiritual, the bodies of women suffered more severely from this perversion of early ascetic propaganda.

The foremost defender of embodied Christianity in late antiquity was the Italian ascetic Jovinian (d. 406). He reacted against the zealots' denigration of the body by attacking their glorification of celibacy. He denied the contention of those ascetics that virginity was a higher vocation than marriage, and he contended that thankful eating was as just good as fasting. He opposed strong and early traditions about the body, including those that prohibited menstruating women and men with nocturnal emissions from approaching the altar.[8] Their less than perfectly contained bodies allegedly failed to mirror the holiness appropriate to Christians.

Among Jovinian's opponents were influential theologians such as Jerome and Augustine. Under Jerome's guidance, Christians were taught to discipline and deny their unruly bodies from early childhood.[9] Augustine was not as vehemently opposed to sexuality. He could hardly be so lest he be called a Manichee,[10] yet he did share some beliefs which were used to denigrate non-celibate life. He taught that the fact that erections could not be controlled by the voluntary muscle system was apt punishment for original sin.[11]

The Passion of Perpetua and Felicity is valuable for contemporary readers because it is a window to a time before Jerome and Augustine, a time when there was an option for holiness not firmly wedded to unmitigated asceticism. This commentary will therefore focus on the prominent mention of the bodies of women. Attention to references to bodies provides clues to the meaning of the story of the martyrs and of the larger Christian story.

Before discussing the story and its implications, it is important to see how the particular message of embodied Christianity has been deemphasized in "scholarly" treatments of the *Passion*.

MARGINALIZATION OF WOMEN'S WISDOM

When academics considered the *Passion*, many discounted the contribution of a woman as author, first, by attacking the claim of a woman's authorship, and then by minimizing the normative value of the text.

Many attributed the final form of the *Passion* to a man, to the prominent African theologian Tertullian (ca. 160–ca. 225). The original connection with Tertullian came from the fact that a copy of the *Passion* was found in a manuscript of Tertullian's works.[12] But proximity does not guarantee authorship. In this case it underlies a once-widespread prejudice in the scholarship of early Christianity. Attributing the text to Tertullian followed the same tradition to which the texts of the Christian Testament were subjected. If the writing had survived and was venerated by Christians, it was considered more valuable if it had been written by a man who was already famous. As the canonical Gospels were attributed to the personal male companions of Jesus, the story of Perpetua was credited to the most well known male writer of her time.

Attribution to Tertullian also relied on the fact that some of the biblical quotations in the *Passion* accorded verbatim with those in Tertullian. However, as Victor Saxer wisely noted, this does not necessarily indicate that Tertullian was the editor but simply that the same translation of the Bible was used by both authors.[13]

Since the publication of the critical edition of the text in 1936, scholars have carefully analyzed the *Passion* and have come to several conclusions about authorship. First, the *Passion* is a composite work. The diary of Perpetua (1.4–10.14) and the report of the vision of Saturus, her comartyr (11.2–13.8) were written by different persons. These two accounts are surrounded and linked by the additions of an editor (1.1–1.3; 11.1; 14.1–21.11), which tell the story of Felicity and the executions of the martyrs.[14]

Second, the editor is not Tertullian. Neither the prose rhythms nor the vocabulary is his.[15]

Third, the original language of Perpetua's diary and of the editor's additions was Latin. Saturus's reports were originally in Greek but were translated into Latin for the composite edition.[16] Scholars now believe that the *Passion* contains the stories of the martyrs in their very own words. Thus the reader has access to the life and world of at least one Christian woman of the very early third century. For no other document can we say: this woman speaks to us in her own words.

After authorship, the second complex of the critical questions concerns the alleged Montanist tendencies of the text. If the text were a Montanist document, whether by Tertullian or not, perhaps an orthodox Christian should spurn its contents. Guilt by association would condemn any insights from this document.

The Montanist movement in early Christianity originated in Asia Minor in the second half of the second century. It was named for Montanus, its first prophet. The chief prophetesses of the movement were Maximilla and Prisc(ill)a. The former was the movement's leader after Montanus. The Montanists inculcated respect for the gift of prophecy. They espoused an apocalyptic eschatology and proclaimed the imminent descent of the holy city, Jerusalem, on their own town of Pepuza. Contemporary church councils in Asia Minor espoused an antimillenarian stance and therefore condemned Montanism.[17]

In its African manifestations, if we are to judge from Tertullian's writings, Montanism encouraged asceticism, discouraged second marriages, and condemned the policy of ecclesiastically sponsored postbaptismal repentance.[18] African Montanism preserved some of the earliest ideas of Christianity which valued the treatment of one's body as symbolic of one's attitude toward the imminent coming of the kingdom. This was in distinct contrast to later ascetics, whose denigration of the body was based on a dualist assumption of a dichotomy between soul and body and the consequent devaluation of the "lower" element, the body.

As long as scholars maintained that Tertullian was the author or editor of the *Passion*, one could assert the Montanist origin of the document because it was taken for granted that Tertullian ended his life as a Montanist. With the date of the execution of the martyrs as 203, the *Passion* conveniently fell into the portion of Tertullian's career in which he began his turn toward Montanism.[19]

If the story of Perpetua and Felicity came from the pen of Tertullian, a promoter of heresy, it was easy to minimize the story as a model for Christian behavior. One could pick and choose elements of the story as Augustine did in his sermons on Perpetua and Felicity's feast day, minimizing enthusiasm for martyrdom and exalting anything that might be construed as a hint of asceticism.[20]

With the link to Tertullian broken, the idea of the Montanism of the *Passion* needed to be reexamined. Scholars have offered two possible links between a *Passion* not by Tertullian and the Montanist movement. First, Perpetua herself might have been a Montanist. Second, the editor might well have been a Montanist without Perpetua having been so and might simply have used the diary selections because they cohered with the editor's Montanist program.[21]

In evaluating the alleged Montanism of the text, contemporary readers need to ask two questions: first, is this a Montanist document? Second, how ought the results of an assessment of the Montanism of the *Passion* to set the agenda for a consideration of the value of the document?

The first question, whether the document is Montanist, invites the reader to render two judgments. The first is whether the *Passion* manifests the distinctive attributes of Montanism. Of all of the *distinctive* traits of Montanism, the only one it seems to include is prophetic speech. Testimony given in ecstatic states is a hallmark of Montanist practice.[22] The *Passion* includes only one example of Perpetua's ecstatic testimony. It occurred immediately after she had been gored by a deliberately provoked cow (20.8). But this is not the dissociative trancelike activity that has been associated with Montanism, but rather hysterical fugue, a temporary dissociation of mind from the condition of the body. This form of self-defense allows the torture victim to continue to function without feeling or remembering disabling bodily pain.[23]

It is true that the *Passion* does manifest some of the other characteristics attributed to the movement. These include the power of the martyrs to intercede to forgive sins (7–8), anticlericalism (13), and happiness regarding impending martyrdom (18.1). Although these features might be Montanist, none of these attributes is *distinctively* Montanist. On the contrary, they are characteristic of African Christianity generally during the second through fourth centuries.[24]

The document does manifest to a high degree one of the other characteristics of Montanist writings: a reliance on dreams for information about the present and the future. The editor of the *Passion* approvingly cited Acts 2:17–18:

> In the last days, says the Lord, I shall pour out my Spirit on all flesh, and their sons and daughters will prophesy; and on my men servants and women servants I shall pour out my Spirit and the young people will see visions and the old will dream dreams. (1.4)

Dreams allowed for the continuing revelation of which the Montanists were prime exponents.

But in early Christianity dreams and visions were part and parcel of *every* Christian's life. Dreams were accessible to all. In fact, according to the early, non-Montanist Tertullian, dreams were the way in which people normally received much of their information about God. They constituted a preparation for death.[25] Christians might ask God for dreams, just as non-Christians who sought them by incubation in the temples.[26] In addition, recourse to dreams and visions (undifferentiated by early Christians[27]) characterizes earlier martyr stories such as Stephen and Polycarp.[28] Dreams remained a standard feature of North African stories.[29]

Perpetua's dreams contain many of the elements of non-Montanist apocalyptic literature to which she was no doubt exposed.[30] Daniel, Acts, Revelation, *The Gospel of Peter*, *The Shepherd of Hermas*, all provide motifs that Perpetua may have appropriated.

Various interpretations of these dreams have been offered: Jungian archetypes of the collective culture, impressions of classical literature, appropriations of biblical and Christian stories, explorations of sacramental themes.[31] But in the explication of Perpetua's dreams, the interpreter must deal not only with particular sources but also with their combination and transformation by individuals under great physical and psychological stress.[32] The spontaneity of the *Passion* and its distinctively personal aspects militate against overloading the symbolism of the dreams.[33] This commentary will concentrate on the context of the *Passion* itself as the hermeneutic key.

In the case of Perpetua, then, even the prominent role of dreams is not of itself a reason to classify the text or even Perpetua's reports as Montanist. The *Passion* lacks the central and distinctive attributes of Montanist literature. The question remains whether one can deem it Montanist for the constellation of peripheral characteristics it shares with Montanism: the ability of martyrs to forgive sin, anti-clericalism, joy in martyrdom, and reliance on dreams. But the *Psssion* shares this constellation of characteristics more with the literature of "orthodox" martyrs than with Montanism.

The second question remains: How ought the results of an assessment of the Montanism for the *Passion* to set the agenda for a consideration of the value of the document. The whole question of the orthodoxy of the *Passion* is nothing but a covert attack on women's wisdom. Many martyr stories share these identical peripheral "Montanist" attributes, but because their protagonists were not women, the charge of heresy is not made. The accusation is a close cousin to the charge leveled against nearly every man deemed heterodox in the ancient (and modern) world: he travels with, consorts with, takes advice from, women. Scholars sometimes fail to recognize the tactic of devaluation by association and spend their time attempting to vindicate or glorify Perpetua the Montanist.[34] But such a defense is not necessary once the nature of the attack is recognized.

On balance, *The Passion of Perpetua* cannot be marginalized as the work of a heretical woman. The *Passion* remains the work whose orthodoxy was never questioned by contemporary local Christians. They even read her diary as scripture on her feast day.[35] She was venerated overseas by Roman Christians under Constantine and by that paragon of North African orthodoxy, Augustine of Hippo.[36]

Even if one were to decide that not only the editor's program but that of Perpetua herself was Montanist, this ought not handicap the investigation of the *Passion*, nor can it invalidate Perpetua's own experience. Finally, it ought not detract from any insight this work gives to the history of this woman and her contemporaries or to an appropriation of that history for contemporary spirituality. Perpetua and Felicity provide models for women under attack, and these models shall not be taken away from them.

THE IDENTITY OF PERPETUA: FROM DEPENDENCE TO INDEPENDENCE

So who was Perpetua? What kind of a person was she? The editor provided a brief description. She was wellborn, well educated, respectably married, with a child not yet weaned. At the time of her arrest she was a Christian cate-chumen about twenty-two years old. Both her parents were still alive. She had two or more brothers, one of whom was perhaps a catechumen like herself (2). Dinocrates, another brother, died at the age of seven, probably of cancer affecting the face (5).

More revealing than the editor's description are Perpetua's relationships with others and the content of her dreams. From Perpetua's own writings the reader comes to know her through her interactions with, first, the men of her family and civic community, and then the men of her church. Within the first group we find her father, her child, her brother Dinocrates, her judge, and her executioner. In each of the relationships with the men of this first group Perpetua began in a situation of dependency. She was defined by her relation-ship with these males. Her faith, however, enabled her to transform each rela-tionship. She strove for a self-definition against these men. Her father lost con-trol of her. She disengaged herself from her infant son who could have con-trolled her when he grew up. Her power determined the eternal repose of her brother. Even her judge could not frighten her for her sentence was not to the beasts but to heaven. Her executioner could not perform his job without her assent and physical assistance.

Less prominent are the men associated with her church community or her dreams of martyrdom: deacons, brother Christians, a bishop and a presbyter, and a fellow martyr. All these men assist her in her approach to martyrdom or defer to her in her capacity as confessor and martyr.

In each case, the narrative mentions prominently aspects of body and its positioning in space.

Perpetua's father and her child play the major roles in the drama of the *Passion*. Four scenes feature dialogue between the daughter and the father.

Most include the son. From one scene to the next readers witness Perpetua's self-definition achieved through bodily experience.

Perpetua, though an adult and a married woman, was according to Roman law, not an independent person. There were two legal possibilities for her status: after her marriage she could have passed *in manu mariti* (literally, into the hand of her husband), and become subject to him, or she could have remained *in patria potestate*, under her father's jurisdiction.[37] The choice would not have been hers but that of her family. Regardless of her legal situation, she might have been living with her natal family if her husband were out of the country or deceased.[38] Perpetua's relationship with her father suggests this latter living arrangement. She was *in patria potestate* legally and in fact.

In Perpetua's first scene with her father (3), the two of them engage in a philosophical dialogue in which Perpetua likens herself to an inanimate object, a vase. As the vase cannot be called by any other name, so she cannot be called or be anything else than what she is, a Christian. Her father's reaction was one of rage. Her response manifested her physical vulnerability. She felt as if he would pluck out her eyes, and she was relieved and comforted when he left along with his diabolical arguments.

A few days later Perpetua was baptized in the prison. The reception of baptism was Perpetua's liberation from fear and domination. Inspired by the experience, she asked for only one thing, *sufferentia carnis*, patient endurance *in the flesh* (3.5).[39] *Sufferentia* was perseverance to the end, the forbearance of the saints in the book of Revelation. But Perpetua marked patient endurance with her own stamp: it became patient endurance *in her own embodied existence*. She would not lose control of her body and of its symbolic value.

After this prayer there is little philosophical dialogue in the *Passion* and little sense of Perpetua as passive object. Instead, one finds a close attention to her body and to Perpetua as active participant in the drama. Attention to the body is, of course, not unusual in stories of torture. But Perpetua's concentration on her own body will provide her the opportunity to assert her personality and her faith in the face of dehumanizing conditions.

Once her father was gone and her baptism was past, Perpetua began to notice conditions in her prison as especially distressing to the body. The darkness, heat, and crowded conditions were oppressive, but what bothered her even more was her separation from her infant son (3.6). She had been nursing him and the infrequency of his visits were a trial for the bodies of both mother and child. The child was nearly starved between visits, while the mother's breast were repeatedly engorged with milk to the point of excruciating pain. She would have been hesitant to express the milk on her own, if she could have done so. This would have been physically difficult to do under the stressful prison conditions. More importantly she would have feared that once she had done so—and relieved her pain—her hungry child would be brought in and she would be unable to satisfy his needs.

After the deacons Pomponius and Tertius bribed the guards, Perpetua and her companions were transferred to a better location within the prison and she was able to have her baby with her. *Then* the prison seemed a palace (3.9).

But this maternal delight was dependent on the money and goodwill of men and bonded her more closely to her male child. However, it was only a short episode in her prison experience. Her brother in prison (not necessarily a sibling from her earthly family) recalled her to the reality of prison life (4.1). He mentioned the concern of the incarcerated Christians. Would their imprisonment end in martyrdom or release? He addressed her with the language of utmost respect, "Lady, sister." He reminded her that by her suffering, by her confinement to prison as a confessor, she had the authority to ask for a dream that would show the future for her true family. Perpetua acknowledged this and agreed to petition God for a vision. She thus became, through her dreams and her visions, through her eyes and heart, the medium of the community, an authority in and for her church.

Perpetua received her answer in a dream (4.8–10), which has been interpreted against both Christian and classical backdrops. (Considering Perpetua's recent conversion, both ought to be explored.) In her dream, she had to scale a ladder, following her comartyr Saturus, who would eventually be executed before her (21.8). The ladder rose all the way to heaven and was flanked by weapons used in torture. Jacob's ladder (Gen 28:12) is an obvious source of the image. One might also be tempted to consider the celestial ladder of Mithraism (Origen, *Contra Celsum* 6.22).[40] While the imagery may come from a very popular source, one ought not to fall prey to the interpretation of Perpetua's ladder fulfilling the same function as the Mithraic ladder with its suggestion of multiple and distinct stages in the process of personal transformation.[41] Perpetua did not undergo a phased transformation but was immediately and radically transformed by this first vision. So whether the image of the ladder came to Perpetua from Christian or non-Christian sources, she has made it her own. The point of the ladder was like torture and martyrdom: it was a means to ascent. It caused neither harm nor fear.

Only at the beginning of the ascent was there any hint of opposition at all. Below the ladder reclined a huge dragon. The dragon, a potent symbol of evil, was nearly ubiquitous in early Christian literature, especially the Bible.[42] As Perpetua approached the ladder, the dragon already feared her. Professing her faith, she stepped on its head with her foot. The gesture is often seen as a reflection of Gen 3:15, but the maneuver is one frequently encountered in biblical and classical writings about any kind of domination.[43] Once she conquered the dragon, the ascent was effortless.

At the top of the ladder, Perpetua entered a heavenly garden. This part of the *Passion* provides a complex of rich imagery. The setting drew as much on pagan as on Christian imagery. She encountered a tall old shepherd. The identification with the Good Shepherd, while initially attractive, is not warranted for two reasons. First, he was represented as milking the sheep. Nowhere was milking the iconographic or literary task of the Good Shepherd (though in reality it would have been the task of actual shepherds). Second, Perpetua drew particular attention to his grey hair, the same color as her own father's hair. The Good Shepherd in Perpetua's time was always a young man, never old.

Marie-Louise von Franz looks at other shepherds such as those of *Poimandres* and *Hermas*. She sees the old man as a spiritual guide who initiated her into the mysteries with milk.[44] But this shepherd guides Perpetua nowhere; she is *already* where she belongs. He offers her no wisdom, only welcome. The identity of the milking man is not the Good Shepherd or even the Guide as Shepherd.

His height especially impressed Perpetua (even though he is seated throughout the interview). Such height was emblematic of a theophany in both Christian and non-Christian literature.[45] Both his age and his commanding position in the midst of the white-robed crowd identified him as the owner of the garden. His commanding identity is strengthened in his welcoming her, calling her his "child." Here we have another clue to his identity. He was Perpetua's master or father. Because there was no hint of servility in the text and because the color of his gray-white hair resembled that of Perpetua's father (5.2), he appeared to be more paternal than imperious. This was a new father. He offered her the product of his milking of a sheep. It was not, as one would expect, milk. It was already partially curdled cheese. It was too late in her religious life for the milk. She is past her baptism when milk would have been sacramentally administered. Perpetua consumes the solid food of an adult Christian. Consuming food in another world, like Proserpina, Perpetua was bound to that other world.[46] The master of that other world can be none other than God envisioned as a good, nourishing father, the antithesis of her abusive earthly father.

When Perpetua woke from her dream, she noticed the taste of sweet curds in her mouth, a sensation no doubt inspired by the sight of her own child's mouth after feedings. She realized that her future was to taste the sweetness of heavenly food through martyrdom. From this crucial point on, her natural father, her child, and the rest of her biological family are of little account in her life. She was fully invested with the gift she sought at Baptism. *Sufferentia carnis*, patient endurance in the flesh, was hers.

In her second dialogue with her earthly father only a few days later (5), the reader sees a distinct change in Perpetua from her first encounter with her father, evidence of her new power. The scene begins with her father standing erect, calling her "daughter, if I am worthy to be called your father." Alvyn Pettersen points out the delicious irony of this statement coming as it does after Perpetua's adoption by her new father in her first dream.[47] Perpetua's natural father pleaded with her, the child he deemed beloved above all his other children, to have pity on his gray hair and to renounce her faith. When she resisted, however, he addressed her in formulas derived from Greco-Roman prayers. He pleaded for the sake of the members of the family. He bent his neck to kiss her hands, and his supplications ended with him at her feet entreating her as his "lady" (*domina*). This is the same word of deference by which her brother in faith had addressed her (4.1). Like the devilish dragon of Perpetua's first dream, her father, the man of diabolical arguments, wound up at her feet. The dream of heaven and the assurance of martyrdom guaranteed *sufferentia* and turned the tables. This time it was he, not Perpetua, who looked for comfort. Perpetua's response was not fear of bodily harm as in her last encounter with him, but pity for him. She knew he would be unhappy to see her suffer.

At their next meeting, which takes place at the forum of Carthage perhaps a few days later (6), we have a combination of the motifs of the first two scenes with her father as well as those of her dream. They are ascent, identity, and placement at the feet of Perpetua. The confessors were "suddenly taken up" to the forum for their hearing. As they were ascending a platform (not a ladder) for their interrogation, Perpetua's father appeared, accompanied by her child, and tried to drag her down the stairs she had already ascended. But Perpetua had already ascended, tasted heaven, and been transformed. She could not turn back in dream or in reality, and he was unsuccessful.

The man who was governor questioned Perpetua about her identification with the Christian name, just as her father had. Like her father, he bade her have pity on her father's gray hair and on the members of her family, but Perpetua had already disengaged herself from the influence of her relatives. In his last attempt at breaking Perpetua's will, the governor ordered her father beaten on the ground (at Perpetua's feet once again). She felt sorry for her father not personally, but for his old age.

As for her son, she had no anxiety, and immediately the discomfort of her milk-engorged breasts ceased. Thus she broke the bond with the last male who might control her within her lifetime according to Roman law. The child went off in the custody of Perpetua's father.

It is at this point that the confessors' judicial fate was sealed and they were condemned to death in the arena. What Perpetua dreamt was now coming true. She had passed from the first stage of being a confessor, confined to prison, to the second stage of martyr, condemned to the beasts. At this point she not only had the authority to ask for dreams about her companions but also the power to use her position for others, as the reader will note in her relationship with her brother Dinocrates.

In her final encounter with her father (9), the old man entered and immediately threw himself at her feet, tearing out his hair (which had been *his* identity) and cursing his years. Perpetua's response was simply to feel sorry for his old age again. Such emotion she could have felt for any stranger.

In the four scenes Perpetua changed from daughter to *domina* and from doting to detached mother. Her emotions mutated from fear to pity to disengagement. She had become a new person, independent of ties to her natural family, united more closely to her family of confessors in prison. Even her body professed that detachment. Her milk supply which had previously troubled her ceased to make her uncomfortable. Many factors might have combined to affect her milk supply: the stress of being in prison, the repeated absence of her child, a diminished water supply, the lack of sunlight in the dungeon cell (confusing the diurnal cycle of the body), and the stress of imprisonment. But these had been insufficient to reduce the supply completely. The final factor, the divinely confirmed desire for martyrdom, was the necessary catalyst. Thus, her faith in her appointed future transformed her relationship with her child as well as her own bodily functions.[48]

The other major family figure in Perpetua's story was her brother, Dinocrates. She had not even thought of him throughout her confinement; however, now after the vision and her condemnation to the beasts, his name came to her lips (7.1). This absent-minded mention of a person was considered to be an omen of some kind in antiquity.[49] But her detachment from him was already apparent in her description of her sibling. Once she had tasted heavenly food in the first vision, he was only her "brother in the flesh." Why then did he enter the story? Perpetua's dreams of Dinocrates provided her with the realization that she was in a privileged position and could pray effectively for him.

The night after her condemnation to the beasts, she dreamed of him (7.4–7). She saw him and many others in darkness. The boy was pale and dirty. Like Dives, he was tormented by thirst. Like Tantalus, refreshment was inches away.[50] The rim of a large pool of water was just too high for him to slake his thirst. Note how the text turns the reader to another body and its appetites.

There was a great distance between Perpetua and Dinocrates, just as between Lazarus and Dives in Luke 16:26 (though the vocabulary is different). The gulf between Perpetua and Dinocrates was not only the distance between the living on earth and the dead below the earth in some sort of Hades or Tartarus. It was also the separation between Perpetua the martyr, proleptically in heaven, and the other dead. For only the martyrs were admitted directly to heaven or so North African Christians believed. All others had to wait until the final judgment.[51]

Perpetua's relationship with Dinocrates was no longer a familial one, one based on a blood relationship, but one of power based on her position as martyr, on a new kind of relationship in blood: she could pray for him and *her* prayers would be answered because she was suffering for her faith. Two traditions entwine here: the first is that the living might effectively pray for the dead; and the second is that those who are confessors might forgive the sins of others. These were found in the Bible of the early Christians and in their other literature, especially in North Africa.[52] So she prayed for him daily, and soon she received another vision in which he was clean, well-dressed, and refreshed (8.1–4). He now enjoyed the cool waters of the pool, the refreshment of those in paradise. In addition, his facial disfigurement was healed. Only a scar remained. Like the child that he was, he splashed the water happily playing in the pool, not only relieved of suffering but also healed in body.

Because of the pool of water in both visions, some commentators see early Christian attitudes toward baptism reflected here. The most developed interpretation in this mode is the allegorization of the scene by Jacqueline Amat, for whom every element in the dream is interpreted biblically and sacramentally. The darkness from which Dinocrates emerges is the outer darkness of the Bible.[53] In her estimation, the pool of water is, without a doubt, a representation of the pool of Bethsaida (John 5:4), which in turn reflects baptism in the North African tradition.[54] His dirty clothes would represent the original sin clinging to his soul before baptism. She out-allegorizes even the Western father of the doctrine of original sin: Augustine himself took the dirty clothes as actual sin.[55]

Marie-Louise Franz, as usual, offers a psychological explanation: Dinocrates' inability to reach the rim of the pool in the first dream represents Perpetua's own unbaptized past or some immature aspect of her development in Christianity. Both Franz and Michel Meslin see the absent-minded mention of Dinocrates as a reflection of Perpetua's unresolved tensions with her non-Christian family.[56]

Perpetua's dreams of Dinocrates may have been influenced by her initiation into Christianity, but linking his sordid state to his lack of baptism would be an unnecessary and anachronistic allegorization. One ought instead to see the scenes as Perpetua herself did. As soon as she remembered him, she reflected on her own situation: "I recognized immediately that I was worthy and that I ought to pray for him" (7.2). In view of her impending death as a martyr, she could, by her intercession, make it possible for her brother to be refreshed with the water of immortality.[57] Her remembrance of her brother represented not Perpetua's residual attachment to her earthly family but recognition of her position of power as confessor. Even in this world, that position was confirmed: after this dream, her guard began to treat her and her companions with a new respect because of "the great power" within them (9.1).

Strangely absent from this web of relationships are Perpetua's mother and her husband. For a while at least, Perpetua entrusted her son to her mother. Apart from this we know nothing of this woman. Perpetua's husband is an even bigger enigma. One presumes that she is married, as the narrator describes her as respectably married. Were her husband deceased she should have been described as widowed. Perhaps her husband is not resident in Carthage at the time of her imprisonment.[58] This might explain not only his absence but the care given to Perpetua's child by her own family and not the father's. Roman children often stayed with their father or their father's relatives in situations such as these.[59] But when Perpetua was in prison, her child was not sent to live with his father. The boy spent part of the time with Perpetua in her cell, but she finally entrusted him to her brother (3.8). The last the reader knows of the child, he was under the control of Perpetua's father, who refused her request to turn him over to the deacon Pomponius (6.7), a representative of the Christian family. Perpetua's husband, if indeed she had one, did not figure in these incidents.[60] His physical absence from Carthage is one likely alternative.

There is another option that might be held either alternatively or simultaneously. The phrase describing her as respectably married, *matronaliter nupta*, may not be as straightforward as it appears. It may not describe her relationship with the legal or natural father of her child. Its possible equivocation would certainly be consonant with the rest of the story. This ambiguity of language regarding familial relationships characterizes all of the *Passion*. Perpetua's own speech echoed new relationships under the vocabulary of family. She called her fellow prisoner "brother" (4.1), while she named her natural sibling "my brother according to the flesh" (7.5). She disengaged herself from both her father and her child. In addition, her father no longer called her daughter, but "domina," while her Father in heaven called her his "child." So whether unmarried, married and separated, or widowed, Perpetua had broken the bonds of the family "according to the flesh." Given all this equivocation, "respectably married" may have nothing to do with legal wedlock but may refer ultimately to an ecclesial relationship.

Besides the evidence of confusion in familial relations throughout the *Passion*, one should also note that the editor spends time twice describing her. These descriptions form an *inclusio*. The first portrayal includes *matronaliter nupta* as part of a string of conventional descriptions delineating her roles toward men in her natural family (2.1). At that point in the story the phrase seemed relatively straightforward. After the confusion of family titles and roles in her own diary, the reader is faced with the editor's second description toward the end of the story. At that point Perpetua is being led into the arena where she will achieve her true identity through her own blood (18.2). There the editor inscribes her with her true identity: "wife of Christ . . . delight of

God." Perhaps "respectably married" applied not to a legal marriage but to her recent transition from adherent to Roman religion, conceived so often as family religion, to baptized Christian, participant in a new family. Then "wife of Christ" makes clear the true meaning of "respectably married."

Even if "respectably married" did refer to a legal husband, Peter Dronke can still properly assert that her husband's absence is an indication of Perpetua's asceticism.[61] Both absence and asceticism might be reconciled in Tertullian's advice to widows not to remarry but to pledge their vows to Christ and join an angelic family.[62] In any case, the absence of her husband from the narrative fits well with Perpetua's forgetfulness of Dinocrates. It emphasized her independence of any man who might control her and limit her blessed freedom as a Christian.

In reporting her final dream, Perpetua told of the completion of her transformation. Like her first dream, her last depicted a transition from this life to the next. In both she was led by a man she knew to another place.[63] In this case, instead of Saturus her companion in martyrdom, we have the deacon Pomponius, dressed like the inhabitants of heaven in the first dream. He took her hand and led her through rough and tortuous places (10.3). Like the passage up the ladder in the first dream, the ascent was potentially dangerous. However, Perpetua did not feel personally threatened. Like Saturus, her guide in the first dream, Pomponius too disappeared when his job was done, and Perpetua walked into the amphitheater alone.

In her dream, Perpetua encountered not the animals she expected, for she had been condemned to the beasts, but an Egyptian opponent accompanied by his attendants. As he rolled in the dust to ready himself for the battle, Perpetua too prepared. Her attendants, handsome young men, stripped her to rub her with oil.[64] As her clothes were removed, she discovered herself to be a man.

Why should Perpetua have envisioned herself as a man? Was this not a betrayal of the identity forged in the face of the men in her life? This temporary transformation was a culturally conditioned affirmation of Perpetua's ultimate victory. In antiquity, as in the twentieth century, the male body was considered the norm.[65] The ambient culture offered models of humanity based on the superiority of the male or on the ideal of the androgyne.[66] Masculine-oriented biblical metaphors flowed from and reinforced prejudice for male superiority (e.g., Eph 4:13; 6:11–17; Rom 13:12). Gnosticism capitalized on it.[67] Since women were unable to become physically male, male and female became metaphors for moral categories.[68] The strong woman as male was a literary topos of late antiquity among both Christians and non-Christians. Men who were not strong were deemed "not virile." Conversely, women who bore up under trial were deemed masculine (4 Macc 15:23).[69]

Perpetua's male body indicated that she has been strengthened and would prevail in her bout with the Egyptian, that is, in her martyrdom. This transformation from female to male represents no enduring change in Perpetua's physical identity. She returned to her former, proper shape as soon as the contest has ended. She was addressed as "daughter" by the judge of the contest (10.13), not the sexually ambiguous "child" of the first dream (4.8). And it was as a woman that she received her reward (10.12–13).

Nevertheless, she fought *as a man*. This is an instance wherein martyrdom was male-defined as policy and masculine-defined in its exercise. Under these circumstances Perpetua was Christian insofar as she conformed to a world constructed by men in their image.

Martyrdom was male-defined as policy in two ways. First, the strategy of persecution as a means of religious and social control was devised by the male authorities of the Roman Empire, usually by local governors. Second, the policy that the Christians as a group would undergo martyrdom rather than flee the city was made by male ecclesiatical authorities.

Martyrdom as suffered in this case was defined by men in masculine terms. The historical Jesus in his male embodiment was not the model.[70] The mode of successful martyrdom was described in generalized masculine terms, soldier or athlete, exemplars with which this recent convert would have been familiar. The only female models offered to North African women like Perpetua and Felicity were non-Christian women: Dido, Cleopatra, the unnamed wife of the Carthaginian general Hasdrubal, and Lucretia, all suicides, women whose *only* option was destruction directly at the hands of men or indirectly through male-approved self-destruction.[71] Like the ethnic Catholic women of the twentieth century, these women could have escaped the decisions made by men about their bodies through death.

Influenced by previous Christian literature, Perpetua's dream used the athletic metaphor for her male body.[72] The referee in the contest was dressed like Pomponius, the deacon, in the robes of heaven. Like the shepherd of the first dream, here was another theophany, towering high above the walls of the arena. Like a trainer of gladiators, he carried the rod of discipline.

The trainer also carried a green branch with golden apples. The resemblance of the branch to the golden bough of Aeneas is attractive but too easy, for that bough is golden (*Aeneid* 6.140-44), not green as in Perpetua's story. More likely, it was suggested by the green boughs bearing fruit which are carried by some of the people in *The Shepherd of Hermas* (*Simil.* 8.1.18). These were the saints who had wrestled with the devil and won, that is, the martyrs (*Simil.* 8.3.6).

Perpetua's identification of the Egyptian with the devil raises the question of ethnic and racial prejudice. Why would she choose an Egyptian? According to Jan den Boeft and Jan Bremmer, Egyptians were considered the athletes *par excellence* of the Roman Empire. Had she wished to identify black in the sense of the race, she could have chosen to describe her opponent as Ethiopian. But the dark pigmentation of the Egyptian promoted an association with the chthonian deities whose color was black.[73] Thus, Perpetua as a member of the early Christian community participated in the tradition of ascribing evil to people with dark pigmentation. Stories like this and especially the iconography they engendered contributed to building later racial (not only color) prejudices. In fact, Perpetua's story adds to the tradition of ascribing evil to the "Other" for the Egyptian begins the contest rolling in the dust, he spends most of the battle at Perpetua's feet, and the battle ends with her stepping on his head. This reinforced the association of black and evil by recalling the biblical prediction of the woman and the serpent (Gen 3:14–15).

All that is evil finds its place at the feet of Perpetua. The dragon at the foot of the ladder, her father with his "diabolical arguments," and the devil Egyptian all tried unsuccessfully to prevent her ascent by striking out at or grasping at her feet (3.3; 4.4–7; 5.5; 6.2; 9.2; 10.11).[74] All failed.

In Perpetua's own self-portrait, the reader sees a young woman who moved from dependence on men to virtuous victory of her own virile image over the devil. In each encounter she took control of her bodily self. Her baptismal prayer for endurance in the flesh was being answered.

PERPETUA ENVISIONED BY A MALE COMPANION

The themes so obvious in Perpetua's own diary continue in the vision of her companion Saturus (11–13). His dream began with ascent. He too entered a heavenly garden (with Perpetua at his side). Again the vision of God was that of a seated aged man with gray-white hair and very tall stature. But this man, though old, had a youthful face. Here and in many of the details of the dreams, one again sees the influence of the visions of *Hermas*, where the old woman, who represents the church, has a progressively more youthful face.[75]

Like the transformed Dinocrates, who was relieved of his suffering and played happily (8.4), Saturus and Perpetua were told to go and play in the marvelous garden.

Significantly, in this dream, this man Saturus did not have the same attitude toward his body as Perpetua had toward hers. In Perpetua's diary, in her experiences and in her dreams, her body was an indicator of her spiritual life. In the dream of Saturus, his body was denied any transformed role. Death was an abandonment of flesh, a release from carnal embodiment: "We died," he said, "and we passed out of the flesh and we began to be carried toward the east by four angels whose hands did not touch us" (11.2). The angels could not touch them, for they had no bodies. He also attributed the abandonment of the body to Perpetua. But even in the remark he placed on her lips in his dream narrative, the reader hears an echo of the ambiguous language of Perpetua herself: "I thank God that however happy I was in the flesh, I am happier here and now" (12.7). If this "here and now" in Saturus's dream was death, it was just as much for Perpetua any moment after her experience of heaven which she had expressed in bodily metaphors.

Perpetua's acceptance by the heavenly shepherd in her first dream had transformed her. The change must have been obvious to her companions, for it was reflected in Saturus's dream (13). Outside the gates of heaven, Saturus and Perpetua met two quarreling ecclesiastics, Optatus the bishop and Aspasius the presbyter. They threw themselves at the feet of the martyrs, but it was Perpetua alone who raised them up and drew them aside to reconcile them. By her own martyrdom she was transformed not only with respect to herself and to her family relations but also in regard to her status as authority with respect to the ecclesiastical hierarchy. She did not trade subjection in her family for subjection in the church. On the contrary, she became a woman of power as she freed the dead from torment, acted as a respected medium, and finally became an authority figure for the quarreling clergy.

THE OTHER WOMAN: FELICITY

The disengagement from family and the transformation of the body obvious in the story of Perpetua are no less evident with her sister-Christian, Felicity. Her description, social status, relationship with the men in her life and with her baby all parallel Perpetua's.

Perpetua's status was ambiguous and so was Felicity's. Perpetua's position was "respectably married" at the beginning of the story (2.1), but her husband never appeared in the narrative. Perpetua's title was complemented at the end of the story with "wife of Christ . . . delight of God" (18.2).

So Felicity began the narrative with an ambiguous title. She was *conserua* or "companion in service" with the catechumen Reuocatus (2.1). There is ambiguity about her service. She might have been slave or concubine of Reuocatus.[76] More likely, they were both slaves of the same owner. Again there is ambiguity whether the owner was an earthly or heavenly one. It is possible they were both slaves in the same household as well as Christians in the same congregation. The ambiguity of their relationship distracts the reader from Felicity's male companion to her own ambiguous identity as a Christian still in the world, not yet martyred. Liminal women have always attracted attention.

Felicity's relationship with the men in her life was analogous to Perpetua's; Felicity too came to exercise power in her life once her martyrdom was a foregone conclusion. When Felicity and her companions were imprisoned, she was eight months pregnant, a very vulnerable state according to biologists of antiquity. As in the story of Perpetua, the father of her child was not mentioned. Unlike Perpetua, she could not have been "respectably married" in the world of Roman law because she was a slave. Her pregnancy, not her marital status, is the focus of her identity when the reader first encounters her. The editor's comments inform the reader that pregnant women were not executed (15.2).[77] Thus, the community of martyrs in the prison was disconsolate that they would have to leave behind the woman who had been their companion (*conserua*) thus far along the road of faith. Felicity and her companions may have feared that as a solitary and lonely woman, she would be unable to suffer bravely and endure to the end.

Knowing the power of prayer, her companions prayed for an early end to the pregnancy so that Felicity might be executed with them. Their prayer was answered three days before the date of their anticipated ordeal. However, as Felicity endured a painful labor and delivery, a prison guard taunted her. If she suffered so much now, he asked, how was she going to bear the sufferings of the arena? The guarantee of impending martyrdom empowered her to reply: in the arena when she was tortured, another inside her would suffer because she was suffering on account of Him. Once the threshold to martyrdom was passed, Felicity, like Perpetua, was a different woman and her bodily reactions proclaimed the new identity. She suffered not in the service of any earthly master, but as *conserua* in a new family.

Like Perpetua, Felicity was forced to work through her relationship with her baby. Perpetua had spent some time with her child and had to disengage herself from the mutual physical dependency of breast-feeding. She had to change from doting to detached mother. She had to break the bonds with her boy, who would grow up to follow her father's religion.

Felicity, on the other hand, might be criticized as lacking in all motherly feeling. To purchase her martyrdom, she was forced to offer the life of her little girl in a risky eighth-month birth.[78] Her baby daughter was taken from her at birth to be raised by her "sister," a Christian. She had no time to bond with her child, but, in truth, she did not need to, because her little girl would grow up in the family of faith.

PARTNERS IN MARTYRDOM

Felicity's disengagement from her child does not seem as complete as Perpetua's. Perpetua's milk dried up when she received the promise of martyrdom, but as Felicity endured her torture and death by the beasts in the arena, this woman's breasts dripped with milk. Reflecting on the cessation of lactation with Perpetua, one might be tempted to think Felicity less a heroine than Perpetua, her transformation less complete. But when one reflects on the probable audience of this story, there is a better answer: Perpetua and Felicity were complementary role models. Through their bodies these two women in their own parts of the story provided alternate models for the women of their audience. Slave or free, pregnant, nursing, or having weaned a child, respectably married or not, women in the audience could identify with one of these women martyrs. Perpetua had no husband at her side; Felicity had her *conseruus*. Perpetua's son was taken by her non-Christian natural family, Felicity's daughter by her family in Christ. As Perpetua was brave in the face of family opposition and Felicity dependent on the support of her comartyrs, each woman in the audience could identify with one woman or the other or with different aspects of either.

The attention of the story to physical surroundings, to family relationships, and to bodily functions and appetites provides opportunities for identification by embodied women, people whose lives—for better or worse—were defined by their particular female embodiments. As the relationships which defined Perpetua and Felicity most closely in their secular world were stripped from them, from their bodies, or willingly cast aside, they became more and more who they truly were.[79] So too the women of the audience could rejoice in becoming who *they* truly were. Like Perpetua, they could be called by no name other than "Christian." Like Felicity, they could anticipate their own brave sufferings knowing that Someone else would suffer for them.

In the final sections of the *Passion*, the editor tells the story of the execution of the martyrs. Even here the bodies of the women proclaim their identity. Their calm step and radiant faces reveal a lack of fear as the final moments approached. Before Perpetua received the assurance that she would be a martyr, she could not look her father in the eye. As she approached death her assurance of her status enabled her to stare down the crowd in the arena (18.2).

In this last hour, however, the martyrs suffered one more assault on their identity. The martyrs were forced to change clothing, to don religious robes of local cults (18.4). Perpetua's (and later the editor's) interest in clothing was part of the sensitivity to the sensual world.

Clothing as an extension of the body and thus as an expression of identity had played a great role in Perpetua's narrative. In her dreams of heaven or of theophanies, she always noticed clothing (4.8; 10.2; 10.8). In the vision of her brother Dinocrates, his dirty and disheveled appearance indicated his sorry state. After her prayers, his clothing as well as his cancer-scarred face was transformed (8.1).[80]

Even the editor continued Perpetua's interest in clothing as the extension of the body, as a means of identity. When the martyrs were brought to the arena, the men were to be dressed as priests of Saturn and the women as priestesses of Ceres. In this final part of their lives, they were to be subject to one last indignity, to have their bodies arrayed as sacrifices to alien divinities, to die with their bodies newly vested and proclaiming a different identity. Only a woman, Perpetua, protested. This woman who could not be called other than Christian (3.2), could not allow her body to be used this way. The military tribune acceded to her demands that the women not be dressed as votaries of Ceres. (We have not one word about what happened to the men.) In a biting reversal of his order (and in line with many martyr stories), the tribune commanded that the women be sent to the arena naked, that is, not in control of their bodies or the way they were perceived. They were to be attacked by a deliberately provoked cow. The editor recognized the choice of the female of the species as a deliberate and diabolical ploy to match powerful women with a more powerful female animal, body to body. This was too much even for the jaded members of the audience at the arena. They were not amused, for they saw only the vulnerability and obvious motherhood in the naked bodies of Perpetua and Felicity. So the two women were robed again in their own clothes as Christians and then they were returned to the arena.

Clothing played a role in Perpetua's second appearance in the arena. After she was attacked by the cow, she took a moment to rearrange her clothing. The editor attributed it to her modesty. But after she repinned her hair, she provided the key to the gesture. It was not prudish modesty but the attempt to portray with her clothed body her estimation of her own situation. On the day of her martyrdom she did not wish to be perceived as in mourning, with torn clothes and disheveled hair, but as properly prepared in her bodily suffering, clad for her hour of glory (20.5). Even when she had been gored and tossed by the cow, she was protected by an episode of hysterical fugue and would not believe she had been attacked until she saw the marks "on her body and her clothing" (20.9). *Sufferentia carnis* placed her beyond suffering. For while she could not control what happened to her body, she could act to control how it was perceived.

In the final scene in the arena, Perpetua was to be beheaded. Her executioner, a novice gladiator, was unable to execute her on the first try. It was Perpetua herself who supplied guidance to the young man. It was she who guided his inexperienced hand so he could cut her throat. The editor commented that she could not be killed unless she herself willed it. Perpetua's one and only baptismal request, perdurance in the flesh, was granted. She remained in some limited control of herself, of her body, of perceptions of her body until the end, even when the end was male-determined and accomplished.

Within the constraints of her social situation, Perpetua's story is a mixture of victory and defeat. Her story begins and ends with her under the control of prison authorities. There is no physical escape. Yet she exercises what little control she does have, reinforced by *sufferentia*. While she cannot control all that happens to her body, she can control how it is interpreted.

In effect, Perpetua's tale is one of limited victory. It tells how to cope, to exercise what minimal control one can have. It is a cautionary tale to encourage others who have no choice but physical suffering. As such, it offers the same sort of solace and strength as the body-centered stories I heard as a child. But those stories were denigrated by the men of my community, who saw no purpose in their telling. They sometimes told the stories their own way—minus the pain and the coping strategies—as something that just happened to women as passive objects. So too *The Passion of Perpetua and Felicity* suffered deformation.

THE TWISTING OF TRADITION

The editor's account of the deaths of Perpetua and Felicity showed that to the final moment their bodies manifested their status as privileged people. But despite the intense interest Perpetua and her editor showed in the body as locus and instrument of holiness, the retelling of this story by ecclesiastical authorities has been one that minimized the bodies of these martyr-mothers.

Augustine led the North African tradition with the often-repeated adage that their martyrdom was more glorious because heroism was harder for them as women. Quodvultdeus of Carthage repeated the idea, which had quickly become a commonplace. Both men took up the notion that the women who suffered martyrdom became not male in body—which was impossible, except in Perpetua's dream—but in spirit.[81] Their female bodies were denied any importance.

When the existence of their bodies could not be denied, their sexuality and maternity were transformed. What even God could not do, according to the medievalists,[82] the church did: Perpetua and Felicity were liturgically rendered virgins. The Sarum missal (ca. 1200) provided for scriptural readings concerning virginity on their feast day.[83] A Franciscan Missal (ca. 1350) went a bit farther. It used the same readings as Sarum and added a caption to their portrait styling them virgins-martyrs.[84] By the sixteenth century their transformation was complete as their status as virgins was integrated into the proper prayers of the Mass. The Missals of the Teutonic Order (printed between 1516 and 1523) and of the Council of Trent (1570) provided for the same celebration of their feast with the common Mass of many holy women, not virgins, but there were special Collect and Secret prayers providing for their mention as "virgins and martyrs."[85] The Missal of Trent also used the parable of the virgins and their lamps for the day.

Eventually even their feast day was taken from them. When Thomas Aquinas was canonized in 1323, Perpetua and Felicity were commemorated second, if at all, on their day, after this later (and male) saint.[86] Calendar reforms of 1908 further devalued these embodied women. They stripped them of their traditional feast day, March 7, the day of their death. Ironically, these bodily women are replaced by a man known as the Angelic Doctor (disguising his own well-known corpulence). Perpetua and Felicity were transferred to March 6.[87] In the reforms of Vatican II, they received their feast day back, and mention of their status as "virgins" was dropped, a gesture to the historical bodiliness of these mothers.

A MODEST SUGGESTION

I suggest one further step, not only for liturgical experts but for hagiographers, historians, and all who value embodied humanity: I propose the reclamation of women's stories of women's bodies. Rather than silently passing over their mention or denigrating them as the men of my childhood did, scholars and storytellers should attend to them, for they represent the attempts of women to control, if not their bodies at least the perception of their bodies, their very selves. Even if the women in these stories have been used to promote martyrdom as a patriarchally endorsed practice, the stories need not serve only that purpose nor need they be only cautionary tales for the present. They can serve also as warnings and counterexamples by exposing the community of discourse which offers death as the only option for women's self-definition. When the stories of women-defined women's bodies take an equal place along with men's stories of men's bodies, readers can begin to see what the *human* body is (as it exists both male and female, not simply as male and male-defined female). Such stories can be used to break the bonds of discourse systems that threaten to destroy all the disempowered peoples of the earth, so that their *sufferentia carnis* can be realized by means other than suicidal martyrdom.

NOTES

1. On the self-defense capabilities engendered by martyr stories, see my article "The Ascetic Body and the (Un)making of the Martyr," *Journal of the American Academy of Religion* 59/3 (1991): 301–13.

2. Elisabeth Schüssler Fiorenza, *In Memory of Her: A Feminist Theological Reconstruction of Christian Origins* (New York: Crossroad, 1983).

3. An outstanding example of the use of epigraphy to move women from the peripheries to the center is Bernadette J. Brooten, *Women Leaders in the Ancient Synagogue: Inscriptional Evidence and Background Issues* (Chico, CA: Scholars Press, 1982).

4. Elisabeth Schüssler Fiorenza, *Bread Not Stone: The Challenge of Feminist Biblical Interpretation* (Boston: Beacon, 1984), 114.

5. The critical edition is *Passio Sanctarum Perpetuae et Felicitatis*, ed. Cornelius Ioannes Maria Ioseph van Beek (Nijmegen: Dekker & Van De Vegt, 1936).

6. Asceticism is bodily discipline or self-denial for some spiritual end. Ascetic practices include dietary restrictions or fasting, flagellation, wearing clothing whose quantity or quality (e.g., hairshirt) contributes to discomfort, maintenance of uncomfortable physical positions. In general, the object of these exercises is the control of the body to permit closer union with the divine.

7. The history of early Christian attitudes toward the body is magisterially detailed by Peter Brown in *The Body and Society: Men, Women, and Sexual Renunciation in Early Christianity* (New York: Columbia University Press, 1988).

8. Dionysius of Alexandria, *Epistula canonica ad Basilidem episcopum*, canon 2 (Migne *PG* 10:1282–83; in translation in *Maenads, Martyrs, Matrons, Monastics: A Sourcebook on Women's Religions in the Greco-Roman World*, ed. Ross S. Kraemer [Philadelphia: Fortress, 1988], 43).

9. See, e.g., Jerome, *Ep.* 107, to his friend Laeta on raising her infant daughter to deny her embodiment (*CSEL* 55:290–305 = Kraemer, pp. 127–37).

10. Manichaeism was a religious movement founded in Persia by Mani (216–276 C.E.). The religion combined elements of Jewish Christianity and Zoroastrianism. It featured a radically dualist cosmology and a gnostic soteriology. Manicheans were opposed to conception, as it imprisoned more souls in matter. Special diets for advanced adherents assisted the liberation of souls from material bondage. Persecuted by Christian rulers and sporadically by Zoroastrians, they continued into the Middle Ages and may have influenced European Christianity up to the fifteenth century.

11. Augustine on penile erections in *De nuptiis et concupiscentia* 1.7 (*CSEL* 42:219–20).

12. The attribution began with Theodoric Ruinart, *Acta Martyrum* (Verona: Tumerman, 1731), 79. Adolf Harnack gave it widespread publicity in *Geschichte der altchristlichen Literatur bis Eusebius* 1 (Leipzig: Hinrichs, 1893). Few noticed that in volume 2 Harnack changed his mind. See the discussion of the history of the attribution in van Beek, *Passio*, 84*–91*.

13. Victor Saxer, *Bible et hagiographie: Textes et thèmes bibliques dans les Actes des martyrs authentiques des premiers siècles* (Berne and New York: Peter Lang, 1986), 94–95.

14. Åke Fridh, *La Problème de la Passion des Saintes Perpétue et Félicité* (Studia Graeca et Latina Gothoburgensia 26; Stockholm: Almqvist & Wiksell, 1968), 45.

15. Some of the early work on this question was done by W. H. Schwering, "Prose Rhythms in the *Passio Perpetuae*," *Journal of Theological Studies* 30 (1929): 56–57; and "En marge de la *Passion des Saintes Perpétue et Félicité*," *Revue Bénédictine* 43 (1931): 15–22. The best analysis is that of Fridh, who concluded that the editor was not Tertullian but a contemporary Carthaginian. The few new arguments proposed between the publication of Fridh's article and 1979 are deftly summarized and analyzed by René Braun, "Nouvelles observations linguistiques sur le rédacteur de la 'Passio Perpetuae,'" *Vigiliae Christianae* 33 (1979): 105–17. See also Luigi Franco Pizzolato, "Note alla 'Passio Perpetuae et Felicitatis,'" *Vigiliae Christianae* 34 (1980): 105–19. There have been no significant addenda to the controversy since 1980.

16. Fridh, *Problèem*, 80, 82–83.

17. On the history of Montanism, see Pierre de Labriolle, *La crise montaniste* (Paris: Leroux, 1913; repr. New York: AMS, 1983). Labriolle's *Sources de l'histoire du montanisme* (Fribourg: University of Fribourg, 1913; repr. New York: AMS, 1980) is corrected and nuanced by Ronald E. Heine, *The Montanist Oracles and Testimonia* (North American Patristics Society Patristic

Monograph Series 14; Macon, GA: Mercer University Press, 1989). See also the article by
Susanna Elm in this volume.

18. See the extensive collection of citations in Heine, *Montanist Oracles*, 62–93.

19. On the dating of the *Passion*, see Timothy D. Barnes, "Pre-Decian *Acta Martyrum*,"
Journal of Theological Studies 19 (1968): 522–25; and Clementina Mazzucco, '*E fui fatta mas-
chio*': *La donna nel cristianesimo primitivo (secoli I-III)* (Università degli Studi di Torino,
Fondo di Studi Parini-Chiro Letteratura 1; Florence: Casa Éditrice Le Lettre, 1989), 119 n. 38.

20. See Augustine's sermons 280–281(b) (Migne *PL* 38:1281–84).

21. Eugenio Corsini, "Proposte per una lettura della 'Passio Perpetuae,'" in *Forma Futuri:
Studi in onore del Cardinale Michele Pellegrino* (Turin: Bottega d'Erasmo, 1975), 485. This
idea is strongly endorsed by Margaret Miles, *Carnal Knowing: Female Nakedness and
Religious Knowing in the Christian West* (Boston: Beacon, 1989), 62. Miles sees Perpetua's
writing as used for agenda she herself would not have supported.

22. Timothy David Barnes provides a fairly complete list of distinctively Montanist characteristics: "1. The naming of Montanus, Prisc(ill)a or Maximilla, or an appeal to Montanist 'oracles'
uttered by them. 2. Reference to the New Prophecy or rebuttal of charges of 'pseudoprophetia'
or of introducing 'nova disciplina'. 3. Commendation of the ecstatic state. 4. Mention of spiritual gifts possessed only by the Montanists. 5. Description of the Holy Spirit as the 'Paracletus.' 6.
'Nos' or 'noster' used to describe things or persons peculiarly Montanist. 7. 'Vos' or 'vester'
used to contrast catholic Christians with Montanists. 8. Abuse of the catholics as 'psychici'"
(*Tertullian, A Historical and Literary Study* [Oxford: Clarendon, 1971], 43–44).

23. Tilley, "Ascetic Body," 306–7.

24. See the discussion of the "Montanism" of *The Passion* in Barnes, *Tertullian*, 71–78; and
Jacqueline Amat, *Songes et visions: L'au delà dans la littérature latine tardive* (Paris: Études
Augustiniennes, 1985), 67. On martyrs being able to forgive sins, see Tertullian, *Mart.* 1 (*CCL*
1:3) in favor of the custom, and *Pud.* 22 (*CCL* 2:1328–29) against it. Cf. *The Martyrs of Lyon* in
Eusebius, *Hist. eccl.* 5.1.45, in *The Acts of the Christian Martyrs*, ed. and trans. Herbert
Musurillo (Oxford: Clarendon, 1972), 76 (= Loeb 1.428). For implied anticlericalism, see
Passio Ss. Maximae, Donatillae et Secundae 1.6 (*Analecta Bollandiana* 9 [1890], 110). On the
response to martyrdom, see *The Acts of the Scillitan Martyrs* 17 (Musurillo, p. 88).

25. *De Anima* 42–48 (*CCL* 2:845–55).

26. *De spect.* 29 (*CCL* 1:251). Incubation is the practice of sleeping in temples, shrines, or
other holy places. Both Christians and non-Christians in antiquity used incubation to attempt to
procure health or the answer to questions about daily life.

27. See Domenico Devoti, "Sogno e Conversione nei Padri: Considerazioni Preliminari,"
Augustinianum 27 (1987): 114–15, for a bibliography on dreams and visions in the ancient
world. Also useful is Jacques Le Goff, *The Medieval Imagination*, trans. Arthur Goldhammer
(Chicago and London: University of Chicago Press, 1988), 193–231.

28. Acts 7:55–56; *Mart. Pol.* 5.2 (Musurillo, p. 6).

29. E.g., *The Martyrdom of Saints Marian and James* 6.5–7.4 and 8.2–11 (Musurillo, pp.
200–206); *The Martyrdom of Saints Montanus and Lucius* 5–8 and 11 (Musurillo, pp. 216–20
and 222).

30. The term "apocalyptic" refers to a genre of literature that was popular in Judaism and
Christianity, especially between 200 B.C.E. and 200 C.E. Apocalyptic writings are usually pseudonymous; that is, they are attributed to famous religious figures of the past, such as Adam, Moses,
or Elijah. In dreams and visions, they reveal secrets about the course and meaning of world history, especially the end-times, manifested in symbolic language. Examples include the
Testaments of the Twelve Patriarchs, the *Sibylline Oracles,* and the books of *Enoch.*

31. Classification of the various interpretations of the dreams with full bibliography is in Mazzucco, *'E fui fatta maschio,'* 130–31.

32. Jacques Fontaine, *Aspects et problèmes de la prose d'art latine au IIIe siècle: La genèse des styles latins chrétiens* (Turin: Bottega d'Erasmo, 1968), 87.

33. Especially careful in this respect is Michel Meslin, "Vases sacrés et boissons d'éternité dans les visions des martyrs africains," in *Epektasis: Mélanges patristiques offerts au Cardinal Jean Daniélou,* ed. Jacques Fontaine and Charles Kannengiesser (Paris: Beauchesne, 1972), 153. Peter Dronke comments perceptively: "Perpetua did not intend to construct spiritual allegories for the benefit of later Christians. Only once at the close of her fourth dream, does she briefly admit an allegorical meaning, and that for one personage only (the Egyptian) among all her dream experiences" (*Women Writers of the Middle Ages* [Cambridge: Cambridge University Press, 1984], 7).

34. E.g., Elaine C. Huber, *Women and the Authority of Inspiration: A Reexamination of the Authority of Inspiration From a Contemporary Feminist Perspective* (Lanham, MD: University Press of America, 1985) in a study of Montanist women and Anne Hutchinson.

35. Augustine, *Sermo* 281 (Migne *PL* 38:1281).

36. The feast of Perpetua and Felicity is recorded in the *Feriale Ecclesiae Romanae,* also known as the *Depositio Martirum* (ca. 336 C.E.). See *Monumenta Germaniae Historica: Auctores Antiquissimi,* ed. Theodore Mommsen (Berlin: Weidmann, 1891), 9.71. Evidence for the celebration of the feast day in North Africa is Augustine, *Sermons* 280, 281 (a) and (b), and 282 (Migne *PL* 38:1281–84). See also Thomas Heffernan, *Sacred Biography: Saints and their Biographers in the Middle Ages* (New York and Oxford: Oxford University Press, 1988), 193 for the spread of the veneration of Perpetua.

37. For the various options available to Roman women, see J. A. Crook, *Law and Life of Rome, 90 B.C.–A.D. 212* (Ithaca, NY: Cornell University Press, 1967), 103.

38. For family arrangements such as these, see Suzanne Dixon, *The Roman Mother* (London and Sydney: Croom Helm, 1988), 217.

39. *Sufferentia* (along with *patientia*) is one of the Vulgate translations of the Christian Testament *hypomone.* Nowhere else in early Christian literature is *sufferentia* or *hypomone* linked to words of the body.

40. Mithraism was an astrological mystery religion popular especially with Roman soldiers from the first century C.E. to the fourth. It featured a savior figure, Mithras (associated with the Persian deity Mithra and the mythic character Perseus). Its ritual and mythology made it superficially similar to Christianity. Its popularity won it the enmity of early Christian writers.

41. This is suggested by Marie-Louise von Franz, "Die Passio Perpetuae: Versuch einer psychologischen Deutung," in *Aion: Untersuchungen zur Symbolgeschichte,* ed. Carl Gustav Jung (Zurich: Rascher, 1951), 413.

42. See, e.g., Gen 3:1–20; Isa 27:1; Rev 12:3, 9; 20:2; *3 Bar.* 4. For a discussion of these texts, see Saxer, *Bible et hagiographie,* 45, 87.

43. E.g., Josh 10:24; Luke 10:19. For a discussion of these passages, see Franz Joseph Dölger, "Der Kampf mit dem Ägypter in Perpetua-Vision: Das Martyrium als Kampf mit dem Teufel," *Antike und Christentum* 3 (1932): 179–81. In the Vulgate the use of the verb of this sentence, *calco,* almost always denotes domination whether of land or people.

44. Franz, "Die Passio," 432.

45. Amat (*Songes et visions,* 78) lists several examples of great height indicating the divine, e.g., *Poimandres* 1.4; Lucian, *Philopseudes* 22; *Secrets of Enoch.* To these I would add the *Gospel of Peter* 10.40 in *New Testament Apocrypha,* 2 vols., ed. Edgar Hennecke and Wilhelm Schneemelcher (Philadelphia: Westminster, 1964), 1:186.

46. See Miles, *Carnal Knowing*, 60, who links eating with permanent residency. But like Proserpina, Perpetua must return to earth out of her dream.

47. Alvyn Pettersen, "Perpetua—Prisoner of Conscience," *Vigiliae Christianae* 41 (1967): 144; see also Dronke, *Women Writers*, 5–6.

48. See Miles, *Carnal Knowing*, 61.

49. See Pierre Courcelle, *Les Confessions de saint Augustin dans la tradition littéraire* (Paris: Études Augustiniennes, 1963), 137–38.

50. On the ancient parallels to the suffering of Dinocrates, see Franz Joseph Dölger, "Antike Parallelen zum leidenden Dinocrates in der Passio Perpetuae," *Antike und Christentum* 2 (1930): 1–40. See also Dronke, *Women Writers*, 10.

51. Tertullian, *De Anima* 55 *ad fin.* (*CCL* 2:862–63).

52. 2 Macc 7:37; 12:43–45; 4 Macc 7:28; 9:24; *Acts of Paul and Thecla* 28–29, in Hennecke and Schneemelcher, 2:360–61, *The Martyrs of Lyon* in Eusebius, *Hist. eccl.* 5.1.45–56 (Musurillo, p. 64 = Loeb 2:428); Tertullian, *Monog.* 10.4 (*CCL* 2:1243). The controversy over the suitability of the confessors forgiving sins was still a major issue at Carthage fifty years later. See Cyprian, *Laps.*, *passim* (*CSEL* 2/1:237-64) and *Ep.* 9 (*CSEL* 2/2:488-89).

53. Amat (*Songes et visions*, 129) cites Prov 4:19, 13 and Lam 3:6. In this vein one would need to consider Matt 22:11–14.

54. Amat, *Songes et visions*, 30. Cf. Tertullian, *Bapt.* 5 (*CCL* 1:281); and Optatus of Milevis, 3.2 (*CSEL* 26:68–69).

55. Augustine, *De orig. anim.* 1.2 (*CSEL* 60:312).

56. Franz, "Die Passio," 445, 448, 446; Meslin, "Vases sacrés," 146–48.

57. Meslin, "Vases sacrés," 146–47.

58. See Dronke, *Women Writers*, 282 n. 3.

59. Dixon, *Roman Mother*, 132–33.

60. Dronke suggests that Perpetua's husband once had a larger role in the story and that the dialogues between Perpetua and her father were transferred from the persona of the husband to the father. He thinks that the absence of the husband makes Perpetua more attractive as an ascetic figure. There are no "editorial seams" or strong literary motifs to warrant this suggestion of transference (*Women Writers*, 282 n. 3).

61. Ibid.; see also Heffernan, *Sacred Biography*, 185, 233–34, who suggests a "renunciation of the marriage debt" following baptism. See Tertullian, *Uxor.* 1.3 and 2.8 (*CCL* 1:35, 392–93).

62. Tertullian, *Uxor.* 1.4 (*CCL* 1:377–78).

63. Franz, "Die Passio," 458.

64. Amat gives this anointing sacramental signification; however, this is an unwarranted construal of the act (*Songes et visions*, 82).

65. Aristotle, *De gen. anim.* 2.1 (732a; Loeb 13.132). Cf. the number of contemporary medical studies which use only male subjects, yet the conclusions of these studies are applied *mutatis non mutandis* to women.

66. On the ambient culture, see Kari Vogt, "'Becoming Male': One Aspect of an Early Christian Anthropology," trans. Ruth Murphy in *Women—Invisible in Church and Theology*, ed. Elisabeth Schüssler Fiorenza and Mary Collins, *Concilium* 182 (Edinburgh: T. & T. Clark, 1985), 80; and Miles, *Carnal Knowing*, 55–56; as well as Dennis R. MacDonald, *There Is No Male or Female* (Philadelphia: Fortress, 1987). On the androgyne, see Wayne A. Meeks, "The Image of the Androgyne: Some Uses of the Symbol in Earliest Christianity," *History of Religions* 13 (1974): 194.

67. Mazzucco, *'E fui fatta maschio,'* 122–23.

68. Vogt, "'Becoming Male,'" 76.

69. Cf. the use of masculine and feminine terms in the patristic documents cited by Vogt, "'Becoming Male,'" 73–79.

70. While the image of Christ as male-embodied savior might be problematic to many contemporary feminists, it would not have been so to Perpetua, even if she had been asked to model her martyrdom on his. Neither she nor her text can solve this twentieth-century problem directly.

71. Tertullian, *Mart.* 4 (Migne *PL* 1:699A–B).

72. Earlier Christian use of the athletic metaphor: 1 Cor 9:25 and 2 Tim 2:5 regarding perdurance in faith; *1 Clem.* 5.1 (Loeb 1.16) about martyrs in general; *Martyrs of Lyon* in Eusebius, *Hist. eccl.* 5.1.19 (Musurillo, p. 66 = Loeb 1.414), describing Blandina.

73. Jan den Boeft and Jan Bremmer, "Notiunculae Martyrologiae II," *Vigiliae Christianae* 36 (1982): 390, with extensive bibliography. On color and ethnic prejudice, see Lellia Cracco Ruggini, "Il negro buono e il negro malvaggio nel mundo antiquo," in *Conoscenze etniche e rapporti di convivenza nell' antichità* (Scienze storiche 21; Contributi dell' Instituto di storia antica 6, ed. Marta Sordi; Milan: Università Cattolica del Sacro Cuore, 1979), 108–35; and Frank M. Snowden, *Before Color Prejudice: The Ancient View of Blacks* (Cambridge, MA: Harvard University Press, 1983); idem, *Blacks in Antiquity: Ethiopians in the Greco-Roman Experience* (Cambridge, MA: Belknap, 1970). The term "chthonian" describes the blood-lusting divinities of the Greco-Roman underworld. The force of the word was to point to dread experienced by people on account of the harm these beings could do.

74. See Dronke, *Women Writers*, 5–6, and Dölger, "Der Kampfe," 179.

75. Compare, *inter alia*, rough places Perpetua trod (10.3) with those of Hermas (*Vis.* 1.1.3); the four angels who bear Saturus and Perpetua to the east (11.2) with the four men who bear the Lady Church to the east (*Vis.* 4.1); and the young face of the old man (12.3), which resembles the progressively younger face of the old woman (*Vis.* 3.10.3). In Hermas, too, familial relations are transformed as Hermas's wife is named as his sister (*Vis.* 2.3.1).

76. Mazzucco rehearses the arguments for this interpretation of the word (*'E gui fatta maschio,'* 190–200).

77. For a discussion of such legislation, see Johannes Quasten, "A Roman Law of Egyptian Origin in the 'Passio Perpetuae et Felicitatis,'" *The Jurist* 1 (1941): 193–98.

78. This is the charge Devoti brings against Perpetua ("Sogno e Conversione," 131–32), and the one which Heffernan deflects from Felicity (*Sacred Biography*, 223–24).

79. See Miles, *Carnal Knowing*, 59.

80. This attention to clothing as an extension of the body was not a significant part of the testimony of the martyr Saturus. In his vision the inhabitants of heaven are merely clothed with the proverbial white robes (12.1).

81. Augustine, *Sermo* 280.1 (Migne *PL* 38:1281) and 281a.1 (Migne *PL* 38:1284); Quodvultdeus, *De tempore barbarico* 1.5 (CCL 60:430–31).

82. See Jerome, *Ep.* 22 (Migne *PL* 22:397), and Thomas Aquinas, *Summa Theologica* I, q. 25, a. 4, cited in *The Power of God: Readings on Omnipotence and Evil*, ed. Linwood Urban and Douglas N. Walton (New York: Oxford University Press, 1978), 67–68; but cf. Peter Damien, *De divina omnipotentia* (Migne *PL* 145:595–622), in *The Power of God*, 59–66.

83. The epistle was 1 Cor 7:25–34, an exhortation to virginity; the Gospel was Matt 25:1–13, the parable of the virgins. See *The Sarum Missal*, ed. J. Wickham Legg (Oxford: Clarendon, 1916; repr. 1969), 256.

84. *The Franciscan Missal Ms. Douce 313 (ca. 1350)* with an introduction by W. A. Hassal (Major Treasures of the Bodleian Library number 6; Oxford: Oxford Microform Publications, 1978), fol. 265r.

85. *Missale adnotulando minorum teutonicorum* (Hagenau: Thomas Anshelm, n.d.), fol. clxx verso, and *The English-Latin Sacramentary for the United States of America* (New York: Benziger Brothers, 1966), p. 49S (not yet showing the influence of post-Vatical II liturgical reform).

86. As exemplar, *Missale Romanum* (Dublin: Coyne, 1833), 415–17.

87. *The Roman Calendar: Text and Commentary* (Washington, DC: United States Catholic Conference, 1976), 49.

RECOMMENDED READINGS

The Acts of the Christian Martyrs. Introduction, texts and translations by Herbert Musurillo. Oxford: Clarendon, 1972.

Brown, Peter. *The Body and Society: Men, Women and Sexual Renunciation in Early Christianity*. New York: Columbia University Press, 1988.

Dronke, Peter. *Women Writers of the Middle Ages*. Cambridge: Cambridge University Press, 1984.

Fridh, Åke. *La Problème de la Passion des Saintes Perpétue et Félicité*. Studia Graeca et Latina Gothoburgensia 26. Stockholm: Almqvist & Wiksell, 1968.

Heffernan, Thomas. *Sacred Biography: Saints and their Biographers in the Middle Ages*. New York and Oxford: Oxford University Press, 1988.

Mazzucco, Clementina. *'E fui fatta maschio': La donna nel cristianesimo primitivo (secoli I-III)*. Università degli Studi di Torino. Fondo di Studi Parini-Chiro Letterature 1. Florence: Casa Editrice Le Lettre, 1989.

Miles, Margaret R. *Carnal Knowing: Female Nakedness and Religious Meaning in the Christian West*. Boston: Beacon, 1989.

Passio Sanctuarum Perpetuae et Felicitatis. Edited by Cornelius Iohannes Maria Ioseph van Beek. Nijmegen: Dekker and Van De Vegt, 1936.

Schüssler Fiorenza, Elisabeth. *In Memory of Her: A Feminist Theological Reconstruction of Christian Origins*. New York: Crossroad, 1983.

Vogt, Kari. "'Becoming Male': One Aspect of an Early Christian Anthropology." Translated by Ruth Murphy. In *Women—Invisible in Church and Theology,* edited by Elisabeth Schüssler Fiorenza and Mary Collins. *Concilium* 182. Edinburgh: T. & T. Clark, 1985.

The Book of Aseneth

ROSS S. KRAEMER ◆

INTRODUCTION

THREE BRIEF PASSAGES in Genesis (41:45, 50–52 and 46:20) assert that Pharaoh gave Joseph a woman named Aseneth, daughter of the Egyptian priest of On, as his wife, and that Aseneth bore Joseph two sons, Manasseh and Ephraim. Despite the fact that prohibitions against intermarriage occur in numerous biblical passages, for the authors and editors of the Bible, this story was apparently unremarkable. While later rabbinic sources have somewhat more to say about this alliance,[1] the marriage receives the most attention in an enigmatic Greek story preserved in a number of versions. Modern scholars frequently title the story *Joseph and Aseneth,* but its ancient title is uncertain. Here I will simply call it *Aseneth.*[2]

Although *Aseneth* has received considerably less attention than many comparable texts, a scholarly consensus of sorts has emerged about its origins, date, provenience, and central concerns. The scholar who first published a Greek text and translation (1889–90) construed it as a Christian text, but it is now universally assumed to be Jewish. It is also assumed to be the work of a single, anonymous (and male) author. *Aseneth* is extant principally in Greek, which was almost certainly the language of its composition, and in Latin, Slavic, Armenian, and Romanian, in manuscripts that date no earlier than the tenth century C.E. Two Syriac manuscripts which date to the sixth or seventh century C.E. contain a translation of *Aseneth* within the Syrian Chronicle of Pseudo-Zacharias,[3] whose history ends with 569 C.E. A preface identifies the translator as a Syrian monk who lived in the second half of the sixth century C.E., strengthening the probability that the Aseneth story was composed in Greek prior to the mid-sixth century.

No ancient fragments of *Aseneth* that antedate the Syriac manuscripts have ever been identified, and no ancient author is known to quote it directly. Apart from the Syriac reference to a Greek text, the earliest allusion to the

Greek stories appears to be in a medieval work by Peter the Deacon of Monte Cassino, entitled *On The Holy Places,* written before 1137; he, in turn, is thought to be quoting from a late fourth (or early fifth) century pilgrimage diary by a woman named Egeria.[4] Despite its late attestion, it is generally assigned a date of somewhere between the first century B.C.E. and the early second century C.E. Virtually all scholars place it within the broad category of a Greco-Roman romance, or novel, whose specific concern is the conversion of Aseneth to Judaism and her subsequent marriage to Joseph. Most consider it a thinly veiled projection of Hellenistic Jewish beliefs (and possibly also practices) back onto the biblical narrative of Genesis.

Since the Greek manuscripts contain significantly different readings, scholars disagree about the precise nature of the "original" text. While some favor the shorter textual reconstruction of Marc Philonenko, a majority have accepted the arguments of Christoph Burchard in favor of a "longer" "original." Interestingly, the differences between the reconstructions proposed by Philonenko and Burchard significantly affect the presentation of Aseneth, particularly around the issue of gender.

Under careful scrutiny, the majority opinion about the most primitive form of this work emerges as unsubstantiated, improbable, or simply wrong. Although space does not permit a detailed defense of my conclusions, I am convinced that the shorter version of the text is by and large earlier than the longer version, that a shorter version was known to the redactor(s) of the longer texts, and that many of the differences are intentional alterations, reflecting specific concerns of the redactor(s). Regarding date, I am more and more inclined to consider both the shorter and the longer versions most comprehensible within the cultural climate of the third and/or fourth centuries C.E. I also now think that the earlier story or stories probably, though not certainly, originate in Jewish circles, and that the longer, later versions may show some signs of subtle Christian editing. Less likely but not impossible would be an author who would have used the self-designation *theosebēs* (one who reveres or fears God), as a technical term for a pagan devotee of the God of Israel.[5] Further, though I have elsewhere argued that the shorter version of *Aseneth* could have been authored by a woman, I am somewhat less inclined to think this so. The redactor(s) of the longer version seem to me almost certainly to be male, on the basis of their revisions of passages that are particularly concerned with constructions of gender.

Behind *Aseneth,* various scholars claim to have detected the influence of everything from Egyptian myths and folktales to Gnostic allegorical dramas. While I agree that *Aseneth* draws heavily on the common cultural currency of the Greco-Roman world, I now believe that previous scholarship has failed to identify and elucidate the three dominant paradigms that undergird these stories and may, for the sake of artifice and convenience, be labeled the midrashic, the magical,[6] and the mystical.

Much (though not all) of the story of Aseneth in the Greek manuscripts appears constructed out of biblical elements and motifs. The basic framework of the text may be derived from the constraints of the biblical story itself (which I believe the author[s] knew). From the need to answer certain basic questions and to resolve certain basic anomalies in that story, the author(s) drew heavily on the language, motifs, and metaphors of traditions that we find in certain biblical books, particularly Genesis, Proverbs, Psalms, and Song of Songs. This process of deriving much of both the narrative framework and the details of the story from the bare bones of the biblical text may be labeled "midrashic."[7] Some previous scholars have acknowledged the general midrashic character of Aseneth, but they have done little more than signal probable biblical parallels. A closer analysis of the language and motifs of both the shorter and longer reconstructions reveals the high degree to which each text relies on these materials and demonstrates the extent to which the longer text expanded this process even further.

Of equal if not more significance for the content and interpretation of *Aseneth* are two other paradigms, the magical and the mystical. The dominant paradigm in the center of the story, which deals with Aseneth's transformation from an Egyptian idolater to a suitable spouse for Joseph, is in fact the magical adjuration of an angel. This phenomenon is familiar to us from such diverse sources as the Greek magical papyri (many of which are intimately connected with Jews and Judaism); Jewish mystical writings called "Hekhalot" texts (from their descriptions of visions of the various heavens or palaces [*hekhalot*] experienced by adept practitioners) and the enigmatic *Sepher ha-Razim* (the *Book of the Mysteries*), a Hebrew work dating probably to the third or fourth century C.E., which contains numerous rituals and spells for compelling angels to do human bidding.

In many ancient sources, the adjuration of angels acquires a strong mystical dimension. In the Greek stories, Aseneth represents the prototypical soul who seeks and attains restoration to a primordial angelic identity, a concept that is probably derived from interpretations of Genesis 1. She is the penitent suffering sinner whose desire for reconciliation with the divine is found in many Psalms. Additional mystical motifs undergird the texts and the authors' choices of narrative structure and detail. For the author of the shorter text, the marriage of Joseph and Aseneth is simultaneously the union of the Wise Man with Wisdom personified as female, and that of the lovers in Song of Songs: it represents and/or enacts the divine union of the heavenly bodies of the Sun (Helios) and the Moon (Selene) and, as the text itself makes clear, of the son and daughter of God. Less obvious but also present underneath the longer text (and perhaps also the shorter) is the paradigm afforded by the primordial couple in Genesis, particularly 1:26–27.

While there is nothing inherently feminist about this analysis so far, a self-consciously feminist perspective allows us to illuminate still other dimensions of the text(s). In my own work, feminist commentary (and feminist critique of any sort) takes gender as a fundamental category of analysis. I read all ancient sources as a historian and as what Howard Eilberg-Schwartz has called a "cultural archaeologist."[8] Texts, for me, may be analyzed as potential evidence for (other) women's experiences, as potential evidence for male perceptions of women and/or women's experiences, and as potential evidence for the history of the cultural construction of gender, that is, the ways in which every community and society ascribe meaning to the categories female and male.

These perspectives generate a laundry list of potential questions to address in a feminist commentary. How are women (and men) presented or portrayed within the text? What cultural constructions of gender are implicit, or even explicit, within the text? How does the text's posture with regard to gender relate to constructions of gender in the larger cultural context? What tensions does the text exhibit around issues of gender? Does it accept prevailing notions of gender (insofar as we are able to establish those)? Does it critique such notions? What does the text say about the real experiences of women (and men)? Are women's experiences perceptible through the text? What difference does the imputed gender of the author or of the audience make to one's analysis of the text?

Many feminists insist that full feminist analysis cannot confine itself to questions of gender alone but must also include attention to issues of race and class. They argue that gender is but one component in the structure of social relationships and that the patterns of dominance and hierarchy that typify most societies are constructed not only out of ideas about gender but also of ideas about other forms of categorizing and ranking human beings.

In the Greco-Roman world, combinations of categories played a fundamental role in the construction of ancient social hierarchy. It mattered whether you were male or female, freeborn, enslaved, or freed from slavery; it mattered whether you were a citizen or a foreigner; it mattered whether you were a Jew, a Christian, or what we call "pagan"; it mattered whether you were a child or an adult. At the top of this hierarchy were free citizen adult males, the vast majority of whom, before the fourth century C.E., would have been pagans. At the bottom were female slaves (whose religious self-identification was probably of less significance than either their gender or their enslavement). Individuals related to one another through complex hierarchical relationships which expressed themselves in a wide range of social behavior: who ate what, when, with whom; who had sex with whom (and in what positions); who wore what; who went where; how space was arranged. All these things reflected constructions of social hierarchy and provided a potent means to express both social conformity and social protest. For reasons which are primarily pragmatic (too little space and not enough time), I have decided to focus my commentary primarily on gender-related questions, noting, where I can, the ways in which other aspects of ancient social hierarchy affect the texts and our readings of them. At the conclusion, I'll propose some brief answers to my laundry list.

COMMENTARY[9]

INITIAL DESCRIPTION OF ASENETH (1.16–2.20)

Aseneth is initially described as an unsurpassingly beautiful virgin of eighteen, attended by seven similarly beautiful virgins, who lives in a large apartment in a high tower within Pentephres' compound. So great is the reputation of her beauty that numerous aristocratic young men seek her as a bride, including the son of Pharaoh. Beautiful virgins who live in high towers and young men who desire them are stock items in folktales, and similar motifs are easily discernible in ancient Greco-Roman romantic novels.[10] Despite the presence of such motifs, the entire description of Aseneth draws heavily on the identifications of Aseneth with Wisdom, the female lover in Song of Songs, the daughter of the king, the penitent sinner, the soul in search of angelic transformation, and even the Strange or Foreign Woman in Proverbs and elsewhere.

For instance, Aseneth's gold and silver, her clothing, jewels, and linens are just such riches as Prov 24:3 assigns to Woman Wisdom: "By Wisdom a house is built: by knowledge the rooms are filled with all precious and pleasant riches." Although Aseneth's rooms allude to Wisdom's house, they initially contain the representations of Aseneth's Egyptian gods and, like Aseneth herself, require transformation. While the presence of such idols is consistent with Aseneth's identity as the daughter of an Egyptian priest and fulfills an important need for the narrative, it also accords with the presentation of the Foreign or Strange Woman in Proverbs, who is the antithesis of Woman Wisdom. The Strange Woman's house is filled with the dead (Prov 9:18). And Aseneth's gods turn out to be just that—dead, deaf, and dumb to boot (Prov 8:5; 12:6).

ASENETH'S VIRGINITY (1.6; 2.12–16)

The emphasis on Aseneth's virginity (a universal trait of heroines in ancient romances) is essential, given the ultimate outcome of the story: it guarantees the legitimacy of Manasseh and Ephraim and the tribes that bear their names.

The extraordinary stress on Aseneth's virginity, buttressed by the claims that she has lived all her life carefully guarded in a tower, out of the sight of men, may also reflect early Jewish stereotypes about the sexual immorality of Gentiles per se, a stereotype that is discernible within this text in the description of the extravagant lust of the Egyptian women for the beautiful Joseph. The claim in 1.8 that Aseneth is in no way like the daughters of the Egyptians, but in all ways like the daughters of the Hebrews, and that her physical attributes are the same as those of the matriarchs Sarah, Rebecca, and Rachel may be intended to dissociate her from such stereotypes. Aseneth's virginity is also consistent with the emphasis on sexual purity required for various magical and mystical experiences in numerous ancient sources.

ASENETH'S RESIDENCE (2.1–20)

Aseneth's walled residence with its garden, fountains, and rivers resonates with Cant 4:12. "A garden locked is my sister, my bride; a garden locked, a fountain sealed." Aseneth's residence within a secure compound may also draw on the imagery of Ps 45:13–14, particularly since the story ultimately develops the image of Aseneth as the daughter of God (the king):

> The daughter of the king, all her glory (is) within . . .
> she is led to the king; behind her, the virgins, her companions . . .
> (Ps 44:14–15 LXX)[11]

Although there are some particular difficulties associated with the translation and interpretation of this verse, it contains some of the central elements of Aseneth's attributes, including her seclusion and her virgin companions. If it is not the impetus for this description of Aseneth, it would at the very least have affirmed the appropriateness of those details.

While exploiting connections with Wisdom and the divine bride, the precise description of Aseneth's residence points to even more complex associations, which are connected to the magical and mystical paradigms. Pentephres' compound may be seen to incorporate paradise (the garden), seven heavens (the seven rooms of the seven virgins), and a divine temple (Aseneth's three chambers). In addition to the similarities between Aseneth's rooms and descriptions of ancient temples (including the Jewish Temple in Jerusalem), the identification of these three rooms with a temple may initially be signaled by Joseph's entrance into the compound from the east, at noon (the hour of the Sun's height), where Joseph represents the divinity entering the temple precincts. This reading is strengthened in subsequent chapters, when it is to these rooms that the angelic being, having the appearance of Joseph, descends to Aseneth.

ASENETH'S VIRGIN COMPANIONS (2.10–11)

Aseneth's seven virgin companions are similarly susceptible to multiple interpretations. At the midrashic level, the biblical Esther also has seven companions (Esth 2:7), and, as noted, Ps 45:14 (44:15 LXX) envisions virgin companions for the king's daughter. That Aseneth's virgin companions specifically number seven also accords with Prov 9:1: "Wisdom has built her house; she has hewn her seven pillars." This association is at best implicit in the shorter text, but it is much clearer in the longer versions, where in 17:6, the angelic figure blesses the seven virgins and explicitly calls them the seven pillars of the City of Refuge.

At the magical and mystical levels, the number seven is extremely significant in both Jewish and non-Jewish symbolic systems in the ancient world. The first-century Jewish philosopher Philo of Alexandria explicitly associated seven with virginity,[12] while numerous texts envision seven heavens, and/or seven palaces. *Sepher ha-Razim* assumes a seven-tiered structure to the divine realms. The seven virgins, whose beauty is explicitly compared to that of the stars in heaven, may thus symbolize residents of the heavenly realms, whose virginity may be integrally associated with their angelic identities. Belief in the virginity of angels, understood as asexuality, is reflected in the Gospel of Matthew: "in the resurrection, they neither marry nor are given in marriage, but are like angels in heaven" (22:30).

The seven virgins are said to serve (*diakoneō*) Aseneth. This word particularly (though by no means exclusively) means to serve meals, and it is frequently used in reference to cultic activities in both pagan and Christian sources. Its usage here may simply point to the ordinary functions of servants, grounded in the reality that elite unmarried women in antiquity would certainly have had female companions. Several passages in *Aseneth* use this term for Aseneth's relationship with Joseph, and another possibility is that it alludes to the service of angels.

ASENETH'S GARMENTS (3.9–11)

Throughout the story, clothing is a crucial device by which the author expresses Aseneth's status. At the outset of the dramatic action, learning that her parents have returned from their ancestral estate, Aseneth adorns herself in clothing and jewelry that has multiple referents. She wears a linen robe the color of hyacinth, woven with gold, and trousers of gold cloth; over these she wears a gold girdle. Her bracelets and necklace are made of precious stones that bear engraved on them the images and names of the gods of Egypt. A tiara rests on her head; a diadem around her temples; a veil on her head completes the arrangement. After her initial encounter with Joseph, Aseneth strips off all this fine, idolatrous clothing and dons, instead, the black robe of mourning she had worn at the death of her younger brother. In 18.3, after her conversion and transformation, Aseneth again adorns herself in clothing and jewelry that are described in almost the same way as her initial bridal garments, except that, unsurprisingly, they contain no images or names of Egyptian gods. While the use of clothing to denote status and to symbolize transformation is more or less a universal cultural fact, the usages of clothing here have parallels in many ancient texts, Jewish and otherwise.

The garments Aseneth wears at the beginning and the end of the story accord well with traditions about Woman Wisdom. In Proverbs 31, the paean to the virtuous woman, the wise woman wears clothing of fine linen and purple (*byssos* and *porphyra*—the same terms that occur in Aseneth). In Sirach, Wisdom wears an ornament of gold, and her bonds are a purple (*hyakinthos*) cord. The wise man will wear her like a robe of glory and put her on like a crown of gladness (Sir 6:30–31).[13] The little-known *Biblical Antiquities* of Pseudo-Philo also associates splendid garments, hyacinth, and purple, with bridal attire (40:6).

Aseneth's clothing instantly brings to mind the dress of ancient royalty, as in the description of the Persian king Artaxerxes in the Greek version of the book of Esther: "He was seated on his royal throne, clothed in the full array of his majesty, all covered with gold and precious stones" (Add. Esth. 15:6). The statues of gods and goddesses in ancient temples, as well as their human priestly attendants were also similarly attired. According to Exod 28:5, the vestments of the Israelite priests were to be made of similar materials: fine linen (*byssos*), purple (*porphyra*), hyacinth, and gold. The high priest was to wear two onyx stones, each one engraved with the names of six of the sons of Israel (Exod 28:9–12). Spectacular clothing characterizes both angels and humans transformed into angels in a variety of ancient Jewish texts. That royalty, priests, and statues of the gods all wore extraordinary clothing is hardly coincidental and points to close associations between the three in ancient conceptualizations. Many ancient writers, including Jews and Christians, utilized clothing as a metaphor for the body encasing the soul.

ASENETH AS BRIDE OF GOD (4.2)

As the text divulges, Aseneth's garments encode all this imagery, including the bridal motif. "And Pentephres and his wife rejoiced in their daughter Aseneth with great gladness, for her parents beheld her adorned as a "bride of [G]od." The meaning of "bride of [G]od" (*nymphē theou*) is not clear and probably carries multiple meanings. Convinced that *Aseneth* draws heavily on Egyptian imagery, Philonenko considered this description an allusion to the possible marriage between Aseneth and the son of Pharaoh, since ancient Egyptians believed Pharaoh to be the divine incarnation, and the son of Pharaoh would presumably one day become that incarnation himself. But if so, the allusion is ironic, for Aseneth will become the bride not of an Egyptian god's son but of the true God's son, Joseph. However, the image of divine bride also reflects the numerous images of sacred marriage (*hieros gamos*) within the story, including the unions of Selene (Moon) with Helios (Sun), Wisdom, and the Wise Man, the lovers in Song of Songs, and so forth.

ASENETH'S DISDAIN OF MEN (2.1)

In 2.1, the author takes up the recurring theme that Aseneth was contemptuous and disdainful of all men, here a gender-specific term. The charge of misandry (hating men) reinforces Aseneth's claim to virginity. But this is not its sole function in the story. Interestingly, in the longer version, though not in the shorter, Aseneth ultimately confesses her hatred of men and their offers of marriage as one of her many sins. The redactor(s) of this version may simply be concerned to make Aseneth's confession comprehensive and consonant with earlier references to her sins. But the initial reference to her hatred of men may itself reflect earlier speculation about the exact nature of Aseneth's sins, in addition to the obvious one of idolatry. This may be one of the few times when the author imputes to Aseneth a characteristic derived more from the author's own perceptions of women than from traditional constellations.

ASENETH'S EXCHANGE WITH HER FATHER (4:5–16)

When Aseneth greets her parents adorned as a bride, it is not surprising that she immediately finds herself in a discussion with her father on the subject of marriage. Aseneth replies to her father's greetings with the same words with which Abraham, Moses, and Samuel answered the divine summons—"Here I am"—and obediently sits between her parents. Pentephres then proposes to marry Aseneth to Joseph, whom he describes as "a man who reveres God" (*theosebēs*) and who is temperate and a virgin like Aseneth herself. Though Aseneth has so far been the model of a dutiful daughter, at this suggestion she responds with horrified anger. Recounting a version of the story of Potiphar's wife, she accuses her father of wishing to enslave her to a foreigner and counters that, rather than marry Joseph, she will instead marry the firstborn son of Pharaoh. The narrator's voice informs us that Pentephres was ashamed to speak any further with his brazen daughter. A courtier interrupts the dramatic action to announce Joseph's arrival, and Aseneth flees back to her tower room to watch Joseph's entrance.

The role that gender plays here (and indeed throughout the text) is significant yet subtle, and it would be unwise to see this scene as a straightforward denigration of women. Instead, the scene offers the answers to a number of unverbalized difficulties that may well have concerned the author(s). It provides a partial answer to the question of why Pharaoh, rather than the respective fathers of the couple, arranged the marriage; it claims that Pentephres attempted to marry Aseneth to Joseph, but she (stubbornly and in ignorance) refused to agree. Later, the text will offer an explanation for why Jacob was not a party to the wedding arrangements. It also expands the portrait of the pre-transformation Aseneth as an exemplar of the Foreign/Strange woman and of the person devoid of wisdom: ignorant (of the truth about Joseph as demonstrated by the false rumors she accepts), foolish, arrogant, and lacking in filial piety.

Read as historical and social verisimilitude, this passage paints an intriguing portrait of ancient familial dynamics. Aseneth's mother remains totally silent throughout this exchange, playing no role in the discussion of her daughter's proposed marriage. The general tenor of ties between Aseneth and her parents is one of warmth and affection, but also of formality and hierarchy. Aseneth repeatedly addresses her father as "my lord and my father," and speaks of him only in the third person, while he addresses her in the more informal (and therefore hierarchically superior) first and second persons. But Aseneth's refusal to marry Joseph and her independent choice of the son of Pharaoh as a preferable husband are presented as filial insolence which shames her father. Such sentiment is characteristic of hierarchical social orders in which the inappropriate behavior of subordinates brings shame and dishonor on their social superiors.

From the standpoint of social realia, it may be interesting that Pentephres does not insist that Aseneth marry Joseph. Roman first marriages were normally arranged by the parents of the couple, and, although daughters' (and sons') consent was needed, the grounds on which a daughter could refuse were limited to claims that the proposed groom was of bad moral character.[14] This is precisely the objection that Aseneth raises here. Similarly, some rabbinic sources suggest that fathers could not marry off their daughters without their consent (*b. Qiddushin* 41a). But it is also the case that accounting for Pharaoh's role in the marriage requires the removal of both Pentephres and Jacob as parties to the betrothal. If that is the driving force behind the construction of the scene, then Pentephres cannot force Aseneth. And while Aseneth's explanation for her refusal may be consonant with marriage customs in the Roman period, her specific accusations against Joseph are clearly drawn from the story of Joseph and Potiphar's wife and serve the further function of demonstrating the degree and ironic nature of her pre-transformation ignorance.

ASENETH FIRST SEES JOSEPH (5.4–6.8)

Joseph's initial appearance in the text is extremely significant for the magical and mystical dimensions of the stories. He is the virtual incarnation of the Sun. Like that body rising, he appears from the east, and the author's portrait of him would have been instantly recognizable as a description of Helios, the Greek deity of the sun. His chariot is gold; its horses are snow-white, with gold bridles. Joseph wears a gold crown with twelve stones—a number fraught with significance in Jewish and pagan symbolic systems (twelve signs of the zodiac—which themselves appear in much ancient Jewish synagogue art; the twelve tribes of Israel, and so forth). While basic elements of this description of Joseph (the chariot of the second in command, the garments of fine linen) clearly come from Gen 41:41-43, they are heavily interlaced with the attributes of Helios. In addition, the author may also draw on an assemblage of images such as those in Psalm 19 (LXX 18), especially vv. 4b–5: "In the heavens he has set a tent for the sun, which comes out like a bridegroom from his wedding canopy, and like a strong man runs its course with joy." The description of Joseph's garments closely (and intentionally) resembles that of Aseneth's with their connections to royalty and perhaps also priesthood.

Aseneth's apperception of Joseph functions as a pivotal point within the story. The narrator tells us that at the sight of him "her soul was pierced excruciatingly, and her insides dissolved and her knees became paralyzed, and her whole body trembled and she was overwhelmed with fright" (6.1). Aseneth's response is not unlike that of other Egyptian women when confronted with Joseph's beauty (namely, all-consuming lust). But this entire description can be read as an expansion of Cant 5:6, "My soul failed me when he spoke." Indeed, the entire scene in Song of Songs (Canticles) may undergird this portion of Aseneth. There the male lover comes to his beloved's garden, where he eats his honeycomb with honey and drinks wine with milk. He knocks at the woman's door but she is sleeping; and when she goes to answer, he has gone, leaving her faint with love. In those ancient circles where this text was read as an allegory of God and the soul, and sleep was viewed as a metaphor for ignorance and the absence of wisdom, the passage from Song of Songs could easily have been profitably exploited.[15]

In any case, at Joseph's appearance, Aseneth knows instantly what she did not know before: hardly the son of a Canaanite shepherd, to be despised and disparaged, Joseph is rather the very son of God, who bears within him the divine light. Rueing the words she hurled at her father moments earlier, Aseneth prays now for nothing more than to be Joseph's slave forever. Joseph's actual entrance into the drama is thus the catalyst for Aseneth's self-knowledge and ultimate transformation and redemption. At once, Aseneth knows herself to have been ignorant and foolish; though by the very utterance of those words, Aseneth demonstrates her newly acquired knowledge and perception. From a feminist vantage point, this is nothing less than a double-edged sword: a female protagonist gains the knowledge and insight that will lead to personal transformation,[16] but the catalyst of that transformation is a male authority figure, and her initial response to her newly acquired wisdom is to pray to be subservient to that male figure for the rest of eternity. In a hierarchical system in which Joseph stands at the top, Aseneth hopes only to assume a position at the very bottom, the precise antithesis of the social position she held only instants earlier, as the virgin daughter of an aristocratic family who aspired to marry the (false) son of (the false) God. Aseneth's wisdom shows her precisely what wisdom usually shows ancient questors: that the world is not at all what it appears to be and is, in fact, exactly the opposite.

Appealing though this reading may be, it has some difficulties. In numerous texts that depict the encounter between humans and angelic or other divine beings, assuming the status of slave or servant to the divine being is presented as a highly appropriate response. Ironically, in virtually all of these examples, the human assuming the status of slave or servant is male (perhaps because Aseneth is one of the few nonbiblical depictions of an encounter between a woman and an angel). Certainly, for later Christian readers of the story, the pious person who seeks to be a slave to God was in the company of such exemplaries as the apostle Paul himself.

THE FIRST ENCOUNTER BETWEEN JOSEPH AND ASENETH (7.2–9.1)

While Aseneth knows the true identity of Joseph the moment she sees him, Joseph ironically makes the same erroneous assumptions about Aseneth that she previously made about him. Fearing that Aseneth will attempt to seduce him, Joseph asks Pentephres to send her away. The narrator informs us that many Egyptian women, including all the wives and daughters of Egyptian officials, were overcome by sexual desire for Joseph, so great was his beauty. Joseph, however, is able to resist the advances of these women by remembering the commandments of his father, Jacob, to stay away from foreign women. Though absent from the biblical text, Jacob's "commandments" are found in some rabbinic sources and in *Jub.* 40:5–8, where the commandment is to stay away from the wives of other men.[17]

Pentephres quickly enlightens Joseph about Aseneth's identity, insisting that she is not a foreigner but Pentephres' own daughter, and a virgin like Joseph; she detests all men, and is Joseph's sister. Joseph seems delighted to hear all this, and agrees to greet Aseneth, declaring his brotherly love for her. The exchange between Joseph and Pentephres over whether Aseneth is a foreign/ strange woman evokes again the imagery of Proverbs.

Viewed midrashically, the designation of Aseneth as Joseph's sister points again to the underlying framework of the traditions in Proverbs and Song of Songs.

> My son, keep my words and store up my commandments with you;
> Keep my commandments and live . . .
> Say to Wisdom, you are my sister
> and call insight your intimate friend,
> that they may keep you from the strange woman
> from the adulteress with her smooth words. (Prov 7:4–5)[18]

Even more relevant is the Septuagint, which seems to speak of only one woman, the "strange and wicked one." This passage accords with several aspects of *Aseneth* here: it equates Wisdom with the wise son's sister, and it connects the father's teachings with the protection of his son (the wise man) from strange women (Aseneth and Potiphar's wife). Further, the future bride is called "my sister, my bride" several times in the Song of Songs (4:9, 10, 12; 5:1).

When her mother then brings Aseneth down to meet Joseph, a slight but significant change appears in the text. Introducing Aseneth to Joseph, Pentephres remarks on the affinity between the two: "Greet your brother, for he is a virgin as you are today, and detests all foreign [strange] women as you detest all foreign men." This is the first time we read that Aseneth detests not simply men, but foreign men, either specifically, or particularly. At least in the shorter version, which does not subsequently catalogue misandry as one of Aseneth's sins, this may mitigate her hatred of men, turning it from a charge of misandry to a virtue and an analogy to the wise son's rejection of strange women.

In the aftermath of her revelation at the sight of Joseph, Aseneth has reverted to the obedient and submissive daughter who now does willingly whatever her father commands, consonant with the idea of filial piety as an aspect of wisdom. When Pentephres instructs Aseneth to come forward and kiss her brother, it is now Joseph who balks. Putting his right hand on Aseneth's chest, he utters a long speech, asserting that "a man who reveres God" (*theosebēs anēr*), blesses God with his mouth, eats blessed bread, drinks a blessed cup and is anointed with blessed oil, cannot possibly kiss a foreign woman, who blesses idols, eats from idolatrous altars, drinks idolatrous libations and is anointed with perditious ointments. Pentephres' assertions aside, Aseneth is still (or once again?) a foreign woman, and Joseph will not have any bodily contact with her.

Into this narrative, the longer version inserts additional problematic language. The shorter text merely indicates that when Joseph goes to stop Aseneth, he puts his hand on her chest. The longer text reads instead: "he stretched out his right hand and put it on her chest, between her two breasts, and her breasts were already standing up like ripe apples." The effect of this reading is to sexualize the scene and depict Aseneth as another of the Egyptian women sexually aroused by Joseph. Though this may initially seem gratuitous and inexplicable, it is, in fact, consistent with the pattern of differences between the two versions, particularly in the tendency of the longer text to make biblical allusions more explicit. Song of Songs exalts the beauty of the woman's breasts several times (4:5; 7:3; see also breast imagery in 8:1, 8–10; and Prov 5:12–20: "rejoice in the wife of your youth . . . may her breasts satisfy you at all times"), most suggestively in the following verse:

> Oh, may your breasts be like clusters of the vine,
> and the scent of your breath like apples. (Cant 7:8)

At Joseph's rejection, Aseneth breaks into tears, wailing aloud, and gazing intently at Joseph. This last detail may have some significance for gender constructions in antiquity. Many ancient authors claim that the gaze of a woman was sexual and highly dangerous to men; they insisted that proper women should never look directly at a man. Typical is Sir 26:9: "The licentiousness of a woman is made known by her raised gaze, and by her eyelids."[19] Aseneth's action here may thus signify her subversion of ancient gendered norms, but it may also be intended to intensify the portrait of her as a woman overcome with sexual desire—though less so in the shorter text, where such a portrait is as false an image of Aseneth as her initial slanders are of Joseph. In any case, Joseph takes pity on Aseneth, showing those (divine?) qualities of gentleness and mercy, and he prays to God for Aseneth's transformation.

JOSEPH'S BLESSING AND ASENETH'S CHOSENNESS (8.10)

The concluding lines of this section take quite different forms in the longer and shorter versions. In the shorter text, Joseph concludes: "And may she drink the cup of your blessing, she whom you chose before she was conceived, and may she enter into your rest, which you have prepared for your chosen ones." The longer reads: "And may she drink the cup of your blessing, and number her among your people, that you have chosen before all (things) came into being," and then reverts to the shorter text.

The notion that Aseneth was chosen by God before her birth raises some difficult problems. From a midrashic perspective, it is consonant with the identification of Aseneth with Wisdom, since several biblical passages are explicit that Wisdom was created by God before the rest of creation (Prov 8:22; Ps 139:16 [LXX 138]). Numerous male biblical figures (Jeremiah, Samuel, Isaac, Samson) are also chosen by God before their birth, and Aseneth's general association with such figures may have already been signaled in the words with which Aseneth responded to her father's greeting, as I noted above. In addition, though, this passage may reflect ancient beliefs, attested in such writers as the third-century Christian Neoplatonist Origen, about the existence of souls prior to their incarnation in bodies. The revisions of the longer text suggest considerable discomfort with the association of Aseneth with preexistent Wisdom and with exalted male figures. The longer version retains the general notion of divine choice prior to creation, but claims that it was not Aseneth but the people of Israel whom God had chosen.

ASENETH'S TRANSFORMATION (10.2–17.6)

Though magical and mystical elements may be detected in virtually all of Aseneth, they become paramount in the structural center of the text, which recounts Aseneth's transformation. Because virtually all scholars have attempted to interpret Aseneth's experiences within frameworks of religious conversion, and because virtually all scholars have dated Aseneth no later than the early second century C.E., they have failed to notice the extraordinary consonance between Aseneth's actions and experiences and encounters with angels represented in a plethora of ancient sources. These sources, which range from magical formulas for the adjuration of angels preserved on papyri to lengthy literary depictions of encounters between angels and humans, constitute evidence for a basic pattern of such encounters, which illuminates many elements of the Aseneth stories.

Such encounters may be initiated by either the divine party or the human: they may involve ascent of the human into the heavenly realms, or descent of the angelic being to earth. Their end result may be as mundane as securing success for the human being in business or love, or as profound as enabling the human being to see the throne of God and participate in the heavenly liturgies which the angels offered to God. While many of these sources are Jewish and/or Christian, many are neither and demonstrate that beliefs about such encounters permeated the entire Greco-Roman world.

The extant sources reveal a basic pattern to these encounters, which included necessary preparation by the human being, specific acts to draw down the heavenly being, or enable the human to ascend to the heavens, appropriate human responses to the divine being(s) and vice versa, the conferral of benefits on the human being, and the ultimate return of the parties to their proper spheres/loci. In intriguing ways which I can only note here, such encounters exhibit the phases of ritual elucidated and analyzed by Victor Turner—namely, separation, liminality, transformation, and reintegration.[20]

Typically, the phase of separation requires the individual to abstain from ordinary human actions and intercourse, including food, drink, sex, and sleep. Often the individual is required to remove all signs of cultural identity, such as clothing and other adornment, consonant with Turner's liminal phase. Symbolically and socially, the individual may be characterized as dead. In some sources, the changes wrought appear to have the intention of transforming the human body into a heavenly body, which is then able to interact with other angelic beings.

Drawing down the divine or ascending to heaven is accomplished in a variety of ways: by performing certain magical acts, including the utterance of powerful commands, or by prayer. Once the human and the angelic or divine beings are together, it is common for the human to experience fear and to lie prostrate: the angelic being typically responds by admonishing the human not to be afraid, and by having the human stand up. At this point, the human being sometimes receives new clothing, and a new name, reflective of the transformation. In the ensuing encounter, the divine being confers some benefit on the human, whether a revelation of the future, or a vision of the highest deity, or even temporary transformation into the divine company. Frequently, the human reciprocates to some extent by offering the divine being a sacrifice, whether in the form of a meal or other offering. At the conclusion of the encounter, the divine being ascends back to the heavens, or the human being descends back to earth and is reintegrated into ordinary human social relations.

Within Jewish sources, the basic outlines of such encounters are already visible in numerous biblical passages, notably in Judges 13, which presents a series of encounters between an angel and the future parents of Samson, a man named Manoah and his unnamed wife. This particular narrative undoubtedly undergirds the story of Aseneth, but like many other biblical elements woven into these texts, it can only partially account for the rich detailing of the stories. To fully comprehend the magnitude of Aseneth's usage of magical and mystical paradigms, it is necessary to compare the Greek texts with such sources as the formulas for the adjuration of Helios in *Sepher ha-Razim,* or in the Greek magical papyri as well as the literary depictions of such experiences in texts ranging from Apuleius's *Metamorphoses* 11 to 2 and 3 *Enoch.* Tantalizingly, many of the sources that most closely cohere with Aseneth are likely to date from the third and fourth centuries C.E.

In its duration and in the specificity of her actions, Aseneth's seven-day penance, prior to the appearance of the angel, is typical of the preparations portrayed in numerous sources. The prescriptions for adjuring Helios in *Sepher ha-Razim,* for example, call for the adept to abstain for seven days from all food, drink, and unclean things. A generic spell from the magical papyri prescribes seven days of abstinence from meat and uncooked food and wine, and it requires the petitioner to go alone to the eastern portion of the house, village, or city, and throw out the leftovers (*PGM* 4.52–60), which is essentially what Aseneth does with her food, and which has no parallel in the biblical passages on which the story also draws. The appearance of the angel in the east on the heels of the morning star, Aseneth's prostration, the angel's initial responses, her change of name and clothing, the angel's revelation of her future, Aseneth's offering to the angel, and the form of his ascension all accord with the ancient magical and mystical traditions. Taken together, they strongly suggest that Aseneth has here compelled Helios to appear in her room, to give her an accurate accounting of her future and to transform her, at least temporarily, into an angelic being, a foretaste of the transformation she will most likely undergo permanently at death.

ASENETH'S CONFESSION (12.1–13.12)

On the eighth day of her repentance, unable to move her limbs, Aseneth offers up an eloquent confession to God. The shorter and longer texts have some particularly interesting differences here. The longer contains two lengthy monologues that are absent from the shorter. The narrative introduction claims that Aseneth was so completely devastated by her seven days of abasement that she is unable to speak, and so utters this first confession in her heart only. At the conclusion of this internal speech, Aseneth regains enough strength to sit up on her knees, but she is still terrified to name the name of God aloud and so silently recites a second speech, expressing her fears about opening her mouth to God and speaking the divine name aloud.

From a feminist perspective, it is quite tempting to see the longer narrative as reflective of ancient ideas about gender and speech. Many ancient sources evince a widely held belief that in women, silence was ideal. "A silent wife is a gift from the Lord" (Sir 26:14). Even more interestingly, many ancient writers also connect women's speech and women's sexuality, drawing a clear analogy between the mouth and the vagina. The chaste woman had a closed mouth and a closed vagina (except, of course, to her licit husband): the unchaste woman opened her mouth to speech and her vagina to illicit intercourse. So closely connected were these mouths seen to be that some writers offer up the public speech of a woman as de facto evidence of her unchastity.[21] Interestingly, the traditions in Proverbs make a somewhat more subtle distinction, by associating Woman Wisdom with speech that leads to righteousness and the Foreign/Strange woman with speech that leads to sexual immorality (on the speech of the Wise Woman, see, e.g., Prov 8:1–8; 31:26; for the Strange woman and the adulterous woman, see 2:16; 5:3; 6:24; 7:4; 7:21).

We might then view the insertions of the longer text as the product of a redactor who is concerned with these issues and who may even intend to connect Aseneth's virginity with her silence here, blurring the fine distinction in Proverbs and stressing the blunter association of women's speech with women's unchastity. This Aseneth might be understood to utter her first two speeches silently to counter the possible implication that the seemingly chaste Aseneth was engaged in unchaste, inappropriate speech. Indeed, much of the second silent speech concerns itself precisely with endowing Aseneth with sufficient courage to open her mouth to God: a mouth that was previously defiled by sacrifices to idols. While Aseneth has already spoken in this story, her prior speech has always either been in private to herself (3.8) or in response to speech initiated by her hierarchical superior (her father or Joseph). All of the silent soliloquies could be generated from the text of the spoken prayer, which contains the seemingly anomalous claim in 12.6 that "I am not worthy to open my mouth before you." Chapter 11 in the longer text could easily have been composed as an answer to the question, How could Aseneth have spoken aloud to God if she was indeed unworthy? The answer is that first she prayed silently, not only confessing her sins but also praying to God for the courage to speak aloud.

Such otherwise intriguing analysis is somewhat undercut by evidence for the use of silent prayer in antiquity, together with the role silence plays in the magical adjuration of angelic and other divine beings.[22] PGM 77:1–5, for instance, calls for silent recitation of the requisite incantation. After his vision of the chariot, the adept Ishmael does not have enough strength to sing a hymn (*3 Enoch* 9:1–10). As one ritually and symbolically dead, Aseneth may have the incapacity for articulate speech, which the ancients often ascribed to the dead. Further, the motif of the repentant sinner or seeker of God who has difficulty speaking occurs in numerous biblical passages. A passage such as Ps 30:11–12 (LXX 29) might well have provided the skeletal framework for this section: "You have turned my mourning into dancing; you have taken off my sackcloth and clothed me with joy, so that my soul[23] may praise you and not be silent."

In chapter 12, which contains material common to both reconstructions, Aseneth catalogues her sins before God: lawlessness, impiety, profane speech. In 12.7, she prays to be delivered from her unspecified persecutors, drawing a parallel between a child who seeks refuge with its father and mother and her own flight to God, who here is thus imaged as both mother and father. Interestingly, the longer text omits the reference to the mother and contains instead a lengthy image of a terrified child finding sanctuary in the arms of a comforting father. Again, we might be tempted to argue here for the hand of a redactor uncomfortable with maternal imagery for the divine, and this may be the case. But this change is also consistent with the pattern of differences between the two versions. Here, unable to find precedent for the imagery of both parents in biblical traditions, the redactor may be attempting to bring the text into closer conformity with existing traditions, particularly Ps 102:13 (NRSV 103), which combines the ideas of the compassionate father and those who fear God: "As a father has pity upon (his) sons; The Lord has pity upon those who fear him."

In chapter 13, Aseneth recapitulates in hymnic form the prior narrative of her abasement. Both texts have Aseneth reiterate that she sinned against God out of ignorance and spoke blasphemy against Joseph. But after the phrase "Pardon me, Lord, because I sinned against you in ignorance," the longer text contains the small but remarkable additional words "being a virgin," which appear to have the effect of connecting Aseneth's ignorance either with her virginity or with her gender. Since all versions of the text repeatedly emphasize Joseph's virginity as well, I am tempted to conclude that this phrase intends to connect Aseneth's ignorance with her gender.

Both versions end with Aseneth's fervent prayer for yet another reversal: that rather than be given to Joseph as an aristocratic wife, she become his servant and wash his feet, forever. The longer text has Aseneth pray also to make Joseph's bed. As I cautioned earlier, this may not be a gender-specific desire to serve Joseph, given the frequency with which ancient magical and mystical texts envision humans as the slaves or servants of divine beings and are themselves aimed at temporarily inverting the relationship, binding the divine being to do the will of the human! Nevertheless, it is interesting that bed-making was typically women's work.

ASENETH'S (UN)VEILING (15.1–2)

When the angelic being first appears in Aseneth's chamber, he instructs her to remove her black mourning garments, to wash in living water, and to change into brand-new clothing. These instructions are consonant both with biblical passages such as Ps 30:11–12 (LXX 29:12–13) and with magical and mystical traditions such as *2 Enoch* 21 (the receipt of new clothing), *Sepher ha-Razim* (washing in living water) and others. Aseneth follows all these instructions. But she adds one thing the figure has not mentioned: she covers her head with a fine veil. When she returns to the figure, he remarks on this immediately: "Lift the veil from your head, because today you are a holy virgin and your head is as a young man's." And Aseneth complies.

Readers well-schooled in early Christian debates about women's headcoverings, which we see first with Paul's tortured arguments in 1 Cor 11:3–16, will immediately wonder what's implied here. Certainly one possibility is that the author intends to signify Aseneth's androgyny, which characterizes the status of initiates in many religious traditions. If so, this verse presumes a social system in which Aseneth's veil symbolizes her gender (and probably also her place within ancient social hierarchy), whereas the absence of the veil symbolizes her distancing from her gender and her (temporary) removal from that same hierarchy. Here we may also have a more specific allusion to the state of the primordial being in Gen 1:26, as being initially without gender differentiation.

Alternatively, the author may have intended to signify Aseneth's transformation into masculinity. Numerous ancient texts utilize the metaphor of becoming male as a stage in the salvation of the soul (which is itself feminine in Greek). Although most of the examples are Christian, Philo utilized this metaphor extensively, including in his account of the women among the monastic Jewish Therapeutic society (*On the Contemplative Life*). It is also conceivable that the Greek translation of Proverbs 31 underlies this tradition. There, for the Hebrew *'ēšet hayil* (the strong/competent/capable woman), the Greek reads *gynē andreia,* which literally means something like the "woman of masculine capabilities." Given the centrality of wisdom traditions and the probable mystical undertones in *Aseneth,* it might be that the author here draws on an interpretation of Aseneth as androgynous Wisdom.

It is interesting that Paul's arguments about women's headcoverings are explicitly supported by his exegesis of the creation of human beings in Genesis 1–3. In 1 Cor 11:7, he argues: "For a man ought not to have his head veiled/covered, since he is the image and reflection/glory of God; but woman is the reflection/glory of man," interpreting Gen 1:26–27 with Gen 2:21–25. For Paul, creation establishes a divine hierarchy of God–man–woman, which he believed had to be preserved in human social relationships as well. If the author of this passage in *Aseneth* had similar concepts in mind, we might infer that since Aseneth's head is like that of a young man, she stands in a human–divine hierarchy as though she were male and as the direct image of the divine, as the primordial *anthropos* in Gen 1:26–27 was the direct image or glory of God and perhaps also androgynous. This, in turn, suggests that the removal of Aseneth's veil symbolizes her temporary angelic transformation, especially since the angelic figure in Aseneth is repeatedly called *anthropos.*

THE DIVINE FEMININE METANOIA (REPENTANCE) (15.7–8)

In keeping with magical traditions where angels are compelled to foretell the future truthfully to those who have successfully adjured them, Aseneth's angel proceeds to tell her that she will become the bride of Joseph and receive the new name of City of Refuge. As City of Refuge, she will shelter all those who devote themselves to God through repentance (Metanoia). The angelic figure then offers a stunning and problematic description of the figure of Metanoia that differs significantly in the two versions.

According to the shorter text, Metanoia is a daughter of the Most High who appeals hourly to God, her father, on behalf of all who repent. This divine daughter is the mother of virgins, who has prepared a heavenly bridal chamber for those who love her, whom she will serve for time eternal. She is herself a very beautiful virgin, pure and holy and gentle: God loves her, and the angels stand in awe of her. The longer text concurs that Metanoia is the daughter of the Most High, exceedingly beautiful, pure, gentle and virgin, who intercedes on behalf of the repentant. God loves her and the angels stand in awe of her. But this version contains subtle differences which materially alter our perception of Metanoia.

The longer text explicitly locates Metanoia in the heavens. Rather than the mother of virgins, Metanoia is here said to be the guardian, or overseer, of virgins. Rather than a bridal chamber, the Metanoia of the longer text prepares a place of rest for the repentant. This Metanoia is not only beautiful, pure, virgin, and meek, but she is always laughing. The narrator's voice claims that it is because of these qualities that God loves Metanoia and the angels stand in her awe. In the prior verses of the longer version, the heavenly figure claimed responsibility for actions the narrator of the shorter version attributes to God. At this point, the figure now separates himself from God, claiming that Metanoia is his sister, whom he loves exceedingly.

As far as I know, this description of Metanoia, and indeed the personification of Metanoia, is unique to the texts of *Aseneth*. In both versions, it has striking affinities with the personification of Wisdom in ancient sources. The addition of sister imagery in the longer text appears consistent with that version's general tendency to elaborate on biblical allusions. Metanoia's attributes are those of Woman Wisdom, particularly in her various virtues, her intercessory functions, and God's love for her and those who love her. "I [Wisdom] love those who love me, and those who seek me diligently find me" (Prov 8:17); "The Lord loves those who love her" (Sir 4:14). Metanoia's hourly petitioning of God on behalf of the repentant resembles Wisdom's daily petitioning of God: "I was daily his delight; rejoicing before him always" (Prov 8:30). This last association may account for the seemingly small detail of her perpetual laughter in some versions of the longer text. In addition, at least in some respects, Metanoia closely resembles the portraits of Sophia and other feminine manifestations of the divine in Gnostic texts.

From a feminist perspective, the longer version may present a diminished portrait of Metanoia more reliant on ancient constructions of the proper woman. This Metanoia is defined not only as the daughter of God but also as the sister of the angelic being, and she is loved by them not for her role in the salvation of the repentant but for her stereotypically female qualities of beauty, chastity, good disposition and meekness. To the extent, though, that this is the result of the addition of traditional details, it is difficult to say whether the redactor's intention was to domesticate the image of Metanoia, or whether the effect is accidental.

Also worth noting, though beyond the scope of this discussion, are the similarities between the figure of Metanoia in Aseneth and that of the angelic Metatron, who figures in many ancient Jewish mystical traditions, including *3 Enoch* and other Hekhalot materials. Finally, the longer text may here reveal traces of Christian redaction, which interweaves the visible figures of Aseneth and Metanoia, and the invisible figures of the virgin Mary and consecrated Christian virgins. At the very least, later Christian readers are likely to have read the text in precisely this way.

THE MYSTERY OF THE HONEYCOMB (16.1–9)

Consonant with both Judges 13 and magical paradigms, after the angel discloses Aseneth's future, she offers to prepare him a meal. The angelic figure tells Aseneth to bring him a honeycomb as well, which she is amazed to discover in her chamber. When Aseneth speculates that the honeycomb might have come from the angel's own mouth, the angel's response confirms Aseneth's wisdom. Putting his hand on her head, the angel says: "Blessed are you, Aseneth, that the secrets of God have been revealed to you; and blessed are those who devote themselves to God in repentance, for they shall eat from this comb. For this honey the bees of the paradise of delight have made, and the angels of God eat of it, and all who eat of it shall not die for eternity," (16.7). And he breaks off a portion of the honeycomb, eats a piece himself and places some in Aseneth's mouth. Aseneth's consumption of angelic food must signify her transformation (or perhaps initiation) into the angelic ranks, and guarantees her ultimate immortality.

In the longer text, this passage is lengthier and repetitive. Before the angel gives Aseneth the honeycomb, he instructs her, saying "eat," and she does. The addition of this small detail allows the story to be read now as an inversion of Genesis 2–3. There, of course, a woman eats the fruit of mortality and shares it with her mate. Here a masculine figure (a double of Aseneth's future husband, Joseph) eats some of the food of immortality and then gives some to the woman. Not only does the angel give the food of immortality to Aseneth, but he explicitly tells her to eat it. In Gen 3:12, Adam says only that Eve gave him the fruit and he ate it. But in Gen 3:17, God says to Adam, "you have listened to the voice of your wife," implying that Eve actually spoke to Adam. Thus, this small detail in the longer version (16.15) reverses the biblical account with careful precision.

This passage is enormously suggestive and problematic. It appears that the divine couple of Joseph and Aseneth restore the damage done by Adam and Eve, affording human beings a means to return to their original angelic state and, indeed, acquiring precisely the immortality which God feared Adam and Eve might aquire had they remained in Eden (Gen 3:22–24). What does this mean for Aseneth's identity as a woman? What, precisely, is Aseneth's role in the reversal of Eve's actions? Must Eve's deeds be compensated for by those of another woman (as some Christian writers intepreted the perfect obedience of Mary as the reversal of Eve's disobedience, e.g., Irenaeus, *Against Heresies* 3.22.4). And what precisely must that compensation be? Gen 3:1–5 and following may be read (and indeed has been so read) to imply that Eve learned of the forbidden fruit not from God directly but rather from Adam, and therefore it is Eve's disobedience *to her husband* that leads to their shared mortality. By contrast, it is Aseneth's obedience to the angelic double of her husband Joseph that obtains immortality for her. Further, although the masculine figure also eats, thus formally reversing the actions of Adam and Eve, he is already an angelic being, and it is hardly necessary for him to eat angelic food in order to receive immortality (though perhaps he must continue to eat it). It is significant that the actions of Aseneth and "Joseph" undo death but not sexuality, as opposed to other ancient interpretations (virtually all Christian) in which angelic identity and/or restoration to the primordial state undid both. But given the inescapable parameter of this story, that Aseneth must marry Joseph and give birth to both Manasseh and Ephraim, we could hardly expect otherwise!

It is fairly obvious that Aseneth here functions as a salvific figure, not only for her reversal of Eve's actions but also for the role she will play as City of Refuge. Female saviors are fairly rare in the religions of the Greco-Roman world, with the important exception of Isis, so that this portrait of Aseneth may be quite significant precisely for its presentation of a salvific female.[24] It is also obvious that Aseneth is depicted in all versions of this story as the recipient of divine mysteries and wisdom. But if my reading of this section of the longer text is correct, its subliminal message is that paradise is restored when women are properly obedient to their husbands. Then do they regain the immortality Eve traded for knowledge. This, too, is consonant with the identification of Aseneth with Wisdom, and of Wisdom with the Virtuous Woman, who is similarly obedient, industrious, and fruitful.

After they eat from the honeycomb, Aseneth observes the mysterious sequence of the bees. In the longer version, some of the bees wish to harm Aseneth. When instructed to go to their place, the benevolent bees do not die but fly directly to the courtyard, while the malevolent bees first die and then are resurrected.

Previous scholars have offered virtually nothing in the way of cohesive interpretation of these passages.[25] From a midrashic perspective, the scene with the bees is reminiscent of the imagery in Ps 118:10 (LXX 117), but I do not think this is its primary origin. Rather, I think the bees enact dramas of death and resurrection consistent with their representation of souls, probably souls awaiting incarnation and/or rebirth. Already in the first century C.E., Virgil associated bees with souls, but the more specific identification of bees as a symbol of (virtuous) souls awaiting incarnation occurs in the writings of the Neoplatonist Porphyry in the third century.[26]

At the conclusion of the drama of the bees, Aseneth asks the angel to bless her seven virgin companions, which he does. Whether this constitutes an act of female solidarity is impossible to determine. He then disappears, while Aseneth sees something like a fiery chariot ascending into the heavens in the east. This imagery recalls both mystical Jewish traditions of the heavenly chariot of fire and the identification of the angel with Helios.

In the wake of the angel's departure, Aseneth utters a brief prayer, asking forgiveness for having spoken evil in ignorance. In the longer text, she is far more self-depreciating. Calling herself audacious and lacking sense (an attribute of the strange woman in Prov 9:13), Aseneth berates herself for having said that an *anthropos* came into her room from out of heaven, and not having realized that it was [G]od. Her final comment here resembles that in the shorter text, but with two subtle differences. First, she says it "in herself," recalling her earlier silent prayers. Second, where the shorter text has her confess to having spoken evil in ignorance, consonant with the earlier scenes in which Aseneth slanders Joseph in ignorance, the longer text claims that she has spoken all her words in ignorance, a broader and more devastating claim.

Aseneth's Final Physical Transformation (18.3–7)

Dressed now in new robes, her head uncovered, Aseneth goes to her rooms and takes out a robe called "first," which has the appearance of lightning. It is clearly the clothing of gods and angels. The longer text adds explicitly that the robe is a wedding gown, a change that may be intended to minimize, though not eliminate, the angelic implications of her clothing. Aseneth puts on this extraordinary robe and a brilliant royal girdle with precious stones, as well as gold trousers, bracelets, a necklace, and a gold crown. Her completed costume is virtually identical to that which she wore when she first expected to meet Joseph, with the notable absence of the stones bearing the images and names of the gods of Egypt. And, as then, she covers her head with a veil.

What this signifies depends, obviously, on the interpretation of the earlier scene in which the angel instructed her to remove the veil. But it is not too difficult to read this detail as signifying Aseneth's return to the role of dutiful woman. The longer text eliminates some of the ambiguity of the veil (testifying to such ambiguity in the first place) by stating that Aseneth covered her head "like a bride."

Aseneth then instructs a young female attendant to bring "pure water from the spring," presumably the spring that runs through the courtyard in 2.20, which alludes to the rivers that watered the Garden of Eden. Looking into her reflection in this water, Aseneth is transfigured: her face is like the sun, and her eyes are like the rising morning star. This constellation of images appears in Cant 6:10: "who is this that looks forth like the dawn, fair as the moon, bright as the sun?"

Taken together with her garment of light, this scene affirms Aseneth's angelic transformation. It may also allude to the transformation of Moses in Exod 34:29–34, which says that when Moses came down from Sinai, he did not know that his face shone because he had been talking to God. Subsequently, he veils his face before the Israelites except when he goes to speak with God. This lends the veiling of Aseneth an alternative interpretation. In subsequent Jewish mystical traditions, Moses' face was believed to shine with the reflection of God's glory. Perhaps we should see Aseneth's veiling as analogous to that of Moses: just as Moses spoke with God face to face and beheld an aspect of God, so Aseneth has conversed with God, or at least with God's manifestation in the form of the angel. Therefore, like Moses, her face shines and requires a veil to protect others from its brilliance. If so, the reading of the longer text, which makes her veil unambiguously that of a bride, intentionally mutes the association of Aseneth with Moses.

JOSEPH AND ASENETH ARE "REUNITED" (19.1–20.4)

In the shorter text, a servant then announces Joseph's arrival. When Joseph sees Aseneth, he calls her to him, saying that he has received good news about her from heaven. They embrace each other for a long time, after which Aseneth invites Joseph into her house and, taking his hand, leads him inside. This scene thus revisits their initial meeting, but whereas then Joseph refused to touch Aseneth, now he embraces her gladly, signifying her transformation into an acceptable spouse for him.

The treatment of this scene in the longer text is consistent with the themes and concerns of prior passages. In the first, the location of the action plays a modest role. From her rooms, which we know are upstairs, Aseneth comes down to meet Joseph. Whether he is still outside the doors of the courtyard or inside them is not specified. After they greet and embrace, Aseneth takes Joseph into "her" house. The longer text displays much more interest in the question of location, repeatedly specifying who is where. In particular, that text clarifies that Joseph and Aseneth meet outside the house, but still inside the courtyard, whose gates have been closed behind Joseph, leaving foreigners outside. This detail suggests redaction sensitive to ancient social norms of gendered space. In many ancient sources, including Jewish writers such as Philo, there is an integral connection between physical space and women's sexuality. Domestic space was considered the proper physical sphere of women, especially virgins. Virginity and chastity were symbolized by enclosure, including walled cities and walled gardens. Respectably married women could venture into certain public spaces provided they were symbolically "housed," either by being accompanied by a retinue of domestic slaves, and/or by wearing clothing which signified their respectability (and concealed their bodies). The still virgin and unmarried Aseneth does not yet leave the confines of the courtyard but remains behind the closed gates.

ASENETH WASHES JOSEPH'S FEET (20.2–4)

In the shorter text, Joseph now sits down on Pentephres' throne, and Aseneth brings water to wash his feet. Joseph proposes that Aseneth let one of the seven virgins do this, since such activity is presumably the responsibility of servants. In ancient society broadly, footwashing was an act of hospitality and a mark of deference. Aseneth insists, claiming that her hands are his hands, and her feet his feet. In the longer text, Aseneth first grounds her response in her identity as Joseph's servant. Here, too, she identifies her feet and hands with Joseph's and claims that their souls are identical. The editor of the longer reconstruction, Burchard, views this as "a poetic expression of loving someone like yourself," while the editor of the shorter text reads it as an illustration of the mystical union of the two. But it may be that Burchard's view is influenced by his textual choices, for certainly Aseneth's claim that she is Joseph's servant emphasizes her subordination to him and mutes the view of the two as one being. It also seems plausible that the shorter text utilizes the primordial human being in Gen 1:26–27 as the dominant paradigm of marital love, whereas the longer text here subtly brings in the subordination of Eve to Adam in Genesis 2–3.

THE WEDDING OF JOSEPH AND ASENETH (20.6–21.7)

The denouement of the story occurs rapidly in both versions. Aseneth is reconciled with her parents, who, returning from their estate, greet the bridal couple with great joy and rejoicing. Pentephres offers to make the wedding, but Joseph demurs, insisting that Pharaoh must do so, because he is Joseph's father. Consistent with its treatment of similarly problematic passages, the longer text has Joseph say that Pharaoh is "like" his father. This undoubtedly reflects an interpretation of Gen 45:8, where Joseph receives the title of "Father to Pharaoh," apparently an ancient title of viziers. Its primary function remains the resolution of the biblical anomaly that has Pharaoh, and not the fathers of the couple, instigate the marriage. Both texts agree that Joseph then remained with Pentephres and did not have sex with Aseneth prior to the celebration of the nuptials, perhaps reflecting debate in some ancient quarters about the point at which a betrothed couple could engage in licit sexual relations. When the celebrations are over, the marriage is properly consummated, and Aseneth conceives and gives birth to Manasseh and Ephraim.

The Postscript (22–29)

Though the story seems as though it should end here, all the complete manuscripts contain a second part, as I noted above. Though it contains a few passages that are interesting from the vantage point of gender, there is simply insufficient space to address them here.

The Usages and Significance of Gender in Aseneth

Within the shorter and the longer versions, the portraits of both women and men are highly artificial. As we have seen, virtually everything about the characters, from their physical and moral attributes, to their actions and speeches, to their clothing and possessions, is constructed from ancient texts and traditions—primarily, though hardly exclusively, Greek Jewish scripture. On the whole, the texts utilize constructions of gender that were fairly conventional in Greco-Roman antiquity. A complex hierarchy, both on earth and in heaven, is the norm. Women are subordinate (and subservient) to men, as are slaves to their owners and subjects to their rulers, though class is clearly a factor: male slaves and servants are subordinate to free aristocratic women. In the cosmos, human beings are subordinate to angels, who are in turn subordinate before God.

Both versions of Aseneth utilize ancient stereotypical associations of gender. It is the female Aseneth who is foolish and ignorant: the male Joseph who is wise. It is the woman who is Other, the male who is Self; the woman who is human, the male who is divine. But none of this is absolute. By drawing particularly on the dichotomy of the Wise and Strange women in numerous wisdom traditions, the authors are able to portray the transformation of Aseneth from foolish and ignorant to wise and discerning, from Other to Self, from mortal human to angelic immortal, from Egyptian idolater to one who reveres the true God.

Does this subtlety intend at least a modest critique of ancient constructions of gender? This is not inconceivable, particularly if we contrast either version of *Aseneth* with more overtly misogynist writings such as The Wisdom of Jesus ben Sira (Sirach). We might argue that *Aseneth*'s relative lack of misogyny is nothing more than a by-product of the author's need to transform her into an acceptable wife for Joseph, and that in the desire to accomplish this, Aseneth's negative femaleness becomes subordinated to her positive *theosebeia*, her inclusion in the community of those who revere God. But such an interpretation becomes less persuasive when we recall that this story isn't the only one told in antiquity to account for the marriage of Aseneth to Joseph. Rabbinic legends (found, interestingly, in sources that are probably fourth century C.E. and later) offered significantly different explanations for the marriage, claiming that Aseneth was only the adopted daughter of Pentephres and was really the daughter of Joseph's niece, Dina, who had been raped by a Canaanite named Shechem according to Genesis 34.[27] It is tempting to propose that these different stories circulated in communities with somewhat different ideas about gender, and with somewhat differing social structures consonant with those ideas.

Additionally, Aseneth's adjuration of the angel and her receipt of heavenly revelation and blessings may also constitute a critique of ancient constructs of gender. But because more information about the true date, author, and social context of *Aseneth* is lacking, this remains hypothetical. It is quite interesting, though, that *Aseneth* is virtually the only such nonbiblical text to narrate such an encounter between a woman and an angel. (The only other example is a brief scene in the *Life of Adam and Eve,* where an angel shows Eve the reception Adam receives in heaven).

Apart from this, the texts don't manifest much tension around issues of gender, although the longer version does consistently demonstrate more discomfort about gender than the shorter version, particularly in places where the shorter version appears to make troubling claims about Aseneth, as in its statement that Aseneth was chosen by God before her birth. Many of the differences between the two versions are to be found at precisely such points, with the longer redaction consistently depicting Aseneth as just a little bit closer to ancient conventions about acceptable women.

Whether the texts say much about the real experiences of women and men is extremely difficult to determine. Even in its own time(s), *Aseneth* is a story about a past far distant from its authors and audiences. To the degree that the story depends heavily on biblical and related traditions, I think it says little about the lives and experiences of "real" persons, though in a general sense, its portrait of ancient social life is consonant with what we know from numerous other sources. But to the degree that it draws on magical and mystical traditions of Greco-Roman antiquity, it may allude more specifically to the worldviews and maybe even some of the actual practices of "real" people.

NOTES

1. Some rabbinic traditions account for the marriage by claiming that Aseneth was the adopted daughter of Pentephres and was biologically the child of Joseph's niece Dinah and a Canaanite named Shechem, who had raped her (according to Genesis 34), on which see the

detailed study by V. Aptowitzer, "Asenath, the Wife of Joseph: A Haggadic Literary-Historical Study," *Hebrew Union College Annual* 1 (1924): 239–306. Aptowitzer's assemblage of rabbinic references is extraordinarily useful, but his conclusions about the relationship between those traditions and our Greek stories are highly improbable.

2. For texts and translations, as well as introductions, see the "Recommended Readings."

3. English translation is available as *The Syriac Chronicle known as that of Zachariah of Mitylene,* trans. F. J. Hamilton and E. W. Brooks (London: Methuen, 1899; reprint, New York: AMS Press, 1979). Unfortunately, it omits a translation of *Aseneth.* See also Marc Philonenko, *Joseph et Aséneth: Introduction, Texte Critique, Traduction et Notes* (Leiden: E. J. Brill, 1968), 12–13.

4. See C. Burchard, "Joseph and Aseneth: A New Translation and Introduction," in *Old Testament Pseudepigrapha,* ed. James Charlesworth (Garden City, NY: Doubleday, 1985), 2:187.

5. The ordinary meaning of *theosebēs* is simply one who fears or reveres God, and it occurs frequently in the Greek translation of the Hebrew Scriptures with that connotation. However, references in some Greco-Roman authors, as well as donative and burial inscriptions suggest that the term at least sometimes signified a pagan who revered the Jewish God but had not formally become a Jew. This is actually a terribly thorny issue, and the recent scholarly literature on the subject is too extensive to identify here.

6. I use the term "magical" here mostly for the sake of convenience and because many of the relevant sources are collected under that rubric. It is, however, a highly problematic term, as pointed out by John Gager, *Curse Tablets and Binding Spells* (New York and Oxford: Oxford University Press, 1993).

7. For a superb presentation of the inner logic of midrash, which provided the impetus for my work here, see James L. Kugel, *In Potiphar's House: The Interpretive Life of Biblical Texts* (San Francisco: HarperCollins, 1990).

8. Howard Eilberg-Schwartz, *The Savage in Judaism: An Anthropology of Israelite Religion and Ancient Judaism* (Bloomington and Indianapolis: Indiana University Press, 1990), 143–44.

9. The commentary follows the shorter text and numbering of Philonenko, utilizing my own translation in *Maenads, Martyrs, Matrons, Monastics: A Sourcebook on Women's Religions in the Greco-Roman World,* ed. Ross S. Kraemer (Philadelphia: Fortress, 1988). As appropriate, I treat the different readings in the longer version as reconstructed by Burchard, where I generally utilize his own English translation, with a few exceptions.

10. See, e.g., Chariton, *Chaereas and Callirhoe,* 1.1.1 (conveniently available in B. H. Reardon, *Collected Ancient Greek Novels* [Berkeley: University of California Press, 1989]).

11. This translation is my literal one, from the Greek. The alternate translation in the NRSV reads: "All glorious is the princess [the daughter of the king] within, gold embroidery is her clothing; in many-colored robes she is led to the king; behind her the virgins, her companions, follow."

12. Philo, *On Creation* 30; *Allegorical Interpretation* 1.4ff.

13. This is the LXX translation; the Hebrew is slightly different.

14. For Roman references, see Beryl Rawson, "The Roman Family," in *The Family in Ancient Rome: New Perspectives,* ed. Beryl Rawson (Ithaca, NY: Cornell University Press, 1986), 21.

15. Rabbinic sources claim that the Song of Songs was interpreted by Rabbi Akiba in the early second century C.E., as a dialogue between God and Israel. Christian allegorical interpretation of the Song of Songs occurs as early as the late second century C.E. (Tertullian and Hippolytus) and becomes widespread after the writings of Origen in the third century. I am

grateful to Jay Treat, who is completing a doctoral dissertation on allegorical interpretation of the Song of Songs at the University of Pennsylvania, for his assistance here.

16. On Aseneth as a tale of quest and self-transformation, see Susan Doty, "From Ivory Tower to City of Refuge: The Role and Function of the Protagonist in 'Joseph and Aseneth' and Related Narratives" (Ph.D. dissertation, The Iliff School of Theology and the University of Denver, 1989).

17. This material is treated extensively in Kugel, *In Potiphar's House*, especially pp. 106–12.

18. Trans. NRSV from the Hebrew, adapted slightly.

19. My translation. On ancient understandings of the gaze, see Blake Leyerle, "John Chrysostom On the Gaze," *Journal of Early Christian Studies* 1 (1993): 2:159–74.

20. Victor Turner, *The Ritual Process: Structure and Anti-Structure* (New York: Cornell University Press, 1969; reprinted 1977).

21. See especially Kathleen E. Corley, *Private Women, Public Meals: Social Conflict in the Synoptic Tradition* (Peabody, MA: Hendrickson, 1993), 24–79, esp. 42–44.

22. See Pieter W. van der Horst, "Silent Prayer in Antiquity," *Numen* 41 (1994): 1–25.

23. NRSV; The Hebrew and Greek more literally read "glory."

24. Gail Paterson Corrington, *Her Image of Salvation: Female Saviors and Formative Christianity* (Louisville: Westminster, 1992).

25. A new doctoral dissertation by Gideon Bohak at Princeton University offers a highly imaginative interpretation of the bees that is quite different from, if not antithetical to, the one I propose here.

26. Virgil, *Aeneid* 6.703–18; see also *Georgics* 4; Porphyry, *On The Cave of the Nymphs* 8.

27. See Aptowitzer, "Asenath."

RECOMMENDED READINGS

Batiffol, P. "Le Livre de la Prière d'Aséneth." *Studia Patristica* I-II (1889-90):1–115.

Betz, Hans Dieter, ed. *The Greek Magical Papyri in Translation, including the Demotic Spells. Volume One: Texts.* Chicago: University of Chicago Press, 1986.

Burchard, C. "Joseph and Aseneth: A New Translation and Introduction." In *The Old Testament Pseudepigrapha,* edited by J.H. Charlesworth, 2:177–247. Garden City, NY: Doubleday, 1985.

Cook, D. "Joseph and Aseneth." In H. F. D. Sparks, ed., *The Apocryphal Old Testament,* 465–503. Oxford: The Clarendon Press, 1984.

Denis, A.-M. *Concordance grecque des pseudépigraphes d'Ancien testament.* Louvain-la-Neuve: Université Catholique de Louvain, 1987.

Kraemer, R. S. "The Confession and Marriage of Aseneth." In *Maenads, Martyrs, Matrons, Monastics: A Sourcebook on Women's Religions in the Greco-Roman World,* 263–79. Philadelphia: Fortress, 1988.

Morgan, Michael, trans. *Sepher Ha-Razim: The Book of the Mysteries.* Texts and Translations 25, Pseudepigrapha Series 11. Chico, CA: Scholars Press, 1983.

Philonenko, M. *Joseph et Aséneth: Introduction, Texte Critique, Traduction et Notes.* Leiden: E. J. Brill, 1968.

Contributors

Mary Ann Beavis earned her Ph.D. in New Testament Studies at Cambridge University. She is the author of *Mark's Audience,* and a number of articles in biblical and related studies. She is currently Acting Director of the Institute of Urban Studies, The University of Winnipeg.

Sheila Briggs is Associate Professor in the School of Religion at the University of Southern California. Her fields are theology and the history of theology, investigated from a feminist perspective.

Elizabeth A. Castelli is Assistant Professor of Religious Studies at Occidental College in Los Angeles. She is the author of *Imitating Paul: A Discourse of Power,* and the co-author and co-editor of the Bible and Culture Collective's *The Postmodern Bible.*

Kathleen E. Corley is Assistant Professor of New Testament and Christianity in the Department of Religious Studies and Anthropology at the University of Wisconsin-Oshkosh. She earned her Ph.D. in New Testament at The Claremont Graduate School in Claremont, California. Dr. Corley is an Episcopalian and in the past has served as a Lay Eucharist Minister and Layreader in local parishes.

Mary Rose D'Angelo is Associate Professor of Theology and Acting Director of the Gender Studies Program at the University of Notre Dame. She is a member of the editorial board of the *Journal of Biblical Literature.* Her recent articles include feminist and historical critiques of the arguments about "*abba*" and "father" as divine titles, and studies of women's partnerships in antiquity, women in Luke-Acts, women and resistance in the context of Jesus, and the divorce sayings as evidence of gender politics in early Christian prophecy.

Joanna Dewey is Associate Professor of New Testament Studies at the Episcopal Divinity School, Cambridge, Massachusetts. She is the author of *Markan Public Debate,* and numerous articles on Mark, the oral media world of the Bible, and feminist approaches to the Bible.

Linda Bennett Elder is Assistant Professor of Religion at Valdosta State University. She has presented a number of papers on Jewish women in the late Second Temple period. Her article "The Woman Question and Female Ascetics at Qumran" is scheduled for publication in *Biblical Archaeologist.*

Lone Fatum was ordained to the ministry of the Church of Denmark (Lutheran) in 1975. Since 1981 she has served as Assistant Professor of New Testament at the Institute of Biblical Exegesis, University of Copenhagen. She has published several works on exegesis and gender hermeneutics.

Ingvild Sælid Gilhus is Professor in the History of Religions at the University of Bergen, Norway.

Deirdre Good is Professor of New Testament at The General Theological Seminary in New York City. She is currently working on a hypertext lexicon of the Greek New Testament and an annotated bibliography of Matthew's Gospel.

Susan Ashbrook Harvey is Associate Professor of Religious Studies at Brown University in Providence, Rhode Island. She is a specialist in early Syriac Christianity.

Margaret D. Hutaff teaches courses in biblical studies in the Graduate Programs in Ministry at Emmanuel College, Boston, Massachusetts.

Karen L. King is Associate Professor of Religious Studies at Occidental College in Los Angeles. Her areas of specialization include women's studies, early Christianity, and Gnosticism. Her publications include *Images of the Feminine in Gnosticism, The Unknowable God, A Reader's Guide to the Nag Hammadi Library in English,* and *Women and Goddess Traditions.* At present she is working on a commentary on the *Gospel of Mary.*

Cynthia Briggs Kittredge is a doctoral student at Harvard Divinity School. Her dissertation is on obedience in the Pauline tradition.

Ross S. Kraemer is the author of *Her Share of the Blessings: Women's Religions Among Pagans, Jews and Christians in the Greco-Roman World,* and the editor of *Maenads, Martyrs, Matrons and Monastics: A Sourcebook on Women's Religions in the Greco-Roman World.* She is Adjunct Associate Professor of Religious Studies at the University of Pennsylvania and is associated with the Center for Judaic Studies at Penn, where she is currently writing a book-length study of *Aseneth,* and a book on Jewish women in the Greco-Roman diaspora.

Rebecca Lesses is a doctoral student in religion at Harvard University. She is finishing her dissertation on early Jewish mysticism and magic and plans to pursue future research on women in early Jewish mysticism. She also writes science fiction.

Amy-Jill Levine is Professor of New Testament at Vanderbilt University Divinity School. Her Ph.D. in religion is from Duke University.

Linda M. Maloney received a Ph.D. in American Studies from Saint Louis University (1968) and a Th.D. in New Testament from Eberhard-Karls-Universität Tübingen (1990). She is Associate Professor of New Testament at the Franciscan School of Theology, Graduate Theological Union, Berkeley, California.

Clarice J. Martin is Associate Professor of New Testament at Colgate-Rochester Divinity School-Bexley Hall-Crozer Theological Seminary. Her teaching and research interests include Luke-Acts, the Synoptic Gospels, the social origins of earliest Christianity and biblical hermeneutics (including womanist hermeneutics). She has published numerous articles on New Testament history, exegesis and literature, including "The *Haustafeln* (Household Codes) in African American Biblical Interpretation: 'Free Slaves' and 'Subordinate Women,'" in *Stony the Road We Trod: African American Biblical Interpretation,* ed. Cain Hope Felder, and "The Rhetorical Function of Commercial Language in Paul's Letter to Philemon (v. 18)," in *Persuasive Artistry: Studies in New Testament Rhetoric in Honor of George A. Kennedy,* ed. Duane F. Watson.

Shelly Matthews is an ordained minister in the United Methodist Church and a doctoral student at the Harvard Divinity School. Her dissertation is on mission and conversion and women in antiquity.

Sheila E. McGinn received her Ph.D. in Early Christianity from Northwestern University/Garrett-Evangelical Theological Seminary. She is Assistant Professor of Religious Studies at John Carroll University.

Anne McGuire is Associate Professor of Religion at Haverford College, where she teaches courses in the history and literature of early Christianity and Gnosticism. She received her Ph.D. in Religious Studies from Yale University (1983) and is presently at work on a book on gender imagery in selected Nag Hammadi texts.

Carolyn Osiek is Professor of New Testament at Catholic Theological Union, Chicago, Illinois. She is New Testament book review editor of *Catholic Biblical Quarterly,* advisory board member of the *Journal of Early Christian Studies,* and one of the editors of *Silent Voices, Sacred Lives: Women's Readings for the Liturgical Year.*

Pheme Perkins is Professor of Theology (New Testament) at Boston College. She is the author of eighteen books as well as some sixty articles in scholarly and popular journals. She has served on administrative committees of learned societies as well as on the editorial boards of several journals. Her most recent books are *Peter: Apostle for the Whole Church,* and *Gnosticism and the New Testament.*

Tina Pippin is Assistant Professor of Bible and Religion at Agnes Scott College. She is the author of *Death and Desire: The Rhetoric of Gender in the Apocalypse of John.*

Adele Reinhartz is Associate Professor in the area of Judaism and Christianity in the Greco-Roman World, in the Department of Religious Studies at McMaster University, Hamilton, Ontario. She has published extensively on the Gospel of John, as well as on biblical narrative and post-biblical Judaism.

Marie-Eloise Rosenblatt is Assistant Professor of Religious Studies at Santa Clara University in northern California, where she teaches courses in New Testament and biblical spirituality. She is editor of *Where Can We Find Her? Searching for Women's Identity in the New Church,* and author of *Paul the Accused: His Portrait in Acts.*

Jane Schaberg is Professor of Religious Studies at the University of Detroit Mercy. She is the author of *The Illegitimacy of Jesus,* and is working on a book on Mary Magdalene traditions. She is also a poet.

Luise Schottroff is Professor of New Testament in Kassel, Germany. Her research focuses on the social history of early Christianity and on feminist liberation theology in the context of Western Europe. In addition to publications in German, her newest book in English is *Let the Oppressed Go Free: Feminist Perspectives on the New Testament.*

Silvia Schroer received her doctorate and habilitation from the Catholic Theology Faculty of Fribourg/Freiburg, Switzerland, in the discipline of Old Testament and Contextual Biblical World Studies. She is engaged in scientific and pastoral work with a focus on ancient oriental iconography and feminist critical exegesis. She is currently participating in a research project sponsored by the Swiss National Foundation (Schweizer Nationalfond).

Elisabeth Schüssler Fiorenza is the Krister Stendahl Professor of Divinity at the Harvard Divinity School. She was the first woman president of the Society of Biblical Literature (1987), is co-editor with Judith Plaskow of the *Journal of Feminist Studies in Religion* and is also an active editor of the international journal *Concilium*. Her book *In Memory of Her: A Feminist Theological Reconstruction of Christian Origins* (1983) has been translated into eight languages. Among her other recent books are *Bread Not Stone: The Challenge of Feminist Biblical Interpretation, Revelation: Vision of a Just World, But She Said: The Rhetoric of Feminist Interpretation for Liberation,* and *Discipleship of Equals: A Critical Feminist Ekklesia-logy of Liberation.* Her latest book is *Jesus: Miriam's Child, Sophia's Prophet: Critical Issues in Feminist Christology.*

Turid Karlsen Seim is Professor of Theology (New Testament) and Dean of the Faculty of Theology at the University of Oslo, Norway. She is the author of many articles and most recently *The Double Message: Patterns of Gender in Luke-Acts.* Her present research is on the language of birth in the Johannine Tradition.

Elsa Tamez, of Mexican heritage, is Professor in the Latin American Biblical Seminary in Costa Rica, and a researcher at the Ecumenical Research Department. Her most recent book is *The Amnesty of Grace: Justification by Faith from a Latin American Perspective.*

Sarah J. Tanzer is a member of the faculty at McCormick Theological Seminary in Chicago, Illinois.

Maureen A. Tilley is a member of the faculty of the Department of Religion at The Florida State University in Tallahassee, where she teaches courses in the history of Christianity in late antiquity. Her areas of interest include Donatism and hagiography in Roman North Africa as well as the history of biblical interpretation.

Elaine Mary Wainwright teaches biblical studies and women's studies courses in the Brisbane College of Theology in Queensland, Australia. She has written a number of articles, and her doctoral thesis was published recently as *Toward a Feminist Critical Reading of the Gospel According to Matthew.*

S. C. Winter directs the religion program at the Eugene Lang College of the New School for Social Research in New York City. She received her Ph.D. from Union Theological Seminary. She is currently writing on the sources and original languages of the Fourth Gospel and figurative language in the book of Zechariah.

Antoinette Clark Wire is Professor of New Testament Studies at San Francisco Theological Seminary and the Graduate Theological Union. Her doctoral thesis at Claremont Graduate School was on Pauline Theology as an Understanding of God: the Explicit and the Implicit. Her recent book *The Corinthian Women Prophets: A Reconstruction through Paul's Rhetoric* extends this study. Her present research focuses on those who generate and orally transmit early Christian traditions. She is also studying oral traditions in recent Chinese Christianity.

COLOPHON

Searching the Scriptures, Vol. 2:
A Feminist Commentary,
was designed by Maurya P. Horgan and Paul J. Kobelski.
The type is 11-point Sabon and was set by
The HK Scriptorium, Inc., Denver, Colorado.